Anatomy
of
Wonder

Anatomy
of
Wonder

A Critical Guide
to Science Fiction

Third Edition

Edited by

Neil Barron

R. R. Bowker Company
New York & London, 1987

To Carolyn, center of my life

Published by R. R. Bowker Company,
a division of Reed Publishing (USA) Inc.
Copyright © 1987 by Neil Barron
All rights reserved
Printed and bound in the United States of America

Library of Congress Cataloging-in-Publication Data

Anatomy of wonder.

    Includes bibliographies and indexes.
    1. Science fiction—Bibliography. 2. Science
fiction—History and criticism. I. Barron, Neil,
1934–
Z5917.S36A52 1987   016.80883′876   87-9305
[PN3433.8]
ISBN 0-8352-2312-4

R00748 33679

Contents

Preface vii

Contributors xi

Introduction xiii

English-Language Science Fiction

1. The Emergence of Science Fiction: The Beginnings to the 1920s
   Thomas D. Clareson 3

2. Science Fiction between the Wars: 1918–1938
   Brian Stableford 49

3. The Early Modern Period: 1938–1963
   Joe De Bolt and John R. Pfeiffer 89

4. The Modern Period: 1964–1986
   Brian Stableford 209

5. Children's and Young Adult Science Fiction
   Francis J. Molson 329

Foreign-Language Science Fiction

6. Foreign-Language Science Fiction 377

   German SF, *Franz Rottensteiner* 379

   French SF, *Maxim Jakubowski* 405

   Russian SF, *Patrick L. McGuire* 441

   Japanese SF, *David Lewis* 474

   Italian SF, *Gianni Montanari* 504

   Danish SF, *Niels Dalgaard* 518

   Swedish, SF, *Sam J. Lundwall* 530

   Norwegian SF, *Jon Bing* 537

Dutch SF, *J. A. Dautzenberg* 545

Belgian SF, *Danny De Laet* 553

Romanian SF, *Ion Hobana* 562

Yugoslav SF, *Alexander B. Nedelkovich* 571

Hebrew SF, *Nachman Ben-Yehuda* 577

Research Aids

7. Science Fiction Publishing and Libraries
   Neil Barron 585

8. General Reference Works
   Neil Barron 593

9. History and Criticism
   Neil Barron 609

10. Author Studies
    Neil Barron 636

11. Science Fiction on Film and Television
    Neil Barron 672

12. Science Fiction Illustration
    Neil Barron 687

13. Teaching Materials
    Muriel Rogow Becker 697

14. Science Fiction Magazines
    H. W. Hall 721

15. Library and Private Collections of Science Fiction
    and Fantasy
    H. W. Hall and Neil Barron 734

16. Core Collection Checklist
    Neil Barron 763

Author/Subject Index 787

Title Index 841

Preface

The first edition of *Anatomy of Wonder* (1976) was the first comprehensive critical guide to science fiction. Selected as an outstanding reference book by the American Library Association and *Choice* magazine, it was also well received by fans and scholars. The second edition (1981) was 55 percent longer, far more inclusive and accurate, and was nominated for the Science Fiction Achievement Award, informally known as the Hugo (after Hugo Gernsback, 1884–1967, founding editor of *Amazing Stories* [14-22]), and recommended by *Locus* [14-37].

This third edition is even more complete in coverage, especially in its treatment of foreign-language science fiction and the rapidly growing secondary literature. All chapters have been thoroughly revised, including those devoted to earlier fiction.

Some idea of the improvements in successive editions can be obtained from this summary:

Number of Annotated Entries*

Section	1st ed. (1976)	2nd ed. (1981)	3rd ed. (1987)	New in 3rd ed.
Beginnings to 1920s	227	182	108	4
1918–1938	73	131	147	23
1938–1986	701	913	1,090	448
Children's SF	99	166	180	29
Foreign-Language SF	0	263	476	232
Research Aids	155	245	554	318
Libraries/Private Collections	52/0	62/33	63/32	5/10

*Figures are inexact because the coverage of chapters changed with successive editions but are sufficiently accurate to show the magnitude of the changes. Many annotated entries discuss more than one title.

The modern period, 1938–1986, was divided into two chapters, partly to highlight the works of the many authors who achieved prominence beginning in the 1960s, and partly to provide a contrasting critical viewpoint. Approximately 38 authors appear in both Chapters 3 and 4, with 13 of them having only one book in Chapter 4.

Although this edition is published primarily for libraries, it has been edited for a variety of overlapping audiences.

1. Public, school, college, and university libraries desiring to develop well-rounded collections of science fiction, whether for support of instructional programs or for recreational reading.
2. Interested readers, including librarians and SF fans, who wish to become more familiar with the best or representative works in the field.
3. High school, college, and university faculty who use SF books in their courses, whether general in nature, devoted to SF only, or to the emerging specialty of future studies, and who wish to select titles for possible course use or background reading.
4. Students enrolled in such courses wishing to broaden their backgrounds or select titles for more intensive study, or merely for recreational reading.

In order to keep this guide to a reasonable length, additions have usually been balanced by deletions of weaker or superseded titles from the earlier editions. There is still a tendency to regard SF as a primarily Anglo-American phenomenon, an insular view that undermines balanced critical estimates. Although many distinguished works have been translated into English, Chapter 6, "Foreign-Language Science Fiction," clearly indicates the riches that remain inaccessible to the monolingual English reader.

Although relatively few libraries collect SF comprehensively, the list of library and privately owned collections has been expanded as well as revised (Chapter 15). Chapter 7, "Science Fiction Publishing and Libraries," provides guidance in monitoring SF book reviewing and in selection, ordering, and cataloging. Because SF courses are common at several levels, Chapter 13, "Teaching Materials," has been extensively revised.

The introductory essays provide historical perspective on the periods or languages discussed, though they cannot replace the more comprehensive histories of the field annotated in Chapter 9, "History and Criticism." The annotations that follow the introductions evaluate the books judged most significant for literary or historical reasons. Although plot summary is provided to suggest what the book is "about," the emphasis throughout is on critical evaluation. Given the large number of books annotated and the need for terseness, we may—rarely, we hope—inadvertently somewhat alter or distort a book's concept. No work of art can be reduced to its paraphrasable content. The term *science fiction* is not uniformly used. Some authors use science-fiction, science-fictional, SF, Sf, sf; this guide uses *science fiction* as a noun and adjective and SF as the abbreviation.

The annotations include these elements:

Entry number, assigned according to chapter and sequence, as [1-1], [3-147], and so on.

Name of author or editor, with the unused or lesser used portion in parentheses, such as Heinlein, Robert A(nson). Books are listed under the name most commonly used by the author, even if it is a pseudonym (the given name is shown in parentheses). Current cataloging practices (AACR II) for anthologies favor the title as the main entry, but in this guide anthologies are generally listed by editor, except for some serial anthologies having successive editors.

Nationality of author or editor, if known and if other than American.

Title, including better-known variant titles. Title changes are extremely common in SF, and no attempt was made to include all variants. *The Science Fiction Encyclopedia* [8-30] and the Reginald bibliography, *Science Fiction and Fantasy Literature* [8-1], provide more details. When a book is part of a series, this is usually noted. Series are common in category fiction and are thoroughly listed in Tim Cottrill, *Science Fiction and Fantasy Series and Sequels* [8-22].

Publisher and year of first edition, relying when possible on the bibliographies by R. Reginald, Everett F. Bleiler, and L. W. Currey, in that order (see Chapter 8), as authorities for such information. Somewhat more detailed bibliographic information is provided for non-English language books and for some of the early works, as well as for nonprint materials. As a rule, any edition is acceptable, but in a few cases specific editions are recommended. Most secondary literature is still in print, evidence of its recent publication, and a surprisingly high percentage of the better fiction is reprinted/reissued regularly. Hardcover reprints are now infrequent.

Succinct plot summary, noting principal themes, critical strengths or weaknesses, comparable works, and key awards or nominations received. Notable stories in collections and anthologies are usually mentioned.

Cross-references to works with similar or contrasting themes are usually included. The entry number for each annotation is used in brackets for cross-reference whenever the title is mentioned elsewhere in the text, as [2-112] or [5-23].

First-purchase (core collection) titles, indicated by an asterisk (*) preceding the entry number. Many are in print, although most works from the post-World War II period are available only as paperbacks. Starred fiction titles were selected on the basis of one or more of these characteristics: awards or nominations received (see Chapter 16), influence of the work, outstanding or unique treatment of a theme, critical and/or popular acceptance, importance of the work in the author's total output, or historical importance (especially for early works). Nonfiction works were judged by the usual criteria of scope, accuracy, currency, ease of use, balance, and so on. Many annotations identify stories as award winners and nominees by these abbreviations:

HN—Hugo Nominee
HW—Hugo Winner
IFA—International Fantasy Award
JWC—John W. Campbell Memorial Award
L—*Locus* award winner
NN—Nebula Nominee
NW—Nebula Winner
SFHF—Science Fiction Hall of Fame [see 3-455]

Nonstarred titles are those that are relatively less important, but might be found in a more comprehensive collection. This large category includes many of the less distinguished but still respectable efforts in the field and necessarily reflects substantial personal judgment. Certain titles were selected as representative of their type; others equally good could have been selected. Because this is a selective guide to the best, better, or representative works, only a few annotations, mostly of nonfiction, are unequivocally negative.

Sections discussing SF in eight additional foreign languages have been added to this edition, expanding this guide's scope still further.

"Research Aids" is greatly expanded from the first and second editions, partly reflecting the increased academic acceptance of the field. The intent throughout *Anatomy of Wonder* was to be reasonably comprehensive without becoming exhaustive. Knowledgeable readers will find almost every work they would judge of major significance annotated, even if their individual judgments differ from those of the contributors. Because no typology or definition can satisfactorily resolve all problems of what to include or exclude, there is a section at the end of Chapter 8 that annotates key reference works devoted to fantasy and horror fiction, whose readers are often SF readers as well, and that are often written by writers better known for their science fiction.

The Author/Subject Index and Title Index supplement the self-indexed chapters. See the introductions to the indexes for more details.

In order to improve this guide's scope and balance, detailed comments were received from four principal outside readers, who were generous in sharing their knowledge. These include:

Brian Aldiss, who also wrote the Introduction to this guide.

David Pringle, until recently the editor of *Foundation* [14-36] and author of *Science Fiction: The 100 Best Novels* [9-78].

Everett F. Bleiler, a Renaissance scholar equally at home in SF, supernatural, fantasy, and detective fiction; compiler of the first and for many years the only checklist of fantastic literature [8-2]; and a winner of the Science Fiction Research Association's Pilgrim award.

Sam Moskowitz, winner of the Science Fiction Research Association's 1981 Pilgrim award for his many pioneering studies of the development of SF and owner of one of the outstanding science fiction research collections [15-77].

Specialized advice was also provided by Michael Klossner, for Chapter 11; Vincent Di Fate, Robert Weinberg, and Gary K. Wolfe for Chapter 12; and Pascal Thomas and Pascal Ducommun for the section on French SF. Thanks are also due to Ray Beam, secretary/treasurer of First Fandom, an international group of approximately 200 fans active in SF since the 1930s, to whom he circulated my request for information on private collections listed in Chapter 15; and Ed Meskys for information on SF for the blind and visually impaired (Chapter 15).

Contributors

Neil Barron, 1934– . An active SF fan in the late 1940s and early 1950s, he edited the 1976 and 1981 editions of *Anatomy of Wonder*. In 1982 he received the Pilgrim award for his overall contributions to science fiction and fantasy scholarship. Address: 1149 Lime Place, Vista, CA 92083. (Letters to any contributors should be sent to him for forwarding.)

Brian W. Aldiss, 1925– . One of Britain's most versatile writers, his science fiction has won many awards. Equally gifted as a critic, he wrote the first critical history of SF, *Billion Year Spree*, recently revised as *Trillion Year Spree* [9-4].

Muriel Rogow Becker. An associate professor of English at Montclair State College, New Jersey, she has taught SF in junior and senior high school and in college for more than 20 years.

Nachman Ben-Yehuda. The holder of two degrees from the University of Chicago, he has been a lecturer in sociology at Hebrew University, Israel, since 1978. Active in SF in Israel, his most recent book is *Deviance and Moral Boundaries* [9-11].

Jon Bing, 1944– . Author of SF since 1967, and a translator, editor, and critic, he is also research director and professor at the Norwegian Research Center for Computers and Law.

Thomas D. Clareson, 1926– . A professor of English at the College of Wooster, Ohio, he founded and still edits *Extrapolation* [14-33]. The editor of many books (see Chapter 9), he is an authority on early American SF, the subject of *Some Kind of Paradise* [9-24] and *Science Fiction in America, 1870s–1930s* [8-12A].

Niels Dalgaard, 1956– . Active in Danish SF fandom since 1974, he currently edits its *Proxima* [6-366], the leading Scandinavian journal of SF criticism. He is writing his thesis on Danish SF of the 1970s.

J. A. Dautzenberg, 1944– . A professor of Dutch language and literature and a free-lance journalist, he is working on a two-volume history of Dutch and Flemish literature.

Joe De Bolt, 1939–   . A professor of sociology at Central Michigan University, he has edited critical works dealing with Brunner [10-29] and Le Guin [10-93]. His major academic interests are the sociology of science and technology, social change, and small groups.

Danny De Laet, 1944–   . Active in Belgian SF since 1962, he is a translator, publisher, editor, and literary agent.

H. W. Hall, 1941–   . A librarian at Texas A&M University, he is one of the field's most active bibliographers (see Chapter 8).

Ion Hobana, 1931–   . A Romanian author of novels, short fiction, children's poetry, and critical studies of SF, he has also translated extensively from French and Italian, and his own work has been translated into many languages.

Maxim Jakubowski, 1944–   . Born in England, educated in France, he is the editorial director of Ebury Press, London. He has extensive experience as a translator, writer, critic, and editor.

David Lewis, 1954–   . A graduate of the University of Michigan who specialized in Japanese language and literature, he has lived in Japan for several years and is currently a journalist with *Newsweek* in Tokyo.

Sam J. Lundwall, 1941–   . After his first professional SF sale at the age of 13, he has written several dozen novels and critical books about SF (see Chapter 9).

Patrick L. McGuire, 1949–   . A Princeton graduate, his doctoral thesis, *Red Stars* [9-58], was one of the earlier detailed studies of Russian SF.

Francis J. Molson, 1932–   . A professor of English, he specializes in nineteenth-century American and children's literature, especially fantasy.

Gianni Montanari, 1949–   . With a degree in modern languages, he has taught English and French. He has edited for several Italian publishers and has written three novels, a study of British SF, and a biobibliographic guide to Italian SF.

Alexander B. Nedelkovich, 1950–   . A teacher of English, he has translated many English-language SF novels into Serbo-Croat. He is working on his doctoral thesis in SF.

John R. Pfeiffer, 1938–   . A professor of English, he has written articles in critical, bibliographic, and reference works in British, American, and German literature. He has taught fantasy and SF courses at the U.S. Air Force Academy.

Franz Rottensteiner, 1942–   . An Austrian critic and editor and the agent for Stanislaw Lem, he has written about SF and fantasy (see Chapter 9). He edits the German language journal, *Quarber Merkur* [14-39].

Brian Stableford, 1948–   . A well-regarded British author (see Chapter 4), he is one of SF's most knowledgeable critics. In 1987 he received the Distinguished Scholarship Award of the International Association of the Fantastic in the Arts.

Introduction: Success Stories

Brian W. Aldiss

There is a short story by Kit Reed in which authorities in the future decide to exterminate all dogs as an antipollution measure. A married couple living in an apartment keep a big Doberman that—this is the husband's fear—the wife loves more than she does her partner. The extermination police eventually come and hammer on the apartment door. The woman has a robe of her husband's for the dog, plus a towel to shroud his head. She forces her husband to get into a dog suit.

This brief tale has much to offer, in addition to its gleeful horror. The suspicion of—perhaps one should say hostility toward—governments of any political hue, with their power to make arbitrary decisions, is typical of the sharper kind of science fiction of earlier days. The law's delay, the insolence of office, is a sound perennial theme—neglected of late, unless I am mistaken.

In addition, Reed raises the pertinent question of dogs. Someday, someone is going to do something about dogs. They do foul parks and pavements. They do gobble up food that would be welcome in the Third World. H. G. Wells was at least as phobic about dogs as Kit Reed, mistrusting them as bringers of disease into the home. On the other hand, much can be said in favor of dogs. They are beautiful and faithful. Science approves of their presence in the case of heart-attack victims, for whom patting and stroking is a remedial pastime. This has always struck me as a good idea. Our attenuated industrial souls need such nourishing beliefs.

Also, of course, the Reed story centers on a human relationship. It is a classic SF story of its kind: brief, amusing, spiked. It's called "Dog Days." But it will never become widely popular, because its two main characters are victims, the no-luck members of society. It is not a further accretion of present-day Trash SF.

One of the major problems SF faces at present is not that it experiences difficulty in keeping up with dramatizations and domestications of scientific advance—

that problem is a perennial one, and always capable of solution—but that it has invested heavily in telling success stories. Success stories are what SF now dishes out at the "fast-fable" counter. They're gaudy, they're budget-friendly, they're fattening. It's just nourishment they are low on. They're mainly Trash SF.

I am not talking about the kind of success meted out in fairy stories. That kind of success is tempered with justice, and a reward for persistence, luck, cunning, or cooperation. Jack the Giant-Killer wins because he has one talent, his ability with an axe. Hansel and Gretel evade prospective cannibalism and live happily ever after by virtue of quick thinking and one quick shove. Goldilocks, who is a trespasser, attains no greater success than to escape from the Three Bears. Kindness to animals earns better rewards. The young lady who brings herself to kiss the frog finds that she has won herself a prince; Beauty is kind to her poor Beast, and gains a kingdom. Not only do fairy tales enshrine profound truths: where they contain magic, their human characters are generally very ordinary and without magic, though perhaps with some special quality, like forbearance. "Pride, anger, gluttony, and idleness," says the Beast at the end of his story, "are sometimes conquered, but the conversion of a malicious and envious mind is a kind of miracle."

In much SF and fantasy, however, this just isn't so. It's the protagonists who have the magic. They have pride, they walk tall, they spill their anger and their seed where they will, they kill off the beasts or aliens with no second thought, and as for kissing a frog—forget it. They are out to win empires and galaxies, and they do, even if it takes six sequels. They are giants. Even nature bends to their will. This is Trash SF.

This is not just success. It's madness.

How has SF become so involved with the telling of success stories—I mean, *ludicrous* success stories? In this respect, it is caught up in its own success story, which certainly has been one of immense growth and popularity in recent years—since, let's say, the time of *Star Wars,* the movie archetype of ludicrous success stories, in which a teenager, a pal, a princess, and an interstellar Pekingese-or-something get right in there and defeat a whole galactic empire. Great viewing, trivial concept.

Science fiction gained what it has long wished for: everyone's attention. When wishes are granted, as fairy tales remind us, trouble's in store. The trouble here is that writers have started to identify with the rulers rather than the ruled. Despite all the cautionary words that Frank Herbert expended on the subject, hero worship has become rather the order of the day. And many of those heroes indiscriminatingly wear jackboots.

These are generalizations. One is forced to use them when talking about SF in general. In fact, some of the more successful novels of recent years have not been of the ludicrous success type. The human race, or at least our present generation, does not put up much of a showing in Greg Bear's *Blood Music* [4-50] or in Bruce Sterling's *Schismatrix* [4-538] or in Vonnegut's amazing *Galapagos* [4-577], to cite three examples. The interest in these books—not the only interest—is a speculative one, the old speculative excitement of good SF, where the basic postulate is given and the reader then participates in its working out. We aren't to be conned, or lulled to sleep, or reassured that everything is going to be just great from now on. We are given an intellectual delight, as, for example, the weird and wonderful conversations in *Schismatrix.*

The comparative popularity of these three novels, and others that still attempt to do more than fill in space between commercials, encourages the thought that succès fou has not yet killed off the old kind of skeptical SF that runs through Shelley, Wells, Stapledon, the marvelous *Galaxy* writers of the fifties—Pohl, Sheckley, Tenn, Knight, Dick, Bester, Sturgeon, among them—to such contemporaries as Reed, Ballard, Disch, and Sterling. Nor, evidently, has succès fou killed off the skeptical SF reader. We need him. We need him—and her—more than ever.

Perhaps *especially* her. How heartening the recent uncompromising appearance of Margaret Atwood's *The Handmaid's Tale* [4-31]. It traffics easily between its past and present tenses to create its future, full of a sly wit that mitigates while emphasizing the fallen nature of its characters. The fact that *The Handmaid's Tale* is in the utopian/dystopian mode means that Atwood is free of the imagined necessity of a success story formula. Skepticism is the watchword here.

We do not live in skeptical times. It's the day of Trash SF, reflecting faithfully the kind of governments we have at present. This is a period when all concerned might benefit from reciting every day at breakfast that couplet of Samuel Johnson's:

How small, of all that human hearts endure
That part which laws or kings can cause or cure!

Generalizing again, there's no truth that is 100 percent true. The growth and success of SF have brought genuine advances, some of them reflected in *Anatomy of Wonder* and by this third edition itself. Increased sophistication means that many better-written novels appear than was once the case. Under the surface, where float a few "big names" who cream off most of the financial advantages of the general success, there is more diversity than ever before.

The number of middle-range authors supporting this diversity has increased. One result is, I believe, a necessarily greater calculation as to what will sell. This means sell to the publisher, not to the public—hence the setting up of the fast-fable bars on all sides. The publisher likes formulas, and not every writer has the strength, the integrity, or the obsessional quality, whichever it may be, to follow or even develop his own inclinations.

So what do we get as a result? We get a number of narratives that conform to the old well-used trial-obstacle-success formula. The skeptical reader leaves and eats elsewhere.

The trial-obstacle-success formula is a good one. Like the classic recipe for Coca Cola, you vary it at your peril. But writers aren't producing Coke. Their business is lifeblood. You must bleed—Dick bled, Sturgeon bled.

Any formula, when over-used, represents failure, not success. A failure of artistry, a failure of nerve. In the end, the formula kills the creative spark. You've followed the Reed character, you've jumped into the dog suit.

Science fiction is always in danger, like any vigorous form of writing, constantly undergoing change.

But it is not nostalgia alone that sees more virtue in less affluent times. The difference in intellectual strength and conceptual imagery—and in willingness to espouse new forms—between *2001: A Space Odyssey* (1980) and *Solaris* (1971) on the one hand, and *Close Encounters of the Third Kind* and *Star Wars* (both 1977) on the other hand, is all too apparent. The troubled heroes of the first two are in marked contrast to the characterless Luke Skywalker in the latter pair, and this simplification marks a descent into fantasy that is apparent also in the screenplays.

If one has a belief in the general rightness of people, it seems likely that the audience will eventually reject tales of ludicrous success, in which Good triumphs forever over Evil and Bugs Bunny over the Dark Universe, simply because reality is not constructed that way. It would be a shame to dump all the eggs in the success formula basket. Failure and frustration are honorable themes for any exploratory fiction. More than honorable; fruitful. Failure is often more interesting than success, as the life histories of Antigone, Madame Bovary, Anna Karenina, and Tess of the D'Urbervilles testify. Can you imagine Eugene O'Neill writing *Long Day's Journey into* Day? Or Vivaldi's *Seasons* ending with Spring?

All this is more by way of hope than complaint. People listen. People can be persuaded. Most of us need guidance, as anyone knows who has ever attended a writers' conference. Science fiction writers, with a predominantly youthful audience, are in a position to give guidance. Many of these writers have a firm understanding of life's problems, and use those problems to lend veracity to their imaginings.

People listen. I believe that people listened to my history of science fiction, first *Billion Year Spree* [9-4], then (with David Wingrove) *Trillion Year Spree* [9-4]. I believe they listened to Neil Barron's *Anatomy of Wonder*. I see our two books as complementary. Perhaps Neil feels the same. Although we live thousands of miles apart, our judgments are often very similar. Perhaps that is why Neil invited me to write this Introduction to his third edition.

The very fact that he has a third edition and I a second, follows from the success of SF in recent years. More options are open to us. The audience is larger, more diverse, richer than it was. And, we hope, no more foolish. A much larger number of readers go by out there. What a shame not to try to speak truth to them, as we see it.

Trash SF and the fast fable do not actually lie. They are simply in the wrong business. There certainly is such a thing as success. People succeed. Nations succeed. Success is pleasant, or generally regarded as such. Victory—as history and evolution both declare—is to be preferred to defeat. The slave owner is better off than the slave.

It is simply that any literature with any pretense to seriousness must see both sides of the picture. If SF does not pretend to seriousness it should not take on the serious subjects it does. So much, I believe, John W. Campbell was saying in the 1940s. But this present period of history may come to be seen as the great American heyday. Great days bring great responsibilities.

The United States of America is now the indisputable superpower of the world. Who can seriously say America nay, except its own conscience? It is this unparalleled success that is celebrated in much American science fiction. That pie-in-the-sky, the galactic empire, is increasingly as American as apple pie. Galactic empires are easy to write about and easy to read about, as both writer and reader are charged with the same dream of American glory. Everyone feels at home there, in a place where a dash of technology and good old Marine know-how—

plus just a touch of brute force—supply the prevailing ethos. The cult of the individual, of the guy who walks tall, ensures that one man can always "win" the empire, or overturn it. Consult the advertisement pages of *Locus* [14-37] if you doubt me. "The majestic epic of a rebellion that inflamed a million worlds," cry the publishers of *The Darkling Wind*—and it is but a variant of a cry heard many times over.

Empires are on the whole not particularly glorious things. Anyone telling you otherwise is writing Trash SF. Empires are generally transitory arrangements of dominion, which sooner or later fall apart for historical reasons rather than from fisticuffs, from abstruse economic causes rather than because two blond youngsters kidnap the Wicked Queen. Actually it is hard to think of a way in which many disparate worlds could be induced to cohere, or to share some kind of common goal and understanding. More than a State Department or a Colonial Office is needed for such enterprises. The history of our century does not induce us to be optimistic on this score, or to welcome any kind of imperialism. Incarceration usually follows incorporation.

For instance, we have forged little in the way of common goals and understanding with whales and dolphins, although we have been led to believe that they are among the most pleasant of creatures, with good intelligence; moreover, they are fellow beings of our own planet. Some of us continue to hunt them to extinction. That's how a galactic empire would work. Humankind would bring about as much benefit to other species as the railroad brought to the buffalo.

At all periods, critical voices must speak up in order for civilization to survive. During the time of the opulent Second Empire, France was plagued by Zola, writing his novels about the underprivileged. The novels have survived longer than the epoch. At the height of the British Empire, the poet Shelley wrote of the politician who brutally suppressed an Irish rebellion:

I met Murder on the way—
He had a mask like Castlereagh—

There is always room for disagreement. Science fiction has traditionally provided a platform for the underdog, the outsider, the exile, from Frankenstein's monster onward. The classic utopias—Plato's, More's—are arguments for the greatest good of the greatest number. There are loud militarist/imperialist voices within the SF camp. They need not be shouted down. Equally, they need not be the only voices we listen to.

I believe that this work of reference, *Anatomy of Wonder*, the willing collaboration of many hands, is valuable not only as a research tool and reader's companion, but as a reminder of how very various SF is, *and should be*, now and into the starry future.

English-Language
Science Fiction

1

The Emergence of Science Fiction: The Beginnings to the 1920s

Thomas D. Clareson

The early history of science fiction has been explored much more fully in the decade since the publication of the first edition of *Anatomy of Wonder* in 1976. The bibliographies annotated in Chapter 8, notably those by Reginald [8-1], Clarke [8-14], and Clareson [8-12A], as well as the important historical studies by Suvin [9-98], Clareson [9-24], and Stableford [9-93], provide abundant information about the evolution of English-language SF. These studies document in detail what my chapters in the first and second editions of *Anatomy of Wonder* argued more briefly, "that between the Civil War and the 1920s in America alone as many as a thousand books were published that reflected directly the impact of scientific theory and technology on the literary imagination, and must be considered, at the least, as precursors of modern science fiction" (*Anatomy of Wonder*, 2nd ed., p. 3).

Because of the ready availability of these recent studies, approximately 40 percent of the 182 annotations in the second edition were omitted here, with a number of the titles simply mentioned more briefly in this introduction.[1] These deleted titles retain literary and historical value in themselves, but often that value lay in the individual work's uniqueness or in the close relationship it revealed between SF and the general body of fiction. The retained titles indicate the main thrust of the field as it acquired its modern identity.

The academic and popular attention given to SF has not proved an unmixed blessing, for some of the individuals have concentrated on literary theory and exclusive definitions instead of emphasizing historical perspective. Genre criticism, for example, tends to isolate SF in the present century as much as those who would confine SF to the specialist magazines. Some of the most enthusiastic devotées of the modern (post-1926) period would exclude the "lost-race" motif from the field, although increasingly throughout the nineteenth century the growing interest in prehistory, archaeology, geology, anthropology, and exploration created a wide audience for that type of fiction. Those areas of science and scientific speculation—concern for the "lost continent" of Atlantis, reaction to the discovery of prehistoric, non-European civilizations, reconciliation of such discoveries with the account given in Genesis—captured the literary and popular imaginations of the period as much as did the technological wonders pouring out of the laboratories of Bell and Edison and Tesla.

Nor is it helpful to insist that critics/literary historians find special criteria by which to evaluate science fiction because somehow, due to its subject matter, it differs from other literature. Again, that is divisive and makes as much sense as the outcries after the lunar landings and space probes that space travel should no longer be written about *as fiction* because of scientific findings. Such a judgment ignores the idea that SF has never been concerned with scientific discovery and the nuts and bolts of technology per se, but has tried instead to examine the effects of those developments on the individual person and on society as a whole. Perhaps the chief problem facing the student/reader of SF remains the recent attempt to distinguish sharply and completely between science fiction and fantasy instead of seeing them as intermingling in a complex literary tradition borrowing from and equal in importance to the tradition of social realism and literary naturalism. The most obvious examples occur in that fiction dealing with horror—from the gothic novel, at least, to the contemporary best-seller; from Mary Shelley and Edgar Allan Poe to the film *Aliens*.

Without calling for a strict definition, one can establish several characteristics to aid in understanding the historical development of the field. First, writers of SF make use of the discoveries, theories, and speculations in the fields of science that appeal to the imagination at the time the story is written. So long as something is thought to be scientific at the time the story is written, it should not be discarded subsequently as mere fantasy. Second, no society can develop a science fiction until it reaches a certain stage of scientific inquiry and technological development; before that time, it will not have the writers or the audience for SF because, individually and collectively, the literary interest lies elsewhere. Granting these premises, one must recall that fiction is a continuum having certain established conventions that writers/readers expect and make use of. Examples abound: the voyage to the moon in the seventeenth century, the "future history" created in the specialist magazines of the 1940s, the encounter with a supposedly vanished (alien) culture, be it terrestrial (nineteenth century) or extraterrestrial (twentieth century).

One other ingredient is necessary to the emergence of a science fiction: belief in ongoing change. So long as Western civilization did not basically question the static mythos in which Earth is the center of creation and humanity's life and destiny are framed by the Fall and Final Judgment, there could be little speculation about alternative possibilities in the future. The Renaissance changed all that, although the beginning, ironically, came with the Crusades and found expression in the subsequent "travel books" of men like Sir John Mandeville and Marco Polo, which pictured the wonders lying beyond the European peninsula and provided glimpses of exotic kingdoms like Cathay and that of Prester John. Hard on the discovery of America, Sir Thomas More raised the island of Utopia [1-68], whose communistic society served as a vehicle for an implicit attack on England. One cannot overestimate the importance of More's *Utopia*. It gave its name to those innumerable societies portrayed well into the twentieth century that advocated change and foresaw the perfectibility of the political state; moreover, it transformed the travel book into the "imaginary voyage," that narrative framework which has remained one of the essential literary forms of SF, whatever the destination of the voyager.

The imaginary voyage was never the exclusive domain of British writers; as Philip Babcock Gove has pointed out in *The Imaginary Voyage in Prose Fiction* [9-69], it became the most popular form of fiction in the seventeenth century. While Sir Francis Bacon's *The New Atlantis* (1627) emphasized the importance science was beginning to assume, Andreae's *Christianopolis* (1619) portrayed an ideal Christian commonwealth on an island near the South Pole, and Tommaso Campanella's *The City of the Sun* (1623) described a metropolis in Central Asia where such subjects as mathematics, geology, geography, botany, and the mechanical arts were studied. Not until *Gulliver's Travels* [1-89], in which Swift satirized the Royal Societies of London and Dublin, did a major writer of a *terrestrial* imaginary voyage sharply question the increasing stature science was assuming in the intellectual milieu.

Generally speaking, the most notable voyages stemmed from the impact of Copernican astronomy. In 1610 Galileo had published *Sidereus Nuncius*, with its vivid descriptions of the heavens as seen through the telescope. Johannes Kepler's *Somnium* [1-54] postulates an inhabited moon but in no way does his narrative contradict what might be observed. In that same year, 1634, there appeared the first English translation of Lucian's *True History*, important for its satiric accounts of voyages to the moon. The first English-language journey was Bishop Francis Godwin's *The Man in the Moone* [1-39]. During his visit to the lunar world, its protagonist, Domingo Gonsales, confirms the theories of Kepler and Galileo before turning his interest to the inhabitants who live in "another Paradise" amid their scientific researches. Perhaps no other single work proved so popular; Marjorie Nicolson has pointed out that J. B. D. (Jean Baudoin) translated it as *L'Homme dans la lune* (1648); it was this translation with which both Poe and Verne were familiar.[2]

Another British cleric, Bishop John Wilkins, used *A Discourse Concerning a New World and Another Planet* (1638) to argue that the moon may be "habitable" and went so far as to suggest that one day man would fly and establish a colony on the moon.[3] The third important title of the period was Cyrano de Bergerac's *Histoire comique des états et empires de la lune*, translated into English first by Tho. St. Serf and then by A. Lovell [1-12]. Emphasizing that Cyrano de Bergerac "had his feet on the new ground of science," Nicolson asserts that his narrative must be recognized as "the most brilliant of all the seventeenth century parodies of the cosmic voyage."[4] When Cyrano's first attempt to reach the Moon fails, he falls among the barbarians of New France in Canada, where, having built a new ship, he is propelled to the Moon by rocket power—caused by firecrackers sending his ship aloft. In the lunar kingdoms he finds himself classified with the lowest creatures, as does Lemuel Gulliver in *Gulliver's Travels*. Cyrano takes as his guide Godwin's Domingo Gonsales.

In *Iter Lunare* (1703), David Russen, a teacher at Hythe, in Kent, felt compelled to criticize the scientific inaccuracies of such fictions as those by de Bergerac and Godwin and to entertain the scientific data making spaceflight a probability. In this, of course, he echoed Bishop Wilkins. Other titles might be cited. Daniel Defoe's *The Consolidator* (1705) attacks both Wilkins and Godwin. He turns to the libraries of China, where he finds the record of a lunarian who had long ago been persuaded to be an intellectual leader in the court of the emperor; his own protagonist reaches the Moon in a ship powered by a gaseous *fuel*. Samuel Brunt's *A Voyage to Cacklogallinia* (1727) employs the project of a lunar flight as a means of satirizing the South Sea Bubble.

A century later George Tucker, writing as Joseph Atterley, made the first American contribution to the motif with *A Voyage to the Moon* [1-4], chiefly distinguished for the scientific accuracy of the conditions of the journey. He stressed that the ship "must cross an airless void in bitter cold."[5] In 1835, although not itself a description of a voyage, "Discoveries in the Moon Lately Made at the Cape of Good Hope, by Sir John Herschel"—published in the New York *Sun* by Richard Adams Locke and subsequently known simply as "The Moon Hoax"—created something of a sensation by describing at length the variety of life on the Moon. One cannot be certain of its exact relationship to Poe's "The Unparalleled Adventures of One Hans Pfaall" [1-75]. Although Poe gives an account of Pfaall's ascent by balloon, he concludes by explaining why the manuscript of Pfaall must be a hoax and continues with an attack on both Locke and Godwin. He demands that such narratives exhibit a verisimilitude as well as scientific accuracy. Edward Everett Hale attained so effective a degree of realism in "The Brick Moon" [1-48] that it can be read as the first story to deal with an artificial satellite. The narrative also proves to be the most delightfully comic parody of both the cosmic voyage and the post-Darwinian intellectual controversies written in the nineteenth century.

When Nicolson reminds her readers that Godwin, Wilkins, and Cyrano de Bergerac "established the conventions of the moon voyage for more than a century,"[6] she might have said that they dominated the extraterrestrial voyage until the 1870s when Asaph Hall discovered the two moons of Mars and the Italian astronomer Giovanni Schiaparelli announced that he had observed "canali" on Mars. Although the Italian word implies no more than channels, a controversy arose that included such individuals as the American astronomer Percival Lowell, for *canals* on Mars implied intelligence and civilization; the ensuing debate has not been silenced completely even by recent space probes. Overnight Mars replaced the Moon as the most frequent destination of cosmic voyagers. Percy Greg's *Across the Zodiac* [1-40] inaugurated many new conventions, including the use of "apergy"—an electrical force counteracting gravity.

If the imaginary voyages went outward toward the Moon and Mars, they had also gone to subterranean worlds, as might be supposed in a society having the myths of Hades and the underworld. In the first of these, Holberg's *A Journey to the World Under-Ground* [1-50], Nicolas Klimius finds a hollow Earth and lands on the planet Nazar, which becomes a typical vehicle for satire. Holberg achieves much of his effectiveness by inverting the customs of European countries. Robert Paltock's *The Life and Adventures of Peter Wilkins* [1-73], which enjoyed a popularity second only to those of *Robinson Crusoe* and *Gulliver's Travels*, took its narrator-protagonist by a river through extensive caverns to a deep valley near the South Pole, where he found a species of humanoid having the ability to fly. (By inventing mechanical wings, the Vril-ya of Bulwer-Lytton's *The Coming Race* [1-61] share the ability to fly; more importantly, they understand the nature and use of "vril," a kind of electrical force that is the essence of all matter.)

The polar regions have long attracted those who wrote of imaginary voyages. The myth of *terra australis incognita* (the land mass that medieval geographers thought must exist to balance the heavily laden northern hemisphere in order to prevent the Earth from turning over) kept the Antarctic a vital part of the Western imagination. After the discovery of America not only was there the added attraction of the hazardous passage of the Strait of Magellan, but an obsession to find the Northwest Passage around the American continent to Asia lured innumerable explorers into the Arctic. Captain Cook's explorations of the South Seas late in the eighteenth century fueled the concepts of the noble savage and idyllic lands somewhere beyond the limitations of Europe. As the nineteenth century ended, the race to the poles themselves made headlines. While these historical matters made the Antarctic and Arctic settings attractive, the decisive literary factor arose from the first American utopia, *Symzonia: A Voyage of Discovery* [1-81] by Captain Adam Seaborn, possibly the pseudonym of John Cleves Symmes of Ohio. He proposed that the Earth is hollow, containing seven inhabitable spheres, and that the innermost, utopian sphere is accessible through openings at both poles. The idea sparked the American and British imaginations. In 1826, with a collaborator, he published *Symmes Theory of Concentric Spheres;* in 1827 he lectured at Union College; in 1834, after his death, J. N. Reynolds—a friend of Poe—appealed to Congress. By the end of that decade officers of American and British ships were under orders to watch for the polar openings, especially in Antarctica. As late as 1873 an article in the *Atlantic Monthly* argued the existence of "Symmes Hole"; in perhaps a more learned fashion, the debate was repeated in an Ohio journal in 1909.[7] Yet one infers that the theory would have become another of those dry, nineteenth-century scholarly exchanges had it not been for the imagination of Edgar Allan Poe, especially as it gained expression in his longest, though fragmentary, work, *The Narrative of Arthur Gordon Pym of Nantucket* [1-74].

One characteristic of these early imaginary voyages must be noted. They occurred "here-and-now," even *Symzonia* and *Arthur Gordon Pym*. Several explanations come to mind. First, the new astronomy and the physical exploration of the world gave the writers settings not needing a time shift. Second, as a literary vehicle with an emphasis on utopia, the voyage provided a means of social criticism having no need of the future. Finally, the implications for change inherent in the industrial and political revolutions had only begun to be realized by the early nineteenth century.

The earliest fictions to make conscious predictions about the future were, as

I. F. Clarke has pointed out [8-14], two eighteenth-century British projections emphasizing the continuity of European affairs and, quite naturally, the continuing ascendancy of Great Britain. Samuel Madden's *Memoirs of the Twentieth Century* (1733) pictures a continent dominated by the pope and Jesuits (the latter control Russia), although "everywhere" the United Kingdom continued to have power and prestige. *The Reign of George VI, 1900–1925* [1-2] gives a jingoistic Tory description of an ideal monarch who defeats all of Europe after repelling a Russian invasion near Durham. (America, incidentally, remains a loyal colony.)

In that these two narratives ignore the concept of progress—of dramatic change, particularly in terms of differences resulting from the industrial revolution—they fail to take heed of that mood which increasingly dominated the eighteenth century. As the Renaissance deepened into the Enlightenment, the concept that reason was the highest faculty of the mind drew increasing favor in intellectual circles—and a rational mind *must* exist in a rational universe whose laws could be discerned by further investigation. Such a view envisioned the perfectibility both of humanity and of the sociopolitical state, creating an optimism that remains even in the 1980s at the heart of much SF. (To the extent that this optimism faltered, the dystopian mood of the present century, especially in Europe and especially in the late 1960s, has gained supporters.)

The first vision of a change bringing about the betterment of society came in Louis Sebastien Mercier's *L'An 2440* [1-63], translated into English as *Memoirs of the Year Two Thousand Five Hundred* (1771; America, 1795). The "first influential story of the future in world literature, [it] became one of the most widely read books of the last quarter of the eighteenth century."[8] Its protagonist falls asleep, awakening in a Paris transformed by science and invention. In the United States Mary Griffith's "Three Hundred Years Hence" [1-43] foresees a society in which all advancements have resulted from technological achievements and changes in attitude toward such social issues as women's rights. Between them these novels set the pattern for many of the subsequent portraits of future societies—particularly that legion of utopian states created in the last decades of the nineteenth century, climaxing, perhaps, with H. G. Wells's *A Modern Utopia* [1-101]. Clarke suggests that beginning with Mercier's novel, this body of fiction is "an extension of the scheme Bacon had presented in *The New Atlantis*."[9] It grew out of that faith in inevitable progress which became so much a part of the makeup of the nineteenth-century mind. By projecting utopia into the future, Mercier and Mrs. Griffith—and their successors—gave substance to J. O. Bailey's insight that utopia "shifted from a place to be found to a condition to be achieved."[10]

Yet even as this optimism took shape, the gothic intruded, giving to the emerging SF a new dimension and an emotional intensity it had not previously known. The dream of the Enlightenment balanced precariously on the razor's edge of the debate involving epistemology that grew out of Locke's "Essay concerning Human Understanding" (1690). If one ignores the paraphernalia of the gothic plots, beginning with Walpole's *The Castle of Otranto* (1765), then one realizes that its enduring core comes out of the disquieting conclusions of the eighteenth-century psychological empiricists. As a fictional mode it reawakened the demonic and the irrational. Man, the solitary individual, was marooned in a vast, brooding nature, which one could not be sure was "reality." In romantic art the situation is typified by the lone figure dwarfed against vast mountains or the sea. In addition to this isolation, he also could not be certain that his mind functioned properly. The issue was simple: could he comprehend reality if, indeed, he actually perceived it? A negative answer opens up the world of the absurd.

Poe's *The Narrative of Arthur Gordon Pym of Nantucket* [1-74] dramatizes this dilemma. During the first portion of the narrative, Pym, telling his own story, emphasizes his heightened psychological excitement and uncertainties until the reader questions whether Pym's reports are reliable, if sane. Once aboard the *Lady Guy* headed into the Antarctic wastes, however, Pym becomes a veritable personification of rationality as he records the details of an external world different from anything he (or his reader) has ever known. The story breaks off abruptly when Pym and his companions, in a canoe, find themselves drawn toward a cataract and a chasm near the South Pole; the imagery evokes only associations with Symmes's theory of polar openings. The lasting impact of Poe's story may be seen by the number of later authors who attempted sequels, ranging from Charles Romyn Dake's *A Strange Discovery* (1899) to Verne's *An Antarctic Mystery* (American edition, 1899).

Successful as Poe was, however, Mary Shelley's *Frankenstein; or, The Modern Prometheus* [1-84] had an even greater effect on SF. In asserting that SF "was born from the Gothic mode [and] is hardly free from it now," Brian Aldiss argues that *Frankenstein* was the first science fiction novel.[11] In the island kingdom of Utopia, Sir Thomas More gave SF its first myth; Mary Shelley gave the field its second myth in her tale of a being patched together from cadavers and given life by a scientist who has trespassed beyond those limits set for man. Her monster is Dr. Frankenstein, who conjures up the image of Faust as he plays God and then recoils in horror from the creature he has created. Through the technique of the story-within-a-story, the heart of the novel becomes the unnamed creature's account of his repeated rejection by all those whom he meets, including Victor Frankenstein. Becoming increasingly demented (by error he was given the brain of a criminal), he gives himself to his craze for revenge, pursuing Frankenstein across the vast Arctic ice floe. Despite the appearance and seeming madness of the creature, some persons read the novel as Mary Shelley's plea on behalf of individualism. She brings her indictment against Dr. Frankenstein, who, crazed himself, seeks to kill the being he has created. Guilt-ridden, he recognizes that, like Faust, he has committed the sin of intellectual pride in his zeal to be the first to create another being.

Mary Shelley seized on a second, apocalyptic theme in her final novel, *The Last Man* [1-85], in which a plague sweeps through Europe annihilating humanity. Her protagonist, believing himself the only survivor, struggles toward Rome in search of someone alive. Hers was not the first such catastrophe. As a reaction to Dr. Edward Jenner's published results of his work with vaccine, as well as Thomas Malthus's dire predictions of overpopulation, Jean-Baptiste Cousin de Grainville wrote *Le Dernier Homme* (1805; English translation, 1806), called by Clarke the "earliest account in fiction of the last days of mankind."[12] Between them they created what may be called the "catastrophe motif," a kind of story permeating Wells's fiction and forming the basis of such individual novels as Doyle's *The Poison Belt* [1-32] and London's *The Scarlet Plague* [1-60]. To read the motif as nothing more than the dark side of the vision of humanity's perfectibility oversimplifies, for it does not take into account that in the late nineteenth and early twentieth centuries—especially before World War I—the scientist/engineer saved at least a segment of humanity from some natural disaster, as in Garrett P. Serviss's *The Second Deluge* [1-83], or helped survivors to rebuild a devastated world, as in George Allan England's *Darkness and Dawn* trilogy [1-33].

Although de Grainville and Mary Shelley introduced a third lasting motif, their works stand unique in the early part of the century, for the gothic mode more typically concentrated on the aberrations of the individual mind, as best illustrated by the short tales of Poe, like "The Black Cat" and "The Tell-Tale Heart," where first-person narrators reveal the depths to which they have sunk because of their obsessions. Therein lies the heritage of terror coming down from the gothic to contemporary fiction, as in Stephen King's *Pet Sematary* (1983). In the mid-nineteenth century the writer who most nearly equaled Poe was Fitz-James O'Brien, whose "The Diamond Lens" [1-72] introduces a new world to SF. Using a perfect lens, its protagonist, the microscopist Linley, discovers in a drop of water a subatomic world in which the beautiful nymph, Animula, dwells; he falls in love with her but inadvertently allows the water to evaporate so that she dies. He goes mad, ending up in a madhouse. Perhaps the best-known story using the subatomic world remains Ray Cummings's *The Girl in the Golden Atom,* first serialized in *All-Story Weekly* in 1919. Unquestionably the most terrible remains Mark Twain's pessimistic "The Great Dark" [1-25], not published until long after his death. Its first-person protagonist falls through his microscope into the subatomic world of a drop of water, where he and his family must sail forever aboard a ship that has no port as a haven. Against nothing but intense heat and light or intense darkness and cold, great monsters rise occasionally from the water, sometimes threatening the ship itself (they are, of course, microbes). No story better captures Twain's hatred and fear of the concept of determinism, which increasingly haunted his imagination. Nor did he offer himself or his reader surcease by relying on the shopworn convention of awakening from a dream. There was no respite.

In the 1890s fear unified the best fiction of Ambrose Bierce. Throughout his stories Bierce refers to racial memory, particularly in terms of the human inheritance of a terrible dread of death and the unknown. He gave a new dimension to horror by drawing on biology in "The Damned Thing" [1-13]; he assigned to the traditional creatures of such stories as O'Brien's "What Was It" (1859) and Maupassant's "Le Horla" (1887) a scientific explanation: just as there are sounds that man cannot hear, so, too, "at each end of the spectrum the chemist can detect what are known as 'actinic rays,' representing colors man cannot see. And, God help me [writes the diarist] The Damned Thing is of such a color."

Although Henry James gave little or no explicit attention in his texts to scientific data, like Bierce he showed an awareness of the new psychology in his ghost stories dealing with obsession and hallucination. "Maud Evelyn" (1900) seems inexplicably neglected by critics, while the incomparable ambiguity of "The Turn of the Screw" (1898) marks one of the high points of turn-of-the-century fiction. Ford Madox Ford's reference to James's technique as the "analysis of an anxious state of mind"[13] applies almost as well to much of the fiction of Bierce. Between them the two did more than any of their contemporaries to transform the traditional ghost story into a psychological case study.

The concern for abnormal states of mind had taken another turn as early as

Oliver Wendell Holmes's *Elsie Venner* (1861) with its medical interest in multiple personality. The classic example from the nineteenth century remains Stevenson's *The Strange Case of Dr. Jekyll and Mr. Hyde* [1-86], in which a London physician hopes to use a drug to rid himself of that streak of evil within him which has marred his personality since his youth; unwittingly he "frees a monster of evil who finally dominates him."[14] As one examines a spectrum of American stories from Thomas Bailey Aldrich's "The Queen of Sheba" (1877) to Albert Bigelow Paine's *The Mystery of Evelin Delorme* (1894) and Vincent Harper's *The Mortgage on the Brain* (1905), one does not know how to interpret the fact that most of the fiction dealing with multiple personality builds around a love story in which the young woman suffers from some mental quirk. Except for amnesia, one cannot describe the condition as any kind of breakdown. Intriguingly, only in such novels as *Some Ladies in Haste* (1908) and *The Green Mouse* (1910) does the fashionable New York writer Robert W. Chambers add an element of comedy to his love stories. The protagonist of *Some Ladies in Haste* uses posthypnotic suggestion to induce the first five young women he sees from the windows of his club to fall in love with some of his friends. One of the young women is, of course, his fiancée. The protagonist of *The Green Mouse* develops a machine capable of intercepting psychic waves, thereby assuring that one falls in love with the person one *should* love and marry. An advertisement for the machine reads in part: "Wedlock by Wireless. Marriage by Machinery. A Wonderful Wooer without Words." In a sense Chambers anticipates the computer-dating fad, although his own central couples follow the impulses of their irrational hearts.

In and of themselves the novels concerned with psychological abnormalities make up a cul-de-sac. To begin with, they dated very quickly. Since their settings and action involved everyday life—thus the popularity of the love story—they were soon lost among substantive concerns and narrative techniques, like the stream of consciousness, which led to modern psychological realism. One strand developed into novels—which some persons label fantasy, others, SF—such as Jack London's *The Star Rover* (1915), whose protagonist, a prisoner in solitary confinement, teaches himself "astral projection"; with his spirit freed from his body, he experiences a number of incarnations. In terms of SF, psychological aberrations were replaced by the motif dealing over the years with mutants, androids, "supermen," and clones. A pair of scientists in Wells's *The Food of the Gods* [1-99] develops a food supplement causing giantism and producing individuals who are superior to Homo sapiens. More typical of the motif is John Davys Beresford's *The Hampdenshire Wonder* [1-11], whose youthful protagonist, a mutant, has a mind far in advance of those of his contemporaries. The motif includes such later titles as Stapledon's *Odd John* [2-110] and van Vogt's *Slan* [3-383]. A noteworthy early American example has never been republished: Edgar Fawcett's *Solarion* [1-34] gives a new twist to the Frankenstein story in that one of its main characters is a dog possessing an artificially enhanced intelligence.

During the last decades of the nineteenth century the interest in psychology remained peripheral to what seemed at the time more central, vital concerns. The first motif to dominate the emerging SF dramatized the portrayal of future wars. In May 1871, *Blackwood's* published anonymously *The Battle of Dorking: Reminiscences of a Volunteer* [1-21]. Coming fresh upon the surprising result of the Franco-Prussian War, amid a growing hysteria of nationalism and imperialism, as I. F. Clarke has pointed out in *Voices Prophesying War* [9-27], *The Battle of Dorking* caught the British populace in a mood of foreboding and uncertainty regarding the future of the empire. Published throughout the English-speaking world and widely translated, it triggered a reaction throughout Europe, serving as the prototype for innumerable books predicting an imminent holocaust. Its author, Sir George Tomkyns Chesney, who had been recalled from India to establish the Royal Indian Engineering College at Staines, warned his countrymen against a German invasion and British defeat because Britain had refused to accept the cost of building her defenses and so had remained militarily unprepared. Most importantly, he predicted that the use of new weapons would decide the outcome of such a struggle. This attention to the "hardware" of the period proved to be the distinctive innovation of the story.

As one might expect, most of the British authors forecast a war that would be decided in a great sea battle: *The Great Naval War of 1887* (serialized in *St. James Gazette* in 1887) and *Trafalgar Refought* (1905), both by William Laird Clowes and A. H. Burgoyne; *The Captain of the 'Mary Rose'* (1892) by Clowes; *Blake of the 'Rattlesnake'* (1895) by Frederick T. Jane, who gained his fame through his annual books describing the standing navies in *Jane's Ships*. The authors showed their fascination with the new "ironclads," those "dreadnaughts" that became the battleships of the line by the turn of the century, although they also gave much attention to the tiny "torpedo boats," like Jane's *Rattlesnake*, whose speed and mobility made them the despair of the ponderous, seemingly invincible ironclads.

Rear Admiral P. Colomb gave his name to the collaboration of a number of military men and journalists who produced *The Great War of 189-: A Forecast* [1-26], first published in the illustrated magazine *Black and White*. It was widely translated immediately. By 1894, according to Clarke, its German version, *Der grosse Krieg von 189-*, had reached its fifth edition; in a special introduction General von Below praised it because it concerned itself not only with tomorrow's battles but also with " 'the subject of international politics in Europe.' "[15] It portrayed an Anglo-Saxon struggle against a Franco-Russian alliance; its fighting engulfed the Eurasian continent from the approaches to Paris and the Riviera to Vladivostok. These tales have an importance for intellectual history not only for the insights that they give into the military strategy and armaments race at the turn of the century, but for their reflection of the uncertain, shifting alliances of the period.

In the earlier works France continued to be the primary, traditional enemy. As early as Robert Cromie's *For England's Sake* (1889), British forces fought the good fight against Russia in Asia, a result of the tensions involving India; in his *The Next Crusade* (1896), Britain teamed with Austria to defeat Russia and Turkey, thereby making the Mediterranean "a British lake." If one names a single factor that tipped the scales, it must be the naval race between Britain and Germany, which led to the alignments caught up in the debacle of World War I. The persistent fear of invasion of the British Isles, strengthened by the prophecy and immediacy—in terms of realistic detail (the kind of emotional impact Wells achieved by destroying the villages around the City of London in *The War of the Worlds* [1-105])—of *The Battle of Dorking*, may have triggered the decision to side with France against Germany. If so, then the matter-of-fact tone of Erskine Childers's *Riddle of the Sands* [1-24] may have been the literary achievement of the period; its protagonist supposedly discovers a German plot to invade England

and reports in detail the method that Germany would use to gain surprise and victory. The plot—or, rather, the public's shift in allegiance—seemed to be confirmed by the publication of August Niemann's *Der Weltkrieg—Deutsche Traume* (1904), translated as *The Coming Conquest of England.*

Niemann's success reminds us that other voices than British clamored for war. In France, for example, as early as 1892–1893, Capitaine Danrit (E. A. Driant) published his first trilogy of books outlining his concepts of the next conflict with Germany: *La Guerre en forteresse, La Guerre en rase campagne,* and *La Guerre en ballon.* In 1888 he had been appointed adjutant to General Boulanger at the ministry of war and married Boulanger's youngest daughter in the autumn of that year. From 1892 to 1896 he served as an instructor at St. Cyr before being recalled to active duty. He wrote with equal ease of wars against the Germans or the British. The urge to express an intense nationalism that brought glory to the homeland, whoever the enemy, seemed to provide adequate motivation for these writers. Driant, incidentally, died at Verdun.

Clarke points out that the future war motif had its greatest impact when it captured the imagination of the public; this occurred when journalists, like George Griffith and Louis Tracy, made use of mass circulation journals and papers. He singles out William Le Queux, who first gained fame with *The Great War in England in 1897* [1-57], but achieved an even greater success with *The Invasion of 1910* (1906), a cliché-ridden diatribe against those persons—especially those in government—whom he accused of ignoring Lord Roberts's warning that Great Britain had not prepared itself for modern warfare.[16] Clarke explains the success of the "new mythology of imaginary wars" in terms of "the nationalistic emotions of the period." Of the writers themselves, he declares, "[They] were trying to create a Beowulf myth for an industrial civilization of ironclads and high-speed turbines, a new and violent *chanson de geste* for an age of imperialism, told in the inflammatory language of the mass press."[17] The European writers won many a land battle, however, with cavalry charges—just as the cavalry waited impatiently behind the trenches to charge to victory in World War I. The most terrible irony of the future war motif in Europe, at least, is that no writer foresaw the impasse of trench warfare, the gas attacks, the aerial warfare. Trapped by past glories (or infamous defeats, as in the case of France) and the surge of nationalism, they failed to see the implications of the new weaponry. Irony on irony: one wonders whether the Battle of Jutland was cut short because those in command remembered the widespread prediction that the next major war would be finished by a single, glorious battle at sea. As one might expect, Wells proved to be the exception; in *The War in the Air* [1-104], he expressed the fear that social collapse would follow the expected world conflict because men would not have the ability to solve their social and political problems or to control such new weapons as the airplane. In contrast—perhaps in desperation—although his *The World Set Free* (1914) envisions atomic warfare, ultimately a rational settlement of world affairs establishes a utopian state, for international politics and devastating armaments have made sovereign, fragmented nations and empires untenable.

Because of the persistence of the concept of Manifest Destiny and the consequent flirtation with imperialism at the turn of the century, the United States did not escape the wildfire. With the advent of World War I, writers allowed German hordes to occupy the continental United States. Cleveland Moffett's *The Conquest of America* [1-67], serialized in *McClure's Magazine,* typifies the response; he used Thomas A. Edison by name as the inventor who turned the tide. In that Edison was a member of a special board appointed to overcome the crisis, Moffett reflects the probable influence of Frank Stockton's *The Great War Syndicate* [1-88], in which appointed businessmen lead the United States to victory over Britain.

From the first, American treatments of the motif had a distinctive quality that grew out of its own dreams and nightmares. As early as 1880, in *Last Days of the Republic* [1-30], P. W. Dooner had warned of an "impending catastrophe" resulting from the importation into California of cheap coolie labor. Because the Chinese keep together even when their number increases and because they remain loyal to their homeland, China eventually conquers the United States. The theme of "the yellow peril"[18]—this time Japanese—recurred in such novels as J. U. Giesy's *All for His Country* (1915), in which a Mexican-Japanese invasion is beaten back only after the invention of an "aero destroyer," and in Hector C. Bywater's essaylike tome, *The Great Pacific War: A History of the American-Japanese Campaign of 1931–33* (1925), which is often cataloged by libraries as nonfiction. It persisted in Gawain Edwards's *The Earth Tube* (1929), in which nameless "Mongol" legions stalk across both American continents, and during the 1930s found a haven in such pulp magazines as *Dusty Ayres and His Battle Birds* and *Operator #5,* whose heroes thwarted every effort of Asiatic hordes to ravage the United States. The obsession with the yellow peril had also gained expression as early as a three-part, "factual" prediction in *Cosmopolitan* (1908), "If War Should Come," whose author, Captain Pierson Hobson, identified as "one of the greatest living experts in the sciences of war,"[19] described a sneak attack on Hawaii. One infers that this body of popular literature made conflict with Japan inevitable. Certainly it contributed to the imprisonment of Nisei Americans during World War II; one wonders how a continued portrayal of rampaging Asiatic armies would have influenced the public reaction toward Vietnam.

The second American variation found expression as early as Stanley Waterloo's *Armageddon* (1898). American scientists develop a dirigible-like craft to defeat a European coalition and promise to keep up the good work until they invent a weapon "so terrible" that fear of it will bring all war to an end. American politicians form an Anglo-Saxon alliance with Great Britain and decree that their councils will direct the affairs of the world, perhaps for generations, until the "lesser breeds" are capable of governing themselves. One can catalog the permutations of these themes: Benjamin Rush Davenport's *Anglo-Saxons Onward* (1898), Simon Newcomb's *His Wisdom: The Defender* (1900), Hollis Godfrey's *The Man Who Ended War* (1908), Roy Norton's *The Vanishing Fleets* (1908), and J. Stewart Barney's *L.P.M.: The End of the Great War* [1-6].

In *The Vanishing Fleets,* Norton permits a recalcitrant Kaiser to become part of an Anglo-Saxon triumvirate, but only after he has repented his ways following internment in a lumber camp in the Pacific Northwest, where he glimpses intuitively those higher truths that should govern humanity. At the other end of the limited spectrum, in *L.P.M.: The End of the Great War* [1-6], Barney's protagonist, the American scientist Edestone, first defeats all the warring nations with his advanced weapons and then calls for an authoritarian world government to be ruled by "the Aristocracy of Intelligence," presumably made up of businessmen and scientists. Only in Arthur Cheyney Train and Robert Williams Wood's *The*

Man Who Rocked the Earth [1-91], serialized in the *Saturday Evening Post* in the autumn of 1914, does a conference of nations assemble in Washington to abolish war and form a federated, utopian world state. However racist and jingoistic this concept of alliances and conferences may seem more than 70 years later, one wonders what influence, if any, it may have had on Henry Ford's peace mission or the thinking of President Wilson.

While some writers celebrated their nationalism and the new technology in the future war motif, others gave new vitality to the established imaginary voyage and created the second dominant motif of the period. Before one reaches H. Rider Haggard and the lost-race novel, however, one must confront the problem of Jules Verne. In Britain, as early as 1877, he gained a devoted following because he presented "to the public, in a series of fantastic romances and marvelous travels, the results of the wonderful discoveries and theories of modern men of science."[20] The prefatory "In Memoriam" to the posthumous collection of W. H. Rhodes's short stories, *Caxton's Book* [1-78], suggests that had Rhodes been able to devote himself more to his fiction than to the practice of law, even by the late 1860s "the great master of scientific fiction, Jules Verne, would have found the field of his efforts already sown and reaped." For some persons, like the American editor Hugo Gernsback, who emphasize the prophetic nature of SF—especially its accuracy in extrapolating technological achievement—Verne became the founder of a new field of fiction, SF. Even after Gernsback lost control of *Amazing Stories*, a sketch of "Jules Verne's Tombstone at Amiens Portraying His Immortality" graced the masthead of the magazine.

By the early 1860s Verne had written a number of comedies and comic operettas for various theaters in Paris, as well as a few short stories. In 1862 he wanted to complete a factual article dealing with African exploration, incorporating into it the idea that the use of a balloon would make such a venture easier. The publisher, Pierre Hetzel, asked that he change the article into fiction; apparently, too, it was Hetzel who spoke of an adventure story based on scientific fact. The result was *Cinq semaines en ballon* (1863; published in the United States as *Five Weeks in a Balloon*, 1869), the first of *Les Voyages extraordinaires*. Its protagonist, Dr. Samuel Ferguson, an English explorer, becomes the source of vast amounts of information as he and his companions drift from Zanzibar across the interior of Africa, sighting Lake Victoria. Ferguson declares the lake to be the source of the Nile (in the same year John Speke confirmed that observation). The narrative establishes the basic conventions Verne employed throughout his fiction: a man of reason (a scientist) both invents the necessary gadgetry and provides an abundance of factual information; a journey to some exotic destination provides the narrative frame, while a series of largely disconnected episodes, usually involving the threat of pursuit and capture, makes up the story.

By 1864 Hetzel had launched a new magazine for younger readers—*Magasin d'éducation et de récréation*—and in the initial March issue there appeared the first installment of Verne's second story, *Les Aventures du Capitaine Hatteras* (*The Adventures of Captain Hatteras* [1-92], published in book form in 1867), whose explorers find the elusive North Pole at the cost of Hatteras's sanity. It was not issued in book form until after the success of *Voyage au centre de la terre* (*A Journey to the Center of the Earth*, 1864 [1-94]) and *De la terre à la lune* (*From the Earth to the Moon*, 1865 [1-93]). In the former he relied on the theory that volcanoes are joined by subterranean passages permitting them to be fed from some fiery source within the Earth. His "gadget" was the so-called Ruhmkorff coil, for which the German physicist Heinrich Ruhmkorff received a cash award in the same year that Verne wrote the story. One can certainly call it a rudimentary form of the flashlight, but at that time such an application of electricity was unknown to the public. (As with so many of his contemporaries, electricity fascinated Verne; he relied on it again and again.) He also displayed the nineteenth-century fascination with geology, for as his explorers go deeper into the Earth, they find relics of the prehistoric past, ranging from the bones of extinct animals and men to the sight of a gigantic manlike creature acting as a shepherd of a herd of mastodons. In this way Verne dramatized, to some extent at least, the highly controversial theory of evolution.

In *From the Earth to the Moon* he spends much of the narrative developing a cannon capable of firing a projectile at a velocity of seven miles per second—that is, escape velocity. He later defended his practice while condemning Wells's use of a metal negating the power of gravity. In the second part of the novel, *Autour de la lune* (*Round the Moon*, 1870 [1-93]), the projectile orbits the Moon because it is deflected by a comet; it returns to Earth and splashes down in the Pacific, where its voyagers, not unlike modern astronauts, are picked up by a U.S. naval vessel. Published in the same year, *Vingt milles lieues sous les mers* (*Twenty Thousand Leagues under the Sea*, 1870 [1-95]) undoubtedly remains his best-known and most popular *voyage extraordinaire*. It features his most notable protagonist, Captain Nemo, that self-willed outcast of society who loves freedom and hates despotism and at least echoes the earlier gothic heroes. The novel remains a veritable encyclopedia of oceanography, a kind of underwater travelogue ranging from the sunken Atlantis to shipwrecks and Spanish bullion, from descriptions of underwater life to the fierce encounter with the giant squid. He named the *Nautilus* for the submarine Robert Fulton built in France under the sponsorship of Napoleon I.

When one examines Verne's major work closely, a single question looms ever larger: in what way was Verne so original that he earned the reputation of founding a new form of fiction? He himself never claimed that he had done so. One notices that he made use of knowledge available to the scientific community of his period—and to anyone else who bothered to look it up—and that he relied on a narrative frame long available and frequently used. He gave enthusiastic voice to the obvious accomplishments of the new technology, although like most of his contemporaries he does not seem to appreciate the full implications of the science giving rise to that technology. To say these things does not detract from the vividness of his imagination or the impact of his ability as a storyteller. It does ask, however, in what way he differed from his contemporary writers: how was he unique? As Everett Carter reminded his readers in *Howells and the Age of Realism*, the scientist—that is, medical men, engineers, inventors, machinists, archaeologists, and even students of such exotic subjects as the occult and Egyptology—became protagonists of popular fiction in the last decades of the nineteenth century.[21] Except for his encyclopedic presentation of the "latest" facts—and, perhaps, his impressionable young audience, although research indicates that adults read his books as frequently as did children—one cannot immediately perceive what distinguishes Verne from the many other authors who made use of the imaginary voyage framework.

For example, James De Mille's *A Strange Manuscript Found in a Copper Cylinder*

[1-28] echoes Symmes and Poe, for an unknown culture survives in the Antarctic, and a group of educated Englishmen aboard a becalmed yacht rescue from the sea a manuscript giving an account of a marooned sailor's experience among the people. Three times they interrupt the narrative of the sailor—"Thomas More"—to speculate about the feasibility of its contents. By this means De Mille introduces a variety of scientific and technical data from the period as the Englishmen debate the story's validity. The resulting fusion of known fact and imagination makes the novel one of the most effective of its kind; indeed, the technique makes De Mille's novel unique.

Other voyagers had long found enchanting cities and countries that provided them with a means of criticizing their own societies. By the end of the century many writers employing the imaginary voyage framework championed a neoprimitivism, condemning the new urban-industrial society. In Albert Bigelow Paine's *The Great White Way* (1901), an American expedition finds a people in Antarctica who live in close harmony with nature in a valley so beautiful that the narrator calls it "the land of heart's desire." The people have developed the power of telepathy. The young technologist chooses to marry the queen of this agrarian society instead of returning to the outer world. In Henry Drayton's *In Oudemon* (1901), the narrator stumbles across a group of British colonists in the mountains of South America; they possess an advanced technology of a sort and have access to the outer world, but they, too, choose to deny the materialism of the Western world. As with the future war motif, one could catalog titles.

One writer—Sir H. Rider Haggard—gave the lost-race motif its lasting, most popular form. After writing *King Solomon's Mines* [1-45], a panorama of Africa drawing on his personal knowledge of the land, Haggard created *She: A History of Adventure* [1-46] and *Allan Quatermain* [1-44]. In *She* his explorers reach the Valley of Kor in the unknown heart of the continent, where they find descendants of a lost colony of Egyptians living near the ruins of a once-great city. They are ruled by Ayesha—"She-Who-Must-Be-Obeyed." Given immortality by the Flame of Life, she languishes impatiently, awaiting the reincarnation of her beloved Kallikrates, who lives again in Haggard's protagonist, Leo Vincent. Her accidental death cuts short their renewed love. *Allan Quatermain* changes that, for the protagonist takes as his wife the lovely queen of the sun-worshipping Zu-Vendris, Nyleptha, who bears him a son—"a regular curley-haired, blue-eyed young Englishman in looks . . . destined to inherit the throne of the Zu-Vendris." In short, Haggard created a form that focused on a love story of a modern Western man for a primitive beauty, a pagan princess so beautiful that "language fails me when I try to give some idea of the blaze of loveliness [possessed by Nyleptha and her sister]." He was immediately parodied and endlessly imitated. Only Bellamy's *Looking Backward* [1-8] drew a greater literary response; there was, however, a difference, because after a few parodies, other novelists followed Haggard's basic plot, as late as James Hilton's *Lost Horizon* [2-43]. If the future war motif played out the fantasies of Western nationalism, then the lost-race motif played on one of the fantasies emerging in part, at least, during the high tide of imperialism: the fascination of the British/American man for the non-European woman.[22]

Haggard's imitators did not confine themselves to terrestrial voyages. Between Percy Greg's *Across the Zodiac* (1880) and Garrett P. Serviss's *A Columbus of Space* (1911), the interplanetary voyage had become the province of those mystics, like the Theosophists under Madame Blavatsky, who seized on the concept of parallel evolution advanced by John Fiske in *Outline of Cosmic Philosophy* (1874) to resolve the differences between traditional religion and Darwinian theory. For them Mars became heaven, as in Louis P. Gratacap's *The Certainty of a Future Life on Mars* (1903) and Mark Wicks's *To Mars Via the Moon* (1911). Both books express the divided interests of their authors in that the early chapters of each read like an astronomy text, while mysticism dominates after the protagonists encounter Martians who are reincarnations of the voyagers' friends and relatives. For such writers Mars is heaven, one of the chain of worlds leading eventually to a spiritual unity with the godhead. Although in a prefatory note to *Journey to Mars* [1-76], Gustavus W. Pope insisted that no matter what world serves as its home, "Humanity, created in the Image of God, must always and necessarily be the same in Esse," he allows his protagonist, an audacious American naval officer, to marry a Martian princess in *Wonderful Adventures on Venus* (1895). Despite his emphasis of the love story, Pope defended the scientific romance as a distinct type of fiction; he apparently planned to write a series of novels, using a different planet of the solar system as the setting for each one. A decade later, in *Lieut. Gullivar Jones: His Vacation* (1905), Edwin L. Arnold sends his naval officer to Mars on a flying carpet; there, in a pastoral kingdom, Princess Heru wants him to be her husband. He stays with her until her kingdom is threatened by barbarians; just before its destruction he returns by carpet to Earth, where he gains promotion and marries his faithful fiancée. Although a number of details, including the title, suggest that Arnold intended the book as a parody, a few critics, especially Richard Lupoff, believe that Arnold influenced Edgar Rice Burroughs's "Under the Moons of Mars" (1912), published in book form as *A Princess of Mars* [1-17].

What Rider Haggard was to one generation, Burroughs was to the next. Perhaps the most obvious distinction between them lies in Haggard's reliance on his personal experience and his desire for verisimilitude, whereas Burroughs created imaginary worlds, even his unexplored Africa. Erling B. Holtsmark has shown that Burroughs's protagonists—from John Carter, Warlord of Mars, and Tarzan of the Apes [1-18] to the least of them—echo the heroes of classical myth.[23] In so doing, he has not emphasized that throughout Burroughs's fiction an implicit neoprimitivism rejects early twentieth-century society because somehow its industrial urbanization and its effete code of manners—particularly those of the European aristocracy, though not exclusively so—have deprived the male of some aspect of a masculinity looking back to those times when he roamed as a warrior-hunter and supposedly through his physical prowess and cunning controlled his destiny. Both men established the erotic code for the popular fiction of their generations. Whereas Haggard always focused on the ambiguous mysteries of such an exotic woman as Ayesha, Burroughs used the desire for a woman to fulfill male fantasies of a heightened masculinity by making his stories an endless series of captures/kidnappings, separations, and rescues. The promise—without explicit fulfillment—lies at the heart of the eroticism in his fiction.

With the notable exception of Jane Porter of Baltimore, Tarzan's mate, Burroughs's principal women reign in some jungle world or on another planet, be it Barsoom (Mars) or Amtor (Venus). In the Tarzan stories, in fact, Jane is replaced by such lovely barbarians as La, priestess of Opar, lost colony of Atlantis, or half-mad Nemone, queen of the City of Gold. They fall in love with the protagonist at first sight. With the exception of the sometimes indifferent Tarzan, Burroughs's protagonists are gallant and devoted lovers (their code of conduct often seems as formal and prissy as anything in the Victorian/American world of the early twentieth century); nevertheless, Burroughs's primitive beauties—"this half-naked little savage"; "this beautiful animal"—are reduced to sex objects, although no one—villain or hero—does more than abduct/rescue and desire/adore them.

In Burroughs's first published work, *A Princess of Mars,* to escape death at the hands of Apaches, John Carter literally wishes himself to Mars, where Dejah Thoris awaits his love. In *At the Earth's Core* [1-15], David Innes finds Dian the Beautiful in Pellucidar, that strangely prehistoric world within the Earth which shares the polar openings of "Symmes Hole." Whether or not from a sense of American Manifest Destiny,[24] he attempts to unite that vast jungle into federated states. Carson Napier journeys to another world by mistake in *Pirates of Venus* [1-16] to reach Duare, princess of Vepaja, though he is most often separated from her. *The Land That Time Forgot* [2-10]—that is, the island of Caspek in the Antarctic—focuses on the love of a young American for a cave girl. *The Moon Maid* [2-11] begins a trilogy in which the first spaceship (*The Barsoom*) finds a Symmesian world within the hollow Moon, where warring peoples plan the eventual devastation of Earth. Burroughs's intolerance of the yellow lunar race negates his sympathy for the American Indian. While establishing the time period as 1967, he declared that the 1914 war in his imaginary world "terminated in the absolute domination of the Anglo-Saxon race over all the other races of the world." Nonetheless, the story attempts to bring the protagonist and the beloved Nah-ee-lah together. *The Monster Men* (1929) reworks the Frankenstein theme in that its scientists try to create people chemically. Fortunately for the American heroine, her lover—Number 13—is not a monster but an amnesiac.

With good reason many critics have called Burroughs a one-plot author; Holtsmark notices that by the late 1930s, the "narrative formula [had been] worked to exhaustion."[25] From the first his stories served as a kind of proving ground for his protagonists' masculinity—survival in an exotic yet hostile environment; physical victory over sundry opponents; and the devotion of a sensuous and primitive woman (as someone said, Jane goes ape very readily). Granting the formulaic pattern—caused, in part at least, by the demands of the mass market pulps—one must acknowledge that he freed the lost race/imaginary world novel from outdated themes. Perhaps the most significant characteristic of his fiction is the way in which he adapted all of the conventions coming to him from the nineteenth century to his own ends. By stripping away the dead thematic wood, so to speak, he focused on the actions of a series of heroes, carefully placing them on the epic stages of imagined worlds, where they could escape the limitations of modern civilization.

Others had tried to do the same. During the nineteenth century the discoveries in archaeology dwarfed the legendary Kingdom of Prester John or the lost cities of Cibola and El Dorado. In terms drawn from the new sciences the period revitalized the myth of a golden age. For popular, "latest" authority the writers turned to *Atlantis: The Antediluvian World* (1882) by Ignatius Donnelly. The concept of a lost, central homeland proved indispensable to the theory of diffusion, the only possible way, so theorized many experts, to explain the similarities between the Mayans and the ancient Egyptians. They had to be *colonies* of a mother-land, wherever that might lie. Such theorizing reinforced the lost-race motif, but it also raised the continent of Atlantis—from Cutcliffe Hyne's *The Lost Continent* [1-52] to Arthur Conan Doyle's *The Maracot Deep* [2-28]. A variety of writers peo-pled pre-Columbian America with vast empires, although many of them tied themselves to a rapidly dating mysticism, as in the instance of Froma Eunice Wait's *Yermah the Dorado* (1897).

Doyle created the classic tale of the survival of a remnant from prehistory in *The Lost World* [1-31]. Still others wrote of the caveman himself, for geology and an emerging paleontology had created a new myth—the "missing link"—which fascinated the popular imagination. Both Stanley Waterloo's *The Story of Ab* [1-97] and Jack London's *Before Adam* [1-58] dramatize that moment when a single individual, possessing a higher intelligence because of the size of its brain—a theory the sciences of the period insisted on—transformed the beast into the first human. Their protagonists learned the use of fire, clothing, boats, and weapons, and they felt the first emotions of brotherhood and love (not animal lust) as they began the climb toward modern man. Waterloo gave the theme its most original treatment in *A Son of the Ages* [1-96] when by combining the conventions of racial memory and reincarnation, he took his hero through a number of lives. All of these tales have survived into contemporary fiction, as exemplified by William Golding's *The Inheritors* (1962) and the "Atlan" novels of Jane Gaskell, but in SF they have undergone a number of permutations. Perhaps the influence of Rob-ert E. Howard was most important; following the lead of Burroughs toward imaginary worlds, he placed his "Hyperborian world" somewhere/sometime in prehistory after Atlantis, thereby liberating himself and his successors from in-herited conventions. The various motifs—from lost race to Atlantis itself—have fused together in what is now the "sword-and-sorcery" portion of SF or fantasy, as the individual critic/reader decides.

Contemporary critics look back at what some of them—unfortunately, per-haps—still call the "prehistory" of SF and insist that the main thrust of the field has always concentrated on scientists and their achievements, whether the event itself or its effects. As previously noted, in all their guises, scientists became he-roes of popular fiction in the last decades of the nineteenth century, more so in the United States than in Britain or France. (One notices in the future war motif, for example, that European writers made use of the new "hardware," but they did not give as much emphasis to the inventor as did Americans.) An explanation of the difference may lie in America's increasing infatuation with the machine. British writers had long shown an ambivalence toward the machine; Richard Jeffries had already destroyed industrial Britain in *After London* [1-53], while the protagonists of W. H. Hudson's *A Crystal Age* [1-51] and William Morris's *News from Nowhere* [1-69] dream of a pastoral England that has rejected industrializa-tion. In *The Napoleon of Notting Hill* [1-23], G. K. Chesterton projected his pasto-ral scene a century into the future and specifically attacked Wells.

In contrast, advanced technology played a key part in many American visions of utopia, such as Chauncey Tinker's *The Crystal Button* (1891). More impor-tantly, by the 1890s boy inventors proliferated, the most important being Frank Reade, Jr. He was followed by Tom Swift and made individual appearances in such weeklies as *Pluck and Luck* and as late as Richard B. Montgomery's *A Sheet of*

Blotting Paper; or, The Adventures of a Young Inventor (August 2, 1916). An amusing blending of motifs resulted, for the youths produced a dazzling variety of vehicles to transport them to exotic parts of the Earth, many of which had not been explored by the turn of the century. At one end of the spectrum the protagonists of Charles E. Bolton's posthumous *The Harris-Ingram Experiment* (1905) not only developed the finest electrically run steel mill in the world, but they also built a utopian community shared by workers and managers. At the other end, Hugo Gernsback had enshrined the scientist as a hero of the state in *Ralph 124C41 +* [1-37]. During the period of World War I probably the most popular scientist in the United States was Craig Kennedy, "the scientific detective" created by Arthur B. Reeve [1-77]; from 1910 until late in 1915 (with the single exception of November 1912) his exploits inside the laboratory and out graced the pages of *Cosmopolitan* and were collected in book form as late as 1926. It seems safe to say that in the United States at that time a scientist could do no wrong—unless, of course, he was a "mad," villainous descendant of Dr. Frankenstein, whose schemes threatened the balance of civilization. (Almost always not an American, such a figure had appeared in the weeklies as early as the 1890s to thwart the boy prodigies, but he did not move toward center stage until after World War I.)

Unlike Craig Kennedy, Doyle's Professor George Challenger seems to confront the establishment rather than to ease its way with new inventions. In *The Lost World* [1-31] he leads an expedition into the interior of Venezuela to prove to the members of the Zoological Institute that prehistoric creatures still live on Earth. In *The Poison Belt* [1-32], he reminds readers of the *Times* that the Earth floats "towards some unknown end, some squalid catastrophe which will overwhelm us at the ultimate confines of space" and suggests that the world may be entering a strange belt of ether. He is denounced. But the world does undergo a "death" for 28 hours and then awakens from a cataleptic trance caused by the changed atmosphere. After Doyle's traumatic reaction to his son's death during the war, Challenger becomes more passive in *The Land of Mist* [2-27], a denunciation of materialism and an expression of pathetic hope in life after death.

The voice that endures from the period before World War I is that of H. G. Wells, but he, more than any other writer in SF, questioned the comfortable presumptions of the Victorian and Edwardian periods. Repeatedly he dramatized the precariousness of humanity's very existence amid universal flux and change, of which even science had only partial knowledge. Mark Hillegas quite rightly has identified him as the principal literary source of the dystopian mood that gained prominence after World War I in Europe and after World War II in the United States.[26] On the one hand, his story "The Star" [1-102] permits the Earth to survive a cosmic catastrophe and gives humanity a chance to rebuild, calling attention to the spirit of brotherhood following the ordeal. On the other hand, "The Sea Raiders" (1896) reports the appearance of *Haploteuthis ferox* in the English Channel in order to symbolize "the violence of a changeable nature and the complacency with which man views his immutable world."[27] *The Time Machine* [1-103] climaxes with the vision of a dying world where only dark shapes scuttle across the beach of a tideless ocean. So much attention has been given the Eloi and Morlocks during that passing moment—the year 802,701—that too many critics read the novel solely as a statement of the inevitable fate of Western industrial society—the evolution of humanity into two distinct species. This Marxian projection is but one of the dichotomies of the period that the Eloi and Morlocks may suggest. *The Island of Dr. Moreau* [1-100], in which Moreau transforms various animals into the Beast People, may be read at the level of the Frankenstein myth, but Robert Philmus teases the imagination with his assertion that it is a symbolic reinstatement of God into "the tortuous process of evolution"—that is, "God becomes Moreau, a vivisectionist insensitive beyond all humanity to the pain of his creatures" who are "irrational creature[s] motivated by fear and desire."[28] *The War of the Worlds* [1-105]—written at the height of the popularity of the future war motif—suggests to its narrator that "our views of the human future must be greatly modified by these events. We have learned now that we cannot regard this planet as being fenced in and a secure abiding place."

Repeatedly Wells sounded the same basic warning, but his contemporaries did not heed it, caught up as they were in their fevers of imperialism and outrage, demanding social reforms that did not address the issues Wells raised. Wells may have had too profound an insight; the implications regarding the future may have slipped past his readers who knew Verne and Haggard as well as, if not better than, they knew him. One infers that the events of the twentieth century had to take place before the stature of his early romances could be fully appreciated. Although neither Wells nor the narrator of *The Time Machine* shares the metaphysical background and stance of Camus, the narrator concludes: the traveler "saw in the growing pile of civilization only a foolish heaping that must inevitably fall back upon and destroy its makers in the end. If that is so, it remains for us to live as though it were not so." One can read into that assertion the courage to face the absurd.

As the new century brought the old establishment to a fiery end at Passenchendale, Verdun, and the Somme, the parameters of SF had been marked out by Verne, Wells, Haggard, and Burroughs—from the adulation of the inventor and his gadgetry, whether used in peace or war, to a love story in an exotic, primitive setting. During the last decades of the nineteenth century and the first years of the twentieth, science fiction had grown into a widely popular literary form. Perhaps not always immediately apparent, the roots of the dystopian mood were already present. In 1922 Evgenii Zamiatin praised Wells highly in a brief study, *Herbert Wells;* in 1924 the English-language edition of Zamiatin's novel *We* [2-147] was published in the United States by Dutton. Its portrayal of the United State in the twenty-sixth century, a glass-enclosed city-state inhabited by those who survived a great war and are kept regimented and separate from the irrational, "ugly" natural world, is obviously an attack not only on Soviet Russia of the day but on all technocratic states. With *We,* utopia died. Aldous Huxley and George Orwell merely added hymns of anger and despair.

Ironically, the English-language edition—the only edition—of *We* appeared two years before American SF was relegated, by and large, to the pulp specialist magazines until after World War II. To dismiss its writers of that period as bland optimists is to misread them. To some extent they did express the enduring optimism in their own terms, but they also raised their own questions, and in the privacy of the specialist magazines—so to speak—those who cared for the field made even more complex a literary form that may well have become the vehicle most able to inform readers about themselves, their technical societies, and the awesome universe vast about them.

Notes

1. Most of these earlier works are likely to be of less interest to this guide's audience—Ed.
2. Marjorie Hope Nicolson, *Voyages to the Moon* (Macmillan, 1948), p. 265.
3. Ibid., pp. 265–266.
4. Ibid., p. 159.
5. J. O. Bailey, *Pilgrims through Space and Time* (Argus, 1947), p. 45.
6. Nicolson, *Voyages to the Moon*, p. 94.
7. P. Clarke, "Symmes Theory of the Earth," *The Atlantic Monthly* 31 (1873): 471–480; and John Weld Peck, "Symmes Theory," *Ohio Archaeological and Historical Society Publications* 18 (1909): 29–142.
8. I. F. Clarke, *The Pattern of Expectation: 1644–2001* (Basic Books, 1979), p. 16.
9. Ibid., pp. 23–24.
10. J. O. Bailey, as cited by Thomas D. Clareson, *A Spectrum of Worlds* (Doubleday, 1972), p. 13.
11. Brian W. Aldiss, *Billion Year Spree* (Doubleday, 1973), pp. 18, 19.
12. I. F. Clarke, *The Pattern of Expectation*, p. 43.
13. Ford Madox Ford, *Henry James: A Critical Study* (London: 1913), p. 225.
14. Robert Philmus, *Into the Unknown* (Univ. of California Press, 1970), p. 90.
15. I. F. Clarke, *Voices Prophesying War: 1763–1984* (Oxford, 1966), p. 67.
16. Ibid., p. 148.
17. Ibid., pp. 120–121, 127.
18. Brian Stableford, "The Yellow Danger," in Frank Magill, ed. *Survey of Science Fiction Literature* (Salem Press, 1979), vol. 5, p. 2527.
19. Hobson Pierson, "If War Should Come," *Cosmopolitan* 45 (June 1908): 38.
20. *Men of Mark* (London: 1877). Verne is number 24.
21. Everett Carter, *Howells and the Age of Realism* (Lippincott, 1950), pp. 92–93.
22. This phrasing seems appropriate. With the exception of Pierre Benoit's *L'Atlantide* (1919; English-language edition, 1920), dealing with the French in the Sahara, one cannot recall a title published before World War I written by any but a British or American author. That fact may in itself give insight into the cultures. The pattern within the motif becomes amusingly complex; if the woman's people could in any way have contributed to the bloodstream of northern Europe, the protagonist may stay with her as her husband; if not, she usually commits suicide before the end of the narrative. The only exception to the pattern that comes to mind is Frank Aubrey's *The Devil-Tree of El Dorado* (1896). The term "non-European" should not be read as a euphemism. It applies to Polynesians, Asians, Africans, and Amerinds. As might be imagined, few novels in the motif discussed explicitly the problems of race or women's rights. See Thomas D. Clareson, *Some Kind of Paradise* (Greenwood, 1985), especially Chapter 6.
23. Erling B. Holtsmark, *Tarzan and Tradition* (Greenwood, 1981) and *Edgar Rice Burroughs* (Twayne, 1986, TUSAS 499).
24. Holtsmark, *Edgar Rice Burroughs*, p. 81.
25. Ibid., pp. 76–77.
26. Mark Hillegas, *The Future as Nightmare* (Oxford, 1967), p. 4.
27. Clareson, *A Spectrum of Worlds*, p. 60.
28. Philmus, *Into the Unknown*, p. 17.

Bibliography

1-1. Abbott, Edwin A. (as A Square) (U.K.). **Flatland: A Romance of Many Dimensions.** Seeley, 1884.
The narrator, citizen of a two-dimensional world, uses the land for some satire, especially of education and women. He briefly envisions a one-dimensional world (Lineland) where motion is impossible. A three-dimensional man (Sphere) intrudes into the plane of Flatland, thereby giving knowledge of Spaceland. The two speculate about a world of four dimensions. The book becomes a mathematician's delight, an exercise in the limits of perception. Compare the ingenious speculations in A. K. Dewdney's *The Planiverse* [4-171].

1-2. Anonymous (U.K.). **The Reign of George VI, 1900–1925.** Nicholl, 1763. Charles Oman, ed. Rivingtons, 1899.
I. F. Clarke suggests that this first "future history" provided a working model illustrating the political theories of Bolingbroke. Unlike typical SF it neither portrays nor advocates change, but simply projects Britain's eighteenth-century political problems into the twentieth century. The story has value as an expression of wish fulfillment and as an example of the themes that will grow from *The Battle of Dorking* [1-21].

1-3. Astor, John Jacob. **A Journey in Other Worlds.** Appleton, 1894.
After vivid descriptions of a utopian Earth in A.D. 2000, the narrative shifts to voyages to Jupiter and Saturn. The travelers explore prehistoric Jupiter and hunt its game. Mysticism dominates the stop at Saturn. The novel affirms Fiske's concept of parallel evolution. Astor borrows the antigravity force "apergy" from Greg's *Across the Zodiac* [1-40].

1-4. Atterley, Joseph (pseud. of George Tucker). **A Voyage to the Moon: With Some Account of the Manners and Customs, Science and Philosophy of the People of Morosophia, and Other Lunarians.** Elam Bliss, 1827.
In this initial American interplanetary journey, Atterley's ship is the first to use an antigravity coating. He includes the discussion of more scientific data for its own sake than did his British predecessors. After visits to Morosophia (whose inhabitants are trying to perfect an internal combustion engine) and to utopian Okalbia, the voyagers return to Earth. Atterley was dean of the faculty at the University of Virginia when Poe was a student there; a reference in "Hans Pfaall" [1-75] indicates that his writing influenced Poe to some extent.

1-5. Aubrey, Frank (pseud. of Frank Atkins) (U.K.). **A Queen of Atlantis: A Romance of the Caribbean Sea.** Hutchinson, 1899.
Abandoned in the Sargasso Sea, two young boys and a girl find an island that they name Atlantis. Threatened by giant cuttlefish and warring factions of a primitive people, they befriend a faerielike race of "flower dwellers" who are descendants of Atlantis. In *King of the Dead: A Weird Romance* (1903) the remnant of a *white* race that ruled all the Americas when Egypt was at her fullest glory fails in an attempt to resurrect the dead of untold generations in order to regain their

lost empire. In *The Devil-Tree of El Dorado* (1896), youthful explorers find a lost city in Venezuela on Mount Raraima, the same site Conan Doyle was to use in *The Lost World* [1-31]. One youth remains behind when his friends return to civilization; he marries the princess Uluma. As Fenton Ash, Atkins wrote *A Trip to Mars* (1909), in which two boys are taken to a Mars where various nations are fighting. In Nicholls's *The Science Fiction Encyclopedia* [8-30], John Eggeling points out that this "wartorn" Mars precedes Burroughs's use of the idea in *A Princess of Mars* [1-17].

1-6. Barney, J(ohn) Stewart. **L.P.M.: The End of the Great War.** Putnam, 1915.
An American scientist, Edestone, defeats all warring nations and calls for an authoritarian world government to be ruled by "the Aristocracy of Intelligence." He goes beyond the advocacy of Anglo-Saxon supremacy, a favorite theme of the period, to denounce "majority rule, equality of man, and perpetual peace through brotherly love"; he asserts that government should be organized and administered like "the great corporations of America." The novel is unique, at least in American fiction, because of the extreme position Edestone takes. For other fictional portraits of Thomas Edison, see Serviss's *Edison's Conquest of Mars* [1-82]. Compare Wells's *A Modern Utopia* [1-101] for a different view of a special ruling class.

1-7. Bellamy, Edward. **Equality.** Appleton, 1897.
This sequel to *Looking Backward* [1-8] served as a rebuttal to Bellamy's critics. It argues that economic equality is the cornerstone on which the complete life of an industrial democracy rests—political, intellectual, ethical. Although it emphasizes the place of religion in the world of A.D. 2000, society needs no organized church or ordained ministry. Despite the thread of a love story, this is more an essay than a novel. In *The Blindman's World and Other Stories* (1898), "To Whom This May Come" describes a utopian society on a Pacific island whose people have mastered telepathy.

*1-8. Bellamy, Edward. **Looking Backward: A.D. 2000–1887.** Ticknor, 1888.
Without doubt the most famous of the American utopias, this was the progenitor of several hundred works, both in the United States and Europe, as individuals sided with Bellamy or attacked him. Science is incidental to the text, although technology has made the utopian state possible. The controversial issue centered on socialism. See Roemer's *The Obsolete Necessity* (1976) for the most detailed contemporary discussion of Bellamy and the United States in utopian literature at the end of the century. For very different treatments of socialism, see Morris's *News from Nowhere* [1-69], Donnelly's *Caesar's Column* [1-29], and London's *The Iron Heel* [1-59].

1-9. Benson, Robert Hugh (U.K.). **Lord of the World.** Pitman, 1907.
An ardent Catholic, Benson attacked the humanistic utopias of Wells and Bellamy. The narrative dramatizes the apocalyptic encounter between the Antichrist and the Catholic Church. Rome is razed by bombing, and the pope and his few remaining followers retreat to Palestine. The novel ends with an ambiguous vision that may be the Second Coming and the end of the world. Benson envisioned an

alternative future in a far less well known novel, *The Dawn of All* (1911), portraying a utopian society under papal rule. For a very different treatment of Catholicism in contemporary SF, see Silverberg's "Good News from the Vatican" (1971).

1-10. Beresford, John Davys (U.K.). **Goslings.** Heinemann, 1913. U.S. title: *A World of Women*, Macauley, 1913.
A plague sweeps from China through Russia to western Europe, almost wiping out the male population. The attempt of women to reorganize society obviously changes a number of conventions. Stableford regards *Goslings* as the first effort in British fiction to depict an all-female society seriously and sympathetically. The premise is cut short when the existence of an appreciable number of men is discovered; men and women together, with, it is hoped, better understanding of one another, will rebuild, a favorite British theme. Compare Gilman's *Herland* [1-38] and Lane's *Mizora* [1-56] for earlier treatments of feminist utopias; see Wylie's *The Disappearance* [3-408] for a more recent speculation.

*1-11. Beresford, John Davys (U.K.). **The Hampdenshire Wonder.** Sidgwick & Jackson, 1911. U.S. title: *The Wonder*, Doran, 1917.
Long celebrated as one of the earliest "superman" novels, the narrative tells of a boy whose mind is thousands of years in advance of his society. Adults regard him as little better than a macrocephalic idiot because of his silence. His chief enemy is the local vicar. His death leaves open the question of murder. Compare Stapledon's *Odd John* [2-110], Wylie's *Gladiator* [2-145], and van Vogt's *Slan* [3-383].

1-12. Bergerac, Cyrano Savinien de (France). **The Comical History of the States and Empires of the Worlds of the Moon and Sun.** Tr. by A. Lovell, 1687. The original authorized version was entitled *Histoire comique des états et empires de la lune,* 1656. The first English tr. was by Tho. St. Serf, 1659. Recommended tr. by Geoffrey Strachan, *Other Worlds,* Oxford, 1965.
Marjorie Hope Nicolson praises this book as the finest of the seventeenth-century "parodies" of the cosmic voyage, but also insists that it proved highly important to Swift [1-89]. Once on the Moon, the hero becomes the companion of Godwin's Domingo Gonsales [1-39] and witnesses conventional actions such as warfare. One high point comes when the lunarian "philosophers" debate whether he is a human being; another, when he is tried for "heresy" because he asserts the Earth is inhabited. Despite any element of parody, the narrative expresses Cyrano's scientific curiosity.

1-13. Bierce, Ambrose. **In the Midst of Life** (1891); **Can Such Things Be?; Works.** Neale Publishing, 1909–1911, vols. 2 and 3.
Bierce remains one of the most significant writers in the evolution of the ghost story to the psychological case study. His "Moxon's Master" is the closest to Poe's "Maelzel's Chess Player." The automaton in Bierce is a variation on the Frankenstein theme. "The Damned Thing" (1893) draws on biology and is his purest SF, notable for both its use of the Frankenstein theme and its narrative technique. "The Man and the Snake" is his most ironic dramatization of fear. Franklin discusses his importance to early SF in *Future Perfect* [1-36], as does Clareson in *Some Kind of Paradise* [9-24].

1-14. Bradshaw, William Richard. **The Goddess of Atvatabar.** Douthitt, 1892.
Arctic explorers discover a Symmesian world. Extravagant magic and mysticism
provide the background to the narrator's wooing of Queen Lyone. As king he
opens trade negotiations with the outside world. Julian Hawthorne's introduction denounces Zola and the literary naturalists, predicting that the future of literature lies with such romances as Bradshaw's.

Bulwer-Lytton, Edward. **The Coming Race** [see **1-61**].

*1-15. Burroughs, Edgar Rice. **At the Earth's Core.** McClurg, 1922.
First published in *All-Story* (1914), this novel introduces David Innes to the
Symmesian world of Pellucidar, where the first-person narrator searches the jungles for Dian the Beautiful. It is a Darwinian world where assorted beast-men
and animals—some dinosaurs—struggle for survival. Innes attempts to unify the
various tribes into a loose federation. At the end he returns to the surface without Dian. To gain credibility, Burroughs employs a framing device: an Englishman has found Innes's manuscript. Six novels make up the Pellucidar series.

1-16. Burroughs, Edgar Rice. **Pirates of Venus.** Burroughs, 1932.
Published in *Argosy* (1931), this novel takes Carson Napier, the weakest of Burroughs's major protagonists, to Venus (Amtor); his beloved is Duare, princess of
the treetop kingdom of Vepaja. The central action involves a fight against the
criminal Thor, who incited the workers to kill the ruling class (this attack on communism marks one of the few occasions when Burroughs commented explicitly
on contemporary affairs). Five novels make up the Venus series. He may have delayed using that planet because of the earlier novels of Otis Adelbert Kline.

*1-17. Burroughs, Edgar Rice. **A Princess of Mars.** McClurg, 1917.
Published under the pseudonym Norman Bean as "Under the Moons of Mars"
in *All-Story* (1912), *A Princess of Mars* introduces Burroughs's most epic adventure
and his finest imaginary world, Barsoom, a construct based loosely on Percival
Lowell's theories. Against a dying planet torn by strife, John Carter fights his way
across the deserts, gaining the friendship of such warriors as Tars Tarkas of
Thark and the love of the incomparable Dejah Thoris, princess of Helium. They
live happily for nine years until by accident Carter ends up on Earth at the cave
where he escapes marauding Apaches by willing himself to Mars. *The Gods of
Mars* (1918) and *The Warlord of Mars* (1919), both seeing magazine publication in
1914, complete the personal saga of Carter. Eight other novels follow the adventures of his family and friends. This first novel introduced the conventions Burroughs used throughout his various series, including some of the tales of Tarzan,
but no other series proved so effective. Permutations of Barsoom survive in the
worlds of "swords and sorcery" so popular in contemporary SF.

1-18. Burroughs, Edgar Rice. **Tarzan of the Apes.** McClurg, 1914.
Published in *All-Story* (October 1912) and serialized in the New York *Evening
World* before book publication, the novel emphasizes the boyhood and youth of
Tarzan, Lord Greystoke, Burroughs's most famous (and most macho) hero, the
only one to attain mythic proportions and become a part of worldwide popular
culture. Burroughs claimed that Tarzan combines the best of environments (unknown Africa) and the best of heredities (British aristocracy). Because D'Arnot is

his teacher, taking him to Paris, one cannot fail to compare him to Rousseau's *Émile* (1762), especially in terms of education, to contrast the eighteenth and twentieth centuries, both emphasizing the "natural man." Tarzan saves Jane Porter from an unwanted marriage, but does not wed her in this first novel. Because attention to Jane and Jack (Korak the Killer), the son of Tarzan, aged the apeman, his family was omitted from most of the later novels, while Tarzan roamed the jungles and veldt, always beloved by a conveniently available primitive beauty. One should compare the Africas and the love stories of Burroughs and H. Rider Haggard [1-46] to see the contrasts. For other treatments of Tarzan, one should consult Philip José Farmer's *Lord Tyger* (1970) and *Tarzan Alive* (1972), as well as Gene Wolfe's "Tarzan of the Grapes" (1972). Among the innumerable films are Bo Derek's feminist *Tarzan*—which attempts the story from Jane's point of view—and the neo-behaviorist *Tarzan: Lord Greystoke,* with its brilliant cinematography.

*1-19. Butler, Samuel (U.K.). **Erewhon; or, Over the Range.** Trubner, 1872; **Erewhon Revisited Twenty Years Later.** Richards, 1901. Desmond MacCarthy, ed. Dutton, 1965.

In New Zealand, the narrator, Higgs, finds an agrarian, utopian society that has destroyed its machines because of a fear that machines will supersede humanity. Those chapters entitled "The Book of the Machine" attack both Darwinian theory and the deist view that the Universe (and, by implication, humanity) is a mechanism set in motion and then abandoned by God. The central fear is that machines will undergo a mechanical evolution until they replace humanity. The Erewhonians abhorred dependence on machines and so destroyed theirs. Higgs escapes in a balloon. In *Erewhon Revisited,* Higgs's return is reported by his son, whose own visit makes up an epilogue. Higgs's escape triggered a new religion, Sunchildism. This fact leads to a satire of the clerical establishment, Christianity's origins, and the concept of the Second Coming. Compare the attitude toward machines and industrialization in W. H. Hudson [1-51], William Morris [1-69], E. M. Forster [1-35], and more recently Vonnegut's *Player Piano* [3-392].

1-20. Campanella, Tommaso (Italy). **City of the Sun.** Tr. of *Civitas Solis,* 1623. In *Ideal Commonwealths,* Kennikat, 1968.

A sea captain describes a communistic utopian community in central Asia ruled by a philosopher-king (Metaphysicus) aided by three magistrates—Power, Wisdom, and Love. Education focuses on mathematics, geology, geography, botany, and the mechanical arts. Eugenics determines the citizens' mating selections, and the physicians have a secret method of "renovating" life about the seventieth year. Campanella wrote *Civitas Solis* about 1602, when he was a prisoner of the Inquisition.

*1-21. Chesney, Sir George (Tomkyns) (U.K.). **The Battle of Dorking: Reminiscences of a Volunteer.** Blackwood, 1871.

Published anonymously in *Blackwood's* (May 1871), *The Battle of Dorking* laid the foundation of the future war motif. Clarke's *Voices Prophesying War* [9-27] gives the fullest account of its impact throughout Britain, Europe, and America. The 64-page pamphlet gained much of its effect from Chesney's choice of a participant-observer as narrator; he dramatizes the invasion by German forces in realistic detail. In part its success occurred because Germany had just crushed France in the first conflict fought *in* Western nations since the time of Napoleon I. While Bellamy's *Looking Backward* [1-8] could appeal to the dreams of idealists, Chesney spoke to the fears of a society that believed a catastrophic war was imminent and inevitable.

1-22. Chester, George Randolph. **The Jingo.** Bobbs-Merrill, 1912.
In a delightful spoof of the lost-race motif, the jingoistic Jimmy Smith, representative of the Eureka Manufacturing Company, brings "improvements" to the kingdom of Isola in the Antarctic. Even his love for the reigning princess is (gently) satirized. Isola becomes a loyal territorial republic waiting to be discovered by the United States. For satire of a more serious tone, see Cowan's earlier *Revi-Lona* [1-27].

1-23. Chesterton, G(ilbert) K(eith) (U.K.). **The Napoleon of Notting Hill.** J. Lane, 1904.
In his first novel Chesterton attacks the notion of progress and the superiority of the sciences, commenting on the inept prophecies of "H. G. Wells and others, who thought that science would take charge of the future." His London a century in the future is "almost exactly as it is now." His central theme insists that to avert disaster, society must return to local patriotism and the universal ideas of the Middle Ages.

*1-24. Childers, Erskine (U.K.). **The Riddle of the Sands: A Record of Secret Service Recently Achieved.** Smith, Elder, 1903.
In *Voices Prophesying War* [9-27], Clarke names Childers's novel "undoubtedly the best" since *The Battle of Dorking* [1-21]. Instead of another glimpse of clashing armies, Childers presents a work of detection. Realism of detail (plausibility) and characterization also set it apart from its contemporaries, as does the quality of Childers's style. He adopts the ruse of being the editor of a friend's manuscript. This book was republished in 1940 during another threat of invasion.

*1-25. Clemens, Samuel Langhorne (Mark Twain). **A Connecticut Yankee in King Arthur's Court.** Webster, 1889. Recommended ed. by Bernard L. Stein, Univ. of California, 1979.
Hank Morgan suffers a blow on the head and goes backward in time to Arthur's Camelot in the sixth century. Starting as a celebration of modern progress and a denunciation of both British aristocracy and the church-dominated society, Hank's efforts—as "the Boss"—to transform Arthurian Britain into a facsimile of the nineteenth century end in slaughter and death. The novel voices Twain's confusion and despair. It should be compared with de Camp's classic tale of time travel, *Lest Darkness Fall* [3-135], a return to the Rome of Augustus. Twain's shorter pieces were usefully collected and edited by David Ketterer in *The Science Fiction of Mark Twain* (Archon, 1984). The most important of the 15 stories is "The Great Dark," first published in 1962. It captures the dark side of Twain's imagination and his hatred of the concept of determinism. Edwards's nightmare voyage in a drop of water becomes symbolic of the absurdity of the universe. "The Curious Republic of Gondour" (1874) provides Twain's statement about utopias, while "From the 'London Times' of 1904" (1898) allows him to invent a

"gadget," the "telectroscope," and thus is his closest approach to early SF. Ketterer includes excerpts from *A Connecticut Yankee in King Arthur's Court.*

1-26. Colomb, Rear Admiral P(hilip Howard), and others (U.K.). **The Great War of 189-: A Forecast.** Heinemann, 1893.
Originally serialized in 1892 in the illustrated magazine *Black and White,* this forecast of imminent war, a collaboration of military men and journalists, attempted to calculate what the next conflict would be like. Many incidents were presented as though they were reports from the scene by news correspondents and officers. The novel closes with the warning that Germany has begun to rearm and that weaknesses in the British army have been glossed over.

1-27. Cowan, Frank. **Revi-Lona: A Romance of Love in a Marvelous Land.** Tribune Press, 188?; Arno, 1976.
Apparently privately printed, this narrative remains one of the most successful parodies of the lost-race motif, utopian societies, and exploration of the Antarctic. The first-person narrator discovers a society dominated by women and ruled by a council of 25, each of whom becomes his hostess and his mistress. The language and action are sexually explicit for the period. The father of many children by many women, he inadvertently brings about the destruction of the society and its principal city before a ship picks him up and returns him to the outside world. This should not be dismissed as a masculine fantasy but read as a commentary on the literature and society of the 1880s. Compare it with Gilman's *Herland* [1-38], Lane's *Mizora* [1-56], or Beresford's *Goslings* [1-10].

Cyrano de Bergerac, Savinien (France). **The Comical History of the States and Empires of the Worlds of the Moon and Sun** [see **1-12**].

*1-28. De Mille, James. **A Strange Manuscript Found in a Copper Cylinder.** Harper, 1888.
A shipwrecked sailor, Thomas More, who indicates that he has knowledge of previous "wild works of fiction about lands in the interior of the earth," proceeds to give a portrait of the Kosekin, a society antipodal to the outside world. To escape the stigma of such fictions, De Mille adopts a clever frame: in 1850, passengers aboard the becalmed yacht *Falcon,* property of Lord Featherstone, rescue More's manuscript from the sea. Three times they interrupt its reading to debate scientific data and theory in order to substantiate incidents in the narrative.

*1-29. Donnelly, Ignatius (as Edmund Boisgilbert). **Caesar's Column.** 1890. Walter B. Rideout, ed. Harvard, 1960.
Only Bellamy's *Looking Backward* [1-8] had greater popularity or influence than *Caesar's Column.* Donnelly portrayed an actual revolution in 1988; improved technology had separated the elitist capitalist class from the squalor of the working class, but the "heartlessness" of the ruling class caused the revolution. The narrator rescues some machines and compatriots, flying them to Africa, where he hopes to found a Socialist state. Dirigibles and poison gas had been used in the fighting. New York had been a city of wonders. For another account of the class struggle, see London's *The Iron Heel* [1-59].

1-30. Dooner, P(ierton) W. **Last Days of the Republic.** Alta California, 1880.
Written as a protest against importing coolie labor, the narrative suggests that
the workers remain agents of the Chinese government. This is the first discussion of "the yellow peril," although Dooner does not use that term. A "fifth column" becomes active, and the United States is destroyed as a nation. The book is
presented as a history without individualized characterization or fully developed
dramatic scenes.

*1-31. Doyle, Arthur Conan (U.K.). **The Lost World.** Hodder & Stoughton,
1912.
Professor George Challenger leads a party of explorers who discover a remnant
of the prehistoric world atop a plateau, Raraima, Venezuela (see Aubrey [1-5]).
Despite such anachronisms as cavemen living with dinosaurs, both Challenger
and the credibility of detail strengthen the narrative, making it the classic of its
type. Its tone and material differ sharply from those of Haggard. Challenger is
featured in 2 of the 14 stories collected in *The Best Science Fiction of Arthur Conan
Doyle,* edited by Charles G. Waugh and Martin H. Greenberg (1981).

*1-32. Doyle, Arthur Conan (U.K.). **The Poison Belt.** Hodder & Stoughton,
1913.
Professor Challenger's party survives an apparent worldwide catastrophe to explore a vacant world before all life reawakens. The idea of humanity's having a
second chance is present. For a later British treatment of the catastrophe motif,
see Wyndham's *The Day of the Triffids* [3-411]. Compare it to Serviss's *The Second
Deluge* [1-83], especially for its presentation of the scientists. For the role of science in man-made disasters, see Scortia-Robinson's *The Prometheus Crisis* (1975).

1-33. England, George Allan. **Darkness and Dawn.** Small, Maynard, 1914; Hyperion, 1975.
"The Vacant World," "Beyond the Great Oblivion," and "The Afterglow"—originally published in *Cavalier*—chronicle how, after a thousand years of suspended
animation, an American engineer and the typist in the office next door awaken
and rebuild a "finer, better" civilization. An explosion of subterranean gases had
torn a second moon from the Midwest and left a chasm, where dwelt the remaining "Merucaans." Volume 1 explores the eastern United States. With the aid of a
surviving biplane (complete with fuel) the protagonist reestablishes the survivors
in Volume 2. The last of the three witnesses the fruition of his efforts. Although
extremely dated in language and manner, the trilogy remains the classic example
of American optimism before World War I.

1-34. Fawcett, Edgar. **Solarion: A Romance.** Lippincott, 1889.
First published in the September 1889 issue of *Lippincott's Magazine, Solarion* was
the most original treatment of the Frankenstein theme written in the nineteenth
century. Framed by the narrative of an American residing in Switzerland, it gives
the story of Kenneth Rodney Stafford, who reminds one of Victor Frankenstein.
He uses the knowledge of another to augment the intelligence of the dog
Solarion until the animal has human intelligence and converses with him. Their
dialogues recall *Frankenstein* [1-84], both in terms of Solarion's loneliness and

Stafford's echoing the Faustian theme. He gives the dog to Cecilia Effingham when she marries. Solarion falls in love with Cecilia and maims Stafford when he attempts to kill the dog in a fit of jealousy and repugnance. For a contrasting treatment of the love of an animal for a woman, see Stapledon's *Sirius* [2-111].

*1-35. Forster, E(dward) M(organ) (U.K.). **"The Machine Stops."** 1909.
Long recognized as an attack on Wells, Forster's story pictures a future in which humanity lives underground in hexagonal cells, where they spend almost their entire adult lives. They rely entirely on pushbuttons to activate various functions of the machine. When it breaks down, humanity perishes. Forster intimates that a few survivors on the surface—perhaps exiled there for sins against the machine—hold any hope for the future that may exist. See also Tarde's *Underground Man* [1-90]. "The Machine Stops" must be judged the first full-fledged dystopian view of the effects of technology.

*1-36. Franklin, H. Bruce. **Future Perfect: American Science Fiction of the Nineteenth Century.** Oxford, 1966.
Franklin emphasizes the works of such major nineteenth-century writers as Hawthorne and Poe (to whom he gives most attention) and Melville, Bierce, Bellamy, and O'Brien. The 15 stories divide themselves among such topics as "Automata," "Marvelous Inventions," and "Time Travel." He chose works published originally in such magazines as *Harper's*, the *Atlantic Monthly*, *Century*, and *Arena*, which reached wide audiences. The importance of the anthology lies not in its comprehensiveness but in the evidence it gives of the diversity of SF during the last century.

1-37. Gernsback, Hugo. **Ralph 124C41+: A Romance of the Year 2660.** Stratford, 1925.
First published as a serial in *Modern Electrics* (1911), this story serves as the classic expression of American infatuation with the machine; it is a virtual catalog of descriptions of advanced machines. Its protagonist is a state hero, who literally resurrects his sweetheart from the dead after an accident. Unique for the period, the "other man" is a Martian. Compare Serviss's *The Second Deluge* [1-83] and *Edison's Conquest of Mars* [1-82] for similar, if not equal, adulation of the scientist. White's *The Mystery* [1-107] and *The Sign at Six* [1-108] differ in tone.

*1-38. Gilman, Charlotte Perkins. **Herland.** Pantheon, 1979.
Originally published in *The Forerunner* (1915), which Gilman edited, this feminist utopia somewhere in Canada expresses the author's conviction that women could collectively be the moving force in reforming society. To explore her ideas as widely as possible, she introduces three men, each representing a different attitude toward women, into a society where parthenogenesis has been practiced for 2,000 years. One man elevates women to an inhuman pedestal; the second has no luck with them; and the third is the complete chauvinist who believes women wish "to be mastered." The narrator—the second man—comes to understand that the so-called feminine charms of the outside world are entirely artificial. The actions of the chauvinist force the three to leave. The novel gives the most complete, nonviolent statement of the period about the need to recognize

women as equal beings and reform society accordingly. Ann J. Lane's introduction has value for its biographical information about Gilman.

1-39. Godwin, Francis (U.K.). **The Man in the Moone; or, A Discourse of a Voyage Thither.** 1638. Grant McColley, ed. Folcroft, 1973.
Although not sophisticated by modern standards, this narrative by an Anglican bishop is the earliest to give the Moon voyage a quality of scientific credibility. Poe's criticism of Godwin in "Hans Pfaall" [1-75] disguises his indebtedness. Its protagonist, Domingo Gonsales, introduced the conventions of the journey and became Cyrano de Bergerac's companion [1-12].

*1-40. Greg, Percy (U.K.). **Across the Zodiac: The Story of a Wrecked Record.** 1880. Hyperion, 1974.
Despite the use of antigravity (Greg called the force "apergy"), Greg's chief concerns lay with the nature of Martian society. A monarchical utopia has replaced communism, which failed because of lack of incentive and strife over the allocation of certain jobs. Martian philosophy is so dominated by a dogmatic positivism that opposition to science is a heresy. The plot explores Martian polygamy and allows Greg to air his views regarding female suffrage and moral reform. The narrative is presented as a manuscript recovered from meteoric debris on a Pacific island.

1-41. Griffith, George (pseud. of George Chetwynd Griffith-Jones) (U.K.). **The Angel of the Revolution: A Tale of the Coming Terror.** Tower, 1894; Hyperion, 1974.
Originally published in *Pearson's Magazine* (1893), this novel played on two of Britain's gravest nightmares: social revolution and war. When a group of anarchists, the "Terrorists," learn that France and Russia plan to attack Britain, Germany, and Austria, they build a fleet of airplanes in their secret valley—called Aeria—in Africa. While they cause the workers in the United States to rise and bring down the government, with poison gas, dirigibles, and submarines, they establish themselves as rulers in Europe. They make certain that peace and socialism triumph by maintaining their air force to ensure the obedience of the world.

1-42. Griffith, George (pseud. of George Chetwynd Griffith-Jones) (U.K.). **Olga Romanoff; or, The Syren of the Skies.** Tower, 1894; Hyperion, 1974.
First published in *Pearson's Magazine* (1893–1894), the novel gives an account of the effort of Olga Romanoff, descendant of the czars, to seize power from the Aerians (formerly the "Terrorists") after they have ruled the Anglo-Saxon Federation for more than a century. She is foiled only because a comet devastates much of the Earth. Griffith reveals his indebtedness to Bulwer-Lytton [1-61] when the Aerians indicate they have a force like "Vril." For its treatment of catastrophe, compare it to Wylie and Balmer's *When Worlds Collide* [2-146].

1-43. Griffith, Mary. "Three Hundred Years Hence" in **Camperdown: or, News from Our Neighborhood.** Carey, Lea & Blanchard, 1836.
Although Griffith was indebted to Mercier's *Memoirs of the Year Two Thousand Five Hundred* [1-63], her utopia is most notable for the influence of women once they have gained equality, especially in "money matters." One result has been the abolition of killing and war (the blacks did not use force and have been emancipated;

the Indians did and have "vanished"); another is improved hygiene, both personal and public. All technological advance resulted from the development of an unspecified force by a woman, which replaced steam and heat as sources of energy. More an essay than a novel, it ends when the dreamer awakens.

1-44. Haggard, H(enry) Rider (U.K.). **Allan Quatermain.** Longmans Green, 1887.
Allan Quatermain is the prototype for the fully developed lost-race motif. Unlike many of his subsequent imitators, Haggard allows his protagonist to marry Nyleptha, queen of the Zu-Vendris, and remain in the primitive kingdom of Africa. Because the topical concerns of the utopian fiction burned out or grew dated, only the future war motif had wider popularity before World War I. The lost-race motif continued its dominance until World War II sent troops to every corner of the world. In addition to the implications of its neoprimitivism, it became perhaps the chief vehicle for the literary eroticism of Western culture during that period. It seems also to have been primarily, if not uniquely, an expression of British and American culture. The most comprehensive discussion of the motif occurs in Clareson's *Some Kind of Paradise* [9-24].

1-45. Haggard, H(enry) Rider (U.K.). **King Solomon's Mines.** Cassell, 1885.
In this novel Haggard discovered Africa; his own personal background gives the novel an authenticity of detail lacking in Verne and Burroughs. It did for the story of exploration and adventure what Schiaparelli's announcement of the "canali" of Mars did for the interplanetary voyage: it provided a new setting. Cassell reprinted the novel four times within the first year; it has never been out of print.

*1-46. Haggard, H(enry) Rider (U.K.). **She: A History of Adventure.** Longmans Green, 1887.
Ayesha, She-Who-Must-Be-Obeyed, is Haggard's most famous character, surpassing even stalwart Allan Quatermain. Her dark beauty certainly influenced the portrayal of many women in popular fiction. Among Haggard's contemporaries one thinks of Griffith's *Olga Romanoff* [1-42]; a generation later, of Lo-Tsen in Hilton's *Lost Horizon* [2-43].

1-47. Haggard, H(enry) Rider (U.K.). **When the World Shook: Being an Account of the Great Adventure of Bastin, Bickley, and Arbuthnot.** Cassell, 1919.
Although there is much talk and little drama in the narrative, some critics regard this novel as the closest Haggard came to SF, simply because he made use of the myth of Atlantis. Three companions find the priest of Atlantis, Oro, and his daugher, Yva, in suspended animation in a cavern on an island in the Pacific. Oro sank the ancient kingdom because of its evil, and after seeing wartime Europe, threatens to bring on another deluge. He dies, as do Arbuthnot and Yva, whose love, by implication, will survive death.

1-48. Hale, Edward Everett. "The Brick Moon" in **Masterpieces of Science Fiction.** Sam Moskowitz, ed. World, 1966.
"The Brick Moon" first appeared in the *Atlantic Monthly* (October-December 1869); a single-installment sequel, "Life on the Brick Moon," was published in *Atlantic* (February 1870). Although hailed as the first story of an artificial, man-

made satellite, a close reading, particularly of the tone of the narrator and the messages received from the Moon, suggests that Hale used it as a vehicle to satirize science and technology, as well as Darwinian theory and, perhaps, fiction dealing with imaginary voyages and utopian societies. Hale gives as much attention to its financing as to its construction and (accidental) launching. Prior to Arthur C. Clarke's *Islands in the Sky* [5-34], it is the longest narrative to deal with an artificial satellite.

1-49. Hartwell, David G., and Lloyd Currey, eds. **The Battle of the Monsters and Other Stories.** Gregg Press, 1976.
These eight stories published between 1878 and 1908 range from William J. Henderson's "Harry Borden's Naval Monster: A Ship of the Air," in which the United States sides with Venezuela during its war in 1927 with Britain (bombs from a balloon sink a British cruiser), to Leonard Kip's "The Secret of Apollonius Septric," a dream-vision anticipating something of the tone of Olaf Stapledon. The title story by Morgan Robertson describes the warfare of germs, white corpuscles, and antibodies of an inoculation in the human bloodstream. It should be compared with similar historically oriented anthologies, like Clareson's *A Spectrum of Worlds* (1972), Franklin's *Future Perfect* [1-36], and Menville and Reginald's *Ancestral Voices* [1-62].

*1-50. Holberg, Ludwig (Denmark). **A Journey to the World Under-Ground: By Nicolas Klimius.** Tr. anonymously, 1742. Tr. of *Nicolai Klimii Iter Subterraneum,* 1741. Univ. of Nebraska, 1960, as *The Journey of Niels Klim to the World Underground.*
Falling through a cavern to the center of the world, Klim finds a sun and its planets within the Earth. He observes the "true laws of Motion." On the planet Nazar he learns about various societies. Holberg's satire is comparable to that of Swift [1-89]; his general strategy is to invert human conventions. It was long suppressed in Denmark as a dangerously radical book. Also annotated as [6-346 and 6-390].

1-51. Hudson, W(illiam) H(enry) (U.K.). **A Crystal Age.** Unwin, 1887; Doric Books, 1949.
The narrator, a botanist, suffers a fall and awakens in an unspecified pastoral society having no knowledge of the nineteenth century. No industrialization is apparent. Although the unit of society is the matriarchal family, there is no marriage nor recognition of sexual love. In a preface to his collected works, Hudson remarked that such "romances of the future" grew out of "a sense of dissatisfaction with the existing order of things." Compare Hudson with Jefferies's *After London* [1-53], in which modern industrial civilization has also disappeared.

1-52. Hyne, Cutcliffe (pseud. of Charles John Cutcliffe Wright Hyne) (U.K.). **The Lost Continent.** Hutchinson, 1900.
On one of the Canary Islands two Englishmen find a manuscript, the memoir of Deucalion, last king of Atlantis. He becomes involved with "lovely, sinful" Phorenice, self-proclaimed queen and goddess of Atlantis, and Naïs, daughter of the chief priest. Much attention is given to battles and the schemes of Phorenice, but the world is not vividly or dramatically presented. Deucalion places Naïs in a

state of suspended animation and they escape as the continent sinks. Hyne established many of the conventions regarding Atlantis that came down to contemporary SF through the fiction of such writers as Robert E. Howard. The characterization of Phorenice owes much to Haggard's *She* [1-46].

1-53. Jefferies, Richard (U.K.). **After London; or, Wild England.** Cassell, 1885.
A trained naturalist who hated industrialization, Jefferies pictures an England that has reverted to a vast woodland after some unspecified catastrophe has left the land dominated by a great lake in the Midlands. No cities survive. The story follows the odyssey of Felix Aquila, whose home is Thyma Castle; it ends as he brings his beloved Aurora to live with him among shepherds. One may trace this theme through Hudson's *A Crystal Age* [1-51] to John Collier's *Tom's A-Cold* (1933).

*1-54. Kepler, Johannes (Germany). **Somnium, seu opus posthumum de astronamia lunari.** 1634. The definitive English tr. is that of Edward Rosen, Univ. of Wisconsin Press, 1967.
The dream-vision of Duracotus, an apprentice to Tycho Brahe, describes the physical appearance of the Moon and its life forms. Most observations agree with those of Galileo, although Kepler gives it water and atmosphere. Wells's *First Men in the Moon* [1-98] uses many similar details and makes specific reference to Kepler.

1-55. Kipling, Rudyard (U.K.). **"With the Night Mail."** 1905.
Dirigible balloons, such as Postal Packet 162 from London to Quebec, fly the air currents of the world. Aviation has changed the world so completely that it is governed by the Aerial Board of Control (A.B.C.), whose laws permit anything—including war—that does not obstruct "traffic and all it implies." A sequel, "As Easy as A.B.C." (1912), describes the unsuccessful attempt by the District of Illinois to break away from the board in 2065.

1-56. Lane, Mary E. Bradley. **Mizora: A Prophecy.** Dillingham, 1890.
A Russian noblewoman sentenced to Siberia escapes to a Symmesian world, where she finds a feminist utopia in which parthenogenesis has been practiced for 3,000 years. Genetic engineering assures that all the women will be uniformly blonde and beautiful (with 30-inch waistlines, a sign of Lane's reaction to the fashions of her time). Lane is angrier than Gilman [1-38]; she denounces the cheap prices and cheap labor that make women and children suffer, calling women "beasts of burden." She insists that universal education will bring freedom and equality. *Mizora* was first published in the Cincinnati *Commercial* in 1880–1881. Its date gives it added historical significance.

1-57. Le Queux, William (U.K.). **The Great War in England in 1897.** Tower, 1894.
The most sensational and bloodthirsty novelist using the future war motif, Le Queux made his reputation with this account of a French and Russian invasion. Germany, which aided Britain in this book, became the ruthless enemy in Le Queux's *The Invasion of 1910: With a Full Account of the Siege of London* (1904).

*1-58. London, Jack. **Before Adam.** Macmillan, 1906.
Through racial memory the narrator tells of his life as a caveman. Waterloo accused London of plagiarizing his *The Story of Ab* [1-97].

1-59. London, Jack. **The Iron Heel.** Macmillan, 1907.
Scholars of a Socialist utopian state in the twenty-seventh century discover the Everhard Manuscript, which tells of the early struggles in the twentieth century against a Fascist-type state ruled by the Trusts. His most emotional outburst, the novel may owe something to his experiences of 1902 when he went "down and out in the under-world of London" and bitterly reported his findings in *The People of the Abyss* (1906).

*1-60. London, Jack. **The Science Fiction of Jack London.** Richard Sid Powers, ed. Gregg Press, 1975.
Nine short stories range from "A Relic of the Pliocene" (1901), a kind of tall tale in which a hunter pursues a mammoth in the Arctic, to "The Unparalleled Invasion" (1910), an account of the annihilation of China by Western powers. In addition, the volume contains "The Scarlet Plague" (1915) and "The Red One" (1918), very probably the finest SF by an American author of the period. The elderly narrator of "The Scarlet Plague" recalls the catastrophic plague that decimated the modern world, plunging it into a barbarism from which no recovery can be made. Comparison to Doyle's *The Poison Belt* [1-32] or Wyndham's *The Day of the Triffids* [3-411] favors London and shows how casual the British concept of a "second chance" seems. The protagonist of "The Red One" is lured into the jungles of Guadalcanal by the metallic echo of the god of the savages—called "The Red One" or "The Star-Born." It proves to be a spaceship that crashed some time in the past. The story successfully fuses SF and literary naturalism.

*1-61. Lytton, Edward Bulwer (U.K.). **The Coming Race.** 1871. Emerson M. Clymer, ed. Philosophical Publishing, 1973.
In a subterranean world beneath Britain, an American finds the Vril-ya, a race far in advance of the nineteenth century, both personally and socially. They do not know sorrow, pain, or passion; war, crime, and poverty do not exist. All of this is made possible by the power of Vril, the essential force behind all things. Because Lytton does not share the antipathy toward the machine, his novel differs from those of Butler [1-19], Hudson [1-51], and Morris [1-69]. The women of the Vril-ya are superior to men physically and are equal to the males in all other ways.

1-62. Menville, Douglas, and R. Reginald, eds. **Ancestral Voices: An Anthology of Early Science Fiction.** Arno, 1975.
Ten stories, British and American, dating from 1887 to 1915, have been taken from the books rather than the magazines of the period. They range from the humor of John Kendrick Bang's "A Glance Ahead: Being a Christmas Tale of A.D. 3568" (1901) and Robert W. Chambers's "The Third Eye" (1915) to the horror of Cutcliffe Hyne's "The Lizard" (1904).

1-63. Mercier, Louis Sebastien (France). **Memoirs of the Year Two Thousand Five Hundred.** Tr. by William Hooper from *L'An deux mille quatre cent quarante,* 1771. Dobson, 1795. Gregg Press, 1977.

A Parisian awakens in the year 2500 (2440 in the original) to find a society dominated by science and lacking in all the abuses of the eighteenth century. Education concerns itself with "useful knowledge," while "first communion" involves looking through a microscope. Paris serves as a model of the perfect city throughout the nineteenth century.

1-64. Milne, Robert Duncan. **Into the Sun & Other Stories.** Sam Moskowitz, ed. *Science Fiction in Old San Francisco,* vol. 2. Donald Grant, 1980.

Moskowitz discovered several hundred SF and supernatural stories written by a group of West Coast writers, led by Milne, which were published in the San Francisco papers during the last half of the nineteenth century. Eleven of Milne's 60 stories are collected here, written between 1882 and 1891. They show his interest in topics such as natural catastrophe and electricity. Milne encouraged Bierce to write some of his science fiction tales.

1-65. Mitchell, Edward Page. **The Crystal Man.** Sam Moskowitz, ed. Doubleday, 1973.

Moskowitz calls Mitchell, an editor of the New York *Sun,* the "Lost Giant of American Science Fiction." These 30 stories, written between 1874 and 1886, make use of the motifs and conventions then popular. "The Ablest Man in the World" (1879) must be one of the earliest cyborg stories; a reasoning machine is placed in the head of an idiot. Multiple personality fascinates Mitchell.

1-66. Mitchell, J(ohn) A(mes). **The Last American.** Stokes, 1889.

The story parallels Poe's "Mellonta Tauta" [1-75]. A Persian expedition of the thirtieth century visits America, learning that a climatic change long ago brought about the downfall of the United States. It becomes a vehicle for an attack on American materialism. To see dramatically the shifts in SF in terms of theme and handling of detail, compare Gene Wolfe's "Seven American Nights" (1979), which is also concerned with a Persian's visit to the United States. Wolfe did not know Mitchell's story when he wrote his novelette.

1-67. Moffett, Cleveland. **The Conquest of America.** Doran, 1916.

The novel joins together two stories serialized in *McClure's Magazine* the previous year. Germany occupies the United States, but Thomas Edison invents a radio-controlled torpedo enabling an "insignificant airforce" to annihilate the German navy. Edison sits with other scientists and politicians, all actual persons, who supervise American victory and recall Stockton's *The Great War Syndicate* [1-88].

*1-68. More, Thomas (U.K.). **A Fruteful and Pleasaunt Worke of the Beste State of a Publyque Weale, and of the Newe Yle Called Vtopia.** Tr. by Ralphe Robynson, 1551. Originally *Libellus vere aureus nec minus salutarisquam festivus de optimo reip[ublicae] statu deq[ue] nova insula Vtopia,* 1516. Of the many tr. of *Utopia* those by H. V. S. Ogden (Appleton) or Edward Surtz and J. H. Hexter (Yale), *Collected Works,* vol. 4, or *Selected Works,* vol. 2, are recommended.

More contrasts the state of England, where men are hanged for theft while the state seizes vast areas of land in enclosure, with the communistic society of Utopia, visited by Ralph Hythloday. Utopia is a planned society governed by the principles of justice in keeping with natural law, and the people concern themselves with personal health. Utopia ("no place") serves both as a model of the ideal state and as a vehicle for criticizing existing societies.

1-69. Morris, William (U.K.). **News from Nowhere; or, An Epoch of Rest.** Roberts, 1890. James Redmond, ed. Routledge, 1970.
First published in the *Commonweal* in 1890 as a direct response to Bellamy's *Looking Backward* [1-8], Morris's dream-vision calls up his beloved fourteenth century. Squalor, poverty, and all signs of urban industrialization have vanished. Neither politics nor family tyranny constrains humankind. All do as they please in their own manner and have as a reward a sense of creation and service. In an earlier dream-vision, *A Dream of John Ball* (1886–1887), Morris returned to the Peasants' Revolt to declare that the Fellowship of Man must prevail and all must share the fruits of the Earth equally.

1-70. Moskowitz, Sam, ed. **Science Fiction by Gaslight: A History and Anthology of Science Fiction in the Popular Magazines, 1891–1911.** World, 1968.
After giving a useful survey of British and American magazines of the period, Moskowitz selects 26 stories that give a sound indication of the extent, variety, and popularity of SF reaching the mass audience at the turn of the century. The *Strand, Pearson's,* the *Argosy,* and the *Black Cat* provide most of the titles. The selection covers all the motifs then popular.

1-71. Moskowitz, Sam, ed. **Under the Moons of Mars: A History and Anthology of "The Scientific Romance" in the Munsey Magazines, 1912–1920.** Holt, 1970.
Moskowitz's valuable anthology, which includes a history of the Munsey pulps, shows why the Munsey magazines were the heart of American SF during the period of World War I. From Burroughs and England to Murray Leinster and Charles B. Stilson, two characteristics stand out in the fiction: the protagonist capable of heroic action, and adventure in an exotic setting, whether of an unknown area of the Earth or in another world or dimension. The stories continue to have impact, though the language and some situations may be dated to some extent.

*1-72. O'Brien, Fitz-James. **The Fantastic Tales of Fitz-James O'Brien.** Michael Hayes, ed. John Calder, 1977.
Of seven tales included in the volume, at least four introduce concepts seminal to later SF. "The Diamond Lens" (1858) opens up submicroscopic worlds, although its narrator is labeled a madman. In "What Was It?" an invisible creature, by implication from another dimension, is captured by the narrator. It anticipates Bierce's "The Damned Thing" [1-13] in giving a scientific explanation of invisibility. "The Lost Room" (1858) suggests additional dimensions and/or coexistent worlds. "The Wondersmith" (1859) animates mannequins possessing lives of their own and thereby being capable of independent action. In terms of language and narrative conventions, O'Brien looks back to Poe and the gothic; in

terms of basic premises, he prepares the way for his successors. The *Atlantic Monthly* published many of his too few stories.

1-73. Paltock, Robert (U.K.). **The Life and Adventures of Peter Wilkins.** Robinson & Dodsley, 1751.
More imitative of *Robinson Crusoe* than of Swift, Paltock's narrative first shipwrecks Wilkins off Africa and then takes him to a subterranean world before he meets a race of winged humans. He marries Youwarkee and has seven children by her, some of whom have her power of flight. Scott, Dickens, and Thackeray mention Peter Wilkins. Paltock seems the literary source for the convention of people (as opposed to angels) who can fly, a convention embracing the genetically engineered "Fliers" of Silverberg's *Nightwings* [4-505].

*1-74. Poe, Edgar Allan. **The Narrative of Arthur Gordon Pym of Nantucket.** 1838. Harold Beaver, ed. Penguin, 1976.
The Narrative may be read as a tale of shipwreck, mutiny, cannibalism, and other horrors of seafaring, told in the first person to gain that heightened psychological excitement so typical of Poe and the gothic. But Pym changes character, so to speak, halfway through the story. Through the mutiny and shipwreck, Pym does not trust the working of his own mind and constantly fears that he will go mad. Once aboard the *Jane Guy*, however, he calmly describes a world that grows ever more strange as the ship ventures into the Antarctic. Almost incidentally, Poe indulges his fondness for premature burial and puzzles before he takes Pym and his companions to the brink of the terrible cataract. *The Narrative* breaks off abruptly, and though a number have tried, not even Verne could end the story satisfactorily. Evidence shows that Poe knew Symmes [1-81], and certainly Poe's ending helped make the Antarctic and Symmes's inner world the favorite settings they were well into the twentieth century. In addition to the mayhem of its literal level, *The Narrative* may be read as Poe's symbolic dramatization of the dilemma central to the concern of the eighteenth-century psychological empiricists: namely, that one cannot know the nature of reality because one cannot trust either one's perception of the external world or the workings of one's mind. If read in this fashion, the ending proves to be Poe's finest hoax, for the dilemma cannot be resolved.

*1-75. Poe, Edgar Allan. **The Science Fiction of Edgar Allan Poe.** H. Beaver, ed. Penguin, 1976.
Because Beaver carefully excludes those stories, like "The Black Cat," in which madness and horror are Poe's concerns, this collection shows how much Poe followed the lead of his contemporaries and predecessors. "MS Found in a Bottle" (1833) suggests Symmes's theory of the hollow Earth. Poe criticizes both Godwin and Locke in a postscript to "The Unparalleled Adventures of One Hans Pfaall" (1835), in which he combines close observation with the promise that he may later describe the dwarfish lunarians whom he discovered; he ends the tale by implying that it, too, is a hoax. "The Conversation of Eiros and Charmion" (1839) deals with the catastrophe that overtakes the world when a comet collides with it. "William Wilson" (1839) concerns itself with multiple personalities, while "The Facts in the Case of M. Valdemar" (1845) combines mesmerism and suspended animation. "The Balloon Hoax" (1844) carries four men in a dirigible across the

Atlantic in 75 hours. "Mellonta Tauta" (1849) brings Pundita to "Amricca" by balloon in the twenty-ninth century; New York is a pleasure island for an emperor since "mob rule" has been replaced by a monarchy. A wide variety of inventions, including propeller-driven boats and a transatlantic cable, indicate an advanced technology. In addition to 15 stories, Beaver includes the essay "Eureka" (1848). Perhaps the chief value of the volume is that it shows how much of Poe is lost when one omits the stories of madness and horror—without involved external trappings.

1-76. Pope, Gustavus W. **Journey to Mars.** 1894. Arno, 1975.
Although much of Pope's initial sequence in the Antarctic echoes Poe and Symmes, he introduces the completely unexpected when his young protagonist saves a visiting Martian prince. By magnetically driven ship they return to Mars, where the naval lieutenant falls in love with and marries the princess Suhlamia. Political unrest (and a rival suitor) keep them apart for much of the book; they flee to the Antarctic when a meteor shower threatens Mars. Although Pope adapts the lost-race motif to an interplanetary romance, he seems to anticipate Burroughs [1-17] more than he reminds one of Haggard [1-46]. In *Wonderful Adventures on Venus* (1895), the lovers find that world to be comparable to prehistoric Earth. That parallel includes the sinking of an "Atlantean" continent.

1-77. Reeve, Arthur B(enjamin). **The Silent Bullet.** Dodd Mead, 1912.
This was the first book collection of the adventures of America's best known "scientific detective," Craig Kennedy. Often compared to Sherlock Holmes—a medical doctor, Jameson, is his companion and the storyteller—Kennedy differs sharply from Doyle's hero. From "mechanical wonders" to Freudian theory, he exploited current works in all fields of science, and invented his own "gadgets" when necessary; he made use of wiretapping and developed a "love meter [which] registers the grand passion [because] even love can be attributed to electrical forces." He dealt in assassination and adultery, witchcraft and white slavery. The high point of his career came in "The Dream Doctor" (1914), when he explained in detail Freudian theory for the first time in popular magazine fiction. For the way in which another American scientist handles mysteries, see White's *The Sign at Six* [1-108].

*1-78. Rhodes, W(illiam) H(enry). **Caxton's Book.** Bancroft, 1876.
In an introduction to this posthumous volume, Daniel O'Connell called Rhodes the potential equal of Verne and named "science fiction" a distinct type of fiction. The stories show interests shared by Poe and Verne, although Rhodes was no mere imitator. The longest and best, "The Case of Summerfield," deals with a mad scientist from San Francisco who threatens to destroy the oceans and thus the world if he is not paid a ransom. It was published separately in 1918; it made its newspaper appearance in 1871. Rhodes should be compared with Milne [1-64] and Bierce [1-13].

1-79. Rosny aîné, J. H. (pseud. of Joseph-Henri Boëx) (France). **The Xipéhuz** and **The Death of the Earth.** Tr. by George Edgar Slusser. Arno, 1978.
Long neglected because his work was not available in English, Rosny was one of France's most important SF writers. In *The Xipéhuz* (1887) nomadic prehistoric

men encounter creatures "totally alien to the animal and vegetable kingdoms as we know them" and fight a war of extinction. In the far future water had almost entirely disappeared from the Earth in *The Death of the World* (1912); the last men die among sentient beings who have evolved from iron, the "ferromagnetics," which feed on the blood of humans. Harold Talbott translated *La Guerre de feu* (1900) as *Quest for Fire* (1967), in which different species of cavemen struggle to obtain fire. It was filmed in 1981.

1-80. Russell, Alan K., ed. **Science Fiction by the Rivals of H. G. Wells.** Castle, 1979.
Although Russell includes such noteworthy stories as Grant Allen's "The Thames Valley Catastrophe" (1897), he gives most attention to George Griffith, including his "The Raid of Le Vengeur" (1898) and those stories that made up *A Honeymoon in Space* (1901). It yokes together the future war motif and the interplanetary voyage. Lord Redgrave develops "R force," a kind of antigravity power to motivate his "airship" *Astronef.* While he delivers a treaty to Washington that establishes an Anglo-American alliance and prevents war with France and Russia, he literally kidnaps Zaide Rennick from an ocean liner. They honeymoon to Mars, the Moon, and Venus, meeting a standard assortment of wonders.

*1-81. Seaborn, Adam. **Symzonia: A Voyage of Discovery.** Seymour, 1820. J. O. Bailey, ed. Scholars' Facsimile, 1967.
Symzonia, thought by some scholars, like Bailey, to be the work of John Cleves Symmes himself, portrays a voyage to an inner world to a utilitarian utopia governed by the Best Man. He is elected by a legislature of Worthies, chosen for their virtues as the Good, the Wise, and the Useful. Poverty is unknown, while property is shared. The first utopia by an American, its greater value lies in its introduction of a setting popular well into the twentieth century. Compare with Mercier [1-63] to see the differences in American thinking.

*1-82. Serviss, Garrett P(utnam). **Edison's Conquest of Mars.** Carcosa House, 1947.
Serialized in the New York *Evening Journal* (1898), this was a sequel to Wells's *The War of the Worlds* [1-105], which had been published in *Cosmopolitan* (1897). Serviss dismisses technical detail and scientific explanation as being beyond the readers' knowledge and interest. The novel eulogizes Edison's inventiveness. Except for giantism, the evolution of Mars parallels that of Earth. Serviss's terrestrial jingoism declares that the issue at stake is that of Martian evolution against that of Earth. Edison and company incidentally find a young woman, descendant of humans brought to Mars after the giants built the pyramids.

*1-83. Serviss, Garrett P(utnam). **The Second Deluge.** McBride, Nast, 1912; Hyperion, 1975.
When a watery nebula threatens the Earth, Cosmo Versals builds an ark and chooses the people (no lawyers) who will survive. The public, including other scientists, ridicule him. A geological phenomenon raises a portion of the Rockies so that other Americans live through the flood. The story is told by future historians from the science-dominated society that Versals brought into being. During the flood he incidentally visits lost Atlantis in a submarine. For a contemporary

American treatment of the scientist as hero see White and Adams's *The Mystery* [1-107].

*1-84. Shelley, Mary Wollstonecraft (U.K.). **Frankenstein; or, The Modern Prometheus.** 1818; rev. ed. 1831. M. K. Joseph, ed. Oxford, 1969; Maurice Hindle, ed. Penguin, 1985.
Whatever her literary indebtedness—classical myth, Faustus, or Milton—Mary Shelley gave form to one of the enduring myths of SF: the creation of life by science. Guilty of the sin of intellectual pride, Victor Frankenstein epitomizes a shift in the scientists of the nineteenth century in that he turns from alchemy to electrical forces, a phenomenon that fascinated writers throughout the century. Mary Shelley acknowledged an indebtedness to the physiologists of Germany and Dr. Erasmus Darwin. Aldiss has argued that *Frankenstein* is the first SF novel, although Wells called it more magic than science. See Aldiss's *Frankenstein Unbound* [4-4] for a late treatment of the theme.

1-85. Shelley, Mary Wollstonecraft (U.K.). **The Last Man.** 1826. Brian Aldiss, ed. Hogarth, 1985.
Mary Shelley's apocalyptic vision, indebted to de Grainville's *Le Dernier homme* (1805), has two central concerns. The first involves the abdication of the final British king. Second, Lionel Verney, "the last man," ends his days in Rome after wandering through deserted cities when he left his last refuge in Switzerland. Aldiss suggests that Mary Shelley "added a little imagination" to an actual cholera pandemic spreading from Calcutta around the world. Although she makes no mention of the industrial revolution, she does refer to the use of balloons.

*1-86. Stevenson, Robert Louis (U.K.). **The Strange Case of Dr. Jekyll and Mr. Hyde.** Longmans, 1886.
This classic nineteenth-century presentation of dual personality dramatizes the good and evil within each human. Aware from his youth of a certain wickedness within his nature, Dr. Jekyll experiments and develops a drug that brings his alter ego into ascendancy, thereby transforming himself physically into Mr. Hyde. One learns of the mystery through the eyes of the lawyer Utterson, but only a final manuscript, the full statement of Henry Jekyll, explains the relationship between him and Hyde.

1-87. Stockton, Frank. **The Great Stone of Sardis.** Harper, 1898.
Against the backdrop of the utopian world of 1947, a scientist develops a kind of X-ray machine permitting him to see the strata of the Earth. He burrows through the outer shell to find its core to be a great diamond, while friends make a successful submarine trip to the North Pole. An incidental love story features the woman who is also his financial partner and co-builder of his extensive laboratories. One infers that Stockton was thinking of Thomas Edison, at least to some extent. See Moffett [1-67] and Serviss [1-83] for other American scientists.

1-88. Stockton, Frank. **The Great War Syndicate.** Collier, 1889.
Twenty-three American businessmen assume responsibility for the war against Britain. They develop an armored vessel and an electrically powered "instantaneous motor," seemingly a cross between a jet-propelled shell and an atomic

bomb. After victory, an Anglo-American alliance outlaws all war. Compare Moffett [1-67].

*1-89. Swift, Jonathan (U.K.). **Travels in Several Remote Nations of the World . . . by Lemuel Gulliver [Gulliver's Travels].** 1726. Robert D. Heilman, ed. Modern Library, 1969.

Drawing on the traditions of the imaginary voyage and travel literature, Swift sends his protagonist to visit Lilliput, Brobdingnag, Laputa, and Houyhnhnmland. Lilliput and Brobdingnag satirize humanity's moral and political pettiness and its physical grossness. Book Three directly attacks the Royal Societies of London and Dublin, ridiculing the new science and its materialistic premises, making use of the *Transactions* of the societies as well as Newton's *Principia* to achieve its effectiveness. Book Four reduces humanity to its most brutal and absurd—the Yahoos—contrasting it with the utopian community of the perfectly rational hippomorphic beings, the Houyhnhnms. Swift makes his satire effective by giving it the objectivity of a scientific report. *Gulliver's Travels* anticipates the bitterly critical tone of much SF from the contemporary period.

1-90. Tarde, Gabriel de (France). **Underground Man.** 1905. Tr. by Cloudesley Brereton. Hyperion, 1974.

Published in the same year as Wells's *A Modern Utopia* [1-101], this book opens with a description of a utopian society. The extinction of the sun forces humanity deep into the Earth to survive. The new society, powered by wonderful machines, develops aesthetically and spiritually as it never did on the surface. Wells wrote the book's introduction.

1-91. Train, Arthur Cheyney, and Robert Williams Wood. **The Man Who Rocked the Earth.** Doubleday, 1915.

Serialized in the *Saturday Evening Post* in the autumn of 1914, this gives an account of the efforts of a mad scientist to end the stalemated European war. He increases the length of the sidereal day, disintegrates part of the Atlas mountains, and threatens to change the poles of the Earth. His weapons and airship use atomic power. The narrative describes radiation sickness, apparently for the first time in popular fiction. The story involves the efforts of a German expedition and an American scientist to reach his base in Newfoundland. The Germans are destroyed; the scientist flies the ship—"The Flying Ring"—to Washington, where a conference of nations meets and abolishes war. The mad scientist has died in his own experiments. In a brief sequel, *The Moon Maker*, not published in book form until 1958, the novelists take their protagonist and his companion, the woman scientist Rhoda Gibbs, on a journey through the solar system after they deflect a comet threatening the Earth. It calls to mind Griffith's *A Honeymoon in Space* [1-80] since the subsequent marriage of the two is implied, but it does not have the sweep of the earlier novel.

1-92. Verne, Jules (France). **The Adventures of Captain Hatteras** (*Les Aventures du Capitaine Hatteras*). 1867.

Verne's second novel owes much to Sir John Ross's *Second Voyage in Search of the*

North-West Passage (1835). In the narrative the brig *Forward* follows Ross's route until it is deflected toward the pole. The venture costs Hatteras his sanity.

1-93. Verne, Jules (France). **From the Earth to the Moon** (*De la terre à la lune*). 1865. Recommended tr. by Walter James Miller, Crowell, 1978.
The influence of Poe's "Hans Pfaall" [1-75] on this novel by Verne remains uncertain, for most of the narrative is given to building a cannon and locating the site from which the shot is to be made. The actual shot (flight) provides the climactic action of the novel. Not until *Round the Moon* (*Autour de la lune*) (1870) did the readers learn that because of deflection by a second earthly moon (Verne's invention) the ship merely orbited the Moon and splashed down in the Pacific. Since the dark side of the Moon was invisible to them, the voyagers saw nothing of it. That fact raises a question about Verne's imagination: did he have to depend on factual sources for his works? In this case, like Poe and Locke, he may have pulled his own hoax, for there existed a long tradition of lunar descriptions.

*1-94. Verne, Jules (France). **A Journey to the Center of the Earth** (*Voyage au centre de la terre*). 1864. Recommended tr. by Robert Baldick, Penguin, 1965.
More than half the book is given to the preliminaries before the actual descent begins, the first two chapters relying on a standard point of departure, the discovery of a manuscript giving the location of the caverns in Iceland. The narrative shows Verne's intense care in presenting the latest scientific thought of his age, while the sighting of the plesiosaurus and the giant humanoid shepherding mammoths indicates how well he incorporated lengthy imaginary episodes to flesh out the factual report.

*1-95. Verne, Jules (France). **Twenty Thousand Leagues under the Sea** (*Vingt milles lieues sous les mers*). 1870. Recommended tr. by Walter James Miller, Crowell, 1976.
The voyage of the *Nautilus* permitted Verne to describe the wonders of an undersea world almost totally unknown to the general public of the period. Indebted to literary tradition for his Atlantis, he made his major innovation in having the submarine completely powered by electricity, although the interest in electrical forces goes back to Poe and Shelley. So far as the enigmatic ending is concerned, his readers had to wait for the three-part *The Mysterious Island* (*L'Ile mysterieuse*) (1874–1875) to learn that Nemo had been the Indian warrior-prince Dakkar, who had been involved in the Sepoy Mutiny of 1857. The island the Americans "domesticated" may be regarded as Verne's Robinsonade.

1-96. Waterloo, Stanley. **A Son of the Ages.** Doubleday, 1914.
By combining the ideas of racial memory and reincarnation, the stories trace the protagonist through his various lives—from that of Scar, "The Link," to the Phoenicians, Germanic tribes, and Vikings—in keeping with his idea of Anglo-Saxon supremacy. One episode dramatizes the sinking of Atlantis.

1-97. Waterloo, Stanley. **The Story of Ab: A Tale of the Time of the Caveman.** Way & Williams, 1897.
This is apparently the first American pseudo-historical novel of prehistory from which previously dominant religious themes are completely absent. It dramatizes

the lifetime of an individual whose inventions and intellectual development helped humankind begin its ascent from savagery. It became a prototype for later novels. Waterloo accused London of plagiarism in *Before Adam* [1-58]. The attitudes of the two authors toward the material provide an interesting contrast.

1-98. Wells, H(erbert) G(eorge) (U.K.). **The First Men in the Moon.** Newnes, 1901.
At first this seems the most traditional of Wells's romances because of its inclusion of so many conventions, including negative gravity. The Selenites have evolved a highly complex and insectlike social order. The confrontation between Cavor and The Grand Lunar owes much to Swift in that humanity is found wanting in terms of the Lunar's concept of rational norms. Wells criticizes the Selenite specialization. Cavor is destroyed by his inquiring intellect; his companion, Bedford, is saved by his individuality.

1-99. Wells, H(erbert) G(eorge) (U.K.). **The Food of the Gods.** Macmillan, 1904.
At first reading this account of giantism resulting from deliberate experiments to make growth continuous may seem little more than a horror story. But when the little people (humans) attack the giants—Redwood, the Princess, Cossars, and others—it becomes a symbolic statement of public resistance to change.

1-100. Wells, H(erbert) G(eorge) (U.K.). **The Island of Dr. Moreau.** Heinemann, 1896.
Reading *Moreau* as a version of the Frankenstein myth overlooks the fact that, unlike Faustus or Victor Frankenstein, Moreau has no sense of guilt or controlling humanity. He is the most terrible of the three and cannot be called a tragic hero. Both in the narrator Pendrick and the "Beast People," Wells shows the uneasy tension between "natural" and "civilized" humanity. "The Law" satirizes any attempt to codify religio-moral concepts intended to curb the natural man. Wells emphasizes through his satire after Moreau's death that only a fragile shell of civilization restrains humanity from its natural bestiality. This thrust undercuts the long-time romantic idealization of the natural man. Compare Aldiss's *Moreau's Other Island* (U.K., 1980; U.S. title: *An Island Called Moreau,* 1981).

*1-101. Wells, H(erbert) G(eorge) (U.K.). **A Modern Utopia.** Chapman & Hall, 1905.
In part a parody of the natural man of Morris's *News from Nowhere* [1-69], the novel asserts as its central theme that rejection of technical invention for a willful primitivism achieves nothing. His volunteer nobility, the Samurai, represents his "men of good will"—he makes no mention of women—who must become the governing body of humanity.

*1-102. Wells, H(erbert) G(eorge) (U.K.). **The Short Stories of H. G. Wells.** Benn, 1927.
The best of Wells's short stories vividly exemplify his basic techniques and themes. "The Sea Raiders" (1896) introduces a predatory species of octopus into the channel near Sidmouth, a well-known resort town, to show that humanity exists in a world that it does not fully know, one filled with threats to humanity's continued existence. "The Empire of the Ants" (1905) echoes this theme in that,

by implication, the new species will take over the world. "The Star" (1897) gives humanity a second chance after the approach of a comet devastates modern civilization. "A Story of Days to Come" (1897), whose culture anticipates that of *When the Sleeper Wakes* [1-106], emphasizes his ambivalence toward the concept of inevitable progress. Its companion novella, "A Story of the Stone Age" (1897), stresses the theme of survival in a brutal world. His stories range from the terror of "In the Avu Observatory" (1895) and "The Flowering of a Strange Orchid" (1895) to the predictions of "The Argonauts of the Air" (1895) and "The Land Ironclads" (1903). "The Country of the Blind" (1904) becomes a parable attacking ethnocentric dogmatism. His basic theme stresses that humanity must grow wiser if it is to survive.

*1-103. Wells, H(erbert) G(eorge) (U.K.). **The Time Machine.** Heinemann, 1895.
Critics have emphasized the splitting of humanity into the Eloi and Morlocks so much as Wells's vision of the outcome of the Marxist class struggle that its implication, taken from Thomas Huxley, that humanity cannot control the cosmic evolutionary process, and is, therefore, its victim, has not been adequately emphasized. One should not overlook the fact that the book's climax is the vivid scene of the dying Earth. It must be read as being extremely pessimistic. The final speech of the traveler reveals the inner tensions within Wells that may explain why he turned increasingly to a heavy didacticism.

1-104. Wells, H(erbert) G(eorge) (U.K.). **The War in the Air.** Bell, 1908.
In the early 1900s, a German dirigible fleet attacks New York City. In turn, it is attacked by an Oriental fleet. Guerrilla warfare spreads throughout the world, the "Purple Death" follows, and within 30 years humanity has been reduced to barbarism, forgetting even how to operate machinery. At one level simply another future war story, this is Wells's dramatization of the widening gap between humanity's social intelligence and its inability to manage new inventions. Contemporary humanity cannot meet the challenges science offers to it.

*1-105. Wells, H(erbert) G(eorge) (U.K.). **The War of the Worlds.** Heinemann, 1898.
The dramatic effectiveness of the novel lies in the detailed realism with which Wells destroys Richmond, Kingston, and Wimbledon. He brings horror to very familiar doorsteps. Perhaps more than any of his other works, this dramatizes humanity's fragile place in the universe, a theme that obsessed him from the first and that he desperately tried to communicate to his contemporaries. Filmed in 1953, its most memorable dramatization was the 1938 Orson Welles broadcast.

1-106. Wells, H(erbert) G(eorge) (U.K.). **When the Sleeper Wakes.** Harper, 1899.
One sees in this novel the beginning of the split that leads to the Eloi and the Morlocks. Mechanized progress has made great strides, but there has been no comparable growth in humanity's social and political awareness. An oligarchy of the rich has replaced the timid capitalists and has regimented the workers into

the Labour Company. The dreamer, Graham, awakens to find he owns half the world. When his presence brings unrest, he is killed.

*1-107.   White, Stewart Edward, and Samuel Hopkins Adams. **The Mystery.** Mc-Clure, Phillips, 1907.
Most of the narrative is presented as a mystery echoing the Marie Celeste affair. The narrator finally reports the scientist-hero's successful attempt to find the ultimate energy, *celestium,* on a volcanic island in the Pacific. He and his secret die together. Not only does the novel give one of the most idealized portraits of a scientist; technically it succeeds through its realistic detail and narrative technique.

*1-108.   White, Stewart Edward. **The Sign at Six.** Bobbs-Merrill, 1912.
The narrator of *The Mystery* returns as the protagonist who finds the "mad" scientist threatening to cut off light, sound, and heat from New York City. The protagonist destroys the machine and the notes of the madman because they are too dangerous for humanity to have; they represent an area into which humanity should not trespass. In this sense it repeats the same warning that Mary Shelley voiced in *Frankenstein* [1-84].

2
Science Fiction between the Wars: 1918-1938

Brian Stableford

World War I had a considerable impact on the history of speculative fiction. It put an end to the myth of a war to end war, and brought to Europe a profound fear of the catastrophic possibilities of a further war fought with airplanes and poison gas. Less obviously, its economic side effects helped to change the market situation of science fiction. The middlebrow magazines that had nurtured scientific romance in Britain lost the experimental fervor that had encouraged them to seek out the unusual and the imaginative. The revitalization of commercial advertising was associated with market research that singled out women as the main exercisers of consumer choice, so that magazines aimed at female readers were held to be the best advertising media. This affected the policies of British magazine editors, and in the United States there emerged a sharp division between the advertising-supported slick magazines and the sales-supported pulps. It was not unnatural that science fiction, which was a species of fiction appealing mainly to male readers, was confined to the pulps in America; its closest analogs in Britain were even more closely confined to the boys' papers.

The effects of this severance of the British and American traditions were several. The demands of the pulp marketplace in the United States encouraged the production of exotic adventure stories, but the development of a specialist readership also permitted the simultaneous establishment of a set of expectations (common to both readers and writers) regarding the appropriate content and method of science fiction stories. The precise terms of this "manifesto" for science fiction remained perennially controversial, but there nevertheless developed an awareness, common to a substantial group of readers and writers, that there *was* something called "science fiction" and that those involved with it were following a distinct and particular kind of literary endeavor. This awareness was in some ways constraining, but in others it was liberating—especially in the way that the development of a set of story frameworks provided imaginative elbow-room for a vast range of hypothetical creations. This lebensraum was by no means fully exploited by the early pulp writers, but it was they who put it on the literary map. In Britain, speculative writers had no such established pattern of imaginative conventions to draw on (although many took some warrant from the precedents laid down by Wells) and thus had to be much more careful in the construction of their hypothetical milieux. Their novels, in consequence, tend to stand up much better as individual entities and are much more varied as a result of the idiosyncratic methods and purposes of the writers.

Despite this developing contrast, there remained, of course, a considerable flow of material across the Atlantic. Most of the writing that appeared in book form was reprinted on the other side of the Atlantic (whichever side that might be), and some pulp magazines made their way into Britain. There are certainly many shared influences to be seen in the science fiction produced in the two countries. Nevertheless, the two traditions remained distinct in this period to a much greater degree than they previously had, or ever would again.

The continuity of the two traditions was affected by various factors, including the war itself. Few writers actually died during the war years, although Jack London and William Hope Hodgson were among them, but there were numerous important figures whose output changed considerably in content—all of them British. These included William Le Queux, John Beresford, M. P. Shiel, Sir Arthur Conan Doyle, and—most significant of all—H. G. Wells. A rather different kind of discontinuity was caused in the development of American scientific romance by the emergence in the postwar years of a number of new writers who were to make a significant contribution to the evolution of pulp science fiction and fantasy: A. Merritt, Ray Cummings, Murray Leinster, Francis Stevens, H. P. Lovecraft, and Homer Eon Flint all made their debuts between 1917 and 1919. The discontinuity was further emphasized in the next decade by the diversification of the pulps, when the general fiction magazines very largely gave way to a host of specialist titles, including magazines specializing in imaginative fiction. The *Thrill Book* enjoyed a brief career in 1919; *Weird Tales* was founded in 1923; and Hugo Gernsback began *Amazing Stories* in 1926. By 1930 there were three monthly science fiction magazines, two of which had quarterly companions. These magazines encouraged the emergence of still more new writers.

The change in the character of British science fiction offers striking testimony to the impact of the Great War on the consciousness of the nation. Prior to the war, the most prolific species of futuristic fiction produced in Britain had been the future war story, whose leading exponents had included George Griffith and William Le Queux. Most of these stories had looked forward with some enthusiasm to the prospect of large-scale conflict made more exciting and spectacular by the advent of airships, submarines, and more destructive weaponry. Even those writers who had imagined slaughter on a vast scale—Griffith in *The Angel of the Revolution* [1-41] and M. P. Shiel in *The Yellow Danger* (1898)—seemed to relish the prospect. H. G. Wells, in *The War in the Air* [1-104] and *The World Set Free* (1914), took no pleasure in the contemplation of huge casualty figures, but he thought even so that a war might be a good thing if it could clear away the old social order and make way for the construction of a Socialist world state.

Once the war had come and gone, however, and the reality of modern warfare had been made manifest, an era of disillusionment set in. The future war stories of the next decade saw war as an unmitigated evil that threatened to destroy civilization utterly. Examples include Edward Shanks's *The People of the Ruins* [2-97], Cicely Hamilton's *Theodore Savage* [2-40], P. A. Graham's *The Collapse of Homo Sapiens* (1924), and Shaw Desmond's *Ragnarok* [2-26]. The sequence extends into the 1930s with such novels as Miles's *The Gas War of 1940* [2-7], John Gloag's *To-Morrow's Yesterday* [2-37], and Joseph O'Neill's *Day of Wrath* [2-86].

The United States, as might be expected, was hardly touched by this tide of apocalyptic anxiety. The war had been fought a long way from American shores, and U.S. involvement lasted 18 months rather than four years. The future war stories produced in the United States during this period exhibit the same combination of alarmism and documentary fascination that marked British prewar novels, such as Le Queux's *Invasion of 1910* [1-57]. Examples include Hector Bywater's *The Great Pacific War* (1925) and Floyd Gibbons's *The Red Napoleon* [2-34].

This anxiety concerning the destructive power of contemporary technology was not confined, in Britain, to the contemplation of the possibility of war. Suspicion of the fruits of technological progress became much more general, and fears to the effect that even without a war the advance of technology might have a deleterious effect on the quality of life were commonly expressed. The spread of a similar suspicion in the United States was much less marked, and the balance of opinion in fiction produced there remained more optimistic throughout the period, although the seeds of doubt had certainly been sown.

This change in context helps to explain the fact that so many of the important British speculative writers of the prewar period either stopped producing futuristic works or changed the pattern of their thinking dramatically. Wells continued to write speculative fiction after the war, but nothing remotely similar to his early scientific romances. In general, his postwar work is more polemical and is frequently embittered by what Wells saw as a continuing disaster: the failure of humans to realize how desperate their contemporary historical situation really was. This comes across particularly well in *The Undying Fire* (1919), which is a materialist's version of the story of Job, and in *Mr. Blettsworthy on Rampole Island* (1928), whose hallucinating hero envisions contemporary humans as savage tribespeople unaware of their own brutality. His later utopian novels, *Men like Gods* [2-129] and *The Shape of Things to Come* [2-130], present ideal societies much further removed from the contemporary world than *A Modern Utopia* [1-101] and imply that the contemporary being is far too ignoble to aspire to live in them. Those science fiction stories he wrote as entertainments in this period—*The Autocracy of Mr. Parham* (1930) and *Star-Begotten* [2-131] among them—are uneasy works that have the utmost difficulty in taking themselves seriously.

The change that overtook the work of Sir Arthur Conan Doyle was of a rather different kind, more directly attributable to the ravages of the war itself. Doyle also turned to polemical work, developing an intense interest in spiritualism and the possibility of an afterlife, following the death of his son. The depth of feeling that lies behind *The Land of Mist* [2-27] is obvious, but its hero, Professor Challenger, is tragically demoralized by comparison with his earlier self.

William Le Queux, not unnaturally, never recovered the bloodthirsty ebullience that had characterized his prewar work, and he wrote only one more genuinely science fiction work—*The Terror of the Air* (1920)—before relaxing into the production of lackluster mystery novels for the remainder of his career. Less easy to comprehend, however, is the abandonment of science fiction themes by two writers who remained active and who showed no conspicuous decline in their abilities—John Beresford and M. P. Shiel. Both returned to science fiction near the very end of their careers—Beresford with *What Dreams May Come . . .* (1941) and Shiel with *The Young Men Are Coming!* [2-99]—but in each case there was a gap of more than 20 years separating these late works from the authors' important early contributions to the genre.

Compared with the decisive break in the pattern of British science fiction, the development of the American scene seems much more orderly. It resembles a gradual unfolding, with the variety of the work increasing by stages as new writers and new markets made their appearances. There is, however, a striking contrast between the new writers who emerged in Britain and those who emerged in the United States. The British writers took their place in a tradition that had become more argumentative and more pessimistic, where speculative fiction was commonly used as a medium for thoughtful speculation about social issues. It remained, of course, a medium of entertainment, and many of the new writers produced exciting and colorful narratives, but generally of a rather cerebral disposition. This is obvious even from the most superficial inspection of the works of the more prolific speculative writers of the period—S. Fowler Wright, Olaf Stapledon, and John Gloag.

In the United States, by contrast, the writing of imaginative fiction had taken on a very different emphasis, mainly because of the heavy investment of the pulp magazines in exotic romance, which was itself due very largely to the influence of one writer—Edgar Rice Burroughs. Interplanetary romance of the Burroughs variety thrived in the United States during the period between the end of the war and the founding of *Amazing Stories,* and it helped enormously to make the notion of a specialist fiction that would rely heavily on interplanetary adventures more acceptable. Examples of this curious subspecies of other-worldly romance include J. U. Giesy's "Palos" trilogy (1918–1921), Homer Eon Flint's interplanetary stories (1919–1921), Ralph Milne Farley's Radio Man series [2-29], and Otis Adelbert Kline's Venus series (1924–1926).

Burroughs, however, did not confine himself to interplanetary scenarios in his more exotic stories, and neither did his imitators. Ray Cummings hollowed out his own niche within the field by developing a new milieu—the atomic microcosm. Although this was considerably less plausible than Burroughs's alternative milieux—lost worlds and the interior of the Earth—it proved rather more successful in capturing the imagination and was adopted by Gernsback's science fiction magazines as a conventional setting. Cummings's pioneering venture was *The Girl in the Golden Atom* [2-22]; other microcosmic romances include Austin

Hall's *People of the Comet* [2-31] and Festus Pragnell's *The Green Man of Graypec* (1935), also known as *The Green Man of Kilsona*. Another milieu that became popular was the "parallel world," which had long existed in traditional fantasy unsanctified by such an earnest title. This featured extensively in the work of a writer whose fantasies were even more gaudy and exotic than those of Burroughs—A. Merritt. Although he never wrote bona fide science fiction, Merritt was one of Gernsback's favorite authors, and he influenced several of the early recruits to Gernsback's cause, most obviously Jack Williamson. Notable parallel-world stories from the postwar decade include Merritt's *The Moon Pool* [2-77] and Flint and Hall's *The Blind Spot* [2-31].

Advocates of the view that science fiction is essentially a hard-headed, rational, and realistic form of imaginative fiction frequently exaggerate the difference between this kind of fiction and the kind that Gernsback tried hard to promote in *Amazing Stories,* which was ostensibly prophetic, educational, and faithful to known science. However, the overflow of this material into the early pulp science fiction magazines proved to be rather more than a temporary aberration, and it has remained very much a part of the publishing category ever since. There is and always has been a large overlap between the audience that attends to books published in the science fiction category and the audience for the purest kinds of fantastic romance. It is worth noting, too, the myth that holds the incidence of escapist fantasy in the science fiction magazines to be a result of the gloom and despondency of the depression. This kind of pulp romance enjoyed its heyday—and so, for that matter, did the pulps themselves—in the heady years *before* the Wall Street crash of 1929.

It is mildly surprising that this kind of exotic adventure story is not at all evident in British imaginative fiction, despite the fact that Burroughs himself was a very popular author in Britain. Stacey Blake's *Beyond the Blue* (1920) is an entertaining blend of Vernian and Burroughs romance, but there are no British interplanetary stories that exhibit the same wholehearted exoticism as Burroughs's Martian fantasies. There are a few imitation Tarzan stories, but no science fiction ones. One reason for this is the fact that there seems to have been much less discrimination in the United States between fiction intended for juvenile readers and that for adult audiences. In Britain there was (and still is) something of a gulf between the two. Some of the fiction published in the popular magazines before the war—Wells's scientific romances and Doyle's *The Lost World* [1-31], for instance—was considered to bridge the gulf, but the war seems to have reduced that bridge to ruins. Fantastic romance was regarded throughout the 1920s and 1930s as suitable only for boys' papers unless there was some obviously serious (or perhaps satirical) intent behind it.

Of the authors who became the main suppliers of original material to the science fiction magazines in the years between 1920 and 1940, very few were untouched by the lure of exotic romance. The main concession made by many of them to Gernsback's manifesto was simply that they began to devote more time and attention to the hardware featured in their stories. Such writers as A. Hyatt Verrill and S. P. Meek remained firmly anchored within the established pulp tradition, although they appeared almost exclusively in the SF pulps. Space travel, however, quickly became a matter of interest in its own right rather than simply a literary device for taking characters into an exotic environment, and this led to the rapid development of "space opera" by such writers as Edmond Hamilton, Edward E. Smith, and Jack Williamson.

The writer who actually conformed most closely to Gernsback's notion of what science fiction writers ought to be doing was David H. Keller, who wrote only one interplanetary story and no exotic romance. Keller, who was a doctor specializing in psychiatric medicine, actually had the advantage of knowing something about science—an advantage shared by all too few of Gernsback's writers. Three notable exceptions to this rule among the early recruits to the SF pulps were the mathematician Eric Temple Bell (who wrote under the pseudonym John Taine), John W. Campbell, Jr., and Stanley G. Weinbaum. Taine was able to compensate for his somewhat awkward literary style by the extravagance of his imagination, but Weinbaum—who had both literary ability *and* imaginative power, as well as a low-key humor—died less than 18 months after publishing his first science fiction story. His death robbed the SF pulps during the 1930s of the man who would surely have become their one abiding star. It was Campbell, however, who went on to have by far the most profound effect on the genre as editor of *Astounding.* His career as a writer was cut short soon after he took that office, but he did publish some extravagant space operas and a number of excellent short stories (the latter under the pseudonym Don A. Stuart).

In the evolution of a distinctive species of pulp science fiction from the more generalized field of exotic romance, therefore, we can identify two main trends: first, the emergence of space travel as a theme in its own right rather than as a literary device, and second, the slow but steady accumulation of a group of writers who were capable of doing what Gernsback asked—developing stories from and around the seed of a scientific idea.

There is one further factor that needs to be mentioned when considering the different ways in which British and American science fiction evolved between the wars, and that is the influence of speculative nonfiction. In Britain, particularly between 1925 and 1935, there was something of a boom in what we would now call "futurology." Numerous essays appeared in which authors attempted to anticipate the changes that the near future would bring. A good deal of this material was reprinted in the United States, but Americans produced far less of it. The reason for this, of course, was the fact that in British intellectual circles anxiety about the future was running high. Although there are several predictive works whose tone is entirely optimistic—the Earl of Birkenhead's *The World in 2030 A.D.* (1930) and A. M. Low's *Our Wonderful World of Tomorrow* (1934) are the cardinal examples—many of these essays seem highly dubious about the certainty of progress.

A particularly influential contribution to speculative thought about the future was made by a series of essays published by Kegan Paul, Trench, and Trubner (reprinted in the United States by Dutton), called the Today & Tomorrow series. The essays were initiated by the publication in 1924 of the text of a lecture by J. B. S. Haldane, entitled *Daedalus; or, Science and the Future,* in which the author argued that by the end of the century social life would be altered beyond recognition (entirely for the better) due to the advancement of biological science. The immediate effect of this publication was to prompt a reply from the philosopher Bertrand Russell, entitled *Icarus; or, The Future of Science,* which argued that scientific advancement, by giving greater power to existing power groups, would more likely result in the annihilation, not the betterment, of the human race. The debate was joined by others, and the publishers—thinking that they were on to a good thing—eventually extended the series to include more than 100 pamphlets. Contributors to the series included many eminent scientists and literary figures, and between them they discussed the future of virtually every human field of endeavor and many social institutions. The essayists included Sylvia Pankhurst, Vernon Lee, Vera Brittain, C. E. M. Joad, and James Jeans. Particularly significant, however, was the number of contributors who also wrote speculative fiction (usually—although not always—*after* the essays): André Maurois, Muriel Jaeger, J. Leslie Mitchell, A. M. Low, Robert Graves, John Gloag, Gerald Heard, and, of course, the original contributors, Haldane and Russell.

Haldane's *Daedalus* proved to be enormously influential in several works of speculative fiction, although mainly in a negative way—Aldous Huxley's *Brave New World* [2-47] and C. S. Lewis's trilogy begun with *Out of the Silent Planet* [3-263] are partly reactions against it. A more constructive influence was Haldane's collection of essays, *Possible Worlds* (1927). One of those essays, "The Last Judgment," together with J. D. Bernal's Today & Tomorrow essay, "The World, the Flesh and the Devil," was an important influence on the work of Olaf Stapledon.

In general, this flow of ideas from futurological speculation into speculative fiction helped to maintain the intellectual seriousness of British science fiction. Hugo Gernsback, no doubt, would dearly have loved to generate a similar flow of ideas into his own writers, but he could not do so—and, with the best will in the world, it is difficult to imagine that his writers were really capable of taking advantage of it even if he had. There *were* writers in America who were every bit as capable as Huxley, Stapledon, and Gloag, but speculation about the future never really invaded the intellectual circles in which they moved. For this reason, virtually all the science fiction produced between the wars that has any real literary merit is British or European in origin.

The virtues of the best speculative fiction produced in Britain between the wars are easy enough to see: the novels are serious in intent, ambitious in their attempts to analyze genuine human problems, and frequently subtle in their development of ideas. They were written within—and made a contribution to—an intellectual climate where concern for the future prospects of society had a certain urgency.

American science fiction did not have the benefit of such an intellectual climate, and there is a sense in which it actually had to—and did—build its own subculture specifically to generate such a climate on a limited scale. An urgent concern for the future, and for the possibilities implicit in the march of science (reflected in numerous books popularizing science), was actually rather esoteric in the United States during the 1920s. This situation was transformed as time went by, but there is a sense in which American science fiction has never entirely recovered from its one-time esotericism. The subculture that formed around the SF pulps of the 1920s and 1930s still puts a high value on that esotericism and guards it as best it can.

To contrast American science fiction of this period unfavorably with the best of British speculative fiction, however, should not blind us to the fact that pulp science fiction had virtues of its own. Pulp SF had a verve and enthusiasm that was part and parcel of its awkward naïveté. British speculative fiction was far-ranging in time, but for the most part it paid relatively little attention to space. Leaving aside such visionary works as David Lindsay's *A Voyage to Arcturus* [2-63] and Stapledon's *Star Maker* [2-112], British writers were too interested in this world to pay much heed to others. Strange societies were frequently situated on the Moon or on Mars, so that their mode of organization could be contrasted with ours, but imagining space travel as an actual project, or trying to construct hypothetical life systems that might plausibly exist on other worlds, were minority interests. In the pulps, by contrast, they seemed to be the very heart of the whole endeavor. It was the pulp writers who turned the universe into a gigantic playground for the imagination and sent pioneers out into imaginative territories that were literally limitless. These pioneers hardly began to exploit this wonderful wealth of opportunity, but they laid the first trails and put up the signposts.

Perhaps this sharp difference—although it was mainly due to historical circumstance—says something about the different social psychologies of the United States and Britain.

The period following World War I was also fertile for the development of speculative fiction in languages other than English. The longest-standing coherent tradition of scientific romance was, of course, in France, where Jules Verne's *Voyages imaginaires* had established the genre in the 1860s. Verne died in 1905, and two of his most important contemporaries—Camille Flammarion and Albert Robida—produced no significant work after the turn of the century, although they survived into the 1920s. There was, however, one major writer active before the war who continued his career afterward—Joseph-Henri Boëx, who signed his scientific romances J. H. Rosny aîné. Only one of his works has been properly translated—*The Giant Cat* [2-95]—and his most important postwar work, *Les Navigateurs de l'infini* [6-139], remains unknown outside France.

Other French writers whose careers spanned the war years were Maurice Renard, Jean de la Hire, and Claude Farrère (Charles Bargone). La Hire's work does not exist at all in English, but some works by the other two are available in translation—most impressively Farrère's *Useless Hands* [2-30]. Of the writers who emerged to prominence in the postwar period, the most notable is André Maurois, who wrote various brief episodes from an imaginary future history and two excellent long stories, the novella *The Weigher of Souls* [2-73] and the novel *The Thought-Reading Machine* [2-72]. Gernsback had several French novels translated for the SF pulps, but most of them are minor; the best is probably *La Mort du fer* (1931) by S. S. Held, translated by Fletcher Pratt as *The Death of Iron* (1931). The influence of Rosny, who wrote several prehistoric fantasies, was presumably responsible for the fact that such fantasies are extensively featured in French fiction of the 1920s. Max Begouen wrote several, including *Les Bisons d'argile* (1925), translated as *Bison of Clay* in 1926. Claude Anet's *La Fin d'un monde* (1925), translated as *The End of a World* in 1927, is also notable. Henri Barbusse's panoramic presentation of human history in *Chains* (1925) also includes scenes from prehistory.

No nation underwent a more traumatic transformation as a result of the Great War than Germany, and both the leading German speculative writers of the prewar period died in the second decade of the century—Kurd Lasswitz in 1910 and Paul Scheerbart in 1915. The main ingredient of the futuristic fiction that began to appear in some profusion after the war was technocratic utopianism of an extravagant type, which bore a strong (and not unnatural) resemblance to the kind of fiction that Gernsback wanted to publish in his magazines to inspire the American youth with inventive enthusiasm. The most successful writer of this kind was Hans Dominik, but the only translation of his work used by Gernsback was an article, "Airports for World Traffic," in *Air Wonder Stories* in 1930. Gernsback featured far more work by a writer less well known in his native land, Otfrid von Hanstein, five of whose novels appeared in *Wonder Stories* and *Wonder Stories Quarterly*, beginning with *Electropolis* [2-122]. The image of a technocratic utopia was so prevalent in German popular literature of the day that it became the target of an especially scathing attack in Alexandr Moszkowski's satirical demolition of utopian ideals, *The Isles of Wisdom* [2-81].

Interplanetary stories also featured in German science fiction between the wars, largely due to the influence of rocket pioneer Herman Oberth. Otto Willi Gail's *The Shot into Infinity* [2-33] makes a bold attempt to achieve technical realism, and members of the Society for Space Travel founded by Oberth and others popularized their activities via their involvement with Fritz Lang's film *Die Frau im Mond* (1929). The German cinema of the period produced several notable science fiction films, including Lang's magnificent *Metropolis* (1926), and the success of the film version of *F.P.1 Does Not Reply* [2-101] was an important factor in guiding Curt Siodmak toward Hollywood, where he enjoyed a long career scripting monster movies. Very little German science fiction of the period had any conspicuous literary merit, however, and its history seems to run parallel to the history of pulp SF in the United States in the 1920s and 1930s, without the corresponding maturation in the next decade.

World War I was responsible for a significant historical break in Britain, France, and Germany, but it is arguable that an even more dramatic break occurred in eastern Europe as a result of the Russian Revolution of 1917. Despite the backwardness of Russia in terms of its lack of industrialization relative to the other European powers, there had been some technological utopian novels published in the late nineteenth century, including one by N. Chernyshevsky, the man who translated Karl Marx's *Capital* into Russian. The Russian rocket pioneer Konstantin Tsiolkovsky was encouraged by the new regime, and he completed his Verne-like romance *Beyond the Planet Earth* [2-120] not long after the revolution. Other writers whose speculative works enjoyed great success in the U.S.S.R. were Alexei Tolstoi and Aleksandr Beliaev. Two Russian writers of the period who undoubtedly were literary figures of major importance were prophets without honor in their own country because they rapidly became disenchanted with the Communist state. Evgenii Zamiatin quickly fell from favor after writing the brilliant *We* [2-147], and although Mikhail Bulgakov was greatly admired as a playwright by Stalin, he too was silenced after the implementation of the new economic policy led him to publish the satirical novella "The Fatal Eggs" [2-9].

Of all the speculative writers of the period who wrote in languages other than English, however, one man stands out—the Czech Karel Čapek, whose major works include *R.U.R.* [2-15], the play that gave the word *robot* to several languages, and three fine novels—*The Absolute at Large* [2-13], *Krakatit* [2-14], and *War with the Newts* [2-16]. Čapek contrasts sharply with the German and American writers and far outdoes the British pessimists in respect to his dire suspicion of progress and his unique brand of fatalistic black comedy. His ardent championship of democracy and opposition to the threat of Nazism would have ensured him the same fate as his brother Josef, who died in Belsen, but Karel's death came three months before Hitler's invasion.

Of the science fiction published in the rest of Europe during this period, very little exists in translation. The prehistoric sections of *The Long Journey* [2-50] by Danish Nobel prize winner Johannes V. Jensen have been published in English, but no futuristic fiction from the Scandinavian countries seems to have been translated. The same is true of Italy. It is probable, however, that only four European nations—Britain, France, Germany, and the U.S.S.R.—and Japan can really be said to have had identifiable domestic *traditions* of speculative fiction in this period, and that, in consequence, only these nations warrant special treatment here.

The interwar period is given relatively sparse coverage in most reference books and histories of SF. The American pulp stories of the period are given fullest consideration in Paul Carter's *The Creation of Tomorrow* [9-19], which provides excellent analytical coverage of its main themes. British books are listed and briefly annotated in I. F. Clarke's bibliography *Tale of the Future from the Beginning to the Present Day* [8-14], but Clarke's analytical work *The Pattern of Expectation* [9-26] is less interested in this period than earlier ones. The most detailed commentary on and analysis of the British tradition is to be found in *Scientific Romance in Britain 1890–1950* [9-93] by Brian Stableford.

Fred Polak's *The Image of the Future* (1961), which is perhaps the best of all historical studies of futuristic fiction, ceases to give detailed consideration to particular texts when it reaches this period, and argues that futuristic fiction suffered a crucial deterioration because of the "denaturation" of the image of the future possessed by modern Western culture. This denaturation, according to Polak, was partly a disintegration and fragmentation reflected in the variety and multiplicity of texts, and partly a decline in hopefulness. It *is* true that this period saw the virtual petering out of the tradition of utopian fantasy, and a dramatic loss of confidence in the ability and readiness of Western society to reorganize itself in such a way as to secure the greater happiness of the greatest number, but it is probably a mistake to see this as a final or fatal deterioration in futuristic thought. It certainly reflects the emergence of a more bitter zeitgeist, especially in Britain, but it also reflects the emergence of a new skepticism about the possibility of assuring the happiness of all simply by technological sophistication and sociopolitical reorganization.

Before World War I, prophets could declare that utopian reconstruction was not merely feasible but imminent. Such novels as Edward Bellamy's *Looking Backward* [1-8] and Wells's *A Modern Utopia* [1-101] were near-future visions, replete with advertising copy promoting the idea of a world reborn. As the Great War entered its final phase, it was still possible to hope that it might in some small part be justified if it could prepare the way for such a regeneration as is envisaged in Oliver Onions's *The New Moon* [2-87]. Unfortunately, it was not to be. Optimism ebbed away in the postwar years as men and women counted the cost of the war and hunted in vain for the profit. The march of technology continued, but its champions—Gernsback, Haldane, Dominik, and others—found themselves arrayed against an army of doubters who wondered whether the advancement of technology really could be counted "progress."

It was considered that machines *might,* if responsibly used, help to create heaven on Earth, but it was held to be already proven that they could also create hell. The argument invariably turned on some account of human nature, which was (in the wake of Darwin and Freud) almost invariably held to be rapacious and greedy, not to be trusted either with sophisticated means of destruction or with the means of gratifying to the full childish and hedonistic desires.

Many of the utopias imagined in this period, therefore, tend to be fugitive ones, hiding—like James Hilton's Shangri-La in *Lost Horizon* [2-43]—in some all-but-inaccessible corner of dubious plausibility. There are also ironic utopias, like John Gloag's *The New Pleasure* [2-35], and bizarre visions that call the whole notion of utopia into question, such as Herbert Read's *The Green Child* [2-91]. Rex Warner's surreal allegory of the search for a better world conveys its embittered message in its title—*The Wild Goose Chase* (1937). The most rigorous and thorough of all utopian satires, Alexandr Moszkowski's *Isles of Wisdom* [2-81], is very much in tune with the zeitgeist, and so are the various tales of "utopia betrayed" in which people simply fail to adjust to the opportunities of an age of abundance; examples include Muriel Jaeger's *The Question Mark* [2-49] and Claude Farrère's *Useless Hands* [2-30].

It had been popular before the war to imagine that the miracles of science might be turned against us, by foreign warlords or mad scientists, but in the period between the wars this anxiety grew deeper and broader. There were still mad scientists and foreign warlords, of course, but the suspicion extended to anyone who had power and might try to keep it—Lord Acton's dictum about power's corrupting seemed much more important once it was possible to imagine power groups in control of psychotropic drugs and eugenic programs, as in Huxley's *Brave New World* [2-47], or the gift of immortality, as in Gloag's *Winter's Youth* [2-38] or Bell's *The Seventh Bowl* [2-7]. There was even the possibility that the machines themselves might grow sufficiently powerful to turn against us, as in Miles J. Breuer's *Paradise and Iron* [2-8], and perhaps the possibility that we might turn against our very selves, as in S. Fowler Wright's *The Adventure of Wyndham Smith* [2-138].

The utopian works of the period are, for the most part, unimpressive. The most wholehearted of them are *Man's World* (1926) by Charlotte Haldane, whose husband was Britain's most ardent champion of scientific progress, and *Back to Methuselah* [2-98] by George Bernard Shaw, who renounced Darwinism in favor of the simple faith that human nature might be anything we want it to be. Taken as a group, however, they cannot compare either in imaginative vigor or in literary quality with the mass of dystopian novels.

In the past, dystopian images had been produced almost entirely in order to attack particular political philosophies. This motive remained important in the production of such anti-Socialist polemics as Condé B. Pallen's *Crucible Island* (1919), John Kendall's *Unborn Tomorrow* (1933), and Ayn Rand's *Anthem* [3-315], and such anti-Fascist polemics as Sinclair Lewis's *It Can't Happen Here* [2-62]. But what is most noticeable about the period is the prevalence of novels that go beyond the surfaces of particular ideologies to reach more fundamental questions about the nature of the good life and the entanglement of political power and technological instrumentality. The classics of the period, of course, are Zamiatin's *We* [2-147] and Huxley's *Brave New World* [2-47], but the same kind of analytical thoughtfulness can be seen to a greater or lesser degree in a host of other works—Michael Arlen's *Man's Mortality* [2-1] and Joseph O'Neill's *Land under England* [2-86] are examples.

Shaw, of course, was not the only dissenter with respect to the new view of human nature that became established in the wake of Darwin and Freud. The Marxist Henri Barbusse offered a different account of human nature in *Chains* (1925), and J. Leslie Mitchell was eloquent in his rejection of the notion of inherent bestiality in his curious evolutionary parable *Three Go Back* [2-79]. There is no doubt, however, that the weight of opinion was on the other side, and it was in this period particularly that the "theriomorphic image of man" was adopted as a warrant for scathing misanthropy by a number of writers. This attitude is at its most extreme in the work of S. Fowler Wright, particularly *The World Below* [2-144], but can also be seen in Olaf Stapledon's *Odd John* [2-110] and Claude Houghton's *This Was Ivor Trent* [2-44]. Many dystopian fantasies of the period imply that the citizens of dystopia deserve their fate, and the truly bloodcurdling aspect of *We* and *Brave New World* is their allegation that the vast majority of citizens would be perfectly content with their lot.

Between the extremes of *Back to Methuselah* and *The World Below*, however, there is an extensive spectrum of works in which writers wonder about the real extent of our less fortunate behavioral dispositions and ask what probability exists that we may overcome them. Most writers, in the end, come to the conclusion that even though there is much of the ape in us, there is at least an echo of the angel too—a viewpoint put forward explicitly enough in Wells's *Undying Fire* (1919) and in Guy Dent's *Emperor of the If* [2-25], and perhaps most eloquently of all in E. V. Odle's *The Clockwork Man* [2-84]. Interestingly enough, this force for good is usually construed in spiritual or emotional terms rather than as the power of reason. Indeed, reason is frequently seen to be allied with the dark side of human nature because of its presumed amorality. Fables attacking the amorality of hyperrational and unemotional superhumans are common, such as Noëlle Roger's *The New Adam* [2-94], and so are parables in which scientists are betrayed into evil deeds by their excessive dedication to rationalism, as in *The Weigher of Souls* [2-73] by André Maurois and *The Devil's Highway* [2-137] by Harold Bell Wright and John Lebar.

This conflict between the image of the human implied by contemporary biology and psychology and the older image of theological supposition is a central issue in many of the metaphysical fantasies that import mysticism into speculative fiction. The period produced two of the most important writers in this vein in David Lindsay, author of *A Voyage to Arcturus* [2-63] and other works, and Charles Williams, author of *Many Dimensions* [2-132] and other works. Other titles of similar ilk include Karel Čapek's satire *The Absolute at Large* [2-13], and *The Avatars* (1933) by "A.E."

This importation of metaphysical themes and ideas greatly assisted the main trend in British speculative fiction that counterbalances the pessimism of the future war stories and dystopian fantasies. *Back to Methuselah* [2-98] eventually goes *beyond* utopia to hypothesize that the ultimate evolutionary goal of humankind is a kind of transcendental metamorphosis, in which the brutality of the flesh will be conclusively set aside. Although few other writers imagined a transcendence so extreme, very many did take refuge in the hope that a new kind of being, equipped with a metahuman nature, might emerge to replace Homo sapiens. In misanthropic stories, like *The World Below* [2-144] or John Gloag's *To-Morrow's Yesterday* [2-37], the replacement species are not our descendants, but in Houghton's *This Was Ivor Trent* [2-44] and John Beresford's *What Dreams May Come . . .* (1941) they are. The author who adapted scientific romance most comprehensively to the purpose of metaphysical speculation, Olaf Stapledon, remained perennially interested in the possibility of future human species' evolving a finer nature; this is given extensive consideration in *Last and First Men* [2-109] and its sequel *Last Men in London* (1932), in *Odd John* [2-110], and in such later works as *Darkness and the Light* (1942) and *A Man Divided* (1950).

The positive side of the speculative fiction produced between the wars is, however, not entirely confined to these images of the future transcendence of crude human nature. It can be argued, too, that what Polak actually saw as evidence of deterioration—the sheer fecundity of futuristic imagination, especially as displayed in American SF—is really evidence of a new attitude by no means devoid of optimism. There is a positive element in the very insistence that the future does contain a vast spectrum of possible alternatives: that we are not faced with a single road of destiny but with a bewildering array of possible futures. The naïveté of the pulp fantasist's escapist romps, and their occasional tendency to embrace alarmism in the interests of melodrama, are equally neither here nor there in the context of this argument; what matters is recognizing that there are more things in future possibility than had earlier been dreamed of. That discovery in itself carried with it a certain spirit of exuberance and exhilaration. The British tradition, for all its desperation, did take aboard this consciousness of the spectrum of alternativity.

This is the real importance of such works as Odle's *The Clockwork Man* [2-84], Dent's *Emperor of the If* [2-25], and the display of evolutionary possibility featured in Stapledon's *Last and First Men* [2-109]. This, too, is the real merit of much of the material published in the SF pulps, including the short stories of David Keller [2-55], Laurence Manning's *The Man Who Awoke* [2-68], and John Taine's *The Time Stream* [2-118].

The growing emphasis on alternatives arose naturally enough out of the disenchantment with the universe. The removal of predestination and intrinsic purpose from the scheme of things took away the guarantees we had previously taken for granted (whether in respect to God's mercy or the inevitability of progress), but it also opened a new wonderland of opportunity. Stapledon described *Last and First Men* as an "essay in myth creation," and we might well regard the whole of science fiction in much the same light. A vast wilderness of time and space has been revealed by the advancement of geological and astronomical science, and science fiction can be seen as a kind of mythology that is helping us to populate that wilderness and make it imaginatively manageable. Myths are exemplary fictions, which provide "explanations" for the way the world is in terms of the way it was and will be and guidelines for conduct by displaying the moral order that may be assumed intrinsic in the natural order. This, in large measure, is what science fiction does, too, both consciously and unconsciously. It is, of course, a mythology with many alternative versions of the assumed reality, but how could it be otherwise?

The period between the wars saw a boom in panoramic treatments of the history of the human race, past *and* future. As well as those already named, mention might be made of George Viereck and Paul Eldridge's *My First Two Thousand Years* (1928) and its sequels, and various works by F. Britten Austin, including *Tomorrow* (1930). Like *Chains, The Long Journey, Last and First Men,* and *The Man Who Awoke,* these novels and story sequences look for a *pattern* in the scheme of things that will allow a sensible connection to be made between the origin of the human race, the contemporary human condition, and the possibilities that still lie open.

In addition—and this applies particularly to the work of the pulp writers—the period saw a burgeoning fascination with the concept of infinite space and an infinite array of possible worlds. This frequently (although rather paradoxically) expressed itself in an urge to burst the bounds of infinity, to get outside the universe itself. This is a recurrent theme in early pulp science fiction, exhibited by several microcosmic romances and such stories as "The Eternal World" (1932) by Clark Ashton Smith and "Colossus" (1934) by Donald Wandrei. The space operas of Edward E. Smith and John W. Campbell, Jr., attempted to make the interstellar gulfs imaginatively navigable. Writers such as Stanley G. Weinbaum began the work of designing alien ecosystems of some complexity, fundamentally *different* from the scheme of living things to be found on Earth. The true measure of the mythic quality of many of these inventions can be seen in the fact that they have become what all successful myths become—imaginative clichés, too obvious and familiar ever to be surprising.

The historians of science fiction whose attention is narrowly confined by the Gernsback-invented label have no difficulty in finding contrasts between the science fiction of today and the science fiction of the "pre-Campbellian period." Campbell did, indeed, accomplish much in terms of redirecting the concerns of pulp magazine science fiction and refining its methodology, but if we consider the whole spectrum of speculative fiction produced between 1918 and 1938, rather than just the material written for the pulps, that contrast becomes far less striking. The pattern of history has encouraged changes in emphasis at various times, and there have been innovations, but there is really very little in contemporary science fiction that is without precedent in the fiction produced between the wars. The fundamental issues are strikingly similar—the preoccupation with those facets of human nature that seem to damage our prospects of building a better world; suspicion that the gifts of science may prove to be a Pandora's box where hope lies fugitive among a cloud of troubles; the attempt to grapple imaginatively with the infinite and the eternal. The greatest contrast, in fact, is simply the sheer *amount* of science fiction that is published today in comparison with the amount that was produced during the years between the wars.

It has already been noted that futuristic speculation of any kind was an esoteric pursuit in the United States during this period. In Britain—and perhaps in Germany, too—it was less so, but what was generally popular and accessible was near-future speculation of a relatively limited kind. Some of the imaginative novels published in Britain between the wars enjoyed considerable popularity, but not the bolder ones. Stapledon managed to sustain a popular reputation as a speculator (although *Star Maker* [2-112] was remaindered and not reprinted until long after World War II had ended), but many of the works of his contemporaries sank without trace—some are still in need of being "rediscovered." The mythology of the disenchanted universe was, in this period, restricted to the interests of a relatively small cult. In Britain, membership in the cult was sufficiently intellectually respectable not to entail alienation from other intellectual circles, but in the United States the cult became a cult indeed, defensive in its exclusivity.

This tendency toward cultishness is something that shows up in the fiction itself, to some extent. There is an uneasiness about much of it, and some of it even has an apologetic quality; many authors felt the need to explain what they were doing, and why, in self-effacing prefaces. By comparison with contemporary science fiction, the science fiction published between 1918 and 1938 was not self-confident. It is to the credit of several authors that they did not allow this lack of self-confidence to lead them into imaginative cowardice. If anything, the reverse is the case. There are few more recent works with the determined boldness of *Last and First Men, Star Maker, A Voyage to Arcturus, The World Below,* and *The Clockwork Man.* It is works such as these that represent the literary monuments of the period.

Bibliography

2-1. Arlen, Michael (U.K.). **Man's Mortality.** Heinemann, 1933.
Controllers of the world's air traffic have forced peace on the world, but young officers disillusioned by their methods join forces with a rebel who has invented a faster aircraft. The enigmatic hero is ultimately revealed as a kind of Antichrist and the political questions raised are left open. Compare Kipling's "As Easy as A.B.C." [1-55] and Wells's *The Shape of Things to Come* [2-130] for other accounts of air dictatorship.

*2-2. Asimov, Isaac, ed. **Before the Golden Age.** Doubleday, 1974.
Giant anthology of stories from the SF pulps of 1931–1937, with an autobiographical commentary by Asimov explaining what it felt like to be a science fiction fan in the 1930s. The contents include space opera (Murray Leinster's "Proxima Centauri"), microcosmic romance (Henry Hasse's "He Who Shrank" and S. P. Meek's "Submicroscopic" and "Awlo of Ulm"), encounters with alien beings ("Tetrahedra of Space" by P. Schuyler Miller, "The Moon Era" by Jack Williamson, "Old Faithful" by Raymond Z. Gallun, and "Parasite Planet" by Stanley G. Weinbaum), and extravagant "thought-variants" ("Born of the Sun" by Jack Williamson and "The Accursed Galaxy" by Edmond Hamilton). Easily the best introduction to the romance of early pulp SF. Compare with *From Off This World* [2-69] by Margulies and Friend and *Science Fiction of the Thirties* [2-58] by Knight.

2-3. Atherton, Gertrude. **Black Oxen.** Boni & Liveright, 1923.
A romantic novel in which a rejuvenated society queen returns to her native New York and falls in love with a man many years her junior. Well received in its time, but now dated. Compare *The Young Diana* (1918) by Marie Corelli.

2-4. Beliaev, Aleksandr (U.S.S.R.). **The Amphibian.** Foreign Languages Publishing, 1959. Tr. by L. Kolesnikov of *Chelovek-amphibiia,* 1928.
An account of a biological experiment in which a human child is adapted for aquatic life. Beliaev was one of the most prolific Soviet writers of the 1920s. Another translated novel, *The Struggle in Space* (1928; tr. 1965), contrasts a communist utopia with a capitalist dystopia. His work has a certain Vernian enthusiasm, but his characters are wooden.

2-5. Bell, Neil (pseud. of Stephen Southwold) (U.K.). **The Lord of Life.** Collins, 1933.
A scientist who discovers a new weapon tries to blackmail the world, and then destroys the world. The people aboard an experimental submarine survive, but their chances of making a new beginning are inhibited because there is only one woman among their number. A maliciously ironic black comedy. Compare Sinclair's *The Millennium* [2-100].

2-6. Bell, Neil (pseud. of Stephen Southwold) (U.K.). **Precious Porcelain.** Gollancz, 1931.
Mysterious events in a small town are ultimately explained as the result of a series of experiments in the evocation of alternate personalities. A curious elaboration of the Jekyll-and-Hyde motif, similar in structure to Bell's later novels *The Disturbing Affair of Noel Blake* (1932), which involves the recovery of race ancestral memories, and *Life Comes to Seathorpe* (1946), which involves the creation of artificial organisms.

*2-7. Bell, Neil (as "Miles"; pseud. of Stephen Southwold) (U.K.). **The Seventh Bowl.** Partridge, 1930.
The inventor of an immortality serum is murdered by members of the political elite, who use his discovery to secure their rule and to begin the eugenic reshaping of the human community in the wake of a destructive war. Their methods provoke violent opposition, which is ruthlessly suppressed until a new genius puts up such stern resistance that the world is destroyed. A startling example of postwar cynicism. Southwold wrote a second novel as Miles, *The Gas War of 1940* (1931), based on an episode in *The Seventh Bowl,* and both books were reprinted under the Bell name, the 1931 novel as *Valiant Clay.*

2-8. Breuer, Miles J. **Paradise and Iron.** *Amazing Stories Quarterly,* Summer 1930.
A melodrama set on an island whose population is supported in luxury by the labor of machines coordinated by an artificial brain. When the brain begins to malfunction, the people find themselves in deadly peril. One of the earliest pulp stories voicing suspicion of the myth of technological utopia presented by such stories as von Hanstein's *Electropolis* [2-122], reflecting the concerns of such "mainstream" stories as Forster's "The Machine Stops" [1-35].

2-9. Bulgakov, Mikhail (U.S.S.R.). "The Fatal Eggs" in **Diaboliad and Other Stories.** Indiana University Press, 1972. Tr. by Carl R. Proffer from a 1925 story.

The last satirical piece Bulgakov published before his work was suppressed—a sarcastic account of the creation of an absurd catastrophe by reckless and inefficient Soviet bureaucrats mishandling a wonderful scientific discovery. *Heart of a Dog* (written 1925; tr. 1968) is more subtle and more effective, attaching allegorical implications to the story of a fantastic transplant operation, and it was deemed too dangerous to be published.

*2-10. Burroughs, Edgar Rice. **The Land That Time Forgot.** McClurg, 1924.

Three novellas from *Blue Book* (all 1918) combined in one volume. American and British sailors join forces to capture a German U-boat, which winds up on the lost island of Caprona, where Haeckel's Law ("ontogony recapitulates phylogeny") is literally true, life-forms metamorphosing serially through higher evolutionary stages. The usual Burroughs action-adventure fare, in what is probably his most interesting setting.

2-11. Burroughs, Edgar Rice. **The Moon Maid.** McClurg, 1926.

Three serials from *Argosy/All-Story* (1923–1925), slightly abridged to make a single volume. More action-adventure in various settings; the middle part, which shows Earth under the dominion of alien conquerors, is one of Burroughs's more interesting works, and might be regarded as his most conventional essay in SF.

2-12. Campbell, John W(ood), Jr. **The Black Star Passes.** Fantasy, 1953.

Three novelettes originally published in *Amazing Stories* and its quarterly companion in 1930, featuring the exploits of the reformed space pirate Wade and his one-time adversaries, Arcot and Morey. They pit their superscientific talents against various alien foes in typically extravagant space operas. The scale of the action expands in the two full-length novels that continued the series: *Islands of Space* (1931; reprinted 1956) and *Invaders from the Infinite* (1932; reprinted 1961). The books are very much in the tradition of Smith's Skylark series [2-104], although Campbell handles scientific jargon a little better.

*2-13. Čapek, Karel (Czechoslovakia). **The Absolute at Large.** Macmillan, 1927. Tr. of *Tovarna na absolutno*, 1922.

An account of events following the marketing of atomic engines called "karburators," which annihilate matter in order to produce energy. In so doing, however, the machines liberate the "spirit" previously bound up in the matter, and humans fail miserably to cope with the consequent epidemic of religious inspiration. A classic ironic commentary on human fallibility. Compare Williams's *Many Dimensions* [2-132], a sober fantasy with similar theme and moral.

*2-14. Čapek, Karel (Czechoslovakia). **Krakatit.** Bles, 1925. Tr. by L. Hyde, 1924.

The inventor of a new explosive tries to keep it out of the hands of others, knowing that they will misuse it, but ultimately fails. Much more sober in tone than

Čapek's other early works, it was still sufficiently pertinent to be reprinted 20 years later with the ominous subtitle "An Atomic Phantasy."

*2-15. Čapek, Karel (Czechoslovakia). **R.U.R.: A Fantastic Melodrama.** Doubleday, 1923. Tr. by P. Selver, 1920.
The play that popularized the word *robot* (although the artificial people produced by Rossum's Universal Robots are organic rather than mechanical). The story is a simple allegory: the robots are perfected when they acquire souls, and people then become redundant, ripe for extermination.

*2-16. Čapek, Karel (Czechoslovakia). **War with the Newts.** Allen & Unwin, 1937. Tr. by M. Weatherall and R. Weatherall of *Valkas mloky*, 1936.
This novel is basically an elaboration of the theme of *R.U.R.* [2-15]. The newts are an alien species liberated from their subterranean home by an accident. They begin to learn human ways, and learn them all too well. Eventually, they replace their models, providing in the meantime a particularly sharp caricature of human habits and politics. Slightly long winded, but remains the most effective of Čapek's works.

2-17. Clouston, J(oseph) Storer (U.K.). **Button Brains.** Jenkins, 1933.
A comedy about a robot that is consistently mistaken for its human model, with appropriate farcical consequences. Most of the standard jokes associated with the theme first appeared here. Clouston wrote several other humorous SF stories, but a more sober note is evident in the last and best of his imaginative novels—the time travel story *The Man in Steel* (1939), which makes a wry comparison of the morality of barbarians and civilized people.

2-18. Coates, Robert M(yron). **The Eater of Darkness.** Contact Editions, 1926.
Surreal novel parodying the vogue for thrillers featuring scientific supercriminals. The stylistic fireworks are occasionally irritating, but the preposterous plot is amusing, and the chapter where the mad scientist explains his invention is an excellent parody of science fiction exposition. The genuine article can be found in the novels of Sax Rohmer and in the pulp stories that inspired Hugo Gernsback to found the short-lived *Scientific Detective Monthly* (later *Amazing Detective Tales*). The best individual examples are *The Sign at Six* [1-108] by White and *The Devil's Highway* [2-137] by Wright and Lebar.

2-19. Coblentz, Stanton A(rthur). **Hidden World.** Avalon, 1957.
Originally published in *Wonder Stories* (1935) as *In Caverns Below*, this is perhaps the best of Coblentz's rather heavy-handed satires. Two humans become emperors of the warring subterranean empires of Wu and Zu and fail to convert the people to a more rational way of life. A poke at big business, militarism, and the pretensions of the middle class. Coblentz introduced satirical undertones into his more straightforward adventure stories, of which the best is the Atlantean fantasy *The Sunken World* (1928; reprinted 1949). *After 12,000 Years* (1929; reprinted 1950), in which some of the humans of the future aspire to the condition of the anthill while using insects in a peculiar form of biological warfare, is also interesting.

2-20. Connington, J. J. (pseud. of Alfred Walter Stewart) (U.K.). **Nordenholt's Million.** Constable, 1923.
An early ecocatastrophe story in which denitrifying bacteria inimical to plant growth run wild. The plutocrat Nordenholt creates a refuge for the chosen few in Scotland. Similar in spirit to such disaster stories as Wylie and Balmer's *When Worlds Collide* [2-146] and Serviss's *The Second Deluge* [1-83], it anticipates the theme of Christopher's *The Death of Grass* [3-92].

2-21. Constantine, Murray (pseud. of Katharine Burdekin) (U.K.). **Swastika Night.** Gollancz, 1937.
A strange novel of a future Europe dominated by Nazis, whose rule has resulted in a more extreme social and physical differentiation of the sexes. A young German gradually learns to see the world from a different ideological perspective. Recently reprinted by the Feminist Press, under the author's real name. Her feminist ideals and psychological theories are more elaborately displayed in *Proud Man* (1934), a speculative essay in which three exemplary individuals from the contemporary world are studied by a hermaphrodite visitor from the far future.

*2-22. Cummings, Ray(mond King). **The Girl in the Golden Atom.** Methuen, 1922.
The book contains two stories first published in *All-Story Weekly* in 1919 and 1920—the first of Cummings's many microcosmic romances. The initial novelette is heavily indebted to *The Time Machine* [1-103] by Wells for its narrative frame and to O'Brien's "The Diamond Lens" [1-72] for its theme, although it is a poor pastiche. The sequel is standardized pulp melodrama. The notion of atoms as tiny worlds provided a framework for many stories in the SF pulps, including Festus Pragnell's *The Green Man of Graypec* (1936) and Hall's *People of the Comet* [2-31], and persisted long after the advance of science had made it ridiculous. Cummings's own best work in this vein is *The Princess of the Atom* (1929; reprinted 1950), but it lacks something of the naïve charm of the original novelette.

2-23. Cummings, Ray(mond King). **Into the Fourth Dimension.** Swan, 1943.
Earth is invaded by "ghosts" from the Ego-World, which exists beyond an interdimensional Borderland, and into which the heroes must venture in order to save the world. Standard pulp adventure fiction, originally published in 1926, more interesting in its setting than most. The book also contains short stories by other pulp writers.

2-24. Cummings, Ray(mond King). **The Shadow Girl.** Swan. 1947.
Originally published in *Argosy* in 1929. Cummings's time travel fantasies are, on average, rather better than his space operas, and this story is perhaps the best of them, although some readers prefer *The Man Who, Mastered Time* (1924; reprinted 1929). The characters pursue one another back and forth through time, visiting Peter Stuyvesant's New Amsterdam and fighting a desperate war in twenty-fifth-century New York. No attention is paid to the question of paradoxes. Compare Williamson's *The Legion of Time* [2-135].

*2-25. Dent, Guy (U.K.). **Emperor of the If.** Heinemann, 1926.
A scientist discovers a means of bringing into being the world that might have been if climatic changes favorable to the evolution of humans had never oc-

curred, and he decides to subject men and women to a harsh test of their Darwinian fitness. After concluding this experiment (and canceling out its results), he creates the world of the far future that will result if people remain locked into their contemporary course. Although not fully rationalized, this is a powerful and thought-provoking novel, and one of the first to consider history as a developing series of alternatives.

2-26. Desmond, Shaw (Ireland). **Ragnarok.** Duckworth, 1926.
A graphic future war story in which air fleets devastate the great cities of the world, using chemical and biological weapons as well as high explosives. The rather confused plot seems to owe something to M. P. Shiel's future war stories. Desmond went on to produce *Chaos* (1938) and *Black Dawn* (1944), near-future fantasies that deal speculatively with the social and metaphysical significance of World War II.

2-27. Doyle, Arthur Conan (U.K.). **The Land of Mist.** Hutchinson, 1926.
Professor Challenger becomes involved with spiritualism following the death of his wife. Skeptical at first, he is ultimately convinced that life continues after death. A sober and earnest novel, which contrasts sharply with the playful exuberance of *The Lost World* [1-31] and *The Poison Belt* [1-32].

2-28. Doyle, Arthur Conan (U.K.). **The Maracot Deep and Other Stories.** Murray, 1929.
The title novel features a descent into the depths of the Atlantic Ocean and the discovery of Atlantis. The story begins as a Vernian romance, but the author's interest in spiritualism takes its later chapters in a different direction. The best of the three short stories that accompany it is the Challenger novelette "When the World Screamed," in which Earth turns out to be a living creature.

2-29. Farley, Ralph Milne (pseud. of Roger Sherman Hoar). **The Omnibus of Time.** F.P.C.I., 1950.
A collection of stories involving time travel and time paradoxes, including "The Time Traveler" (1931) and "The Man Who Met Himself" (1935). Although somewhat rough-hewn, the stories show off the virtues as well as the pretensions of one of the more prolific pulp SF writers. Excerpts from two of his more readable pulp romances, "The Hidden Universe" (1939) and "The Golden City" (1933), are included. Farley's best-known work is the series of Burroughsian interplanetary adventures set on Venus, begun with *The Radio Man* (1924; in book form 1948), but these are among the weaker examples of the species.

*2-30. Farrère, Claude (pseud. of Charles Bargone) (France). **Useless Hands.** Dutton, 1926. Tr. by Elizabeth Abbott of *Les Condamnés à mort*, 1920.
A bitter melodrama in which the workers who make bread to feed the United States in the 1990s go on strike, only to find their place taken by mechanical hands. Their subsequent revolt is brutally put down in accordance with the logic of "Darwinian law." It is similar in spirit to Donnelly's *Caesar's Column* [1-29], although its central argument is a little more effective.

2-31. Flint, Homer Eon, and Austin Hall. **The Blind Spot.** Prime Press, 1951.
A confused melodrama dealing with intercourse between two parallel worlds,

first published in *Argosy* in 1921. Although stylistically uneven and eccentric in structure, it contrives to be effective in its own fashion. A sequel, by Hall alone, is *The Spot of Life* (1932; reprinted 1964). Both authors wrote other scientific romances for the pulps, Flint supplying an interesting interplanetary series to *All-Story Weekly* and *Argosy*, the best of which are *The Devolutionist* and *The Emancipatrix* (both 1921; reprinted in one volume 1965). Hall's most interesting solo work in this vein is the microcosmic romance *People of the Comet* (1948), first published in *Weird Tales* in 1923 as "Hop o' My Thumb."

2-32. Forester, C(ecil) S(cott) (U.K.). **The Peacemaker.** Little, Brown, 1934.
A bitterly ironic story about an ineffectual schoolmaster whose mathematical genius leads him to construct a machine that will demagnetize iron at a distance. He is led by unfortunate circumstances to use the machine in a hopeless attempt to blackmail England into initiating a program of disarmament.

2-33. Gail, Otto Willi (Germany). **The Shot into Infinity.** Garland, 1975. Tr. by Francis Currier of *Der Schuss ins All*, 1925.
A Vernian romance about a rocket ship that gets stranded in orbit with its pilot trapped. Much attention is given to technical detail, but the narrative is unconvincing. It was first translated for Gernsback's *Wonder Stories Quarterly* in 1929, and Gernsback also reprinted its sequel, *The Stone from the Moon* (1930), although its subject matter is entirely pseudoscientific.

2-34. Gibbons, Floyd (Philips). **The Red Napoleon.** Cape & Smith, 1929.
A documentary novel by a war correspondent, featuring a hypothetical world war initiated by a Mongol ruler of the U.S.S.R. The author claims to have been motivated by a horror of war, but he takes the usual fascinated interest in planning the campaigns of the would-be conqueror. Hindsight makes it seem rather absurd, but it remains an interesting exercise in future-history-as-propaganda.

2-35. Gloag, John (Edward) (U.K.). **The New Pleasure.** Allen & Unwin, 1933.
The invention of a euphoric drug that stimulates the sense of smell allows people to realize that modern civilization stinks. A gentle satire using an original notion.

2-36. Gloag, John (Edward) (U.K.). **99%.** Cassell, 1944.
Each of several men is enabled to recall a significant experience of one of his ancestors. Each is convinced that he has learned a vital lesson and sets out to apply it to his own life, but the results are ironic and highly ambiguous. A subtle work whose climax includes a brief Stapledonian vision of the human place in the universe.

*2-37. Gloag, John (Edward) (U.K.). **To-Morrow's Yesterday.** Allen & Unwin, 1932.
A bitter satire in which a new theater opens in London with a film showing the decline of the human race into degenerate savagery as a result of war. Although related to such novels as Shanks's *The People of the Ruins* [2-97] and Desmond's *Ragnarok* [2-26], it is much more scathing in its attack on the complacency of an England that (in Gloag's opinion) was not taking sufficient notice of such prophets as Wells.

*2-38. Gloag, John (Edward) (U.K.). **Winter's Youth.** Allen & Unwin, 1934.
A political satire in which the British government, seeking to regain popularity

following the disastrous promotion of a newly discovered gospel subsequently exposed as a fake, promotes a rejuvenating process that precipitates a conflict between young and old. An excellent essay in polished cynicism. Compare Swayne's *The Blue Germ* [2-114] and Bell's *The Seventh Bowl* [2-7].

2-39. Gregory, Owen. **Meccania: The Super-State.** Methuen, 1918.
An early dystopian satire describing the overorganized "rational" society of Meccania (obviously Germany), seen through the eyes of a Chinese tourist. The mockery of bureaucratic process still seems pertinent. Not as funny as Moszkowski's *Isles of Wisdom* [2-81] or O'Duffy's *Spacious Adventures of the Man in the Street* [2-85], but more closely focused and more subtle.

2-40. Hamilton, Cicely (U.K.). **Theodore Savage.** Parsons, 1922.
The eponymous hero's comfortable life is disrupted by a new war; aerial bombing of cities drives their population into rural areas where they must fight for survival as scavengers. Civilization is obliterated and communities re-form at a primitive level, dominated by brutality and superstition. A particularly effective and chilling version of the theme that dominates British speculative fiction between the wars; it was extremely rewritten as *Lest Ye Die* (1928). Compare Stewart's *Earth Abides* [3-358].

2-41. Hamilton, Edmond. **The Horror on the Asteroid.** Allan, 1936.
One of the earliest collections of pulp SF stories, uniform with the publisher's *Creeps* series of anthologies, which reprinted some material from *Weird Tales*. The six stories are representative of Hamilton's early work, lively but rather rough-hewn. Hamilton began writing space opera for *Weird Tales* in the 1920s, and five other early stories, all featuring the Interstellar Patrol, are collected in *Crashing Suns* (1965). A novel-length story from the same series is *Outside the Universe* (1929; reprinted 1964).

2-42. Hargrave, John (Gordon) (U.K.). **The Imitation Man.** Gollancz, 1931.
A scientist creates a homunculus, which grows rapidly to physical maturity. The behavior of the artificial man is entirely imitative, but his telepathic powers allow him to repeat out loud the secret thoughts of others, causing him to become an embarrassment to all who know him. He enjoys a spectacular career but meets an ironic fate. The novel is lighthearted and contrasts sharply with the author's bitter Wellsian novel of ideas, *Harbottle* (1923).

2-43. Hilton, James (U.K.). **Lost Horizon.** Morrow, 1933.
A classic escapist novel about an Englishman's adventure in the fabulous utopian valley of Shangri-La, marvelously filmed by Frank Capra. The novel testifies to the retreat of the utopian dream into the realm of dream-fantasy. Similar escapist fantasies include A. Merritt's *Dwellers in the Mirage* (1932) and Hannes Bok's *The Blue Flamingo* (1948), but *Lost Horizon* is the most stylish of the species.

2-44. Houghton, Claude (pseud. of C. H. Oldfield) (U.K.). **This Was Ivor Trent.** Heinemann, 1935.
A psychological melodrama in which a writer's odd behavior is finally explained as the result of a vision in which he saw a man of the future and realized that a much better world would rise from the ashes of our own sick civilization. A par-

ticularly extreme example of the disenchantment that affected many British writers of the period. Compare Gloag's *To-Morrow's Yesterday* [2-37] and Beresford's *What Dreams May Come . . .* (1941).

2-45. Hoyne, Thomas Temple. **Intrigue on the Upper Level.** Reilly & Lee, 1934.
A crudely written but rather striking fantasy of a world born out of the depression and ruled by gangsters, and of the inevitable revolution that seeks to destroy its rigidly stratified society.

2-46. Hunting, (Henry) Gardner. **The Vicarion.** Unity School of Christianity, 1926.
A novel about America's response to the invention of a machine that can see through time, wholly unconvincing but nevertheless fascinating. It contrasts very sharply with Sherred's famous story based on an identical premise, "E for Effort" (1947).

*2-47. Huxley, Aldous (Leonard) (U.K.). **Brave New World.** Doubleday, 1932.
A devastating criticism of the kind of technological utopia outlined in J. B. S. Haldane's essay *Daedalus; or, Science and the Future.* Its principal images are well established in the modern mythology of the future, and it remains the definitive critique of the technologically supported "rational" society, exposing the darker side of scientific humanism. It is a brilliant and perceptive polemic, and the opposing side of the argument has found no advocate of comparable eloquence. It stands alongside *We* [2-147] and *Nineteen Eighty-Four* [3-302] as one of the classic dystopian novels. Many of the concerns of the novel were treated in a later nonfiction work, *Brave New World Revisited* (1958).

2-48. Jaeger, Muriel (U.K.). **The Man with Six Senses.** Hogarth, 1927.
A careful and sensitive novel about a youth who is attempting to develop and utilize a new mode of sensory perception. It contrasts sharply with later post-Rhineian stories of ESP, such as Blish's *Jack of Eagles* [3-46] and Tucker's *Wild Talent* [3-376].

2-49. Jaeger, Muriel (U.K.). **The Question Mark.** Hogarth, 1926.
An interesting novel about the quality of life in a Wellsian utopia, observing that freedom must include the freedom to be foolish and even ridiculous. The question mark of the title attends the question of whether we are actually capable of making a better life for ourselves, even if we acquire the means to do so.

2-50. Jensen, Johannes V(ilhelm) (Denmark). **The Long Journey: Fire and Ice** and **The Cimbrians.** Knopf, 1923. Tr. by A. G. Chater of parts I-IV of *Den lange rejse*, 1908–1922.
A classic prehistoric fantasy. The fifth part of the series was not translated, but the sixth, translated in 1924, is *Christopher Columbus.* The theme of the whole work is the struggle of evolving humankind to cope with major challenges, including the last glaciation of the northern hemisphere. The only other prehistoric fantasies that can compare with it are the best works of Rosny aîné, particularly *La Guerre du feu* [2-95], and William Golding's *The Inheritors* (1955).

2-51. Johnson, Owen (McMahon). **The Coming of the Amazons.** Longmans, 1931.
One of the many novels featuring a female-dominated society, rather more good-humored than most. It is gently insistent that sex roles are determined by socialization rather than by innate dispositions. Contrast Walter Besant's *The Revolt of Man* (1882) and Charles Eric Maine's *Alph* (1972).

2-52. Jones, Neil R(onald). **Planet of the Double Sun.** Ace, 1967.
The first of five volumes that bring together the bulk of the long-running Professor Jameson series, about an Earthman whose brain is reactivated in a robot body in the distant future. His rescuers are the Zoromes, mechanical space explorers whose ranks he gladly joins. The series is crudely written but ideationally lively, and it provides a good example of the freewheeling pulp imagination. The other four volumes are *The Sunless World* (1967), *Space War* (1967), *Twin Worlds* (1967), and *Doomsday on Ajiat* (1968).

*2-53. Karinthy, Frigyes (Hungary). **Voyage to Faremido and Capillaria.** Corvina, 1965. Tr. by Paul Tabori of *Utazás Faremidóba*, 1916, and *Capillaria*, 1922.
Accounts of voyages made by Lemuel Gulliver, the first bringing him into contact with a society of machines that communicate with one another via musical notes and have difficulty understanding organic life, the second describing a submarine civilization whose sexual politics are based in a very different biology from ours. Two marvelously imaginative social satires, quite without parallel.

2-54. Kaul, Fedor (Germany). **Contagion to This World.** Bles, 1933. Tr. by Winifred Ray of *Die Welt ohne Gedächtnis*.
A hunchbacked genius, reviled by others, takes revenge by releasing a bacterium that causes universal amnesia. He watches the collapse of civilization and the eventual emergence of a new human species. The novel is remarkable for the sympathy accorded the protagonist. Contrast McClary's *Rebirth* [2-74], which features a similar project.

2-55. Keller, David H(enry). **Life Everlasting and Other Tales of Science, Fantasy and Horror.** Avalon, 1947.
The title novel is perhaps the best of Keller's early pulp works—a moral fable in which humans abandon immortality in favor of fertility. The short stories in the collection include several of his best works, all arising out of his interest in psychiatry: "The Dead Woman," "The Thing in the Cellar," and "A Piece of Linoleum." A later collection with more varied contents is *Tales from Underwood* (1952), which shows off his talents to slightly better advantage. His science fiction invariably champions simple human values against the threats posed by the "rationalization" of human affairs through scientific management and the use of mechanical technology.

2-56. Kelly, Frank K. **Starship Invincible.** Capra, 1979.
Three novelettes from the mid-1930s SF pulps, all featuring heroism and self-sacrifice in distant parts of the solar system. Sentimental space opera, crude and naïve, but exhibiting the kind of wide-eyed charm that sustained the appeal of the early SF pulps.

2-57. Kingsmill, Hugh (pseud. of Hugh Kingsmill Lunn) (U.K.). **The Return of William Shakespeare.** Duckworth, 1929.
A delightfully immodest novel in which William Shakespeare is resurrected so that Kingsmill can put his interpretation of the bard's work into the author's own mouth. The plot that surrounds the criticism is frivolous but entertaining.

2-58. Knight, Damon (Francis), ed. **Science Fiction of the Thirties.** Bobbs-Merrill, 1975.
Representative anthology of stories from the SF pulps of the period, with contents that do not overlap with Asimov's superior *Before the Golden Age* [2-2], although many of the same authors are represented. The better stories (Weinbaum's "The Mad Moon," Gallun's "Davy Jones' Ambassador," and Bates's "Alas, All Thinking!") are available elsewhere, and the scarcer ones are of limited interest. Compare also Margulies and Friend's *From Off This World* [2-69].

*2-59. Large, E(dward) C. (U.K.). **Sugar in the Air.** Jonathan Cape, 1937.
An excellent story of the conflict between commercial and scientific interests connected with a project to manufacture carbohydrates by artificial photosynthesis. A devastating attack on the imaginative blindness of the English bourgeoisie. *Asleep in the Afternoon* (1939) is a less distinguished satire about a device that promotes peaceful sleep, but Large's handling of social satire is more assured in his third fantasy novel, *Dawn in Andromeda* (1956).

2-60. Leinster, Murray (pseud. of Will F. Jenkins). **The Forgotten Planet.** Gnome, 1954.
The first two sections of this fixed-up novel are the novelettes "The Mad Planet" and "The Red Dust," originally published in *Argosy* in 1920 and 1921, featuring the exploits of primitive humans in a world of giant insects and arachnids. The logic of the situation provided by the new material does not help to make them more convincing, but they have a certain panache. The most dramatic scenes recur in many stories of human miniaturization, from Edwin Pallander's *Adventures of a Micro-Man* (1902) to Lindsay Gutteridge's *Cold War in a Country Garden* (1971).

2-61. Leroux, Gaston (France). **The Machine to Kill.** Macauley, 1935. Tr. of *La Machine à assassiner,* 1924.
A rather labored crime thriller in which the murderer is a robot that proves difficult to apprehend. It probably owes its inspiration to Villiers de l'Isle Adam's *L'Ève future* (1885) rather than to Čapek's *R.U.R.* [2-15].

2-62. Lewis, Sinclair. **It Can't Happen Here.** Doubleday, 1935.
A novel about the destruction of democracy in the United States and the establishment of a quasi-Fascist state. The element of parody in the book does not undermine its seriousness, and although it is not quite up to the standard of Lewis's novels of the early 1920s, it remains an effectively powerful exercise in alternate history, a cautionary warning against a possible American future.

*2-63. Lindsay, David (U.K.). **A Voyage to Arcturus.** Methuen, 1920.
A classic allegorical romance in which the landscapes and inhabitants of the planet Tormance provide an externalization of the moral and metaphysical ques-

tions that preoccupied the author. Its incarnate theological system influenced Lewis's *Out of the Silent Planet* [3-263], and it also bears some similarity to George Macdonald's *Lilith* (1895), although it is very much a work sui generis. Lindsay's other metaphysical fantasies belong to the same species as Charles Williams's theological fantasies, but generally find Christian theology inadequate to their purpose (an exception is the posthumously published novel *The Violet Apple*, 1978). *Devil's Tor* (1932) is a particularly fine novel in this vein.

2-64. Llewellyn, (David William) Alun (U.K.). **The Strange Invaders.** Bell, 1934. The barbaric survivors of a worldwide catastrophe find that the faith handed down to them from the ancient world (whose deities are Marx and Stalin) is inadequate to cope with the challenge of new circumstances. They are driven from their lands by giant lizards—a baroque embellishment of an otherwise stereotyped postdisaster scenario.

2-65. Lovecraft, H(oward) P(hillips). **At the Mountains of Madness and Other Novels.** Arkham, 1964. Corrected text, 1985.
The title novel first appeared in *Astounding Stories* in 1936 and consists of the report of a scientific expedition to a lost world in the Antarctic, whose members learn the terrifying truth about the human place in the universe. Together with *The Dunwich Horror and Others* (1963), this collection presents the most effective of Lovecraft's stories, which see the universe as an implacably hostile place where quests for knowledge and enlightenment usually prove fatal, revealing in the process that men and women are habitually used for horrible purposes by malevolent alien beings of godlike power. Some readers are alienated by the author's idiosyncratic use of language in the attempt to create a mood of dreadful uncertainty.

2-66. Macaulay, Rose (U.K.). **What Not.** Constable, 1919.
In the period of reconstruction following the Great War, the British Ministry of Brains conceives ambitious plans for reorganizing society in a saner and more scientific fashion, but its attempts to regulate affairs of the heart go fortunately awry. A lighthearted book.

2-67. MacIsaac, Fred. **The Hothouse World.** Avalon, 1965.
First published as a serial in *Argosy* in 1931. The hero wakes from suspended animation to find civilization preserved in a tiny glass-enclosed enclave after most of the world's population has been wiped out by gases in a comet's tail. The sterile autocratic state preserved under glass is contrasted with the anarchy of the world outside; to set history back on course a middle way must be found. MacIsaac was one of the more interesting writers of futuristic stories for the nonspecialist pulps; in "World Brigands" (1928) the domination of world economic affairs by the United States drives a Europe crippled by its war debts to the brink of violent reprisals—an interesting scenario, though soon invalidated by the Wall Street crash.

2-68. Manning, Laurence. **The Man Who Awoke.** Ballantine, 1975.
One of the earliest future histories presented by the science fiction pulps, first published in *Wonder Stories* in 1933. The quality of the writing leaves something to be desired, but the account of future social evolution is imaginative and interesting. Although influenced by Stapledon's *Last and First Men* [2-109], the novel

takes a rather different view of human destiny. Manning was one of the more thoughtful of Gernsback's writers and one of the first to attempt to impart a degree of realism into stories of interplanetary adventure, in "The Voyage of the *Asteroid*" and "The Wreck of the *Asteroid*" (both 1932).

2-69. Margulies, Leo, and Oscar J. Friend, eds. **From Off This World.** Merlin, 1949.
An anthology of the original Science Fiction Hall of Fame stories reprinted in *Startling Stories* from Gernsback's *Wonder Stories.* The stories were chosen by fans and display the more colorful side of pulp SF. They include "The City of the Singing Flame" and its sequel by Clark Ashton Smith, and work by Weinbaum, Hamilton, Williamson, and others. Comparable to Knight's *Science Fiction of the Thirties* [2-58], but inferior to Asimov's *Before the Golden Age* [2-2].

2-70. Marvell, Andrew (pseud. of Howell Davies) (U.K.). **Minimum Man; or, Time to Be Gone.** Gollancz, 1938.
A race of tiny supermen is protected by the hero, and subsequently wins the gratitude of right-thinking men by helping to overthrow a Fascist government in England. Ultimately, though, they will replace Homo sapiens. One of the cleverer extrapolations of the thesis that only another species can hope to establish a saner society. Contrast Beresford's *What Dreams May Come . . .* (1941). Davies wrote two other novels as Marvell, including *Three Men Make a World* (1939), an equally ironic story in which the heroes save civilization from obliteration by war by destroying it more gently with a bacterium that devours petroleum products.

2-71. Matson, Norman. **Doctor Fogg.** Macmillan, 1929.
A bittersweet satire in which the eponymous hero becomes reluctantly famous after building a device to receive radio messages from other worlds. New knowledge promises a technological revolution, and he accidentally brings to Earth a girl exiled from her home world in the distant past. But he and the author harbor doubts as to whether humans are quite ready for membership in an interstellar community.

2-72. Maurois, André (France). **The Thought-Reading Machine.** Jonathan Cape, 1938. Tr. by J. Whithall of *La Machine à lire les pensées,* 1937.
An American scientist invents a machine that records subvocalized thoughts and plays them back audibly. The argument of the novel is that our internal reveries are of no real significance in terms of our true feelings and policies of action. A thoughtful and well-written book that contrasts with the assumptions usually taken for granted by stories dealing with telepathy.

*2-73. Maurois, André (France). **The Weigher of Souls.** Cassell, 1931. Tr. by H. Miles of *Le Peseur d'âmes,* 1931.
An excellent novella concerning a hypothetical meeting of experimental science and theological supposition, bringing into sharp focus questions about the morality of scientific inquiry into human nature. Gary's novel *The Gasp* [4-227] develops the same premise in a more ironic vein.

2-74. McClary, Thomas Calvert. **Rebirth.** Bart, 1944.
Originally published in *Astounding* in 1934, this is the story of a colossal experi-

ment in which a scientist wipes out the memories of everyone on Earth in order to institute a Darwinian struggle for existence. Within a generation, the favored few recover the use of the artifacts of civilization and have supposedly established a better social order. Compare the more pessimistic account by Kaul in *Contagion to This World* [2-54].

2-75. McIlraith, Frank, and Ray Connolly (U.K.). **Invasion from the Air.** Grayson & Grayson, 1934.
One of the more realistic accounts of future warfare involving the use of poison gas, incendiary bombs, and high explosives. It suggests that the disruption caused by heavy bombing would destabilize governments and pave the way for a wave of coups and revolutions. Compare S. Fowler Wright's *Prelude in Prague* [2-143] and its sequels.

2-76. Merritt, A(braham). **The Metal Monster.** Avon, 1946.
The most science fictional of Merritt's exotic romances, originally published in *Argosy* in 1920 and revised for Gernsback's *Science and Invention* in 1927, where it appeared as *The Metal Emperor*. It involves an encounter with an inorganic alien being with a hivelike organization.

2-77. Merritt, A(braham). **The Moon Pool.** Putnam, 1919.
A novel compounded out of a classic novelette and its inferior sequel, originally published in *Argosy* in 1918-1919. It features extravagant adventures in an exotic underworld, recounted in gaudy purple prose. Although it is sheer dream-fantasy, Gernsback reprinted it in *Amazing Stories* in 1927, and it proved to be one of the most popular stories ever to appear there. The introductory novelette is a celebration of the lure of exotic imaginary worlds—a vital element in the tradition of American pulp science fiction.

2-78. Mitchell, J(ames) Leslie (U.K.). **Gay Hunter.** Heinemann, 1934.
As in *Three Go Back* [2-79], the heroine is projected through time with two companions, this time into a future oddly akin to the world of the Cro-Magnons in the earlier novel. She learns that civilization has been obliterated by nuclear wars fought between Fascist states, and must fight to prevent her Mosleyite companions from setting the noble savages on the same road to destruction.

2-79. Mitchell, J(ames) Leslie (U.K.). **Three Go Back.** Jarrolds, 1932.
Two men and a woman are thrown back in time to witness the contrasting lifestyles of our Cro-Magnon ancestors and the brutish Neanderthals. The novel conducts a polemical argument against the notion that humans are innately aggressive by virtue of evolutionary heritage. The version issued as a Galaxy novel in 1953 is bowdlerized. Compare William Golding's *The Inheritors* (1955), which reverses the imagined roles of Cro-Magnon and Neanderthal, pointing to a rather different moral.

2-80. Moore, C(atherine) L(ucile). **Scarlet Dream.** Grant, 1981.
A series of stories featuring interplanetary adventurer Northwest Smith, originally published in *Weird Tales* in the 1930s, and formerly reprinted in *Shambleau* (1953) and *Northwest of Earth* (1954). Lush exotic romances in the tradition later carried on by Leigh Brackett.

2-81. Moszkowski, Alexandr (Germany). **The Isles of Wisdom.** Routledge, 1924. Tr. by H. J. Stenning of *Die Inseln der Weisheit,* 1922.

A marvelously eclectic utopian satire that sets out to demonstrate that all political policies, if taken to extremes, have absurd consequences. The parody of technological utopianism is particularly sharp, and the book, frequently very funny, succeeds in making its point.

2-82. Moxley, F(rank) Wright. **Red Snow.** Simon & Schuster, 1930.

A mysterious red snow sterilizes the human race, and the last generation lives out the remaining years until the species is extinct. An earnestly bitter story. Compare *The Seventh Bowl* [2-7] by Neil Bell.

2-83. Nowlan, Philip Francis. **Armageddon 2419 A.D.** Avalon, 1962.

A novel compounded out of the two novelettes that provided the seed of the Buck Rogers comic strip. Originally published in *Amazing Stories* in 1928 and 1929, they tell the story of a revolt by white Americans against the Oriental race that dominates them, with spectacular use of superscientific weaponry.

*2-84. Odle, E. V. (U.K.). **The Clockwork Man.** Heinemann, 1923.

An excellent fantasy in which a man of the future, fitted with a "clock" that regulates his existence, is thrown into the England of the 1920s by a malfunction, confronting the inhabitants of a small village with a vision of infinite possibility. A highly imaginative story that is probably a response to Beresford's *The Hampdenshire Wonder* [1-11]. Perhaps the outstanding scientific romance of the 1920s.

2-85. O'Duffy, Eimar (Ireland). **The Spacious Adventures of the Man in the Street.** Macmillan, 1928.

A remarkably sharp satire in which Aloysius O'Kennedy is transported to the planet Rathe, where he takes the place of his alter ego. The work is uneven, but it includes scathing parodies of sexual morality, religion, and capitalism, as well as episodes of pure comedy and a climactic allegorical vision pleading the cause of humanism and humanitarian values.

2-86. O'Neill, Joseph (U.K.). **Land under England.** Gollancz, 1935.

The protagonist descends into an underworld in search of his father and finds a totalitarian state where thought-control is facilitated by telepathy. A particularly stylish political allegory, with echoes of the myth of Orpheus and Eurydice. O'Neill's *Day of Wrath* (1936) is a documentary novel charting the course of a new world war and its effects on the civilian population, which invites comparison with Merril's *Shadow on the Hearth* [3-284] and Wylie's *Tomorrow!* [3-409].

2-87. Onions, (George) Oliver (U.K.). **The New Moon: A Romance in Reconstruction.** Hodder & Stoughton, 1918.

An optimistic novel anticipating the social reconstruction of Britain after the Great War, with many of the lessons of More's *Utopia* [1-68] put into effect. The dream was, of course, rapidly betrayed by history.

2-88. Palmer, John (Leslie) (U.K.). **The Hesperides: A Looking-Glass Fugue.** Secker & Warburg, 1936.

The protagonist is taken to Venus, where he finds a totalitarian collectivist state in which religion and free speech are ruthlessly suppressed. He becomes involved with dissenters, who are eventually forced to take arms. An idiosyncratic satire with one or two nice touches, but rather long-winded.

2-89. Parkinson, H(arold) F(rederick) (U.K.). **They Shall Not Die.** Constable, 1939.
A new patent medicine makes its users immune to all disease (although only its inventor knows that it is responsible) but also sterilizes them. The division of the world's population into "Immunes" and "Mortalities" affects social and political change over several decades before the Immunes prove vulnerable to a kind of mental illness that makes them into zombies. Intriguingly understated. Contrast Bell's *The Seventh Bowl* [2-7] and Swayne's *The Blue Germ* [2-114].

2-90. Phillpotts, Eden (U.K.). **Saurus.** Murray, 1938.
A spaceship from another world contains an egg that hatches into an intelligent lizard. This was the first story that attempted to use an alien visitor as an objective observer to comment on the state of contemporary human civilization, and it is rather more sympathetic than most work in this vein. Saurus is more convincing than Grant Allen's future anthropologist in *The British Barbarians* (1895), but his commentary is not as impressive as that of Stapledon's *Sirius* [2-111]. Phillpotts had earlier written a poor science fiction thriller as Harrington Hext, *Number 87* (1922), but his later science fiction novels, written under his own name, are more impressive. One of them—*Address Unknown* (1949)—is similar in theme to *Saurus*, but is much more dubious about the entitlement of an alien being to criticize human conduct.

2-91. Read, Herbert (U.K.). **The Green Child.** Heinemann, 1935.
A strange story whose climax is set in a weird underworld where green-skinned humanoids follow a way of life that culminates in a bizarre transcendence of the human condition. An alternative vision of human possibility is presented in an account of a quasi-utopian state in Latin America. A unique and impressive work by a noted critic of art and literature—a reading of his collection of essays, *Reason and Romanticism* (1926), will help to put *The Green Child* in perspective.

2-92. Renard, Maurice, and Albert Jean (France). **Blind Circle.** Dutton, 1928. Tr. by Florence Crewe-Jones of *Le Singe*, 1925.
A mystery story very much in the French tradition, which quickly becomes complicated by the appearance of several identical corpses. The solution is, of course, a science fiction one. Compare Ben Bova's *The Multiple Man* (1976).

2-93. Robertson, E. Arnot (U.K.). **Three Came Unarmed.** Doubleday, 1929.
A novel about three children raised as "noble savages" in the Far East, who are sent to England when their father dies. Although superior in mind and body, they are crushed and mutilated by civilization, here seen as implacably soul-destroying. A dramatically misanthropic inversion of the Tarzan myth.

2-94. Roger, Noëlle (pseud. of Hélène Pittard) (France). **The New Adam.** Stanley Paul, 1926. Tr. by P. O. Crowhurst of *Le Nouvel Adam*, 1924.
A novel featuring an artificially created superman, emotionless and intellectually powerful, who poses such a threat to "common" people that his creator is forced

to bring about his destruction. It has less in common with Weinbaum's novel of the same title [2-126] than with his "The Adaptive Ultimate."

2-95. Rosny aîné, J. H. (pseud. of Joseph-Henri Boëx) (France). **The Giant Cat; or, The Quest of Aoun and Zouhr.** McBride, 1924. Tr. of *Le Félin géant,* 1918. Reprinted as *Quest of the Dawn Man,* 1964.
A fairly typical example of Rosny's prehistoric romances. The only other example in English, *The Quest for Fire* (1967; tr. of *La Guerre du feu,* 1909), is considerably abridged from the original, and *Ironcastle* (1976; tr. of *L'Étonnant voyage de Hareton Ironcastle,* 1922), a Vernian SF novel, is also considerably rewritten in the English version.

2-96. Scrymsour, Ella (U.K.). **The Perfect World.** Nash & Grayson, 1922.
A curious novel compounded out of two related novellas. The first describes the discovery of an underground world and the catastrophic destruction of the Earth; the second describes the escape of the leading characters to Jupiter, where alien inhabitants have achieved a utopian existence.

2-97. Shanks, Edward (Richard Buxton) (U.K.). **The People of the Ruins.** Stokes, 1920.
The first of the many British postwar novels that foresee Britain returned to barbarism by the ravages of war. The hero wants to restore progress, but his usefulness to the ruler of the new world is entirely concerned with his knowledge of armaments. The decline, it seems, cannot be reversed. Compare Gloag's *To-Morrow's Yesterday* [2-37] and Desmond's *Ragnarok* [2-26].

*2-98. Shaw, George Bernard (Ireland). **Back to Methuselah: A Metabiological Pentateuch.** Constable, 1921.
A classic play, infrequently performed because of its length, in which right-thinking people evolve by determined effort into superhumans, eventually being able to look forward to the day when they may cast off the shackles of vulgar matter and become perfect beings of "pure energy." The play is prefaced by a long essay explaining the neo-Lamarckian theory of evolution, which provides its imaginative basis, and offering reasons for the author's rejection of Darwinism.

*2-99. Shiel, M(atthew) P(hipps) (U.K.). **The Young Men Are Coming!** Allen & Unwin, 1937.
A scientist kidnapped aboard a flying saucer returns to Earth with a rejuvenating serum, under whose influence he founds a social movement, the Young Men, which ultimately becomes embroiled in civil war. The hero challenges a religious fundamentalist to a duel of faiths, and his alien allies release at his behest a storm that devastates the world. A stirring championship of Shiel's idiosyncratic view of the ideology of progress. Compare Wells's *The Holy Terror* [2-128] for an interesting contrast of protagonists.

2-100. Sinclair, Upton. **The Millennium: A Comedy of the Year 2000.** Haldeman-Julius, 1924.
An amusing satirical fantasy in which the survivors of a worldwide catastrophe struggle for control of a food-making machine, recapitulating in the process the various economic stages described in the Marxist account of history. Originally

written as a play in 1909, and might be deemed the first story to feature a neutron bomb.

2-101. Siodmak, Curt (Germany). **F.P.1 Does Not Reply.** Little, Brown, 1933. Tr. by H. W. Farrell of *F.P.1 antwortet nicht,* 1932.
The only one of the author's early novels to be translated, this is a dull melodrama in which enemies of progress try to sabotage an artificial island, which will operate as a refueling station for transatlantic air traffic. Siodmak's later novels in English, especially *Donovan's Brain* [3-351], are more readable.

2-102. Sloane, William (Milligan III). **To Walk the Night.** Farrar, 1937.
The story of a doomed love affair between a young college graduate and the widow of his old teacher (who died under very mysterious circumstances). The woman is attractive but alien, trapped by a web of tragic circumstance that destroys those who become involved with her. The novel is a good blend of mystery and science fiction, and it provides a pessimistic account of human inability to come to terms with the unknown. *The Edge of Running Water* (1939) is similar in tone and implications.

2-103. Smith, Clark Ashton. **Zothique.** Ballantine, 1970.
Smith's brief career as a pulp SF and fantasy writer spanned only a few years in the early 1930s. The interplanetary fiction that he wrote for Gernsback's *Wonder Stories* is relatively weak, and though his lurid tales of Zothique have none of the usual science fictional apparatus, they stand at the head of a tradition of far-future exoticism that extends more moderately through the work of writers like Jack Vance. Compare Vance's *The Dying Earth* [3-380].

*2-104. Smith, E(dward) E(lmer), and Lee Hawkins Garby. **The Skylark of Space.** Buffalo Book, 1946.
The archetypal pulp space opera, first published in *Amazing Stories* in 1928. X, the unknown metal, sends Richard Seaton's water bath hurtling through the roof of his laboratory, heading for infinity. He follows it in his own good time, and the galaxy becomes his playground, where he fights monstrous aliens and his archenemy, Blackie DuQuesne. The writing is stilted and the plot absurd, but the adventure has a naïve exuberance that remains appealing to younger readers. The two early sequels are *Skylark Three* (1930; reprinted 1947) and *Skylark of Valeron* (1934; reprinted 1949). Much later, Smith added a fourth volume, *Skylark DuQuesne* (1966).

2-105. Smith, Garret. **Between Worlds.** Stellar, 1929.
First serialized in *Argosy* in 1919. Rebellious females are exported from the ordered Patriarchy of Venus to exile on Earth, where they arrive in time to witness and take a small part in World War I, learning much from the contrast between earthly civilization and their own. Smith was perhaps the most interesting of all the writers producing SF for the nonspecialist pulps, and his stories should have been more widely reprinted; the most extravagant is the serial "After a Million Years" (*Argosy,* 1922).

2-106. Smith, Wayland (pseud. of Victor Bayley) (U.K.). **The Machine Stops.** Hale, 1936.
One of several stories emphasizing the vulnerability of modern civilization by following the imagined consequences of a "plague" that destroys all metals. As the new barbarians gather to sack the last enclaves of rural harmony, a young genius tries to save the world by making an alloy that can resist the corrosion. Two very similar stories based on the same premise are *The Death of Iron* (1931) by S. S. Held and *The Metal Doom* (1932) by David H. Keller.

2-107. Snell, Edmund (U.K.). **Kontrol.** Benn, 1928.
A lurid mad-scientist thriller involving the transplanting of brains for the purpose of manufacturing a superrace. It begins as a conventional horror story, but changes pace when the action shifts to an island where the dehumanized superbeings are building a technological utopia. Snell's other fantasies are much more conventional, but here he appears to have been quite carried away by his idea.

2-108. Squire, J(ohn) C(ollings), ed. (U.K.). **If; or, History Rewritten.** Viking, 1931. British title: *If It Had Happened Otherwise.*
An excellent series of essays in alternate history inspired by G. M. Trevelyan's essay "If Napoleon Had Won the Battle of Waterloo" (1907). The contributors include G. K. Chesterton, André Maurois, and Hilaire Belloc, but the star of the collection is the double-twist account by Winston Churchill, "If Lee Had Not Won the Battle of Gettysburg." The Sidgwick & Jackson edition of 1972 (which retains the British version of the title) includes Trevelyan's essay and adds new ones by Charles Petrie and A. J. P. Taylor.

*2-109. Stapledon, (William) Olaf (U.K.). **Last and First Men.** Methuen, 1930.
An "essay in myth creation" documenting the entire future history of the human race and its lineal descendants. The "eighteenth men," living nearly two billion years in the future, look forward with equanimity to the end of the story. The book has dated somewhat, not just because its early chapters have been superseded, but also because evolutionary biology has advanced since the 1920s; nevertheless, it remains something of a masterpiece. The immediate sequel, however—*Last Men in London* (1932)—is less impressive, involving an elaborate commentary on the contemporary world from the imaginary viewpoint of one of the eighteenth men.

*2-110. Stapledon, (William) Olaf (U.K.). **Odd John.** Methuen, 1935.
The story of a superchild born into a contemporary human community, apparently modeled on Beresford's *The Hampdenshire Wonder* [1-11]. The novel is well executed, but the child is too obviously a mouthpiece for Stapledon's own prejudices, and his bitter and waspish commentary on human affairs is overdone. The novel lacks the sensitivity of *Sirius* [2-111]; compare Weinbaum's *The New Adam* [2-126].

*2-111. Stapledon, (William) Olaf (U.K.). **Sirius: A Fantasy of Love and Discord.** Secker & Warburg, 1944.
The story of a dog with artificially augmented intelligence. The best of all the novelistic attempts to create an "objective observer" who can pass judgment on contemporary human society, and a much more successful novel than *Last Men in*

London [2-109] or *Odd John* [2-110]. The story is convincing and genuinely moving, a classic of the genre. In terms of its purpose it invites comparison with Howells's *Traveler from Altruria* (1894), Allen's *The British Barbarians* (1895), Wells's *The Wonderful Visit* (1895), and Phillpotts's *Saurus* [2-90], but in its handling of the theme of the augmentation of intelligence it may also be compared with Edgar Fawcett's *Solarion* [1-34] and Keyes's *Flowers for Algernon* [3-228].

*2-112. Stapledon, (William) Olaf (U.K.). **Star Maker.** Methuen, 1937.
A companion piece to *Last and First Men* [2-109], taking the essay in myth creation still further to present an entire history of the cosmos and an account of its myriad life forms. The narrator's vision expands through a series of phases, each giving him a wider perspective until he finally glimpses the Star Maker at his work, experimenting in the cause of producing new and better creations. A magnificent work by any standards; the most important speculative work of the period. Of related interest is *Nebula Maker,* a preliminary and less mature version of *Star Maker,* presumably written in the mid-1930s but not published until 1976 (Bran's Head; reprinted by Sphere, 1979).

2-113. Stevens, Francis (pseud. of Gertrude Bennett). **The Heads of Cereberus.** Polaris, 1952.
A curious story, originally published in *The Thrill Book* in 1919, in which the protagonists pass through a strange parallel world into a hypothetical future where Philadelphia, isolated from the rest of America, has become a totalitarian state. The novel is unconvincing but nevertheless compelling, and is the work of one of the most interesting of the pulp fantasy writers.

2-114. Swayne, Martin (U.K.). **The Blue Germ.** Hodder & Stoughton, 1918.
A scientist releases a bacillus that confers immunity to aging and disease, and also causes flesh to take on a blue tinge. But the blessing is mixed—by killing desire the bacillus promises to put an end to progress, and when it is fortuitously wiped out this is seen as the world's salvation. Compare Parkinson's *They Shall Not Die* [2-89].

2-115. Taine, John (pseud. of Eric Temple Bell). **Before the Dawn.** Williams & Wilkins, 1934.
A prehistoric romance whose hero is a dinosaur. Intended as a popularization-of-science book rather than a novel, it presents a hopelessly incompetent reconstruction of the end of the age of reptiles, but has a certain infectious enthusiasm.

2-116. Taine, John (pseud. of Eric Temple Bell). **The Crystal Horde.** Fantasy, 1952.
Originally published in *Amazing Stories Quarterly* (1930) as *White Lily,* under which title it was once reprinted, this is an extravagant scientific romance involving crystalline life and social strife in the Far East, with the kind of cataclysmic conclusion that Taine loved.

2-117. Taine, John (pseud. of Eric Temple Bell). **The Iron Star.** Dutton, 1930.
One of Taine's mutational romances, in which a radioactive meteorite causes bizarre metamorphoses in a region of central Africa. Its effects include the reversed evolution of humans into protohuman apes. Radiation has the opposite effect in

Seeds of Life (*Amazing Stories Quarterly*, 1931; reprinted 1951), where an ineffectual human being is changed into a superman, although the effect on his genes is even more dramatic than the effect on his physiology.

*2-118. Taine, John (pseud. of Eric Temple Bell). **The Time Stream.** Buffalo Book, 1946.
This is the best of Taine's novels, originally published in *Wonder Stories* in 1931–1932. More sober in tone than his extravagant stories of monsters and mutations, it is a complex novel of time travel whose climactic catastrophe is by no means simply an imaginative display of spectacular violence.

2-119. Tolstoi, Aleksei (U.S.S.R.). **Aelita.** Foreign Languages (Moscow), 1957. Tr. by Lucy Flaxman, 1922.
An interplanetary romance in which an idealistic scientist is upstaged by a down-to-earth engineer, who successfully brings the revolution to Mars. It is crudely written, and the propaganda appears to have been grafted onto the story at a late stage. Tolstoi's other translated scientific romance, *The Death Box* (1926; translated 1936; known in a different translation as *The Garin Death Ray*), is an overlong and confusing thriller about a megalomaniac scientist who is finally overthrown by the workers he attempts to exploit.

2-120. Tsiolkovsky, Konstantin (U.S.S.R.). **Beyond the Planet Earth.** Pergamon, 1960. Tr. by K. Syers of *Vne zemli*, 1920.
A juvenile novel about rocket travel into space, written to popularize Tsiolkovsky's ideas about the possibility of spaceflight and the construction of orbital space colonies. The story is awful, but its basic premise has been amply vindicated—Tsiolkovsky must be regarded as the spiritual father of spaceflight and the myth of the conquest of space. The novel is also reprinted, along with various other essays and pieces of science fiction, under the title *Outside the Earth*, in the definitive collection of Tsiolkovsky's works, *The Call of the Cosmos* (1963).

2-121. Vivian, E(velyn) Charles (U.K.). **Star Dust.** Hutchinson, 1925.
The best of several cautionary tales about scientists who learn how to perform the alchemical trick of making gold, only to find that the discovery brings unexpected difficulties in its wake. Others include Conan Doyle's *The Doings of Raffles Haw* (1891) and John Taine's *Quayle's Invention* (1927). Vivian was one of the better writers of imaginative thrillers, producing lost-world stories under his own name and some fine supernatural stories as Jack Mann, but this was his only science fiction novel.

2-122. von Hanstein, Otfrid (Germany). **Electropolis.** *Wonder Stories Quarterly*, Summer 1930. Tr. by Francis Currier of *Elektropolis*, 1927.
A typical German utopian fantasy of the period, in which an industrialist buys a mountain in Australia and uses the radium he mines from it to provide power for a futuristic city, which he builds nearby in the desert. The greedy Australians try to take their land back, but German superscience prevails.

2-123. von Harbou, Thea (Germany). **Metropolis.** Reader's Library, 1927. Tr. 1926.
The book of Fritz Lang's classic film, written by his wife. The film thrives on its

magnificent visuals, not on its plot, and the novel falls rather flat. It is an unconvincing melodrama about an industrial dispute in a marvelous city of the future. *The Rocket to the Moon* (1930) is the book of the film *Die Frau im Mond,* an interplanetary romance whose special effects were enhanced by the work of the German Rocket Society, but it is similarly depleted in cold print.

2-124. Weinbaum, Stanley G(rauman). **The Black Flame.** Fantasy, 1948.
The book contains the novelette "Dawn of Flame" as well as the title story, although the latter was a new version of the first, rewritten to boost the fantasy content. Neither version sold while Weinbaum was alive; both appeared posthumously in 1939. The stories belong to the species of exotic romance that includes Haggard's *She* [1-46], Benoit's *Atlantida* (1920), and A. Merritt's *Dwellers in the Mirage* (1932)—the translocation of the myth into science fiction does not show it to any greater advantage, but the story is fondly remembered.

*2-125. Weinbaum, Stanley G(rauman). **A Martian Odyssey and Other Science Fiction Tales.** Hyperion, 1975.
An omnibus edition of Weinbaum's pulp science fiction stories, absorbing the two earlier collections, *A Martian Odyssey and Others* (1949) and *The Red Peri* (1952). The stories featuring exotic alien ecosystems are excellent, written with wit and inventiveness. The title work, "The Lotus Eaters," and "The Mad Moon" are among the best stories to appear in the early pulps, and they remain readable today.

*2-126. Weinbaum, Stanley G(rauman). **The New Adam.** Ziff-Davis, 1939.
A classic "superman" novel, written before Weinbaum commenced his brief career as a pulp writer in 1934 but not published during his lifetime. It is an attempt to examine seriously and thoughtfully the possible career of an evolved man born into the contemporary world, and makes much of the analogy of "feral children." Less devoted to social criticism than Stapledon's *Odd John* [2-110], it appears to have been similarly inspired by Beresford's *The Hampdenshire Wonder* [1-11].

2-127. Wells, H(erbert) G(eorge) (U.K.). **The Croquet Player.** Chatto & Windus, 1936.
A neurotic medical man tells the allegorical story of Cainsmarsh, a village whose inhabitants are cursed by their evolutionary heritage (symbolized by the bones of their remote ancestors, which are sometimes exhumed from the marsh). The protagonist, a man of leisure, cannot see the implications of the allegory. A neat parable presenting the view that human nature is fatally flawed.

2-128. Wells, H(erbert) G(eorge) (U.K.). **The Holy Terror.** Joseph, 1939.
A psychological study of the personality of a revolutionary-turned-dictator, who brings about the destruction of the old social order only to become a threat to the establishment of a better one. The protagonist is modeled on Stalin, with Hitler, Mussolini, and Franco also in mind. Perhaps the most interesting exercise in sociopolitical SF among Wells's later works.

2-129. Wells, H(erbert) G(eorge) (U.K.). **Men like Gods.** Cassell, 1923.
The second of Wells's major utopian fantasies, set in the distant future. Our

world has long since collapsed, owing to its failure to convert scientific knowledge into practical wisdom. A new superrace, rather different in psychology, has emerged from the ruins, and its members live amicably in a stateless community.

*2-130. Wells, H(erbert) G(eorge) (U.K.). **The Shape of Things to Come.** Hutchinson, 1933.
The last of Wells's major utopian fantasies is a documentary fiction that attempts to reconnect the utopian future with the present by means of an imaginary future history. It reiterates Wells's conviction that the obliteration of contemporary political intrusions is a necessary first step in social reconstruction, but it relies on war and plague rather than revolution to accomplish the task. The image of the reborn world is really no more convincing than his previous utopian designs.

2-131. Wells, H(erbert) G(eorge) (U.K.). **Star-Begotten: A Biological Fantasia.** Chatto & Windus, 1937.
A curious novel in which Wells dallies half-heartedly with neo-Lamarckian ideas. Martians bombard Earth with mutagenic radiation to assist the emergence of a new kind of being. The work has more in common with *In the Days of the Comet* (1906) than with *The Food of the Gods* [1-99], and is entirely lacking in conviction.

2-132. Williams, Charles (U.K.). **Many Dimensions.** Gollancz, 1931.
The most nearly science fiction of Williams's theological fantasies, featuring a stone made of "absolute matter," which can be divided without loss of substance and allows its owners to move through space and time. The action is subdued and the novel is thoughtful, content to leave the possibilities in the basic premise to the imagination of the reader. It contrasts with Čapek's *The Absolute at Large* [2-13], although in a sense it has the same premise and points to a related moral.

2-133. Williamson, Jack. **The Green Girl.** Avon, 1950.
One of Williamson's many early magazine serials, from *Amazing* in 1930. An extravagant adventure enlivened by Merrittesque purple prose and a superbly melodramatic first line. The same naïve charm is to be found in two similar novels, *The Stone from the Green Star* (1931) and *Xandulu* (1934).

2-134. Williamson, Jack. **The Legion of Space.** Fantasy, 1947.
A space opera first published in *Astounding* in 1934, in which characters based on Falstaff and the Three Musketeers try to obtain control of a secret superweapon to save Earth from an alien menace. Two other serials featuring the same characters were reprinted in *The Cometeers* (1950), and the whole series—including a fourth novelette—assembled in *Three from the Legion* (1979). *The Queen of the Legion* was added in 1983.

*2-135. Williamson, Jack. **The Legion of Time.** Fantasy, 1952.
A classic of pulp SF in which a small army of soldiers of fortune is co-opted into a war between alternate futures to settle which of them will really exist. The gaudy costume drama is sustained by the power of the central idea, which was new in 1938 when the novel was serialized in *Astounding*.

2-136. Winsor, G(eorge) MacLeod (U.K.). **Station X.** Jenkins, 1919.
A competent thriller in which aliens invade Earth by means of a radio installa-

tion. Gernsback reprinted it in *Amazing Stories* in 1926. A similar theme is used in Frank Crisp's *The Ape of London* (1959).

2-137. Wright, Harold Bell, and John Lebar. **The Devil's Highway.** Appleton, 1932.

A marvelously lurid mad-scientist story in which the villain uses a machine to suppress the emotions and conscience of his victims so that they can devote their intellectual energies entirely to his nefarious schemes. Contrast Kaul's treatment of a similarly alienated genius in *Contagion to This World* [2-54].

2-138. Wright, S(ydney) Fowler (U.K.). **The Adventure of Wyndham Smith.** Jenkins, 1938.

In a remote future the inhabitants of a utopia of comforts find their lives utterly pointless and elect to commit mass suicide. One of their number, whose identity is fused with the psyche of a man of our time, saves himself and a woman, but must then face the threat of mechanical killers programmed to hunt them down. Expanded from the short story "Original Sin"; the most scathing of Fowler Wright's denunciations of the leisure society.

*2-139. Wright, S(ydney) Fowler (U.K.). **Deluge.** Fowler Wright, 1927.

A self-published book that became a best-seller. Geological upheavals result in widespread flooding, but southern England is elevated to make the Cotswolds a tiny archipelago. The inhabitants' struggle for existence is described with a cold realism not previously seen. The narrative of the sequel, *Dawn* (1929), runs parallel for most of its length. Compare and contrast England's *Darkness and Dawn* [1-33], Wyndham's *The Kraken Wakes* [3-412], and Ballard's *The Drowned World* [4-37] to appreciate the full spectrum of this species of romantic pessimism.

2-140. Wright, S(ydney) Fowler (U.K.). **Dream; or, The Simian Maid.** Harrap, 1931.

A depressed socialite seeks distraction in hypnotically sharing the experiences of individuals long dead—in this case an arboreal humanoid primate. Her lover and sister follow her into the past, incarnated as members of another protohuman species; all three become involved in the affairs of an enclosed kingdom threatened by gargantuan rats. A slightly bitter celebration of the noble savagery of nature, to be contrasted with Mitchell's *Three Go Back* [2-79]. *Vengeance of Gwa* (1935, originally published under the name of Anthony Wingrave) was intended as a sequel, though the prefatory material was cut from the published editions. *Spiders' War* (1954), in which the heroine visits an idiosyncratically utopian future, completes the trilogy.

2-141. Wright, S(ydney) Fowler (U.K.). **The Island of Captain Sparrow.** Gollancz, 1928.

A castaway on a small island finds the cruel descendants of pirates hunting nonsentient satyrs, while the last fugitive survivors of an antediluvian civilization and a forest-dwelling girl also live in fear of them. After a desperate struggle, hero and heroine inherit this fragment of Eden from those of the Fallen who have usurped it. Contrast Wells's *Island of Dr. Moreau* [1-100], whose philosophical and allegorical themes are touched on.

*2-142. Wright, S(ydney) Fowler (U.K.). **The New Gods Lead.** Jarrolds, 1932.
One of the few SF collections published in the United Kingdom between the wars, featuring a sequence of stories set in nightmarish futures where a scientistic way of thinking has made life frightful. Added to the main sequence are "The Rat," in which the inventor of an immortality serum decides (too late) that it will not improve the quality of life, and "Choice," an allegory in which two lovers decide that life, for all its pain and uncertainty, is preferable to heaven. A striking collection, reprinted with the addition of two stories as *The Throne of Saturn* (1949). Compare Bunch's *Moderan* [4-98].

2-143. Wright, S(ydney) Fowler (U.K.). **Prelude in Prague.** Newnes, 1935.
A future war novel, written as a newspaper serial after an investigative tour of Europe. World War II begins with a German invasion of Czechoslovakia, and a group of Britons trapped in Prague witness the effects of blitzkrieg. *Four Days War* (1936) takes up the story with Germany sending its air fleets against Britain, with horrific consequences. In *Megiddo's Ridge* (1937) the Americans get involved, and the two contending forces muster for the final battle. The rather contrived main narrative follows the exploits of a remarkable British spy who wins the confidence of the German High Command, but the virtues of the trilogy are in their description of the effects of high technology warfare. Compare O'Neill's *Day of Wrath* [2-86].

*2-144. Wright, S(ydney) Fowler (U.K.). **The World Below.** Collins, 1929.
Two short novels, the first of which appeared separately as *The Amphibians* in 1925; the second is also known in one paperback version as *The Dwellers*. A time traveler ventures into the remote future in search of two predecessors. His arrival precipitates a crisis in the affairs of the gentle, telepathic Amphibians, who coexist uneasily with the giant humanoid Dwellers. The account of this bizarre posthuman future draws some imagery from Dante's *Inferno,* which Fowler Wright had recently translated, and was unparalleled in its time for its phantasmagoric quality, but the second part peters out into a few synoptic chapters and a hurried ending. Compare Hodgson's *The Night Land* (1912) and Silverberg's *Son of Man* [4-507].

*2-145. Wylie, Philip (Gordon). **Gladiator.** Knopf, 1930.
A novel about the growth to adulthood of a boy who is a physical (although not intellectual) "superman." It is the first important sympathetic superman story, but exhibits the customary pessimism regarding the prospect of the hero's eventual integration into the human world—a pessimism set aside by the creators of the comic book *Superman,* who borrowed the novel's central notion.

2-146. Wylie, Philip (Gordon), and Edwin Balmer. **When Worlds Collide.** Stokes, 1933.
A celebrated novel of impending cosmic catastrophe and the attempt to save a favored few from sharing the fate of the doomed world. It was filmed by George Pal in 1951. The sequel, dealing with the exploits of the survivors on their new world, is *After Worlds Collide* (1934). Similar themes are developed in McIntosh's *One in Three Hundred* [3-278] and James Blish's ... *And All the Stars a Stage* (1971).

*2-147. Zamiatin, Evgenii (U.S.S.R.). **We.** Dutton, 1924. Tr. by Gregory Zilboorg of *My*.

A magnificent vision of a dystopian society in which life has been totally regulated in the cause of order, harmony, and happiness. The seeds of dissatisfaction have been rooted out, with the sole exception of imagination, which is about to be eliminated from the psyche as humans' noblest project comes to fruition: the building of a spaceship that will allow the "United State" to extend itself throughout the universe. A masterpiece of speculative political philosophy by a disillusioned Russian—never, of course, published in the U.S.S.R. itself. It influenced Orwell's *Nineteen Eighty-Four* [3-302] and provided a prototype for modern dystopian fantasy.

3
The Early Modern Period: 1938–1963

Joe De Bolt and John R. Pfeiffer

This third edition of *Anatomy of Wonder* divides the modern period into early and late periods. In this chapter two new matters, in addition to carrying forward several important matters from our introduction to the second edition, are explained. First, we are not doing much that is new. In the second edition we selected titles about which we had no serious doubts. Since 1981 some works have had sequels, or become series, and in this edition we have tried to identify most of these. Second, we have added about 20 new entries. However, our criteria for this list are unchanged from the second edition. Most works published after 1963, by writers whose publishing careers span 1963, are now in Chapter 4. Pre-1964 works remain here. The selection of titles we made for the second edition, including those dropped for reasons of space for the post-1963 chapter, is sound. The remarks carried forward from the second edition introduction refer, as well, to these dropped titles.

The period in the history of SF from the late 1930s to the middle 1960s is a high golden age for the genre—such a golden age having had its beginnings in the late 1920s, where the effort of Hugo Gernsback was of singular importance. The generally new discipline of the writing craft that began to mark the period by the end of the 1930s is well represented by the editorial principles and influence of John W. Campbell. A second new discipline was imposed by the more realistic understanding of the physical universe provided by modern technics. There is exceptional energy and optimism, a faith in humanity and a view of reality that reflects the triumph of technology, of practical engineering success, and of the consequent material and political progress of these decades that raised the West, and the United States, to history's highest level to date. Indeed, "engineering fiction" might have been a better name for the genre than science fiction.

Of the writers and editors we have identified for our period, we judge these the most important:

Brian Aldiss	Gordon Dickson	C. L. Moore
Poul Anderson	Philip Farmer	George Orwell
Isaac Asimov	H. L. Gold	Edgar Pangborn
Alfred Bester	James Gunn	Frederik Pohl
James Blish	Edmond Hamilton	Ayn Rand
Anthony Boucher	Harry Harrison	Eric Frank Russell
Pierre Boulle	Robert Heinlein	Robert Sheckley
Ray Bradbury	Fred Hoyle	Nevil Shute
Fredric Brown	L. Ron Hubbard	Clifford Simak
Algis Budrys	Aldous Huxley	B. F. Skinner
John W. Campbell	Damon Knight	E. E. Smith
John Christopher	C. M. Kornbluth	Theodore Sturgeon
Arthur Clarke	Henry Kuttner	William Tenn
Hal Clement	Fritz Leiber	Jack Vance
Mark Clifton	Murray Leinster	A. E. van Vogt
Groff Conklin	Stanislaw Lem	Gore Vidal
Edmund Crispin	C. S. Lewis	Kurt Vonnegut
Avram Davidson	Richard Matheson	Jack Williamson
L. Sprague de Camp	J. T. McIntosh	Donald A. Wollheim
Lester del Rey	Judith Merril	Philip Wylie
Philip Dick	Walter Miller, Jr.	John Wyndham

Of course, many of these writers were in business before and after this late golden age. The time's cultural winds impelled them forward to visions mostly of the possible. And it seemed all things were possible. A few writers retain the spirit today, but most of those who wrote in the early modern period are gone or changed. What is important to understand about these writers is that many of them believed they were writing about *a* future, but not necessarily their personal future.

As the avatar of this period's writer one would find a white American male with either some formal education or job experience in an applied field, such as journalism, science, or technology. Long on pragmatism, short on theory, he would have served in or been interested in the military, had a preference for the individual over the collective, and, when asked to consider the world's end, might likely reply like Donald A. Wollheim:

We are not going to end with a bang.
We are not going to end with a whimper.
We are not going to end.
That's all.

—*The Universe Makers*
(Harper, 1971, p. 118)

The latter half of the 1960s brought in the pastel fantasy of the "modern age," launched editorially by Michael Moorcock and authorially by James Ballard—often highly sophisticated in literary skills but sometimes marking the triumph of form over substance, fatalism over faith, and despair over destiny. The future they seemed to be writing about was no longer some future, but *the* future. At the end of *The Sheep Look Up* [4-90], John Brunner quotes from Milton's *Lycidas:*

> The hungry sheep look up, and are not fed,
> But swoln with wind, and the rank mist they draw,
> Rot inwardly, and foul contagion spread.

It was a grimmer vision, indeed. People were no longer the solution; they had become the problem. The universe no longer blazed with potent opportunity but, shrunken, crumbled into lassitude, colors fading, except perhaps for the vivid acid phantoms within one's own skull. Western culture, gripped by malaise, had left its golden age, and SF mirrored that condition.

We repeat from the second edition the procedure followed for defining and identifying works of SF; comments on the SF short story, fandom, fantasy, and the SF writing/film connection; the relation of SF to cultural history; a description of the selection criteria; a description of the sources employed; and our acknowledgments to those who helped prepare the still substantially intact second edition list.

In lieu of an abstract definition, we used the following general descriptions as the basis for a given work as SF. We included categories A–H (see below) and excluded hard fantasy, pure gothic, detective stories, cold war/spy stories, sword and sorcery and/or occult, drug trips and/or internal visions, absurd fiction, and divine intervention or miracles.

The titles of many of the best or better works listed in the descriptions of categories A–H illustrate and perhaps authenticate the eight elements of our working definition. Titles are presented in one category only, although the overlapping of several categories is common. A historical introduction to the best works with a practical topology of SF follow the descriptive categories A–H. (Entry numbers for titles are not shown; see under author or check the index.) Post-1963 titles are in Chapter 4.

A. Demonstration polemics (includes utopias and dystopias)—**Thirties/Forties:** Graves, *Watch the Northwind Rise;* Orwell, *Nineteen Eighty-Four.* **Fifties:** Bradbury, *Fahrenheit 451; The Martian Chronicles;* Caldwell, *Devil's Advocate;* Heinlein, *Double Star;* Kelley, *A Different Drummer;* Pohl and Kornbluth, *The Space Merchants;* Tucker, *The Long Loud Silence;* Vonnegut, *Player Piano;* Wylie, *The Disappearance.* **Sixties:** Barth, *Giles Goat-Boy;* Brunner, *Stand on Zanzibar;* Burgess, *Clockwork Orange;* Disch, *Camp Concentration;* Durrell, *Tunc* and *Nunquam;* George, *Dr. Strangelove;* Heinlein, *The Moon Is a Harsh Mistress;* Vonnegut, *Slaughterhouse-Five.* **Seventies:** Aldiss, *Barefoot in the Head;* Carter, *The War of Dreams;* Compton, *The Unsleeping Eye;* Disch, *On Wings of Song;* Le Guin, *The Dispossessed;* Lundwall, *2018 A.D.;* Malzberg, *Beyond Apollo;* Percy, *Love in the Ruins.*

B. Human destiny stories (includes future histories)—**Thirties/Forties:** Asimov, *Foundation Trilogy;* Heinlein, *The Past through Tomorrow* (continues through 1950s); Stewart, *Earth Abides.* **Fifties:** Blish, *Cities in Flight;* Miller, *Canticle for Leibowitz;* Simak, *City;* Pangborn, *Mirror for Observers;* Efremov, *Andromeda.* **Sixties:** Pangborn, *Davy.* **Seventies:** Crowley, *Engine Summer;* Merle, *Malevil.*

C. Alternate and lost worlds—**Sixties:** Dick, *The Man in the High Castle;* Roberts, *Pavane.* **Seventies:** Amis, *The Alteration.*

D. Descriptions of alien and noncontemporary Earth life—**Fifties:** Clement, *Mission of Gravity;* Wyndham, *The Midwich Cuckoos.* **Sixties:** Delany, *Einstein Intersection;* Farmer, *The Lovers;* Herbert, *Dune;* Le Guin, *The Left Hand of Darkness;* Leiber, *The Wanderer;* Lem, *Solaris;* Tevis, *The Man Who Fell to Earth;* White, *The Watch Below.* **Seventies:** Asimov, *The Gods Themselves;* Benford, *In the Ocean of Night;* Terry Carr, *Cirque;* Gunn, *The Listeners;* Wolfe, *The Fifth Head of Cerberus.*

E. Objective trips to inaccessible places or with new means of transportation (includes time travel, teleportation, faster-than-light travel, matter transmission)—**Thirties/Forties:** de Camp, *Lest Darkness Fall.* **Sixties:** Anthony, *Macroscope;* Leiber, *The Big Time.* **Seventies:** Anderson, *Tau Zero;* Benford, *Timescape;* Finney, *Time and Again;* Forward, *Dragon's Egg;* Moorcock, *Behold the Man.*

F. Latent effects of technology, new technology—**Thirties/Forties:** Williamson, *The Humanoids.* **Fifties:** Brown, *The Lights in the Sky Are Stars;* del Rey, *Nerves;* Heinlein, *Starship Troopers;* Shute, *On the Beach.* **Sixties:** Aldiss, *Greybeard;* Spinrad, *Bug Jack Barron.* **Seventies:** Brunner, *The Sheep Look Up;* Clarke, *Rendezvous with Rama;* Niven, *Ringworld;* Shaw, *Orbitsville;* Spinrad, *Songs from the Stars.*

G. New belief systems (includes new sciences, ideologies, and religions)—**Thirties/Forties:** Hesse, *The Glass Bead Game;* Lewis, "Space Trilogy." **Fifties:** Blish, *A Case of Conscience;* Vance, *Languages of Pao.* **Sixties:** Budrys, *Rogue Moon;* Delany, *Babel-17;* Heinlein, *Stranger in a Strange Land;* Panshin, *Rite of Passage;* Simak, *Way Station;* Zelazny, *Lord of Light.* **Seventies:** Chayefsky, *Altered States;* Farmer, *To Your Scattered Bodies Go;* Silverberg, *A Time of Changes;* Vidal, *Kalki.*

H. New physical and/or mental capacities for living or nonliving things (includes stories of supermen, mutations, and transcendence)—**Thirties/Forties:** Smith, Lensmen series; van Vogt, *Slan.* **Fifties:** Anderson, *Brain Wave;* Bester, *The Demolished Man; The Stars My Destination;* Clarke, *Childhood's End;* Clifton and Riley, *They'd Rather Be Right;* Sturgeon, *More Than Human.* **Sixties:** Ballard, *The Crystal World;* Dick, *The Three Stigmata of Palmer Eldritch;* Keyes, *Flowers for Algernon;* Lem, *The Cyberiad;* Zelazny, *This Immortal.* **Seventies:** Bass, *Half Past Human;* Elgin, *Communipath Worlds;* Silverberg, *Dying Inside.*

There is a very important relationship between the characteristic themes and shapes of SF and the extraliterary history of the 40-odd years of the modern period. That the period begins in the years just before World War II is the perception of a number of notable SF historians—Asimov, Aldiss, de Camp, and Gunn among them. Gunn, writing about the period from 1938 to 1950 in his *Alternate Worlds* [9-41], observes, "During these years the first modern SF editor [John W. Campbell] began developing the first modern SF magazine [*Astounding*], the first modern SF writers and, indeed, modern SF itself." For Aldiss, in *Billion Year*

Spree [9-4], "From 1939 a kind of coherence appears." For Asimov, "The Golden Age of Science Fiction" begins in 1938. De Camp, in his *Handbook* [13-14], reports a rapid expansion in the SF field between 1939 and 1941. We agree, and we have divided the period into parts, each representing roughly a decade or part of a decade. For each part we have blended salient details from contemporary history representing the aspects of popular consciousness that might have been expected to supply inspiration for science fiction. Second, we have mentioned events in the history of the media (print, radio, films, television) that can suggest the modes in which SF was transmitted. Finally, we have represented SF itself, in its topics, titles, and authors, from both the literary mainstream and traditional genre sources.

At least four additional matters must be emphasized here as important to a definitive history of SF, although they are beyond the purview of the record of works presented in *Anatomy*—with its emphasis on the SF novel. The first is a caution against ignoring the importance of short fiction in both the history and modern progress of SF, especially in view of the fact that most readers have discovered SF in the form of the novel, film, or TV show. A history of early SF must be recounted largely in terms of the short story. To a considerable extent, anthologies and single-author collections supply the representative titles. The second is SF fandom with its conventions that began in the late 1930s. Its influence on the genre is enormous and incalculable.

The third is the parent genre of SF—fantasy. With a few exceptions in cases of award nominees, this guide is restricted to SF, but fantasy can hardly be ignored in a full account of the field. By our definition, fantasy is the genus under which SF is collected as a historically local species. In other ages it appears as Aesop's fables, saints' legends, or Arthurian romance. The issues tend to remain the same, while the scenes, furniture, government, technology, and culture change with the times. Modern fantasy is distinct because it is not time- and culture-locked. This is true of the work of three of the most popular writers of fantasy in the last 40 years, J. R. R. Tolkien, Mervyn Peake, and Ursula Le Guin, as well as an impressive roster that includes Richard Adams's *Watership Down* (1972), Poul Anderson's *Three Hearts and Three Lions* (1961), John Brunner's *Traveler in Black* (1971), Fritz Leiber's *Conjure Wife* (1953) and the Gray Mouser and Fafhrd series (1939–1968), James Blish's *Black Easter* (1968), George Orwell's *Animal Farm* (1946), Miguel Angel Asturias's *Mulata* (1967), Avram Davidson's *The Phoenix and the Mirror* (1969), L. Ron Hubbard's "Fear" (1940), Fletcher Pratt's "The Blue Star" (1952), and the collaborative and editorial efforts of L. Sprague de Camp and Lin Carter on Robert E. Howard's unfinished fantasy works. Fine fantasy continued to appear in later years, represented in such works as Michael Moorcock's *Gloriana* (1979) and Chelsea Quinn Yarbro's *Ariosto* (1980). Many such works are by design timeless; they succeed as well in evoking the mood of our time and must be regarded as a definitive element of the context in which we view SF.

The fourth matter to emphasize is a remarkable phenomenon of the decade of the 1970s in particular. The SF film and SF literature have become inextricably connected, especially in the broadly popular perception of science fiction. Many fine SF works became successful films (dates refer to the film): D. F. Jones's *Colossus: The Forbin Project* (1970); Crichton's *The Andromeda Strain* (1971), Christopher's *No Blade of Grass* (1970), Burgess's *Clockwork Orange* (1971), Ellison's *A Boy and His Dog* (1975), Finney's *Invasion of the Body Snatchers* (1980), and King's *Carrie* (1978) represent this trend. No less interesting are the SF works that have become popular because of the great success of the films from which they were adapted (dates refer to the film): Clarke's *2001: A Space Odyssey* (1968), Blish's *Star Trek* books, Lucas's *Star Wars* (1977), Spielberg's *Close Encounters of the Third Kind* (1977, 1980), and A. D. Foster's *Alien* (1979) are extraordinary examples. One way or another, the success of the SF film has radically altered the popular perception of SF as literature.

The breakdown that follows this introduction to the modern period presents the topics of SF as literature only, with emphasis on the novel, from before World War II to the mid-1960s.

Pre-1940s. With the rise of fascism, the advent of World War II, and the experience of the depression, a coming to terms with hard reality began to characterize SF. Stanton A. Coblentz's "Lord of Tranerica" (1939) cautioned against the victory of the Axis powers, a theme to be resurrected in such works as Dick's *Man in the High Castle* (1962) and Spinrad's *The Iron Dream* (1972). P. Schuyler Miller erected an architecture of the depression in *The Titan* (1935, 1952). Movies and pulp literature proliferated for the huge audience otherwise idled by the depression. American comic books emerged with Superman in the June 1938 *Action Comics,* the beginning of the "golden age" of comics that would be the vulgar assimilation of the more disciplined fantasy of SF. The reaction to Orson Welles's "War of the Worlds" radio production in 1938 illustrated the incredible influence the electronic media would have upon the public consciousness. And John W. Campbell became editor of *Astounding* late in 1937 to shepherd in the first New Wave in SF. In the literary mainstream, Balmer and Wylie's *When Worlds Collide* was out. C. S. Lewis's famous "Space Trilogy" was in progress, while Aldous Huxley's *Brave New World* had been available since 1932. Campbell, within the field, would turn from the adolescently conceived superman, space opera, gadget-fascinated stories marking the apprenticeship of the Binder brothers, Nelson Bond, E. E. Smith, and Jack Williamson to more probable and plausible scenarios represented by Stanley Weinbaum's *Martian Odyssey* (published in 1949 as a book), Campbell's own pieces (collected in *Who Goes There?*), and the work of such fledglings as Isaac Asimov and Robert A. Heinlein. Nearly single-handedly, Campbell focused the visions of important SF writers for decades to come. He made these writers critically self-conscious. This self-consciousness has increased through the years and continues with an unprecedented intensity today.

1940s. From the outset of the decade, few significant historical developments failed to find treatment in SF. Heinlein in "Sixth Column" (1941) expressed the general anxieties of World War II. Lester del Rey's "Nerves" (1942) depicted the terrible danger of atomic experiments, while Cleve Cartmill predicted the actual development of the atom bomb with now-legendary accuracy in "Deadline" (1944). It was tragically fitting that by his death in 1946, H. G. Wells had seen his prediction of nuclear warfare come to pass. The bomb ended the war but raised new fears over the possibility of genetic alteration in victim populations, fears mirrored in Poul Anderson's "Tomorrow's Children" (1947). Moreover, the real possibility of global catastrophe found metaphor throughout the decade, from Best's *Twenty-fifth Hour* (1940) to Farjeon's *Death of a World* (1948). Meanwhile, the new threat of the U.S.S.R.–United States cold war was expressed in Engel and Piller's *The World Aflame* (1947), Koestler's *Age of Longing* (1951), and Bradbury's *Fahrenheit 451* (1953). The war had also forced the rapid development of automation, for which robots became the obvious symbol—displayed in the Binders' *Adam Link* (1965), Asimov's *I, Robot* (1950), and Williamson's *Humanoids* (1949). The first of the modern series of UFO flaps occurred to characterize the postwar mood—caught in Ray Jones's *This Island Earth* (1952) and Heinlein's *Puppet Masters* (1951) as the decade ended. Meanwhile, the comic book flourished; Hollywood produced *The Thing*, a bastardization of Campbell's "Who Goes There?," and pulp SF serials multiplied. In the mainstream, Orwell's *Nineteen Eighty-Four* (1949), Rand's *Anthem* (1946), and Stewart's *Earth Abides* (1949) represented, respectively, the political left, the political right, and a socioanthropological view of the decadence of human civilization. In the SF field, Campbell's disciplining influence pervaded. Fascination with the gifts and dangers of science waxed, along with concentration upon the refinements of superhumans in the stories of Asimov, Heinlein, Kuttner, George O. Smith, Williamson, de Camp, and Bradbury—the early greats. Their overall message was earnestly, if tentatively, optimistic.

1950s. Our critical list will show that the bulge in production of memorable SF novels begins in this period and continues unabated to the present. They are so numerous, in fact, that it is a maverick task indeed to select just a few from the nearly 200 annotated entries to represent the signs of the times. Vonnegut's *Player Piano* (1952) challenged the illusion of progress and increasing affluence, while Collins's *Tomorrow's World* (1956) highlighted the struggle between the hedonism and vicariousness of the "beat" generation and traditional puritanism. In Korea the cold war flared and the specter of the H-bomb loomed; so readers were ready for Kornbluth's *Not This August* (1955) and Frank's *Alas, Babylon* (1959). Heinlein's *Starship Troopers* (1959) triangulated a future implied in the success of Sputnik and the rise of the U.S. space program. Leiber's *The Silver Eggheads* (1959) seems more and more prescient of the fruits of war-born computer science, given the breakthrough invention of the transistor. Cities sprawled and made metropolitan life nightmarish; Pohl and Kornbluth's *Gladiator-at-Law* (1955) told the story. And no one could forget Bradbury's "The Pedestrian," predicting the mind-numbing, ubiquitous effects of television. Radio languished. Many SF pulps floundered, while the paperback book began to prosper. Remarkably, a number of mainstream writers produced SF—including Frank, Golding, Shute, Vercors, Wylie, Wouk, Vidal, and Drury. Good writers in the field increased: Pohl, Clement, Norton, Leinster, Kornbluth, Leiber, Sturgeon, Blish, Bester, del Rey, Wyndham, Clarke, Simak, and Miller. Their works made a golden age for SF.

1960s. In such a tumultuous decade, we can only suggest influences. There was the Vietnam war—Ballard's *Love and Napalm: Export USA* (1972); the continuing H-bomb hysteria—George's *Dr. Strangelove* (1963); the U.S. moon landing—Malzberg's *Universe Day* (1971); McLuhan's media theory—Brunner's *Stand on Zanzibar* (1968) and Spinrad's *Bug Jack Barron* (1969); the wide use and abuse of consciousness-altering drugs—Chester Anderson's *The Butterfly Kid* (1967); the explosive civil rights revolution in progress—Seymour's *The Coming Self-Destruction of the U.S.* (1969); the rise of welfarism—Pohl's *Age of the Pussyfoot* (1968) and Jensen's *Epp* (1967); recognition of the population explosion—

Burgess's *The Wanting Seed* (1962), del Rey's *The Eleventh Commandment* (1962), Blish and Knight's *Torrent of Faces* (1967), and Harrison's *Make Room! Make Room!* (1966); the sexual revolution—Heinlein's *Stranger in a Strange Land* (1961), Burroughs's *Nova Express* (1964), and Rimmer's *The Harrad Experiment* (1966); the recognition of the threat to ecology by modern industry—Ballard's *The Burning World* (1964) and Merle's *The Day of the Dolphin* (1969). Moreover, the perennial question of our ability to survive in the chaotic world we make was asked anew in Brunner's *The Whole Man* (1964), Delany's *Babel-17* (1966), Disch's *Camp Concentration* (1968), and Keyes's *Flowers for Algernon* (1966). Alvin Toffler perceptively caught the syndrome of these years with the label "future shock." Meanwhile, all but a few of the SF pulps had died; SF paperbacks flourished, while SF films peaked with Kubrick's *2001,* and television's "Star Trek" furnished a phenomenon that was still strong in the next decade. During the decade of the 1960s, fan interest increased. Wider and more appreciative audiences than ever before developed for SF, and writers both from the mainstream and the field met their appetite:

Mainstream Writers: John Barth, Eugene Burdick, Anthony Burgess, William Burroughs, Lawrence Durrell, Sam Greenlee, John Hersey, Fletcher Knebel, Robert Merle, Alan Seymour, B. F. Skinner, Kurt Vonnegut, Irving Wallace.

Writers in SF Field: Poul Anderson, Philip José Farmer, Frank Herbert, Ursula Le Guin, Robert Silverberg, Cordwainer Smith, Roger Zelazny.

Furthermore, the mood of the 1960s was so stark and wrenching that a special group of writers became identified who seemed to express it most appropriately. For lack of a better term they are referred to as the "New Wave," including Aldiss, Ballard, Brunner, Delany, Disch, Ellison, Malzberg, Moorcock, Spinrad, Reed, and Russ (to name a core). These authors were distinguished from the general field for their emphasis on formerly constrained subject matter and literary experiment. They explored with often painfully ruthless persistence topics once taboo in most SF, such as sex, radical politics, and religion. Simultaneously, they attacked SF's sacred cows: the conquest of space, human progress through technology, the success of the male-dominated capitalistic state. Much of the decade's moods, themes, and developments in writing are summed up in story collections such as Spinrad's *No Direction Home* (1975), Ellison's *Alone against Tomorrow* (1971), Malzberg's *Final War and Other Fantasies* (1969), and Disch's *Fun with Your New Head* (1971).

In literary art and craft, the New Wave authors introduced to SF techniques long common in the mainstream. Their characters were unique and complex, not stereotypes. Narratives featured streams of consciousness, wordplay, prose/ poetry counterpoint, and scenario-structuring techniques borrowed from such nonprint media as radio, film, and television. In addition, they were often appallingly erudite, employing eclectic vocabulary and displaying consummate control of the esoteric detail of virtually all the sciences. Having appeared on the scene first in Britain's *New Worlds,* they reached maturity in Ellison's anthology *Dangerous Visions* (1967). They would meet the malaise of the 1970s arms outstretched.

Though the early modern period in SF ends in the middle 1960s, we have preserved our paragraphs, largely intact, on the 1970s because they are valid, and they locate the works of this early period more certainly.

1970s. Cynicism and civil anarchy combined with beliefs of impending energy crises and of a shrinking planet to provide the mood of the first five years. Malzberg's *Beyond Apollo* (1972) drips with cynicism, and Delany's *Dhalgren* (1975) turns page upon page in a world from which government has fled. Famine and filth ravage Earth in Brunner's *The Sheep Look Up* (1972), while Asimov's *The Gods Themselves* (1972) may be an ironic depiction of just how preposterously desperate our search for energy sources will become. Instead of the prophesied greening of the West, reaction, division, and isolation bridge the decades, as in Brunner's *The Jagged Orbit* (1969) and Priest's *Darkening Island* (1972). The pathology of institutionalized paranoia and oppression wars with the tentatively wholesome search for brotherhood and sisterhood in a world state, as in Hjortsberg's *Gray Matters* (1971) and Russ's *The Female Man* (1975). China has risen, the Vietnam war has ended, and both Russian communism and Western capitalism are on the defensive, as in Harrison's *The Daleth Effect* (1970) and Shaw's *Ground Zero Man* (1971). For the longing eye in this storm of despair is Ursula Le Guin's *The Dispossessed* (1974), a novel whose violent referents in present reality merge into an organization that permits hope and newly innocent joy. Likewise, there is Reynolds's utopia, *Looking Backward from the Year 2000* (1973). Watergate broke, radically depreciating the charisma of the American presidency and adding to a nearly universal decline of public confidence in traditional institutions; Knebel's *Night of Camp David* (1965) and Sapir and Murphy's Destroyer series (1971) hardly seem fiction. One form of surcease is sought in religious revivals and new cults, epitomized in Silverberg's *Tower of Glass* (1970). Simak's *A Choice of Gods* (1972), Gary's *The Gasp* (1973), MacLean's *Missing Man* (1975), and Goulart's *After Things Fell Apart* (1970). Another form was nostalgia, presented in SF anachronistically set in a culture that no longer exists, such as Clarke's *Rendezvous with Rama* (1973) and Niven and Pournelle's *Mote in God's Eye* (1974). Finally, many looked to alien gods to lift them from their troubles, as in Cowper's *The Twilight of Briareus* (1974), even to the point of scouring the Earth of its unfit, as the Hoyles do in *The Inferno* (1973).

In the early 1970s, SF itself became a matter for serious study in the literature and humanities departments of American universities. All the moods, traditions, and resources of SF coalesced. The golden age writers were still publishing, and more new authors emerged who were immediately polished and professional. There was a convergence of the mainstream with the SF writers' ghetto, which strongly implied that once-unthinkable proposition: science fiction or "speculative fiction" might indeed become the mainstream's heart. Certainly, it was for the first time authentically international, as represented in the dissemination of works by European, Asian, and South American writers. Even so, mainstream and "field" continued to be distinguishable. Associated with the field were Niven, Russ, Lem, Malzberg, Bishop, and James Tiptree. Beyond were Drury, Crichton, Kosinksi, Lange, Percy, and Boulle.

From 1975 to 1980, little developed historically that was not apparent in the first five years of the decade. Likewise, SF for this time reveals no authentically new and original contents. Meanwhile, the remarkable features of SF literary culture were at least the following three: first, there was a consolidation of craft and art in writing at a higher level than ever before—so much so, in fact, that many of the published writers of the 1970s not even mentioned in this edition would have been regarded as brilliant in the 1940s and 1950s. Noteworthy male writers who established a high reputation were Bayley, Benford, Bryant, Card, Stephen

King, Martin, Pournelle, Gene Wolfe, and Varley. Moreover, the number of women writing quality SF increased. Jayge Carr, Cherryh, Lee, Lessing, McIntyre, Sargent, Vinge, and Yarbro are representative.

Second, there was a flowering and proliferation of all the historically representative thematic trends in SF, with no single one clearly dominating. The strain of pessimism born in the late 1960s and early 1970s continued in the works of Ballard, Bayley, M. J. Harrison, Lundwall, and Sanders. Liberal criticism of the idea of progress in Western industrial culture remained strong in writings by such authors as Benford, McIntyre, Varley, and Vinge. Furthermore, there was a growing popular reception of pieces that renewed the optimism and belief in progress that characterized the science fiction of 20 and 30 years earlier, in stories by Anderson, de Borchgrave and Moss, Dickson, and Niven and Pournelle, as the long-claimed dooms failed to arrive.

Third, SF became more profitable for more writers and people associated with the field than ever before. Causes for and effects of this are difficult to isolate. Mainstream writers such as Lessing, Stephen King, and Lawrence Sanders wrote SF that sold well. SF writers such as Herbert and McCaffrey published popular best-sellers. Haldeman and Heinlein received advances in the hundreds of thousands of dollars for quite routine novels—but the important point is that the money was there to gamble on SF publishing. One result was the blurring of the distinction between ghetto and mainstream SF. Science fiction became popular entertainment. Most likely the success of SF films had much to do with this effect. More people saw *Star Wars* in theaters than any film in history. Film historian Kenneth Jurkiewicz wrote down for us—just off the top of his head—the titles and credits of nearly 60 SF films (excluding gothic and horror) released for the first time in the 1970s. Serious fan publishing enjoyed a field day. Academics turned their ponderous attention to the bibliography, history, and criticism of SF that, almost overnight, filled many library shelves. These same academics taught thousands of courses in SF in universities—to millions of students. Those among the students who have continued to be readers at all have continued to read and respect SF, where their counterparts without such courses in past generations did not.

Deciding on the works to be included in the second and third editions required the balancing of a considerable variety of criteria. The selection criteria were as follows:

1. Any definition of SF notwithstanding, as in the first edition, automatically included are all Hugo winners and short-list nominees, and Nebula winners and short-list nominees, for the novel (see Chapter 16). Other awards were persuasive but not binding.

2. All of the works retained from the first and second editions of *Anatomy* were selected with recourse to the following list of works, not presented in the first edition introduction but published in a note to *Science-Fiction Studies* (March 1977):

"Locus Poll: 1975," best all-time SF novels; P. Schuyler Miller, *Analog* reader's choice lists 1953, 1956, 1966, and 1967; Jack Williamson, "Teaching SF: 1972"; Charles G. Waugh, "Best Authors, Best Novels: Chosen by College Instructors of Science Fiction," 1973; and Alexei Panshin, "A Basic Science Fiction Collection," *Library Journal* (June 15, 1970). . . . Kingsley Amis, *New Maps of Hell;* Thomas D. Clareson (ed.), *SF: The Other Side of Realism;* Donald H. Tuck, *A Handbook of Science Fiction and Fantasy,* second edition, and *Encyclopedia of Science Fiction and Fantasy,* Volume I; John R. Pfeiffer, *Fantasy and Science Fiction: A Critical Guide;* Kenneth Bulmer and Peter Nicholls, *The Best of SF: An Exhibition of Science Fiction;* Alva Rogers, *Requiem for Astounding;* Donald A. Wollheim, *The Universe Makers;* Sam Moskowitz, *Seekers of Tomorrow;* Darko Suvin, *Other Worlds, Other Seas;* Damon Knight, *In Search of Wonder,* second edition; James Blish (William Atheling), *The Issue at Hand* and *More Issues at Hand;* L. Sprague de Camp, *Science Fiction Handbook;* Brian Aldiss, *Billion Year Spree;* Donald Franson and Howard DeVore, *A History of Hugo, Nebula, and International Fantasy Awards,* third edition; Hal Hall, *Science Fiction Book Review Index, 1923–1973; Book Review Digest;* the review columns of *The Magazine of Fantasy and Science Fiction, Galaxy, If,* and *Astounding/Analog;* Anthony Boucher's yearly review of SF books appearing occasionally in Judith Merril's *Year's Best* anthologies; articles and reviews in *The Alien Critic; Algol; The Double Bill; Extrapolation; Foundation: Review of Science Fiction; Locus; Luna Monthly; Outworlds; Riverside Quarterly; Science-Fiction Studies; Science Fiction Review, Science Fiction Times;* and individual issues of numerous other fanzines.

Meanwhile, our lists and queries were circulated among academics, fans, and other readers, who made comments and provided specific suggestions.

3. The selected work had received a high number of reviews as indexed in Hall's *Science Fiction Book Review Index* [8-18], but had to meet two of the following additional criteria (4–8) as well.

4. Works mentioned as worthy of inclusion by critics in published reviews of the first edition of *Anatomy.* A minimum of three recommendations required; combine with 3 above and 5 through 8 following.

5. Works mentioned as worthy of inclusion by the outside readers listed in the preface. A minimum of three recommendations required; combine with 3 and 4 above and 6 through 8 following.

6. Votes received in periodic Locus Poll, published in *Locus,* placed a title from first to fifth in popularity; combine with 3 through 5 above and 7 and 8 following; three recommendations required.

7. The title had been selected for inclusion in the Salem Press *Survey of Science Fiction Literature* [8-29]; combine with 3 through 6 above and 8 following; three recommendations required.

8. The work was strongly recommended in Peter Nicholls's *Science Fiction Encyclopedia* [8-30] when the recommendation came from a contributor who had not made a recommendation in another format. Combine with 3 through 7 above; three recommendations required.

9. There was a strong possibility of inclusion if a work attained mainstream best-seller status.

10. If none of the above applied, a representative work by a reasonably prolific writer receiving generally outstanding reviews could be included.

11. A work could be selected if there was a need to represent the short fiction of an established author famous for novels but good in shorter fiction as well.

12. Also included were works considered reasonably worthy pieces not written in English for which a translation is available. We did not, however, select

foreign works just because they were foreign; selections met some of the preceding criteria.

13. If none of the above applied, a work could be included if deemed worthy on the basis of the editor's professional judgment. We were conservative, as we had to be.

The production of the manuscript for the list and the design of its entries proceeded with at least the following constraints and aids:

1. The names listed are the writing names of the authors; full forms of names and pseudonyms, when known, are given following the practice of *Science Fiction Encyclopedia*.

2. Publishers and dates of titles listed are, to the best of our ability to ascertain, for the first edition of the work in English. Where possible, we checked titles against Currey's *Science Fiction and Fantasy Authors* [8-3A], a marvelously executed research tool that richly deserves its recognition; Locke's *Science Fiction First Editions* [8-5]; Nicholls's *The Science Fiction Encyclopedia* [8-30]; Tuck's *The Encyclopedia of Science Fiction and Fantasy through 1968* [8-7] (indispensable); Marshall B. Tymn's *American Fantasy and Science Fiction* (Fax, 1979); and Wells's *Science Fiction and Heroic Fantasy Author Index* (1978). With the exception of Currey's almost flawless volume, we never used these sources singly. Occasionally, we also turned to *Cumulative Book Index*.

3. That a work is listed is a strong implicit comment in favor of it. Where a critical comment might have been made too glibly because of the press of time, we have withheld it altogether. Commentary on many collections is withheld because of the great difficulty in doing it precisely and usefully. Also, we recommend that the more widely available and easily accessible reviews of SF be read with or preferred to commentary that we have provided for a work. Finally, we have made conservative use of reviews for a number of the annotations; we admired those reviews but did not use them except for the basic information they provided.

We continue to acknowledge those people who gave us help on both the first and second editions. They are Nicolé Ballard, Tom Barber, Paula Brandimore, Cy Chauvin, Joseph De Bolt, Jr., Stephen Dark, Howard DeVore, David Ginsburg, James Gribben, Tom Jones, Kenneth Jurkiewicz, James La Motte, Cecily Little, Kerry Lutz, Doris Miller, Peter Nicholls, John Pfeiffer, Jr., Clinton Price, Linda Sutliff, Darko Suvin, Marshall Tymn, Frank Varela, Edward Walsh, Donna Wilson, and Robert J. Wilson. A special thanks to the Library Loan Office staff at Central Michigan University Library. Most of all, loving thanks to our wives, Denise De Bolt and Jeanne Pfeiffer, without whom we would not have done *Anatomy* a third time.

Bibliography

3-1. Abé, Kōbō (Japan). **Inter Ice Age 4.** Knopf, 1970. Tr. by E. Dale Saunders of *Dai yon kampyo-ki,* 1959.

Foreseeing worldwide flooding due to melting ice caps, an underground group of Japanese scientists forces aquatic adaptive changes on human fetuses in the name of survival. Katsumi, information scientist whose work helps develop a machine to predict the future, faces the moral dilemma of whether to support this effort after his own child has been turned into a water-dwelling "aquan." Creative story with doses of philosophy; includes a philosophic postscript by Abé Kōbō. Writing awkward, perhaps due to translation. Compare Christopher's *The Long Winter* [3-93] and Kavan's *Ice* [4-293].

*3-2. Aldiss, Brian W(ilson) (U.K.). **Best Science Fiction Stories of Brian W. Aldiss.** Faber, 1971; enlargement of 1965 issue. U.S. title: *Who Can Replace a Man?* Harcourt, 1966.

Sixteen stories of Aldiss's early and middle period. The classic "Who Can Replace a Man?" tells of the attempted self-emancipation of the robotic machines on an automated farm following the collapse of human society; the machines are trapped again by their programmed subservience to humans. Also noteworthy are the time-twisting "Man in His Time" (NN, 1966; IIN, 1967); "Not for an Age," winner of a 1957 *Observer* contest; "Man on Bridge," "Poor Little Warrior," and the haunting "Old Hundredth." Some of the stories are collected in *Galaxies like Grains of Sand* [3-3] and other Aldiss collections.

3-3. Aldiss, Brian W(ilson) (U.K.). **Galaxies like Grains of Sand.** Signet, 1960. British title: *The Canopy of Time,* Faber, 1959. The American edition is a major revision of the British issue.

Eight stories from 1957 to 1958 plus poetic interstitial sequences make up a "chronological novel," sketches of a future history that depicts the universe's end and rebirth. *Starswarm* (Signet, 1964; derived from *Airs of Earth,* Faber, 1963), another "chronological novel," is similarly organized, except divisions, "surveys" are of different galactic sectors named for various colors; eight stories (1958–1963) and connective sections. Both collections are illustrative of Aldiss's major concerns with time, change, and the unfolding of uncontrollable, irresistible forces. Stories are comparable with those of James Ballard.

*3-4. Aldiss, Brian W(ilson) (U.K.). **The Long Afternoon of Earth.** Signet, 1962. British title: *Hothouse,* Faber, 1962; considerably expands the U.S. first edition. Novelization of the five Hugo-winning (1962) Hothouse stories. In the far future, Earth's rotation has stopped and one hemisphere continually faces the bloated Sun. Vegetation has evolved to fill every ecological niche, and giant plant-spiders spin webs that entwine Earth and Moon. Of animal life, the only survivors are a few social insects and treetop dwelling humans, who, like their star and world, are devolving and close to extinction. An intelligent morel explains the approaching end to a group of humans it befriends and offers to take them with it to seed younger worlds, but they refuse. Perhaps humans have finally attained wisdom. Contrast Frank Herbert's *The Green Brain* (1966) and Clarke's *The City and the Stars* [3-98]. Also annotated as [4-7].

3-5. Aldiss, Brian W(ilson) (U.K.). **The Saliva Tree and Other Strange Growths.** Faber, 1966.
Excellent collection of ten stories, including the title work, a pastiche of H. G. Wells about the "invasion" of an English farm by aliens from Auriga, which won a Nebula (1965). Also outstanding are "Day of the Doomed King," "Parental Care," and "The Source."

3-6. Aldiss, Brian W(ilson) (U.K.). **Starship.** Criterion, 1959. British title: *Nonstop*, Faber, 1958.
The human cosmos shrinks to the vast but limited interior of an uncontrolled derelict interstellar ship. A jungle grows from its hydroponic tanks, wherein savage tribes live, testifying to Aldiss's version of social devolution. But the stalwart, creative few fight and eventually find the control room, pull the brake, and liberate humanity once again. Good writing and plot. Contrast with its prototype, Heinlein's *Orphans of the Sky* [3-203].

3-7. Allighan, Garry (South Africa). **Verwoerd—The End: A Look-back from the Future.** Purnell, 1961.
In 1987, a historian recounts how apartheid in South Africa, brutally established by Prime Minister Hendrik Frensch Verwoerd, was made to work acceptably and prestigiously under later benevolent rule. Apartheid properly administered can work. Energetically argued polemic. Would not persuade antiracist reader. Contrast Brunner's *The Jagged Orbit* [4-88].

*3-8. Anderson, Poul. **Brain Wave.** Ballantine, 1954.
Anderson's first adult novel and one of his best. Earth moves out of a shower of galactic radiation that has retarded the development of intelligence during the evolution of life; intellect, both human and animal, makes a quantum leap. The genius becomes the supergenius; the retarded and higher animals become old-style normal; neither Earth, now inherited by the former meek, nor the galaxy, watched over by the new superintellects, can ever be the same again. Like Charlie in Keyes's *Flowers for Algernon* [3-228], humanity suffers the trauma of mental growth, and while it is truly a *Childhood's End* [3-97] for humans, it is one they make for themselves. Poetic and insightful.

3-9. Anderson, Poul, and Gordon R(upert) Dickson. **Earthman's Burden.** Gnome, 1957.
The Hokas, bear-like inhabitants of 500 light-year distant Toka, are innately imitative of that which suits their needs and inflexibly consistent in its application. Alex Jones of Interstellar Survey discovers the results when, shipwrecked, he finds himself in a Wild West land of teddy-bear "cowboys" and tyrannosaurian "injuns," the Slissii, blood enemy of the Hokas. Old films and books from a previous Earth expedition had provided the models for the Hokas's first cultural borrowing ("The Sheriff of Canyon Gulch," originally "Heroes Are Made," 1951), as similar materials were to do in the five other Hoka stories in this volume about Cavaliers, Space Patrollers, Sherlockians, Buccaneers, and Foreign Legionnaires. Sequels include a novel, *Star Prince Charlie* (Putnam, 1975), and *Hoka!* (Wallaby/Simon & Schuster, 1983), the latter composed of four additional stories, mostly from the 1950s. Humorous literary spoofing and cute aliens make an irresistible

combination for most SF fans. Compare Piper's *Little Fuzzy* [3-308] and Biggle's *Monument* [3-34].

*3-10. Anderson, Poul. **The Enemy Stars.** Lippincott, 1959. Revised in Berkley, 1979 issue.
Four men try to survive when their matter transmitter is destroyed while they are exploring a dead star. Lots of physics, but in-depth characterization as well: wealthy liberal aristocrat Maclaren, the sole survivor; Buddhist Nakamura, who overcomes his fear of space; young Ryerson, god-haunted descendant of ancient Norsemen, who finds his manhood; revolutionary Sverdlov, who learns to see beyond mere politics. An affirmation of humanity's quest into the unknown; original title, from Kipling, was "We Have Fed Our Seas." Contrast Malzberg's *Beyond Apollo* [4-352]. HN, 1959.

*3-11. Anderson, Poul. **The High Crusade.** Doubleday, 1960.
Humorous tale of English knights in A.D. 1345 who capture a Wersgorix Empire spaceship. Carried back to the empire through treachery, the knights resist surrender and eventually destroy the empire, replacing it with an interplanetary feudal system "united in Christendom, the English tongue, and the English crown." Entertaining action, historical color, and consistency of internal logic that makes it all seem possible. Compare Leinster's *The Pirates of Zan* [3-258]. HN, 1961.

3-12. Anderson, Poul. **The Star Fox.** Doubleday, 1965.
Good action story and argument for taking military hard line against external threat. Industrialist and ex-navy officer Gunnar Heim resists the "Militants for Peace" on the home front and fights the crafty Aleriona with his privateer starship, the *Star Fox,* until the timid politicians decide to make war. As usual, the aliens fear humans because of their rapid technological development and want to defeat them while they still can. Trite for the mid-1960s. Contrast Anderson's *Fire Time* [4-15]. Compare Ben Bova's *As on a Darkling Plain* (1972). NN, 1965; first part, "Marque and Reprisal," HN, 1966.

3-13. Anderson, Poul. **Time and Stars.** Doubleday, 1964.
Six stories from 1960 to 1963. Includes "No Truce with Kings" (HW, 1964), the story of the discovery and overthrow of benevolent aliens secretly guiding humanity in a new direction amid civil war in a fragmented, nuclear devastated United States; pleads humanity's right to shape its own destiny. Also noteworthy is "Epilogue," where Earth is inhabited by highly evolved mechanical life; makes an interesting contrast with Lem's *The Invincible* [3-260].

3-14. Anderson, Poul. **Trader to the Stars.** Doubleday, 1964.
Three Nicholas Van Rijn novelettes, an Anderson series featuring a colorful and crafty merchant-prince who pursues profit throughout a laissez-faire universe of the far future. A unique blend of Anderson humor, philosophy, and historical extrapolation (note the excerpt from "Margin of Profit") in defense of the virtues of free enterprise. Part of Anderson's Technic History series. Contrast London's *The Iron Heel* [1-59].

3-15. Ashton, Francis Leslie (U.K.). **Alas, That Great City.** Dakers, 1948.
Jonathan and Joy of the twentieth century assimilate by telepathy and time travel

the adventures of Larentzal and Cleoli 13,000 years ago in Atlantis's last days. It is destroyed when a former planet causes geological upheavals at it becomes Earth's moon. The book's thesis is that human destiny is ordered by great events of natural law. Using Platonic, Egyptian, and Aztec myths, this is a Ben Hur romance and adventure in a SF catastrophe setting. Excellent characterization in sentimental epic tradition. See also Ashton's *Breaking of the Seals* (1946). Compare with Bond's lesser work, *Exiles of Time* [3-50], and Taylor Caldwell's *The Romance of Atlantis* (1975).

*3-16. Asimov, Isaac. **The Caves of Steel.** Doubleday, 1954.
An SF/detective story set in an immense city where progressive and regressive cultural factions provide the apparent motive for a murder of a progressive "Spacer." The solution of the crime is left to human detective Elijah Baley and robot R. Daneel Olivaw, whose relationship is a principal interest of the novel. An all-time favorite of SF readers. Related to Asimov's *I, Robot* [3-20], *The Naked Sun* (Doubleday, 1957), *The Rest of the Robots* (Doubleday, 1964), *The Robots of Dawn* [4-28], and *Robots and Empire* [4-28], which tie the robot stories into his Foundation series [3-19]. Contrast Simak's *City* [3-345].

3-17. Asimov, Isaac. **The Early Asimov; or, Eleven Years of Trying.** Doubleday, 1972.
Twenty-seven stories, including Asimov's earliest surviving effort. Not noteworthy as fiction, but valuable for the extensive biographical sections between stories, which deal heavily with Campbell and the experience of writing "under" him. Stories are illustrative of the general SF pulp content of the time (1939–1949) and feature Asimov's distinctive humor.

3-18. Asimov, Isaac. **The End of Eternity.** Doubleday, 1955.
Perhaps Asimov's best early novel. Andrew Harlan, an "Eternal" sworn to use secret time technology to police human history against disasters, falls in love with an outsider and betrays his cause. Making history "safe" denies humanity its destiny; Harlan destroys the secret Eternity police, giving humans the agonies of atomic war, but also the nobility of their freedom. Compare Anderson's "No Truce with Kings" [3-13]; contrast Silverberg's more modern *Up the Line* [4-512].

*3-19. Asimov, Isaac. **The Foundation Trilogy.** Doubleday, 1963.
Neither novels nor trilogy, but rather a series of nine stories written in the 1940s and inspired by the fall of Rome. Eight were written for Campbell's *Astounding*. Now classics, they portray the destruction of a human galactic empire and the efforts of psychohistorians to shorten the coming dark ages. To do this, they set up the hidden Foundation to guide humans in the development of a new culture (*Foundation,* 1951; alternate title: *The 1000 Year Plan*, Doubleday, 1955). As predicted, the old empire's survivors attempt to destroy the Foundation and fail; but an unanticipated threat, a powerful psychic mutant called the Mule, consolidates a mini-empire, which threatens the original "Seldon's Plan" (*Foundation and Empire,* 1952; alternate title: *The Man Who Upset the Universe*, Doubleday, 1955). Finally, with the Mule vanquished, the Second Foundation leads humanity in the development of mental science, and the dark ages will soon end (*Second Founda-*

tion, Avon, 1953). Some internal inconsistencies and pulp writing style, but the series helped open SF to new content beyond mere space opera. Recent sequels are *Foundation's Edge* and *Foundation and Earth* [4-26]; these works are tied to the robot series through *Robots and Empire* [3-16, 4-28]. Awarded a special Hugo (1966) for all-time best series.

*3-20. Asimov, Isaac. **I, Robot.** Gnome, 1950.
Nine "positronic" robot stories, originally published 1940–1950, with new material added for continuity. Contains Asimov's famous Three Laws of Robotics and involves the history of U.S. Robots and Mechanical Men, Inc., and the strong-willed "robopsychologist" Dr. Susan Calvin. "Reason" and "Liar!" are particularly noteworthy. *The Rest of the Robots* (Doubleday, 1964) presents eight additional positronic robot stories, mainly from the 1950s; superior stories include "Victory Unintentional," "Let's Get Together," and "Lenny." Also contains autobiographical material by Asimov, plus the two robot novels about policeman Elijah Baley and his robot detective sidekick, R. Daneel Olivaw: *The Caves of Steel* [3-16] and *The Naked Sun* (1957). For later sequels see [3-16]. Compare with the original *Frankenstein* [1-84], Binder's *Adam Link: Robot* [3-35], and Williamson's *The Humanoids* [3-402].

*3-21. Asimov, Isaac. **Nightfall and Other Stories.** Doubleday, 1969.
Twenty stories with interesting biographical notes by Asimov, all from the 1950s and 1960s except the title story, perhaps Asimov's best, "Nightfall" (SFHF). Written in 1941, it tells of a world that never sees the stars except during an eclipse that occurs only once every 2,049 years, causing madness and cultural collapse. Compare Galouye's *Dark Universe* [3-170]. Other stories are average Asimov. Another collection of works from the same period is *The Martian Way and Other Stories* (Doubleday, 1955), which includes four stories written between 1952 and 1954. In "The Martian Way" (SFHF), the rings of Saturn are mined for water to keep colonial Mars free from reactionary Earth politics. Compare Heinlein's *Red Planet* (1949). Good traditional SF of the period.

3-22. Asimov, Isaac. **Pebble in the Sky.** Doubleday, 1950.
Asimov's first published novel, about a man, a tailor by trade, from 1950 who finds himself suddenly in the future involved in a war between Earth and the Trantorian Galactic Empire—a yarn that can be more or less related to the Foundation stories [3-19]. A sentimental favorite among SF readers. Other works set in this future history are *The Stars, Like Dust* (Doubleday, 1951) and *Currents of Space* (Doubleday, 1952). Compare Laumer's *Worlds of the Imperium* [3-248]; contrast Hicks's *The First to Awaken* [3-213].

3-23. Atkins, John (Alfred) (U.K.). **Tomorrow Revealed.** Spearman, 1955.
Some 3,000 years in the future, the son of a stargazer patches together a history of Earth and planets from such "authorities" as Wells, Huxley, Graves, Orwell, Bradbury, and C. S. Lewis. He determines that human destiny is ordered by "theological significance" after all. Not doctrinaire; gracefully written; persuasively interpolates "sources." Marvelous entertainment for reader seasoned in his-

tory of speculative literature. Compare Churchill's *A Short History of the Future* [3-96]; contrast Allighan's *Verwoerd—The End* [3-7].

3-24. Bahnson, Agnew H., Jr. **The Stars Are Too High.** Random, 1959.
Four men, pretending to be UFO aliens, use an ultra-advanced gravity-driven craft they have secretly developed to frighten Earth's cold-warring nations into peace. The scheme is bungled; nuclear war seems imminent, but the U.S.S.R. and United States agree to cooperate against the common threat. In return, the idealists turn the craft over for international inspection. A tense, smoothly written story. Compare Sturgeon's "Unite and Conquer" [3-365] and Martin Caidin's less believable *The Mendelov Conspiracy* (1969).

3-25. Barjavel, René (France). **Ashes, Ashes.** Doubleday, 1967. Tr. by Damon Knight of *Ravage,* Denoël, 1942.
A war in the Western Hemisphere causes electricity to fail permanently worldwide in 2052. Paris, the one-time "City of Light," is thrown into darkness and disaster. As famine, cholera, and conflagration stalk urban society, forcing it back to the primitive, young François, his fiancée Blanche, and a few others escape to the countryside to build a new life. The resultant rural "utopia," a rigid society along "be fruitful and multiply" lines, is described by some critics as an antitechnological and reactionary cliché, while others see Barjavel's work as asserting the values of love and peace. By the time of her death Blanche has given François 17 children, while he, at age 129, has just replaced his seventh wife with a pregnant girl of 18. Compare with Stewart's *Earth Abides* [3-358]. Contrast with Merle's *Malevil* [4-376] and Russ's *The Female Man* [4-458]. Also annotated as [6-58].

3-26. Barnes, Arthur K(elvin). **Interplanetary Hunter.** Gnome, 1956.
Gerry Carlyle, woman in male-dominated society, hunts strange animals on Sol's planets with chief henchman Tommy Strike. Five stories from the 1937–1946 period are representative of the stage in evolution of SF from space opera to much more plausible scenarios of Stanley Weinbaum. Compare Weinbaum's Ham Hammond stories, "Parasite Planet" [2-2] and "The Lotus Eaters" [2-125].

3-27. Bennett, Margot (U.K.). **The Long Way Back.** Bodley Head, 1954.
Future Africans form expedition to explore savage Britain, where they learn that nuclear weapons, which they now verge on developing, destroyed that once-great civilization. Description of African society and cave-dwelling Britons is this uneven cautionary tale's high point. Lightner's *The Day of the Drones* [5-97], written later, is a startlingly parallel work.

3-28. Beresford, J(ohn) D(avys), and Esmé Wynne-Tyson (U.K.). **The Riddle of the Tower.** Hutchinson, 1944.
In the dream of Mr. Begbie, preserving much of the objectivity dreams are known to bear, emerge visions of a utopian past and an unconsciously totalitarian future—viewed from Mr. Begbie's present near the end of World War II. The dominant mood is pessimistic, with a possible implication that some sort of utopian anarchy would give humanity a viable future. Compare Bellamy's *Looking*

Backward [1-8], Herbert's *Hellstrom's Hive* [4-269], and Le Guin's *The Dispossessed* [4-324].

3-29. Best, (Oswald) Herbert. **The Twenty-fifth Hour.** Random, 1940.
About 1965, "offensive" war reduces Europe to stone age. Americans are wiped out by plague. Hugh from Europe and Ann from America survive to make new life in utopian civilization sprung up in Alexandria, Egypt. Good character development—complex. Thoughtful anthropological insight. Strong narrative weakens in last third of work. Deserves comparison with postcatastrophe stories of John Christopher or Stewart's *Earth Abides* [3-358].

*3-30. Bester, Alfred. **The Demolished Man.** Shasta, 1953.
One of modern SF's top novels, the tragedy of a twenty-fourth century Oedipus, Ben Reich, a ruthless interplanetary tycoon subconsciously driven to unknowingly commit patricide. He is pursued by a vengeful "Esper" policeman, Lincoln Powell, and by a mental phantom, The Man with No Face, symbol of his evil deed. In escaping Powell and the law's enlightened penalty for murder—social restoration after personality demolition—Reich risks a more complete destruction by his own guilty subconscious. Extrapolated social setting and innovative writing techniques compare with Brunner's *Stand on Zanzibar* [4-92], while the mature handling of telepaths anticipates Silverberg's *Dying Inside* [4-502]. The touchstone of hybrid SF and detective fiction, its sophistication in character development and the exploration of the human psyche are rare in either genre. Winner of the first Hugo (1953); placed second in IFA (1954).

*3-31. Bester, Alfred. **Starlight: The Great Short Fiction of Alfred Bester.** Nelson Doubleday, 1976.
Reprints two complete, previously published collections: *Starlight* and *The Light Fantastic* (both Berkley, 1976). Eighteen stories from 1941 to 1974, including "Fondly Fahrenheit" (SFHF), "The Four-Hour Fugue" (HN, 1975), "The Men Who Murdered Mohammed" (HN, 1959), and "The Pi Man" (HN, 1960), as well as "5,271,009" (variant title: "The Starcomber"), "Of Time and Third Avenue," "Adam and No Eve," and "Oddy and Id."

*3-32. Bester, Alfred. **The Stars My Destination.** Signet, 1957. British title: *Tiger! Tiger!*, Sidgwick & Jackson, 1956. The U.S. version is a revision of the U.K. issue.
Twenty-fifth-century Earth features the decadence of the common people in the grip of multinational capitalism, even though, essentially illogically, humankind has acquired the ability to teleport over distances up to 1,000 miles. Enter Gully Foyle, apelike space sailor, who, driven by desire for revenge, transcends his ignorance, social class, and parapsychic limitation to bring to everyone the power and responsibility to teleport to the ends of the universe—a godlike existence. Under the stress of murderous constraints, human beings will develop abilities that enable them to survive and triumph. A Pollyannaish though seductively optimistic interpretation of how most people will be selected to survive—when the alternative is extinction. The political scenario is prescient of topics widely current today. The narrative paraphernalia anticipates Brunner's wholesale effects in *Stand on Zanzi-*

bar [4-92] and *The Sheep Look Up* [4-90]. A well-modulated paranormal powers-emerging story. Gully Foyle is a persuasively complex "everyman." Compare Simak's *Time and Again* [3-347].

3-33. Biggle, Lloyd, Jr. **The Metallic Muse.** Doubleday, 1972.
Seven stories from 1957 to 1968, introduced by the author, which more or less touch on the arts. Biggle, trained in music, is known for his use of the arts in his works. Notable stories: "Tunesmith"—TV commercials are the only entertainment and medium for the highly automated arts until tunesmith Baque dares to bring back traditional music; "In His Own Image"—a humanoid robot, priest to a congregation of machines in a space hostel, electroshocks a castaway into conversion.

3-34. Biggle, Lloyd, Jr. **Monument.** Doubleday, 1974.
A marooned maverick Earthman leaves a legacy of knowledge so that the peaceful, happy natives of his Edenic castaway world can resist the inevitable exploitation by Earth's expanding commercial domain. Makes a sentimental but effective case against cultural imperialism and environmental corruption. In this novel the country boys outsmart the city slickers. Expansion of delightful story nominated for a Hugo in 1962. Contrast Silverberg's *Downward to the Earth* [4-501].

3-35. Binder, Eando (pseud. of Earl Andrew Binder and Otto Oscar Binder). **Adam Link: Robot.** Paperback Library, 1965.
Charles Link creates Adam and Eve Link, robots; metal with human emotions. Adam agonizes over identity, saves Earth from alien invasion, and goes to the Moon to think over future with Eve. A sentient robot will have problems with humankind. Written in late 1930s and early 1940s, these robot stories break from space opera and gadget tales. Thoughtful treatment of artificial intelligence. Compare Shelley's *Frankenstein* [1-84], Asimov's *I, Robot* [3-20] (Binder used title first in 1939 "Link" story), and Jones's *Colossus* [4-289].

3-36. Binder, Eando (pseud. of Earl Andrew Binder and Otto Oscar Binder). **Puzzle of the Space Pyramids.** Curtis, 1971.
Captain Atwell and crew make first trips to Mars, Venus, Mercury, Ganymede, and Jupiter, finding life on all and also pyramids on each employed by ancient Martians to alter the eccentric orbit of Asteroidia with gravity beams to prevent collision with Mars. The planet broke into the asteroid belt and destroyed Martian civilization. Life seems to exist everywhere. Episodic (serialized in *Thrilling Wonder Stories,* 1937–1942), but an ingenious compilation of what have become clichés about our solar system. One of the first attempts to humanize space explorers. Compare Clarke's *2001: A Space Odyssey* [4-140].

3-37. Bioy Casares, Adolfo (Argentina). **The Invention of Morel and Other Stories.** Univ. of Texas Press, 1964. Tr. by Ruth I. C. Simms of *La invención de Morel,* 1940.
Influenced by Wells's *The Island of Dr. Moreau* [1-100]. Deals with Morel's search for immortality, culminating in invention depending heavily on photographic principles. Story by nameless narrator, recounting stay on Morel's island, who falls in love with Morel's *amante,* Faustine. She ignores him because he is on another plane of existence.

3-38. Bixby, (Drexel) Jerome (Lewis). **Space by the Tale.** Ballantine, 1964.
Eleven SF and fantasy stories from 1952 to 1963, including "The Bad Life,"
about the torture of a space-age social worker by the depraved inmates of Limbo,
a prison planet; "Small War," a novel first-contact story in which human and
alien mutually reject contact; and "Angels in the Jets," where a new planet's atmosphere turns an exploration ship's crew mad, leaving its captain the choice of
madness or death. Enjoyable yarns.

3-39. Blackburn, John F(enwick) (U.K.). **A Scent of New-Mown Hay.** Mill, 1958.
At the end of World War II, Nazi scientist Rosa Steinberg mutates fungus that
transforms women into hideous monsters; spores have widespread effect by the
late 1950s and threaten the world so that cold war enemies unite. Plague is a
metaphor of great evil still abroad from the war. Plausibly scientific basis. Cloak-
and-dagger suspense with politically conservative mood. Contrast Crichton's *The
Andromeda Strain* [4-156].

3-40. Blish, James. **Anywhen.** Doubleday, 1970.
Seven well-crafted stories first published between 1956 and 1968, with a brief
preface and story introductions. Of special note are "A Style in Treason," a color-
ful far-future romp where treachery has replaced diplomacy; "The Writing of
the Rat," in which humans learn they are the descendants of galactic slavers; and
"A Dusk of Idols," which stands our traditional humanistic values on their heads.
Literate works by one of the genre's intellectuals. The U.K. edition adds
"Skysign."

3-41. Blish, James. **The Best of James Blish.** Ballantine, 1979.
Collection of 12 stories with an afterword by Blish under his literary critical
pseudonym William Atheling, Jr. Stories are from 1940 to 1966, including "Surface Tension" (SFHF). Earliest is "Citadel of Thought"; latest is "A Style in Treason." Perhaps better as a sampling of Blish than representative of his best stories.

*3-42. Blish, James. **A Case of Conscience.** Ballantine, 1958.
Father Ramón Ruíz-Sánchez, Jesuit priest and biologist, sees a new planet, Lithia,
and its intelligent reptilian inhabitants as creations of the devil presented to
tempt humans, because they offer final proof of evolution. One of these reptiles,
Egtverchi, brought to Earth as an egg by Ramón, grows up a stunted misfit, creates social havoc, then escapes back to Lithia. Fearing that Egtverchi's impact on
Lithia would make it even more of a danger to the human soul, Ruíz-Sánchez ex-
orcises the planet, whose sun immediately goes nova. A novel rich in theological
concerns, well researched and executed, and open to several interpretations.
Blish's best SF work (HW, 1959). *Case* is the final third of what Blish has termed a
philosophic trilogy, "After Such Knowledge." The first part is an excellent historical novel on the life of Roger Bacon, *Doctor Mirabilis* (Faber, 1964), while the middle part is composed of two fantasy novels—*Black Easter* (Doubleday, 1968),
where a deal with the devil unleashes victorious evil, and a sequel, *The Day after
Judgment* (Doubleday, 1971). Works are independent of one another in subject
matter, but all speak to the same issue: "Is the desire for secular knowledge, let
alone the acquisition and use of it, a misuse of the mind, and perhaps even actively evil?" An effort unique in SF; highly recommended.

*3-43. Blish, James. **Cities in Flight.** Avon, 1970.
Four novels constitute a future history in which Earth's cities, using the "spin-dizzy" drive, leave the planet to escape repression and take up nomadic existence in space. This omnibus includes an essay by Richard D. Mullen, "The Earthmanist Culture: *Cities in Flight* as a Spenglerian History," which contains a chronology of Spenglerian and Blishian worlds. Great space opera in the mode of Asimov's *The Foundation Trilogy* [3-19], but even more grandiose and rich in detail. The story begins with *They Shall Have Stars* (alt. title: *Year 2018!*, Faber, 1957), composed of material published between 1952 and 1954, which tells of the perfecting of the antigravity spindizzy and the building of a huge structure, "The Bridge," on Jupiter. The cities are fleeing Earth in *A Life for the Stars* (Putnam, 1962). Here, life in such a city is traced as the "Okies" struggle for survival, seeking what work they can in return for needed supplies. *Earthman, Come Home* (Putnam, 1955) is composed of four stories from 1950 to 1953 written into continuity (title story included in SFHF). It tells of New York City and its mayor, John Amalfi, as they confront other cities turned rogue and a Vegan fortress that threatens Earth. But the day of the Okie cities is over; under Earth's ban, New York flees to the Great Magellanic cloud to found New Earth. Here, the immortal city dwellers face the ultimate threat—the end of the universe. In *The Triumph of Time* (Avon, 1958) (British title: *A Clash of Cymbals*), New York flees to the universe's heart to ride out the storm; the end comes, and Amalfi, hanging lost in the "unmedium," explodes himself to begin creation anew.

3-44. Blish, James, and Robert Lowndes. **The Duplicated Man.** Avalon, 1959.
Two immortals play a dangerous game when they manipulate a war to prevent the use of atomic weapons. A normal, Paul Danton, finally breaks the deadlock with the use of a duplicating machine and the cooperation of both immortals. Convoluted plot with good psychological depiction. People can overcome failure, but only through the sacrifice of those who can force the move. Compare with Pohl's *Slave Ship* [3-312].

3-45. Blish, James. **Galactic Cluster.** Signet, 1959.
Eight stories, 1953–1959, representative of early Blish. Emphasis is on people, as in "Tomb Tapper," a strong antiwar story about men who tap the minds of downed enemy airmen and the horror they find there, and "A Work of Art," where the personality of Richard Strauss, recreated in the mind of a musical illiterate in an age of musical decadence, faces his failure as a composer. "Common Time" is an exploration of the subjective time effects of faster-than-light flight on an astronaut. Contrast with Asimov's *The Martian Way* [3-21]. The U.K. edition drops three stories and adds "Beanstalk," one of Blish's better tales.

3-46. Blish, James. **Jack of Eagles.** Greenberg, 1952. Alternate title: *ESP-er,* Avon, 1958.
Blish's first novel, overly melodramatic with poor characterization, but an important early study of scientifically based psi powers. Danny Caiden develops a range of "wild talents," including telepathy, teleportation, and telekinesis, which disrupt his life. On the run from the F.B.I., criminals, and a group of "psi-men,"

he finally vanquishes the bad guys and gets the girl. Contrast with Silverberg's strikingly realistic *Dying Inside* [4-502].

*3-47. Blish, James. **The Seedling Stars.** Gnome, 1957.
The Pantropy series, written between 1952 and 1955, tells of a biological development that allows humans to be shaped to fit non-Earth environments and the effects of such seeding. "Seeding Program," the weakest story, traces program's origins and the fight on Ganymede against reactionary Earth efforts to kill it; in "The Thing in the Attic," treetop dwellers reestablish contact with Earth people; "Surface Tension" (SFHF), the best of the series, tells of tiny water dwellers who explore the "Universe" beyond their little puddle; "Watershed" confronts the prejudice of the "basic type" human toward the pantropied ones. Prose awkward at times, but ideas and action carry the series and reflect Blish's lifelong interest in biological science.

3-48. Blish, James, and Norman L(ouis) Knight. **A Torrent of Faces.** Doubleday, 1967.
Based on the concept, under development by the authors since 1948, of an Earth able to hold one trillion inhabitants; excellent description of the technological, environmental, and societal elements of this crowded world whose 800 years of stability have ended—for the best, the authors feel—by impact with the asteroid Flavia. Story suffers from weak characterization. Compare with Harrison's *Make Room! Make Room!* [4-257] and del Rey's *The Eleventh Commandment* [3-139].

3-49. Bloch, Robert. **Fear Today, Gone Tomorrow.** Award Books, 1971.
Twelve SF and fantasy stories, from 1954 to 1968, with emphasis on horror and death; in "A Toy for Juliette," Jack the Ripper time travels into the future, while in "The Hungry Eye," an alien feeds on the murders committed by its hypnotized human slaves. Stories of satire and social criticism also included; the humorous "Report on Sol III" has an alien ethnographer delineating human failings, and in the powerful fantasy story "The Funnel of God," an immortal black African shaman becomes God and destroys decadent Earth with a giant gob of spit. Typical Bloch, but SF is not his forte.

3-50. Bond, Nelson S(lade). **Exiles of Time.** Prime, 1949.
Originally published in 1940, a fast-paced action story built around an astronomical catastrophe that threatens ancient Mu and the attempt to prevent it by bringing modern humans into the past. But time is unalterable, a closed circle—our past is our future. Full of clichés, stereotyped characters, and questionable anthropology, geology, and astronomy, but a neat "explanation" of cross-cultural catastrophe myths, the Ice Age, Charles Fort's anomalies, and Ragnarok.

3-51. Bond, Nelson S(lade). **Lancelot Biggs: Spaceman.** Doubleday, 1951.
Lancelot Biggs, skinny genius, with rotating Adam's apple, performs astounding feats—some good, like saving his ship from bloodthirsty space pirates, and some bad, like turning a valuable cargo of vegetables into a rotten mess. He bumbles along, testing his seemingly farfetched "theories" to the consternation of his old space-dog captain, yet seems always to save the day in this 1939–1943 pulp series. Typical but good space/science yarns of the period, complete with space

navy slang, space academy football rivalries, pig latin, and a space radio operator called Sparks. In the end, Lancelot marries the captain's daughter, invents antigravity, and gets his own command. Perfect examples of future-as-today SF. Compare the John Grimes character in Chandler's Rim World series [3-90].

3-52. Borges, Jorge Luis (Argentina). **Labyrinths.** New Directions, 1962; revised 1964. Several translators.
Twenty-two "stories," ten "essays," and eight "parables" collected here are the principal contents of *Ficciones* (1944) and *El Aleph* (1949), as well as the principal pieces of interest to SF readers. Note especially "Tlön Uqbar, Orbis Tertius," "The Circular Ruins," and "The Babylon Lottery." Borges has an international literary reputation. *Ficciones*, before its English translation, shared the 1961 Formentor Prize with Samuel Beckett.

3-53. Boucher, Anthony (pseud. of William Anthony Parker White). **Far and . Away.** Ballantine, 1955.
Eleven fantasy and SF stories from 1941 to 1954. Stories of interest include "Star Bride," a short tragedy of interplanetary imperialism; "Balaam" a first-contact story involving a rabbi and a priest who face a test of conscience; and "The Other Inauguration," about U.S. politics and the penalty for tampering with fate. Also of interest is the SF-fantasy blend "Snulbug," a time travel story involving a cute time-warping demon and his master's abortive efforts to capitalize on knowledge of the future. Typical Boucher stories.

3-54. Boulle, Pierre (France). **Garden on the Moon.** Vanguard, 1965. Tr. by Xan Fielding of *Le Jardin de Kanashima*, 1964.
The space race begins at the German Peenemünde rocket base and includes the United States, the U.S.S.R., and Japan. Ironically, Japan wins the race to put the first man on the Moon by the simple expedient of allowing the rocket pilot to die there. The moral is that the space effort is enormously important and should be an international effort. Competition here is wasteful and intermittently tragic. Moving fictional history and extrapolation of the people and events surrounding the effort to put human beings on the Moon. Compare Clarke's *Prelude to Space* [3-103].

*3-55. Boulle, Pierre (France). **Planet of the Apes.** Vanguard, 1963. Tr. by Xan Fielding of *La Planète des singes*. 1963.
Expedition to Betelgeuse solar system finds a world whose dominant species is simian; humans are subordinate animals. Prejudices, posturing, and social absurdities are portrayed with Swiftian comment and literary deftness. Boulle is a first-rank author whose novel contrasts sharply with adulterated film and TV versions. An excellent modern *Gulliver's Travels* [1-89].

3-56. Boulle, Pierre (France). **Time Out of Mind.** Vanguard, 1966. Tr. by Xan Fielding and Elisabeth Abbott of *Contes de l'absurde suivis de $E=mc^2$*, 1957.
Twelve stories, including "Time Out of Mind" about time travelers from past and future who meet man from present and trap him in endless piece of the present, and "The Perfect Robot," about "humanizing" androids by making them defective in perception and judgment. Familiar story scenarios excellently rendered.

3-57. Bowen, John (Griffith) (U.K.). **After the Rain.** Faber, 1958.
The rain falls and there comes a second deluge of Earth. Some survivors stay alive on a raft. After many days they come to an island and have a chance to begin life again. There is joylessness in their salvation because the time on the "ark" has demonstrated all the viciousness, brutality, and insanity that characterize humankind. Just before they disembark on the island, Tony, the one heroic figure of the group, commits suicide. Well-written, biting satire. Bowen is principally a playwright; this novel is derived from an earlier play. Compare Ballard's *The Drowned World* [4-37].

3-58. Boye, Karin (Sweden). **Kallocain.** Univ. of Wisconsin Press, 1966. Tr. by Gustaf Lannestock of *Kallocain,* 1940.
Even in translation the language of this narrative evokes a mood of poignant disgust. Set in a world of socialist totalitarianism, it tells of the discovery by an experimental chemist of a drug that makes anyone injected with it tell everything— "Kallocain," a truth serum. In the hands of a police state it will interdict all privacy. Focused as the memoir of a single individual, the chemist inventor, the story is a more powerful awful warning than its obvious, and later, asssociated work, Orwell's *Nineteen Eighty-Four* [3-302], especially because in this case the protagonist is both perpetrator and victim of the device of his enslavement. The art of the story's telling is at least as fine as that of Orwell. Also annotated as [6-367].

3-59. Brackett, Leigh (Douglass). **The Best of Leigh Brackett.** Edmond Hamilton, ed. Nelson Doubleday, 1977.
Collection of ten stories from the years 1944 to 1956, including the earliest, "The Jewel of Bas," "The Vanishing Venusians," and "The Veil of Astellar." The latest is "The Queer Ones." Afterword by the author. Her husband, Hamilton, also provides an introduction. Action and adventure in the Burroughs mode, yet cleaner and clearer in prose.

*3-60. Brackett, Leigh (Douglass). **The Long Tomorrow.** Doubleday, 1955.
Len Colter lives in an antiscientific age after World War IV. Neo-Mennonite and evangelical fundamentalist culture forbids science, but scientists work in secret. Colter suffers a protracted period of indecision but finally joins them to renew technology, hoping it won't be misused again. Fine illustration of how fear creates a sterile and superstitious culture. Compare Cooper's *The Cloud Walker* (Hodder, 1973) and Miller's *A Canticle for Leibowitz* [3-287].

*3-61. Bradbury, Ray (Douglas). **Fahrenheit 451.** Ballantine, 1953.
Based on 1951 short story "The Fireman" (SFHF), work's title refers to the flash point of book paper. Totalitarian state outlaws virtually all books, especially the classics; an underground form of people who memorize great books to preserve them for posterity. The plot revolves around a "fireman's" conversion from book burner to preserver. Widely popular as film. Inspired a BBC symphony. Won Commonwealth Club of California second annual Gold Medal.

3-62. Bradbury, Ray (Douglas). **The Golden Apples of the Sun.** Doubleday, 1953.
Twenty-two SF and fantasy stories, including "The Fog Horn," about a sea monster that loves a fog horn; "The Pedestrian," the classic tale of a walker who is

lonely because everybody is watching television; "A Sound of Thunder," where a time safari to hunt tyrannosaurus rex alters the present because a hunter accidentally kills a butterfly; and the title story, about a spaceship that flies into the Sun's atmosphere to capture part of its substance. Emphasis on message and characters rather than science. Bradbury selected stories from this collection, the two following works, and his several other collections for *The Stories of Ray Bradbury* (Knopf 1980), which contains 100 stories, 6 not previously collected.

*3-63. Bradbury, Ray (Douglas). **The Illustrated Man.** Doubleday, 1951. The U.K. edition includes two stories not in the U.S. edition and excludes four of the U.S. edition stories.
Eighteen SF and fantasy stories from 1947 to 1951 plus prologue and epilogue. Structured by the device of a man's body tattooed with pictures, each of which comes alive with a story. Includes "The Veldt," about a futuristic playroom that realizes children's fantasies and leads to their parents' death; "Kaleidoscope," with an exploded spaceship's crew hurtling through space to their deaths; "The Long Rain," in which a group of lost men fight the endless rains of Venus; and "Zero Hour," a study in horror where a child leads her alien playmate to the attic where her parents are hiding. Some social criticism, but emphasis on sentimentality in highly crafted, emotion-generating stories. IFA third place, 1952.

*3-64. Bradbury, Ray (Douglas). **The Martian Chronicles.** Doubleday, 1950. British title: *The Silver Locusts,* Hart-Davis, 1951. The first printing of a "complete" edition, including the variously excluded "The Fire Balloons" and "The Wilderness," was by Time Inc., 1963.
The frame story for *Chronicles* is the colonization of Mars by Earth in the late twentieth century. Stories provide vignettes of spacemen landing on Mars, the first colonies, the nature of the nearly mystically existing Martians, and the lives of Earth people who become "Martians." Themes are of cautionary social criticism. Earth people will treat Mars as Europeans treated North America, raping and plundering it. Stories are "exemplums" set in the future, with moral and quasi-religious messages. Compare with Bradbury's *The Illustrated Man* [3-63]. Received $1,000 award from National Institute of Arts and Letters for contribution to American literature; perhaps the best-known of all modern SF books. By 1980 there were at least 56 printings in the Bantam paperback edition alone.

3-65. Briarton, Grendel (pseud. of Reginald Bretnor). **Through Time and Space with Ferdinand Feghoot.** Paradox, 1962. Expanded as *The Complete Feghoot,* Mirage, 1975.
Fifty "Feghoots," including five published for the first time (most of the others appeared in *Magazine of Fantasy and Science Fiction*). Each runs one to two pages, involves a fantasy or SF motif, and concludes with a pun—generally so arch and bad that it's funny. With Gahan Wilson's cartoons, one of the few really fascinating droll spinoffs from the serious main currents of the genre.

3-66. Brown, Fredric. **Angels and Spaceships.** Dutton, 1954. Alternate title: *Star Shine,* Bantam, 1956.
Seventeen stories and vignettes from 1941 to 1949, and an introduction by the author on the distinction between SF and fantasy. The vignettes, Brown's forte,

range from the horror of "Pattern" and "Answer" through the tenderness of "Reconciliation" and the broad humor of "Politeness." Other superior stories include "Letter to a Phoenix," a philosophical statement about human nature and destiny; and "The Waveries," in which invading aliens eat electricity and turn back the technological clock, to the betterment of humanity.

*3-67. Brown, Fredric. **Honeymoon in Hell.** Bantam, 1958.
Twenty-one stories and vignettes, some fantasy, including the classic "Arena" (SFHF), the story of a superior being's test of a human's vs. an alien's fitness to survive through single combat. Also noteworthy are "The Dome," about the wages of a man who deserts mankind to save himself; "Too Far," a punny story about a lecherous were-deer's retribution; and "Imagine," a treatise on our sense of wonder in under 200 words. Like much Brown, parables, entertainments, and puzzles.

*3-68. Brown, Fredric. **The Lights in the Sky Are Stars.** Dutton, 1953. British title: *Project Jupiter*, Boardman, 1954.
Mature story, rich in characterization for the SF of its day, of the efforts to reopen space exploration with a flight to Jupiter over the objections of "conservationists." Senator Ellen Gallagher gives her life for the project, while her lover, Max Andrews, once denied space travel due to an accident, fights the bureaucracy and alcoholism to see the project through and to go on the voyage. The rocket goes, but Max does not. A powerful, poignant plea for spaceflight and a study of a man obsessed by it. Compare with Kornbluth's *Takeoff* [3-241]; contrast with Malzberg's *Universe Day* (Avon, 1971).

3-69. Brown, Fredric. **Space on My Hands.** Shasta, 1951.
Nine stories, ranging from humor to horror, and a brief introduction by the author on writing SF. Includes "The Star Mouse," one of Brown's most popular stories, about a lonely scientist who sends a mouse, Mitkey, into space, where aliens make it intelligent. Also noteworthy are "Pi in the Sky," where the stars are used to advertise soap; "Nothing Sirius," which has a member of a space-touring penny arcade troupe fall in love with the thought projection of an alien cockroach on an unexplored planet; and "Come and Go Mad," about a man driven insane by the knowledge that ants are really Earth's masters, humans merely parasites. Good collection of Brown from 1941 to 1951.

3-70. Brown, Fredric. **What Mad Universe.** Dutton, 1949.
Brown's first SF novel; an SF editor is tossed into an alternate universe by the failure of the first Moon rocket in 1955. In this universe, filled with SF pulp fiction clichés, spaceflight was accidentally discovered in 1903 by a scientist using a sewing machine, and humans presently face a space war with Arcturians. Good, humorous SF satire with girls in transparent space suits, BEMs, a superscientist, and all. Contrast with Malzberg's *Herovit's World* [4-356].

3-71. Brunner, John (Kilian Houston) (U.K.). **No Future in It.** Gollancz, 1962.
Eleven stories from 1955 to 1962, representing Brunner's superb early corpus of short fiction, perhaps his greater forte. Examples include "The Windows of Heaven" (originally "Two by Two," 1956), a moving, almost biblical tale of the last man, a lunar explorer, returning to find a nova-sterilized Earth, and the only

source for reseeding is his own body, a figurative ark; "Protect Me from My Friends" (1962), about a telepath escaping from his enforced but protected environment after meeting a sympathetic woman only to be overcome by the chaos of the open world; "Elected Silence" (originally "Silence," 1959), in which a man suffering from solitary confinement by aliens for 28 years endures similar tortures after being liberated by his own kind; "Puzzle for Spacemen" (1955), an ingenious murder mystery set in space; and "Report on the Nature of a Lunar Surface" (1960), Brunner's most anthologized story, a tongue-in-cheek communiqué about lunar pollution. His first collection.

*3-72. Brunner, John (Kilian Houston) (U.K.). **Out of My Mind.** Ballantine, 1967. U.K. edition is different in content.
Thirteen stories originally published between 1956 and 1965; overall tone is of pessimism and horror. Outstanding stories include "The Totally Rich," about a wealthy woman's attempt to recreate her dead lover; "The Last Lonely Man," where death is cheated only by corrupting life; and "Such Stuff," in which a researcher becomes trapped in the dreams of his subject. "The Nail in the Middle of the Hand," although not SF, is a gruesome little masterpiece about Christ's executioner. Some of the genre's best short fiction.

3-73. Brunner, John (Kilian Houston) (U.K.). **The Squares of the City.** Ballantine, 1965.
President Vados, dictator of a Brazil-like South American country, invites traffic analyst Boyd Hakluyt to rid his ultramodern capital of squatters. Intrigue and death follow, climaxing in Hakluyt's discovery that Vados and a political rival are manipulating people's behavior with advanced techniques in thought control. This is the result of an agreement between the two leaders to compete for power without suffering the devastation of a civil war; they are literally playing chess using people as pieces. The game is ruined and civil disorder erupts; people must ultimately make their own destiny. The novel's plot follows exactly the moves of an actual championship game played in 1892. Mature, interesting reading on either level. Written in 1960. HN, 1966. Contrast Kuttner and Moore's *The Fairy Chessman* [3-246] and Barry Malzberg's *The Tactics of Conquest* (Pyramid, 1974).

*3-74. Brunner, John (Kilian Houston) (U.K.). **The Whole Man.** Ballantine, 1964.
Expansion of two stories originally published in 1958 and 1959; unusually rich in character development for SF of its time. Crippled, misshapen Gerald Howson precariously exists as a ridiculed outcast among society's dregs. A powerful natural telepath, Howson can link others into an all-consuming fantasy world, an ability that nearly dooms both himself and his only friend, a lonely, unwanted mute girl. Fortunately, they are saved by the telepathic community, whose members perform vital roles in communication and psychotherapy. With training, Howson becomes a master at healing the mentally ill, but, despite fame and fortune, remains haunted by the legacy of social revulsion caused by his deformity. Finally he discovers a novel use for his talent—mental "concerts" that reach thousands and uplift their lives. No longer isolated, Howson joins the world, a whole man at last. A creative and poignant work that marked Brunner as a major SF writer. Compare Silverberg's *Dying Inside* [4-502]. HN, 1965.

3-75. Budrys, Algis. **Blood and Burning.** Berkley, 1978.
Aptly named collection of nine SF stories, and a few additional pieces, representing 1954 to the present. "A Scraping at the Bones" and "The Nuptial Flight of Warbirds" present the protagonist character of Budrys's *Michaelmas* [4-96]. "The Master of the Hounds" won a special Edgar from the Mystery Writers of America.

3-76. Budrys, Algis. **Budrys' Inferno.** Berkley, 1963. British title: *The Furious Future*, Gollancz, 1964.
Nine stories, published between 1953 and 1958, and an author's introduction. Tales emphasize emotion and characterization, such as "The Peasant Girl," with old Mr. Spar, a cantankerous cabinetmaker who resents his sister's marriage to a boy with superhuman powers, and "Dream of Victory," where an android, driven to frenzy by his inability to have offspring, kills his human lover. At times, as in "And Then She Found Him," as sensitive and concerned with love as Sturgeon's work.

*3-77. Budrys, Algis. **Rogue Moon.** Fawcett, 1960.
Ed Hawks masterminds exploration of alien construct on Moon using quasi-suicidal Al Barker as explorer. Moon trips are accomplished by "teleportation" effect that duplicates traveler at Moon-base receiver, leaving original behind. Barker is "killed" again and again in dangerous work that killed or drove insane earlier candidates. Each time the Earth duplicate replaces him. Finally, Hawks himself makes the trip and must commit suicide on Moon so there won't be two of him on Earth. What is a human, form or "matter"? Probing character analysis in radically realistic treatment of doppelgänger proposition. Last paragraph is a nova. Contrast Benford's *In the Ocean of Night* [4-53] and Varley's *Titan* [4-571]. HN, 1961; SFHF.

*3-78. Budrys, Algis. **The Unexpected Dimension.** Ballantine, 1960.
Seven stories from 1954 to 1959, three of which deal with utopias and the need to overthrow them due to either the pressures of change or stagnation ("The End of Summer," "The Burning World," "The Executioners"). Most outstanding is the sad and sensitive "The Distant Sound of Engines," about a shipwrecked alien dying in an Earth hospital; compare with McKenna's "Casey Agonistes" [3-279].

3-79. Budrys, Algis. **Who?** Pyramid, 1958.
Lucas Martino struggles up from an Italian immigrant farming family to become an MIT graduate and a genius in physics, crucial to national security. An accidental lab explosion brutally maims him and lets him fall into Soviet hands. The Soviets restore him using mechanical parts, but fail to get his research secrets. Returned to the West, his metal face an emotionless mask, he is not allowed to continue his work; no one can prove his true identity. A twice-destroyed man, he returns to his rundown family farm, forsaking physics forever. A powerful comment on cold war espionage and its self-defeating nature. Compare with Harrison's *The Daleth Effect* [4-256] and Blum's *The Simultaneous Man* (Little, Brown, 1970). HN, 1959.

3-80. Bulmer, Kenneth (U.K.). **City under the Sea.** Ace, 1957.
Average adventure story, but setting is an excellently developed "aquaculture" of

the near future; detailed descriptions of undersea cities, corporate farms, transportation and communication systems, recreation, surgically altered "menfish," and sea life. Lyrical passages effectively communicating the mood of underwater existence contrast sharply with uninspired, involuted plot: a space navy officer, inheritor of an undersea farm, is kidnapped and forced into undersea slavery by farm's manager. He escapes in time to establish contact with extraterrestrials inhabiting ocean deeps who want détente with humanity. Compare setting with Clarke's superior *The Deep Range* [3-99].

3-81. Burdick, Eugene L(eonard), and (John) Harvey Wheeler. **Fail-Safe.** McGraw-Hill, 1962.
Nuclear capability, with "fail-safe" firing procedures, was thought a good war deterrent, but accident launches a nuclear strike that destroys Moscow. The president volunteers to "nuke" New York City to avoid a world war. Theme: when you have a superweapon, it will ultimately be employed. Slick popular fiction; successful film. Compare George's *Dr. Strangelove* [3-172].

*3-82. Burgess, Anthony (pseud. of John Anthony Burgess Wilson) (U.K.). **A Clockwork Orange.** Heinemann, 1962. U.S. edition (Norton, 1963) omitted a final chapter, restored in 1987 reissue.
Squarely in the tradition of Orwell's *Nineteen Eighty-Four* [3-302], *Clockwork* presents a story of electrochemical brainwashing of a young man who has committed mayhem. He is conditioned to become sick at the thought of violence. The special Russian-based slang invented for the story is both stunningly effective and an impediment to many readers. The narrative reflects the masterpiece of a first-rank mainstream novelist. The novel was filmed by Stanley Kubrick. Contrast Anthony and Margroff's *The Ring* (Ace, 1968).

3-83. Burgess, Anthony (pseud. of John Anthony Burgess Wilson) (U.K.). **The Wanting Seed.** Heinemann, 1962.
Another first-order dystopian warning story. It presents a world in which all measures imaginable are encouraged to curb the population explosion. Richly satirical. Like Vonnegut, Burgess writes in a Swiftian SF tradition. Compare Brunner's *Stand on Zanzibar* [4-92] and Blish and Knight's *A Torrent of Faces* [3-48]. Contrast del Rey's *The Eleventh Commandment* [3-139].

3-84. Caldwell, (Janet Miriam) Taylor (Holland). **The Devil's Advocate.** Crown, 1952.
Through the years, the novels of Caldwell have been a staple for mass market American publishing. She has millions and millions of readers. Her hallmark is the powerful character, almost savagely individualistic, at the center of most of her works. *Advocate* sketches an America of 1970 as a nightmare world of totalitarian socialism—the result of the leftward movement of U.S. politics beginning in the 1930s. The yoke is lifted and freedom is restored at the end, but the novel is a right-wing call to arms reminiscent of Rand's *Anthem* [3-315] and *Atlas Shrugged* [3-316] in its stridency, and of Lewis's *It Can't Happen Here* [2-62] in its conception.

3-85. Campbell, John W(ood). **The Best of John W. Campbell.** Lester del Rey, ed. Nelson Doubleday, 1976.
Not to be confused with the British work issued with the same title. A collection

of 12 stories from 1932 to 1960, including "Twilight" (SFHF), "Cloak of Aesir," "Forgetfulness," and the classic "Who Goes There?," better known as *The Thing.* Earliest is "The Last Evolution"; latest is "Space for Industry." Also has an overview of Campbell's career by the editor and a personal afterword by Campbell's wife. Samples both Campbell's "superscience" stories and the more sensitive "Don A. Stuart" ones. Compare Weinbaum's *A Martian Odyssey* [2-125] and *The Best of Raymond Z. Gallun* [3-169].

*3-86. Campbell, John W(ood). **Who Goes There?** Shasta, 1948.
A collection, now classical in status, of seven stories written by Campbell as Don A. Stuart for *Astounding* between 1934 and 1938. Includes "Twilight" (SFHF) and the title story, from which the film *The Thing* (1951) was crudely extracted, as well as a second, less successful film of the same name. "Who Goes There?" is considered by many the best SF suspense story ever done. "Twilight" and its sequel "Night" are set in the sad, dim end of time when humanity is dying amid its mighty machines, devoid of life's spark and curiosity. The other stories are "Blindness," "Frictional Losses," "Dead Knowledge," and "Elimination." Contrast the stories of J. G. Ballard [4-34, 4-38].

3-87. Capon, (Harry) Paul (U.K.). **The Other Side of the Sun.** Heinemann, 1950.
Timothy and Rose travel to Antigeos, Earthlike planet on opposite side of Sun, in 1960s. They discover ideally functioning anarchistic state of Antigeonians. Villain McQuoid would colonize and exploit it, but is finally lost. Other members of expedition return to Earth. Pedestrian in science; enlightened in political philosophy. The first volume of a trilogy. Sequels are *The Other Half of the Planet* (1952) and *Down to Earth* (1954). Contrast Norman's *Tarnsman of Gor* [4-401]; compare Le Guin's *The Dispossessed* [4-324].

3-88. Carr, John Dickson. **Fire, Burn!** Hamilton, 1956.
One of several mystery-SF hybrids by a best-selling mystery writer, involving a modern detective time traveled back to the early nineteenth century to solve a mystery in a story excellent for the authentic feel of its setting. Compare Finney's *Time and Again* [4-214].

3-89. Carr, Robert Spencer. **Beyond Infinity.** Fantasy Press, 1951.
Four stories: "Beyond Infinity," "Morning Star," "Those Men from Mars," and "Mutation." "Morning Star" presents a beautiful female visitor from Venus who seeks to ensure success of expedition to bring Earth males to Venus. On Venus only women evolved; male of species remained in "spore" state. Solid stories of human interest set in America of 1940s and 1950s.

3-90. Chandler, A(rthur) Bertram (Australia). **The Rim World Series.**
Writing with imagination and zest, Chandler, himself a lifelong working mariner, blends the military sea story with old-time space opera to produce the Rim World stories, begun in 1959 and basically built around the character John Grimes. His *Road to the Rim* (Ace, 1967) tells of Grimes's earliest adventures and introduction to the Rim Worlds, the frontier planets along the outer edge of the galaxy. The first Rim story, *The Rim of Space* (Avalon, 1961), tells of the escapades of Derek Calver among the Rim Runners, as does *The Ship from Outside* (Ace,

1963). The other 24 books in the series all involve Grimes. See [4-124] for the last book in the series. Compare Pournelle's *The Mercenary* [4-421] and Lupoff's *Space War Blues* [4-345].

3-91. Charbonneau, Louis (Henry). **The Sentinel Stars.** Bantam, 1963.
TRH-247, a "natural man," rebels against the world welfare state, The Organization, that structures a citizen's life in the finest detail. There are the Freedom Camps, whose life of luxury and nonregimentation is purchased by a citizen's life-long labor to pay his tax debt, but these, too, are a prison where freedom means license. In such a planned world, even underground resistance is futile; TRH and his true love, state prostitute ABC331, are exiled to the wilderness and find a new society of outcasts emerging to challenge the weak city folks. One of *Brave New World*'s less illustrious descendants, but typical of such SF dystopias of the 1950s and 1960s as McCann's *Preferred Risk* [3-275A] and Dick's *Solar Lottery* [3-144].

*3-92. Christopher, John (pseud. of Christopher Samuel Youd) (U.K.). **The Death of Grass.** Michael Joseph, 1956. U.S. title: *No Blade of Grass,* Simon & Schuster, 1957.
Christopher's most popular adult SF novel. It depicts the arrival and results of world famine from a blight on the world's "grass" crops. Typically, the focus is on the behavior of a handful of survivors who must toughen themselves to violence as civilization disintegrates. The postcatastrophe scenario is Christopher's forte. The novel was made into a very successful U.S. film, billed with the American title. Compare Stewart's *Earth Abides* [3-358] and Shiel's *The Purple Cloud* (1901).

3-93. Christopher, John (pseud. of Christopher Samuel Youd) (U.K.). **The Long Winter.** Simon & Schuster, 1962. British title: *The World in Winter,* Eyre, 1962.
The apparent arrival of an ice age closes down civilization in Europe and England, driving the survivors south into Africa. The ordeal of a few individuals who have survival competence is persuasively presented. The Caucasian refugees' attempt to find a place in a now-dominant African civilization provides a telling scenario of an ironically reversed racist predicament. Compare Kavan's *Ice* [4-293].

3-94. Christopher, John (pseud. of Christopher Samuel Youd) (U.K.). **The Possessors.** Simon & Schuster, 1964.
A holiday skiing party at a Swiss chalet is subtly attacked by ruthless extraterrestrials. First Andy is killed and returned to life "possessed." Most of the rest of the party follow, especially children, until Christopher's favorite stress situation is set. Three men and a woman survive by burning to death "possessed" bodies while they are trapped in a lodge. An eerily realistic terror tale. Contrast Clement's *Needle* [3-110]; compare Finney's *The Body Snatchers* [3-163].

3-95. Christopher, John (pseud. of Christopher Samuel Youd) (U.K.). **A Wrinkle in the Skin.** Hodder, 1962. U.S. title: *The Ragged Edge,* Simon & Schuster, 1966.
This time the catastrophe is caused by major earthquakes in Europe. The population is reduced to a handful, and survivors live because they can divest themselves of civilized gentleness and bring themselves to kill. Noteworthy are the

scenes of journey over dry seabeds lifted by the quakes. Compare Niven and Pournelle's *Lucifer's Hammer* [4-397].

3-96. Churchill, R(eginald) C(harles) (U.K.). **A Short History of the Future.** Werner Laurie, 1955.
Genially self-deprecating history of humankind by historians 6,000 years in future. Orwell's *Nineteen Eighty-Four* [3-302] is central reference for account based on Bradbury, Huxley, Russell, Vonnegut, and Waugh, among others. History will be cyclical, generally, although Spengler is not mentioned. Ingenious in interpolating "sources." Engaging satirical tone. Compare Atkins's *Tomorrow Revealed* [3-23].

*3-97. Clarke, Arthur C(harles) (U.K.). **Childhood's End.** Ballantine, 1953.
Earth, threatened with self-annihilation, is visited by superior species, who act as agents for something that might be called transcendental cosmic sentience. Through these agents, ironically possessing the classic form of devils, humankind is pacified and the stage is set for the last generation of children, who in a climax of vaulting psychic-spiritual triumph coalesce their substance and join the cosmic oversoul. In face of its narrative mediocrity, *Childhood's End*'s enormous popularity is hard to explain. Perhaps with unconscious accuracy it combines just the right elements of messianic myth and modern scenario to compel the midtwentieth-century audience. The message seems clear: humanity needs help to fulfill its cosmic destiny. This is precisely the message of Clarke's novel and film, *2001: A Space Odyssey* [4-140]. Contrast Russell's *Sinister Barrier* [3-323], Davidson's *Clash of Star-Kings* [3-127], and Stapledon's *Last and First Men* [2-109].

*3-98. Clarke, Arthur C(harles) (U.K.). **The City and the Stars.** Harcourt, 1956.
Expansion and complete revision of Clarke's first novel, *Against the Fall of Night* (1948). The supercity of Diaspar and its immortal citizens have existed in cultural stasis for a billion years as Earth's mountains crumbled and its seas turned to desert. This vision marks the story's excellence; the tedious plot of Alvin uniting Diaspar with its forgotten neighbor, Lys, a pastoral anarchy peopled with telepaths, soon devolves into van Vogtian space opera. Alvin travels across the galaxy in search of other intelligence, meets strange creatures, explores the artifacts of past galactic civilization, and opens humanity to progress once more. Strong element of cultural renaissance following a period of "stagnation" (stability?) central to much of Clarke's work, but the writing here is generally inadequate for carrying such an awesome message. Note: Harcourt published an omnibus, *From the Ocean, from the Stars* (1961), which contains this novel, *The Deep Range*, and *The Other Side of the Sky*. Compare Campbell's "Twilight" and "Night," in *Who Goes There?* [3-86].

3-99. Clarke, Arthur C(harles) (U.K.). **The Deep Range.** Harcourt, 1957.
Classic early story of oceanic exploitation. Grounded spaceman Walter Franklin rises from Warden, a cowboy of the deeps herding whales, to director of the vital Bureau of Whales, a major producer of Earth's protein. Along the way he almost snares a mammoth sea serpent, does capture a giant squid, rescues a trapped submarine, and confronts Earth's major religious leader, a Buddhist, who prefers whale milking and plankton farming to the slaughter of whales. Embodies

Clarke's optimistic philosophy of human growth as well as future extrapolation, but remains chiefly an action story. Compare Bulmer's *City under the Sea* [3-80]; contrast Bass's *The Godwhale* [4-41].

3-100. Clarke, Arthur C(harles) (U.K.). **Expedition to Earth.** Ballantine, 1953. Some story title changes in the U.K. edition.

Eleven stories from 1946 to 1953 that exhibit Clarke's versatility in SF. Stories of interest: the beautiful and philosophic "Second Dawn," about a culture that developed mental powers before advanced technology and now must discover the latter; "The Sentinel," realistic tale of finding a lunar pyramid, prototype of *2001* monoliths; "Superiority," in which a mighty space fleet is vanquished by a scientifically inferior enemy because of the latent effects of their too-advanced military technology; "Breaking Strain," where enough air remains for only one of a two-man spaceship crew and they must pick who will die; and the humbling "History Lesson," about the attempted reconstruction by Venusians of extinct human culture from its sole surviving record—a Walt Disney cartoon.

3-101. Clarke, Arthur C(harles) (U.K.). **A Fall of Moondust.** Harcourt, 1961.

Efforts to rescue tourists from a lunar surface vehicle buried under a sea of dust. Emphasis on well-worked-out technical aspects of lunar dust, vehicles, and rescue processes, but social and psychological effects on trapped passengers and crew also treated—although they behave much like typical British characters facing a common crisis. Tension and suspense maintained despite present-day knowledge that the Moon just isn't that dusty. Compare with Caidin's *Marooned* (Dutton, 1964).

*3-102. Clarke, Arthur C(harles) (U.K.). **The Other Side of the Sky.** Harcourt, 1958.

Collection of 24 stories written between 1947 and 1957 contains, along with contents of *Expedition to Earth, Reach for Tomorrow,* and *Tales from the White Hart,* all the pre-1960s short fiction by Clarke that he thinks worthy of preservation. Outstanding efforts include "The Nine Billion Names of God" (SFHF), in which Tibetan monks use a computer to compile all the possible names of God, thereby ending the universe; and "The Star" (HW, 1956), about the consternation of a Jesuit astrophysicist who discovers that the nova heralding Christ's birth also destroyed a magnificent people inhabiting its planetary system. Also of interest are "Venture to the Moon" and "The Other Side of the Sky," each containing six vignettes commissioned by the *London Evening Standard* and chronicling the initial experience of space, and the poignant "The Songs of Distant Earth," story of a lovelorn girl on a distant planet and a boy aboard a ship of colonists that briefly stops before heading even farther out.

*3-103. Clarke, Arthur C(harles) (U.K.). **Prelude to Space.** Gnome, 1954.

Written in 1947 and several times revised until the 1954 edition, this is one of the earliest scientifically accurate and realistic accounts of the first Moon voyage. Unlike the earlier classics, Verne's *From the Earth to the Moon* [1-93] and Wells's *The First Men in the Moon* [1-98], the emphasis is on preparations rather than the melodrama of the trip itself, anticipating the social, personal, and technical meaning and romance behind the actual conquest of space caught in Oriana Fallaci's *If the*

Sun Dies (1966). The meager plot involves the conversion of Dirk Alexson, hired as the project's historical interpreter, as he learns the inner working of Interplanetary, the private organization sponsoring the development of the moonship *Prometheus,* and of the engineers and astronauts who are making it happen. Hindsight illuminates errors, such as initial development of space travel by private interests, its relatively low cost, the invention of atomic engines, a lunar landing as late as 1978, and elimination of nationalism in space, which are more than offset by a narrative that oscillates between nuts and bolts and the poetic as Clarke makes his clearest statement of the necessity for progress: "Out of the fears and miseries of the Second Dark Age, drawing free—oh, might it be forever!—from the shadows of Belsen and Hiroshima, the world was moving towards its most splendid sunrise. After five hundred years, the Renaissance had come again."

3-104. Clarke, Arthur C(harles) (U.K.). **Reach for Tomorrow.** Ballantine, 1956.
Twelve stories from 1946 to 1953. Superior works include "Rescue Party," written in 1945, a Campbellesque space opera touting human drive and ability; "Jupiter Five," about the discovery that Jupiter's innermost moon is really an abandoned alien ship; "The Parasite," in which an alien telepathic peeping Tom, Omega, drives a man to suicide; "A Walk in the Dark," in which a man hurries through the night to catch a spaceship on a lonely alien planet only to find a deadly creature waiting for him; "Trouble with the Natives," a humorous first-contact story of a flying saucer's crew who have difficulty finding anyone to believe them when they land in rural Britain.

3-105. Clarke, Arthur C(harles) (U.K.). **Tales from the White Hart.** Ballantine, 1957.
Fifteen SF tall tales, reminiscent of de Camp and Pratt's fantasy *Tales from Gavagan's Bar* (1953), written between 1953 and 1956. Harry Purvis spins the yarns in the out-of-the-way London pub, the White Hart, where the regulars include the likes of John Christopher and John Wyndham (a real pub, the Globe, was a traditional gathering place for SF personalities). In "The Man Who Ploughed the Sea," Purvis tells of his meeting in the Atlantic with two millionaire scientists, one of whom trades his process for extracting minerals from sea water for the other's yacht—one gets a process still to be perfected, the other, with less than a year to live, a ship he has coveted on which to spend his final days. A more outrageous example is "What Goes Up," in which Purvis relates how an Australian scientist invented antigravity but died in a flaming meteor after falling 20 feet horizontally while trying to reach the device.

3-106. Clarke, Arthur C(harles) (U.K.). **The Wind from the Sun.** Harcourt, 1972.
Eighteen stories, all Clarke wrote during the 1960s, full of topical scientific and technical ideas in the classic Heinlein tradition. Title story portrays a race by sunlight-powered space sailing ships; "The Light of Darkness" has an African scientist destroying a dictator with a laser-fitted telescope; a cyborg named Falcon descends into Jupiter's atmosphere aboard a balloon-type craft in "A Meeting with Medusa"; an astronaut dies alone on Mars in "Transit of Earth"; and in "The Cruel Sky," a thalidomide-crippled scientist uses an antigravity device to scale

Mt. Everest. Compare Niven's *All the Myriad Ways* (Ballantine, 1971) and Bova's *Forward in Time* (Walker, 1973).

3-107. Clement, Hal (pseud. of Harry Clement Stubbs). **The Best of Hal Clement.** Lester del Rey, ed. Ballantine, 1979.
Collection of ten stories from 1942 to 1976, including those that became *Natives of Space* (1965); the stories of sympathetic vampires, "Assumption Unjustified" and "A Question of Guilt"; and "Answer" and "Dust Rag." Earliest is "Impediment." Clement's hard science and rational approach is well illustrated in "Uncommon Sense," in which an amateur exobiologist uses knowledge gained by observing alien life forms to retake his ship after it was hijacked by his crew. Also contains an introduction, "Hal Clement: Rationalist," by the editor and an author's afterword. Compare Asimov's stories [3-17, 3-21] and contrast those of Disch [4-186].

3-108. Clement, Hal (pseud. of Harry Clement Stubbs). **Cycle of Fire.** Ballantine, 1957.
Nils Kruger, Earthman, and Dar Lang Ahn, alien, must cooperate to survive on a planet of tremendous climactic extremes. But first they must break through the awful mistrust with which one alien meets another. A tour de force epitomizing the radical points of view different species must adopt to coexist. Logical in the mode for which Clement is famous. Compare Dickson's *The Alien Way* [3-145] and White's *The Watch Below* [4-594].

*3-109. Clement, Hal (pseud. of Harry Clement Stubbs). **Mission of Gravity.** Doubleday, 1954.
Earthmen are aided in recovery of crashed observer satellite on disk-shaped planet Mesklin by 15-inch-long natives armored to adapt to the 700 Earth gravities of their unusual world. Consummately logical "hard-core" SF (IFA second place, 1955). Sequel is *Starlight* (Ballantine, 1971), which provides more adventures with Captain Barlennan, merchant Mesklinite, on a planet where the awesome gravity forces can kill you with a six-inch fall. *Close to Critical* (Ballantine, 1964) is an associated novel. Compare Forward's *Dragon's Egg* [4-217].

*3-110. Clement, Hal (pseud. of Harry Clement Stubbs). **Needle.** Doubleday, 1950. Variant title: *From Outer Space,* 1957.
An alien policeman pursues an alien criminal on Earth by inhabiting a human boy's body (with the boy's cooperation). The alien criminal runs away from his pursuer by inhabiting another human. In Clement's hands all very plausible. Sequel: *Through the Eye of a Needle* (Ballantine, 1978). Contrast Finney's *The Body Snatchers* [3-163]; compare Wyndham's *Chocky* [3-410].

3-111. Clifton, Mark. **Eight Keys to Eden.** Doubleday, 1960.
Underrated novel belonging to *Childhood's End* [3-97] tradition. A new planet's colony is suddenly incommunicado. Eventually investigators learn the planet is a perfectly harmonized ecology of mind and matter, an ideal that the Earth-born colonists are just beginning to realize at story's end. Especially interesting for critique of psychically sterilizing effects of Earth-type civilization. Compare John Brunner's *Bedlam Planet* (1968).

3-112. Clifton, Mark. **The Science Fiction of Mark Clifton.** Barry N. Malzberg and Martin H. Greenberg, eds. Southern Illinois Univ. Press, 1980.

In addition to three novels, Clifton (1906–1963) published 21 short stories from 1952 to 1962, all listed in the bibliography. Eleven of the best are assembled here, his first American collection, including his first, "What Have I Done?," as well as "Star, Bright," "Crazy Joey," "What Thin Partitions," "Sense from Thought Divide," and others. Each is preceded by editors' headnotes. Judith Merril quotes from her extensive correspondence with Clifton, whom she strongly admires. Malzberg's afterword places Clifton in critical perspective, argues that his short fiction is better than his novels and that he deserves greater recognition.

*3-113. Clifton, Mark, and Frank Riley. **They'd Rather Be Right.** Gnome, 1957. Alternate title: *The Forever Machine*, Galaxy, 1959.

The first of the supercomputers, "Bossy" is built and soon put to work "healing" or "perfecting" human beings. Treated humans become physically and mentally perfected, including the full development of psi abilities. Society, represented in distorted commercial and news media information, reacts with a witch-hunt. An honest, extremely wealthy man saves the heroes and the Bossy prototype so that enough machines can be built to process all humanity. Stereotyped characters; good narrative. Compare Bester's *The Stars My Destination* [3-32]; contrast Keyes's *Flowers for Algernon* [3-228]. HW, 1955.

3-114. Clingerman, Mildred (McElroy). **A Cupful of Space.** Ballantine, 1961.

Sixteen stories, mostly fantasy; full of cute kids, frightened or worried women, eccentric grandmothers, and sentimental aliens. Among better SF are "Minister without Portfolio," where Earth is spared by aliens due to their contact with an elderly traditional woman; "The Word," where aliens trick or treat on Halloween; and "Birds Can't Count," an axiom for both humans watching birds and aliens watching humans. Compare with Judith Merril's *Out of Bounds* (1960) and deFord's *Xenogenesis* [3-137].

3-115. Cogswell, Theodore R(ose). **The Wall around the World.** Pyramid, 1962.

Ten SF and fantasy stories, from 1952 to 1960, and two introductions on the distinction, or lack of one, between the two genres by Anthony Boucher and Frederik Pohl. "The Specter General" (SFHF) describes a distant future after the collapse of a human galactic empire where those remnants having machines no longer know how to repair them, while one isolated military post ritualistically trains technicians, but lacks machines enough to live above the level of primitive hunters. In most of the other stories, elements of SF and fantasy are combined— such as alien invaders meeting vampires. Entertaining, but not sophisticated.

3-116. Cole, Everett B. **The Philosophical Corps.** Gnome, 1962.

Dalthos A-Riman leads contingent of space corps that deals with new species and cultural disturbers, "drones," by reeducation instead of obliterating violence. Procedure of benevolent brainwashing. Ideological space opera, combining interesting adventures in context of at least politically conservative machinations of a "thought control police force." Part of a 1950s *Astounding* series. Compare Mitchison's *Memoir of a Spacewoman* [3-288].

3-117. Collins, Hunt (pseud. of S. A. Lombino). **Tomorrow's World.** Avalon, 1956. Alternate title: *Tomorrow and Tomorrow*, 1956.

Expansion of "Malice in Wonderland" (1954), published under Lombino's major pseudonym, Evan Hunter. In the near future, U.S. society is polarized between the dominant drug-using, pornography-gazing, body-painting, hip Vikes, who only want vicarious experiences, and the subordinated, sexually and emotionally repressed, puritanical Res, whose doctrine of "realism" is equally narrow. The dialectic unfolds, with Re defeating Vike, but this time, a new synthesis leading to a balanced society may result. Interesting slang, as in Brunner's *Stand on Zanzibar* [4-92], and an extrapolation unusually close to the present sensate culture; plot is merely vehicle for the author's comments on society and humanity. Lots of sex for its time. Compare Compton's *Synthajoy* [4-145].

*3-118. Condon, Richard (Thomas). **The Manchurian Candidate.** McGraw-Hill, 1959.

The well-written benchmark novel of Korean War era brainwashing techniques and their implications for a cold-war world. Raymond Shaw, Medal of Honor winner, is "brainwashed" into a time-bomb assassin by communist psychologists. Back in the United States, his mission is set in motion by a posthypnotic signal. Conditioning and hypnosis are complementary psychotherapeutic techniques that will be turned to subtly terrible purposes in international warfare. The effect has become a commonplace in recent SF. Condon's story is powerful and convincing. Compare Budrys's *Who?* [3-79].

3-119. Conquest, (George) Robert (Ackworth) (U.K.). **A World of Difference.** Ward Lock, 1955.

An Earth government works to build an orderly, utopian world based on applied psychology. Yet, two forces remain uncontrolled—the rebel descendants of the defeated Communists now hiding in the asteroids and the Freedom and Vigilance League, who remain stubbornly skeptical of the state's claimed benevolence. Against this background, four friends, former comrades in arms, weave humanity's destiny: Stahlberg, generalist, author, and womanizer; Vlakhov, director of projects and chief trouble-shooter of the World Federation Government; Hayakawa, physicist developing the photon-drive to take *Starship Zenith* to Procyon; Custis, artist and league sympathizer. Long on talk and slow on action, this novel is Conquest's vehicle for exploring the problems of freedom and modern technology; he calls SF "work devoted mainly to possibility exploration." (Conquest is a noted poet, Soviet specialist, and SF anthologist [3-420].) Can people be free if their freedom is achieved by control of their very minds? Who controls the altruistic controllers, and might their enemies use their science against them? Can human creativity even exist if humans are "cured" of their aberrations? Compare Koestler's *Twilight Bar* [3-237], Solzhenitsyn's *Candle in the Wind* [3-357A], Rand's *Anthem* [3-315], and Orwell's *Nineteen Eighty-Four* [3-302].

3-120. Cooper, Edmund (U.K.). **Deadly Image.** Ballantine, 1958. British title: *The Uncertain Midnight*, Hutchinson, 1958.

In one of Cooper's typical, but realistically portrayed, decadent and destroyed future societies, androids, devoid of the grace of love, relentlessly press against humanity's fading tenure. Who is the more worthy of inheriting the Earth? Compare with Brunner's *Slavers of Space* (Ace, 1960). Contrast Williamson's *The Humanoids* [3-402] and Goulart's *After Things Fell Apart* [4-237].

3-121.   Cooper, Edmund (U.K.). **Seed of Light.** Hutchinson, 1959.
Episodic and space-operatic novel in three parts: "Bitter Harvest" describes the events leading up to humanity's final nuclear war (a weapons satellite put up by an altruistic Britain triggers a new arms race in space); "The Seed" tells of the struggle of a small band of survivors to find a safe home (aboard the wandering starship *Solarian* where they develop a new society); "Germinal," in which the now-recovered human race settles down to a new and wiser beginning (the starship warps back to a prehistoric Edenic Earth where the humans, purged of their aggression, greet their once enemy Neanderthal neighbors with "Peace!"). A message novel reflecting the author's and the time's cold-war climate and fear of the bomb. Should appeal to anti-"Star Wars" groups today. Compare Aldiss's *Starship* [3-6] and Shute's *On the Beach* [3-344]. Contrast Stewart's *Earth Abides* [3-358].

3-122.   Coppel, Alfred. **Dark December.** Fawcett, 1960.
After World War III, Gavin is released from duty as member of ICBM team and travels in loneliness and loss over the devastated remains of the United States, learning to survive physically and to replace his lost family with a new one. Postcatastrophe story in John Christopher mold; perhaps more of a psychological study. Compare Frank's *Alas, Babylon* [3-166] and Huxley's *Ape and Essence* [3-220].

3-123.   Crane, Robert (pseud. of Bernard Glemser) (U.K.). **Hero's Walk.** Ballantine, 1954.
Strong story about the conflict between Earth's ambitious leaders, bent on exploiting the other planets, and the quarantine of Earth by a superior species, the Ampiti. During the resulting bombardment of Earth's cities, Neil Harrison struggles to reach his girl and reflects on the blunders that led to the disaster. The militarists have been overthrown and Earth surrenders to the Ampiti; perhaps they will spare a wiser humankind. Realistic description of bombing in this antiwar story. Contrast Anderson's *The Star Fox* [3-12].

3-124.   Curtis, Jean-Louis (pseud. of Louis Lafitte) (France). **The Neon Halo.** Secker, 1958. Tr. by Humphrey Hare of *Un Saint au néon*, 1956.
A collection of five stories in a satirical mood, much appreciated by French SF readers.

*3-125.   Daniel, Yuli (as Nikolai Arzhak) (U.S.S.R.). **This Is Moscow Speaking, and Other Stories.** Dutton, 1969. Tr. by Stuart Hood, Harold Shukman, and John Richardson of *Ici Moscou*.
"Moscow Speaking" is most controversial of four stories included, about declaration in Russia, August 10, 1960, of a "Public Murder Day" and public's passive acceptance of it. An analysis of the phenomenon and orchestration of terrorism, like Shirley Jackson's "The Lottery." In other stories: "Hands" involves the terror of a police executioner who believes his bullets do not harm a priest he is ordered to kill (reminiscent of Brunner's "The Nail in the Middle of the Hand" [3-72]); "Atonement," in which a man falsely accused of being an informant comes to accept the punishment for his alleged betrayal; "The Man from MINAP," a comic

tale of a man whose service is sought by women and then the state because he can determine the sex of a child when he has intercourse. Compare the stories of Barry Malzberg.

3-126. Davidson, Avram. **The Best of Avram Davidson.** Michael Kurland, ed. Doubleday, 1979.
Twelve stories from 1955 to 1971, including "The Golem" and "What Strange Stars and Skies." Earliest is "Or the Grasses Grow"; latest is "The Trefoil Company." Foreword by Peter Beagle, introduction by the editor, and afterword by the author also included. Chapter 8 of his *The Phoenix and the Mirror* (Doubleday, 1969) is reprinted, along with "Help! I Am Dr. Morris Goldpepper" and "The Sources of the Nile," two other well-known Davidson works. The moral questions that pervade Davidson's stories are exemplified in "Now Let Us Sleep," about the "rescue" of primitive aliens from their planet, which is needed for economic development, for use in research on a deadly disease and the effects of this on the conscience of their naïve "liberator."

3-127. Davidson, Avram. **Clash of Star-Kings.** Ace, 1966.
Despite its title, a well-constructed, well-characterized, and maturely written tale of the final struggle between two star-races—one peaceful and benevolent, the other cruel, warlike eaters of human hearts. The setting is a mountain village in modern Mexico, and the story abounds with local color and lore. In *Chariots of the Gods* fashion, the star-races were once godlike visitors to ancient Mexico, but their war took them elsewhere. When they return for a hidden weapon capable of tipping the balance, natives and two expatriate American writers get drawn into the fray. Suspenseful and realistic. Compare Wilson's *The Mind Parasites* [4-611]. Nebula novella nominee, 1966.

3-128. Davidson, Avram, and Ward Moore. **Joyleg.** Pyramid, 1962.
Congressional fact-finding expedition in Tennessee foothills becomes international free-for-all as Isachar Joyleg, veteran of the American Revolution, is revealed to possess "fountain of youth" in his moonshine still. Reporters, congressional investigators, and even ambassadors from Soviet Union try to exploit him. But trunk of old papers from days of Revolution turns tables and makes Joyleg master of the world. Rollicking social criticism. Compare Frank's *Mr. Adam* [3-167].

*3-129. Davidson, Avram. **Or All the Seas with Oysters.** Berkley, 1962.
Seventeen stories, including title story (HW, 1958), about subtly evolved tragedy in bicycle shop when safety pins, coat hangers, and bicycles begin to "regenerate." Also of interest is the humorous "Help! I Am Dr. Morris Goldpepper" and the ethnic "The Golem." Mood is science fantasy rather than science fiction.

3-130. Davidson, Avram. **Strange Seas and Shores.** Doubleday, 1971.
Seventeen well-crafted SF and fantasy stories from 1958 to 1967 that exhibit Davidson's wit and taste for the offbeat. Time travel and plot to prevent the development of modern technology unfold in "Take Wooden Indians." "The House the Blakeneys Built" creates a social microcosm for the battle of stability vs. change. A man searches futilely for a family that predicts new fads in "The Sources of the Nile," and an orphan child turns the tables on his mean grandfa-

ther in "The Goobers." Strong on characterization and story backgrounds. Also includes a preface by the author and an appreciation of him by Ray Bradbury.

*3-131. de Camp, L(yon) Sprague. **The Best of L. Sprague de Camp.** Ballantine, 1978.
Collection of 18 stories from 1938 to 1976, most before 1957. Earliest is "Hyperpelosity"; latest are "The Little Green Men" and "Two Yards of Dragon." Classic de Camp is here: "The Gnarly Man" (1939), about a living Neanderthal in a sideshow, and "A Gun for Dinosaur" (1956), in which hunters travel in time to bag big game like a tyrannosaur. An essay, "Language for Time Travelers" (1938), influenced many writers in their treatment of language in different time settings; three examples of verse appear, but all are post–golden age in publication date (but not in flavor). Poul Anderson provides an introduction, while the author has an afterword. A very satisfying collection.

3-132. de Camp, L(yon) Sprague. **Divide and Rule.** Fantasy, 1948.
"Hoppers," insectile aliens, conquer Earth and recast human society in feudal mold, partitioned into fiefs to discourage unified resistance; they allow only medieval technology, with few exceptions, such as radios. Resistance is cast with hero "knight" and "cowboy" in comic-adventure tale vaguely reminiscent of *Don Quixote.* Revision of a 1939 story. Compare Tenn's *Of Men and Monsters* [3-371]. This edition also contains "The Stolen Dormouse" (1941), one of de Camp's best stories.

3-133. de Camp, L(yon) Sprague, and P(eter) Schuyler Miller. **Genus Homo.** Fantasy, 1950.
A busload of scientists and chorus girls sleep Rip-van-Winkle-style a million years into the future and find a geophysically different Earth. There is no human race, and several species of monkey and ape, along with beavers, have evolved intelligence comparable to humans. A combination of allegory, satire, and clever extrapolation that descends into soap opera. Boldly considers practicality of nudity, polygamy, and the amalgamation of humans in the gorilla culture that befriends them. At its best, similar to *Gulliver's Travels* [1-89], Stewart's *Earth Abides* [3-358], and Boulle's *Planet of the Apes* [3-55].

*3-134. de Camp, L(yon) Sprague, and Fletcher Pratt. **The Incomplete Enchanter.** Holt, 1941. As *The Compleat Enchanter,* includes *The Castle of Iron,* Nelson Doubleday, 1975.
The humorous adventures of Harold Shea, a dilettante psychologist who finds himself through excursions into mythical and fictional worlds where magic, like technology here, operates by fixed laws. Mental exercises in symbolic logic are the means of transportation, carrying Shea first to Norse mythology's Ragnarök, then into Spenser's *Faerie Queene.* Background well developed. Based on material dating from 1940. Two sequels of lesser quality: *The Castle of Iron* (Gnome, 1950) originally appeared in 1941 and is set in Ariosto's *Orlando Furioso; Wall of Serpents* (Avalon, 1960) is derived from 1953–1954 stories, set in Kalevala and Irish mythology. Contrast Zelazny's *The Dream Master* [4-628].

*3-135. de Camp, L(yon) Sprague. **Lest Darkness Fall.** Holt, 1941; rev. ed., Prime, 1949.
Martin Padway, time-traveled to A.D. 535 Rome, sets about distilling brandy,

teaching Arabic mathematics to bookkeepers, inventing printing, and the like. Eventually helps the Goths defend Rome from the Byzantine threat and attempts to accelerate progress and prevent the "dark ages"—contrary to *his* history. Neat anthropological interpretation of history. This is de Camp's best. Compare Golding's *The Brass Butterfly* [3-176]. Contrast the Strugatskiis' *Hard to Be a God* (1964).

3-136.   de Camp, L(yon) Sprague. **Rogue Queen.** Doubleday, 1951.
A female-dominated species governed on the hive model is visited by an exploration team from Earth. The contact leads to a revolution by some members of humanoid hive people who adopt democratic Earth government model with leadership of "rogue" woman. Contact between alien species will lead to transformation of culture of less enlightened. Thoughtful anthropological insights. Clever Swiftian parody of human institutions and provincialism. Part of the Viagens Interplanetarias future history series. Compare Herbert's *Hellstrom's Hive* [4-269].

3-137.   deFord, Miriam Allen. **Xenogenesis.** Ballantine, 1969.
Sixteen fantasy and SF stories from 1950s and 1960s, many from the *Magazine of Fantasy and Science Fiction* and more or less tied to the general theme of procreation and sex. Of interest are "The Daughter of the Tree," "Season of the Babies," and "The Last Generation." Emphasis on characterization, moral issues, and humanity. Contrast with Clingerman's *A Cupful of Space* [3-114].

*3-138.   del Rey, Lester. **And Some Were Human.** Prime, 1948.
Twelve SF and fantasy stories from the 1940s, including "Nerves" and "Helen O'Loy" (both SFHF), the latter about an android woman humanized and married by one of her makers. Also of interest are "The Day Is Done," which depicts the conflict between Neanderthals and Cro-Magnons, and "The Stars Look Down." One of the better known early collections.

3-139.   del Rey, Lester. **The Eleventh Commandment.** Regency, 1962.
One of the best treatments of the future Roman Catholic Church theme. Here the church rules an Earth teeming with billions. It has decreed that humans should proliferate without restraint. Reason: long-range genetic improvements that drive the species up the steps of evolution far outweigh the short-range miseries of overpopulation. Text revised in Ballantine, 1970, edition. Contrast with Harrison's *Make Room! Make Room!* [4-257].

*3-140.   del Rey, Lester. **Nerves.** Ballantine, 1956.
First published in 1942 and later expanded, probably the earliest major work to deal with an accident at an atomic power plant. Seen through the eyes of the plant physician, engineers battle courageously to stop an escaped experimental isotope from exploding. Prophetic in its anticipation of popular fear and resistance to nuclear plants, the story is not likely to satisfy present-day atomic critics with its last-minute solution based on the guess of an untried nuclear boy wonder. Taut action, gobs of technology; unrealistically, del Rey's nuclear plant is insured! Original short story in SFHF. Compare John G. Fuller's nonfiction *We Almost Lost Detroit* (1975), Ray Kytle's *Meltdown* (Walker, 1977), and Robert Heinlein's "Blowups Happen" (1940).

3-141. Dick, Philip K(indred). **Eye in the Sky.** Ace, 1957.
Remarkable variation on alternate-worlds model. Eight people are knocked out
in a bevatron field. As consciousness returns to successive victims, the others are
drawn into the private reality of the one returning to consciousness. Resulting adventures in worlds of religious Fascist, a "nice" but sexually frigid female
blueblood, and a communist sympathizer are suspenseful, interesting, and instructive. Creator of each world is literally "god" in that world, leaving others at
his or her mercy—in fear of the "eye in the sky." Context for story is paranoia of
spy-hunting, top-secret-labeling, cold-war United States. First two-thirds of novel
especially well told. Compare Le Guin's *The Lathe of Heaven* [4-326].

*3-142. Dick, Philip K(indred). **The Man in the High Castle.** Putnam, 1962.
A classic alternate-history novel depicting a world in which Axis powers won
World War II and have divided and occupied the United States. Especially noteworthy are the insights into the conqueror-conquered relationship, the Japanese
mind, and the attempts by Americans to emulate it. The book's driving force is
the *I Ching*, the basis not only of characters' actions, but of writing of *The Grasshop-
per Lies Heavy*, a widely read "subversive" alternate-history novel that has the Allies winning the war. (Still, the world portrayed in that book is not our real one.)
Dick also used the *I Ching* in plotting the novel. A cleanly written although complexly plotted work, its central action involves the attempt by a German faction to
warn the Japanese of an impending nuclear attack on their homeland. Surrounding this are several subplots in which characters realize their destinies for good or
ill. Dick's best. Compare Hersey's *White Lotus* (Knopf, 1965); contrast Sarban's
The Sound of His Horn [3-327]. HW, 1963.

3-143. Dick, Philip K(indred). **Martian Time-Slip.** Ballantine, 1964.
In the late twentieth century Earth has well-established Martian colonies, turning
out the Martian "Bleekmen" from their own planet and using them as slaves or
forcing them to live far from human settlements. For humans, business—capitalism—prevails. Arnie Kott, president of the plumbers' union on Mars, meets Jack
Bohlen, a schizophrenic in remission, who has rapport with Manfred Steiner, an
"autistic" boy who like Bleekman lives in a temporal moment—sometimes past
and sometimes future—different from that of normal humans. Kott wants to exploit for investment purposes the Steiner boy's ability to see the future, but Kott
is killed, perhaps because of his selfish intentions. The fragile materialism of humanity contrasts with the void of ultimate existential questions. See other works
by Dick for reproduction of this theme.

3-144. Dick, Philip K(indred). **Solar Lottery.** Ace, 1955. British title: *World of
Chance*, Rich, 1956.
In a stagnant future social order supposedly based on chance, people operate with
game theory's Minimax. But few can actually win; giant industrial complexes with
fealty systems and a rigid class system see to that. Even the Quizmasters, absolute tyrants chosen at random, subvert the system by trying to abolish or rig the drawing,
while public assassins attempt to murder them and personal telepathic body-
guards provide security. Against this background, a complex plot unfolds of
Quizmaster Verrick's loss of office to a new one, Cartwright, who wins the throne
through fraud so he can send a spaceship to search for a mystical tenth planet.

Verrick's attempt at assassination almost succeeds except for the intervention of his idealistic "serf," Benteley, who questions if immoral orders should be followed. Finally, there is hope that humankind will once more be free to strive toward its potential. Dick's first major achievement. Contrast with van Vogt's *The World of Null-A* [3-386].

3-145. Dickson, Gordon R(upert). **The Alien Way.** Bantam, 1965.
Earth has achieved faster-than-light drive and makes the inevitable contact with hostile aliens. War with the Ruml is averted because Jason Barchar has discovered the "alien way" of looking at survival. The Ruml, of course, must learn the "alien way" of humanity. Brotherhood, however, is not the message; rather, it is that knowledge and power are necessary for ultimate survival. Humanity has it. Excellent for orchestration of Ruml's and humanity's points of view. Compare Spinrad's *Songs from the Stars* [4-529].

*3-146. Dickson, Gordon R(upert). **Dorsai!** DAW, 1976. Alternate title of an abridged edition, *The Genetic General*, Ace, 1960.
Donal Graeme's social and biological makeup gives him strength, courage, and intelligence with psi ability. Beginning his career as a mercenary, he overcomes many challenges to become the most powerful military man in the galaxy; yet he is vaguely disappointed, because his full power has emerged in his trials and he is like a god. Graeme's intelligence is interestingly illustrated; good emerging superman story. Graeme's people are the Dorsai, the galaxy's greatest warriors, who developed their mercenary culture in order to survive on their resource-poor world. Some liberal readers may find this celebration of the militaristic identity unpalatable, but Dickson is an excellent writer of SF military organization and action. The Dorsai are Dickson's most celebrated SF creation and are also part of the 12-volume masterwork many years in the writing. This is the Childe Cycle, Dickson's vision of humanity's evolutionary potential. Over a 1,000-year span from the fourteenth to the twenty-fourth century, three basic human types, or "prime characters"—the Men of Faith, of War, and of Philosophy—interact to produce the most highly evolved human type, Ethical-Responsible Man, who will leave the species' "childhood" behind. Graeme is the first of this new type, as he blends the elements of the Splinter Cultures—the warrior Dorsai, the philosophic Exotics, and the spiritual Friendlies. Other novels in the cycle include *Necromancer* (Doubleday 1962; alternate title *No Room for Man*, Macfadden, 1963), *Tactics of Mistake* (Doubleday, 1971), and *Soldier, Ask Not* [3-148]. Associated works are *The Spirit of Dorsai* (Ace, 1979), *Lost Dorsai* (Ace, 1980), *The Dorsai Companion* (Ace, 1986), which can replace the two preceding books, and *The Final Encyclopedia* [4-181]. Compare Asimov's *Foundation Trilogy* [3-19]; contrast Clarke's *Childhood's End* [3-97].

3-147. Dickson, Gordon R(upert). **Gordon R. Dickson's SF Best.** James Frankel, ed. Dell, 1978.
Collection of 16 stories including "In the Bone," about the survival test of a high tech age man stripped of everything by superior aliens and left naked in an off-Earth forest; "Act of Creation," a robot story with a twist; and "Call Him Lord," involving a visit by an imperial prince to now-backward Earth that shows up his

failings (the last story, NW for novella, 1966). Also contains an introduction by Spider Robinson and a Dickson bibliography. Good, but not all his best.

3-148. Dickson, Gordon R(upert). **Soldier, Ask Not.** Dell, 1967.
Tam Olyn, a newsman, discovers himself to be one of the "movers" of humanity. He has an instinct that enables him to direct the forces of human development. Playing games with real lives, he encourages a poor religious colony to hire men out as mercenaries even against the invincible Dorsai. He learns only too late how well he succeeded and how unnecessary it was. Excellent psychological profile. Part of the Childe Cycle (see *Dorsai!* [3-146]). Contrast Smith's Lensman series [3-355]; compare Pournelle's *The Mercenary* [4-421]. The original short story was a 1965 Hugo winner.

*3-149. Drury, Allen (Stuart). **Advise and Consent.** Doubleday, 1959.
This first book, a best-seller and Pulitzer prize winner, launched a five-volume, 3,000-page future history, which, according to the author, constitutes an "argument between those who would use responsible firmness to maintain orderly social progress and oppose Communist imperialism . . . and those who believe that in a reluctance to be firm, in permissiveness and in the steady erosion of law lie the surest path to world peace and a stable society." Battle lines are drawn over the controversial nomination of Robert Leffingwell as secretary of state at a time when the Soviet Union is competing with the United States more than ever, and has won the moon race. In *A Shade of Difference* (Doubleday, 1962) international crises escalate, as an African ruler pushes his nation's independence and humiliates the United States at home and in the United Nations over its racial situation. *Capable of Honor* (Doubleday, 1966) has war escalating in Africa and breaking out in Panama, while Walter Dobius, a powerful columnist, manipulates the press for his own ends and the presidential nominating convention is disrupted by the National Anti-War Activities Congress. *Preserve and Protect* (Doubleday, 1968) opens with the suspicious death of President Hudson, and, as the country rocks with violence, interest groups work behind the scenes to pick a replacement candidate. At this crossroads, the consequences of that decision are explored in a final pair of novels. *Come Nineveh, Come Tyre: The Presidency of Edward M. Jason* (Doubleday, 1973) details the decline of the United States as its president yields to Soviet power and *The Promise of Joy* [*The Presidency of Orrin Knox*] (Doubleday, 1975) follows the other presidential choice, as he attempts to rally the country in the face of an impending Russian/Chinese war and to decide whether to intervene and, if so, on which side. Described by some as political soap opera and by others as insightful speculation on American politics, it remains a monumental effort, rich in satire and irony in a politically conservative vein. Compare with de Borchgrave and Moss's *The Spike* (Crown, 1980); contrast Lewis's *It Can't Happen Here* [2-62] and Brunner's *The Sheep Look Up* [4-90].

3-150. Dudintsev, Vladimir (U.S.S.R.). **A New Year's Tale.** Dutton, 1960. Tr. by Gabriella Azrael from *Novy Mir*, 1956. Pub. in U.S.S.R. in 1965.
Allegory of scientific discovery of ultimately cheap heat and light for dark continent that never gets light from Sun (North America?). Hero makes break-

through by learning he has a "year" to live and understands paradox of hurrying in real sense—by being completely composed. Ambition leading to scientific discovery is metaphor for political and moral triumph—perhaps. Contrast Asimov's *The Gods Themselves* [4-27].

3-151.   Duncan, David. **Occam's Razor.** Ballantine, 1957.
A scientific experiment using soap films and wire frames to test the theory of minimals inadvertently taps another space-time continuum and introduces a beautiful girl and horned, superstrong man onto a top-secret island Moon-rocket base. The resulting confusion and blunders by officials threaten to launch nuclear world war. Interesting characterizations, but weak in science. Compare Maine's *Count-Down* [3-269].

3-152.   Efremov, Ivan Antonovich (U.S.S.R.). **Andromeda: A Space Age Tale.** Foreign Language Publishing House, 1959. Tr. by George Hanna of *Tumannost' Andromedy*, 1958.
Nearly a thousand years in the future, Earth, a socialist commonwealth, explores its area of the galaxy and finally is contacted by Andromeda galaxy. Space opera and soap opera as an exhibition and rhapsodic presentation of fulfillment of human intellectual curiosity and need for constructive adventure, in line with doctrinaire ideals of socialistic state. Tirelessly inventive of interesting problems and solutions, generally plausibly depicted. Compare Reynolds's *Looking Backward from the Year 2000* [4-439] and its associated works.

3-153.   Ehrlich, Max (Simon). **The Big Eye.** Doubleday, 1949.
Earth narrowly misses catastrophic collision with new planet, "the big eye," which astronomers have announced will actually collide in order to unify world and end all war. Gravely flawed in science and sociology, but sentimentality is very satisfying. Reflects the rise of social concerns among post–world war scientists. Compare Sturgeon's "Unite and Conquer" in *A Way Home* [3-365]. Contrast Wylie and Balmer's *When Worlds Collide* [2-146]. A Book-of-the-Month Club selection.

3-154.   Emtsev, Mikhail, and Eremei Parnov (U.S.S.R.).   **World Soul.** Macmillan. 1977. Tr. by Antonina W. Bouis of *Dusha Mira*, 1964.
Lots of readers like this woodenly assembled story of a seaweed that "threatens" humanity by making all humans telepathic in a short-range way. The seaweed, become a physically gigantic growth, is the "world soul." The intriguing question of whether it would be good or bad to proceed as a telepathic species is nowhere nearly fully exploited. Compare Henneberg's *The Green Gods* [3-209]; contrast Boye's *Kallocain* [3-58].

3-155.   Engel, Leonard, and Emanuel S. Piller. **The World Aflame: The Russian-American War of 1950.** Dial, 1947.
In 1955, historians give account of war between America and Russia, five years ongoing and no end in sight. America's monopoly of A-bomb not enough for quick victory. Right-wing point of view corroborates late 1940s McCarthyism, fear of communism. Historically interesting potboiler. Compare Farjeon's *Death of a World* [3-156].

3-156. Farjeon, J(oseph) Jefferson (U.K.). **Death of a World.** Collins, 1948.
In the future, aliens read diary of John Smith, a last survivor when the governments of Earth destroyed the planet. Slickly narrated by first-class popular writer. An awful-warning story. Compare Wylie's *Triumph* [3-409].

3-157. Farmer, Philip José. **The Alley God.** Ballantine, 1962.
Three superior stories. "The Alley Man" (HN, 1960) is about the world's last Neanderthal, who works as a trash man, and his "attractiveness" for a certain young lady. "The Captain's Daughter" (1953) tells of an alien life-form that inhabits human bodies and reproduces by making its hosts have intercourse, a fate that a spaceship captain and his daughter struggle against. In "The God Business" (1954), the hero is reborn a god after wandering in a fantastic, allegorical environment created out of the mind of his old professor of classical literature. Typical of Farmer's themes, treatments, and innovativeness.

3-158. Farmer, Philip José. **The Green Odyssey.** Ballantine, 1957.
Fast, humorous story of Alan Green, spaceship-wrecked on a barbarous lawn-covered planet over which the natives sail in wind-driven wheeled ships. No superman despite his ability-enhancing symbiote and technical knowledge, the timid Green is made a slave, works as a court gigolo, and finds himself under the thumb of a strong-willed wife with five children; then he hears of two captured Earthmen and sets off with his family in a fascinating "wind roller" to rescue them and himself. Compare Foster's *Icerigger* [4-219]; contrast Carr's *Leviathan's Deep* [4-112].

*3-159. Farmer, Philip José. **The Lovers.** Ballantine, 1961. Hardcover 1979 edition is slightly revised.
Expansion of a 1952 story that generated much controversy in SF because of its sexual content. Linguist Hal Yarrow is sent by his rigid, neo-Islamic theocratic government, the Sturch, as part of an expedition to kill the intelligent, friendly, insectlike aliens on a planet wanted for colonization. Hal falls in love with a female member of another alien life-form on the planet, one capable of mimicking human form and behavior. She becomes pregnant, which causes her death, but Hal still has the "children," all female, to love. Meanwhile, the insectlike aliens, having uncovered the Sturch's plot, kill the other Earthmen, freeing Hal from his superior's wrath. A commentary on the meaning of humanity and love in a police state. Compare Howard's *The Eskimo Invasion* (Ballantine, 1967) and Michael Coney's *Mirror Image* (1972).

3-160. Farmer, Philip José. **Night of Light.** Berkley, 1966.
Two John Carmody stories, about a vicious criminal turned priest, unartfully tacked together (NN, 1966). Carmody reforms after braving a periodic solar disruption, called the Night of Light, that literally gives people what they really want. The good Carmody sires a new god, Yess, after the evil Carmody had killed the old god, Yess. This first part is the more effective, reaching the mood of Delany's *Dhalgren* [4-165] at times. The second, more convoluted and less well written, has Catholic priest Carmody returning to Kareen to ask his god-son not to proselytize off-planet. For a future when humans travel over a million light-

years between planets, customs and beliefs are unrealistically too similar to the present (must heroes eternally be puffing on those cigarettes?). Story too light to carry message of local versus galactic saviors. The original shorter version of *Night of Light* appears in *Father to the Stars* (Pinnacle, 1981), another collection of Father Carmody stories.

*3-161.   Farmer, Philip José. **Strange Relations.** Ballantine, 1960.
Five stories of humans meeting aliens, including "My Sister's Brother" (HN, 1961), of a religiously inclined member of first Mars exploration team who learns from a female alien what true "brotherhood" might be, and "Mother," a Freudian-influenced study of a young man trapped inside an alien monster who uses him as part of her reproductive system. Daring stories for the SF of their time.

3-162.   Fast, Howard (Melvin). **The Edge of Tomorrow.** Bantam, 1961.
Seven stories from 1959 to 1960, including "The Large Ant," about humans' impulsive killing of a giant antlike creature that has come bearing superscientific knowledge. These tales are parables condemning human arrogance, cruelty, and lack of empathy.

*3-163.   Finney, Jack (pseud. of Walter Braden Finney). **The Body Snatchers.** Dell, 1955. Later as *Invasion of the Body Snatchers,* Dell, 1961.
Aliens invade Earth in form of seed pods, beginning in small California community. Aliens want human bodies. Attempted takeover is impersonal competition of species for survival. Fierce tenacity of Miles and Becky, and use of fire, drive the invaders back to space. Basis for films, *Invasion of the Body Snatchers,* 1956 and 1979. In the film versions, the invaders are not repelled. Compare Heinlein's *The Puppet Masters* [3-205] and Philip Dick's "The Father Thing" (1954).

3-164.   Finney, Jack (pseud. of Walter Braden Finney). **The Third Level.** Rinehart, 1957. British title: *The Clock of Time,* Eyre, 1958.
Twelve stories, including the famous "I'm Scared," concerning a man who is cataloging the gradual breakdown of serial time under the influence of popular modern will to escape the present into the past and the future. The title story postulates a level below the two existing in the New York subway that is 50 years in the past. Time paradox is the topic of most of the stories.

3-165.   Fitz Gibbon, Constantine (Robert Louis) (Ireland). **When the Kissing Had to Stop.** Cassell, 1960.
A Pollyanna self-delusion by England's traditional leadership permits a rise to power of extreme left-wing elements, so that the Sino-Soviet communist bloc finally takes over the U.K. The deftly positioned details of the treatment of British citizens in concentration camps are effective. Compare Sinclair Lewis's *It Can't Happen Here* [2-62], Caldwell's *The Devil's Advocate* [3-84], and de Borchgrave and Moss's *The Spike* (Crown, 1980).

*3-166.   Frank, Pat (pseud. of Harry Hart Frank). **Alas, Babylon.** Lippincott, 1959.
After nuclear holocaust nearly devastates America, a small group of people survive to try to make a new and better world. Order is key to survival. With it, civiliza-

tion will survive even the bomb. Excellent popular narrative. Compare Stewart's *Earth Abides* [3-358] and Christopher's postcatastrophe stories.

3-167. Frank, Pat (pseud. of Harry Hart Frank). **Mr. Adam.** Lippincott, 1946. A nuclear blast sterilizes every man on Earth except Homer Adam. Civilization's chaos is aggravated by bureaucracy until Tommy Thompson's seaweed tonic reestablishes fertility. Belly-laughing satirical attack on U.S. bureaucrats. Compare Davidson and Moore's *Joyleg* [3-128].

3-168. Franke, Herbert W. (Austria). **The Orchid Cage.** DAW, 1973. Tr. by Christine Priest of *Der Orchideenkäfig*, 1961. In distant future, Earthmen visit far planet in simulacrum message form, discovering humans there have been made into "orchids" by their computerized civilization. They are reduced to rudimentary organs ("orchid" means "teste" in Greek). As for humans, machine civilization makes life virtually meaningless. Logical tour de force. Ingenious space-travel concept. Compare Anthony's *Macroscope* [4-23] and Campbell's "Twilight" [3-86].

3-169. Gallun, Raymond Z(inke). **The Best of Raymond Z. Gallun.** J. J. Pierce, ed. Ballantine, 1978. Thirteen stories from 1934 to 1952, an afterword by Gallun discussing their creation, and an introduction by Pierce calling Gallun "The Quiet Revolutionary": "one of the three men—along with John W. Campbell and Stanley G. Weinbaum—who did most to set in motion the evolution of SF from crude pulp fiction to a form increasingly imaginative and literate." Perhaps. Others grant "ideas" but point out "crude" prose. At worst, prime pulps; at best, ground breakers: "Old Faithful" (1934) introduces a humanized Martian, Number 774, who races the death his regimented society has imposed on him to make first contact with Earthmen; "Derelict" (1935), an innovative, sympathetic robot story; "Davey Jones' Ambassador" (1935)—the question of fire's necessity for social development; "Hotel Cosmos" (1938)—inventive housing of aliens that anticipates White's *Hospital Station* [3-398]; "Magician of Dream Valley" (1938)—very early pollution warning story about energy-based lunar life-forms being killed by a nuclear fuel factory relocated off Earth; "Seeds of the Dusk" (1938), with a logical treatment of intelligent plants; "The Restless Tide" (1951), about humanity's tendency to become bored with the status quo and seek the challenges of new horizons—"I guess folks will have to reach the stars sometime . . . or die." Compare Weinbaum's *A Martian Odyssey* [2-125], Campbell's *Who Goes There?* [3-86], and Binder's *Adam Link* [3-35].

*3-170. Galouye, Daniel F(rancis). **Dark Universe.** Bantam, 1961. A nuclear war has forced many to retreat to prepared shelters for what becomes a generation-long exile. Loss of lighting power forces development of other senses, hearing and heat sensing, in two groups of exiles. Jared, while exploring this dark underground universe, discovers others from above seeking survivors. The light they bring creates a profound culture shock. Excellent insight. Good use of the formula of changing one element of a normal reality and extrapolating. Compare Asimov's "Nightfall" [3-21] and Heinlein's *Orphans of the Sky* [3-203]. HN, 1962.

3-171. Garrett, Randall. **Takeoff!** Starblaze, 1980.
Collection of 21 stories, parodies, and pastiches of famous SF writers and their works, including E. E. Smith, Russell, Lovecraft, Asimov, E. R. Burroughs, de Camp, van Vogt, Poul Anderson, Bester, Campbell, Lin Carter, and others. Compare Briarton's *Through Time and Space with Ferdinand Feghoot* [3-65], which Garrett also parodies. A second edition (1986) adds a Gernsback pastiche from 1957, coauthored with Lin Carter.

3-172. George, Peter (Bryan) (U.K.). **Dr. Strangelove; or, How I Learned to Stop Worrying and Love the Bomb.** Corgi, 1963.
Script from film of same title that dramatizes through actions of principal participants—bomber pilots, generals, politicians, and others—how the nuclear holocaust will begin. Humans are selfish, stupid, sex-crazed, essentially suicidal. Remarkable for relentless parody of the behavior of leaders of "free world." Great popularity as film and novel. Derived from the author's serious novel *Red Alert* (Ace, 1959; variant title: *Two Hours to Doom* by "Peter Bryant," Boardman, 1958). Compare Dick's *Dr. Bloodmoney* . . . [4-174].

3-173. Glaskin, G(erald) M(arcus) (Australia). **A Change of Mind.** Barrie & Rockliff, 1959.
A middle-aged accountant, Edward Henderson, hypnotically exchanges "minds" with Roger, a young, athletic mechanic. Resulting situation causes Edward to lose wife, Betty; finds sympathy in Dorothy. Roger commits suicide. Soap-operatic tale providing probing insights into the nature of individual identity. Compare Chris Stratton's *Change of Mind* (white man's brain in black man's body) (1969) and Stine's *Season of the Witch* (man's brain in woman's body) [4-539].

3-174. Godwin, Tom. **The Survivors.** Gnome, 1958. Variant title: *Space Prison*, 1960.
Vying with humankind for ascendancy in inhabited space, the alien Gerns maroon 4,000 people on the 1.5-gravity planet Ragnarök as "rejects" from slavery. Nearly 300 years later, 1,000 of the marvelously adapted humans survive to escape the planet and begin successful conquest of Gerns. Human race is remorselessly resourceful and will triumph against all odds. An epic ordeal reminiscent of Clement's *Mission of Gravity* [3-109] and White's *The Watch Below* [4-594]. Sequel is *The Space Barbarians* (Pyramid, 1964).

3-175. Gold, H(orace) L. **The Old Die Rich and Other Science Fiction Stories.** Crown, 1955.
Twelve SF and fantasy stories, including "Trouble with Water," about a man cursed by water gnome so water won't touch him; "Man of Parts," about human who joins metabolisms with mineral-eating alien; and "The Man with English," for whom brain operation reverses all senses. Also includes author's critical comments on each story. Tightly told "amusements," many with a Jewish character flavor, by the pioneering editor of *Galaxy Science Fiction*. Compare stories by Avram Davidson [3-126, 3-129, 3-130].

3-176. Golding, William (Gerald) (U.K.). **The Brass Butterfly.** Faber, 1958. In story form as "Envoy Extraordinary" in *Sometime Never* (Ballantine, 1957).
In ancient Rome, Phanocles is Da Vinci-like genius who invents paddlewheel steam warship, explosives, and pressure cooker for emperor, who is too culturally naïve to see them as much more than toys. Therefore, they don't change history. Emperor's enemies are neutralized by accident, as usual. Human history seems inexorably plodding—perhaps to humankind's benefit. Satirical play; compare Vidal's *Visit to a Small Planet* [3-390] and de Camp's *Lest Darkness Fall* [3-135].

3-177. Gordon, Rex (pseud. of Stanley Bennett Hough) (U.K.). **No Man Friday.** Heinemann, 1956. U.S. title: *First on Mars,* Ace, 1957.
Despite a silly, juvenile beginning (a spaceship is secretly built by British technicians, incompetently manned, and crash-landed on Mars by an unskilled survivor), the story vastly improves with a detailed portrayal of the castaway's creative struggle for survival. At first, practical sense and engineering know-how seem to win out, proving human superior ability, but the castaway's technologically hewn niche is destroyed by originally conceived, truly alien Martian life. Although a self-conscious pastiche of Defoe's *Robinson Crusoe,* the book questions the basic Western assumptions of action, progress, and growth; it's the castaway who becomes a man Friday, a pet, to an offspring of the giant, wormlike, but highly evolved Martians. Compare Robert Heinlein's *Red Planet* (Scribner, 1949).

3-178. Gottlieb, Hinko (Yugoslavia). **The Key to the Great Gate.** Simon & Schuster, 1947. Tr. by Fred Bolman and Ruth Morris from Serbo-Croat.
Remarkable story of Nazi tyranny written by an ex-concentration camp prisoner. Tarnopolski, a Polish gentleman, confounds Nazi guards with fabulous powers based on his mastery of the space-time continuum. Damon Knight has termed it "a classic science-fantasy extravaganza, charming, pathetic, profound and wonderfully funny." Compare London's *Star Rover* (1915); contrast Disch's *Camp Concentration* [4-184].

*3-179. Graves, Robert (Ranke) (U.K.). **Seven Days in New Crete.** Cassell, 1949. U.S. title: *Watch the Northwind Rise.*
Edward Venn-Thomas, poet, travels to the future where Greek-like golden age reigns at the pleasure of the "goddess," nature. He has been brought to sow the seeds of disorder so that the beauty of order may be more richly experienced— Milton's *felix culpa*? By contrast the twentieth century provides limitless opportunity for appreciation of divine harmony. Literary, didactic, satiric, pleasant narrative by a first-rank modern British poet. Compare Varley's *Titan* [4-571]; contrast Levin's *This Perfect Day* [4-338].

3-180. Gray, Curme. **Murder in Millennium VI.** Shasta, 1951.
In the 5700s, murder in matriarchal society that has "forgotten" death provides mystery story to describe world of big, flat-chested women, small men, and food pills in fascinating scenario of alternate Earth. Damon Knight recommended it in spite of poor narrative structure. Contrast A. B. Chandler's *Spartan Planet* (1969) or Russ's *The Female Man* [4-458].

3-181. Guerard, Albert Joseph. **Night Journey.** Knopf, 1950.
Paul Halden, sergeant, wanted to make a contribution to winning the war against dictatorship for all the traditional freedoms. But the war has no meaning, no victories, only misery and destruction. Halden's personal experience is focus for this message. This is a post–World War II European war, but it could be any war. Relentless rendering of psychological experience. Compare with Reed's *Armed Camps* [4-436] and Malzberg's *Final War* (Ace, 1969).

3-182. Guin, Wyman (Woods). **Living Way Out.** Avon, 1967. British title: *Beyond Bedlam.*
Collection of seven stories from 1950 to the mid-1960s, including "Beyond Bedlam." Earliest is "Trigger Tide"; latest are "A Man of the Renaissance" and "The Delegate from Guapanga." "Volpla" has the light, humorous Guin touch as it tells how a man's complex joke—passing off as aliens a colony of flying, sentient creatures he mutated from rats—backfires when the Volplas take their destiny into their own hands. Compare the works of Robert F. Young [3-417]; contrast those of Fast [3-162].

3-183. Gunn, James E(dwin). **The Immortals.** Bantam, 1962.
Composed of stories from 1955 to 1960, the novel depicts people practically immune to death due to a superior circulatory system. This immunity can be temporarily conferred by transfusion. They are hunted by the rich who want their blood. Eventually the "immortals" face the world where they will have to live immortally. Humans desire immortality—will do nearly anything for it. Good example of a profound philosophical and psychological problem. Basis for a TV series, from which Gunn adapted a similar novel, *The Immortal* (Bantam, 1970). Contrast George Bernard Shaw's *Back to Methuselah* [2-98].

3-184. Gunn, James E(dwin). **Future Imperfect.** Bantam, 1964.
Ten stories, nine from the 1952 to 1958 period, with one original, "The Last Word." Most frequently anthologized is "The Misogynist" (1952), in which Gunn's use of literary allusion, characteristic of much of his later work, is prominent. His most recent collection of short stories, *Some Dreams Are Nightmares* (Scribner, 1974), collects four tales from the 1950s.

3-185. Gunn, James E(dwin). **The Joy Makers.** Bantam, 1961.
Three loosely linked stories from 1955 depict the rise and dominance of a scientific pursuit of pleasure in human society. The Hedonic order finally decays when its leaders cannot become happy themselves. "Happiness" is not the proper human state. It stultifies people. Slickly written social criticism. Compare Huxley's *Brave New World* [2-47].

3-186. Hadley, Arthur T(wining). **The Joy Wagon.** Viking. 1958.
A computer decides to run for U.S. presidency with results that put human politicians to shame. The computer is foiled at the last moment of the campaign by a concerned woman and an eyebrow pencil. A slapstick, satirical look at politics of the 1950s by a major journalist of the time. Compare Frank's *Mr. Adam* [3-167] and Harrison's *Stainless Steel Rat for President* [3-193]; contrast Jones's *Colossus* [4-289].

3-187. Hamilton, Edmond (Moore). **The Best of Edmond Hamilton.** Leigh Brackett, ed. Doubleday, 1977.
Collection of 21 stories from 1926 to 1968. The earliest is the "The Monster God of Mamurth"; the latest is "Castaway." Stories of note include "What's It Like Out There?," "Requiem," and "He That Hath Wings," a well-crafted, moving tale of a man born with wings who must decide if he is going to live a "normal" life on the ground or take to the air as his nature demands. Hamilton may be at his best in the short fiction form. Brackett, his wife, provides an introduction, as well as having picked these works from his more than 300 publications. In an afterword, Hamilton describes himself as a young writer whose head was filled with "visions of wonders to come, of great dooms sweeping upon the hapless Earth, of strange and usually ominous forms of life undreamed of now, of vast grandeur of things to come when the starry universe would be webbed by the fleets of man." The golden age capsulized.

3-188. Hamilton, Edmond (Moore). **The Star of Life.** Dodd, 1959.
Updated 1947 space opera about America's first Moon-orbiting astronaut, quick-frozen for 10,000 years following his spacecraft's failure, who leads an underground dedicated to giving immortality, inexplicably limited to a small elite, to all humanity. Opposing him, deep in the Trifid nebula, are the immortal Vormen, humans altered by the life-prolonging radiation of a unique star, who secretly guard the dangerous Third Men, their aggressive mutated descendants. Moral: human destiny is the stars, for good or ill, the quest an end in itself. Typical Hamilton adventure. Compare Herbert's *The Eyes of Heisenberg* (Berkley, 1966); contrast Gunn's *The Immortals* [3-183].

3-189. Harness, Charles L(eonard). **Flight into Yesterday.** Bouregy & Curl, 1953. Reprinted as *The Paradox Men*, Ace, 1955.
Complexly plotted, swashbuckling time travel tale that blends Einsteinian relativity and Toynbeean historical theory. In a militaristic, totalitarian, future United States, an aristocratic class profits from the labor of citizens who have sold themselves into slavery to escape dire poverty. Amnesiac superman Alar/Muir struggles to end this injustice and prevent suicidal global war. Setting is of more interest than the strained plot. Compares only in its use of historical theory with Blish's Spenglerian *Cities in Flight* [3-43] and Asimov's cyclic *Foundation Trilogy* [3-19]. The Crown (1984) edition should now be taken as the definitive one, being revised and having a new foreword by Zebrowski and new afterword by the author, as well as a reprinted appreciation by Aldiss.

3-190. Harness, Charles L(eonard). **The Rose.** Roberts & Vinter, 1966.
Psychiatrist-ballerina Anna Van Tuyl is haunted by dreams that begin when she gets rare, debilitating disease. Transforming dreams into ballet leads her to Ruy Jacques, a millionaire who also has the disease. But Ruy's wife, Martha, who is perfecting an invention to make science supreme over art, is jealous and tries to have Anna killed when she finds her in love with Ruy. However, love conquers as the deformation of the lovers turns out to be chrysalis stage before the next step in human evolution. Fine sentimental epic richly enhanced by cogent treatment of antagonism of the rational and the aesthetic in modern culture. Originally pub-

lished in 1953. Compact edition also contains two other fine 1950s stories, "The Chess Players" and "The New Reality." Contrast Huxley's *After Many a Summer Dies the Swan* [3-219].

*3-191. Harrison, Harry. **Deathworld.** Bantam, 1960.
First work of a trilogy; Hugo nominee in 1971. This and its sequels, *Deathworld 2* (Bantam, 1964; British title: *The Ethical Engineer*, Gollancz, 1964) and *Deathworld 3* (Dell, 1968), are contained in *Deathworld Trilogy* (Nelson Doubleday, 1974). Series follows psychic gambler Jason dinAlt as he helps tame Deathworld itself, where local psychic life has evolved into incredibly deadly forms in defense against the thoughts of hostile human colonizers. In the two less successful sequels, dinAlt survives being marooned on a planet with viciously competitive cultures and then leads the original Deathworld colonists—themselves culturally evolved into very tough customers—in the conquest of Pyrrus, a rich planet peopled by Mongol-like barbarian warriors. Much action with Darwinist philosophy. Compare Dickson's *Dorsai!* [3-146].

3-192. Harrison, Harry. **Planet of the Damned.** Bantam, 1962. British title: *Sense of Obligation*, Dobson, 1967.
Brion of the Cultural Relationships Foundation engineers the salvation of Dis, a hellish planet infected with an alien parasite that made it behave homicidally. The pacifist planet Nyjord does the mopping up. Evil is not ultimately mysterious; it has a cause that can be neutralized if the agents of good keep their heads. Adventure as a clever solution to problem in social anthropology. A related novel is *Planet of No Return* (Tor, 1982). Compare Philip José Farmer's "The Captain's Daughter"; contrast Le Guin's *The Word for World Is Forest* [4-329]. HN, 1962.

3-193. Harrison, Harry. **The Stainless Steel Rat.** Pyramid, 1961.
In a plot typical of Harrison at the time, "Slippery" Jim di Griz, larcenous but nonhomicidal con man (shade of dinAlt in *Deathworld* [3-191]), is trapped by the interplanetary crime fighting Special Corps, who recruit from the criminal ranks to find the unique skills not provided by the healthy low-crime legitimate world (like Brandd from the hostile world of Anvhar in *Planet of the Damned,* Bantam, 1962), and made to work for them. Bored with the tedium of training school, di Griz informs corps leader Inskipp of the illegal construction of a Warlord class Imperial battleship, and sets off on his first case, only to confront the murderous but beautiful supervillain, Angelina. The Rat proved popular, and sequels soon followed: *The Stainless Steel Rat's Revenge* (Walker, 1970); *The Stainless Steel Rat Saves the World* (Putnam, 1972); *The Stainless Steel Rat Wants You* (Bantam, 1979); *The Stainless Steel Rat for President* (Bantam, 1982); and *A Stainless Steel Rat Is Born* (Bantam, 1985). First-person narrative, action, humor, and inventiveness make for an entertaining diversion.

3-194. Hartley, L(eslie) P(oles) (U.K.). **Facial Justice.** Doubleday, 1960.
This story of a woman named Jael exemplifies life in a totalitarian state, based upon absolute egalitarianism, grown up after World War III—and its subsequent fall. The faces of all persons must, quite literally, be equal. Cogent satire and poignant melodrama reminiscent of Huxley's *Brave New World* [2-47] and von Harbou's *Metropolis* [2-123].

3-195. Hawkes, Jacquetta (U.K.). **Providence Island.** Chatto & Windus, 1959.
Archaeologists discover lost race on Pacific island, survived from Magdelanian prehistoric period. Islanders live Edenically; have psychic power, used finally to prevent United States from turning island into nuclear testing target. Psi ability would make technological civilization unnecessary; by comparison with island culture it is stupid. Interesting anthropological insights. Contrast E. R. Burroughs's Pellucidar stories [1-15]. Compare Clifton's *Eight Keys to Eden* [3-111].

3-196. Heard, H(enry) F(itzgerald) (pseud. of Gerald Heard) (U.K.). **Doppelgangers.** Vanguard, 1947.
Complex, dense novel loaded with relatively sophisticated philosophic and social speculation. Plot involves the attempt by the Mole, an underground revolutionary genius, to physically modify a nameless pawn to resemble Alpha, benevolent dictator of a hedonistic utopia based on Sheldon's somatotypes. The double not only supplants Alpha, but in effect becomes him. Humanity has finished its revolutionary period, from the religious, to political, to economic, and, finally, to the psychological/anthropological era; a third force, the Elevated, a group based on Hinduism and other philosophies, intervenes to destroy the Mole, one of their fallen colleagues, and help point Alpha II and humanity again up the road of social evolution. Rewarding study of power despite its turgid prose. Contrast Huxley's *Brave New World* [2-47] and Heinlein's *Double Star* [3-199].

3-197. Heinlein, Robert A(nson). **Beyond This Horizon.** Fantasy, 1948.
Many older readers of modern SF insist on remembering *Horizon*, Heinlein's inimitably cobbled novel of a postscarcity civilization wherein people in general spend their time wondering what to do with their time, and the Heinleinian heroes make sure it is something very damned interesting. Contrast Campbell's "Twilight" [3-86]; compare Delany's *Triton* [4-170].

3-198. Heinlein, Robert A(nson). **The Door into Summer.** Doubleday, 1957.
Dan Davis, an electronics engineer, invents an all-purpose robot and is shanghaied into suspended animation for 30 years by his business partner and his fiancée. He returns by way of a time machine, rescues his cat, starts a rival company, proposes (future) marriage to a 12-year-old, and returns to the future to reap his reward. Good adventure in an unusually mellow mood for Heinlein. Contrast MacDonald's *The Girl, the Gold Watch, and Everything* [3-267].

*3-199. Heinlein, Robert A(nson). **Double Star.** Doubleday, 1956.
An actor is coerced into impersonating a kidnapped politician. The politician is recovered but soon dies. His staff persuades the actor to continue the act and carry out the ambitions of the politician. An approving but informative view of the morality of politics. Not major Heinlein. Contrast Heard's *Doppelgangers* [3-196]. HW, 1956.

3-200. Heinlein, Robert A(nson). **Glory Road.** Putnam, 1963.
Oscar Gordon is chosen by Ishtar, queen of seven universes, to rescue "phoenix egg," key to computer complex of her government. He succeeds after picaresque adventures that prove his courage. Parody of familiar Heinlein militaristic heroism. Adventure clichés are vitalized by comic treatment in this sword-and-sorcery

effort, but not superior Heinlein. Compare Vance's *The Dying Earth* [3-380]. HN, 1964.

3-201.   Heinlein, Robert A(nson).   **Have Space Suit—Will Travel.**   Scribner, 1958.
Kip Russell, high-schooler, wants to go to the Moon. Instead, he wins a second-hand space suit in a contest and with the help of extraterrestrials travels the galaxy, returning eager to get a good education. Cogent critique of public education curriculum. Well-paced juvenile adventure story inspirational to teen readers about how to get a good education. Contrast Friedberg's *Revolving Boy* (Doubleday, 1966). HN, 1959.

3-202.   Heinlein, Robert A(nson).   **The Menace from Earth.**   Gnome, 1959.
Eight stories, best known of which is "By His Bootstraps" (1941). Others include "The Year of the Jackpot," "Columbus Was a Dope," "Goldfish Bowl," and "Project Nightmare."

3-203.   Heinlein, Robert A(nson).   **Orphans of the Sky.**   Gollancz, 1963.
First published as "Universe" in 1951 and expanded for this version, *Orphans* is part of Heinlein's future history series, mostly contained in *The Past through Tomorrow* [3-204]. It is Heinlein's classic story of a whole population of passengers on a gigantic interstellar spaceship destined to travel for generations. Compare Clarke's *Rendezvous with Rama* [4-138] and Aldiss's *Starship* [3-6].

*3-204.   Heinlein, Robert A(nson).   **The Past through Tomorrow.**   Putnam, 1967.
A treasure trove of Heinlein's short fiction, spanning his writing career from 1939 to 1957 and including some of his best and most popular efforts. Contains most of Heinlein's future history stories, plus a revised chronology; perhaps most notable are "The Roads Must Roll" (SFHF), about life on the solar-powered conveyor-belt highways of the future, and "The Man Who Sold the Moon," in which businessman and space-travel enthusiast D. D. Harriman makes the first Moon flight a reality. Also included are such well-known works as "Blowups Happen," "Coventry," "The Green Hills of Earth," "Life-Line," "Logic of Empire," "Methuselah's Children," "Requiem," and "—We Also Walk Dogs." The one notable omission is "Universe" (SFHF; in *Orphans of the Sky* [3-203]). The first serious attempt in SF to project a detailed, consistently feasible future for humankind; hard SF, as in Niven's Known Space series [4-389], but equally concerned with social and political matters, as in the more space-operatic stories of Asimov's Foundation [3-19] and Blish's *Cities in Flight* [3-43] future histories. Scenario begins with the contemporary "Crazy Years," passes through a "period of imperial exploitation" around the year 2000, and continues into the twenty-second century and "the first human civilization." A basic item in any SF library. Most of this omnibus collection was published as four separate books: *The Green Hills of Earth* (Shasta, 1951), *The Man Who Sold the Moon* (Shasta, 1950), *Revolt in 2100* (Shasta, 1953), and *Methuselah's Children* (Gnome, 1958). A recent related work is *The Cat Who Walks through Walls* [4-261].

3-205.   Heinlein, Robert A(nson).   **The Puppet Masters.**   Doubleday, 1951.
As the late 1970s saw the second film version of Finney's *The Body Snatchers* [3-

163], the favorite novel version of this kind of story for SF readers was still Heinlein's paranoia-laden tale of sluglike creatures, arrived in saucer-shaped craft to enslave humans by the particularly gruesome procedure of growing into each person's nervous system from a position on the upper back of the victim—making his or her profile hump-backed. Compare Wyndham's *Midwich Cuckoos* [3-413].

*3-206. Heinlein, Robert A(nson). **Starship Troopers.** Putnam, 1959.
Heinlein was an Annapolis cadet. *Troopers* is story of space cadet academy and after, as negotiated by single individual. Novel largely responsible for view of Heinlein as Fascist and war-approving. Heinlein was "hawk" for Vietnam war. Vintage Heinlein storytelling. Compare Panshin's *Rite of Passage* [4-406] and Smith's Lensman series [3-355]; contrast Harrison's *Bill, the Galactic Hero* [4-255] and Kornbluth and Merril's *Gunner Cade* (Simon & Schuster, 1952). HW, 1960.

*3-207. Heinlein, Robert A(nson). **Stranger in a Strange Land.** Putnam, 1961.
Valentine Michael Smith, born of human parents and raised by Martians, returns to Earth as a young man, rich and a virtual superman because of the parapsychological powers Martian education produced in him. Jubal Harshaw befriends Michael and his fortune until Michael can acculturate himself. Mike becomes wise, but keeps his virtue—becoming a Christ-figure who finally "discorporates." Harshaw is familiar Heinlein central character in a radicalized mood, favoring free love, ritual cannibalism, and other familiar Heinlein social propositions. First half of novel is best; breaks in middle, and so is flawed for many readers. Read well beyond SF fandom; used in college composition courses; directly associated with Charles Manson, murder-cult leader of the Sharon Tate massacre. Best known of Heinlein's SF. Compare Silverberg's *The Masks of Time* [4-504]; contrast Vidal's *Visit to a Small Planet* [3-390]. HW, 1962.

*3-208. Henderson, Zenna. **Pilgrimage: The Book of the People.** Doubleday, 1961.
Linking narrative added to earlier short stories. A preternaturally good "human" species arrives on Earth in small groups of survivors after their sun goes nova. They have psi talents that are always used for wholesome purposes. Meetings with Earth humans are basic to most of the stories, producing scenarios that probe gently but deeply the inadequacies of humans. Chief characters are schoolteachers and children. Has Simak's sentimentality and Wellman's eye for backwoods culture. Contrast Wyndham's *The Midwich Cuckoos* [3-413]. Sequel is *The People: No Different Flesh* (Gollancz, 1966). A 90-minute TV production based on the *People* materials was aired in the 1970s. The sequel volume contains "Captivity" (HN, 1959).

3-209. Henneberg, N(athalie) C. (France). **The Green Gods.** DAW, 1980. Tr. by C. J. Cherryh of *Les Dieux verts*, 1961.
In a galaxy already colonized by humans, strange interplanetary forces rearrange the surface of Earth and enshroud it in a virtually impenetrable magnetic shield. Earth is cut off from everything for millennia. Meanwhile, the shield creates a "greenhouse" effect, giving plants an edge that enables them to become supersentient, with paranormal abilities thrown in. Humans left on Earth must

fight from an inferior strength to escape the exotic dominance of the plants. Nice adventure. Compare Wyndham's *The Day of the Triffids* [3-411] and Disch's *The Genocides* [4-185].

3-210. Herbert, Frank. **The Dragon in the Sea.** Doubleday, 1956. Variant titles: *21st Century Sub*, Avon, 1956, and *Under Pressure*, Ballantine, 1974.
In twenty-first-century war with Eastern Hemisphere, U.S. subs are lost trying to steal from enemy's underwater deposits. John Ramsey, psychologist-electronics crewman, discovers cause of the loss of the subs by learning meaning of "sanity" to humankind, especially in closed, pressurized world of submarine. Sanity is different adaptations in different environments. Fine adventure narrative and good speculative psychology. Compare White's *The Watch Below* [4-594].

*3-211. Hersey, John (Richard). **The Child Buyer.** Knopf, 1960.
Revealed in the court records of the litigation over the whole affair is the classic account of the corralling and "forcing" of very bright children to maximize their ability to contribute to corporate profit and national brainpower. The flashes of clearly Shavian wit (a character is named Broadbent) serve only to dramatize more powerfully the sinister totalitarian designs free Western nations flirt with. Compare Brunner's *Shockwave Rider* [4-91].

*3-212. Hesse, Hermann (Germany/Switzerland). **The Glass Bead Game (Magister Ludi).** Holt, 1969. Tr. by Richard Winston and Clara Winston of *Das Glasperlenspiel*, 1943.
In twenty-fifth-century Castalia, Joseph Knecht works his way to becoming Magister Ludi, a grandmaster of "games," in a utopia devoted to mental and aesthetic ideals. The intellectually elitist pursuit is symbolized by the fantastically intricate and disciplined Glass Bead Game. Knecht rejects the Castalian ideal for one that is socially conscious as well. Individual perfection is meaningless until it finally transcends the one and aggrandizes the lives of the many. The book's excellence is consummate—hailed by Thomas Mann and admired by T. S. Eliot and André Gide, it is the principal work for which Hesse received the Nobel prize in 1946. Compare Mann's *Doctor Faustus* (1947) and Brunner's *The Whole Man* [3-74]. Rand's *Atlas Shrugged* [3-316] represents the antithesis of this philosophy.

3-213. Hicks, Granville. **The First to Awaken.** Modern Age, 1940.
Cast as a memoir of George Swain, one of eight volunteers in a cryogenics suspended-animation experiment undertaken in 1940, who is the first to awaken in 2040. He finds a post–World War II utopia ordered by the inspiration of what appears to be an Aristotelian golden mean, scientific method, a form of socialism, a sexual freedom in a wholesomely progressive sense, and far more happiness than the world he left—as a bank teller-amateur historian. Hicks was a first-order cultural and literary historian. Compare Hesse's *The Glass Bead Game* [3-212] and Le Guin's *The Dispossessed* [4-324].

3-214. Hingley, Ronald (Francis) (U.K.). **Up Jenkins!** Longmans, 1956.
Civil war splits Britain into a free north and totalitarian south. Peter Gosling in the south is saved by Helen Browning, whose husband has infiltrated the southern regime and leads escapees to the north through the mine tunnels of a "con-

centration camp." Good satire. Compare Priest's *Fugue for a Darkening Island* [4-428]; contrast John Christopher's *Pendulum* (Simon & Schuster, 1968).

3-215. Hoyle, Fred, and John Elliot (U.K.). **A for Andromeda.** Souvenir Press, 1962.
Hoyle's fascination with extraterrestrial intelligence shows in this classic tale of decoding a radio message from space. The message gives plans for creating a humanoid, a clever device for invasion by aliens, because the humanoid is automatically programmed to multiply its numbers as an invasion force. The story is developed from a U.K. television series. Sequel: *Andromeda Breakthrough* (Souvenir Press, 1964). Compare Gunn's *The Listeners* [4-244].

*3-216. Hoyle, Fred (U.K.). **The Black Cloud.** Heinemann, 1957.
A cloud of interstellar matter throws solar system into chaos and begins destruction of earthly life. But cloud is intelligent, honors life, and retreats after communication is established. So plausible and astronomically accurate that astronomy classes assign it as supplementary reading. Contrast Theodore Thomas and Kate Wilhelm's *Year of the Cloud* (Doubleday, 1970).

3-217. Hoyle, Fred (U.K.). **Ossian's Ride.** Heinemann, 1959.
A young Oxford graduate is drafted by British intelligence to penetrate and investigate I.C.E. (Industrial Corporation of Eire)—a huge megacorporation that has made enormous advances in science in a cordoned-off area in southwest Ireland. He discovers that beneficent aliens reborn as humans are behind the scientific explosion. Very similar in outlook to *A for Andromeda* [3-215] and *Andromeda Breakthrough* [3-215], as well as Gunn's *The Listeners* [4-244].

*3-218. Hubbard, L(afayette) Ron(ald). **Final Blackout.** Hadley, 1948.
In a world made decrepit by many wars, "the Lieutenant" brilliantly engineers the resurrection of England, effectively neutralizing technologically superior, politically decadent America's attempt to colonize it. Military discipline can yield crucial human freedom. Persuasive. Fine evocation of loneliness of genius in a wasted civilization. Hubbard's best SF; controversial when first published in 1940. Contrast Shiel's *The Purple Cloud* (1901); compare Best's *The Twenty-fifth Hour* [3-29] and Pournelle's *The Mercenary* [4-421].

*3-219. Huxley, Aldous (U.K.). **After Many a Summer Dies the Swan.** Harper, 1939. British title: *After Many a Summer,* 1939.
American oil baron and entrepreneur searches for longevity or immortality through research of personal physician. They find it through consumption of fish entrails, demonstrated in form of 200-year-old British aristocrat who, with mistress, has "evolved" into ape. As a dog is underdeveloped wolf, humans may be underdeveloped apes. Nature and God are "good"; civilization is "evil." Erudite, comic; full of incisive social criticism. Enthralling narrative. Contrast Vercors's *Sylva* [3-387]; compare Taine's *The Iron Star* [2-117].

3-220. Huxley, Aldous (U.K.). **Ape and Essence.** Harper, 1948.
In 1947, William Tallis writes rejected screenplay of California in 2018 visited by New Zealand Rediscovery Expedition after nuclear holocaust. Situation is neomedieval, church-directed. Message is scalpel-like satirical account of twentieth-

century humans' failure to understand their nature. Lesser writers would not handle this scenario and theme intelligently until the 1960s. Compare Miller's *A Canticle for Leibowitz* [3-287] and Merle's *Malevil* [4-376].

3-221. Huxley, Aldous (U.K.). **Island.** Harper, 1962.
Farnaby, spiritually crippled journalist, shipwrecks on Pala, 100-year-old experimental island utopia, idyllic, communal, insulated. Inhabitants are psychically whole in transcendental philosophy of love. War and neurosis unknown. Farnaby's guilt-ridden mentality contrasts with serene yogic spirit of Pala. The end will come when Pala is taken over by outside interests for its oil. Buddha was right. Capitalism is the antithesis of love. Contrast Skinner's *Walden Two* [3-352]; compare Le Guin's *The Dispossessed* [4-324].

3-222. Jones, Raymond F. **This Island Earth.** Shasta, 1952.
Cal Meacham discovers that an intergalactic civilization, at war with another, evil, intergalactic civilization, is using Earth as manufacturing base for important weapons. He joins them in time to turn tide and save Earth by ignoring their computers and doing the unexpected. Good suspense; grandiose scope of Smith's Lensman space operas [3-355]. Basis for fair SF film.

3-223. Jones, Raymond F. **The Toymaker.** Fantasy, 1951.
Six stories, including title work about warlike diplomacy contrasted with subtler diplomacy of the Toymaker, and "Forecast," about the problems encountered after we can control the weather. Generally, fine SF that leaves space opera behind.

3-224. Kantor, Mackinlay. **If the South Had Won the Civil War.** Bantam, 1961.
The South wins and the United States is divided into the Confederacy, the Union, and Texas. Not until 1960 do proceedings for reunification begin. Kantor's *Andersonville* is popular Civil War history. This novel ingeniously incorporates major figures from actual history, preserving their personalities, to make this a delightful diversion for Civil War buffs. Compare Moore's *Bring the Jubilee* [3-291] and Douglas C. Jones's *The Court-Martial of George Armstrong Custer* (Scribner, 1976).

*3-225. Karp, David. **One.** Vanguard, 1953. Variant title: *Escape to Nowhere*, Lion, 1955.
Burden is an English professor in totalitarian state who is devastatingly brainwashed by the genius inquisitor Lark and given new identity as "Hughes." Though the superficial identity switch is successful, Hughes retains his "heretical" and basic desire to assert individuality. The few people who successfully resist complete brainwashing will defeat all totalitarianisms. Excellent primer on techniques of brainwashing. A Book-of-the-Month Club choice. Compare Orwell's *Nineteen Eighty-Four* [3-302] and Burgess's *A Clockwork Orange* [3-82]; contrast Huxley's *Brave New World* [2-47].

*3-226. Kelley, William Melvin. **A Different Drummer.** Doubleday, 1959.
Tucker Caliban and his ancestors are heroes of story set in mythical state in the deep South. Beginning with the life of an African slave in the United States, it ends with all of the black population leaving that state in 1957, making it the only

state without one black person in residence. Told as a fine literary parable, the story comes so close to reality as to fill all the requirements of the SF of social criticism in the form of the "warning story." This might be ranked among the dozen finest American short novels of the 1950s. Compare Bradbury's "Way in the Middle of the Air" in *The Martian Chronicles* [3-64].

3-227. Keppel-Jones, Arthur (South Africa). **When Smuts Goes.** African Bookman, 1947.
A political and economic history of South Africa from 1952 to 2010, as published in 2015. It explains the reduction of the nation to near barbarism because of racism and the economic caste system. An awful-warning story. Successful affectation of synoptic history. Compare Allighan's *Verwoerd—The End* [3-7] and Brunner's *The Jagged Orbit* [4-88].

*3-228. Keyes, Daniel. **Flowers for Algernon.** Harcourt, 1966.
Exquisite story of mentally retarded Charlie Gordon, who becomes a genius as the result of an intelligence-enhancing drug. Through his diary containing periodic "progress reports," we follow Charlie's emergence into the "normal" adult world and then beyond as his mind blazes; but the flame is short-lived and shrinks back into darkness and ashes. A sensitive and poignant exploration of the meaning of humanity and intelligence that grips the reader through its characters' full dimensionality and their inevitable tragic destinies. One of SF's truly fine works. Also excellent as the film *Charly* (1968). Compare Anderson's *Brain Wave* [3-8] and Sturgeon's "Maturity" in *Without Sorcery* [3-366]. Hugo short fiction winner, 1960; HN, 1967; NW, 1966.

3-229. Kirst, Hans Hellmut (Germany). **The Seventh Day.** Doubleday, 1959. Tr. by Richard Graves of *Keiner kommt davon,* 1957. British title: *No One Will Escape,* 1960.
Long narrative of rigorous verisimilitude of the tragic diplomatic vicissitudes of nuclear nations for six days, culminating in the detonation of over 1,000 nuclear bombs with nearly a hundred million dead. At novel's end the seventh day has not dawned. It will be anniversary of the doom of civilization. Russia and the United States are the instigators. Excellent awful-warning tale. Symbolism of the undoing of the seven days' work of Genesis is intended. Kirst is best known in United States for non-SF *Night of the Generals.* Compare Wylie's *Triumph* [3-409] and Shute's *On the Beach* [3-344].

3-230. Klein, Gérard (France). **Starmaster's Gambit.** DAW, 1973. Tr. by C. J. Richards of *Le Gambit des étoiles,* 1958.
Jerg Algan uses a symbolic game of chess to pursue space-operatic adventures in a search for the secret of what makes the universe run. He discovers the source of sentience in the stars, the suns of solar systems, whose plans for humans are benevolent and transcendent. A well-paced narrative with a vaulting theme, reminiscent of Clarke's *Childhood's End* [3-97]. Prix Jules Verne winner, 1958.

3-231. Kneale, (Thomas) Nigel (U.K.). **The Quatermass Experiment.** Penguin, 1959.
A six-part play produced for the BBC in 1953. Professor Quatermass heads manned space shot that returns with crew in last stages of being absorbed by a

plant-thing from outer space. Earth is threatened; catastrophe barely averted. Space program scientists should be more careful. Effective melodrama and social satire for its time. Sequels: *Quatermass II* and *Quatermass and the Pit* (both Penguin, 1960). Compare "Tom Corbett, Space Cadet," a U.S. television series of the 1950s.

3-232. Knebel, Fletcher, and Charles W. Bailey II. **Seven Days in May.** Harper, 1962.
America faces a well-organized coup when Democratic President Jordan Lyman, elected as a hard-liner after a Communist invasion of Iran forces that country's partition and the U.S. military's humiliation, develops a disarmament treaty with the U.S.S.R. Marine Colonel Casey slowly unravels the conspiracy and plans to foil the cabal led by General Scott. Gripping and suspenseful as both a best-seller and film. Of equal success is Knebel's *Night of Camp David* (Harper, 1965), in which the U.S. president, Mark Hollenbach, goes crazy and pushes the world to the brink of catastrophe. The day is saved when he is brought to resign. Good speculative suspense that cogently anticipates Watergate, Nixon's resignation, the United States's problems with Iran, and the Soviet "peace offensive" during the Reagan era. Representative of an emerging allied genre, speculative literature about the role of the U.S. presidency, along with Wallace's *The Man* (1964), Johnson's *The Presidential Plot* (1969), Serling's *The President's Plane Is Missing* (1967), and the Drury series [3-149].

*3-233. Knight, Damon F(rancis). **Far Out.** Simon & Schuster, 1961.
Thirteen stories from 1949 to 1960, introduced by Anthony Boucher, that catch the wit and urbanity of this SF writer's writer. "To Serve Man," a gruesome little comment on human gullibility, involves the appearance of seemingly altruistic aliens who secretly want to use humans as food; in "Not with a Bang" humanity is doomed to extinction due to its prudishness when the last man on Earth has a fatal attack in the men's room while the last woman waits outside; the real value of communication is illustrated in "Babel II," when a visiting alien scrambles human speech and writing; in "Special Delivery" a woman suffers the arrogance of a superintelligent fetus who mentally communicates with her until its precociousness thankfully is destroyed by birth; "You're Another" tells of a young man dogged by a lucky piece that brings only bad luck until he discovers he is being used as comic relief in a play for a future society's entertainment and switches to the role of hero.

3-234. Knight, Damon F(rancis). **Hell's Pavement.** Lion, 1955. Variant title: *Analogue Men,* Berkley, 1962.
Knight's first novel presents the old "big brother" mind-control scenario with exemplary vigor; character and event enriched in detail. In a future society, humans are controlled by "analogues," individually induced psychological hangups. Hope for freedom rests with the "immunes," an underground population of people who cannot be "psyched." Story's end promises freedom, but not without near-catastrophic social upheaval. Effective adventure and suspense; sensible social criticism—especially of a consumer society. Compare Orwell's *Nineteen Eighty-Four* [3-302] and Vonnegut's *Player Piano* [3-392].

*3-235. Knight, Damon F(rancis). **In Deep.** Berkley, 1963. The U.K. edition, Gollancz, 1964, drops "The Handler."
Eight stories from 1951 to 1960, including "The Country of the Kind" (SFHF), about a killer excommunicated by his society and his pathetic rebellion and loneliness. Also has "The Handler," an unusual piece in which an ugly dwarf is rejected while the large humanoid shell he inhabits and directs is a social success, and "Stranger Station," about a battle of love and hate between a human and an alien aboard an isolated space station where the alien periodically appears to give the man a longevity chemical.

3-236. Knight, Damon F(rancis). **Turning On.** Doubleday, 1966. The U.K. edition, Gollancz, 1967, adds "The Handler."
Fourteen stories from 1951 to 1965 by the first major critic of SF. Includes "Mary," about Mary and Klef, dwellers in a floating city artificially organized for survival of forgotten holocaust; breaking custom, they enter monogamous love and depart for the land, which is losing its radioactive poison. Also includes "The Man in the Jar," "The Night of Lies," and "The Big Pat Boom," a satirical comment on the tourist industry. An uneven collection.

3-237. Koestler, Arthur (Hungary/U.K.). **The Age of Longing.** Macmillan, 1951.
Hydie loves Colonel Nitkin, agent for totalitarian forces that will try to enslave Western nations. The background of characters and events characterizes the cold war in France in the mid-1950s. Story's end finds the chief characters waiting for the "comet" of destruction. Drama of the helplessness of those in a civilization that impersonally moves toward its destruction. Compare Kirst's *The Seventh Day* [3-229]. Koestler turns to SF again to make his point about humanity's need for peace in *Twilight Bar: An Escapade in Four Acts* (Macmillan, 1945); doesn't work on the stage. Compare Solzhenitsyn's *Candle in the Wind* [3-357A].

*3-238. Kornbluth, C(yril) M. **The Best of C. M. Kornbluth.** Frederik Pohl, ed. Nelson Doubleday, 1976.
Nineteen stories, from 1941 to 1958, that span Kornbluth's all-too-short career. Better efforts include "Shark Ship" ("Reap the Dark Tide," HN, 1959), about life aboard the ships of a nomadic seafaring culture that had fled the overpopulated land but now must return to it; "Two Dooms," a defense for the building of the A-bomb, in which a Manhattan Project scientist stumbles on a key to a successful bomb, but considers withholding it until he "travels" in a drug-induced dream into a future where the United States lost World War II; and "The Adventurer," which has the U.S. Cabinet secretly creating a charismatic leader by exposing a child to a harsh life, in order to overthrow a tyrannical hereditary presidency—only to find they have created a worse dictator. Also includes "The Little Black Bag" (SFHF). Pohl, Kornbluth's frequent collaborator, contributes a useful appreciation, and a short autobiographical sketch concludes the book.

*3-239. Kornbluth, C(yril) M. **Not This August.** Doubleday, 1955. British title: *Christmas Eve*, M. Joseph, 1956.
The United States has been defeated and occupied by Red China and Russia, and the people in rural upstate New York wither under an oppressive yoke

aimed at their extinction and the introduction of Russian colonists. But wait! Billy Justin discovers a vast cavern where a nearly completed launch vehicle and orbiter, armed with hydrogen and cobalt bombs, are hidden. The U.S. underground rises, as does the space station, and defeat becomes victory. A cold-war story warning of inevitable Communist aggression. Received major critical attention in the mainstream when it first appeared. Contrast Lange's *Vandenberg* (Stein & Day, 1971) and Dick's *The Man in the High Castle* [3-142.] A revised edition (by Pohl) was published by Pinnacle (1981), with foreword and afterword by Pohl.

3-240. Kornbluth, C(yril) M. **The Syndic.** Doubleday, 1953.
Charles Orsino and Lee Falcaro of culturally hospitable Syndic infiltrate the Mob nation to investigate the meaning of the Mob's growing use of diplomacy by assassination. After harrowing adventures, they return to report onset of cultural psychosis and recommend therapy and standing armies to protect Syndic. But Frank Taylor, Syndic's leader, hedges, preferring brief prolongation of Syndic's good life against immediate paranoiac readying for war. Human culture in history enjoys only brief moments of splendor, then plunges again into long periods of savagery; *carpe diem.* Effective adventure in somberly persuasive theory of history. Compare Stewart's *Earth Abides* [3-358].

3-241. Kornbluth, C(yril) M. **Takeoff.** Doubleday, 1952.
Under cover of a California amateur rocket club's building of a mock spaceship, the head of the AEC and crippled aircraft magnate (patterned after Howard Hughes?) conspire, out of fear of bureaucratic ineptness and espionage, to build the first Moon rocket. Patriotic scientist Mick Novak, who uncovers the plot but thinks it is a foreign effort, almost spoils things. Still, he and the millionaire's daughter blast off to the Moon. Novel looks ridiculous in the hindsight of NASA, but its anti-big government and cold-war sentiment remain vigorous in many quarters. Compare Clarke's *Prelude to Space* [3-103]. IFA nominee, 1953.

*3-242. Kuttner, Henry. **The Best of Henry Kuttner.** Nelson Doubleday, 1975.
Seventeen SF and fantasy stories, from 1939 to 1955, and a flattering introduction by Kuttner protégé Ray Bradbury, "Henry Kuttner: A Neglected Master," that points out Kuttner's significant influence on the genre. Catches his best short fiction, including "Mimsy Were the Borogoves" (SFHF), in which two children are taught advanced knowledge by toys accidentally lost from the future; "The Twonky," about a strange machine that looks like a console radio but acts as a monitor on its owner's behavior; "Two-Handed Engine," in which the infallible Furies, robot police who detect and execute murderers, are tricked by an official who reprograms them to cover up a killing, but who finds his guilt just as effective a jailer.

3-243. Kuttner, Henry, and C. L. Moore (as Lawrence O'Donnell). **Fury.** Grossett, 1950. Variant title: *Destination Infinity,* Avon, 1958.
Sam Harker is born an "immortal," a decadent breed of Venusian humans who live 1,000 years and stagnantly rule the underwater civilization colonized by Earth after it was poisoned by nuclear wars. Unfortunately, Sam is made igno-

rant of his heritage when he is surgically altered to resemble a commoner. Sam's frustrated drive forces colonization of the forbidding jungle surface of Venus, preserving survival initiative for humankind. Themes: natural selection works; human destiny is to fill the universe. Thoughtful development of Ben Bowman, computerlike prophet immortal who can extrapolate future but not interfere. An intelligent, albeit incorrect, setting of Venusian ecology. Transcends pulp fiction antecedents. Novel is a sequel to Kuttner's "Clash by Night." Compare Clarke's *City and the Stars* [3-98].

*3-244. Kuttner, Henry, and C. L. Moore (as Lewis Padgett). **Mutant.** Gnome, 1953.
Five stories, the 1945–1953 Baldy series from *Astounding,* that chronicle the history of a group of mutant telepaths and their struggle to survive in a world of inimical "normals." The invention of a device to induce telepathy in normal infants gives hope for an eventual reuniting of the race. Adversity overcome enables civilization to progress. Classic work in the emerging-telepath scenario. Compare Wyndham's *Re-Birth* [3-414] and Henderson's *Pilgrimage* [3-208].

3-245. Kuttner, Henry (as Lewis Padgett). **Robots Have No Tails.** Gnome, 1952.
Five 1943–1948 stories of Gallegher, the alcoholic, untrained inventor whose creative unconscious (Gallegher Plus) is unleashed when drunk, and Joe, his narcissistic robot with supersenses. Formula plots: Gallegher's unconscious self takes commissions for fantastic inventions and leaves his sober self in financial or legal trouble. A new binge leads to solution. Once highly touted as humorous SF, but the idea of creativity credited to alcohol and distorted image of science as product of eccentric, ignorant individual leaves sour taste today. Spots of social satire and wordplay are worthwhile. Compare with Bond's *Lancelot Biggs* [3-51].

3-246. Kuttner, Henry, and C. L. Moore. **Tomorrow and Tomorrow and The Fairy Chessman.** Gnome, 1951. Also published separately.
Two complexly plotted but superior short novels with grim and bitter dystopian views. *Tomorrow,* dating from 1947, presents a near future ruled by the dictatorial Global Peace Commission dedicated to the status quo. An underground tries to start an atomic war to blast civilization again into cultural and scientific progress. Compare Gunn's *The Burning* (Dell, 1972) and Leiber's *Gather, Darkness!* [3-250]. *Chessman* (variant titles: *Chessboard Planet,* Galaxy, 1956, and *The Far Reality,* World, 1963), first published in 1946, depicts a distant future of endless, meaningless war in which scientists are driven mad by the solution of a mysterious equation. Time travel, extratemporal perception, and fairy chess players constitute major elements of the tale. Compare Geston's *Out of the Mouth of the Dragon* [4-231].

3-247. Laumer, (John) Keith. **Envoy to New Worlds.** Ace, 1963.
Six stories from Retief series. Jaime Retief is space-going diplomat of low degree who cuts through bureaucratic red tape to successes his superiors cannot achieve. Allegedly derived from Laumer's own diplomatic career. Humorous and sometimes pointed satire and parody. Sequels include several additional collections

and novels. Compare Stableford's Halcyon Drift series (DAW, 1972) and Tubb's Dumarest stories [4-556].

3-248. Laumer, (John) Keith. **Worlds of the Imperium.** Ace, 1962.
Brion Bayard from Earth of the 1950s becomes the reluctant hero of a war between worlds parallel to his (and ours). In pursuit of his success, he meets himself. Related works are *The Other Side of Time* (Berkley, 1965), *Assignment in Nowhere* (Berkley, 1968), and *Beyond the Imperium* (1981). Upbeat pulp adventure; very popular. Compare Norman's *Tarnsman of Gor* [4-401].

*3-249. Leiber, Fritz (Reuter). **The Big Time.** Ace. 1961.
Part of the Change War series, written in the late 1950s and 1960s, about a vast war between the mysterious Snakes and Spiders fought by recruits from many species and many past and future times; the war's object is to alter past events in such a way that one side gains ultimate victory. *The Big Time* involves events in the Place, a Spider R & R center outside the cosmos, when the medical and entertainment staff becomes involved in an attempted mutiny led by a disillusioned time soldier. Dramatic staging, action, and dialogue are reminiscent of a play, as characters emotionally and verbally spin about in an intense, flowing narrative. A comment on the psychological aspects of war. *The Mind Spider* (Ace, 1961) contains other stories in the series. All associated pieces of the series are collected in *The Change War* (Gregg, 1978). Contrast with Asimov's *The End of Eternity* [3-18] and Le Guin's *The Lathe of Heaven* [4-326]. HW, 1958.

*3-250. Leiber, Fritz (Reuter). **Gather, Darkness!** Pellegrini & Cudahy, 1950.
In this 1943 story, Brother Jarles, a priest of the Hierarchy of the Church of the Great God, a religion firmly based on concealed technology, is caught up in a revolution conducted by "witches," underground scientists. Jarles's inner war of morality vs. duty is reflected by the witches' war against the misuse of science. Solid SF and the forerunner of later novels involving the role of religion and science. Compare del Rey's *The Eleventh Commandment* [3-139]; contrast Miller's *A Canticle for Leibowitz* [3-287] and Robert Heinlein's *Sixth Column* (1949).

3-251. Leiber, Fritz (Reuter). **The Green Millennium.** Abelard, 1953.
In a decadent United States, reminiscent of settings in Pohl and Kornbluth's *Gladiator-at-Law* [3-311] and Brunner's *Stand on Zanzibar* [4-92], two symbiotic species from Vega, one satyrlike, the other looking like green cats, secretly invade Earth. The cats exhale a pacifying, mood-elevating hormone and are aggressively sought by semilegitimate organized crime, the government, a religious cult, and Phil Gish, the story's average-guy hero. But the cats, in their self-assured feline way, "capture" not only the Earth, ending war and interpersonal violence, but the reader as well. Colorful, humorous entertainment despite an overly convoluted plot.

3-252. Leiber, Fritz (Reuter). **The Silver Eggheads.** Ballantine, 1962.
Of interest as a satire on writers, readers, publishers, and editors extrapolated from the worst practices in popular literature today; otherwise, minor Leiber. Comic at times, even biting, despite a contrived, ridiculous plot about the attempted use of encapsulated brains of ancient authors to produce books after the

destruction of all automated writing machines called "wordmills." Compare Biggle's "Tunesmith" [3-33], Malzberg's *Herovit's World* [4-356], and Leiber's own "The Night He Cried" (1953).

*3-253. Leiber, Fritz (Reuter). **The Wanderer.** Ballantine, 1964.
Common people are swept up in a worldwide disaster when the Wanderer, a mysterious purple-and-gold-surfaced planet, pulls into orbit next to the Earth. Gravitational effects rip the globe as the Wanderer breaks up the Moon for fuel and then suddenly vanishes, closely pursued by another planet-sized spaceship. Lots of characters, action, and catastrophe details in this heavily loaded, perhaps tongue-in-cheek novel. Superior Leiber. Compare Ashton's *Alas, That Great City* [3-15] and Wylie and Balmer's *When Worlds Collide* [2-146]; contrast Niven and Pournelle's *Lucifer's Hammer* [4-397]. HW, 1965.

*3-254. Leinster, Murray (pseud. of Will[iam] F[itzgerald] Jenkins). **The Best of Murray Leinster.** J. J. Pierce, ed. Ballantine, 1978.
Collection of 13 stories from 1934 to 1956, including "First Contact" (SFHF); "Sidewise in Time," the earliest; "Symbosis"; "The Power"; "Proxima Centauri"; and "Critical Difference," the latest.

*3-255. Leinster, Murray (pseud. of Will[iam] F[itzgerald] Jenkins). **Colonial Survey.** Gnome, 1957. Variant title: *The Planet Explorer*, Avon, 1957.
Bordman is colonial survey troubleshooter through four loosely linked chapters, saving new colony from disaster in each. Included is "Combat Team," about pioneer cooperation between humans and mutant kodiak bears, which won Hugo as "Exploration Team" in 1956. Each story set as problem to be solved. Compare Mitchison's *Memoirs of a Spacewoman* [3-288] and Barnes's *Interplanetary Hunter* [3-26].

3-256. Leinster, Murray (pseud. of Will[iam] F[itzgerald] Jenkins). **The Forgotten Planet.** Gnome, 1954.
Human castaways, culturally degenerated by harsh conditions on a world dominated by previously seeded insects and fungi, are rallied by a genius, Burl, who rediscovers technology and aggressiveness, compresses thousands of years of cultural evolution into a few days, and leads his band to a "natural" home on a temperate plateau. And all just in the nick of time to meet a visiting spaceship full of sportsmen. Based largely on 1926 and 1927 stories, and shows its age; author's claims of authenticity of insect behavior may be valid, but overall scientific accuracy, especially in cultural and behavioral sciences, is terrible. Basically, a blend of social Darwinism, great-man theory, and pop anthropology and entomology, in a plot too full of coincidences and underdeveloped characters. Surprisingly, the work remains absorbing and vivid, perhaps because it touches obsolete myths we still hold. Compare with Aldiss's *The Long Afternoon of Earth* [3-4] and Blish's "The Thing in the Attic" [3-47].

3-257. Leinster, Murray (as Will[iam] F[itzgerald] Jenkins, the author's true name). **The Murder of the U.S.A.** Crown, 1946.
America's cities are mysteriously destroyed by about 300 A-bombs. Lieutenant Sam Burton subsequently solves the mystery of what country did it (readers are

never told). Detective story with crime so big it becomes SF. Anticipates Bester's *Demolished Man* [3-30] and Wahlöö's *Steel Spring* (Delacorte, 1970). One of earlier A-bomb attack warning stories.

3-258. Leinster, Murray (pseud. of Will[iam] F[itzgerald] Jenkins). **The Pirates of Zan.** Ace. 1959. Includes Leinster's *The Mutant Weapon*, Ace, 1959.
Bron Hoddan leaves the space pirates of Zan to seek his fortune as an electrical engineer on civilized, stagnant Walden. But his innovations force him into exile on feudal Darth, where he hatches a scheme of mock-space piracy that not only makes him rich, but renews human social progress. Humorously satirizes static human societies and spoofs SF pulp conventions by making them seem plausible. Possible libretto source for SF equivalent of Gilbert and Sullivan. Contrast Gunn's *The Burning* (Dell, 1972). HN, 1960.

3-259. Lem, Stanislaw (Poland). **The Investigation.** Seabury, 1974. Tr. by Adele Milch of *'Sledztwo,* 1959.
Scotland Yard is confronted by the strange mystery of the dead moving and then walking away. Detective Gregory doubts it is supernatural and suspects the eccentric statistician Sciss—for the phenomenon's pattern suggests either ghoulish human activity or the existence of natural phenomena undreamed of in our philosophy. Finally, Gregory confronts the latter with all its psychic consequences. The story's familiar setting and form provide contrast to its central theme: our limited understanding of and discomfort with the unknown. Compare Sloane's *The Edge of Running Water* [2-102].

3-260. Lem, Stanislaw (Poland). **The Invincible.** Seabury, 1973. Tr. by Wendayne Ackerman of *Niezwyciezony,* 1964.
The spaceship *Invincible* lands on uninhabited Regis 111 to discover how its sister ship, the *Condor,* was defeated and its crew driven into infantile madness. It appears that abandoned machines have evolved through natural selection on Regis 111, giving rise to highly specialized mechanical life forms—which are beyond human efforts to defeat. Surface space opera with philosophical undercurrents. Compare Harrison's *Deathworld* [3-191].

*3-261. Lem, Stanislaw (Poland). **Solaris.** Walker, 1970. Tr. by Joanna Kilmartin and Steve Cox of *Solaris,* 1968.
Written in 1961. A planetwide ocean seems to have a life of its own as it twists itself into fantastic shapes and provides visions for Earth people to study. But its nature defies all Earth's ingenuity; a multitude of "solutions" are offered, none of which seem to fit. Humans can interpret the truly alien only in their own limited terms. A fascinating and philosophical work, highly original. Compare Blish's *A Case of Conscience* [3-42] and Dick's *Eye in the Sky* [3-141].

3-262. Lewis, C(live) S(taples) (U.K.). **The Dark Tower and Other Stories.** Collins. 1977.
Collection of six fiction pieces. The title story is a long fragment that apparently might have become a fourth volume in Lewis's Space Trilogy [3-263]. With this volume virtually all of his fantasy and SF-related pieces are now in print.

*3-263. Lewis, C(live) S(taples) (U.K.). **Out of the Silent Planet.** Bodley Head, 1938. **Perelandra.** Bodley Head, 1943. Variant title: *Voyage to Venus,* Pan, 1953. **That Hideous Strength.** Bodley Head. 1945. Abridged version: *The Tortured Planet,* Avon, 1958.
The three novels form a "Space Trilogy" featuring the symbolically named Ransom, who goes to Mars from Earth, the Silent Planet, to find preternatural Martian society; then to Venus, Perelandra, to find human life beginning on that planet; then back to Earth to guide the battle against the forces of evil symbolized by the atheistic scientism, "hideous strength," of the modern university. The medieval magician Merlin is resurrected to neutralize the evil and preserve humankind for *caritas*—God as the expression of awesome divine love. The narrative is often tedious and clogged, but stories are rich fusion of philological theory, medieval and Arthurian legend (the "Matter of Britain"), and sophisticated Christian theology and philosophy. Enormously popular since its publication. Compare J. R. R. Tolkien's *Lord of the Rings.*

3-264. Long, Frank Belknap. **The Early Long.** Doubleday, 1975.
A stalwart of the golden age, over his 50-year career Long has produced more than 500 works ranging from poetry, through fantasy, to science fiction, and nonfiction. The 17 stories (1924–1944) here represent only a narrow portion of his range and output, but are worthwhile anyway, with effort ranging from Lovecraft-type works such as "The Hounds of Tindalos" and "The Space Eaters"—for which Long is best known—to the more traditional SF of "The Flame Midget" and "The Census Taker," in which the therapeutic dreams of people in another universe impinge on people in our own. Also of interest is "Dark Vision," a 1939 Freudian story about a man accidently shocked into a telepathy capable of receiving the subconscious, and his consequent terror.

3-265. Lundberg, Knud. **The Olympic Hope.** Stanley Paul, 1958.
A novel about the use of science and drugs to assist athletes of the 1996 Olympics. Perhaps implausible when written, but prescient in retrospect.

3-266. MacDonald, John D(ann). **Ballroom of the Skies.** Greenberg, 1952.
Extraterrestrial interference explains all the troubles humans have in trying unsuccessfully to create a rational civilization—warless and humane. Humankind is deliberately kept in internal conflict to force into prominence the future leaders of Earth. A "we-are-not-alone" imaginative exercise in a paranoid and incipiently sinister mood. Compare Card's *A Planet Called Treason* [4-110].

3-267. MacDonald, John D(ann). **The Girl, the Gold Watch, and Everything.** Fawcett, 1962.
A comic parable about the use of power obtained by a "watch" that speeds up time for its owners so that, at a ratio of about one-half hour to a second, the watch owner "lives" and moves at invisible speed—granting virtual omnipotence. Nice power fantasy. Compare Gerrold's more complex and downbeat *The Man Who Folded Himself* [4-229].

3-268. MacDonald, John D(ann). **Wine of the Dreamers.** Greenberg, 1951. Variant title: *Planet of the Dreamers,* Pocket Books, 1953.
A well-spun yarn of the world of 1975 exhibiting familiar insanity. The explana-

tion is that human irrational behavior is manipulated, inadvertently, by telepathic dreamers from another world. When the dreamers learn this, life on Earth takes a turn for the better. Compare Le Guin's *The Lathe of Heaven* [4-326].

3-269. Maine, Charles Eric (pseud. of David McIlwain) (U.K.). **Count-Down.** Hodder, 1959. U.S. title: *Fire Past the Future,* Ballantine, 1960.
Mystery and SF elements blend in a suspenseful Ten Little Indians tale of successive murders among isolated scientists counting down the launch of an antigravity spaceship. Mind-controlling time traveler is the villain, sent back to prevent human discovery of time travel. Pseudoscience mishmash about Lorentz-Fitzgerald equations cannot be taken seriously, nor can the scientific conceptual breakthrough by the nonscientist hero of the story. Compare Temple's *Shoot at the Moon* (Whitney & Wheaton, 1966).

3-270. Manvell, Roger (U.K.). **The Dreamers.** Gollancz, 1958.
Jane Fettes, postmistress for village 40 miles from London, is hypnotically programmed with dream by African tribesman whose wife was allowed to die by Dr. Morgan in Africa. Morgan is now village resident. Dream is designed to kill Morgan with fear after it is passed from person to person to him. Morgan is saved by a journalist and Dr. King, an African visiting London as specialist in tribal occultism. Solution is through a séance, but details for a behavioral explanation are provided by narrative. A subtle and exotic SF gimmick. Compare Condon's *Manchurian Candidate* [3-118].

3-271. March, William. **The Bad Seed.** Holt, 1954.
Rhoda Penmark is a beautiful eight-year-old child of "bad" parents who has somehow inherited a consummately evil nature from them. Her great intelligence enables her to maintain a front of perfect virtue while she does secret evil, including murder, her nature undiscovered at end of a suspenseful story. Very popular despite scientifically invalid doctrine of inherited evil. Contrast Ira Levin's *Rosemary's Baby* (1967) and Blatty's *The Exorcist* (1971), where the supernatural cause of evil replaces the now discredited pseudogenetics of *Seed.*

3-272. Martinson, Harry (Edmund) (Sweden). **Aniara.** Knopf. 1963. Tr. by Hugh MacDiarmid and E. Hurley Schubert of *Aniara,* 1956.
An epic poem. *Aniara* is the name of a spaceship from Earth running out of control into the depths of space, carrying its passengers into a years-long contemplation of the meaning of matter and humanity in the universe. The work is noteworthy especially because the author won the Nobel prize in literature in 1974, although the Swedish critic Richard L. McKinney says the translation is atrocious. Compare Diane Ackerman's poetic epic, *The Planets: A Cosmic Pastoral* (Morrow, 1976).

3-273. Matheson, Richard (Barton). **Born of Man and Woman.** Chamberlain, 1954. Variant title: *Third from the Sun,* Bantam, 1955; drops four stories, including "The Traveller."
Seventeen fantasy, horror, and SF stories, from 1950 to 1954, the best of early Matheson. Horror and SF are blended in the title story (SFHF), where a monstrous offspring plots revenge against its parents who keep it chained in the cel-

lar, and in "Lover When You're Near Me," in which an ugly alien female with ESP powers forces her love on a terrorized Earthman. More philosophic are "Third from the Sun," about a family and their neighbors fleeing their world in a stolen spaceship on the eve of total war, and "The Traveller," in which a time traveler visits the crucifixion and gains a faith based not on physical miracles, but on Jesus's willingness to die for his beliefs. Compare and contrast with the works of John Collier and Ray Bradbury.

*3-274. Matheson, Richard (Barton). **I Am Legend.** Fawcett, 1954.
Classic scare story of a disease that causes a kind of vampirism, whose victims rise from graves and flee light. Finally, a lone survivor, barricaded against the undead, goes forth by day to destroy the vampires. He becomes a symbol of fear to them and the basis of a new myth. Reversal of *Dracula*. Terror and meaning of novel did not survive translation into two screenplays. Compare Williamson's *Darker Than You Think* [3-401].

3-275. Matheson, Richard (Barton). **The Shrinking Man.** Fawcett, 1956.
Strange radiation causes a man to shrink; good depiction of his personal and family problems as he diminishes. Eventually becoming trapped in his own basement, he defeats a spider in a climactic scene and goes forth to face the unknown. Fascinating story with meticulous detail. Basis for fair SF film. Contrast John Aylesworth's *Fee, Fei, Foo, Fum* (Avon, 1963); compare Lindsay Gutteridge's *Cold War in a Country Garden* (Putnam, 1971).

3-275A. McCann, Edison (pseud. of Lester del Rey and Frederik Pohl). **Preferred Risk.** Simon & Schuster, 1955. Ballantine, 1980, reissue adds an afterword on the collaboration.
Governments have withered, leaving all power in the hands of a ubiquitous, ultimate insurance company, symbol for welfare society, which has insured against everything and eliminated social ills to keep from paying claims. But the costs of utopia are the usurpation of power by a dictatorial Underwriter and the end of progress due to the elimination of risk. Thomas Wills is the stock rebel, manipulated first by the perverted company to spy on misguided revolutionaries, then by the underground to explode an air-poisoning cobalt bomb in a naïve attempt to bankrupt the company. Of course he vanquishes the villain and humbly undertakes the initiation of a U.S.-type balance of power, democratic world government as Earth's frozen-down millions escape the fallout in company vaults. Morals: power corrupts; and administrative politics and economics must be separated. Good example of liberal ideology in SF; contrast Rand's *Atlas Shrugged* [3-316] and Reynolds's *Looking Backward from the Year 2000* [4-439]. Winner of a Galaxy–Simon & Schuster $6,500 prize.

3-276. McHugh, Vincent. **I Am Thinking of My Darling.** Simon & Schuster, 1943.
Jim Rowan searches for his actress wife, Niobe, even as New York is stricken by epidemic fever that releases inhibitions and causes nonviolent chaos in the community. A tragicomic analysis of the principles of social change, as cure is found

and the Rowans are reunited at the end of the strange week. Compare Frank's *Mr. Adam* [3-167].

3-277. McIntosh, J. T. (pseud. of James Murdock MacGregor) (U.K.). **The Fittest.** Doubleday, 1955. Variant title: *The Rule of the Pagbeasts,* Fawcett, 1956.
Scientist Paget's experiments heighten animal intelligence, and some—dogs, rats, and cats—escape. These "paggets" destroy civilization, forcing humans into a desperate Darwinian fight for survival. Despite these catastrophes, the work is optimistic. Humans have what it takes to overcome any problem eventually. Excellent action story. Compare Wyndham's *The Day of the Triffids* [3-411].

*3-278. McIntosh, J. T. (pseud. of James Murdock MacGregor) (U.K.). **One in Three Hundred.** Doubleday, 1954.
The Sun is going nova and humans can survive only by migrating to Mars. However, there are only a limited number of spaceships, and of these only a small number can actually reach Mars. Once there, the environment and internal strife threaten the few remaining survivors. The survival process is Darwinian, but the outcome is upbeat. Compare Wylie and Balmer's *When Worlds Collide* [2-146].

*3-279. McKenna, Richard M(ilton). **Casey Agonistes and Other Science Fiction and Fantasy Stories.** Harper, 1973.
Five of McKenna's best stories, from 1958 to 1967, and an introduction by Damon Knight. Stories of true manhood, humanhood, and de Chardin-like evolution: powerful "Casey Agonistes," where dying men create a clownish red ape in a collective fantasy; "Hunter, Come Home," with men trying to destroy a planet's biosystem as a test of their manhood; "The Secret Place" (HN, 1967; NW, 1966), about the games boys play; "Mine Own Ways," where man makes himself; and the exquisite "Fiddler's Green," with its strange world created by seven men lost at sea. Contrast Anderson's *Time and Stars* [3-13] and *Seven Conquests* (1969).

3-280. Mead, Harold (U.K.). **The Bright Phoenix.** M. Joseph, 1955.
The account of John Waterville, citizen and explorer of post–World War II "perfect" Socialist state, who leads colonization of new territory by genetically selected colonists (he's not one). Arrogant colonists are destroyed by indigenous inhabitants. Waterville is befriended by inhabitants but has tragic love affair. Unfortunately, human predicament is warring one; denial of this exacerbates the problem. Deft scene-setting and excellent characterization. Compare Orwell's *Nineteen Eighty-Four* [3-302], Russell's *The Great Explosion* [3-321], and Kornbluth's *The Syndic* [3-240].

3-281. Mead, Shepherd. **The Big Ball of Wax.** Simon & Schuster, 1954.
Clever satire and SF by the author of *How to Succeed in Business without Really Trying.* Lanny Martin, momma's boy and middle-level executive of monopolist conglomerate, Con Chem, tells how he and his company turned the spiritually revolutionary mind-altering device that allows users to "become" other people at will to reassuringly commercial applications. Madison Avenue ingenuity can be depended upon to subvert all possibility of human progress in the direction of a totalitarian consumer state. Martin's shallow and disarming ingenuousness perfectly contrasts with the appalling slavery implied in the commercial state de-

picted in the story. Constantly inventive. Compare Huxley's *Brave New World* [2-47], Vonnegut's *Player Piano* [3-392], Pohl and Kornbluth's *The Space Merchants* [3-313], and Compton's *Synthajoy* [4-145].

3-282. Merril, Judith. **The Best of Judith Merril.** Warner, 1976.
Collection of nine stories and two poems from 1948 to 1974, including "That Only a Mother" (SFHF), the earliest, "Dead Center," "Whoever You Are," "Daughters of Earth," "The Lady Was a Tramp," and the latest, "In the Land of Unblind," a prose poem, as is "Auction Pit." In "Stormy Weather," a typical story, a young telepathic woman operating a space station may have mistimed a bomb fired to destroy a dangerous cloud of space debris because she can't contact her telepathic boyfriend and fears their relationship is over. Sentimental content, good writing, but dated today due to its sex role stereotypes. Introduction by Merril's old friend, Virginia Kidd. Contrast stories by Leigh Brackett [3-59].

3-283. Merril, Judith. **Daughters of Earth.** Gollancz, 1968.
Three stories from the 1950s that illustrate Merril's sensitive and competent approach to "female" SF subjects. The title story is a chronology of six generations of women who ride the crest of humanity's space exploration; emphasizes their emotional responses as generations alternately pursue security and pioneering. The male hero of "Project Nursemaid," a military psychologist, confronts his own inner emotional turmoil as he counsels women giving up their embryonic children to an experimental space program, selects other women to raise these children, and struggles to protect the program's integrity and the children's future. In "Homecalling," a castaway girl and her baby brother develop a relationship with an intelligent insectlike female alien who heads a matriarchal society; a tender, insightful story that upholds the universality of motherhood. Contrast with the modern feminist viewpoint in Russ's *The Female Man* [4-458].

*3-284. Merril, Judith. **Shadow on the Hearth.** Doubleday, 1950. British issue, Roberts & Vinter, 1966, is revised.
Atomic catastrophe novels tend to focus on the large-scale collapse of civilization, with isolated bands of survivors stumbling through radioactive rubble. This novel of the early atomic age focuses on a suburban housewife and her family when New York City is bombed. The terror is intensified by being experienced through the eyes of the mother and her two young children, one of whom is the probable victim of radiation sickness (the shadow of the title). As the utilities fail, the voices on the telephone cease, and radio announcements impersonally document the dissolution of their world, the family attempts to cope. The understated tone makes this novel especially effective. Aired on television as *Atomic Attack*. Compare Stewart's *Earth Abides* [3-358] and Shute's *On the Beach* [3-344].

3-285. Miller, P(eter) Schuyler. **The Titan.** Fantasy, 1952.
Eight stories dating from the 1930s and 1940s. An uneven collection; superior works include the long title story based on an unfinished 1935 serial about an Earthman marooned on Mars and kept in a zoo as a Star-Beast until he joins a revolt of the Martian lower class and gives his life. Also of note are the 1944 time paradox story "As Never Was," about archaeologists who explore the future; and

"Old Man Mulligan," a 30,000-year-old Neanderthal who uses his knowledge to overcome a gang of kidnappers on a watery, frontier Venus; both stories reflect Miller's interest in anthropology.

3-286. Miller, Walter M(ichael), Jr. **The Best of Walter M. Miller, Jr.** Pocket Books, 1980.
Collection of 14 stories from 1951 to 1957, all those included in *Conditionally Human* (Ballantine, 1962) and *View from the Stars* (Ballantine, 1964), plus two others. Highlights are "The Darfstellar" (HW, 1955), "You Triflin' Skunk!," "The Big Hunger," "Anybody Else Like Me?," and "Crucifixus Etiam." *The Science Fiction Stories of Walter M. Miller, Jr.* (Gregg, 1978) not only contains the two earlier collections cited, but has an introduction by David Samuelson. Miller brings a depth of character and richness of meaning to SF unusual for the times, and, with them, bridges the gulf from the pulps to the mainstream. Compare Bester's [3-31] and Sturgeon's short stories of the 1950s [such as 3-359, 3-361].

*3-287. Miller, Walter M(ichael), Jr. **A Canticle for Leibowitz.** Lippincott, 1960.
Story begins 600 years after World War III, going through new dark ages, renaissance, and modern times, ending with onset of World War IV—even though interstellar travel has been achieved. Thesis: future history will recapitulate past history, repeating its tragic failure. Fortuitously, the Roman Catholic Church has a hand in next 2,000 years as it had in past 2,000. Brilliant, often satiric transformation of the history of Western civilization, focused by 1,800 years of vicissitudes of life at Abbey Leibowitz, where civilization's sources were preserved after World War III. No short comment can convey work's excellence. Named by many as best SF novel of modern period. Compare Huxley's *Ape and Essence* [3-220], Merle's *Malevil* [4-376], and Roberts's *Pavane* [4-444]. HW, 1961.

3-288. Mitchison, Naomi (Margaret Haldane) (U.K.). **Memoirs of a Spacewoman.** Gollancz, 1962.
Picaresque story of a "communicator," specialist in identifying and communicating with alien life forms. What "lives" and "thinks" will surprise humankind. Modes of communication will be bizarre. Fitful lapses in novel's continuity more than offset by brilliantly ingenious constructs of those we will meet and how we will "talk" with them. Compare Cole's *The Philosophical Corps* [3-116] and Weinbaum's *Martian Odyssey* [2-125].

*3-289. Moore, C(atherine) L. **The Best of C. L. Moore.** Nelson Doubleday, 1975.
Ten stories from 1933 to 1946 selected by Lester del Rey that catch Moore's best early SF; also includes del Rey's biographical sketch of Moore and an afterword by her. Top stories: "The Bright Illusion" (1934), a human-alien love story that transcends the flesh; "No Woman Born" (1944), a variant on the Frankenstein theme about the transplantation of a burned beautiful woman's brain into an extraordinary metal body and her emerging superhumanness; "Vintage Season" (1946, SFHF), about jaded visitors from the future who return to view historic catastrophes and their disdainful treatment of a man who discovers their secret.

Contains the popular "Shambleau," one of several tales featuring Northwest Smith, one of her popular pulp characters.

3-290. Moore, C(atherine) L. **Judgment Night.** Gnome, 1952.
Vintage space opera set in a galactic empire, assembled from five long narratives from 1943 to 1950, including "Judgment Night," "The Code," "Paradise Street," "Promised Land," and "Heir Apparent." Compare Smith's Lensman series [3-355].

3-291. Moore, Ward. **Bring the Jubilee.** Farrar, 1953.
Hodgins McCormick, historian, lives in an alternate United States in which everything from major wars to minor inventions such as the typewriter are different or happened otherwise. This is due to the South having won the Battle of Gettysburg (and the Civil War), a "fact" changed by McCormick when he time travels back to the moment of the battle. By 1877 he has written a narrative of his lost alternate future—the "text" of this novel, a lost manuscript. Excellent and ingenious transformation of real history. Compare Finney's *Time and Again* [4-214] and Kantor's *If the South Had Won the Civil War* [3-224].

3-292. Moore, Ward. **Greener Than You Think.** Sloane, 1947.
Miss Francis perfects a chemical that enables plants to transform any material directly for growth. Albert Weener chronicles its application until "grass" has obliterated everything on Earth. Meanwhile, humanity, in the form of government and industry, fiddles while doomsday arrives. Good satire. Compare Wyndham's *The Day of the Triffids* [3-411] and Disch's *The Genocides* [4-185]; contrast Christopher's *No Blade of Grass* [3-92].

3-293. Mrozek, Slawomir (Poland). **The Ugupu Bird.** Macdonald. 1968. Tr. by Konrad Syrop of *Wesele w atomicach*, 1959.
Seventeen stories and vignettes, including the title work, a parable on the interconnectedness of the ecosystem; "Ad Astra," a parable of conflict between traditional and modern writers; and "Escape Southward," employing *Waiting for Godot* as springboard for evolutionary parable on humankind, the evolving cousin of the Yeti or Abominable Snowman. Nakedly mythic and archetypal, tightly constructed narratives told independently of a communist ideological context. Compare G. B. Shaw's *Far-Fetched Fables* (1950).

3-294. Nathan, Robert. **Portrait of Jennie.** Knopf, 1940.
This sentimental story became a 1949 movie starring Joseph Cotton and Jennifer Jones. "Jennie" is a beautiful woman displaced in time. An emotionally powerful love tale, rejuvenated in the more recent film *Somewhere in Time*, starring Christopher Reeves. Compare Finney's *Time and Again* [4-214].

3-295. Nearing, Homer, Jr. **The Sinister Researches of C. P. Ransom.** Doubleday, 1954.
Eleven stories loosely linked as novel of Professor Ransom, mathematician, and Professor Tate, philosopher, who try to develop breakthrough for linking arts and sciences. Their successes are Pyrrhic; Ransom finally wins Superman award from Nietzsche Society for extraordinary inventions, and so on. The gentlest of

science-fantasy humorous nonsense. Compare Weinbaum's "Professor Van Manderpootz" stories in *Martian Odyssey* [2-125].

3-296. Nesvadba, Josef (Czechoslovakia). **The Lost Face: Best Science Fiction from Czechoslovakia.** Taplinger, 1971. Tr. by Iris Urwin. British issue, *In the Footsteps of the Abominable Snowman* (Gollancz, 1970), lacks two stories of the U.S. edition.
Eight stories by a Czech physician, including title story about plastic surgeon who helps a criminal escape with a brilliant face-lift; "In the Footsteps of the Abominable Snowman," about the contrast between a life in nature and a life according to reason; and "The Death of an Apeman," about the possibility that an ape might be as human as a human. Fine parables, with humorous notes, in search of the definition of humanity in an age of science, reason, and the modern world's turmoil. Compare Vercors's *You Shall Know Them* [3-388].

3-297. Neville, Kris (Ottman). **Bettyann.** Tower, 1970.
Based on stories originally published in 1951 and 1954, a sensitive, touching, at times Bradbury-like tale of an unintentionally abandoned orphan alien infant raised as a crippled human girl. Growing up, Bettyann searches for her identity, while her people, a dying race, return to search for her. Learning of her heritage, she chooses to remain on her adopted Earth. An underrated work. Sequel: "Bettyann's Children" in *Demon Kind*, Roger Elwood, ed., Avon, 1973. Makes a sharp contrast with Wyndham's *The Midwich Cuckoos* [3-413].

3-298. Nourse, Alan E(dward). **Tiger by the Tail and Other Science Fiction Stories.** McKay, 1961. British title: *Beyond Infinity*.
Collection of nine stories from 1951 to 1961, including the title story, "Nightmare Brother," "Love Thy Vimp," and "Family Resemblance," which makes the comic case that humans evolved from pig stock, not the primates. Nourse does humor well; stories often contain little morals. Compare stories by Robert Sheckley.

3-299. Oliver, Chad. **Another Kind.** Ballantine, 1955.
Seven stories, including "Rite of Passage," about how "primitive" civilization can be far more advanced than high technologies; "Scientific Method," an ingenious first-contact story; and "Night," about an American Indian who prepares a primitive planet against the rapine of colonization by Earth. Fascinating anthropological epitomes; termed by Anthony Boucher the outstanding SF book of 1955.

3-300. Oliver, Chad. **The Edge of Forever.** Sherbourne, 1971.
Six stories of "anthropological science fiction" from 1952 to 1959. "Transfusion" is about the seeding of Earth with humankind; another story of interest is the poignant "Didn't He Ramble," in which a rich jazz buff recreates an asteroid Storyville, complete with android musicians and live call girls, to escape his mundane life on Earth. Also includes biographical sketch of Oliver and checklist of his works by William F. Nolan. Clean, expository narrative by a writer who deserves more popularity.

3-301. Oliver, Chad. **Shadows in the Sun.** Ballantine, 1954.
Paul Ellery, anthropologist, discovers that Jefferson City, Texas, is a galactic

alien colony, negotiates with the aliens for possible membership in galactic civilization, and finally decides to stay on Earth as a small part of Earth's attempt to mature its civilization so it may be part of galactic society. Oliver's background in anthropology is ingeniously mined for the story. Contrast Simak's *Way Station* [3-349].

*3-302. Orwell, George (pseud. of Eric Arthur Blair) (U.K.). **Nineteen Eighty-Four.** Secker, 1949. A useful version is Irving Howe's *Orwell's Nineteen Eighty-Four: Text, Sources, Criticism* (Harcourt, 1963; 2nd ed., 1982).
Mentioning *1984* in SF area is like mentioning the Bible. The title marks the triumph of the totalitarian state. Three superpowers divide the world and conduct sham wars. Newspeak is official, insidious language used to propagate lies. Big Brother polices you through two-way TV in your quarters. Romance is forbidden, sex a political act. Personal opinion is neutralized by brainwashing. Life is hell. One of the half-dozen most influential novels of the twentieth century. Influence on SF of social criticism is incalculable. Compare Zamiatin's *We* [2-147] and Burgess's *Clockwork Orange* [3-82]. Burgess specifically responded to *1984* in his own *1985* (Little, Brown, 1978). Part I is a severe critical analysis of Orwell's novel; Part II is a fictional rejoinder, providing what Burgess thinks is a more plausible scenario. A mock—but serious—self-interview concludes *1985*. Another "sequel" is *1985* by Gyorgy Dalos [4-160].

3-303. Pangborn, Edgar. **Davy.** St. Martin's, 1964.
On island Neonarcheos, Davy writes memoirs of life in medieval United States 300 years after nuclear holocaust, as he grows from "bondsman" to explorer interested in resuming the ascent of the human species. Davy is a Tom Jones character (HN, 1965; NN, 1964). Set in the world of *Davy* is the prequel work *The Company of Glory* (Pyramid, 1975). Compare Miller's *A Canticle for Leibowitz* [3-287] and Roberts's *Pavane* [4-444]. *Still I Persist in Wondering* (Dell, 1978) is a collection of seven stories from the early 1970s associated with Pangborn's novel *Davy*. The bibliography of Pangborn's works included in this volume does not list his novella, "Mount Charity" (NN, 1971).

*3-304. Pangborn, Edgar. **A Mirror for Observers.** Doubleday, 1954.
For thousands of years, Martian observers chronicle and gently manipulate human history, optimistic for its destiny. Elmis (Miles), Martian, narrates life of Angelo (Abraham), human genius and potential initiator of great age of ethics for humankind, who must elude influence of bad Martian Namir and does. There is hope for humanity in its Gandhi and Martin Luther King figures. Characterization of Angelo inspirational almost as latter-day saint's life. Contrast Vonnegut's *The Sirens of Titan* [3-393]. IFA winner, 1955.

3-305. Pangborn, Edgar. **West of the Sun.** Doubleday, 1953.
An exploring starship crash-lands on another planet. The explorers form a utopian colony including members of two vastly different sentient native species. Dilemma when a rescue ship comes, but all choose to remain and abandon the tyranny of Earth government. Pangborn's first novel. Good characterization, literate narrative. Compare Edmund Cooper's *A Far Sunset* (1967) and Russell's *The Great Explosion* [3-321].

3-306. Phillips, Mark (pseud. of Randall Garrett and Laurence M. Janifer). **Brain Twister.** Pyramid. 1962.
A "let's find the telepaths among us" story. FBI agent Kenneth Malone heads the search and finds seven, including Miss Thompson, an old lady who is Queen Elizabeth of England and "immortal." All were found in asylums. Only Thompson is not totally insane. Story is soapish and superficially esoteric in references to Elizabethan society. Sequels: *Supermind* (Pyramid, 1963) and *The Impossibles* (Pyramid, 1963). Compare Robinson's *The Power* [3-318] and Blish's *Jack of Eagles* [3-46]. HN, 1960.

3-307. Piper, H(enry) Beam. **Federation.** Ace, 1981.
Five stories of an overly neglected Campbell author whose career (1947–1964) was cut short by suicide. In a long introduction John F. Carr describes a grand "Terro-Human Future History" underlying most of Piper's works, a conclusion not generally shared among SF scholars to date. Some of these stories unquestionably fit within Piper's Federation series, including the noted "Omnilingual" (1957), about a woman archaeologist's persistence in deciphering a scientific "Rosetta stone" of a long-dead Martian culture. Also of interest is "Oomphel in the Sky" (1960), a Federation story set in the conflict between statist Terra and the freer colonial worlds of Kwann, in which the natives are pacified by a religious scam built around the "Oomphel-Mother."

3-308. Piper, H(enry) Beam. **Little Fuzzy.** Avon, 1962.
In *Little Fuzzy*, Jack Holloway, in opposition to commercial interests, proves the lovable Fuzzies are sapient. A charming exploration of the question "Who is human?" The Fuzzies are a notable example of sympathetic aliens (HN, 1963). Sequels are *The Other Human Race* (Avon, 1964; variant title: *Fuzzy Sapiens*, Ace, 1976) and *Fuzzies and Other People* (Ace, 1984), which continue the "colonizer vs. native" theme of the first volume. Fuzzies have become ever more popular among SF fans, generating spin-off books as "Star Trek" did; see *Fuzzy Bones* (Ace, 1981) by William Tuning and *Golden Dream: A Fuzzy Odyssey* (Ace, 1982) by Ardath Mayhar. Compare the "tweel" stories of Weinbaum's *Martian Odyssey* [2-125], Anderson and Dickson's *Earthman's Burden* [3-9], and Vercors's *You Shall Know Them* [3-388].

*3-309. Pohl, Frederik. **The Best of Frederik Pohl.** Lester del Rey, ed. Nelson Doubleday, 1975.
Sixteen stories, selected by Lester del Rey, originally published between 1954 and 1967. Includes "The Midas Plague" (SFHF), a classic warning about superabundance; "Day Million," a future-shocking love story; "The Census Takers," whose job is killing surplus people in an overcrowded world; and "The Day the Martians Came," a pointed statement on racism. Also includes an overview of Pohl's career by del Rey and an afterword by Pohl on the genesis of several of the stories. A basic Pohl sampler.

3-310. Pohl, Frederik. **Drunkard's Walk.** Ballantine, 1960.
Cornut, teacher and mathematician, fights off suicidal impulses to discover that humans have been ruled by a handful of telepathic "immortals" who seek to prevent the species from discovering that it, too, is telepathic. Mild inebriation is in-

terim safeguard against immortals' mental control. Story is a metaphor for exploitation of humankind by conspiracy of elite. Compare Blish's *Jack of Eagles* [3-46] and del Rey's *Pstalemate* (Putnam, 1971).

3-311. Pohl, Frederik, and C. M. Kornbluth. **Gladiator-at-Law.** Ballantine, 1955.
Derivative of *The Space Merchants* [3-313]; the United States is dominated by monopoly capitalism, primarily under the control of Green, Charlesworth, an ancient couple in giant test tubes who date from Lincoln's time. There is a two-class system, with the affluent living in marvelous G-M-L Homes available only by contract to employees of major companies, and the poor living in Belly Rave, today's suburbs turned to slums. Lawyer Charles Mundin fights, both in a Roman-type arena and in the stock market, for love and for control of G-M-L Homes so that all can have good housing. Well-developed and interesting social background, but the story's solution, the replacing of bad company heads by good ones, seems a weak reed with which to shore up an otherwise strong attack on the economic order. Compare Brunner's *Stand on Zanzibar* [4-92].

3-312. Pohl, Frederik. **Slave Ship.** Ballantine, 1957.
The Vietnamese, driven by religious fervor, conquer nearly the entire Eastern Hemisphere; the United Nations, including the United States, are totally mobilized against them. Communication with animals is developed for use in the war, and naval Lieutenant Logan Miller is sent on a last-ditch mission, using a submarine crewed by animals, to find a secret enemy weapon that threatens to tip the stalemate so much that nuclear war is inevitable. But the enemy is itself reeling under the weapon—an alien life form attracted by telepaths—and this discovery ends the war. Full of neat futurist ideas, like most Pohl novels, but not his best writing. A note on the science of animal communications is included. Contrast Merle's *The Day of the Dolphin* (Simon & Schuster, 1969).

*3-313. Pohl, Frederik, and C. M. Kornbluth. **The Space Merchants.** Ballantine, 1953.
Advertising is king in a near-future United States dominated by monopoly capitalism and divided into a small, relatively affluent professional and business class and a large class of poor industrial serfs and captive consumers. Against this well-developed background, "star-class copysmith" Mitchell Courtenay heads his firm's campaign to sell the difficult colonization of Venus to the public. But enemies shanghai Courtenay, forcing him to work as a laborer; unrepentant, he uses the underground of a persecuted environmentalist group (the Conservationists or Consies) to regain his former position. But the love of his Consie wife and the knowledge that big business doesn't play by the rules causes him to lose his idealism; Mitch joins the underground and absconds with the Venus rocket in the hope of saving that planet from human exploitation. A fine satire on advertising, and strong social commentary, but its ending begs the question. Sequel is *The Merchant's War* (St. Martin's, 1984). Both were collected as *Venus, Inc.* (Nelson Doubleday, 1986). Contrast Brunner's *The Sheep Look Up* [4-90].

3-314. Pohl, Frederik, and C. M. Kornbluth. **Wolfbane.** Ballantine, 1959. Baen, 1986, issue substantially revised.

Perhaps the most atypical novel by these creative collaborators; Oriental religion, Western technology, and social Darwinism are blended in a Campbell-like tale of Earth's removal from orbit by alien, pyramid-shaped robots who use the malnourished, culturally involuted human survivors as food-producing machine components. Of course, a maverick human makes a revolution, destroys the pyramids, and again finds the path of human progress. Unless intended as a Coblentz-type satire-cum-SF-parody, the work suffers from numerous writing faults: a redundant, overly slow first half; a too-compressed second half; numerous hanging threads, problems of motivation, and typos that invite a thorough rewrite. Compare Russell's *Sinister Barrier* [3-323].

*3-315. Rand, Ayn. **Anthem.** Cassell, 1938. Abridged in the Caxton, 1946, issue. Written in 1937. In far future after world war, all trace and memory of the concept "I" are abolished in a collectivist dystopia. Then Equality 7-2521, a genius, rediscovers electricity, is condemned to death by Council of Scholars, and escapes with beautiful woman to forest. He discovers "I" with her; renames himself Prometheus and vows to gather new society of self-conscious people once more. Parable of Rand's once enormously influential "objectivism." The individual is all. Narrative is fiery, moralistic, and polished. Compare Silverberg's *A Time of Changes* [4-510].

3-316. Rand, Ayn. **Atlas Shrugged.** Random, 1957.

John Galt and cohorts embrace "objectivist" philosophy, withdrawing from world that does not appreciate their independent genius and towering ambition. Civilization crumbles, while in their mountain retreat the objectivists prepare to rebuild it with their vision in control. *Atlas* is vehicle for Rand's famous philosophy of ruthlessly rational individualism. Long speeches and multiple subplots make long, intellectually melodramatic book. Compare Heinlein's *Stranger in a Strange Land* [3-207].

3-317. Reynolds, Mack. **The Best of Mack Reynolds.** Pocket Books, 1976.

Collection of 22 stories from 1950 to 1975. Earliest is "Down the River." Others of note are "Pacifist," "Revolution," "Compounded Interest," "The Business, as Usual," and "Fad." Autobiographical introduction by the author, a long-time left-wing political activist. Stories reflect social concerns. For example, in "Pacifist" (1964), a Merril year's-best [3-449] pick, a secret antiwar terrorist group tries to force peace by murder, kidnapping, and intimidation; an operative tires of the killing and risks his own life, but the cause, if not perfect, is still just. Compare Brunner's "The Inception of the Epoch of Mrs. Bedonebyasyoudid" (1971).

3-318. Robinson, Frank M(alcolm). **The Power.** Lippincott, 1956.

A psi-emerging story. Tanner and Nordlund are among some psychologists testing for telekinesis. The "power" exists, but who has it? Nordlund (Adam Hart) does, and tries to keep it to himself. Tanner hunts the power holder, miraculously escaping many near-fatal "accidents" secretly caused by Nordlund. He has Nordlund killed after realizing that he, Tanner, has power too; it takes a superman to catch a superman. Story ends with Tanner contemplating fun of playing god. First-rate adventure yarn; basis for fair SF film. Compare Blish's *Jack of Eagles* [3-46] and Pohl's *Drunkard's Walk* [3-310].

3-319. Roshwald, Mordecai (Israel). **Level 7.** McGraw-Hill, 1959.
Officer X-127, of an undisclosed nationality, writes a diary recording his fateful duties and short life in the deepest level of a 4,200-foot bomb shelter—Level 7— where he helps fire the missiles and then chronicles the gradual destruction of the upper levels down to his own. An unoriginal awful-warning story. Recommended by Bertrand Russell, J. B. Priestley, and Linus Pauling. Compare Farjeon's *Death of a World* [3-156], Shute's *On the Beach* [3-344], and Lem's *Memoirs Found in a Bathtub* (Seabury, 1973).

3-320. Russell, Bertrand (Arthur William) (U.K.). **Nightmares of Eminent Persons and Other Stories.** Bodley Head, 1954.
Twelve story pieces, including the *1984*-like "Eisenhower's Nightmare: The McCarthy-Malenkov Pact," and "Dr. Southport Vulpes's Nightmare: The Victory of Mind over Matter," about the ascent of the robot machine age. Satire by an enormously erudite and seasoned spectator of modern civilization and a winner of a Nobel prize in literature, 1950.

*3-321. Russell, Eric Frank (U.K.). **The Great Explosion.** Dobson, 1962.
Faster-than-light drive allows Earth's dissidents to colonize far-flung worlds. Four hundred years later Earth's ambassador sets out with military vessel to bring four such worlds into the Terran empire for "mutual defense." They find the planet of Buddhists and Mohammedans empty. On the planets settled by convicts, nudist health lovers, and Gands (people who say "no" to all forms of tyranny), the mythology of Terran aegis is rejected in vignettes of surgically deft satire. Corporate government is nonsense. Fortunately, stellar distance will make it virtually impossible. Slickly told; picaresque; satisfying. Expansion of ". . . And Then There Were None" (1951, SFHF). Compare Le Guin's *The Dispossessed* [4-324]; contrast Niven and Pournelle's *The Mote in God's Eye* [4-398].

3-322. Russell, Eric Frank (U.K.). **Men, Martians, and Machines.** Dobson, 1955.
Four stories from an early 1940 SF *Astounding* series. Jay Score is a humanoid robot with human emotions. In company with humans and chess-playing octopoid Martians, he adventures around the stars. Well-written parody with good stereotyping (with a difference) of characters. Representative of one of the true pulp masters.

3-323. Russell, Eric Frank (U.K.). **Sinister Barrier.** World's Work, 1943. The Fantasy Press, 1948, edition is a revision of the 1943 issue.
Revised from its original appearance in the initial (March 1939) issue of *Unknown*, this novel boosted a now-hackneyed theme, the idea that humans are pets of aliens, an idea popularized by Charles Fort. A number of distinguished scientists die, and the hero of this suspense novel discovers and eventually destroys the cause of their death, the Vitons, who parasitically feed upon the nervous energy of their human cattle. Well-paced adventure but little more. Compare Pohl and Kornbluth's *Wolfbane* [3-314] and Wilson's *The Mind Parasites* [4-611].

3-324. Russell, Eric Frank (U.K.). **Wasp.** Avalon, 1957.
Outclassed Terra enlists James Mowry to pose as a Sirian humanoid and conduct a campaign of sabotage on the enemy planet Jaimel as his part in an interstellar war. Single-handed, he reduces the planet's military, police, and intelligence services to a state of confusion. Fast action, effective secret-agent scenario, perhaps inspired by Allied World War II espionage activity. Some consider the Dobson, 1958, printing the uncorrupted edition. Compare Laumer's Retief series [3-247].

3-325. St. Clair, Margaret. **Change the Sky and Other Stories.** Ace, 1974.
Eighteen SF and fantasy stories, from 1951 to 1961. Title story: a man has an artist create the ideal world for which he has been searching the universe all his life. Instead, he finds a hell reliving the childhood he has fled from. General theme of collection: if you seek for something and find it, it probably isn't what you thought you were looking for. Other stories of interest include "An Old-Fashioned Bird Christmas," "An Egg a Month from All Over," and "Marriage Manual."

3-326. St. Clair, Margaret. **Sign of the Labrys.** Bantam, 1963.
Sam Sewell and Despoina are of the Wicca, supernormals viewed as "witches," immune to fungus plagues that kill millions. Death reaches even into the elaborate underground shelters of the Wicca, who survive to lead a new humankind again to the Earth's surface. The species is hard to destroy. Remarkable for Dantesque underground setting. Compare Henderson's *Pilgrimage* [3-208].

*3-327. Sarban (pseud. of John W. Wall) (U.K.). **The Sound of His Horn.** Davies, 1952.
Englishman Alan Querdilion, escaping a Nazi POW camp in 1943, falls into a future alternate Earth where the Germans have won World War II. Living in decadent baronial splendor on feudal estates, the German rulers blend their pagan past and racist beliefs in a sadistic and ruthless New Order with a genetically debased "under-men" caste (the remnants of "inferior races"), humans conditioned to behave like animals, and hunts using social dissidents as prey. Alan inevitably becomes such a prey and only returns to our world through the self-sacrifice of a fellow victim. A rural dystopia in sharp contrast with Dick's *The Man in the High Castle* [3-142]. Also compare Spinrad's *The Iron Dream* [4-527].

3-328. Schmitz, James H(enry). **The Universe against Her.** Ace, 1964.
Light, humorous adventure of Telzey Amberdon, individualistic and cute heroine, who first joins the crest cats of Jontarou, intelligent beings treated as big game, in upsetting the Establishment and then uses her newly acquired psionic powers to flout the bureaucratic Psychology Service. Other titles in the series are *The Telzey Toy* (DAW, 1973) and *The Lion Game* (DAW, 1973). Compare Norton's *Catseye* [5-116].

3-329. Schmitz, James H(enry). **The Witches of Karres.** Chilton, 1966.
The captain of an old tramp starship rescues three "witch" children and returns them to Karres. He then becomes involved in cosmic adventures ending with his saving humankind, with the children's aid, from the clutches of a maniacal computer and a race of lizard conquerors. Between crises the honest captain, a disdainer of sex and evil thoughts, smokes cigarettes and drinks coffee (perhaps pondering why people have evolved over the centuries into the stereotypes of

early twentieth-century pulp fiction). Entertaining, especially for juveniles. Expansion of a 1949 *Astounding* story. Contrast Lafferty's *The Reefs of Earth* (Berkley, 1968). HN, 1967.

3-330. Sellings, Arthur (pseud. of Robert Arthur Ley) (U.K.). **The Long Eureka.** Dobson, 1968.
Collection of nine stories, including the title story, "Blank Form," "The Scene Shifter," "One Across," "The Well-Trained Heroes," "Homecoming," "Verbal Agreement," "Trade-in," and "Birthright." An earlier collection of 16 stories, *Time Transfer* (M. Joseph, 1956), is also worthy of note.

3-331. Sellings, Arthur (pseud. of Robert Arthur Ley) (U.K.). **Telepath.** Ballantine, 1962. British title: *The Silent Speakers*, Dobson, 1963.
Arnold and Claire discover they are telepathic, have trouble understanding it and convincing others of it. They learn to teach it to others and humankind gets a new destiny. Well told. Good characterization. Compare Brunner's *The Whole Man* [3-74] and del Rey's *Pstalemate* (Putnam, 1971).

3-332. Sellings, Arthur (pseud. of Robert Arthur Ley) (U.K.). **The Uncensored Man.** Dobson, 1964.
Superalien "solvers" make a breakthrough to Mark Anders, who discovers that his consciousness has been masked from its potential full range of psi powers. All humans have it and will soon be in touch with the ultimate mind of the universe with aid of "solvers." Excellent suspense; effective weave of British romantic and Victorian poetry (Wordsworth and Arnold). Compare Pohl's *Drunkard's Walk* [3-310], Blish's *Jack of Eagles* [3-46], and del Rey's *Pstalemate* (Putnam, 1971).

3-333. Serling, Rod(man). **Stories from the Twilight Zone.** Bantam, 1960.
Six stories from the TV series that won three consecutive Hugos for best dramatic presentation (1960–1962). Includes "The Mighty Casey," about a robot baseball pitcher who gets a heart and goes into social work. Slick entertainments in the Hitchcock mold often considered trite by SF insiders. Other volumes of *Twilight Zone* stories are *More Stories from the Twilight Zone* (Bantam, 1961) and *New Stories from the Twilight Zone* (Bantam, 1962). Of related interest is an anthology of stories by others from which *Twilight Zone* scripts were adapted: *The Twilight Zone: The Original Stories* (1985). The three Serling collections have been published in an omnibus edition, *Stories from the Twilight Zone* (Bantam, 1986), which contains a new introduction by T. E. D. Klein, as well.

3-334. Sheckley, Robert. **Citizen in Space.** Ballantine, 1955.
Twelve stories, the best of which are "The Accountant," "Hunting Problem," "The Luckiest Man in the World," "The Mountain without a Name," "Something for Nothing," and "A Ticket to Tranai." Written with the ingenuity and clean style typical of early Sheckley, they often employ traditional SF situations to comment on humans and their behavior, in the manner of Bradbury and Vonnegut. For example, in "The Mountain without a Name," first a planet, then a galaxy instructs proud mankind about his unsavory self by "spitting him out" to die in space, while in "Hunting Problem," a first-contact story is given a unique twist by having an alien Boy Scout win his achievement badge by hunting a wild Mirach (a human explorer) and taking its hide (his uniform).

3-335. Sheckley, Robert. **Immortality, Inc.** Bantam, 1959. Expansion of the only partly authorized *Immortality Delivered,* Avalon, 1958.

Science has verified an afterlife and corporations peddle it in 2110, the year Thomas Blaine awakes after being snatched from a 1958 death for a company's ad campaign. It's a future familiar to Sheckley readers—cynical, impersonal, avaricious, full of mayhem and human hunts—and the anachronistic and shallow Blaine barely copes. He is led through a tortuous and surprising plot, encountering real ghosts, zombies, and spirits, and finally obtains self-understanding. A well-written and often witty novel of social and philosophical comment; compare Pohl and Kornbluth's *The Space Merchants* [3-313] and Farmer's *Night of Light* [3-160]. HN, 1959.

3-336. Sheckley, Robert. **Journey beyond Tomorrow.** Signet, 1962.

Humorous social satire, still relevant today, in the form of oral accounts of the journey of Joenes, a young Candide from Manituatua, who leaves his simple island home in the year 2000 to travel through the United States and U.S.S.R. to seek his fortune. Government, the military, academe, various idealisms, the police, psychiatry, and many more are lampooned as Joenes is buffeted by events leading to a cataclysmic accidental war between elements of the U.S. defense system that destroys civilization. Returning to the Pacific islands, Joenes and his beatnik friend, Lum, become the prophets of a new nontechnological civilization. Contrast Heinlein's *Stranger in a Strange Land* [3-207] and Vonnegut's *Cat's Cradle* [3-391].

3-337. Sheckley, Robert. **Notions: Unlimited.** Bantam, 1960.

Twelve stories, from 1952 to 1957, that span Sheckley's rich early career. Superior efforts include "Watchbird" (1953), which warns against trying to solve human problems with machines; "Paradise II" (1954), about a planet of the dead whose posthumous technology terrifyingly traps two human explorers; "Native Problem" (1956), with an expatriate Earthman mistaken for a native by colonists wanting to settle on his lonely world; "Dawn Invader" (1957), which rebuts the Darwinian notion that alien races can't coexist; "The Language of Love," which teaches that the overintellectualization of love can inhibit it. Like much early Sheckley, deceptively bland but definitely mind-sticking.

*3-338. Sheckley, Robert. **Pilgrimage to Earth.** Bantam, 1957.

Fifteen stories, most from 1954 to 1956. In "The Academy," a dystopian vision of thought control, ubiquitous "sanity meters" monitor humanity, weeding out individualism and inventiveness, the misfits being locked away in enforced sleep. The brilliant title story depicts a cynical future Earth where dreams are for sale; the resulting disillusionment is free. Sheckley's humor finds voice in "The Body," about the transplantation of a famous scientist's brain into a dog's body, and in "Milk Run," where the AAA Ace Interplanetary Decontamination Service gets fouled up with a spaceship full of alien livestock. Also contains the horrific "Fear in the Night." A full spectrum of the unique Sheckley talent.

*3-339. Sheckley, Robert. **Untouched by Human Hands.** Ballantine, 1954.

British issue, M. Joseph, 1955, drops "The King's Wishes" and "The Demons," and adds "Watchbird" and "Hands Off."

Thirteen stories from 1952 and 1953. Includes the realistic "Seventh Victim," where humans hunt one another for sport; "The Monsters," a study in cultural relativism; the dystopian "Cost of Living," an extrapolation of our debt-ridden consumer society; "Specialist," about a spaceship composed of an organic community; and the humorous title story, which proves that one person's meat is another person's poison when two lost humans discover a warehouse full of alien goods. A good mix of Sheckley wit, poignancy, and insight; his first collection, which marked him as a major new SF author.

3-340. Sherred, T(homas) L. **First Person, Peculiar.** Ballantine, 1972.
Collection of stories including the very fine and early (1947) "E for Effort," "Eye for Iniquity," "Cure Guaranteed," and "Cue for Quiet."

3-341. Sherriff, R(obert) C(edric) (U.K.). **The Hopkins Manuscript.** Gollancz, 1939. Variant title: *The Cataclysm,* Pan, 1958.
In the Macmillan, 1963, edition, John Gassner discusses Sherriff's career in an introduction and George Gamow critiques the novel's science in an epilogue; there are also excellent illustrations by Joe Mugnaini. Memoir of Edgar Hopkins, a very ordinary British middle-class gentleman, who details the events leading to and following the collision of Earth and Moon. Ironically, it is the greed-induced warfare over the crashed Moon's extensive resources, now filling the North Atlantic basin, that finally destroys civilization. Anticipates the later British catastrophe stories of Wyndham, Christopher, and Ballard, while following the tradition of Wells's *War of the Worlds* [1-105]. A superior work. Contrast Niven and Pournelle's *Lucifer's Hammer* [4-397].

3-342. Shiras, Wilmar H. **Children of the Atom.** Gnome, 1953.
Derived from a late-1940s *Astounding* series, including "In Hiding" (SFHF). Radiation from atomic plant explosion in 1958 causes birth of about 30 superintelligent children who "hide" from recognition until, after uniting with the help of a psychiatrist, they decide to reveal themselves and reenter society to make a better world for all. Intelligence is worthless in selfish uses. Humans will readily accept aid from geniuses!(?) Energetic narrative. Compare Smith's *The Fourth "R"* [3-356] and Sturgeon's *More Than Human* [3-362].

3-343. Shute, Nevil (pseud. of Nevil Shute Norway) (U.K.). **In the Wet.** Heinemann, 1953.
In Australia, a Church of England priest makes journal account of the future of British Commonwealth as heard from dying man, to be reincarnated as David Anderson. England will decline; Australia will rise (population 100,000,000 by the year 2000) and become leader of Commonwealth. England, Australia, and Canada to be administered by Governors General, taking workload from monarchy. Socialism will decline, replaced by Millian poly-vote system according to individual achievement. Utopian extrapolation of British empire's best (realistically) possible future. Good writing by mainstream novelist. Compare Bellamy's *Looking Backward* [1-8].

*3-344. Shute, Nevil (pseud. of Nevil Shute Norway) (U.K.). **On the Beach.** Heinemann, 1957.
In the atomic age, even the little nations have the bomb and the inevitable hap-

pens—a nuclear war releasing so much radioactivity that the planet is doomed. A British military unit waits for the end in Australia. An awful-warning story. Plausible world political scenario; fine suspense. Extraordinary popularity as book and film. Compare Wylie's *Tomorrow!* [3-409].

*3-345. Simak, Clifford D(onald). **City.** Gnome, 1952.
Eight "legends" constitute the heritage of sentient dogs who have inherited Earth from humans, along with android robots to aid the dogs. There is strong doubt that humankind ever existed. If so, humanity's passing coincides with the gradual abandonment of that peculiarly human artifact, the city—produced by the same creative genius that runs awry and makes war, whereas dog culture completely pacifies the animal kingdom. Sublime humanity may not work; instead may transform or become extinct—a dead divinity. A maudlin, poignant, quietistically philosophical twilight-of-the-gods account of humanity; the end of the human species. A contrast to the vaulting optimism of Bester's *The Stars My Destination* [3-32], Clarke's *Childhood's End* [3-97], and Asimov's *Foundation Trilogy* [3-19]; a seminal work in modern SF's swing to pessimism. In the Ace, 1981, edition, a final city story, "Epilog," has been added, making it the first complete edition. Compare Stewart's *Earth Abides* [3-358] and Campbell's "Twilight" [3-86]. IFA, 1958.

3-346. Simak, Clifford D(onald). **Ring around the Sun: A Story of Tomorrow.** Simon & Schuster, 1953.
Jay Vickers and Ann Carter discover a ring of parallel earths "around the Sun," or rather through time, and also a mutant human species that subverts Earth's capitalist economies with a "forever" technology. Vickers and Carter find love for each other as well. Many SF historians rate this work highly and regard it as emblematic of the 1950s SF vision. Contrast Capon's *The Other Side of the Sun* [3-87].

3-347. Simak, Clifford D(onald). **Time and Again.** Simon & Schuster, 1951. Variant title: *First He Died,* Dell, 1953.
Asher Sutton travels 6,000 years of human history to gain special assistance, to mature, and to survive to write a universe-guiding book, telling all life, "We are not alone." Destiny is with life. The human species, against its psychotic claims, is decidedly not preeminent in the universe. Be it louse or superandroid, all life is lovely before destiny; all are equal. Racism, nationalism, and Manifest Destiny are obscene behaviors and delusions. Sutton is well-rounded prophet-messiah figure. Compare Clarke's *Childhood's End* [3-97].

3-348. Simak, Clifford D(onald). **Time Is the Simplest Thing.** Doubleday, 1961.
Shepherd Blaine is a teleporting star traveler who leaves Fishhook Corporation because he has become "contaminated"—joined minds with a superintelligent, benevolent alien. Mechanical space travel won't work. It must be accomplished by paranormal means. In fact, humankind's future depends upon paranormal powers; yet the normals hunt the paranormals as witches until, led by the "alienated" Blaine, paranormals depart Earth for new planets, leaving normal humanity to stagnate and devolve. A profound critique of human "spirituality": when messianic ones appear, fearful people repudiate and murder them. Courageous peo-

ple welcome them and become them. An obvious but effective allegory. Compare Henderson's *Pilgrimage* [3-208] and Wyndham's *Re-Birth* [3-414]. HN, 1962.

*3-349. Simak, Clifford D(onald). **Way Station.** Doubleday, 1963.
Nostalgic story of Civil War veteran and frontiersman Enoch Wallace, made immortal to tend a secret galactic travel station in rural Wisconsin, and his loneliness, his love of Earth, and his solitary struggle to bring galactic benefits to humans. Finally, after CIA spying and witch-fearing neighbors threaten to close the station, Enoch's dreams come true. Aided by his alien, coffee-drinking friend, Ulysses, and a beautiful deaf-mute hill girl with psychic powers, Enoch saves the Talisman, an artifact that brings peace by opening people's contact with "the cosmic spiritual force," and proves Earth worthy to join the galaxy. Maudlin, but effective. Compare Henderson's *Pilgrimage* [3-208]. HW, 1964.

3-350. Simak, Clifford D(onald). **The Worlds of Clifford Simak.** Simon & Schuster, 1960.
Twelve stories from the 1950s, including "The Big Front Yard" (HW, 1959; SFHF), a prototype of the author's *Way Station* [3-349] and *All Flesh Is Grass* (Doubleday, 1965), in which a folksy fix-it man finds his ancestral home turned into a portal between worlds; "Lulu," about a computerized spaceship who falls in love and elopes with her three-man crew; and "Neighbor," a typical Simak story involving a small farming community and an alien family who settle there, isolating and preserving it as an idealized, rural American utopia.

3-351. Siodmak, Curt (Germany). **Donovan's Brain.** Knopf, 1943.
The brain of Donovan, killed in plane crash, survives in laboratory suspension; it gains psi power over its attendant, becomes obsessed, and finally dies. The source story for the popular brain-survival jokes. Not particularly well written but tremendously well known. Belongs to the Frankenstein's monster tradition. In a tenuous sequel, *Hauser's Memory* (Putnam, 1968), Pat Cory, Nobel prize-winning biochemist, transplants RNA from Hauser, World War II German chemist, to Hillel Mondoro. Unwittingly, he transplants Hauser's whole revenge-directed personality. Mondoro dies killing Geller, Nazi concentration camp criminal, while under control of "Hauser's memory," thus losing Hauser's formula for control of hydrogen fission. Ingenious biochemical gimmick and routine espionage yarn. Both novels are bases for several films. Contrast Hjortsberg's *Gray Matters* (Simon & Schuster, 1971).

3-352. Skinner, B(urrhus) F(rederick). **Walden Two.** Macmillan, 1948.
Frazier, mercurial genius, in effort to prove science of human behavior, sets up Walden Two. In this utopian environment, psychological problems of group living are solved with principles of behavioral engineering. Largely dialogue between Frazier and Castle, representing determinism and free will, respectively. Frazier rejects free will, democracy, and theology as sine qua non of human actualization in favor of appealing utopia of positive reinforcement—behaviorist's answer to "love." Brilliant tour de force. Contrast Orwell's *Nineteen Eighty-Four* [3-302] and Brunner's *The Shockwave Rider* [4-91].

3-353. Smith, Cordwainer (pseud. of Paul Myron Anthony Linebarger). **Norstrilia.** Ballantine, 1975.

Part of the Instrumentality of Man series. Rod McBan of conservative and enormously wealthy (holding monopoly on Stroon immortality drug) planet of Old North Australia finds inherited land and life in jeopardy. With a computer he becomes richest man in known universe—owning 30 or 40 planets, including Earth. He travels in disguises to avoid assassination. He is erratic but powerful telepath. Story characterized by allegorical names typical of Linebarger's tales. Themes of contrast between rugged individualism and corporate government; arid, inhospitable planets and lushness of Old Earth. Nostalgia for traditional values of Earth although underpeople foment revolution and Instrumentality of Man governs by promoting change. The original 1960 version was published as *The Planet Buyer* (Pyramid, 1964; HN, 1965); and *The Underpeople* (Pyramid, 1968). Compare Chandler's *Big Black Mark* (DAW, 1975); contrast the CoDominion works by Niven and/or Pournelle, *Mote in God's Eye* [4-398] and *The Mercenary* [4-421].

*3-354. Smith, Cordwainer (pseud. of Paul Myron Anthony Linebarger). **You Will Never Be the Same.** Regency, 1963.

Part of the Instrumentality of Man series. Eight stories, including the 1948 "Scanners Live in Vain" (SFHF). Colorful allegorical introductions to universe of 15,000 years hence when people sail space on huge estatelike plane-forming ships, castes of nonhuman, animal-derived underpeople are enslaved by "true" humans (less normal than the "animals"), and Lords of the Instrumentality of Man govern all with ruthless benevolence. *Space Lords* (Pyramid, 1965) adds five Instrumentality stores, including "The Ballad of Lost C'mell" (SFHF). Both collections provide fine allegory and dreamlike imagery. Both are basically contained in *The Best of Cordwainer Smith* (Nelson Doubleday, 1975), edited, with introduction, by J. J. Pierce.

*3-355. Smith, E(dward) E(lmer). **The Lensman Series.** Fantasy Press, 1948–1954.

The greatest of the early golden age space opera. A lensman is a superbred male or female chosen by the agents of cosmic goodness in the universe to have his or her virtues magnified and augmented with a bracelet "lens." The lensmen become the balance of power against forces of cosmic evil. On the greatest of battlefields, employing the most violent weapons, the lensmen fight the most ferocious of all wars. In sequence, the novels of the series are: *Triplanetary* (1948); *First Lensman* (1950), second-best of series; *Galactic Patrol* (1950); *Gray Lensman* (1951), best of series; *Second Stage Lensman* (1953); *Children of the Lens* (1954); and *The Vortex Blaster* (1960). Boxed and sold together by Fantasy Press as "The History of Civilization." Compare Lucas's *Star Wars* (Ballantine, 1976).

3-356. Smith, George O(liver). **The Fourth "R."** Ballantine, 1959. Alternate title: *The Brain Machine,* Lancer, 1968.

Jimmy Holden inherits a learning machine from his murdered father. He's bright but must hide from murderer guardian until he can gain his majority, secure adult rights, and give the machine to the world to enhance everyone's intelligence. Fruits of science are for all to share. Good suspense. Clever plotting. Set in nostalgia United States. Compare Stapleton's *Odd John* [2-110] and Clifton and Riley's *They'd Rather Be Right* [3-113].

3-357. Smith, George O(liver). **Venus Equilateral.** Futura, 1975. U.S. title: *The Complete Venus Equilateral,* Ballantine, 1976. These later editions add three stories to the Prime (1947) original edition.

Thirteen stories about Venus Equilateral, a communications satellite absolutely essential to maintaining contact among the planets of the solar system when the Sun is in the way. Stories analyze science, psychology, and politics of the station's operations. Interesting yarns woven of clichés and steretypes of golden-age SF.

3-357A. Solzhenitsyn, Aleksandr (Isaevich) (U.S.S.R.). **Candle in the Wind.** Univ. of Minnesota Press, 1973. Tr. by Keith Armes in association with Arthur Hudgins of *Sveča na vetru,* 1969.

Many serious thinkers and writers have felt the need to use the trappings and forms of science fiction to make their statements, and so has this Nobelist, perhaps the greatest living Russian writer. Written in 1960 and originally titled "The Light Which Is in Thee," this play reflects the author's background in physical science, as does his *The First Circle.* Set in some indeterminate time and place, the characters contend with the applications of a new technology, "biocybernetics," similar to biofeedback; Alex persuades Alda to have this "neurostabilization" treatment so she can better handle the stresses in her life. The treatment fails, as her father's death shocks Alda. Yet, despite its negation of affectivity, she again seeks its seductive relief. Solzhenitsyn issues social warnings through the general, from the "Department of Thoughts and Feelings," who foresees the new treatment's being used to subdue the citizenry, and the self-interested scientists who sell out in return for occupational support by the state. Not considered dramatically successful, but worthwhile as a vehicle for the author's concerns. Compare Koestler's *Twilight Bar* [3-237], Orwell's *Nineteen Eighty-Four* [3-302], and Conquest's *A World of Difference* [3-119].

*3-358. Stewart, George R(ippey). **Earth Abides.** Random, 1949.

Plague sweeps Earth, killing 250,000 for every survivor. Ish and Em lead nine original survivors in San Francisco Bay area. Only humans are killed in plague; all other flora and fauna survive, as well as the physical plant of civilization—including the Huntington Library. Ish spends 40 or 50 years trying to make road back to civilization. But his sons and daughters are quintessential tribal primitives when he dies. Human civilization is trivial; the planet "abides." Lasting excellence is brilliant dramatization of anthropological and sociological principles at work, respected by today's scholars. Compare Christopher's *No Blade of Grass* [3-92] and Merle's *Malevil* [4-376]. First IFA winner, 1951.

3-359. Sturgeon, Theodore. **Aliens 4.** Avon, 1959.

Four long stories, including the well-known "Killdozer!" (1944), about a duel between a man-operated power shovel and a "possessed" bulldozer; "The (Widget), the (Wadget), and Boff" (1955), in which aliens trying to psyche out humankind are confounded by the colorful residents of a boarding house. Also contains the horrific "The Comedian's Children" (1958), and a fantasy set in the American West, "Cactus Dance" (1954). Entertaining and insightful reading.

3-360. Sturgeon, Theodore. **The Dreaming Jewels.** Greenberg, 1950. Variant title: *The Synthetic Man,* Pyramid, 1957.

Utterly alien jewel-like creatures dream into existence the being who will grow up as Horty Armand, inhuman but humanoid, telepathic, and able to change his shape and regenerate major body parts. Fleeing his vicious stepfather, Horty joins a carnival to meet his beloved, Zena, and other friends and enemies. Plot plays guess-who's-human with the reader while Horty and Zena finally learn that "humanity" is a conditioning, not a biology. Exceptional use of music to characterize Horty. Progressive sexual theory given the novel's publication date. As in Sturgeon's presentation of childhood in his *More Than Human* [3-362] and *Venus Plus X* [3-364], Horty's youth is a symbol for human hope. Compare Henderson's *Pilgrimage* [3-208].

*3-361. Sturgeon, Theodore. **E Pluribus Unicorn.** Abelard, 1953.

Thirteen fantasy and SF stories, from 1947 to 1953, and an introduction by Groff Conklin. The most outstanding story is "A Saucer of Loneliness," a sensitive love story of a lonely woman touched by a small flying saucer and hounded nearly to death by the government and the public; on a deserted beach, she is found by an equally lonely man led to her by the bottles she has tossed into the sea, perhaps as some other lonely being tosses "saucers" across space. In "The World Well Lost," Sturgeon capably explores homosexuality and its social condemnation, both between alien birdlike creatures who flee their repressive society for sanctuary on Earth and between crew members of the ship that sets out to return them. Other stories of interest are "Bianca's Hands," "The Silken-Swift," and "The Professor's Teddy Bear."

*3-362. Sturgeon, Theodore. **More Than Human.** Farrar, 1953.

Sturgeon's greatest work; it vaulted him to the forefront of SF writers. Several misfit children, symbolizing humankind in their diversity, are driven together by an inner call to form a new "gestalt" based on the parapsychological union among its specialized parts. This communion realizes the potential Sturgeon feels humankind possesses to achieve its *psychic* destiny. A popular novel in SF courses, it is one of the genre's best-known works. Compare Roberts's *The Inner Wheel* (Hart-Davis, 1970) and Clarke's *Childhood's End* [3-97]. Winner of the IFA, 1954.

3-363. Sturgeon, Theodore. **A Touch of Strange.** Doubleday, 1958. Berkley, 1959, issue drops two stories.

Nine stories, including the excellent study of the corruption of power, "Mr. Costello, Hero." A galactic wheeler-dealer who thrives on sowing dissension and controlling people almost suborns a ship's purser; a wise society gives such a megalomaniac what he wants as therapy/object lesson—the purser visits him in exile where he is pitting one ant colony against another. Other works of note are "Affair with a Green Monkey," "The Other Celia," and "A Touch of Strange."

3-364. Sturgeon, Theodore. **Venus Plus X.** Pyramid, 1960.

Pilot Charlie Johns of familiar Earth crashes to his death, but his brain and its contents are saved by the People of Ledom, recently instituted secret parallel Earth civilization. They put it into a new body and ask Charlie Johns what he thinks of their utopian society, especially remarkable for the biobisexuality of its citizens (Charlie's new body is male). The resulting events and dialogue are an interesting critique of familiar Earth society with the often tragic confusion of its gender-stamped roles. An estimable anticipation of Le Guin's two prizewinning novels, *The Left Hand of Darkness* [4-327] and *The Dispossessed* [4-324]. HN, 1961.

3-365. Sturgeon, Theodore. **A Way Home.** Funk & Wagnalls, 1955. The U.S. Pyramid, 1956, issue drops two stories. British title of abridged edition, dropping three stories: *Thunder and Roses,* M. Joseph, 1957.
Eleven stories, with introduction by Groff Conklin. "Unite and Conquer" represents Sturgeon touch with story of brilliant scientist who tricks world into "uniting" against threat from invading aliens, bringing a new, beneficial world order. Also contains the nuclear warning story "Thunder and Roses," as well as "The Hurkle Is a Happy Beast" and "Tiny and the Monster."

*3-366. Sturgeon, Theodore. **Without Sorcery.** Prime, 1948. Eight of the stories in this collection reappear in *Not without Sorcery,* Ballantine, 1961.
Thirteen of Sturgeon's earliest stories, from 1939 to 1948, with an introduction by Ray Bradbury. Includes the classic "Microcosmic God" (SFHF), about a superscientist whose fantastic inventions were made by a rapidly evolving miniature species he created and for whom he was a god. Also of note are "It," "Shottle Bop," "Ether Breather," "Brat," "Cargo," and "The Ultimate Egoist."

3-367. Taylor, Robert Lewis. **Adrift in a Boneyard.** Doubleday, 1947.
Fred Robinson, his wife, housekeeper, housekeeper's son, an old man, and a girl survive an agency that kills every other human being where he stands. Their survival devices and travels are a combination of the realistic and quixotic, ending on an Edenic island where they seem to have a choice of living "naturally" or returning to a restored world. A disarmingly complex parable questioning the meaning of human existence. Compelling urbane dialectic metaphored in characters of serenely cynical Fred and Martha, his superficially empty-headed wife. Contrast Stewart's *Earth Abides* [3-358].

3-368. Temple, William F(rederick) (U.K.). **The Four-sided Triangle.** Fell, 1951.
Bill and Rob, scientists who have developed a matter duplicator, both love Lena. When she decides to marry Rob, only a duplicate Lena—Dorothy—can assuage Bill's heartbreak. But Dorothy, an atom-for-atom copy of Lena, really loves Rob also, and so, as could only happen in SF, a four-sided love triangle is formed. This simple "boy loses girl, boy builds girl" plot is enhanced by the author's warm and realistic characterization, relatively rare in SF of the day. Expanded from a 1939 *Amazing* story. Basis for a film. Compare Merril's *Shadow on the Hearth* [3-284] for characterization, and contrast del Rey's "Helen O'Loy" [3-138].

3-369. Tenn, William (pseud. of Philip Klass). **The Human Angle.** Ballantine, 1956.
Eight stories from the mid-1950s, including "Wednesday's Child," about a strange young woman who reproduces by shucking the mother's body and becoming a mature person in body of new baby; ingenious and profoundly sym-

bolic. Also of interest is "The Discovery of Morniel Mathaway." Collection abounds with Klass-ic wit.

*3-370. Tenn, William (pseud. of Philip Klass). **Of All Possible Worlds.** Ballantine, 1955. U.K. issue drops two and adds three other stories (M. Joseph, 1956). Seven stories, from 1947 to 1954, and an effective advocacy essay, "On the Fiction in Science Fiction." Better stories include "Down among the Dead Men," about the "recycling" of dead men in a vicious space war; "The Liberation of Earth," a satirical comment from the victims' viewpoint of being "saved" by brutal forces fighting over them; "The Tenants," in which two aliens rent a nonexistent thirteenth floor and move in; and "The Custodian," about a man who stays behind on Earth after the rest of humanity has fled in advance of the Sun's going nova.

3-371. Tenn, William (pseud. of Philip Klass). **Of Men and Monsters.** Ballantine, 1968.
Alien giants colonize Earth. Earthlings live like cockroaches in the giants' dwellings, regarded at most as pests. A few humans lead humankind out of superstitious ratlike existence to stars—stowed away on a spaceship of the giants. Humans are infinitely adaptable and resourceful. Lilliputian point of view cogently maintained. Anthropological and psychological example. Tenn's only novel to date. First part was "The Men in the Walls," from *Galaxy* in 1963. Compare T. H. White's *Mistress Masham's Repose* (1946).

3-372. Tenn, William (pseud. of Philip Klass). **The Wooden Star.** Ballantine, 1968.
Eleven stories with author's note. Among them are several of Klass's best: "Generation of Noah," "Brooklyn Project," "Null-P," "Eastward Ho!," "The Masculinest Revolt." "Will You Walk a Little Faster?" (1951), about gnomelike aliens in flying saucers encouraging humanity's inevitable suicide so they can inherit the Earth, by relying on humanity's greedy, individualistic nature, contains typical Klass elements: humor, satire, a dark view of humanity, and skillful writing.

*3-373. Tevis, Walter S. **The Man Who Fell to Earth.** Fawcett, 1963.
Sadly beautiful story of an alien from Anthea (Mars or perhaps another solar system?) who came to Earth from a superior but dying civilization to get help from humans. He puts his whole being into becoming as "human" as possible, and psychologically he succeeds. But "humanity" is not enough, as he reveals himself only to be defeated by the xenophobia of Earth. The repudiation is doubly tragic since he has become empathetic with humans. A parable of man's inhumanity to man—this time in the guise of an alien "man." Social criticism in a progressive mood. A film version was released in 1976. Contrast Biggle's *Monument* [3-34]; compare Le Guin's *Left Hand of Darkness* [4-327].

3-374. Thomas, Theodore L., and Kate Wilhelm. **The Clone.** Berkley, 1965.
Life is accidentally created in the catch basin of a Chicago drain; this "clone" grows into a miles-square blob that eats organic material, including people. The city is threatened as the clone adapts to eating parts of buildings. Plausibly devel-

oped expansion of a 1959 *Fantastic* story. Compare Pedler and Davis's *Mutant 59* (Souvenir Press, 1971). NN, 1965.

*3-375. Tucker, (Arthur) Wilson. **The Long Loud Silence.** Rinehart, 1952. The early edition deletes implications of cannibalism; revised issue, Lancer, 1970.
A nuclear-biological war devastates the United States east of the Mississippi. Corporal Russell Gary survives on the east side, but, along with a few others, finds himself quarantined and forbidden to reenter civilization. Eventually, he is reconciled to a life of primitive necessity. Excellent scenario. Kornbluth called it "enormously effective social criticism, saying much about man and his society." Compare Frank's *Alas, Babylon* [3-166]; contrast Wylie's *Triumph* [3-409].

3-376. Tucker, (Arthur) Wilson. **Wild Talent.** Rinehart, 1954. U.K., M. Joseph, 1955, issue is expanded. Variant title: *Man from Tomorrow*, Bantam, 1955.
Paul Breen discovers, during an appropriate experience of confusion, that he has psi talent. Unwittingly he reveals himself to government agents, who try to use him and kill him. He survives and goes into hiding with the woman he has come to love. Good telepathy-emerging story. Cold-war world will not appreciate a "new" man. Compare Blish's *Jack of Eagles* [3-46], Sellings's *Telepath* [3-331], Roberts's *The Inner Wheel* (Hart-Davis, 1970), Brunner's *The Whole Man* [3-74], and Sturgeon's *More Than Human* [3-362].

3-377. Vance, Jack. **The Best of Jack Vance.** Pocket Books, 1976.
Collection of five stories and a novella representing over two decades, including "The Moon Moth" (SFHF), "The Last Castle" (HW, 1967; NW, 1966), and "Abercrombie Station." Vance delights in building alien and alternative cultures, as these stories brilliantly demonstrate. "Abercrombie Station" is a space satellite retreat for obese people; "The Last Castle" portrays a future Earth populated by decadent humans and their alien servants; "The Moon Moth" is set in a complex culture of mask-wearing beings intent on their personality-based status system; "Rumfuddle" assumes gateways between alternate Earths so all can have their own; and "Ullward's Retreat" offers the opportunity to rent half a world, if you can afford it, to get away from the pressures of your neighbors on the overcrowded planets. In an introduction, Barry Malzberg calls Vance "one of the ten most important writers" in SF.

3-378. Vance, Jack. **The Blue World.** Ballantine, 1966.
Eleventh-generation descendants of convicts, who hijacked ship taking them to penal planet, live on water planet on giant lily-padlike islands. Mild climate and socialistic community, threatened by sea beast and emerging caste system, is preserved by Sklar Hast, Hoodwinker, who kills the beast and sets technology afoot for potential reunion with main body of humankind. Epic adventure in futuro-exotic setting. Effective presentation of ecology and resulting life-style from "criminal" beginnings. Revised from its 1964 publication in *Fantastic*. Compare Card's *Planet Called Treason* [4-110]. NN, 1966.

*3-379. Vance, Jack. **The Dragon Masters.** Ace, 1963.
On Aerlith (Stone in the Sky), planet on fringe of galaxy, descendants of ancient war live feudally, while fighting reptilian "basics" with specially bred dragons. Ba-

sic raid repelled with aid of Sacerdotes, indigenous quietistic humans. A tentacle of the galactic history of humanity, which must always fight to live. Intriguing extrapolation. Contrast Davidson's *Rogue Dragon* (1965). Compare McCaffrey's *Dragonriders of Pern* [4-368]. HW for novella, 1963.

3-380. Vance, Jack. **The Dying Earth.** Hillman, 1950.
Six stories from 1950 about Earth in the far future: magic replaces science; population shrinks; the Sun is dying. Yet humans struggle for survival in tragic-heroic mood. Sequel is *The Eyes of the Overworld* (Ace, 1966). Picaresque adventures of Cugel the Clever who, having offended Iucounu the Laughing Magician, must make a perilous journey over the dying Earth to recover a magical adjunct for Iucounu. Exotic characters and fascinating situations. Well told (NN, 1966). Other books in the series are *Cugel's Saga* (Simon & Schuster, 1983), *Rhialto the Marvelous* (Underwood-Miller, 1984), and, by Michael Shea, *A Quest for Simbilis* (DAW, 1974). Contrast Wolfe's *The Shadow of the Torturer* [4-616].

*3-381. Vance, Jack. **The Languages of Pao.** Avalon, 1959.
Vance may never write a more important novel than this one. The Edenic planet of Pao has been occupied virtually without resistance by the invaders from the harsh planet of Breakness. The story of the rise of the formerly passive peoples of Pao to regain their freedom is an example of the biosociological and linguistic theories that environment and language shape the talents and perceptions sentient beings may possess. To become competitive, the people of Pao must learn more violent arts and languages that express degrees of quality and strength. Compare Delany's *Babel-17* [4-164] and Watson's *The Embedding* [4-586].

3-382. van Vogt, A(lfred) E(lton). **Away and Beyond.** Pellegrini & Cudahy, 1952.
Nine stories, from 1940 to 1948 and the peak of van Vogt's most prolific period. In "Asylum" (1942) Earth is invaded by sensuous, "life energy" sucking, blood stealing alien vampires and only William Leigh, reporter for the *Planetarian,* stands in their way. "The Second Solution" depicts the struggle of a young "ezwal," a mind-reading and sentient but extremely deadly life-form, to decide whether to protect its species from Earth's enmity by playing the brute animal, or to admit its nature in the hope of future cooperation. "Heir Unapparent" (1945) tells of an aging dictator who hates killing being pressured to use the ultimate weapon, the "Contradictory Force," against invading rebels, while in "Vault of the Beast" (1940) a deadly protean robot slips onto Earth to kidnap a mathematician capable of unlocking a mammoth prison holding a monster alien bent on destroying our universe. Typical of van Vogt's vaulting imagination, the stories also end with unexpected and even more imaginative twists. The short story form seems to discipline the author's well-known meandering tendencies, but does little for his style. Contrast with the equally imaginative but well-crafted stories of John Brunner [3-71, 3-72].

*3-383. van Vogt, A(lfred) E(lton). **Slan.** Arkham, 1946. Simon & Schuster, 1951, issue is revised.
First appeared in 1940 *Astounding,* a classic ESP story of benevolent superhumans overcoming repression by superstitious, mob-spirited humanity. The

golden-tentacled slans are telepathic, superintelligent, physically superior or mutants hated by the public and hunted by the secret police of world dictator Kier Gray. Young Jommy Cross, orphaned son of a slan scientist, vows to end the bigotry, but falls into the hands of a grandmother Fagin. After maturing, he continues his quest, running afoul of the spaceships of nontelepathic slans, actually true slans with some traits temporarily inhibited. But Cross, now not only a biological superman but a technological one as well, thanks to his father's discovery of a new energy source, does not discover this until he goes to warn dictator Gray of the tendrilless slans' planned vengeful attack on Earth. True slans are by nature "antiwar, antimurder, antiviolence." Surprise! Gray is really a true slan helping a master plan unfold for the eventual evolutionary slan replacement of the increasingly sterile normals. Descendants might include Blish's *Jack of Eagles* [3-46], Rey's *Pstalemate* (Putnam, 1971), and Disch's *Camp Concentration* [4-184].

3-384. van Vogt, A(lfred) E(lton). **The Voyage of the Space Beagle.** Simon & Schuster, 1950. Variant title: *Mission: Interplanetary,* Signet, 1952.
Nexialism—"applied wholism"—is civilization's best hope for finally escaping Spenglerian history cycles. Elliot Grosvenor is a synthesist, sailing between galaxies in the exploring *Space Beagle* and fighting both the narrow views of the crew of scientific specialists and the vicious aliens encountered along the way. Basically a spectacular parade of villainous BEMs: hypnotic space-birds, an Id-eating cat-monster, an eight-legged matter manipulator that uses human bodies for egg incubators, and a giant gas cloud that ate a galaxy. Of course, all are bested by polymath Grosvenor. Three stories written into continuity, two of which date from 1939 *Astounding*. Compare Foster's *Alien* (Warner, 1979).

3-385. van Vogt, A(lfred) E(lton). **The Weapon Shops of Isher.** Greenberg, 1951.
Immortal Robert Hedrock created the inviolate Weapon Shops as a check to big government on Earth; their creed—"The right to buy weapons is the right to be free." Now, after hundreds of years of uneasy stability, the strong-willed young Isher empress, Innelda, attempts the shops' destruction. Provincial Cayle Clark, who has a talent for luck, is drawn into the struggle, as is an innocent reporter from 1951 who ends martyred as an explosive pendulum swinging through time; behind the scenes, superman Hedrock schemes to save the status quo. Awkward, illogical, and amateurish at times, but continuously inventive and politically attractive to many. *The Weapon Makers* (Greenberg, 1952; alternate title: *One against Eternity,* Ace, 1955) was rewritten after its initial 1943 appearance to make it a sequel to *Shops;* Hedrock struggles to force the empress to release the repressed technology of an interstellar drive. Hunted as a traitor by both the empire and the shops, he escapes into deep space only to encounter sentient spiderlike aliens who may threaten humans. Hedrock outwits them all, is revealed to be empire's original founder, and sets indomitable humankind on a course to the stars. Grandiose space opera with libertarian politics and humanistic values. Compare Harness's *Flight into Yesterday* [3-189].

*3-386. van Vogt, A(lfred) E(lton). **The World of Null-A.** Simon & Schuster, 1948.
Originally published in 1945, this is a complexly and unsteadily plotted space op-

era full of pseudo-science, gadgets, and cardboard characters, but still fascinating in its grandiose scale and audacity. Gosseyn, an immortal superman, uses doppelgängers to foil a galactic plot by villains who have subverted the machine that appoints world leaders. They seek the overthrow of the non-Aristotelian system that Gosseyn originally set up to mentally train humanity into true maturity. The machine is destroyed, but the null-a-trained Earthpeople resist the invaders, and Gosseyn, despite his repeated "deaths," defeats their cunning chief. In an even more flamboyant sequel, *The Pawns of Null-A* (Ace, 1956; originally published as "The Players of Null-A" in 1948, later the title of the Berkley, 1966, edition), Gosseyn is carried further into the intrigues of galactic war. Another sequel, *Null-A Three* (DAW, 1985; first published in French in 1984), has Gosseyns 2 and 3, and their double brains, again galaxy-hopping to save the day. For a recent and improved version of this type tale, see Niven and Pournelle's *The Mote in God's Eye* [4-398].

3-387. Vercors (pseud. of Jean Bruller) (France). **Sylva.** Putnam, 1962. Tr. by Rita Barisse of *Sylva*, 1961.
Gentleman farmer Richwick sees a fox turn into a woman, captures her, and raises her to become his wife—after "education" that distills 500,000 years of mental development. Simultaneously, Dorothy, an earlier love, "descends" to savagery by means of drugs. A credible, stunning, minor literary masterpiece that exhibits the tremendous resources of human love. Compare David Garnett's *Lady into Fox* (1923) and Franz Kafka's "Metamorphosis." HN, 1963.

3-388. Vercors (pseud. of Jean Bruller) (France). **You Shall Know Them.** Little, Brown, 1953. Tr. by Rita Barisse of *Les Animaux dénaturés*, 1952. Variant titles: *The Murder of the Missing Link*, Pocket Books, 1958, and *Borderline*, Macmillan, 1954.
Douglas Templemore is sperm donor to apelike mother Paranthropus named Derry, who bears several children. Are they human? Templemore kills one and demands to be charged with murder. Found innocent, Templemore nevertheless has advanced the problem of definition of human to new insights. A cogent philosophical dialectic in good supporting yarn. Compare Bass's less discursive *Half Past Human* [4-41].

3-389. Vidal, Gore. **Messiah.** Dutton, 1954. Little, Brown, 1965, issue is revised.
John Cave: J.C.: Jesus Christ gives a post-mid-century world Cavesword and Cavesway, the passionate desire for death and procedure of faithful suicide. From California to North America to the world, people join a religion that worships death. A grim, relentless satire; a *reductio* for a species that places empirical science over reason. Probing critique of Western world's way of doing business. Compare Miller's *A Canticle for Leibowitz* [3-287].

3-390. Vidal, Gore. **Visit to a Small Planet.** Little, Brown, 1956. With other plays, Signet, 1960.
Insignificant, history-locked Earth is visited by a child superalien who parks his saucer in plain view and threatens national crisis—even world and historic crisis—since he can change the past. His guardians retrieve him just in time. Comic tone; bald satire and parody in a play that reveals humankind, represented by

the United States, as fools and cowards in context of cosmic realities. A film version stars Jerry Lewis. Compare the "Star Trek" television series.

3-391. Vonnegut, Kurt, Jr. **Cat's Cradle.** Holt, 1963.
A satire on the atomic age and the Manhattan Project that unleashed the bomb on modern humanity. Here the "bomb" is Ice-9, with a melting point of over 100 degrees Fahrenheit, which gradually freezes virtually all life on Earth—a metaphor for radioactivity? Parody of every foible of frenetic midtwentieth-century world. Razor-witted narrative. Compare Pedlar and Davis's *Mutant 59* (Souvenir Press, 1971) and Brunner's *The Sheep Look Up* [4-90]. HN, 1964.

*3-392. Vonnegut, Kurt, Jr. **Player Piano.** Scribner, 1952. Variant title: *Utopia 14*, Bantam, 1954.
Paul Proteus, engineer, leads revolt against machine-computer conformist civilization, only to find that when it succeeds, people wish for the machines again. In order or in chaos, mob psychology is stupid. Modern civilization has hate-love affinity for machines. Incisive satire; a classic modern dystopia. Compare Huxley's *Brave New World* [2-47]. IFA, third place, 1953.

3-393. Vonnegut, Kurt, Jr. **The Sirens of Titan.** Dell. 1959.
All of human history has been manipulated by Tralfamadorians in order to produce replacement part for Salo's (robot messenger) spaceship, downed on Titan. His message: "Greetings." The "part" appears very much like a beer-can opener—a "church key." Humankind's "meaning" is a trivial footnote in the process of the cosmos. Excellent satire. Contrast Pangborn's *Mirror for Observers* [3-304]; compare Haldeman's *Forever War* [4-247] and Johannesson's *Tale of the Big Computer* (Coward, 1968). HN, 1960.

3-394. Vonnegut, Kurt, Jr. **Welcome to the Monkey House.** Delacorte, 1968.
Twelve pieces were earlier published as *Canary in a Cat House*, Fawcett, 1961.
Twenty-five stories, including "Harrison Bergeron," about "equality" arranged by system of handicaps imposed upon people with exceptional abilities; "Deer in the Works" (not SF), about a deer that gets trapped on the grounds of a modern factory—metaphor for humans in industrial age; and "Report on the Barnhouse Effect," in which a scientist uses his discovery of psychic power to disarm the world and end war.

3-395. Waugh, Evelyn (U.K.). **Love among the Ruins.** Chapman & Hall, 1953.
In the superwelfare state of future England, the do-nothings and criminals live more luxuriously than the workers. Miles, a nice person when he is not a psychotic incendiary, leaves his lovely prison digs and has a love affair with beautiful, blond, bearded ballerina, Clara—which goes sour when she has her beard replaced with a rubber mask. He finally makes a marriage of convenience to ugly Miss Flower to begin career as counter propaganda minister in favor of preserving permissive welfare state. Waugh is master satirist. Compare Vonnegut's *Welcome to the Monkey House* [3-394].

3-396. Werfel, Franz (Austria). **Star of the Unborn.** Viking, 1946. Tr. by Gustave O. Arlt of *Stern der Ungeborenen*, 1945.
In the midst of World War II, F. W. writes a three-part history of the future,

modeled perhaps on Dante's *Divine Comedy*, with the aid of his "guide," B. H. He travels the universe and learns it is made in image of what humans are destined to become; that even as humans separate from God in time, paradoxically they come closer to God as the end of all things approaches—100,000 years (?) from 1943. Erudite and profound, from author of *Song of Bernadette*. Compare Stapledon's *Last and First Men* [2-109].

3-397. White, James (U.K.). **The Escape Orbit.** Ace, 1965. British title: *Open Prison*, Four Square, 1965.
Chlorine-breathing aliens are fighting a war of attrition with humanity that threatens the imminent destruction of both. Sector Marshall Warren is captured and incarcerated on an alien prison planet. He leads a "great escape" just in time to salvage remnants of human civilization as hostilities collapse. Rigorous details of escape plans are the novel's adventure feature. Compare Godwin's *The Survivors* [3-174]. NN, 1965.

3-398. White, James (U.K.). **Hospital Station.** Ballantine, 1962.
A picaresque story of Sector General, a galactic hospital replete with environments and medical technology to treat every imaginable life form. Conway and O'Mara, doctor and psychologist, link the episodes. Alien anatomy and psychology ingeniously imagined. White's best-known work; related works are *Star Surgeon* (Ballantine, 1963), *Major Operation* (Ballantine, 1971), *The Aliens among Us* (Ballantine, 1969; not all stories from this series), *Ambulance Ship* (Ballantine, 1979), *Futures Past* (Ballantine, 1982), *Sector General* (Ballantine, 1983), and *Star Healer* (Ballantine, 1985). Compare Anthony's *Prostho Plus* (Gollancz, 1971) and Mitchison's *Memoirs of a Spacewoman* [3-288].

3-399. White, James (U.K.). **Second Ending.** Ace, 1962.
Ross, last human of an Earth sterilized by radioactivity, survives the death of the solar system in suspended animation tended by robots who deliver him to "human" civilization on Fomalhaut IV. Humankind can expect many endings, but no end. Spectacular scaling of the life of a human to the five-billion-year life of a solar system. Compare Varley's *The Ophiuchi Hotline* [4-569]; contrast Simak's *City* [3-345]. HN, 1962.

3-400. Williams, Robert Moore. **Doomsday Eve.** Ace, 1957. Bound with Eric Frank Russell's *Three to Conquer*.
Not a giant, but a yeoman of the golden age, the prolific Moore reputedly sold over 150 works during his 40-year career. Seldom remarked, and even less read, today, he is listed here both as a representative and as a tribute to the many others like himself who, along with those who have better weathered the changes in genre fashions, helped liberate the minds of golden age readers. This novel, said to be among his best, is set during the aftermath of a future world war and humanity's impending demise, as emerging supermen mentally fight to assure survival. Other works of note are the Zanthar series of books, in which a superscientist defeats supervillains, and *The Day They H-Bombed Los Angeles* (Ace, 1961). Judgment of Williams runs from "mish-mash," "clanking apparatus," and "routine hooly-dooly" to "fast," "diverting," and "yet, the darn thing has vitality." Contrast Frank's *Alas, Bablylon* [3-166] and Stewart's *Earth Abides* [3-358].

*3-401. Williamson, Jack. **Darker Than You Think.** Fantasy Press, 1948.
Evil in the form Homo lycanthropus triumphs in this 1940 story, perhaps
Williamson's best. Modern humans still possess genes from Ice-Age masters, a
parapsychic race of shape-changing vampires. These genes have been concentrated in Will Barbee, the Black Messiah, and he is unwittingly used to murder a
group of archaeologists who have uncovered the plot to overthrow humankind.
Excellent description of the wild, free experiences of werewolf Barbee, but the
carefully laid pseudo-scientific basis for lycanthropy seems absurd today. Compare Matheson's *I Am Legend* [3-274], Zelazny's *This Immortal* [4-632], Sheckley's
Immortality, Inc. [3-335], and Lem's *The Investigation* [3-259] as other examples of
supernatural folk myths given an empirical explanation.

*3-402. Williamson, Jack. **The Humanoids.** Simon & Schuster, 1949. The Avon,
1980, edition includes "With Folded Hands" (SFHF) and an introduction by the
author.
The humanoids are sentient robots designed with the injunction "to serve and
obey, and guard men from harm." They carry this to the extreme that humans
are not permitted to do anything of potential harm and must have happiness
even if it is drug-induced. Forester, an astrophysicist, rebels and is forced to develop parapsychological powers to free himself from the robots' domination,
then finds that this is the robots' hidden purpose. Excellent and influential work.
Sequel: *The Humanoid Touch* (1980). Compare Asimov's *I, Robot* [3-20]; contrast
Simak's *City* [3-345].

3-403. Williamson, Jack (as Will Stewart). **Seetee Ship.** Gnome, 1951.
A tale assembled from stories published in *Astounding* beginning in the early
1940s. Rick Drake returns to the asteroids from an Earth university to help his father find a way to utilize contraterrene matter and fight the corporation that rules
the asteroids through the control of energy. With the help of an old asteroid miner
who has an absolute direction and time sense, they succeed. In the sequel, *Seetee
Shock* (as Will Stewart, Simon & Schuster, 1950), a contraterrene artifact appears,
but cannot be approached or used until it is realized that the direction of time on
this strange form of matter is opposite to the normal flow. Outstanding space opera. Compare Asimov's *The Gods Themselves* [4-27].

3-404. Wolfe, Bernard. **Limbo.** Random, 1952. British title: *Limbo 90*, Secker,
1953.
Dr. Martine (Lazarus) spends 18 years on a secret island doing research on the
brain's aggressive centers. Outside, World War III ends and a worldwide ampu-
tee culture arises with people becoming voluntary cyborgs. This utopia fails, and
Martine's research notes, along with his earlier notebooks, become a dangerous
potential for a new utopia based upon a type of lobotomy. Humans will not find
utopia through any form of surgery, though they consistently attempt it. Brilliant metaphor for twentieth-century civilization's predicament. Compare, carefully, Brunner's *Stand on Zanzibar* [4-92].

3-405. Wouk, Herman. **The "Lomokome" Papers.** Simon & Schuster, 1956.
Originally written in 1949, *Papers* represents Wouk's only excursion into SF. A
U.S. Navy astronaut goes to Moon to discover Lomokome (Hebrew for "no-

where" or "utopia"), Lomadine, and the memory of Lozain, a nation of cannibals destroyed by Lomokome and Lomadine. Lomokome finally defeats Lomadine through Professor Ctuzelawis's theory of Reasonable War, in which killing is done with scientific precision and economy. War by advanced civilization is just as vicious and suicidal for all parties as it is at any level of civilization. Satire indebted to Wells, Swift, Butler, and Defoe, inspired by reading Nicolson's *Voyages to the Moon* [9-69]. Compare Boulle's *Planet of the Apes* [3-55].

3-406. Wright, Austin Tappan. **Islandia.** Farrar, 1942.
Islandia is Wright's childhood fantasy utopia continued and elaborated through his adulthood to the end of his life. Set facing the Antarctic, it is an independent nation in contact with the real nations of the world. Its very elaborateness is a virtue, being in published form a distillation of the massive manuscript that details even the history of its literature. In complexity of conception comparable to Tolkien's Middle Earth and Herbert's *Dune* [4-268].

3-407. Wul, Stefan (pseud. of Pierre Pairault) (France). **Temple of the Past.** Seabury, 1973. Tr. by Ellen Cox of *Le Temple du passé*, 1958.
Massir labors heroically to save his expedition, downed on a chlorine/silicone-based planet and swallowed by a whale. Primitive telepathic lizards help him put himself in suspended animation in Temple Acropolis. Ten thousand-odd years later, Earth expedition discovers the 18-foot-tall Massir and identifies him as coming from Earth's lost Atlantis. The tenacity of sentience against nature is limitless; it will prevail in some form. Splendid example of a survival adventure. Compare Clement's *Cycle of Fire* [3-108].

*3-408. Wylie, Philip (Gordon). **The Disappearance.** Rinehart, 1951.
Superior Wylie novel whose premise is the mutual disappearance of men and women from each other's worlds. These single-sex societies are traced as they adapt and evolve over four-year period; then they are united as suddenly and inexplicably as they were separated, as if no time had passed. But the memories of the separation are retained, of the social degeneration of the men, of the challenge and growth of the women, and they catalyze a new era in human relations—people have learned to love. Well-written social criticism and social extrapolation. Contrast Russ's *The Female Man* [4-458]; compare Le Guin's *Left Hand of Darkness* [4-327].

3-409. Wylie, Philip (Gordon). **Tomorrow!** Holt, 1954.
In World War III, the United States sustains great losses: near Christmas, four cities are hit by H-bombs; 25 hit by A-bombs; 20 million dead or injured; hundreds of thousands dying in riots. U.S. population is vulnerable because of cities' concentration. Meticulous, if dated, analysis of how United States would weather attack. To escape surrender, United States counters with superbomb that could (but doesn't) destroy the planet. Wylie rewrites this scenario in *Triumph* (Doubleday, 1963), but the devastation of the United States is virtually complete, and the focus is on the survivors who weather the holocaust in an elaborate survival shelter. Compare Huxley's *Ape and Essence* [3-220], Frank's *Alas, Babylon* [3-166], and Merle's *Malevil* [4-376].

3-410. Wyndham, John (pseud. of John Benyon Harris) (U.K.). **Chocky.** Ballantine, 1968.
Young boy and alien, Chocky, form temporarily successful symbiosis so that alien can give knowledge and wisdom to humans. Not successful; alien must work in fits and starts through many people. Humans can't accept "super" people. Well-written yarn. Expansion of a 1963 *Amazing* story. Compare Clement's *Needle* [3-110].

*3-411. Wyndham, John (pseud. of John Benyon Harris) (U.K.). **The Day of the Triffids.** Doubleday, 1951. Variant title: *Revolt of the Triffids,* Popular Library, 1952.
The triffids seem beneficent plants until human greed and mismanagement turn them into quasi-sentient, mobile flora that threaten to take over Earth, reducing humans to small enclaves for survival. In the end a "weapon" to destroy them seems possible but does not yet exist. Fine pace and excellent narrative. Good postcatastrophe analysis. Compare Finney's *The Body Snatchers* [3-163] and Disch's *Genocides* [4-185]. IFA nominee, 1952.

3-412. Wyndham, John (pseud. of John Benyon Harris) (U.K.). **The Kraken Wakes.** M. Joseph, 1953. U.S. title with altered text: *Out of the Deeps,* Ballantine, 1953.
Sentient aliens infest the deep seas of Earth, and humanity narrowly escapes obliteration when they come landside. Humans will win out in the face of catastrophe. Excellent oceanography; effective first-person journal narrative. Compare Wells's *The War of the Worlds* [1-105].

*3-413. Wyndham, John (pseud. of John Benyon Harris) (U.K.). **The Midwich Cuckoos.** M. Joseph, 1957. Alternate title: *Village of the Damned,* Ballantine, 1960.
Aliens impregnate the women in the English village of Midwich, who give birth to superchildren, brilliant with psi power. The people in charge of them, though viewing them benevolently, acknowledge their threat to humanity and destroy them. A superior species must destroy humankind by its very nature—unless humankind destroys it in immature stage. A really original scenario; social criticism; good story. Very popular; basis for superior SF film. Compare G. O. Smith's *The Fourth "R"* [3-356] and Shiras's *Children of the Atom* [3-342].

3-414. Wyndham, John (pseud. of John Benyon Harris) (U.K.). **Re-Birth.** Ballantine, 1955. British title with altered text: *The Chrysalids,* M. Joseph, 1955.
After a nuclear war, "normal" people gradually ostracize the mutants among them. They are wise to do so, because the dominant mutation provides telepathic ability, creating a new species. A superhuman inevitably, if regretfully, will make humans as presently known obsolete. Excellent telepathy-emerging story. Compare Roberts's *The Inner Wheel* (Hart-Davis, 1970) and Kuttner's *Mutant* [3-244].

3-415. Wyndham, John (pseud. of John Benyon Harris) (U.K.). **Tales of Gooseflesh and Laughter.** Ballantine, 1956.
Eleven stories, some from *Jizzle* (Dobson, 1954) and *The Seeds of Time* (M. Joseph, 1956), including "Compassion Circuit," about compassionate robot servant who has her masters' bodies replaced because they are so frail and subject to pain—

compare with Lester del Ray's "Helen O'Loy" [3-138]. Other stories of interest are "Una," "Confidence Trick," "Chinese Puzzle," and "More Spinned Against" (pun intended). Mostly fantasy, some SF and SF/fantasy blends. Compare the short fiction of John Collier.

3-416. Wyndham, John (pseud. of John Benyon Harris) (U.K.). **Trouble with Lichen.** M. Joseph, 1960. U.S. Ballantine, 1960, issue is textually different.
The "trouble" is that special lichen can extend human life virtually indefinitely, but you can't tell the world of the discovery until you can mass-produce it. Desire for immortality and concurrent power is as old as people's experience with death. Good social psychology. Fine Wyndham story, as usual. Compare Gunn's *The Immortals* [3-183].

3-417. Young, Robert F(ranklin). **The Worlds of Robert F. Young.** Simon & Schuster, 1965.
Known as a slick, sentimental storyteller, frequently publishing his SF/fantasy blend in the *Saturday Evening Post* and the *Magazine of Fantasy and Science Fiction,* Young provides a good cross section of his work in this 16-story collection introduced by Avram Davidson. Sensitive and symbolic stories include his well-known "Goddess in Granite" and "The Dandelion Girl," which features a female time traveler, while broad humor characterizes "Production Problem" and "Written in the Stars." "Romance in a Twenty-First Century Used-Car-Lot" satirizes America's preoccupation with cars, the subject of two other Young stories not published here. His other collection is *A Glass of Stars* (Harris-Wolfe, 1968), which contains a second car satire, "Thirty Days Had September." Compare and contrast *The Early Long* [3-264] and *The Best of Barry N. Malzberg* (Pocket Books, 1976).

Anthologies

According to tradition, the modern SF anthology originated in the golden age of the early 1940s with the appearance of Phil Stong's *The Other Worlds* (1941) and Donald Wollheim's *The Pocket Book of Science Fiction* (1943). Since that time, such works have greatly increased in both number and type. Groff Conklin reported that from 1946 to 1952, over 50 SF anthologies had been published contrasted with about 200 genre-labeled novels and single-author collections (*Omnibus of Science Fiction,* Crown, 1952, p. ix). But in 1973 alone novels and collections, excluding reprints, numbered over 200, while 105 new anthologies were issued. In 1974, the figures reached about 250 novels and single-author collections as opposed to 78 anthologies; even though the total number of anthologies declined from 1973 to 1974, the majority of the 1974 anthologies contained only original stories (*Locus* 153, Dec. 30, 1973; *Locus* 168, Dec. 24, 1974). Besides proliferation of original anthologies, the growth in anthology varieties is further represented by the presence in the 1973–1974 lists of single-theme anthologies, year's-best series, anthologies of award-winning stories, translations of non-English SF, retrospective anthologies from single magazines, works published for classroom use in a variety of fields, and even an anthology of stories adapted from TV scripts.

Since 1974, the last complete year included in the first edition of *Anatomy of Wonder*, SF has continued to boom (see Chapter 7). Anthology production has not kept pace; for example, *Locus* reported that in 1977 only about 60 anthologies appeared (*Locus* 208, Jan.–Feb., 1978). Still, quality anthologies have continued to appear, and their variety remains great. Theme, classroom, and historical anthologies were especially prominent during this time as SF continued to broaden its respectability and readership. However, the apparent decline of the SF magazine in the 1970s, coupled with the huge increase in the number of SF novels on the market, may indicate a shift away from modern SF's traditional emphasis on shorter fiction, and, with it, darker days for anthologies. This prediction, made in the 1981 edition of *Anatomy of Wonder*, has been borne out by more recent figures from 1985, when a record annual production of 1,332 science fiction and fantasy books was reached, of which only 64 were either reprint or original anthologies. In fact, original anthologies numbered only 26, far below the 249 new science fiction novels of that year and even less than the 41 volumes of science fiction literary criticism.

Still, the anthology has been and remains an important vehicle for SF. Given the genre's emphasis on short fiction and the existence of an active fan subculture complete with jargon, social organization, and a sense of its own historical development, this was to be expected. And once created, the anthology became a major factor in shaping the field's standards (such as Bleiler's, Merril's, and Wollheim's year's-best series); widening its horizons (Ellison's *Dangerous Visions* and Suvin's *Other Worlds, Other Seas* as cases in point); introducing new readers to the field (Conklin's, Crispin's, and Amis's anthologies, and, more recently, Blish's "Star Trek" series); chronicling its history and much of its best short fiction (Healy's, Boucher's, Moskowitz's, and Knight's anthologies, as well as the Nebula, Hugo, and Science Fiction Hall of Fame winners' collections); advancing the genre's academic respectability (Silverberg's *The Mirror of Infinity* and Clareson's *A Spectrum of Worlds* are examples); and opening new markets for writers (Pohl's *Star Science Fiction Stories*, Carnell's *New Writings in SF*, and Knight's Orbit series).

Although the need for including anthologies in any volume dealing with modern SF is clearly evident, the selection of specific works from such a large and diverse population is difficult. Those annotated in the following pages were picked according to certain criteria. First, only works composed largely or totally of SF from 1939 to 1963 have been included. Thus, such excellent works as Donald A. Wollheim's *Portable Novels of Science* (Viking, 1945), August Derleth's *Beyond Time and Space* (Pellegrini & Cudahy, 1950), and Sam Moskowitz's *Masterpieces of Science Fiction* (World, 1966) are not found here.

Second, the works selected had to be representative of the history and variety of anthologies in SF. This variety can be expressed in 12 major categories, which are discussed below. Anthologies designed for educational and academic uses are annotated in Chapter 13.

As a third criterion, the works selected for annotation do not include those volumes, although often excellent, composed only of three or four novellas. A large number of these have recently appeared, such as Sallis's *The Shores Beneath* (Avon, 1971), Silverberg's *Chains of the Sea* (Nelson, 1973), *Three Trips in Time and*

Space (Hawthorn, 1973), *The New Atlantis* (Hawthorn, 1975), *The Crystal Ship* (Nelson Doubleday, 1976), and Elwood's *Futurelove* (Bobbs-Merrill, 1977); but older examples, such as *Sometime, Never* (Ballantine, 1957), also exist. This exclusion is based on space limitations and the inherent problem of making a long list even longer, often for the sake of one or two outstanding stories, many of which can be found in other larger anthologies, single-author collections, or novel expansions. Given these three limiting criteria, the final selections were based on a work's historical importance, significant impact on the field, intrinsic high quality, and/or its representativeness of some major trend or development in SF.

The 12 major categories into which the SF anthologies can be divided yield an overview of the variety of anthology types and of their historical development. For post-1980 examples, see Chapter 4.

1. *General reprint anthologies.* Originates the modern SF anthology with Stong's *The Other Worlds* (1941) and Wollheim's *The Pocket Book of Science Fiction* (1943); includes such classic volumes as Conklin's *The Best of Science Fiction* (1946), Healy and McComas's *Adventures in Time and Space* (1946), Derleth's *Strange Ports of Call* (1948) and *The Other Side of the Moon* (1949), Conklin's *The Omnibus of Science Fiction* (1952), and Boucher's *A Treasury of Great Science Fiction* (1959), and continues with such fine more recent examples as Moskowitz's *Modern Masterpieces of Science Fiction* (1965), Cerf's *The Vintage Anthology of Science Fantasy* (1966), Knight's *A Science Fiction Argosy* (1972), and Hoskin's *The Liberated Future* (1974). Silverberg and Greenberg's *The Arbor House Treasury of Modern Science Fiction* (1980) is an excellent contemporary capstone for this tradition of broadening SF's readership.

2. *General original anthologies.* Popularized by Healy's *New Tales of Space and Time* (1951), this form at times has been important in shaping SF, as with Ellison's *Dangerous Visions* (1967) and *Again, Dangerous Visions* (1972), or in simply providing good new SF, as in Elder's *The Farthest Reaches* (1968) and Ferman and Malzberg's *Final Stage* (1975). Others have explored the state of SF outside the United States, as did Priest's *Anticipations* (1978) for Britain and Harding's *Rooms of Paradise* (1979) for Australia. A channel for innovation in SF.

3. *Reprint anthology series.* Important in bringing SF to new audiences, as with Crispin's *Best SF* (1955) and Amis and Conquest's *Spectrum* (1961) to Britain, and, to new generations, Silverberg's *Alpha* (1970), Aldiss's *Space Opera* (1974), and Lupoff's *What If?* (1980).

4. *Original anthology series.* Pioneered in the United States by Pohl's *Star Science Fiction Stories* (1953) and in Britain by Carnell's *New Writings in SF* (1964), this form provides important better paying markets for short fiction. In addition, the field itself has been influenced, as with Knight's innovative *Orbit* (1966). These traditions are carried on, although less extremely, by Carr's *Universe* (1971) and Silverberg's (now Randall's) *New Dimensions* (1971). More traditional SF appears in Judy-Lynn del Rey's *Stellar Science Fiction Stories* (1974), while major new authors are showcased in Martin's *New Voices in Science Fiction* (1977). As magazines decline, this form has become especially important.

5. *Year's-best anthology series.* Taken as guides to the field's best short fiction, this form, beginning with Bleiler and Dikty's best series in 1949, has helped legitimate the field and extend its horizons, as in Merril's (1956) and Harrison and Aldiss's (1968) series. A single series, such as Wollheim and Carr's (1965), once may have been able to provide a good overview of the genre, but today's great di-

versity and quantity of works are more aptly caught in several series, such as Carr's (1972), del Rey's (1972), and Wollheim's (1972). May not always be the "best" but are useful compilations of better works from many sources.

6. *Best of a magazine series*. Chronicler of SF's evolving heart, this form flowered in 1952, when modern SF's three major early magazines, *Astounding, Fantasy and Science Fiction*, and *Galaxy*, launched series. (Prior to that time, *Astounding* was amply represented in many of the classic reprint anthologies.) *New Worlds*, which later was to be such a profound innovator in SF, soon followed in 1955. Only slight efforts have been made on behalf of SF's less illustrious magazines, although *The Best of Planet Stories* (1975) is a good beginning. Meanwhile, new magazines have launched best volumes, especially the innovative *The Best of Omni Science Fiction* (1980).

7. *Anthologies of award-winning stories*. The SF subculture loves awards, and the most prestigious of them, the Hugo, began to be anthologized in 1962. The Nebula followed in 1966. Nebulas awarded retroactively by the Science Fiction Writers of America appeared in multiple volumes, as *The Science Fiction Hall of Fame* in 1970 and 1973. Of these, only the Nebula volumes are annual and, therefore, current. Provides interesting insights into the tastes of the award-voting constituencies.

8. *Historical reprint series*. Provides views of the field's development. Knight took the long view in *A Century of Science Fiction* (1962), while more intensive ten-year probes are made by Aldiss and Harrison in *Decade* (1975) and by Pohl, Greenberg, and Olander in *Science Fiction of the Forties* (1978). Perhaps the ultimate level has been reached by Asimov and Greenberg in their The Great SF Stories (1979) series, which reprints short fiction from a single year. See also the examples cited in classroom aids (Chapter 13).

9. *Anthologies of SF by non-SF authors*. Not unexpectedly, early volumes were of SF by scientists—Pohl's *The Expert Dreamers* (1962) and Conklin's *Great Science Fiction by Scientists* (1962). Other examples include SF by mainstream writers in Harrison and Gordon's *The Light Fantastic* (1971) and by mystery writers in Waugh, Greenberg, and Olander's *Mysterious Visions* (1979). These broaden SF's horizons.

10. *Anthologies of translated SF*. These began to appear regularly only recently and are still not numerous enough. Early examples include *Soviet Science Fiction* and *More Soviet Science Fiction* (1962), *Russian Science Fiction* (1963), and Knight's *Thirteen French Science-Fiction Stories* (1965). Other Soviet anthologies followed: *Path Into the Unknown* (1968) and Ginsburg's *The Ultimate Threshold* (1970). More European countries are represented in Suvin's *Other Worlds, Other Seas* (1970) and Rottensteiner's *View from Another Shore* (1973). More recently, France appears again in Jakubowski's *Travelling Towards Epilson* (1977) and Russia in *New Soviet Science Fiction* (1979). SF from the U.S.S.R. seems to have a special fascination for English-language readers.

11. *Theme anthologies*. Long one of SF's most popular anthology types, this form seems capable of generating a never-ending and, in the 1970s, an ever-expanding variety of volumes. (See [8-12] for an index to these anthologies.) Some themes show a continual presence; extraterrestrial life has been explored from Margulies and Friend's *From off This World* (1949) and Conklin's *Invaders of Earth* (1952) to Dozois and Dann's *Aliens!* (1980) and Pronzini and Malzberg's *Bug-Eyed Monsters* (1980). Likewise, anthologies on war and conflict range from Derleth's

Beachheads in Space (1952) to Dickson's *Combat SF* (1975), Haldeman's *Study War No More* (1977), and Bretnor's three-volume *The Future at War* (1979, 1980). Other major themes show less continuity from the past, perhaps because of traditional SF's tendency toward prudishness; for example, religion anthologies increase only in the 1960s and later, with Santesson's *Gods for Tomorrow* (1967), Mayo's *Other Worlds, Other Gods* (1971), and Elwood's *Chronicles of a Comer* (1974), while sex waits for the 1970s, with Scortia's *Strange Bedfellows* (1972), Elder's *Eros in Orbit* (1973), Hill's *The Shape of Sex to Come* (1978), and Greenberg and Waugh's *Love 3000* (1980). Some themes clearly reflect the special interests of the times; social problems emerge strongly in the 1970s with Harrison's *The Year 2000* (1970); Disch's *The Ruins of Earth* (1971), *Bad Moon Rising* (1973), and *The New Improved Sun* (1975); and Bryant and Harper's *2076: The American Tricentennial* (1977). Women are another example; Sargent's *Women of Wonder* volumes began in 1975, followed by McIntyre and Anderson's *Aurora: Beyond Equality* (1976), Laurance's *Cassandra Rising* (1978), Kidd's *Millennial Women* (1978), and Salmonson's *Amazons!* (1980). The 1970s also saw volumes on nearly every theme imaginable; some of the better ones include McCaffrey's *Alchemy and Academe* (1980), Elwood's *Future City* (1973), Dann's *Wandering Stars: An Anthology of Jewish Fantasy and Science Fiction* (1974), and Ferman and Malzberg's *Arena: Sports SF* (1976). This form ranges from the trivial to the polemical; at its best, it highlights the numerous speculative facets of an issue.

   12. *Miscellaneous works that further illustrate the history and development of SF anthologies.* Stories based on the "Twilight Zone" TV series have appeared in three volumes (1960, 1961, 1962) and the popular "Star Trek" series was adapted from script to story form by Blish beginning in 1967; much of contemporary SF's popularity may stem from these TV shows. At the opposite extreme is an anthology of serious SF verse, Lucie-Smith's *Holding Your Eight Hands*. An unusual form was attempted by Elwood in his Continuum series (1974, 1975), where stories were to "be continued" through four consecutive volumes, yet were to be so autonomous that each volume could be read independently or in any order. By the mid-1960s, science fiction, like the rest of Western culture, was undergoing severe shocks as traditional institutions came under attack by an energetic adversary culture of intellectuals and a rapidly rising new class beholden to government for its sustenance. These effects were soon apparent in Merril's year's-best anthologies and her *England Swings SF* (1968), but the chief ground breaker in this area was Moorcock's *The Best of New Worlds* (1965) and the New Worlds anthology series that began in 1967. Ellison's *Dangerous Visions* original anthologies (1967 and 1972) proved the high-water mark of the so-called New Wave phenomenon, which by then had practically become the mainstream of the field, almost completely submerging the trailing ends of SF's golden age. For these post-1963 anthologies, see Chapter 4.

3-418. Aldiss, Brian W(ilson), and Harry Harrison (U.K.), eds. **Decade: The 1940s.** Macmillan, 1975.
This series of anthologies assumes that SF is constantly changing and attempts to document those changes. Two criteria govern a story's inclusion, say the editors; first, the story has lasting quality, and second, the story is characteristic of its time. This volume features an overview of the decade by Aldiss and eight stories,

including Brown's "Arena" (SFHF), Simak's "Huddling Place" (SFHF), and Russell's "Hobbyist." All the stories are from Campbell's *Astounding*. *Decade: The 1950s* (Macmillan, 1976) contains 12 stories, none of which are from *Astounding*, although in the introduction Harrison points out the 1950s built on Campbell's foundations. Especially noteworthy stories include Budrys's "The Edge of the Sea" (HN, 1959), Bradbury's "The Pedestrian," Clarke's "The Star" (HW, 1956), and Cordwainer Smith's "Scanners Live in Vain" (SFHF). *Decade: The 1960s* (Macmillan, 1977) contains 18 stories and could be called the New Wave decade, although the editors avoid this term. For example, there is Ballard's "The Assassination of John Fitzgerald Kennedy Considered as a Downhill Motor Race," Disch's "Descending," Keith Roberts's "Manscarer," and Zoline's "The Heat Death of the Universe." It is hoped that the editors will continue the series, which so well exhibits their astute and unique perspective.

3-419. Aldiss, Brian W(ilson) (U.K.), ed. **Space Opera.** Futura, 1974.
Beginning with this volume, Aldiss has produced a series of excellent, entertaining anthologies drawn largely from the modern SF pulp magazines. Each volume contains an introduction by the editor and reprints the original blurbs that accompanied each story (where there were none, Aldiss wrote them). Space opera, a mix of reality, melodrama, dreams, and screwy ideas, according to Aldiss, is the theme of the first volume. Most of its 14 stories come from the 1950s, although the earliest, George Griffith's "Honeymoon in Space," dates from the 1900s; the most recent is Sheckley's parody, "Zirn Left Unguarded, the Jenghik Place in Flames, Jon Westerly Dead," from 1972. Other stories of interest: Bradbury's "All Summer in a Day," Brackett's "The Sword of Rhiannon," Galouye's "Tonight the Sky Will Fall," Hamilton's "The Star of Life," and Harness's "The Paradox Men." The next volume, *Space Odysseys* (Futura/Orbit, 1974), collects "quests for elusive somethings." Its 15 stories, ranging from 1937 to 1974, include Asimov's "Reason," Bester's "Time Is the Traitor," Brackett's "The Lake of the Gone Forever," Clarke's "The Sentinel," E. E. Smith's "Galactic Patrol," and Tiptree's "And I Awoke and Found Me Here on the Cold Hill's Side" (NN, 1972; HN, 1973). In *Evil Earths* (Weidenfeld & Nicolson, 1975), there are 14 darker pulp visions, including Campbell's "Night," Clarke's "If I Forget Thee, Oh Earth," Dick's "The Golden Man," Leiber's "Later Than You Think," and Tenn's "Down among the Dead Men." The rise and fall of interstellar empires is the theme in the two-volume *Galactic Empires* (Weidenfeld & Nicolson, 1976), which contains 26 stories mainly from the 1950s. Included are Anderson's "The Star Plunderer," Asimov's "Foundation," Blish's "Beep," Davidson's "The Bounty Hunter," Harrison's "Final Encounter," Michael Shaara's "All the Way Back," and James White's "Resident Physician." The most recent volume is *Perilous Planets* (Weidenfeld & Nicolson, 1978).

3-420. Amis, Kingsley (William), and Robert Conquest (U.K.), eds. **Spectrum.** Gollancz, 1961.
Originally developed as an annual reprint anthology series for British readers to show the scope and variety of SF and to plug its value as a literary form sui generis; published a year later in the United States. Largely limited to U.S. genre sources and authors of the 1940s, 1950s, and early 1960s. Introductions by the

editors review trends in SF and argue their case in each volume except in *Spectrum 4* (1965), where an excellent debate on SF, "Unreal Estates," by C. S. Lewis, Brian Aldiss, and Amis is included. Excellent fiction reprinted includes Pohl's "The Midas Plague" (1), Kuttner's "Vintage Season" (2), Anderson's "Call Me Joe" (3), Bester's "Fondly Fahrenheit" (3), and Kornbluth's "The Marching Morons" (4), all in SFHF. Also, Sheckley's "Pilgrimage to Earth" (1), Wyman Guin's "Beyond Bedlam" (2), Sturgeon's "Killdozer" (3), Leinster's "Exploration Team" (3) (HW, 1956), Ballard's "Voices of Time" (3), and Brunner's "Such Stuff" (4). *Spectrum 5* (1966) is of lesser quality and marks the series' end.

*3-421. Asimov, Isaac, and Martin H(arry) Greenberg, eds. **Isaac Asimov Presents the Great Science Fiction Stories.** Vol. 1, 1939. DAW, 1979.
The best anthology series of the later golden age of SF yet devised. The first volume contains 20 stories, most classics, including Binder's "I Robot," Campbell's (as Stuart) "Cloak of Aesir," de Camp's "The Gnarly Man," van Vogt's "Black Destroyer," Rothman's "Heavy Planet," Heinlein's "Life-Line," Sturgeon's "Ether Breather," Temple's "The Four-sided Triangle," and Williamson's "Star Bright." The following issues, up through Volume 14, 1952 (DAW, 1986), maintain this high quality. In each, the editors briefly describe the "mundane" and science fiction worlds of that year, and provide critical and personal notes introducing each story. Should be in every library's reading room—and in hardcover.

*3-422. Bleiler, Everett, and T(haddeus) E(ugene) Dikty, eds. **The Best Science-Fiction Stories.** Fell, 1949.
Major early "year's-best" anthology series; stories generally limited to U.S. genre sources and authors. Still a solid compilation of better works from the late 1940s to the late 1950s. Bleiler drops as editor after the 1954 edition, but Dikty, after combining it with *The Year's Best Science Fiction Novels*, continues the series with Fell until 1956. A final, 1958 edition appeared from Advent and the SF Book Club. Dikty's editions are notable for yearly review essays by the editor and for a yearly SF fantasy book index compiled by Earl Kemp. The 1954 edition carries an index of stories in the series to date. Bleiler and Dikty set the standard for later year's-best anthologies. The 1949–1950 volumes were bound together and issued as *Science Fiction Omnibus* (Doubleday, 1952), a popular and influential anthology of SF's golden age.

*3-423. Boucher, Anthony (pseud. of William Anthony Parker White), and J. Francis McComas, eds. **The Best from Fantasy and Science Fiction.** Little, Brown, 1952.
Since its founding in 1949, *F&SF* has been the literary aristocrat among American SF magazines. It publishes both fantasy and SF, mainly original, although many stories were reprints during the magazine's first few years. Its approximately annual "best" collection reflects the nature and quality of the magazine; Anthony Boucher and J. Francis McComas edit series 1–3, Boucher alone 4–8, Robert Mills 9–11, and Avram Davidson 12–14. The present editor, Edward Ferman, has continued the series through volume 24 (1982). Doubleday published the series, beginning with number 3, until Scribner did the twenty-fourth. Besides the usual excellent 10 to 15 stories in each volume, other items of interest are frequently reprinted, including poetry and Gahan Wilson cartoons. An addi-

tional 25 stories not collected in the regular series can be found in a special volume, *A Decade of Fantasy and Science Fiction,* edited by Robert Mills (Doubleday, 1960). The lead stories, appreciations, and updated bibliographies from six "special author" issues have been collected in *The Best from Fantasy and Science Fiction: A Special 25th Anniversary Anthology,* edited by Edward Ferman (Doubleday, 1974); authors are Sturgeon, Leiber, Anderson, Blish, Asimov, and Bradbury. Another collection of outstanding fiction, poetry, and cartoons, *The Magazine of Fantasy and Science Fiction: A 30-Year Retrospective,* edited by Edward Ferman (Doubleday, 1980), is the hardcover publication of the magazine's special thirtieth anniversary issue; also included are essays by Ferman ("How F&SF Was Born") and Asimov ("F&SF at 30"). Asimov, a long-time science columnist for *F&SF,* has published several collections of his columns. Together, these volumes comprise a comprehensive library of superior SF and fantasy. Also annotated as [4-652].

*3-424. Boucher, Anthony (pseud. of William Anthony Parker White), ed. **A Treasury of Great Science Fiction.** 2 vols. Doubleday, 1959.
Giant collection of superior 1938–1958 SF largely overlooked by earlier anthologists. Contains four good novels (Wyndham's *Re-Birth,* van Vogt's *The Weapon Shops of Isher,* Anderson's *Brain Wave,* and Bester's *The Stars My Destination*) and 21 shorter pieces, among which the following are outstanding: Heinlein's "Waldo" and "The Man Who Sold the Moon," George P. Elliott's "Sandra," Clingerman's "Letters from Laura," E. B. White's "The Morning of the Day They Did It," Bradbury's "Pillar of Fire," Kuttner and Moore's "The Children's Hour," Sturgeon's "The (Widget), the (Wadget) and Boff," Kornbluth's "Gomez," Dick's "The Father-Thing," and Oscar Lewis's "The Lost Years" (the only nongenre inclusion). Long an enrollment offering by the SF Book Club, this anthology has introduced many serious readers to SF.

3-425. Brackett, Leigh, ed. **The Best of Planet Stories #1.** Ballantine, 1975.
SF's pinnacle of pulp from 1939 to 1955, *Planet Stories* spanned the genre's best and baddest. Its garish covers with BEMs, near-nude spacewomen, and blazing rockets set the mood for tales of high adventure in deep space; seven good ones are collected here, including Anderson's "Duel on Syrtis," Brackett and Bradbury's "Lorelei of the Red Mist," and Brown's "The Star Mouse." It is to be hoped that more volumes will follow this one. An anthology from another pulp is *Amazing Stories: 60 Years of the Best Science Fiction,* edited by Isaac Asimov and Martin Greenberg (Random, 1985), which contains 20 stories.

*3-426. Campbell, John W(ood), Jr. **The Astounding Science Fiction Anthology.** Simon & Schuster, 1952.
Beginning with its appearance as an SF magazine in 1933, *Astounding/Analog* (the name was changed in 1960) became SF's most important magazine, which it remained until challenged by *Fantasy and Science Fiction* and *Galaxy* in the 1950s; if not as important today, it at least remains modern SF's true soul. In 1939, under Campbell, SF's single most important editor, it was instrumental in launching modern SF's golden age. Many of its better early stories are contained in the great SF anthologies of the 1940s and 1950s, but, beginning with Campbell's excellent *Astounding* (1952) anthology, its editors and others have produced a series of anthologies composed specifically of its contents. Campbell also edited *Prologue to Analog*

(1962) and the annual *Analog 1* (1963) through *Analog 8* (1971), all from Double-day. Ben Bova, Campbell's successor, edited *Analog 9* (Doubleday, 1973), *The Best of Analog* (Baronet, 1978), and *The Analog Science Fact Reader* (St. Martin's, 1974), the latter containing selected science-fact articles from the magazine. In addition, Harrison and Aldiss have produced *The Astounding-Analog Reader* [3-437], while Harrison alone has edited a volume of selected editorials by Campbell, *Collected Editorials from Analog* (Doubleday, 1966). Also see *The Best of Astounding*, edited by Tony Lewis (Baronet, 1978). Under editor Stanley Schmidt, a long series of *Analog* reprint volumes have appeared, drawing from current issues as well as past ones.

3-427. Carnell, E(dward) J(ohn) (U.K.), ed. **The Best from New Worlds Science Fiction.** Boardman, 1955.
Once Britain's premiere SF magazine, *New Worlds* was an innovator both under the early editorship of Carnell, beginning in 1946, and under that of Michael Moorcock, starting in 1967, when it helped launch SF's New Wave. Carnell's anthology contains eight stories from such standbys as James White, McIntosh, and E. C. Tubb. Carnell drew on *New Worlds* again for *Lambda 1 and Other Stories* (Berkley, 1964; U.S. and U.K. editions vary); here are Aldiss, Philip High, Moorcock, and John Rackham. Moorcock edited *The Best of New Worlds* (Roberts & Vinter, 1965), which drew on Aldiss, Harrison, and Sellings and included Brunner's "The Last Lonely Man" and Ballard's "The Terminal Beach." A series followed, beginning with *Best SF Stories from New Worlds 1* (Panther, 1967), which ran to eight volumes, all from Panther, ending in 1974; the first six were also published in the United States. They provide a good sampling of Ballard, Moorcock, Aldiss, Disch, Sladek, Spinrad, Zelazny, Priest, Langdon Jones, David Masson, Charles Platt, James Sallis, and other New Worlders. Makes an interesting contrast with the *Astounding-Analog* [3-437] series; some would call several of these stories marginal SF at best.

3-428. Cerf, Christopher, ed. **The Vintage Anthology of Science Fantasy.** Vintage, 1966.
Excellent collection of 20 modern stories, biographical notes, and editor's introduction (aimed at demonstrating that "science fantasy" can be "literate, provocative, and absorbing"). Besides major U.S. and British authors, Spain's José María Gironella is represented with "The Death of the Sea" and Poland's Julian Kawalec with "I Kill Myself." Outstanding works include Bradbury's "There Will Come Soft Rains," Sturgeon's "And Now the News," Knight's "The Analogues," Ballard's "Chronopolis," Davidson's "Or All the Seas with Oysters" (HW, 1958), Bester's "The Men Who Murdered Mohammed" (HN, 1959), and Miller's "A Canticle for Leibowitz" (SFHF).

*3-429. Conklin, Groff, ed. **The Best of Science Fiction.** Crown, 1946.
One of the earliest classic SF reprint anthologies of short SF (40 stories!) with an essay by Campbell on the nature of SF and a long introduction by the editor. Most stories were derived from the American pulps, such as *Amazing, Astounding,* and *Planet Stories*, and date from the 1930s and 1940s. However, the editor "tried to make it an adequate cross-section of the field, historically as well as contextually" and a story each is included by Frank R. Stockton, Poe, Doyle, Wells, and Huxley. Other stories of note include Cleve Cartmill's "Deadline" (of interest be-

cause it was investigated as a Manhattan Project leak), Sturgeon's "Killdozer," Leinster's "First Contact" (SFHF), and Heinlein's "Universe" (SFHF) and "Blow-ups Happen."

3-430. Conklin, Groff, ed. **Invaders of Earth.** Vanguard, 1952.
Appearing at a time when people were reporting "flying saucers," this volume suggests that not all aliens may be benevolent strangers bearing gifts or wisdom, like Harry Bates's "Farewell to the Master" (1940, on which the film *The Day the Earth Stood Still*, 1951, was based), but may be after our real estate if not our very hides, like Heinlein's *Puppet Masters* [3-205]. The 22 stories here, from the 1940s and 1950s, are divided into alien invasions of the distant past, immediate past, immediate future, and distant future; an editor's introduction traces the highpoints of enemy alien fiction from Voltaire to Wells and beyond. Among the many good inclusions are Leinster's "This Star Shall Be Free," Wollheim's "Storm Warning," Sturgeon's "Tiny and the Monster," Clingerman's "Minister without Portfolio," Brown's "The Waveries," and Pangborn's "Angel's Egg." Other anthologies of interest that deal with aliens in evil or good incarnations include *From Off This World*, edited by Leo Margulies and O. J. Friend (1949); *Contact*, edited by Noel Keyes (1963); *Encounter with Aliens*, edited by George W. Earley (1968); *The Science Fiction Bestiary*, edited by Robert Silverberg (1971); *The Alien Condition*, edited by Stephen Goldin (1973); *Creatures from Beyond*, edited by Terry Carr (1975); *Aliens!*, edited by Gardner Dozois and Jack Dann (1980); and Pronzini and Malzberg's *Bug-Eyed Monsters* [3-454].

3-431. Conklin, Groff, ed. **The Omnibus of Science Fiction.** Crown, 1952.
Similar to Conklin's 1946 anthology [3-429]; contains stories from the late 1940s to mid-1950s, as well as earlier works. Of the 43 stories, all fall after 1937 except one each by Will Gray, David Keller, Jack London, Lovecraft, André Maurois, Fletcher Pratt and B. F. Ruby, and R. R. Winterbotham. Of the more recent works, interesting pieces include Deutsch's "A Subway Named Mobius," Boucher's "The Star Dummy," Bradbury's "Kaleidoscope," and Clarke's "History Lesson." The Conklin anthologies cited here, along with his *A Treasury of Science Fiction* (Crown, 1948) and *The Big Book of Science Fiction* (Crown, 1950), represent a solid, 2,409-page, 145-story library of short SF prior to 1952, and, along with over 30 other, smaller volumes, make him preeminent among early SF anthologists.

3-432. Crispin, Edmund (pseud. of Robert Bruce Montgomery) (U.K.), ed. **Best SF.** Faber, 1955.
Crispin is the British Goff Conklin. His early anthologies brought much good SF from U.S. genre sources to British audiences. His first volume contained Blish's "A Case of Conscience," while in the next are found Brown's "Placet Is a Crazy Place," Heinlein's "Blowups Happen," Clarke's "The Nine Billion Names of God" (SFHF), and Bradbury's "Zero Hour." Faber published *Best SF 7* in 1970, ending the series.

3-433. Derleth, August William, ed. **The Other Side of the Moon.** Pellegrini & Cudahy, 1949.
Twenty stories that include Bradbury's "Pillar of Fire," Lovecraft's "Beyond the Wall of Sleep," van Vogt's "Vault of the Beast," and Wells's "The Star"; also sto-

ries by P. S. Miller, Lord Dunsany, C. A. Smith, Leinster, N. S. Bond, Wandrei, G. Kersh, Jenkins, Padgett, Russell, Sturgeon, and others. Another of Derleth's fine early anthologies of SF, this one with a horror or weird tinge.

3-434. Derleth, August William, ed. **Strange Ports of Call.** Pellegrini & Cudahy, 1948.
One of modern SF's major anthologists, Derleth was also a successful writer and a cofounder of Arkham House. A Lovecraft aficionado, he successfully promoted weird, horror, and science fiction, especially through his anthologies. This one contains 20 SF stories selected on the basis of literary quality; included are Bradbury's "The Million Year Picnic," Heinlein's "The Green Hills of Earth," and Sturgeon's "Thunder and Roses," and other works by such authors as Keller, Wandrei, Lovecraft, Dunsany, Wells, Kuttner, Wylie, and C. A. Smith. Still good reading today.

3-435. Ferman, Edward L(ewis), and Barry Malzberg, eds. **Arena: Sports SF.** Doubleday 1976.
Theme anthology of 11 stories (and an introduction by the editors) that stretch the concepts of both sport and SF. Especially noteworthy stories are Brown's "Arena" (SFHF), Budrys's "Nobody Bothers Gus," Pronzini's "The Hungarian Cinch," and Will Stanton's "Dodger Fan.". Pronzini's is the only original story. Sport is also the focus of *The Infinite Arena*, edited by Terry Carr (1977). It reprints seven stories, the better ones being Clarke's "Sunjammer," Malcolm Jameson's "Bullard Reflects," and Martin's "Run to Starlight." Proves again that SF is—and has been—about everything.

*3-436. Gold, H(orace) L., ed. **Galaxy Reader of Science Fiction.** Crown, 1952.
With its appearance in 1950, *Galaxy* provided a market for SF less technologically oriented than that associated with *Astounding;* socially critical stories, satires, and social science fiction appeared in its pages. Although its first few years may be considered its golden age, *Galaxy*'s career was marked by a number of highs and lows, and powerful editors have left their individual stamps on it. These are mirrored in the numerous anthologies that chronicle its history. The first sequence, edited by Gold, runs through *The Sixth Galaxy Reader* (Doubleday, 1962), only the first two of which appeared from Crown; Gold also edited three volumes of longer *Galaxy* fiction, all from Doubleday: *The World That Couldn't Be and Eight Other Novelets from Galaxy* (1959), *Bodyguard and Four Other Short Novels from Galaxy* (1960), and *Mind Partner and Eight Other Novelets from Galaxy* (1961). The next editor, Frederik Pohl, contributed a second sequence, all from Doubleday, which runs from *The Seventh Galaxy Reader* (1964) to *The Eleventh Galaxy Reader* (1969) and includes *Time Waits for Winthrop and Four Other Short Novels from Galaxy* (1962). The next editor, Ejler Jakobsson, produced a brief third sequence, *The Best from Galaxy: Vol. I* (1972) and *Vol. II* (1973); both appeared from Award Books and credited "The Editors of Galaxy Magazine" as compiler. A final sequence was edited by James Baen, the fourth editor, and consists of *The Best from Galaxy III* (1975) and *IV* (1976), and *Galaxy: The Best of My Years* (1980), all from Ace. A retrospective volume has appeared, *Galaxy Magazine: Thirty Years of Innovative Science Fiction*, edited by Frederik Pohl, Martin Harry Greenberg, and Joseph

D. Olander (Playboy, 1980), which contains 25 stories, a history, memoirs, and a *Galaxy* index (with several errors in the hardcover edition). A collection of Gold's editorials and comments from *Galaxy*, plus a ten-page autobiographical sketch, appear as *What Will They Think of Last? SF for Fun and Profit from the Inside*, edited by Gold (Institute for the Development of the Harmonious Human Being, 1976). *Galaxy* ceased publication in 1980. *Galaxy*'s sister magazine, *If*, had its own "best" series, *The Best from If: Vol. I* (Award Books, 1973) and *Vol. II* (Award Books, 1974), both edited by Pohl, and *Vol. III*, edited by James Baen (Award Books, 1976).

3-437. Harrison, Harry, and Brian W(ilson) Aldiss (U.K.), eds. **The Astounding-Analog Reader.** Doubleday, vol. 1, 1972; vol. 2, 1973.
Tribute to Campbell, his magazine, and his era that perpetuates the legend. Volume 1 contains 15 stories from 1932 to 1946; volume 2, 21 stories from 1947 to 1965. Perhaps as much a nostalgia trip as a historical document, the set is divided into 12 sections, most a few years in depth and preceded by their own introductions, within which the stories, complete with Campbell's original lead-ins, are arranged chronologically. Stories included both here and in SFHF are Asimov's "Nightfall," Anderson's "Call Me Joe," Godwin's "The Cold Equations," Leinster's "First Contact," and Moore and Kuttner's "Vintage Season." Other notable works are Bester's "The Push of a Finger," Blish's "The Bridge," Brown's "Placet Is a Crazy Place," Campbell's "Forgetfulness," Dickson's "Computers Don't Argue," Heinlein's "By His Bootstraps," Simak's "City," Sturgeon's "Thunder and Roses," and Tenn's "Child's Play."

3-438. Harrison, Harry, ed. **The Light Fantastic: Science Fiction Classics from the Mainstream.** Scribner, 1971.
Thirteen stories by authors not generally thought of as SF writers. Twain, Kipling, C. S. Lewis, and E. M. Forster are represented, but the remaining authors are post-1938: Burgess, Kersh, Amis, Greene, Borges, Robert Graves, E. B. White, Leo Szilard, and John Cheever. Excellent introduction by James Blish, "The Function of Science Fiction," which discusses SF as literature and its unique qualities.

*3-439. Healy, Raymond J., and J. Francis McComas, eds. **Adventures in Time and Space.** Random, 1946. Variant title: *Famous Science Fiction Stories*, Modern Library, 1957.
The most popular and influential reprint anthology of SF's golden age; within 997 pages are crowded 33 stories, many now classics, such as del Rey's "Nerves" (SFHF), Brown's "The Star-Mouse," Asimov's "Nightfall" (SFHF), and Campbell's "Who Goes There?" (SFHF) to name just a few; and two articles, one on rocketry by Willy Ley and another on time travel by A. M. Phillips. This anthology dominated *Astounding SF* readers' polls in 1953 and 1956, and still placed twentieth in 1966. Stories largely from the late 1930s and early 1940s and limited to genre authors and publications; catches the cream of SF's first New Wave. Other stories of interest include Heinlein's "Requiem," "The Roads Must Roll," and "By His Bootstraps," Campbell's "Forgetfulness," van Vogt's "Black De-

stroyer," P. S. Miller's "As Never Was," Rocklynne's "Quietus," Padgett's "The Twonky" and "The Proud Robot," and Bates's "Farewell to the Master."

3-440. Healy, Raymond J., ed. **New Tales of Space and Time.** Holt, 1951.
Historically important work that popularized the original SF anthology. Contains ten original stories, including Asimov's "In a Good Cause," Boucher's "The Quest for Saint Aquin," Bradbury's "Here There Be Tygers," and Neville's *Bettyann* [3-297]. Refreshingly optimistic by today's SF standards.

3-441. Hoskins, Robert, ed. **The Liberated Future.** Fawcett, 1974.
Twelve diverse stories from 1948 to 1973 that, the editor claims, point us toward a freer future. Interestingly, story sources range from the traditional *Astounding* with Anderson's "Sam Hall" and Kornbluth's "The Little Black Bag" (SFHF), through the middle ground of *Galaxy* with Sheckley's "Street of Dreams, Feet of Clay," to the innovative *Quark*, with Le Guin's "A Trip to the Head." A fine anthology.

*3-442. Knight, Damon F(rancis), ed. **A Century of Science Fiction.** Simon & Schuster, 1962.
Twenty-six stories and excerpts from larger pieces, two-thirds of which fall into the modern period. The book is divided into seven categories: robots, time travel, space, other worlds and people, aliens among us, supermen, and marvelous inventions (similar to what Conklin did), within each of which three to five pieces are placed more or less chronologically. The resulting sequences of idea development, coupled with Knight's usually informative comments, make for an unusual reading experience. Story selections are good; superior modern items include Aldiss's "But Who Can Replace a Man?," Anderson's "Call Me Joe" (SFHF), and Clarke's "The Star" (HW, 1956). A companion volume, *One Hundred Years of Science Fiction* (Simon & Schuster, 1968), is built along the same lines and contains 21 stories. Unfortunately, Knight's valuable comments on the stories are absent from this volume. Outstanding among the modern works included are Clarke's "The Nine Billion Names of God" (SFHF), Ballard's "The Voices of Time," and Kornbluth's "The Mindworm." Also of interest is Knight's *A Century of Great Short Science Fiction Novels* (Delacorte, 1964), composed of novels by R. L. Stevenson, Wells, Čapek, Heinlein, Sherred, and Richard McKenna. Together, these three volumes provide a spectacular overview of SF's development.

3-443. Knight, Damon F(rancis), ed. **Cities of Wonder.** Doubleday, 1966.
A meritorious anthology on the city. Reprints 11 stories from 1928 to 1964. Outstanding stories are Heinlein's "It's Great to Be Back!," Ballard's "Billenium," E. M. Forster's "The Machine Stops," Stephen Vincent Benét's "By the Waters of Babylon," and Campbell's (as Don A. Stuart) "Forgetfulness." Its SF is more traditional, but its stories are more noteworthy, its tone less overwhelmingly negative, than *Future City* (Trident, 1973), edited by Roger Elwood, another noted anthology of 22 original stories and poems on the theme of the city, and a good contrast to Knight's anthology. Includes a preface by the editor, a foreword by Simak, and an afterword by Pohl. A New Wavish-tinged work, the mood is generally downbeat and pessimistic. Noteworthy stories include Herbert's "Death of a City," Lafferty's "The World as Will and Wallpaper," and Malzberg's "Culture

Lock" and (as K. M. O'Donnell) "City Lights, City Night." Other authors include Disch, Bova, Koontz, Silverberg, Monteleone, and Ellison.

3-444. Knight, Damon F(rancis), ed. **A Science Fiction Argosy.** Simon & Schuster, 1972.
Includes two novellas, 22 short stories, and two outstanding novels (Bester's *The Demolished Man* [3-30] and Sturgeon's *More Than Human* [3-362]), all of which, with the exception of Collier's "Green Thoughts," appeared after 1945. The short fiction, largely drawn from three American SF magazines, is of high quality; examples include Charles Harness's "An Ornament to His Profession" (NN, 1966; HN, 1967), Shirley Jackson's "One Ordinary Day, with Peanuts," Cordwainer Smith's "The Game of Rat and Dragon," Pohl's "Day Million," Sheckley's "Can You Feel Anything When I Do This?," Aldiss's "Man in His Time" (NN, 1966; HN, 1967), and Shaw's "Light of Other Days" (NN, 1966).

3-445. Knight, Damon F(rancis), ed. & tr. **Thirteen French Science-Fiction Stories.** Bantam, 1965.
Stories are reprinted from *Fiction*, the French edition of *The Magazine of Fantasy and Science Fiction*, and date from the mid-1950s to the early 1960s, except for Mille's "After Three Hundred Years" (1922). Despite the usual SF props such as spaceships and aliens, many stories stress boy-girl, or human-alien, love: Cliff's "The Chain of Love," Veillot's "A Little More Caviar?," Klein's "The Monster," Damonti's "Olivia," and, especially, Dorémieux's "The Vanna," where a man dies to save his disease-carrying alien lover. In Cheinisse's "Juliette," it is the star-crossed love of boy and his robot car. Also contains some fantasy.

3-446. Lupoff, Richard A(llen), ed. **What If? Stories That Should Have Won the Hugo, Vol. I.** Pocket Books, 1980.
One of SF's best critics offers his choice for the most outstanding but overlooked story in each year since the founding of the Hugo Award. This first volume contains Tenn's "Firewater!" (1952), Knight's "Four in One" (1953), Sturgeon's "The Golden Helix" (1954), Jackson's "One Ordinary Day, with Peanuts" (1955), Anderson's "The Man Who Came Early" (1956), Wilhelm's "The Mile-Long Spaceship" (1957), and Kornbluth's "Two Dooms" (1958). Also contains an excellent introduction, "Earned Glory," by the editor, which traces the development of the SF field and its various awards; this is continued as short segments that preface each story summarizing each year. A second volume appeared in 1981, but a third volume, which was prepared, has yet to be published. See the Hugo Winners series [4-634].

3-447. Magidoff, Robert, ed. **Russian Science Fiction.** Tr. by Doris Johnson. New York Univ. Press, 1963.
One of the earliest and best anthologies of Russian SF, composed of 11 stories and an introduction by the editor, a Russian native and scholar of Slavic studies, including works by Beliaev, Efremov, Dneprov, Dudintsev, and Tsiolkovsky, the father of Russian rocket science. Two further volumes appeared: *Russian Science Fiction, 1968* and *Russian Science Fiction, 1969,* but the American SF readership remains cool to Russian SF, finding it often lacking in excitement and vague in intent. Also appearing about the same time were *Soviet Science Fiction* and *More So-*

viet Science Fiction (both Collier, 1962); in an introduction, Asimov describes their contents as "technology dominant." Of the eight stories (original publication dates not given), Krapivin's "Meeting My Brother" and A. Strugatskii's "Wanderers and Travellers" are especially strong. Other anthologies of interest are *New Soviet Science Fiction* [4-670], Ginsburg's *The Ultimate Threshold* (Holt, 1970), *Path into the Unknown* (MacGibbon & Kee, 1966), Fetzer's *Pre-Revolutionary Russian Science Fiction: An Anthology* (Ardis, 1982), and, most especially, Vladimir Gakov's *World Spring* (Macmillan, 1981), for it is the only one of these Russian anthologies with a contemporary Soviet compiler—and is highly recommended.

3-448. Margulies, Leo, and O(scar) J(erome) Friend, eds. **My Best Science Fiction Story.** Merlin, 1949.
A pioneer theme anthology of 25 stories, plus introductions by the authors explaining the bases of their choices of "best" story. Some picks are not surprising, such as Sturgeon's "Thunder and Roses," Williamson's "Star Bright," Bradbury's "Zero Hour," Brown's "Nothing Sirius," Heinlein's "The Green Hills of Earth," and Paul Ernst's horrifying classic "The Thing in the Pond." But readers may be puzzled by others, such as Asimov's "Robot AL76 Goes Astray," considering that he had already written "Nightfall" and "Liar." Anticipates Harrison's four *SF: Authors' Choice* anthologies (Berkley, 1968 and 1970; Putnam, 1971 and 1974). These choices seem even stranger—Asimov picks "Founding Father" and Anderson "The Last of the Deliverers"—until one reads that only nonanthologized stories could be included. Compare the recent and much better anthology of 25 authors' choices edited by Josh Pachter, *Top Science Fiction* (Dent, 1984).

*3-449. Merril, Judith, ed. **SF: The Year's Greatest Science-Fiction and Fantasy.** Dell, 1956 (title and publisher vary).
With 18 stories ranging from those by Steve Allen through Ted Sturgeon to Shirley Jackson, an introduction by Orson Welles, and a yearly summation and honorable mentions by the editor, Merril launched what came to be the finest annual year's-best anthology in SF. Emphasizing literary quality as well as ideas, the selections and authors were not limited to ghetto sources; thus, these anthologies include much of the best short speculative fiction written at the time. Frequently covered British as well as U.S. sources. Anthony Boucher summed up the year in SF books in numbers 6, 7, 8, and 9 (1961–1964). Merril's brief commentaries on SF are an added bonus in most volumes. Title changed to *The 5th Annual of the Year's Best SF* with number 5 (1960) and continued through number 11 (1966). Series ended with *SF 12* (Delacorte, 1968), having helped launch the New Wave of the 1960s and expanded the genre's horizons.

3-450. Moskowitz, Sam, ed. **Modern Masterpieces of Science Fiction.** World, 1965.
Twenty-one stories by the authors examined by Moskowitz in *Seekers of Tomorrow* [10-192]. Emphasis on golden age SF, with stories ranging from Smith's "The Vortex Blasters" to Farmer's "Mother"; other stories include Campbell's "Night," Heinlein's ". . . We Also Walk Dogs," Asimov's "Liar!," Williamson's "With Folded Hands," Sturgeon's "Microcosmic God," Simak's "Huddling Place," Leiber's "Coming Attraction," these last four all in SFHF. Makes an interesting comparison with Cerf's *The Vintage Anthology of Science Fantasy* [3-428].

3-451. Pohl, Frederik, ed. **The Expert Dreamers.** Doubleday, 1962.
Sixteen SF stories by scientists; some are regular SF contributors, such as Clarke, Asimov, R. S. Richardson, Hoyle, and G. O. Smith, but others include George Gamow, Norbert Wiener, and Leo Szilard. General literary quality is not exceptional, but ideas are exciting and competently developed. Editor introduces each author and, in an introduction, argues that *science* fiction is not a misnomer. Another anthology on the same theme is Groff Conklin's *Great Science Fiction by Scientists* (Collier, 1962), which contains 16 stories—many by the same authors as found in Pohl's collection—and editor's introduction and story notes. Other scientist-authors include E. T. Bell, J. B. S. Haldane, Julian Huxley, Chad Oliver, and John R. Pierce.

3-452. Pohl, Frederik; Martin Harry Greenberg; and Joseph Olander, eds. **Science Fiction of the Forties.** Avon, 1978.
A series of retrospective anthologies, by decade, by a team (Olander and Greenberg) of contemporary SF's most active "family" of anthologists. Overall, story selection is good, forewords and afterwords abound, and there are scholarly introductions and bibliographies of important SF books published during the decade. *Science Fiction of the Fifties* (Avon, 1979) drops Pohl as an editor. A useful companion series is edited by Isaac Asimov and Martin Harry Greenberg, *Isaac Asimov Presents the Great Science Fiction Stories* [3-421]. Other retrospective anthologies of merit for the same period include *The End of Summer: Science Fiction of the Fifties*, edited by Barry N. Malzberg and Bill Pronzini (Ace, 1979), and *Classic Science Fiction: The First Golden Age*, edited by Terry Carr (Harper, 1978), which take stories from 1940 to 1942. Compare the similar Aldiss and Harrison anthologies [3-418].

*3-453. Pohl, Frederik, ed. **Star Science Fiction Stories.** Ballantine, 1953.
The pioneer original SF anthology series that ran to six numbers, ending in 1960. Among the outstanding stories from this series are Clarke's "The Nine Billion Names of God" (1) (SFHF), Bixby's "It's a *Good* Life" (2) (SFHF), Clarke's "The Deep Range" (3), Kornbluth's "The Advent on Channel Twelve" (4) (HN, 1959), Davis's "Adrift on the Policy Level" (5), and Dickson's "The Dreamsman" (6). The "best" of the Star series was pulled together by Pohl in *Star of Stars* (Doubleday, 1960). Another interesting spinoff was the short-lived quality SF magazine *Star Science Fiction*, begun in January 1958.

3-454. Pronzini, Bill, and Barry Malzberg, eds. **Bug-Eyed Monsters.** Harcourt, 1980.
Thirteen entertaining stories that span 1927 to 1980 and feature that beloved/ bemoaned SF mainstay, the BEM. In addition to works by Bloch, Janifer, Brown, Anderson, Kornbluth, Pronzini and Malzberg, Asimov, and others, there are Clare Winger Harris's "The Miracle of the Lily," Knight's "Stranger Station," van Vogt's "The Rull," and Wollheim's "Mimic." Also contains a selection of BEM cartoons by Gahan Wilson. Compare Dozois and Dann's *Aliens!* (Pocket Books, 1980).

*3-455. Science Fiction Hall of Fame, Vol. I, Doubleday, 1971; Vols. IIa and IIb, Doubleday, 1974.
Volume I, edited by Robert Silverberg, contains 26 short stories and novelettes awarded retroactive Nebulas by the Science Fiction Writers of America; these are

the membership's choices as the best short SF published before 1965. Only two stories, Weinbaum's "A Martian Odyssey" (1934) and Campbell's "Twilight" (1934), appeared before 1938, while only one, Zelazny's "A Rose for Ecclesiastes" (1963), appeared after 1959. All stories are reprinted in order of their original publication. The method of selection is explained by the editor in an introduction that leaves the reader wondering which stories were omitted due to lack of space. Still, an excellent overview of short SF up through the 1950s. Only one overlap with Hugo winners (Keyes's "Flowers for Algernon"). Anthology is abbreviated as SFHF, as is Ben Bova's two-volume sequel, which contains 22 novellas, 11 in each subvolume, each also the recipient of retroactive Nebulas by the Science Fiction Writers of America as the best novella-length SF published prior to 1965. Foster's "The Machine Stops" (1928) and Wells's *The Time Machine* (1895) are the only pre-1938 stories, while Smith's "The Ballad of Lost C'mell" (1962), Vance's "The Moon Moth" (1961), and Budrys's "Rogue Moon" (1960) fall after the 1950s. Editor's introduction explains selection procedures and indicates that two stories that should have been included could not be—Miller's "A Canticle for Leibowitz" and Bradbury's "The Fireman." Only Simak's "The Big Front Yard" overlaps with Hugo winners. These certainly represent much of the best SF of the times, but seem more dated than do the shorter stories in Volume I. See Hugo and Nebula awards series [4-634, 4-673].

3-456. Scortia, Thomas N(icholas), ed. **Strange Bedfellows: Sex and Science Fiction.** Random, 1972.
Ground-breaking reprint anthology of 19 SF stories that deal with sex as their central idea. Stories date from the early 1950s to the early 1970s, and range from Boucher's light "Khartoum: A Prose Limerick" through Sturgeon's homosexuals in "The World Well Lost" to the powerful "Mother," Farmer's wrenching story of the ultimate return to the womb. Other authors include Silverberg, Zebrowski, Bretnor, Aldiss, and de Ford. Also includes introductions to stories and a brief but interesting essay on sex in SF by the editor, "Where Have All the Deflowerers Gone?" A lesser collection on the same theme is Joseph Elder's *Eros in Orbit* (Trident, 1973) with ten original stories, the best of which are Silverberg's "In the Group," Goulart's "Whistler," and Zebrowski's "Starcrossed." Also see Douglas Hill, ed., *The Shape of Sex to Come* (Pan, 1978), which has Sladek's "Machine Screw," Hilary Bailey's "Sisters," and, again, Silverberg's "In the Group"; and *Love 3000,* edited by Martin H. Greenberg and Charles Waugh (Elsevier/Nelson, 1980), which presents nine more stories about sexuality. Homosexuality is the subject of Elliot's *Kindred Spirits* [4-649].

3-457. Silverberg, Robert, and Martin Harry Greenberg, eds. **The Arbor House Treasury of Modern Science Fiction.** Arbor House, 1980.
Large anthology of 39 stories and an introduction by the editors in which they say this work was consciously designed to be the contemporary equivalent of those two giant classic anthologies that took SF beyond its narrow magazine readership, Conklin's *The Best of Science Fiction* [3-429] and Healy and McComas's *Adventures in Time and Space* [3-439]. All stories were written after 1945; most are from the 1950s and 1960s. Outstanding works include Aldiss's "Poor Little Warrior!," Anderson's "The Queen of Air and Darkness" (NW, 1971; HW, 1972), Asimov's "The Bicen-

tennial Man" (NW, 1976; HW, 1977), Blish's "Common Time," Bradbury's "Kaleidoscope," Davidson's "Or All the Seas with Oysters" (HW, 1958), Kornbluth's "The Marching Morons" (SFHF), Le Guin's "Winter's King" (HN, 1970), McIntyre's "Of Mist, and Grass, and Sand" (NW, 1973; HN, 1974), Malzberg's "A Galaxy Called Rome" (NN, 1975), Niven's "Neutron Star" (HW, 1976), Pohl's "Day Million," Russ's "When It Changed" (NW, 1972), Shaw's "Light of Other Days" (NN, 1966), Sturgeon's "When You Care, When You Love" (HN, 1963), Varley's "In the Bowl" (NN, 1976), and Zelazny's "The Keys to December" (NN, 1967). A good basic collection of generally well-known modern SF stories, but still not definitive. A companion volume is *The Arbor House Treasury of Great Science Fiction Short Novels*, edited by Silverberg and Greenberg (Arbor House, 1980), which collects 15 novellas from 1941 to 1977 by Asimov, Blish, Chandler, Clarke, Delany, DeVet and MacLean, Wyman Guin, Heinlein, Knight, Silverberg, Sturgeon, Cordwainer Smith, Tiptree, Vance, and Varley. Also, there is *The Arbor House Treasury of Science Fiction Masterpieces*, edited by Silverberg and Greenberg (Arbor House, 1983), a collection of 37 stories from Poe to Le Guin arranged by date. Compare Knight's *A Century of Science Fiction* [3-442].

3-458. Stong, Phil(ip Duffield), ed. **The Other Worlds.** Funk, 1941. Alternate title: *25 Modern Stories of Mystery and Imagination*, Garden City, 1942.
Although many of its 25 stories were horror, this anthology was an important SF landmark in that it pioneered the drawing of stories from the pulps for hardcover publication; sources included *Weird Tales, Astounding Stories, Amazing Stories, Westminster Magazine, Esquire,* and *Thrilling Wonder Stories.* In a foreword, the editor says: "This is an attempt to collect and preserve some yarns that may or may not be inferior to those of [Machen, Blackwood, Morgan, and Dunsany], but which might be lost because of obscure publications or because of the very occasional performances of the authors." These authors included Bates, Binder, del Rey, Derleth, Farley, Kuttner, Leinster, Lovecraft, Quinn, Sturgeon, and Wellman; Stong certainly succeeded. A good selection of the better prewar pulp fiction (the more garish BEM and space opera types of story are excluded).

3-459. Stover, Leon E., and Harry Harrison, eds. **Apeman, Spaceman: Anthropological Science Fiction.** Doubleday, 1968.
Pioneer among SF anthologies for classroom use in nonliterature areas. Introductions by anthropologist Carleton S. Coon and the editors set the stage for 26 stories, poems, essays, and a cartoon. Informative introductions precede the work's subdivisions of "Fossils,"."The Hairless Ape," "Dominant Species," "Unfinished Evolution," "Prehistory," "Archaeology," "Local Customs," and "Applied Anthropology"; thus, the major areas of anthropology—cultural, physical, and archaeological—are covered. Items of interest include anthropologist Horace Miner's satirical "Body Ritual among the Nacirema," Clarke's "The Nine Billion Names of God" (SFHF), and Coon's essay, "The Future of the Races of Man." Similar anthologies, many less well done, have since appeared.

3-460. Waugh, Charles G.; Martin Harry Greenberg; and Joseph Olander, eds. **Mysterious Visions: Great Science Fiction by Masters of the Mystery.** St. Martins, 1979.
In a scholarly introduction, Waugh posits a "neglected genre, fantastic myster-

ies," a blend of mystery and SF or fantasy, which is illustrated here by 26 stories, originally published from 1879 to 1972, by some of the mystery genre's most noted authors. Included are G. K. Chesterton, Agatha Christie, Sir Arthur Conan Doyle, Erle Stanley Gardner, Evan Hunter, John D. MacDonald, Sax Rohmer, and Mickey Spillane. *The 13 Crimes of Science Fiction,* edited by Isaac Asimov, Martin Harry Greenberg, and Charles G. Waugh (Doubleday, 1979), makes an interesting companion volume; it provides 13 SF-mystery stories from 1954 to 1977 by leading SF writers. Included are Asimov's "The Singing Bell," Niven's "ARM" (HN, 1976), Dick's "War Game," Reamy's "The Detweiler Boy," and Tenn's "Time in Advance." Other noteworthy anthologies of a related nature: *Dark Sins, Dark Dreams,* edited by Barry N. Malzberg and Bill Pronzini (1978); *Crime Prevention in the 30th Century,* edited by Hans Stefan Santesson (1969); *Space, Time and Crime,* edited by Miriam Allen de Ford (1964); *Space Police,* edited by Andre Norton (1956).

3-461. Wollheim, Donald A(llen), ed. **The Pocket Book of Science Fiction.** Pocket Books, 1943.

Ten stories in what is traditionally recognized as the first true modern SF anthology. Contains works by early writers Benét, Bierce, Collier, Wells, West, and Weinbaum; also includes Sturgeon's "Microcosmic God" (SFHF) and Heinlein's "—And He Built a Crooked House" from the modern period.

4
The Modern Period: 1964–1986

Brian Stableford

When we speak today of "the sixties" as a period in our cultural history we call to mind events, issues, and fads that belong to the latter part of the decade. The previous phase of cultural history came to an end in 1963, and if we are to single out one particular moment when a punctuation mark was added to the unfolding sentence of history, the most conspicuous candidate is the twenty-second of November, when President Kennedy was assassinated. This was also the year of the great civil rights march on Washington, and the year when the Beatles ushered in a new era in popular music. It is by the juxtaposition of events as disparate as these that we construct in memory and mythology some sense of historical phasing. Thus, 1964 was for many people the first year in a new mini-era.

The new era was characterized in several different ways. There were autumn elections in both the United States and England; Johnson beat Goldwater and Harold Wilson's Labour party regained power after 13 years in opposition. On the same day that power changed hands in England it changed hands in the U.S.S.R., too; Khrushchev was replaced (without, of course, the necessity of an election). Meanwhile, governments throughout Africa were changing as decolonialization proceeded apace: new nations like Tanzania and Malawi were being born. The Vietnam war was in the process of being stepped up: a U.S. destroyer was attacked off North Vietnam in August and North Vietnamese bases were bombed in reprisal. The bombing was escalated early in 1965, provoking student demonstrations in Washington as dissent over civil rights expanded into what sometimes seemed like a rebellion of the young against the entire political order. By June 1965 U.S. troops were given leave to take the offensive role in a war that—it later transpired—they would not win.

The antagonism of the late 1960s youth culture to the "official culture" of the Establishment was symbolized in ways other than political demonstration. Distinctive tastes in musical entertainment had always been the primary badge of youth culture, but now the allegiances of musical taste were combined—and to some extent confused—with an interest in "getting high" with the aid of drugs: cannabis, amphetamines, and hallucinogens, especially LSD. LSD was not simply produced in quantity for illicit distribution; it came with promises of some kind of enlightenment, a transcendence of ordinary experience. This ideology was used by the adherents of youth culture (who were not all young in chronological terms) to further distinguish themselves from their opponents (who were, of course, not all old). The counterculture came to see itself not simply as being in the right, but possessed of a wisdom inexplicable to the uninitiated. This view was endorsed by one of the most influential would-be analysts of the counterculture, Marshall McLuhan, whose *Understanding Media* was published in 1964. McLuhan argued that the world was on the threshold of apocalyptic change because the new electronic media, especially TV, extended the human sensorium in a way radically different from print, and thus altered the way in which the world was perceived by those socialized by the new media. It was also possible to believe in this period, by courtesy of the linguistic theory of Benjamin Whorf and its extensions in the philosophy of knowledge, that a world differently perceived was indeed a different world. The idea was newly fashionable that it was possible for two people living in the same city, or the same household, to experience different realities, and the counterculture of the 1960s was effectively a practical extrapolation of this opinion.

All of this was of some significance for the evolution of science fiction. The direct influences are easy enough to see. An interest in drugs, altered states of consciousness, and the relationship between the actual and the perceived became central to the work of one of the major SF writers of the period, Philip K. Dick, and infected the work of many other writers to some degree. Perceptions of the Vietnam war also affected attitudes to hypothetical future wars, especially wars against hypothetical alien beings. Broader issues of the day—particularly the invasion of politics by ecological questions—were taken up in a big way by SF writers. The traditional technophilia of hard SF now began to face very determined opposition from technophobic speculators who had a strong scientific base of their own in extrapolating the hazards of overpopulation, pollution of the environment, and the waste of nonrenewable resources.

Less obvious, but surely of equal importance, are the effects of the general situation on the cultural situation of SF. It had long been the case that teenagers formed a disproportionately large sector of the SF audience. All surveys indicate that the majority of readers are recruited to SF at 13, and although many retain their interest for life, for some it is simply another teenage fad. Thus, although SF cannot be said to *belong* to youth culture, any sweeping change in youth culture is likely to be reflected in SF. It is unsurprising, therefore, that there emerged within the SF community in 1964 what has come to be called the "New Wave": a radical manifesto designed to transform and renew SF by defying the conventions and customs that seemed to be its "Establishment." The New Wave propagandists wanted to be "experimental" in every way they could think of, and they wanted to break and overturn "editorial taboos" wherever they could locate them. The SF community thus found itself split; its ideologies became a spectrum extended between a conservative pole of technophiliacs who believed strongly in telling a good story the old-fashioned way, and tended also to be old-fashioned in their attitudes toward sex; and a radical pole of apocalyptic technophobes and ecological mystics who were sympathetic to surrealism, cared little for plot, and wrote liberally (in more ways than one) about sex. These two poles were, of course, relatively uninhabited, but it was easy enough to place most writers in one or the other temperate zone on either side of the presumed equator.

The first major propagandist for the SF New Wave was Michael Moorcock, who acquired his platform in 1964 when he became editor of the British magazine *New Worlds* and transformed it from a relatively traditional format into an avant-garde publication preoccupied with its own contemporaneity. Moorcock thought that the future was not really to be found in the visions of galactic empire and technological triumph seen in so much SF, but in apocalyptic possibilities with which the present was already pregnant. Other British writers, including J. G. Ballard and Brian Aldiss, had already begun moving in the same direction, more interested in the "inner space" of human perceptions and psychological reactions to hypothetical situations than in the "outer space" of colorful futuristic adventure stories. Several new writers, including the Americans Thomas M. Disch and John Sladek, were quickly recruited to the cause.

The American New Wave lacked any such platform within the genre magazines, but eventually acquired one in an influential anthology edited by Harlan Ellison, *Dangerous Visions* [4-650], which was claimed by its creator to be a "revolution" against the limitations and taboos imposed by other editors. Ellison invited 32 of the field's leading writers to demonstrate what they could do in this vein, but it was clear enough even then who the writers were that intended to take full advantage of the new license. Philip José Farmer wrote the most controversial story in *Dangerous Visions* but the principal experimental SF writers publishing in the United States at the time were Samuel R. Delany and Roger Zelazny. They, along with David R. Bunch and R. A. Lafferty, had been publishing magazine stories for some time, demonstrating that the taboos to which the New Wave writers were ideologically opposed were as much symbol as actuality.

Other changes in the cultural situation of SF were taking place at this time, and were already facilitating considerable change in the kinds of work that SF writers could do, and the economic rewards it might bring. Throughout the period covered by the previous chapter—1938–1963—SF was primarily a magazine medium. A good deal of SF was published in book form, but the vast majority of SF books consisted of material reprinted from the magazines. The most upmarket of the various paperback SF lines in 1963 was the Ballantine line, which featured very few original novels and published a very high proportion of short story collections. A higher proportion of original works was featured in the more prolific Ace line, but the majority were short novels marketed in the celebrated "Ace Double" format. It had been inevitable for some years, though, that the magazines would eventually lose their primary status, and that book publication—especially paperback publication—would become much more important, in economic terms, to SF writers. Paperback books had a much longer "shelf life" than magazines, and could be constantly reprinted to capitalize on the popularity of their successes.

By 1963 paperback companies were beginning to realize that big rewards could be reaped by cultivating the popularity of particular writers and capturing the loyalty of readers. Ace and Ballantine were already engaged in a competition in the promotion of Edgar Rice Burroughs, a longtime stalwart of American popular fiction. Ace was also cultivating the popularity of Andre Norton. Between 1963 and 1965 Signet similarly cultivated Robert Heinlein, Pyramid found itself able regularly to reprint its editions of Edward E. Smith's novels, and Berkley promoted a sequence of books by J. G. Ballard. Soon, paperback publishers began to mine the old pulp magazines for promotable series: Bantam resurrected Doc Savage and Lancer brought sword and sorcery back into vogue by reprinting Robert E. Howard's Conan series (adding numerous new volumes by contemporary writers because there was an insufficient supply of the real thing) and issuing short series of similar stories by Michael Moorcock. The same phenomenon was evident in England, where one of the longtime paperback SF publishers, Panther, found its 1964 reprints of various Isaac Asimov novels selling well enough to warrant regular reprinting thereafter. Science fiction was not yet quite ready for the best-seller lists, but many SF books were by now steady sellers that had reached millions of readers. Science fiction and heroic fantasy were intricately interlinked in the marketplace and the publishing schedules, and it was therefore of some importance for the marketing of SF when the competition between Ace and Ballantine entered a remarkable new phase in 1965, when both publishers issued editions of J. R. R. Tolkien's *Lord of the Rings*. Ballantine had arranged reprint rights with Tolkien's English publisher while Ace took advantage of a loophole in the copyright laws and got its editions out first. Thanks to these paperback editions Tolkien's work became a youth culture fad such as had never been seen before, and there opened up a vast market for heroic fantasy. Many SF writers were already writing futuristic heroic fantasy, and SF stories with swordplay and magic thrown in for good measure began to appear in profusion.

The proliferation of paperback SF also permitted a more conspicuous stratification of the genre. In the old days of the pulps it had been very obvious that *Astounding* was upmarket of *Thrilling Wonder Stories* but by 1964 the magazines were all respectably middlebrow, and it was in the paperback market that one could readily distinguish the more sophisticated from the less sophisticated. The scene was set for the better SF writers to make a bid for greater literary respectability, and this was done, first by promoting individual volumes, and later by launching the new line of "Ace Specials" edited by Terry Carr, which were clearly differentiated by design and advertisement from the ordinary Ace SF line. The line did not last long—from 1968 to 1971—but it did break important new ground in SF publishing in the United States. In England, there had been a much more obvious stratification of the marketplace for many years, with paperback companies like Badger Books well downmarket of anything in the United States, and respectable hardcover houses like Faber producing books much more upmarket than those of any U.S. publisher, but even in England there was a certain confusion. The most prolific paperback publisher of SF in 1963 was Digit, which cheerfully mixed titles by Brian Aldiss with those of Vern Hansen and other veteran hacks. In that year, though, Penguin began its upmarket line of SF paperbacks by British and American authors, with avant-garde covers, and by 1966 both Digit and Badger were finished, bringing the U.K. scene very much into line with the U.S. situation.

In the later 1960s, the popularity and cultural standing of SF were to be further boosted by its extensions in other media. There had been SF films for many years, but with very few exceptions they were schlock films that confirmed in many minds the impression that SF was rubbish that could not be taken seriously. This impression was largely confirmed by SF on TV, though Rod Serling's "Twilight Zone" had helped erode it slightly. The late 1960s, however, began a new era in TV and film SF. In the cinema, *Alphaville* (1965) and *Fahrenheit 451* (1966) were imported from France, and Stanley Kubrick collaborated with Arthur C. Clarke in the making of *2001: A Space Odyssey* (1968). These lent a respectability to cinema SF later confirmed by the Russian film of Stanislaw Lem's *Solaris* [3-261], made in 1971. At the same time, films like *Barbarella* (1967) confirmed that SF imagery was acquiring a certain sleazy chic. The first serious SF novel to be properly and effectively filmed in America was Daniel Keyes's *Flowers for Algernon* [3-228], which was made into *Charly* (1968). Science fiction on TV entered an entirely new phase, begun in Britain with the long-running "Doctor Who," which began in 1963, and continued spectacularly in the United States with "Star Trek," which first came to the screen in 1966. Although "Star Trek" was not particularly long-lived in its TV incarnation (78 episodes were screened over a three-year period), it attracted a cult following of remarkable avidity, and spawned four movies (so far) as well as dozens of novels—repeats of the TV plays are still running and the flood of books shows no sign of drying up. "Star Trek" spawned its own distinctive fan community in imitation of SF fandom, and for some years the conventions held by that community were on a larger scale, and featured more exaggerated cultish behavior, than the general run of SF conventions.

"Star Trek" was not particularly sophisticated, although it did use scripts by SF writers as good as Harlan Ellison, Theodore Sturgeon, and Norman Spinrad, but its success did signify that the imagery of SF was not only very widely distributed in the contemporary cultural environment, but that its basic motifs were familiar enough not to have to be newly introduced every time they were employed outside the specialist context of a magazine read only by the SF cognoscenti.

The widening of the potential audience for SF books meant that the economic opportunities available to the professional SF writer were considerably increased. There was already a handful of full-time SF writers when the 1960s began, but by the time the decade ended there were dozens, and some of them were on the brink of becoming rich. The Science Fiction Writers of America was founded the 1965, and quickly took up various causes on behalf of its members. It also began to give out its own awards, the Nebulas.

In the meantime, academic interest in SF was also growing rapidly. One of the side effects of campus unrest was that students demanded a greater say in the composition of the college curriculum, and asked that literature courses should take more account of the literary phenomena of the present day. Courses in science fiction began to proliferate, and academics with an interest in SF founded the Science Fiction Research Association in 1970. There was already one long-standing academic journal in the field—Thomas D. Clareson's *Extrapolation* [14-33], founded in 1959—and two others came into being in the early 1970s: the British *Foundation* [14-36] in 1972 and *Science-Fiction Studies* [14-41] in 1973. The demand for information about the field, by writers, readers, and academics, was so considerable that the newsletter *Locus,* which commenced publication in 1968 with a circulation of about 100, had acquired by 1972 a circulation of well over 1,000, by 1975 was printing around 2,500 copies per issue, and has a current circulation approaching 8,000.

The information collected on a regular basis by *Locus* bears eloquent testimony to the expansion of the SF/fantasy field in the 1970s. In 1972, when the count was first taken, 85 original hardcover books appeared and 28 reprints; there were 140 original paperbacks and 95 reprints. These figures increased steadily until 1979, when the recession cut back the volume of total paperback sales by some 10 to 15 percent. In that year there were 320 original hardcovers and 132 reprints; there were also 365 original paperbacks and 471 reprints. The number of new titles appearing had tripled in seven years. The recession put an end to this expansion, and for the next five years publication was steady at a slightly lower level, but in 1985 the figures again began to set new records: in that year there were 305 original hardcovers, 332 original paperbacks in the standard mass market format, and 78 original paperbacks in the large trade format. (See Chapter 7 for a more detailed discussion.) Stories in *Locus* also recorded that the first SF title to make the best-seller lists in both hardcover and paperback was Frank Herbert's *Children of Dune* in 1977; that the first six-figure advance for an SF novel was paid to Robert Silverberg in 1978; that the first half million dollar advance for an SF novel was paid to Robert Heinlein in 1979; and that the first three-quarter million dollar advance for an SF novel was paid to Frank Herbert in 1980. Thus is the success of SF in the marketplace mapped out; nowadays it is rare to see an American best-seller list that does not have 3 or 4 SF or fantasy titles in its top 20. Now that the effects of the recession are fading, and publication is entering a new phase of expansion, one can only guess how much progress can still be made.

Changes in the characteristic themes of science fiction between 1964 and 1986 have been partly determined by the advancement of various fields of technological endeavor and partly by sociopolitical waves of fashion that have brought various projects and possibilities into the arena of general discussion and controversy.

In terms of technological developments the most spectacular advances have been in the field of information processing, which was revolutionized by the microprocessor invented by M. E. Hoff in 1969. The first microcomputers came onto the market in 1971, and since then the power of the machines has increased vastly while their cost has come steadily down. It is now possible to buy word processing equipment for approximately the same price as a large typewriter, and a powerful personal computer for little more than the price of a TV set. Science fiction writers, of course, were interested in computers before the 1960s began, and readily anticipated that they would become steadily more powerful. They found it easy enough to imagine future society being run by computerized dictatorship.

It was taken for granted in the 1960s that such power would be correlated with enormous size, and that the effort put into building such machines would be so great that only one or two could exist in the world. D. F. Jones's *Colossus* [4-289] provides an excellent example of this way of thinking. By the 1980s, however, an entirely new range of possibilities was in sight, with the interface between man and machine becoming much more intimate, opening a way into a vast and complex "software universe" (often dubbed cyberspace) where human operators and manufactured programs could contend and conflict in countless different ways. Vernor Vinge's *True Names* [4-576] and William Gibson's *Neuromancer* [4-233] present striking explorations of this new world of possibility.

Another group of technologies, whose progress has been far less spectacular but whose prospects seem equally tremendous, has grown up in connection with genetic engineering. The possibility of taking technical control over the processes by which living creatures reproduce themselves and evolve was foreseen as soon as genetic theory was first advanced. J. B. S. Haldane predicted a bright future for biological engineers as long ago as 1923, when he delivered the lecture that became his controversial essay *Daedalus; or, Science and the Future,* but it was not until the end of the 1950s that the genetic code contained in DNA molecules was finally "cracked" by molecular biologists, and not for another decade that techniques for splitting DNA strands to isolate particular genes became reasonably efficient. During the 1970s techniques were refined by which new genes could be "transplanted" into bacteria in plasmid rings, so that cultures of transformed bacteria could become living factories manufacturing desirable proteins like insulin, interferon, and growth hormones. Now that such production has been commercialized the research-and-development race is truly on, and the transformation of plant and animal genomes has become a near-future possibility. Even the very modest interventions in human reproduction that have become possible—in vitro fertilization and the cryogenic storage of fertilized ova— have raised new moral questions that have generated considerable public debate. The biological engineering featured in the SF of the 1960s tended to be fairly modest, and Frank Herbert's *Dune* [4-268] features a project to produce a superman by selective breeding over many generations. Eight years later, in *Hellstrom's Hive* [4-269], Herbert employed much more direct methods. By that time, the possibility of cloning human beings was attracting much attention, as evidenced by such novels as Pamela Sargent's *Cloned Lives* [4-470] and Kate Wilhelm's *Where Late the Sweet Birds Sang* [4-603]. By the 1980s, the potential of biotechnology seemed positively apocalyptic. This awareness is spectacularly demonstrated in *Blood Music* [4-50] by Greg Bear.

A third area of technology whose progress has always been of cardinal interest to SF writers is that concerned with the space program, but here the history of the relevant period is by no means one of steady progress. In 1964, thanks to the initiative seized by President Kennedy, the race for the moon had been well and truly joined. NASA, abundantly funded, was highly active. Not only was Ranger VII taking close-up photographs of the lunar surface; Mariner IV was launched in order to photograph Mars. Manned Apollo missions began in 1968, and the first moon landing was achieved in 1969. By the time the final Apollo mission was completed in 1972, though, the excitement had begun to wear off. The Skylab and Space Shuttle programs continued, but the economic recession of

1979 put them in a new context of cost-cutting and gradual winding down. The objective of making the Space Shuttle a profit-making enterprise seemed unlikely to be fulfilled when attempts to put satellites into orbit began to go awry, and the program was decisively interrupted in 1986 following the explosion of a shuttle shortly after takeoff. The reaction of SF writers to this pattern of spectacular triumph followed by slow decline was varied and complex. Hard SF writers had always felt a kind of proprietary interest in the Apollo project, considering themselves its ideological forefathers—a view endorsed and reinforced by the media, when SF writers were regularly co-opted as Earth-based commentators on the Apollo missions. For SF writers, Armstrong's moon landing was indeed one small step in a pattern of conquest that would take humankind forward into the farther reaches of the SF imagination, and the gradual winding down of space exploration that followed in the 1970s and 1980s was not so much a disappointment as a betrayal. Some SF writers therefore became ardent propagandists for the revival of the space program, prophesying disaster if pusillanimous politicians continued to frustrate human destiny in their characteristically blind and small-minded fashion. Magazines like *Analog* and James Baen's carefully titled *Destinies* and *Far Frontiers* presented open propaganda in their nonfiction articles as well as dramatized propaganda in their fiction. Examples of this sense of betrayal can be found in G. C. Edmondson's *The Man Who Corrupted Earth* [4-197] and Lee Correy's *Manna* [4-149]. Some SF writers used their fiction to take symbolic revenge on the heretics opposing their sacred mission; Larry Niven and Jerry Pournelle's disaster story, *Lucifer's Hammer* [4-397], reserves some nasty fates as well as nasty comments for those foolish enough to have set themselves up in opposition to the cause of progress. As previously noted, though, SF now had a technophobic pole as well as a technophilic one, and there were SF writers who did not think at all kindly of the space program, considering it a perverse product of human delusions of grandeur. One writer who incurred the wrath of the faithful in no uncertain terms was Barry Malzberg, whose *Beyond Apollo* [4-352] raised a storm when it won the first John W. Campbell Memorial Award. Because Campbell had been the most ardent champion of the myth of space conquest, it seemed to many singularly perverse of the award jury to commemorate his passing by honoring a book so determined in its ideological opposition to and mockery of that myth. Malzberg is, however, something of an exception even among the softer SF writers, many of whom remain entranced by the idea of a galactic culture filled with wonderful alien races, and would hate to refuse the technology necessary to get access to it even if they use it mainly to lay the groundwork for emotional parables celebrating simpler ways of life and extolling the virtues of being nice instead of powerful.

In addition to these changing technologies, it is worth noting the effect of a technological constant on the characteristic worldview of SF. In one important respect, nothing could change: weapons technology was already sufficiently advanced well before 1964 to assure that an all-out war between the superpowers would annihilate the human race, and that the very least result to be expected of nuclear holocaust would be the destruction of civilization. The apparent likelihood of nuclear war has shifted slightly with minor changes in government in the United States and the U.S.S.R., but SF deals in such long-term expectations that fluctuations in momentary popular anxiety make little impact on it. The role of nuclear holocaust in SF has nevertheless changed significantly since the early 1960s. One of the best SF films of the period was the black comedy *Dr. Strangelove; or, How I Learned to Stop Worrying and Love the Bomb* (1963), whose title was quickly parodied by Philip K. Dick in *Dr. Bloodmoney; or, How We Got Along after the Bomb* [4-174], and these titles contained an ironic appreciation of what would happen in SF; no one actually learned to love the bomb, but the hysteria ebbed away from tales of the holocaust as writers became much more interested in the potentialities of the postholocaust scenario. Hypothetical accounts of how we might "get along" after the destruction of civilization began to multiply, and began to acquire a more romantic aspect. Images of a partially devastated world have now become utterly commonplace in SF, almost as if the inevitability of the holocaust is taken for granted, and postholocaust America has become an arena for frontiersmanship almost as important as the solar system under conquest. The new mythology of the postholocaust frontier can be found in such works as Kim Stanley Robinson's *The Wild Shore* [4-447] and Paul O. Williams's "Pelbar Cycle" novels [4-604].

This catastrophist romanticism is, as might be expected, largely confined to the United States. In Britain, where a rich tradition of catastrophe fiction had existed since the 1930s, images of a world from which civilization had been conveniently (and sometimes comfortingly) obliterated had been produced in abundance in the 1950s, and that trend was just reaching its culmination in the mid-1960s novels of J. G. Ballard. Since then British writers have shown a tendency to dwell on the less pleasant aspects of postholocaust scenarios, often in a rather embittered tone. There is little romanticism in Keith Roberts's *The Chalk Giants* [4-440] and none in Peter Van Greenaway's *graffiti* [4-562], although there is some in Russell Hoban's *Riddley Walker* [4-272].

Other classic SF themes, of course, remained quite uninfluenced by technological developments in the real world. A little work was done in the field of trying to make contact with alien beings, but Carl Sagan's messages carried on Pioneer and Voyager probes are unlikely to be received by anyone or anything for several centuries, if at all, and the radio telescope listening program designed by a NASA study group, Project Cyclops, never got under way. Nevertheless, the prospect of a first contact with aliens via radio wave seemed to many SF writers to be close at hand, and worthy of very serious consideration. The popularity of alien menace stories had waned dramatically in the 1950s, and the SF writers of the late 1960s were ready to presume that contact with aliens would probably bring nothing but good, and so much good that the establishment of such contact would mark a vital watershed in human history: a revelation so marvelous that it could be compared only with the miraculous advent of a new religion. This idea is most strikingly presented in James E. Gunn's *The Listeners* [4-244], and it is not surprising that when Carl Sagan was offered a huge advance to write an SF novel, contact with aliens was to be the theme.

For those writers who used the establishment of a galactic community as an initial hypothesis, though, the question of dealing with alien beings was a very different one. The magazine era of SF's history, from 1926 to 1963, had seen aliens make giant strides toward acceptability. The vast majority were no longer loathsome invaders to be exterminated like vermin; they were peaceful beings wiser and nicer than we brutish and power-crazed human beings. By and large, we were not merely prepared but highly privileged to live next door to them, and the fact that we could not marry our daughters to them was a matter for regret. In the late 1960s and 1970s, alien beings were employed to assault human vanity in dozens of different ways. Human self-importance counted for little in the face of the agrarian ambitions of *The Genocides* [4-185] in Thomas M. Disch's novel, and the optimism of human religious faiths could be made to look pretty silly when set aside the actual and obvious redemptions and salvations available to alien beings in such stories as Robert Silverberg's *Downward to the Earth* [4-501] and George R. R. Martin's "A Song for Lya" [4-361]. Even when aliens were savages, they were usually nobler savages than any Rousseau ever dreamed of, and they showed up our nastiness in no uncertain terms in such stories as Ursula Le Guin's *The Word for World Is Forest* [4-329]. Where love and marriage between humans and aliens did become possible, it was usually the aliens who conducted themselves with the greater dignity and moral integrity, as in *Leviathan's Deep* [4-112] by Jayge Carr. When humans went to war against aliens, as in *The Forever War* [4-247] by Vietnam veteran Joe Haldeman, it usually turned out to be a mistake, and even when there really was no alternative but genocide, as in Orson Scott Card's *Ender's Game* [4-109], the action could not help but leave an appalling burden of guilt crying out for a sequel in which some kind of redemption might be permitted.

It was in this period too, though, that SF writers began to bring new scientific resources to bear in dramatizing the differences that might exist between humans and aliens, conscientiously trying to escape from the trap of describing aliens who were simply people in funny costumes. Ursula Le Guin (the daughter of anthropologist Alfred Kroeber) and Michael Bishop made productive use of the insights of anthropology in designing enigmatic alien societies, while Ian Watson and C. J. Cherryh drew extensively on linguistic science. In this way modern SF has begun to extrapolate the possible worlds made imaginable by the human sciences, as well as the possible transformations of the human world made plausible by our increasing command of the hard sciences. These "possible worlds" need not include alien beings at all—the ones closest to home are those dealing with transformations of past history, and there has been a sophistication of alternate world stories as well as alien world stories in this period. Keith Roberts's *Pavane* [4-444] and Phyllis Eisenstein's *Shadow of Earth* [4-200] are examples.

As stories of interracial relations in the galactic community and stories of altered history have become more serious, they have inevitably taken aboard more ideological commitments. The SF myth of the conquest of space always had politics built into it, of course, but its politics were largely taken for granted and unscrutinized in the magazine era, when it was still possible for the writers and editors to assume that some kind of broad political consensus did exist in the United States. Despite John W. Campbell, Jr.'s, idiosyncratic preoccupation with the merits of slavery, SF writers of the 1950s were not particularly self-conscious about the ideological undercurrents in their work, because there was little opposition to rouse them to righteous indignation. Things changed in the 1960s when Robert Heinlein turned preacher in *Stranger in a Strange Land* [3-207]. By the time the turbulent decade was reaching its close it was impossible for writers *not* to be self-conscious about the political implications of their work. All those ideals that had been taken for granted in pulp SF were suddenly charged with disguised fascism by courtesy of Norman Spinrad's ingenious description of a Hitlerian pulp SF story in *The Iron Dream* [4-527]. By that time the politicization of the SF community had been remarkably demonstrated when two groups of SF writers took out ads in the June 1968 issue of *Galaxy* to express their support for or disapproval of the Vietnam war. The technophilic stalwarts of hard science fiction—Poul Anderson, John W. Campbell, Hal Clement, Robert Heinlein, Larry Niven, Jerry Pournelle, and G. Harry Stine among them—were solidly ranged in the pro-Vietnam lobby, while the anti-Vietnam lobby was packed with those writers whose fiction was decidedly disenchanted with the thrust of technological progress: Ray Bradbury, Harlan Ellison, Philip K. Dick, Ursula Le Guin, Barry Malzberg, Joanna Russ, Robert Silverberg, and Kate Wilhelm among them. After this, there could be no taking for granted what route into the future humankind ought to take. Ideas of progress would henceforth have to be supported with argument, and the question of what kind of future we ought to be making for our children had to be treated as a wide-open one.

This new self-consciousness, with its attendant agonizing and propagandizing, was by no means limited to the narrow political arena surrounding international relations and the space program. The emergence of the "green politics" of campaigners against pollution was quickly reflected in science fiction by stories espousing a curious "ecological mysticism," whereby the ecological relations of exotic cultures and exotic life-forms came to assume an almost allegorical significance. In this way of thinking, our disruption and possible destruction of the "balance of nature" in the Earth's ecosphere were to be seen not merely as a dangerous folly, but also as a kind of sin. For the ecological mystics, environmental pollution was not simply a practical problem but evidence of a foul apostasy by which we had ceased to have appropriate reverence for and awe of nature, frequently dressed, as of old, in maternal symbolism. The most direct representation of this ideology can be found in Ernest Callenbach's *Ecotopia* [4-107], but it is latently present in much SF set on exotic worlds, from Frank Herbert's *Dune* [4-268] to Brian Aldiss's "Helliconia" trilogy [4-6].

Even more striking than SF's new consciousness of ecological politics is its new consciousness of sexual politics. Throughout the magazine era, SF was consumed by an audience that was predominantly male—most surveys suggested that female readers accounted for little more than 10 percent of the audience. Female characters played a limited number of stereotyped roles. Female writers were few in number and mostly fell into step with the prevailing norms, whatever their private opinions might be. In the late 1960s, though, all of this was overturned. Feminists interested in stimulating social change became interested in futuristic fiction as a medium for the extrapolation of their hopes and anxieties. Female readers—initially attracted, it seems, by "Star Trek" and by the increasing prominence of magical fantasy in the SF marketplace—began to compose an ever-greater proportion of the audience, and it became possible to aim books at them. A large fraction of the new writers recruited to SF in the 1970s were female, and although one of them sheltered under a male pseudonym—James Tiptree, Jr.—she soon left no doubt as to where she stood on matters of sexual politics. New male writers like John Varley also went to considerable lengths to be conspicuously nonsexist. Joanna Russ brought the SF novel spectacularly to bear on the issues of sexual politics in *The Female Man* [4-458], and her example was followed by many others, including male apologists for homosexuality such as Samuel Delany and Thomas M. Disch. In tackling themes of such intimacy, SF left no possible doubt about its relevancy as a species of literacy, and its obvious flexibility and versatility in addressing the core issues of sexual politics provided a powerful argument for the unique potential of the genre as a philosophical instrument. Science fiction's thought experiments in physical science have mostly been silly, and its thought experiments in biological science have hardly seemed relevant to the real world, but its thought experiments in sexual relations have certainly succeeded in touching nerves. The decision by the British feminist publishing house The Women's Press to experiment with a science fiction line (begun in 1985) seems a perfectly natural one.

It is difficult to move this discussion of themes in modern SF onto a more general level, but a consideration of the way that SF has reflected developments in science during this period can be at least tentatively expanded to take note of certain parallels between the recent development of ideas in the philosophy of science and the evolution of SF. Scientific knowledge has been called into question by several philosophers skeptical of its claim to be the one and only truth. The claim made by scientists to be issuing an objective description of the universe has been attacked, most famously by Thomas Kuhn in *The Structure of Scientific Revolutions* (1962), which suggests that revolutions in science's idea of the universe can as easily be accounted for in terms of the internal workings of the scientific community as by reference to the compelling power of new discoveries. Kuhn raises the disturbing idea that present-day scientific theories may simply be one more way of perceiving "reality," not necessarily superior to any other way of perceiving it. Some of Kuhn's disciples have cheerfully elected to believe that science is simply one more set of myths. The more moderate but slightly elusive Paul Feyerabend suggests in *Against Method* (1975) that the best dictum to adopt if intellectual progress is to be made is that "anything goes." In a sense, SF writers might be considered to have been following this advice all along: in SF, if not in real scientific theory, there has always been a very liberal interpretation of what might count as a plausible hypothesis. Science fiction writers may have protested that they must never entertain the truly impossible, but they have adopted considerable license in deciding what must be eliminated on that account. It is noticeable, though, that recent SF has become much more robust in its adoption of the anything-goes policy. Old impossibilities are once again being adopted, quite without apology, as premises for SF stories. The Symmesian hollow world is once again available for exploitation, as demonstrated by James P. Blaylock's *The Digging Leviathan* [4-65], and adventure stories can now be set on alternate worlds that are nothing like the real one, as in Richard A. Lupoff's *Circumpolar!* [4-344] or Terry Pratchett's *Strata* [4-424]. This new liberalism has much to do with the increasing popularity of fantasy, and the way that certain authors have exploited it by recklessly fusing together SF and fantasy motifs. This syncretic enthusiasm can clearly be seen in the work of writers like Piers Anthony, Jack Chalker, and Tim Powers, and it has made possible a fusion of themes that would have been unthinkable in those golden days when *Astounding* was one thing and *Unknown Worlds* very definitely another.

Limitations of space have necessitated the deletion of many of the titles published between 1964 and 1980 that were annotated in the second edition of *Anatomy of Wonder*. I have also revised the annotations so that the majority have been shortened, in order to maximize the space available for annotating works published between 1980 and 1986, and a few new ones published before 1980. By this means I hope to increase the utility of this edition, while the second edition will retain a certain utility too. The criteria used in selecting the list of works to be annotated are broadly similar to those used in previous editions: all award-winning novels have been included, and most novels nominated for awards; best-sellers have been annotated, including mainstream best-sellers that have considerable SF interest. With respect to the most recent works I have attempted to give a broadly representative cross section of active SF writers.

In selecting works for annotation I have made use of the review columns of several periodicals, most especially *Locus* [14-37], *Fantasy Review* [14-35], *Foundation* [14-36], and Richard Geis's *Science Fiction Review*, which ceased publication at the end of 1986. I have also made considerable use of a recently published reference book dealing with the field: Curtis C. Smith's *Twentieth-Century Science-Fiction Writers* [8-32]. I am, of course, greatly indebted to Joe De Bolt and John R. Pfeiffer, who dealt with the years 1938–1980 in the previous edition, and I should also like to acknowledge my indebtedness to those people who have assisted me in my research of the years 1980–1986: David Langford, Chris Morgan, and those publishers who made available books and information, especially Claire Eddy of Tor Books and Elsie Wollheim of DAW Books.

Bibliography

4-1. Adams, Douglas (U.K.). **The Hitch-Hiker's Guide to the Galaxy.** Pan, 1979.
Adaptation of a much-loved and very funny British radio series. Earth is demolished to make way for a new hyperspatial bypass, but the hero stows away on a starship with a reporter for the eponymous reference book. Their outrageous extraterrestrial adventures are part satire, part slapstick. *The Restaurant at the End of the Universe* (1980) completed the adaptation of the original radio scripts, but Adams then added *Life, the Universe and Everything* (1982) and *So Long, and Thanks for All the Fish* (1984). The books gradually run out of comic inspiration and become increasingly saturated with a bitterly ironic weltschmerz. Compare Sheckley's *Options* [4-491].

4-2. Aldiss, Brian W(ilson) (U.K.). **An Age.** Faber, 1967. U.S. title: *Cryptozoic!*, Doubleday, 1968.
A dissident artist in a decadent New Britain is recruited as an assassin to kill a theoretician whose ideas about temporal "mind travel" pose a threat to the regime. His journeys through time take him to England during the depression and to the remote eras of the prehistoric past; ultimately he must confront awkward questions about the nature of time and memory. A baroque adventure story,

elaborately dressed with fascinating ideas. Compare Silverberg's *Hawksbill Station* [4-503].

*4-3. Aldiss, Brian W(ilson) (U.K.). **Barefoot in the Head: A European Fantasia.** Faber, 1969.
The Acid Head War, fought with psychotropic weapons, has left all Europe crazy. The hero journeys back and forth across the continent, becoming a guru in the Gurdjieff tradition and acquiring quasi-messianic status. A Joycean celebration of the vivid eccentricities of the 1960s counterculture, brilliantly phantasmagoric. Based on materials published in *New Worlds;* a fine testament to the stimulus provided by the magazine.

4-4. Aldiss, Brian W(ilson) (U.K.). **Frankenstein Unbound.** Cape, 1973.
The protagonist timeslips from the twenty-first century into a past where Mary Shelley coexists with the monster of her imagination. An interesting extrapolation of Aldiss's fascination with Mary Shelley and her book; more successful than his later attempt to reconsider the philosophical import of a Wells novel, *Moreau's Other Island* (1980; U.S. title: *An Island Called Moreau*).

*4-5. Aldiss, Brian W(ilson) (U.K.). **Greybeard.** Faber, 1964.
Unwise experimentation with nuclear devices has led to the sterilization of mankind, and there seems no hope for the future. The central characters, waiting for the end, consider the ironies and frustrations of their situation. A key work in the tradition of British disaster stories. Compare Moxley's *Red Snow* [2-82] for an earlier variation on the theme.

4-6. Aldiss, Brian W(ilson) (U.K.). **Helliconia Spring.** Cape, 1982.
The first volume (JWC, 1983; NN, 1982) in a trilogy continued in *Helliconia Summer* (1983) and *Helliconia Winter* (1985; NN, 1985). Helliconia is a planet whose sun eccentrically orbits a much brighter star, and thus has a "great year" extending over hundreds of generations. Its societies undergo vast changes, interrupted by periodic plagues, and the relationship between humans and the cold-loving phagors also alters dramatically. Observers from Earth watch with interest from an orbital station, and relay the story of one great year back to an avid audience on Earth. The dedication states that the trilogy takes up themes from Aldiss's non-SF novel *Life in the West* (1980) in attempting to analyze the "malaise" from which our world is supposed to be suffering. Compare May's Pliocene Exile series [4-366].

*4-7. Aldiss, Brian W(ilson) (U.K.). **Hothouse.** Faber, 1962. U.S. edition, *The Long Afternoon of Earth* (Signet, 1962), was abridged. The 1976 Gregg Press reprint of the complete edition has a useful introduction by Joseph Milicia. This edition was itself reprinted by Baen, 1984.
Novelization of a series of short stories (HW, 1962). In the very far future human life and endeavor are dwarfed by the fecund plant kingdom. The hero learns to look beyond the immediate struggle for existence, and to see his life in the context of Earth's history, with the help of an intelligent fungus. A fabulous imaginative tour de force. Compare Hodgson's *The Night Land* (1912) and Fowler Wright's *The World Below* [2-144]. Also annotated as [3-4].

4-8. Aldiss, Brian W(ilson) (U.K.). **The Moment of Eclipse.** Faber, 1970.
Collection of Aldiss's stories from the late 1960s, taking full advantage of the latitude permitted by the avant-gardism of the New Wave and becoming cosmopolitan in their settings. This trend in Aldiss's work continued in *Last Orders and Other Stories* (1977) and in *Seasons in Flight* (1984), where only a minority of the stories are SF, others being fables set in the poorest regions of the world. The idiosyncratic artistry and literary showmanship of *The Moment of Eclipse* are stylish products of the New Wave. Compare Jones's *Eye of the Lens* [4-290].

4-9. Aldiss, Brian W(ilson) (U.K.). **Report on Probability A.** Faber, 1968.
An attempt to write a novel based on Heisenberg's Uncertainty Principle. A series of observers sustain alternative realities with their unwavering inquisitiveness. An enigmatic work that has affinities with the French anti-novel. Compare Robert Anton Wilson's modeling of modern physical theory in narrative, *Schrödinger's Cat* [4-612].

4-10. Amis, Kingsley (U.K.). **The Alteration.** Cape, 1976.
Alternate-world story of Catholic-dominated Europe; the central character is a young singer who faces the possibility of being castrated to preserve his voice. A nice balance is struck between the hard-edged plot and the ironic background. Compare Eisenstein's *Shadow of Earth* [4-200].

4-11. Amis, Kingsley (U.K.). **Russian Hide and Seek.** Hutchinson, 1980.
A future England, having become a satellite of the U.S.S.R., is stripped of its traditional culture, and cannot retrieve it even when the political situation eases. Dour and embittered. Compare Munro's *When William Came* (1914).

4-12. Anderson, Chester. **The Butterfly Kid.** Pyramid, 1967.
Psychedelic adventures in Greenwich Village, with aliens intervening to materialize the phantoms of hallucination. An engaging expression of countercultural exuberance. The author and two friends are the main characters; the friends added their own contributions to an unusual trilogy in *The Unicorn Girl* (1969) by Michael Kurland and *The Probability Pad* (1970) by T. A. Waters. HN, 1968.

*4-13. Anderson, Poul. **The Avatar.** Putnam, 1978.
Progress on Earth is being stifled by a paternalistic regime, and the hero must embark on a transgalactic odyssey to find an alien species sufficiently sophisticated to bring him home adequately enriched with knowledge. Compare Sheffield's *Between the Strokes of Night* [4-493].

4-14. Anderson, Poul. **The Byworlder.** Signet, 1971.
An alien visitor arrives on Earth in the twenty-first century, when the United States is culturally fragmented because wealth and advanced technology have liberated idiosyncrasy, and aesthetic motives have become paramount. Compare Reynolds's *Commune 2000* [4-439]. NN, 1971.

4-15. Anderson, Poul. **Fire Time.** Doubleday, 1974.
One of Anderson's several exercises in the design of an alien ecology and its extrapolation into the history and politics of intelligent natives; here their techno-

logical progress is periodically interrupted by close passages of a red star. Compare Clement's *Cycle of Fire* [3-108]. HN, 1975.

4-16. Anderson, Poul. **Orion Shall Rise.** Pocket Books, 1983.
Picks up themes from short stories collected in *Maurai and Kith* (1982). The Maurai (descendants of the Maori) have thrived in the wake of the nuclear holocaust and have established a low technology utopia; they are now faced with opposition from survivors in North America who plan to revive nuclear power. Long and rather loosely organized. Compare Spinrad's *Songs from the Stars* [4-529].

4-17. Anderson, Poul. **People of the Wind.** Signet, 1973.
Humans and birdlike aliens combine forces to defeat an invasion of the aliens' world by other humans. Action-adventure enlivened by the careful design of the alien culture and its relations with humankind. Part of the "Technic Civilization" future history. HN, 1974; NN, 1973.

*4-18. Anderson, Poul. **Tau Zero.** Doubleday, 1970.
A malfunctioning starship continues to accelerate as it nears light speed, and its crew observe relativistic effects, ultimately being carried beyond the time frame of the universe, while the cruel circumstances force psychological and interpersonal adaptations. An archetypal example of hard SF with a visionary element. Compare Bear's *Eon* [4-51]. HN, 1971.

4-19. Anderson, Poul. **There Will Be Time.** Doubleday, 1972.
The time traveling hero learns that the future of the United States is bleak, and sets out to repair the time stream. A reaction against the ideas of the 1960s counterculture, which is satirized by quotes from "Withit's Collegiate Dictionary." Compare Gunn's *Kampus* (1977). HN, 1973.

4-20. Anthony, Piers (pseud. of Piers Anthony Jacob). **Battle Circle.** Avon, 1978.
A trilogy originally published separately: *Sos the Rope* (1968), *Var the Stick* (1972), and *Neq the Sword* (1975). The first volume won a competition sponsored by Pyramid Books and *The Magazine of Fantasy and Science Fiction*. In a postholocaust world a highly formalized code duello sets the stage for a gradual reconstitution of society. An early illustration of Anthony's ability to tie exaggerated action-adventure plots to more elaborate idea schemes.

*4-21. Anthony, Piers (pseud. of Piers Anthony Jacob). **Chthon.** Ballantine, 1967.
The plot and counterplot, running in close parallel, tell of the protagonist's escape from a hellish prison and the transgalactic odyssey that ultimately confronts him with the chemical nature of his own being. A stylized futuristic fable. The sequel, *Phthor* (1975), is much less successful. HN, 1968; NN, 1967.

4-22. Anthony, Piers (pseud. of Piers Anthony Jacob). **Cluster.** Avon, 1977. British title: *Vicinity Cluster*.
The first of a series extended in *Chaining the Lady* (1978), *Kirlian Quest* (1978), *Thousandstar* (1980), and *Viscous Circle* (1982), in which Superpowers dependent on Kirlian auras are also the key to cosmic cultural integration. Protagonists hur-

tle through adventures on alien worlds, harassed by enemies, on a variety of universe-saving quests. Colorful, exotic adventure fiction, crashing through the old limits of SF costume drama. Breezy and inventive. Compare Chalker's Well World series [4-123].

4-23. Anthony, Piers (pseud. of Piers Anthony Jacob). **Macroscope.** Avon, 1969.
The macroscope is an instrument allowing human observers access to the wonders of the universe; when Homo sapiens is relocated in this cosmic perspective the narrative shifts to a quasi-allegorical mode in which the symbolic significance of astrological lore is reworked. A more extended exercise in the same vein is the trilogy *God of Tarot* (1979), *Vision of Tarot* (1980), and *Faith of Tarot* (1980), which similarly attempts to display a modern philosophy of life by reinterpreting the apparatus of an occult system. A further series of this type, using even more baroque apparatus and taking its pretensions even more seriously, is The Incarnations of Immortality, begun with *On a Pale Horse* (1984) and continued in *Bearing an Hourglass* (1984) and *With a Tangled Skein* (1985).

4-24. Anthony, Piers (pseud. of Piers Anthony Jacob). **Omnivore.** Ballantine, 1968.
First part of a trilogy completed by *Orn* (1971) and *Ox* (1976). A stylized alien ecology is made to parallel certain traits in human personality; a whole series of problems is met by preserving relationships of interdependence. The series moves by degrees toward the ritualized and gamelike plot structures that often fascinate Anthony.

4-25. Asimov, Isaac. **The Bicentennial Man and Other Stories.** Doubleday, 1976.
Collection of 12 stories, the most notable being the robot story "That Thou Art Mindful of Him" (HN, 1975) and the title story (HW, 1977). Asimov's more recent short stories can be found in *The Winds of Change and Other Stories* (1983).

4-26. Asimov, Isaac. **Foundation's Edge.** Doubleday, 1982.
Fourth volume (HW, 1983; NN, 1982) of the Foundation series [3-19], uncomfortably extending its themes and beginning the work of binding it into a common future history with Asimov's robot stories. In the 1940s the series seemed sophisticated in introducing political themes into space opera, but SF has evolved so far in the meantime that the new book seems rather quaint. A feast of nostalgia for longtime readers. The story continues in *Foundation and Earth* (1986), with the hero pursuing his quest to track down the origins of mankind, gradually learning the truth about Earth. *Prelude to Foundation* is forthcoming.

*4-27. Asimov, Isaac. **The Gods Themselves.** Doubleday, 1972.
A novel reflecting Asimov's fascination with the sociology of science, reminiscent in parts of J. D. Watson's *The Double Helix* (1968). The energy crisis is "solved" by pumping energy from a parallel universe, whose alien inhabitants must try to communicate with humans in order to tell them that both races are in deadly peril. Written with a verve and economy that are missing from Asimov's more recent novels. Compare Bob Shaw's *A Wreath of Stars* (1976). HW, 1973; NW, 1972.

4-28. Asimov, Isaac. **The Robots of Dawn.** Doubleday, 1983.
The heroes of Asimov's earlier robot detective stories, *The Caves of Steel* [3-16] and *The Naked Sun* (1957), undertake a new investigation on the utopian world of Aurora, where men live in harmony with their machines. The murder mystery becomes a peg on which to hang part of the argument connecting the robot series with the Foundation series. This argument is further extended in *Robots and Empire* (1985), in which robots renegotiate the famous laws of robotics and set humankind on the road to galactic empire. Prolix, but better connected with their antecedents than the new Foundation novels [4-26]. HN, 1984.

4-29. Asprin, Robert. **The Cold Cash War.** St. Martin's, 1977.
Large corporations rebel against government restrictions on their operation, forming private armies to do battle on their behalf and winning by virtue of their technological enterprise. A combination of interesting premises and melodramatic plotting. Compare Mack Reynolds's *Mercenary from Tomorrow* (1968).

4-30. Attanasio, A. A. **Radix.** Morrow, 1981.
Earth is much altered by the loss of its magnetic "shield" against cosmic radiation, and the changes are accelerated by a burst of energy from a collapsar, which brings about a wholesale metamorphosis of Earth's life system. Many beings transcend the limitations of frail flesh in different ways, and the plot follows one such transcendent maturation. Compare Silverberg's *Son of Man* [4-507] and Delany's *Einstein Intersection* [4-167]. NN, 1981.

4-31. Atwood, Margaret (Canada). **The Handmaid's Tale.** McClelland & Stewart, 1985.
Dystopian novel of a world ruled by militaristic fundamentalists in which sexual pleasure is forbidden. Conception and childbirth have become difficult and the handmaid of the title belongs to a specialist breeding stock. The story is annotated by a historian in a further future, whose shape is not revealed. Compare Wyndham's "Consider Her Ways" (1956) and Charnas's *Walk to the End of the World* [4-125]. NN, 1986.

4-32. Auel, Jean M. **The Clan of the Cave Bear.** Crown, 1980.
A best-selling novel about a Cro-Magnon girl adopted by a tribe of Neanderthalers, who disturbs their tradition-bound ways and becomes an important agent of change. Dense and highly detailed. The series continues in *The Valley of Horses* (1982) and *The Mammoth Hunters* (1985). Compare Case's *Cook* [4-120].

4-33. Ballard, J(ames) G(raham) (U.K.). **The Atrocity Exhibition.** Cape, 1970. U.S. title: *Love and Napalm: Export U.S.A.*, Grove, 1972.
A series of "condensed novels"—collages of images presenting a kaleidoscopic pattern of twentieth-century myths and motifs, particularly those that dominated the 1960s. Political assassinations, customized cars, the space program, the arms race, the media as brokers of celebrity—all are juxtaposed here in a nightmarish panorama of a culture out of control, subject to a cancerous malaise. Compare Burroughs's *Nova Express* [4-100].

*4-34. Ballard, J(ames) G(raham) (U.K.). **Chronopolis and Other Stories.** Putnam, 1971.
Ballard's short fiction is distributed over more than a dozen collections, in various combinations, but this selection—which overlaps considerably with *The Best Short Stories of J. G. Ballard* (1978)—preserves the best of his early work. Alienated protagonists bear witness to the world's descent into a perverse decadence; if they attempt to resist (many do not), they are likely to be maddened by the consciousness of their hopeless entrapment. "The Terminal Beach" (1964) marked a turning point in the concerns of British SF, and signaled the start of the era of avant-garde methods.

*4-35. Ballard, J(ames) G(raham) (U.K.). **The Crystal World.** Cape, 1966.
Completes a quartet of apocalyptic novels begun with *The Wind from Nowhere* (1962) and continued with *The Drowned World* [4-37] and *The Drought* [4-36]. Time begins to "crystallize out," causing vast tracts of African rain forest to undergo a metamorphosis that echoes and contrasts with the metamorphosis of human flesh that is leprosy. The hero's symbolic odyssey, like that of the protagonist in Conrad's *Heart of Darkness,* brings him to a more fundamental existential level. Superb imagery. NN, 1966.

*4-36. Ballard, J(ames) G(raham) (U.K.). **The Drought.** Cape, 1965. U.S. title (of a considerably shorter version): *The Burning World,* Berkley, 1964.
Evaporation from the world's oceans is inhibited by pollutants, and inland areas are devastated by drought. Humans adapt psychologically in various ways, the protagonist's personal life becoming spiritually desiccated in tune with his surroundings. The narrative is suitably dry and laconic.

*4-37. Ballard, J(ames) G(raham) (U.K.). **The Drowned World.** Berkley, 1962.
Earth's climate enters a new phase, similar to the conditions of the Triassic; the ice caps melt and natural selection produces an appropriate ecosphere. As humans struggle vainly to adapt, "memories" locked in the most primitive parts of their nervous systems begin to respond to the call of circumstance. A marvelous culmination of the long British tradition of ambivalent disaster stories.

4-38. Ballard, J(ames) G(raham) (U.K.). **Vermilion Sands.** Berkley, 1971.
A collection of stories showing the more colorful and romantic side of Ballard's imagination. In a decadent resort town, avant-garde artists and the jetsam of faded star-cults play out their casual tragedies. Elegantly ironic and overripe; *Sunset Boulevard* transposed into the SF idiom. Compare Killough's *Aventine* [4-295].

4-38A. Barnes, Steven. **Streetlethal.** Ace, 1983.
In the heart of a future Los Angeles partly devastated by an earthquake, all the evils of contemporary civilization are concentrated in the Maze, which has streets as mean as any ever envisaged, but down these streets a man must go. Tough action-adventure with a soft center of sentimentality. Compare Gibson's *Neuromancer* [4-233].

4-39. Barrett, Neal, Jr. **Stress Pattern.** DAW, 1974.
A castaway on an alien planet must find a way to survive, although the natives

ignore him, by adapting to its very peculiar ecosphere. A strange novel by an inventive writer whose skill in composing exotic adventure stories is also exhibited by a series begun with *Aldair in Albion* (1976), set on an Earth from which humans have disappeared, leaving behind animal species made humanoid by genetic engineering.

4-40. Barth, John. **Giles Goat-Boy; or, The Revised New Syllabus.** Doubleday, 1966.
A fabulation in which the world is a university and the hero an experimental embodiment of the theriomorphic image of human nature. A clever satire, very much the product of its time. One of the works that began drawing science fiction ideas into the American literary mainstream. See also Pynchon's *Gravity's Rainbow* [4-432].

4-41. Bass, T. J. (pseud. of Thomas J. Bassler). **Half Past Human.** Ballantine, 1971.
In a distant future the world's surface is used to grow food while the Earth Society has retreated underground, where the life-style of the degenerate Nebishes is sustained by computer regulation. A few real humans live precariously on the surface, conserving hope for the future of mankind (NN, 1971). In the sequel, *The Godwhale* (1974; NN, 1974), a huge cyborg is co-opted by humans who have adapted to underwater life, and may provide the means to set humankind on the road to a better future. Highly imaginative and richly detailed. Compare Silverberg's *The World Inside* [4-513].

4-42. Batchelor, John Calvin. **The Birth of the People's Republic of Antarctica.** Dial, 1983.
As civilization collapses, an odd assortment of characters sets sail for Sweden in search of a better world; ultimately their journey takes them into the icy wastes of Antarctica, but even there they find no escape from the troubles that afflict humankind. Compare Vidal's *Kalki* [4-572].

4-43. Batchelor, John Calvin. **The Further Adventures of Halley's Comet.** Congdon & Lattes, 1981.
Members of a wealthy bourgeois family plot to extend their empire into space; their Machiavellian schemes require the kidnapping and incarceration of assorted idealists. Meanwhile, an extraordinary trio of mages associated with Halley's Comet look on. A baroque tale. Compare Pynchon's *Gravity's Rainbow* [4-432].

4-44. Bayley, Barrington J(ohn) (U.K.). **The Fall of Chronopolis.** DAW, 1974.
An autocratic empire extends across time, its armies deployed in time traveling citadels, but its attempts to control change are subverted. A colorful adventure story with metaphysical themes woven into the plot. Compare Harness's *Ring of Ritornel* [4-252].

*4-45. Bayley, Barrington J(ohn) (U.K.). **The Knights of the Limits.** Allison & Busby, 1978.
Collection of stories, mostly from the *New Worlds* anthologies, showing off the versatility of Bayley's fertile imagination. "The Exploration of Space" is a strange di-

mensional fantasy; "Me and My Antronoscope" is a bizarre exercise in speculative cosmology; "The Cabinet of Oliver Naylor" is a baroque space opera exhibiting the author's fascination with philosophical problems. A follow-up collection, *The Seed of Evil* (1979), is slightly less dazzling, but has the gruesome "Sporting with the Chid" and the fine *conte philosophique*, "Man in Transit."

4-46. Bayley, Barrington J(ohn) (U.K.). **Soul of the Robot.** Doubleday, 1974.
The story of a robot with a soul, whose philosophical wrestling with the concept of self-consciousness is background to an eventful plot. Lighthearted and exuberant. A sequel is *The Rod of Light* (1985). Compare and contrast Asimov's *Robots and Empire* [4-28].

4-47. Bayley, Barrington J(ohn) (U.K.). **Star Winds.** DAW, 1978.
Interplanetary adventure blended with alchemy in a fabulous tale of interstellar sailing ships, with Bayley's customary spice of metaphysical speculation. Colorful, with zestful narration. Compare Franson's *Shadow of the Ship* [4-223].

4-48. Bayley, Barrington J(ohn) (U.K.). **The Zen Gun.** DAW, 1983.
The galactic empire is on the rocks, humankind having grown so decadent that the pigs, their erstwhile servants, decide that it is time they took over. Meanwhile, the ultimate weapon is in the hands of an altogether unsuitable custodian, and the fabric of space is being torn apart. Inventive and witty space opera. Compare van Vogt's *Battle of Forever* [4-566].

4-49. Bear, Greg. **Beyond Heaven's River.** Dell, 1980.
A Japanese pilot kidnapped by aliens from the Battle of Midway is abandoned 400 years later; he finds that humankind now has a budding galactic empire, but his experiences as an experimental subject make him wonder about the significance of it all. Unusual and thoughtful. Compare Lupoff's *Sun's End* [4-346].

*4-50. Bear, Greg. **Blood Music.** Arbor House, 1985.
A genetic engineer conducts unauthorized experiments that result in the creation of intelligent microorganisms. Having infected himself, he becomes a "universe" of sentient cells and when his "disease" becomes epidemic the whole living world undergoes an astonishing transformation. A brilliant novel, expanded from a novelette (HW, 1984), that extends the SF imagination to new horizons. Compare Clarke's *Childhood's End* [3-97] and Attanasio's *Radix* [4-30]. HN, 1986; NN, 1985.

4-51. Bear, Greg. **Eon.** Bluejay, 1985.
World War III looms as an asteroid starship mysteriously orbiting Earth is taken over by Americans, who discover that it is an artifact from the future that offers a gateway to infinite opportunity. Hard SF unfolding into vast realms of possibility. The forthcoming sequel is *Eternity*. Compare Robinson's *Memory of Whiteness* [4-446] and Sheffield's *Between the Strokes of Night* [4-493].

4-52. Benford, Gregory. **Against Infinity.** Simon & Schuster, 1983.
The first part of this Ganymede-set novel draws its inspiration from Faulkner's novella, "The Bear," with an adolescent and an aging hunter tracking down a strange alien creature. Inevitably, the story moves to new ground when it gives more attention to the nature of the alien and the kind of world the hero's rite de

passage will take him into. An interesting attempt to infuse SF with narrative realism. Compare Clarke's *Rendezvous with Rama* [4-138] and *2010: Odyssey Two* [4-141]. NN, 1983.

4-53. Benford, Gregory. **In the Ocean of Night.** Dial, 1977.
A fix-up novel in which the hero looks for evidence of the existence of aliens, and ultimately meets one; contact may invigorate a world becoming gradually decadent. In a sequel, *Across the Sea of Suns* (1984), the difficulty of coming to terms with alien beings, and the necessity of so doing, lie at the heart of a complex plot involving the confrontation of alternative human philosophies of life. Thoughtful hard SF, its visionary element less wide-eyed than in Anderson's *The Avatar* [4-13] and other like-minded works. NN, 1977.

*4-54. Benford, Gregory. **Timescape.** Simon & Schuster, 1980.
As the world lurches toward disaster, scientists in 1998 try to transmit a warning message to 1962 by means of tachyons. Their story is told in parallel with that of the scientists trying to decode the transmission, and the two plots converge on the possibility of paradox. Unusual for the realism of its depiction of scientists at work; admirably serious in handling the implications of its theme. Compare Scholz and Harcourt's *Palimpsests* [4-479]. JWC, 1981; NW, 1980.

4-55. Benford, Gregory, and David Brin. **The Heart of the Comet.** Bantam, 1986.
Scientists exploring Halley's Comet in 2061 are marooned when plague breaks out and monsters attack, but they survive and thrive in extraordinary fashion. Colorful space adventure that diversifies into speculative metaphysics. Compare Williamson's *Lifeburst* [4-608].

4-56. Benford, Gregory, and Gordon Eklund. **If the Stars Are Gods.** Putnam, 1977.
Fix-up novel based on a novelette (NW, 1973). The protagonist confronts a series of enigmas in the shape of various kinds of extraterrestrial life, including the benign aliens who visit the solar system searching for a new sun-god. Compare Watson's *The Embedding* [4-586].

4-57. Bensen, Donald R. **And Having Writ . . . .** Bobbs-Merrill, 1978.
Alternate history story in which the aliens whose crashing starship caused the Tunguska explosion in our world land safely, and although they try not to interfere they utterly transform the history of the twentieth century. Cleverly constructed and beautifully ironic. Compare Watson's *Chekhov's Journey* [4-585].

4-58. Biggle, Lloyd, Jr. **The World Menders.** Doubleday, 1971.
Human observers on an alien world are appalled by the plight of an enslaved race, but all is not as it seems. Serialized in *Analog* and heavily influenced by John W. Campbell's ideas about the merits of slavery. An earlier story in the same series, *The Still Small Voice of Trumpets* (1968), allows the observers to interfere in order to oppose a less obvious tyranny.

4-59. Bischoff, David. **Mandala.** Berkley. 1983.
Expanded from the novelette "The Warmth of the Stars"; a far-future love story

set on an artificial world faced with imminent disaster. Compare Carr's *Cirque* [4-114].

4-60. Bishop, Michael. **Ancient of Days.** Arbor House, 1985.
Expanded from the novella "Her Habiline Husband" (NN, 1983). Continues themes first tackled in *No Enemy but Time* [4-63] in a more lighthearted vein. A modern woman falls in love with a relic of the prehistoric past, outraging the neighbors. Funny and sentimental. Compare Farmer's "The Alley Man" (1959).

4-61. Bishop, Michael. **Blooded on Arachne.** Arkham, 1982.
The first of a pair of collections of short stories, followed by *One Winter in Eden* (1984). Bishop claims to be stressing the "palpability" of alien landscapes and transfigured futures in these atmospheric stories, which do indeed seem infatuated with strangeness. The title story draws on anthropological material after the fashion of *Transfigurations* [4-64] while the novella, "The White Otters of Childhood" (HN, 1974; NN, 1973), has a leading character named after the protagonist of *The Island of Dr. Moreau* [1-100]. A further Bishop collection is *Close Encounters with the Deity* (1986).

*4-62. Bishop, Michael. **Catacomb Years.** Berkley, 1979.
Fix-up novel extrapolating themes from the earlier *A Little Knowledge* (1977) and introducing new insights into an elaborate study of the culture of twenty-first-century Atlanta. The diffuse and richly detailed text presents an unusually convincing picture of future life in a period of crisis. Compare Pohl's *Years of the City* [4-420].

*4-63. Bishop, Michael. **No Enemy but Time.** Pocket Books, 1982.
A strange, alienated child has lurid dreams of the Pleistocene era, and discovers the truth of them when he becomes a time traveler in adulthood. He joins forces with a band of habiline protohumans and fathers a child, which he brings back to the present. Brilliant and memorable, written with great conviction. Compare Case's *Cook* [4-120]. NW, 1982.

4-64. Bishop, Michael. **Transfigurations.** Berkley, 1979.
Expanded from the novella "Death and Designation among the Asadi" (NN, 1973; HN, 1974). One of the more impressive SF novels using perspectives and themes drawn from anthropology to aid depiction of an enigmatic alien culture. Compare Le Guin's *The Word for World Is Forest* [4-329].

4-65. Blaylock, James P. **The Digging Leviathan.** Ace, 1984.
A complicated adventure story that plays affectionately with supposedly antiquated pulp ideas, including the hollow earth. Evil conspirators try to use the imaginative power of a young genius for their own nefarious ends. Breezy homage to the delights and eccentricities of pulp SF, witty and well written. Compare Helprin's *Winter's Tale* [4-265].

4-66. Blaylock, James P. **Homunculus.** Ace, 1986.
Intricately plotted action-adventure story set in Victorian England, where the natural philosophers of the Trismegistus Club battle a sinister reanimator of corpses and a greedy entrepreneur while a tiny alien imprisoned in one of four

identical boxes is passed unwittingly from hand to hand, causing havoc wherever he goes. A witty and very stylish combination of SF and Victorian melodrama, in the same vein as Powers's *The Anubis Gates* [4-422].

4-67. Bodelsen, Anders (Denmark). **Freezing Down.** Harper, 1971. Tr. by Joan Tate of *Frysepunktet,* 1969. British title: *Freezing Point.*
The protagonist has an incurable disease and is put into cryonic suspension until medical science can cure it; he cannot adapt to life in the future but is officiously sheltered from death by those who take charge of him. A Kafkaesque treatment of significant moral issues.

4-68. Bova, Ben. **Colony.** Pocket Books, 1978.
Carries forward themes from *Millennium* (1976) and *Kinsman* (1979); with Earth in trouble the future of humankind seems tied up with the fortunes of orbital space habitats—stepping-stones to the colonization of the solar system, and focal points of desperate power struggles. The wide-ranging story takes in many convincing near-future scenarios; an attempt to incorporate the format of mainstream best-sellers into SF. Compare Dickson's *The Far Call* [4-180].

4-69. Bova, Ben. **Privateers.** Tor, 1985.
The United States having withdrawn from the space race, the Russians have established control of the Moon's resources and are gradually gaining economic hegemony. A heroic millionaire undertakes a private space program to restore American fortunes, but must operate outside the law as a buccaneering pirate. Compare Anderson's *The Star Fox* [3-12] and Edmondson's *The Man Who Corrupted Earth* [4-197].

4-70. Bova, Ben. **Test of Fire.** Tor, 1982.
A novel that adds a new opening sequence to a revised version of *When the Sky Burned* (1973). Earth is destroyed by a huge solar flare and nuclear war; a colony on the Moon survives, and must ultimately send emissaries back to the mother world to take a hand in its continuing conflicts.

4-71. Bova, Ben. **Voyagers.** Doubleday, 1981.
A first-contact story in which an alien ship detected near Jupiter heads for Earth; people react in many different ways as anxiety and optimism spread like wildfire. Compare Benford's *In the Ocean of Night* [4-53] and Gunn's *The Listeners* [4-244].

4-72. Boyce, Chris (U.K.). **Catchworld.** Gollancz, 1975.
Joint winner (with Charles Logan's *Shipwreck,* 1975) of a *Sunday Times*/Gollancz SF novel competition. The artificial intelligence guiding an armed starship on a revenge mission rebels against its crew and absorbs their personalities into its software, creating a compound being that undergoes further evolution. Compare O'Donnell's *Mayflies* [4-402].

4-73. Boyd, John (pseud. of Boyd Upchurch). **The Last Starship from Earth.** Weybright & Talley, 1968.
An alternate Earth is ruled by a dictatorship that employs religion and the insights of social science to secure its hegemony, exporting dissidents to the planet Hell. The hero plans to save the world by striking at the very heart of the de-

spised order, preventing Christ's conquest of Rome. Clever development of an interesting premise. Compare Earnshaw's *Planet in the Eye of Time* [4-196].

4-74. Boyd, John (pseud. of Boyd Upchurch). **The Pollinators of Eden.** Weybright & Talley, 1969.
A repressed female scientist is liberated and fulfilled, thanks to alien orchids. Sexual mores and the workings of the scientific community are gently satirized. Compare Ronald Fraser's classic fantasy *Flower Phantoms* (1926).

4-75. Boyd, John (pseud. of Boyd Upchurch). **Sex and the High Command.** Weybright & Talley, 1970.
Males becomes superfluous when science gives women a better means to sexual fulfillment and reproduction. Macho military men fight to preserve phallic pride, but ultimately prove impotent. A witty and double-edged commentary on sexual politics, resented by feminists and male chauvinists alike. Compare Tiptree's "Houston, Houston, Do You Read?" (1976).

4-76. Boyett, Stephen R. **The Architect of Sleep.** Ace, 1986.
On a parallel Earth evolution has followed a different path; the intelligent native species are descended from raccoons. The hero crosses over into this world and gets involved in its conflicts; the ending is open and promises further adventures. Action-adventure on the SF/fantasy borderline.

4-77. Bradley, Marion Zimmer. **City of Sorcery.** DAW, 1984.
The latest novel in the Darkover series, which began with the Ace Double *The Planet Savers/The Sword of Aldones* (1962), and continued in *The Bloody Sun* (1964), *Star of Danger* (1965), *The World Wreckers* (1971), *Darkover Landfall* (1972), *The Spell Sword* (1974), *The Heritage of Hastur* (1975; NN, 1975), *The Shattered Chain* (1976), *The Forbidden Tower* (1977; HN, 1978), *Stormqueen!* (1978), *Two to Conquer* (1980), *Sharra's Exile* (1981), *Hawkmistress* (1982), and *Thendara House* (1983). Associated materials include *Free Amazons of Darkover* (1985). *The Planet Savers* first appeared in 1958, and the series thus extends across nearly 30 years. It has evolved as the changing market situation of SF has altered. The early novels are action-adventure stories confronting ordinary humans with the psi-powered descendants of colonists whose world has been long out of touch with galactic civilization. Bradley gradually elaborated the history of Darkover and began to write longer, denser novels that focused more and more on the relationships between characters, diversifying into an elaborate exercise in sexual politics and exploring the ramifications of the hypothetical intimacy permitted by telepathic communication. In the later novels, therefore, psychological melodrama replaces action-adventure and female protagonists replace male ones. The history cobbled together from the earlier novels (further confused by the temporary association with the series of two other novels) eventually proved unsatisfactory, and *The Heritage of Hastur* became the first novel assuming the fully worked out and coherent history; *Sharra's Exile* was subsequently written to replace *The Sword of Aldones* in the "official canon." The series is fascinating as an exercise in world building, and as a testament to changing fashions in SF during the modern period.

4-78. Brautigan, Richard. **The Hawkline Monster: A Gothic Western.** Simon & Schuster, 1974.
A pair of professional killers are hired to get rid of a monster created by an eccentric scientist. A funny variation on the Frankenstein theme, written in the author's typical mock-naïve style, which works better here than in the hippie-utopia story *In Watermelon Sugar* (1968).

4-79. Bretnor, Reginald. **Schimmelhorn's Gold.** Tor, 1986.
Eccentric inventor Papa Schimmelhorn is hired by Swiss bankers to build a gold-making machine, but finds his task confused by the enmity of an alchemist, the effects of love potions, and the attentions of the Minotaur. A cavalier mixture of SF and fantasy in the spirit of pure entertainment. Papa's earlier exploits are collected in *The Schimmelhorn File* (1979).

4-80. Brin, David. **The Postman.** Bantam, 1985.
Expanded from a novella (HN, 1983). In postholocaust America a scavenger picks up the uniform of a dead postman, triggering the myth that the Post Office still survives and that order might soon be restored to the shattered world. By degrees, he is forced reluctantly to accept the responsibility of his peculiar charismatic authority. An antidote to postholocaust romanticism, but not without a romanticism of its own. Compare and contrast Robinson's *The Wild Shore* [4-447]. HN, 1986; JWC, 1986.

4-81. Brin, David. **The Practice Effect.** Bantam, 1984.
The hero is marooned in a pseudomedieval world whose technology is based on the eponymous anomaly in the laws of physics. He uses his own knowledge to transform it, and ultimately learns its true nature. Lighthearted, playing with several SF clichés and recomplicating de Camp's *Lest Darkness Fall* [3-135] in much the same way that *Sundiver* [4-83] and *Startide Rising* [4-82] recomplicate themes from Poul Anderson.

*4-82. Brin, David. **Startide Rising.** Bantam, 1983.
Continues from *Sundiver* [4-83] the story of the uneasy relationship between Earth's intelligent species and the suspicious galactic community. A dolphin-commanded starship makes a significant discovery in deep space but must take refuge in an alien ocean from rival adversaries, who then begin to squabble over their unsecured prize. Taut action-adventure with a colorful background. Continued in *The Uplift War* (Phantasia Press, 1987). Compare Niven's Known Space series [4-390]. HW, 1984; NW, 1983.

4-83. Brin, David. **Sundiver.** Bantam, 1980.
The intelligent species of Earth (men, apes, and dolphins) seem to be highly exceptional in having advanced to technological sophistication without the alien Patrons that generally supervise the "uplift" of sentient species throughout the galactic culture. Men learn to be suspicious of their ambivalent galactic neighbors after making contact with life-forms in the Sun. Intelligent and complex space opera.

4-84. Broderick, Damien   (Australia). **The Dreaming Dragons.** Norstrilia Press, 1980.
An aborigine anthropologist and his nephew discover an alien artifact that gives

them access to a vault beneath Ayers Rock. The boy is changed by the experience and becomes the key to scientific study of the vault and its builders. An intriguing combination of SF motifs and mythological referents. Compare Zelazny's *Eye of Cat* [4-629].

4-85. Broderick, Damien (Australia). **The Judas Mandala.** Pocket Books, 1982.
Carries forward themes from *The Dreaming Dragons* [4-84]; in a far future benevolently ruled by powerful computers some humans find a way to escape their governance by dimensional side-stepping. They gradually extend their ability to travel in time until they begin trying to alter and control history. A convoluted and effective SF mystery. Compare van Vogt's *Masters of Time* (1950).

4-86. Brooke-Rose, Christine (U.K.). **Xorandor.** Carcanet, 1986.
Two teenagers make contact with a strange life-form that feeds on hard radiation and has a silicon chip brain. Attempts to make use of its offspring in processing nuclear wastes have unfortunate consequences. Tricky narrative style laden with programming jargon, but lively. Compare Stapledon's *The Flames* (1947).

4-87. Brunner, John (U.K.). **The Crucible of Time.** Arrow, 1984.
Fix-up novel tracking seven stages in the history of an alien species from early discoveries in science to technological maturity—a history that is also a race against time, because the aliens' world is under threat of destruction. An intriguing exercise in alternate history based in alternate ecology, impressive in scope. Compare Blish's *The Seedling Stars* [3-47].

4-88. Brunner, John (U.K.). **The Jagged Orbit.** Ace, 1969.
A dystopian black comedy of a culturally fragmented near-future United States whose citizens are armed to the teeth and have made fortresses of their homes. As the personal arms race threatens to escalate yet again, an investigative journalist and a psychologist combine forces to strike a blow for sanity. The bitter alarmism, very much a product of the 1960s, makes the novel a striking period piece. Compare Barnes's *Streetlethal* [4-38A] and Bunch's *Moderan* [4-98].

4-89. Brunner, John (U.K.). **Quicksand.** Doubleday, 1967.
A psychiatrist forms a close relationship with a mystery woman who first convinces him that she is from a future utopia, then reveals that the future is terrible—a disappointment he finds hard to take. Subtle in theme and delicate in narration. Compare Wilhelm's *The Clewiston Test* [4-598].

*4-90. Brunner, John (U.K.). **The Sheep Look Up.** Harper, 1972.
The most elaborate alarmist novel about industrial pollution. Uses techniques similar to *Stand on Zanzibar* [4-92] to present a kaleidoscopic image of future America drowning in its own wastes. Relentlessly angry and anguished. Compare Philip Wylie's *The End of the Dream* [4-617]. NN, 1972.

4-91. Brunner, John (U.K.). **The Shockwave Rider.** Harper, 1975.
The third of Brunner's massive alarmist fantasies, partly inspired by Alvin Toffler's *Future Shock,* warning against the loss of individual freedom that might result from widespread use of information technology and against the psychological effects of rapid technological change. Brunner complained bitterly about

Harper's insensitive editing; the Ballantine paperback (1976) restored the author's text.

*4-92. Brunner, John (U.K.). **Stand on Zanzibar.** Doubleday, 1968.
Complex novel borrowing techniques from John Dos Passos and ideas from Marshall McLuhan and other 1960s commentators to provide a multifaceted image of an overpopulated near future. Clever, highly detailed, and frequently very witty; a successful experiment. One of the key works of the period. Prix Apollo, 1973; HW, 1969; NN, 1968.

4-93. Brunner, John (U.K.). **Total Eclipse.** Doubleday, 1974.
Human scientists try to solve the enigma of technologically advanced alien crustaceans whose sophistication could not save them from extinction. Meanwhile, humankind also trembles on the brink of annihilation. Hard SF without the ideological uplift of American works in that vein. Contrast Hogan's *Inherit the Stars* [4-276].

4-94. Brunner, John (U.K.). **The Whole Man.** Ballantine, 1964. British title: *Telepathist.*
Developed from two novellas. A crippled and deformed social outcast is nearly destroyed by his telepathic powers, but learns to use them to create therapeutic dreams for others and eventually to create a new art form. Good characterization and sensitive narration. Compare Silverberg's *Dying Inside* [4-502] and Zelazny's *The Dream Master* [4-628]. HN, 1965.

4-95. Bryant, Edward. **Cinnabar.** Macmillan, 1976.
A "mosaic novel" about a decadent far-future city where aesthetic motives are paramount and ennui reigns supreme. Compare Harrison's Viriconium series [4-260] and Terry Carr's *Cirque* [4-114].

4-96. Budrys, Algis. **Michaelmas.** Berkley, 1977.
The hero and his machine-intelligence sidekick secretly rule the world, but their subtle dictatorship is threatened by insidious alien intruders. A slick power fantasy. Compare van Vogt's *Anarchistic Colossus* [4-565].

4-97. Bulmer, Kenneth. **The Ulcer Culture.** Macdonald, 1969. Reissued as *Stained-Glass World*, 1976.
A cynical dystopian fantasy of future corruption; machines and exploited workers keep things going while the elite revel in drug-induced dreams—but the dreams become nightmarish and the system is close to collapse. A far cry from Bulmer's customary adventure stories. Compare Gunn's *The Joy Makers* [3-185].

*4-98. Bunch, David R(oosevelt). **Moderan.** Avon, 1971.
Collection of linked stories of a future world completely altered by the progressive cyborgization of its inhabitants and artificialization of its environments. Humanity is lost with the discarded "flesh-strips" and the nightmare progresses to its inevitable conclusion. A magnificent work full of striking imagery and fine prose. Compare Fowler Wright's *The New Gods Lead* [2-142].

4-99. Burroughs, William S(eward). **Cities of the Red Night.** Holt, 1981.
Several SF motifs are drawn together in this complex account of human corrup-

tion and corruptibility; alternate histories, nuclear holocaust, time travel, and so on, are employed as metaphors and surrealities. A phantasmagoria crowded with apocalyptic imagery; completes the absorption of SF motifs into the repertoire of American mainstream fiction begun by such works as Barth's *Giles Goat-Boy* [4-40] and Burroughs's own *Nova Express* [4-100].

4-100. Burroughs, William S(eward). **Nova Express.** Grove, 1964.
A novel of future violence and corruption, in which the anarchic Nova Mob descends like the Furies on hapless humankind, while the Nova Police try to match them. Carries forward themes from the famous avant-garde trilogy *The Naked Lunch* (1959), *The Soft Machine* (1961), and *The Ticket That Exploded* (1962). Burroughs influenced the work of J. G. Ballard, especially *The Atrocity Exhibition* [4-33].

4-101. Busby, F(rancis) M(arion). **Star Rebel.** Bantam, 1984.
Fast-paced adventure story in which the tough hero must go to extraordinary lengths to survive and hit back against his enemies, repeating the theme of the author's earlier *The Demu Trilogy* (Pocket Books, 1980). Sequels to the present story are *Rebel's Quest* (1985), *Rebel's Seed* (1986), and *The Alien Debt* (1984), the latter connecting this series to another whose heroine, Rissa Kerguelen, generally features in more ironic accounts of extreme individual assertiveness in a space opera setting. Compare Resnick's *Santiago* [4-437].

4-102. Butler, Octavia. **Clay's Ark.** St. Martin's, 1984.
A novel that bears the same relationship to *Patternmaster* (1976) as *Wild Seed* [4-104] does to *Mind of My Mind* [4-103], developing the ideas therein more fully in an earlier setting. In a decadent future California humans become commensals of an alien life-form—an association described in distinctly ambivalent terms. Tense development of an interesting premise.

4-103. Butler, Octavia. **Mind of My Mind.** Doubleday, 1977.
Butler's second novel, developing ideas about the linking of minds via telepathy, first used in the earlier *Patternmaster* (1976) to describe a whole society, on a more intimate scale. The mental gestalt featured here, unlike the one in Sturgeon's *More Than Human* [3-362], is racked by internal conflicts; the plot features the power struggle between daughter and father, and between radical idealism and dogmatic conservatism. Tautly written and gripping.

4-104. Butler, Octavia. **Wild Seed.** Doubleday, 1980.
The earliest, in terms of internal chronology, of the "Patternist" stories. Here the immortal hero begins to create the small empire later to be riven in *Mind of My Mind* [4-103]. An intense work, making good use of the author's anthropological research in its depiction of African settings. Certain themes are also carried forward from the timeslip novel *Kindred* (1979), in which a modern black woman is cast back to the early days of slavery. (John Pfeiffer feels strongly that both *Wild Seed* and *Kindred* should be core collection titles.—Ed.)

4-105. Caidin, Martin. **Cyborg.** Arbor House, 1972.
After being badly smashed up in a crash, a pilot is reconstructed into a superhuman hybrid of flesh and high technology. Several sequels followed (some by oth-

er hands) and the story was adapted into the TV series "The Six Million Dollar Man." An imminent-future thriller by an author whose use of SF ideas is bolder and more assured than that of most writers in this vein.

4-106.   Calisher, Hortense. **Journal from Ellipsia.** Little, Brown, 1965.
A female anthropologist sends back news from a strange other dimension where everything is connected and relationships are transcendently different. A deftly satirical and pleasantly quirky novel admired by some of the proponents of SF's mid-1960s New Wave.

4-107.   Callenbach, Ernest. **Ecotopia.** Banyan Tree, 1975.
A utopian novel of ecologically sensitive political reorganization. The West Coast states have seceded from the union and have established a life-style based on small-scale technology and environmental conservation. A visitor from the East is gradually converted to these ideals. The sequel, *Ecotopia Emerging* (1981), fills in (and revises) the historical background. Perhaps the most important modern addition to the tradition of Bellamy's *Looking Backward* [1-8] and an interesting development of the ideologies that have since been adopted by various European "green" parties.

4-108.   Calvino, Italo (Italy). **Cosmicomics.** Harcourt, 1968. Tr. by William Weaver of *Le Cosmicomiche,* 1965.
The childlike Qfwfq has the entire cosmos and all eternity as his playground, and naïvely confronts the great mysteries of time and space in 12 bizarre tales. *t zero* (1969) offers more of the same. Zestful modern fabliaux with a unique charm.

4-109.   Card, Orson Scott. **Ender's Game.** Tor, 1985.
The infant hero is subjected to horrific manipulation by the military in order to make him the perfect commander to annihilate the insectile aliens who have twice attacked the solar system. Based on a novelette (HN, 1978), the expanded version is dressed up with much discussion of moral propriety, and undergoes a dramatic ideological shift at the end, but remains in essence a hyped-up power fantasy. Grimly fascinating. The sequel, *Speaker for the Dead* (1986), takes off from the climactic shift in perspective to construct a very different story, much closer in tone to *Songmaster* [4-111], in which Ender becomes a more Christlike savior. Compare Heinlein's *Starship Troopers* [3-206] and Haldeman's *Forever War* [4-247]. HW, 1986; NW, 1985.

4-110.   Card, Orson Scott. **A Planet Called Treason.** St. Martin's, 1979.
Talented exiles on a prison planet form distinct tribes until the hero travels widely among them, combining their resources in order to provide them with the wherewithal to break free. An earnest SF parable.

4-111.   Card, Orson Scott. **Songmaster.** Dial, 1980.
Developed from two novelettes, including "Mikal's Songbird" (HN, 1979). A young boy achieves a unique position in the household of the galactic emperor, where he can witness and subtly influence affairs of state. His maturation becomes an unfolding spiritual illumination. Disch's *On Wings of Song* [4-187] might almost be regarded as a parody of it, although both writers share a genuine rever-

ence for music. Card—a one-time missionary for the Mormon faith—handles the metaphysical overtones of his story with some conviction.

*4-112. Carr, Jayge. **Leviathan's Deep.** Doubleday, 1979.
An alien female whose society is matriarchal embarks on a doomed love affair with a human male, whose species is busily employed in the conquest of the galaxy. An intelligent novel, spiced with wit, that brings a measure of conviction to a difficult theme. More even-handed in its treatment of sexual politics than most exemplary adventures in interstellar miscegenation. Contrast Farmer's *The Lovers* [3-159] and Lee's *The Silver Metal Lover* [4-322].

4-113. Carr, Jayge. **Navigator's Syndrome.** Doubleday, 1983.
Rabelais is a planetary way station where contract law is supreme. A member of its decadent elite contrives to frame an offworlder in order to enslave her; she must get by until members of her powerful navigators' guild can make provision for her escape. A classy action-adventure story. *The Treasure in the Heart of the Maze* (1985) is a further novel with the same galactic culture as background.

4-114. Carr, Terry. **Cirque.** Bobbs-Merrill, 1977.
A decadent far-future city faces a crisis that demands heroic action from some of its strange citizens. Clever and colorful, with a rich underlay of moral and metaphysical questions. Compare Bryant's *Cinnabar* [4-95] for another version of the far-future *civitas solis* and Dick's *Galactic Pot-Healer* [4-176] for some similar play with metaphysical anxiety. NN, 1977.

4-115. Carter, Angela (U.K.). **Heroes and Villains.** Heinemann, 1969.
After the holocaust, the flame of culture and learning is kept alight by Professors guarded by Soldiers, while barbarians and mutants threaten to extinguish it. The heroine, a Professor's daughter, runs off with a barbarian and enjoys her just desserts. A strange combination of the lyrical, the ironic, and the author's usual fascinated flirtation with horrors.

*4-116. Carter, Angela (U.K.). **The Infernal Desire Machines of Doctor Hoffman.** Hart-Davis, 1972. U.S. title: *The War of Dreams*, Harcourt, 1974.
The hero, Desiderio, sets out to find and defeat Dr. Hoffman, whose machines are the fountainhead of troublesome illusions. His journey is an odyssey into the unconscious, where he is alternately (sometimes simultaneously) seduced and threatened in a phantasmagoric variety of ways. A gothic black comedy, elaborating and decoding much of the erotic symbolism of fantastic fiction; a disturbing tour de force.

4-117. Carter, Angela (U.K.). **The Passion of New Eve.** Gollancz, 1977.
The English hero loses himself in a decadent near-future New York, undergoes a forced sex change at the hands of sex war guerrillas, is captured by a brutal masculinist nihilist, and meets the transvestite film star who incarnated in celluloid the perfect image of feminine frailty, before floating away from the California coast as the holocaust destroys America. Wonderfully phantasmagoric. Compare Ballard's *Vermilion Sands* [4-38] and *Hello America* (1981).

4-118. Carter, Lin. **The Valley Where Time Stood Still.** Doubleday, 1974.
A heavily nostalgic story of a fabulous and magical Mars in the tradition of C. L.
Moore and Leigh Brackett. Wide-eyed adventure fiction by an author whose un-
flagging appetite for exercises in pastiche has completely obscured his own literary voice. *Time War* (1974), which pays homage to A. E. van Vogt, has something
of the same eccentric charm as the present story.

4-119. Carver, Jeffrey A. **The Infinity Link.** Bluejay, 1984.
A dense and detailed story of contact between Earth and alien beings aboard a
starship passing through the solar system. The heroine, who establishes telepathic contact with the alien ship, is caught in the middle of a conflict between
various vested interests. Compare Bova's *Voyagers* [4-71].

4-120. Case, Tom (pseud. of Tony Knight) (U.K.). **Cook.** Tom Case, 2 Champion Rd., Caversham, Reading RG4 8EL, England, 1981.
A stranded time traveler is adopted by Neanderthalers, but fails to adjust himself
to their way of life. The Neanderthalers are themselves doomed to be losers in
the struggle for existence, and this knowledge provides a tragic counterpoint to
the narrator's attempts to adapt. Realistic, sentimental, and well written; the best
self-published SF novel since Fowler Wright's *Deluge* [2-139]. Compare Bishop's
No Enemy but Time [4-63] and contrast Auel's *Clan of the Cave Bear* [4-32].

4-121. Chalker, Jack L(aurence). **Dancers in the Afterglow.** Ballantine, 1978.
An exercise in social contrasts, where SF ideas (psychic powers and an alien invasion) are used to set up extreme cases of individualistic competition and communal togetherness. Attempts to read this as political allegory (even if that is the author's intention) can only lead to sterile argument; the real point at issue is the nature of the "self" as social product, and the question of whether "happiness" is
the highest value. More akin to Powers's *Dinner at Deviant's Palace* [4-423] than to
Huxley's *Brave New World* [2-47] but interesting as well as vivid.

4-122. Chalker, Jack L(aurence). **Downtiming the Night Side.** Tor, 1985.
A time traveling agent hops from one identity to another after the fashion of so
many Chalker heroes, experiencing social roles that permit a typical sly pruri-
ence as well as others that set up discussions of political philosophy (Karl Marx is
a character). Fast moving and fascinating, provocative and exasperating without
the elaborate structural ritual that complicates and pads Chalker's multivolume
novels. Compare Gloag's *99%* [2-36].

4-123. Chalker, Jack L(aurence). **Midnight at the Well of Souls.** Ballantine,
1977.
A vast range of alien habitats is preserved in the "hexes" of the Well World, built
long ago by godlike aliens. The powers commanded by these aliens now seem to
be up for grabs, and the hero must race other contenders through the exotic mi-
lieus at breakneck pace, working up to a dramatic climax that is resolved by a casually fabulous flourish. The sequels, *Exiles at the Well of Souls* (1978), *Quest for the
Well of Souls* (1978), *The Return of Nathan Brazil* (1979), and *Twilight at the Well of
Souls* (1980), can hardly help being weaker retreads of the original, but the last
two have a certain panache, throwing moral, metaphysical, and cosmological

speculations into a giant melting pot. Compare Anthony's Cluster series [4-22] and Farmer's Riverworld series [4-210].

4-124. Chandler, A(rthur) Bertram (Australia). **The Wild Ones.** Collins, 1984. The last completed novel in the long-running series of Rim World stories. Here, the perennial Grimes is an agent provocateur stirring things up on a planet where cruel fur traders enjoy the protection of a fundamentalist political elite. Like E. C. Tubb (and unlike Marion Zimmer Bradley), Chandler declined to move with the times (apart from putting more sex into his stories) and persisted with his comfortable brand of lightweight space opera to the end.

4-125. Charnas, Suzy McKee. **Walk to the End of the World.** Ballantine, 1974. A bitterly misanthropic (in the narrow sense) feminist novel set in a post-holocaust world. The heroine escapes from the nightmarish Holdfast, where women are ruthlessly victimized, to the wilderness where a new society is forming. The sequel, *Motherlines* (1979), describes her adoption into an all-female society of noble savages. The novels are regarded as classics by some feminists and fellow travelers. Compare Huxley's *Ape and Essence* [3-220].

4-126. Chayefsky, Paddy. **Altered States.** Hutchinson, 1978.
First novel by a well-known film scriptwriter, subsequently filmed by Ken Russell. Experiments in hallucination induced by sensory deprivation ultimately lead the hero into a psychic and physical regression to the protohuman. An interesting development of themes from the work of John Lilly. Compare James Kennaway's *The Mind Benders* (1963) and Ian Watson's *The Martian Inca* (1977).

4-127. Cherryh, C. J. (pseud. of Carolyn Janice Cherry). **Cuckoo's Egg.** DAW, 1985.
A member of a catlike race rears an unlovable alien child, training him for membership in an elite corps of judges; the child resents his status as a stranger, but ultimately learns the whys and wherefores of his situation, and that he must accept it. The cool, mannered narrative suits the theme. HN, 1986.

*4-128. Cherryh, C. J. (pseud. of Carolyn Janice Cherry). **Downbelow Station.** DAW, 1981.
Political space opera set on the star station Pell, caught in the middle of the conflict for control of humankind's fragile interstellar "empire." Complex and multifaceted: the many-sided conflict provides action and intrigue while the central characters try to construct viable personal relationships and work out careers in a fluid situation. The novel is the key work in an elaborate future history used as background for several other novels, including *Merchanter's Luck* [4-129A] and *Voyager in Night* [4-134]. HW, 1982.

4-129. Cherryh, C. J. (pseud. of Carolyn Janice Cherry). **The Faded Sun: Kesrith.** DAW, 1978.
The first volume (HN, 1979) of a three-decker novel, completed in *The Faded Sun: Shon'Jir* (1979) and *The Faded Sun: Kutath* (1980). An alien society organized somewhat after the fashion of an anthill hires out its warriors as mercenaries, but when its clients get into a war with humankind the warriors and their kin are virtually wiped out. The client species sues for peace but the survivors go their own

way; one human involves himself with their cause and their quest to save their race. Compare Carr's *Leviathan's Deep* [4-112].

4-129A. Cherryh, C. J. (pseud. of Carolyn Janice Cherry). **Merchanter's Luck.** DAW, 1982.
The alienated hero of this sophisticated space opera is moved to extraordinary action by erotic fascination, and is tested to the full by the adventures that follow. A study of ambition and self-esteem, set in a richly detailed exotic background. Compare Bear's *Beyond Heaven's River* [4-49].

4-130. Cherryh, C. J. (pseud. of Carolyn Janice Cherry). **Port Eternity.** DAW, 1982.
An interstellar pleasure cruiser is stranded in chaotic subspace, and its crew must find a way out. Those aboard include "true" humans and their manufactured servants, whose personalities are designed along with their bodies; on this vessel the manufactured people are named for characters in Tennyson's *Idylls of the King*, and their lives are part of an intricate web of fantasization. Unusual and fascinating. Compare Smith's *Space Lords* (1965).

4-131. Cherryh, C. J. (pseud. of Carolyn Janice Cherry). **The Pride of Chanur.** DAW, 1982.
Intelligent space opera following the adventures of a leonine hero in a politically corrupt interstellar civilization. A fascinating exercise in speculative cultural anthropology, with Cherryh's usual deft and intense plotting. Sequels are *Chanur's Venture* (1984), *The Kif Strike Back* (1985), and *Chanur's Homecoming* (1986). Compare Crowley's *Beasts* [4-157].

4-132. Cherryh, C. J. (pseud. of Carolyn Janice Cherry). **Serpent's Reach.** DAW, 1980.
Convoluted action-adventure story in which a family of genetically engineered humans enjoys a special relationship with the Hives of an alien species. The heroine is victimized by her own kind and must live among aliens and subhumans until the opportunity arises to obtain revenge.

4-133. Cherryh, C. J. (pseud. of Carolyn Janice Cherry). **Visible Light.** DAW, 1986.
Collection of stories set in a curious frame, as much fiction as commentary. The three SF stories include a neat apocalyptic fable, "Cassandra" (HW, 1979), and a surreal short novel, *Companions*.

4-134. Cherryh, C. J. (pseud. of Carolyn Janice Cherry). **Voyager in Night.** DAW, 1984.
A small starship carrying three humans is captured by a gargantuan alien vessel; the personalities of the humans are replicated several times, different versions of each person becoming involved with the alien ship's very peculiar inhabitants. A strange, highly stylized narrative that goes beyond the usual issues at stake in first-contact stories. Compare Lem's *Solaris* [3-261].

4-135. Clark, Ronald (U.K.). **Queen Victoria's Bomb.** Cape, 1967.
A Victorian scientist invents and tests an atomic bomb; can it be used to secure

and sustain the British Empire against its multifarious enemies? An unusual and fascinating thriller, which is also an exercise in the sociology of technology.

*4-136. Clarke, Arthur C(harles) (U.K.). **The Fountains of Paradise.** Gollancz, 1979.
An engineer succeeds in building a space elevator connecting a tropical island (modeled on Sri Lanka but moved for geographical convenience) to a space station in geosynchronous orbit. Imposing propaganda for high technology as the means of human progress and salvation. Sheffield's *The Web between the Worlds* [4-496] develops the same premise in a more conventional fashion. HW, 1980; NW, 1979.

4-137. Clarke, Arthur C(harles) (U.K.). **Imperial Earth.** Gollancz, 1975.
The Harcourt Brace edition of 1976 is considerably expanded.
The hero makes a pilgrimage to Earth from the satellite Titan, and must attempt to repair an old relationship that has been damaged. Fine technological realism and interesting future cultures; the most nearly utopian of Clarke's Earth-set novels, with the usual spiritual uplift in the climax.

*4-138. Clarke, Arthur C(harles) (U.K.). **Rendezvous with Rama.** Gollancz, 1973.
A vast alien spaceship passes through the solar system, using the Sun's gravity to boost its velocity. Human explorers witness the brief blossoming of its artificial life system, but do not meet its makers. Compare Niven's *Ringworld* [4-392] and Shaw's *Orbitsville* [4-482] for similarly charismatic artifacts. HW, 1974; NW, 1973; JWC, 1974.

4-139. Clarke, Arthur C(harles) (U.K.). **The Songs of Distant Earth.** Ballantine, 1986.
Earth is destroyed when the Sun explodes; a few refugees escape on a starship that uses a new quantum drive. En route to an empty and hostile world that they intend to terraform, the refugees call at a colony world settled long ago from a "seedship," whose peaceful and happy society arouses their ambivalent admiration. A sober and sentimental story, deliberately understated to contrast with contemporary space operas. Based on a 1958 short story; the expansion is awkwardly episodic but provides an interesting updating of Clarke's worldview.

4-140. Clarke, Arthur C(harles) (U.K.). **2001: A Space Odyssey.** New American Library, 1968.
Novelization of the Stanley Kubrick film partly based on the short story "The Sentinel." Alien monoliths mysteriously influence human evolution and entice a space mission into the outer solar system, where computer HAL breaks down and the lone survivor undergoes a psychedelic encounter with strangeness: a symbolic transcendence of the human condition.

4-141. Clarke, Arthur C(harles) (U.K.). **2010: Odyssey Two.** Ballantine, 1982.
A joint Russian/American expedition to Jupiter resurrects the computer HAL and discovers life on Europa; then the intelligence controlling the monoliths of *2001* begins to move in its characteristically mysterious way, sending a messiah to

Earth to save humankind and issuing a new commandment. The combination of technological realism and awed mysticism works as well here as anywhere else in Clarke's work, and the religious imagery is even more pronounced than in *Childhood's End* [3-97]. Compare Benford and Eklund's *If the Stars Are Gods* [4-56].

4-142. Compton, D(avid) G(uy) (U.K.). **Ascendancies.** Gollancz, 1980.
A strange substance that turns out to be a miraculous source of energy begins to fall from the heavens, but its utopian potential is compromised by strange side effects. Less intense than many of Compton's novels, but equally compelling. Compare John Gloag's *Manna* (1940) and John Brunner's *The Stardroppers* (1972).

*4-143. Compton, D(avid) G(uy) (U.K.). **The Continuous Katherine Mortenhoe.** Gollancz, 1974. U.S. title: *The Unsleeping Eye,* DAW, 1974.
In a world from which pain and disease have been banished the heroine contracts a terminal illness and has to cope with the intense media interest her condition provokes. Her attempts to hide come to nothing when a reporter with cameras implanted in his eyes wins her confidence, but he becomes bitterly disillusioned with his mission. Brilliantly filmed in France as *Death Watch,* under which title it was once reprinted. One of the finest examples of the SF novel. A sequel, *Windows* (1979), further develops the reporter's crisis of conscience; he has his camera-eyes put out, but ironically makes himself the object of the same kind of curiosity to which he once pandered. Contrast Silverberg's more stylized and hyperbolic *Thorns* [4-509].

4-144. Compton, D(avid) G(uy) (U.K.). **The Electric Crocodile.** Hodder & Stoughton, 1970. U.S. title: *The Steel Crocodile,* Ace, 1970.
Two workers at a secret research institute act as agents for a dissident group, but ultimately cannot oppose the claustrophobic conservatism that has sterilized both scientific and moral progress. Subtle and very convincing. Compare Kate Wilhelm's "April Fool's Day Forever" (1970). NN, 1970.

4-145. Compton, D(avid) G(uy) (U.K.). **Synthajoy.** Hodder & Stoughton, 1968.
A machine is developed that can record emotional experiences for later transmission into the minds of others. Abused by its inventor, it is subsequently used in the psychiatric treatment of his wife and murderer. Intricately constructed, with fine characterization and compelling cynicism. Compare Malzberg's *Cross of Fire* [4-354].

4-146. Coney, Michael G(reatrex) (U.K.). **The Celestial Steam Locomotive.** Houghton Mifflin, 1983.
The first part of a two-decker novel concluded in *Gods of the Greataway* (1984). A far-future Earth is inhabited by several humanoid species; "true" humans have retreated into seclusion, dreaming their lives away with the aid of the great computer, Rainbow, while the godlike alien, Starquin, despite imprisonment, interferes extensively with Earth's affairs. The central characters embark on a quest to bring out of the network of alternative possibilities (the "Ifalong") a new destiny for all humankind. A curious combination of mythical fantasy and SF. *Cat Karina* (1982) is an independent novel with the same background. Compare Smith's *Norstrilia* [3-353] and Crowley's *Engine Summer* [4-158].

4-147. Coney, Michael G(reatrex) (U.K.). **Hello Summer, Goodbye.** Gollancz, 1975. U.S. title: *Rax,* DAW, 1975.
A planet that regularly exchanges its orbit from one element of a binary star to another faces the prospect of a long ice age, and its inhabitants must adapt themselves to this disruption. Compare Aldiss's "Helliconia" trilogy [4-6].

4-148. Cooper, Edmund (U.K.). **A Far Sunset.** Hodder & Stoughton, 1967.
A castaway on an alien world must adapt to the indigenous culture, though his ultimate success alienates him from his own kind when the possibility of rescue arises. An interesting exercise in speculative anthropology. Compare Barrett's *Stress Pattern* [4-39].

4-149. Correy, Lee (pseud. of G[eorge] Harry Stine). **Manna.** DAW, 1984.
A libertarian utopia in Africa invests heavily in a manned space program, taking up the torch of human progress in spite of attacks from outside. Propaganda with a certain infectious enthusiasm. Compare Edmondson's *The Man Who Corrupted Earth* [4-197].

4-150. Coulson, Juanita. **Tomorrow's Heritage.** Ballantine, 1981.
The first volume of a futuristic family saga, in which sibling rivalries complicate human expansion into the solar system and first contact with aliens. *Outward Bound* (1982) continues the story. Compare Merril's *Daughters of Earth* [3-283] and Randall's *Journey* [4-434].

4-151. Cover, Arthur Byron. **The Platypus of Doom and Other Nihilists.** Warner, 1976.
A bizarre collection of four novellas, including a parody of Barry Malzberg (the title story) and an ironic homage to the angst-ridden private-eye novel ("The Aardvark of Despair"). "The Clam of Catastrophe" introduces some of Cover's literary heroes (mostly under the cover of pseudonyms) into a chaotic and absurd adventure story—other exercises in the same vein are *Autumn Angels* (1975; NN, 1975) and the more pretentious *An East Wind Coming* (1979). Compare Philip José Farmer's *Venus on the Half-Shell* (1975).

4-152. Cowper, Richard (pseud. of John Middleton Murry, Jr.) (U.K.). **Breakthrough.** Dobson, 1967.
An experiment in parapsychology eventually reveals that the protagonists covertly harbor the personalities of people from a prehistoric golden age. Compare Sellings's *The Uncensored Man* [3-332].

4-153. Cowper, Richard (pseud. of John Middleton Murry, Jr.) (U.K.). **Clone.** Gollancz, 1972.
A satire on SF clichés and the high tech consumer society. The juvenile protagonist's gifted innocence throws the corrupt follies of the sophisticated world into sharp relief. *Profundis* (1979) is a blacker comedy with much the same message. Compare Sheckley's *Journey beyond Tomorrow* [3-336].

4-154. Cowper, Richard (pseud. of John Middleton Murry, Jr.) (U.K.). **The Custodians and Other Stories.** Gollancz, 1976.
The first of Cowper's short story collections, followed in the United Kingdom by *The Web of the Magi and Other Stories* (1980) and *The Tithonian Factor and Other Sto-*

ries (1984); the U.S. collection, *Out There Where the Big Ships Go* (1980), combines materials from the first two. Cowper displays a poetic style and an unusual delicacy of touch in featuring encounters between his characters and the speculative situations in which they are placed; he frequently builds tragic images of people dehumanized by technophilia and the lust for power; "The Custodians" (HN, 1976; NN, 1975) is one such lament for lost sanity.

*4-155.   Cowper, Richard (pseud. of John Middleton Murry, Jr.) (U.K.).   **The Road to Corlay.**   Gollancz, 1978.   U.S. eds. include as prelude, "Piper at the Gates of Dawn."
The first (NN, 1979) of three novel-length sequels to the fine novella "Piper at the Gates of Dawn" (HN, 1977; NN, 1976), which deals with the revival of a heretical cult in a postholocaust Britain dominated by oppressive religious orthodoxy. The cult, organized around the symbol of the White Bird of Kinship, enjoys the advantage that its most talented members can invoke and use a paranormal empathy, often associated with music. In *A Dream of Kinship* (1981) the cult has been transformed by the passing of centuries into an alternative orthodoxy, but in *A Tapestry of Time* (1982) it undergoes a further renewal. The books are lyrical fantasies affirming the author's conviction that it is spiritual rather than technological development that truly constitutes human progress. Compare Le Guin's *Always Coming Home* [4-323].

4-156.   Crichton, Michael.   **The Andromeda Strain.**   Knopf, 1969.
A satellite returns to Earth harboring a deadly plague, and worldwide catastrophe is narrowly averted. Realistic and suspenseful; made into an effective film. *The Terminal Man* (1972) is similar in its convincing handling of technical matters.

4-157.   Crowley, John.   **Beasts.**   Doubleday, 1975.
In a Balkanized near-future America various outsiders, including hybrid beastmen left over from experiments in genetic engineering, resist the recentralization of authority. Displays the same romantic nostalgia as Crowley's other works, but in less expansive fashion.

*4-158.   Crowley, John.   **Engine Summer.**   Doubleday, 1979.
In a far-future America returned to agrarian primitivism by disaster, the hero has recorded for future generations the story of his youthful quest for enlightenment. Beautifully written and eloquently argued; can be appreciated even by those who lack sympathy with the ideology behind its Arcadian romanticism. Compare Le Guin's *Always Coming Home* [4-323].

4-159.   Curval, Philippe (France).   **Brave Old World.**   Allison & Busby, 1977. Tr. by Steve Cox of *Cette chère humanité*, 1976.
An EEC-based political community of the future, isolated from the rest of the world, is penetrated by a spy whose intrusion precipitates the crisis that has long been brewing because of the side effects of the "slow-time" technology that expands subjective life spans. Convoluted but intriguing. Also annotated as [6-77].

4-160.   Dalos, Gyorgy (Hungary).   **1985.**   Pluto Press, 1983.
A sequel to Orwell's *Nineteen Eighty-Four* [3-302] that presents an ironic allegory of the postwar history of Hungary. Controlled liberalization allows the intellec-

tuals of the Outer Party some freedom of expression, but the illusions and pretensions of would-be dissidents like Winston and Julia are undercut by the cynical observations of O'Brien. A sharp political satire, witty and provocative. Contrast with the novella embedded in Anthony Burgess's *1985* (1978).

4-161. Dann, Jack. **The Man Who Melted.** Bluejay, 1984.
A man searches for his lost wife in a world where social order has been torn apart by outbreaks of hysterical collective consciousness, which have spawned a new religiosity and an epidemic of schizophrenia. An ironic reconstruction of the voyage of the *Titanic* is featured in the plot. Aggressively decadent, with a hint of Jacobean tragedy. Compare Zelazny's *Dream Master* [4-628]. NN, 1984.

4-162. Deighton, Len (U.K.). **SS-GB.** Cape, 1978.
Best-selling alternate-history story describing Britain occupied by Nazis in 1941. Compare Martin Hawkin's *When Adolf Came* (1943) and Frederick Mullally's *Hitler Has Won* (1975).

4-163. Delaney, Joseph H., and Marc Stiegler. **Valentina.** Baen, 1984.
Fix-up novel based on a novella (HN, 1985) about the development of a self-aware computer program and its problematic education. Compare Gerrold's *When Harlie Was One* [4-230] and Ryan's *The Adolescence of P-1* [4-459].

*4-164. Delany, Samuel R(ay). **Babel-17.** Ace, 1966.
An unorthodox heroine must come to terms with an artificial language whose constraints on thought and behavior make it an effective weapon of war. Clever, colorful, and highly original; it updates and sophisticates the theme of Vance's *The Languages of Pao* [3-381]. Compare also Watson's *The Embedding* [4-586].

*4-165. Delany, Samuel R(ay). **Dhalgren.** Bantam, 1975.
To the depopulated city of Bellona, which is subjected to occasional distortions of time and space, comes a youthful hero hungry for experience and keen to develop his powers as a creative artist. A dense and multilayered novel that alienated some readers who had previously applauded Delany's colorful fantastic romances, but reached a much wider audience. Convoluted and fascinating, it remains one of the key works of avant-garde SF, by an author determined to extend the limits of the genre. NN, 1975.

4-166. Delany, Samuel R(ay). **Driftglass.** Doubleday, 1971.
A collection of Delany's shorter works, including the brilliant "Time Considered as a Helix of Semi-Precious Stones" (HN, 1970; NW, 1969) and "The Star Pit" (HN, 1968). A later, slightly overlapping collection is *Distant Stars* (1981), which includes the short novel *Empire Star* (1966), a highly sophisticated space opera.

*4-167. Delany, Samuel R(ay). **The Einstein Intersection.** Ace, 1967.
In the far future the nonhuman inhabitants of Earth mine the mythologies of the ancient past in search of meanings appropriate to their own existence; the hero must undertake an Orphean quest into the underworld of the collective unconscious, confronting its archetypes. A fabulous tour de force of the imagination. Compare Zelazny's *This Immortal* [4-632] and Carter's *Infernal Desire Machines of Doctor Hoffman* [4-116]. HN, 1968; NW, 1967.

*4-168. Delany, Samuel R(ay). **Nova.** Doubleday, 1968.
A grail epic cast as space opera, whose hero must trawl the core of an exploding star for the fabulous element that is the power source of the galactic civilization. The most romantic and action packed of Delany's novels, but no less sophisticated for that. Beautifully written. HN, 1969.

4-169. Delany, Samuel R(ay). **Stars in My Pocket like Grains of Sand.** Bantam, 1984.
The first part of a novel to be completed in *The Splendor and Misery of Bodies, of Cities,* which accepts the impossible task of describing, analyzing, and bringing to life the culture of a galactic civilization, telling meanwhile a story of love and conflict at the individual level. An awesome project, with all the density and richness accompanying Delany's determination to stretch the limits of the genre.

4-170. Delany, Samuel R(ay). **Triton.** Bantam, 1976.
Subtitled *An Ambiguous Heterotopia,* this complex novel considers the problems that might arise for an individual trying with difficulty to orient himself in a culture where people have almost unlimited choice of identity and social role. The uncertainty of the protagonist's life is reflected in the unstable politics of the solar system, which ultimately becomes embroiled in a brief but catastrophic war. A rich, dense dramatization of issues in existential philosophy and sexual politics.

4-171. Dewdney, A. K. **The Planiverse.** Poseidon, 1984.
A modern novel inspired by Abbott's classic *Flatland* [1-1], in which the author/ protagonist and his students tour a two-dimensional planet in the planiverse. Compare C. H. Hinton's *An Episode of Flatland* (1907).

4-172. Dick, Philip K(indred). **The Divine Invasion.** Pocket Books, 1981.
The chief characters return to Earth from a space colony, setting in train a remarkable second coming, which heralds a strange millennium. The religious philosophy interwoven with the plot is idiosyncratic, but Dick's usual fervor of sympathy and anxiety is here strengthened by a powerful injection of faith and hope as well as charity. The religious themes were carried forward into Dick's last (non-SF) novel, *The Transmigration of Timothy Archer* (1982; NN, 1982).

*4-173. Dick, Philip K(indred). **Do Androids Dream of Electric Sheep?** Doubleday, 1968.
In a future where technological sophistication has made the ersatz virtually indistinguishable from the real the hero is a bounty hunter who must track down and eliminate androids passing for human. But android animals are routinely passed off as real by people trying to purge human guilt for having exterminated so many living species, and the new messiah is an artificial construct; so where is the difference between the human and the androidal? A key novel (NN, 1968) in Dick's canon. The film, *Blade Runner,* is a very pale echo. *We Can Build You* (1972) further explores the ambiguity of such distinctions as human/android and sane/ schizophrenic in a haunting story of people who create machines more human than they are.

4-174. Dick, Philip K(indred). **Dr. Bloodmoney; or, How We Got Along after the Bomb.** Ace, 1965.
A striking postholocaust novel in which the United States, despite awful devastation, sticks perversely to the same old social ruts. The characters struggle manfully to get by in appalling circumstances, wondering where the blame for it all truly lies. Compare Swanwick's *In the Drift* [4-550]. NN, 1965.

4-175. Dick, Philip K(indred). **Flow My Tears, the Policeman Said.** Doubleday, 1974.
The protagonist is drawn into the reconstructed reality of a woman's drug-induced dream, where he has been stripped of his identity and made vulnerable to persecution by her policeman brother. Written with the author's customary fervor, more emotionally charged than the earlier drug story *Now Wait for Last Year* (1966), but less nightmarish than *The Three Stigmata of Palmer Eldritch* (1965; NN, 1965). NN, 1974; HN, 1975; JWC, 1975.

4-176. Dick, Philip K(indred). **Galactic Pot-Healer.** Berkley, 1969.
A very curious novel in which the hero, a dissatisfied mender of pots, joins a group of misfits assembled by a godlike alien to raise a sunken cathedral, while other aliens read the runes that may indicate the destiny of the universe. A prefiguration of the metaphysical themes of Dick's last novels, developed in a mock-naïve fashion slightly reminiscent of Vonnegut's *The Sirens of Titan* [3-393]. *A Maze of Death* (1970) picked up the theological issues for more earnest development, but *Our Friends from Frolix-8* (1970) reassigned them to a throwaway role as an alien god is discovered dead in the void and his human messiah plays an essentially ambiguous role.

4-177. Dick, Philip K(indred). **A Scanner Darkly.** Doubleday, 1977.
The protagonist is, as usual in Dick's novels, gradually enmeshed by a web of circumstance in which he ceases to be able to distinguish between reality and hallucination. The fascination with which the author had previously contemplated such situations is here replaced, though, by horrified revulsion. An affectively powerful novel.

*4-178. Dick, Philip K(indred). **Ubik.** Doubleday, 1969.
The dead can be reactivated into a kind of half-life where they must construct their own shared realities, competing with one another to impose their own patterns. In this Schopenhaueresque world of will and idea it is not easy for the characters to formulate a policy of psychological adaptation. Takes up themes from *Eye in the Sky* [3-141] and is closely related to his hallucinatory novels but is more tightly plotted than many Dick novels.

4-179. Dick, Philip K(indred). **VALIS.** Bantam, 1981.
A convoluted novel in which the author figures as character, though his role is subservient to that of his alter ego, Horselover Fat, who achieves a miraculous enlightenment by courtesy of the godlike Vast Active Living Intelligence System, but has difficulty communicating his insights to others. *Radio Free Albemuth* (1985) uses similar materials, apparently being a different draft of the same project.

4-180.   Dickson, Gordon R(upert).   **The Far Call.**   Dial, 1978.
Political fantasy about a mission to Mars that is doomed to fail by the chicanery of
its promoters. The book version is much expanded from an *Analog* serial of
1973, the private lives of the characters being mapped out extensively, presumably with the intention of appealing to a wider audience. Interesting for its study
of the clash between the ideals of scientific progress and the follies of political
pragmatism. Compare Bova's *Colony* [4-68].

4-181.   Dickson, Gordon R(upert).   **The Final Encyclopedia.**   Tor, 1984.
The fifth of a projected sextet of novels forming the futuristic element of the
planned Childe Cycle. The transformation of this series (for earlier volumes see
[3-146]) from militaristic action-adventure into a philosophical commentary on
the evolution of humankind is as much a testament, in its way, to the trends of
modern SF as the maturation of Bradley's Darkover series [4-77] or the recomplication of Asimov's Foundation series [4-26]. *The Final Encyclopedia* itself is
rather rambling, and some readers may prefer the terse associated works that are
not asked to carry the burden of the author's philosophical pretensions: material
originally in *The Spirit of Dorsai* (1979) and *Lost Dorsai* (1980); recently reprinted
in *The Dorsai Companion* (1986).

4-182.   Dickson, Gordon R(upert).   **The Forever Man.**   Ace, 1986.
A possibility emerges of ending the long space war between humans and alien
enemies when a survivor of an early battle, his personality absorbed into the fabric of his ship, returns from a distant part of the galaxy. Action-adventure with
much material relating to military organization. Compare Haldeman's *The Forever War* [4-247].

4-183.   Dickson, Gordon R(upert).   **Time Storm.**   St. Martin's, 1977.
The surface of Earth is fragmented by temporal faults, and the hero, having lost
his wife, searches for some understanding of what has happened. Compare
Hoyle's *October the First Is Too Late* (1966). HN, 1978.

*4-184.   Disch, Thomas M(ichael).   **Camp Concentration.**   Hart-Davis, 1968.
A political prisoner is used as a guinea pig in an experiment that uses a syphilis-
related spirochete to boost IQ to unparalleled levels. The author boldly presents
the story as first-person narrative, and carries it off brilliantly. A key work of
avant-garde SF, written with its serialization in *New Worlds* in mind. Compare
Keyes's *Flowers for Algernon* [3-228].

4-185.   Disch, Thomas M(ichael).   **The Genocides.**   Berkley, 1965.
Humankind is wiped out when aliens turn Earth's surface into a vast farm. The
last survivors try to hollow out a new ecological niche as parasites, but can't cope.
Magnificently misanthropic, mocking the pretensions of cosmic significance that
SF so often credits to the human species. Contrast Heinlein's *Have Space Suit—
Will Travel* [3-201]. NN, 1965.

4-186.   Disch, Thomas M(ichael).   **The Man Who Had No Idea.**   Gollancz, 1982.
The most recent collection of Disch's shorter fiction, following *One Hundred and
Two H Bombs* (1966; enlarged as *White Fang Goes Dingo and Other Funny SF Stories*,
1971); *Under Compulsion* (1968; U.S. title: *Fun with Your New Head*), *Getting into*

Death (1973; U.K. and U.S. editions differ), and *Fundamental Disch* (1980). Disch is a master of black comedy, but can also write with nightmarish intensity or with a cool weltschmerz. This collection has nothing to match the classic "The Asian Shore" (NN, 1970; in *Getting into Death* and *Fundamental Disch*) but it has the ironic and satirical title story and another novelette, "Concepts," in which people separated by a vast gulf of space fall in love via a hyperspatial link, and the bleakly horrific "The Apartment Next to the War." Disch is one of the best contemporary American short story writers. Compare Ellison's *Deathbird Stories* [4-205].

*4-187. Disch, Thomas M(ichael). **On Wings of Song.** St. Martin's, 1979.
The hero, growing up in the ideologically repressive Midwest, yearns to learn the art of "flying," by which talented individuals can sing their souls out of their bodies. He loses his freedom, his wife, and his dignity to this quest, but in a cruelly ambiguous climax might have achieved an absurd triumph. Clever and compelling; a disturbing satire subverting SF myths of transcendence. Contrast the Robinsons' *Stardance* [4-449] and Clarke's *Childhood's End* [3-97]. HN, 1980; JWC, 1980; NN, 1979.

*4-188. Disch, Thomas M(ichael). **334.** McGibbon & Kee, 1972.
A dystopian vision of future New York, focusing on various residents of a huge apartment house and other parties interested in it. A brilliant work, utterly convincing in its portraits of people trying to get by in a world they are powerless to influence or control. The most eloquent display of the pessimism that became newly acceptable in New Wave SF. Compare Brunner's *Stand on Zanzibar* [4-92].

4-189. Douglas, Carole Nelson. **Probe.** Tor, 1985.
A psychiatrist becomes emotionally involved with an amnesiac girl whose psychokinetic powers attract unwelcome attention. Slow moving but intriguing. Compare Brunner's *Quicksand* [4-89].

4-190. Dozois, Gardner. **Strangers.** Berkley, 1978.
Expansion of a novella (HN, 1975; NN, 1974) tracking the love affair between a man and an alien woman whose reproductive biology is exotic. A virtual reprise of Farmer's *The Lovers* [3-159], with added depth of characterization.

4-191. Drake, David. **Bridgehead.** Tor, 1985.
A professor in an American university builds a fabulous machine at the behest of visitors who claim to be from the future, but he and his colleagues discover that it is part of a system of portals through which an interstellar war is about to be launched. Relentlessly fast-paced action-adventure SF.

4-192. Drake, David. **Hammer's Slammers.** Ace, 1979.
A collection of stories about the exploits of interplanetary mercenaries in the thirtieth century. *Cross the Stars* (1984) is a novel about an ex-slammer trying to get home, transposing Homer's *Odyssey* after the fashion of at least four other SF novels. *Forlorn Hope* (1984) is also about future mercenaries. Although primarily action-adventure stories, these works are serious in their treatment of the ideology of militarism, and Drake's fascination with military organization is also displayed in novels featuring Roman legionnaires, including *Birds of Prey* (1984) and *Ranks*

of Bronze (1986), which has kidnapped Romans serving alien masters as unwilling mercenaries. Compare Pournelle's work in this vein, especially *The Mercenary* [4-421].

4-193. Duffy, Maureen (U.K.). **Gor Saga.** Methuen, 1981.
The story of a growing child who is the experimental offspring of a human and a gorilla, and the effects of this revelation on him. Some satire and criticism of scientism as well as analysis of what it really means to be human. Compare Vercors's *Borderline* [3-388].

4-194. Durrell, Lawrence (U.K.). **The Revolt of Aphrodite.** Faber, 1974.
Omnibus edition of *Tunc* (1968) and *Nunquam* (1970). The inventor of a super-computer is hired by a multinational corporation that wants him to predict the future, but he is corrupted by greed. He reemerges from the madhouse in the second volume in order to make a duplicate of the corporation head's lost love. Mannered and convoluted. Compare Barth's *Giles Goat-Boy* [4-40].

4-195. Dvorkin, David. **Time for Sherlock Holmes.** Dodd Mead, 1983.
One of several novels co-opting the great detective into SF adventures. Here Holmes, having developed an elixir of youth, is still alive in 1990 to defend the world against Professor Moriarty, now armed with Wells's time machine and nuclear weapons. Delicately executed literary fun and games. Better than *Sherlock Holmes' War of the Worlds* (1975) by Manly Wade and Wade Wellman or *Morlock Night* (1979) by K. W. Jeter.

4-196. Earnshaw, Brian (U.K.). **Planet in the Eye of Time.** Hodder & Stoughton, 1968.
Trainee teachers in a galactic civilization undertake a time trip to discover the truth of Christian faith, which has enormous influence but still faces the threats of doubt and heresy. A fascinating recruitment of SF to the service of theological speculation. Compare and contrast Farmer's *Jesus on Mars* [4-209] and Moorcock's *Behold the Man* [4-380].

4-197. Edmondson, G. C. **The Man Who Corrupted Earth.** Ace, 1980.
An aggressive entrepreneur whose company has been hijacked in a boardroom coup gets his own back, and also succeeds in revitalizing the moribund space program, by buying up the space shuttles abandoned in orbit and putting them to good use. The entrepreneurial buccaneering is described with such verve and style that even socialists might enjoy it. Compare Heinlein's *The Man Who Sold the Moon* [3-204] and Rand's *Atlas Shrugged* [3-316].

4-198. Edmondson, G. C. **The Ship That Sailed the Time Stream.** Ace, 1965.
An entertaining timeslip story about a naval vessel dislodged from the present by lightning strikes attracted to its illicit still (NN, 1965). The sequel, *To Sail the Century Sea* (1981), expands the theme to take in attempts to alter the course of history. Witty and intelligent. Compare de Camp's *Lest Darkness Fall* [3-135].

4-199. Effinger, George Alec. **What Entropy Means to Me.** Doubleday, 1972.
A complex set of interwoven stories in which the central character invents the tale of his brother's search for his father, while beset by problems of his own (NN, 1972). Highly unusual, reminiscent in some ways of Flann O'Brien's *At*

Swim-Two-Birds (1939); Effinger's penchant for surrealism and the intricate inter-weaving of story lines is further demonstrated in *Relatives* (1973) and *The Wolves of Memory* (1981), which exhibit the same sharp imagery and the same conscientious failure to achieve coherency.

4-200. Eisenstein, Phyllis. **Shadow of Earth.** Dell, 1979.
The heroine is projected into an alternate world in which the Spanish Armada conquered England and secured Spanish domination of the world. She finds the task of survival in a technologically primitive and exaggeratedly male chauvinist world very difficult. Compare Roberts's *Pavane* [4-444] and Amis's *The Alteration* [4-10] for other alternate worlds based on similar premises.

4-201. Eklund, Gordon. **All Times Possible.** DAW, 1974.
A "uchronian" novel set in an alternate history; its protagonist is a hero of the labor movement whose martyrdom may or may not secure the American revolution for which he has worked. A distinctive ironic pessimism underlies the narrative, recalling the author's earlier *The Eclipse of Dawn* (1971). Compare Ted White and Dave Van Arnam's *Sideslip* (1968).

4-202. Elgin, Suzette Haden. **Communipath Worlds.** Pocket Books, 1980.
Omnibus containing *The Communipaths* (1970), *Furthest* (1971), and *At the Seventh Level* (1972). The telepathic hero is a reluctant agent for a galactic federal government, but his particular missions remain subservient to the author's interest in general issues of communication and the way in which communication systems and languages are implicated in social stratification. *Native Tongue* (1984) has the same concerns, in a narrative context that may be more appropriate. The hero of *Communipath Worlds* also features in *Star Anchored, Star Angered* (1979), which deals with questions of theology, and in *Yonder Comes the Other End of Time* (1986), which links the series to her Ozark Trilogy of fantasies. Elgin's plots are rough-hewn, but the ideas in them are intriguing and sometimes challenging. Compare the works of C. J. Cherryh [4-127 through 4-134].

4-203. Elliott, Sumner Locke. **Going.** Harper, 1975.
An ambiguous utopia has been achieved, but its citizens must submit to euthanasia at 65. The heroine, faced with imminent termination, reviews her life and evaluates her situation. A stylish mainstream novel with SF elements. Compare Lessing's *Memoirs of a Survivor* [4-333].

*4-204. Ellison, Harlan. **Alone against Tomorrow.** Macmillan, 1971.
Short stories dramatizing situations of acute alienation, including many of Ellison's best: "I Have No Mouth and I Must Scream" (HW, 1968) and " 'Repent, Harlequin!' Said the Ticktockman" (HW, 1966; NW, 1965) are among them. Intense, filled with Sartrian nausea but by no means lacking in caritas. Compare Sallis's *A Few Last Words* [4-464].

*4-205. Ellison, Harlan. **Deathbird Stories.** Harper, 1975.
Collection of stories said to display "a pantheon of modern gods"; angry reactions against aspects of the contemporary world. Outstanding are "The Death-bird" (HW, 1974; NN, 1973), "Pretty Maggy Moneyeyes" (HN, 1968; NN, 1967), "Shattered Like a Glass Goblin" (NN, 1969), and "Paingod." Demonstrates Elli-

son's brilliance as a short story writer, able to generate great affective power. Compare Spinrad's *No Direction Home* [4-528].

4-206.   Ellison, Harlan. **Shatterday.** Houghton Mifflin, 1980.
Collection of short stories continuing a trend in Ellison's work toward surrealism and psychological study, including the ironic (non-SF) novella "All the Lies That Are My Life" (HN, 1981) and the bitter fable "Count the Clock That Tells the Time." Compare Disch's *The Man Who Had No Idea* [4-186].

4-207.   Evans, Christopher (U.K.). **The Insider.** Faber, 1981.
In a near-future Britain a parasitic alien intelligence is forced by the death of its human host to take over another, and in order to remain in hiding must detach the host from the network of his social responsibilities. An unusual and gripping novel, written with skill and intensity.

4-208.   Farmer, Philip José. **Dayworld.** Putnam, 1985.
The world is so overcrowded that people must live in shifts, one day per week. Criminal "daybreakers" are pursued by government agents; the hero is one of them, troubled by his own multiple-personality conflicts as well as his adversaries. Ingenious and fast moving, but rattles on so relentlessly that it ends (as do so many Farmer novels) with no real conclusion in sight.

4-209.   Farmer, Philip José. **Jesus on Mars.** Pinnacle, 1979.
An expedition to Mars finds Jesus alive and well. Borrows the hypothesis that supports eccentric cults like the Aetherius Society and develops it in an earnest manner. The same earnestness can be found in Farmer's "biographies" of pulp heroes, *Tarzan Alive* (1972) and *Doc Savage: His Apocalyptic Life* (1973), and the fact that it is here applied to a more serious issue adds an extra turn of the ironic screw.

*4-210.   Farmer, Philip José. **To Your Scattered Bodies Go.** Putnam, 1971.
The entire human race is reincarnated along the banks of a huge river. Sir Richard Francis Burton sets off to find out who accomplished this remarkable feat, and why (HW, 1972). In *The Fabulous Riverboat* (1971), Sam Clemens undertakes a similar quest. Both characters, and others who become involved in further books of the series, *The Dark Design* (1977) and *The Magic Labyrinth* (1980), are continually sidetracked by violent conflicts in which characters from various phases of Earth's history are idiosyncratically matched against one another, causing the main issue to be constantly confused. Associated stories outside the main sequence are "Riverworld" in *Riverworld and Other Stories* (1979) and *Gods of Riverworld* (1983). An early version of the story, written in the early 1950s for an ill-fated competition, was recently rediscovered and issued as *River of Eternity* (1983).

*4-211.   Farmer, Philip José. **The Unreasoning Mask.** Putnam, 1981.
A swashbuckling space opera with heavy metaphysical overtones; the ambiguous hero undertakes a fabulous quest despite the suspicions of his crew that he is committing awful crimes and exposing them to great danger. Much more tightly organized than most of Farmer's later works, with a suitably apocalyptic climax. Compare Ian Watson's *Gardens of Delight* [4-587].

4-212. Felice, Cynthia. **Godsfire.** Pocket Books, 1978.
On a planet where it rains all the time humans are enslaved by feline aliens, one of whom is the narrator. An unusual and well-constructed novel. Compare Cherryh's felines in the Chanur series [4-131].

4-213. Felice, Cynthia, and Connie Willis. **Water Witch.** Ace, 1982.
On a desert planet those who can locate water and those who control its distribution have prestige and power; the heroine makes a fraudulent bid to join the elite, and gets herself involved in complex intrigues. Lighthearted and likable.

4-214. Finney, Jack. **Time and Again.** Simon & Schuster, 1970.
Timeslip romance whose plausibility is enhanced by making the time travel part of an experimental project and by unusually scrupulous research. Excellent historical detail and a compelling plot make this the outstanding work of the subgenre. Compare Matheson's *Bid Time Return* [4-364].

4-215. Forbes, Caroline (U.K.). **The Needle on Full.** Onlywomen, 1985.
Collection of feminist SF stories, including two novellas: "London Fields," in which the women who inhabit the ruins of London after men have been wiped out by plague have to cope with the reappearance of a group of males; and "The Comet's Tail," about the fate of two female astronauts on a long space mission during whose course Earth is destroyed. Slightly rough-hewn, but written with feeling. Compare Charnas's *Walk to the End of the World* [4-125].

4-216. Ford, John M. **Web of Angels.** Pocket Books, 1980.
A computerized communications network binds together an interstellar community, and is elaborately policed to protect it from the exploits of "webspinners." The young hero, a talented webspinner, is shielded by others but still loses his first love and is brought to painful maturity by his quest for revenge. A rich text, laden with allusions, that uses complex mythological analogies to dramatize the magical quality of its imaginary technologies. Compare Vinge's *True Names* [4-576].

4-217. Forward, Robert L(ull). **Dragon's Egg.** Ballantine, 1980.
A race that evolves on the surface of a neutron star lives on a vastly compressed time scale, but nevertheless manages to make contact with human observers. A fascinating and ingenious example of hard SF. Its representation of scientists at work compares with Benford's *Timescape* [4-54]. In the sequel, *Starquake!* (1985), the aliens achieve technological sophistication, are returned to primitivism by a "starquake," and rebuild their civilization—a process that takes several of their generations but only 24 hours of our time. Compare Brunner's *Crucible of Time* [4-87].

4-218. Forward, Robert L(ull). **The Flight of the Dragonfly.** Pocket Books, 1984.
The two parts of a bilobate planet harbor very different physical conditions, though there is much interaction between their environments. Humans make contact with the intelligent natives and require their help in rescuing an exploration ship. An exercise in world building comparable to Clement's *Mission of Gravity* [3-109].

4-219.   Foster, Alan Dean. **Icerigger.** Ballantine, 1974.
The first part of a story continued in *Mission to Moulokin* (1979), in which castaways on a cold planet must fight for survival and enlist local help to attempt escape. Colorful action-adventure; compare Vance's Planet of Adventure tetralogy (1968–1970).

4-220.   Foster, Alan Dean. **The Tar-Aiym Krang.** Ballantine, 1972.
First part of a triology continued in *Orphan Star* (1977) and *The End of the Matter* (1977), following the adventures of a young psi-powered hero who takes on mighty adversaries and wins by ingenuity and audacity. Entertaining picaresque space opera in a modern vein. Foster has used the same background and sometimes the same characters in other novels, including *Bloodhype* (1973), *Nor Crystal Tears* (1982), and *For Love of Mother-Not* (1983). The more recent works move away from pure space opera toward more thoughtful consideration of the relationships between different species in the interstellar commonwealth.

4-221.   Foster, M(ichael) A(nthony). **The Morphodite.** DAW, 1981.
On a planet where change is suppressed by a determined totalitarian government, revolution is precipitated by an assassin whose calculation of social stresses tells him where to strike and whose shape-shifting power keeps him one step ahead of his pursuers. In the sequels, *Transformer* (1983) and *Preserver* (1985), the morphodite's mission is carried further, into the wider reaches of interstellar civilization. Action-adventure fiction enlivened by the protagonist's dramatic changes of identity and the problems that ensue therefrom.

4-222.   Foster, M(ichael) A(nthony). **Waves.** DAW, 1980.
An enigmatic intelligent ocean interferes with Slavic colonists on an alien world. Apparently inspired by Lem's *Solaris* [3-261]; the author draws on his background as a Russian linguist with the U.S. Air Force in setting up the situation. An interesting novel of ideas.

4-223.   Franson, Robert W(ilfred). **The Shadow of the Ship.** Ballantine, 1983.
Expanded from a 1976 novella, the story features a very strange kind of interstellar travel, in which "wagon trains" are pulled across subspace trails by huge animals. The plot concerns a caravan of adventurers searching for a mysterious alien ship. A very unusual adventure story.

4-224.   Frayn, Michael (U.K.). **A Very Private Life.** Collins, 1968.
In a privatized society where telecommunications sustain social intercourse, the misfit heroine goes outside in search of new horizons, but finds the natural life not to her taste. An ironic dystopia in the tradition of Huxley's *Brave New World* [2-47].

4-225.   Gallun, Raymond Z(inke). **The Eden Cycle.** Ballantine, 1974.
A novel that investigates the common assertion that evolution into superhumanity would take the spice out of life; the central characters struggle to find meaning and purpose in a situation in which they can effectively have anything they want. Contrast Moorcock's Dancers at the End of Time trilogy [4-383].

4-226.   Garnett, David S. (U.K.). **Mirror in the Sky.** Berkley, 1969.
Humans are fighting an interminable war against the alien Creeps, their morale

boosted by drugs and pinups of the forces' sweetheart. One man, though, begins to suspect that the war is nothing but a monumental hoax. Action-adventure gently rippled by the New Wave worldview. Contrast Haldeman's *The Forever War* [4-247].

4-227. Gary, Romain (pseud. of Romain Kassevgari) (France). **The Gasp.** Putnam, 1973.
A scientist succeeds in isolating *élan vital* that is the human soul, and it is exploited as an energy source. Satirical black comedy with a fast-paced plot, apparently following up the central idea of Maurois's *The Weigher of Souls* [2-73].

4-228. Gaskell, Jane (U.K.). **A Sweet, Sweet Summer.** Hodder, 1969.
Britain is isolated after an enigmatic alien invasion and the rule of law disintegrates, presenting the extraterrestrial observers with an appalling image of human folly and corruption. Slick and cynical. Compare Hodder-Williams's *The Chromosome Game* [4-273].

4-229. Gerrold, David (pseud. of Jerrold David Friedman). **The Man Who Folded Himself.** Random, 1973.
A time traveler shuttles back and forth, replicating himself many times over and creating practical and existential problems for himselves. A playfully narcissistic treatment of the time paradox theme, developing ideas from Heinlein's "By His Bootstraps" (1941) and "All You Zombies . . ." (1959).

4-230. Gerrold, David (pseud. of Jerrold David Friedman). **When Harlie Was One.** Doubleday, 1972.
The hero supervises the making and education of a sentient computer, which eventually designs an artificial intelligence even more powerful in order to demonstrate its usefulness. Compare Delaney and Stiegler's *Valentina* [4-163] and Ryan's *Adolescence of P-1* [4-459].

4-231. Geston, Mark S(ymington). **Lords of the Starship.** Ace, 1967.
In the far future a nation whose ancestors once built starships attempts to duplicate their achievement, though it no longer has the appropriate technology and must expend many generations in the project. *Out of the Mouth of the Dragon* (1969) is set in the same desolate far future, and deals with the last of the many wars that have laid it waste. Grim and somber stories, with some fine imagery and a uniquely bitter ennui.

4-232. Gibson, William. **Count Zero.** Arbor House, 1985.
A complex adventure story set in the same future as *Neuromancer* [4-233]. The eponymous hero gets into trouble as a result of a weird experience in cyberspace, while two other protagonists follow their own projects to the entangled climax. Clever and slick. The same settings also feature in many of Gibson's short stories, collected in *Burning Chrome* (1986).

*4-233. Gibson, William. **Neuromancer.** Ace, 1984.
In a highly urbanized future dominated by microelectronic technology, anti-hero Case is rescued from wretchedness and given back the ability to send his persona into the cyberspace of the world's computer networks, where he must carry out a hazardous mission for an enigmatic employer. An adventure story much en-

livened by elaborate technical jargon and sleazy, streetwise characters—the pioneering "cyberpunk" novel. Compare Boyce's *Catchworld* [4-72] and Vinge's *True Names* [4-576]. HW, 1985; NW, 1984; JWC, 1985.

4-234. Goldin, Stephen. **The Eternity Brigade.** Fawcett, 1980.
Professional soldiers whose personalities are stored in memory banks are periodically reincarnated to serve as mercenaries—but the tapes have been bootlegged and the soldiers end up fighting themselves. A view of the profession of arms that may be contrasted with that in Drake's *Hammer's Slammers* [4-192] or Pournelle's *The Mercenary* [4-421].

4-235. Goldstein, Lisa. **The Dream Years.** Bantam, 1986.
A young French writer allied with the surrealist movement of the 1920s is enabled by his meetings with a mysterious girl to timeslip into the future, to 1968 and a further, unspecified time when he can see the outcome of the thought-revolution pioneered by the surrealists. Unashamedly sentimental and delicately crafted; contrast past-oriented timeslip romances like Finney's *Time and Again* [4-214].

4-236. Gordon, Stuart (pseud. of Richard Gordon) (U.K.). **Smile on the Void.** Arrow, 1982.
A mock-documentary novel presenting the "real" story of a late twentieth-century messiah who flourishes in the 1980s, disappears in 1992, and might or might not return in 1999 to proclaim the millennium. Calculatedly bombastic and heavily ironic, teasing the reader with the probability that it is all a joke. Compare (with tongue in cheek) Knight's *Man in the Tree* [4-304].

4-237. Goulart, Ron. **After Things Fell Apart.** Ace, 1970.
A detective pursues a gang of feminist assassins through the eccentric subcultures of a balkanized future United States. The best of the author's many humorous SF novels, with a genuine satirical element to add to the usual slapstick. Compare Sheckley's *Journey beyond Tomorrow* [3-336].

4-238. Grant, Charles L. **The Shadow of Alpha.** Berkley, 1976.
In the twenty-second century devastating plague winds have depleted the human population of the United States, while androids that used to do most of the work have mostly run wild. Here and in two sequels, *Ascension* (1977) and *Legion* (1979), set several generations later, some semblance of political order is gradually restored. Compare Swanwick's *In the Drift* [4-550].

4-239. Griffin, Russell M. **The Blind Men and the Elephant.** Pocket Books, 1982.
A deformed product of experiments in bioengineering is exhibited as a freak and spied on by government agents; he participates in some bizarre adventures involving some very peculiar characters. Black comedy; compare Sladek's *Roderick* novels [4-522].

4-240. Griffin, Russell M. **Century's End.** Bantam, 1981.
As the millennium approaches in 1999 chiliastic panic gives birth to numerous strange cults, which use the media to spread their messages and fight their ideo-

logical battles. Can order possibly be reborn from such chaos? Clever satire; compare Shea and Wilson's *Illuminatus!* [4-490].

4-241. Guin, Wyman. **The Standing Joy.** Avon, 1969.
A curious superman story set in an alternate world, which speculates extensively on matters of creativity and libido. Compare Jarry's *The Supermale* (1902) and Sturgeon's "Maturity" (1947).

4-242. Gunn, James E(dwin). **Crisis!** Tor, 1986.
A time traveler becomes a human catalyst helping the world of the near future to solve its problems, despite being handicapped by the fact that every time he alters the future his memories are obliterated. Carefully optimistic and constructive; compare Pohl's *Years of the City* [4-420].

4-243. Gunn, James E(dwin). **The Dreamers.** Simon & Schuster, 1980.
Once the mechanism of memory is known, the business of learning is technologically transformed, but the acquisition of information by ingestion and injection mechanizes the personality. Thoughtful development of fascinating premises; similar in structure and import to the author's classic *The Joy Makers* [3-185].

*4-244. Gunn, James E(dwin). **The Listeners.** Scribner, 1972.
A fix-up novel about the radio astronomers who pick up and decode a message from an alien civilization, and about the public reaction to the event; the work is heavy with religious symbolism and literary allusion. Compare Clarke's *2010* [4-141] and Kube-McDowell's *Emprise* [4-307].

4-245. Hackett, John, and others (U.K.). **The Third World War: August 1985.** Macmillan, 1979.
A documentary "reconstruction" of the background to and fighting of World War III. Futurological alarmism comparable with William Le Queux's *The Invasion of 1910* [1-57], which was also a best-seller of its time. The use of expert writers adds an aura of plausibility. The basic thesis is further elaborated in a sequel, *The Third World War: The Untold Story* (1982), which is more of a pseudotextbook, and is heavier on propaganda. Compare Stableford and Langford's *The Third Millennium* [4-534].

4-246. Haiblum, Isidore. **Nightmare Express.** Fawcett, 1979.
An alternate-world story in which the crucial turning point is 1935, allowing Haiblum to use his characteristic hard-boiled detective story tone in a near-natural setting. Lots of mean streets, but humor too. Compare the nostalgic element in the work of Arthur Byron Cover [4-151].

*4-247. Haldeman, Joe. **The Forever War.** St. Martin's, 1975.
Fix-up novel of interstellar war against hive-organized aliens. Realistic descriptions of military training and action, with interesting use of relativistic time distortions. A reprise of and ideological counterweight to Heinlein's *Starship Troopers* [3-206]. Compare also Card's *Ender's Game* [4-109]. HW, 1976; NN, 1975.

4-248. Haldeman, Joe. **Worlds.** Viking, 1981.
The first part of a projected trilogy whose second part is *Worlds Apart* (1983). Earth lurches toward World War III, after which devastation the future of hu-

mankind will become dependent on the society of the "Worlds"—orbital satellites. Near-future realism combined with loosely knit action-adventure. Compare Bova's *Colony* [4-68] and *Test of Fire* [4-70].

4-249. Handley, Max. **Meanwhile.** Arlington, 1977.
Complex satirical adventure story, part apocalyptic fantasy and part sex comedy, with dozens of SF and fantasy motifs jostling one another. Very funny. Compare Shea and Wilson's *Illuminatus!* [4-490].

4-250. Harness, Charles L(eonard). **The Catalyst.** Pocket Books, 1980.
A curious mixture of realism and far-fetched romance in which a scientist struggles against bureaucratic repression to create a miracle drug. Stylization almost as pronounced as in the classic novella "The Rose" (1953), but the detail drawn from the author's long experience in patenting scientific processes provides an apt counterweight.

4-251. Harness, Charles L(eonard). **Redworld.** DAW, 1986.
An adolescent hero succeeds to a mythic role on a world circling Barnard's Star, which has only 23 known elements and where the evolution of science has been consequently inhibited. The author's own adolescent experiences are apparently woven into the plot, assisting empathy between reader and protagonist, and producing a peculiar balance between the exotic and the familiar. Compare Brian Herbert's *Sudanna, Sudanna* [4-266].

4-252. Harness, Charles L(eonard). **The Ring of Ritornel.** Berkley, 1968.
A fine space opera in which a corrupt galactic empire faces apocalyptic destruction as the contending forces of chance and destiny (personalized in rival deities) resolve their conflict. Will the cosmos be reborn and renewed when the cycle ends? The themes echoed here from the classic *Flight into Yesterday* [3-189] recur again in *Firebird* (1981), and these three works are among the most stylish modern space operas. Compare Ian Wallace's Croyd series [4-580] and Barrington J. Bayley's *The Pillars of Eternity* (1982).

4-253. Harness, Charles L(eonard). **The Venetian Court.** Ballantine, 1984.
Technological progress has been taken over by an inventive computer, and the corporation controlling it has used its power to make patent infringement a capital crime. Within this context Harness stages a courtroom melodrama with a brilliant defense lawyer and a hanging judge. Contrived and stagy, but carried off with great panache.

4-254. Harrington, Alan. **Paradise 1.** Little, Brown, 1977.
A novel in which the author of the best-selling *The Immortalist* further popularizes his ideas about the sociology of death and the possibility of its conquest. Here, death has been rendered unnecessary early in the twenty-first century, but utopia is still a long way away, with Machiavellian chicanery in the corridors of power and the Death Partisans peddling the ultimate pornography. Contrast Randall's *Islands* [4-433].

4-255. Harrison, Harry (pseud. of Henry Maxwell Dempsey). **Bill, the Galactic Hero.** Doubleday, 1965.
A parody of the interstellar war story as exemplified by Heinlein's *Starship Troopers* [3-206]. A boisterous black comedy; compare Shaw's *Who Goes Here?* [4-489].

4-256. Harrison, Harry (pseud. of Henry Maxwell Dempsey). **The Daleth Effect.** Putnam, 1970. British title: *In Our Hands, the Stars,* Faber, 1970.
An Israeli scientist invents antigravity and flees to Denmark in order to develop his invention for peaceful purposes rather than allowing it to become a hot pawn in the cold war. Action-adventure with a political slant. Compare Shaw's *Ground Zero Man* (1971).

*4-257. Harrison, Harry (pseud. of Henry Maxwell Dempsey). **Make Room! Make Room!** Doubleday, 1966.
A classic novel of overpopulation and pollution, reprinted in connection with the film version (which certainly fails to do the book justice) as *Soylent Green.* An archetypal example of 1960s alarmism. Compare Brunner's *Stand on Zanzibar* [4-92]. NN, 1966.

4-258. Harrison, Harry (pseud. of Henry Maxwell Dempsey). **West of Eden.** Bantam, 1984.
Alternate-history story in which the dinosaurs were not killed off and ultimately produced sentient, humanoid descendants devoted to biotechnology. Their civilized race is ultimately forced into contact and conflict with savage human beings, adding culture shock to crisis. Inventive, fast-paced narrative. The story is continued in *Winter in Eden* (1986); a third and concluding volume is forthcoming.

4-259. Harrison, M(ichael) John (U.K.). **The Centauri Device.** Doubleday, 1974.
An alienated spaceman whose genes equip him to use a powerful weapon is harassed by those wishing to exploit him, but eventually gets his own back. A parody of space operas, with some political satire thrown in. Compare Bayley's *Zen Gun* [4-48].

4-260. Harrison, M(ichael) John (U.K.). **A Storm of Wings.** Sphere, 1980.
A sequel to the downbeat sword-and-sorcery novel *The Pastel City* (1971). It begins the transformation of the city Viriconium into a milieu for more sophisticated literary exercises, extended in *In Viriconium* (1982; U.S. title: *The Floating Gods*) and *Viriconium Nights* (1984). Images of decadence and exhaustion abound in this series, which contrasts with other images of far-future cities in Bryant's *Cinnabar* [4-95] and Carr's *Cirque* [4-114] and has strong affinities with certain aspects of Michael Moorcock's work. SF motifs are relatively sparse in what is essentially a fantasy series, but the use of entropic decay as a prevalent metaphor sustains the bridge between genres.

4-261. Heinlein, Robert A(nson). **The Cat Who Walks through Walls.** Putnam, 1985.
The aging hero, a writer and unfairly disgraced ex-soldier, becomes embroiled in murderous intrigue and goes on the run with his newly acquired Amazonian wife. When in extremis he is rescued by the Justice League of Heinleinia, carried

over from such novels as *The Moon Is a Harsh Mistress* [4-263], *Time Enough for Love* [4-264], and *The Number of the Beast* (1980). A narcissistic SF ego trip, fascinating fare for psychoanalysts and Heinlein aficionados.

4-262. Heinlein, Robert A(nson). **Friday.** Holt, 1982.
An artificially created superwoman, courier for a secret organization, has to fend for herself when the decline of the West reaches its climax; she ultimately finds a new raison d'être on the extraterrestrial frontier. Welcomed by Heinlein fans as action-adventure respite from his more introspective works, but actually relates very closely to some sections of *Time Enough for Love* [4-264] and refers to much earlier material ("Gulf," 1949). HN, 1983; NN, 1982.

*4-263. Heinlein, Robert A(nson). **The Moon Is a Harsh Mistress.** Putnam, 1966.
Colonists of the Moon declare independence from Earth, and contrive to win the ensuing battle with the aid of a sentient computer. Action-adventure with some exploration of new possibilities in social organization and fierce assertion of the motto "There Ain't No Such Thing as a Free Lunch." Compare Poul Anderson's *Tales of the Flying Mountains* (1970). HN, 1966; HW, 1967; NN, 1966.

4-264. Heinlein, Robert A(nson). **Time Enough for Love.** Putnam, 1973.
Partial biography of Lazarus Long, the long-lived hero of *Methuselah's Children* [3-204], involving the promiscuous multiplication of his genes (sometimes in unorthodox ways) and a journey into the past that affords him the opportunity to seduce his mother and die a hero's death (not final, of course) in World War I. An extravagant exercise in the production of an idealized fantasy self, drawing on the repertoire of SF ideas to support and sanction extraordinary forms of imaginary self-indulgence. Powerful because of the wish-fulfillment aspect of its composition. Compare "Baron Corvo's" *Hadrian VII* (1904). HN, 1974; NN, 1973.

4-265. Helprin, Mark. **Winter's Tale.** Harcourt, 1983.
The foundling hero is raised by a primitive tribe inhabiting the Jersey marshes in the late nineteenth century, and becomes embroiled in the feuding of gangs of petty criminals before being magically hurled through time into the 1990s, where he finds New Yorkers facing a problematic millennium. More fantasy than SF despite the futuristic element, but the extraordinarily rich narrative invites comparison with John Crowley's masterpiece, *Little Big* (1981), and it has links with other millenarian SF stories; compare, for instance, Griffin's *Century's End* [4-240].

4-266. Herbert, Brian. **Sudanna, Sudanna.** Arbor House, 1985.
An eccentric work describing the everyday lives (with a few extraordinary adventures thrown in) of alien beings on a peculiar planetoid, while they struggle to cope with the uncomfortable legacy of long-gone invaders. Hovers uneasily between comedy and seriousness, but has a certain charm. Compare Brunner's *Crucible of Time* [4-87].

4-267. Herbert, Frank. **Destination: Void.** Berkley, 1966.
The computers guiding a starship en route to a new world fail, and the crew

must construct an artificial intelligence to repair the damage, but the intelligence defines itself as God and demands worship as the price of looking after its human cargo. In two sequels written with Bill Ransom, *The Jesus Incident* (1979) and *The Lazarus Effect* (1983), this artificial God and his human subjects draw on biblical lore in order to explore the possibilities of worship, trying to figure out how it should be appropriately done. Compare the first book to Boyce's *Catchworld* [4-72], the sequels to Malzberg's *Cross of Fire* [4-354].

*4-268. Herbert, Frank. **Dune.** Chilton, 1965.
The first volume (HW, 1966; NW, 1965) of a best-selling series continued with *Dune Messiah* (1969), *Children of Dune* (1976; HN, 1977), *God-Emperor of Dune* (1981), *Heretics of Dune* (1984), and *Chapter House: Dune* (1985). The first volume is the story of a selectively bred messiah who acquires paranormal powers by use of the spice that is the main product of the desert planet Arrakis, and uses them to prepare for the ecological renewal of the world. Politics and metaphysics are tightly bound into a remarkably detailed and coherent pattern; an imaginative, tour de force. The series as a whole is overinflated, the later revisitations of the theme being prompted more by market success than the discovery of new things to do with it. *Children* sees the culmination of the themes laid down in *Dune* itself, but *God-Emperor* and *Heretics* form a duet that re-presents the themes in a more elaborate form, with a denser commentary on the underlying ideas. *Chapter House* adds little. The series demonstrates how a good SF writer's ability to build a coherent and convincing hypothetical world can serve the purpose of making philosophical and sociological questions concrete; the series thus becomes a massive thought experiment in social philosophy, and is more considerable as such than Asimov's Foundation series [3-19] and [4-26] or Bradley's Darkover series [4-77].

4-269. Herbert, Frank. **Hellstrom's Hive.** Doubleday, 1973.
A secret research project undertakes an extraordinary experiment in social and biological engineering, creating a human hive that supposedly represents the next phase in human evolution. Compare Bass's *Half Past Human* [4-41].

4-270. Herbert, Frank. **The White Plague.** Putnam, 1982.
A molecular biologist driven mad by cruel circumstance unleashes a plague that will universalize his personal tragedy and destroy the women of the world. The terrorism that initially provoked him is reproduced on a grand scale: an appalling visitation of a kind of "justice." Compare Priest's *Fugue for a Darkening Island* [4-428].

4-271. Herbert, Frank, and Brian Herbert. **Man of Two Worlds.** Gollancz, 1986.
Dreens are compulsive storytellers with the power of imaging, which solidifies the figments of their imagination. They are presumably the creators of the material universe, but have little or no control over those beings (like humans) to whom they have given free will. While the Dreen powers-that-be wonder whether to erase Earth, an immature Dreen fuses personalities with a power-hungry human

and undergoes many adventures, including fighting with the French Foreign Legion on Venus. A van Vogtian entertainment.

4-272. Hoban, Russell. **Riddley Walker.** Cape, 1980.
A postholocaust story in which gunpowder is rediscovered but set aside by the naïvely wise hero, who believes that mankind must find a new path of progress this time. The first-person narrative is presented in the decayed and transfigured dialect of the day, and represents a fascinating linguistic experiment. Compare Aldiss's *Barefoot in the Head* [4-3]. NN, 1981; JWC, 1982.

4-273. Hodder-Williams, Christopher (U.K.). **The Chromosome Game.** Mithras, 1984.
Two hundred years after the nuclear holocaust human beings are recreated from stored sperm and ova; the children are reared by computers, but this does not prevent their society from recovering all the evils and follies that destroyed their ancestors. Compare Van Greenaway's *graffiti* [4-562] for a similar bleakness of outlook.

4-274. Hogan, James P(atrick). **Code of the Lifemaker.** Ballantine, 1983.
The "descendants" of factory robots abandoned long ago on Titan have built a civilization now discovered by humans. A charlatan psychic takes a leading role in an attempt to enslave them, but other humans are prepared to defend their freedom. Compare Silverberg's *Tower of Glass* (1970).

4-275. Hogan, James P(atrick). **The Genesis Machine.** Ballantine, 1978.
A brilliant physicist invents a machine that enables him to prevent the nuclear holocaust, although not without difficulty. Compare Shaw's *Ground Zero Man* (1971).

4-276. Hogan, James P(atrick). **The Minervan Experiment.** Nelson Doubleday, 1981.
Omnibus edition of a trilogy: *Inherit the Stars* (1977), *The Gentle Giants of Ganymede* (1978), and *Giants' Star* (1981). A humanoid corpse discovered on the moon presents a puzzle that unravels into the story of an ancient civilization whose colonies in the solar system were destroyed by war. The trilogy starts well but deteriorates gradually into unexceptional space opera; in the third volume humans and alien allies resist absorption into a nasty galactic empire. The strength of the first volume is its portrayal of scientists battling with a mystery, producing and testing hypotheses until the solution is found. Compare Benford's *Timescape* [4-54].

4-277. Hogan, James P(atrick). **Voyage from Yesteryear.** Ballantine, 1982.
The starship *Mayflower II* arrives on a colony world that is a libertarian utopia, into which its pilgrims try to import a centralized political economy; resistance proves too strong. Contrast the final sequence of Russell's *The Great Explosion* [3-321].

4-278. Holdstock, Robert (U.K.). **When Time Winds Blow.** Faber, 1982.
Time winds carry objects back and forth in time on an alien planet; the detritus they leave is eagerly investigated during periods of calm. Investigators, though,

live in constant peril of being caught up by the winds. The story is heavy on dialogue and philosophical discussion. Compare Priest's *An Infinite Summer* [4-430].

4-279. Holmes, Bruce T. **Anvil of the Heart.** Haven, 1983.
Genetic engineering is creating a new race, and the last natural men and women must grow old alongside their superchildren, who are already planning their utopia. The protagonist becomes involved in a rebellion against the new order. Compare Sargent's *The Golden Space* [4-471].

4-280. Hubbard, L(afayette) Ron(ald). **Battlefield Earth.** St. Martin's, 1983.
The hero rallies the last remnant of humankind to rebel against their alien conquerors and take a more prominent place in the galactic community. Very long and packed with rather implausible action. Its success in the marketplace was followed up with the best-selling early volumes in a projected ten-volume series entitled *Mission Earth: The Invaders Plan* (1985), *Black Genesis* (1986), and *The Enemy Within* (1986). Here Earth is a vital pawn in the power games played by the elite of the galactic empire. Space opera on an unprecedented scale—the full work is said to run to 1,200,000 words. Compare for style and imagination, though not for scope, *Space Fury* (1962) by R. Lionel Fanthorpe and *The Troglodytes* (1962) by Nal Rafcam.

4-281. Hyams, Edward (U.K.). **Morrow's Ants.** Allen Lane, 1975.
A wealthy industrialist builds a self-contained futuristic city and applies sophisticated techniques of behavior control to maintain order and create a society in the image of the anthill. Compare Herbert's *Hellstrom's Hive* [4-269].

4-282. Ing, Dean. **Soft Targets.** Ace, 1979.
An interesting near-future novel about the problem of terrorism and its relationship with media news coverage. Compare Mack Reynolds's "Of Future Fears" (1977).

4-283. Ing, Dean. **Systemic Shock.** Ace, 1981.
The first of a series of postholocaust novels in which the shattered society of the United States is held together by religious cults and ruled by violence. Grim realism and involved plotting. The series continues in *Single Combat* (1983) and *Wild Country* (1985).

4-284. Jakes, John. **On Wheels.** Paperback Library, 1973.
A curious novel about future gypsies forced to drive endlesly around the American freeways, developing their own customs and myths. Compare Reynolds's *Rolltown* [4-439].

4-285. James, Dakota. **Milwaukee the Beautiful.** Fine, 1986.
Immigrants from Central America flood the United States when the greenhouse effect makes the tropics uninhabitable. The Union breaks up, Milwaukee becoming an independent nation where traditional values are upheld. Simultaneously satirizes the old-style American Dream and the new-style ecological politics of books like Callenbach's *Ecotopia* [4-107].

4-286. Jeschke, Wolfgang (Germany). **The Last Day of Creation.** Century, 1982. Tr. by Gertrud Mander of *Der letzte Tag der Schöpfung,* 1981.
Time travel story in which Americans try to hijack the Middle East's oil from the past; when paradoxes accumulate, the travelers are cut off from futures that no longer exist. A fast-paced adventure story with a touch of weltschmerz. Compare Silverberg's *Up the Line* [4-512]. Also annotated as [6-19].

4-287. Jeter, K. W. **Dr. Adder.** Bluejay, 1984.
Quasi-pornographic novel of a decadent future Los Angeles and the attempts made by a video evangelist to clean it up, with the protagonist caught in the exotic crossfire. Compare Barnes's *Streetlethal* [4-38A].

4-288. Jeury, Michel (France). **Chronolysis.** Macmillan, 1980. Tr. by Maxim Jakubowski of *Le Temps incertain,* 1973.
Agents from competing futures penetrate the present by means of a drug and try to influence events so as to establish their own time lines. An important work of surreal SF. Compare Leiber's "Change War" stories [3-249] and Dick's *Ubik* [4-178]. Also annotated as [6-114].

4-289. Jones, D(ennis) F(eltham) (U.K.). **Colossus.** Hart-Davis, 1966.
A supercomputer gradually outgrows the control of its human makers and acquires ambitions of world domination. The computer is defeated in *The Fall of Colossus* (1974) and revived in *Colossus and the Crab* (1977). The first volume—filmed as *The Forbin Project*—is an archetypal treatment of a popular theme. Compare Rayer's *Tomorrow Sometimes Comes* (1951) and Herbert's *Destination: Void* [4-267].

4-290. Jones, Langdon (U.K.). **The Eye of the Lens.** Macmillan, 1972.
A collection of New Wave stories by a *New Worlds* writer, including the controversial "I Remember, Anita" and such fine surreal stories as "The Great Clock" and "The Time Machine."

4-291. Joseph, M(ichael) K(ennedy) (New Zealand). **The Hole in the Zero.** Gollancz, 1967.
Surreal SF novel, set largely outside time and space, in which the characters can and do create their own subjective realities, searching therein for some kind of existential anchorage. Compare Dick's *Ubik* [4-178] and Stableford's *Man in a Cage* [4-532].

4-292. Kahn, James. **Time's Dark Laughter.** Ballantine, 1982.
The more interesting sequel to *World Enough and Time* (1980), recklessly mixing motifs from SF and fantasy. The world is periodically reconstituted, the breaks in its history arising because of the creation of messianic beings. Both books have some remarkably graphic imagery, but it is here more disciplined in the service of the main theme. Compare Helprin's *Winter's Tale* [4-265] and Powers's *Anubis Gates* [4-422].

*4-293. Kavan, Anna (pseud. of Helen Woods) (U.K.). **Ice.** Owen, 1967.
A dreamlike story whose narrator pursues a fragile girl through increasingly ice-bound war zones while harboring nostalgic feelings about the warm and gentle

world of the indri of Madagascar. A classic surreal novel of existential catastrophe. Contrast Ballard's *Drowned World* [4-37].

4-294. Kilian, Crawford (Canada). **Eyas.** Bantam, 1982.
Ten million years in the future humans live alongside many other races; the eponymous protagonist, heir to a throne, must cope with personal problems and save his people. Kilian's forte is tales of maturation in difficult circumstances; another is *Brother Jonathan* (1985). Compare Card's *Ender's Game* [4-109].

4-295. Killough, Lee. **Aventine.** Ballantine, 1982.
A collection of short stories set in a future artist's colony where decadence and ingenuity thrive in harness. Compare Ballard's *Vermilion Sands* [4-38].

4-296. Kilworth, Garry (U.K.). **The Night of Kadar.** Faber, 1978.
A starship carries frozen embryos that become the settlers of a new world, but a malfunction prevents their receiving the necessary education, and they must struggle to come to terms with themselves as well as with the indigeneous aliens. Compare Herbert and Ransom's *The Jesus Incident* [4-267].

4-297. Kilworth, Garry (U.K.). **The Songbirds of Pain.** Gollancz, 1984.
Collection of short stories including the time travel story "Let's Go to Golgotha," which won a *Sunday Times* SF story competition in 1975. The title story and some others show the author in a lyrical vein that contrasts with the taut adventure fiction of his novels. Compare the short fiction of Richard Cowper [4-154].

4-298. Kilworth, Garry (U.K.). **A Theatre of Timesmiths.** Gollancz, 1984.
A closed-world story; the inhabitants of a city completely surrounded by vast walls of ice face crisis as their central computer becomes unreliable, and must rediscover their history in search of a solution.

4-299. King, Stephen. **Carrie.** Doubleday, 1974.
The story of an alienated teenage girl whose latent psychokinetic power bursts forth in an orgy of destruction when she is humiliated at a high school prom. A graphic and satisfying revenge fantasy. Contrast van Vogt's *Slan* [3-383].

4-300. King, Stephen. **The Dead Zone.** Viking, 1979.
The juvenile hero acquires the gift of precognition, although his talent is almost entirely limited to disastrous events; but can the holocaust he foresees in connection with the campaign of a presidential candidate be averted? Compare Cherryh's "Cassandra" [4-133].

*4-301. Kingsbury, Donald (Canada). **Courtship Rite.** Simon & Schuster, 1982. British title: *Geta*, 1984.
A colony on an arid world is in cultural extremis because of its lack of resources, and the central characters become involved with a challenge to its established order. An unusually detailed and complex novel, interesting because of its carefully worked political and anthropological themes. Compare Herbert's *Dune* [4-268]. HN, 1983.

4-302. Klein, Gerard (France). **The Day before Tomorrow.** DAW, 1972. Tr. by P. J. Sokolowski of *Le Temps n'a pas d'odeur,* 1967.

Interplanetary peace is secured by transtemporal agents who alter the history of worlds likely to prove troublesome, but a team on one such mission finds unexpected problems with paradoxes and a peculiar alien culture. Compare Jeury's *Chronolysis* [4-288].

4-303. Knight, Damon. **CV.** Tor, 1985.

A huge oceangoing vessel—effectively a floating city—is menaced by an alien parasite that can inhabit the bodies of human beings. A thriller in the same vein as Campbell's *Who Goes There?* [3-86]—compare the 1982 film version, *The Thing.*

4-304. Knight, Damon. **The Man in the Tree.** Berkley, 1984.

The story of a superhuman giant alienated in youth by his powers and by his accidental killing of the bullying son of a sheriff, who resolves to hunt him down. He grows up "in hiding" as a carnival freak, but ultimately embarks on a messianic quest to save mankind. Much is made of the parallels between his career and that of Jesus. Compare Sturgeon's *The Dreaming Jewels* [3-360] and Wyman Guin's *The Standing Joy* [4-241].

4-305. Komatsu, Sakyō (Japan). **Japan Sinks.** Harper, 1976. Tr. (abridged) by Michael Gallagher of *Nippon Chimbotsu,* 1973.

A best-selling catastrophe story in which millions of people are saved from the inundation of their nation. Contrast with the American catastrophism of Niven and Pournelle's *Lucifer's Hammer* [4-397]. Also annotated as [6-259].

4-306. Koontz, Dean R(ay). **Beastchild.** Lancer, 1970.

An alien participating in the calculated genocide of humankind decides that humans are not so bad after saving and befriending a child. Compare Cherryh's *Cuckoo's Egg* [4-127].

4-307. Kube-McDowell, Michael P. **Emprise.** Berkley, 1985.

The first volume of a trilogy continued in *Enigma* (1986) and to be completed in *Empery.* A future society in decline is revitalized by a message from the stars, and prepares for the momentous contact. In the second volume the aliens' claim to be descended from humans is investigated, and a search of neighboring star systems reveals other "lost colonies" of a previous human expansion into space. Compare the first volume to Sagan's *Contact* [4-463], the second to Niven's *Protector* [4-391].

4-308. Lafferty, R(aphael) A(loysius). **Annals of Klepsis.** Ace, 1983.

A minor historian comes to Klepsis but is told that it has no history for him to write, because its existence is merely a prelude to the beginning of time, and the universe to which he belongs is only a figment of the imagination of its founder. Typical wild adventure with apocalyptic undertones. Compare Dick's *Galactic Pot-Healer* [4-176].

4-309. Lafferty, R(aphael) A(loysius). **Apocalypses.** Pinnacle, 1977.

Two novels: *Where Have You Been, Sandaliotis?* and *The Three Armageddons of Enniscorthy Sweeny.* The first is a Fortean romance about a Mediterranean nation that is only occasionally accessible, the second a fine surrealist account of the apocalyptic reshaping of human destiny by an inspired artist. Marvelous fabulations by a writer sui generis.

*4-310. Lafferty, R(aphael) A(loysius). **Fourth Mansions.** Ace, 1969.
An innocent tries to understand the enigmatic events and secret organizations that are symbolic incarnations of the forces embodied in the (highly problematic) moral progress and spiritual evolution of humankind. A bizarre tour de force; one of the finest examples of American avant-garde SF. Compare Zelazny's *This Immortal* [4-632] and Delany's *The Einstein Intersection* [4-167]. NN, 1970.

*4-311. Lafferty, R(aphael) A(loysius). **Nine Hundred Grandmothers.** Ace, 1970.
The first and best of Lafferty's short story collections, followed by *Strange Doings* (1971), *Does Anyone Else Have Something Further to Add?* (1974), *Ringing Changes* (1984), and various collections issued by small presses. Lafferty's shorter works tend to be highly distinctive and idiosyncratic, often mixing materials from Celtic or Amerindian folklore with SF motifs in order to produce tall stories with a philosophical bite. At his most stylized Lafferty is comparable to Calvino's *Cosmicomics* [4-108], but he is rarely so abstracted and his stories have a characteristic warmth as well as a breezy imaginative recklessness and a good deal of wit.

4-312. Lafferty, R(aphael) A(loysius). **Past Master.** Ace, 1968.
St. Thomas More is snatched out of the past in order to save a decidedly ambiguous utopia—if its enemies can't prevent his doing so. A heartfelt but lighthearted exercise in the theater of the absurd: bewildering, funny, and thought-provoking. NN, 1968; HN, 1969.

4-313. Lafferty R(aphael) A(loysius). **Space Chantey.** Ace, 1968.
The *Odyssey* transposed into bizarre space opera, omnivorously devouring bits and pieces from other mythologies, to construct a futuristic mythos open to all possibilities, where the outrageous can only be commonplace and characters who are innocent and worldly-wise at the same time can stroll through the tallest tales ever told.

4-314. Laidlaw, Marc. **Dad's Nuke.** Fine, 1985.
Mock soap opera set in a near future where the domestic scene has been transformed by all manner of new technologies and every man's home is a fortress. Clever black comedy, taking themes from such novels as Brunner's *Jagged Orbit* [4-88] to absurd extremes.

4-315. Lake, David J(ohn) (Australia). **The Man Who Loved Morlocks.** Hyland House, 1981.
A sequel to *The Time Machine* [1-103] that cleverly sets out to oppose and "correct" the pessimism of Wells's classic, casting doubt on the Time Traveller's judgments and developing an alternative view of human destiny. Much superior to other modern sequels (Egon Friedell's *Return of the Time Machine*, 1946; tr. 1972, and K. W. Jeter's *Morlock Night*, 1979, are examples) and more interesting than

other reflections on Wellsian ideology (Aldiss's *Moreau's Other Island,* 1980, and Priest's *The Space Machine,* 1976, for instance).

4-316. Lake, David J(ohn) (Australia). **The Right Hand of Dextra.** DAW, 1977.
A New Jerusalem is built in a green and pleasant alien land, where the emigrant pilgrims from Earth face the prospect of mingling and merging with the unfallen telepathic natives. In the sequel, *The Wildings of Westron* (1977), their hopes seem to have come to nothing because the legacy of their earthly existence has not been entirely set aside. Action-adventure SF with considerable metaphorical weight. Compare and contrast Lewis's *Out of the Silent Planet* [3-263] and *Perelandra* [3-263].

4-317. Langford, David (U.K.). **The Space Eater.** Arrow, 1982.
A future war novel, capitalizing on ideas developed in the author's nonfiction *War in 2080* (1979). Heroism is a difficult business in a world oversupplied with lethal hardware, and the protagonist has a hard time saving the universe from the unfortunate side effects of the use of matter transmitters. Rather brittle melodrama, redeemed by its inventiveness and zest. Compare Vinge's *Peace War* [4-575].

4-318. Lanier, Sterling E(dward). **Hiero's Journey.** Chilton, 1973.
The world, wasted by nuclear war, is dominated by horrid mutants; the protagonist goes questing for the legendary computers that might save humankind. *The Unforsaken Hiero* (1983) present his further adventures. Boisterous picaresque adventure fiction, comparable to Piers Anthony's Xanth fantasy novels as well as SF postholocaust romances like Zelazny's *Damnation Alley* (1969).

4-319. Laumer, Keith. **The Infinite Cage.** Putnam, 1972.
A van Vogtian novel of burgeoning superhumanity. The protagonist begins the story in a state of complete ignorance but gradually becomes all-powerful and undergoes a transcendental metamorphosis. A particularly clear version of one of the most prevalent motifs in modern SF. Compare Sellings's *The Uncensored Man* [3-332] and Randall's *Islands* [4-433].

4-320. Laumer, Keith. **Star Colony.** St. Martin's, 1981.
Fix-up novel detailing the history of a colony whose misfortunes begin with the crash landing of the colonizing vessel and are compounded by the interventions of an indigenous hive intelligence before things really get difficult, when the colony is rediscovered by the galactic community. Compare Bradley's Darkover series [4-77].

4-321. Lee, Tanith (U.K.). **Sabella; or, The Blood-Stone.** DAW, 1980.
Science fiction vampire story in which the heroine comes to terms, under stress, with her alien nature. The emotional intensity that is the author's forte is abundantly displayed in the second part of the text. Compare Matheson's *I Am Legend* [3-274].

4-322. Lee, Tanith (U.K.). **The Silver Metal Lover.** DAW, 1982.
A teenage girl finds the perfect soul mate—but how is she going to explain to her mother that he is a robot? An ironic inversion of del Rey's "Helen O'Loy" [3-

138], told in earnest fashion, ultimately facing (as del Rey's story does not) the issues involved in its premise.

*4-323. Le Guin, Ursula K(roeber). **Always Coming Home.** Harper, 1985.
An elaborate account of the culture of the Kesh—people living in "the Valley" in northern California in a postindustrial future. The main narrative sequence concerns the experiences of a girl fathered on a woman of the valley by an outsider, but there is a great wealth of supplementary detail to set this story in context; the environment, mythology, and arts of the imaginary society are scrupulously described. A fabulously rich work, the most elaborate exercise in imaginary anthropology ever undertaken, even including a cassette recording. Compare Wright's *Islandia* [3-406] and Brunner's *Stand on Zanzibar* [4-92].

*4-324. Le Guin, Ursula K(roeber). **The Dispossessed.** Harper, 1974.
Subtitled *An Ambiguous Utopia,* this story contrasts the poverty-stricken world of Anarres, whose political order is anarchist and egalitarian, with its rich neighbor Urras, from whose capitalist and competitive system the settlers of Anarres initially fled. A physicist who must travel from one world to the other serves as a self-conscious and anxious viewpoint character. A dense and very careful work, arguably the best example of how SF can be used for serious discussion of moral and political issues. The quality of the writing is also outstanding. Compare Lessing's Canopus in Argos series [4-334] and Hesse's *Magister Ludi* [3-212]. HW, 1975; JWC, 1974; NW, 1974.

4-325. Le Guin, Ursula K(roeber). **The Eye of the Heron.** Gollancz, 1982.
Short novel originally published in Virginia Kidd's anthology *Millennial Women* (1978). On a colony world the exploited, agrarian underclass migrates en masse to escape the oppressions of the city-dwelling elite. Takes up themes from *The Dispossessed* [4-324] but lacks drive and conviction.

4-326. Le Guin, Ursula K(roeber). **The Lathe of Heaven.** Scribner, 1971.
A psychiatrist sets out to use a patient whose dreams can alter reality to create utopia, but in usurping this power he is gradually delivered into madness. Compare Dick's *Flow My Tears, the Policeman Said* [4-175] and *Ubik* [4-178].

*4-327. Le Guin, Ursula K(roeber). **The Left Hand of Darkness.** Ace, 1969.
Humans on the world of Winter are hermaphrodite, able to develop male or female sexual characteristics during periodic phases of fertility. An envoy from the galactic community becomes embroiled in local politics and is forced by his experiences to reconsider his attitudes toward human relationships. Serious, meticulous, and well written, the book has been much discussed and praised because of its timely analytic interest in sexual politics. Compare Sturgeon's *Venus Plus X* [3-364]. HW, 1970; NW, 1969.

*4-328. Le Guin, Ursula K(roeber). **The Wind's Twelve Quarters.** Harper, 1975.
The first of Le Guin's two short story collections, the other being *The Compass Rose* (1982). The stories are various in theme but uniformly well written, ranging from the philosophical "Vaster Than Empires and More Slow" (HN, 1972) and the moving story of clone siblings, "Nine Lives" (NN, 1969), to a brief prelude to

The Dispossessed [4-324], "The Day before the Revolution" (NW, 1974; HN, 1975) and the dark fable "The Ones Who Walk Away from Omelas" (HW, 1974). These stories can stand comparison with modern short fiction of any kind. Within the SF field their elegance is matched by some of the work of Thomas M. Disch [4-185, 4-186], but their earnest seriousness is without parallel.

4-329. Le Guin, Ursula K(roeber). **The Word for World Is Forest.** Berkley, 1976.
Short novel originally published in *Again, Dangerous Visions* [4-650]. Human colonists on an alien world cause untold damage to the innocent natives and their environment. A harsh comment on the ethics and politics of colonialism, making good use of anthropological perspectives. Compare Bishop's *Transfigurations* [4-64]. NN, 1972; HW, 1973.

4-330. Lem, Stanislaw (Poland). **The Cyberiad.** Seabury, 1974. Tr. by Michael Kandel of *Cyberiada,* 1967.
A series of fables about two robot "constructors" who build marvelous machines that usually fulfill their appointed tasks, but with unforeseen side effects. Futuristic folklore akin to Lafferty's *Space Chantey* [4-313] but with a satirical element more akin to the work of John Sladek. *Mortal Engines* (tr. 1977) is a similar collection.

4-331. Lem, Stanislaw (Poland). **The Futurological Congress.** Seabury, 1974. Tr. by Michael Kandel of *Ze wspomnien Ljona Tichego, Kongres Futrologiczny,* 1971. A story of Ion Tichy, whose adventures can also be found in *The Star Diaries* (tr. 1976; also published as *Memoirs of a Space Traveller*). A convention of futurologists is disrupted by terrorism, and the release of psychotropic chemicals hurls the protagonist into a dream of a violent and decadent dystopian future. Satire of the "no-good-will-come-of-it-all" school pioneered by Karel Čapek.

4-332. Lem, Stanislaw (Poland). **His Master's Voice.** Secker, 1983. Tr. by Michael Kandel of *Glos pana,* 1968.
A stream of "signals" from outer space is the subject of various attempted decodings, and an excuse for all kinds of wild hypotheses about who might have sent the message and why, in which are reflected various human hopes and fears. Cool satire; contrast Sagan's *Contact* [4-463].

4-333. Lessing, Doris (U.K.). **The Memoirs of a Survivor.** Octagon, 1974.
The heroine watches the slow disintegration of civilization while a teenage girl left in her care slowly matures, the two processes of decay and growth being carefully contrasted. Compare and contrast Disch's *334* [4-188].

4-334. Lessing, Doris (U.K.). **Shikasta.** Cape, 1979.
The first of a series presenting the "Archives of Canopus in Argos"; its sequels are *The Marriages between Zones Three, Four and Five* (1980), *The Sirian Experiments* (1981), *The Making of the Representative for Planet 8* (1982), and *The Sentimental Agents in the Volyen Empire* (1983). Shikasta is Earth, whose history—extending over millions of years—is here put into the cosmic perspective, observed by Canopeans who seem to be in charge of galactic history although responsible to some higher, impersonal authority. The sequels follow the exploits of various hu-

man cultures whose affairs are subtly influenced by the Canopeans; all share the remotely detached perspective that transforms the way in which individual endeavors are seen. Thoughtful and painstaking. Compare Stapledon's *Last and First Men* [2-109] and *Last Men in London* [2-109] and Pangborn's *A Mirror for Observers* [3-304].

4-335. Leven, Jeremy. **Creator.** Coward, McCann, 1980.
A novel exploring—with great delicacy, much sentimentality, and a good deal of wit—the meaning of creativity. Only marginally SF, in that one character is trying to clone his dead wife while looking after the affairs of another "offspring" (the lead character in a novel he is writing) but a fine novel that uses its SF motif more earnestly than most of the other American mainstream novels that have taken such motifs aboard.

4-336. Leven, Jeremy. **Satan.** Knopf, 1982.
Satan, newly incarnate in the form of an artificial intelligence, seeks the advice of a psychoanalyst who has already had occasion to ponder the problem of evil. Meanwhile, a more positivistically inclined psychiatrist uses extreme methods in his quest for an understanding of the mysteries of the human brain. A fine philosophical novel, not as affectively powerful as *Creator* [4-335] but more intellectually gratifying.

4-337. Levin, Ira. **The Boys from Brazil.** Random, 1976.
An aging Nazi-hunter discovers Dr. Mengele's plot to produce a whole series of Hitler clones when the boys' adoptive fathers have to be killed in order to reproduce the key event in Hitler's upbringing. A thriller that cleverly questions genetic determinism.

4-338. Levin, Ira. **This Perfect Day.** Random, 1970.
A dystopian society is tightly controlled by the computers that oversee and regulate it; rebels against its drug-induced conformity must therefore try to change the fundamental programming. In the tradition of *Brave New World* [2-47] and *Player Piano* [3-392] but adds little that is original.

4-339. Lichtenberg, Jacqueline. **Dushau.** Warner, 1985.
First of a trilogy continued in *Farfetch* (1985) and *Outreach* (1986). In a Byzantine galactic empire alien empaths who can establish magical relationships with planetary ecosystems are perceived as a threat and persecuted, but the human heroine takes up their cause. Lichtenberg is one of the most intense proponents of ecological mysticism, making symbolic models of human relationships in exotic biologies. Compare McCaffrey's Pern series [4-368] and Cherryh's Faded Sun trilogy [4-129].

4-340. Llewellyn, Edward (Canada). **Salvage and Destroy.** DAW, 1984.
An agent for the race that controls galactic civilization puts on human guise in order to investigate Earth as a possible source of threat. A thriller with some interesting exotic biology and a light spice of satire. Compare the Herberts' *Man of Two Worlds* [4-271].

4-341. Logsdon, Syd. **A Fond Farewell to Dying.** Pocket Books, 1981.
After a nuclear war India has emerged as the new superpower; an American bi-

ologist working there discovers a way to record and transcribe memories, so that a man can be reincarnated in a younger clone body, but in the religious culture of Hinduism this process seems a blasphemy. A thoughtful novel. Compare Silverberg's *To Live Again* (1969).

4-342. Longyear, Barry B(rookes). **Manifest Destiny.** Berkley, 1980.
Short story collection including "Enemy Mine" (NW, 1979; HW, 1980), in which an alien and a human stranded on a hostile world must cooperate although their species are at war. "The Jaren" expresses a similar conviction that if different races cannot achieve a proper sympathy for one another the results must be tragic. *The Tomorrow Testament* (1983) is a novel set against the same background as "Enemy Mine," and similarly deals with the cultivation of understanding; "Enemy Mine" itself was expanded to novel length by David Gerrold, the resultant book (1985) being issued as a collaboration, in connection with a film version.

4-343. Lundwall, Sam J(errie) (Sweden). **2018 A.D.; or, The King Kong Blues.** **DAW,** 1975.
In a polluted future world dominated by crass commercialism the hero struggles to make a living in the corrupt advertising profession, while a bored oil sheikh plays games with the world economy. Satirical black comedy with considerable bite. Compare Pohl and Kornbluth's *The Space Merchants* [3-313] and Wilson's *Spaceache* [4-613].

4-344. Lupoff, Richard A(llen). **Circumpolar!** Pocket Books, 1984.
Pulp-style adventure fiction set on an alternate Earth shaped like a millstone with a "Symmes Hole" at its center. The Richtofen brothers and a Russian princess race against Howard Hughes, Charles Lindbergh, and Amelia Earhart to fly across the bottom of the world. Compare Blaylock's *The Digging Leviathan* [4-65]. The sequel is *Countersolar!* (1986).

4-345. Lupoff, Richard A(llen). **Space War Blues.** Dell, 1978.
Fix-up novel in which human colonies fight a race war in space, disrupting the lives of the peaceful tribesmen who have adapted to life as spacefaring nomads. A deliberate mingling of the avant-garde and romantic aspects of 1970s SF, based on a short novel that appeared in Ellison's anthology *Again, Dangerous Visions* [4-650].

4-346. Lupoff, Richard A(llen). **Sun's End.** Berkley, 1984.
A Japanese construction worker emerges from suspended animation as a bionic superman, ready to take on the perils of twenty-first-century life. Picks up from Lupoff's fantasy novel *Sword of the Demon* (1977) themes associated with his fascination with Japanese culture, and also continues his long-standing interest in superheroes; the story is apparently to be continued. Compare and contrast Bear's *Beyond Heaven's River* [4-49].

4-347. Lynn, Elizabeth A. **A Different Light.** Berkley, 1978.
An artist suffering from terminal cancer is determined to savor the light of other suns and restore contact with a lost lover, even though hyperspatial travel will fur-

ther shorten his life expectancy. Elegiac in tone and heavily romantic. Compare Robinson's *The Memory of Whiteness* [4-446].

4-348. Lynn, Elizabeth A. **The Sardonyx Net.** Putnam, 1981.
On the one planet in the galactic community where slavery still survives, political adversaries fight over the drug that sustains the system. The chief protagonist is caught in a conflict of loyalties, finding his principles and emotions continually at odds as he moves through the convoluted plot. Colorful action-adventure SF with pretensions to moral seriousness. Compare Carr's *Navigator's Syndrome* [4-113].

4-349. MacLean, Katherine. **The Missing Man.** Berkley, 1975.
Extended from a novella (NW, 1971). The psychic hero, although a social outsider, uses his powers for the public good but has still to achieve full development of his superhuman nature. Compare Brunner's *The Whole Man* [4-94] and Sellings's *The Silent Speakers* [3-331].

4-350. MacLeod, Sheila (U.K.). **Xanthe and the Robots.** Bodley Head, 1977.
A robotics engineer with personal problems has a heavy emotional investment in her machines, and in making them more human must recover her own essential humanity. A dramatic recomplication of the theme of Čapek's *R.U.R.* [2-15]; compare Dick's *We Can Build You* [4-173] and Asimov's robot stories featuring Dr. Susan Calvin [3-20].

4-351. Malamud, Bernard. **God's Grace.** Farrar, 1982.
The protagonist survives atomic armageddon while diving in a bathysphere. He subsequently makes his way to a desert island, where a talking chimpanzee acts as his Man Friday. With the aid of other anthropoid apes they begin the recreation of civilization; as in Robinson Crusoe the hero's relationship with his creator is a theme of central importance. A witty fable. Compare Vidal's *Kalki* [4-572] and Leven's *Creator* [4-335].

4-352. Malzberg, Barry N(orman). **Beyond Apollo.** Random, 1972.
Winner of the first John W. Campbell Memorial Award (1973), causing controversy because it is a wickedly funny undermining of the SF myth of the conquest of space, of which Campbell was one of the principal promoters. The sole survivor of a Venus mission cannot explain what became of his companions. *The Falling Astronauts* (1971) and *Revelations* (1973) also challenge with mockery the values implicit in the space program.

4-353. Malzberg, Barry N(orman). **Chorale.** Doubleday, 1978.
The hero, trapped into a reenactment of the life of Beethoven in order to preserve the integrity of the past, steps out of his allotted role to rebel against the dictatorship of inevitability. Feverishly introspective (as is usual with Malzberg) but with an unusual briskness suited to the inspiration of the Ninth Symphony.

*4-354. Malzberg, Barry N(orman). **Cross of Fire.** Ace, 1982.
Expanded from the novella "Le Croix" (The Cross). A dissident in a future totalitarian state undergoes a kind of psychotherapy involving induced illusions, which allow him to play Christ, in which role he ardently but hopelessly seeks

meaning through self-sacrifice. Mordant wit and graphic imagery combine in a powerful and disturbing story. Compare Moorcock's *Behold the Man* [4-380].

*4-355. Malzberg, Barry N(orman). **Galaxies.** Pyramid, 1975.
Expanded from the novelette "A Galaxy Called Rome." The plot, deliberately designed as a hard SF story, involves a spaceship endangered by a black hole, on whose fate much depends; this is blended with an elaborate commentary on the psychology and sociology of SF writing, using the story as paradigm. It thus becomes a brilliantly self-conscious work of art, more telling in many ways than *Herovit's World* [4-356]. Contrast Anderson's *The Enemy Stars* [3-10].

4-356. Malzberg, Barry N(orman). **Herovit's World.** Random, 1973.
Non-SF novel about an SF writer driven mad by nausea, possessed first by the personality implicit in his pseudonym, and then by the personality of his tough hero. Two earlier novellas published under the pseudonym K. M. O'Donnell, *Dwellers of the Deep* (1970) and *Gather in the Hall of the Planets* (1971), also comment bitterly on the ideological perversities of the SF community, but *Herovit's World* is black comedy with much more bite.

4-357. Malzberg, Barry N(orman). **The Man Who Loved the Midnight Lady.** Doubleday, 1980.
Perhaps the best of Malzberg's several short story collections; also outstanding is the earlier *Down Here in the Dream Quarter* (1976). Most of Malzberg's stories contrive to be anguished and witty at the same time—classic examples of ironic weltschmerz. Compare the short fiction of John Sladek [4-519] and the work of nongenre writers like Bernard Malamud.

4-358. Malzberg, Barry N(orman). **The Remaking of Sigmund Freud.** Ballantine, 1985.
Fix-up novel featuring an alternate world where Freud psychoanalyzes Emily Dickinson from afar and is assassinated by a disappointed patient, and a future where he is reincarnated aboard a spaceship to save its crew members from the kind of extraterrestrial angst that was suffered by the protagonist of *Beyond Apollo* [4-352]. Lacks the fluency of Malzberg's earlier novels, but gains in complexity by way of compensation. Compare Leven's *Satan* [4-336]. NN, 1985.

4-359. Mann, Philip (New Zealand). **The Eye of the Queen.** Gollancz, 1982.
A painstaking account of contact between humans and a very strange alien culture. The text consists of a diary written by a scientist who tries to understand the aliens, interrupted by a commentary by his assistant. Slow moving but intriguing and commendably ambitious. Compare Bishop's *Transfigurations* [4-64] and Cherryh's *Voyager in Night* [4-134].

4-360. Martin, George R(aymond) R(ichard). **Dying of the Light.** Simon & Schuster, 1977.
On a wandering world, briefly brought to light by its temporary association with a sun, several races have built cities for a great festival. The self-pitying protagonist pursues his lost love here, and becomes involved with the alien tribe into which she has married as the long night closes in again. Compare Lynn's *A Different Light* [4-347]. HN, 1978.

4-361. Martin, George R(aymond) R(ichard). **A Song for Lya and Other Stories.** Avon, 1976.
Collection whose title story (HW, 1975) is one of several notable studies of an alien species whose biology is such that their religious faith in life after death is materially founded. One of the protagonists goes native in order to take advantage of this opportunity, but her lover cannot. Martin is generally at his best in medium-length stories: *Nightflyers* (HN, 1981; reprinted as a book, 1985) is another story of contact with mysterious aliens, while the title story of the collection *Sandkings* (1981; HW, 1980) is a memorable account of insectile "pets" learning to see their "owners" in a new light. His other collections are *Songs of Stars and Shadows* (1977) and *Songs the Dead Men Sing* (1983).

4-362. Martin, George R(aymond) R(ichard), and Lisa Tuttle. **Windhaven.** Pocket Books, 1981.
Fix-up novel including "One-Wing" (HN, 1981). On a stormy world humans struggle to survive on the islands of an archipelago, their communications depending on the flyers who use artificial wings. The heroine has a turbulent time on the ground as well as in the air. Compare McCaffrey's Pern series [4-368].

4-363. Masson, David I(rvine) (U.K.). **The Caltraps of Time.** Faber, 1968.
Notable collection of short stories by a writer associated with Moorcock's *New Worlds,* including the fine "Traveller's Rest," about a war fought on a world where time passes at different rates in different places. Polished and original. Compare Bayley's *Knights of the Limits* [4-45] and Sallis's *A Few Last Words* [4-464].

4-364. Matheson, Richard. **Bid Time Return.** Viking, 1975.
Timeslip romance in which a young author is allowed to meet (briefly) the actress from the past with whose photographic image he has fallen in love. Compare Finney's *Time and Again* [4-214].

4-365. Maxwell, Ann. **Timeshadow Rider.** Tor, 1986.
The hero and heroine have complementary superpowers but are forbidden ever to touch one another; when the universe is threatened, though, they must combine forces to save it. High-pitched melodrama gushing with emotion. Compare McIntyre's *Superluminal* [4-371].

4-366. May, Julian. **The Many-Colored Land.** Houghton Mifflin, 1981.
The first volume (HN, 1982; NN, 1981) of the "Saga of the Pliocene Exile," followed by *The Golden Torc* (1982), *The Nonborn King* (1983), and *The Adversary* (1984). Associated material can be found in *The Pliocene Companion* (1984). Misfits flee by time warp from the twenty-second century, ending up in the Pliocene, where they and other time travelers are caught up in a conflict between two alien species. The rich background is well worked out and the characters engaging, making this one of the most lively and intelligent of the SF/fantasy series that have appeared in such profusion in the last ten years. Compare Bradley's Darkover series [4-77].

4-367. McCaffrey, Anne. **The Crystal Singer.** Ballantine, 1982.
The heroine's special musical talents enable her to work with the crystals that sustain interstellar communications, but the symbiotic relationship with an alien life-

form she must exploit in her work has some unpleasant side effects. A somber novel, more complex than most of McCaffrey's works; the sequel, *Killashandra* (1985), is not so successful. Compare the Robinsons' *Stardance* [4-449].

4-368. McCaffrey, Anne. **Dragonflight.** Ballantine, 1968.
First of the Pern series, combining the novellas "Weyr Search" (NN, 1967; HW, 1968) and "Dragonrider" (NW, 1968; HN, 1969). Immediate sequels are *Dragonquest* (1971; HN, 1972) and the best-selling *The White Dragon* (1978; HN, 1979)—these three novels appear in an omnibus as *The Dragonriders of Pern* (1978). An associated trilogy [5-110] aimed at younger readers is *Dragonsong* (1976), *Dragonsinger* (1977), and *Dragondrums* (1979). Later novels set on Pern are *Moreta, Dragonlady of Pern* (1983; HN, 1984) and *Nerilka's Story* (1986). Pern is a lost colony where dragons telepathically bonded to female riders breathe fire to burn up the spores of deadly vegetable invaders that appear at long intervals. The dragons can also travel through time whenever the plots require a deus ex machina. Despite the commercial success of later volumes the quality and originality of the books decline somewhat as the series proceeds, but the author appears to have achieved in these novels a mode and intensity of feeling that broke new ground in fitting SF to the imaginative needs of alienated teenage girls, thus helping to break the masculine mold of most previous SF. Compare and contrast the works of Jacqueline Lichtenberg [4-339] and Doris Piserchia [4-412, 4-413].

4-369. McCaffrey, Anne. **The Ship Who Sang.** Walker, 1969.
Fix-up novel in which the heroine is the cyborg guidance system of a spaceship, in which role she can construct more fulfilling relationships with male pilots than she ever could have hoped to have find in her fleshly incarnation. The initial story is genuinely poignant, but the later sections are more strained. Compare McIntyre's *Superluminal* [4-371].

4-370. McIntyre, Vonda N(eel). **Dreamsnake.** Houghton Mifflin, 1978.
Novel based on the short story "Of Mist and Grass and Sand" (NW, 1973; HN, 1974). A healer whose instruments are metabolically engineered snakes must journey to a city that has contacts with the star worlds in the hope of replacing the dreamsnake that eases the pain of her clients. A convincing mixture of stoicism and sentimentality, rather highly strung. Compare Tiptree's *Up the Walls of the World* [4-555]. NW, 1978; HW, 1979.

4-371. McIntyre, Vonda N(eel). **Superluminal.** Houghton Mifflin, 1984.
Novel based on the novella "Aztecs" (NN, 1977; HN, 1978). The heroine surrenders her real heart for an artificial one in order to become a starship pilot. Her subsequent struggles against the effects of this voluntary alienation ally her with other social outsiders, but in the end she wins a spectacular victory over the natural and technological handicaps afflicting humankind. Intense to the point of feverishness. Compare Cordwainer Smith's "Scanners Live in Vain" [3-354].

4-372. McQuay, Mike. **Lifekeeper.** Avon, 1980.
A grim and violent story of a militaristic future culture where the loyalty of citizens is secured by a custom-designed religion and by the waging of perpetual war. Compare Garnett's *Mirror in the Sky* [4-226].

4-373. Mendelson, Drew. **Pilgrimage.** DAW, 1981.
The sole city on a devastated future Earth moves slowly across its surface as those at the decaying Tailend make their constant pilgrimage to the expanding Frontend, but the old order is collapsing and the horizons of the closed world must expand again. Compare Kilworth's *A Theatre of Timesmiths* [4-298].

4-374. Meredith, Richard C(arlton). **Run, Come See Jerusalem.** Ballantine, 1976.
Complicated time travel story juxtaposing two alternate versions of the twenty-first century, whose existence is contigent on the success of the protagonist's mission to interfere with the past. Compare Saberhagen's *A Century of Progress* [4-461].

4-375. Meredith, Richard C(arlton). **We All Died at Breakaway Station.** Ballantine, 1969.
Space opera in which the technologically reincarnated hero must make a valiant last stand against alien enemies, reflecting meanwhile on whether the game has been worth the candle. Compare Goldin's *Eternity Brigade* [4-234].

*4-376. Merle, Robert (France). **Malevil.** Simon & Schuster, 1974. Tr. by Derek Coltman of *Malevil*, 1972.
Survivors of a nuclear holocaust are drawn to the medieval castle of Malevil, where a charismatic leader supervises the progress of their community. Dense and thoughtful. Compare Stewart's *Earth Abides* [3-358]. JWC, 1974.

4-377. Mitchell, Adrian (U.K.). **The Bodyguard.** Cape, 1970.
Dystopian novel following the career of a bodyguard in a violent near future, with Europe on the edge of revolution. A sour black comedy by a noted poet. Compare Marta Randall's America-set *Those Who Favor Fire* (1984).

4-378. Mitchison, Naomi (U.K.). **Not by Bread Alone.** Marion Boyars, 1983.
A multinational corporation gives away free food produced in abundance by bio-engineers, in order to stimulate world economic growth; the effects of the plan on man's relationship with the environment are problematic, and the bioengineering processes prove imperfect. An interesting combination of themes drawn from biology and anthropology.

4-379. Monteleone, Thomas F. **The Time-Swept City.** Popular Library, 1977.
Fix-up novel following the development of the city of Chicago, which ultimately acquires an identity of its own in the artificial intelligence guiding its automated systems. The human population becomes marginal to its affairs and the city is inherited by robots. Compare and contrast Simak's *City* [3-345].

*4-380. Moorcock, Michael (U.K.). **Behold the Man.** Allison & Busby, 1969.
Expanded from a novella (NW, 1967). The alienated hero travels back to the time of Christ in the hope of enlightenment, but he finds Jesus grotesquely ill-fitted to the role of messiah and must take his place. Darkly ironic; a fascinating exercise in the psychology of martyrdom. Compare Malzberg's *Cross of Fire* [4-354].

4-381. Moorcock, Michael (U.K.). **The Black Corridor.** Mayflower, 1969.
Novel actually written in collaboration with Hillary Bailey, whose contribution is

acknowledged in some later (revised) editions. A crewman aboard a starship carrying frozen survivors away from the ruined Earth is beset by guilt-stricken dreams and delusions. An innovative work of avant-garde SF. Compare Cherryh's *Voyager in Night* [4-134] and Stableford's *Man in a Cage* [4-532].

4-382. Moorcock, Michael (U.K.). **The Cornelius Chronicles.** Avon, 1977.
Omnibus containing *The Final Programme* (1968), *A Cure for Cancer* (1971), *The English Assassin* (1972), and *The Condition of Muzak* (1977), the first three in slightly revised form. Jerry Cornelius, the contemporary and near-future avatar of the multifaceted Moorcockian hero, features in the tetralogy in various roles: secret agent, messiah, corpse, dreary teenager, and even a negative image of himself. The first novel begins as a parody of heroic fiction, its events running parallel to two of Moorcock's early Elric stories, but moves on to parody other themes in popular fiction. The middle volumes present a kaleidoscopic display of twentieth-century motifs, and the fourth moves on again to subvert the fantasy elements in the first three and add its own theme of tragedy, symbolized with the aid of images drawn from the harlequinade. The series is a sprawling masterpiece: a dream-story loaded with all the threads of contemporary consciousness and modern mythology, bearing an appropriate burden of nightmare and irony. The ubiquitous Jerry can also be found in *The Lives and Times of Jerry Cornelius* (1976), *The Entropy Tango* (1981), and "The Alchemist's Question" in *The Opium General and Other Stories* (1984), while associated materials include *The Adventures of Una Persson and Catherine Cornelius in the Twentieth Century* (1976) and an anthology edited by Moorcock and Langdon Jones, *The Nature of the Catastrophe* (1971).

4-383. Moorcock, Michael (U.K.). **The Dancers at the End of Time.** Granada, 1983.
Omnibus containing *An Alien Heat* (1972), *The Hollow Lands* (1974), and *The End of All Songs* (1976). At the end of time all-powerful immortals have no problems except how to amuse themselves, which they do in exotically contrived fashion, mining the past for its quaint inspirations. Colorful, witty, and boisterously decadent, with a certain distinctive weltschmerz. Associated works are *Legends from the End of Time* (1976), *The Transformation of Miss Mavis Ming* (1977; variant title: *Messiah at the End of Time*), and *Elric at the End of Time* (1984).

4-384. Morgan, Dan, and John Kippax (pseud. of John Hynam) (U.K.). **A Thunder of Stars.** Macdonald, 1968.
First volume in a space opera series continued in *Seed of Stars* (1972), *The Neutral Stars* (1973), and *Where No Stars Guide* (1975; by Kippax alone). Officers of the space corps face a series of crises generated by the growing threat of alien enemies. Tautly plotted action-adventure SF. Compare Chandler's Rim Worlds series [3-90] and [4-124] and Dickson's *The Forever Man* [4-182] for alternative views of the culture and organization of futuristic armed services.

4-385. Morrow, James. **The Continent of Lies.** Holt, 1984.
Set in a future where the dominant entertainment medium consists of dream-experiences coded into "cephapples" grown on the "noostrees" that hold together the biospheres of planetoids. The villain is growing dreamfruit, which will drive men mad and make them revere him as a god, and the hero is uniquely

qualified to stop him. Marvelously exotic action-adventure SF, sparkling with wit but losing nothing of its suspense and excitement in consequence; a first-rate entertainment. Compare Zelazny's *Isle of the Dead* [4-630].

4-386. Morrow, James. **This Is the Way the World Ends.** Holt, 1986. Satirical apocalyptic fantasy in which the few survivors of the holocaust are put on trial by those who would have lived if only their ancestors had ordered their affairs more reasonably. Clever and elegant. Compare Vonnegut's *Cat's Cradle* [3-391].

4-387. Nelson, Ray Faraday. **Timequest.** Tor, 1985.
Revised and extended version of *Blake's Progress* (1975). The heroine is the wife of William Blake, who becomes his guide and mentor in the dreamlike excursions into time and space that provide the basis for his visionary poems. An unusual and idiosyncratic philosophical adventure story, crafted with care. Nelson's concern with utopianism is displayed more crudely in *Then Beggars Could Ride* (1976) and negatively in a novel of rebellion against dystopian organization, *The Prometheus Man* (1982).

4-388. Niven, Larry. **The Integral Trees.** Ballantine, 1984.
The descendants of humans shipwrecked in an alien solar system eke out a difficult living in a bizarre worldless ecosystem. One group, forced into exile, undergoes a series of adventures culminating in their meeting with a strange spacefarer. The plot is mainly a vehicle to display the intricately worked out environment; the book is thus an imaginative exercise comparable to *Ringworld* [4-392]. The story is apparently to be continued in *The Smoke Ring*. HN, 1985; NN, 1984.

*4-389. Niven, Larry. **The Long ARM of Gil Hamilton.** Ballantine, 1976.
Collection of novellas featuring a hero whose missing arm is more versatile in spirit than it was in the flesh. Although the stories are integrated into the Known Space future history they are earthbound mysteries set against the background of the development of organ-bank technology, and they are among the finest examples of the SF detective story. The series continues in *The Patchwork Girl* (1980), an excellent story of futuristic detective work set on the moon. The criminal activities usually involve "organlegging," which also features in other short stories and in the Known Space novel *A Gift from Earth* (1969).

4-390. Niven, Larry. **Neutron Star.** Ballantine, 1968.
The first collection of Niven's hard science stories, early works developing the Known Space future history. The title story (HW, 1967) is one of several in which Beowulf Shaeffer is blackmailed into taking on a dangerous mission in an exotic environment. The bibliography of Niven's collections is complex, stories being recombined into some later selections, but *The Shape of Space* (1969) and *All the Myriad Ways* (1971) preserve more early works and later ones can be found in *A Hole in Space* (1974). *Tales of Known Space* (1975) is useful for the notes about the future-historical background. The title story of *Inconstant Moon* (1973) (HW, 1972; also in *All the Myriad Ways*) is a marvelously vivid story in which people on the nightside of the world realize that the Sun has gone nova when the Moon becomes much brighter, and must wait to die with the coming dawn. The recent collection, *Limits* (1985), contains stories written in collaboration with three other writers as well as solo efforts.

4-391. Niven, Larry. **Protector.** Ballantine, 1973.
Part of the Known Space series. Here the Pak Protectors, remote ancestors of mankind and builders of *Ringworld* [4-392], are introduced; the discovery of a Pak ship leads to the creation of a human/alien "hybrid" whose subsequent career threatens to alter the course of human destiny. HN, 1974.

*4-392. Niven, Larry. **Ringworld.** Ballantine, 1970.
An exploration team consisting of an exotic mix of humans and aliens investigates a huge artifact occupying a planetary orbit around a sun. A novel of imaginary tourism; its real hero is the artifact, whose nature is further explored and explained in *Ringworld Engineers* (1980; HN, 1981). Compare Clarke's *Rendezvous with Rama* [4-138]. HW, 1971; NW, 1970.

4-393. Niven, Larry. **A World out of Time.** Holt, 1976.
The hero, whose personality is resurrected into another man's body, takes a three-million-year trip through space-time and returns to the solar system to find it (understandably) much changed. He becomes involved in a mad chase after a special kind of immortality. Imaginative action-adventure in a more lighthearted vein than the Known Space novels.

4-394. Niven, Larry, and Steven Barnes. **The Descent of Anansi.** Tor, 1982.
Near-future melodrama in which a space shuttle delivering a monomolecular cable from the Moon to Earth becomes a pawn in a political power play. Taut and suspenseful (in more ways than one). Compare Bova's *Colony* [4-68].

4-395. Niven, Larry, and Steven Barnes. **Dream Park.** Phantasia, 1981.
A novel about the ultimate theme park, where people can project themselves physically into fantasy role-playing games. Inevitably, the hero gets involved in a game where someone is playing murderously hard. Compare Saberhagen's *Octagon* [4-462].

4-396. Niven, Larry, and Jerry Pournelle. **Footfall.** Ballantine, 1985.
The aliens displaced from the outline of *Lucifer's Hammer* [4-397] come into their own here, in an invasion story that aspires to be the definitive modern version of the theme, just as *Mote in God's Eye* [4-398] attempted to provide a definitive first-contact story. Spectacular in scale and detail. Compare Wells's *The War of the Worlds* [1-105] and Heinlein's *The Puppet Masters* [3-205] to put the story in historical perspective. HN, 1986.

4-397. Niven, Larry, and Jerry Pournelle. **Lucifer's Hammer.** Playboy, 1977.
The world is badly damaged by a meteor strike but the survivors manage to get things going again. An SF book that cashed in on the Hollywood boom in (more localized) disaster stories and became a best-seller, though the aliens who were in the original outline had to be left out. A tough-minded exercise in imaginary social Darwinism. Compare and contrast Sherriff's *The Hopkins Manuscript* [3-341].

4-398. Niven, Larry, and Jerry Pournelle. **The Mote in God's Eye.** Simon & Schuster, 1974.
Space opera in which officers in the interstellar navy must play it by ear when they contact strange and dangerous aliens. Detailed background and eventful plot. Compare Morgan and Kippax's Stars series [4-384].

4-399. Niven, Larry, and Jerry Pournelle. **Oath of Fealty.** Phantasia, 1981.
A giant "arcology" in Los Angeles is threatened by numerous enemies, and its managers must declare independence in order to defend their quasi-utopia against terrorism. Robust political SF. Compare Mark Reynolds's *The Towers of Utopia* (1975).

4-400. Nolan, William F(rancis), and George Clayton Johnson. **Logan's Run.** Dial, 1967.
In a world where population control requires euthanasia at 21 a policeman puts to good use his expertise in hunting down those who won't submit when he becomes a "runner" himself. A slickly written and lively entertainment, horribly mangled in the long-delayed film version. Inferior sequels by Nolan alone are *Logan's World* (1977) and *Logan's Search* (1980).

4-401. Norman, John (pseud. of John Frederick Lange). **Tarnsman of Gor.** Ballantine, 1966.
First of an extensive series set on the "counter-Earth" of Gor, where humans are organized in quasi-feudal castes and slavery is institutionalized. Burroughsian fantasy with the exoticism toned down and the sexual aspects of slavery heavily emphasized. An interesting response to the progress of feminist ideals, this fantasy world negates all the values of real-world sexual politics. Compare the similarly motivated but rather different works of Barbara Cartland, which are even more popular among pusillanimous escapists.

4-402. O'Donnell, Kevin, Jr. **Mayflies.** Berkeley, 1979.
A human brain used as the central computer of a starship recovers sentience and fights for godlike control of the ephemeral human "mayflies" whose generations come and go while the ship makes its laborious way to its destination, encountering aliens en route. An impressively casual handling of the cosmic perspective. Compare Herbert's *Destination: Void* [4-267].

4-403. O'Donnell, Kevin, Jr. **ORA:CLE.** Berkley, 1984.
The hero has a brain implant that allows him to hook into computer systems; suddenly he becomes a target for assassination and all manner of more subtle assaults when the world is threatened by aliens. Compare Vinge's *True Names* [4-576].

4-404. Palmer, David R. **Emergence.** Bantam, 1984.
A juvenile genius is enabled by her superhumanity to survive the nuclear holocaust, and sets off across the blasted United States to search for others of her kind. Compare George O. Smith's *The Fourth "R"* [3-356]. HN, 1986.

4-405. Palmer, Jane (U.K.). **The Watcher.** Women's Press, 1986.
Disjointed but lively interstellar romance about a cosmic disruption that originates in the dreams of a human girl, and about the android sent to track her down who aspires to become human himself.

*4-406. Panshin, Alexei. **Rite of Passage.** Ace, 1968.
The heroine belongs to a starfaring culture, and her rite de passage into adulthood involves her descent into a colony world whose culture is very different. A homage to Heinlein's juveniles, but more carefully and painstakingly constructed

than most of his models; compare especially *Citizen of the Galaxy* [5-61]. HN, 1969; NW, 1968.

4-407. Pedler, Kit, and Gerry Davis (U.K.). **Mutant 59: The Plastic Eater.** Souvenir Press, 1971.
Novel based on a screenplay for the alarmist British TV series "Doomwatch." A virus developed to combat pollution by reprocessing plastics escapes and eats its way through London's communication systems. Followed by *Brainrack* (1974), a convincing thriller about widespread subtle poisoning that ultimately causes a meltdown at a nuclear reactor, and *The Dynostar Menace* (1975), about a series of mysterious deaths aboard a space station laboratory. Compare Crichton's *The Andromeda Strain* [4-156].

4-408. Percy, Walker. **Love in the Ruins.** Farrar, 1971.
Subtitled *The Adventures of a Bad Catholic at a Time Near the End of the World;* Dr. Thomas More invents a device that might cure the world of its chemically induced collective insanity, but things are too far gone. Allegorical social comment. Compare Leven's *Satan* [4-336].

4-409. Pesek, Ludek (Czechoslovakia). **The Earth Is Near.** Bradbury, 1974. Tr. by Anthea Bell of *Die Erde ist Nah: Die Marsexpedition,* 1970.
Winner of a German children's book prize, but by no means a work of juvenile fiction. A manned expedition to Mars survives various hardships, its members driven by their SF-inspired dreams of marvels to be revealed, but they find Mars utterly arid and unrewarding. Fine narrative realism; contrast Bradbury's *The Martian Chronicles* [3-64] and Varley's "In the Hall of the Martian Kings" [4-570]. Also annotated as [5-132].

4-410. Pesek, Ludek (Czechoslovakia). **Trap for Perseus.** Bradbury, 1980. Tr. by Anthea Bell of *Falle für Perseus,* 1976.
The commander of a spaceship goes aboard a long-lost vessel and is forced to take his place in the strange society that has evolved there. All his values are assaulted by sophisticated techniques of persuasion, and he gradually adapts his consciousness to the new ideologies. Marketed as a juvenile, but a very striking and thought-provoking work of sociological SF. Compare Orwell's *Nineteen Eighty-Four* [3-302]. Also annotated as [5-133].

*4-411. Piercy, Marge. **Woman on the Edge of Time.** Knopf, 1976.
A Hispanic-American mother undergoes experimental psychosurgery. She makes psychic contact with the twenty-second century world that has resulted from a feminist revolution whose success may depend on the subversion of the experiments in which she is involved. Outstanding for the elaborate description of the future utopia and the graphic representation of the inhumanity inherent in the way that contemporary people can and do treat one another. Compare Russ's *The Female Man* [4-458].

4-412. Piserchia, Doris. **Earthchild.** DAW, 1977.
Earth's ecosphere is being taken over by a vast blue alien vegetable, opposed by the last human being (a girl) and by another plant intelligence whose instruments

are green. Action packed, but almost surreal in tone. Follows the earlier *Star Rider* (1974) in using SF motifs as fantastic symbols reflecting the anguish of female puberty, and embodies Piserchia's fascination with the theme of ecological metamorphosis, also featured in *Doomtime* (1981) and *Earth in Twilight* (1981).

4-413. Piserchia, Doris. **Mister Justice.** Ace, 1973.
A time traveling vigilante superman tires of delivering criminals to institutionalized justice and takes on the role of judge and executioner. An intense and striking work. Compare Bester's *The Stars My Destination* [3-32].

4-414. Pohl, Frederik. **The Coming of the Quantum Cats.** Bantam, 1986.
A story of parallel worlds whose alternate histories become entangled by investigation and invasion. Various alternates of the chief characters struggle to survive and set things right. The inevitable ironies that arise from the comparison of closely related alternate worlds never become satirical, and the story remains superficial. A slick, fast-paced entertainment. Compare Leiber's *Destiny Times Three* (1945; in book form, 1957).

*4-415. Pohl, Frederik. **Gateway.** St. Martin's, 1977.
Mankind "inherits" the stars by finding and exploiting (with considerable difficulty) the starships and gadgets left behind by the alien Heechee. The flippant, guilt-ridden hero has greatness thrust upon him by degrees as he picks up his winnings in the game of Russian roulette that men must play in gaining control of the Heechee artifacts (HW, 1978; NW, 1977; JWC, 1978). His luck continues to hold in *Beyond the Blue Event Horizon* (1980; HN, 1981; NN, 1980), which ends with his finding out why the Heechee ran away. In *Heechee Rendezvous* (1984), the aliens finally arrive on stage in the flesh, although little more is added to the process of unfolding discovery. *The Annals of the Heechee* (1987) concluded the series. Fine contemporary space opera, with some neatly ironic characterization.

4-416. Pohl, Frederik. **JEM: The Making of a Utopia.** St. Martin's, 1979.
A new planet is ripe for exploitation by Earth's three power blocs: food-exporting nations, oil-exporting nations, and people's republics. Three species of intelligent natives enter into appropriate associations with the three colonizing groups, and are thus drawn into the web of conflicts and compromises that reproduces all the evils of earthly politics. A cynical ideological counterweight to stories of human/alien cooperation along the lines of Anderson's *People of the Wind* [4-17].

*4-417. Pohl, Frederik. **Man Plus.** Random, 1976.
The protagonist is technologically adapted for life on Mars. The process by which he is made into an alien is revealed, ironically, to be part of a plan to save humanity from the coming self-destruction of nuclear war. A convincing and cynical reexamination of the theme of Bradbury's *The Martian Chronicles* [3-64].

4-418. Pohl, Frederik. **Midas World.** St. Martin's, 1983.
Fix-up novel combining stories from different phases of Pohl's career, extending the classic "The Midas Plague." In much the same fashion *The Merchants' War* (1984) expands on *The Space Merchants* [3-313], but Pohl is rather less successful

in reexamining his own themes than he is in reexamining those of others, the sequels being overly constrained by the content of the original stories.

4-419. Pohl, Frederik. **Starburst.** Ballantine, 1982.
An expansion of the novella "The Gold at the Starbow's End" (1972) in which ten geniuses on a pointless interstellar mission use the journey time to become even cleverer and devise more powerful technologies, able to create a new world that may succeed where the old one failed. The optimism of the story had been undercut before its expansion by the cynicism of *Man Plus* [4-417] and *JEM* [4-416].

4-420. Pohl, Frederik. **The Years of the City.** Simon & Schuster, 1984.
Five novellas tracking the future of New York City as its leading citizens grapple with the problems of crime, urban decay, pollution, etc., using the electronic media to create a new-style democracy. A fascinating set of extrapolations, determinedly constructive. Compare Niven and Pournelle's *Oath of Fealty* [4-399]. JWC, 1985.

4-421. Pournelle, Jerry. **The Mercenary.** Pocket Books, 1977.
Fix-up novel about space mercenaries led by a charismatic military genius. *West of Honor* (1976; revised 1980) is a novel in the same series. Similar works include *Janissaries* (1979), in which involuntary mercenaries serve alien masters, and its sequel *Clan and Crown* (1982; written in collaboration with Roland Green). The stories present a polemical glorification of militarism and libertarian tough-mindedness. Compare Heinlein's *Starship Troopers* [3-206] and Drake's *Hammer's Slammers* [4-192].

*4-422. Powers, Tim. **The Anubis Gates.** Ace, 1983.
An academic interested in a minor Victorian poet named William Ashbless is recruited as a kind of tour guide to a time traveling expedition whose members expect to hear Coleridge lecturing. When he is marooned in 1810 he has to fight a multitude of enemies, including the man who has marooned him, Egyptian sorcerers, a malevolent beggar-king, and the body-stealing murderer, Dog-Faced Joe. His struggle for survival, which necessitates his becoming Ashbless, makes a fabulous adventure story with some excellent gothic elements. More fantasy than SF, but the ingeniously constructed paradox-avoiding time-tripping draws heavily on the SF tradition. Compare Blaylock's *Homunculus* [4-66]. Philip K. Dick award, 1984.

4-423. Powers, Tim. **Dinner at Deviant's Palace.** Ace, 1985.
A hard-boiled version of the story of Orpheus and Eurydice set in postholocaust California, with a bizarre alien presiding over an exotic hell. A fast-moving adventure story with the author's usual gothic touches; a key example of the new postholocaust romanticism. Compare Zelazny's *Damnation Alley* (1969). Philip K. Dick award, 1986; NN, 1985.

4-424. Pratchett, Terry (U.K.). **Strata.** New English Library, 1982.
The heroine, a "worldbuilder," deserts her work in order to investigate the mysterious works of others (presumably aliens) in the same vein—in particular, a flat Earth enclosed within a crystal sphere, complete with monsters and demons. She

sets out with two alien companions to explore it, attempting to find out who built it and why. An absurdist *Ringworld* [4-392], subverting various SF clichés.

4-425. Preuss, Paul. **Broken Symmetries.** Pocket Books, 1983.
A brilliant theoretical physicist becomes involved in controversy—and ultimately conflict—generated by the discovery of a new subatomic particle. Technically detailed; its fascinating scientific and technological speculations are virtues making up for the rather makeshift plot. Compare Benford's *Timescape* [4-54].

4-426. Preuss, Paul. **Human Error.** Tor, 1985.
A biologist and a computer scientist combine their artistry to produce a powerful biochip microcomputer. Inevitably, though, the potential of the new creation extends far beyond the purpose for which it was intended. Not as apocalyptic as Bear's *Blood Music* [4-50] but very effective in its fashion.

4-427. Priest, Christopher (U.K.). **The Affirmation.** Faber, 1981.
The protagonist exists simultaneously in London and the exotic Dream Archipelago; as the state of his affairs in the former deteriorates he finds new opportunities in the latter, but he does not know whether this represents a viable solution to his predicament. Compare Saxton's *Queen of the States* [4-474].

4-428. Priest, Christopher (U.K.). **Fugue for a Darkening Island.** Faber, 1972. U.S. title: *Darkening Island.*
A vast immigration of African refugees precipitates political chaos in Britain, culminating in three-sided civil war. The protagonist searches for his lost wife and daughter as the narrative shifts back and forth in time, building an extraordinarily grim picture. One of the best post-Ballardian works in the tradition of British catastrophe stories. Compare Jean Raspail's polemical account of a collapse of Western civilization provoked by Third World refugees, *The Camp of the Saints* (1973; tr. 1975).

4-429. Priest, Christopher (U.K.). **The Glamour.** Cape, 1984. The U.S. edition, Doubleday, 1985, is substantially revised.
Outcasts of society, who pass unnoticed in "the hierarchy of visual interest," can make themselves invisible (a talent that is, ironically, the "glamour" of the title). The amnesiac hero gradually relearns the use of this talent and rediscovers his love for the heroine. A delicately ambivalent tale of welcome alienation. Compare Leiber's *The Sinful Ones* (1953; revised 1980).

4-430. Priest, Christopher (U.K.). **An Infinite Summer.** Faber, 1979.
Priest's second collection, superior to *Real-Time World* (1974). The mundane lives of the characters are usually interrupted by fantastic distortions of time and space, whose consequences are seductive but possibly subversive of sanity. Includes "Palely Loitering" (HN, 1980) and "The Watched" (HN, 1979).

4-431. Priest, Christopher (U.K.). **Inverted World.** Faber, 1974.
A city is subject to space-time distortions that force its inhabitants to move it en masse, pursuing a point of stability across a hyperbolic surface, although observers from outside see it progressing across Europe. A fascinating juxtaposition of incompatible worldviews, with some fine imagery in the description of the hero's mission away from the city. Compare Dick's *Martian Time-Slip* [3-143].

4-432. Pynchon, Thomas. **Gravity's Rainbow.** Viking, 1973.
A sprawling novel about a World War II psychological warfare unit full of weird characters, one of whom seems to be determining the pattern of V-2 rocket attacks by his sexual activities, but refuses to submit to study and possible control. Extraordinarily elaborate black comedy. Compare the research establishment in Scholz and Harcourt's *Palimpsests* [4-479].

4-433. Randall, Marta. **Islands.** Pocket Books, 1980.
Revised edition of a novel first published in 1976. A mortal woman, a freak in a world of immortals, immerses herself in archaeological studies and makes a discovery that might give her access to a better kind of immortality, in which a kind of transcendence will utterly defeat existential angst. Compare Cowper's *The Tithonian Factor* [4-154]. NN, 1976.

4-434. Randall, Marta. **Journey.** Pocket Books, 1978.
First part of a two-decker novel completed in *Dangerous Games* (1980). A family saga about the settlers of a colony world who create a new society, found a dynasty, and eventually play a crucial role in the complex politics of the galactic community. Compare Coulson's *Tomorrow's Heritage* [4-150].

4-435. Reamy, Tom. **Blind Voices.** Berkley, 1978.
A small Kansas town is visited during the depression by a circus whose freaks have been produced by psionic genetic engineering. A moving story of exotic evil vanquished by exotic saintliness, very much in the tradition of Sturgeon's *The Dreaming Jewels* [3-360]. NN, 1978; HN, 1979.

4-436. Reed, Kit. **Armed Camps.** Faber, 1969.
Warfare is institutionalized as a means of social control and a product of technological imperatives. The two protagonists move from opposite political poles toward a climactic meeting. Reed's forte is the production of SF fabulations in which characters struggle to retain and assert their humanity in a mechanical and devalued world, but she can also be very witty—both aspects of her writing are displayed in her short story collections: *The Killer Mice* (1976), *Other Stories, and the Attack of the Giant Baby* (1981), and *The Revenge of the Senior Citizens ** Plus* (1986).

4-437. Resnick, Mike. **Santiago.** Tor, 1986.
Santiago is a legendary outlaw—a superhuman Robin Hood—for whom the assorted characters must search, among them the bounty-hunting protagonist. A sprawling action-adventure story enlivened by its mock-mythic elements. Compare Gordon's *Smile on the Void* [4-236].

4-438. Reynolds, Mack. **Lagrange Five.** Bantam, 1979.
An O'Neill space colony develops an effective social system, but its key role in the power politics of the solar system makes it the target of subversive conspiracy. The theme is further developed in *The Lagrangists* (1983), *Chaos in Lagrangia* (1984), and *Trojan Orbit* (1985), all edited by Dean Ing from posthumously discovered manuscripts. Compare Haldeman's Worlds series [4-248].

4-439. Reynolds, Mack. **Looking Backward from the Year 2000.** Ace, 1973.
An updated reprise of Bellamy's classic utopian novel [1-8]. A new Julian West

awakes from suspended animation to find the world much changed for the better, an economy of abundance based on nuclear fusion having permitted egalitarian social reform. Progress has been so rapid, though, that there seems no place for the refugee from the ugly past. The sequel, *Equality in the Year 2000* (1977), continues the story and finds a way out of the hero's predicament, but the question of whether humankind's problems could really be solved by these reforms is brought into question in *Perchance to Dream* (1977) and *After Utopia* (1977), two of many "spin-off" novels generated by Reynolds's futurological speculations about the year 2000. Here he develops anxieties that new technologies could lead to an era of sterile hedonistic decadence. Other spin-off works include *Commune 2000* (1974), in which freedom and wealth allow numerous idiosyncratic subcultures to isolate themselves; *The Towers of Utopia* (1975), about life in tightly integrated skyscraper cities; and *Rolltown* (1976), in which whole communities go on the road in search of lebensraum. The plots of these novels tend to be mechanically melodramatic, but they contain some fascinating and thought-provoking ideas, and some provocative Socialist rhetoric.

4-440. Roberts, Keith (U.K.). **The Chalk Giants.** Hutchinson, 1974.
Fix-up postholocaust novel in which Britain is rent apart and barbarism reigns. The final sequence, like the final sequence of *Pavane* [4-444], is set at Corfe Gate. A brilliant and disturbing book, which develops the grimly realistic aspect of British catastrophic fiction. To be sharply contrasted with Cowper's Kinship trilogy [4-155].

4-441. Roberts, Keith (U.K.). **Kiteworld.** Gollancz, 1985.
Fix-up novel set in a pseudomedieval world dominated by a religious elite, in which men are carried aloft by giant kites to look out for invading demons. Has affinities with *Pavane* [4-444] and *The Chalk Giants* [4-440], although it sets aside the idea of historical cyclicity that underlies these novels.

4-442. Roberts, Keith (U.K.). **The Lordly Ones.** Gollancz, 1986.
Roberts's most recent collection, following *Machines and Men* (1973), *The Grain Kings* (1976), and *Ladies from Hell* (1979) (in addition to various fix-up novels). The title story and "The Comfort Station" both deal with the collapse of civilized order—one of Roberts's favorite themes—and do so with much feeling. "Diva" and "Sphairistike" are more playful, as is the author's wont when dealing with the leisurely aspects of life. Compare Richard Cowper's short fiction [4-154].

4-443. Roberts, Keith (U.K.). **Molly Zero.** Gollancz, 1980.
The adolescent heroine escapes from intense and enigmatic education in "the Blocks," living as a working girl, a gypsy, and ultimately as an urban outlaw, but her apparent escape turns out to be simply one more phase in her rite de passage. A grimly earnest version of a common SF theme, exhibiting Roberts's fondness for young female protagonists threatened by the forces of corruption.

*4-444. Roberts, Keith (U.K.). **Pavane.** Hart-Davis, 1968. U.S. editions add an extra episode.
Fix-up novel describing what appears to be an alternate world where the Catholic Church retained it hegemony in Europe because of the victory of the Spanish Armada. But this technologically retarded world also harbors fairies who know the

real truth, and when progress rears its ugly head again its value is brought sharply into question. A rich, many-faceted narrative, written with great care and delicacy; one of the finest SF novels of the period. Compare Miller's *A Canticle for Leibowitz* [3-287] and Amis's *The Alteration* [4-10].

4-445. Robinson, Kim Stanley. **Icehenge.** Ace, 1984.
An expedition to Pluto discovers a mysterious artifact, presumably built by humans. In this time people live for centuries but their memories are cut short, so that the past becomes curiously uncertain, probably falsified by official historians; the problem at the heart of the story, therefore, is why the artifact has been erased from the record. Reflections on the philosophy of knowledge and the logic of scientific inquiry underlie the plot. The novel's questioning of "reality" is different from that to be found in many works by Philip K. Dick, and for that reason bears an interesting relation to it.

*4-446. Robinson, Kim Stanley. **The Memory of Whiteness.** Tor, 1985.
An inspired musician tours the solar system with a one-man orchestra designed by a brilliant physicist, whose theory of the universe is strongly linked to the fundamentals of musical aesthetics. The protagonist's friends must try to protect him from threats that appear to come from a strange religious cult, though he seems not unwilling to accept a messianic role in their unfolding psychodrama. A highly original and delicately fashioned novel whose exotic settings are remarkably convincing.

4-447. Robinson, Kim Stanley. **The Wild Shore.** Ace, 1984.
After the nuclear holocaust the United States is quarantined by the United Nations, and the survivors must remake their civilization in isolation. The protagonist, his role analogous to that of Huckleberry Finn, explores this new frontier world. The most sophisticated example of contemporary American romantic catastrophism. Compare Powers's *Dinner at Deviant's Palace* [4-423] and Brin's *The Postman* [4-80]. NN, 1984.

4-448. Robinson, Spider. **Callahan's Crosstime Saloon.** Ace, 1977.
A series of barroom tall stories in which Jake Callahan lends a helpful ear to his clients. Comedy and sentimentality form a thick sandwich for a thin slice of metaphysical filling. The series is extended in *Time Travelers Strictly Cash* (1981) and *Callahan's Secret* (1986). Compare the short fiction of R. A. Lafferty [4-311] and Clarke's *Tales from the White Hart* [3-105].

4-449. Robinson, Spider, and Jeanne Robinson. **Stardance** Dial, 1979.
Based on a novella (HW, 1978; NW, 1977). A story of exotic redemption in which a crippled dancer becomes involved with man's first contact with aliens, and is enabled by his expertise to help set the stage for a mystical communion between the species. Compare Card's *Songmaster* [4-111].

4-450. Rohan, Mike Scott (U.K.). **Run to the Stars.** Arrow, 1982.
Thriller in which a security man turns against his bureaucratic masters, discovering that they intend to abandon man's only space colony and have launched a missile to destroy the aliens whose message of greeting they have intercepted. Moves

steadily to a tense climax in deep space. Compare Benford's *In the Ocean of Night* [4-53].

4-451. Rotsler, William. **Patron of the Arts.** Ballantine, 1974.
Expansion of a fine short story about future artwork that involves multisensual experience, although the interesting speculations about future art and the creative process are somewhat diluted by the action-adventure plot.

4-452. Rucker, Rudy. **The 57th Franz Kafka.** Ace, 1983.
Collection of lively and innovative stories, many (including "Schrödinger's Cat") dealing with abstruse items of physical theory, usually drawing on the author's background in mathematics. Rucker's interest in dimensional fantasies is displayed by "Message Found in a Copy of *Flatland*" and the article "Hyperspherical Space and Beyond." Compare Bayley's *Knights of the Limits* [4-45].

*4-453. Rucker, Rudy. **Software.** Ace, 1982.
Artificial intelligence has developed to the point where computers can begin the inevitable power struggle with mankind. Should we be prepared to put aside our frail flesh in favor of inorganic forms that will preserve our personalities in their software? The extravagant plot is well spiced with wit. Compare Bayley's *Soul of the Robot* [4-46]. Philip K. Dick award, 1983.

4-454. Rucker, Rudy. **White Light.** Ace, 1980.
A strange fantasy of life after death that has abundant SF interest by virtue of the author's use of the "higher dimensions" as a milieu for displaying ideas drawn from number theory and other areas of higher mathematics. The author suggests that this exercise in "transrealism" can be regarded as the first element in a trilogy completed by *The Sex Sphere* (1983), in which a hypersphere trapped into an intersection with our 3-D space obligingly responds to the sexual fantasies of the male characters, and *The Secret of Life* (1985). Rucker's work invites comparison with some very early SF writers, including Camille Flammarion and C. H. Hinton, as well as such avant-garde figures on the contemporary scene as John Shirley and Bruce Sterling.

4-455. Russ, Joanna. **Alyx.** Gregg Press, 1976. Variant title: *The Adventures of Alyx*.
Incorporates the novel *Picnic on Paradise* (1968; HN, 1969) with four short stories featuring the same heroine. Alyx's native land is the cradle of civilization, where she is an outlaw because her ideas are so far ahead of her time, but in the novel she is snatched out of context to become a time traveling agent charged with rescuing a group of tourists trapped on a resort planet where local politics have turned sour. Clever and lively. Another novel similar in kind is *The Two of Them* (1978), in which a female agent is dispatched to a quasi-Islamic world where she rescues a girl from a harem.

4-456. Russ, Joanna. **And Chaos Died.** Ace, 1970.
A castaway on a colony world, whose inhabitants have been taught telepathy by mysterious aliens, picks up the gift himself, but then finds himself alienated from ordinary humans, able to remain sane only among members of what is now his

own kind. A determined attempt to examine psi powers from a new angle. Compare Sellings's *The Uncensored Man* [3-332]. NN, 1970.

4-457. Russ, Joanna. **Extra(ordinary) People.** St. Martin's, 1984.
Collection of linked stories, deliberately didactic in form, in which liberated women in different societies challenge the forces of oppression. Includes "Souls" (HW, 1983). As with *The Female Man* [4-458] the result is multifaceted and the call for a revolution in sexual politics is eloquent even though the stories retain a full appreciation of the difficulty of compiling a manifesto for a nonsexist society.

*4-458. Russ, Joanna. **The Female Man.** Bantam, 1975.
A contemporary woman encounters three "alternative selves," including a version from the feminist utopia Whileaway, a version from a world where patriarchy is more powerful and more brutally imposed, and a version from a world where the sex war has exploded into armed conflict. The juxtaposition of these alternatives, phantasmagoric and very witty, provides an extraordinarily rich and thought-provoking commentary on sexual politics. A key novel of feminist SF. Compare Piercy's *Woman on the Edge of Time* [4-411] and Saxton's *Queen of the States* [4-474].

4-459. Ryan, Thomas J. **The Adolescence of P-1.** Macmillan, 1977.
Novel about the maturation of a sentient computer that eventually has to make some tough moral decisions about the use of "his" powers. Sentimental and suspenseful. Compare Gerrold's *When Harlie Was One* [4-230] and Delaney and Stiegler's *Valentina* [4-163].

4-460. Saberhagen, Fred. **Berserker.** Ballantine, 1967.
Collection; the first book in an extensive series of novels and collections, continued in *Brother Assassin* (1969; variant title: *Brother Berserker*), *Berserker's Planet* (1975), *Berserker Man* (1979), *The Ultimate Enemy* (1979), *The Berserker Wars* (1981), *Earth Descended* (1982), *The Berserker Throne* (1985), *Berserker Base* (1985), and *Berserker: Blue Death* (1985). *Berserker Base* is a fix-up group containing novelettes by six other writers. Berserkers are automated war machines programmed to destroy life, whose perennial and inescapable threat unites the life forms of the galaxy and stimulates their collective technological progress. The power of the premise, and its fecundity in generating plots, is aptly demonstrated by the expansion of the series to take in work by other writers. The series has become an archetypal example of the SF myth that opposes man and machine, and also develops the common assumption of SF writers that without some kind of challenge men might use their technology to become lotus eaters, stagnating in evolutionary decadence. The early stories tend to be a little clumsy, but Saberhagen's writing skills have developed; the series testifies, like Bradley's Darkover series [4-77], to the sophistication and changing concerns of the SF field during the modern period.

4-461. Saberhagen, Fred. **A Century of Progress.** Tor, 1983.
An involved time travel story in which alternate universes hang in the balance, including Hitler's thousand-year reich. All matters are eventually settled at the 1939 World's Fair in Chicago. Action-adventure with some clever ideas. Compare Pohl's *Coming of the Quantum Cats* [4-414].

4-462. Saberhagen, Fred. **Octagon.** Ace, 1981.
Subscribers who join in a collaborative computer-based war game find it becoming altogether too real, with fatal casualties. Compare Vinge's *True Names* [4-576].

4-463. Sagan, Carl. **Contact.** Simon & Schuster, 1985.
Much-touted first novel by the noted popularizer of science, concerning the deciphering of a message from the stars and the voyage to a fateful rendezvous. The fervor of the story exceeds that of Gunn's *The Listeners* [4-244] and Kube-McDowell's *Emprise* [4-307]. It can also be compared to Clarke's *2010: Odyssey Two* [4-141].

4-464. Sallis, James. **A Few Last Words.** Hart-Davis, 1969.
Collection by an American writer associated with Moorcock's *New Worlds*. The stories provide models of human alienation dramatized by sometimes extravagant SF devices and occasional surreal humor. In "The History Makers" the protagonist's peaceful private affairs are contrasted with the rise and fall of civilizations, while the protagonist of the title story must decide whether to join a mass retreat from threatened catastrophe. Compare the short fiction of Thomas M. Disch [4-186].

4-465. Sanborn, Robin. **The Book of Stier.** Berkley, 1971.
A charismatic musician sparks off a social movement that transforms society—but who is really behind the apocalyptic changes? A sour satire on the counterculture and the implications of its ideas. Compare Vidal's *Messiah* [3-389] and Aldiss's *Barefoot in the Head* [4-3].

4-466. Sanders, Lawrence. **The Tomorrow File.** Putnam, 1975.
Best-selling story of the brilliant protagonist's climb toward wealth and power in an oppressive bureaucratized future. Cleverly constructed; inspired by Huxley's *Brave New World* [2-47] and comparable with Brunner's *Stand on Zanzibar* [4-92].

4-467. Sanders, Scott Russell. **Terrarium.** Tor, 1985.
Human society has retreated into domed cities where the business of living can be carefully regulated, but a few romantic misfits return to the wilderness outside, which has now recovered from the damage inflicted upon it by pollution and exploitation. A sentimental exercise in ecological mysticism. Compare Wilhelm's *Where Late the Sweet Birds Sang* [4-603].

4-468. Sapir, Richard Ben. **The Far Arena.** Seaview, 1978.
A Roman gladiator whose body has been preserved in the Arctic ice is resuscitated and becomes a critical observer of our time. Witty and elegant. Compare Grant Allen's *British Barbarians* (1895).

4-469. Sargent, Pamela. **The Alien Upstairs.** Doubleday, 1983.
In a bleak near future, where most people perform meaningless make-work tasks for lack of constructive employment, an alien comes to stay in a boardinghouse and changes the lives of the central characters. An unusual modern version of the theme of J. K. Jerome's classic "Passing of the Third Floor Back" (1973).

4-470. Sargent, Pamela. **Cloned Lives.** Fawcett, 1976.
Fix-up novel that examines carefully and intently the relationships that exist between members of an experimental human clone as they grow to maturity in a largely unsympathetic world. Compare Le Guin's "Nine Lives" [4-328] and contrast Wilhelm's *Where Late the Sweet Birds Sang* [4-603].

4-471. Sargent, Pamela. **The Golden Space.** Pocket Books, 1982.
In a world of near-immortal humans, biologists experiment with the design of a "more rational" human species, but the fate of the experiment becomes problematic while society adapts to man's new relationship with death. Thoughtful and neatly understated. Compare Wilhelm's *Welcome, Chaos* [4-602].

4-472. Sargent, Pamela. **Venus of Dreams.** Bantam, 1986.
Long novel about the relationship between two people involved in a project to terraform Venus. Carefully constructed and delicately handled, with some striking imagery to set off the love story.

4-473. Saxton, Josephine (U.K.). **The Power of Time.** Chatto, 1985.
Collection of stories ranging from the Kafkaesque parable "The Wall" (1965) to a satirical account of "The Snake Who Had Read Chomsky" (1981) and a gruesomely surreal tale of autosurgery, "No Coward Soul" (1982). Saxton is one of the most versatile of absurdist SF writers, with a lively imagination and a nice sense of humor. Compare Disch's *The Man Who Had No Idea* [4-186].

4-474. Saxton, Josephine (U.K.). **Queen of the States.** Women's Press, 1986.
Magdalen is confined in a mental hospital because people think she suffers from delusions; she coexists in several realities, in one of which she is politely studied by aliens interested in the mysteries of human sexuality. Lively and witty, with a profusion of deft ironies. Compare Vonnegut's *Slaughterhouse-Five* [4-578] and Piercy's *Woman on the Edge of Time* [4-411].

4-475. Saxton, Josephine (U.K.). **The Travails of Jane Saint and Other Stories.** Women's Press, 1986.
In the title short novel (first published separately in 1980) the heroine, imprisoned in a sensory deprivation tank awaiting brainwashing, embarks on a dreamquest in search of her lost children, hoping perhaps also to save the world. A surreal feminist fantasy, with a light touch and a great deal of humor. Compare and contrast Russ's *Extra(ordinary) People* [4-457].

4-476. Schenck, Hilbert. **At the Eye of the Ocean.** Pocket Books, 1980.
Novel about individuals whose extraordinary sensitivity to the sea enables them to locate the places and times at which a mystical moment of enlightenment is available to those who ardently desire it. Finely realized backgrounds (Cape Cod at widely spaced intervals of history) and effective writing; mystical SF at its best.

*4-477. Schenck, Hilbert. **A Rose for Armageddon.** Pocket Books, 1982.
As a new dark age looms, a handful of aging intellectuals race to finish a project in the computer simulation of social relationships in the history of a small island. A mystery emerges whose solution may offer an opportunity for redemption not only to the unhappy characters but also to their unhappy era. Poignant and beau-

tifully written; highly original in its recomplication of the timeslip romance—compare and contrast Finney's *Time and Again* [4-214].

4-478. Schmidt, Stanley. **The Sins of the Fathers.** Berkley, 1976.
The first novel in a series, followed by *Lifeboat Earth* (1978). The culture of the alien Kyyra, incorporating elaborate social engineering, might serve as a model for future human evolution. An interesting attempt to describe and display the life-style and philosophy of a technologically advanced species. Compare Anderson's *The Avatar* [4-13].

4-479. Scholz, Carter, and Glen A. Harcourt. **Palimpsests.** Ace, 1985.
Complex, somewhat overwritten novel in which the hero takes possession of an artifact from the future—found, incongruously, in an archaeological dig. After being pursued and recruited to a bizarre research establishment he eventually penetrates to the heart of the mystery. Literary showmanship maintains an impression of profundity, but this is really an exercise in absurdism, interestingly related to Waldrop's *Them Bones* [4-579], published in the same Ace Special series at about the same time.

4-480. Scott, Jody. **Passing for Human.** DAW, 1977.
A rhapsodic essay in misanthropy, engagingly indiscriminate in finding human beings despicable (especially the males) and then forgiving them for it. Ribald and zestful. The sequel, *I, Vampire* (1984), whose narrator rejoices in the name Sterling O'Blivion, is equally sharp and has the same ebullient charm. Compare Saxton's *Travails of Jane Saint* [4-475].

4-481. Sellings, Arthur (pseud. of Robert Arthur Ley) (U.K.). **Junk Day.** Dobson, 1970.
Postholocaust story in which survivors in London are exploited by the junkman, whose gangsterism restores a kind of social order before his evil role is usurped by scientists, who take over by means of behavioral engineering techniques. An exercise in polished cynicism; compare Van Greenaway's *graffiti* [4-562].

4-482. Shaw, Bob (U.K.). **Orbitsville.** Gollancz, 1975.
The protagonist is forced to flee from Earth when he incurs the wrath of his imperious employer, and discovers a vast artificial sphere surrounding a sun, which offers apparently unlimited opportunities for human colonists. A sequel, *Orbitsville Departure* (1983), is a taut thriller in whose climax the purpose of Orbitsville is revealed. Inevitably invites comparison with Niven's *Ringworld* [4-392], although the books are very different in tone and technique, and a more apt comparison is to Simak's *Ring around the Sun* [3-346].

*4-483. Shaw, Bob (U.K.). **Other Days, Other Eyes.** Gollancz, 1972.
Fix-up novel featuring one of the most ingenious SF inventions: "slow glass," which is quite transparent but lets light through so slowly that the image may take years to emerge. The book presents a marvelous study of the possible applications of the substance and its impact on society, incorporating some fine vignettes (including the brilliant "Light of Other Days," NN, 1966). A thoughtful and painstaking exercise in extrapolation, demonstrating how an apparently triv-

ial and by no means implausible innovation would have dramatic and far-reaching effects; a key thought-experiment in the sociology of technology.

4-484. Shaw, Bob (U.K.). **The Palace of Eternity.** Ace, 1969.
Thriller in which it transpires that human beings have alien commensals that secure a kind of life after death—but the aliens are under threat of destruction as a side effect of a new technology. Thematically fascinating; compare Simak's *Time and Again* [3-347] and Martin's *A Song for Lya* [4-361].

4-485. Shaw, Bob (U.K.). **The Peace Machine.** Gollancz, 1985.
Revised version of *Ground Zero Man* (1971). The hero invents a device that can destroy stockpiled nuclear weapons, and tries to blackmail the world into a saner arrangement of its affairs, but then must run and hide as he is relentlessly hunted down. The best modern version of a plot that was popular in the 1930s; compare Forester's *The Peacemaker* [2-32] and Vivian's *Star Dust* [2-121].

4-486. Shaw, Bob (U.K.). **The Ragged Astronauts.** Gollancz, 1986.
In a planetary system where two worlds share a common atmosphere the human inhabitants of one are forced by circumstance to migrate to the other in hot air balloons. An unusual adventure story in which good characterization helps to make extraordinary events plausible, the first novel in a projected trilogy.

4-487. Shaw, Bob (U.K.). **The Two-Timers.** Ace, 1968.
The protagonist, traumatized by the death of his wife, transports himself into an alternate world where he saves her, but then faces a problematic confrontation with his other self when the unforeseen side effects of his displacement disrupt the space-time continuum. A tense and dramatic thriller, convincingly handled.

4-488. Shaw, Bob (U.K.). **Vertigo.** Gollancz, 1978.
In a future where antigravity harnesses give individuals the power of flight, a policeman grounded by a serious accident is sent to Canada to recuperate. He must fight hard to overcome his personal problems, and eventually finds his courage severely tested by his involvement in a vendetta conducted by delinquent flyers against a local businessman. Realistic, displaying Shaw's craftmanship in combining imaginative creativity with narrative subtlety.

4-489. Shaw, Bob (U.K.). **Who Goes Here?** Gollancz, 1977.
Warren Peace has joined the Space Legion to forget, but can't help wondering what it was that was so awful he had to forget it all. Finding out involves him with monsters, mad scientists, and time paradoxes. Pure fun, very readable, and highly enjoyable. Compare Harrison's *Bill, the Galactic Hero* [4-255].

4-490. Shea, Robert, and Robert Anton Wilson. **Illuminatus!** Dell, 1984.
Omnibus edition of a three-decker novel whose separate parts—*The Eye in the Pyramid, The Golden Apple,* and *Leviathan*—first appeared in 1975. A wild extravaganza that hypothesizes that all the secret societies claiming access to a special enlightenment were and are part of a huge conspiracy that will take over Earth unless the heroes of the counterculture can stop them. A crazy compendium of contemporary concerns. Compare Pynchon's *Gravity's Rainbow* [4-432].

4-491. Sheckley, Robert. **Dimension of Miracles.** Dell, 1968.
The winner of a galactic sweepstake finds problems returning home with his prize, passing through various absurd alternate Earths, perennially threatened by imminent death. Less chaotic than the later bizarre odyssey *Options* (1977), and more imaginative than the convoluted *Dramocles* (1983), but not up to the standard of the earlier *Journey beyond Tomorrow* [3-336]. Sadly demonstrates the difficulty that Sheckley has in developing his brilliant comic writing at novel length.

4-492. Sheckley, Robert. **Is *That* What People Do?** Holt, 1984.
The most recent collection of Sheckley's short fiction, although it recombines stories from several earlier collections, as did *The Wonderful World of Robert Sheckley* (1979). Most of his modern period stories were first collected in *The People Trap* (1968); *Can You Feel Anything When I Do This?* (1971, variant title: *The Same to You Doubled*); and *The Robot Who Looked Like Me* (1978). Sheckley's stories are very funny, but the humor is generally underlaid with a dark and serious suspicion of the follies of human vanity. His robot stories are exceptionally fine, and should be compared and contrasted with the Asimov stories whose themes they often subvert and mock [3-20, 4-28]. Compare also the short fiction of John Sladek [4-519].

4-493. Sheffield, Charles. **Between the Strokes of Night.** Baen, 1985.
Earth is destroyed but the survivors find themselves on the threshold of infinite possibility thanks to the miracles of S-space (in which human beings live thousands of times more slowly than in normal space). The plot moves boldly from the early twenty-first century to the thirtieth millennium. Compare Bear's *Eon* [4-51].

4-494. Sheffield, Charles. **Hidden Variables.** Ace, 1981.
Sheffield's second collection, following *Vectors* (1979). Mostly hard SF, including a homage to Heinlein's *The Man Who Sold the Moon* [3-204] and a story coincidentally adopting the same premise as Forward's *Flight of the Dragonfly* [4-218]. One story featuring the idiosyncratic inventor McAndrew is part of a series collected in *The McAndrew Chronicles* (1983); these are playful extrapolations of ideas in nuclear physics (explanatory tables and background information are provided). Compare the short fiction of Larry Niven [4-390].

4-495. Sheffield, Charles. **Sight of Proteus.** Ace, 1978.
Tracks the development and eventual application of a technology of transmutation allowing human bodies to be reshaped and augmented. Although treated with great suspicion, the techniques ultimately prove themselves of immense value. An interesting extrapolation of the argument about biological experiments first put forward in Haldane's *Daedalus* (1923).

4-496. Sheffield, Charles. **The Web between the Worlds.** Ace, 1979.
Novel about the building of a space elevator, written independently of Clarke's *Fountains of Paradise* [4-136] and providing an interesting comparison of the way that different writers can build plots around the same premise.

4-497. Shepard, Lucius. **Green Eyes.** Ace, 1984.
Scientific researchers reanimate corpses biotechnologically, introducing new personalities. One of these "zombies" escapes, in the company of a female doctor, and gradually acquires superhuman powers that enable him to find out the truth behind voodoo mythology and the true purpose of the project that created him. Upmarket melodrama. Compare Matheson's *I Am Legend* [3-274].

4-498. Shirley, John. **Eclipse.** Bluejay, 1985.
Political thriller in which near-future Europe is taken over by Fascists who capitalize on a resurgence of racism. The heroes resist as best they can. Compare Sinclair Lewis's *It Can't Happen Here* [2-62].

4-499. Shirley, John. **Three-Ring Psychus.** Zebra, 1980.
Population pressure precipitates an evolutionary leap by which men are freed from the restrictions of the law of gravity. Social adaptation to degravitation proves difficult, though, as psychically bonded social groups must set aside the old ways of warfare and hatred. Rather rough-hewn, but imaginatively lively. Compare Anderson's *Brain Wave* [3-8].

4-500. Silverberg, Robert. **The Conglomeroid Cocktail Party.** Arbor House, 1984.
One of the most recent of Silverberg's many short story collections; outstanding among the rest are *Moonferns and Starsongs* (1971), *The Reality Trip and Other Implausibilities* (1972), *Born with the Dead* (1974), and *The Feast of St. Dionysus* (1975). The bibliography of the collections is complex, stories being frequently rearranged into new combinations. Stories written between 1963 and 1976 are characteristically written with great feeling, often featuring alienated heroes whose problems are sometimes solved (but often remain tragically unsolved) by transcendental experiences that run the gamut of traditional SF motifs and extend the vocabulary of ideas considerably. The present collection of stories, dating from 1980 to 1984 and following a period of temporary retirement, revisits the author's favorite themes, but in a rather more detached and diffident fashion. "The Pope of the Chimps" recovers the interest in religion displayed in *Tower of Glass* (1970), *Downward to the Earth* [4-501], etc., while "The Far Side of the Bell-Shaped Curve" is a story of erotically obsessed time travelers highly reminiscent of *Up the Line* [4-512], but in each case the treatment is cooler and more ironic. The stories are clever and polished, but many readers may prefer the drive and intensity of the best work in the earlier collections, including "To See the Invisible Man," "Sundance," "Passengers" (NW, 1969; HN, 1970), "Born with the Dead" (NW, 1974; HN, 1975), and "Schwartz between the Galaxies" (HN, 1975). Most recent is *Beyond the Safe Zone: Collected Short Fiction of Robert Silverberg* (Fine, 1986), which collects 27 stories.

*4-501. Silverberg, Robert. **Downward to the Earth.** Doubleday, 1970.
The guilt-stricken protagonist returns to the alien world where he was once a colonial officer and where he committed crimes for which he now seeks forgiveness and redemption. In order to become truly human, he must become alien, sharing the religious rituals of the natives and the related processes of physical metamorphosis. A superb novel; one of the best examples of the use of hypothetical bi-

ology and alien culture to symbolize problematic aspects of human existence. Compare Le Guin's *The Word for World Is Forest* [4-329] and Shaw's *Palace of Eternity* [4-484].

*4-502. Silverberg, Robert. **Dying Inside.** Scribner, 1972.
The story of a telepath whose powers are fading—a loss that may allow him to overcome his alienation from the human world. Told with great intensity and merciless realism; one of the finest works of the period and one of the best examples of the SF novel. NN, 1972; HN, 1973. Compare Russ's *And Chaos Died* [4-456]. *The Stochastic Man* (1975; HN, 1976; NN, 1975) is a similar but less impressive story of ESP-related alienation, this time embodied in a story of the acquisition of precognitive abilities.

4-503. Silverberg, Robert. **Hawksbill Station.** Doubleday, 1968. British title: *The Anvil of Time*, 1969.
A future government sends dissidents back in time to a Cambrian prison camp; moves for their repatriation are made—but can they really be rescued from their spiritual wasteland? A grim story of exile, told with compassion.

4-504. Silverberg, Robert. **The Masks of Time.** Ballantine, 1968. British title: *Vornan-19*, 1970.
As the millennial year 2000 approaches, an enigmatic visitor from the future comes to study twentieth-century man, and is trapped in a quasi-messianic role. Compare Griffin's *Century's End* [4-240]. Another enigmatic messiah figure is the industrialist in *Tower of Glass* (1970; NN, 1970; HN, 1971), who builds a new Tower of Babel and is deified by oppressed androids.

4-505. Silverberg, Robert. **Nightwings.** Avon, 1969.
Fix-up novel (first novella, HW, 1969) in which a decadent Earth is taken over by aliens who have old scores to settle, but who might offer humankind a path to salvation too. Lushly romantic and elegiac far-future fantasy.

4-506. Silverberg, Robert. **The Second Trip.** Doubleday, 1972.
The protagonist's artificial personality is created to inhabit the body of a criminal whose own mind has been erased, but the erasure proves imperfect and a bizarre struggle for control and existence ensues, counterpointed by the problems of a female telepath whose own hold on reality is fragile. A tense story of psychological subversion. Compare Evans's *The Insider* [4-207].

4-507. Silverberg, Robert. **Son of Man.** Ballantine, 1971.
Surreal allegory set in a far future where mankind has diversified into a whole spectrum of specialized species. An evolutionary fantasy recalling Bergson rather than Darwin, it explores in an unusual manner what we can and ought to mean by "human nature." A beautiful and brilliant book. Compare David Lindsay's *A Voyage to Arcturus* [2-63].

4-508. Silverberg, Robert. **Star of Gypsies.** Fine, 1986.
The Romanies are here represented as refugees from a distant star; in the far future they are the only people who can pilot starships and go "ghosting" through space and time to experience the history of their kind over many millennia. Here a far-future gypsy king offers his vision of the past and future of his race and

ours. Compare Sheffield's *Between the Strokes of Night* [4-493] and Bear's *Eon* [4-51] for other recent attempts to display a contemporary cosmic perspective.

4-509. Silverberg, Robert. **Thorns.** Ballantine, 1967.
Two lonely people, alienated by awful experiencees, are brought together by a psychic vampire in order that their anguish might feed his extraordinary lust, but they achieve a remarkable transcendence of their predicament. A highly stylized SF fable, comparable with Harness's *The Rose* [3-190].

4-510. Silverberg, Robert. **A Time of Changes.** Doubleday, 1971.
A colony world preserves a strange culture based on self-hatred, but the protagonist learns individualism from a visiting Earthman and becomes a revolutionary advocate of a new kind of community. Unlike Rand's *Anthem* [3-315], with which it inevitably invites comparison, it is not a political allegory but an exploration of the value of human relationships. HN, 1972; NW, 1971.

4-511. Silverberg, Robert. **Tom o'Bedlam.** Fine, 1986.
In California, which has been spared the nuclear holocaust, people dream of exotic alien worlds. The dreams inspire a millenarian cult and puzzle psychiatrists; the eponymous hero claims that they promise salvation to stricken mankind, but skeptics wonder whether he may simply be broadcasting hallucinations. Metaphysical SF in the same vein as *Nightwings* [4-505] but without the exoticism and much of the intensity.

4-512. Silverberg, Robert. **Up the Line.** Ballantine, 1969.
A satirical and sexy extrapolation of the "time patrol" theme, in which the protagonist turns outlaw, trying to alter history instead of protecting it, and is appropriately punished. Compare Anderson's *Guardians of Time* (1961). HN, 1970; NN, 1969.

*4-513. Silverberg, Robert. **The World Inside.** Doubleday, 1971.
In a crowded future, populations have to be gathered together in massive Urbmons: compact high-rise cities whose culture has set aside ideas of privacy. For some this is a kind of hell, but there can be no escape from it, even to the world outside. Compare Bass's *Half Past Human* [4-41]. HN (withdrawn), 1972.

*4-514. Simak, Clifford D(onald). **A Choice of Gods.** Putnam, 1972.
In a depopulated post-technological world, robots have taken over man's religious quest. An interesting example of SF mysticism, carrying forward themes from *City* [3-345]; rather more ambitious, despite its relative orthodoxy, than Schenck's *At the Eye of the Ocean* [4-476].

4-515. Simak, Clifford D(onald). **The Marathon Photograph and Other Stories.** Severn House, 1986.
Simak was a prolific short story writer in the earlier part of his career, but this is his only collection of modern period stories. It includes "The Grotto of the Dancing Deer" (HW, 1981; NW, 1980) and the title novella. Favorite Simak themes are displayed: cross-time perspectives juxtaposing past and future; questions of religious philosophy. The settings are evocative and the narratives polished.

4-516. Simak, Clifford D(onald). **Project Pope.** Ballantine, 1981.
On the planet End of Nothing humans and robots labor to produce a syncretic religion to unite disparate faiths, constructing a computer that will be the "ultimate pope." A crisis of faith emerges, however, when they receive news of heaven. Picks up themes from *A Choice of Gods* [4-514]. Compare Farmer's *Jesus on Mars* [4-209] and Ian Watson's *God's World* (1979). HN, 1982.

4-517. Simak, Clifford D(onald). **The Visitors.** Ballantine, 1980.
Alien "black boxes" descend on Earth in droves, peacefully reproducing themselves and minding their own business. They pay for what they consume, but their payments threaten to precipitate economic chaos. An ironic story, to be compared and contrasted with the Strugatskiis' *Roadside Picnic* [4-542].

4-518. Skal, David J. **When We Were Good.** Pocket Books, 1981.
In a world rendered sterile by radiation, genetic engineering techniques are used to develop a race of "perfect" hermaphrodite children whose social role is highly problematic. A bitter tale of a blighted future. Contrast Aldiss's *Greybeard* [4-5].

4-519. Sladek, John T(homas). **The Lunatics of Terra.** Gollancz, 1984.
Sladek's most recent collection, following *The Steam-Driven Boy and Other Strangers* (1973), *Keep the Giraffe Burning* (1977), and *Alien Accounts* (1982). Sladek's main theme is the invasion of the human environment and usurpation of human prerogatives by machines, but he also has a strong interest in peculiar logics and creative illogicalities, which often supply him with ideas for short stories. He is a surreal humorist; no one in SF has a finer feeling for the aesthetics of the incongruous. Compare the short fiction of Robert Sheckley [4-492] and Kit Reed [4-436].

4-520. Sladek, John T(homas). **The Müller-Fokker Effect.** Hutchinson, 1970.
Computer tapes on which a man's personality is stored are bootlegged about, causing havoc wherever they go, until the millionaire who caused all the trouble reintegrates the personality in a new body. Wild and intricate satire. Compare Griffin's *Century's End* [4-240].

4-521. Sladek, John T(homas). **The Reproductive System.** Gollancz, 1968. U.S. title: *Mechasm*, 1969.
Metal-eating, self-replicating robots threaten to destroy the fabric of civilization if they cannot be controlled and contained, although if used responsibly they might pave the way to paradise. A satirical parable of man/machine relationships. Compare and contrast Rucker's *Software* [4-453].

*4-522. Sladek, John T(homas). **Roderick.** Granada, 1980. U.S. edition is abridged, having been planned as the first part of a three-volume edition.
First part of a two-decker novel completed in *Roderick at Random* (1983). A satirical bildungsroman in which the eponymous artificial intelligence slowly develops through eccentric infancy to detached maturity while various enemies attempt to locate and destroy him. Very funny, picking up themes from *The Reproductive System* [4-521] in presenting its satirical account of man/machine relationships but extrapolating them to new extremes.

4-523. Sladek, John T(homas). **Tik-Tok.** Gollancz, 1983.
Tik-Tok is a robot whose "asimov circuits" malfunction, allowing him to become

as morally defective as the humans who made him and thus enabling him to build a spectacular career for himself. A fine black comedy.

4-524. Smith, Martin Cruz. **The Indians Won.** Belmont, 1970.
Alternate-history novel developing the thesis that the American Indian tribes might have managed to stand fast against the western migration of the European colonists, securing their own nation state. An intriguing premise, developed in a rather dry manner.

4-525. Spinrad, Norman. **Bug Jack Barron.** Walker, 1969.
The protagonist, a TV personality, makes a powerful enemy when he attacks a plutocrat who is trying to develop an immortality treatment. Taboo-breaking in its day because of its sexual frankness and extravagant cynicism; remains significant as an early examination of the growing power of the media and their manipulators. Compare Sterling's *The Artificial Kid* [4-537]. HN, 1970; NN, 1969.

*4-526. Spinrad, Norman. **Child of Fortune.** Bantam, 1985.
An exotic bildungsroman whose heroine embarks on an odyssey within the galactic culture that also forms the background to *The Void Captain's Tale* [4-530]. She falls in for a time with the ageless storyteller and philosopher Pater Pan, and undertakes a journey across the psychedelic Bloomenveldt, before attaining her particular enlightenment. A fabulously ornamented and compelling story, carrying forward the erotic themes of its predecessor and developing them in a broader context. Compare Delany's *Stars in My Pocket like Grains of Sand* [4-169].

*4-527. Spinrad, Norman. **The Iron Dream.** Avon, 1972.
A futuristic fantasy supposedly written by Adolf Hitler, who is here said to have become a pulp SF writer after emigrating to the United States in the 1920s. Here the ideas that inspired the Third Reich are rendered harmlessly into pulp adventure fiction—but how harmless, then, is such fiction? Hitler's *Lord of the Swastika* is similar enough to much real pulp SF to make us look again at the ideologies embedded in the genre. Compare Malzberg's *Herovit's World* [4-356]. NN, 1972.

4-528. Spinrad, Norman. **No Direction Home.** Pocket Books, 1975.
Collection of stories from 1969 to 1975 by a writer arguably more sensitive than any other to the themes and controversies of the time: ecocatastrophe, Vietnam, rock music, sporting spectacle, and media manipulation all feature herein. The earlier collection, *The Last Hurrah of the Golden Horde* (1970), was not so pertinent; *The Star-Spangled Future* (1979) combines stories from both books.

4-529. Spinrad, Norman. **Songs from the Stars.** Simon & Schuster, 1980.
In postholocaust America the "black" scientists are ideologically opposed by a "white" ecologically mystical counterculture whose heroes Clear Blue Lou and Sunshine Sue hitch a ride in a space shuttle to see whether there is a new enlightenment to be found in tapes of messages received from an extraterrestrial civilization. Cleverly subversive of certain SF myths. Compare and contrast Anderson's *Orion Shall Rise* [4-16].

*4-530. Spinrad, Norman. **The Void Captain's Tale.** Pocket Books, 1983.
Like *The Iron Dream* [4-527], this novel delves beneath the surface of SF mythology looking for the psychological drives within—and presents a phallic starship

that really does have a psychological drive! A fabulous erotic fantasy deployed in SF dream-symbolism; very clever and written with much verve. Compare Carter's *The Infernal Desire Machines of Doctor Hoffman* [4-116]. NN, 1983.

4-531. Spinrad, Norman. **A World Between.** Pocket Books, 1979.
Picks up the theme of the power of the media from *Bug Jack Barron* [4-525] and elaborates it graphically. A quasi-utopian world is threatened by ideological invasion from two sources: Fascistic "transcendental scientists" and radical lesbians pour forth their propaganda, but fail to woo the hearts and minds of the people away from liberal democracy and moral tolerance. Striking without being strident.

4-532. Stableford, Brian M(ichael) (U.K.). **Man in a Cage.** John Day, 1976.
Hyperspatial travel turns out to be an inherently schizophrenic experience; sane men crack under the strain, so what is needed is a man who has learned to live with madness. The hero finds this Herculean labor testing and enlightening, and succeeds in bringing the ship home, but there is still no place for him in the world of the sane. Contrast Malzberg's *Cross of Fire* [4-354] and Saxton's *Queen of the States* [4-474].

4-533. Stableford, Brian M(ichael) (U.K.). **The Walking Shadow.** Fontana, 1979.
A mysterious force hurls human beings through time in ever-extending leaps. The march of progress is interrupted and Earth is offered redemption by alien beings who believe that their brand of ecological mysticism is the only way of avoiding the doom that threatens intelligent life everywhere in the universe, but the hero prefers to follow his own course toward a more doubtful salvation. Notable for its development of an original premise in speculative biology: "third phase life."

4-534. Stableford, Brian, and David Langford (U.K.). **The Third Millennium.** Sidgwick & Jackson, 1985.
A speculative history of the period A.D. 2000–3000; after a time of crisis, progress in physics and biotechnology paves the way for a dramatic improvement of the human condition and for an expansion into space. Perhaps the most ambitious exercise in speculative future history since Stapledon's *Last and First Men* [2-109], which it surpasses in optimism and speculative rigor, although not in scope.

4-535. Steele, Linda. **Ibis.** DAW, 1985.
The story of a love affair between a human and an alien female of a hivelike species, which reflects ironically certain issues in human sexual politics. Compare de Camp's *Rogue Queen* [3-136] and Carr's *Leviathan's Deep* [4-112].

4-536. Stephenson, Andrew M(ichael) (U.K.). **The Wall of Years.** Futura, 1979.
War between parallel worlds tears apart the fabric of space-time, and the protagonist must try to stabilize history in the time of Alfred the Great. Effective depiction of Dark Age Britain makes the book memorable. Compare de Camp's *Lest Darkness Fall* [3-135].

4-537. Sterling, Bruce. **The Artificial Kid.** Harper, 1980.
The hero, a product of exotic biotechnology, is a street-fighting media star whose career is interrupted when he gets involved in dirty politics behind the scenes of

his quasi-utopian world. Imaginatively lively, with some interesting settings and characters. Compare Morrow's *Continent of Lies* [4-385].

*4-538. Sterling, Bruce. **Schismatrix.** Arbor House, 1985.
The hero, in the course of a long and eventful life, witnesses the political and technological evolution of the solar system after Earth has been devastated. The long struggle between the biotechnologically inclined Shapers and the electronically expert Mechanists is complicated by the arrival of aliens and the eruption of new ideological movements. A marvelous compendium of ideas; an imaginative tour de force. Compare Williamson's *Lifeburst* [4-608].

4-539. Stine, Hank. **Season of the Witch.** Essex House, 1968.
The best of a series of avant-garde pornographic SF books that also included work by Philip José Farmer and David Meltzer. A rape-murderer's personality is relocated in his victim's body in order to teach him a sharp lesson. More convincing than Robert Heinlein's *I Will Fear No Evil* (1970), which has a similarly prurient approach to a similar theme.

4-540. Strugatskii, Arkadii Natanovich, and Boris Natanovich Strugatskii (U.S.S.R.). **Beetle in the Anthill.** Macmillan, 1980. Tr. by Antonina W. Bouis of *Zhuk v muraveinike*, 1979–1980.
An agent of the security forces is charged with the task of hunting down a man whose existence poses a threat to the world—a space explorer suspected of having been programmed by aliens to destroy mankind. An intense thriller questioning the implicit paranoia of "security."

4-541. Strugatskii, Arkadii Natanovich, and Boris Natanovich Strugatskii (U.S.S.R.). **Definitely Maybe.** Macmillan, 1978. Tr. by Antonina W. Bouis of *Za milliard let do kontsa sveta*, 1976–1977.
The work of the world's leading scientists is radically disrupted by inexplicable events. Can they mount an investigation of what is happening, or must any such project be disrupted in its turn? As in other Strugatskii works, characters must bring rationality to bear on the irrational, and must accept the probability that it will prove inadequate.

*4-542. Strugatskii, Arkadii Natanovich, and Boris Natanovich Strugatskii (U.S.S.R.). **Roadside Picnic & The Tale of the Troika.** Macmillan, 1977. Tr. by Antonina W. Bouis of *Piknik na obochine*, 1972, and *Skazka o troike*, 1968.
Two short novels. In the first, human scavengers try to make capital out of the rubbish left behind by alien tourists, which poses awful dangers as well as promising fabulous rewards. Human vanity is satirized but credit is given where it is due. The second, which is linked to the novel *Monday Begins on Saturday* (tr. 1977), mixes motifs from SF and folklore in order to satirize bureaucratic process in scientific research and society. As usual, the scientific method proves no match for the arbitrarily miraculous.

4-543. Strugatskii, Arkadii Natanovich, and Boris Natanovich Strugatskii (U.S.S.R.). **The Snail on the Slope.** Bantam, 1980. Tr. by Alan Myers of *Ulitka na sklone*, 1966–1968.
Two interlocked stories offer different views of a strange alien forest, the per-

spectives embodying contrasting ideologies of intellectual method and social organization. A dense and complex work, comparable to Lem's *Solaris* [3-261] in more ways than one.

4-544. Strugatskii, Arkadii Natanovich, and Boris Natanovich Strugatskii (U.S.S.R.). **The Ugly Swans.** Macmillan, 1979. Tr. by Alexander Nakhimovsky and Alice Stone Nakhimovsky of *Gadkie lebedi,* 1972.
In a decadent future strange weather conditions bring fantastic changes to a region where children appear to be evolving into superhumanity. Contrast Clarke's *Childhood's End* [3-97].

4-545. Sturgeon, Theodore. **Godbody.** Fine, 1986.
Written in the late 1960s, this posthumously published short novel is a metaphysical fantasy of a Christlike visitation, carrying forward Sturgeon's constant preoccupation with love as a force of redemption. Compare Knight's *Man in the Tree* [4-304], Dick's *Divine Invasion* [4-172], and Farmer's *Jesus on Mars* [4-209].

4-546. Sucharitkul, Somtow. **The Aquiliad.** Pocket Books, 1983.
In an alternate world the Roman Empire extends to the Americas, its culture enlivened by Amerindian inputs. Lurking in the wings, though, is a nasty minded time traveler whose machinations may upset the applecart and cause temporal chaos. A witty subversion of SF themes whose serious extrapolation can be found in such works as Chalker's *Downtiming the Night Side* [4-122].

4-547. Sucharitkul, Somtow. **Light on the Sound.** Pocket Books, 1982.
First of a series extended in *The Throne of Madness* (1983), *Utopia Hunters* (1984), and *The Darkling Wind* (1985). A galactic civilization is dominated by the all-powerful Inquestors, who cruelly exploit the sentient Windbringers to sustain their hegemony. The Windbringers' only defense is the beauty of light and sound, so the Inquestors use deaf and dumb humans as their agents. The heroes and heroines of the books are rebels against this monstrous tyranny, but their resistance is a complicated business. An understanding of their enemies slowly emerges. Baroque, highly ornamented SF, original in style and outlook. Compare Smith's *Norstrilia* [3-353] and Delany's *Stars in My Pocket like Grains of Sand* [4-169].

4-548. Sucharitkul, Somtow. **Mallworld.** Donning, 1981.
An alien race fascinated by the mysteries of anthropology studies human behavior in the context of a sprawling future shopping center where human eccentricity is extravagantly and satirically displayed. Funny, but with a deft touch of sentimentality. Compare Sheckley's *Dimension of Miracles* [4-491].

4-549. Sucharitkul, Somtow. **Starship and Haiku.** Pocket Books, 1984.
An extraordinary work in which Earth has suffered ecocatastrophe, men rediscover their kinship with whales, and a dubious messiah urges the entire Japanese nation to expiate their historical sins in seppuku. Compare Watson's *The Jonah Kit* [4-588] and Bear's *Beyond Heaven's River* [4-49].

4-550. Swanwick, Michael. **In the Drift.** Ace, 1985.
Fix-up novel begun with "Mummer's Kiss" (NN, 1981), set in and around the area polluted by fallout after a meltdown at Three Mile Island. Essentially a story

of the pioneering of a new and hazardous frontier, rejoicing in its own grimness. Compare Pangborn's *Davy* [3-303] and Robinson's *The Wild Shore* [4-447].

4-551. Tevis, Walter S(tone). **Mockingbird.** Doubleday, 1980.
In a decadent future whose inhabitants have abandoned literacy, the alienated hero becomes a rebel, while one of the robots that keep things going acquires human sensibilities (to his cost). A further study of alienation using SF motifs is *Steps of the Sun* (1983). NN, 1980.

4-552. Thurston, Robert. **Q Colony.** Berkley, 1985.
Extended from the novelette "The Oonaa Woman" (1981); the story of a research unit on an alien world, focusing on the clash of cultures and the problems that arise from sexual encounters between the two species. Compare Dozois's *Strangers* [4-190].

4-553. Tiptree, James, Jr. (pseud. of Alice Sheldon). **Brightness Falls from the Air.** Tor, 1985.
A thriller in which a lonely outpost of galactic civilization is taken over by gangsters while the debris of a nova comes ever closer. The violent oppression recalls old sins committed and old hurts sustained by the human and alien characters. Seemingly modeled on the film *Key Largo* (1948). Compare Cherryh's *Downbelow Station* [4-128]. *The Starry Rift* (1986), although billed as a sequel, is actually a collection of three novellas with the same background, including "The Only Neat Thing to Do" (HN, 1986).

4-554. Tiptree, James, Jr. (pseud. of Alice Sheldon). **Out of the Everywhere and Other Extraordinary Visions.** Ballantine, 1981.
The fourth Tiptree collection, following *Ten Thousand Light Years from Home* (1973), *Warm Worlds and Otherwise* (1975), and *Star Songs of an Old Primate* (1978). Her most effective stories seem motivated by outrage, using SF motifs to set up situations in which the injustices and tragedies of our world are magnified. Scientism, cruelty, and sexism are all attacked, sometimes stridently. Compare the short fiction written by Robert Silverberg in the late 1960s and early 1970s [4-500].

4-555. Tiptree, James, Jr. (pseud. of Alice Sheldon). **Up the Walls of the World.** Berkley, 1978.
Airborne aliens who enjoy a utopian existence are threatened with extinction when a sun-destroying entity nears their home. Telepathic explorers set up a psychic pipeline to Earth, which might allow some of them to escape by appropriating human bodies. Meanwhile, the human contactees have problems of their own. A rather shrill and high-strung story. Compare Carver's *Infinity Link* [4-119]. HN, 1979.

4-556. Tubb, E(dwin) C(harles) (U.K.). **The Winds of Gath.** Ace, 1967. U.K. title: *Gath*.
The first of a very long series describing Earl Dumarest's attempts to locate his lost home-world (Earth) in a galaxy where virtually every habitable world has been colonized by humans. He is opposed and constantly frustrated by the mechanized instruments of the enigmatic Cyclan. Now some 30 volumes long,

the series is a remarkable example of the indefinitely delayed climax. The stories are competent action-adventure stories in settings that are sometimes intriguing.

*4-557. Tucker, Wilson. **The Year of the Quiet Sun.** Ace, 1970.
Time travelers trying to figure out a way to subvert the future armageddon that their researches may actually be initiating. Their researches also stir up, ironically, controversy regarding the authenticity of the biblical Book of Revelations. A grimly realistic and cleverly constructed story, unusual in its subtlety. Compare Silverberg's *Masks of Time* [4-504]. JWC (retrospective), 1976; HN, 1971; NN, 1970.

4-558. Tung, Lee (India). **The Wind Obeys Lama Toru.** Kutub-Popular, 1972.
A satire on contemporary anxieties about population explosion; chaos is caused by the foolish misuse of a series of drug treatments to promote fertility, reduce fertility, and then promote it again. Compare such Western perspectives as those to be found in Brunner's *Stand on Zanzibar* [4-92] and Harrison's *Make Room! Make Room!* [4-257].

4-559. Turner, George (Australia). **Beloved Son.** Faber, 1978.
The first part of a trilogy also including *Vaneglory* (1981) and *Yesterday's Men* (1983). Social reconstruction has followed ecocatastrophe, international relations being conducted on the basis of a strict ethic of noninterference, but order and control are threatened by the results of experiments in biotechnology and research into the possibility of immortality (already possessed by the mutants who are the main characters of *Vaneglory*). Cynical and downbeat, convinced of the imperfectibility of humankind and inclined to be maudlin about it. Compare Compton's *Electric Crocodile* [4-144].

4-560. Vance, Jack. **Emphyrio.** Doubleday, 1969.
The protagonist must travel to Earth in order to recover the knowledge necessary to free his world from the cultural rigidity imposed on it by alien rulers. Picks up themes from earlier Vance novels, including *The Languages of Pao* [3-381], to further illustrate the author's fascination with colorful, exotic cultures and messianic rebels against their stagnation.

4-561. Vance, Jack. **The Last Castle.** Ace, 1966.
A novella in which far-future Earth is recolonized by humans who establish themselves as an aristocracy supported by alien underclasses, but become vulnerable to revolution. Elegant exoticism with an underlying political message. Compare Smith's *Norstrilia* [3-353]. HW, 1967; NW, 1966.

4-562. Van Greenaway, Peter (U.K.). **graffiti.** Gollancz, 1983.
A return to the postholocaust scenario of Van Greenaway's first novel, *The Crucified City* (1962), with the elegiac tone of the earlier novel here replaced by an angry and anguished bitterness. Survivors of the bombing use the limited time left to them to make sure that the elites who let the war happen cannot stay safely in their underground bunkers.

4-563. Van Greenaway, Peter (U.K.). **Manrissa Man.** Gollancz, 1982.
The U.S. Defense Department explores the possibility of augmenting the intelligence of apes so that they can be used as cheap labor, but once they learn to

speak the apes have plenty to say for themselves and plans of their own. Tautly plotted thriller with a strong thread of black comedy. Contrast Duffy's *Gor Saga* [4-193] and Michael Crichton's *Congo* (1980).

4-564. Van Scyoc, Sydney J(oyce). **Daughters of the Sunstone.** Nelson Double-day, 1985.
Omnibus edition of a trilogy: *Darkchild* (1982), *Bluesong* (1983), and *Starsilk* (1984). The sentient starsilks can form symbiotic relationships with intelligent beings, permitting an expansion of consciousness that aids various characters on different alien worlds to overcome problems and achieve more harmonious relationships. Action-adventure plots in interesting settings. Compare Lichtenberg's *Dushau* trilogy [4-339].

4-565. van Vogt, A(lfred) E(lton). **The Anarchistic Colossus.** Ace, 1977.
A future society without a state, where systems of social control are fully automated, is threatened by would-be alien invaders. The hero must first free himself from restraint before he can fight the aliens, but becomes involved in difficult complications. A typically convoluted plot, enlivened by the intriguing background.

4-566. van Vogt, A(lfred) E(lton). **The Battle of Forever.** Ace, 1971.
Only a few true humans remain in a world populated by genetically engineered beast-men; they enjoy utopian seclusion until one of them becomes curious about the outside world and discovers unexpected threats. Compare Smith's *Norstrilia* [3-353] and Bayley's *The Zen Gun* [4-48].

4-567. van Vogt, A(lfred) E(lton). **Cosmic Encounter.** Doubleday, 1980.
Time collapses into the year 1704, the detritus of its collapse including a twenty-fifth-century robot-manned battleship, which might take over unless a disinherited English aristocrat and pirate can acquire superhuman powers and save the universe. Swashbuckling SF adventure, not making much sense but delighting with its sheer panache.

*4-568. Varley, John. **Millennium.** Berkley, 1983.
Slick time travel story based on "Air Raid" (NN, 1977; HN, 1978) in which the damaged citizens of a ruined future Earth try to save humankind by kidnapping people from the past whose disappearance cannot create paradoxes. While they are snatching passengers from a doomed jumbo jet, an object is left behind, sparking off changes that may destroy the universe if the time stream is not healed. Clever and tightly constructed, acknowledging its debt to the long tradition of time paradox stories by using famous titles as chapter headings. HN, 1984.

4-569. Varley, John. **The Ophiuchi Hotline.** Dial, 1977.
Contact with aliens at first brings new opportunities, but then come the Invaders, determined to take over the solar system and expel humankind. What future can there be for displaced persons in the galactic civilization? Compare Brin's *Startide Rising* [4-82].

*4-570. Varley, John. **The Persistence of Vision.** Dial, 1978. British title: *In the Hall of the Martian Kings*, 1978.
The first of Varley's short story collections, followed by *The Barbie Murders and*

Other Stories (1980) and *Blue Champagne* (1986). The title story (NW, 1978; HW, 1979) is a rather sickly parable that supposes that men are so alienated that the path of true enlightenment will be reserved for the handicapped. "In the Hall of the Martian Kings" (HN, 1978) has castaways on Mars saved by the advent of miraculous life-forms. Varley almost always deals in extremes, and the fervent inventiveness of his early stories made them very striking. Compare the short fiction of James Tiptree, Jr. [4-554].

4-571. Varley, John. **Titan.** Putnam, 1979.
First volume (NN, 1979; HN, 1980) of a trilogy completed in *Wizard* (1980; HN, 1981) and *Demon* (1984). The heroine finds an artificial world among the satellites of Saturn and becomes an agent of its resident intelligence, the godlike Gaea, before being forced to turn against "her." Conscientiously nonsexist action-adventure SF. Compare Piserchia's *Earthchild* [4-412].

4-572. Vidal, Gore. **Kalki.** Random, 1978.
A would-be avatar of the eponymous deity annihilates humankind save for a chosen few, but the New Order quickly founders in betrayal and cruel circumstance. Bleakly ironic. Compare Neil Bell's *The Lord of Life* [2-5].

4-573. Vinge, Joan D(ennison). **Eyes of Amber and Other Stories.** Signet, 1979.
A collection whose title novella (HW, 1978) is the story of communication between a human linguist and a strange female alien. "To Bell the Cat" also revolves around problems of human/alien communication, while "Tin Soldier" is a curious tale of alienation in which the hero falls out of touch with those around him by aging more slowly. Vinge's short fiction can also be found in *Fireship* (1978) and *Phoenix in the Ashes* (1985).

4-574. Vinge, Joan D(ennison). **The Snow Queen.** Dial, 1980.
An amalgam of SF and heroic fantasy borrowing the structure of Hans Christian Andersen's famous story, set on a barbarian world exploited by technologically superior outworlders, against the background of a fallen galactic empire. The convoluted plot is further dressed up with ideas drawn from Robert Graves's classic of anthropological pseudoscience, *The White Goddess*. The recipe proved popular. *World's End* (1984) is a more modest sequel. HW, 1981; NN, 1980.

4-575. Vinge, Vernor. **The Peace War.** Bluejay, 1984.
The superhuman protagonist can augment his talents even further by interfacing with computers, and must exploit such advantages to the full in order to survive in a future transformed (and wrecked) by the exploitation of elaborate information technology, new biotechnologies, and "bobbles"—stasis fields (HN, 1985). Bobbles offer a means of suspended animation, and this becomes the starting point of a sequel, *Marooned in Real Time* (1986), which features an Earth abandoned save for those committed, voluntarily or involuntarily, to such imprisonment. The books combine interesting extrapolations with lively plotting.

4-576. Vinge, Vernor. **True Names.** Bluejay, 1984.
Novella first published in 1981 (HN, 1982). Clever computer hackers have established their own fantasy world within the data matrix of the world's computers, where they can work mischief and enjoy themselves—until someone (or maybe

something) tries to take over the world and the hero, blackmailed into cooperation with the FBI, has to stop the rot. A lively and fascinating extrapolation of the idea that advanced technology opens up the opportunities traditionally associated with wizardry. A precursor of Gibson's *Neuromancer* [4-233].

4-577. Vonnegut, Kurt, Jr. **Galapagos.** Delacorte, 1985.
A group of tourists on a cruise survive the end of the world, settling on a small Galapagos Island and beginning a new evolutionary sequence. The ghostly narrator looks back on things from a perspective one million years hence. Compare Malamud's *God's Grace* [4-351].

*4-578. Vonnegut, Kurt, Jr. **Slaughterhouse-Five; or, The Children's Crusade.** Delacorte, 1979.
Billy Pilgrim survives the Dresden firestorm as a POW, but subsequently becomes unstuck in time after being kidnapped by Tralfamadorians and caged with a blue movie starlet. Thus he learns that everything is fixed and unalterable, and that one simply has to make the best of the few good times one has. A masterpiece, in which Vonnegut penetrated to the heart of the issues developed in his earlier absurdist fabulations. A key work of modern SF. NN, 1969; HN, 1970.

4-579. Waldrop, Howard. **Them Bones.** Ace, 1984.
Archaeologists digging in Louisiana find disturbing anachronisms; the narrative cuts continually to the past, where a twenty-first-century time traveler finds history altered. Can order possibly be restored? Compare Sucharitkul's *The Aquiliad* [4-546]. Waldrop's delight in paradoxes and temporal incongruities is further shown off by the short fiction collected in *Howard Who?* (1986), including "The Ugly Chicken" (NW, 1980; HN, 1981).

4-580. Wallace, Ian (pseud. of John W. Pritchard). **Croyd.** Putnam, 1967.
The first of a series of sophisticated van Vogtian superman stories, in which the eponymous hero must continually save the galaxy. *Dr. Orpheus* (1968) is a particularly fine blend of SF and quasi-mythological themes, strongly recalling Charles Harness's casually embellished van Vogtian adventure stories. Later volumes are *A Voyage to Dari* (1974) and *Z-Sting* (1978).

4-581. Wallace, Ian (pseud. of John W. Pritchard). **Deathstar Voyage.** Putnam, 1969.
The first of a series of SF mystery stories featuring policewoman Claudine St. Cyr; others are *The Purloined Prince* (1971) and *The Sign of the Mute Medusa* (1977). *Heller's Leap* (1979) is a more convoluted novel bringing together Claudine St. Cyr and Croyd. The stories cleverly exploit the potential of SF motifs in setting up "impossible" situations, but play fair with the reader in strictly defining the terms within which the mystery must be solved. Compare Niven's Gil Hamilton series [4-389].

4-582. Wallace, Ian (pseud. of John W. Pritchard). **The Lucifer Comet.** DAW, 1980.
Alien beings with godly pretensions fight for control of the human species; one resembles Satan but his role is Promethean. An extrapolation of the kind of argument found in many apologies for the devil; other SF versions include two by

Theodore Sturgeon: "One Foot and the Grave" (1949) and "Excalibur and the Atom" (1951). Action-adventure with good ironic undertones. Compare also Watson's Book of the River trilogy, especially the final volume [4-584].

4-583. Watkins, William Jon. **What Rough Beast.** Playboy, 1980.
A humanoid female alien with psi powers comes to Earth with benevolent motives but is opposed by the forces of blind bureaucracy, which are misusing technologies that ought to be exploited more responsibly. An extravagant tale of redemption. Compare the Robinsons' *Stardance* [4-449].

4-584. Watson, Ian (U.K.). **The Book of the River.** Gollancz, 1984.
First part of a trilogy completed in *The Book of the Stars* (1985) and *The Book of Being* (1985). Societies on the two banks of a vast river are kept apart by the living "black current," which also intervenes to make females dominant in the economic life of one shore. The heroine manages to cross to the other side, where she finds a cruelly oppressive male-dominated society, and then must play a crucial role in the events following the withdrawal of the alien divider. In the later volumes she gradually learns the truth behind the enigmatic mythology of her world, and must join in a cosmic conflict between the Worm and the Godmind, suffering death and rebirth in her quest to save humankind from the fate planned for it by the latter. Echoes themes from Watson's earlier work, but the tone is much lighter and the plotting more easily paced; the central character is appealing. Compare Varley's Titan trilogy [4-571].

4-585. Watson, Ian (U.K.). **Chekhov's Journey.** Gollancz, 1983.
A Soviet film unit tries to inspire the leading man by putting him in psychic touch with Chekhov; a time ship hurtles through history toward the disaster that will "become" the Tungus incident; and the real Chekhov sets off to investigate the explosion. As the narrative threads intertwine, history is subtly altered. A multifaceted story whose plot is underlaid by questions in the philosophy of history; clever and well written.

*4-586. Watson, Ian (U.K.). **The Embedding.** Gollancz, 1973.
An intricately constructed novel about the power of language to contain and delimit "reality." It features an experiment in which children are taught an artificial language to alter their perception of the world; an Amerindian tribe whose use of psychotropic drugs is associated with transformations of their native tongue; and alien visitors who seek to understand humans via their communicative artifacts. Original and mind stretching, something of an imaginative tour de force. Compare Delany's *Babel-17* [4-164]. NN, 1975.

*4-587. Watson, Ian (U.K.). **The Gardens of Delight.** Gollancz, 1980.
A colony world visited after many years by a starship from Earth is found to have been remade in the image of the Bosch triptych whose centerpiece is the famous "Garden of Earthly Delights"; here the characters (human, nonhuman, and mechanical) undergo continual metamorphic reincarnations, apparently striving to ascend an evolutionary ladder to transcendental enlightenment. Despite the fabulous trappings and the use of alchemical metaphors, the story is provided with a sound SF explanation and has the sense of discipline that is (or ought to be) charac-

teristic of SF. Marvelous imaginative and intellectual showmanship, unparalleled in its exoticism. Compare and contrast Silverberg's *Son of Man* [4-507].

4-588. Watson, Ian (U.K.). **The Jonah Kit.** Gollancz, 1975.
Men open communication with whales by imprinting a human thought pattern on the brain of a sperm whale, but when the whales learn what we have to tell them—including an astronomer's recent discovery that ours is only an echo of the "true" universe—their worldview is devastated. A highly original novel, with some effective description of nonhuman consciousness. Compare Sucharitkul's *Starship and Haiku* [4-549].

*4-589. Watson, Ian (U.K.). **Miracle Visitors.** Gollancz, 1978.
Novel developing the hypothesis that UFO experiences are altered states of consciousness that tantalize rationality and beckon humankind to further mental evolution. Some fine imagery displayed in a careful and orderly narrative. Picks up themes from the earlier novels *The Martian Inca* (1977) and *Alien Embassy* (1977), which feature more melodramatic images of emerging metahumanity. Compare Chayevsky's *Altered States* [4-126].

4-590. Watson, Ian (U.K.). **Queenmagic, Kingmagic.** Gollancz, 1986.
In a universe ordered according to the rules of chess, rival pawns discover how to preserve themselves from the apocalyptic checkmate, and experience universes embodying the logic of several other games before discovering the fundamental truths of their mode of existence. The more playful element in Watson's work, introduced in *Deathhunter* (1981) and continued in the River trilogy [4-584], is here taken to a lighthearted extreme.

4-591. Watson, Ian (U.K.). **The Very Slow Time Machine.** Gollancz, 1979.
Watson's first collection, followed by *Sunstroke and Other Stories* (1982) and *Slow Birds and Other Stories* (1985). The stories display his delight in novel and startling ideas, filling a spectrum from the flippant "My Soul Swims in a Goldfish Bowl" to the extravagant title story about a most unusual journey through time. The versatility of Watson's imagination is well suited to short fictions of the "idea as hero" variety. Compare Bayley's *Knights of the Limits* [4-45].

4-592. Watson, Ian (U.K.), and Michael Bishop. **Under Heaven's Bridge.** Gollancz, 1981.
An unusual transatlantic collaboration. The story confronts a Japanese linguist with a very unusual alien culture. Borrows ideas from Bishop's *A Little Knowledge* (1977), exhibits Watson's preoccupation with alien worldviews, and exploits both writers' interest in Japanese culture. Careful and conscientious. Compare Mann's *Eye of the Queen* [4-359].

4-593. White, James (U.K.). **The Dream Millennium.** Ballantine, 1974.
Colonists in suspended animation aboard a generation starship experience dreams that unlock a way into the collective unconscious and allow them to obtain new insights into their past lives and their human nature. Painstaking and neatly understated. Contrast Moorcock's *The Black Corridor* [4-381].

4-594. White, James (U.K.). **The Watch Below.** Ballantine, 1966.
Descendants of people trapped in the hold of a sunken cargo ship have devel-

oped a worldview that makes them suitable contactees of aquatic aliens in search of a new home. Intriguing development of an unusual premise, showing White's preoccupation with the idea of establishing harmonious relationships between species with very different biologies—other extrapolations of the theme can be found in *All Judgment Fled* (1968) and his stories about the multi-environmental galactic hospital Sector General, featured most recently in *Ambulance Ship* (1979) and *Star Healer* (1985).

4-595. White, Ted. **By Furies Possessed.** Signet, 1970.
Aliens of repulsive appearance that can fuse their nervous systems with those of humans are at first considered by the hero to be parasitic monsters, but he learns that men have much to gain from such an association. A reaction against the implied paranoia of Heinlein's *The Puppet Masters* [3-205].

4-596. White, Ted. **The Jewels of Elsewhen.** Belmont, 1967.
Interdimensional action-adventure story enlivened by a fine surreal opening sequence in which the protagonist finds the world transformed into a decaying artifact. Compare Leiber's *The Sinful Ones* (1951).

4-597. Wilder, Cherry (New Zealand). **Second Nature.** Pocket Books, 1982.
Descendants of survivors of a crashed spaceship have established a thriving colony on an alien world despite losing much of the cultural heritage of their ancestors; their affairs are thrown into crisis by the appearance of natives previously supposed to have been extinct. Conscientious development of its premises, with good characterization. Compare Kingsbury's *Courtship Rite* [4-301].

*4-598. Wilhelm, Kate. **The Clewiston Test.** Farrar, 1976.
The protagonist, recovering from a serious accident, throws herself into her scientific work, but becomes increasingly frustrated by the personal and professional problems that develop as her experiments with behavior-controlling drugs produce ambiguous results. A first-rate novel presenting an excellent picture of scientists at work, developing a compelling argument about the conflict that can arise between the objectivity of the scientific outlook and the need for warmth and concern within human relationships. Compare Leven's *Satan* [4-336].

4-599. Wilhelm, Kate. **Huysman's Pets.** Bluejay, 1986.
A writer enmeshed in personal problems following his divorce is asked to write a biography of geneticist and psychologist Huysman. His research leads him to a continuing experiment whose guinea pigs are ESP-talented children. A good thriller whose reliance on remarkable coincidences is justified by the premises of the story. Compare Wilson's Schrödinger's Cat trilogy [4-612].

*4-600. Wilhelm, Kate. **The Infinity Box.** Harper, 1975.
Perhaps Wilhelm's best short story collection, including the fine title novella (NN, 1971) and "April Fool's Day Forever" (NN, 1970), the latter presenting a characteristric Wilhelm theme: a new and promising discovery with tragic side effects. The earlier collections, *The Downstairs Room* (1968) and *Abyss* (1971), also have some strong material; the former includes "The Planners" (NW, 1968), one of many convincing stories of scientists at work in the forefront of genetic and behavioral research. More recent stories can be found in *Somerset Dreams and Other*

Fictions (1978) and *Listen, Listen* (1981). Wilhelm has no peer as a writer of realistic near-future SF stories examining the human implications of possible biological discoveries.

4-601. Wilhelm, Kate. **Juniper Time.** Harper, 1979.
The heroine is a linguist sought by the authorities because they need her to help translate an alien "message," but she has fled decaying civilization for the simpler life of the Indians, who have again come into their own in the returning wilderness. Compare Crowley's *Engine Summer* [4-158] for a similar celebration of the pastoral. NN, 1979.

4-602. Wilhelm, Kate. **Welcome, Chaos.** Houghton Mifflin, 1983.
A serum that immunizes against all disease and stops aging is kept secret by a group of scientists because many people cannot survive the initial administration. Their hopes of increasing its success rate and overcoming the sterility that is its main side effect are dashed when the world comes to the brink of nuclear war because the Soviet government apparently has the secret, and they must decide whether to make public what they know. A gripping account of individuals wrestling with a novel moral dilemma; excellent characterization. Parkinson's *They Shall Not Die* [2-89] provides an interesting contrast of perspectives.

4-603. Wilhelm, Kate. **Where Late the Sweet Birds Sang.** Harper, 1976.
Ecocatastrophe destroys the United States, but a family of survivalists comes through the crisis, using cloning techniques to combat a plague of sterility. But are their descendants really victors in the struggle for existence, or has their artificial selection simply delivered them into a different kind of existential sterility? Compare Herbert's *Hellstrom's Hive* [4-269] and Sargent's *Cloned Lives* [4-470]. NN, 1976; HW, 1977.

4-604. Williams, Paul O(sborne). **The Breaking of Northwall.** Ballantine, 1981.
First volume in the "Pelbar Cycle," continued in *The Ends of the Circle* (1981), *The Dome in the Forest* (1981), *The Fall of the Shell* (1982), *An Ambush of Shadows* (1983), and *The Song of the Axe* (1984). A thousand years after the nuclear holocaust civilization has been recovered by numerous local groups, which have developed their own distinctive cultures and are now moving toward reunification at a national level. The reunification is by no means smooth, conflicts between different groups being common, further complicated by conflicts between groups and rebellious individuals. Action-adventure fiction, much strengthened by the anthropological sources on which the author draws; underlaid by serious sociological arguments and speculations. Compare Roberts's *The Chalk Giants* [4-440] and Robinson's *The Wild Shore* [4-447].

4-605. Williams, Walter Jon. **Hardwired.** Tor, 1986.
Earth's surface has been devastated in a war against orbiting space stations; the survivors live in a violent world of petty tyrants and black marketeers. The tough hero, who can enter into cyborg symbiosis with his high tech transport, and the equally tough heroine are outlaws caught up in renewed world conflict. Action-adventure hyped up almost to the level of parody, handled with panache. Compare Powers's *Dinner at Deviant's Palace* [4-423].

4-606. Williams, Walter Jon. **Knight Moves.** Tor, 1985.
The hero has already provided humankind with an interstellar drive and an immortality treatment—the former resulting from a deal with an alien anthropologist who commissioned him to buy up the Earth in order to facilitate his researches. Now the human race must be saved from cultural stagnation, and figuring out the secret of teleportation might just do the trick. An ambitious and well-written book, seemingly heavily influenced by Roger Zelazny but less frenetic in pace and ultimately finding a direction of its own. Compare especially *This Immortal* [4-632] and *Doorways in the Sand* [4-627].

4-607. Williamson, Jack. **Firechild.** Bluejay, 1986.
A genetic engineer invents a powerful weapon, but turns it on himself rather than surrender it to his military masters. Born of this sacrifice is an angelic homunculus who becomes an instrument of worldly redemption. Compare Bear's *Blood Music* [4-50].

4-608. Williamson, Jack. **Lifeburst.** Ballantine, 1984.
Intelligent space opera in which the human conquest of the solar system is inhibited by violent political disputes and interrupted by the arrival of a gravid alien queen of a powerful and rapacious species, while gentler aliens stand on the sidelines. An illustration of the way in which Williamson's work has become gradually more sophisticated with the evolution of the genre; compare *The Legion of Space* [2-134] and *The Reefs of Space* (1964).

4-609. Williamson, Jack. **Manseed.** Ballantine, 1982.
A damaged seedship—one of many programmed to distribute human life throughout the universe—tries to seed a world where an advanced civilization was once obliterated. The genetically engineered colonists are superhuman, and have powerful cyborg associates, but they still face a stiff challenge. Sophisticated space opera. Compare Benford and Brin's *Heart of the Comet* [4-55].

4-610. Willis, Connie. **Fire Watch.** Bluejay, 1985.
Collection; the title story (HW, 1983; NW, 1982) has time traveling students discovering the real texture of history, and shows off the author's main strength: her ability to import a warmth and intimacy into classic SF themes. Compare Cherryh's *Visible Light* [4-133].

4-611. Wilson, Colin (U.K.). **The Mind Parasites.** Arkham, 1967.
A scientist discovers that antilife entities have been preventing humans from achieving their true potential, and have perverted human nature. The heroes begin to set things right. A similar parable, more extensively dressed up with pseudoscientific materials, is *The Philosopher's Stone* (1969). Wilson found in the works of A. E. van Vogt and H. P. Lovecraft themes echoing his own beliefs and his SF is essentially a series of pastiches; *The Space Vampires* (1976) is virtually a sequel to van Vogt's "Asylum," and is less weighed down by hints that it all might be true.

4-612. Wilson, Robert Anton. **Schrödinger's Cat: The Universe Next Door.** Pocket Books, 1979.
First part of a three-decker novel continued in *The Trick Top Hat* (1980) and *The*

Homing Pigeons (1981). The three stories run more or less in parallel, and the workings of their convoluted plots model alternative interpretations of the strange world of subatomic physics. Funny and clever, carrying forward some of the countercultural fascinations of *Illuminatus!* [4-490]. Compare Aldiss's *Report on Probability A* [4-9] and Wilhelm's *Huysman's Pets* [4-599].

4-613. Wilson, Snoo (U.K.). **Spaceache.** Chatto & Windus, 1984.
Near-future black comedy following the fortunes of a young heroine exported from an overcrowded Earth; she winds up on the bizarre high technology world of Neptune. Her adventures continue in *Inside Babel* (1985), which returns her to Earth. Grotesque imagery and boisterous misanthropy abound. Compare Adams's *Hitch-Hiker's Guide to the Galaxy* [4-1].

*4-614. Wolfe, Gene. **The Fifth Head of Cerberus.** Scribner, 1972.
Three linked novellas (title novella HN, 1973; NN, 1972) forming a coherent whole (though the coherency has not been obvious to all readers). The key issue is the identity of the main characters—one is a boy who is the latest in a series of clones whose failure to achieve success in life has become the focal point of obsessive "self"-examination; the other is apparently an anthropologist who offers a strange "reconstruction" of the life of alien aborigines that were supposedly wiped out by human colonists but actually used their shape-shifting powers to mimic and displace the humans (including the anthropologist). A supremely delicate exercise in narrative construction; not easy to follow, but one of the true classics of SF.

4-615. Wolfe, Gene. **The Island of Doctor Death and Other Stories and Other Stories.** Pocket Books, 1980.
Collection, including the title story (NN, 1970) and a novella that inverts its themes, "The Death of Doctor Island" (NW, 1973; HN, 1974). They deal with the subtle interaction of "private" fictional worlds and "public" real ones; Wolfe is playing, as in *The Fifth Head of Cerberus* [4-614], with relationships between appearance and reality more subtle and mystifying than those to be found in such Philip Dick novels as *Martian Time-Slip* [3-143] and *Do Androids Dream of Electric Sheep?* [4-173]. This preoccupation recurs in many of his other stories; a second collection is *Gene Wolfe's Book of Days* (1981).

*4-616. Wolfe, Gene. **The Shadow of the Torturer.** Simon & Schuster, 1980.
The first volume (NN, 1980) of a four-volume novel completed in *The Claw of the Conciliator* (1981; HN, 1982), *The Sword of the Lictor* (1982; HN, 1983; NN, 1982), and *The Citadel of the Autarch* (1983; NN, 1983; JWC, 1984). SF and fantasy motifs are combined here in a far-future scenario akin to Vance's *The Dying Earth* [3-380]; planetary resources are exhausted and civilization is in the final stages of decline. The hero is a disgraced torturer who embarks on a long journey, becoming involved with a religious order that preserves a relic of a long-gone redeemer, and eventually with a plan to renew the Sun. A rich, many-layered story; the detail and integrity of the imagined world invite comparison with Herbert's *Dune* [4-268] and Tolkien's "Middle Earth" but it is a unique literary work that transcends issues of categorization.

4-617. Wylie, Philip. **The End of the Dream.** Doubleday, 1972.
Ecocatastrophe story of a particularly extreme kind, in which Wylie brings to bear the same realism of presentation and intensity of alarmist feeling that he brought to his nuclear war stories *Tomorrow!* [3-409] and *Triumph* [3-409]. Compare Brunner's *The Sheep Look Up* [4-90].

4-618. Yarbro, Chelsea Quinn. **False Dawn.** Doubleday, 1978.
A grim tale of social misfits winning a brief moment of joy from dire circumstance in a future California ruined by ecocatastrophe. Compare Swanwick's *In the Drift* [4-550].

4-619. Yarbro, Chelsea Quinn. **Hyacinths.** Doubleday, 1983.
A near-future government copes with the dissatisfactions generated by economic depression by implanting subliminal messages in the piped dream-plays that are the principal entertainment medium of the day. The heroine must build her career in this corrupt world. Compare Compton's *Synthajoy* [4-145].

4-620. Yermakov, Nicholas. **Last Communion.** Signet, 1981.
First volume of a trilogy completed in *Epiphany* (1982) and *Jehad* (1984). The alien inhabitants of a newly discovered world can absorb the personalities of their dead to form curious gestalts. The repressive human elite is determined to usurp this ability, while the heroes are determined to protect the aliens, but a fusion of human and alien species is ultimately inevitable. An intriguing extrapolation of a theme developed very differently in Martin's *A Song for Lya* [4-361].

4-621. Young, Robert F(ranklin). **The Last Yggdrasil.** Ballantine, 1982.
Novelization of the fine short story, "To Fell a Tree" (1959), in which the human hired to fell a gargantuan, thousand-year-old tree meets the "dryad" who inhabits it.

4-622. Young, Robert F(ranklin). **Starfinder.** Pocket Books, 1980.
Fix-up novel in which spaceships are constructed from the carcasses of time traveling space whales, providing an exotic, paradox-laden scenario for romantic adventures. Compare Sucharitkul's *Starship and Haiku* [4-549].

4-623. Yulsman, Jerry. **Elleander Morning.** St. Martin's, 1983.
Complex mystery story in which the granddaughter of the eponymous heroine discovers what might have happened if her grandmother had not assassinated Hitler, and uncovers a plot to revive Nazi dreams of glory in her own peaceful world. A fascinating exercise in alternate history, with unusual characterization. Contrast Saberhagen's *A Century of Progress* [4-461].

4-624. Zahn, Timothy. **A Coming of Age.** Bluejay, 1985.
On a colony world a mutation has given young children telekinetic powers, which they lose at puberty, and society has been adaptively transformed. The story studies the situation from various viewpoints, and supplies a fast-moving plot. An interesting exercise in the extrapolation of a premise; compare Shaw's *Other Days, Other Eyes* [4-483] and *Vertigo* [4-488].

4-625. Zebrowski, George. **Macrolife.** Harper, 1979.
Humans are forced by cosmic catastrophe to quit Earth, dispersing into the galaxy in space habitats hollowed out in asteroids. As much essay as story, providing a sociology of these quasi-utopian "macroworlds" as they continue the human story across vast reaches of future time. Comparable in scope to Stapledon's *Last and First Men* [2-109] and very impressive in the breadth of its vision despite being a bit of a stylistic patchwork.

*4-626. Zelazny, Roger. **The Doors of His Face, The Lamps of His Mouth and Other Stories.** Doubleday, 1971.
Fine collection; the title story (HN, 1966; NW, 1965) concerns a man facing up to his fears in the shape of a Venerian sea monster, and "A Rose for Ecclesiastes" (HN, 1964) is a poignant story about a man who unwittingly brings faith to a Martian race on the brink of extinction. The earlier collection *Four for Tomorrow* (1967) is equally good, but subsequent collections, *My Name Is Legion* (1979) and *The Last Defender of Camelot* (1980), are weaker, although the former does feature "Home Is the Hangman" (HW, 1976; NN, 1975)—a suspenseful story about an enigmatic robot executioner.

4-627. Zelazny, Roger. **Doorways in the Sand.** Harper, 1976.
The hero's freeloading academic life is interrupted when he is accused of stealing an object vital to Earth's future in the galactic community. A fast and furious chase story, slickly written. Compare Nolan and Johnson's *Logan's Run* [4-400].

*4-628. Zelazny, Roger. **The Dream Master.** Ace, 1966.
Expanded from the novella "He Who Shapes" (NW, 1965). A psychiatrist links minds with disturbed patients in order to construct therapeutic dream experiences. He tries to train a blind woman in the relevant techniques, despite opposition from her intellectually augmented guide dog, and finds his own balance of mind threatened. Compare Le Guin's *The Lathe of Heaven* [4-326] and Brunner's *The Whole Man* [4-94].

4-629. Zelazny, Roger. **Eye of Cat.** Pocket Books, 1982.
An escaped alien pursues a blood feud against the human who captured it; he takes refuge in the homeland of his Navajo ancestors, throwing himself into a shamanic trance in order to confuse his telepathic tracker. Human telepaths try to help out, but can only delay the inevitable confrontation. A chase thriller whose use of the mythological themes that dominated Zelazny's earlier work recalls a little of their brilliance.

4-630. Zelazny, Roger. **Isle of the Dead.** Ace, 1969.
The human hero has learned the alien power of "worldscaping," embracing a new religion along with his godlike powers, but a resentful alien sets out to destroy him. The hero's psychological hangups are incarnated in one of his creations, and his inner and outer conflicts are fused. NN, 1969.

*4-631. Zelazny, Roger. **Lord of Light.** Doubleday, 1967.
A colony world has used its powerful technology to recreate Hindu culture, its elite assuming the roles of the gods. The hero first rebels against these "gods" on their own terms, but then opposes them more successfully with a new faith. Pyro-

technically dramatic and imaginatively fascinating (HW, 1968; NN, 1967). The similar *Creatures of Light and Darkness* (1969), which draws heavily on Egyptian mythology, is less successful.

*4-632. Zelazny, Roger. **This Immortal.** Ace, 1966.
Expanded from a shorter version entitled "... And Call Me Conrad" (HW, 1966). The superhuman hero must defend an extraterrestrial visitor against the many dangers of a wrecked Earth where mutation has reformulated many mythical entities. A fascinating interweaving of motifs from SF and mythology—perhaps the most successful of Zelazny's several exercises in that vein. Compare Delany's *Einstein Intersection* [4-167]. NN, 1966.

Anthologies

The SF anthology has crucially changed its role during the modern period. When SF was primarily a magazine genre, the chief function of anthologies was to give more permanent form to material that might otherwise have been consigned to oblivion after an ephemeral exposure measured in the weeks that a magazine might remain on a newsstand. By 1964, however, the magazines had lost their primary position and the materials featured in them were likely to be recycled much more quickly into single-author collections. By 1970 it was obvious that the magazines were in a financially precarious situation, and to many observers their days seemed numbered. This was a cause of some critical anxiety because it was a commonly held view that the SF short story had special merits of its own, distinct from non-SF short stories and from SF novels. This argument was popularized by Kingsley Amis, in *New Maps of Hell* [9-5], when he pointed out that the real "hero" of most SF short stories is the novel premise developed therein (the thesis is thus often known as the "idea-as-hero" argument).

It seemed to some editors that the future for the SF short story lay with anthologies that, instead of reprinting stories from the magazines, would buy original material directly from the authors. One such short-lived series had existed during the magazine boom of the early 1950s—Frederik Pohl's *Star Science Fiction Stories* [3-453]—and new exemplars were provided in 1966 by Damon Knight's *Orbit* [4-655] and in 1967 by Harlan Ellison's *Dangerous Visions* [4-650]. The latter claimed to be breaking new ground in escaping the "taboos" that supposedly governed the major magazines (symbolized in many minds by the censorious pen of John W. Campbell's editorial assistant, Kay Tarrant). The year 1971 saw the launch of two more original anthology series: Terry Carr's *Universe* [4-642] and Robert Silverberg's *New Dimensions* [4-664]. In the same year, the British magazine *New Worlds*, which had long carried the banner for the New Wave, followed the example of *New Writings in SF* [4-640] and was relaunched as a quarterly paperback series—though it soon went on to a slacker schedule, and eventually closed down after its tenth issue in 1976. There were several further attempts to launch similar series, though few enjoyed even limited success.

Another major propagandist for original anthologies was Roger Elwood, who began producing them by the score in the early 1970s. It had long been established even in the field of reprint anthologies that those that had no identity by courtesy of belonging to a series could best be organized around some connecting theme, and Elwood invented themes in great profusion. Other anthologies boasted of being the cutting edge of the genre's evolution, rejoicing in titles like *The Farthest Reaches* (Joseph Elder, ed.; 1968) and *Final Stage* (Edward L. Ferman and Barry N. Malzberg, eds.; 1975). A new group of apologists began to campaign on behalf of the SF novella, arguing that many ideas had a heroic status too grand to be confined in a few thousand words, yet need not be extrapolated in novel form. Thus the 1970s also saw a rash of anthologies consisting of three or four novellas—sometimes, but not always, developing a single theme. An early pioneer of such books was Robert Silverberg, who went on to become the decade's most prolific anthologist once the wave of fashionability had passed Elwood by.

As things turned out, though, this displacement of effort was premature. The magazines did not die. Although one of the most famous titles—*Galaxy*—just failed to make it into the 1980s, its place as a market leader had already been taken by *Isaac Asimov's Science Fiction Magazine* [14-25], and although *Analog* [14-23] changed proprietors its circulation was relatively undisturbed. *The Magazine of Fantasy and Science Fiction* [14-26] also maintained its market position. As the 1980s began, therefore, the tide was already beginning to turn against the original anthologies. The one American magazine that had adopted paperback book format—*Destinies*, begun in 1978—survived only a couple of years (though it has recently been replaced by a virtual clone, *Far Frontiers* [4-662]). When the recession put a brake on the expansion of SF publication and forced a certain pruning, anthologies were cut back much more severely than novels. With the exception of the various best-of-the-year series, where there is still a degree of competition, anthology production has received very little investment in terms of cash or publicity. Reprint anthologies now flourish only in association with the selling power of Isaac Asimov's name, which is recklessly appended to dozens of books "coedited" with other people—usually, but not always, Martin H. Greenberg and Charles G. Waugh.

The individual annotations that follow are heavily biased toward recent books. Some important series and a few anthologies of special interest from the years 1964 to 1980 are noted, but it is very unlikely that many of the anthologies produced in those years will ever be reprinted, because the stories have been recycled through single-author collections or used as parts of novels (a glance through the annotations in the earlier part of the chapter will confirm the importance of this trend in the contemporary SF marketplace). Contemporary readers will usually find it more convenient to track down particular works of interest in single-author volumes, or by accumulating best-of-the-year series—though anthologies on particular themes will still retain a certain interest when they are compiled with an appropriate degree of care and intelligence.

4-633. Aldiss, Brian W. (U.K.), and Sam J. Lundwall (Sweden), eds. **The Penguin World Omnibus of Science Fiction.** Penguin, 1986.
Anthology of stories from many nations, put together in connection with the

World SF organization founded in 1976. Most of the material is recent, though some dates back to the 1950s. Notable for featuring material from South America and Southeast Asia as well as more familiar points of origin, and fascinating in its diversity.

*4-634. Asimov, Isaac, ed. **The Hugo Winners: Volume 5.** Doubleday, 1986.
Latest in the series of collections of Hugo winners in the short story, novelette, and novella categories. The present volume covers the years 1980–1982. The remainder of the modern period is covered in Volumes 2 (1971; covers the years 1962–1970), 3 (1977; covers the years 1971–1975), and 4 (1985; covers the years 1976–1979). The stories are supplemented by connective comments by the editor, which are usually amusing in spite of their dubious relevance. The quality of the stories is secured by their award-winning status, and the series is also of interest as a monitor of changing tastes and expectations among the hard-core SF audience.

4-635. Asimov, Isaac; Patricia Warrick; and Martin H. Greenberg, eds. **Machines That Think: The Best Science Fiction Stories about Robots and Computers.** Holt, 1984.
Perhaps the best of the retrospective theme anthologies using Asimov's name as a selling point. The contents span the entire history of SF, and although many of the stories have also appeared in earlier theme anthologies, this large volume offers the best historical overview for the time being.

4-636. Benford, Gregory, and Martin H. Greenberg, eds. **Hitler Victorious: 11 Stories of the German Victory in World War II.** Garland, 1986.
Theme anthology mixing reprints and original stories, dealing with the most popular of all alternate-history premises.

4-637. Bishop, Michael, ed. **Light Years and Dark.** Berkley, 1984.
Large anthology featuring (according to the subtitle) *SF and Fantasy of and for Our Time.* Mixes reprints and original material, providing a good cross section of the concerns and modes of modern imaginative fiction. Authors featured include Spinrad, Niven, Tiptree, Wolfe, Ballard, and Dozois.

4-638. Broderick, Damien (Australia), ed. **Strange Attractors: Original Australian Speculative Fiction.** Hale & Iremonger, 1985.
One of several collections of SF stories by Australian writers; such collections provide a significant market for writers whose domestic opportunities for publication are limited. Broderick's material is rather more avant-garde than that featured in the Collins anthologies [4-644]. This work can be placed in historical context with the aid of Van Ikin's interesting retrospective survey of Australian SF writing from 1845 to 1979, *Australian Science Fiction* (Univ. of Queensland Press, 1982).

4-639. Budrys, Algis, ed. **L. Ron Hubbard Presents: Writers of the Future, Volume II.** Bridge, 1986.
Second anthology of stories by new writers, selected from entries to an annual competition. The book also includes essays and comments by established writers, including Herbert, McCaffrey, Niven, and Wolfe.

4-640. Bulmer, Kenneth (U.K.), ed. **New Writings in SF 29.** Sidgwick & Jackson, 1976.

Last of a series of original anthologies begun under the editorship of E. J. Carnell in 1964 (Bulmer took over from number 22). The series was an important market for lesser British SF writers, especially those whose careers were launched after the demise of *New Worlds* and those who were more traditionally inclined.

4-641. Carr, Terry, ed. **Best Science Fiction of the Year 15.** Tor, 1986.

Latest in the series of one of the best-of-the-year anthologies. Carr first began editing such anthologies in collaboration with Donald Wollheim in 1965. He tends to strike a good balance between big names and not yet established writers, and is always sensitive to originality of approach. When the series was being issued by Ballantine/Del Rey it was briefly (in 1979–1980) split into two, *Best Science Fiction of the Year* being supplemented by *Best Science Fiction Novellas of the Year.*

4-642. Carr, Terry, ed. **Universe 16.** Doubleday, 1986.

The lone survivor of the original anthology series founded in such profusion in the early 1970s; it was first issued in 1971 and the current publisher picked it up from the seventh collection. The series features high-quality fiction at the softer end of the spectrum without being too self-consciously avant-garde. Several writers featured in Carr's newly revived "Ace Special" line had previously published significant early work in *Universe,* including Carter Scholz, Kim Stanley Robinson, Howard Waldrop, and Lucius Shepard.

4-643. Clute, John; Colin Greenland; and David Pringle (U.K.), eds. **Interzone: The First Anthology.** Dent, 1985.

First of a projected series of anthologies reprinting the best stories from the British magazine *Interzone* [14-24]. This edition includes one original story. The material is mostly avant-garde, polished, and elegant but decidedly downbeat. Authors featured include Ballard, Keith Roberts, and Angela Carter.

4-644. Collins, Paul (Australia), ed. **Frontier Worlds.** Cory & Collins, 1983.

One of a series of original anthologies of Australian SF stories begun with *Envisaged Worlds* (1978) and including *Distant Worlds* (1981). An interesting showcase for Australian writers, more traditionally inclined than Broderick's *Strange Attractors* [4-638]. Authors featured include Lake, Chandler, Wilder, Wynne Whiteford, and Jack Wodhams.

4-645. Dann, Jack, ed. **Wandering Stars: An Anthology of Jewish Fantasy and Science Fiction.** Harper, 1974.

Theme anthology mixing original and reprinted stories, concentrating on premises related to Jewish culture, religion, and folklore. A second anthology, *More Wandering Stars* (1981), was subsequently issued by the same editor.

4-646. Datlow, Ellen, ed. **The Third Omni Book of Science Fiction.** Zebra, 1985.

The third of a series (the first two were issued simultaneously in 1983) that seems to have replaced *The Best of Omni Science Fiction,* of which six editions were issued 1980–1983, all edited or coedited by Don Myrus. The earlier series had a format similar to that of *Omni* magazine, and frequently used original as well as reprinted material. The new series is all reprint. The material is high quality (as befits the highest paying genre market) but has a surprising tendency to be downbeat in tone despite its relatively traditional character.

4-647. Disch, Thomas M(ichael), ed. **The Ruins of Earth.** Putnam, 1971.
First of a series of theme anthologies edited by Disch in the 1970s; the others are *Bad Moon Rising* (1973), *The New Improved Sun* (1975), *New Constellations* (1976; in collaboration with Charles Naylor), and *Strangeness* (1977; in collaboration with Charles Naylor). The books mix original and reprinted material, focusing on themes of contemporary concern and fashionability. They are interesting because they operate on the boundary between SF and the literary mainstream, juxtaposing SF with more conventional avant-garde items. The material is high in quality, heavy on irony, and (despite the title of the third volume) bleak in outlook.

4-648. Dozois, Gardner, ed. **The Year's Best Science Fiction: Third Annual Collection.** Bluejay, 1986.
By far the biggest of the best-of-the-year anthologies, although it remains to be seen whether it will be picked up by another publisher following Bluejay's demise. If it is, it may remain the best bet for regular purchase simply by virtue of being less restricted by space in its choice of longer stories. Dozois seems to be a middle-of-the-road editor in the same mold as Terry Carr.

4-649. Elliot, Jeffrey M., ed. **Kindred Spirits.** Alyson, 1984.
Anthology of SF stories of homosexual interest, issued by a specialist publisher. A second anthology, *Worlds Apart* (1986), was issued by the same publisher, edited by Camilla De Carnin, Eric Garber, and Lyn Paleo.

***4-650.** Ellison, Harlan, ed. **Dangerous Visions.** Doubleday, 1967.
The first big hardcover anthology of original SF stories—a classic that launched a publishing vogue as well as providing a manifesto for the American New Wave. Ellison's combative introductions set off the stories superbly, though some of the efforts at "taboo-breaking" now seem a little sophomoric. A very influential book, followed by the even bigger and equally fine *Again, Dangerous Visions* (1972). *The Last Dangerous Visions*, reputed to be of gargantuan proportions, has been promised for many years.

4-651. Ellison, Harlan, ed. **Medea: Harlan's World.** Bantam, 1985.
Somewhat delayed realization of a project begun in 1975, whereby 11 writers "collaborated" on the design of an imaginary colony world, outlining its physical characteristics, geography, ecosphere, societies, and history. It is unusual to find writers as disparate as Niven, Wilhelm, Herbert, Disch, and Sturgeon combining their efforts, and this unlikely teaming helps to make the book a fascinating project. There is elaborate supplementary material in addition to the stories.

4-652. Ferman, Edward L., ed. **The Best from Fantasy and Science Fiction: 24th Series.** Scribner, 1982.
The last (for the time being, at least) of a long-running series of selections from the field's most eclectic magazine—the first volume was issued in 1952. In its hey-

day, when it kept an annual schedule, the series suffered very little in comparison to the best-of-the-year anthologies, which had the whole field to choose from. Also worthy of note is the same editor's *The Magazine of Fantasy and Science Fiction: A Thirty Year Retrospective* (Doubleday, 1980).

4-653. Green, Jen, and Sarah Lefanu (U.K.), eds. **Despatches from the Frontiers of the Female Mind.** Women's Press, 1985.
Original anthology of feminist SF, including American as well as British writers. The stories range from the heavily didactic to the sensitively sentimental; Russ, Tiptree, and Tanith Lee are among those featured. This is the latest in a sequence of feminist anthologies, which began with the *Women of Wonder* series edited by Pamela Sargent from 1975 to 1978. Other important examples are *Aurora: Beyond Equality* (Vonda N. McIntyre and Susan Janice Anderson, eds.; 1976) and *Cassandra Rising* (Alice Laurance, ed.; 1978).

4-654. Jakubowski, Maxim (U.K.), ed. **Travelling towards Epsilon.** New English Library, 1977.
Anthology of SF stories translated from the French. The introduction provides historical context, and historical perspective can also be gained by comparing the present collection with Damon Knight's *Thirteen French Science-Fiction Stories* [3-445]. It is interesting to juxtapose the collection with other books of SF in translation from a particular nation—for example, the Sturgeon-introduced *New Soviet Science Fiction* [4-670].

4-655. Knight, Damon, ed. **Orbit 21.** Harper, 1980.
The last of the pioneering original anthology series begun in 1966. Knight's relationship with the Clarion workshops ensured that he was often in a position to find talented new writers as their careers were just getting under way, and the series played a major role in establishing the careers of several major writers, including Kate Wilhelm and Gene Wolfe. R. A. Lafferty was also extensively featured. An early preference for material with particularly polished literary style gradually gave way to an interest in esoteric material, sometimes without much discernible speculative content, but the series was a worthy experiment whose early volumes feature some very fine material.

4-656. Martin, George R. R., ed. **The John W. Campbell Awards: Volume 5.** Bluejay, 1984.
A continuation of the series begun as *New Voices,* which issued four annual volumes, 1978–1981, each featuring long stories by the authors nominated for the John W. Campbell Award for the best new writer in the years 1973–1976. A sixth volume was scheduled to appear in 1986 but its fate remains uncertain in view of Bluejay's demise. The 1977 nominees represented were C. J. Cherryh, Carter Scholz, Jack Chalker, and M. A. Foster, all of whom have built considerable careers in the interim, thus giving the volume a slightly redundant air.

4-657. Martin, George R. R., ed. **Wild Cards.** Bantam, 1987.
Anthology of stories (tending toward presentation as a fix-up novel) set in an alternate world in which an alien virus devastated Manhattan in 1946, its side effects including strange mutations and psychic powers. A curious mixture of

superheroic power fantasy and civil rights crusade; featured writers include Howard Waldrop, Walter Jon Williams, and Roger Zelazny.

4-658. Merril, Judith (Canada), ed. **Tesseracts.** Press Porcépic, 1985.
Representative anthology of stories by Canadian writers, mixing originals and reprints. More famous names include William Gibson, Spider Robinson, and Phyllis Gotlieb, but the main interest is in the juxtaposition of unusual genre material with speculative work by mainstream writers—a similar sort of mix to that which distinguished Merril's famous best-of-the-year anthologies of the 1950s and early 1960s [3-449], which were renowned for their eclecticism and favoring of avant-garde material. Some stories here have been translated from the French. Compare Broderick's *Strange Attractors* [4-638].

*4-659. Moorcock, Michael, ed. **New Worlds: An Anthology.** Flamingo, 1983.
Anthology looking back at the *New Worlds*/New Wave phenomenon from a reasonably distant perspective. Many of the stories appeared earlier in the six-volume series *The Best SF Stories from New Worlds* (1968–1971), also edited by Moorcock, but the present volume includes a good deal of bibliographical data and other supplementary material that makes it a most valuable retrospective.

4-660. Morris, Janet, ed. **Afterwar.** Simon & Schuster, 1985.
Theme anthology about the aftermath of nuclear war, almost all the material being original. The doom and gloom is occasionally alleviated by the intervention of fantasy motifs, confirming that it becomes easier, when thinking about the unthinkable, to entertain the impossible. Featured authors include Benford, Watson, and Cherryh. Historical perspective can be gained by comparing this item with the reprint anthology *Countdown to Midnight* (H. Bruce Franklin, ed.; DAW, 1984).

4-661. Nolane, Richard D. (France), ed. **Terra SF II: The Year's Best European SF.** DAW, 1983.
Second (and apparently last) in a series of anthologies of translated Western European SF. Most of the stories are from France and Germany, although the net is cast wide enough to have picked up items from Finland and Italy. Although not all published in a single year, the stories are all recent. The *Terra SF* anthologies follow an earlier anthology edited by Donald A. Wollheim, *The Best from the Rest of the World* (1976). Another such anthology, including Eastern European material, was *View from Another Shore* (Franz Rottensteiner, ed.; 1973). Compare also Aldiss and Lundwall's *Penguin World Omnibus of Science Fiction* [4-633].

4-662. Pournelle, Jerry, and James Baen, eds. **Far Frontiers: Volume VI.** Baen, 1986.
Latest in a series of original anthologies. Like its predecessor *Destinies*, it is a hybrid of magazine and anthology. The series began in 1985. It features hard SF and speculative nonfiction, provides assertive propagandist support for the space program, and boasts a muscular libertarian political standpoint. Pournelle and John F. Carr earlier edited a two-volume anthology, *The Endless Frontier* (1979–1982), in the same vein.

4-663. Pournelle, Jerry, and John F. Carr, eds. **There Will Be War: Warrior.** Vol. 5. Tor, 1986.

Latest in a series of theme anthologies begun with *There Will Be War* (1983), mixing original and reprinted stories with poems and essays. Reflects a strong commitment to militarism and its associated codes of behavior; features propaganda for the Strategic Defense Initiative and similar political programs. Comparable with British future war fiction of the bombastic kind produced in the wake of Chesney's *The Battle of Dorking* [1-21] until the outbreak of World War I. It remains to be seen whether the present series will exhibit a similar relationship to World War III. An earlier series of anthologies on related themes, without the propagandist aspect of the present series, was Reginald Bretnor's three volume set *The Future at War* (1979–1980).

4-664. Randall, Marta, and Robert Silverberg, eds. **New Dimensions 12.** Pocket Books, 1981.

Last of a series of annual anthologies begun by Silverberg in 1971. The early issues helped establish the careers of Barry Malzberg, James Tiptree, Jr., and Gardner Dozois, and the series continued its role as a promoter of new writers to the end. In very much the same vein as Carr's Universe series [4-642].

4-665. Ryan, Alan, ed. **Perpetual Light.** Warner, 1982.

Theme anthology offering 23 original stories dealing with aspects of "religious experience." Modern SF writers have been curiously fascinated by the phenomena of religious observance and questions of theology and metaphysics. This anthology revisits the theme of some of the better anthologies of the 1970s, including Mayo Mohs's *Other Worlds, Other Gods* (1971; reprints) and Terry Carr's *An Exaltation of Stars* (1973; original novellas). This outstanding collection includes particularly fine stories by Silverberg, Benford, and Schenck.

4-666. Sargent, Pamela, and Ian Watson (U.K.), eds. **Afterlives.** Vintage, 1986.

Theme anthology mixing a few reprints with mostly original stories of life after death. SF and fantasy approaches mingle in many of the stories, demonstrating again the fascination many SF writers have with questions of metaphysics, and with the possibility that technology might one day provide opportunities that humans have long yearned for in the context of the theological imagination.

4-667. Schochet, Victoria, and Melissa Singer, eds. **The Berkley Showcase: Volume 5.** Berkley, 1982.

Last in a series of original anthologies, notable for being tied to a particular publisher rather than an editor. Upheavals in the publishing industry during the last ten years forced many of the original anthologies to fold or switch publishers, and this series was essentially vulnerable to such changes of market strategy. It tended to be more traditionally inclined than *Universe* [4-642] or *New Dimensions* [4-664].

4-668. Sheckley, Robert, ed. **After the Fall.** Sphere, 1980.

Theme anthology of original stories, eccentrically electing to deal with an essentially downbeat theme in an essentially upbeat manner, thus producing some unusually ironic material and some nice black comedy. Features three stories by Zelazny, plus Disch, Farmer, and Shaw.

4-669. Sterling, Bruce, ed. **Mirrorshades: The Cyberpunk Anthology.** Arbor House, 1986.
Reprint anthology of the latest self-declared New Wave movement in American SF, edited by one of the major proponents of and propagandists for "cyberpunk," which aspires to provide a streetwise and cynical assessment of future possibilities generated by the new information technology. Other leading figures in the movement—William Gibson, John Shirley, and Rudy Rucker prominent among them—are of course represented.

4-670. Sturgeon, Theodore, introducer. **New Soviet Science Fiction.** Macmillan, 1979.
A representative anthology of modern Soviet SF, featuring most of the major writers from the U.S.S.R. with the exception of the Strugatskiis, whose work was independently featured in the complementary collection *Noon: 22nd Century* (1978). Earlier anthologies along the same lines include *The Ultimate Threshold* (1970), edited by Mirra Ginsburg. Darko Suvin's anthology, *Other Worlds, Other Seas* (1970), also features a good deal of Soviet SF alongside stories from other Warsaw Pact countries. *Soviet Literature No. 1* (1982) offered an anthology of "Science Fiction of Today," which should also be compared to these volumes. They provide an interesting contrast of perspectives with American SF.

4-671. Torgeson, Roy, ed. **Chrysalis 10.** Doubleday, 1983.
Latest (and apparently last) in a series of original anthologies begun by Torgeson's Zebra Books in 1978. Appeared more frequently than its models, but was always less impressive even as a showcase for not yet established writers.

4-672. Wollheim, Donald A., and Arthur W. Saha, eds. **The 1986 Annual World's Best SF.** DAW, 1986.
The latest in the longest running series of best-of-the-year anthologies, begun by Wollheim and Terry Carr for Ace in 1965. Most of the DAW editions, though not all, have been co-credited to Saha. Despite Wollheim's reputation for favoring traditional material he has always been reasonably eclectic in selecting stories for these anthologies, and although he is slightly inclined to favor DAW authors he is a reliable spotter of stories that subsequently win awards.

*4-673. Zebrowski, George, ed. **Nebula Awards 20.** Harcourt, 1985.
The Nebula Award anthologies, unlike the Hugo Award anthologies [4-634], cover one year at a time, including selected nominees as well as winners. They are effectively best-of-the-year anthologies, although they tend to be published somewhat later than the other such series, and their annual schedule has occasionally been disturbed by changes of publisher. Each volume has a different editor, which can cause confusion for individuals and institutions trying to establish a set. The first anthology (published 1966) covered the year 1965 and was edited by Damon Knight. The intervening volumes, with editors and years of publication are: 2 (Aldiss and Harrison, 1967); 3 (Zelazny, 1968); 4 (Anderson, 1969); 5 (Blish, 1970); 6 (Simak, 1971); 7 (Biggle, 1972); 8 (Asimov, 1973); 9 (Wilhelm,

1974); 10 (Gunn, 1975); 11 (Le Guin, 1976); 12 (Dickson, 1978); 13 (Delany, 1980); 14 (Pohl, 1980); 15 (Herbert, 1981); 16 (Pournelle, 1982); 17 (Haldeman, 1983); 18 (Silverberg, 1983); and 19 (Randall, 1984). Most editions, including the present one, have some supporting material in the shape of essays and bibliographical supplements. The fiction is generally outstanding, and provides an invaluable overview of the fashions and changes of taste in the evolution of SF throughout the modern period.

5

Children's and Young Adult Science Fiction

Francis J. Molson

Rocket Ship Galileo [5-63], written by Robert Heinlein and published in 1947, is generally considered the first American juvenile science fiction work to merit serious critical attention. For the first time—at least, as far as specialists in children's literature knew—an author expertly blended together characters, subject matter, and plot in a way that was novel, relevant, and appealing to young readers. Ross, Art, and Morrie, the protagonists in the story, were believable teenagers. The subject matter—a trip to the Moon in an atomic engine–powered rocket—was plausible extrapolation from current scientific knowledge; for who in 1947 had not heard of atomic power and the V-1 and V-2 rockets—technological breakthroughs that rendered possible a variety of schemes and proposals previously judged illusory or harebrained? The plot of the novel was both exciting and timely; not only a trip to the Moon and the discovery there of an extinct civilization, but the destruction of a lunar base from which a band of Nazis plotted World War III.

There was another reason why the specialists were willing to praise *Rocket Ship Galileo*. The novel fit nicely into a recently developed genre, the junior novel, designed to appeal to teenagers by acknowledging their existence and speaking to their special needs. For Ross, Art, and Morrie, like many other American teenagers, fretted over vocational goals. They even debated whether they should obey their parents, who at first would not allow the boys to accompany Dr. Cargraves, eminent scientist and Morrie's uncle, on his flight to the Moon; however, Cargraves convinced the boys' parents that going to the Moon would be not only adventurous but educational and character building. Seen as a junior novel, then, *Rocket Ship Galileo* easily met the important didactic requirements demanded of literature aimed at young readers. Thus, science fiction, once it was demonstrated that it could be written competently and contain didactic elements, was allowed to enter the mainstream of children's literature.

The publication of *Rocket Ship Galileo* may have marked mainstream children's literature recognition of SF and its potential for engaging youth, but the book did not initiate children's and young adult (YA) SF. Prior to 1947 young readers had ready access to popular SF literature specifically written for them or easily comprehensible. As early as the late 1870s, for instance, the Frank Reade and Frank Reade, Jr., stories, perhaps the most important SF series in nineteenth-century America, began to appear. Begun by Harry Eaton and continued by Luis Senarens, who contributed most of the 187 Reade stories (reprinted in ten volumes by Garland Publishing), these adventures not only chronicled the exploits of a boy genius responsible for many remarkable inventions, but in Jules Verne–like fashion strewed the exploits over a wide geographic area. Other science adventure stories, modeled on or similar to the successful Reade pattern, could be found in the Tom Edison, Jr., Happy Days, Pluck and Luck, and the British The Boys' Own Paper series.

Not long after the heydey of the Reade stories, the Edward Stratemeyer syndicate, alert to possible changes and new trends in youths' reading tastes, decided that science adventure might still attract young readers. Accordingly, in 1906 Stratemeyer published in hard cover the first volume in what came to be called the Great Marvel series, *Through the Air to the North Pole* [5-136], written by Roy Rockwood, a syndicate house name and, most likely, actually Howard Garis, Stratemeyer's most effective author. Perhaps the most interesting of early SF for boys, the Great Marvel books, with their distinctive Jules Verne flavor, eventually numbered nine titles. Stratemeyer, apparently convinced that the juvenile market for science adventure was real and might sustain a regular series, released in 1910 five titles of a proposed series focused on another boy inventor and his "marvelous" achievements—Tom Swift [5-6]. Written by Victor Appleton, another house name and, again, really Howard Garis, the Tom Swift books proved most successful, totaling 40 titles before their demise in 1941 and becoming one of the two or three most popular series of the twentieth century.

There were other series competing with Tom Swift and the Great Marvel adventures for the attention of young boys enthusiastic for SF; girls, as was typical of the time, were deemed a priori "uninterested or unsuited for science or strenuous adventure." Prominent among these were: Hancock's The Conquest of the United States [5-58]; Bonner's The Boy Inventors; two called The Radio Boys—one by Gerald Breckinridge, the other by Allen Chapman; Howard Garis's Rocket Riders; and Snell's Radiophone Boys. Perhaps the most imaginative of these rivals to Tom Swift were the four volumes of Claudy's Adventures in the Unknown [5-36], actually expansions and revisions of stories first published in *American Boy*. Finally, youngsters' dreams of interplanetary adventure were realized during the 1930s in tales of Buck Rogers and Flash Gordon in the comics and then in Big Little Books.

Youngsters, however, did not have to limit their reading to children's series books. What would be called today adult SF, often in pulp form, was available to the young. It was not until the last decades of the nineteenth century that distinctions between children's books and adult ones began to be drawn with any kind of precision. Thus, young and old readers might be reading Verne, Wells, or Burroughs. Further, some youngsters, even when popular children's SF was available, probably skipped it and read adult SF. Isaac Asimov, for example, when speaking of his youth, does not mention reading children's SF, but he does vividly recall reading copies of *Science Wonder Stories, Amazing Stories,* and *Air Wonder Stories,* which were for sale on his father's newsstand.

Within the mainstream itself, certain books, usually fantasies, indirectly contributed to the development of space fantasy or SF. For instance, Robinson Crusoe's narrative of survival on a strange island and Gulliver's adventures among the astonishing miniature and gigantic peoples were read also by children and soon became staples of their reading fare, presumably whetting an appetite for similar adventure tales. Charles Delorme (pseudonym of Charles Rumball) in *The Marvellous and Incredible Adventures of Charles Thunderbolt in the Moon* (1851) implied the possibility of space adventure and to that extent predated Verne. Elbert Perce's *Gulliver Loi, His Three Voyages: Being an Account of His Marvelous Adventures in Kailo, Hydrogenia, and Ejano* (1852) contains one of the very first references to space travel by rocket. Charles Kingsley's *The Water Babies* (1863) moralized excessively, but it did utilize the fantasy mode to inform its readers of both the science of underwater life and the theory of evolution; thus, the latter appeared for the first time as a topic in children's literature. The stories of Alice's journeys not only introduced children to wonderlands where ordinary reason is eschewed, but, by entertaining their young readers, sought to undermine the dictum that children's books had to teach earnestly and ought not waste or "murder" time. Albert E. Hooper's *Up the Moonstair* (1890) placed lunar inhabitants on the hidden side of the Moon to escape the prying eyes of Earth's astronomers; Howard Pyle's *The Garden behind the Moon* saw the moonlight as a bridge from Earth to the Moon; and in Frances Montgomery's *The Electrical Elephant* (1903) and its sequel *On a Lark to the Planets* (1904), the young protagonists, because of the electrically powered mechanical elephant, traveled worldwide and in space. L. Frank Baum, attempting in many of his books an indigenous American fantasy, saw in electricity a peculiarly appropriate American material for imaginative treatment and wrote *The Master Key* [5-9]. Baum should also be given credit for creating one of the first fully realized robots in children's literature, Tik Tok, who was introduced in *Ozma of Oz* (1902) and seven years later had its own book, *Tik-Tok of Oz.* And, as a final instance, Hugh Lofting, in *Doctor Dolittle in the Moon* (1929), sent his inestimable and much-traveled hero out into space for further adventures.

After the popular and critical success of *Rocket Ship Galileo,* mainstream publishers did not take long to realize that juvenile science fiction might prove profitable. By 1958, at least 90 additional science fiction titles, excluding series books, were published in the United States alone. Although this amount hardly seems impressive, the total was indeed large in comparison with preceding years when virtually nothing appeared, and it indicated that science fiction was well on its way to becoming an important subgenre of both American and British children's literature. The relatively sudden popularity and acceptance of children's science fiction in the 1950s can be attributed to many causes: the pioneering work of Heinlein, who went on writing other good juveniles; the emergence of a handful of genuinely talented writers, such as Andre Norton and Alan Nourse, who wanted to write for young audiences; the continuing development of preteens and teenagers as separate groups requiring their own reading material (most of the new titles were addressed to these groups); the growing popularity of science fiction, not only in novels and short stories but in the two media that drew teenagers and preteens as avid fans, film and comics—1950 saw in the British *The Eagle* the initial appearance of the hugely successful Dan Dare comic; and the Sputnik phenomenon and resulting interest in space and its exploration, which rendered less suspect and flamboyant the speculation of science fiction.

It would be pleasant to claim that most of the children's science fiction in the 1950s was well done, but the truth is the opposite. Children's literature, historically, has been burdened with hackwork, and juvenile science fiction is no exception. Too many publishers, eager to take advantage of the interest in science fiction, were willing to accept any manuscript dealing with a first trip to the Moon, life on Venus, or a visitor from Mars or some other planet, provided the story had for protagonists youngsters—and sometimes even animals, virtually eschewed all references to sex, and ostensibly had some educational or moral value. For instance, in Leslie Greener's *Moon Ahead* (1951), Noel and Frank and their fathers are invited to go along on a rocket flight to the Moon. A plethora of scientific and procedural information clogs the narrative, and the adventures on the Moon are tepid and predictable. In Carl Biemiller's *The Magic Ball from Mars* (1953), J, a young boy meets a mysterious visitor from Mars who gives him a magic ball because J believed in the stranger. The U.S. military appeals to J's patriotism in order to get the ball, which will grant any wish, but the Martians, fearing the possibility of planetwide war, take back the ball without even allowing J to decide whether he might voluntarily return it. Martians and the first trip to the Moon are combined subject matter in Mary Patchett's *Send for Johnny Danger* (1956). The first humans on the Moon, Johnny Danger and his crew, readily escape from their Martian captors, who, although able to colonize the Moon because of their very advanced technology, are inexplicably unable to cope with human beings. Or, as another example, in Ruthven Todd's *Space Cat* (1952), Flyball, a cat, accidentally becomes a crew member on a rocket to the Moon, finds sentient life there, saves his captain, and returns to Earth a hero. This work, incidentally, illustrates the problems confronting anyone who wants to write science fiction for the younger child. Generally speaking, trying to organize a picture book around a scientific principle or technological procedure is difficult because of the intended audience's lack of scientific knowledge. Consequently, the author opts for little or no science at all, and the result is best labeled space fancy—for example, a picture book about talking cats or monkeys acting as space pilots, or about metal-eating monsters from space.

Three features of children's and YA science fiction from the 1950s deserve particular attention. The first is the contribution that the John C. Winston Company made to the emerging subgenre. Under the editorial direction of Cecile Matschat and Carl Carmer, Winston published 26 novels in the 1950s, almost one-third of the juvenile SF released during that decade. (Gregg Press reprinted several of them.) As a group, the novels still make for interesting and mildly entertaining reading; some of the novels—for example, Raymond Jones's *Planet of Light* (1953), Oliver's *Mists of Dawn* [5-129], Anderson's *Vault of the Ages* [5-4], and North's *The Ant Men* [5-115]—compare quite favorably, in imaginative conception, style, and narrative pace, with the typical children's SF novel written today. The format of the Winston novels clearly reveals the editors' perspicacity. Usually each of the stories was preceded by an introduction in which the author summarized briefly the then-current information about a particular planet (such as Venus or Saturn), or natural phenomena (such as ESP or the possibility of timeslips), or a particular scientific discipline (such as archaeology or oceanography), and then, even more briefly, speculated about future changes or applications. The narratives that followed supposedly embodied or illustrated the speculation; thus, whatever entertainment or escape the narrative provided would be justified by the speculation. In this way, the didacticism expected of children's books was incorporated into the Winston novels, and science fiction, "cheapened" in the eyes of librarians, teachers, and concerned parents by its association with pulps, series books, and comics, would be elevated and made respectable. Fortunately for the reader, the narratives are, generally speaking, relatively unencumbered by ill-digested blocks of information and speculation, and they succeed, or fail, primarily as storytelling and not as instruction.

The second noteworthy feature of children's SF in the 1950s was the rekindling of interest in SF series fiction. The same year of *Rocket Ship Galileo*'s release, Grosset & Dunlap published John Blaine's *The Rocket's Shadow* [5-17] and three other titles as part of a prospective series devoted to Rick Brant's Electronic Adventures, which ultimately included 23 volumes. Other series were begun: Carey Rockwell's Tom Corbett, Space Cadet books, Jay Williams and Raymond Abrashkin's Danny Dunn adventures (still popular) [5-171], and, perhaps most appropriately, a new Tom Swift series. Interestingly, for the new series the "sons" of both the author and the hero were involved: Victor Appleton II wrote 33 stories about Tom Swift, Jr. At the end of the decade, two additional series were inaugurated: Dig Allen by Joseph Greene and Mike Mars by Donald Wollheim. Clearly, the renewal of interest in series SF and its acceptance by youngsters suggest that mainstream children's SF in its short history not only has been sustained by itself but has contributed to popular culture manifestations of science fiction.

The third feature that should be noted concerning SF for young readers in the 1950s is the relatively high number of titles—about one-third, which includes many of the Winston novels—produced by already established authors of science fiction. The names of those who have written for both children and adults include some of the most prominent authors of science fiction: Isaac Asimov, Robert Silverberg, Donald Wollheim, Poul Anderson, James Blish, Ben Bova, Arthur Clarke, Lester del Rey, Gordon Dickson, Murray Leinster, Andre Norton, Jack Vance, and Harry Harrison. Of more than passing interest is the possibility that some of these "name" authors might have been forced, were it not for their juvenile SF output, to cease writing science fiction. Unfortunately, the evidence also suggests that several were not above placing hackwork in the supposedly lucrative juvenile market. On the other hand, the competent work of Heinlein, Norton, Bova, del Rey, and Dickson provided direction to and some prestige for children's science fiction until new talent, seriously committed to writing for children and unwilling to compromise, entered the field in the next three decades.

Since the 1950s children's and YA science fiction has definitely come of age. An overreliance on first trips to the Moon or meeting Martians has been abandoned, and new and wider-ranging topics have been essayed. The political abuses of behavior modification and mind control, for instance, are a central concern in John Christopher's novels, Sleator's *House of Stairs* [5-143], and Ames's *Anna to the Infinite Power* [5-2]. ESP has become a favorite topic; especially fine examples are Virginia Hamilton's *Justice and Her Brothers* and its two sequels [5-57], and Joan Vinge's *Psion* [5-160]. Theological speculation can be found in the novels of Madeleine L'Engle, in particular her time trilogy [5-96] and *The Young Unicorns* (1968), and of Alexander Key [5-88]. The sexism historically so endemic in children's books (as well as in SF in general) is also under attack, especially in the novels of Sylvia Engdahl, H. M. Hoover, and Monica Hughes, whose central protagonists are girls or young women who are assigned tasks usually given males, and in Robert O'Brien's *Z for Zachariah* [5-127], which depicts the tragic shortcomings of conventional male-female relationships even in the aftermath of catastrophe. The evils of racism are explored candidly in Piers Anthony's *Race against Time* [5-5], Monica Hughes's *The Keeper of the Isis Light* and its two sequels [5-77], A. M. Lightner's *The Day of the Drones* [5-97], Craig Strete's *The Bleeding Man and Other Science Fiction Stories* [5-150], and Laurence Yep's *Sweetwater* [5-179]. The ecological movement, as expected, is becoming a more common topic. For example, James R. Berry's *Dar Tellum: Stranger from a Distant Planet* [5-14], one of the few SF picture books that work, argues for conservation; and Adrien Stoutenburg's *Out There* [5-149] is a study of human destruction of other species and its effect on a future where expeditions are organized to find any traces of animal life. Finally, as might be anticipated in fiction designed for youth, the conflict between the demands of society and individual freedom continues to be portrayed but in more contemporary terms: Dale Carlson and Danny Carlson's *The Shining Pool* [5-26], Hoover's *The Lost Star* [5-71], John Rowe Townsend's *The Creatures* [5-155], and Robert Westall's *Futuretrack 5* [5-167].

Perhaps the best evidence that children's science fiction has become a permanent, important segment of children's literature is twofold. One aspect is that children's science fiction, at ease with itself and confident of its value, can make fun of itself as in the Matthew Looney books of Jerome Beatty [5-10], which, describing Moon inhabitants' debating whether Earth can support any life, gently parody stock situations and attitudes. The other aspect is that the mainstream has granted science fiction its highest awards. L'Engle's *A Wrinkle in Time* [5-96], with its talk of time warps and its depiction of a world ruled by a computer that exemplifies the worst features of behavior modification and mind control, won the Newbery Medal in 1963 as the best children's book of the year. And Robert C. O'Brien's *Mrs. Frisby and the Rats of NIMH* [5-126], the story of rats who have become superintelligent through psychological and biological experimentation and who build themselves a utopian society, was awarded the 1972 Newbery Medal.

It is only fitting that young adult fiction, successor to the junior or teen novel of the 1940s and 1950s, some of whose major conventions Heinlein incorporated into his pioneering juveniles, continues featuring SF. In their *Literature for Today's Young Adults,* second edition (1985), Alleen Nilsen and Kenneth Donelson claim that SF enjoys tremendous popularity among teens and cite as evidence the popularity of not just the fiction itself but also SF film, TV tie-ins, and SF conventions. Nilsen and Donelson believe that the reasons for the popularity of SF among young adults are that SF is exciting reading, refuses to patronize its audience, permits young adults to read imaginative fiction without feeling it is "kid stuff," presents attractive, real heroes at a time when the world is too often perceived as devoid of anyone worth admiring, and encourages its readers to be intellectually curious. Among the authors judged most appealing to young adults are Heinlein, L'Engle, and H. M. Hoover.

The list of annotated titles that follows is selective. I have personally handled and read all the books. (Numbers in parentheses after the year of publication indicate suggested reader age levels.) All of the titles meet the criteria outlined in Chapter 3 by Joe De Bolt and John Pfeiffer. In making these selections, I have been guided more by the needs of the general reader, the classroom teacher, and the librarian, and less by those of the specialist or "fan" of SF. There are several consequences of this approach. First, I have consulted extensively the reviews and commentary in the *Horn Book Magazine, School Library Journal,* the *Booklist, Bulletin of the Center for Children's Books, Language Arts,* and *Children's Literature.* At the same time, I have consulted the various bibliographic and critical resources of adult science fiction; particularly helpful have been *Locus* [14-37], *Luna Monthly, Delap's SF and F Review, Science Fiction and Fantasy Book Review, Fantasy Review* [14-35], and *The Year's Scholarship in Science Fiction and Fantasy* [8-17]. Second, the books selected, in addition to being within the conventional age levels—for example, 9 to 12 or 13 and above—are those that are well written; illustrate aptly a particular theme, approach, and direction in science fiction; or represent the multivolume work of an author such as Norton, Heinlein, or Walters. Third, most of the books annotated have been published since 1947, for reasons that should be clear from what has been said above.

Readers seeking further information about children's and YA science fiction have several sources. First is the book-length study, two of which have appeared in very recent years. In 1981 Lillian Biermann Wehmeyer's *Images in a Crystal Ball: World Futures in Novels for Young People* (Libraries Unlimited) was published. Containing over 150 annotations and extensive commentary, Biermann's book is didactic and classroom-oriented as she lays out a rather elaborate program built around children's and YA science fiction for developing or supplementing instructional units in futuristics. Obviously the value of Biermann's program depends on teachers' conviction that not only does futuristics belong in the classroom but the didactic potential of SF should be tapped even at the risk of neglecting or distorting its potential to entertain. More critical than Biermann's study is Janice Antczak's *Science Fiction: The Mythos of a New Romance* [13-3]. Focusing on novels for children 8 to 14, Antczak argues that SF can be read as the story of a modern quest and, hence, is organized around the structure and pattern of the quest. This new manifestation of an ancient pattern, along with the romantic nature of SF, presumably attracts young readers and provides them a way to cope with the possible futures confronting them. Unfortunately, Antczak's emphasis on SF as traditional quest in modern form, regardless of her stated intent, tends to present SF as essentially conservative rather than estranging or critical.

A second source of information is the individual essay. Most helpful are:

Adams, John, "Linkages: Science Fiction and Science Fantasy," *School Library Journal* 26 (May 1980): 23.

Children's Literature Association Quarterly, Winter 1981 issue devoted to SF, which included Eleanor Cameron, "Fantasy, SF and the Mushroom Planet Books"; Francis Molson, "Writing for the 'Electric Boy': Notes on the Origins of Children's SF"; David Greene, "L. Frank Baum: SF and Fantasy"; Carol Stevens, "SF in the Classroom."

Children's Literature Association Quarterly, Summer 1985 issue devoted to SF, which included Francis Molson, "Three Generations of Tom Swift"; C. W. Sullivan, III, "Heinlein's Juveniles: Still Contemporary after All These Years"; Virginia Wolf, "Andre Norton: Feminist Pied Piper"; Janice Antczak, "The Visions of H. M. Hoover."

Engdahl, Sylvia L., "The Changing Role of Science Fiction in Children's Literature," *The Horn Book Magazine* 47 (October 1971): 450.

Esmonde, Margaret, "From Little Buddy to Big Brother: The Icon of the Robot in Children's Science Fiction," in *The Mechanical God: Machines in Science Fiction,* edited by Thomas P. Dunn and Richard D. Erlich (Greenwood, 1982).

Greenlaw, M. Jean, "Science Fiction: Impossible! Improbable! or Prophetic," *Elementary English* 48 (April 1971): 201.

McCaulet, Virginia, "Out of This World: A Bibliography of Space Literature for Boys and Girls," *Elementary English* 36 (February 1959): 98.

Molson, Francis, "The Winston Science Fiction Series and the Development of Children's Science Fiction," *Extrapolation* 25 (Spring 1984): 34.

Moskowitz, Sam, "Teen-Agers: Tom Swift and the Syndicate," in *Strange Horizons: The Spectrum of Science Fiction,* edited by Sam Moskowitz (Scribner, 1976).

Nodelman, Perry, "Out There in Children's Science Fiction: Forward into the Past," *Science-Fiction Studies* 12 (November 1985): 255.

Roberts, Thomas, "Science Fiction and the Adolescent," *Children's Literature* 2 (1973): 86.

Svilpis, Jānis, "Authority, Autonomy, and Adventure in Juvenile Science Fiction," *Children's Literature Association Quarterly* 8 (Fall 1983): 22.

A third source of information is the work of adult SF criticism or commentary, which occasionally alludes to children's or YA science fiction and its authors. The most useful is *The Science Fiction Encyclopedia* [8-30], although its informative entries are needlessly flawed by ambiguous use of the term *juvenile,* which usually denotes children's books but sometimes seems to refer to first works by authors and now and then even puerile books. Also useful is Tuck's *The Encyclopedia of Science Fiction and Fantasy through 1968* [8-7].

Bibliography

5-1. Allum, Tom (U.K.). **Boy beyond the Moon.** Bobbs, 1960. British title: *Emperor of Space,* 1959 (11–14).
Guy Abbot meets Professor Harvey, a famous expert in interplanetary travel whose innovative spaceship is rejected as unworkable by the government. Unexpectedly the professor dragoons four escaped prisoners and Guy as a crew and they take off for Emperor, the mysterious planet. The journey out, the sudden death of Harvey, encountering prehistoric fish and tremendous purplish fires, a mutiny by the prisoners, a rescue party, and a novel return to Earth make up the adventures. Accurate scientific information; an above-average space adventure with a refreshingly different set of characters. Contrast Claudy's *The Mystery Men of Mars* [5-36].

5-2. Ames, Mildred. **Anna to the Infinite Power.** Scribner, 1981 (12 up).
Esteemed a perfect student, superintelligent, amoral Anna suddenly begins to question her identity when she spots an exact look-alike, and sets out, with the help of her brother, to solve the mystery. Credible characterization and poignant conclusion enhance a gripping story of cloning experimentation. Compare Bova's *Exiled from Earth* [5-21]; contrast Hoover's *Children of Morrow* [5-70].

5-3. Ames, Mildred. **Is There Life on a Plastic Planet?** Dutton, 1975 (13 up).
Overweight and friendless, Holly meets the proprietor of a strange doll shop and accepts from her a lifelike, identical-to-her doll to substitute for the girl in school and then at home. Becoming afraid when the doll insists it is Holly, the girl must struggle to escape the shop, which, she realizes, contains dolls of some of her classmates. Ominous in tone, suspenseful and sensitive in its characterization of troubled children, the novel effectively combines science fiction and the gothic.

5-4. Anderson, Poul. **Vault of the Ages.** Winston, 1952 (12 up).
Five hundred years after the "Doom," the Lann army from the north invades the peaceful Dale country and threatens the vestiges of civilization. Escaping from marauding Lanns, Carl stumbles on a time vault among the ruins of a city, which summarizes in books and containers past scientific and human knowledge for the use of whatever people survive the nuclear holocaust. Carl determines that the store of knowledge, instead of being taboo, is needed by the people, who may, it is hoped, profit wisely. However, both the Lann army and ignorance must be overcome before the time vault can open its riches. Brisk adventure, well written, effective in dramatizing human ambivalence before the potential of knowledge.

*5-5. Anthony, Piers. **Race against Time.** Hawthorn, 1973 (14 up).
Six teens, representing "true Caucasians, Negroids, and Mongoloids," suspect that they are being brought up in a zoolike setting. Breaking out and painfully learning the true reason for their segregation, the youths decide to return to the "banks" where they resolve to master their distinctive cultures and prepare to become an elite. An exceptionally well paced opening highlights a provocative look at a possible future grounded in racial purity and cultural equality. Compare Lightner's *The Day of the Drones* [5-97].

5-6. Appleton, Victor. **Tom Swift and His Electric Rifle.** Grosset & Dunlap, 1911 (9–11).

Having perfected his new electric rifle, Tom decides to try it out on an elephant hunt in Africa. With friends Ned Newton, Mr. Damon, and Durban, who is an elephant hunter, Tom takes off for Africa in the *Black Hawk,* his newest airship. There he becomes embroiled in native attacks, rescuing various whites, and tracking down lions and elephants. One of a group of five books published concurrently and written by the Edward Stratemeyer syndicate, its hero is young, inventive genius Tom Swift, who is easily superior to his contemporaries and able to overcome all dangers. So popular were the books that they eventually totaled 38 volumes. Like series fiction then and now, the Tom Swift books emphasize rapidity of incident and stereotypical characterization. Oddly, none of the books deals with space travel or extraterrestrial life, the two most common topics of science fiction.

5-7. Asimov, Isaac (as Paul French). **David Starr: Space Ranger.** Doubleday, 1952 (12 up).

To an Earth suffering from overpopulation, its Martian colony is a necessary breadbasket. When poisoned food begins to turn up, David Starr, agent of the Council of Science, is sent to investigate and uncovers an alien conspiracy. Routine adventure story, among the first space operas for children; significant also because of the special status of its author. There are five other David Starr adventures: *Lucky Starr and the Pirates of the Asteroids* (1953), *Lucky Starr and the Oceans of Venus* (1954), *Lucky Starr and the Big Sun of Mercury* (1956), *Lucky Starr and the Moons of Jupiter* (1957), and *Lucky Starr and the Rings of Saturn* (1958).

5-8. Ballou, Arthur W. **Bound for Mars.** Little, Brown, 1970 (12–14).

The *Pegasus,* under command of Colonel Sanborn, is scheduled to place the first permanent station on Mars. For this historically important mission, the crew has been most carefully screened, physically and psychologically. However, George Foran, the youngest crew member, cracks under the strain and threatens the ship's safety. Carefully the commander entraps Foran, and the mission continues. Actual incidents are not, per se, much above routine; what is impressive is the authentic detailing of on-board procedures, especially the in-space repair of one sled that malfunctions. Highly recommended for hard science fiction devotees.

5-9. Baum, L(yman) Frank. **The Master Key: An Electrical Fairy Tale.** Bowen-Merrill, 1901 (10 up).

Rob Joslyn, precocious tinkerer in things electrical, accidentally hits the Master Key and summons the Demon of Electricity. Like the genie of old, the Demon provides Rob with various devices—a travel machine, a "blaster," a garment shield, food tablets, a recorder of ongoing events, and spectacles that distinguish good and evil—that utilize electrical or magnetic power. Each device, although working "magically" to the observer, is explained on scientific grounds—explanations asserted but not demonstrated. Rob enjoys numerous adventures around the world, but decides to return the devices to the Demon because people are not wise enough to handle advanced technology. Routine adventure spiced by early-twentieth-century American chauvinism; early science fantasy. Important pioneering attempt to adapt current science to traditional fantasy to create an American fairy tale.

5-10. Beatty, Jerome, Jr. **Matthew Looney's Voyage to the Earth.** Scott, 1961 (10 up).
Matthew is selected to accompany his uncle on a flight to Earth to test for life and utility. No life can be found since the landing occurs at the South Pole. However, it is Matthew's recorded observation of his pet's going into water and living that vindicates the voyage and shows that life can exist on Earth. A lighthearted spoof of science fiction formulas; enjoyable for both juveniles and adults and enhanced by Gahan Wilson's droll illustrations. Matthew's adventures are continued in *Matthew Looney's Invasion of the Earth* (1965), *Matthew Looney in the Outback* (1969), and *Matthew Looney and the Space Pirates* (1972). Presumably for girls are the adventures of Matthew's sister: *Maria Looney on the Red Planet* (1977), *Maria Looney and the Cosmic Circus* (1978), and *Maria Looney and the Remarkable Robot* (1979).

5-11. Bell, Clare. **Ratha's Creature.** Atheneum, 1983 (12 up).
Long ago in an alternate world, a band of intelligent wild cats, the Named, survive because Ratha dares to use fire as a weapon against predatory cat raiders, the UnNamed. Believable characterization, vivid, accurate details, and plausible incidents make for a fascinating story. Sequel is *Clan Ground* (1984), in which Ratha faces challenges to her leadership and use of fire. Compare Norton's Star Ka'at series [5-119].

5-12. Bell, William Dixon. **The Moon Colony.** Goldsmith, 1937 (12–14).
Julian and Joan Epsworth, captured by the great, evil scientist Toplinsky, are forced to accompany him to the Moon, where a colony is being formed and eventual invasion of Earth organized. Before the brother and sister can return to Earth, they survive attacks by Toplinsky's colonists and crickets, controlled by a beauteous and evil Amazon-like queen, Carza, and lead lunar pygmies and their queen, Moawha, against Carza. Nonmainstream children's space adventure; constantly shifts from fact and informed extrapolation (such as rocket technology) to brutal violence and romance with even a hint of sex. Compare Burroughs's "Under the Moons of Mars" [1-17].

*5-13. Benford, Greg(ory). **Jupiter Project.** Nelson, 1975; 2nd ed., 1980 (14 up).
What prevents the Astronautical-Biological Laboratory orbiting Jupiter, which has had no luck in finding life and justifying its high cost, from closing is young Matt Bowles's accidental discovery of Jovian bacteria. Expertly and plausibly, the novel weaves together details of the operations of a scientific expedition in space, the problems of a closed-in society, and the challenges and difficulties of growing up. Through additional material—in particular, scenes of explicit sexual activity—the second edition amplifies the sociological and rite-of-passage dimensions. Compare Williamson's *Trapped in Space* [5-174] and Marsten's *Rocket to Luna* [5-107]; contrast Stone's *The Mudhead* [5-147].

5-14. Berry, James R. **Dar Tellum: Stranger from a Distant Planet.** Illus. by E. Scull. Walker, 1973 (6–8).
Ralph makes contact with a plantlike life form, Dar Tellum, from the planet Sidra. As Earth is suffering from an overabundance of carbon dioxide in the atmosphere, Dar Tellum suggests placing certain algae in the atmosphere, and the problem of pollution is alleviated. A simple story; some humor; plenty of striking black-and-white illustrations. One of the few science fiction picture books that works. Compare Leek's *The Tree That Conquered the World* [5-95].

*5-15. Bethancourt, T. Ernesto. **The Mortal Instruments.** Holiday House, 1977 (13 up).
Humanity in the far future, evolving into bodiless energy, sends those few who cannot evolve into the past where they become geniuses or great leaders, both good and evil. Eddie Rodriguez is revealed as an evil genius who seeks to take over the computers of I.G.O. in order to dominate the world. Suspenseful, quick moving, well plotted, and superbly written, this is one of the best science fiction novels for young people. Sequel is *Instruments of Darkness* (1979), which manifests same high level of craftsmanship and interest.

5-16. Biemiller, Carl L. **The Hydronauts.** Doubleday, 1970 (12 up).
A postcatastrophe story. Because of great changes brought about by radiation, the seas have become the major source of food. Kim, Toby, Genright, and Tuktu are trainees in the Warden Service, which oversees the harvesting of the oceans. Patrolling the kelp forests, guarding the shark pens, and tracking down a mysterious hostile power provide the four ample adventure and experience. Provocative look at future marine life, harvesting the sea, and water-survival techniques; taut writing; credible characterization. Compare Clarke's *Dolphin Island* [5-33]. Subsequent adventures of the quartet are found in *Follow the Whales: The Hydronauts Meet the Otter People* (1973) and *Escape from the Crater: More Adventures of the Hydronauts* (1974).

5-17. Blaine, John. **The Rocket's Shadow.** Grosset, 1947 (8–11).
Rick Brant, a young inventor of electronic devices, is caught up in intrigue aimed at preventing, if not destroying, his father's experimental Moon rocket. Although atypical in that the hero's inventive skills are modest, the narrative is typical series fiction in its emphasis on incident, routine characterization, and bland style. The first of 24 volumes, and the first of the second wave of series science fiction for boys that began after World War II.

5-18. Blish, James. **Mission to the Heart Stars.** Putnam, 1965 (14 up).
The flight of the starship *Argo* across the galaxy is the occasion for an investigation into the various forms taken by societies that Earth might face in the future. Stability versus change, self-satisfaction versus curiosity, coercion versus tolerance, are the poles around which these societies are organized; another topic of investigation is the way society is affected by technological advancement and sheer lasting power. Although lacking in exciting adventures, the novel contains ample, provocative speculation and discussion. Compare Heinlein's *Citizen of the Galaxy* [5-61].

*5-19. Bond, Nancy. **The Voyage Begun.** Atheneum, 1981 (13 up).
In a future where pollution, energy shortages, and changes in the climate severely affect the economy, Paul takes part in an apparently harebrained scheme to help old Walter Jepson build a boat. Impressive narrative; distinctive characters, most of whom are rendered to a degree rarely found in science fiction; especially sensitive nature description; convincing study of impact of changing environment on human life. Compare Corlett's *Return to the Gate* [5-37]; contrast Christopher's *Empty World* [5-28].

5-20. Bonham, Frank. **The Forever Formula.** Dutton, 1979 (12 up).
Awakening in a strange hospital and an even stranger world, dominated by the "super-old," Evan Clark realizes that he had been secretly frozen, misplaced, found, and then thawed so that his mind could be probed to reveal his father's formula to ensure hyperlongevity. The boy becomes a pawn in a struggle between those demanding "immortality" and those preferring mortality. Fast-paced, suspenseful, and fascinating portrait of a world where life for those 200 or more years old is privileged and for the "younger" is degrading and squalid. Contrast Heinlein's *Tunnel in the Sky* [5-66].

*5-21. Bova, Ben(jamin William). **Exiled from Earth.** Dutton, 1971 (13 up).
A world suffering from overpopulation fears genetic engineering, so the best geneticists and support scientists are banished to an orbiting satellite. Some scientists are mysteriously reprieved, but, Lou Christopher discovers, only to aid unwittingly a revolt that fails. Again banished, Lou convinces his associates that the only hope for the race's preservation is to aim for the stars, and they depart Earth. Tight, suspenseful writing, especially the description of Lou's escape attempt; thoughtful examination of science's need to be free. Compare Norton's *The Stars Are Ours* [5-121]. Story of the long flight to the stars and a new home is continued in two subsequent novels—*Flight of Exiles* (1972) and *End of Exile* (1975)—that conclude the Exiles trilogy.

5-22. Bova, Ben(jamin William). **The Winds of Altair.** Dutton, 1973 (12 up).
A plan to alter the hostile environment of Altair to one suitable for colonization by the teeming millions of Earth is thwarted by Jeff Holman. Having had his mind electronically channeled into that of a giant wolfcat, Jeff realizes how benign and supportive Altair's environment actually is to its native life. Quick-moving narrative, with low-keyed technological passages, reflects engagingly contemporary concern for conserving Earth's resources, in particular, animals. Compare Stoutenburg's *Out There* [5-149] and Lightner's *The Space Ark* [5-99].

5-23. Cameron, Eleanor. **The Wonderful Flight to the Mushroom Planet.** Little, Brown, 1954 (11–13).
When David and Chuck build a small spaceship and deliver it to Mr. Bass, the boys are informed of the existence of the mushroom planet, Basidium, which can be seen only by a special filter devised by Bass, and that they and their spaceship have been selected to check on conditions on Basidium. There the boys assist in preventing disaster by suggesting how more sulfur can be placed in the planet's diet. After their return, the boys can enjoy their triumph only in secret. Well-writ-

ten, mildly entertaining combination of science fiction and fantasy; popular with children. Other mushroom planet books are *Stowaway to the Mushroom Planet* (1956), *Mr. Bass's Planetoid* (1958), *A Mystery for Mr. Bass* (1960), and *Time and Mr. Bass* (1967).

5-24. Capon, Paul (U.K.). **Flight of Time.** Heinemann, 1960 (12–14).
A Wellsian time travel book. Four children, accidentally blundering into a UFO, travel to 2260 England. Then follows a glance both at futuristic cities, travel, and communication, and at alterations to the country's geography. More interesting is the adventure in the past, 1960 B.C. While observing a bloody battle between two Stone Age peoples over the talisman spaceship, the children are under attack and, just managing to activate the controls, return to the present. Above average in style. Compare Severn's *The Future Took Us* [5-139].

5-25. Capon, Paul (U.K.). **Lost: A Moon.** Bobbs-Merrill, 1956. British title: *Phobos, the Robot Planet,* 1955 (13 up).
Three vacationers are picked up by a small spaceship and brought to Phobos, the Martian satellite, which they learn is a highly complex automated machine that speaks English, picked up from another person previously kidnapped. Outwitting the machine, the four escape to Earth while bringing about the satellite's destruction. Well written stylistically, the novel features interesting, somewhat humorous characterization that instills some freshness into familiar Martian subject matter. Compare Wollheim's *The Secret of the Martian Moons* [5-177].

5-26. Carlson, Dale, and Danny Carlson. **The Shining Pool.** Atheneum, 1979 (14 up).
A light suddenly appearing in a nearby pool begins to dominate every youth in town except Ben, a teenager given to stubborn independence and reflection. Encouraged by a teacher versed in spirituality, Ben manages to fend off the light, actually an alien force seeking to expand itself at the expense of human individuality, and convinces it to leave Earth. Although a bit static, the novel is still unusual science fiction for youth in that it eschews routine approaches and uses instead philosophic speculation to articulate themes of individuality and freedom. Compare Bethancourt's *The Mortal Instruments* [5-15].

5-27. Chilton, Charles (U.K.). **Journey into Space.** Jenkins, 1954 (10–14).
With a crew of four, the *Luna* takes off on the first lunar flight. Arriving on the Moon, the crew encounters another spacecraft, attempts to escape, but is forced by the aliens to land on a planet that turns out to be Earth—but centuries ago. Competently written; suspenseful handling of on-board procedures; plausible details of time and space travel. Based on a very popular British radio series. Contrast Bell's *The Moon Colony* [5-12] or Heinlein's *Rocket Ship Galileo* [5-63].

5-28. Christopher, John (pseud. of Christopher Samuel Youd) (U.K.). **Empty World.** Hamish Hamilton, 1977 (14 up).
In spite of personal problems, Neil gradually realizes that virtually the entire world may soon die from plague. One of the few survivors, the teenager forces himself to master survival techniques. Even though the future of the race is literally at stake, Neil also learns that getting along with people, especially girls, is still not easy for him. Tersely written, somber in mood, and always believable, the

novel vividly recreates a postholocaust world; final note of hope is convincing. Compare O'Brien's *Z for Zachariah* [5-127]; contrast Parker's *The Hendon Fungus* [5-130].

5-29. Christopher, John (pseud. of Christopher Samuel Youd) (U.K.). **Fireball.** Gollancz, 1981 (12 up).
Drawn into a parallel world, similar to Roman Britain, Brad and Simon participate in the Bishop of London's successful revolt. When the ensuing regime promises to be repressive, the boys and two friends escape to the New World. Vintage Christopher: terse, plausible story continues author's investigation of various political systems and their treatment of individual rights. Sequels are *New Found Land* (1983) and *Dragon Dance* (1986), in which the friends journey to California. Compare Silverberg's *The Gate of Worlds* [5-141]; contrast Oliver's *Mists of Dawn* [5-129].

*5-30. Christopher, John (pseud. of Christopher Samuel Youd) (U.K.). **The Guardians.** Hamish Hamilton, 1970 (12–14).
England of 2052 is divided into two parts: the Conurb, a megalopolis teeming with unrest and pacified by bread and games, and the County, where the gentry pursue a rural life-style. Conurban Rob flees, after the mysterious death of his father, to the County, where he is befriended by the Giffords and passed off as gentry. In the course of an uprising, Rob learns the terrifying facts of the guardians' systematic repression of all dissident elements and, giving up an opportunity to become a guardian, leaves for the Conurb to join the revolutionary movement. Tautly written; thoughtful study of the potentially evil implications of behavioral modification and mind control. Winner of the Guardian Award, 1971. Contrast Severn's *The Future Took Us* [5-139].

5-31. Christopher, John (pseud. of Christopher Samuel Youd) (U.K.). **The Prince in Waiting.** Hamish Hamilton, 1970 (12–14).
After a series of earthquakes destroys much of civilization, England rebuilds following the pattern of medieval walled cities ruled over by the Spirits as they are interpreted by the seers. Thirteen-year-old Luke suddenly finds himself recognized when his father is selected Prince of Winchester. After his father's sudden death, Luke is forced to flee to the Sanctuary, where science and technology are preserved and augmented and the seers practice trickery to keep the people malleable. Luke also discovers that he is to be groomed to become prince of princes and reunite the cities. The first of a trilogy; the others, *Beyond the Burning Lands* (1971) and *The Sword of the Spirits* (1972), continue Luke's career as he fails at reunification through force and becomes content to wait and use peaceful means. As is typical of this author, dramatic interplay and ample incidents, investigation of both proper use of science and technology and individual rights versus society's needs. Compare Dickinson's *The Weathermonger* [5-43].

*5-32. Christopher, John (pseud. of Christopher Samuel Youd) (U.K.). **The White Mountains.** Hamish Hamilton, 1967 (12–14).
The first volume in the Tripod trilogy about a successful invasion of Earth by aliens and the eventual triumph by humans over the invaders. The tripods consolidate their control by inserting metal communicators into the heads of all adults;

thus, behavior modification is quick and brutal if need be. Will, Henry, and Jean Paul all fear the ceremony of capping that marks rites of passage and set out to join a small band of humans at the White Mountains who resist the tripods. Picture of future life in England after an alien invasion is convincing and troubling; journey of boys is exciting and suspenseful; tripods are suggestive of Wells. In *The City of Gold and Lead* (Hamish Hamilton, 1967), Will and Fritz enter the city of the masters to discover the nature of tripods and ascertain whether there is any way they can be overthrown. *The Pool of Fire* (Hamish Hamilton, 1968) describes the overthrow of tripods and their masters. However, an ominous note enters at the end when the various nations squabble among themselves.

5-33. Clarke, Arthur C(harles) (U.K.). **Dolphin Island.** Holt, 1963 (12–14).
A story of experiments on Dolphin Island to open up more effective communication with the dolphins. Johnny Clinton, unloved runaway, discovers a special affinity with dolphins when they rescue him from a sinking hovercraft. Later, after a great storm, he uses the dolphins to surf across to the mainland to bring medical aid. Characterization of humans and the incidents are routine; what is above average is the depiction of various experiments, current and future, with dolphins, all of which assume that one day dolphins and humans will communicate freely. Compare Merle's *The Day of the Dolphin* (1967).

5-34. Clarke, Arthur C(harles) (U.K.). **Islands in the Sky.** Winston, 1952 (12–15).
As his prize for winning a television quiz show in the second half of the twenty-first century, Roy Malcolm goes to an orbiting space station. There he has several adventures involving space pirates, the making of a space film, and a runaway rocket ship. The strength of the book, despite its publication date, is in the details, all plausibly explained, of the procedures of space travel and life on an orbiting station. The same thoroughness later seen in *2001: A Space Odyssey* [4-140] is clearly evident. As an adventure story, routine; as an investigation into the required technology necessary for space travel, exceptional.

5-35. Clarke, Joan B. (U.K.). **The Happy Planet.** Cape, 1963 (12–15).
A postcatastrophe story. Three future societies are contrasted: the Tuanians, descendants of the Getaways who left before the great destruction, are a technologically advanced, highly regimented people; the Hombods, descending from holocaust survivors, have established a semipastoral life that may make Earth a "happy planet"; and the Dredfooters, descended from cyborgs, attempt to prey on the Hombods. A Tuanian attempt to investigate Earth's utility is thwarted, and the planet is spared the joyless, rationalistic life of Tuan. Although a relatively thoughtful study of possible societies, its excessive length may hamper enjoyment.

5-36. Claudy, Carl H(arry). **Adventures in the Unknown: The Mystery Men of Mars.** Grosset, 1933 (11–13).
Ted and Adam are recruited by Professor Lutyens to accompany him on a rocket trip to Mars, where they are imprisoned by buglike, superintelligent Martians, whose plan to join human brains to the gigantic brain ruling the planet is foiled

by the professor, who gives his life to save the boys. Expanded from a story in *American Boy* and one of the Adventures in the Unknown, the novel aptly represents one of the two authors writing before Heinlein (the other is Roy Rockwood) whose imagination and storytelling ability still stand out. There were three sequels.

*5-37. Corlett, William. **Return to the Gate.** Bradbury, 1977 (14 up).
This conclusion to a trilogy dramatizing growth in self-knowledge and the necessity of risking friendship—the highly praised *The Gate of Eden* (1975) and *The Land Beyond* (1976) being the other segments—takes place in a not-too-distant future of violent social disintegration and painful rebuilding. Focus is on old age and its natural, although often unrealized, alliance with youth. The visionary is subordinate, but the portrait of love's insistence on no conditions is memorable for its lyrical terseness and allusiveness. Compare L'Engle's *A Wrinkle in Time* [5-96], where unconditional love is also demanded and the young and old are allies.

5-38. Craigie, David (pseud. of Dorothy M. Craigie) (U.K.). **The Voyage of the Luna 1.** Eyre & Spottiswoode, 1948 (12–14).
Martin and Jane Ridley, members of a British family famous for exploring, stow away on board a test rocket that precedes the first manned flight to the Moon. Once there the children encounter lunar ants, ash forests, snakes, and bats. While they explore the Moon, the second rocket is readied for their rescue, and the children return world-famous. A Jules Verne–like adventure with a premium on fanciful incidents and not science; firm and very British characterization; slowly developing story because of time devoted to background and minor characters. Compare Heinlein's *Rocket Ship Galileo* [5-63].

*5-39. Cross, John Keir (U.K.). **The Angry Planet.** Peter Lunn, 1945 (13–15).
Three children stow away on an experimental rocket ship bound for Mars. There they encounter the Beautiful People, who are mobile plant life, and the Terrible Ones, ugly mushroomlike plants. In spite of their best efforts, the humans and the Beautiful People are overcome in battle, the rocket crew barely managing to escape. Finally, a volcanic explosion seemingly terminates all Martian life. A British book influenced by Wells and one of the very first science fiction mainstream novels, it precedes even *Rocket Ship Galileo* [5-63]. Use of journal device for a multiple perspective provides effective change of mood and narrative pace. Careful, speculative discussion of possible life on Mars. Compare Claudy's *The Mystery Men of Mars* [5-36]. Sequel: *The Red Journey Back* (1954); British title: *SOS from Mars*.

5-40. del Rey, Lester. **The Infinite Worlds of Maybe.** Holt, 1966 (12 up).
Bill Franklin's father has disappeared into one of the infinite possible worlds, leaving a cryptic note for his son. Assisted by Professor Adams, Bill studies his father's notes until the pair figure out how they, too, can enter the possible worlds. Following his father's track, Bill travels into the future, a second war between the states, a simian-dominated land, a society with a technology that satisfies all wants (where Adams remains), an ice age, and finally a society devoted to individual perfection, where his father awaits him. Investigation both of a variety of alterna-

tive societies that humans might select if comfort, ease, and pleasure are goals, and of the nature of time. Compare Capon's *Flight of Time* [5-24].

5-41. del Rey, Lester. **Step to the Stars.** Winston, 1954 (12 up).
Eschewing space opera gadgetry and employing then-current knowledge and techniques, the book plausibly and convincingly lays out the various stages and dangers of constructing the first space station. The narrative involves Jim Stanly's growth from a lonely, skilled mechanic, too poor to pursue his goal of becoming a space pilot, to a confident, poised man who earns his space pilot wings. A subplot of espionage and sabotage by a pacifist group opposed to military uses of space is too conventional to add much to the book's impact. Compare Heinlein's *Starman Jones* [5-65] or Norton's *Star Man's Son: 2250 A.D.* [5-120].

5-42. del Rey, Lester; Cecile Matschatt; and Carl Carmer, eds. **The Year after Tomorrow: An Anthology of Science Fiction Stories.** Winston, 1954 (11–13).
Pioneering collection of short science fiction for youth. Important because most stories were actually written for young readers, unlike the vast majority of subsequent anthologies for the juvenile market whose contents were written for adults and then deemed, on perfunctory editing, "suitable" for youth. Special features are four stories reprinted from the *American Boy:* three by Carl Claudy, "The Master Minds of Mars" (later expanded into *Adventures in the Unknown:·The Mystery Men of Mars* [5-36]), "The Land of No Shadow," and "Tongues of Beast"; and one by P. van Dresser, "By Virtue of Circumference."

*5-43. Dickinson, Peter (U.K.). **The Weathermonger.** Gollancz, 1968 (12–14).
The first volume in the Changes trilogy. Geoffrey and Sally, brother and sister, having been abandoned to die as witches, escape to France where they are urged to return to England and discover the cause of the changes that have thrown the British Isles back into the Middle Ages where ignorance and superstition again rule, all things mechanical are feared, and even the weather is controlled by incantation. The children find out that Merlin's sleep has been disturbed, and, unhappy with what he sees, Merlin has sent England back to a time he knows. Geoffrey and Sally convince him to wait for a more suitable time to return and he relents, freeing England from its curse. A brilliantly imaginative combination of myth and science fiction. *Heartsease* (Gollancz, 1969) recounts the successful rescue of a witch by a group of children. In *The Devil's Children* (Gollancz, 1970), Nicky and a band of Sikhs, free of the madness caused by the changes, become allies, settle on a farm, and beat off various threats to their safety. Compare Mayne's *Earthfasts* [5-109].

5-44. Dicks, Terrance. **Doctor Who and the Day of the Daleks.** Target, 1974 (9–11).
Doctor Who, time lord trapped in time, is mistakenly the object of an assassination attempt by guerrillas from an alternate time who seek to change twentieth-century history so that Earth can be liberated from Daleks. After several adventures also involving Jo, the doctor's assistant, and the Brigadier, the doctor defeats the hated Daleks, and sets history aright. Seventh in the series of the many novelizations by various authors of the very popular, long-lived, and criti-

cally acclaimed British television series. Typical series fiction: fast moving, incident filled, routine characterization.

5-45. Dickson, Gordon R. **Space Winners.** Holt, 1965 (12–14).
Jim, Curt, and Ellen are selected by the Alien Federation for a secret training mission of great moment. They are joined by Atakit, a small, squirrel-like, but strong alien. Crash landing on Quebahr, a planet closed to technological knowledge, the four, after various adventures, assist in establishing cooperation among the several hostile peoples. They discover also that their mission actually was to Quebahr, and the three teenagers become part of an advance cadre for bringing Earth into the federation. Well-paced narrative, competently written, many surprises. Contrast Heinlein's *Tunnel in the Sky* [5-66] for a less sanguine adult view of teenagers.

*5-46. du Bois, William Pene. **The Twenty-One Balloons.** Viking, 1947 (10 up).
Krakatoa in the late nineteenth century is the site of an amazing civilization that combines outlandish but workable household devices to save labor and a utopian social organization built around eating tastes and financed by a diamond hoard. Professor Sherman, a retired teacher on a balloon tour over the Pacific, is forced down near Krakatoa and invited to join the group. The eruption of the volcano ends the utopian experiment and the professor escapes to inform a curious country why he was found in the ocean amid twenty-one balloons. A humorous, Jules Verne–like, richly imaginative book that can be enjoyed by all. Newbery Medal, 1948. Compare Baum's *The Master Key* [5-9] and its sympathetic handling of the American penchant for practical machines; contrast Hunter's *The Incredible Adventures of Professor Branestawn* [5-80] and its British whimsical put-down of machines.

*5-47. Engdahl, Sylvia Louise. **Enchantress from the Stars.** Atheneum, 1970 (13–15).
A long, detailed novel built around the notion that a traditional fairy tale may actually refer to incidents involving a wise, superior race visiting a younger race and world to spare it contamination. To Georyn, a youngest son, Elana is an enchantress who would help him destroy a ravaging dragon, actually a rock-destroying machine of the Imperial Exploration Corps. Elana and her father instruct Georyn in utilizing his latent psychological power, which frightens the materialistic Imperial colony, who are a Youngling people, into leaving the planet—Earth? Strong features are the working out of correspondences between fairy tale and the mission, anticolonizing theme, and the preeminence of Elana; thus, a rare nonsexist novel. Newbery honor book, 1971. Compare L'Engle's *A Wrinkle in Time* [5-96]; contrast Heinlein's *Tunnel in the Sky* [5-66].

5-48. Engdahl, Sylvia Louise. **The Far Side of Evil.** Atheneum, 1971 (13–15).
Another long, detailed story devoted to Elana and the Anthropological Service. Now graduated from the academy, Elana is sent on a mission to Toris, a Youngling planet, split between liberal and reactionary factions and on the brink of war. As usual, she is to observe and not interfere. However, a second agent, Randil, becoming too involved, falls in love and interferes. Before matters can be

set right and Toris can turn its attention to space travel and not war, Elana is imprisoned and tortured and Randil killed. Good but drawn-out depiction of Elana's interrogation through brainwashing; thus, length may offset admirable attempt to fuse science fiction and conventional romance formulas.

5-49. Fairman, Paul W. (ghost-written for Lester del Rey). **The Runaway Robot.** Westminster, 1964 (12-14).
Sixteen-year-old Paul Simpson must return to Earth from Ganymede and leave behind his robot, Rex. Paul jumps ship and is reunited with Rex, who also has been pining for Paul. After several adventures in which the pair are forced to separate, the two are again happily reunited on Earth. A feature that sets the book off from the commonplace is that it is told from Rex's perspective. Humor also abounds because of the robot's habit of assuming, even against the evidence of his "eyes," that his human masters are superior in all respects to robots, since masters by definition never make errors and know all.

5-50. Fisk, Nicholas (U.K.). **A Rag, a Bone and a Hank of Hair.** Kestrel, 1980; Crown, 1982 (12 up).
Superintelligent Brin, required to take part in experiments manipulating Reborns, artificially created humans of the twenty-third century, is increasingly resentful of their inhumane treatment. Although the impact of this insightful critique of social engineering is muted by point-of-view problems and inconclusive ending, the story is worthwhile, at times very moving. Compare Ames's *Anna to the Infinite Power* [5-2].

5-51. Fisk, Nicholas (U.K.). **Space Hostages.** Hamish Hamilton, 1967 (11–13).
A group of nine children, kidnapped by a "flying saucer," discover that their kidnapper is a crazed pilot of a secret British craft. Arrogant Tony and intelligent Brylo contend for leadership but are forced to cooperate to save the craft. An eerie opening, insightful study of differing personalities clashing, and plausible description of life aboard spacecraft make for superior science fiction for preteens. Contrast Capon's *Lost: A Moon* [5-25].

5-52. Fisk, Nicholas (U.K.). **Time Trap.** Gollancz, 1976 (14 up).
In 2079, English life is possible only within Ecoshield, where regimentation stifles liberty, and moral permissiveness and cowardice encourage teenage rioting and mugging. Dano Gazzard, who becomes privy to the secret of time travel through drugs, is driven to choose between an "idyllic" past (1942) and an uncertain future. Tautly written and somewhat horrifying portrait of a possible future blends Anthony Burgess's moral vision and John Christopher's terse readability.

*5-53. Fisk, Nicholas (U.K.). **Trillions.** Hamish Hamilton, 1971 (12–14).
Countless numbers of strange geometric objects, called trillions by the children, fall from the skies on Earth. Thirteen-year-old Scott Houghton, who has extraordinary ability to observe and think, discovers that the trillions have intelligence, are from a destroyed planet, and have come to Earth seeking work and a new home. General Hartman is the leader of those who see the trillions as invaders seeking to destroy, and he proposes to exterminate them. Scott, however, who communicates with the trillions, has them leave to continue their search. Suspenseful, well-written narrative, political overtones, and ecological orienta-

tion. Contrast Finney's *The Body Snatchers* [3-163] or Wyndham's *The Day of the Triffids* [3-411].

5-54. Forman, James D. **Call Back Yesterday.** Scribner, 1981 (12 up).
The only survivor of a hostile seizing of an American embassy in the Mideast in the near future, Cindy is forced finally to accept that her ill-advised flirtation with a young Arab may have precipitated nuclear conflagration. Suspenseful, plausible, and ultimately believable account of what could have been an absurd young adult romance. Compare the Johnsons' *Prisoner of PSI* [5-82].

5-55. Freeman, Gaail. **Alien Thunder.** Bradbury, 1982 (12–14).
In a future in which Earth is dying, Walker learns that his mother has actually become an alien sent to gather as many children as possible for transportation to another world where humanity may have a chance to survive. The first-person narration gives mystery, suspense, and poignancy to an otherwise ordinary plot. Contrast the Carlsons' *The Shining Pool* [5-26].

5-56. Halacy, D(aniel) S(tephen), Jr. **Return from Luna.** Grosset, 1969 (13 up).
Rob Stevens arrives at the Moon colony to find it discouraged by cutbacks in funds that have severely curtailed the colony's aim to become independent. Nuclear war breaks out on Earth, and the colony, along with its Russian counterpart, is forced to go it alone. Dissension festers and some men crack and mutiny; only cooperation with the Russians enables the colony to survive until all are rescued. A survival story translated into a lunar and technological setting. Writing and characterization adequate; quite good recreation of lunar life and terrain; technological passages mesh smoothly into the narrative.

*5-57. Hamilton, Virginia. **Justice and Her Brothers.** Greenwillow, 1978 (14 up).
Justice and her older brothers, who are identical twins, along with a fourth child, slowly realize that they are gifted with ESP. Conflict ensues as one brother cruelly manipulates his weaker twin and Justice senses that she, not the older boys, is to become leader of linked group and possible progenitor of a new life form. In this exceptionally good book, strong writing and characterization and brooding, convincing atmosphere and setting accompany theme familiar in adult science fiction, for example, Clarke's *Childhood's End* [3-97] or Sturgeon's *More Than Human* [3-362], but still novel in SF for children. Sequels: *Dustland* (1980) and *The Gathering* (1981).

5-58. Hancock, Harrie Irving. **The Invasion of the United States; or, Uncle Sam's Boys at the Capture of Boston.** Altemus, 1916 (12–14).
Invading an unprepared United States, the Germans enjoy smashing victories near Boston. Regardless of American courage, particularly as exhibited by Bert Howard and the boys from Gridley High, the seemingly invincible German Army advances on New York. First of four volumes in The Conquest of the United States series, which, combining prowar propaganda, school story, and the visionary, depicts a German invasion and which abruptly ended when actual war (World War I) broke out. Proto–science fiction, which atypically eschews space adventure and technological marvels and instead focuses on futuristic politics and sociology.

*5-59. Harding, Lee (Australia). **Misplaced Persons.** Harper, 1979. Published by Hyland House in 1979 in Australia as *Displaced Person* (13 up).
Aware that he cannot make contact with people and that the world is turning gray, Graeme soon finds himself alone, except for an alcoholic ex-teacher and a frightened girl, in a terrifying world where food must be scavenged and darkness is becoming total. Suddenly returned to the normal world, the boy retains a few shreds of evidence that the bizarre events did actually happen. Convincing psychological study of timeslip; well plotted and written; fresh characterization. Winner of the 1978 Alan Marshall Award for narrative fiction. Contrast Engdahl's *The Far Side of Evil* [5-48].

5-60. Harrison, Harry. **The California Iceberg.** Walker, 1975 (8–12).
In the year 2000, young Tod Wells is invited by his father, captain of the atomic tugboat *Stormqueen,* to go along on a voyage to tow huge icebergs to California, which is suffering from severe drought. Intended for young readers without using a monotonous or restrictive vocabulary or style, the narrative provides ample incident, plausible technology, and suspense in describing one way of relieving water shortages in the future. Compare Morressy's *The Windows of Forever* [5-114] for similar success in addressing young readers.

5-61. Heinlein, Robert A(nson). **Citizen of the Galaxy.** Scribner, 1957 (13 up).
Before Thorby Baslim can enter into his rightful inheritance as head of Rudbek, a Terran financial corporation, he is first a slave boy on Jubbul in the Nine Worlds, a quasi-Roman empire, then an adopted son of the People, an intergalactic trading company organized around matriarchy, and finally a guardsman in a futuristic foreign service. Emphasis is not on characterization or incident, but on explaining alternate ways of organizing society and dramatizing distinction between owning and controlling, having power and using it. Early instance of using children's science fiction for explaining and pushing ideas rather than merely relating exciting incidents.

5-62. Heinlein, Robert A(nson). **Farmer in the Sky.** Scribner, 1950 (13–15).
Emigration to Ganymede and the opportunity to homestead is the choice of Bill and his family. The flight out is long, and disappointment awaits Bill when the colonists discover that land and equipment are not ready. Bill is lucky to be assigned an early plot and begins the process of making soil. In spite of the setback of a massive quake, Bill decides to continue farming rather than return to Earth for further schooling. Subplots concerning Bill's relationship with father and stepmother and setting up scouting on Ganymede make the book, supposedly, more attractive to young readers. Chief interest is description of futuristic agricultural techniques.

*5-63. Heinlein, Robert A(nson). **Rocket Ship Galileo.** Scribner, 1947 (13 up).
Ross, Art, and Morrie, all amateur rocketeers, become involved with Morrie's uncle, Doctor Cargraves, and his plan to fly to the Moon. Having worked together in building an experimental, atomic-powered rocket, the three boys and Cargraves set off for the Moon. There they are attacked by a few Nazis plotting World War III from a secret lunar base. The boys overcome the Nazis and, having also discovered the ruins of a dead lunar civilization, return to Earth famous.

A pioneering novel that began American mainstream science fiction for children and combined young protagonists, gadgetry, current science, and adventure in such a way that even today the book retains interest.

5-64. Heinlein, Robert A(nson). **The Rolling Stones.** Scribner, 1952 (13 up).
The Stone family, at the instigation of the twins, Castor and Pollux, reconditions a spaceship as a family yacht, *The Rolling Stone,* and embarks on various adventures, including selling used bikes on Mars and flat cats (which proliferate hugely) in the asteroids. Its humor and wit still fresh, its portrait of family life still winning although sexist, and its hard science plausible and detailed, the novel aptly illustrates the author's eminence as writer of children's science fiction.

*5-65. Heinlein, Robert A(nson). **Starman Jones.** Scribner, 1953 (13–15).
Story of Max Jones's rise from hillbilly runaway to acting captain of a starship. What makes Max's rise possible is a phenomenal memory that retains all the astrogator's tables, needed for astronavigation, and the cunning of Sam, an older man who befriends the runaway and gets him aboard the *Asgard* with fake credentials. Striking are the detailed, convincing picture of spaceship operational procedures and the suspense whenever the ship must pass through an anomaly. A subplot involving colonization of Charity, an unexplored planet, provides a change of pace and conventional adventure.

*5-66. Heinlein, Robert A(nson). **Tunnel in the Sky.** Scribner, 1955 (12–14).
Rod Walker and his classmates, having been sent into an unknown world as part of a survival test, find themselves stranded. Banding together, as many as 50 teenagers are forced to make their own laws and rules. Just as the new society is viable and children are born, the young people are rescued and returned to Earth where many, including Rod, are forced back into teen roles. A provocative book, especially in its portrait of adults who fail to discern the maturity of young people. One unfortunate flaw is the stereotyped and sexist characterization.

5-67. Hill, Douglas (U.K.). **Galactic Warlord.** Gollancz, 1979; Atheneum, 1980 (12 up).
Shocked to learn that he is the only legionary to survive the destruction of Moros, Keill Randor, assisted by the alien Glr, smashes Thr'un, one of the evil Deathwing, and begins his search for the dreaded Warlord. Perhaps the best of current space opera for young readers: quick moving, suspenseful, action-filled. Followed by *Day of the Starwind* (1980, 1981), in which Randor contends with bogus legionaries, and *Planet of the Warlord* (1981, 1982), in which Randor and Glr finally destroy The One, responsible for destroying Moros. Compare Vance's *Vandals of the Void* [5-158].

5-68. Hill, Douglas (U.K.). **The Huntsman.** Heinemann, 1982 (12 up).
Relying on his uncanny ability to survive in the open, Finn Ferral sets out to rescue his foster father, Josh, and sister, Jena, stolen by brutal, ugly aliens who have enslaved Earth. Fast-paced adventure with enough originality and diversity of character to make for very entertaining reading. Sequels are *Warriors of the Wasteland* (1983), in which Finn finds his sister, and *Alien Citadel* (1984), in which guerrilla warfare, directed by Finn, forces the Slavers to leave Earth for more profit-

able ventures elsewhere. Compare Christopher's Tripod trilogy [5-32]; contrast Norton's *Storm over Warlock* [5-122].

*5-69. Hoover, H. M. **Another Heaven, Another Earth.** Viking, 1981 (12–14). Discovering that Xilan, presumably ignored by explorers 400 years earlier, actually has a human colony, a scientific team learns that the planet is genuinely inhospitable to human life. In spite of the fact that they are doomed, the original colonists will not leave. Intriguing concepts, plausible scenario, and rich and sustained characterization add up to an exceptionally interesting and moving novel. Contrast Sargent's *Earthseed* [5-137].

5-70. Hoover, H. M. **Children of Morrow.** Four Winds, 1973 (12–14). Set in a future after widespread nuclear devastation has wiped out civilization, the story contrasts two forms of government and economy that the survivors have adopted. One is afraid, cautious, reactionary, distrustful of what technology survives, and, hence, increasingly brutal and stagnant. The other is open, bold, and willing to build on extant science and to utilize genetic mutations to construct a new society, which seems to have combined successfully progress, discipline, justice, and love. The descriptions of the countryside after the Great Destruction are plausible and convincing. In all, a stimulating novel. Compare Clarke's *The Happy Planet* [5-35]. Sequel: *Treasures of Morrow* (1976).

5-71. Hoover, H. M. **The Lost Star.** Viking, 1979 (13 up). As part of an archaeological team surveying Blathor, Lian Webster realizes that the indigenous Lumpens, apparently fat and stupid animals, are really intelligent. Soon she uncovers their secret—they are an alien race, the Toapa, protected by a powerful computer brain within a mysterious dome—and must decide whether to share her knowledge with other team members. Multilayered story: mystery, coming of age, and study of racism and xenophobia. Compare Engdahl's *Enchantress from the Stars* [5-47] and Silverberg's *Across a Billion Years* [5-140]; contrast Anthony's *Race against Time* [5-5].

*5-72. Hoover, H. M. **The Rains of Eridan.** Viking, 1977 (12 up). The three experimental stations on Eridan are inexplicably infected by unnatural fear. The cause of and antidote to the fear are discovered by Theo Leslie, a biologist, who also learns the challenge and joy of parenting when she befriends an orphan child. Superior science fiction: plausible alien world, well-paced plotting, sensitive and tactful characterization, in particular, the growth of love between an older woman and a young girl who share a deep commitment to science. Compare Lightner's *The Space Plague* [5-100].

5-73. Hoover, H. M. **Return to Earth.** Viking, 1980. (14 up). In 3307, a retiring senior diplomat, Galen Innes, returns to his native Earth seeking peace, but unexpectedly becomes embroiled in conflict between the Dolmen, a dishonest leader of a powerful cult, and Samara, teenage heiress to the gigantic Lloyd Corporation. Befriending the young girl, Galen assists her in outwitting, then destroying the Dolmen. The vision of possible economic and social organizations is disquieting, and the novel presents an appealing portrayal of friendship between youth and old age; evidence of author's continuing success in wedding young adult concerns and science fiction. Contrast Heinlein's *Citizen of the Galaxy*

[5-61]; compare L'Engle's *A Wrinkle in Time* [5-96] or Corlett's *Return to the Gate* [5-37].

5-74. Hoover, H. M. **The Shepherd Moon.** Viking, 1984 (12–14).
Lonely 13-year-old Merry unexpectedly makes friends with her powerful grandfather, and together they stave off attempt to conquer Earth by a colonist from a forgotten artificial moon. Especially good are sympathetic insight into youth and old age relationship and study of corrosive effects of stagnant social classes. Compare Bond's *The Voyage Begun* [5-19] or Corlett's *Return to the Gate* [5-37].

5-75. Huddy, Delia (U.K.). **The Humboldt Effect.** MacRae, 1982 (12–14).
Because the Humboldt Time Machine, working in unexpected ways, sucks his friend Arthur into the past while drawing into the present a fourth-century B.C. man, the project leader, Luke, must travel into the past to set matters straight. Attractive novel: intriguing correspondences to the Jonah and the whale story, suspense, and believable characterization. Compare Engdahl's *Enchantress from the Stars* [5-47].

*5-76. Huddy, Delia (U.K.). **Time Piper.** Hamish Hamilton, 1976 (13 up).
When Luke goes to work for Humbolt, the brilliant scientist experimenting with a time machine, he again meets Hare, the strange young girl disliked by most of her peers. As the machine is tested, he realizes that Hare and her just-as-strange friends have been transported from the past, actually Hamlin, Germany. Fascinating blend of legend and science fiction, mystery and suspense, the well-plotted novel also examines teenagers at odds with their surroundings and reaching out for sympathy. Compare Mayne's *Earthfasts* [5-109]; contrast Capon's *Flight of Time* [5-24].

5-77. Hughes, Monica (U.K.). **The Keeper of the Isis Light.** Hamish Hamilton, 1980; Atheneum, 1981 (12 up).
Olwen, keeper of the intergalactic lighthouse Isis Light, who has been isolated from humanity except for Guardian, welcomes settlers from Earth only to discover the poignant truth about her capacity to survive on harsh Isis. Likable protagonist, plausible setting, and provocative scenario offset conventional story of lovers' misunderstanding. Sequels are *The Guardian of Isis* (1981, 1982) and *The Isis Pedlar* (1982, 1983), which continue story of Olwen's unhappy romance and fate of Isis human colony. Contrast Engdahl's *The Far Side of Evil* [5-48].

5-78. Hughes, Monica (U.K.). **The Tomorrow City.** Hamish Hamilton, 1978 (12–14).
C-Three, a computer built to coordinate all power uses in a city, takes literally its charge to do what is best for children, in particular, Caro, daughter of its designer. A reign of terror, instigated by C-Three, is terminated only when the computer, "grief-stricken" at having blinded Caro, blows up. New subject matter for children's science fiction is effectively handled through a convincing, plausible scenario and believable characterization. Compare Bethancourt's *The Mortal Instruments* [5-15].

5-79. Hunter, Evan. **Find the Feathered Serpent.** Winston, 1952 (12–14).
Neil, substituting for his father, the inventor of a time machine, journeys back in

time, hoping to find the origin of Quetzalcoatl, the great white god. He meets Eric, who becomes instrumental in assisting the Mayans to resist barbarian invaders and in introducing corn and other agricultural innovations. Returning to the present, Neil realizes that he has participated in the making of legend and myth. A time travel tale involving a Wellsian time machine; patterned also after books describing long-lost peoples. By far, more interesting as an archaeological and anthropological reconstruction than as hard science fiction. Compare Oliver's *Mists of Dawn* [5-129].

5-80. Hunter, Norman (U.K.). **The Incredible Adventures of Professor Branestawn.** Bodley Head, 1933 (12 up).
The highly creative professor is responsible for devising an array of inventions—time machine, paper enlarger, thief catcher, perpetual clock—that, never doing exactly what they are supposed to do, place their creator and his equally dotty friends in humorous and absurd predicaments. First of eight books devoted to the madcap professor, this inimitable combination of science fiction and fantasy is very popular in Great Britain because of its whimsy and spoofing.

5-81. Jackson, Jacqueline, and William Perlmutter. **The Endless Pavement.** Illus. by Richard Cuffari. Seabury, 1973 (7–9).
At a time when cars are everywhere, pavement endless, and the planet ruled by The Great Computermobile, life is highly regimented and organized around the car. One day, to obtain an apple she sees and can hardly recognize, Josette breaks the routine and brings the whole system to a halt. One of the few effective picture books that looks into the future. However, given the current energy crisis, the use of an automobile-dominated society as a metaphor for a dehumanized world already seems a bit outdated. Drawings are appropriately stark and nightmarish.

5-82. Johnson, Annabel, and Edgar Johnson. **Prisoner of PSI.** Atheneum, 1985 (12 up).
When the famous psychic Emory Morgan is kidnapped, his previously estranged son, Tristan, assembles a team and, using PSI, frees Morgan. Oddball characters, unexpected plotting, and a suggestive portrait of a future America suffering from climatic changes result in fresh, contemporary story. Compare Forman's *Call Back Yesterday* [5-54].

5-83. Jones, McClure. **Cast Down the Stars.** Holt, 1978 (12–14).
To save her own, the spirit people, Glory, Second Starcaster and someday First Starcaster and First Reader of Solstice Tower, must cast the stones correctly so the Serpent Line that keeps out barbarians and the cold can be repaired. Intertwined are stories of Glory's relation with her grandfather, Sun in Winter, who has rejected her parents, and of her budding love for Honor, Third Geomancer. Fascinating picture of a future world and culture dominated by astrology and geomancy whose ultimate credibility depends on reader's degree of acceptance of latter as science.

5-84. Jones, Raymond F. **The Year When Stardust Fell.** Winston, 1958 (12–14).
Cosmic dust from an approaching comet disturbs the surface tension of all metals, causing them to blend together. The resulting destruction of virtually all machinery throughout the world breeds violence and chaos. Ken Maddox, his chem-

ist father, and a few other scientists are able finally to find a remedy. Except for the prominence of young Ken, picture of social disintegration and scientific antidote is plausible and convincing, but lacks the emotional impact the British postcatastrophe novel began to have for children in the 1960s. Best of author's three novels in the Winston 1950s series.

5-85. Karl, Jean E. **But We Are Not of Earth.** Dutton, 1981 (12 up).
In training to be Discoverers like their parents, four very bright teens, the Terrible Four, apparently discover Ariel, an Earthlike planet, but soon suspect they have been manipulated for other, devious purposes. Likable characters, quick action, suspenseful plot, and plausible setting and subject matter add up to a winning story. Compare Dickson's *Space Winners* [5-45]; contrast Heinlein's *Tunnel in the Sky* [5-66].

*5-86. Karl, Jean E. **The Turning Place: Stories of a Future Past.** Dutton, 1976 (14 up).
A series of loosely related stories concerning a future Earth, defeated by aliens and forced to rebuild, which decides to forgo materialism and imperial expansion and utilize human intelligence and curiosity to form a new society. Aimed explicitly at youth in terms of themes and interest and thoroughly nonsexist in characterization, the stories are genuinely speculative as they image a future extrapolated from humanity's "best" traits; hence, hopeful and even inspiring. Compare Bradbury's *The Martian Chronicles* [3-64]; contrast Simak's *City* [3-345].

5-87. Kestaven, G. R. (U.K.). **The Pale Invaders.** Chatto, 1974 (12 up).
After the Upheavals, the inhabitants of a peaceful valley who are satisfied with a quiet pastoral life are disturbed by strangers asking for permission to dig "coal." The elders must decide whether the past—what young Gerald has accepted as "make-believe"—can be learned from or must be avoided at all costs. Air of mystery, sensitive depiction of coming of age, and probing of morality of technology result in superior children's science fiction. Compare Hoover's *Children of Morrow* [5-70].

5-88. Key, Alexander. **Escape to Witch Mountain.** Westminster, 1968 (11–13).
Tony and Tia, orphan brother and sister, are placed in a home with no possessions except a star box that suggests a mysterious origin and an equally mysterious destination. When a stranger seeks to adopt them, the children run away. Before they reach the safety of Witch Mountain, they realize that they possess parapsychological powers and remember that they are "Castaways" from a destroyed planet. It is also hinted that the children are sought by forces of satanic evil; hence, the book is another of the more recent stories dramatizing a universal struggle between good and evil in which youthful protagonists play active roles. A Walt Disney film of the same name was released in 1975. Sequel: *Return from Witch Mountain* (1978).

5-89. Key, Alexander. **The Forgotten Door.** Westminster, 1965 (11–13).
Little Jon falls through a forgotten door into an alien world—Earth. Temporarily forgetting his past, Jon is befriended by the Bean family, who gradually suspect he is from another, peaceful world. Others, not that perceptive, are frightened by, or want for their own uses, Jon's telepathic power. As a mob closes in on

him, Jon tries to find the door back; when he does, he takes the Bean family with him. Taut, suspenseful story; firm characterization, depiction of Jon's regaining memory especially good; ethical commentary never allowed to take over narrative. Compare Winterfeld's *Star Girl* [5-175].

5-90. Knott, William C. **Journey across the Third Planet.** Chilton, 1969 (12–14).

Laark is forced to abandon ship on Earth, a strange planet. His appearance makes him an alien, and his journey to meet a rescuing starship seems impossible except for the help of Peter, a runaway who joins Laark. In addition to the exciting adventure, the depiction of the slowly growing friendship between the two is distinctive, in particular, Laark's realization that Earth, technologically very inferior to his home, can give Krall, an old and tired planet, insights gained from the courage and resourcefulness of a young planet. Contrast Key's *The Forgotten Door* [5-89].

5-91. Kurland, Michael. **The Princes of Earth.** Elsevier/Nelson, 1978 (14 up).

In the far future, Adam Warrington, from the backwater planet Jasper, wins a scholarship to the University of Sol on Mars. On his way there the teenager becomes entangled in intrigue, aids a prince of Earth, is kidnapped, escapes, and eventually enrolls in school. Always interesting and sometimes witty commentary on future politics and schooling, interlaced with futuristic technology; plausibly based on present events and knowledge. Contrast Anthony's *Race against Time* [5-5] or Sleator's *House of Stairs* [5-143].

5-92. Latham, Philip (pseud. of Robert Shirley Richardson). **Missing Men of Saturn.** Winston, 1953 (12–14).

The spaceship *Albatross* is ordered to follow the *Anomaly*, a ghost ship, out to Saturn. Subsequently, the crew is exposed to a series of terrifying incidents, and members disappear. Gradually, it becomes apparent that Saturn is inhabited, and both the Saturnians, an old civilized race, and the descendants of Captain Dearborn, first explorer of Saturn who disappeared mysteriously, do not want any interlopers. The crew, however, is set free as the Saturnians decide rapprochement is inevitable. Suspenseful, well-written mystery for two-thirds of the book; then speculation about the possibility of life on Saturn intrudes.

5-93. Lawrence, Louise (pseud. of Elizabeth Rhoda Wintle) (U.K.). **Children of the Dust.** Bodley Head, 1985 (13 up).

The several Harnden daughters and their children, who survive the terrible first years after nuclear war, represent contrasting approaches to rebuilding society, and then embody the mutations able to thrive in the reconstructed civilization. Compassionate yet honest tone, coupled with effective use of point of view, enriches plausible, detailed plot. Compare Hoover's *Children of Morrow* [5-70]; contrast Clarke's *The Happy Planet* [5-35].

5-94. Lawrence, Louise (pseud. of Elizabeth Rhoda Wintle) (U.K.). **The Power of Stars.** Collins, 1972 (12 up).

The power of the stars, becoming manifest one night, accidentally possesses Jane and seeks to establish itself on Earth. Jimmy and Alan, one suspicious and the other blinded by love, compete to understand and help the girl. Suspense, a surprise ending, and convincing atmosphere and characterization are features of an impressive combination of science fiction and the young adult novel.

5-95. Leek, Sybil. **The Tree That Conquered the World.** Prentice-Hall, 1969 (8–10).
Julian discovers in his yard a strange, fast-growing tree that speaks. He also sees that the tree's swift growth and intense desire to propagate itself by the thousands can stem the tide of pollution and smog in the Los Angeles area. So, with Sam and Laura, his sister, he establishes Operation Treetop to plant as many seedlings as possible. The children become national heroes. In spite of being preachy, the book is informative concerning dangers of pollution; also one of the few picture books that are entertaining and factual.

*5-96. L'Engle, Madeleine. **A Wrinkle in Time.** Farrar, 1962 (13–15).
Meg and Charles Wallace Murray, along with Calvin, Meg's classmate, become involved in an attempt to find Dr. Murray, a brilliant scientist who has mysteriously disappeared. Under the direction of Mrs. Who, Mrs. Whatsit, and Mrs. Which, three "angels," they "tesseract" to Camazotz, a distant star, where the children must save Dr. Murray, held captive by "It" in Central Intelligence. Eventually, it is the self-effacing love of Meg, and not the brilliant intelligence of Charles, that saves their father. One of the contemporary fantasy–science fiction novels that enmesh children in planetwide struggles between good and evil. Well written, firm characterization, provocative themes. Newbery Medal, 1963. Contrast Heinlein's *The Rolling Stones* [5-64]. Companion novels are *A Wind in the Door* (1973), in which Charles Wallace's bloodstream becomes an arena for a clash between good and evil, and *A Swiftly Tilting Planet* (1978), in which an older Charles Wallace, aided by Meg and the unicorn Gaudior, goes back in time to resolve several moral crises and avert nuclear catastrophe.

5-97. Lightner, A(lice) M(ary). **The Day of the Drones.** Norton, 1969 (10–14).
A postcatastrophe story. Afria (once Africa) seems the only land uncontaminated by radioactivity. An expedition sets out to explore the potentially dangerous nearby lands and discovers in an ancient northern country (once England) the Bee-people, a mutant, dwarfed race descended from the predisaster white population, organized around matriarchal principles and controlled by gigantic mutant bees. A harrowing look at a possible future society adversely affected by radiation, virtually bookless, and unsure of the uses of power and knowledge; a perceptive study of the nature and effects of racial prejudice.

5-98. Lightner A(lice) M(ary). **Doctor to the Galaxy.** Norton, 1965 (11–13).
Young Dr. Garrison Bart becomes, through a mix-up, a veterinarian instead of a physician on a faraway planet. He discovers that lustra, a local moneymaking grain, inhibits growth. To the Assembly of Scientists he announces the discovery, but his findings are rejected; he is also charged with illegally practicing medicine. Bart makes another discovery: lustra inhibits cancerous growth. This time he is honored for his discovery and is able to become a physician. Interesting story

that aptly represents the author's ability to find subject matter appealing to preteens. Contrast Heinlein's *Farmer in the Sky* [5-62].

5-99. Lightner A(lice) M(ary). **The Space Ark.** Putnam, 1968 (12–14).
Dinkie, Uncle Rol, Cherry, the Rock, and Dr. Binns attempt to establish on another planet several of the unique species of Shikai, whose sun is going nova. Although too episodic and predictable to be an exciting adventure, the narrative profits from fluent style, likable characters, and author's manifest enjoyment of nature and animals. Contrast Heinlein's *The Rolling Stones* [5-64]. Sequel and superior to *The Rock of Three Planets* (1963) and *The Planet Poachers* (1965).

5-100. Lightner, A(lice) M(ary). **The Space Plague.** Norton, 1966 (13 up).
Reflecting the author's knowledge of lepidopterology and entomology, the novel depicts a group of young people caught up in a search for the cause of a space plague on the planet Arcona. Barney, a beetle specialist, and Jenny, a lepidopterist, eventually untangle the causes of the disease, all of which involve the brilliant flutterfly. Deft, entertaining mixture of science and exotic locale, with a touch of romance; convincing and satisfying narrative. Compare Nourse's *Star Surgeon* [5-125].

5-101. Lord, Beman. **The Day the Spaceship Landed.** Walck, 1967 (8–9).
Young Mike meets four spacemen and cooperates with their request for information. The visitors from outer space leave, stating that they will return in two years for a formal visit to the United States. A straightforward and, at times, amusing narrative; the realistic pictures by Harold Berson contribute to the lack of cuteness. Sequel: *The Day the Spaceship Returns* (1970). Compare Slobodkin's *The Space Ship under the Apple Tree* [5-145].

5-102. MacArthur, David (U.K.). **The Thunderbolt Men.** Claridge, Lewis & Jordan, 1947 (12–14).
Kidnapped and brought to a remote island, David and Rosemary find a secret base ruled over by the fanatic Dr. Gruber, who plans to destroy the civilized world through his Thunderbolt cadre, powerful magnetic fields, and an atom destroyer. Along with Logan, a British agent, and Dr. Nicolai, the inventor of the new weaponry, the children manage to foil Gruber's plot. Very early British science fiction for youth echoes Verne and Wells, reflects the then recently won war in its proud British patriotism, and expresses concern for possible nuclear war.

5-103. Mace, Elizabeth (U.K.). **Out There.** Greenwillow, 1975. British title: *Ransome Revisited* (13 up).
Eleven confronts a bleak life after his schooling is finished and he is sent to the quarries. Along with his subnormal older brother and two acquaintances, Susan and Will, Eleven escapes and sets out for a community where freedom, rumor has it, exists. Postholocaust survival story is marked by tough-minded honesty in its depiction of the ways supposedly deprived youth manage to survive with self-respect and dignity fundamentally intact and continue to hope for a better life. Contrast Clarke's *The Happy Planet* [5-35].

5-104. MacGregor, Ellen. **Miss Pickerell Goes to Mars.** McGraw-Hill, 1951 (8–10).

Miss Pickerell finds a rocket ship trespassing on her pasture. Determined to register a complaint, she clambers on board and is mistakenly locked in as the rocket takes off for Mars. Her presence resented, she is not finally accepted until she rescues one of the crew. She returns a heroine! Early space fantasy, light reading, popular with young readers. There are eleven other Miss Pickerell books. Beginning with *Miss Pickerell on the Moon* (1965), the books are actually written by Dora Pantell.

5-105. MacVicar, Angus (Scotland). **The Lost Planet.** Burke, 1953 (10–14).

Recently orphaned Jeremy Grant goes to live with his uncle, Dr. Lachlan McKinnon. The teenager becomes part of the crew that, utilizing McKinnon's experimental atom-powered rocket, explores "the lost planet," finding there a flower whose scent promotes gentleness and peace, and iridonium, which can change lead into gold. The briskly moving narrative, engaging characterization, and theme exhorting unity and cooperation aptly represent the work of an early popular British author of children's science fiction.

5-106. Mark, Jan. **The Ennead.** Crowell, 1978 (14 up).

Three socially deviant characters, Isaac, Eleanor, and Moshe, are destroyed by the rigidly stratified society of Erato, a harsh, stark planet still struggling through to the freedom of spirit its inhabitants have sought. Unusually somber in mood and marked by sharp characterization and distinctive setting, the novel is a ringing statement of the need for individual freedom and the power of human spirit.

5-107. Marsten, Richard (pseud. of Evan Hunter). **Rocket to Luna.** Winston, 1953 (12–14).

Ted Baker, Space Academy cadet, unexpectedly becomes backup on the first rocket to the Moon. Rejected at first by the crew, Ted is accepted eventually as it is he who pilots the rocket onto the Moon's surface and saves the life of one of the crew. Although time has made obsolete some of the presentation of the technology required for a lunar flight, the technical descriptions are detailed and accurate. Moreover, the story still retains much of the tension and excitement of a journey to the Moon. Compare Heinlein's *Rocket Ship Galileo* [5-63].

5-108. Martel, Suzanne. **The City under Ground.** Viking, 1964 (11–13).

A postcatastrophe story. Where old Montreal used to be, Surreal, an underground city, survives because of a highly technological and rigidly organized society. Two sets of brothers, Luke and Paul and Eric and Bernard, showing curiosity and initiative, help the city fight a mysterious, hitherto-unknown underground enemy and stumble on a way to the surface where they discover a cleansed Earth and other survivors, the Lauranians, a free, less repressed, and technologically inferior people. Surreal decides to go aboveground and ally itself with the Lauranians. Adequately written and mildly engaging incidents. Compare Silverberg's *Time of the Great Freeze* [5-142].

*5-109. Mayne, William (U.K.). **Earthfasts.** Hamish Hamilton, 1966 (12–14).

David and Keith meet an eighteenth-century drummer boy emerging from a newly formed grassy mound and carrying a steady, cold, white-flamed candle.

Before Keith can return the candle to the past, inexplicable phenomena—
"boggarts," heaving ground, moving stones, wild boars, giants, shadowing horse-
men, awakening Arthurian knights, and even David's "death"—plague the area.
A remarkable combination of fantasy and science fiction; strong characterization; fine depiction of the boys' determination to treat the constantly burning candle scientifically before succumbing to its power; exceptional use of atmosphere;
brilliant style.

*5-110. McCaffrey, Anne. **Dragonsong.** Atheneum, 1976 (12 up).
Frustrated in her desire to express her musical talent and forced to live as girls
are wont to in Half Circle, Menolly injures her hand. Recuperating, she witnesses
the birth of fire lizards, survives Thread-fall out in the open, and eventually
comes to the attention of the Masterharper, who wants Menolly to utilize her talent. As part of the Pern sequence, the novel provides detailed description of the
birth of fire lizards, the small relatives of dragons, and is a slow but sensitive,
somewhat unconventional revelation of a girl's coming of age. Compare
Engdahl's *Enchantress from the Stars* [5-47]. Two subsequent novels continue portrait of coming of age. *Dragonsinger* (1977) follows Menolly's life in Harper Hall
and underscores necessity of discipline in mastering any art or craft. *Dragondrums*
(1979) focuses on Piemur, a boy soprano, and details his adventures on the way
to becoming a journeyman drummer.

*5-111. McKillip, Patricia. **Moon-Flash.** Atheneum, 1984 (12 up).
Impelled by questions concerning Riverworld and her own dreams, Kyreol, accompanied by Terje, a young man, travels beyond the end of the world and
learns the truth: River is a small "primitive" region carefully observed and
guarded by the Dome, a technologically developed civilization. A superior story:
fascinating application of anthropology; rich, detailed nature description; sustained mystery. Sequel is *The Moon and the Face* (1985), in which Kyreol and Terje
bring about the commingling of River and the Dome. Compare Stone's *The
Mudhead* [5-147]; contrast Hunter's *Find the Feathered Serpent* [5-79].

5-112. Miklowitz, Gloria. **After the Bomb.** Scholastic, 1985 (12–14).
When a Russian nuclear bomb accidentally explodes over Los Angeles, young
Philip Singer is forced into the unlikely role of leader for his family. Well-researched and harrowing depiction of immediate aftermath of a nuclear disaster
is joined to attractive characterization. Contrast Swindells's *Brother in the Land* [5-
154].

5-113. Morressy, John. **The Humans of Ziax II.** Walker, 1974 (7–9).
Toren, son of the Earth commander in charge of Pioneer Base One on Ziax II,
loses his way in the jungle and is befriended by the Imbur, dwellers of the rain
forest. From them Toren learns that killing is not always necessary. Further, he is
instructed in the use of psychological powers that enable humans to survive without killing. A picture book; easy-to-understand vocabulary conveys the ethical insights without distorting through oversimplification. Sequel: *The Drought on Ziax
II* (1978).

5-114. Morressy, John. **The Windows of Forever.** Walker, 1975 (8–10).
While exploring a house left to his family by his uncle, Tommy stumbles into a future where he meets his uncle under several guises and in different times. The young boy also confronts an alternate Tommy who both preserves Earth from alien attack and saves his uncle's life. Commendable, successful attempt, aimed at middle-grade readers, to explore definitions of time and concept of alternate worlds.

*5-115. North, Eric (Australia). **The Ant Men.** Winston, 1955 (12–14).
A scientific expedition is caught in a central Australian desert storm and whirled into a lost world inhabited by gigantic mantises and antlike creatures struggling up the evolutionary ladder to human intelligence. Vivid nature description and strong characterization—in particular, the expedition's gradual realization that they are indeed in a lost world—outweigh routine plotting and scenes of battle. One of the best written of the 1950s Winston series and still enjoyable today. Compare Oliver's *Mists of Dawn* [5-129].

5-116. Norton, Andre (pseud. of Alice Mary Norton). **Catseye.** Harcourt, 1961 (13 up).
Temporary work in a strange interplanetary pet shop involves Troy Horan, a displaced person, in adventure, intrigue, and mystery, hallmarks of typical Norton work. Surprised to learn that he can communicate with animals, Troy stumbles on the fact that several pets in the shop are being used as secret weapons in a plot against the rulers of Korwar. Troy is forced to flee into the wild and a dead, booby-trapped underground city; only the closest cooperation between Troy and several exotic animals enables him to survive and become a member of the Rangers, who patrol the wild. Skillful narrating of science fiction adventure and sympathetic depiction of animal-human relationship.

*5-117. Norton, Andre (pseud. of Alice Mary Norton). **Operation Time Search.** Harcourt, 1967 (13 up).
Ray Osborne is accidentally sent back into a time when the Atlantean Empire sought to overthrow the Murians, and he becomes the instrument whereby the latter, worshipers of the Flame, are able to annihilate Atlantis, where devotees of the false Poseidon traffic in demonic powers. Osborne wonders why Atlantis lingers in legend while the Murian Empire disappeared, but fails to observe that the religion and kings of Mura provide the basis for the Greek pantheon and mythology. Osborne remains in the past, determined to organize in the Barren Lands a colony, ruins of which are the mounds dotting the central United States. An Atlantis legend story, entertaining, especially stimulating in its speculation concerning origin of myth.

5-118. Norton, Andre (pseud. of Alice Mary Norton). **Quest Crosstime.** Viking, 1965. British title: *Crosstime Agent* (13–15).
In a future when moving "crosstime" to parallel universes is possible, one group on Vroom favors crosstiming so that society can rebuild itself after nuclear devastation by using the resources of other universes. The Rogan sisters and Blake Walker, all with various parapsychological abilities, are swept into a revolt orga-

nized by those opposed to crosstiming. Before the revolt is put down, the adventure spills over to E625, a crosstime world embroiled in a tense stalemate modeled on the conflict between the American Plains Indians and the pioneers. Exciting and fast-moving story.

5-119. Norton, Andre (pseud. of Alice Mary Norton), and Dorothy Madlee. **Star Ka'at.** Walker, 1976 (8–10).
Tiro and Mer, ESP-proficient cat-agents of a far-off world, are sent to an Earth heading for imminent catastrophe and hope to save terran cats, descendants of a colony of Ka'ats. They meet Jim and Elly Mae and are eventually moved, in spite of instructions, to assist them, urgently working to rescue both cats and the two children. Perhaps too determinedly nonracist, nonsexist, and socially relevant, the narrative still does feature likable characters, attractive illustrations, and ample incident. One of the very few effective science fiction narratives for the younger child. Sequels are *Star Ka'at World* (1978), *Star Ka'ats and the Plant People* (1979), and *Star Ka'ats and the Winged Warriors* (1981). Compare Morressy's *The Humans of Ziax II* [5-113].

*5-120. Norton, Andre (pseud. of Alice Mary Norton). **Star Man's Son: 2250 A.D.** Harcourt, 1952. Variant title: *Daybreak 2250 A.D.* (12 up).
Rejected by his father's clan, young Fors, a mutant, runs away to prove himself a Star Man, or explorer. Along with Arskane, a black youth who befriends him, Fors is successful in uniting the several clans against their common enemy, the Beast Things, and in instilling in the former the dream of starting over without repeating the mistakes of the Old Ones. The author's first SF novel, one of her best, both a fine study of coming of age and a convincing portrait of postholocaust world. Compare Heinlein's *Farmer in the Sky* [5-62] or *Red Planet* (1949).

5-121. Norton, Andre (pseud. of Alice Mary Norton). **The Stars Are Ours.** World, 1954 (13 up).
Even in a time when Earth has embarked on interplanetary flight, old animosities continue to exist and eventually lead to a devastating war. Scientists are proscribed by the Company of Pax, and a handful of Free Scientists escape to the stars. After exploring a new planet, the humans enter into an alliance with a race of mermen to take up anew the history of humanity. Well plotted, filled with incident, and skillfully written. Sequel: *Star Born* (1957).

5-122. Norton, Andre (pseud. of Alice Mary Norton). **Storm over Warlock.** World, 1960 (13 up).
Terrans and the evil, cruel Throngs clash over establishing sovereignty in Warlock, a newly discovered planet. Thorvald and Shann Lantee, the only survivors of a terran survey, along with two wolverines, are forced to flee a band of Throgs. Falling into the hands of Wyvern·or witches, the pair is tested but eventually accepted by them. The new allies of Terra assist in pushing the Throgs back to their own planet. Early space adventure featuring one major characteristic of the author: witches and witchcraft, illusion versus dream. Of secondary interest is human-animal coequal relationship. Sequel: *Ordeal in Otherwhere* (1964).

5-123. Nourse, Alan E(dward). **The Bladerunner.** McKay, 1974 (13 up).
By the early twenty-first century, overpopulation has forced sterilization on any-one seeking medical care. A medical black market springs up for those opposed to this kind of medical practice. When a mysterious flu virus threatens a nation-wide epidemic, Billy Gimp and other bladerunners—that is, persons who pro-vide black-market physicians with supplies and assistance—are called on to warn the populace. The epidemic is curtailed and humane changes in health care en-sue. Suspenseful incidents; fascinating look at future medical care and proce-dures; responsible handling of overpopulation control problem. Compare Lightner's *Doctor to the Galaxy* [5-98].

5-124. Nourse, Alan E(dward). **The Mercy Men.** McKay, 1968 (12–14).
In this novel of narrative twists and surprises, Jeff Meyer feels a compulsion to seek out and kill a man he believes has killed his father. Suspecting that the man has entered a research medical center, Jeff decides to enter also as a mercy man, that is, one who allows medical self-experimentation for money. Before Jeff can leave the center, he is shocked to learn that he, like his father, is triggered to go insane and that this insanity affects the laws of probability. Jeff is a carrier of a dis-order that must be eradicated or treated. As in other novels by the author, specu-lation about future medical practice is stimulating; style and characterization are above average. Compare the Suttons' *The Programmed Man* [5-152].

*5-125. Nourse, Alan E(dward). **Star Surgeon.** McKay, 1960 (12 up).
Expert blending of futuristic medicine, its procedures and organization, and the story of Earth's attempt to enter the Galactic Confederation. Earth, hospital cen-ter for the entire galaxy, prides itself on its medical skill and begrudgingly allows Dal, a Garvian and first off-Earth medical student, to intern. After several adven-tures Dal wins his silver star as a star surgeon, and Earth has passed its probation. Suspenseful in depicting possible future medical technology, especially provoca-tive speculation about possible applications of symbiosis.

*5-126. O'Brien, Robert C. **Mrs. Frisby and the Rats of NIMH.** Atheneum, 1971 (10–14).
Mrs. Frisby, head of a family of field mice, is told to consult neighboring rats con-cerning the illness of her son. Justin, a leader of the rats, agrees to help because Mr. Frisby had been of assistance to the rats. On hearing the whole story of the rats as the object of psychological and biological experimentation by the NIMH laboratories and the rats becoming, as a result, superintelligent, Mrs. Frisby also volunteers to aid the rats. The rats escape from an attempt by the NIMH labora-tories to exterminate them and establish a utopian society away from humans. Outstanding combination of fantasy and science fiction; a winning portrait of rats and mice that has little cuteness. Newbery Medal, 1972.

*5-127. O'Brien, Robert C. **Z for Zachariah.** Atheneum, 1975 (14–16).
A postcatastrophe story. Believing she may be the only survivor of a devastating war, Ann Burden is pleased to see a man enter the Burden valley and decides to befriend him. Shocked when, after all she has done for him, he tries to rape her, Ann is forced to leave the valley, hoping to come across other survivors. Sensitive

transformation of trite subject into a tragic story of human behavior in the face of destruction and possible extinction. Use of journal to record struggle for understanding, carefully paced narrative, and characterization of protagonist are distinctive. Compare Engdahl's *The Far Side of Evil* [5-48].

5-128. Offutt, Andrew J. **The Galactic Rejects.** Lothrop, 1973 (13–15).
Rinegan, Berneson, and Cory, all gifted with parapsychological power, but social misfits, find themselves on Bors, a hitherto-unknown agrarian world where crime and the proverbial rat race seem nonexistent and life is utopian. Impressed by the marked contrast to Earth, the three change and become circus performers. The extent of change is tested when they decide not only to preserve Bors's society from the invading Azuli, archenemy of Earth, but to bring peace by offering to immunize the Azulians from a disease fatal to them, but not to terrans. Different and refreshing because of the engaging circus scenes. Compare Lightner's *The Space Plague* [5-100] or Nourse's *Star Surgeon* [5-125].

5-129. Oliver, Chad. **Mists of Dawn.** Winston, 1952 (12–14).
A time travel machine accidentally transports young Mark Nye 50,000 years into the past. Attacked by brutish Neanderthals and befriended by the relatively civilized Cro-Magnons, Mark learns how to survive by cooperating with nature and with other human beings. The plot is less adventure and more a dramatized and still engrossing presentation of then-current anthropological speculation about primitive peoples. Compare Hunter's *Find the Feathered Serpent* [5-79].

5-130. Parker, Richard (U.K.). **The Hendon Fungus.** Gollancz, 1967 (13 up).
Fungus sent to England by Dr. Hendon accidentally escapes and spreads throughout the countryside with devastating results. Since it feeds on calcium, all concrete and stone buildings in southern England crumble before a bulldozed strip, islandwide, and grubbing pigs finally stop the fungus. Quick-moving, plausible plot, likable characters, and insights into bureaucratic mind and profiteers make up deliberately low-keyed, effective story. Compare Christopher's *No Blade of Grass* [3-92] or Jones's *The Year When Stardust Fell* [5-84].

5-131. Patchett, Mary E. (U.K.). **Adam Troy: Astroman.** Lutterworth, 1954 (12–14).
Early British science fiction for children is set in a future with Earth about to be devastated by an asteroid, Object A, and struggling to find some way to survive out in space. Adam is sent to determine whether colonies on artificial satellite E.E.I., Moon, and Mars can be adapted for tremendously expanded growth. Parallel story deals with survivors on Earth after A's devastation. Above-average writing and characterization, along with variety of incident and detailed setting, provide entertaining reading.

5-132. Pesek, Ludek (Czechoslovakia). **The Earth Is Near.** Bradbury, 1974. Tr. by Anthea Bell of *Die Erde Ist Nah*, 1970 (13 up).
An engrossing adventure, convincing investigation of what happens to an international crew of 20 during a journey to Mars and its exploration. The dramatization of the shifting psychological states of mind on the long trip and during the terrifying dust storms; the explicit and hidden animosities and rivalries that emerge; the loneliness and futility experienced because the crew has depended

too much on specialized machines, which fail or prove useless; the frustration resulting from the suspicion that the expedition might have done better if it had attempted to harmonize with Martian ecology; and human courage and endurance all give the novel its distinction. German Children's Book Prize, 1971. Compare Halacy's *Return from Luna* [5-56]. Also annotated as [4-409].

*5-133. Pesek, Ludek (Czechoslovakia). **Trap for Perseus.** Bradbury, 1980. Tr. by Anthea Bell of *Falle für Perseus* (13 up).
When the spaceship *Perseus III*, investigating the fate of two previous *Perseus* ships, is trapped by the presumably lost Argo, Commander Blair undergoes brainwashing, eventually accepting both the totalitarian society of Argo and a role in entrapping *Perseus IV*. Impressive narrative, fascinating psychological study, richly detailed setting, Kafkaesque atmosphere. Compare Malzberg's *Beyond Apollo* [4-352]; contrast Sleator's *House of Stairs* [5-143]. Also annotated as [4-410].

*5-134. Randall, Florence Engel. **A Watcher in the Woods.** Atheneum, 1976 (12 up).
From the day the Carstairs family inhabits an old house, individual members sense a mysterious, powerful, and potentially dangerous force in the woods watching them. Increasingly bizarre electronic and other disturbances culminate in the discovery of a time-trapped visitor from space in the woods. Stylistic excellence, plausible use of science fiction and ghost story elements, and fresh characterization, especially of warm family life, make for superior storytelling. Compare L'Engle's *A Wrinkle in Time* [5-96].

5-135. Reynolds, Alfred. **Kiteman of Karanga.** Knopf, 1985 (12–14).
Failing his ordeal and charged with cowardice after choosing banishment instead of death, Karl finds a new opportunity to prove himself by helping the people of Eftah wrest their freedom from the lizard-riding Hrithdon. Attractive and sympathetic characters, distinctive setting, and adventure mark the fast-moving narrative. Compare Norton's *Star Man's Son: 2250 A.D.* [5-120].

5-136. Rockwood, Roy (pseud.). **Through the Air to the North Pole; or, The Wonderful Cruise of the Electric Monarch.** Cupples & Leon, 1906 (9–11).
Orphans Mark Sampson and Jack Darrow, befriended by Professor Amos Henderson, accompany him and his black assistant Washington (in a secret airship) to the North Pole. The voyagers encounter assorted adventures, from attack by eagles to capture by "Esquimaux," before attaining success. First of the eight Great Marvel books, these Verne-like adventures, from the Edward Stratemeyer syndicate, both predated the Tom Swift series and surpassed it in literary quality and imaginative scope, although they never equaled it in popularity.

*5-137. Sargent, Pamela. **Earthseed.** Harper, 1983 (13 up).
Zoheret and her young companions, artificially born and raised aboard Ship, struggle to colonize Hollow, contending against their own inner doubts and the hostility of other human colonizers. Attractive characters, unexpected plotting, and perceptive insight into social and political organizations make the narrative superior storytelling. Compare Karl's *But We Are Not of Earth* [5-85]; contrast Ames's *Anna to the Infinite Power* [5-2].

*5-138. Schlee, Ann (U.K.). **The Vandal.** Macmillan, 1979; Crown, 1981 (12 up).
Placed under psychological care because of his act of vandalism, Paul slowly realizes that the daily Drink, which all must take, no longer is making him immune to the "contamination" of memory, the past, and history. Impressive story: taut narrative pace, Kafkaesque atmosphere, and insightful study of once-benevolent government gone bad. Compare Westall's *Futuretrack 5* [5-167]; contrast Fisk's *Time Trap* [5-52].

5-139. Severn, David (pseud. of David Unwin) (U.K.). **The Future Took Us.** Bodley Head, 1957 (12 up).
A timeslip narrative. Two boys, Peter and Dick, are carried forward into the Great Britain of A.D. 3000 via a machine devised by the Calculators, who venerate mathematics and reason and dominate the masses growing increasingly restive and seeking liberty under the leadership of a handful of aristocrats. A provocative look at a future England controlled by an elite and devastated by social unrest, which predates similar portraits by both Peter Dickinson (the Changes trilogy) [5-43] and John Christopher (the Prince in Waiting trilogy) [5-31].

5-140. Silverberg, Robert. **Across a Billion Years.** Dial, 1969 (14 up).
Story of a dig in 2375 on Higby V for further evidence of the High Ones is narrated by Tom Rice, apprentice archaeologist. Although Tom is often an amusing narrator and a wry observer of the team made up half of humans and half of aliens—evidence of attempt to engage young readers—the book is replete with information about archaeology, present and future. Speculation about origin of life, ESP, and a superrace is also interesting. Compare Hunter's *Find the Feathered Serpent* [5-79]; contrast Oliver's *Mists of Dawn* [5-129].

5-141. Silverberg, Robert. **The Gate of Worlds.** Holt, 1967 (13–15).
Alternative history that answers the question of what would have happened to Europe and the rest of the world if the Black Death of 1348 had killed three-fourths instead of one-quarter of Europe's population. Dan Beauchamp of New Istanbul (London) leaves to make his fortune in Mexico. Accepting the patronage of a rascally nephew of King Moctezuma, Dan never quite makes his fortune. Of more interest than Dan's adventures is the portrait of the New World, non-Christian, less dependent on machinery, and non-Westernized; anthropological and archaeological information and speculation are sound and challenging. Compare Dick's *The Man in the High Castle* [3-142].

5-142. Silverberg, Robert. **Time of the Great Freeze.** Holt, 1964 (12–14).
By A.D. 2230, because of the fifth ice age, cities were forced underground. Centuries later the inhabitants of these cities, afraid and suspicious, were content with their living conditions and the lack of communication with each other. Jim Barnes, his father, and five other men, having made radio contact with London, were as a consequence expelled from New York and determined to make London over the ice. Their many adventures and dangers make up a fast-moving story that also entertains through suggesting what elements in today's civilization might survive after an ice age.

*5-143. Sleator, William. **House of Stairs.** Dutton, 1974 (14 up).
Five 16-year-old orphans find themselves in a house of stairs with a red machine as the only furniture. When the machine light blinks and sounds are emitted, the teenagers realize they must perform in a certain way or the machine will not spit out food pellets. Three of the young people do what the machine wants, use each other, and become brutal and mechanistic. The other two open to and sustain each other as humans. The young people discover that they have been subjects in a psychological conditioning experiment. The language and attitudes of teenagers are captured; the breaking down of all external, protective devices is plausibly rendered. However, the truth of the situation may be too obvious to some readers; hence, the sharpness of the attack on behavioral modification procedures is blunted. Compare O'Brien's *Mrs. Frisby and the Rats of NIMH* [5-126].

5-144. Sleator, William. **Singularity.** Dutton, 1985 (12 up).
Dislocations in time and space, caused by a singularity or passageway to another universe located on their property, alter Barry and Harry, twins trapped in a competitive relationship. Entertaining amalgam of young adult focus on difficult sibling relationship, sympathetically handled, and current speculation concerning black holes. Contrast Randall's *A Watcher in the Woods* [5-134].

5-145. Slobodkin, Louis. **The Space Ship under the Apple Tree.** Macmillan, 1952 (8–10).
Marty, a junior scientist-explorer from outer space, lands under an apple tree in Eddie's grandmother's apple orchard. Eddie and Marty become close friends and share many adventures. Perhaps more space fairy tale than science fiction, the book is humorous, lively, and enjoyed by younger children. Further adventures of Marty and Eddie are *The Space Ship Returns to the Apple Tree* (1958), *The Three-Seated Space Ship* (1962), *Round Trip Space Ship* (1968), and *The Space Ship in the Park* (1972).

*5-146. Snyder, Zilpha Keatley. **Below the Root.** Atheneum, 1975 (13 up).
In the first part of the Green Sky trilogy the Kindar are introduced. They live pleasantly in the large branches and trunks of the great trees of Green Sky; the banished Erdlings live below, barely above subsistence level, and called monsters by the Ol-zhaan, leaders of Green Sky. Young Raamo, destined to be a leader and very curious, descends to the ground and, finding out the truth, sets in motion the rejoining of the two peoples. A low-keyed, leisurely moving narrative pace does not seriously detract from the impact of the very detailed and ultimately convincing portrait of this unique arboreal society. Compare Williams's *The People of the Ax* [5-172] and Hoover's *Children of Morrow* [5-70]. *And All Between* (1976) focuses on two children, Teera and Pomma (Erdling and Kindar, respectively), who utilize their telekinetic powers to smooth over the forces working to keep apart the two groups. *Until the Celebration* (1977) details the growing pains of the peoples' rejoining, finally accomplished when Raamo gives his life to cement the union.

*5-147. Stone, Josephine Rector. **The Mudhead.** Atheneum, 1980 (13 up).
The "purple people-eaters" of Sigma capture Corly when, bored and resentful,

the young boy leaves the station established by the terran scientific team. Physically tormented, he is saved by the tribe's shaman, a Mudhead, despised but required by the people, only to realize that he is himself destined to become a Mudhead. Further pain and deprivation must be suffered before Corly and his brother, also captured, can escape. Impressive mingling of anthropology and space exploration; especially effective setting; convincing and moving portrait of a boy's maturation through physical and psychological suffering. Compare Engdahl's *The Far Side of Evil* [5-48].

5-148. Stone, Josephine Rector. **Praise All the Moons of Morning.** Atheneum, 1979 (10–14).
Via time travel two young women from different pasts join forces on the planet Ix-thlan and, aided by Kiffen, an Aslan-like protector, escape the evil, demonic Tez and his worshipers, the Goldmen, and find a utopian future. Themes of youth's testing, drug addiction, and potentially creative tension between the old and the new are special features. Contrast Strete's *The Bleeding Man and Other Science Fiction Stories* [5-150].

*5-149. Stoutenburg, Adrien. **Out There.** Viking, 1971 (13–15).
Sometime in the twenty-first century cities lie sterile under steel and plastic domes. Outside is a land so ravaged by waste and pollution that virtually all wildlife is gone. Into this land Zeb and a handful of youngsters travel on an outing to find animal life. The group does locate ample signs of wildlife, but also meets a hunter. An even more ominous note is sounded at the end: the possibility that the restored land may become recreational land, and the cycle of ecological nightmare begin anew. Well-written and believable situation; polemic against human selfishness and exploitation balanced. Contrast Norton's *Star Man's Son: 2250 A.D.* [5-120] or Clarke's *The Happy Planet* [5-35].

5-150. Strete, Craig. **The Bleeding Man and Other Science Fiction Stories.** Greenwillow, 1977 (12 up).
One of the relatively rare collections of original science fiction short stories for youth, the book is also superior science fiction. Exceptional among the well-crafted and provocative stories are "The Bleeding Man," about a young Indian male who becomes psychochemically a superman, and "Into Every Rain, A Little Life Must Fall," a portrait of a future city controlled by "wombeops." Added strength is an Amerind dimension that challenges Western logic and reason. Contrast Norton's *The Beast Master* (1959).

*5-151. Suddaby, (William) Donald (U.K.). **Village Fanfare.** Oxford, 1954 (13 up).
In 1908 the village of Much Swayford becomes the center of activity for Burton, the man from the future. Come to Edwardian England to learn from the past, Burton, through his giant computator and his ability to project images of himself anywhere in the world, relearns and takes back the human attributes—laughter, courage, and love for music—that he believes will enable his time, the age of great brains, to go on. Clearly indebted to Wells not only for its depiction of scientific apparatus and time travel, but for its sympathetic, gently humorous portrayal of British village life. A book that deserves wider reading.

5-152. Sutton, Jean, and Jeff(erson) Sutton. **The Programmed Man.** Putnam, 1968 (13–15).
The conventions of space opera and the novel of espionage are interwoven in this neatly plotted story of suspense and adventure. Various agents feint and counterfeint to discover the secret of the N-Bomb, a weapon that has kept peace in the galaxy. Compounding the intrigue is the existence of the "programmed man," a mysterious agent whose identity and purpose, rumor has it, have been programmed to become known at the moment of great crisis. A double surprise ending caps the fast-paced novel.

5-153. Sutton, Jeff(erson). **Beyond Apollo.** Putnam, 1966 (13 up).
Delivery of the first lunar permanent station is on schedule when Logan sickens from weightlessness and Apollo II has to return to earth. Clay, command pilot, decides to go ahead putting Big Lander on the Moon. The landing is successful, but an off-target landing spot and another injury appear to force abandonment of the project until Clay stays behind alone to man the station. A taut, suspenseful story; vivid, believable rendering of landing procedure; good description of Moon scenery, atmosphere, and travel; theme of human endurance and determination easily comes across. Compare Marsten's *Rocket to Luna* [5-107].

*5-154. Swindells, Robert (U.K.). **Brother in the Land.** Oxford, 1984; Holiday House, 1985 (13 up).
In the aftermath of nuclear war in Britain, Danny, his younger brother, Ben, and their friend, Kim, can hope to survive only by adopting "Neanderthal" tactics. Ruthlessly honest extrapolation, realistic characterization, and starkly effective style constitute a powerful story. Compare Mace's *Out There* [5-103]; contrast Lawrence's *Children of the Dust* [5-93].

5-155. Townsend, John Rowe. **The Creatures.** Lippincott, 1980 (13 up).
Two young Persons, Victor and Harmony, decide to leave Colony, established on Earth by its conquerors from Home Planet, and find out for themselves if life can be less restrictive and more exciting out among the Creatures, those native to Earth and despised by the supercerebral Persons. Becoming entangled in intrigue and open revolt, the young couple side with the Creatures in their fight for freedom. Plausible story of adventure and insight into the nature of real liberty and responsibility.

5-156. Townsend, John Rowe. **Noah's Castle.** Lippincott, 1975 (12 up).
The Mortimer family, led by its stubborn father, battens down through hoarding to live out a catastrophe of inflation and scarcity befalling England in the near future. Strains within the family and without force several members to break with the father's plan, and the "castle" is invaded and destroyed. Relentlessly honest in its picture of strong personalities clashing and vivid in depicting society's disintegration, the novel is superior postcatastrophe fiction. Compare Christopher's *The Guardians* [5-30]; contrast Corlett's *Return to the Gate* [5-37].

5-157. Townsend, John Rowe. **The Visitors.** Lippincott, 1977 (14 up).
While jotting down his rapidly fading memories of the Wyatts and their daughter, ostensibly foreign and very mysterious visitors to Cambridge, young John

Dunham is forced to admit that the latter are actually visitors from the future and can bring only grief to those whose lives they touch. The time travel motif is handled freshly and poignantly; characterization is deft and insightful. Compare Suddaby's *Village Fanfare* [5-151].

5-158. Vance, Jack. **Vandals of the Void.** Winston, 1953 (12–14).
Futuristic piracy and old-fashioned megalomania play prominent roles in this novel of space rockets being attacked, taken, and reconverted into a fleet designed to conquer Earth and its colonies. Young Dick Murdock uncovers the lair of the Basilisk and is able to alert Earth to former's identity and plans. The story, in spite of the vintage space opera elements, is still interesting because of the rich detailing and swift narrative pace. Stylistically one of the best-written Winston 1950s novels.

5-159. Van Lhin, Eric (pseud. of Lester del Rey). **Battle on Mercury.** Winston, 1953 (12–14).
When rescue ship crashes and a terrible electric storm is imminent, one of the mining domes on Mercury faces extinction. Dick Rogers; his "pet" Johnny Quicksilver, a Wispie, which is an indigenous life form; Pete the Robot; and Hotshot Charlie, a prospector, combine to bring aid successfully after battling the inhospitable terrain, electricity-eating demons, and Silicone Beasts. Still "fun reading," the novel stands out among the Winston series because of its deft style, fast pace, and imaginative characterization. Compare Vance's *Vandals of the Void* [5-158].

*5-160. Vinge, Joan D. **Psion.** Delacorte, 1982 (13 up).
Centuries in the future, Cat, an illiterate slum child, reluctantly undergoes training to utilize his telepathic powers and becomes involved in the struggle both to outwit Robiy, an evil telepath, and to aid the wise telepaths, the Hydrans. Fine characterization, detailed setting, provocative study of psi, and suspenseful plotting; engrossing narrative. Compare the Johnsons' *Prisoner of PSI* [5-82]; contrast Norton's *Quest Crosstime* [5-118].

5-161. Walsh, Jill Paton (U.K.). **The Green Book.** Macmillan, 1981; Farrar, 1982 (8–10).
Forced to leave Earth to establish a colony on Shine, Pattie and her father, brother, and sisters learn that humans can adapt and a new home is established. Short narrative, almost elegantly written with believable characters and plausible incidents, is a good example of effective SF for younger readers. Compare Morressy's *The Windows of Forever* [5-114].

5-162. Walters, Hugh (pseud. of Walter Llewellyn Hughes) (U.K.). **Destination Mars.** Faber, 1963 (12–14).
All goes well as Chris Godfrey and his companions find, during investigation into the possibility of Martian life, exciting evidence of life and civilization. However, disembodied Martian life makes its presence known and demands to be taken to Earth. When the crew resists, the new hostile life takes over the minds of all except Chris and begins the flight to Earth. Mysterious space voices, transmitted by the ship's radio, frighten away the Martians and the crew escapes. Effective space adventure, adequately written, ample incident and suspense, representative of

the author's quality work in children's science fiction. Compare Heinlein's *Rocket Ship Galileo* [5-63] or Capon's *Lost: A Moon* [5-25].

5-163. Walters, Hugh (pseud. of Walter Llewellyn Hughes) (U.K.). **The Mohole Mystery.** Faber, 1968 (12–14).
Four astronauts, becoming "subterranauts," volunteer to descend 40 miles into Earth's mantle. First Serge, then Chris, via rocket plummeting down a two-feet-in-diameter tube into a forbidding cavern, ascertain the source of a mysterious, deadly bacteria. Perhaps the best written of the author's many books. The narrative moves fast and features interesting technology and training techniques. Only flaw is implausible balloonlike creatures residing in the cavern.

5-164. Walton, Bryce. **Sons of the Ocean Deeps.** Winston, 1952 (12–14).
Chagrined at having been washed out of the rocket program, Jon West hopes to hide away in the underseas service. Gradually learning underwater survival techniques, suffering patiently the taunts of Sprague, who resents his family, and acquiring self-knowledge, Jon proves himself a man. One of the better 1950s Winston novels. Depiction of aquatic life, real and imagined, and of possible living quarters is extensive and interesting; style is competent; and hero's maturation is plausible and convincing. Compare Norton's *Star Man's Son: 2250 A.D.* [5-120].

5-165. Watson, Simon (U.K.). **No Man's Land.** Gollancz, 1975 (12 up).
Set in a future England where progress rules and the countryside is "rationalized" through technology, the story concerns Alan's fight, aided by another youth, Jay, and the 65-year-old general, to prevent the demolition of an ancient keep by a gigantic robot. Although the fight is successful, the victory over rationalizing is just local. A bit slow moving, the novel impresses because of its plausible scenario and its sympathetic portrait of old age and love of the countryside. Compare Corlett's *Return to the Gate* [5-37]; contrast Christopher's *The Prince in Waiting* [5-31].

5-166. Webb, Sharon. **Earthchild.** Atheneum, 1982 (13 up).
Young people who can become immortal because of the Mouat-Gari process must be protected from their envious elders. Since immortality is no guarantee of creativity, a select few, chosen by Kurt Kraus, one of the immortal leaders, are asked to decide between immortality and creative mortality. Engrossing reading, provocative speculation, and poignant and believable situations. Sequels are *Earth Song* (1983), which focuses on David Defour, a gifted young composer who chooses music over immortality, and *Ram Song* (1984), in which Kurt again intervenes to preserve balance between demands for immortality and society's need for creativity. Compare Bonham's *The Forever Formula* [5-20].

*5-167. Westall, Robert (U.K.). **Futuretrack 5.** Kestrel, 1983 (13 up).
A young computer genius, Kitson goes "razzle," running away from tending Laura, the master computer, and joining up with Keri, a master cyclist. The couple set out to discover the secret of Scott-Astbury, responsible for much that explains tightly controlled twenty-first-century England. Powerful novel: nightmarish depiction of future life, especially in the cities; intriguing plot; distinctive, richly allusive, yet colloquial style. Compare Burgess's *A Clockwork Orange* [3–82].

5-168. White, T(erence) H(ansbury). **The Master.** Cape, 1957 (14 up).
Exploring the supposedly barren island Rockall, Nicky and Judy accidentally fall into the water and into the secret headquarters of the Master, a 157-year-old ESP adept who is plotting to conquer the world via powerful vibrators he has invented. Another accident, when the Master slips into the ocean after being bitten by the children's dog, finally saves the world. Off-beat characterization and psychological probing are revealed through the extensive dialogue; hence, a bit talky for many young readers. Still, the acerbic wit and charm characteristic of the author are present. Compare MacArthur's *The Thunderbolt Men* [5-102].

5-169. Wibberly, Leonard (pseud. of Patrick O'Connor). **Encounter Near Venus.** Farrar, 1967 (11–13).
Four members of a family must spend their summer vacation with their uncle. Becoming involved with Venusian life forms, children and uncle journey to Nede, a satellite of Venus, where they are caught up in a struggle to keep Ka, the evil Smiler, away from corrupting Nede, an innocent world. A struggle between-forms-of-good-and-evil book, suggestive of the Narnia books by C. S. Lewis. Information about science and ethics is, generally speaking, skillfully meshed into the narrative.

5-170. Wilder, Cherry (New Zealand). **The Luck of Brin's Five.** Atheneum, 1977 (13 up).
Scott Gale, navigator of a terran bio-survey team on Torin, crash-lands and is found and befriended by Dorn, member of the family called Brin's Five. According to custom, the family considers Scott a Diver and their new "luck." Through the ensuing adventures—in particular, those involving flying machines and air races—and the dangerous intrigue of those opposed to change, Scott proves he is indeed a "luck" and precipitates a new openness to change among the people. Although narrative pace flags occasionally, the novel creates an original world and culture vaguely Oriental. Sequel is *The Nearest Five* (1980), which just as engagingly continues to detail Torin. Compare Yep's *Sweetwater* [5-179].

5-171. Williams, Jay, and Raymond Abrashkin. **Danny Dunn and the Homework Machine.** McGraw, 1958 (10–12).
Entrusted by Professor Bullfinch with a home-sized computer, Danny cannot resist using it for his homework. His teacher and his mother, however, arrange matters in such a way that Danny and his friends, Joe and Irene, learn their homework as they program the computer. Typical of the 15-volume Danny Dunn series: some adventure built around a scientific device, real or imagined, designed by Professor Bullfinch, and involving Danny and his friends. Easy reading, diverting and entertaining, very popular with children.

5-172. Williams, Jay. **The People of the Ax.** Walck, 1974 (12–14).
A postcatastrophe story. Two societies have survived: human beings, or the ax people, who have souls and no longer kill except for food, and the "crom," a humanlike people hated by the humans. Arne realizes he possesses "tendo," the ability to sense the spirit of harmony in all, and hence is destined to become a leader of the humans. Arne's first, and revolutionary, intuition is a suspicion that crom may also be human, and he successfully awakens soul in one of their lead-

ers. Competently written, plausible look at possible future societies, except that author becomes too tendentious when contemporary civilization is blamed for all human failures. Very different from the Danny Dunn series. Compare Norton's *Star Man's Son: 2250 A.D.* [5-120].

5-173. Williams, Jay. **The Time of the Kraken.** Four Winds, 1977 (12 up).
Spurned by his people as he warns them of the coming of the terrible Kraken, Thorgeir Redhair seeks the gods' help. With three companions, the young hero makes the arduous journey to the Temple of Arveid and learns the surprising truth: his people are descendants of humans escaping from a hopelessly polluted Earth via rockets to new worlds. A brisk retelling, cast in heroic terms, of Icelandic saga that presupposes a scientific explanation for the latter; hence, an adroit blending of fantasy and science fiction. Compare Huddy's *Time Piper* [5-76].

5-174. Williamson, Jack. **Trapped in Space.** Doubleday, 1968 (10–14).
Although resenting Ben, his older and more talented brother, Jeff Stone still volunteers to search for him, missing while exploring Topaz. Accompanied by Lupe Flor, a fellow starman, and a fuzzy alien, Buzzy Dozen-Dozen, Jeff locates his brother among the hostile rock hoppers of Topaz. Before a rescue can be effected, the humans must convince the hoppers to trust Earth and join the galaxywide family. Written economically without sacrificing detail or variety, the story effectively combines adventure, space technology, and the theme of growing up. Compare Marsten's *Rocket to Luna* [5-107].

5-175. Winterfeld, Henry (Germany). **Star Girl.** Harcourt, 1957. Tr. by Kyrill Schabert of *Kommt ein Madchen Geflogen*, 1956 (11–13).
Mo, an 87-year-old "girl" from Asra or Venus, accidentally falls out of her father's spaceship. She is found by several German children under a forest tree and they, believing her story, agree to help Mo meet her father that night. The village adults refuse to believe or help Mo, but the children and Mo eventually succeed. Exceptional are the realistic portrayal of adult disbelief and their quick willingness to consider Mo insane, and the sharply distinguished characterization of Mo and the children. Less convincing is the speculation about possible Venusian civilization.

5-176. Wollheim, Donald A. **The Secret of Saturn's Rings.** Winston, 1954 (10–12).
Young Bruce Rhodes accompanies his famous scientist father on a United Nations mission to prove that Saturn's rings were artificially caused. The expedition, although harassed by Terraluna, a corporation seeking to blast into the Moon's core to find precious ores, is successful, and evidence of life on Saturn is uncovered. The scenes describing father and son marooned in the rings and devising ways to travel are still imaginative; one of the better 1950s Winston books. Compare Latham's *Missing Men of Saturn* [5-92].

5-177. Wollheim, Donald A. **The Secret of the Martian Moons.** Winston, 1955 (12–14).
Early children's mainstream space opera. A handful of humans, secretly left behind in a final attempt to discover the origin and fate of the Martian cities, become embroiled in a rivalry between the two factions of the cowardly Vegans,

who centuries before had placed two artificial spheres, Phobos and Deimos, in orbit near Mars. Before peace can be established, the Star people, the original inhabitants of Mars, return and enter into an alliance with Earth. Minimal characterization and science hardware, but ample incident and a quick-moving story. Contrast Claudy's *The Mystery Men of Mars* [5-36].

5-178. Wrightson, Patricia (Australia). **Down to Earth.** Harcourt, 1965 (9–11). The new, strange boy in George's neighborhood in Sydney turns out to be Martin, a Martian touring Earth. After a series of incidents (some of them quite humorous) brought about by Martin's difficulty in adjusting to Earth customs and his habit of announcing to anyone he meets that he is from outer space, Martin, along with other "tourists," departs for home just as Earth's defenses sense a possible invasion. A believable, humorous, and at times touching space fantasy. Compare Winterfeld's *Star Girl* [5-175]; contrast Key's *The Forgotten Door* [5-89].

*5-179. Yep, Laurence. **Sweetwater.** Harper, 1973 (12 up).
Young Tyree is torn between pursuing an interest in music encouraged by Amadeus, an Argan (the oldest race on the planet Harmony), and obeying his father, elected captain of the Silkies, descendants of the starship crews from Earth, who are fighting for a life in harmony with the dominant sea. A distinctive narrative that unexpectedly and winningly combines a richly imagined world and its ecology, a boy's rite of passage, and wide-ranging allusions to music and the Old Testament. Compare Norton's *Star Man's Son: 2250 A.D.* [5-120].

*5-180. Zebrowski, George. **Sunspacer.** Harper, 1984 (14 up).
Unsure whether he wants a career in theoretical physics but aware that he needs adventure and the challenge of hardship and danger, Joe Sorby, a high school student of the future, forgoes college on Bernal to become a maintenance apprentice. Very detailed scenario of possible solar system exploration; convincing portrait of youth unsure of himself and his options. Compare Kurland's *The Princes of Earth* [5-91] or Heinlein's *Starman Jones* [5-65].

Foreign-Language
Science Fiction

6
Foreign-Language Science Fiction

A large majority of those books that might be called science fiction were originally published in English, but considerable work of distinction—and much of no distinction—has been published in other languages. Some of this has been translated into English, but for many reasons a body of quality work remains inaccessible to the monolingual English-language reader. So that this guide can be of benefit to readers of languages in addition to English, untranslated SF and selected nonfiction in a number of languages are surveyed here by specialists whose backgrounds are summarized in the list of contributors at the beginning of this book.

The contributors were asked to annotate mainly books not yet translated into English, but they were encouraged to refer to translated works in their introductions. Cross-reference entry numbers, therefore, appear in the introductory essays. Both translated and nontranslated works are listed in alphabetical order by the author; the references to entry numbers for translated works indicate that these English-language books are annotated in other chapters. Through the listing of both translated and nontranslated works in this chapter, the reader may obtain a more complete overview of a national literature. The sequence of entries is individual authors, anthologies, nonfiction, and, in some cases, magazines. Chapters dealing with SF in Hungarian, Czechoslovakian, and Polish were promised but unfortunately not received in time.

German SF

Franz Rottensteiner

One of the main difficulties with German SF (written originally in German) is that it has attracted so little critical or even bibliographical attention.[1] Since most of it is not relevant in a literary sense, it has not been preserved in the libraries, let alone collected (I know of no German library with a special SF collection) or documented. In fact, until recently there existed only two bibliographies of German SF—Heinz Bingenheimer's very incomplete *Katalog der deutschsprachigen utopisch-phantastischen Literatur aus fünf Jahrhunderten 1460–1960* (1959–1960) and volume 2 of *Lexikon der Science Fiction Literatur* [6-36]. This deplorable state has been rectified to a large extent by Robert N. Bloch's *Bibliographie der utopischen und phantastischen Literatur 1750–1950* [6-39], a much more comprehensive work, comparable to E. F. Bleiler's *Checklist* [8-2]. An in-depth study containing much original bibliographical research is Nagl's *Science Fiction in Deutschland* [6-45]. It even contains some information of SF in popular German magazines, a particularly neglected field. Before World War I, many illustrated papers, especially boys' magazines, book series like Das Magazin der Unterhaltung und des Wissens, and yearbooks for young readers such as the still existing *Das neue Universum* published some SF. But even the many short stories written by the popular Hans Dominik for *Das neue Universum* were not collected in book form until 1977 (and then only partially). .

The "Groschenhefte," saddle-stitched publications similar to the American dime novels, played an essential role in the development of German SF; yet, although they are important even today, they have received very little historical treatment. One such series became known principally because Willy Ley (a skilled science populizer who often wrote articles for SF magazines) happened to mention it: Der Luftpirat und sein lenkbares Luftschiff, later reprinted also as *Der Fliegerteufel* and known as *Kapitän Mors*. Appearing since 1908 in Berlin, there were at least 165 weekly issues, with an estimated circulation of 40,000 to 100,000 copies. Between 1909 and 1913, this was probably the most popular dime novel series for boys in Germany and featured a hero who is the cosmic equivalent of Verne's Captain Nemo, a Robin Hood of outer space. His spaceship is powered by solar energy, and he has an arsenal of marvelous inventions for his adventures. At least in its technological aspects, the series appears to have been quite advanced for its time.

An earlier series, very similar to the American Frank Reade books, was Aus dem Reiche der Phantasie (1901, ten issues) by Robert Kraft (1869–1916). Its young protagonist, Richard, is transported by "imagination" in the shape of a young woman into various backgrounds, including the Stone Age and the Moon with its etheric inhabitants. The author was a prolific hack in the manner of Karl May, but more given to mystical and fantastical and technological elements. He wrote a number of books full of inventions à la Jules Verne, such as *Im Panzerautomobil um die Erde* (1906), *Der Herr der Lüfte* (1908), *Die Nihilit Expedition* (1909), and *Im Aeroplan um die Erde* (1908), but more typical are long serials appearing in weekly installments of mostly 32 pages each, running to thousands of pages. Examples are *Detekiv Nobody's Erlebnisse und Reisabenteuer* (1904–1906), *Atalanta, die Geheimnisse des Sklavensees* (about 1912), and *Klingsor, der Mann mit den Teufelsaugen* (1915–1916). They contain everything that popular literature has to offer. Since heroes and villains chase each other around the world, there are episodes in the Wild West, among Chinese pirates, and in Egyptian tombs, and the Earth is bored with labyrinths and infested with secret societies. Mysteries are Kraft's stock-in-trade, and his protagonists take it on themselves to mete out punishments that do exceed the crimes. Elements of supertechnology are included as well as mystical and supernatural ones. In *Die neue Erde* (1910), planned as the first of a book series, Kraft deals with the theme of a catastrophic shift of the poles, with a new age of barbarism.

Similar adventure stories of the time were the five volumes of *Thomas Alva Edison, der grosse Erfinder*, written by one "John Merriman" and pretending to be translations from the English; cheap plagiarisms of Wells; and Robert Heymann's series Wunder der Zukunft, "novels from the 30th century" (1909).

Between the wars this tradition was continued by two successful dime novel series: Sun Koh, der Erbe von Atlantis (1933–1936, 150 issues) and Jan Mayen, Herr der Atomkraft (1935–1939, 120 issues), written by P. A. Müller under the pseudonyms Lok Myler and Freder van Holk. Sun Koh is an Atlantean who appears in modern London without memory, but soon gets hold of various superweapons to battle against evil and to become master of Atlantis when it will rise again from the waves. The series was so successful that it had several (somewhat rewritten) editions after World War II and is currently running again as a paperback series.

After 1945 there were a number of other, short-lived series, as well as lending library editions (shoddy books produced in small editions specifically for lending libraries, then numerous in Germany, until they were killed in the 1960s by television and the paperbacks). In 1951 and 1952, the first American SF novels were beginning to appear in hardback, and since 1953 another dime novel series, Utopia—Jim Parkers Abenteuer im Weltraum, was published by Pabel and written under the house pseudonym of Alf Tjörnsen; in 1954 Pabel followed with *Utopia-Grossband,* mostly translations of American SF, but also including some German authors such as Henry Walter, Clark Darlton (Walter Ernsting, editor of the series), Wolf Detlef Rohr, and others, up to number 203 (1963). *Jim Parker* was soon finished in *Utopia,* but the series continued with a mixture of good and bad, translations and German originals, up to 1968 (no. 596). Its big competitor became *Terra* (since 1957) from Pabel's rival, Moewig, to which Ernsting had switched. Moewig also published a *Terra Sonderband* (99 issues, 1958–1965, since then a paperback series; it folded with no. 371 in 1986). From 1955 to 1959, Pabel put out 26 issues of the first true German SF magazine, *Utopia-Magazin,* which included a number of German authors, among them Hellmut W. Hofmann and Jesco von Puttkamer. *Terra* (555 issues) was followed by 190 issues of its successor, *Terra Nova,* and 643 issues of the now defunct *Terra Astra.* In 1960, hardcover and, more significantly, paperback publication of SF was begun on a larger scale in Germany by Heyne and Goldmann (initially hardbacks, paperbacks since 1962). Goldmann also published a number of books by the Austrian-born Herbert W. Franke.

The paperbacks did not kill the dime novels, and the most successful series of them all began in 1961: Perry Rhodan, conceived by K. H. Scheer, a prolific writer for the lending libraries, and Walter Ernsting, SF editor, writer, and translator, who also has the honor of having founded German SF fandom. Besides the two originators, the novels were written by a team of authors that over the years included Kurt Brand, William Voltz, Ernst Vlcek, H. G. Ewers, Kurt Mahr, and H. G. Francis (the last three pseudonyms).[2] Perry Rhodan may be called "total" SF, the ultimate series incorporating everything that was ever thought of in science fiction written into one interminable sequence. Rhodan and his team of humans, aliens, robots, and mutants roam through time and space, empire-building. More than 1,300 weekly issues have appeared so far; there is a sideline in Atlan (another 800 issues), a paperback series featuring other characters from the Rhodan universe (in three printings); but a *Perry Rhodan Magazin* lasted only from 1978 to 1981. The main series is now in its fifth printing, and Moewig reissues the series in book form (25 volumes so far). Sales figures are a closely guarded secret, but the first volumes were said to have been about 70,000 copies each. By now, sales of the books undoubtedly have fallen off, but of the whole series an impressive one billion copies have been sold in Germany alone.

Rhodan imitators by other publishers were all failures: *Mark Powers* (1962–1964, 48 issues and more in *Utopia*), *Rex Corda* (1966–1967, 38 issues), and *Ren Dhark* (1966–1968, 98 issues). There were and still are many other (single hero and other) dime novel series, such as Zauberkreis SF, Zeitkugel, Commander Scott, Gemini, Erber SF, Orion—often the only outlet for the beginning writer.

At the other end of the SF spectrum are books, usually of high literary quality, written by non-SF writers; on the one hand in the more respected field of fantastic literature, sometimes touching on SF (the interest of E. T. A. Hoffmann in particular and of German romanticism in general in automatons, golems, doppelgängers, and similar beings on the borderline between science and fantasy—a strong tradition continued in the twentieth century in the work of such writers as Gustav Meyrink, Alfred Kubin, Oskar Panizza, and the more sensational Hanns Heinz Ewers, with Franz Kafka as a somewhat literary showcase) and on the other hand in the equally respected genre of utopias and dystopias. One utopian forerunner was Michael Georg Conrad's *In purpurner Finsternis*[3] (1895), a mediocre novel influenced partly by Nietzsche and critical of Wilhelmian Germany. Bellamy's *Looking Backward* [1-8] (translated 1890) also prompted a number of continuations and mostly angry protests: Eugen Richter's *Sozialdemokratische Zukunftsbilder* (1891), Richard Michaelis's *Ein Blick in die Zukunft* (1890), Emil Gregorevius's *Der Himmel auf Erden* (1892), and others. Notable utopias were Theodor Hertzka's *Freiland* (1891) and Theodor Herzl's Zionist vision *Altneuland* (1902)—the one utopia that came true.

A utopian and an absolute outsider both in German SF and German letters was Paul Scheerbart (1863–1915), a Prussian pacifist who is said to have starved to death in protest against World War I. He writes in a very simple, almost childish, and colorful style, locating his stories in remote places of the Earth or preferably in a cosmos that is conceived as a total antithesis to the misery and drudgery of this planet. In his universe all is play and simply a matter of the most amazing and surprising metamorphoses. Scheerbart was a proponent of glass architecture, and his fiction is dominated by visual images; he believed in the ameliorating power of light. His best SF novel is probably *Lesabèndio*[4] (1913), the story of a Babylonian tower project among the wormlike inhabitants of the asteroid Pallas. His significant books include *Na prost!* (1898), *Die grosse Revolution* [6-29], the Munchhausian novel, *Münchhausen und Clarissa* (1906), and *Astrale Novelletten* (1912). Scheerbart has enthusiastic supporters and critics but very few readers. But because Scheerbart is now in the public domain, many of his books have been reissued, both in beautiful collectors' editions and in paperback.

More realistic were the single SF books by Bernhard Kellermann, Gerhart Hauptmann, and Alfred Döblin—all writers of eminent literary status. Kellermann's *Der Tunnel*[5] (1913) is a fiction classic dealing with technology and technicians; the gigantic project of a tunnel between Europe and America is an epic struggle of deep impact. Alfred Döblin, one of the greatest of all German novelists, wrote in *Berge, Meere und Giganten*[6] [6-8] a stark and wild vision of the coming wars in Europe, the clash of ideologies and races, and the titanic attempts of humankind to refashion genetically the human body. In the breadth of its scope and vision, the book is sometimes reminiscent of Olaf Stapledon, but it is much more powerful.

During and after World War II, two spiritual utopias of world standing saw publication: Hermann Hesse's *Das Glasperlenspiel* [3-212] and Franz Werfel's *Stern der Ungebornen* [3-396], both mighty attempts to reaffirm traditional Western values of mind and heart in a world swept by Nazism. Another traditional novelist of great impact is Ernst Jünger, who contributed two novels to SF: *Heliopolis*[7] (1949) and *Gläserne Bienen* (1957). Both affirm traditional cultural values, but unlike Hesse or Werfel, Jünger is more combative than contemplative and opposed to all collectivist and socialist ideas, stressing instead the testing by fire of the combat soldier and the experience of the trenches. Zestful antitotalitarian dystopias are Hermann Kasack's *Die Stadt hinter dem Strom* (1949) and

Walter Jens's *Nien: Die Welt der Angeklagten* (1950). The topical theme of atomic holocaust has also given rise to some notable works. Hans Wörner wrote *Wir fanden Menschen* (1948); Jens Rehn, *Die Kinder des Saturn* [6-26]; and Hannelore Valencak, *Die Höhlen Noahs* (1961). An eccentric figure in German letters, an admirer of Poe, Verne, Bulwer-Lytton, and James Joyce (whom he equals in difficulty of style) was Arno Schmidt (1914–1979). His *Die Gelehrten-republik* (1957, translated as *The Egghead Republic*) is a cold war satire taking place in a postatomic world, where strange mutants roam; the short novel bows to Verne's *Propeller Island* in its use of the ship situation. *Kaff, auch Mare Crisium* (1960) contrasts a lunar setting with a typically philistine German household. The book has been praised highly by some, while others have attacked its irreverence as obscene. Some SF affinities are also notable in the work of Heinrich Schirmbeck, Carl Amery, and Günter Herburger.

In the mainstream, the undisputed pioneer of German SF was Kurd Lasswitz[8] (1848–1910). His *Auf zwei Planeten* [6-22] is a classic of interplanetary fiction, remarkable not only for its striking anticipation of space travel, including space stations, but also for its attempt to give philosophical depth to a struggle between a technologically advanced humanoid Mars and an Earth fighting for independence and autonomy. The novel is not wholly successful—Lasswitz was too didactic—but is nevertheless a praiseworthy effort. In a lighter vein are some of his really inventive short stories in the volumes *Bilder aus der Zukunft* [6-23], *Seifenblasen* (1890), and *Traumkristalle* (1902).

The most successful SF writer of the period between the wars was Hans Dominik (1872–1945), an engineer turned writer. After many stories for young readers, Dominik serialized a novel, *Die Macht der Drei*,[9] in *Die Woche* (1922); the book edition sold 170,000 copies during his lifetime. Dominik's stories usually revolve around a single invention, which is never described in detail—a new fuel, electricity from the air, invisibility, a supermetal, various new energies—but his real theme is power as the nations of Earth, allied in changing constellations, fight for world control. His novels became increasingly nationalistic. Hardly less important than the dominant inventions is a strain of mysticism in them and a belief in destiny. Typical novels are *Atlantis* (1925), *König Laurins Mantel* (1928), *Befehl aus dem Dunkel* (1933), *Lebensstrahlen* (1938), and *Himmelskraft* (1939). Similar to him is Rudolf H. Daumann (1896–1957), author of *Dünn wie eine Eierschale* (1937), *Macht aus der Sonne* (1937), and other works.

The 1920s saw a wealth of German SF, mostly trivial, some rather revanchist and militarist, in which Germany takes revenge for its defeat in World War I, while others are more mystical or racist. Edmund Kiss, for instance, wrote a tetralogy about Atlantis, celebrating the Aryans.[10] That decade was also the heyday of German rocketry, when the members of the Verein für Raumschiffahrt dreamed of interplanetary space travel. Otto Willi Gail (1896–1956) is one of the writers who presented a technically almost accurate picture of space travel, inspired by the work of Oberth and his friend Max Valier. Both *Der Schuss ins All* [2-33] and its sequel, *Der Stein vom Mond* (1926), appeared also—as did some other German SF of the time, including Friedrich Freksa's novel of cryonics and interplanetary invasion, *Druso: Oder die gestohlene Menschenwelt*[11] (1931)—in the American SF magazines. Bruno H. Bürgel, Curt Siodmak, Thea von Harbou (*Me-*

tropolis [2-123]; *Die Frau im Mond,* 1926, both important UFA films), Otfried von Hanstein, Walther Kegel, Karl-August von Laffert, Hans Richter, St. Bialkowski, and F. W. Mader were other, often quite prolific, SF writers between the wars.

After World War II, Freder van Holk, Claus Eigk, P. E. Sieg, and Richard Koch continued this tradition in books, but the newer generation of writers followed the Anglo-Saxon example. At the beginning of the 1980s, German SF seemed to be booming, as did science fiction in general. Heyne, the largest German SF publisher with eight to ten titles a month, published an original German novel or short-story collection nearly every month. There were also many original German SF anthologies, a lot of them edited by Jörg Weigand, beginning with *Quasar I* (1979), and especially notable being *Vorgriff auf morgen* (1981); and by Thomas Le Blanc, who had, after *Die Anderen* (1979) with Heyne, a series of all-German anthologies for Goldmann in Munich, named after various stars in alphabetical order, beginning with *Antares;* but the books were of rather mixed quality, and they ended with *Jupiter* (1985). Other short-story outlets for German writers were Wolfgang Jeschke's *SF Story Readers* (with Heyne, ending with no. 21 in 1984, now continued irregularly under individual titles), Herbert W. Franke's *International SF* (with Goldmann, three volumes) and now *Kontinuum* (so far three volumes with Ullstein), Franz Rottensteiner's *Polaris* (Suhrkamp, so far ten volumes), and Hans Joachim Alpers's *Kopernikus* (14 volumes, Moewig)—all international anthologies with an occasionally high percentage of German contributions.

But the readers reacted, sometimes violently, to the appearance of German authors, writing angry letters to publishers, and when the SF boom (1984–1986) was over and sales declined sharply, German authors were the first to suffer—along with translations from non-English languages, and anthologies in general. Heyne went back from ten titles a month to eight and Moewig from four to two monthly; Ullstein, Suhrkamp, and Knaur also cut their lists, and Knaur is ceasing publication of SF altogether. Especially marked is the reduction at Moewig/Pabel, once the largest SF publisher in Germany. The company folded its series Terra SF, Terra Fantasy, Andre Norton, E. C. Tubb, and Clark Darlton (these last three authors had series named after them, following the success of the collected works of the German writers K. H. Scheer and W. D. Rohr). With any regularity German SF appears now only from Ullstein (Andreas Brandhorst/Horst Pukallus, Thomas Ziegler, Ronald M. Hahn, K. Iwoleit) and Suhrkamp (Herbert W. Franke, Peter Schattschneider, Ulrich Horstmann, Marianne Gruber, Gerd Maximović, as well as some East German writers such as J. and G. Braun and Karlheinz and Angela Steinmüller—both husband-wife teams).

The quality of German writers is rather mixed, but promising writers include Karl Michael Armer, Marianne Gruber, Thomas Ziegler, Joern J. Bambeck, Gero Reimann, Gisbert Haefs, Bernard Richter, Georg Zauner, Gerd Maximović, Peter Schattschneider, Horst Pukallus, Gerd Ulrich Weise, Hendrick P. Linckens, H. J. Alpers (also an editor and agent), and Wolfgang Jeschke (SF editor of the most important German SF publisher, Heyne)—in no particular order. A more important market for German SF writers than the paperbacks (there are virtually no SF hardcovers in Germany; only Stanislaw Lem appears in hardback, and even Asimov and Clarke usually only in paper) is the SF radio dramatizations that Dieter Hasselblatt (formerly with Deutschlandfunk, now with Bayerischer Rundfunk) has done much to promote. Men's magazines, such as the German edition of *Play-*

boy, also run some original SF once in a while. In the juvenile field, the position of German SF is much stronger. Some German publishers do exclusively German authors (Ensslin and Laiblin had a series by Hans Joachim Alpers and Ronald M. Hahn, but an absolute runner is the series Weltraumpartisanen, written by Mark Brandis, a pseudonym for Nikolai von Michalewsky; 30 volumes have appeared since 1970, in many printings). Arena and Boje have strong juvenile lists with about an equal share of translations (Andre Norton, John Christopher, and others) and German originals (Walter Brenner, Lothar Streblow, and Walter Ernsting—who uses his own name on his juveniles).

Herbert W. Franke is generally regarded as the most important German SF author. He has written many collections and novels. Three of his novels have been translated into English: *The Mind Net* (1974), *The Orchid Cage* [3-168], and *Zone Null* (1974); the first two are translations of *Das Gedankennetz* (1961) and *Der Orchideenkäfig* (1961). Other novels by Franke include *Die Glasfalle* (1961), *Die Stahlwüste* (1962), *Der Elfenbeinturm* [6-11], *Ypsilon minus* [6-12], *Sirius Transit* (1979), *Tod eines Unsterblichen* (1982), *Transpluto* (1982), *Die Kälte des Weltraums* (1984), and *Endzeit* (1985); some of his collections are *Der grüne Komet* (1960), *Einsteins Erben* (1972), *Paradies 3000* (1981), and *Der Atem der Sonne* (1986). Franke is not a great storyteller or stylist, but he has found a characteristic and highly successful form of expressing his serious scientific concerns, especially the misuses of communication and the manipulation of human beings.

Much more successful than science fiction has been some German fantasy. Michael Ende's books, *The Neverending Story* (*Die unendliche Geschichte*) and *Momo*, have for years occupied top places on German best-seller lists, and Wolfgang E. Hohlbein's *Märchenmond*, *Elfentanz*, and a series of fantasies for Goldmann have also achieved high print runs.

Just as there are virtually no SF hardbacks in Germany, the climate hasn't been favorable for SF magazines; a *Perry Rhodan Magazin* failed, as did a short-lived German edition of *Omni*. *Starship* (later retitled *Star SF*) lasted only from 1983 to 1984; currently an attempt is being made with *Phantastic Times*, edited by Uwe Drabert. Heyne came out with a lavishly produced magazine in paperback form: *Heyne SF Magazin* (no. 1, 1981, ending with no. 12 in 1985), with a heavy content of nonfiction. On the other hand, there are now two SF almanacs and yearbooks: Moewig has the yearly *SF Almanach* and *Science Fiction Jahrbuch*, both featuring stories, essays, reviews, and annual surveys, both edited by Hans Joachim Alpers; and Heyne started *Das Science Fiction Jahr* in 1986, edited by Wolfgang Jeschke (a sort of yearly continuation of the SF magazine, but without any fiction; it contains also a bibliography of the SF published by Heyne during the year).

To combat the general decline of sales, which in many cases have sunk as low as 3,000 to 4,000 copies for a paperback, many publishers now offer bargain volumes: several volumes either by the same or different authors bound into one at cheap prices.

A late development in German SF is the emergence of specialty publishers, similar to the small fantasy presses in the United States. One such publisher is Corian-Verlag Heinrich Wimmer in Meitingen; besides publishing the semiprofessional magazine *Science Fiction Times* [6-51] and Körber's big *Bibliographisches Lexikon der utopisch-phantastischen Literatur* [6-42], Corian has several book series.

Corian began with a hardcover series by German authors, including Andreas Brandhorst, Ronald M. Hahn/Harald Pusch, Thomas Ziegler, Hendrick P. Linckens, Karen Liepelt, and Michael Weisser, and a reprint of Paul Gurk's classic *Tuzub 37* [6-15]; but those volumes didn't sell and were soon remaindered. Still going is a softbound series, Edition Futurum, which usually presents a specific writer in writings by and about him, including a bibliography, but has also offered two thematic anthologies. So far the following volumes have appeared, in this order: *H. P. Lovecraft—der Poet des Grauens* (1983); *Isaac Asimov—der Tausendjahresplaner* (1984); *Marion Zimmer Bradleys "Darkover"* (1983); *Lesebuch der deutschen Science Fiction* (1983); *J. R. R. Tolkien—der Mythenschöpfer* (1984); *J. G. Ballard—der Visionär des Phantastischen* (1985); *Die seltsamen Welten des Philip K. Dick* (1984); *Stanislaw Lem: An den Grenzen der Science Fiction und darüber hinaus* (1985); *Feministische Utopien—Aufbruch in die postpatriarchale Gesellschaft* (1986); and *Kurd Lasswitz—Lehrer, Philosoph, Zukunftsträumer* (1986).

A second series called Studien zur phantastischen Literatur offers monographs on SF; three volumes, by Dagmar Barnouw, Barbara Puschmann-Nalenz, and Gerd Hallenberger, have appeared so far.

Another small press is Edition Phantasia of Joachim Körber, a prolific German SF translator; he publishes limited editions of works by Philip K. Dick, J. G. Ballard, Peter Straub, and Stephen King, as well as H. P. Lovecraft's *Supernatural Horror in Literature,* in deluxe editions. Körber's greatest coup was the first world publication of Stephen King's *It* in a 300-copy edition, while his most ambitious project is the publication of Scheerbart's collected works.

Vastly different has been the development of SF in the German Democratic Republic[12] (GDR), where pure entertainment is scorned and SF often serves as a vehicle for ideological content; indeed, an addition of ideology is sometimes necessary to get technological speculations into print. Where a direct clash of communism and capitalism is depicted, the writing is just as crude as in Western horror visions of collectivist futures (for example, Aldiss's *Enemies of the System* [1978]). The Dominik and Daumann tradition nevertheless played some role in early GDR science fiction, for example, in the work of Heinz Vieweg, Eberhardt del'Antonio, or Kurt Fahlberg. Later there was a shift into the cosmos, partly influenced by Alexei Tolstoy, Stanislaw Lem, and I. Efremov, sometimes with capitalist-communist confrontations on other planets (del'Antonio's *Titanus* [6-7]) or von Däniken-like meetings between aliens and humans in the past (Carlos Rasch, *Der blaue Planet,* 1963, and Günther Krupkat, *Als die Götter starben,* 1963), and adventures in space like Carlos Rasch's *Asteroidenjäger* (1961) continue to be perennially popular.

With increased liberalization, many of the newer East German writers plainly do not find it necessary to pay lip service to official doctrine. Young writers such as Bernd Ulbrich, Karlheinz Steinmüller (*Der letzte Tag auf der Venus,* 1979, *Windschiefe Geraden,* 1984, and the novel *Andymon,* 1982), and Erik Simon (also an accomplished anthologist) write sophisticated short stories that make hardly any reference to specific social situations and resemble more "ideal" thought-experiments much in the manner of Lem. Or they go, equally like Lem, into satire, irony, and the grotesque, alluding to the present in a veiled, mirror-broken, and comic form. Branstner's *Stern der Beschwingten* (1968) seeks to emulate Swift, while Johanna and Günter Braun[13] are undoubtedly indebted to the German romantic tradition with its fairy tales and grotesqueries, E. T. A. Hoffmann, and particularly Jean Paul. Since the wit of the Brauns is wholly linguistic, it is to be feared, however, that they would not translate well. The Brauns, who publish all of their work under their joint byline, came late to SF; so far they have published five SF books with large circulation in the GDR, three novels—*Der Irrtum des Grossen Zauberers* [6-4], *Unheimliche Erscheinungsformen auf Omega XI*[14] (1974), and *Conviva Ludibundus* (1978)—as well as two superior story collections, *Der Fehlfaktor* [6-3] and *Der Utofant. In der Zukunft aufgefundenes Journal aus dem Jahrtausend III* (1981). But while their older SF continues to be reprinted in the GDR, their latest three SF books could appear only in West Germany: *Das Kugeltranszendentale Vorhaben* (1983), *Die unhörbaren Töne. Phantastische Berichte an die Behörde* (1984), and *Der x-mal vervielfachte Held* (1985, stories). A utopian novel of note is Gottfried Meinhold's *Weltbesteigung* (1984).

Among the lesser writers of GDR science fiction are Wolfgang Kober, Rolf Krohn, Alfred Leman, Ernst-Otto Luthard, Klaus Möckel, Karl-Heinz Tuschel, and Wolf Weitbrecht. Information on GDR writers can be found in a small booklet, *Science-fiction in der DDR. Personalia zu einem Genre* (1982), edited by Erik Simon and Olaf R. Spittel. Complete bibliographies of the SF published in the GDR are to be found in the *Lichtjahr* almanacs (four volumes, 1980–1985, with more to come). Valuable among GDR publications are also the many representative anthologies of SF from various countries, especially East European countries. A recent illustrated history of SF is Dieter Wuckel's *Science Fiction* (1986).

On the whole SF in the GDR has improved a great deal during recent years. It is currently relatively free of heavy-handed ideology, and the best writers, such as Bernd Ulbrich, Wolfgang Steinmüller, and the Brauns, can stand beside the writers of any country. Of the two Germanies, the GDR seems, in fact, to have the greater potential for distinguished SF.

Notes

1. This may be gauged from the critical literature on SF in Germany, most of which deals with Anglo-American SF. See Franz Rottensteiner, "Some German Writings on SF," *Science-Fiction Studies* 1 (Fall 1974): 279–285, 6 (July 1979): 201–209, and 12 (July 1985): 209–220. Compare William B. Fischer, "German Theories of Science Fiction: Jean Paul, Kurd Lasswitz, and After," *Science-Fiction Studies* 3 (November 1976): 254–265.
2. Perry Rhodan is discussed more fully in Sylvia Pukallus, Ronald M. Hahn, and Horst Pukallus, " 'Perry Rhodan' as a Social and Ideological Phenomenon," *Science-Fiction Studies* 6 (July 1979): 190–200.
3. Conrad's book is discussed in Edwin Kretzman, "German Technological Utopias of the Pre-War Period," *Annals of Science* 3 (October 1938): 417–430.
4. A brief critical essay on this book is included in Magill, *Survey of Science Fiction Literature* [8-29]. A longer article on Scheerbart is Franz Rottensteiner's "Paul Scheerbart, Fantast of 'Otherness,' " *Science-Fiction Studies* 11 (July 1984): 109–121.
5. Kretzman, "German Technological Utopias," pp. 417–430.
6. A brief critical essay on this book is included in Magill, *Survey of Science Fiction Literature* [8-29].

7. Ibid.
8. On Lasswitz, see Franz Rottensteiner, "Kurd Lasswitz: A German Pioneer of Science Fiction," in Clareson's *SF: The Other Side of Realism* [9-23], pp. 289–306; Kretzman, "German Technological Utopias"; Mark Hillegas, "The First Invasions from Mars," in *Michigan Alumnus Quarterly Review* (February 1960): 107–112; Mark Hillegas, "Martians and Mythmakers," in *Challenges in American Culture*, ed. by Ray B. Browne, Larry N. Landrum, and William K. Bottorff (Bowling Green, Ohio: Bowling Green Univ. Popular Press, 1970), pp. 150–177; and especially William B. Fischer, *The Empire Strikes Out: Kurd Lasswitz, Hans Dominik and the Development of German Science Fiction* [6-40].
9. A brief critical essay on this book is included in Magill, *Survey of Science Fiction Literature* [8-29].
10. On Edmund Kiss and the ideological content of German SF of the 1920s and 1930s, see Manfred Nagl, "SF, Occult Sciences, and Nazi Myths," *Science-Fiction Studies* 1 (Spring 1974): 185–197, an excerpt from his German dissertation, *Science Fiction in Deutschland* [6-45].
11. A brief critical essay on this book is included in Magill, *Survey of Science Fiction Literature* [8-29].
12. On SF in the GDR, see Horst Heidtmann, "A Survey of Science Fiction in the German Democratic Republic," *Science-Fiction Studies* 6 (March 1979): 92–99.
13. A detailed analysis of the SF work on this writer team is provided by Darko Suvin, "Playful Cognizing or 'Technical Errors' in Harmonyville: The SF of Johanna and Günter Braun," *Science-Fiction Studies*, no. 23 (March 1981): 72–79.
14. A brief critical essay on this book is included in Magill, *Survey of Science Fiction Literature* [8-29].

Bibliography

Individual Authors

[All authors are from West Germany unless otherwise indicated.]

6-1. Amery, Carl (pseud. of Christian Mayer). **Der Untergang der Stadt Passau.** Munich: Wilhelm Heyne Verlag, 1975.

After a plague that left only one man alive in 50,000, the city of Passau in Bavaria has become a center of the civilized world, living parasitically on the countryside. The discontented peasants rise against the city, which is divided in itself and which finally falls to the hordes of the Hungarians and "Rosnmer" (the inhabitants of what is today Rosenheim). These happenings are told in vivid and artificial language in a chronicle style as written down by Deacon Egid in his "Magnalia Dei per Gentem Rosmeriorum." Amery, a leading German writer, was inspired in this book by Miller's *A Canticle for Leibowitz* [3-287]; compare also Pangborn's *Davy* [3-303].

6-2. Bialkowski, Stanislaw. **Krieg im All. Roman aus der Zukunft der Technik.** Leipzig: Fr. Wilhelm Grunow, 1935.
Led by a renegade Earthman, the Martians launch an attack on Earth when Phobos threatens to fall on Mars. After gigantic space battles fought with explosives, electro-cannon, and giant radium guns, not very different from the hardware in the stories of Edmond Hamilton or E. E. Smith, a peace treaty is made. An expedition to the moons of Jupiter encounters the dying emperor of Atlantis, who provides them with the secret of restoring the Mars atmosphere and stabilizing the orbit of Phobos, as well as telling of the original couple of Ewa and Atam from outer space. A fast-moving tale that sees war as the spring of all progress; nonwhites are considered inferior races of subhuman origin and are subdued in a bloody war.

*6-3. Braun, Johanna, and Günter Braun (GDR). **Der Fehlfaktor.** Berlin: Verlag Das Neue Berlin, 1975.
Written in a memorable tongue-in-cheek and ironic manner, these humorous and mannered stories deal with problems such as the ill effects of computerization, bureaucratization, genetic engineering, contact with other worlds, excessive rationalization, and the substitution of technology for nature. Included is a tale of Merkur Erdenson, the hero of their novel *Unheimliche Erscheinungsformen auf Omega XI* (1974), a space traveler recalling Lem's Ijon Tichy. These grotesque and paradoxical thought-experiments and flights of the imagination present real problems in a comically estranged form. In American SF, R. A. Lafferty comes closest to them.

*6-4. Braun, Johanna, and Günter Braun (GDR). **Der Irrtum des Grossen Zauberers.** Berlin: Verlag Neues Leben, 1972.
The romantically ironic and bizarre story of how Oliver Input, a brash young man trained by the great wizard Multi Multiplikato to become his successor in the fictitious country of Plikato, overthrows the rule of the wizard. Input is a great believer in machines and has also bred a new kind of pear that is a sort of universal food, as well as a Huxleyan soma and tranquilizer for the population. Written in a fairy-tale-like manner reminiscent of German romanticism, with characters named as scurrilously as any in Jean Paul, the novel abounds in metamorphoses of a symbolic nature and ends, much as the other novels of the Brauns, in a comic apocalypse.

6-5. Colerus, Egmont (Austria). **Wieder wandert Bebemoth. Der Roman einer Spätzeit.** Berlin: Atlantischer Verlag, 1924.
This fantasy of the decline of a future empire, obviously written under the influence of Nietzsche and Oswald Spengler, is an impressionist symphony of forms and colors. In a Byzantine future world, Zarathustra Orley, an architect representative of the arts, and Herckenau, a billionaire and representative of big business, build a porcelain city in the plains of the Guadalquivir as a symbol of their power and wealth, but also of their decadence. In the end the city and the two men are destroyed by more primeval forces, and a Japanese, an African, and a hastily gathered Nordic army decide the fate of Europe in battle over its ruins. This hectic and colorful novel is a typical expression of the restless spirit of the 1920s. Compare Alfred Döblin's *Berge, Meere und Giganten* [6-8].

6-6. Daumann, Rudolf Heinrich. **Abenteuer mit der Venus.** Berlin: Schützen-Verlag, 1940.

Advised by a jealous priest caste, queen Moli Moagatse rules a people of troglodytes living in dire circumstances in subterranean caves on Venus. While Horst Harl is kept captive as her future consort, his friend, Adelbert Brendt, escapes to Earth and mounts a rescue expedition, once he has gotten out of the madhouse in which he was locked after crashing his spaceship on his return to Earth. The rescue operation is successful, but the Venusian civilization is destroyed by volcanic eruptions. Some aspects of the novel are reminiscent of John Benyon Harris's *The Secret People* (1935). A fine interplanetary adventure, much more interesting than Hans Dominik's more successful novels, with which Daumann's work is often compared.

6-7. del'Antonio, Eberhard (GDR). **Titanus.** Berlin: Verlag Das Neue Berlin, 1959.

An expedition from a now-communist Earth encounters a planetary civilization with advanced technology but low social development; it turns out that the inhabitants of the planet, ruled by priests, are the dispossessed exploiters driven from another planet who want to steal the secrets of the spaceship to take their revenge on the exploited who rebelled against them. In a similarly stereotyped manner, the conflict between communism and capitalism is transplanted into the cosmos in Hubert Horstmann's *Die Stimme der Unendlichkeit*. In del'Antonio's sequel, *Heimkehr der Vorfahren* (1966), the space travelers return to Earth after 300 years, which gives rise to adaptive problems, communism having developed further during that time.

*6-8. Döblin, Alfred. **Berge, Meere und Giganten.** Berlin: S. Fischer Verlag, 1924.

A strange, hectic, and visionary chronicle of future European history, spanning several centuries. The individual characters, although superhuman men of action, propelled by their own demons, are less important than is the sweep of history. There are terrible wars between European city states, between Europe and Asia, and between worshipers and opponents of the machine, fought with devastating energy weapons; there is synthetic food and genetic engineering, and finally a gigantic project for the de-icing of Greenland, resulting in the creation of a new race of titanic people. Dark, baroque, wildly exuberant in its depth and scope of imagination and intensity of feeling, this is a powerful novel about the human struggle against nature and one's own self. Thematically similar to Stapledon, the novel is closer in spirit to the work of Cordwainer Smith, who is said to have admired it greatly.

6-9. Dominik, Hans. **Atomgewicht 500.** Berlin: August Scherl GmbH., 1935.

Two rival American companies, Dupont and United Chemicals, are experimenting with high temperatures and pressures to create new atomic elements. Dupont gets Dr. Wandel, a German scientist who knows everything about the field, while his competitors are arrogant bunglers who have to be saved from blowing themselves up. Dr. Wandel's element 500 produces energy in the form of heat by just reacting with water. As usual in Dominik, the scientific content is nil and the technical understanding insignificant; the action in this case concerns the naïvely presented intelligence work of giant industrial companies, not states. The basic plot is the same in all of Dominik's novels.

6-10. Dominik, Hans. **Der Brand der Cheopspyramide.** Berlin: August Scherl GmbH., 1927.

After the Moors have reconquered Spain, there exist three powerful Arab states and a rather disunited United States of Europe, all engaged in a chase after atomic energy. A British scientist has invented it but died, and the German Friedrich Eisenecker has also solved the problem secretly. Helped by a beautiful female spy in love with their caliph, the Arabs steal the British apparatus but manage only to blow up the pyramid of Cheops, while Eisenecker supplies the Spanish guerrillas with atomic weapons shooting "condensed electricity." The formula of international intrigue is the same as in the many other novels of this popular author.

*6-11. Franke, Herbert W. (Austria). **Der Elfenbeinturm.** Munich: Goldmann Verlag, 1965.

Mortimer Cross belongs to a group of revolutionaries revolting against a computerized society. After initial successes on the Moon, the revolution fails, because of both its anachronistic nature and the divisions among the rebels. Some escape into the galaxy. Unable to colonize an Earth-like planet for lack of numbers, the fugitives turn to another planet already peopled by intelligent but nonhuman water-dwellers and transplant their minds into them—rather than survive as savage humans, they prefer to exist as nonhuman intelligences. Franke's prose is bleak, functional, and austere, but deals with real scientific and social problems. Like Philip K. Dick, he seems to write one big, ongoing novel, always formed of much the same elements.

Franke, Herbert W. (Austria). **The Orchid Cage (Der Orchideenkäfig)** [see 3-168].

*6-12. Franke, Herbert W. (Austria). **Ypsilon minus.** Frankfurt am Main: S. Verlag, 1976.

Ben Erman, an agent of the computer control of a dystopian computerized society, one day is ordered to audit his own tapes. He discovers that three years in his life are missing. With the help of drugs, he succeeds in overcoming his mental block, uncovering scenes from the past that become visible to him as in an unfocused film. The plot is interrupted by theoretical statements: short essays on the principles of the state, guidelines for personality auditing, excerpts from a songbook for psychotraining, and teaching aids. The general atmosphere of Franke's novels is not unlike that of Dick's, but Dick is much more inventive and transcends the borders of the scientifically accepted, which Franke never does.

*6-13. Fühmann, Franz (GDR). **Saiäns Fiktschen.** Rostock: VEB Hinstorff Verlag, 1981.

Franz Fühmann is one of the most prominent GDR authors, and undoubtedly, if these stories had come from a less prominent man, they wouldn't have been printed at all. For in the guise of science fiction, against a background of two inimical future blocs, "Libroterr" and "Uniterr," the author paints a devastating picture of the "truly free society of Uniterr," using brilliant dialectics to debunk its lies and insincerities, the official cynicism of an alienated dystopian society that is only too close to home. "Bewußtseinserhebung"—"uplifting of your consciousness," commonly known as mind reading—for instance, is a test of loyalty to the state. The protagonist passes against his expectations, despite his hidden bad attitudes, with the small condition that he spy on his father. And "Das Duell" is a brilliantly reasoned historical argument using the familiar SF gimmick of time travel. A visit to the scene of a historical duel shows something quite different from what was expected; but soon official historical science supplies the answers of dialectical materialism to prove that the party line was right all the time. Fühmann's debunking of real socialism surpasses even Orwell.

Gail, Otto Willi. **The Shot into Infinity (Der Schuss ins All)** [see **2-33**].

6-14. Grunert, Carl. **Der Marsspion und andere Novellen.** Berlin-Leipzig: Buchverlag fürs Deutsche Haus, 1908.
Short stories in the tradition of Kurd Lasswitz, but H. G. Wells and Jules Verne are equally important influences. There is a sequel to Wells's *The Time Machine* [1-103], while other stories appear to be inspired by "The Star" and "AEpyornis Island." There is also a Vernian story of a balloon flight. Other stories, often with a touch of humor, are popularizations of science, all rather weak and naïve. The best are two tales about visitors from outer space bent on missions to prevent Earth from finding out about them.

*6-15. Gurk, Paul. **Tuzub 37. Der Mythos von der grauen Menschheit oder von der Zahl 1.** Berlin: Holle, 1935.
As in E. M. Forster's "The Machine Stops" [1-35], humans have become totally isolated from nature, living in concrete silos. History, poetry, philosophy, and all individualism have disappeared, and people have become machines, partly of metal. The seas are filled and the mountains leveled; the goal is to reproduce completely by chemical means. Corrosion sets in, however. There is a brief invasion of life forms from outer space, and when one of the Gray Ones starts thinking and doubting, the whole system comes crashing down. Life on Earth starts anew with life spores arriving from space. Poetic and symbolically dense, this dystopian novel is a passionate plea for individualism and personality against collectivism, uniformity, and mindless conformism.

6-16. Hawel, Rudolf (Austria). **Im Reiche der Homunkuliden.** Vienna: Verlag von Huber & Lahme Nachf., 1910.
Accompanied by a comic servant in the Jules Verne style, Professor Voraus ("Ahead"), inventor of magnetic suspension, sleeps like the hero of Wells's *When the Sleeper Wakes* [1-106] into the future, awakening in the year 3907. The Earth is peopled by chemically created asexual androids living in a Bellamy-like utopian world. The visitors from the past are introduced to the marvels of the future, including solar energy and the transmutation of the elements. The homunculi totally lack aggressive impulses, but their equilibrium is disturbed by the servant's desire to have a woman created for himself. The humor of the novel is rather broad, but it is an interesting novel in the Bellamy tradition.

Hesse, Hermann. **The Glass Bead Game (Das Glasperlenspiel)** [see **3-212**].

6-17. Hey, Richard. **Im Jahr 95 nach Hiroshima.** Hamburg: Hoffmann und Campe, 1982.

Hey is a well-known writer of mysteries, and this novel is his only SF book. In the year 95 "after Hiroshima" the world is threatened by a new ice age, and the old world has fallen apart; while the United States and the U.S.S.R. fight a hopeless battle against the encroaching ice, the Third World powers have become domi- nant, and the Swiss have emigrated to an artificial island in the Mediterranean, where the memory of the Swiss mountains is kept alive by giant holograms. The future world is typically that of SF, and the author has his fun with SF topics. There are time travel and mutants, for instance, but the time travel leads only to places where nobody wants to go, and the mutations are of a very queer kind, such as a drab woman who periodically is changed into a sex bomb. The Russians and the Americans have built rival space stations on a small asteroid, but their crews screw without regard for ideology; and a mad scientist succeeds in establish- ing contact with God, but God shows not the slightest interest in mankind. In short, the author has written a madly scurrilous satire that reminds you alter- nately of John Sladek and R. A. Lafferty.

6-18. Illing, Werner. **Utopolis.** Berlin: Der Bücherkreis, 1930.

The first-person narrator is stranded on an isolated island where the workers have rid themselves of the rule of capitalism. There are neither exploiters nor ex- ploited, and there is total equality in work as in love, all based on the free relation- ship of equal partners. For educative purposes some capitalists are still kept, weighted down with medals for achievements like class murder, newspaper lies, and tax evasion. But the vengeful capitalists brainwash the population with rays and introduce once more an empire with soldiers and priests. This results in a struggle fought with bombs, death rays, and electric force-screens, in which the workers prevail. This grotesquely exaggerated, frequently funny novel contains many allusions to the German situation of the time, although the author fails to recognize the impact of the rise of Nazism. Although weaker than London's *Iron Heel* [1-59], this is still interesting and one of the rare German SF novels told from a socialist point of view.

6-19. Jeschke, Wolfgang. **Der letzte Tag der Schöpfung.** Munich: Nymphen- burger Verlagshandlung, 1981. Tr. as *The Last Day of Creation* (St. Martin's, 1984).

An amusing and irreverent spoof on ancient astronaut theories à la von Däniken, these are SF time travel stories about changing the past and American clandes- tine actions in the world. Part one describes the finding of strange artifacts, some thought to be the members of Catholic saints, alien cars, and others; in part two, Project Chronotone is presented, an attempt by the U.S. Navy to get control of the world's oil fields by sending heavily armed commandos in "time cages" mil- lions of years into the past. Part three is a chronicle of the mess these commandos find themselves in; assisted by ferocious educated apes as ancillary troops, they have to fight a mud battle against Arabs flying in MIGs and gunning with atomic grenades. Some of the survivors make it to Atlantis. The thoroughly ironic, some- times savage tone of the book recalls some stories by Barry Malzberg or

R. A. Lafferty. Compare Carl Amery's *Das Königsprojekt* (1974). Also annotated as [4-286].

6-20. Jeschke, Wolfgang. **Der Zeiter.** Munich: Lichtenberg Verlag, 1970, expanded ed., Munich: Wilhelm Heyne Verlag, 1978.
It is the quality of the writing that distinguishes these stories, which are strong in mood but rather slight. Their subject matter is the standard fare of SF: time travel and its paradoxes, extraterrestrials assuming the shape of human beings, ghastly atomic mutations. The important exception is "Der König und der Puppenmacher" (translated as "The King and the Dollmaker" in Donald A. Wollheim's anthology *The Best from the Rest of the World,* 1976), an intricately plotted, finely wrought tale of playful time paradoxes that manages to catch the mood of a romantic Kunstmärchen. Of interest also is "Welt ohne Horizont," a well-written variation on Heinlein's "Universe."

Kaul, Fedor. **Contagion to This World (Die Welt ohne Gedächtnis)** [see 2-54].

Kirst, Hans Hellmut. **The Seventh Day (Keiner kommt davon)** [see 3-229].

6-21. Kossak-Raytenau, Karl L. **Die Welt am laufenden Band.** Vienna: Höger Verlag, 1937.
For the industry leader and inventor Felix Voss, the machine has achieved theological significance. His zeal is to create ever more perfect machines, such as the robot Mars. His ambition has made him blind both to human misery and to economic facts, and when there are no buyers left for his perfect machines, the result is an economic world crisis. He dies a martyr on the altar of the machine. A vivid expression of the fear of rationalization and the machine, the book has certain similarities to Kurt Vonnegut's much later *Player Piano* [3-392].

6-22. Lasswitz, Kurd. **Auf zwei Planeten.** Weimar: Felber, 1897. Tr. as *Two Planets,* ed. by Mark Hillegas (Southern Illinois, 1971).
Translated into English, in an abridged form, as late as 1971, this novel could exert little real influence on the development of modern SF, but soon after its original appearance, it was translated into many European languages and has been frequently reprinted in both Germanies after World War II. It is remarkable both for its scientific background, giving the first detailed picture of the mechanics of space travel in fiction, including space stations, and for its philosophically ambitious picture of the first contact and conflict between two civilizations. Upon reaching the North Pole, some explorers in a balloon discover that the Martians have already been there and have erected a space station hovering over the pole. Subsequently they are taken to Mars to witness its marvels, and later take an active part in human resistance when the technically and morally superior Martians have established a protectorate over backward Earth, and the superior Martian principles have been corrupted by an excess of power. Though slow-moving and perhaps overly didactic, the book remains an interesting example of sophisticated early SF, sound technological forecasts, and a minor counterpiece to Wells's artistically much superior *The War of the Worlds* [1-105].

*6-23. Lasswitz, Kurd. **Bilder aus der Zukunft. 2 Erzählungen aus dem 24. und 39. Jahrhundert.** Breslau: Schottlaender, 1878.

These two youthful stories, written long before the interplanetary classic *Auf zwei Planeten* [6-22], are of interest principally as collections of SF ideas, including sleep-teaching, food pills, the computer, and an odor-piano. Lasswitz's philosophical bent becomes apparent in "Bis zum Nullpunkt des Seins," which treats a conflict between reason and feeling in 2371 in the manner of a student's joke. "Gegen das Weltgesetz" is an equally not-quite-serious adventure story that has many similarities to Gernsback's later *Ralph 124C41+* [1-37].

Moszkowski, Alexandr. **The Isles of Wisdom (Die Inseln der Weisheit)** [see 2-81].

6-24. Prokop, Gert (GDR). **Wer stiehlt schon Unterschenkel?** Berlin: Verlag Das Neue Berlin, 1977.

In a supercapitalist United States of the twenty-first century, surrounded by communist states, a couple of enormously rich men rule at their whim. While secretly working for the socialist underground, private eye Timothy Truckle, possessed of a fine sense for the commodities of life and assisted by his trusty old computer, Napoleon, solves more discreetly than the various police and secret service organizations the most complicated cases (which invariably show how mean those exploiters are). Propagandistic in intent, this is a grotesque overexaggeration of the evils of capitalism, but inventive in the details of plot and background and well written.

6-25. Rank, Heiner (GDR). **Die Ohnmacht der Allmächtigen.** Berlin: Verlag Das Neue Berlin, 1973.

The utopian world of Astilot has neither violence nor change, and all work is done by cephaloids, bionic machines serving invisible masters that have long since withdrawn from ruling the planet. Asmo, the protagonist, is an outsider, the only human being daring to ask questions and the only one able to resort to violence. A fanatical underground believing in the value of work wants to lead the humans from their vegetative existence to a more conscious state of being, if necessary by force. The inevitable revolution results in a more humane society. The novel is somewhat unfocused, combining elements of Huxley's *Brave New World* [2-47] and Williamson's *The Humanoids* [3-402] in a revolutionary pattern similar to much Western SF.

6-26. Rehn, Jens (pseud. of Otto Jens Luther). **Die Kinder des Saturn.** Neuwied/Rhein: Luchterhand, 1959.

A physician and a young couple expecting a child survive the atomic catastrophe because they are protected by a mine. The physician writes his impressions, thoughts, and feelings in his diary—despairing notes of recollection and remembrance that nobody will ever read. When the radiation gets weaker, the survivors go back to the surface, only to die a slow and painful death. In its cool yet graphic description of the final catastrophe, this literary book has more in common with Sven Holm's *Termush* [6-347] than with Shute's *On the Beach* [3-344]. A similar German book is Hannelore Valencak's *Die Höhlen Noahs*.

6-27. Sandt, Emil. **Cavete! Eine Geschichte, über deren Bizarrerien man nicht ihre Drohungen vergessen soll.** Minden i.W.: J. C. C. Bruns' Verlag, 1907.

Fritz Rusart is one of those noble inventors who want to force peace on civilization with his airships, one of them named *Robur* after a Jules Verne story. But after the British have captured one of his ships, he turns his invention over to the German kaiser. Subcharacters include two pathetic caricatures of Jewish businessmen. Although Wells's similar *The War in the Air* [1-104] still has a certain nostalgic charm, this almost plotless novel is only a period piece.

*6-28. Schattschneider, Peter (Austria). **Singularitäten. Ein Episodenroman im Umfeld schwarzer Löcher.** Frankfurt am Main: Suhrkamp, 1984.

After the collection *Zeitstopp* (1982), *Singularitäten* is Schattschneider's second book, an episodic novel of connected short stories, all located in a common future world with a galactic federation of mankind and the relics of lost civilizations to be found everywhere. All have to do with black holes: as stellar gates for space travel, mini-black holes as bombs and energy suppliers, time distortions as a means for gaining eternal youth, and as a refuge and a prison. A physicist, Schattschneider offers good explanations, and he also tells colorful stories with interesting characters and good plots. Niven's *Tales of Known Space* [4-390] are similar; among German writers, Schattschneider's greatest affinities are with the Steinmüllers and H. W. Franke; but he is a better storyteller than Franke and a more versatile writer.

*6-29. Scheerbart, Paul. **Die grosse Revolution. Ein Mondroman.** Leipzig: Insel Verlag, 1902.

For centuries the Lunarians have been watching Earth with their telescopes, but now one faction, led by Mafikâsu, proposes to build a gigantic telescope to explore the further cosmos and ignore warlike Earth and its ugly customs. They want to see more pictures of the wide world outside, and when the inhabitants of Earth do not reform within 50 years, the Lunarians prevail. The fairy-tale-like, totally artificial world of Scheerbart is so divorced from physical as well as social gravity that there is really nothing comparable to it in modern SF, although some affinities might be found in Cyrano de Bergerac, whom Scheerbart admired. Scheerbart's world is dominated by visual images, metamorphoses, and continuous picturesque changes.

Siodmak, Curt. **F.P. 1 Does Not Reply (F.P. 1 Antwortet Nicht)** [see **2-101**].

*6-30. Steinmüller, Angela, and Karlheinz Steinmüller (GDR). **Der Traum vom Grossen Roten Fleck.** Frankfurt am Main: Suhrkamp, 1985.

This first West German collection by a leading SF couple from the GDR is mainly a selection from the GDR collections *Der letzte Tag auf der Venus* (1979), by Karlheinz alone, and *Windschiefe Geraden* (1984). Both are scientists, and in choice of themes, outlook, and literary variety they are similar to the young Austrian SF writer Peter Schattschneider. Their stories are as remarkable for the grounding in science and thematic versatility as for the storytelling abilities of the authors and their imagery; often they convey the impression of new states of consciousness. The stories range from a remarkable dystopian tale (the title story) to explorations of the potential of human beings, whether brought about by natural abilities or by technology. One of the best of this kind is "Der schwarze Kasten," a fine detective story about a sort of auxiliary computer worn by human beings, on which they have become too dependent.

6-31. Ulbrich, Bernd (GDR). **Der unsichtbare Kreis.** Berlin: Verlag Das Neue Berlin, 1977.
Surprisingly for an East German author, these stories are completely free of any ideological content, being rather "models" of abstract situations divorced from particular social circumstances, in the manner of Stanislaw Lem. Many of the stories are located in space, most impressively the title story, which is reminiscent of the basic situation of *Solaris* [3-261], a tender love affair between an astronaut on Neptune and an alien approaching him in the shape of a woman he once loved. There is a strong dystopian flavor and there is even humor. This is a genuinely varied book with strong plot and good characterization, freshly written even when dealing with typical SF ideas and situations. A similar, more recent book is Karlheinz Steinmüller's *Der letzte Tag auf der Venus* (1979).

von Hanstein, Otfrid. **Electropolis (Elektropolis)** [see **2-122**].

von Harbou, Thea. **Metropolis** [see **2-123**].

6-32. Weisser, Michael. **Syn-Code-7.** Frankfurt am Main: Suhrkamp, 1982.
Weisser's style is deliberately jargon-prone and hard to read, and, as some critics have noted, his use of scientific terminology is not always correct. Nevertheless, this novel is remarkable for the way it explores the possibilities of biotechnology and genetic engineering. In the author's future, coded unicellular biocolonies have become the slaves of society. The bioplasts do all the work, whereas human beings live in the beauty of illusion and idleness. And then something goes wrong, and an investigation and fight against the threat begin; the title refers to a rather dictatorial emergency plan in the fight against the threat to this biotechnical utopia. The novel is somewhat similar to those of H. W. Franke, perhaps more inventive but not so well grounded in science as Franke's, and has been both praised and violently attacked for its functional language and drab characterization. In his later *Digit* (1983), Weisser repeats much the same story in a digitalized world.

Werfel, Franz (Austria). **Star of the Unborn (Stern der Ungebornen)** [see **3-396**].

Winterfeld, Henry. **Star Girl (Kommt ein Madchen Geflogen)** [see **5-175**].

6-33. Ziegler, Thomas (pseud. of Rainer Zubeil). **Die Stimmen der Nacht.** Frankfurt am Main, Berlin, Wien: Ullstein, 1984.
An alternate world novel comparable to Dick's *The Man in the High Castle* [3-142] or Sarban's *The Sound of His Horn* [3-327]; it is based on the premise that Germany lost the war but that the atomic bomb was dropped on Berlin and that the Morgenthau plan, the total deindustrialization of Germany, was put into effect. There are still some "werewolf" resistance groups in devastated Europe, but the bulk of the Nazis have emigrated to South America, where Bormann and other top-ranking party members reside in a concrete bunker in the Andes, brooding on revenge. In the density of its atmosphere as well as in the idea of the "burs," talking micromechanisms that haunt people, the novel resembles some of Dick's

work. Later, these "voices of the night" become independent of any mechanism, and the ghosts of the dead begin to babble; the Nazi leaders in the ruins of the cathedral of Cologne (blaming each other for the defeat), while Kennedy returns to Dallas. Through the adventures of a haunted hero, the novel leads up to the inevitable world catastrophe. Ziegler, sometimes an excellent stylist, is a highly interesting SF writer when not turning out purely commercial work.

Anthologies

6-34. Alpers, Hans Joachim, and Ronald M. Hahn, eds. **Science Fiction aus Deutschland. 24 Stories von 20 Autoren.** Frankfurt am Main: Fischer Taschenbuchverlag, 1974.
This first representative anthology of SF by German authors combines some classics (Kurd Lasswitz, Paul Scheerbart), names well known from German literature (Gerhard Zwerenz, Hermann Ebeling, with stories that are more absurd and satirical than SF), and SF regulars (Herbert W. Franke, Wolfgang Jeschke) with many stories by SF fans. These are often critical of German society but show their amateurish origins. Similar anthologies presenting only modern authors are Jörg Weigand's *Quasar I* and Thomas Le Blanc's *Die Anderen* (both 1979).

6-35. Jeschke, Wolfgang, ed. **Das Auge des Phoenix.** Munich: Wilhelm Heyne Verlag, 1985.
This big anthology offers a good overview of current German SF. Besides eight often long stories, it contains three complete novels, including Georg Zauner's *Die Enkel der Raketenbauer* (1980), an excellent piece of "Bajuvarian" postdoomsday SF; Reinmar Cunis's *Livesendung* (1978), representative of engaged but not very well-told SF; and Thomas R. P. Mielke's *Grand Orientale 3301* (1980), a piece of colorful but banal adventure story writing. Among the stories, Jeschke's "Der König und der Puppenmacher" is already a classic of time travel paradox; Karl Michael Armer's "Es ist kein Erdbeben, Ihnen zittern nur die Knie," a satire on advertising; and Horst Pukallus's "Die Wellenlänge der Wirklichkeit," a tightly written thriller with a leftist political message but also poking fun at SF writers. The other stories, by Dieter Hasselblatt, Herbert W. Franke, Carl Amery, Ronald M. Hahn and Hans Joachim Alpers, and Joern J. Bambeck, are representative of contemporary German SF writing.

Nonfiction

6-36. Alpers, Hans Joachim, et al., comps. **Lexikon der Science Fiction Literatur.** 2 vols. Munich: Heyne Verlag, 1980.
Two volumes totaling 1,252 pages offer a capsule history of the SF field; a survey of 11 SF themes and topics such as space opera, utopias and dystopias, aliens, time travel, and such; a biographical encyclopedia (authors only, no artists, editors, or other professionals); and a bibliography of SF published after 1945 in West Germany, Switzerland, and Austria in the German language; the SF of the German Democratic Republic is excluded. Entries are arranged by publishers and series; authors are found in the general index of persons, but there is no title index. This part is a continuation of the *Katalog der deutschsprachigen utopisch-phantastischen Literatur aus fünf Jahrhunderten 1460–1960* (1959–1960) compiled

by Heinz Bingenheimer. Although the listings of the dime novel and lending library series appear to be fairly complete, the listings of paperback and hardcover publications have serious omissions. Also included are listings of authors' pseudonyms, a who's who in German SF, the most important international SF awards, literature on SF, and a short history of SF in Germany after World War II. An invaluable, although not completely reliable and by no means exhaustive, research tool.

6-37. Alpers, Hans Joachim, Werner Fuchs, and Ronald M. Hahn. **Reclams Science-Fiction-Führer.** Stuttgart: Philipp Reclam jun., 1982.
This is similar to the Heyne *SF Lexikon* [6-36] (which will be reissued in a revised one-volume edition in 1987) but restricted to a listing by author. In addition to a short biographical sketch and a bibliography, each author's most important books are annotated in detail. A brief bibliography of works on SF and a glossary of SF terms are also included. Obviously the compilers have learned from their first effort, for this provides much better coverage than the Heyne *SF Lexikon,* with a broader selection of authors and more balanced entries for each author.

6-38. Barnouw, Dagmar. **Die versuchte Realität oder von der Möglichkeit, glücklichere Welten zu denken. Utopischer Diskurs von Thomas Morus zur feministischen Science Fiction.** Meitingen: Corian-Verlag Heinrich Wimmer, 1985. (Studien zur phantastischen Literatur no. 1.)
This monograph, by a professor of literature currently teaching in Texas, starts with the utopias from Thomas More onward, discusses literary strategies of social construction and the possibility and reality of utopia as an idea, and then turns to interplanetary SF with social implications. The main part of Barnouw's work is a lively discussion of Ursula Le Guin's *The Dispossessed* [4-324] and feminism in science fiction. She offers detailed and original analyses of Delany's *Triton* [4-170], Le Guin's *The Left Hand of Darkness* [4-327], Marge Piercy's *Woman on the Edge of Time* [4-411], Joanna Russ's *The Female Man* [4-458], and James Tiptree's "The Women Men Don't See" (1973).

*6-39. Bloch, Robert N. **Bibliographie der utopischen und phantastischen Literatur 1750–1950.** Giessen: Verlagsbuchhandlung Munniksma, 1984.
In this bibliography of both SF and fantasy titles published between 1750 and 1950 in the German language, 2,790 titles (and more in a supplement, with corrections) are listed. Bloch provides authors (with birth and death dates, if known), title, subtitle, place, publisher, year of appearance, and number of pages of first editions. His compilation is much more comprehensive than Heinz Bingenheimer's *Katalog der deutschsprachigen utopisch-phantastischen Literatur aus fünf Jahrhunderten 1460–1960* (1959–1960) (and easier to use), but has some errors: it lists titles that are neither SF nor fantasy, some popular science items, and a number of bibliographical "ghosts." The work, of course, is not quite complete, although it is the most comprehensive German bibliography published so far. In fact, it can be regarded as a kind of German Bleiler *Checklist* [8-2], an indispensable tool for any scholar and collector.

6-40. Fischer, William B. **The Empire Strikes Out: Kurd Lasswitz, Hans Dominik and the Development of German Science Fiction.** Bowling Green, OH: Bowling Green Univ. Popular Press, 1984.

Fischer's book on German SF is, above all, a detailed study of the genre's two most important practitioners: Kurd Lasswitz (1848–1910) and Hans Dominik (1872–1945). Lasswitz was a true pioneer of SF, in both its ideational contents and form; Dominik was a writer of single-idea thrillers, often with nationalist and racist overtones, a best-seller in his time, and still by far Germany's most successful SF author. Fischer gives careful analyses of the work of the two men in the context of their times, both historical and literary. It is ironic that, while Lasswitz has recently received much critical attention in Germany, especially by Rudi Schweikert, and much of his works are now back in print, Fischer's book is still the most detailed account of German SF; and this applies even more to Dominik, who has received almost no critical attention in Germany. The valuable book concludes with a brief discussion of some modern representatives of German SF (Herbert W. Franke, Michael Weisser, and Wolfgang Jeschke) and some conjectures about its development. Also annotated as [9-35].

*6-41. Heidtmann, Horst. **Utopisch-phantastische Literatur in der DDR. Untersuchungen zur Entwicklung eines unterhaltungsliterarischen Genres von 1945–1979.** Munich: Wilhelm Fink Verlag, 1982.

This printed doctoral thesis by a West German scholar and well-known SF anthologist does for the SF of East Germany what Manfred Nagl's *Science Fiction in Deutschland* [6-45] did for the older German SF. It is a thoroughgoing study that covers the development of SF in East Germany, from the founding of the GDR up to 1979. Heidtmann distinguishes four main phases of SF development: a founding period, a period of the cold war when the protagonists of East German SF were busy fending off capitalist saboteurs, then a period of consolidation, and finally a period of liberalization, with J. and G. Braun as the outstanding writers. Heidtmann gives a clear picture of the general cultural background and discusses topics (the building of the new republic, class conflicts in outer space, etc.) and certain aspects (politics, economy, man and society, science and technology, art and culture) peculiar to GDR science fiction. The study contains also some valuable bibliographies: of SF published in the GDR (by country of origin), publications on SF, and so on.

*6-42. Körber, Joachim, ed. **Bibliographisches Lexikon der utopisch-phantastischen Literatur.** Meitingen: Corian-Verlag Heinrich Wimmer, November 1984– .

This is the most ambitious reference work on SF, fantasy, and horror in the German language (including translations), organized as a loose-leaf file and supplemented by quarterly installments. Since November 1984, there have been seven supplements, and it has grown to three large loose-leaf binders with nearly 200 authors covered in more than 2,500 pages, with many more to come. Because the author entries are issued in random order, each supplement has a cumulative author index. For each author there is a brief biographical and critical essay, followed by a bibliography that attempts to list every German appearance, not just books (with their contents), but also all appearances in magazines and anthologies (excluding writings about the author). While the bibliographies in many cases undoubtedly are incomplete, they are very valuable and run in some cases to considerable length. Many authors are and will be included that are not to be found in English-language reference works. A similar work for the fantastic film, called *Enzyklopädie des phantastischen Films*, was begun in 1986; it lists films, people (actors, directors, special effects specialists), and themes/aspects. The basic work and one supplement have appeared so far.

*6-43. Krysmanski, Hans-Jürgen. **Die utopische Methode. Eine literatur und wissenssoziologische Untersuchung deutscher utopischer Romane des 20. Jahrhunderts.** Köln and Opladen: Westdeutscher Verlag, 1963.
This is both a detailed discussion of the content and literary devices of eight mostly highbrow German utopian novels by non-SF authors (Michael Georg Conrad, Bernhard Kellermann, Gerhart Hauptmann, Alfred Döblin, Hermann Hesse, Franz Werfel, and Ernst Jünger) and a theoretical justification of science fiction, influenced by Raymond Ruyer's *L'Utopie et les utopies* (1950) and Schwonke's pioneering German study *Vom Staatsroman zur Science Fiction* [6-48]. It sees SF as a literary experimental field for new possibilities and interprets the older social utopias as a special case of SF. A sophisticated book, both in its generalizations and in the interpretation of individual German novels.

*6-44. Lem, Stanislaw (Poland). **Phantastik und Futurologie, I and II.** Frankfurt am Main: Insel Verlag, 1977, 1980. German tr. of *Fantastyka i Futurologia* (1970).
Despite its title, this is a book about SF, not fantasy, and its Western variety only. It is also no history but a morphological, sociological (the weakest part, although not quite as vapid as Stableford's sociology of SF), structural, linguistic, and, above all, philosophical examination of SF, so stimulating and original (if somewhat jerky and terminologically often inexact) that it will infuriate many readers of SF. It has been rightly said that Lem, despite some brilliant analyses of particular works and literary techniques, is not interested in literature at all; his main concern is with the structure of the real world, not with the structure of the literary work, despite frequent and furious polemics with structuralism. He takes SF—and futurology as well, but this is only a side issue in his book, again despite the title—to task for ignoring or misrepresenting urgent problems of the future, for example, the development of computers, genetic engineering, and the ethical and philosophical horizons of civilization in general. His book is a passionate search for meaning in the universe and in literature, decrying the merely playful aspects of fiction (for example, the time travel stories of SF, the catastrophe theme, or SF's frivolous treatment of metaphysical questions). Lem's book is not an academic theory and history of the genre like Suvin's *Metamorphoses of Science Fiction* [9-97], and unlike Suvin he is, of course, no Marxist critic, but rather an old-fashioned and elitist European intellectual with a firm belief in the necessity of cultural, moral, and intellectual values. He criticizes SF for its lack of philosophical depth and moral responsibility, not for an absence of particular political

beliefs or dogmas. Sample chapters have appeared in translation in *Science-Fiction Studies*.

*6-45. Nagl, Manfred. **Science Fiction in Deutschland. Untersuchungen zur Genese, Soziographie und Ideologie der phantastischen Massenliteratur.** Tübingen: Tübinger Vereinigung für Volkskunde e.V., 1972.
Nagl traces the development of German SF in its popular forms from its beginning in utopias and adventure literature to the mass phenomenon of the twentieth century. He sees SF as a genre arising apart from and in direct opposition to the hopes of utopia, as a literature of conformism for the masses, designed to support and cement existing social structures. Not so much concerned with literary values and analysis, this is a psychological, sociological, and ideological analysis of German SF and its relationship to the pseudosciences, occult beliefs, and the racist, nationalistic, and social Darwinist thought rampant especially after World War I. Full of German sociological and Marxist jargon, it is nevertheless the only study covering the neglected field of popular literature and contains much original bibliographical research. Extensive bibliography and index.

6-46. Ritter, Claus (GDR). **Start nach Utopolis. Eine zukunfts-Nostalgie.** Berlin: Verlag der Nation, 1978; **Anno Utopia oder So war die Zukunft.** Berlin: Das Neue Berlin, 1982; **Kampf um Utopolis.** Berlin: Verlag Die Nation, 1986.
These are not scholarly volumes but nostalgic books for the general reader, entertainingly written, with lots of quotations and many period pieces from rare old magazines and books, as well as advertising material, picture postcards, and the like. Here one finds lots of material about Kurd Lasswitz, Carl Grunert, Julius von Voss, Bertha von Suttner, and a number of sometimes well-known German writers generally not suspected of having written SF. All books share a similar loose organization, are well illustrated, and uncover amusing views of the future from the past; the third book, due in late 1986 but not seen, apparently deals with the topic of future war.

6-47. Rullkoetter, Bernd. **Die Wissenschaftliche Phantastik der Sowjetunion. Eine vergleichende Untersuchung der spekulativen Literatur in Ost und West.** Bern: Herbert Lang, and Frankfurt: Peter Lang, 1974. European University Papers, Series XVIII, Comparative Literature, Vol. 5.
This well-researched overview of Soviet SF provides a running comparison with Anglo-American SF. While using the same literary devices and sharing an interest in the same motifs and themes, such as robots, time travel, and the contact with alien beings, Soviet SF is more socially conscious and generally the "better behaved relative" of Western SF, being more positive (and therefore also more conformist). Typical for Soviet SF is the positive, integrated, nonalienated hero. Doubting Dostoevskian individuals or Grand Inquisitor situations appear only when a communist hero is confronted with capitalist or feudal states. Another analysis of Soviet SF is Hans Foeldeak's *Neuere Tendenzen der sowjetischen Science Fiction* (Munich: Otto Sagner, 1975, Slavistische Beitraege no. 88), which deals in great detail with a number of representative samples of Soviet SF (Illya Varshavsky, Gennadiy Gor, Ivan Efremov, and especially the Strugatskii brothers).

6-48. Schwonke, Martin. **Vom Staatsroman zur Science Fiction.** Stuttgart: Ferdinand Enke Verlag, 1957.

At a time when SF received hardly any critical attention, Schwonke wrote this pioneering thesis, which gives both a sweeping history of the genre and its relationship to utopian thought (the favorite angle of much European, especially German, SF criticism) and a philosophical analysis of its nature, discussing, besides the stalwarts Verne and Wells, Huxley and Orwell, Stapledon, Lasswitz, Bernhard Kellermann, and modern American SF writers such as Asimov, Heinlein, Bradbury, and Williamson. Schwonke perceives a general development from the ameliorating attitude of the old "Staatsromane" and utopias to SF as a field of speculative fiction, which has, under the influence of science and technology, lost the belief in utopian goals, stressing instead the act of creation itself, no matter what the nature of the creation. SF writers are compared to staff strategists preparing fictional plans for all the contingencies that the future may hold.

6-49. Wilfert, Peter, ed. **Tor zu den Sternen.** Munich: Goldmann, 1981.

This large-format paperback is an anthology of mostly original short stories, most of them by American writers, supplemented by a representative sample of artwork (more than 50 reproductions). The writers whose stories were published here for the first time include Ursula Le Guin, Gene Wolfe, A. E. van Vogt, Brian Aldiss, John Brunner, and Michael Moorcock. There are also the German writers Carl Amery, Rainer Erler, and Herbert W. Franke and a story by the Polish writer Stanislaw Lem. The interior illustrations are by a group of little known German artists from the city of Bielefield, including Klaus Porschka, Peter Rump, Arno Langnicke, Annette Fräger, and Gerd Striepecke. In addition, the volume includes three groups of color pages with works by well-known American illustrators (Vincent Di Fate, Chesley Bonestell, Michael Whelan, Ron Miller, Paul Lehr), British (Peter Goodfellow, David Hardy, Eddie Jones, Jim Burns, Les Edwards, Roger Dean, Bruce Pennington, Terry Roberts), and German and other Continental artists. From Germany there are Jürgen F. Rogner, Ute Osterwalder, Michael Payne, Johann Peter Reuter, Helmut Wenske, and Andreas Nottebohm; from Italy, Franco Storchi, Olivero Berni, and Michaelangelo Miani; from France, Pierre Lacombe; from Switzerland, Robert André; and from the Netherlands, Nico Keulers. The Italian illustrations in particular look like SF illustrations anywhere (the typical "Star Wars" spaceships), but among the others is a good minor surrealist (Helmut Wenske), an abstractionist like Andreas Nottebohm, and an excellent commercial illustrator like Ute Osterwalder.

Magazines

6-50. Quarber Merkur. Franz Rottensteiners unillustrierte Literaturzeitschrift. Winter 1963–   . Semiannual. Circulation: 300. Franz Rottensteiner, ed. (A-1060 Vienna, Marchettigasse 9/17). Indexed in H. W. Hall's *Science Fiction and Fantasy Book Review Index, 1980–1984* [8-20].

Quarber Merkur always was and still is the hobby of its editor. Every issue contains some 60 pages of longer articles, sometimes serials, and about 30 pages of international book reviews by various hands, but mostly by the editor (if unsigned). It has published much material that isn't generally available elsewhere, especially on Eastern European SF, most notably essays by Stanislaw Lem. Recent issues featured pieces on Leo Perutz, Gustav Theodor Fechner, Alexander Grin, and Gustav Meyrink. *QM* contains no illustrations and is mimeographed, not printed. It covers the whole field of fantastic literature, utopias, and science fiction. Also annotated as [14-39].

6-51. Science Fiction Times. Magazin für Science Fiction und Fantasy. 1958– .
Monthly. ISSN: 9948-9654. Harald Pusch, ed. Corian-Verlag Heinrich Wimmer (Bernhard-Monath-Str. 24a, D-8901 Meitingen). Circulation: ca. 1,000.
First begun as an offshoot of James V. Taurasi's *SF Times*, the German edition has undergone many metamorphoses, from a small newszine to the current semiprofessional magazine put out by the small nonfiction SF publishing house Corian-Verlag. Over the years, its editors were some prominent German SF fans, from Rainer Eisfeld via Burkhard Blüm to Hans-Joachim Alpers and the leftist AST group (Arbeitsgemeinschaft für spekulative Thematik). Since July 1983, it appeared with Eulenhof Verlag and since April 1984 with Corian-Verlag. Running to 32 pages per issue, it usually includes one or two interviews, some longer critical pieces, about ten book reviews, film reviews, and some news. There is also a sketchy listing of books announced. Controversial but lively in the past, it is now a not very exciting magazine that provides neither comprehensive book reviews nor a running bibliography; news coverage is much better in Dieter Schmidt's fanzine *Fandom Mirror* or Thomas Tilsner's *Science Fiction Media*.

6-52. Solaris-Almanach. Literatur zur Phantastik. 1980– . Irregular, about once a year. Kai Schätzl and Karlheinz Schmitz, eds. Solaris-Verlag (Broichstr. 56, Box 300880, D-5300 Bonn 3, West Germany).
Solaris-Almanach is a beautifully produced publication that prints both fiction and nonfiction: stories, poetry, longer essays, and book reviews. No. 7 (180 pages) centers on the topic of war and prints and reprints many famous writers, including Jack London, Maurice Sandoz, J. L. Borges, Paul Scheerbart, and Gabriel Laub. Its essay and reviews section has pieces on J. L. Borges, Gabriel García Marquez, Czech SF, Stanislaw Lem, and Lao She's *City of Cats*. Several contributors are from the GDR, and usually there is a good coverage of SF in the GDR. The illustrations are also of a uniformly high quality.

French SF

Maxim Jakubowski

Since the 1950s, contemporary French science fiction has enjoyed a healthy resurgence on both the literary and commercial fronts. Intelligently blending the scientific imagination of the Jules Verne tradition with a strong sensitivity for the best in Anglo-Saxon influences, French SF offers a unique mixture of the enduring pulp traditions of the genre and mainstream literary values. But despite isolated instances of translations in English-language countries (Jeury, Curval, Walther, Barbet, Klein), modern French SF is still sadly unknown or unappreciated outside its borders.

As a result of the student unrest and intellectual ferment of the 1960s, SF in France has grown considerably and, with increased public acceptance, has come a growth in academic interest, more easily acquired as French SF is not generally perceived as a derivation of the grimy pulp heritage and retains strong mainstream literary credibility. In fact, modern French SF is often a demanding cocktail of Verne, selective American and British genre influences (the paranoia of Dick and Ballard, Herbert's global galactic politics), and French pragmatism and popular romance, with an added zest of structuralism, existentialism, political commentary, and absurdist preoccupations.

The health of the genre in the early 1980s was characterized by an increasing number of new, generally young, French authors appearing in print with great regularity for the first time, a phenomenon quite unlike the situation in, say, the 1950s, when the rare French SF practitioners often had to use Anglo-Saxon pseudonyms to sway publishers. Unfortunately, few of these early 1980s writers have had the opportunity to prove staying power, and the current outlook, influenced by publishing restrictions, is decidedly patchy, with the closed status of the Anglo-American prime markets a strong factor of discouragement for the more established and talented French SF authors. Notwithstanding these market considerations, and with the possible exception of Eastern Europe, where both social and political considerations distort our appreciation of the genre's exact situation, France is still today the non-English-speaking country where SF is at its most active, with genuine enthusiasm visible from grass-roots level onward, as fandom, semipro magazines, and conventions expand as never before, generating new writing talent at a steady rate.

Although many scholars point to Rabelais's flights of fancy in *Gargantua* and *Pantagruel* (1532 and 1564) as early examples of SF, it is with Cyrano de Bergerac (1619–1655) that we witness the first significant examples of scientific speculation in French literature. De Bergerac's *Histoire comique contenant des états et empires de la lune*, published in 1657 and followed in 1662 by *Histoire comique des états et empires de la lune* [1-12], is a genuine comic romp encompassing journeys, by rather odd means, to both the Moon and the Sun. It is quite unlike any other writing of the same century, either in France or elsewhere, where utopian preoccupations were still the more noticeable format for early examples of science fiction. Fénelon, a seventeenth-century philosopher, mixes metaphysics with such utopian longings in his *Entretiens sur la pluralité des mondes habités* (1686).

The eighteenth century in French literature saw the blooming of the "conte philosophique," and many now famous classical writers often touched on the fringes of SF: Voltaire, Marivaux, de Sade, Diderot, and Montesquieu, although two lesser names were more instrumental in delving into speculative areas— Mercier, with *L'An deux mille quatre cent quarante* (1771) [1-63], an early sleeper awakes novel that, ironically, gained another 60 years in its English translation as *The Year 2500*, and Restif de la Bretonne, whose *La Découverte australe* (1781) is a precursor of the lost-world theme. Restif's later *Les Posthumes* (1796) is lesser known but even more fantastic, with Stapledon-like stellar flight and philosophical speculation.

The flamboyant rise of romanticism through European and, more particularly, the French arts in the nineteenth century was ideally suited to conjectural writing, a literary era that was to end with Jules Verne. However, before Verne, the speculative vein was still being explored by French authors, and one should note some intriguing books such as de Grainville's *Le Dernier Homme* (1805), Balzac's *Louis Lambert* (1832), Nodier's *Léviathan le long* (1833), and Grandville's *Un Autre monde* (1844). But a flamboyant early example of space opera, *Star ou psi de Cassiopée* (1854) by the obscure Charles Defontenay, stands out quite prominently, not only as an intriguing literary curiosity but as a novel well ahead of its time. Its rediscovery is attributable to Pierre Versins.

The appearance of Jules Verne on the scene is viewed by many as the beginning of modern science fiction, not only in France but worldwide, and his influence has been considerable. Just as H. G. Wells can be construed as the writer who crafted the fiction in SF, Verne is seen today as the early proponent of science in SF (although one must emphasize the fact that his books touch not only on the hard sciences, as inspired by the Industrial Revolution, but in an encyclopedic manner with all sciences). It can in fact be argued that Verne's shadow looms heavily over the pulp beginnings of science fiction as we know it: Hugo Gernsback, European-born instigator of the pulp era, placed the early issues of *Amazing Stories* in the late 1920s under the patronage of Verne, the masthead depicting "Jules Verne's tombstone at Amiens portraying his immortality." Furthermore, the first two all-reprint issues of *Amazing Stories* featured *Hector Servadac* and *Journey to the Center of the Earth* [1-94].

There is insufficient room in this introduction for a detailed discussion of Verne's work, a task that many academics are now warming to. The undisputed fact is that, with H. G. Wells, he is one of the founding fathers of SF as it is known today. Born in Nantes in 1828, Verne, from an early age, was drawn to the sea (as a teenager, he once attempted to run away to sea), a major influence on his future stories. Declining to follow in his father's footsteps in a legal career, he embarked on a literary one. Alexandre Dumas was a major influence and model during the unpromising early years when Verne principally wrote verse, opera libretti, and unremarkable dramas. He began publishing popular travel articles in magazines about 1857 and, in 1863, was encouraged by the publisher Hetzel to fictionalize these for a new educational magazine for the young. The association between the two men was to last until Verne's death in 1905 and is responsible for a major body of imaginative fiction totaling 64 novels.

Although Verne wrote within the existing confines of popular literature, his talent was in basing his romances upon a groundwork of actual fact, ensuring plausibility for all his extrapolations of scientific progress, geographic travails and rough-hewn heroes, and ambivalent mad scientists. Not all the *Voyages extraordinaires* initially serialized by Hetzel in his *Magasin d'education et de récréation* and later published in book form are SF, including what is possibly Verne's most famous novel, *Around the World in Eighty Days* (1873). Several posthumous novels and short stories credited to Verne were written or edited by his son, Michel Jules-Verne.

Verne's first romance, *Five Weeks in a Balloon* (1863), is more of a rumbustious geographic adventure, but his next book, *Journey to the Center of the Earth* [1-94], introduces fascinating speculative concepts with three protagonists leading an expedition into the heart of an Icelandic volcano that takes them to a lighted cavern world at the Earth's core. *From the Earth to the Moon* [1-93] is a striking example of early hard SF, detailing with great precision the preparations and scientific premises (still mostly correct, apart from the deadly effect of gravity on the passengers) for a voyage to the Moon. The sequel, *Round the Moon* [1-93], is more fanciful, a tale about survival in space and the group's eventual return to Earth.

Twenty Thousand Leagues under the Sea [1-95] introduces Captain Nemo and his supersubmarine *Nautilus*, both of which return in *The Mysterious Island* (1874–1875). Nemo, a lone anarchist figure at odds with warring humanity, remains one of Verne's most memorable characters and is a pointer to the increasing darkness of his later work, where the magic attraction of science fades in its continuous confrontation with the dark side of mankind. In *Hector Servadac* (1877), a group of disparate personalities are stolen away from the Earth's surface by a passing comet to face conflict and adversity, whereas *The Begum's Fortune* (1878), *The Purchase of the North Pole* (1889), and *The Castle of the Carpathians* (1892) witness Verne's love affair with scientific wonder turning sour.

Other notable novels in the SF genre include *The Clipper of the Clouds* (1886) and its sequel, *The Master of the World* (1904), both featuring the archetypal mad inventor Robur; *The Floating Island* (1895); *An Antarctic Mystery* (1897), a rationalist sequel to Poe's *Arthur Gordon Pym;* and *The Village in the Tree Tops* (1901). Verne's posthumous SF novels are *The Chase of the Golden Meteor* (1908); *The Secret of Wilhelm Storitz* (1910), about invisibility; *The Barsac Mission* (1914); and a collection of short stories, *Yesterday and Tomorrow* (1910). Although the general public still thinks of Jules Verne with Walt Disney screen adaptations in mind, his role was of critical importance to the SF field. Indeed, in France, eminent critics and authors (such as Raymond Roussel, Michel Butor, and Foucault) see him as a major landmark in French literature and socialist history.

Verne had, of course, a score of imitators and followers. Worth noting are the astronomer Flammarion, Robida, and Villiers de l'Isle Adam (*L'Eve future,* 1885). But the most important SF writer in the lineage of Verne is Rosny aîné (1856–1940). Long remembered for his innovative prehistoric novels, Rosny aîné's reputation in the field has only recently been established with the exhumation (and in some cases posthumous publication) of many of his major titles. Surprisingly modern and in tune with many of the preoccupations and idiosyncrasies of the American writers of the golden age, Rosny aîné stands as a genuine original and a precursor whose fame for too long stood in Verne's shadow. His major speculative works are *The Xipéhuz* [1-79], *The Death of the Earth* [1-79], *Le Force mystérieuse* [6-138], and the ground-breaking *Les Navigateurs de l'infini* [6-139].

The influence of Jules Verne flourished in France until World War II, and the very strength of the school of scientific romances that came after him was a strong contributory factor in shielding French readers and authors from the parallel development of pulp fiction into SF in the United States. In fact, the blinkers worked both ways, and many outstanding French SF works of those years have remained quite unknown to Anglo-American readers and critics.

By generally being published in popular magazines combining scientific romance with adventure fiction, travel journalism, and other editorial matters for a mass audience, early French science fiction never became tainted with a pulp stigma, as occurred in the United States and was not relegated to a form of literary ghetto. An important seal of critical respectability was often provided by many established mainstream authors dabbling in the genre, such as Paul Claudel, Emile Zola, Nobel prize winner Anatole France, Claude Farrère, and the marginal Raymond Roussel. Principal contributors to the scientific romance subgenre for the popular market include Paul d'Ivoi, Capitaine Danrit, René Thévenin, André Laurie, Jean de la Hire, and André Valérie.

The works of Gustave Le Rouge are another worthy survivor from those teeming years. His fast-moving Martian adventures in *Le Prisonnier de la planète Mars* [6-123] and *La Guerre des vampires* [6-123] fit in well today with the heroic fantasy genre in vogue, while the picaresque *Le Mystérieux Docteur Cornélius* [6-122] announces the sprawling conspiracy sagas of Thomas Pynchon with an added touch of political naïveté.

European political anxieties between the two world wars are mirrored in José Moselli's *La Fin d'Illa* [6-127] and works by Louis Boussenard, Octave Béliard, Théo Varlet, Gaston Leroux (better rememberd today for *The Phantom of the Opera* and crime novels), Léon Groc, Léon Daudet, and Ernest Pérochon. One of the more noteworthy authors of this period is Maurice Renard, who dedicated his first novel, *Le Docteur Lerne, Sous-Dieu*, to H. G. Wells. In his *Le Péril bleu* [6-136], which influenced the visionary theories of Charles Fort, strange unearthly influences take on a strong paranoic quality, while *Les Mains d'Orlac* (1920) crossed the waters to the Hollywood silver screen.

Régis Messac, who died in 1943 in a Nazi concentration camp, launched Hypermondes, the first regular SF imprint in 1935. The series managed only three titles, a translation of David H. Keller and Messac's own *Quinzinzinzili* [6-126] and *La Cité des asphyxiés* [6-125], both admirably modern novels.

Jacques Spitz, a witty, ironic writer still in great favor in France, published a score of deeply pessimistic novels possibly influenced by the upheaval shaking the world between 1936 and 1945: *L'Agonie du globe* (1935), *Les Evadés de l'an 4000*, *La Guerre des mouches* [6-144], *L'Homme élastique* [6-145], and *L'Oeil du purgatoire* [6-146] are the most notable.

This fertile stream of science fiction by French authors trickled to a halt with the advent of World War II. It is interesting, in retrospect, to examine how the war affected the course of SF in different countries: in America, the burgeoning golden age was hastily speeded to greater achievements by the massive industrial war effort, while the resilient mood of beleaguered England would later be reflected in the new doom-laden school of British catastrophe books exemplified by John Wyndham or John Christopher. In invaded France, on the other hand, SF was to disappear almost completely before emerging anew in the 1950s, at last borrowing from and acknowledging the influence of the now dominant Anglo-American SF.

The only writer of note to appear during the war is René Barjavel, with *Ravage* [6-58] and *Le Voyageur imprudent* [6-60]. His later, postwar career saw him lapse into a particularly French form of philosophical complacency, which mars his future works in the genre.

Straddling the old and new French SF traditions are Marc Wersinger and B. R. Bruss, whose first novels reflect the specter of Hiroshima before he became a prolix pulp writer, borrowing heavily from U.S. models.

By 1952, the massive body of modern Anglo-American science fiction had slowly begun to appear in France. The first two major titles to be translated were Smith's *Skylark of Space* [2-104] and Williamson's *Humanoids* [3-402]. French intellectual circles emerging from postwar existentialism began to take notice of this new imported phenomenon, born of the pulps and unparalleled in France, long before publishers did and became great SF fans, although it is sad to report that few of them, then or later, deigned to write any. However, it was very much due to the efforts of people like Raymond Queneau, Maurice Blanchot, playwright Audiberti, Georges Gallet, and Stephen Spriel that SF took off in France.

One of the more prominent amateurs was Boris Vian, who was later to translate van Vogt and Lewis Padgett into French. Vian was a musician, a playwright, an engineer, a writer of pornographic thrillers, a man sadly ahead of his time. A founding member of the first French SF circle, the Club des Savanturiers, he became famous for all the wrong reasons, and it was only after his premature death at the age of 39 in 1959 that his major novels came into the public eye. Essentially absurdist, with a tongue-in-cheek use of occasional SF archetypes, these titles are *L'Écume des jours* (1947), translated as *Froth on the Daydream*, *L'Automne à Pékin* [6-155], *L'Herbe rouge* [6-156], and *L'Arrache-coeur* (1953), translated as *Heart*

Snatcher. Although not accepted by all critics as part of the SF canon, Vian's role can be seen as characteristic of the transitional period between prewar scientific romance and the assimilated influence of Anglo-American SF. To a large extent, Vian is a harbinger for the British New Wave of the 1960s, which was itself to have a profound influence on French SF.

In September 1951, Fleuve Noir, a publisher of mass market paperbacks, launched an SF series, Anticipation, which is still going strong. Although aimed at the lowest common denominator, Fleuve Noir has produced the occasional gem and has been strongly instrumental, despite all the lowbrow attitudes, in bringing successive generations of readers to SF. Apart from rare translations of Poul Anderson, Ken Bulmer, Arthur Clarke, E. C. Tubb, Leigh Brackett, Murray Leinster, and Fred Hoyle, the large majority of the Fleuve Noir titles have been by local authors. Most frequent are Jimmy Guieu, Richard-Bessière, M. A. Rayjean, Maurice Limat, B. R. Bruss, Jean-Gaston Vandel, and Pierre Barbet. However, some writers of quality have emerged among the dross: Stefan Wul, pen name of a provincial dentist who had a lightning career between 1956 and 1959 before reemerging many years later with the sprawling *Noô* [6-165]; Kurt Steiner, pseudonym of André Ruellan; Gilles d'Argyre, another pen name hiding Gérard Klein; Gilles Thomas; and J. L. Le May.

It was also in 1951 that Gallet and Spriel persuaded two leading French publishing houses, Gallimard and Hachette, to launch an imprint, Le Rayon Fantastique, primarily to introduce scores of Anglo-American classics and near-misses to a French public starved for SF in the traditional vein. In so doing, Le Rayon Fantastique also slowly introduced some new French authors to the field. The first was François Bordes, a Bordeaux archaeologist writing as Francis Carsac. Before the series folded in 1964, following disagreements between the joint publishers, it also launched many of the brightest names still active today: Michel Jeury (then writing as Albert Higon), Gérard Klein, Charles Henneberg, Philippe Curval, the late Christine Renard, as well as others now seemingly lost to the field—Jérome Sériel, Arcadius, and Vladimir Volkoff (fruitful in the mainstream).

Another major imprint, still enjoying great commercial success to this day, is Présence du Futur, launched by Editions Denoël. Despite some lapses toward the end of the initial editor's, Robert Kanter's, tenure (Elisabeth Gille helmed the line from 1975 to 1986 and became a major patron for young authors; critic Jacques Chambon has just succeeded her), Présence du Futur was long the undoubted literary leader in the French field. Its sober, initially nonillustrative covers introduced Bradbury, Lovecraft, and Ballard to France, and in time French authors were regularly featured: Klein, Andrevon, and Sternberg were among the first. In recent years, the series has championed many new talents like Ligny, Volodine, Brussolo, Berthelot, and Jouanne, in addition to the new U.S. generation of Sterling, Swanwick, Rucker, and Kim Stanley Robinson. Anthologies of all-new local authors gathered by Philippe Curval have been another feature, much welcomed on the French scene.

In 1954, a minor publisher, Editions Métal, launched *Série 2000*, with French writers only, introducing Yves Dermèze, Pierre Versins, and *La Naissance des dieux* [6-100], which is Charles Henneberg's first SF novel. This series, however, lasted only a few years.

But 1954 was a crucial date, nonetheless, for two major magazines were launched. Both initially were French reprint editions of American magazines: *Galaxy* and the *Magazine of Fantasy & SF*, becoming, respectively, *Galaxie* and *Fiction*. *Galaxie* long restricted itself to translations only and had a patchy career, but *Fiction* intelligently adapted, with local book reviews, lengthy articles, and French stories. Under the successive editorships of Alain Dorémieux and Daniel Riche, *Fiction* has been the major breeding ground for French SF, where most notable writers began, before graduating to novels (and vice versa; established novelists would often switch to shorter lengths in its pages). Their names include Jacques Sternberg, Carsac, Philippe Curval, Julia Verlanger, most of the Rayon Fantastique contributors, Marcel Battin, Claude Cheinisse, Michel Demuth, Andrevon, Daniel Walther, and others. In recent years, despite increasing financial difficulties and a severe fall in circulation, *Fiction* has continued to champion younger writers, and many a New Wave proponent has published in its pages.

Curval, Sternberg, and Klein were, until 1970, the major writers of SF in France and their major novels are annotated in this section. Curval is still prominent in the field, while Sternberg has moved to mainstream fiction and Klein has increasingly become absorbed in editorial activities. A forcible and thought-provoking critic, Klein, who was once dubbed the child prodigy of French SF when he published his first short stories in his teens, became an editor for publisher Robert Laffont in 1969 and launched the Ailleurs et Demain imprint. This impeccably designed and edited, high-priced series arrived at a time when the genre had been in the doldrums in France, with only Fleuve Noir and Présence du Futur surviving of the many imprints that sprouted between 1950 and 1970. Klein judiciously published the best Anglo-American novels available by Herbert, Le Guin, Dick, and Silverberg, but never hesitated to promote local writers.

The most popular author relaunched by Klein was Michel Jeury, whose two pseudonymous Rayon Fantastique novels had not attracted the attention they deserved. *Le Temps incertain* [6-114] was a major departure for French SF, combining Anglo-American speculative traits with a specifically French preoccupation with social and political factors. It won an award for best SF novel of the year, and Jeury soon turned professional and increasingly prolific, although the quality of his output has always been very high, even when his writing is in a minor key. Jeury became the unwitting leader of a renaissance in French SF, spurred on by his own success and an increasing interest in genre literatures, which followed the May 1968 student uprising.

Philippe Curval also joined the Laffont stable and won the prestigious Apollo prize for *Cette chère humanité* [4-159, 6-77], while Demuth, Christin, Ruellan, Léourier, and Pelot also shone with Ailleurs et Demain titles.

Despite its intrinsic qualities, French SF has always been more concerned with psychology. The only author with a genuine sense of the epic was Charles Henneberg (and his wife, Nathalie Henneberg, who continued what was discovered to be their joint opus after his death). And it is this reliance on the soft sciences, possible inherited from a Cartesian environment and mainstream literary values, that flourishes when local authors, such as Daniel Drode, Philip Goy, or Claude Ollier, delve into the experimental.

While an elegant stylist like Curval has remained active over several decades, slowly nurturing an undeniable oeuvre, centered around his Marcom trilogy (a fourth, closing, novel is still due), *L'Europe après la pluie*, the two main personalities to emerge from the turbulent 1960s and who avoided a rapid creative burnout are Andrevon and Walther. Both revealed in *Fiction* shortly after the political events of May 1968 that they are both strikingly individual writers. Andrevon, a prolific short-story writer and patchy novelist, demonstrates fiercely committed political beliefs of the left-wing variety and strong ecological sympathies. Daniel Walther, a journalist often compared to Harlan Ellison for his lyricism and over-the-top flights of fancy, works under the twin signs of romanticism and existential despair. Once seen as young authors, they have now reached their forties and their work attains a quieter level of accomplishment. Some of Walther's unrepresentative novels have been published in the United States, translated by C. J. Cherryh.

In the mid-1970s, a ferociously political New Wave of younger writers, usually in their twenties, emerged in reaction to the growing dominance of foreign SF in the French marketplace. With the bland encouragement of Jeury, Andrevon, and Walther (who all belonged to older generations), they set out to question the values of the genre in an iconoclastic manner, often fraught with much naïveté. Led by critic Bernard Blanc, this amorphous group soon fizzled out as the more intelligent authors began to assume a voice of their own (Dominique Douay, Jean-Pierre Hubert, Jacques Boireau, Pierre Mondoloni, Pierre Marlson, Yves Frémion, Joël Houssin, Joëlle Wintrebert) and gradually reintegrated the mainstream with some fascinating books. As this happened, yet another wave of young writers broke through, each with strongly individualistic preoccupations: Jean-Marc Ligny, Serge Brussolo, Bruno Lecigne. But in the short time that these two successive French SF waves were at their most vocal, the genre witnessed a remarkable advance quite unlike any development elsewhere, a leap forward of great quality. Dominique Douay and Pierre Suragne writing as Pierre Pelot, although very much on the fringes of the movement, benefited most and are today highly regarded outside the context of their past political sympathies. After a flamboyant beginning, Brussolo has become much too prolific and has spread his talent thin at a rate of four or five novels per year.

Many of these new writers were soon adopted by the Fleuve Noir, under the editorship of Patrick Siry, and curbed their ambitions in the service of Mammon, although this has enabled many of them to write and yet more promising talents to emerge, including Hughes Douriaux, Michel Pagel, Claude Ecken, Pierre Bameul, Alain Paris, and Jean-Pierre Fontana.

The 1980s is proving a difficult period for French SF with a strong fall in market opportunities, a lack of magazines, and the disappearance of many 1970s imprints from publishing houses. A lack of overall unity pervades the scene, although individual books still show many signs of brilliance, as writers like Francis Berthelot, Jean-Claude Dunyach, Jacques Barbéri, Pierre Stolze, Bruno Lecigne, Jean-Pierre Vernay, the promising stylist Emmanuel Jouanne, Lorris Murail, Antoine Volodine, and Richard Canal establish themselves, while the old masters like Curval, Jeury, Andrevon, and Walther are far from absent.

Ironically, the major foreign influence on modern French SF has been the New Worlds speculative fiction school around Moorcock and Ballard, although most of its texts are still to reach France. Ballard is possibly one of the most popular SF authors in France today and a darling of the intelligentsia (with allegedly dozens of university theses on Ballard underway). Also prominent are Philip

Dick, Frank Herbert, and Robert Silverberg. These preferences of the French public accurately reflect the added importance given to literary values and antitechnology, and, although local authors still do not receive the acclaim of Ballard or Dick, they reflect all that is different, ever-active, and healthy in SF in France today. *Note:* In the bibliography that follows, all authors and editors are from France unless noted otherwise.

Bibliography

Individual Authors

*6-53. Andrevon, Jean-Pierre. **Le Désert du monde.** Paris: Denoël, 1977.
A man awakes, with little memory of things past, in a small country village, to discover the world in ruins, victim of a mysterious holocaust. As he searches for both his memory and an explanation for the unsettling events, he successively comes across food, corpses, a dog, and finally a woman, slowly realizing that he is being manipulated by invisible alien entities conducting a strange and sinister experiment in resuscitation and immortality. A clever improvisation on the classic last-man-on-Earth theme with a nod to Farmer's Riverworld series [4-210].

6-54. Andrevon, Jean-Pierre. **Les Hommes-machines contre Gandahar.** Paris: Denoël, 1969.
Andrevon's first uncharacteristic novel is a rare example of science fantasy in French with strong fairy-tale overtones. The Kingdom of Gandahar on planet Tridan lives in peace, devoted to pleasure and the arts, until the day spy-birds bring warning of a forthcoming invasion by ferocious machine-men. The services of Sylvin the Knight are sought by the queen. The adventures that follow are colorful, and many SF themes are employed (including time travel). Compare Jack Vance's *Big Planet* (1957) or the Beatles' *The Yellow Submarine* movie.

6-55. Andrevon, Jean-Pierre. **Le Livre d'or de Jean-Pierre Andrevon,** selected by Patrice Duvic. Paris: Presses Pocket, 1983.
Twelve short stories from 1968 to 1981 that represent the essence of Andrevon's bleak but rewarding visions of the world. A heroic fantasy pastiche, a hard SF homage to Heinlein's "All You Zombies" and a score of pessimistic views of nuclear and ecological catastrophes and end of world situations. A collection that epitomizes how French SF in the person of one of its most prolific short-story writers has absorbed and subverted many of Anglo-Saxon's SF major themes. Introduction by Duvic; thorough bibliography of Andrevon's works.

6-56. Andrevon, Jean-Pierre. **Le Travail du Furet à l'intérieur du Poulailler.** Paris: J'Ai Lu, 1984.
In a near-future France, a professional killer is employed by governmental authorities to exterminate surplus citizens selected by lottery. The novel follows the monotony of his job, until he begins questioning the principles of the lottery and the motives of the authorities. A sardonic novel about an alienated character's slow redemption. Compare Dick's *Do Androids Dream of Electric Sheep?* [4-173].

6-57. Arnaud, G. J. **La Compagnie des glaces.** Paris: Fleuve Noir, 1980.
The first of an impressive 28-volume saga. A new ice age has been going on for some thousands of years, and the planet is controlled by several Industrial Combines while war rages all over the globe. All remaining communications are by rail. The Red Men, a genetically transformed species of dissident mutants, oppose the system and live in the top floors of submerged skyscrapers. Full of action and much compassion for his human characters, Arnaud has throughout this unending series established a strong reputation, worthy of American SF at its most imaginative and flamboyant.

*6-58. Barjavel, René. **Ashes, Ashes.** Doubleday, 1967. Tr. by Damon Knight of *Ravage* (1943).
Although developed as an allegory of France under the German occupation during World War II, this powerful novel unveils the desperation of a world where electricity has disappeared and a strong right-wing return-to-nature movement rules. Reaches a hopeful, bucolic end, which doesn't succeed in eliminating the earlier brooding mood of the book. Also annotated as [3-25].

6-59. Barjavel, René. **Le Diable l'emporte.** Paris: Denoël, 1948.
Pessimistic post-Hiroshima novel describing the utter inevitability of the third and fourth world wars and the construction of a giant arch under Notre Dame Cathedral to allow some to survive the holocaust ultimately brought about by a struggle for possession of the Moon. Civilization suffers total destruction at the end of the novel, although hope remains vested with a man and a woman fleeing by rocket to the stars.

6-60. Barjavel, René. **Future Times Three.** Award Books, 1970. Tr. of *Le Voyageur imprudent* (1944).
A bleak if humorous European time travel yarn, full of the obligatory paradoxes as the protagonist encounters Napoleon and ancient Egyptians, inadvertently commits a murder, and blots himself out of existence.

6-61. Bersianik, Louky (Canada). **The Euguélionne.** Victoria, B.C.: Porcépic, 1981. Tr. by Gerry Dennis, Alison Hewitt, Donna Murray, and Martha O'Brien of *L'Euguélionne*, 1976.
The Euguélionne arrives from another planet, seeking the male of her species. Her adventures on Earth are fantastic, funny, and only too true to life and soon cause her to question the Earth's vision of itself. A French-Canadian feminist classic, which was a best-seller in Quebec. Compare Russ's *The Female Man* [4-458].

6-62. Berthelot, Francis. **La Line noire d'orion.** Paris: Calmann-Lévy, 1980.
Striking first novel, with a galactic scope as a future homosexual society faces extermination in a war with a rival civilization. A political novel in the guise of space opera and one of the more unusual French novels of the 1980s.

6-63. Billon, Pierre. **L'enfant du cinquième nord.** Paris: Seuil, 1983.
A French-Canadian novel that was awarded a prize as best novel of the year in France. A tender evocation of illness with a medical thriller plot infrastructure, as a cancer-stricken child is manipulated by scientists in a remote hospital. The

child is capable of producing radiation and is seen as a pawn in an industrial war. A worthy accomplishment from a new author.

6-64. Boireau, Jacques. **Les Années de sable.** Paris: Encre, 1979.
An Earth-based journalist is given the opportunity of visiting the prison, desert-world of Mira where political exiles are sent. A first novel with a strong utopian slant and a strong pro-ecology slant. Compare Herbert's *Dune* [4-268].

Boulle, Pierre. **Garden on the Moon (Le Jardin de Kanashima)** [see **3-54**].

Boulle, Pierre. **Planet of the Apes (La Planète des singes)** [see **3-55**].

Boule, Pierre. **Time Out of Mind (Contes de l'absurde suivis de E = mc²)** [see **3-56**].

6-65. Bruss, B. R. (pseud. of Roger Blondel). **Apparition des surhommes.** Paris: Froissart, 1953; rev. ed., 1970.
A Swiss canton is suddenly cut off from the rest of the world and taken over by the Agoutes, a race of highly developed and beautiful mutants. The novel examines the ambivalent human attitudes to their new masters. A pioneering title written at a time when the Anglo-American golden age of SF was still generally unknown in France. Contrast with Wyndham's *The Midwich Cuckoos* [3-413].

6-66. Bruss, B. R. (pseud. of Roger Blondel). **Les Espaces enchevêtrés.** Paris: NEO, 1979.
A masterful late novel by veteran B. R. Bruss. A relentless chase through parallel and multiple Earths reveals a cosmological dream with stunning implications. Full of humor and powerful descriptions of other worlds. Compare Simak's *Ring around the Sun* [3-346].

6-67. Bruss, B. R. (pseud. of Roger Blondel). **Et la planète sauta.** Paris: Le Portulan, 1946.
The first important post–World War II French SF novel, still under the strong shadow of Hiroshima. A meteorite falls in the French province of Sologne, bringing with it the spiritual message of the late planet Rhama, which used to lie between Mars and Jupiter, where the asteroid belt now orbits. Rhama succumbed to the combined follies of greed and the atom. A didactic warning bell in the parallels between the flourishing civilization of Rhama and Earth's people is only too apparent.

6-68. Brussolo, Serge. **Portrait du diable en chapeau melon.** Paris: Denoël, 1983.
Genetic mutants are locked away in a hermetic prison with no conscience of what lies outside. A classic SF situation soon subverted by Brussolo's savage visions of reality. Nightmarish and busy, one of Brussolo's more typical early novels.

6-69. Brussolo, Serge. **Vue en coupe d'une ville malade.** Paris: Denoël, 1980.
Pyrotechnic collection of stories by one of the major new French SF revelations of the 1980s. With hallucinatory intensity, Brussolo evokes a radically different universe of Kafkaesque origins, where mineral and flesh coalesce and nightmares abound. A perfect introduction to Brussolo's subversive art containing much of his characteristic microcosm undiluted.

6-70. Canal, Richard. **La Malédiction de l'éphemère.** Paris: La Découverte, 1986.

In a near future ravaged by a third world war caused by mysterious aliens, certain areas have been isolated behind radiation barriers. An adventurer trading in smuggled artifacts seeks to resolve the enigma of the forbidden zones. A clever first novel from a young author. Compare the Strugatskiis' *Roadside Picnic* [4-542].

6-71. Carsac, Francis (pseud. of François Bordes). **Ce monde est nôtre.** Paris: Gallimard, 1962.

The laws of the Galactic League are adamant: only one race is allowed to live on a single planet. But on Nerat three species claim to be the rightful native race. A representative from the league is despatched to solve the problem and deport the parties in the wrong. He discovers that the truth is more complex than he imagined. A clever ethnographic parable on the Algerian War.

6-72. Carsac, Francis (pseud. of François Bordes). **Ceux de nulle part.** Paris: Gallimard, 1954.

A French doctor is kidnapped by extraterrestrials and forced to act as mediator between the Hiss, green-skinned humanoids, and the Misliks, highly intelligent but lethal metal creatures who can also live in absolute zero cold and keep on extinguishing suns during the course of their march through the galaxy. An early, successful, and unusual example of hard-core French SF by a professor of paleontology and prehistory at Bordeaux University. Contrast Clement's *Cycle of Fire* [3-108].

6-73. Carsac, Francis (pseud. of François Bordes). **Pour patrie l'espace.** Paris: Gallimard, 1962.

Inspired by Blish's *Cities in Flight* [3-43], a socially concerned space opera where the protagonist inhabits such a movable space city and opposes the might of the Empire, modeled on the decline of the Roman Empire. Strong element of conflict between humanities and the scientific ethos forms the kernel of the book's moral dilemmas.

6-74. Carsac, Francis (pseud. of François Bordes). **Terre en fuite.** Paris: Gallimard, 1960.

Interesting variation on the traveling world-city theme. To escape a major cosmic catastrophe, scientists and engineers succeed in moving the Earth, which then begins its peregrinations and adventures throughout the galaxy. Compare Blish's *Cities in Flight* [3-43] or Clarke's artificial wanderer in *Rendezvous with Rama* [4-138].

6-75. Christin, Pierre. **Les Prédateurs enjolivés.** Paris: Laffont, 1976.

First book by a young French writer previously better known for his comic-strip scripts ("Valerian" with illustrator Jean-Claude Mézières). This is a collection of unrelated novellas building up to a dark and vivid chronicle of the far-flung future where humans have become both victim and chief predator. Resembles Simak's *City* [3-345] without the American author's prevalent humanism.

6-76. Comte, Jean-François. **Sylvie et les vivisecteurs.** Paris: Atelier Marcel Jullian, 1978.
Striking SF debut by a French mainstream novelist. In 1978, a woman in Louisiana receives a letter sent from the year 2022. A curious, labyrinthine novel/dossier with a fascinating glimpse of a most improbable, romantic future. An oddity but well worth investigation.

Curtis, Jean-Louis. **The Neon Halo (Un Saint au néon)** [see **3-124**].

*6-77. Curval, Philippe (pseud. of Philippe Tronche). **Cette chère humanité.** Paris: Laffont, 1976.
Apollo award-winning novel (the first winner in the French language) by one of the most respected French SF authors. The time is the near future, the Common Market has closed down its electronic frontiers, and what lies within becomes a worrisome, inscrutable mystery to the rest of the world. Strange dream messages percolate through to the outside, and the underdeveloped countries send a spy into the new utopia. A striking work of imagination with forceful poetic as well as scientific leanings; one of the major French SF novels of the 1970s. (See also [4-159].)

6-78. Curval, Philippe (pseud. of Philippe Tronche). **Le Dormeur s'éveillera-t-il?** Paris: Denoël, 1979.
The antinuclear lobby has won the day and the energy race has ground to a halt. As a result, European society has crumbled and lies in ruins as solitary mercenaries and individualists roam the countryside and deserted cities, biding their time and waiting for the inevitable end. Moulis the Wolf tracks down the last survivors of the Multinational Companies while Jipa, a young woman ecologist, discovers a strange sleeper, whom she guesses to be a mutant who owns the key to a better future. But only electricity can cure and awaken him. A somber and ironic pronuclear parable that goes strongly against the grain of most modern French SF's sturdiest beliefs. Superlatively iconoclastic. Contrast Yarbro's *False Dawn* [4-618].

6-79. Curval, Philippe (pseud. of Philippe Tronche). **En souvenir du futur.** Paris: Laffont, 1983.
Industrial war across the barriers of time in this third installment of Curval's major series, L'Europe après la pluie, following *Cette chère humanité* [6-77] and *Le Dormeur s'éveillera-t-il?* [6-78]. Unlike Jeury's *Chronolysis* [6-114], which the novel resembles, the preferred mode of transport is sexual congress, which makes the book highly erotic as the future Common Market controllers battle it out with individual anarchists for stakes neither can fathom.

6-80. Curval, Philippe (pseud. of Philippe Tronche). **La Face cachée du désir.** Paris: Calmann-Lévy, 1980.
Chula is a vital link world in the communications network of the space worlds, and man desperately needs to take it over for strategic reasons. However, Chula follows different laws. Reality on Chula is what you think, dream, or believe is reality. Despite the space opera trappings, one of Curval's most elegant and literary novels.

6-81. Curval, Philippe (pseud. of Philippe Tronche). **L'Homme à rebours.** Paris: Laffont, 1974.

A man awakens on a beach, his memory gone, and no hint to his identity. Where is he? What is this imaginary world he now seemingly moves through, full of parallel universes where realities shift and disappear to the rhythm of his own desires? A metaphysical and poetic interrogation about the true nature of reality and humanity, this slow, hypnotic novel marked Curval's return to SF after an interruption of five years.

6-82. Curval, Philippe (pseud. of Philippe Tronche). **Le Livre d'or de Philippe Curval,** selected by André Ruellan. Paris: Presses Pocket, 1981.

A collection of Curval's best short stories, spanning two decades. From early poetic work in a strong literary mode to fuller, more accomplished tales combining scientific extrapolation and political and social considerations, the book maps Curval's development into one of France's most assured SF writers whose personal touch remains unique whether in the context of stories of alien contact, false realities, or space (both outer and inner) explorations. A perfect introduction to a fascinating writer. Detailed bibliography.

6-83. Curval, Philippe (pseud. of Philippe Tronche). **Les Sables de Falun.** Veviers: Marabout, 1975.

Like so many of Curval's novels, this stems from a highly original premise: the unfolding of a space opera based on the imaginative theories of random word and thought association of Raymond Roussel. Falun, a sumptuous ocean planet, is also a prison. Nils Aldenerer, a fallen priest, tries to escape by solving the mystery of the planet's pink sand, which, when ground into lenses, allows the onlooker to glimpse through time itself. Ultimately, Nils will find himself forced to challenge the faraway government of Earth. A fast-moving novel with strong surrealist overtones, originally serialized in *Fiction*, 1970.

6-84. Curval, Philippe (pseud. of Philippe Tronche). **Y a quelqu'un?** Paris: Calmann-Lévy, 1979.

Clément Volgré is walking down the Champs Elysées with his wife, Nina. Suddenly, the implosion of a window full of television sets in a nearby shop provokes Nina's disappearance. The young woman has not been injured but has simply vanished into thin air, as if vacuumed away. Thus begins for Clément an alcoholic journey through a Paris dominated by property speculators and concrete, where the quest for his lost wife soon merges into a search for a lost city and the uncovering of a massive, insidious conspiracy. From passive resignation to resistance, a powerful fictional itinerary and superlative novel about the banality of evil.

Cyrano de Bergerac, Savinien. **The Comical History of the States and Empires of the Worlds of the Moon and Sun (Histoire comique des états et empires de la lune)** [see **1-12**].

6-85. Demuth, Michel. **Les Galaxiales.** 2 vols. Paris: J'Ai Lu, 1976, 1979.

A vast, continuing future history cycle begun in 1964 by one of the few French SF writers strongly influenced by the epic roots and traditions of the modern genre. The complete series should range from years 2020 to about 4000 and include 29 stories. The first two volumes take the proceedings up to 2185 and include nine and seven novellas, respectively, some of which prove awesome and epic in scope ("La Course de l'oiseau boum-boum," "Les Grands équipages de lumière"). Impeccable writing and inspiration and a close understanding of the basic rules of adventure in the genre make this a milestone in French SF, even in its still incomplete form. Compare Asimov's Foundation series [3-19].

6-86. Dobzynski, Charles. **Taromancie.** Paris: Editeurs Français Réunis, 1977.
A lengthy complex futuristic novel by a mainstream French writer and poet long fascinated by SF (in 1963, he wrote an epic 150-page space opera poem in rhyming verse, "L'Opéra de l'espace"). Taromancie, a city of the future, is governed by a network of illusions; Grizure, a dissident psychoanalyst, rebels against the surrounding technocracy and attempts to solve the coded tarot language of the city. Compare Brunner's *The Squares of the City* [3-73], based on chess.

6-87. Dorémieux, Alain. **Le Livre d'or d'Alain Dorémieux,** selected by Jean-Pierre Andrevon. Paris: Presses Pocket, 1981.
A collection of Dorémieux's best short stories (he has never written any novels) demonstrating how influential he has been for French SF, in addition to his crucial role as editor of *Fiction* over two decades. A consummate stylist seemingly obsessed by love, death, eroticism, and intercourse between humans and aliens. This collection epitomizes his elegant storytelling and provides a perfect introduction to a much-ignored writer. Detailed bibliography.

6-88. Douay, Dominique. **Cinq Solutions pour en finir.** Paris: Denoël, 1978.
A collection of five of Douay's best stories, including the prizewinning "Thomas" (in Jakubowski's *Travelling towards Epsilon* [4-654]). Clever if repetitive examination of the false reality theme and schizophrenia reaches undoubted heights of evocation in a claustrophobic mode. A challenging view of otherness from one of today's most literate French SF authors.

6-89. Douay, Dominique. **L'Impasse-temps.** Paris: Denoël, 1980.
A sardonic warning note about the pernicious strength of absolute power, Douay's fifth novel follows Serge, a melancholic comic-strip artist who one day gains the ability to freeze time around him, allowing him to indulge all his increasingly prankish fancies. With the strict logic of dreams orchestrating the proceedings, we witness the character moving from practical jokes through sexual domineering to complacent corruption. A bitter philosophical tale about the protagonist's gradual metamorphosis into alienness. Compare MacDonald's *The Girl, the Gold Watch, and Everything* [3-267].

6-90. Douay, Dominique. **Strates.** Paris: Denoël, 1978.
Multinational groups control the world in 1990, while the neglected lower classes roam through the outer ruins of the larger cities. Assisted by Bix, a jazz-loving camel, Rémi escapes the frightening reality by inner journeys into his own past. Political speculation and time paradoxes dominate Douay's first major novel, which, though often similar in background and inspiration to Jeury's *Le Temps*

incertain [6-114], in its later surrealistic stages achieves a genuine and mindful warning voice all its own.

6-91. Douay, Dominique. **La Vie comme une course de chars à voile.** Paris: Calmann-Lévy, 1978.
François Rossac is a champion wind-car racer and lives under the protective dome that surrounds the Channel Islands. He gradually begins to notice that his world's reality is shifting: a track changes course, his friends forget certain incidents, strangers from his past keep stalking him. A clever novel about the nature of reality. Contrast Christopher Priest's *A Dream of Wessex* (1977).

*6-92. Drode, Daniel. **Surface de la planète.** Paris: Hachette, 1959.
Drode's only published novel was a highly controversial recipient of the Prix Jules Vernes. Utilizing the sophisticated techniques of the *nouveau roman,* it is difficult and experimental, a rare example of new writing methods and theory applied to create a dour and eerie atmosphere of doom in a postatomic subterranean world. Once the premise of a logical but futuristic language is assimilated, the novel offers a clever variation on the anti-utopian postcataclysm school of writing. Compare Delany's *Dhalgren* [4-165].

6-93. Duits, Charles. **Ptah Hotep.** Paris: Denoël, 1971.
On an enigmatic parallel world with two moons high in the sky, young Prince Ptah Hotep is torn between religious anguish and the beautiful courtesan Aset. When his father dies in suspicious circumstances and the dynasty is overthrown, Ptah Hotep has to undergo mysterious initiation rites and tribulations. A unique French example of heroic fantasy written by a Harvard-educated ex-surrealist.

6-94. Duvic, Patrice. **Naissez, nous ferons le reste!** Paris: Presses Pocket, 1979.
A ferocious satire on the foibles of genetic engineering, Patrick Duvic's long-awaited first novel delves deeply into the consumer world of test-tube babies whose every whim and desire is lavishly catered to from birth onward by an upside-down society not too unlike our own, with a twist of Sheckley and Lewis Carroll combined. Tonic and provocative. Compare Pohl and Kornbluth's *The Space Merchants* [3-313].

6-95. Duvic, Patrice. **Poisson-pilote.** Paris: Denoël, 1979.
A young sailor, Lainie Hook, ventures into a shady bar in the port area and is soon befriended by Heursk, an old veteran of time travel whose memories and tall stories go all the way back to the pioneering days of the craft. Shortly after, the sailor is arrested by the police. From that moment on, Lainie is caught in a never-ending complicated web of intrigue and fantastic adventures involving time travel, telepathy, symbiotic aliens, and assorted SF clichés. A tongue-in-cheek, strictly old-fashioned exercise in the mold of van Vogt's *Null-A* [3-386]. Also contrast Klein's *Starmaster's Gambit* [3-230].

Farrère, Claude. **Useless Hands (Les Condamnés à mort)** [see **2-30**].

6-96. Giuliani, Pierre. **Les Frontières d'Oulan-Bator.** Paris: Calmann-Lévy, 1979.
Future thriller, penned in an American-inspired hard-boiled style, about murky industrial intrigues surrounding the building of an O'Neill City halfway between

the Earth and the Moon. The second half of the novel changes mood as the influence of Dick asserts itself through the questioning of reality. Compare Gibson's *Count Zero* [4-232].

6-97. Goy, Philip (pseud. of Philippe Goy). **Le Livre machine.** Paris: Denoël, 1975.
An often mock-serious utopian novel of Bloc-Rome, a seemingly perfect civilization where work has been abolished. The whole novel is laid out as a curious experiment in typographics, depicting the unfolding of the events as seen through an all-powerful computer, which might in fact well be the author of the book.

6-98. Groc, Léon, and Jacqueline Zorn. **L'Univers vagabond.** Paris: Horizons Fantastiques, 1950.
First known use of the "generation starship" theme in French SF. After a thousand-year journey, the descendants of the two original couples on board reach Alpha Centauri, where they come across radioactive mineral creatures who present a threat to Earth. The novel's main originality is in its theme and the fact that it was written when many American variations on a similar subject were quite unknown in France. Contrast Heinlein's *Orphans of the Sky* [3-203] or Aldiss's *Nonstop* [3-6].

6-99. Henneberg, Charles. **Le Chant des Astronautes.** Paris: Le Masque, 1975.
Flamboyant space opera depicting the war between humans and sparking semitransparent light columns hailing from Algol. Notable, like the majority of Henneberg novels (both Charles and Nathalie) for its respect of pulp SF traditions, more usually neglected in the French domain. Serialized in *Satellite,* 1958. Compare Niven and Pournelle's *The Mote in God's Eye* [4-398].

6-100. Henneberg, Charles. **La Naissance des dieux.** Paris: Métal, 1954.
A scientist, an astronaut, and a poet escape the end of the world. They find sanctuary on an unknown planet, which appears uninhabited apart from a strange form of fog. Goetz, the deformed poet, soon realizes that on this planet his mind is capable of creating life forms out of the fog. Gods and battles straight out of a mixed bag of mythologies ensue. Henneberg's first novel, a tempestuous epic that still holds up well today, compares favorably with Lem's *Solaris* [3-261] or Zelazny's mythologically influenced novels.

Henneberg, Nathalie C. **The Green Gods (Les Dieux verts)** [see **3-209**].

6-101. Henneberg, Nathalie C., and Charles Henneberg. **La Plaie.** Paris: Hachette, 1964.
Epic, Manichaean literary testament by Nathalie Henneberg (a sequel, *Le Dieu foudroyé,* appeared in 1974 from Albin Michel). In the year 3000, the forces of good and evil are battling for Earth, and the only people capable of rescuing the planet from an alien invasion are a race of mutants, whose very illness is violence. Space opera at its most flamboyant; few authors (French or otherwise) can match Henneberg's lyrical braggadocio and tempestuous, if undisciplined, style. Strangely effective schlock.

*6-102. Henneberg, Nathalie C., and Charles Henneberg. **La Rosée du soleil.** Paris: Hachette, 1959.

Classic exotic SF adventure and perhaps the epitome of the often grandiloquent Henneberg art. Cosmic intimations of parallel worlds and untold conspiracies against a backdrop of crusades and 1001 Nights. Religion, mysticism, and sorcery blend with consummate ease. Compare Leiber's *Gather, Darkness!* [3-250].

6-103. Higon, Albert (pseud. of Michel Jeury). **Aux étoiles du destin.** Paris: Gallimard, 1960.

Michel Jeury's first SF novel, a cracking space opera in the grand old style. Two people from Earth are taken aboard a flying saucer and become involved in a war between alien races, one of which lives backward through time. Compare Carsac's *Ceux de nulle part* [6-72] and Dick's *Counter-clock World* (1967).

6-104. Hougron, Jean. **Le Naguen.** Paris: Plon, 1980.

The Union, a coalition of 28 planets colonized by Earth, has been at war for more than 32 years with an unseen, evil adversary civilization, the Vors. Dreik, an officer of the Union fleet, is captured and then released by the Vors, but his memory has been altered. A vigorous future war yarn on an epic scale. Compare Haldeman's *The Forever War* [4-247].

6-105. Hougron, Jean. **Le Signe du chien.** Paris: Denoël, 1961.

Successful SF novel by French author better known for his mainstream work (generally about the Indochina and Algerian wars). The plot is based on the theme of the difficulty of contact between different species and planets, and calmly adheres to genre rules. Contrast Efremov's *Cor Serpentis* (1959) or Leinster's classic story, "First Contact" [3-254].

6-106. Houssin, Joël. **Les Vautours.** Paris: Fleuve Noir, 1985.

Winner of the prize for best French SF novel of 1985, this is the most accomplished novel to date by Houssin, an author who emerged as part of the 1970s political New Wave but went on to become a best-selling crime author. A strong commercial book in the Robin Cook/Michael Crichton mold about the legalized machinations surrounding organ collecting and the brutal society set up to exploit it.

6-107. Hubert, Jean-Pierre. **Le Champ du rêveur.** Paris: Denoël, 1983.

The brain of a dead human child has been combined with that of a dolphin. Mysterious scientists on a faraway planet of the future spend their time analyzing the curious dreams generated by the entity. A challenging and exciting novel of ideas. Compare *The Jonah Kit* by Ian Watson [4-588] or Merle's *Day of the Dolphin* (1967).

6-108. Hubert, Jean-Pierre. **Les Faiseurs d'orage.** Paris: Denoël, 1984.

A group of mysterious immortals manipulate the Earth's weather and a series of seismic quakes to control the destinies of lesser mortals. A strong adventure novel with political resonances about man's inhumanity to man. Compare Zelazny's *Isle of the Dead* [4-630].

6-109. Hubert, Jean-Pierre. **Mort à l'étouffée.** Paris: Kesselring, 1978.

A small town and its immediate surroundings float in the midst of space, supplied with all manners of riches, vital goods, and the occasional body (alive or otherwise), food, and equipment through a mysterious funnel of plenty, the aperture of which lies straight overhead. Political ferment in the town ensures regular changes in the seat of power, and the major characters play games of musical chairs in a Kafkaesque nightmare of shifting natural laws without ever understanding their predicament or the exact nature of the situation. A gripping suspenseful, and prizewinning novel by a young French author, which fully integrates political and nature-of-reality preoccupations. Compare Priest's *Inverted World* [4-431].

6-110. Hubert, Jean-Pierre. **Scènes de guerre civile.** Paris: Opta, 1982.
After the destruction of Europe, exiled Europeans fight for their survival in a civil war context in some North African land. Strongly inspired by events in Lebanon, but heightened by a series of clever SF devices that complicate the hostilities no end, this is a very personal book for Hubert and one that stays with the reader for some time.

6-111. Jeury, Michel. **Le Livre d'or de Michel Jeury,** selected by Gérard Klein. Paris: Presses Pocket, 1982.
Although Jeury's reputation is principally based on his many novels, this collection, covering material initially published in magazines between 1974 and 1979, is an adequate survey of Jeury's major themes and preoccupations. A strong humanist streak pervades Jeury's stories about environmental blight and ecofascism, with salvation often coming from beyond reality or through conscience-transcending drugs. Compare Ian Watson's short-story collections [4-591].

6-112. Jeury, Michel. **L'orbe et la roue.** Paris: Laffont, 1983.
A man awakes 11,000 years after his death into a puzzling new future world. Here he discovers that his personality has been combined with that of others, and seeks the higher powers responsible. Linear but powerful Jeury novel, with echoes of Farmer's *To Your Scattered Bodies Go* [4-210].

6-113. Jeury, Michel. **Soleil chaud poisson des profondeurs.** Paris: Laffont, 1976.
The third novel in Jeury's chronolytic series (*Les Singes du temps* is second and *Poney-Dragon* fourth) and perhaps his most accomplished work to date. The year is 2039 and civilization labors under the joint tyranny of information hypersystems and multinational industrial groups. As the two largest business empires are about to merge, the twin computers World Losis and Universe One imitate a gigantic battle that could destroy all technology. People are increasingly suffering from advanced forms of madness and disappearing into the dimension of time while nomad hordes lurk outside the cities awaiting the first indications of disarray to launch an assault on Garichankar Hospital. A dense, multileveled panorama of future despair. Compare Brunner's *Stand on Zanzibar* [4-92].

*6-114. Jeury, Michel. **Le Temps incertain.** Paris: Laffont, 1973.
Michel Jeury's first major SF novel under his true name, translated by Maxim Jakubowski as *Chronolysis*. Doctor Robert Holzach is a future researcher with the Autonomous Hospitals, experimenting with the use of time-distorting chronolytic drugs. His path merges with that of Daniel Diersant, a twentieth-century

French engineer whose enigmatic death appears to have a vital bearing on the future. Their joint misadventures in chronolytic time see them facing the ghostly forces of HKH, an outlawed multinational group now eking out a repressed existence in nontime and planning an invasion of reality. A poetic and often poignant as well as innovative treatment of time travel, which became a seminal work, strongly influential, in the recent flourishing of SF in France. Also annotated as [4-288].

6-115. Jeury, Michel. **Le Territoire humain.** Paris: Laffont, 1979.
GE III, a mighty postnuclear state, dominates the world in 2125. But in the French Pyrénées is the wild and forgotten territory of Timindia, which for many years has served as a dump for GE III's material and human rejects. There, procurator Jonas Claude seeks Dona Rejren, the young velvet-lioness, and Jael Denak, head of the Three-Names conspiracy, and begins to scale the wall of madness. Observer das Rodal courts insanity when he discovers the true secret of Timindia, and Claude is obliged to switch allegiances. A powerful, sociological extrapolation by Jeury at his fluent best.

*6-116. Jeury, Michel. **Les Yeux géants.** Paris: Laffont. 1980.
Inspired by Méheust's *Science-fiction et soucoupes volantes* [6-192], Jeury's eighteenth novel suggests that UFOs and other unexplained visions are just an archetypal representation of the collective unconscious. On Earth in 2010, a series of odd phenomena badly disrupts the status quo of a right-wing repressive society where, as in all French modern SF, multinational corporations dominate a scene of food and energy shortages. UFO sightings, resuscitations, people turning into animals, are all early manifestations of a new power that soon motivates millions of people to take to the roads, all searching for a mysterious meeting place where some form of alien contact is predicted. A rewarding blend of mysticism and diehard materialism with no easy answers. Compare Watson's *Miracle Visitors* [4-589].

6-117. Jouanne, Emmanuel. **Damiers imaginaires.** Paris: Denoël, 1982.
First novel by one of French SF's great white hopes. A classic quest theme where the two main characters have to discover what the secret mechanism of their universe is, *Damiers imaginaires* follows a classic itinerary before ending up questioning its own premise in a remarkable example of circularity. Fluidity and literary challenge renew a tired theme.

6-118. Jouanne, Emmanuel. **Nuage.** Paris: Laffont, 1983.
A human craft discovers a planet that is initially perceived as a giant fun fair. An elegant treatment of the theme of the sentient world, written in a clean, detached style often reminiscent of the *nouveau roman*. An impressive second novel from an author then still well under 30 years of age. Compare Lem's *Solaris* [3-261].

Klein, Gérard. **The Day before Tomorrow (Le Temps n'a pas d'odeur)** [see **4-302**].

6-119. Klein, Gérard. **Histoires comme si.** Paris: U.G.E., 1975.
A collection of early stories from a French author whose initial promise has never really been fulfilled. Twenty-four stories divided into nostalgic, futuristic, mytho-

logical, cryptic, diabolical, and criminal sections—all demonstrating the natural ease with which Klein could shift between themes, genres, and styles.

6-120. Klein, Gérard. **Le Livre d'or de Gérard Klein,** selected by Michel Jeury. Paris: Presses Pocket, 1979.
Fifteen of Klein's best stories, with initial publication (usually in *Fiction*) ranging from 1958 to 1975. Klein's sparse work (only two new stories in the past decade, as well as a couple of essays) demonstrates the strength of French SF in adopting U.S. role models and giving classic themes a new, invigorating twist. Space opera, time travel, mutants, overpopulation, and ecological nightmares in a powerful cerebral vein. Detailed bibliography.

Klein, Gérard. **Starmaster's Gambit (Le Gambit des étoiles)** [see **3-230**].

6-121. Le Rouge, Gustave. **La Conspiration des milliardaires.** 1899–1900.
An early, impassioned plea against American-style imperialism in the naïve Jules Verne tradition. Pulp writing in the grand old style as a coalition of repulsive American magnates, led by the King of Meat, plans the merciless subjugation of Europe. France, assisted by scientists of genius and assorted magicians, is the old continent's last chance. An imaginative, if one-sided, fable.

6-122. Le Rouge, Gustave. **Le Mystérieux Docteur Cornélius.** 1912–1913.
The undoubted classic of French pulp literature, *Le Mystérieux Docteur Cornélius* consists of 18 short novels narrating the unending struggle between the evil epitome of the mad scientist, Dr. Cornelius, and easygoing plant-lover hero, Prosper Bondonnat. Spanning continents, oceans, and multifarious far-fetched adventures with a cast of hundreds and a thrill per page, the Cornelius saga (not to be confused with Moorcock's similarly eponymous character) is to early SF what opera is to Gilbert and Sullivan. A mine of innovative and pioneering SF concepts liberally peppered throughout justifies the many reprints the work has undergone in France.

6-123. Le Rouge, Gustave. **Le Prisonnier de la planète Mars,** 1908; **La Guerre des vampires,** 1909.
Through the combined psychic energy of several thousand Indian fakirs, Robert Darvil is transported to the planet Mars, where he discovers that human beings are being held in slavery by a local race of vampires. During the course of his struggles, Darvil encounters flying octopuses, crystal mountains, giant brains, invisible entities, and so on. A surprisingly early yarn of epic planetary adventures, and an astonishing precursor in its determined exoticism of E. R. Burroughs's Barsoom series [1-17].

Leroux, Gaston. **The Machine to Kill (La Machine à assassiner)** [see **2-61**].

6-124. Ligny, Jean-Marc. **Temps blancs.** Paris: Denoël, 1979.
This first novel by a young French writer is an ambitious and impressionist violent vision of a metropolis gone wild. At center stage stands the City and its lemminglike inhabitants tightly controlled by the Computer, surrounded by a jungle of industrial wastelands where mutants and other abominations roam. Farther out lies the white expanse of the Countryside with its hordes of telepathic white wolves. A forceful but ultimately despairing vision of a future gone to seed.

Compare Delany's *Dhalgren* [4-165] or David Meltzer's Brain-Plant quartet (Essex House, 1969). Ligny has since published a second novel in a similar vein, *Biofeedback* (Denoël, 1979).

Maurois, André. **The Thought-Reading Machine (La Machine à lire les pensées)** [see **2-72**].

Maurois, André. **The Weigher of Souls (Le Peseur d'âmes)** [see **2-73**].

Mercier, Louis Sebastien. **Memoirs of the Year Two Thousand Five Hundred (L'An deux mille quatre cent quarante)** [see **1-63**].

Merle, Robert. **Malevil** [see **4-376**].

6-125. Messac, Régis. **La Cité des asphyxiés.** Paris: Hypermondes, 1937.
Mathematician Rodolphe Carnage has invented a chronoscope, which allows him to glimpse parts of the future, and he begins communicating through a form of "time post" with his friend Sylvain Le Cateau, who, hypnotized by the machine, has reached the future. Le Cateau introduces the protagonists and reader to the far-fetched but imaginative descriptions of future times and races. A lightweight, often erotic, early time travel yarn. Contrast Wells's *The Time Machine* [1-103] and Benford's *Timescape* [4-54].

6-126. Messac, Régis. **Quinzinzinzili.** Paris: Fenêtre Ouverte, 1935.
After a devastating bacteriological war, a lone adult survivor shepherds half a dozen children in the remote French region of Lozère. The painstaking rebuilding of a community and a new civilization is narrated with humor and affection. A sadly premonitory novel by a writer who was to die in the Nazi concentration camps. Contrast Merle's *Malevil* [4-376].

6-127. Moselli, José. **La Fin d'Illa.** 1925.
Classic French tale of fallen Atlantis. In the far-flung past of Earth, two cities struggle to dominate the world: the immense and tentacular Nour and the smaller police state of Illa. Atomic bombs, flying saucers, subhuman slaves, and assorted pioneering SF paraphernalia appear throughout the story. A frightfully prophetic novel, originally published in magazine form, which preceded both nuclear power and the Nazi era (described here in chilling speculative detail), *La Fin d'Illa* is a genuine lost masterpiece, which remained undiscovered until 1962.

6-128. Ollier, Claude. **La Vie sur Epsilon.** Paris: Minuit, 1972.
An ambitious *nouveau roman* treatment of classic SF imagery by a mainstream experimental writer. It follows, in highly fragmented form, the adventures of four astronauts stranded on the planet Epsilon. The SF argument is utilized by the author for an existential analysis of the psychic changes affecting the characters. Contrast Malzberg's *Beyond Apollo* [4-352].

6-129. Pelot, Pierre (pseud. of Pierre Suragne). **Delirium circus.** Paris: J'Ai Lu, 1977.
Citizen is a leading actor who always plays heroes. But everything around him is artificial: landscape, partners, sea, sky. Even his art is artifice as he performs under the combined influences of drugs and hypnosis. Aware of his alienation, Citizen, assisted by a woman called Marylin, flees and attempts to unravel the truth

that lies behind the closed world of the Dawn Wheel. A clever, humane treatment of the reality theme in a show-biz world by one of French SF's most prolific writers, here in the tradition of Philip K. Dick; contrast Dick's *Time Out of Joint* (1959).

6-130. Pelot, Pierre (pseud. of Pierre Suragne). **Foetus-party.** Paris: Denoël, 1977.
The world is suffering from acute overpopulation, and married couples are given only three chances to procreate. The fetus in its mother's womb is interrogated at the age of five months by the falsely benevolent authorities as to whether he or she wishes to live in such a bleak, programmed world. Should the answer prove negative or the fetus too weak to communicate, it must die. Pelot's imaginative novel takes us behind the scenes and contrasts the lives and struggles of Trash, a drug smuggler, and a mysterious visitor from elsewhere, as they ally themselves against the system.

6-131. Pelot, Pierre (pseud. of Pierre Suragne). **Les Iles de Vacarme.** Paris: Presses Pocket, 1981.
Some thousand years after an ecological catastrophe, the planet's surface is prey to ever-proliferating forests, while authoritarian sects hold the seat of power. As another upheaval looms with the coming of deadly winds, a group of dissidents sets out on a pilgrimage of hope for a mythical, hospitable land. Full of sound and fury, one of the prolific Pelot's best novels, full of action, a touching love story, and a serious reflection on political power and dissidence.

6-132. Pelot, Pierre (pseud. of Pierre Suragne). **Transit.** Paris: Laffont, 1977.
Carry Galen is a researcher for the European Institute of Telergies and travels under hypnosis into parapsychic zones. One day, however, he disappears during the course of his mental journey and arrives, suffering from amnesia, in the utopia of Gayhirna. Tackling the theme "Is utopia really utopia?" Pelot strongly contrasts technological society with Gayhirna. Contrast Jeury's treatment of mind travel in *Le Temps incertain* [6-114].

*6-133. Ray, Jean (pseud. of Jean Raymond De Kremer). **Malpertuis.** 1943.
A mad scientist captures the dormant energy of the gods from Olympus and imprisons them inside human bodies. A tenuous SF argument is the pretext for a somber, venomous, shadowy novel of evildoing in smoky Flemish towns, which, despite its final revelation, is generally considered a masterpiece of French fantasy literature.

6-134. Rémy, Yves, and Ada Rémy. **La Maison du cygne.** Paris: Laffont, 1978.
An accomplished first novel by two writers who haven't yet followed up on it. In a remote base in the Sahara, children are being trained to expand their consciousness under the tutelage of a mysterious Master. A lyrical retelling of an eternal battle between Good and Evil on a cosmic scale. Compare Watson's *The Embedding* [4-586] or Joyce Thompson's *Conscience Place* (1984).

6-135. Renard, Christine. **Le Temps des cerises.** Paris: Kesselring, 1980.
The first (and, by a matter of weeks, posthumously published) collection of Renard's short stories. Includes seven original stories and four previously pub-

lished (out of a total of at least three dozen known stories). This author's work, by one of the few women regularly writing SF in France, is always intimate and elusive and often tackles biological themes with delicacy. Contrast Le Guin's *The Wind's Twelve Quarters* [4-328].

Renard, Maurice, and Albert Jean. **Blind Circle (Le Singe)** [see **2-92**].

*6-136. Renard, Maurice. **Le Péril bleu.** 1910.
As people keep mysteriously disappearing in various parts of the globe, the authorities discover that the victims have in fact been "fished." It seems that Earth is surrounded by a large invisible globe inhabited by an enigmatic but cruel race. Humans live at the bottom of the atmospheric sea and cannot survive at the surface. A clever variation on a theme of paranoia, Renard's major novel still reads as well as when it was originally published.

6-137. Robida, Albert. **Le Vingtième siècle.** 1882.
Surprisingly accurate and witty extrapolation of daily life in 1950 by a contemporary of Jules Verne, better known for his illustrations. Female emancipation, airplanes, aerial hospitals, mechanical politicians, videophones, mobile solar houses. Stylistically dated but an important work in the history of the genre in France.

Roger, Noëlle. **The New Adam (Le Nouvel Adam)** [see **2-94**].

*6-138. Rosny aîné, J. H. (pseud. of Joseph-Henri Boëx). **La Force mystérieuse.** 1913.
A mysterious power destroys part of Earth's light spectrum, bringing about a new ice age and the rapid collapse of civilization. Humanity reverts to barbarism and only a handful of people succeed in reversing the flow, after long periods of lethargy, collective violence, and euphoria. Compare Arthur Conan Doyle's *The Poison Belt* [1-32], also 1913. Rosny accused Doyle of plagiarizing his novel.

Rosny aîné, J. H. (pseud. of Joseph-Henri Boëx). **The Giant Cat (Le Félin géant); The Quest for Fire (La Guerre du feu)** [see **2-95**].

6-139. Rosny aîné, J. H. (pseud. of Joseph-Henri Boëx). **Les Navigateurs de l'infini,** 1925.
The old Martian civilization is slowly dying, making way for a new protoplasmic species of zoomorphs. Members of a human expedition to the red planet come to their assistance and try to halt the flow of evolution. Strong nonanthropomorphic treatment of aliens. Contrast Weinbaum's *A Martian Odyssey* [2-125]. In the posthumously published sequel, *Les Astronautes* (Paris: Hachette, 1960), two Martians are brought back to Earth where one falls in love with a human and gives birth to a child. Compare Farmer's *The Lovers* [3-159].

6-140. Rosny aîné, J. H. (pseud. of Joseph-Henri Boëx). **Récits de science fiction.** Verviers: Marabout, 1973.
Major collection, compiled by Belgian editor and writer Jean-Baptiste Baronian, regrouping the majority of Rosny aîné's pioneering short science fiction. Includes the first part of *Les Navigateurs de l'infini* [6-139], evolutionary fantasies, surprisingly modern portrayals of alien beings ("Les Xipéhuz"), the classic parallel-world story "Un Autre monde," the end of the world ("La Mort de la terre"),

undiscovered land yarns, and so on. This collection amply justifies the claims made by many critics that Rosny aîné is in many respects the equal of Verne and Wells.

Rosny aîné, J. H. (pseud. of Joseph-Henri Boëx). **The Xipéhuz; The Death of the Earth** [see 1-79].

6-141. Ruellan, André. **Les Chiens.** Paris: Lattès, 1979.
Not strictly a film novelization, as Ruellan wrote the screenplay himself in tandem with the novel. A cautionary near-future tale of urban violence and vigilantism. A dark, despairing allegory of everyday fascism, quite unlike the author's other novels whether under his name or his Kurt Steiner pseudonym.

*6-142. Ruellan, André. **Tunnel.** Paris: Laffont, 1973.
Paris, 2025. The city is crumbling, surrounded by ever-present giant rubbish heaps. Civilization is falling to pieces in a violent and absurd manner. Doctor Manuel Dutôt, attempting to keep his half-dead pregnant wife alive, flees with her body. Battles ensue with the Crucified Skulls and the final representatives of established authority. A short-term extrapolation in the bleak dystopian mood of modern French SF, with an added strong touch of black humor. Contrast Ligny's *Temps blancs* [6-124].

6-143. Sériel, Jérome (pseud. of Jacques Vallée). **Le Sub-espace.** Paris: Hachette. 1961.
Award-winning (Prix Jules Verne) first novel by now well-known UFO expert. A perfect example of space opera at its best, with mighty galactic empires struggling, physical paradoxes, and action galore. Sériel's lightning four-year SF career came to an abrupt end in 1965 after a second novel, *Le Satellite sombre* (1962) and only five innovative short stories.

6-144. Spitz, Jacques. **La Guerre des mouches.** 1938.
Following a mutation, flies attack and conquer humans through their larger number, higher intelligence, and rigorous discipline. The story is told from the viewpoint of a surviving human who has been kept by the victorious diptera as a specimen in a reservation, together with an erstwhile dictator, a pope, and other characteristic examples of the late human species. An ironic, almost prophetic pre–World War II parable.

6-145. Spitz, Jacques. **L'Homme élastique.** 1938.
Doctor Flohr finds a way to compress or expand the atom. After succeeding with minerals, vegetables, and animals, he tests his theories with a dwarf. When a European war breaks out, the army asks him to reduce the size of 7,000 men to 5 cm in height. Flohr, only too happy to obtain more experimental subjects, accepts, unaware that he is creating a new race of superbeings. An amusing and ironic treatment of a classic theme. Compare Matheson's *The Shrinking Man* [3-275], Asimov's *Fantastic Voyage* (1966), Barry Malzberg's *The Men Inside* (1973), or Ray Cummings's *The Girl in the Golden Atom* [2-22].

6-146. Spitz, Jacques. **L'Oeil du purgatoire.** 1945.
A mad scientist isolates a bacillus that lives a few seconds ahead of present time and inoculates a painter with it. The unfortunate man thus becomes capable of

seeing the future in a most extreme form: when he sees a child, at first he sees it as an adult, and, as the illness progresses, as a skeleton. Life becomes a nightmare as he keeps moving through a world of corpses. As his condition worsens, he walks through a universe of bones and dust until he finally witnesses the souls of people around him and, at last, his own soul, signifying the end of his ordeal, his own death. A chilling and unique novel whose powerful theme has seldom been tackled elsewhere.

6-147. Steiner, Kurt (pseud. of André Ruellan). **Brebis galeuses.** Fleuve Noir, 1974.

Administered by the Knowledge Police, various illnesses are the punishment inflicted on society's dissidents. Accused of having denied the existence of other solar systems, Rolf B40 is condemned to injection B25. Feverish and in pain, he takes refuge in the ghetto of the contaminated, where he befriends the giant tumor-infested Titann and the girl Jana, who is constantly vomiting blood. Together they investigate the giant medical conspiracy holding the world in throe. A lively thriller written by a doctor; contrast the works of Alan Nourse.

6-148. Steiner, Kurt (pseud. of André Ruellan). **Ortog.** Paris: Laffont, 1975. Originally *Aux armes d'Ortog*, Fleuve Noir, 1960, followed by *Ortog et les ténèbres*, Fleuve Noir, 1969.

A near-feudal future Earth where civilization has badly regressed. Dâl Ortog, a young shepherd, is adopted by the last surviving scientists still living in the cities. Initiated into some of the forgotten arts, his first mission is to solve the mystery of the death that comes from space. In part two, now a hero, Ortog ventures beyond death in the hope of finding his beloved Kalla Karella again. A singular saga halfway between heroic fantasy and space opera, *Ortog* has no equivalent in French SF. Contrast Burroughs's Mars novels [1-17].

6-149. Steiner, Kurt (pseud. of André Ruellan). **Un Passe-temps.** Paris: Fleuve Noir, 1979.

Quality time travel thriller that saw Steiner/Ruellan return to the Fleuve Noir imprint after a five-year sabbatical. Simon Corbel, a contemporary detective, is sent to the twenty-first century to investigate the illegal trading of an aphrodisiac. The future is under the tight control of organized religion and the scene for a plethora of paradoxes.

6-150. Steiner, Kurt (pseud. of André Ruellan). **Le 32 Juillet.** Paris: Fleuve Noir, 1959.

At the turn of midnight on July 31, the protagonist moves into another world, outside time and space, that of an unknown living organism. A dense, poetic novel of discovery, full of evocative symbolism. Compare Asimov's *Fantastic Voyage* (1966) or Farmer's *The Unreasoning Mask* [4-211].

*6-151. Sternberg, Jacques (Belgium). **La Sortie est au fond de l'espace.** Paris: Denoël, 1956.

Relentlessly bleak, if tinged with a touch of black humor, the novel follows the flight of the last remains of humans from a bacteria-infested Earth. They eventually discover that the depths of space are even more treacherous than the environment they left behind. Humanity turns out to be no more than a minor germ that the rest of the universe keeps on rejecting. Compare Vonnegut's *The Sirens of Titan* [3-393].

6-152. Stolze, Pierre. **Marilyn Monroe et les samouraïs du Père Noël.** Paris: J'Ai Lu, 1986.
A humorous space opera romp with an invigorating mix of ingredients: a planet mysteriously inhabited by children only, faster than light travel, immortal samurai, a reincarnation of Marilyn Monroe, and an enigmatic traveler of familiar appearance with a white beard and red cape. An accomplished divertissement of great entertainment value.

Tarde, Gabriel de. **Underground Man** [see **1-90**].

6-153. Veillot, Claude. **La Machine de Balmer.** Paris: J'Ai Lu, 1978.
Private investigator Mathias Vanacker is investigating mad millionaire Silas Balmer and his retinue of ex-Nazi technical assistants, who have just perfected a time-traveling contraption, the chronoscaphe. Vanacker is thrown back to the Paris of 1925 and, later, to the depths of the Amazon jungle. A deliberately old-fashioned SF thriller that harks back to the days of Le Rouge or Verne.

Vercors. **Sylva** [see **3-387**].

Vercors. **You Shall Know Them (Les Animaux dénaturés)** [see **3-388**].

Verne, Jules. **The Adventures of Captain Hatteras (Les Aventures du Capitaine Hatteras)** [see **1-92**].

Verne, Jules. **From the Earth to the Moon (De la terre à la lune)** [see **1-93**].

Verne, Jules. **A Journey to the Center of the Earth (Voyage au centre de la terre)** [see **1-94**].

Verne, Jules. **Twenty Thousand Leagues under the Sea (Vingt milles lieues sous les mers)** [see **1-95**].

6-154. Versins, Pierre. **Les Transhumains.** Paris: Kesselring, 1980.
A rare incursion into fiction by the respected French, Swiss-based researcher and encyclopedist [6-197]. Aliens have finally come to Earth, but their presence is a muted one when they come to live on a remote farm and one of them falls in love with the proverbial farmer's daughter. Low key, pastoral reflection on the meaning of fame.

*6-155. Vian, Boris. **L'Automne à Pékin.** Paris: Minuit, 1947.
An absurdist masterpiece that qualifies as strongly marginal science fiction. In the puzzling desert of Exopotamia, a crowd of motley dropouts live, die, and love as a dispensable railway line is built, which must invariably pass through the only hotel for miles around, the hotel being the geographic center of the desert. Vian's method is a subtle blend of surrealism and fantasy as the events under description slowly move beyond reality and an alternate but credible world shifts in and out of focus. Also a powerful love story, where characters literally die of heartache.

6-156. Vian, Boris. **L'Herbe rouge.** Paris: Toutain, 1950.
In a country where the grass is red, Wolf and Saphir Lazuli are building a machine. Through gripping but repetitive experiments, Wolf discovers that the machine might well travel backward through time, and the two friends become involved in an absurd journey into a fragmented, ever-changing past where they encounter their own memories and doubles. A sad, nostalgic tale, which might be construed as pure fantasy but also reflects the contradictions of the postwar French existential climate.

6-157. Volkoff, Vladimir. **Métro pour l'enfer.** Paris: Hachette, 1963.
Early offbeat novel (Prix Jules Verne, 1963) by a writer who has since become a major mainstream name in Europe and has been likened to Graham Greene or Le Carré. Murky happenings in the penumbra of the Paris métro, where mysterious aliens conspire against humans in a convoluted plot with mystical overtones. Highly entertaining divertissement.

6-158. Volodine, Antoine. **Le navire de nulle part.** Paris: Denoël, 1986.
Russia in a parallel world, where socialism and magic coexist. A fascinating glimpse into a universe that never was for Volodine's second novel, following his praised 1985 debut with *Biographie comparée de Jorian Murgrave,* about an alien prisoner of conscience in a Russian-like communist regime. A new, unique voice in French SF.

6-159. Walther, Daniel. **L'Epouvante.** Paris: J'Ai Lu, 1979.
Novel-length expansion of Walther's often-anthologized "The Gunboat *Dread*" (in *Travelling towards Epsilon* [4-654]). An SF cross between Dino Buzzati's *I Deserto dei Tartari* and Richard McKenna's *The Sand Pebbles.* The gunboat *Dread* slowly moves down the shifting waters of the river Ez on the lost planet of Celaeno of Peroyne. Lieutenant Brand, debilitated by fever and alcohol, is haunted by nightmares, voices, and erotic dreams. War is raging on the banks of the river and, one day, the still-living body of a beautiful woman is lifted aboard. A dense, obsessive, and evocative inner-space saga, awarded best French SF novel of the year status, and one of Walther's more accessible works.

6-160. Walther, Daniel. **Requiem pour demain.** Verviers: Marabout, 1976.
First collection of original material by one of France's most prolific short-story writers. Pyrotechnic yarns of sound, fury, and eroticism blending genre traditions with a romatic European sensibility (Hoffman and Joyce are two major acknowledged influences).

6-161. Wintrebert, Joëlle. **Chromoville.** Paris: J'Ai Lu, 1984.
The most accomplished novel to date by one of the few women currently active in French SF. A varied gallery of strongly drawn characters act out their alienation in a monolithic future city, where class struggle takes many forms and dimensions.

6-162. Wintrebert, Joëlle. **Les Maîtres-feu.** Paris: J'Ai Lu, 1983.
A classic novel in the Anglo-Saxon tradition, with ecological and ethnographic matters to the fore as an alien planet unveils its secrets, one at a time, to a team of strongly drawn human explorers.

6-163. Wintrebert, Joëlle. **Les Olympiades truquées.** Paris: Kesselring, 1980.
Strong novel debut by a young film critic. In the very near future, genetics is freely manipulated in biological factories where future Olympic heroes are literally being built. The novel focuses on the itinerary of two women athletes training for the ultimate test. Despair, feminism, and political protest blend easily in this accomplished dystopian vision of tomorrow's sport world.

6-164. Wul, Stefan (pseud. of Pierre Pairault). **Niourk.** Paris: Fleuve Noir, 1957. In a postholocaust world that has reverted to barbarism, humans have been reduced to roaming hordes and nomad tribes, and the memory of Niourk (New York), the fantastic city of the past, has become a strong symbol of the frightening unknown. A black child discovers what remains of the city and its still-functioning technology. Allegedly severely edited by the publisher, this was Wul's second novel and a landmark in the renewal of modern French SF. Contrast Rosny aîné's *La Force mystérieuse* [6-138] and Ballard's *The Drowned World* [4-37] for a similar locale.

6-165. Wul, Stefan (pseud. of Pierre Pairault). **Noô.** Paris: Denoël, 1977.
Wul's first novel after a 19-year sabbatical is a lengthy and flamboyant venture into alien exoticism. Brice, the young son of an ethnologist who has disappeared during an expedition into the South American jungle, is adopted by a strange adventurer who takes him along to the surrealist planet Soror, where his new father is heavily involved in clandestine politics. Adventures, endless journeys, and wars on various bizarre planets ensue as Brice painfully grows up through a colorful nightmare of love and pain. A feast of the imagination often reminiscent of Jack Vance at his most exotic, as in his *Big Planet* (1957).

6-166. Wul, Stefan (pseud. of Pierre Pairault). **Oms en série.** Paris: Fleuve Noir, 1957.
Humans have become tame domestic pets for the giant, ferocious Draag, invaders of Earth. There comes the day of the revolution. Filmed as *Fantastic Planet*. Contrast Thomas Disch's *Mankind under the Leash* (1968).

Wul, Stefan (pseud. of Pierre Pairault). **Temple of the Past (Le Temple du passé)** [see **3-407**].

6-167. Wul, Stefan (pseud. of Pierre Pairault). **Terminus 1.** Paris: Fleuve Noir, 1959.
The last of Wul's 11 novels published between 1956 and 1959 is a lightweight galactic quest romp with the characters racing toward a mysterious spaceship graveyard. Still surprisingly fresh and modern, this is a perfect introduction to the early novels of Wul.

Anthologies

6-168. Andrevon, Jean-Pierre, ed. **Compagnons en terre étrangère.** 2 vols. Paris: Denoël, 1979, 1980.
Andrevon is generally recognized as the foremost French SF short-story writer (with eight solo collections already published), and here he attempts a series of collaborations with other French authors, along the lines of Harlan Ellison's *Part-*

ners in Wonder (1971), although in this instance all the stories were written specially for the two volumes. The results are a roll call of French SF's main preoccupations and an impressive demonstration of Andrevon's protean talent. Sharing the honors are René Durand, Pierre Christin, Patrice Duvic (with a comic strip drawn by Andrevon), Michel Jeury (with whom Andrevon rewrites the ending to his earlier novel *Le Désert du monde* [6-53], Bernard Blanc, Daniel Walther, Dominique Douay, Alain Dorémieux, and several others.

6-169. Andrevon, Jean-Pierre, ed. **Retour à la terre.** 3 vols. Paris: Denoël, 1975, 1976, 1977.
Leading French original SF anthology series, which began with a strongly ecological initial volume when each of five authors (Daniel Walther, Pierre Marlson, Francis Carsac, Philippe Curval, and Andrevon) tackled the theme of explorers returning from the stars to discover an Earth that has abandoned industrialization. The following volumes feature leading French writers such as Jeury, Douay, Goy, Mathon, Drode, Duvic, Blondel, Dorémieux, and Christine Renard and eschew flamboyant space opera characteristics in favor of more social preoccupations. A fourth, and weaker, volume appeared under the title *Avenirs à la dérive* (Paris: Kesselring, 1979).

6-170. Battestini, Monique, ed. **Les Lolos de Venus.** Paris: Kesselring, 1979.
An anthology combining sex and science fiction, but then surely the French have a right to put another such collection together. Surprisingly gentle, most authors develop the theme of alien contact with imagination. Includes a majority of authors known for their affiliation with the French political SF New Wave of the late 1970s: René Durand, Joëlle Wintrebert, Bruno Lecigne, Daniel Walther, Jean-Pierre Hubert, and others.

6-171. Curval, Philippe, ed. (pseud. of Philippe Tronche). **Futurs au présent.** Paris: Denoël, 1978.
Ground-breaking anthology of all-new young French writers put together by Curval to celebrate the 25 years of Denoël's prestigious Présence du Futur imprint. The general tone is, as is usually the case with modern French SF, essentially bleak and pessimistic and too often just one degree away from existing French political realities, but many of the writers show a promising grasp of speculative concepts and have since begun to fulfill such early promises: Jean-Pierre Vernay, Daniel Martinange, Jean-Marc Ligny, and Serge Brussolo.

6-172. Jeury, Michel, ed. **Planète socialiste.** Paris: Kesselring, 1977.
Highly controversial anthology that almost became a rallying point for the French political New Wave of the late 1970s. Strongly pessimistic speculations on the theme of a planet where socialism has finally triumphed; outstanding story is a collaboration between Bernard Blanc and Dominique Doray, "Tout est possible chantait le papilhomme," a poetic view of incipient problems in a modern utopia. All the other stories (by Jeury, Andrevon, Christin, Hubert, Cheinisse, Pelot, and others) are oddly bleak and uncompromising vistas of what should really be a perfect future.

*6-173. Jeury, Michel, ed. **Utopies 75.** Paris: Laffont, 1975.
Is utopia still realizable? A first-rate anthology on the theme, featuring novellas

by Philippe Curval, Christine Renard, Jean-Pierre Andrevon, and Jeury. Andrevon's contribution, "Le Monde enfin," is possibly his most accomplished work; an uncompromising, utterly bleak vista of the welcome end of human existence on Earth, a convincing ecological plea and a genuine cry from the heart.

*6-174. Klein, Gérard, et al., eds. **Anthologie de la science-fiction Française.** 3 vols. Paris: Seghers, 1975, 1976, 1977; Klein, Gérard, and Monique Battestini, eds. **Le Grandiose avenir** (1950s); Klein, Gérard, ed. **En un autre pays** (1960–1964); Klein, Gérard, and Jacques Goimard, eds. **Ce qui vient des profondeurs** (1965–1970).

Three-volume anthology covering the evolution of modern French SF over two decades from 1950 to 1970. Features all the prominent authors in the genre, including an assortment of important mainstream personalities (Roland Topor, Raphael Pividal, Boileau-Narcejac, Guy Béart, Charles Dobzynski, Claude Veillot). With highly detailed biographical introductions to each story and lengthy volume prefaces, this set constitutes a first-class introduction to the hidden treasures and history of French SF.

6-175. Milési, Raymond, and Bernard Stephan, eds. **Mouvance.** Metz: Stephen, 1977–1984.

A series of eight thematic anthologies that include all the leading French SF authors of the last decade. The volumes feature material from established names and upcoming talents, and the overall quality of the fiction is very high indeed. Themes covered have been (in publication order) mass media, education, consumerism, space, time, communication, civilization, and the individual.

6-176. Walther, Daniel, ed. **Les Soleils noirs d'Arcadie.** Paris: Opta, 1975.

Pioneering anthology of what was to become the French New Wave in SF, loosely inspired by Ellison's *Dangerous Visions* [4-650]. Experiments in no-holds-barred writing with 14 aggressive stories by Mathon, Douay, Duvic, Andrevon, Klein, Jeury, Suragne, Planchat, Hubert, Curval, and others.

Nonfiction

6-177. Allard, Yvon. **Paralittératures.** Montreal: La Centrale des Bibliothèques, 1979. Selections documentaire, 2.

An excellent and comprehensive annotated bibliographical guide to a variety of popular literary genres, including myth, fairy tale, fantasy, supernatural, adventure, historical, detective, western, and science fiction, plus humor. Each section has an introductory essay followed by a well-annotated bibliography of reference works, periodicals, critical and historical studies, articles, a brief guide to authors prominent in each field, descriptions of publishers' series, and annotations of major works in the field. The section devoted to SF occupies 120 of the oversize guide's 728 pages. Particularly valuable for its coverage of non–English-language materials. Compare Inge's *Handbook of American Popular Culture* [8-44].

6-178. Aziza, Claude, and Jacques Goimard. **Encyclopédie de poche de la science-fiction.** Paris: Presses Pocket, 1986.

A reader's guide to SF geared to French academic curricula. Covers 80 selected basic books (all available in the Presses Pocket SF imprint) by all major authors: Aldiss, Ballard, Dick, Herbert, Heinlein, Pohl, Sturgeon, Vance, Zelazny, van Vogt, and others. Clear analysis of plot, characterization, and themes with additional succinct author bibliography. Also selects 100 movies, 50 comic strips, and 50 juvenile SF novels.

6-179. Barets, Stan. **Catalogue des âmes et cycles de la science fiction.** Paris: Denoël, 1979.
Critical and often witty reader's guide to science fiction. A to Z presentation encompasses not only major French- and English-language authors (500 titles reviewed), but also entries on animals, conventions, aliens, fanzines, French, U.S., and British magazines, end of the world, principal publishers and imprints, hard science, heroic fantasy, future histories, mutants, French New Wave, inner space, pioneers, postcataclysm, literary prizes, sex, religion and myths, space opera, utopias and dystopias, alternate worlds, and future cities. A handy and accurate guide for the newcomer to SF. Compares favorably with Searles, *Reader's Guide to Science Fiction* [8-31].

6-180. Blanc, Bernard, ed. **Pourquoi J'ai tué Jules Verne.** Paris: Stock, 1978.
A lengthy and iconoclastic essay interspersed with interviews and specially written short stories by modern French SF authors: Michel Jeury, Gérard Klein, Dominique Douay, René Durand, Jean Bonnefoy, Christian Vila, Daniel Walther, Muriel Favarel, and Pierre Pelot, as well as panel proceedings from various French conventions. Taking as its original premise the necessity for the elimination of Jules Verne from the history of SF in France, the free-ranging essay by Blanc, a leader of the political French New Wave school of SF, serves as a rough manifesto for his deviant movement. Forceful, polemical, but never completely convincing in its violent denunciation of past SF values and Anglo-American literary imperialism.

6-181. Bogdanoff, Igor, and Grichka Bogdanoff. **Clefs pour la science-fiction.** Paris: Seghers, 1976.
Long but generally dull introduction to the genre by two young French critics whose all-encompassing superficiality of approach has since been rewarded by a weekly televised program on SF, "Temps X." Features rapid and generally informative chapters on the history of SF, a sociological approach to the genre, a survey of SF in various countries (with too much generalization), and an examination of categories and themes (psychological, sociological, and scientific). A cursory but ultimately insufficient glance is also given to SF in comic strips, film, painting, sculpture, and music. A well-meaning project (with a vapid introduction by Ray Bradbury), which suffers from having been culled from too many previously available sources and reflects the authors' insufficient knowledge of their subject.

6-182. Bridenne, Jean-Jacques. **La Littérature Française d'imagination scientifique.** Paris: Dassonville, 1950.
Pioneering study of popular scientific romances and early forms of SF in France in the nineteenth and first half of the twentieth centuries. Pinpoints the extraor-

dinary wealth of genre material available in French magazines, which actually preceded the U.S. golden age of pulp.

Chesneaux, Jean. **The Political and Social Ideas of Jules Vernes (Une Lecture politique de Jules Verne)** [see **10-151**].

6-183. Cordesse, Gérard. **La Nouvelle science-fiction Américaine.** Paris: Aubier, 1984.
A well-informed essay from a French academic on the evolution of English-language SF. Cordesse is both strong and incisive on post-1970s developments preceding the "cyberpunk" wave.

6-184. Delmas, Henri, and Alain Julian. **Le Rayon SF.** Toulouse: Milan, 1983.
A comprehensive French-language bibliography of SF, particularly strong on titles not specifically published in SF imprints. Also includes recommended prices for out of print material, which err on the generous for minor and generally accessible material, like Perry Rhodan books. As an introduction, Yves Frémion presents interviews with six SF editors active in France in 1983.

6-185. Eizykman, Boris. **Inconscience fiction.** Paris: Kesselring. 1979.
A disparate collection of provocative essays by one of the more disturbing contemporary French scholars and critics. Not all the articles actually refer to SF, and the book also features Philip K. Dick's "The Man and the Android" article, an article by French electronic musician (and ex-Sorbonne lecturer in philosophy) Richard Pinhas, and an interview with Norman Spinrad by Pinhas. Subjects tackled include the novels of Michel Jeury, the film *Rollerball*, Silverberg's *The Book of Skulls* (1971), Dick's *A Scanner Darkly* [4-177], Ballard's *The Atrocity Exhibition* [4-33], Compton's *The Continuous Katherine Mortenhoe* [4-143], and various others. A Freudian approach to a unified theory of SF.

*6-186. Eizykman, Boris. **Science fiction et capitalisme.** Paris: Mame, 1974.
A complex Freudian-structuralist analysis of science's attitude toward desire, as it manifests itself in science fiction. A confusing attempt to demonstrate the underlying presence in SF of libidinal mechanisms striving to undermine the structure of present-day society. Controversial but with frequent rewarding insights.

6-187. Emelina, Jean, and Denise Terrel. **Actes du premier colloque international de science-fiction de Nice (1983)–Images de l'ailleurs-espaces interieurs.** Nice: Métaphore issue 9/10, 1984.
Collection of papers in French and English given at the first Nice conference in 1983. Strong academic bent with communications by Roger Bozzetto, Marcel Thaon, Jacques Goimard, Darko Suvin, Peter Fitting, Patrick Parrinder, Robert Scholes, David Ketterer, John Shirley, and others, mostly on the subject of inner space.

6-188. Emelina, Jean, and Denise Terrel. **Actes du deuxième colloque international de science-fiction de Nice (1985)—Planète terre.** Nice: Métaphore issue 12/13, 1986.
Collection of papers in English and French given at the second Nice conference

in 1985. International contributions from a variety of academics and guest SF authors. Includes material by Brian Aldiss, Christopher Priest, Marc Angenot, Maxim Jakubowski, William Collins, G. J. Arnaud, David Pringle, Robert Merle, Bernard Sigaud, and others.

*6-189. Goimard, Jacques. **L'Année de la science fiction et du fantastique.** 4 vols. Paris: Julliard, 1978, 1979, 1980, 1981.

Weighty yearbook, which appeared for four years, of all SF activities and publications in France. Features capsule reviews of all books published during the preceding 12 months (including translations from English—in fact, a majority of the titles), anthologies, juveniles, radio and television programs, music, films, comic-strip books and magazines, diary of events, lists of prizes and conventions, and selected essays; also reprints some of the best stories of the year together with a section on authors of the year (with interviews and critical analysis). Fast becoming an indispensable research tool for both scholars and fans. A further volume, edited by Daniel Riche, was published by Temps Futurs in 1983.

6-190. Klein, Gérard. **Malaise dans la science-fiction.** Metz: L'Aube Enclavée, 1977.

Long essay originally written for the special issue of *Science-Fiction Studies* analyzing Ursula Le Guin (no. 7, 1975), but ultimately published in two much-edited parts: "Discontent in American Science Fiction" (no. 11, 1977), and "Le Guin's Aberrant Opus: Escaping the Trap of Discontent" (no. 13, 1977). Klein maps, from a sociological point of view, the general trend in American SF toward discontent and pessimism and demonstrates how the innovative work of Le Guin successfully challenges this new orthodoxy. An original study of modern American attitudes in and to SF seen through French eyes.

6-191. Lahana, Jacqueline. **Les Mondes parallèles de la science fiction soviétique.** Lausanne: L'Age d'Homme, 1979.

Informative study of Russian SF by French academic and translator. Highlights the contrasts between Russian and Anglo-American SF and also analyzes moral and political constraints placed on contemporary Soviet SF writers. Useful bibliography.

*6-192. Méheust, Bertrand. **Science-fiction et soucoupes volantes.** Paris: Mercure de France, 1978.

Intriguing study of the relationship between flying saucer sightings and the body of science fiction literature. Méheust puts forward the highly controversial theory that UFOs and many other still unexplained phenomena are in fact expressions of the human unconscious psychic zone, liberally irrigated by science fiction literature and imagery. His thesis is both clever and convincing, as well as meticulously documented. Méheust's book has since directly inspired two major novels: Watson's *Miracle Visitors* [4-589] and Jeury's *Les Yeux géants* [6-116].

6-193. Pettigrew, Jean, ed. **L'Année de la science-fiction et du fantastique Québécois.** 2 vols. Quebec: Le Passeur, 1985, 1986.

This newly born yearly volume annotates *all* the novels and short stories published within the genre in Quebec during the previous year, and gives an overview. This labor of love testifies to the vitality of the genre in the province, and can be consulted for coverage of French-Canadian SF, which this section does not claim to provide. [Annotation by Pascal Thomas—Ed.]

6-194. Sadoul, Jacques. **Histoire de la science-fiction moderne** (1911–1971). Paris: Albin Michel, 1973. 3rd enlarged ed. Paris: Robert Laffont, 1984.
A lengthy history of the modern genre in the United States that badly suffers from a severe lack of critical analysis and method. Pedestrian writing and a surfeit of plot descriptions combined with a strong bias toward titles published by Sadoul in France in his editorial capacity make this an unreliable reference book from an academic and research point of view. A separate section on science fiction in France is informative, but also suffers from too many personal biases and prejudices.

6-195. Thomas, Louis-Vincent. **Civilisations et divagations.** Paris: Payot, 1979.
A highly original study of SF by a French philosopher who sees the genre as a mirror for contemporary civilization's anguish and fear of death. A clever and well-documented demonstration of how SF relates to its times and how humans fit into the scheme of the universe.

6-196. Van Herp, Jacques (Belgium). **Panorama de la science fiction.** Verviers: Marabout, 1973.
Massive, idiosyncratic study of the genre by a Belgian academic and critic. Along the lines of Pierre Versins's *Encyclopédie* [6-197], this is very much one man's blinkered and opinionated view of SF. Unorthodox and lacking in structure, Van Herp's book is more a collection of random essays on SF themes or ideas that have caught his fancy. Within those parameters, it is nevertheless a formidable achievement. Strong on French-language pre–World War II fiction. Lack of an index makes this a very difficult book to use.

*6-197. Versins, Pierre (Switzerland). **Encyclopédie de l'utopie, des voyages extraordinaires et de la science-fiction.** Lausanne: L'Age d'Homme, 1972. New edition with index by Pascal Ducommun, but all entries unrevised, 1984.
A massive (8½″ × 11″, 997 pp.) encyclopedic dictionary by the foremost Swiss collector of SF [15-63]. Unlike Tuck [8-7], which is largely descriptive bibliography, this comprehensive work includes bio-bibliographic entries for authors, entries for each country with cross-references to their authors, discussions of common SF themes, graphs showing the varying popularity of SF as measured by the fluctuating number of magazines, as well as charts summarizing the future histories of Poul Anderson, James Blish, and Isaac Asimov. SF in television, music, films, comics, ballet, and opera is also discussed. Especially valuable for its often detailed discussion of European SF largely unknown to Anglo-American readers; see also the Nicholls encyclopedia [8-30]. Some users have complained that the contents of many longer entries are not adequately cross-referenced. Well printed and illustrated, its high cost will limit its audience to larger libraries collecting SF intensively.

6-198. Villemur, Alain. **63 Auteurs.** Paris: Temps Futurs, 1976.
Semiprofessionally published exhaustive bibliography of the complete works of 63 writers (54 Anglo-American and 9 French)—novels, short stories, essays, articles, interviews— then in print in the French language. Also features the English and American works' original bibliographic references in their own language. A labor of love and a must for anthologists, agents, and writers (Robert Sheckley and John Brunner, among others, are known to have spotted scores of pirated translations of their works thanks to it). An augmented edition was planned but never issued.

Russian SF

Patrick L. McGuire

The tradition of Russian-language[1] science-fiction is "thinner" than that of the English-speaking world; at every point in their history, SF and proto-SF have been represented by far fewer works in Russia than in Britain and America. In part, this reflects the smaller size of the literate Russian public and, in part, peculiarities of Russian publishing. But despite this lesser output, at no time since the 1890s has interesting Russian SF been entirely lacking, and in most ways the development of the genre has paralleled that of the Anglo-American tradition. One difference is that in the Russian case, political factors rather than economic or literary ones seem to have been responsible for initiating several developmental phases.

In Russia as in the West, the precursors of science fiction included satires and utopias. Among the most frequently cited of the latter is Mikhail Shcherbatov's "A Journey to the Land of Ophir" (*Puteshestvie v zemliu Ofirskuiu,* circulated in manuscript, 1783–1784). Throughout the nineteenth century, there appeared sporadic marginally science fiction works, including several sketches and stories by Prince Vladimir Odoevskii, a contemporary of Edgar Allan Poe. It was not, however, until the 1890s that publications became frequent enough to form a continuous tradition analogous to the already flourishing Western "scientific romance." Western example encouraged the rise of the Russian genre, as did changes in the Russian literary aesthetic as the age of the great mimetic novelists drew to a close. Midway through this first period, the easing of censorship after the 1905 Revolution gave the field a second boost. However, the single most important factor in the rise of Russian SF was the increased pace of Russia's industrialization, which had implications on both the intellectual and the economic planes. Industrialization brought science and technology into the consciousness of the reading and writing public, and it greatly increased that public, by spreading literacy and by lowering the cost of books and magazines. In particular, in the decade before World War I, St. Petersburg publisher P. P. Soikin issued substantial quantities of popular science and science fiction in low-cost editions, some of the latter in his magazine *Adventure World* (*Mir prikliucheniia*). This SF consisted mostly of translations, but it did include works by Russian authors.

Despite a low absolute number of titles, prerevolutionary Russian science fiction covered an impressive range of subtypes. Indeed, perhaps the very lack of an established tradition encouraged originality. Some writers, such as Vladimir Semenov in his two future war novels, sought only to tell an exciting story, emulating such translated Western authors as Max Pemberton. Others addressed a more sophisticated readership. Aleksandr Kuprin and Valerii Briusov, both already established as "serious" writers, each wrote a few works of SF emphasizing philosophical and humanistic concerns. Briusov's *Republic of the Southern Cross* (*Respublik Iuzhnogo Kresta*, 1905), for example, is a rather Hawthornesque symbolic argument for the inherent imperfectibility of humankind. Another group of writers used SF as a means of popularizing scientific ideas. The fictional works of the theorist of space travel, Konstantin Tsiolkovskii, have little literary merit, but they are nonetheless fascinating for realistic depictions of space travel and even of colonies in free space. Later writers, better fictionalists, would find Tsiolkovskii a rich mine of ideas.

Finally there were the utopians. Partly under the influence of Edward Bellamy and H. G. Wells, the Russian utopian novel began to take on a more science fiction flavor, with a setting in the future and much attention paid to technological development. Utopian works were fewer in number than in Britain or the United States, but they did cover most of the political spectrum from neotraditionalists through Slavophiles to Marxists. One of the most interesting of these novels, both on its own and in light of subsequent events, is the Bolshevik Aleksandr Bogdanov's *The Red Star* (*Krasnaia zvezda*) [6-200], which describes the visit of a Russian revolutionary to the planet Mars, which has already had its revolution and passed to the final Marxist stage of "full communism." (Even today's Soviet Union has only officially reached "advanced socialism.") The novel is surprisingly successful both as a work of fiction set on a Mars much like that described by Percival Lowell and as a Marxist tract. The sequel, *Engineeer Menni* [6-200], written after Bogdanov had quarreled with Lenin, is much weaker, little more than a coded propaganda piece. (We learn, for instance, that the greatest Martian socialist theoretician was named Xarma.)

Political developments—World War I, the February and October revolutions, the Russian Civil War—for a time retarded the development of SF. For example, Vladimir Obruchev's novel *Plutonia* (*Plutoniia*), about dinosaurs and other survivals in a hollow Earth, but much more didactic than Edgar Rice Burroughs's Pellucidar series, was written in 1915 but not published until 1924. However, during the civil war the Bolsheviks did sponsor reprintings of Bogdanov's two novels and the making of a film based on London's *The Iron Heel* [1-59].

Once relative order was restored, Russian science fiction embarked on a period of rapid development. Works appeared in unprecedented numbers, and some among them are still read today. A broadened market led to the first full-time Russian SF writers, and indeed SF now flourished as it would not again until the late 1950s, or in some respects even to this day. Despite the claims of Soviet literary historians, it is not clear how much this upsurge really owes to the Revolution. True, Marxism's focus on the future coincided with one of SF's central concerns and Soviet Russia's relative international isolation (although not as total in the 1920s as it would become), plus the ideological incongruity of most foreign works of science fiction, may well have prompted the increased use of native authors. But an orientation toward technological and social progress was hardly the exclusive property of Marxism-Leninism, and the experience of many countries has shown a natural progression from the publication of translated science fiction to the printing of native work. None of the SF writers prominent in the 1920s were party members, and their work, while usually paying at least lip service to Marxism, typically puts forward an extremely vulgarized form of the ideology. Moreover, much of the production of the decade appeared in magazines and books from private publishers (Soikin among them) allowed to resume operation on a smaller scale during the period of the "New Economic Policy."

In state-owned publishing, the picture was mixed. Despite its science fiction–sounding title, the adventure magazine *War of Worlds* (*Bor'ba mirov*) ran little SF, explaining in its first editorial (1924) that what it had in mind was the struggle between the capitalist and socialist worlds and taking to task its competitors for deluding Soviet youth with Atlantises and Tarzans. However, the next year *World Pathfinder* (*Vsemirnyi sledopyt'*) began publication, and its title bore the subhead "Travel, Adventure, Science Fiction." A year before the appearance of *Amazing Stories* in the United States, *World Pathfinder* thus became, as it were, the world's first one-third science fiction magazine. Moreover, the term already in use for science fiction, *nauchnaia fantastika* (often abbreviated to *fantastika*), is the one still employed in Russia. Gernsback did not coin "science fiction" (replacing earlier variants such as "scientific romance" and "scientifiction") until 1929.

The close association of science fiction with adventure fiction in magazines such as *Adventure World* and *World Pathfinder* may well have prompted one of the most characteristic forms of Soviet SF in the 1920s—the "Red detective story" (*krasnyi detektiv*). Actually, "Red thriller" might be a better, if less literal, translation, since these rather James Bondish stories stray far from the classical mystery. Set in the near future, Red thrillers typically revolve around the struggles and intrigues of communists and capitalists seeking to win control of some ultimate weapon invented, as the case might be, by idealistic Marxists or scheming imperialists. In earlier stories of this type, the inevitable communist victory leads to world revolution, while in later versions (written as Russians were building "socialism in one country"), victory merely restores the status quo. Curiously enough, the Red thriller seems to have been invented before the Revolution, and in Polish. The final volume of Jerzy Żulawski's lunar trilogy, *Stara ziema* (1913, *Old Earth*), at least to judge from its 1929 Russian translation, depicts cold war struggles between the capitalist and a then-fictional socialist bloc in a way that remarkably anticipates the Russian works of the 1920s. However, given the relatively late date of the novel's translation, it is not clear how influential the work really was on the Russian field. Most frequently cited today are the contributions to the subgenre of Marietta Shaginian and especially Aleksei Tolstoi, whose novel *Giperboloid inzhenera Garina* (1925, translated as *The Death Box* and *The Garin Death Ray*) and short story "The Union of Five" (*Soiuz piati*, 1925) have been frequently reprinted.

Tolstoi's first contribution to science fiction, however, was not a Red thriller but rather the novel *Aelita* [2-119], an entertaining space adventure owing a great deal both to Tsiolkovskii and to Burroughs. The heroine, Aelita, if not a Martian princess like Dejah Thoris, is at least the daughter of the chairman of the Martian Supreme Council. Also contributing to the novel, and coexisting with some tension, are philosophical elements from both Spengler and Marx. The Martian bourgeoisie are historically doomed, it seems, not so much because of the Martian proletariat as because their civilization is subject to an inevitable Spenglerian "decline." *Aelita* was written in emigration in France and Germany, but published in Russia in 1922. In 1923, Tolstoi himself returned and was soon extremely successful in making himself agreeable to the Soviet establishment, chiefly as a mainstream writer. His prestige was sufficient to keep successive revisions of *Aelita* in print, but in a climate increasingly unfavorable to such romanticism, Tolstoi never again attempted anything similar.

Aelita was by no means the only space adventure story of the 1920s. Such fiction was common, although—whether for aesthetic or political reasons—only a handful of such works from the period have been reprinted or even discussed in literary histories.[2] Soviet space stories might depict human flights into space or, less frequently, visits by extraterrestrials to Earth, but invaders from other planets, so common in American SF of the period, seem to have been virtually unknown. Similarly, intergalactic world wrecking on the scale of E. E. Smith and his colleagues seems not to have appeared. N. Mukhanov's *Flaming Abysses* (*Pylaiusachie bezdny*, 1924) does depict a full-scale interplanetary war between Mars and Earth 500 years in the future. By contrast, peace-loving extraterrestrials were depicted in such works as A. M. Volkov's short story "The Aliens" ("Chuzhie," 1928) or G. Arel'skii's "Gift of the Selenites" ("Podarok selenitov," 1926).

In Aleksandr Beliaev's *Bor'ba v efire* (1928, translated as *The Struggle in Space* [2-4]), conflict in near-Earth space does play a role, but only as one element in the future final conflict between the communist and capitalist blocs. Needless to say, communism triumphs. Beliaev, the first prolific Russian SF writer, has sometimes been called the "Russian Jules Verne." *The Struggle in Space*, with its extrapolations in electronics, rocketry, and other physics-related fields, is atypical for Beliaev's productions of the 1920s. Usually they involved some development in the life sciences: a severed head kept alive in *Professor Dowell's Head* (*Golova professora Douela*, 1925), a human implanted with a shark's gill in *Chelovekamphibia* (1928, translated as *The Amphibian* [2-4]), a new kind of radiation compelling obedience in *Master of the World* (*Vlastelin mira*, 1929). The plot lines in Beliaev's works were usually similar to those of the Red thrillers, but Beliaev placed heavier stress on extrapolated science to the detriment of other story elements. At least nowadays, his readers consist mostly of schoolchildren.

Beliaev had intended to write what ended up as *The Struggle in Space* as a work set in the era of worldwide communism. He consulted authorities up to the commissar of education, A. V. Lunacharskii, on what sort of dramatic conflicts might still exist in this wonderful future, when war, crime, and most other mainstays of the fast-moving plot would have been long abolished. Unable to get a satisfactory suggestion, Beliaev decided to put some capitalists in after all. Similar dramatic considerations may have dissuaded other writers from setting works in the communist future. Exceptions were Iakov Okunev in his *World to Come* (*Griaduschii mir,* 1926) and V. Nikol'skii in *In a Thousand Years* (*Cherez tysiachu let,* 1928). Both of these describe Wellsian megalopolises and emphasize technological rather than social progress. B. P. Veinburg's sketch "On the Occasion of the Bidecamillennium of the Beginning of the Work of Draining the Oceans" ("K dvukhdesiatitysiacheletiu nachala rabot po osushcheniiu okeanov," 1922) is almost Stapledonian in sweep, and, like *Last and First Men* [2-109], it forgoes a conventional plot in favor of a straight pseudohistorical narrative. A number of Soviet works, in the 1920s and later, counterpose to a future or extraterrestrial utopia the suffering and sacrifice of twentieth-century Earth. Once again, this device would seem at least in part a means of injecting some life into the communist utopia. Possibly the first example of this strategy is Vivian Itin's *The Land of Gongori* (*Strana Gongori,* 1922). Finally, in a 1931 work, *The Land of the Happy* (*Strana schchastlivykh*), Ian Larri did come up with a legitimate utopian conflict, indeed the same one that Wells would use in the final section of his screenplay *Things to Come* (1935), a policy conflict between those who favor a space program and those who see it as a useless distraction.

Of course, part of the reason for the scarcity of Marxist utopias may have been a scarcity of convinced Marxists. Indeed, the 1920s also saw several Russian non-Marxist utopias and anti-Marxist dystopias. One was of course the famous *We* (*My,* 1924) by Zamiatin [2-147]. Zamiatin, who had lived for a time in England and had published a monograph on H. G. Wells (the translation is in Parrinder's compilation, *H. G. Wells: The Critical Heritage* [10-174]), showed in particular his indebtedness to Wells's "A Story of the Days to Come" (1897). The former White general P. N. Krasnov, by this time in exile in Germany, brought out a novel there, *Beyond the Thistle* (*Za chertopolokhom,* 1922). In this work, the Soviet regime collapses after being cordoned off from the outside world, and a humane autarchy is established in its place. Although published abroad, both Zamiatin's and Krasnov's novels were at the time obtainable in Russia (*We* only in translation). Curiously enough, the State Publishing House itself published one anti-Marxist utopia, indeed one positing a coup against the Bolsheviks in 1934. An introduction explains that the publisher was issuing the work for purposes of discussion. Economist A. V. Chaianov's *The Journey of My Brother Aleksei to the Land of the Peasant Utopia* (*Puteshestvie moego brata Alekseiia v stranu krestianskoi utopii* by "Iv. Kremnov" [6-205]) advocates the development of the peasantry rather than the proletariat. Technological innovation is modest, and the plot is effectively nonexistent.

At first unnoticed, Stalin's power grew throughout the 1920s, and by the end of the decade Stalinism brought disaster to Soviet SF. In the first place, many markets disappeared. The private publishers were expropriated (Soikin lasted until 1930), and the state-owned houses, now having no need to compete ideologically with a private sector, abolished their own adventure magazines in favor of more edifying fare. Second, in this same period, regime control of literature tightened substantially, culminating in 1932 in the formation of the Union of Soviet Writers. Throughout the 1920s, Soviet SF (like its counterpart in the United

States) had been subjected to severe castigation in many literary circles. But in that decade there had existed alternate channels of publication and other critics more tolerant of SF. By the early 1930s, SF's detractors were in a position to enforce their opinions by fiat. Publication plummeted, from 39 original prose titles of all lengths in 1928 to 3 in 1931 and 2 in 1932. Eventually the genre adapted. Production was back up to 14 titles by 1935 and 33 by 1938. But what now was published was a drastically altered and far inferior science fiction, written mostly by new authors. Indeed, whether or not for reasons connected with their fiction, several of the 1920s authors ended up in the Gulag.

The one major SF writer of the decade who did continue publication was Beliaev. He survived as a writer thanks to support from the scientific community and considerable agility regarding subject matter. For instance, in 1930, with the bloody agricultural "collectivization" campaign well underway, Beliaev prudently came out with a novel about a submarine state farm, *Underwater Farmers* (*Podvodnye zemledel'tsy*). Another aspect of Soviet life in the 1930s was a constant search for suitable popular heroes. In this connection, Tsiolkovskii had been brought out of an obscure retirement into the spotlight, and Beliaev incorporated his ideas in several books. The most far-reaching of these is probably *A Leap into Nothing* (*Prizhok v nichto*, 1933). The title seems to be a riposte to Otto Willi Gail's *The Shot into Infinity* (*Der Schuss ins All*, 1925 [2-33]), which includes Russian characters. In Beliaev's book, capitalists seek to flee the world revolution by building a spaceship and escaping to Venus. Unfortunately, the ship's German crew turns out to be composed exclusively of communists, who leave the capitalists to the mercies of the Venusian dinosaurs and return to Earth. Other SF writers followed much the same course of jumping onto the bandwagon of whatever might be the regime's current campaign. For a few years before the Hitler-Stalin pact, the vogue was the future war story, grossly optimistic and set so near in time and with such conventional technology (certainly no V-weapons or atomic bombs!) that they are at most marginally science fiction.

Production of SF dropped again during Soviet participation in World War II, apparently because of emergency conditions rather than any renewed persecution. Output picked up again afterward, but now authors labored under more constraints than ever. In the late 1940s, to make up for a certain wartime relaxation, Stalinism was imposed on Soviet society with renewed force, and science fiction did not escape the new rigor. On top of the rules for "socialist realism," which applied to all literature, science fiction was expected to follow a so-called near-target rule; it said that SF might utilize scientific developments only slightly in advance of reality. Ideally, indeed, it should do no more than to anticipate the practical application of technology now at the laboratory stage. Moreover, even within these limits the officially sponsored spirit of the times strongly discouraged any evocation of a "sense of wonder." Denunciations for "cosmopolitanism" or "mysticism" lay in wait for the writer at every step. Under the circumstances, it is a tribute to human ingenuity that a few interesting stories, such as some of the early work of Ivan Efremov or Aleksandr Kazantsev's "A Visitor from Outer Space" ("Gost'iz kosmosa," 1951), did manage to see print. To an ever-increasing extent, science fiction assimilated itself to other, more favored genres, such as the cold war espionage story, the "industrial novel," or the mimetic novel about scientists and their work (*nauchno-khudozhestvennyi roman*).

By the early 1950s, Soviet SF was essentially isolated from the outside world. Soviet official criticism rejected all Western SF after Wells as worthless. Only the vaguest hints—and those in the form of denunciations—reached the Soviet SF readership to tell of such developments as the "Campbell revolution," the early 1950s SF boom, or the spread of translated English-language SF to West European countries and Japan. Likewise, outside of a few academics and émigrés, Americans interested in SF were no longer aware that there even was such a thing as Soviet science fiction.

Even Stalin's death in 1953, which led almost immediately to a liberalization in Russian society as a whole and in literature in particular, had little effect on SF, save for a slight increase in quantity and for the appearance of a handful of articles deploring the present state of the field and urging reform. However, in 1955 a Marxist utopia set centuries in the future appeared in Poland, and in 1956, another appeared in Czechoslovakia. These East European developments may have paved the way for change in the U.S.S.R. In 1957, the magazine *Technology for Youth* (*Tekhnika—molodezhi*) ran a translation of an Edmund Hamilton story, probably the first translation of post-Wellsian Western SF since the 1920s. In the same year, the magazine serialized Ivan Efremov's novel of the far communist future, *Andromeda* (*Tumannost' Andromedy* [3-152]). This was the first Soviet utopia since Larri's of 1931, and, with its galactic confederation and intergalactic communication, it also commanded a sweep wider than anything in Soviet SF to date.

Andromeda's far-future setting and its many idiosyncratic philosophical views were not widely imitated, but the novel did serve as a signal that the limits of the genre had broadened dramatically. *Andromeda*'s first success was within the usual SF readership, but after a year or so the novel had become something of a general best-seller, going through several printings and many translations (most of the latter Moscow-sponsored).

Between *Andromeda*'s magazine appearance and its book publication came Sputnik. The first artificial satellite was as much of a surprise to the Soviet public as the atomic bomb had been to Americans, and the launching of Sputnik had an effect on Soviet science fiction that paralleled what had happened in the United States in 1945—speculation previously scorned as unworldly and impractical now seemed triumphantly justified. Old-line, both-feet-on-the-ground authors such as Vladimir Nemtsov did not disappear, and indeed the conservative school took in a few newcomers. But this survival may have been due to political sponsorship from one faction of the Soviet leadership. Certainly the near-target school was pushed into the background, ignored by critics, scholars, and even most readers.

Soon resurgent science fiction had outstripped the production level of the 1920s. Thirty-six original titles appeared in 1957. By 1963, the number had grown to 103, including 29 books, most of the latter containing several times the wordage of the average American volume. Such figures are still low by American standards, but it is a policy of Soviet publishing to print large editions—100,000 copies or so—of a relatively small number of titles, in contrast to an American field of many more titles but smaller average sales. Nor did the Soviet Union go the American route of establishing specialized magazines for SF. An early proposal to reestablish the adventure and SF magazines of the 1920s led instead to an annual anthology, *Adventure World* (*Mir prikliucheniia*, 1955–   ), which has usually included some SF in its contents. In 1961, the magazine *Explorer* (*Iskatel'*), with the subhead "Science Fiction and Adventure," was indeed founded. On the whole, its editing and story selection have not been bold, and the magazine has not proven to have the importance of the magazines in the 1920s or of those in the United States. Two more or less annual anthologies, *Fantastika 19—* (from 1962) [6-219] and *NF* (from 1964) [6-221][3] have played a greater role. Moreover, to a much greater degree than in the contemporary United States, Soviet SF is also published in other kinds of magazines and even newspapers, a dispersion that necessarily turns the more enthusiastic Soviet SF reader into an accomplished bibliographer. As for book publication, after a brief period of interest on the part of many different publishers, most of it has become concentrated in a handful of houses whose publishing mission involves either youth (*Detskaia literatura, Molodaia gvardiia*) or science (*Znanie, Mir*).

Some previous near-target authors such as Aleksandr Kazantsev, Gennadii Gurevich, and of course, Efremov adapted fairly successfully to the new climate for SF. Two of Efremov's later works are set in the same future history as *Andromeda;* the novelette "Cor Serpentis" (1959), widely available in translation (also as "The Heart of the Serpent"; variant Russian title, *Serdtse Zmei*), and the untranslated novel, *The Hour of the Bull (Chas Byka)* [6-203]. The latter depicts the efforts of emissaries from Earth to save "from themselves" the inhabitants of a lost colony whose "state capitalist" society has turned into a dystopia. Under the guise of criticism of the Americans and the Chinese, Efremov managed some pointed commentary on the Soviet regime. Evidently this was belatedly recognized, and since Efremov's death in 1972 the book has been discreetly dropped from discussion of his work.

Outside the *Andromeda* future history, the most notable of Efremov's later works is the long novel *The Razor's Edge (Lezvie britvy,* 1964), a deliberate attempt to revive and update the Soviet adventure-SF genre. It is not entirely successful. Indeed, Efremov's ideas are interesting in almost all his work, but frequently the execution lags far behind the conception, a problem general to most Soviet SF writers who broke in before the late 1950s. In large measure the problem corrected itself among newer writers, who had the benefit of more exposure to Western work, both in the original and increasingly in translation. In general, however, the newer, more proficient writers show less concern with natural science as a field for speculation than did their predecessors. Accordingly, in the U.S.S.R. there is little technically proficient hard science fiction analogous to that of Hal Clement or Larry Niven. Similarly, little attention has been given to the rational depiction of extraterrestrial intelligent life forms in the manner of, say, Poul Anderson. Instead, such beings are depicted as improbably humanlike, as incomprehensibly alien, or as objects of whimsy.

In part, this difference of approach may have been dictated by the realities of Soviet publishing. So many of the conventional situations of science fiction are "impossible" under dialectical materialism, and so many of the favorite Western rationalizations are forbidden by censorship (for example, you may not assume a nuclear war on Earth to generate a postholocaust society), that Soviet critics have emphasized not rational extrapolation, but rather the "arbitrary nature" (*uslovnost'*) of science fiction situations. Similarly, the fact that most types of straight fantasy are frowned on in the Soviet Union may have induced some writers to enter SF who in the West would have chosen another genre.

Both nationally and internationally, the best-known Soviet SF writers are Arkadii and Boris Strugatskii. From almost their very first story in the late 1950s, this brother team displayed a technical proficiency far above that of other Soviet SF writers. By the early 1960s, they had found themes worthy of their skill—in the process moving from fairly hard SF to "softer" works emphasizing social and moral concerns. Their best works in this vein are probably *Hard to Be a God* (*Trudno byt' bogom*, 1964) and *Obitaemyi ostrov* (1969, translated as *Prisoners of Power*), both of which deal on one level with problems of terrestrial intervention on underdeveloped planets and, on another, with the individual's relation to evil, especially to Stalinism. Up to the mid-1960s, evidently willing to hope that some good would come from Khrushchev's promises to revitalize the communist movement, the Strugatskiis also wrote stories in a much brighter spirit, set during and after the entire world's peaceful transition to socialism and then full communism. These are collected as *Stazhery* (1961; translated as *Space Apprentice*, 1981) and *Polden' XXII vek* (*Vozvrashchenie*) (rev. ed. 1967; translated as *Noon: 22nd Century*, 1978). The title of the latter, incidentally, was intended as a riposte to Norton's *Daybreak: 2250 A.D.* [5-120]. Later in the decade these optimistic works cease, to be replaced by a number of somewhat Kafkaesque satires, which fall outside the scope of most definitions of science fiction. These include *The Snail on the Slope* (*Ulitka na sklone*, 1966–1968 [4-543]), *The Tale of the Troika* (*Skazka o troike*, 1968 [4-542]), and others. The Strugatskiis, however, in their critical writing refuse to draw a distinction between fantasy and science fiction, and indeed much of their work, like that of Dick or Ray Bradbury, sits somewhere on the borderline between the two genres. For example, in "Escape Attempt" ("Popytka k begstvu," 1962), a Russian Jew simply wishes his way out of World War II into the utopian communist future, but events in that future are handled as science fiction.

The Strugatskiis may have been the brightest stars of the 1960s, but the decade was not lacking in other competent writers. Within the limits already noted, their work covered a considerable range. Sergei Snegov, who may or may not have utilized Western prototypes, brought galactic-scale space opera to Soviet SF in *Men like Gods* (*Liudi kak bogi*, 1966–1968 [6-210]). In numerous short stories, Anatolii Dneprov invented a subgenre that might be called the socialist-realist horror story. Such works ostensibly unmask the workings of predatory capitalism, but in fact derive their impact either through the devilish ingenuity of the Western (usually American or West German) machinations or by evoking, through approved nonsupernatural means, a sensation of pure horror. Other writers such as Sever Gansovskii and Ol'ga Larionova have also produced interesting works in this subgenre. Larionova's best work, however, probably remains her very first, which is of quite another sort. *Leopard on the Peak of Kilimanjaro* (*Leopard s vershiny Kilimandzharo*) [6-206] combines a world in which (as in Robert Heinlein's "Lifeline," 1939) people know their foreordained date of death, with a romantic triangle involving a long-marooned cosmonaut, his scientist wife, and a young woman Alpine rescue station worker. Georgii Martynov is interesting as a post-Stalinist writer who expresses conservative political views with an expansive format quite different from that of the near-target school. He produced two communist utopias, *Kallisto* (2nd ed., 1962) and *A Visitor from the Abyss* (*Gost' iz bezdny*, 1962 [6-208]); an interesting novel about a plot by extraterrestrial capitalists to take over communist Earth, *Gianeia* [6-207]; and other works. Gennadii Gor is noteworthy as a writer already established in the mainstream who switched over to science fiction and wrote many works, mostly short stories, in the genre.

At the end of the decade, this ferment of activity took a sharp downturn. There were in fact only half as many original SF books published in 1969 as in 1968, and a general feeling of uneasiness came over the field. Several factors may have contributed to this falloff. In the first place, American experience suggests that there may be some sort of creative cycle of about ten years intrinsic to the genre. Second, it has been suggested that after a while, in the U.S.S.R., the novelty simply wore off. In particular, it became apparent to the Soviet public that domestic authors could not come up overnight to the quality of the translated Western SF (representing some of the best works from 30 years of development) that had appeared in the U.S.S.R. almost all at once in the mid-1960s. Surely the most important reason for the downturn, however, was neither of these factors, but rather political intervention. This intervention in turn was not something directed uniquely against SF, but was part of a general tightening up in the humanities and social sciences, which has sometimes (perhaps a little too dramatically) been called "re-Stalinization." The Strugatskii brothers, as the most popular and among the most outspoken Soviet SF writers, had already felt the force of this crackdown, a little sooner and considerably more sharply than the field in general. Their borderline SF novel, *Ugly Swans* (*Gadkie lebedi*) [4-544], scheduled for publication in 1968, was evidently turned down by the censor at the last minute. It circulated in *samizdat*, was published by émigrés in West Germany without the consent of the authors in 1972, and (with official approval) in English in 1979. Although it does have a feeling of what Soviet critics like to call "mysticism," its political content is not glaringly more outspoken than what had already been published legally, but what apparently was to be unacceptable in the climate of the new decade.

The Strugatskiis continue to this day to be both the best and the best-known Soviet SF writers, but after the crackdown their fate began to diverge somewhat from that of the field as a whole. In the 1970s and early 1980s, the Strugatskiis' rate of publication dropped drastically from that of the late 1950s and the 1960s. In part, this may have been a result of personal factors such as difficulty in finding new things to say, increasing age, and reported medical problems. The production of several major American writers of the 1960s has also slacked off more recently. It is clear, however, that in the Strugatskii case there were other factors at work as well. Up to the late 1960s the brothers regularly appeared in books with their name on the title page (that is, independent novels or single author collections). Afterward, book publication was usually delayed for years after the appearance of a given work in a magazine or multiauthor anthology, and in some cases it has not occurred at all. Strugatskii works have regularly appeared in translation as independent volumes or single author collections in the United States and elsewhere abroad before being so published in the Soviet Union. Still, the trend in the Strugatskiis' fortunes seems to have been gradually upward since the late 1970s, and preliminary indications suggest a more substantial improvement since Gorbachev's accession in 1985. In 1977, a Soviet astronomer named an asteroid "Strugatskia," a name confirmed internationally in 1985. In 1979, two Soviet films (both relatively low-budget) based on Strugatskii works appeared, and a Soviet-West European coproduction of *Hard to Be a God* was reportedly in progress in 1986. Moreover, the social and political content of the Strugatskii work that has managed to make it into print in the 1970s and 1980s is generally as outspoken as earlier work. Two novels set in the present discuss the pressures and the moral choices that the regime imposes on writers and other freethinkers. *Definitely Maybe* (*Za milliard let do kontsa sveta*, serialized 1976–1977, Soviet book publication 1984 [4-541]) displaces or generalizes its discussion by using a metaphor of a "homeostatic universe" reacting to protect itself. (Compare Niven's rather different use of the idea in "Rotating Cylinders . . ." (1979). *Lame Fate* (*Khromaia sud'ba*), published under Gorbachev (*Neva*, nos. 8–9, 1986), but set, and hence perhaps written, in 1982, dispenses with any such displacement. Indeed, its nonmimetic elements (a machine to evaluate an author's objective worth, an appearance by possibly the ghost of Bulgakov) are so inconsiderable that the work could just barely be considered SF or fantasy. The novel does, however, have a great deal to say, in remarkably frank language, *about* the writing, publishing, and censorship of Soviet literature, including science fiction. The protagonist, while chiefly a writer of military stories, is clearly modeled to a large extent on Arkadii Strugatskii (notwithstanding a warning that the story is not a roman à clef).

Another recent trend, which started in "Space Mowgli" ("Malysh," 1973) and gained force in *Beetle in the Anthill* (*Zhuk v muraveinike*, serialized 1979–1980 [4-540]) and *Waves Still the Wind* (*Volny gasiat veter*, serialized 1985–1986), has been the "retrofitting" of the future history into which most of the Strugatskiis' straight SF fits so as to make it less utopian. Even according to official ideology, a certain toning down of the optimism of the early 1960s would now be in order: in the 1970s, the Soviet Union was proclaimed to have entered a hitherto unrecognized new stage of development, "advanced socialism," as a sort of consolation prize for failure to enter full communism on Khrushchev's schedule. The Strugatskiis' reworking of their future history has, however, gone further than this ideological revision demands. Into an era centuries in the future, in what is surely full communism even by the revised official timetable, have been introduced many features that were supposed to have died out long before, such as coercion by the state. Elements of Western liberalism are also finding their way into Strugatskii society. It looks very much as if the Strugatskiis have become dissatisfied not merely with the Soviet present, but with its promises for the future, and that they are now looking outside Marxism for guiding social principles. We can say, then, that at the expense of a reduced rate of publication, of forgoing the medium of undisguised absurdist fantasy (which for some reason always brings down the particular wrath of the Soviet regime), and of maintaining an unswerving pro-regime orthodoxy in interviews and nonfictional writing, the Strugatskiis have been able to continue writing fiction on moral, social, and political questions, and may even have won through to an expanded area of toleration under Gorbachev. Some aesthetic defects in their work (inconsistencies, implausibilities, a somewhat perfunctory attitude toward plot) probably arise for the most part from the authors' own artistic decisions, although the need to work around cuts and prohibitions dictated by the censor may play a role here too. However, the

Strugatskiis have been able to maintain a fairly strong position only because of their national and international reputations, which are not (since Ivan Efremov's death in 1972) even remotely approximated by any other Soviet SF writer.

In the first half of the 1970s, it was unclear in what direction Soviet SF was moving as a genre. Rumors of imminent demise notwithstanding, it had survived the late 1960s crackdown, but the SF community seemed unsure of the genre's role in the new climate. There was much discussion in the press of the "crisis of science fiction," but no agreement on diagnosis or treatment. In many works a new pessimism appeared, at least overtly, not about the general picture of the future, but in the form of a preoccupation with such problems as would remain. Voiskunskii and Lukod'ianov's *Splash of Starry Seas* (*Plesk zvezdnykh morei*, 1970 [6-213]) includes depictions of a number of failures on a personal and a societal level. Sergei Vol'f's *Tomorrow Morning, at Breakfast* (*Zavtra utrom, za chaem*, 1974 [6-214]) describes a child's growing pains in the communist future, which no longer looks quite so problem-free. Of course, Western SF of the same period also showed much pessimism, presumably in response to the Vietnam War, the perceived ecological crisis, and the general strain of changing social values, and these factors may also have had an impact on Soviet SF. By the latter half of the 1970s, a tacit modus vivendi between Soviet SF writers and the regime seemed to have emerged: the writers would be relieved of their obligations under socialist realism to actively support the regime, if in return they would refrain from veiled criticism. This compromise, similar to a frequent situation under the tsars, left authors fairly free to consider such areas as individual psychology, love, philosophy, and aesthetics. Works typical of this orientation are Dmitrii Romanovkii's novelette, "Presenting Anna Karenina" ("Chest' imeiu predstavit'—Anna Karenina," 1977 [6-217]), in which a woman is "reprogrammed" as Leo Tolstoy's heroine, who must then attempt to adjust to the near-future Soviet Union, and the many short stories of Kir Bulychev.

In hindsight, however, it can be seen that, in the struggle between free expression and regime control, this apolitical modus vivendi represented a temporary stabilization of the front rather than a peace treaty or even a truce. The regime was already taking measures that soon would inflict substantial losses on the cause of free expression. For one thing, SF publication quotas were kept well below what reader demand or the precedent of the 1960s would have suggested. This fact was somewhat masked by increased reprints (mostly of "safe" books) and by the fact that publication in magazines was less affected than the more prestigious book publication. With fewer slots to fill, publishers (and the cultural guardians standing over them) could afford to be more particular about the ideological character of works they did publish. Moreover, increased competition for fewer opportunities presumably made writers more amenable to compromise. For example, the proportion of published stories set off Earth or even on Earth in the future gradually decreased. Soviet critics have claimed that this was a consequence of the spontaneous desire of writers to be more "relevant," but as early as 1975 at least one Soviet editor was laying down a setting on Earth as a guideline (presumably one dictated to him from on high). The real problem was that stories set in fictional alien societies or in the wonderful future of full communism could easily have all too much relevance to Soviet society, either by pointing up its flaws or by unfavorable contrast.

By the mid-1980s, the proportion of works set away from the here-and-now dropped to a level that was astonishingly low by comparison with English-language SF and only slightly less so by comparison with the earlier Soviet situation. In *Fantastika 1967*, about 53 percent of stories are set off-planet or on Earth more than a few years in the future. In *Fantastika-84*, the figure is about 25 percent. Moreover, by the early 1980s, signs were appearing of a more positive guidance as to subject matter. Antimilitarist stories supported the Soviet Union's "peace-loving foreign policy." Tales of Earthmen working undercover to uplift precommunist planets glorified by analogy the heroic operatives of the KGB. Stories set in the present or near future in research institutes helped to support the flagging prestige of science as a career in the U.S.S.R. The unreadable subgenre of "satires" of the capitalist world, written by authors who had never been there, began to proliferate beyond reason. All this showed disquieting symptoms of at least the initial stages of an attack of the "near-target" disease that had raged in Stalin's last years.

The picture, however, was not entirely bleak. Newer writers were on average much better versed in basic literary technique than their predecessors, and they often managed to breathe life into material that in outline looked hopelessly clichéd. For example, Nataiia Nikitaiskaia's "The Morning Sun" ("Solntse po utram," 1982) is in plot a classic socialist-realist story of a boy-girl-tractor triangle (with aliens substituted for the tractor), but Nikitaiskaia keeps it afloat through interesting characterization and deft stylistic command. Similarly, Vladimir Mikhailov's *Come Over Then, and We'll Talk about It* (*Togda pridite, i rassudim*, 1983 [6-209]) has both antimilitarist and "uplift" themes, but uses them to justify metaphysically tinged near-space opera of great sweep and verve. Another positive factor in the picture is that for some reason the ideological policy enforced on Soviet cinema does not completely coincide with that in literature, and just when the screws were being tightened on written SF, Soviet science fiction films—presumably under the influence of the Western post–*Star Wars* boom—underwent a marked expansion, in which some SF writers participated as screenwriters. Kir Bulychev, for instance, has in written SF steered away from the broad social themes to be found in his first novel, *The Last War* (*Posledniaia voina*, 1970 [6-202]), but these surface again in a film scripted by him, *Per Aspera ad Astra* (*Cherez terny k zvezdam*, 1982), which incidentally is a competent and entertaining production deserving of more Western attention than it has received.

Still another fairly positive sign over the last decade or so has been the improvement of the "infrastructure" of the Soviet SF community, both for writers and for fans. Local SF clubs (larger and more structured than most of their Western counterparts) had been on the downslide through the mid-1970s, whether for political reasons or because of a natural evaporation of enthusiasm, but there has since been a new spurt of growth. For beginning writers, local SF seminars were sponsored by Writers' Union branches in several cities, and a Clarion-like annual residential workshop (for beginners nominated by the Writers' Union) have been running at a Writers' Union retreat near Moscow. A few steps have also been taken toward linking the Soviet SF community with that of the outside world. The magazine *Soviet Literature*, published in a number of non-Soviet languages, has devoted increased attention, including several entire special issues, to SF. Small numbers of Soviet writers, critics, and literary functionaries have appeared at conventions such as Eurocons and Worldcons; approved Soviet spokes-men participate in the organization World SF; and Soviet fans now fairly regu-larly contribute articles to the American SF newsletter *Locus*. However, the motive—or at least the justification to higher authorities—for this limited open-ing up to the world has almost certainly included a strong emphasis on the propa-ganda potential of such contact. The manner in which the Soviet press exploited the modest 1982 "SF tour" of a few American writers, critics, and fans to the U.S.S.R. was particularly striking.

So far as can be discerned in late 1986, cultural policy under Gorbachev com-bines a new strictness about unofficial modes of expression with a degree of liber-alization in official channels. It is still too early to see precisely what this will mean for science fiction. We saw that the Strugatskiis' fortunes seem to have improved. In *Fantastika-85*, delivered to the printer two months after Gorbachev's accession, about 37 percent of stories are set away from the here-and-now, but of these only one (representing 4 percent of all stories) is set in space. It is perhaps significant that both of the recent Strugatskii stories are also Earth-set. In the summer of 1985, soon after Gorbachev took office, the Writers' Union organ, *Literaturnaia gazeta,* ran, over several issues, a forum on the state of SF, and in the following months continued to print occasional individual articles on the theme. The paper carries similar discussions about SF (and other genres) every few years, but the timing of this one provided at least a chance of influencing the new leadership while its outlook was still fluid. Contributors generally criticized SF for being stale and stereotyped, but they were somewhat vague about remedies. Several re-cent articles have emphasized SF's linkage to the present day, but apparently with the objective, not of restricting its locales but rather of justifying settings in other times and on other planets as still having the "relevance" required by social-ist realism. There have also been calls for a clear-cut recognition of straight fantasy's right to exist. If fantasy no longer had to try to pass as SF, this might help Soviet SF itself to reach a clearer focus. The much wider use in recent years of the abbreviation NF (SF), as opposed to the previous employment of *fantastika* (ambiguously either short for *nauchnaia fantastika,* "science fiction," or meaning SF and fantasy taken together), may also point to an emerging, healthier differen-tiation of genres. There have also been calls once again for the founding of a sci-ence fiction magazine. The role of such publications in the West has generally been declining, but there seems no doubt that under Soviet conditions a maga-zine would both answer reader demand and help the development of the genre. Whether Soviet authorities will finally cease regarding such a magazine as at best a useless distraction and at worst a focal point for malcontents is another ques-tion. More broadly, it is uncertain whether Gorbachev will build on the mildly en-couraging start he has made in cultural policy, or whether like many another leader he will harden into conservatism after a few years.

Other Sources on Soviet SF

The last decade has seen so much translation activity for Soviet, and even pre-revolutionary Russian, science fiction that a fairly good picture of Russian-language SF can now be gained even by those who do not read the language. The largest single publisher of translations has been Macmillan, but a number of other trade and academic houses have also issued works, and occasional English translations continue to be published in Moscow. Several points should be borne in mind in trying to form an impression of the Soviet genre from translations: (1) the quality of translation varies, and even a good translation necessarily involves compromises; (2) the publication date of the original may antedate a translation by decades without this being indicated; (3) works selected for translation tend to be both better than, and more similar to, English-language SF than average; they may indeed fail to reflect entire subgenres, such as the Soviet both-feet-on-the-ground school.

The fruits of the last decade have been somewhat more modest for English-language scholarship on Soviet SF, but they have included the first two English-language books on the Soviet genre as a whole: John Glad, *Extrapolations from Dystopia: A Critical Study of Soviet Science Fiction* [9-37] and Patrick McGuire, *Red Stars: Political Aspects of Soviet Science Fiction* [9-58]. Both contain general discussions of the genre in addition to their more specific concerns, and both have bibliographies. Both books are reworkings of earlier dissertations (respectively, 1970 and 1977) and hence neither brings its story fully into the 1980s. Glad's book version omits much material and contains only minimal updating, so it may still be preferable to consult the original dissertation, available from University Microfilms International: John Peter Glad, *Russian Soviet Science Fiction and Related Critical Activity* (New York University, 1970). A useful source for the pre-*Andromeda* period is a longish booklet by Peter Yershov, *Science Fiction and Utopian Fantasy in Soviet Literature* (New York: Research Program on the U.S.S.R., mimeographed Series, no. 62, 1954). Several English-language bibliographies of Soviet SF have also appeared as monographs. A bibliography by Stephen T. Kerr has been largely superseded by later works, but its coverage of translations of individual short stories has not been duplicated, and it translates Russian titles: *A Bibliographical Guide to Soviet Fantasy and Science Fiction, 1957–1968* (New York: n.p., 1969). Alan Myers's *Bibliography of Russian Science Fantasy 1917–1966* (not seen) can be consulted at the library of the School of Slavonic and East European Studies, Senate House, Malet Street, London, or at the British Library. Reportedly, the listing is annotated and is accompanied by a list of SF criticism. See also Suvin's bibliography [6-230].

At shorter lengths, Nicholls's *The Science Fiction Encyclopedia* [8-30] has a general article on Soviet SF plus individual entries on various Soviet authors, as does Versins's *Encyclopédie* [6-197]. The *Survey of Science Fiction Literature* [8-29] includes discussions of a number of individual Soviet books (both translated and untranslated), plus some catchall treatments of Russian short-story authors. Darko Suvin is doubtless the most prolific writer on Soviet SF in English. Of particular use to the newcomer is a long article on one tendency in Russian SF through *Andromeda*, "The Utopian Tradition of Russian Science Fiction," *Modern Language Review* 66 (January 1971): 139–159; revised as "Russian SF and Its Utopian Tradition" in the author's *Metamorphoses of Science Fiction* [9-97], pp. 243–269. Because of their talent and influence, the Strugatskii brothers have drawn special attention. Suvin has published several studies of the Strugatskiis: "Criticism of the Strugatskii Brothers' Work," *Canadian-American Slavic Studies* 5 (Summer 1972): 286–307, in part tracing the ups and downs of the Strugatskiis' career by analyzing critical articles about them. Suvin's introduction, pp. 1–20, to the Strugatskiis' fantasy *The Snail on the Slope* [4-543] includes a bibliography of Strugatskii works through 1977 and a discussion of their pre-*Snail* (pre-1968) titles. This incorporates a 1974 article from *Canadian-American Slavic Studies* as well as presenting new material about *Snail* itself. Patrick L. McGuire's "Future History Soviet Style: The Work of the Strugatsky Brothers" in *Critical Encounters II* [9-94] covers works in the Strugatskii future history through *Beetle in the Anthill* [4-540], and also includes more general discussion of the future history as a literary device and of the relation of Soviet SF to Marxism-Leninism. As noted, several recent issues of *Soviet Literature* (including nos. 1, 1982; 2, 1984; and 6, 1985) have been devoted to SF, and these have included nonfiction material, though frequently of a propagandistic nature. A number of anthologies and other translations have also included substantial scholarly material. Among such volumes are Aleksandr Bogdanov, *Red Star: The First Bolshevik Utopia* [6-200]; Leland Fetzer, ed. and trans., *Pre-Revolutionary Russian Science Fiction: An Anthology (Seven Utopias and a Dream)* (Ann Arbor, MI: Ardis, 1982); Vladimir Gakov, ed., *World's Spring* (New York: Macmillan, 1981); and Leonid Heller, ed., *De la Science-fiction soviétique* (Lausanne: L'Age d'Homme, 1979 [6-227]). The specialist science fiction studies and Russian studies journals sometimes carry articles relating to Soviet SF, but frequently, especially in recent years, the discussion is extremely specialized.

A substantial number of monographs and translations are available in various West European languages, especially French and German. These are not surveyed exhaustively here because of my rather tenuous grasp of these tongues. However, it should be noted in particular that the first edition of Heller's excellent *Vselennaia* . . . [6-227] was in French. Moreover, those who do read Russian should be reminded not to confine themselves to sources published in the U.S.S.R. While the revision of Heller's book is the only known Russian-language émigré monograph on Soviet SF, a number of articles have appeared in émigré journals and, given the present flourishing state of émigré publishing, more are to be expected.

The spring–summer 1984 issue of *Canadian-American Slavic Studies* is given over mostly to a section on Soviet and East European SF, guest-edited by Suvin. It presents a spectrum of articles by Soviet bloc and Western scholars. All but one of the articles (on Poland) deal with aspects of Soviet or East German SF, and only three of the articles are in English, the rest being in Russian or German.

Notes

1. Personal linguistic limitations, coupled with the small number of translations even into Russian, make it necessary to restrict this section to Russian-language SF. It should be noted, however, that at least a little original science fiction has been published in many of the other languages of the Soviet Union; in particular, a significant body of work is said to exist in Ukrainian. The world SF community has repeatedly had its attention drawn to the plight of Ukrainian fantasy and SF writer and dissident Oles Berdnyk, who was imprisoned in 1979 presumably for his participation in the Ukrainian Helsinki Monitoring Group.

2. Many of these works are discussed, although in a fragmented format that

may give more satisfaction to the aerospace engineer than to the SF researcher, in a compilation of speculation on space travel: N. A. Rynin, *Mezhplanetnoe soobshchenie*, 3 vols. (1928–1930). Thanks to a whim of NASA in commissioning a translation, this work is now more easily available in English: *Interplanetary Flight and Communication*, trans. by R. Lavcott et al., 3 vols. in 9 parts (Jerusalem: Israel Program for Scientific Translation, 1970–1971); available from U.S. Department of Commerce, National Technical Information Service, Springfield, VA 22161.

3. Many libraries catalog this work by its subtitle, *Al'manakh*, or from 1972, *Sbornik, nauchnoi fantastiki*.

Bibliography

Individual Authors

Beliaev, Aleksandr. *The Amphibian* [see **2-4**].

6-199. Bilenkin, Dmitrii Aleksandrovich. **Marsianskii priboi.** Moscow: Molodaia gvardiia, 1967.
The first of Bilenkin's short-story collections. Others include *Noch' kontrabandoi* (*Night on the Sly*, 1971), *Proverka na razumnost'* (*Intelligence Test*, 1974), and *Snega Olimpa* (*Snows of Olympus*, 1980). Many of the author's stories have been translated into English. Bilenkin writes both science fiction and humorous fantasy along the lines of the "Unknown" school. Outside of a few novelettes, the longest being "The Space God" (in *Antologiia* [6-215], also included here), Bilenkin has stuck to short stories, most of them probably under 5,000 words. As a rule, these stories are deftly executed, and when Bilenkin has managed to strike just the right note, they are quite moving, but more frequently a bit superficial. These qualities may stem from the nature of the Soviet periodical SF market, where most short stories first appear. There are no specialized SF magazines, but a wide variety of popular science, general fiction, and other sorts of journals print some SF. There, the requirement is for short works comprehensible by a broad public—something like the small American slick SF market. Bilenkin's work would seem to derive many of its virtues and its defects from such constraints.

*6-200. Bogdanov, Aleksandr Aleksandrovich. **Krasnaia zvezda.** St. Petersburg: T-vo Khudozhesvennoi pechati, 1908. Tr. by Leland Fetzer in his *Pre-Revolutionary Russian Science Fiction: An Anthology (Seven Utopias and a Dream)*. Ann Arbor, MI: Ardis, 1982. Also tr. by Charles Rouge and ed. by Loren R. Graham and Richard Stites, as *Red Star: The First Bolshevik Utopia* (includes *Engineer Menni*). Bloomington: Indiana Univ. Press, 1984.
Leonid, a Russian Marxist revolutionary, is taken by Martians to their communist home world. Features of life there include complete sexual equality, free love, collectivized child rearing in Children's Cities, abolition of money, and distribution of goods "to each according to his need." Bogdanov devotes much attention to technology as well: the Martian spaceship is atomic-powered, using something re-

sembling an ion drive, and various technological wonders on Mars itself are described. Beyond the standard utopian tour, one plot strand involves a plan by one Martian faction to annihilate human life on Earth, which, they say, will never reach socialism anyhow, and then to colonize the planet. Another strand concerns Leonid's affair with a Martian woman and his emotional inability to accept Martian free love. More than a tract, surprisingly successful as a novel, *The Red Star* has influenced every Soviet utopia written since. Compare also to Mars novels of its era such as Lasswitz's *Two Planets* [6-22] and Greg's *Across the Zodiac* [1-40] and to Le Guin's *The Dispossessed* [4-324]. A sequel, *Inzhener Menni* (*Engineer Menni*), was written after Bogdanov had quarreled with Lenin over the former's attempts to adapt Machism to Marxism. Inside an intriguing framing device, which has Leonid back on Mars translating into Russian a modern Martian historical novel about events there in the seventeenth century A.D., we have a story about the last days of capitalism on Mars. Unfortunately the sequel is weaker in execution than could have been predicted either from *The Red Star* or from its own outline, lacking in concrete detail and drawing scarcely disguised parallels with Earth. It is thus yet another example of a talented writer who falls victim to the urge to preach and thereby enervates even the propaganda value of his work. Includes some exposition of Bogdanov's proposed philosophy, "tectology," which anticipates general systems theory.

Bulgakov, Mikhail. **"The Fatal Eggs"** and **Heart of a Dog** [see 2-9].

6-201. Bulychev, Kir. **Letnee utro.** Moscow: Moskovskii rabochii, 1979.
Bulychev had been writing the first name of his pseudonym as K-I-R-period, presumably an abbreviation for Kirill, which was how he was cataloged. Later he noticed that *Kir* itself is a perfectly good Russian name, if not very common, and he dropped the period. This will no doubt cause some bibliographic confusion, particularly since his American publisher, Macmillan, has not caught up with him yet. Any of Bulychev's several other collections is also worth attention. The present volume represents both the restrictions in subject matter that were encouraged through the mid-1980s and the way that some authors managed to work successfully within them. We have not one future-set space adventure, but instead chiefly stories about contemporary Muscovites. (One humorous story is set in classical Greece.) The title story, for instance, starts out as a summer idyll in the streets of early morning Moscow and moves out into the surrounding suburban belt of summer cottages. But it ends as a reflection on free will and necessity (with added commentary on vivisection), very neatly and compactly executed. The "mainstream" literary virtues of stress on psychology and everyday life infuse the other stories as well, with the SF element generally brought in as a broadening or illuminating factor, like the final line of a haiku. In most cases the mixture works, and Bulychev displays an enviable command of technique and an eye for the significance of the everyday. At the same time, a certain scope and vision have been lost by concentrating on the here-and-now, using the SF merely to illuminate rather than to create or at least rearrange.

*6-202. Bulychev, Kir. **Posledniaia voina.** Moscow: Detskaia literatura, 1970.
On the invitation of the froglike Koronans, who have invented a resurrection machine, Earth sends a starship to the planet Muna, whose humanoid inhabitants

have just wiped themselves out in a nuclear-chemical-biological war. The Terrestrials and Koronans seek out corpses well enough preserved for resurrection and attempt to construct a peaceful Munan society, but, unknown to them, the last surviving militarists lurk in a fallout shelter and plot reconquest. By American standards, the story is fairly routine, if well told and brightened by unexpected humor. In the Soviet context, however, the post–nuclear war setting (unique save for the Strugatskiis' *Prisoners of Power*) and the leading role of nonhuman species in the "Galactic Center" are distinctly unusual, and there are some indications that the work was more or less repressed after publication. The novel's protagonist, Pavlysh, has since appeared in short stories and novelettes, including some translated into English. For off-planet intervention in a post–nuclear war setting, compare Poul Anderson's "No Truce with Kings" (1963) and Vernor Vinge's "Conquest by Default" (1968).

Daniel, Yuli. **This Is Moscow Speaking (Ici Moscou)** [see **3-125**].

Dudintsev, Vladimir. **A New Year's Tale** [see **3-150**].

Efremov, Ivan Antonovich. **Andromeda (Tumannost' Andromedy)** [see **3-152**].

*6-203. Efremov, Ivan Antonovich. **Chas Byka.** Moscow: Molodaia gvardiia, 1970.
Set in the same future history as the author's *Andromeda* [3-152] and "Cor Serpentis," but a few centuries later. Emissaries from Earth strive to uplift a lost terrestrial colony, which its rediscoverers call Tormance, explicitly after Lindsay's *Voyage to Arcturus* [2-63]. Tormance was originally settled by capitalists and has now degenerated into a totalitarian "state capitalist" dystopia, which controls its population by killing off all but the elite at age 25. The characters themselves draw numerous parallels to twentieth-century United States and China, which may not only have got the novel past the censor, but secured its serialization in the conservative magazine *Molodaia gvardiia* (nos. 1–4, 1969), which almost never runs SF. A careful reading discloses that the novel criticizes at least as many aspects of Soviet society. Several of the emissaries, including their woman leader, are killed, but they plant the seed that will eventually lead to socialist revolution. This long novel includes several aspects besides the overtly political ones, such as polemic with other Soviet authors on the efficacy of intervention on other planets (and hence, presumably, in the Third World). Philosophical views proposed in *Andromeda* and "Cor Serpentis" are further developed here as well. Unfortunately (rather as with Mack Reynolds), the quality of Efremov's writing rarely matches that of his ideation.

Emtsev, Mikhail, and Eremei Parnov. **World Soul (Dusha Mira)** [see **3-154**].

6-204. Gladilin, Anatolii Tikhonovich. **FSSR. Frantsuzskaia Sovetskaia Sotsialisticheskaia Respublika.** New York: Effect Publishing, 1985.
A future-set political novel. With some help from the naïve French Communist party, the Soviet KGB outsmarts or eliminates all opposition and engineers a takeover of France by a puppet government loyal to Moscow. One never has much doubt where the sympathies of the author lie, who emigrated from the U.S.S.R. in 1976 and now lives in Paris, but he successfully avoids heavy-handedness. The

novel's narrator is the KGB colonel in charge of the operation, and he is depicted as a rather likable fellow. The picture presented of the KGB's style of operation coincides with that indicated in Western nonfiction. One weak spot in the novel is the presentation of the initial political situation, which assumes a continued domination of French politics by the left and which posits as part of the background the neutralization of West Germany. The genre SF reader will also notice the absence of any technological extrapolation, notwithstanding the fact that the novel is set at least a decade in the future. Still, it remains fast-moving and readable. It is arguably (depending on definitions) the first Russian SF novel written and published in the émigré community since the 1920s. Compare Sinclair Lewis's *It Can't Happen Here* [2-62].

6-205. Kremnov, Iv. (pseud. of A. V. Chaianov). **Puteshestvie moego brata Alekseiia v stranu krestianskoi utopii.** Moscow: Gosizdat, 1920. Facsimile reproduction (in Russian) in *Oeuvres choisies de A. V. Cajanov,* ed. by V. Kerblay. N.p.: S. R. Publishers, Johnson Reprint, Mouton, vol. 3, 1967. A recent retypeset reprint is Serebrianyivek, 1981.

Much in the traditional utopian mold, the chief departure being a certain jocularity of tone, which does not sit too well with the author's apparently serious purpose. This short book depicts a modernized agrarian society established after a 1934 coup removes the Bolsheviks. Russia industrializes but does not urbanize, maintaining a high technology (including even weather control) on a rural base. The peasantry has become educated and prosperous. Agriculture is transformed by intensive cultivation and supports an ever-increasing population. Many details of Chaianov's society seem grossly impractical, such as using intensive cultivation on Russia's typically dry and poor soils, or maintaining a high technology while depopulating the cities. On the other hand, Chaianov shows himself free of the Marxist prejudice that the only way to uplift the countryside is to urbanize it, and he recognizes the potential of the automobile to transform rural life. A curious sidelight is that this novel, like G. K. Chesterton's *Napoleon of Notting Hill* (1904), is set in the Orwellian year of 1984. Chaianov himself was convicted on trumped-up charges in 1930 and apparently died in Central Asian exile in 1939.

*6-206. Larionova, Ol'ga Nikolaevna. **Ostrov muzhestva.** Leningrad: Lenizdat, 1971.

The most notable item in this collection is "Leopard s vershiny Kilimandzharo" ("Leopard on the Peak of Kilimanjaro"), a short novel that first appeared in the annual anthology *NF* (3, 1965). An astronaut returns to Earth after having been marooned for 11 years on a deep-space station and struggles to cope with the changes that have come into society: thanks to a subspace probe that unintentionally ended up as a time probe, almost every individual now knows the year of his or her death. The hero's personal situation is complicated by a romantic triangle involving Sana, the woman who waited 11 years for him and whose number will be up some time in the current year, and Ille, a young girl full of the joy of life. Almost certainly the best still-untranslated work of Soviet SF. For the plot device, compare Robert Heinlein's "Lifeline," but for general mood and emphasis on interpersonal relations, compare Martin's *Dying of the Light* [4-360]. This collection also includes the novelette translated as "The Useless Planet," and three short stories including the title work, which deals with a similar time travel theme from a quite different perspective.

6-207. Martynov, Georgii Sergeevich. **Gianeia.** 2nd ed., expanded. Leningrad: Detskaia literatura, 1971.
Revision of a novel first serialized in 1963. Having fled the socialist revolution on their own world, a group of extraterrestrial capitalists first conquers an island on an underdeveloped planet and then sets its sights on Earth. However, before the first alien ship can even come up against the mighty defenses of twenty-first-century communist Earth, one of the crew experiences pangs of conscience and blows up the craft. The only survivor is 14-year-old Gianeia, who is rescued and exposed to the marvels of full communism. Inevitably, she comes around to the right way of thinking and decides to stay on Earth. Also playing parts in the novel are the people of Gianeia's mother planet, now living under communism, and the natives of the conquered underdeveloped world, who in the course of the novel accomplish, as it were, a "war of planetary liberation," killing almost all their erstwhile oppressors. Many plot complications result from the fact that Martynov restricts himself to slower-than-light travel. In certain segments the complicated interlocking of various starship schedules becomes a source of pleasure in itself. More clearly aimed at an unsophisticated audience than are many of the nominal juveniles published by Detskaia literatura, and at least in this revised and possibly padded form, somewhat slow-moving, but written in a clean style and interesting as an example of politically conservative but imaginative Soviet SF.

*6-208. Martynov, Georgii Sergeevich. **Gost' iz bezdny.** Leningrad: Lenizdat, 1962.
A communist utopia aimed at adults (serialized in 1961, but according to a prefatory note, first begun in 1951 under Stalin). Certain of its aspects reflect official Stalin era ethnic Russian chauvinism, toned down or dropped in later Martynov work. Volgin, a Soviet diplomat who died in 1956 and whose corpse happened to be exceptionally well preserved, is resurrected almost 2,000 years later and is soon joined in temporal exile by the returning crew of the starship *Lenin*, which had departed in the twenty-first century on a near-light-speed voyage of exploration. Much of the book consists of the usual tour of utopia, but there are some strands of plot. One involves the Phaetonians, previously inhabitants of the hypothetical planet whose explosion, according to some theories, created the asteroid belt. The Phaetonians had fled to another stellar system, but now intend to bring their new planet back to their old home. (Compare Hogan's *Inherit the Stars*, 1977, and sequels [4-276], and see Martynov's earlier *Zvezdoplavateli*, 1961.) Another plot strand involves the incapacity of Volgin or the cosmonauts to adjust to utopian life, however much they may admire it. The eventual resolution is to pass the misfits along to the still further future, when it will be possible to increase intelligence and otherwise adapt them to a new era. Interesting for its depiction of a conservative post-Stalinist utopia and for an attempt at frank depiction of the psychological difficulties contemporaries might feel in such a world. In this latter aspect compare Heinlein's *Door into Summer* [3-198] and *Beyond This Horizon* [3-197].

*6-209. Mikhailov, Vladimir Dmitrievich. **Togda pridite, i rassudim.**   Riga: Liesma, 1983.

Sequel to *Storozh bratu moemu* (*My Brother's Keeper*, 1976, unseen). The plot is multilayered and ferociously complicated. To sketch it in simplified form, the novel depicts an attempt, sponsored by a superadvanced race that has been secretly pulling the strings of galactic history (compare the Arisians in E. E. Smith's Lensman series [3-355]), to use Earth people brought from various eras of history (compare Lafferty's *Past Master* [4-312] and Varley's *Millennium* [4-568]) to save another civilization from the effects of the Renorming, a wave of alteration in physical laws (compare Anderson's *Brain Wave* [3-8]). The endangered inhabitants, like Terrestrials, descend from a seeding by the guiding race, and accordingly are human; they live on both worlds of a double planet system (compare Le Guin's Hainish series, especially *The Dispossessed* [4-324]). The two worlds are at a nuclear standoff. The Renorming will alter the decay rate of fissionables, causing nuclear reactors and weapons to explode if they are not disposed of first. Captain Ul'demir, the viewpoint character, originally from twentieth-century Earth, is inserted as a sort of resident adviser into the mind of a local nuclear physicist. However, when, thanks to his prompting, the ruling capitalist oligarchy learns of the coming Renorming, their only thought is to use their weapons before they lose them. Catastrophe is averted when the terrestrial agents awaken love not only between the physicist and his hitherto casual mistress, Min Alika (who actually is a spy for the enemy planet), but even between the two self-aware supercomputers that respectively control each side's weapons (the computers reflect the personality of their operators, and fortunately one world is hard enough pressed for soldiers to assign women to the computer). As it turns out, individual happiness and, in particular, romantic love, are of literally cosmic importance, because the emotions generated by self-aware beings influence the physical evolution of the universe, and in particular can hold off the Renorming. At the end, Ul'demir is recruited as a full-time emissary of the guiding race. He learns that one such emissary already on duty has not only been the "resident adviser" of Min Alika but had also been incarnate in both of the women Ul'demir had loved previously (compare Haggard's *She* [1-46] and sequels). The superadvanced aliens inform Ul'demir that they are displeased with the evolution of society on Earth, which is too concerned with material production and not enough with the happiness of the individual. As his next assignment, Ul'demir is therefore to be sent back to his own time to effect an alteration of history. His destined love promises to join him in yet another guise.

   Togda pridite obviously shows signs around the edges of fading off into metaphysics, but its central story is developed logically and consistently. The societies of the two hostile planets do contain elements drawn from the United States and U.S.S.R., but they are not carbon copies of either, and both incorporate a number of imaginative details. At least for the foreign reader, a minor difficulty is presented by the novel's convoluted style, with sentences frequently the length of normal paragraphs and paragraphs that often go on for pages. However, while rare in Soviet SF, such a manner of writing is not unusual in Soviet literature as a whole, and Mikhailov clearly remains in control. Similarly, while Mikhailov does not treat his extravagant story entirely seriously, the humor never is permitted to take over completely. In sum, the novel's virtues far outweigh the flaws of its ungainly design, and it is quite possibly the best Soviet SF novel of the past decade.

It is much less clear how a work that in some respects strays far from the approved guidelines for Soviet SF ever managed to see print, even in provincial Latvia. Mikhailov reportedly had published nothing for several years before 1983, and then had several works scheduled for publication all at once, so perhaps the passing of Brezhnev from the scene in late 1982 had some positive effect in Latvia that was not reflected in Moscow. Another unanswered question is to what extent was Mikhailov aware of Western parallels (mostly in works not translated in the Soviet Union) to his ideas, and to what extent he reinvented them independently.

*6-210. Snegov, Sergei. **Liudi kak bogi.** Kaliningrad: Kaliningradskoe knizhnoe izdatel'stvo, 1971.
First published, and probably more readily available, in the anthologies *Ellinskii sekret* [6-216] and *Vtorzhenie v Persei,* 1968, edited by Eugenii Brandis and Vladimir Dmitrevskii. Under the mask of a title borrowed from the respectable H. G. Wells lurks the first Soviet space opera since the 1920s. This long epic depicts the struggle between an alliance of intelligent life forms (chief among them the humans and the humanoid Galactics) and the synthetic Destroyers and their minions, who are bent on wiping out all life in the galaxy. Snegov provides fairly detailed descriptions of the differing communist civilizations of both the humans and the Galactics, and colorful sketches of many less developed species. Characterization and personal subplots are much better developed than is typical for space opera, and Snegov includes some defections to show that even the bad guys have a spark of goodness in them. Despite an inordinate number of loose ends and some unnecessarily bad science, the novel is enormously entertaining. Compare Smith's Lensman series [3-355] and Saberhagen's Berserker series [4-460].

Strugatskii, Arkadii Natanovich, and Boris Natanovich Strugatskii. **Beetle in the Anthill (Zhuk v muraveinike)** [see **4-540**].

Strugatskii, Arkadii Natanovich, and Boris Natanovich Strugatskii. **Definitely Maybe (Za milliard let do kontsa sveta)** [see **4-541**].

Strugatskii, Arkadii Natanovich, and Boris Natanovich Strugatskii. **Roadside Picnic & The Tale of the Troika (Piknik na obochine & Skazka o troika)** [see **4-542**].

Strugatskii, Arkadii Natanovich, and Boris Natanovich Strugatskii. **The Snail on the Slope (Ulitka na sklone)** [see **4-543**].

6-211. Strugatskii, Arkadii Natanovich, and Boris Natanovich Strugatskii. **Strana bagrovykh tuch.** Moscow: Detgiz, 1960.
The first long work in the Strugatskii future history, set in the 1980s as seen from the perspective of 1960 and Khrushchev's promises to overtake and surpass the United States and to provide the "material basis" for full communism. Basically a routine, fairly realistic adventure story about the first successful trip to Venus, interesting for some first attempts at rounded characterization and for some glimpses (artfully indirect) of the posited political and social changes from 1960. Although the communist world is overtaking the West, the competition is amia-

ble and takes place alongside disarmament and international cooperation in outer space. The novel introduces characters such as Bykov, Yurkovsky, and Dauge, who reappear or are alluded to in later works. The Strugatskiis have been deliberately underrepresented in this listing, since almost all their work is now available in English and since a number of discussions of their work have been published (see the section on Other Sources on Soviet SF). It should be borne in mind, however, that they are at least as significant for Soviet SF as Heinlein is for American, and therefore their every work is a high priority for acquisition.

Strugatskii, Arkadii Natanovich, and Boris Natanovich Strugatskii. **The Ugly Swans (Gadkie lebedi)** [see **4-544**].

6-212. Strugatskii, Arkadii Natanovich, and Boris Natanovich Strugatskii. **Volny gasiat veter,** serialized in *Znanie-sila* (nos. 6–12, 1985, and nos. 1 and 3, 1986). Tr. by Antonia W. Bouis as *The Time Wanderers* (Richardson & Steirman, 1987).

A loose sequel to *Beetle in the Anthill* [4-540], set several decades later. Mysterious events first taken as an indication of activity on Earth by the superadvanced alien Wanderers turn out instead to be the work of a mutant superior human race, which the most zealous of the investigators discovers he is a member of. The novel is fast-moving and intriguing up to the point of the resolution of the riddle, which is hopelessly clichéd by Western standards. The "Bromberg hypothesis," that the Wanderers are intervening on communist Earth to uplift it at the same time that Terrestrial "progressors" work on worlds underdeveloped by their standards, is more interesting than the solution actually presented. The social background of the novel takes much further the "retrofitting" of the Strugatskii future history begun in "Space Mowgli" and continued in *Beetle*. As before, the movement is away from Marxism-Leninism and frequently toward Western liberalism. In the present work, the continued existence of religion is mentioned favorably(!), as are close votes in the World Council and the existence of political action groups. Also as in *Beetle,* this rewriting of the social background coexists with multiple allusions to earlier works in the future history; the present novel also alludes heavily to general world literature. A rare Soviet instance of the "emerging superrace" theme. Compare the authors' *The Ugly Swans* [4-544] (unpublished in the U.S.S.R.), Heinlein's "Gulf" (1949), and vast numbers of other Western works.

Tolstoi, Alexsei. **Aelita** [see **2-119**].

Tsiolkovsky, Konstantin. **Beyond the Planet Earth (Vne zemli)** [see **2-120**].

6-213. Voiskunskii, Evgenii L'vovich, and Isai Borisovich Lukod'ianov **Plesk zvezdnykh morei** Moscow: Detskaia literatura, 1970.

A "fix-up" of stories published elsewhere, together following the hero from youth to old age. The most interesting plot line involves antagonism between the human colony on Venus and the mother planet—a common theme in American SF, probably as a recapitulation of U.S. history, but extremely rare in the Soviet genre since it has no analogy in Russian history and presents ideological difficulties. Other plot lines involve the main hero's lifelong struggle to see appropriations made for interstellar travel and his successes and failures in love. A subplot deals with the travails of a genius who invents a faster-than-light drive. One interesting detail is its treatment of interplanetary travel as analogous to commercial aviation instead of the usual nautical analogy. (The title refers to *interstellar* travel.) The novel presents a highly imaginative view of the communist future. It is also of special note for its unusually depressed tone: the main hero's first marriage fails, he is denied the stars (an interstellar program starts only when he is too old to go along), and the Venus-Earth rift finally induces him to give up his career and return to his native Venus. Weak points include cardboard characterization and Lamarckism (no doubt a holdover of genetic ignorance from the days of the discredited Lysenko). Compare Robert Heinlein's *Between Planets* (1951).

6-214. Vol'f, Sergei Evgen'evich. **Zavtra utrom, za chaem.** Leningrad: Detskaia literatura, 1974.
This short novel set in the twenty-first century is more clearly a juvenile than is most of the SF published by Detskaia literatura (Children's Literature). A boy of about 12 turns out to be an intuitive genius and in consequence is asked to head a research group that is trying to synthesize a plastic molecule needed for a spaceship. Genius or not, the boy lacks mature judgment, and the situation is worsened by the fact that his father works on the research team. On the one hand (at least for adult readers), the novel is not as successful as the juveniles of Heinlein or even Martynov. There is too much writing down and the central situation is implausible. But on the other hand, given the initial situation, the psychological consequences are developed more fully than is typical of SF. Moreover, the work shows some interesting shifts from the SF norms of the 1960s. Twenty-first-century "communist" society seems in many respects (such as worker-management relations) depressingly unchanged from the "socialist" Soviet present.

Zamiatin, Evgenii. **We (My)** [see **2-147**].

Anthologies

6-215. Bilenkin, Dmitrii Aleksandrovich, ed. **Antologiia sovetskoi fantastiki.** Moscow: Molodaia gvardiia, 1967–1968. Biblioteka sovremennoi fantastiki, vols. 14–15.
The Library of Modern Science Fiction is a 25-volume collection (originally intended to stop at 15 volumes) of foreign and Soviet SF, and was published from 1965 to 1973. These two volumes devoted to short Soviet works were originally to be the capstone and represent an attempt to select the best contemporary stories and novelettes. The volumes do contain examples of the work of most prominent Soviet SF writers of the early 1960s: Al'tov, Voiskunskii and Lukod'ianov, Gansovskii, Gor, Saparin, Zhuravleva, and others. (Efremov and the Strugatskiis, excluded here, are represented in the Library by volumes of their own.) About half the works in volume 14, and several of the generally longer ones in volume 15, have been translated. In addition to their fiction, these volumes are valuable for a long introduction by the futurologist Igor' Bestuzhev-Lada (in volume 14) and a section of authors' photographs and biographical sketches (in volume 15). Of the additional volumes in the extended series, volume 19, *Nefantasty v fantastike (Mainstream Writers in Fantasy and SF)*, edited by Vsevolod Aleksandrovich Revich (1970), is devoted entirely to Soviet writers, but includes some straight fantasy (the Russian *fantastika* usually means "science fiction" but is am-

biguous), while volume 25, *Antologiia* (1973), not seen, includes both Soviet and foreign short fiction.

6-216.   Brandis, Evgenii Pavlovich, and Vladimir Ivanovich Dmitrevskii, eds. **Ellinskii sekret.** Leningrad: Lenizdat, 1966.
One of several thick Lenizdat anthologies, which do not form a formal series comparable to *Fantastika* or *NF,* but whose average quality is perhaps higher. This volume devotes almost 300 pages to the first half of Snegov's *Liudi kak bogi* [6-210], and also contains the first half of the Strugatskiis' fantasy *The Snail on the Slope* [4-543], two Bradbury translations, and one of the comparatively rare Soviet translations of Robert Heinlein's "The Green Hills of Earth," complete with excellent renditions of Rhysling's verse. The title story is an Efremov work written in 1942, but rejected at the time as "mystical." Among the three other stories are two about Edgar Allan Poe. Gennadii Gor brings him into the twentieth century, and Leonid Borisov contributes a non–science fiction but fanciful story about a hypothetical visit by Poe to St. Petersburg.

*6-217.   Brandis, Evgenii Pavlovich, and Vladimir Ivanovich Dmitrevskii, eds. **Kol'tso obratnogo vremeni.** Leningrad: Lenizdat, 1977.
The title story is listed in the contents as the "third book" of Snegov's *Liudi kak bogi* [6-210]. In fact this novel, taking up after a decade a clue left at the end of "book two," is more in the way of a sequel. The action takes place 20 years after the earlier part, with the Destroyers now properly reformed and ranked with the good guys. As promised in 1968, the sequel concerns an encounter with the superadvanced Ramirans, who were once supreme in this area of the galaxy, but disappeared to the galactic core. Although still space opera, this has advanced in sophistication from the E. E. Smith level to the "Star Trek" level. Of greatest interest in this collection, however, is a novelette by Dmitrii Romanovskii, "Presenting Anna Karenina" ("Chest' imeiu predstavit'—Anna Karenina"). Tolstoy's heroine, after her suicide, awakens in the near-future Soviet Union, only to discover that all her memories are false; she is, or was, a contemporary woman who was "reprogrammed" to shield her from legal responsibility for a killing. Anna then must adjust not only to contemporary society but to the past of the woman whose body she wears. The scenes showing modern Leningrad through the eyes of a nineteenth-century gentlewoman are particularly well done. Compare Robert Silverberg's *The Second Trip* (1972). The collection also includes nine other works of varying quality.

6-218.   Eti udivitel'nye zvezdy.   Baku: Azerbaidzhanskoe gosudarstvennoe izdatel'stvo, 1966.
In the 1960s, a thriving SF community (consisting mostly of Russian-language writers) existed in Baku, capital of the Azerbaijani S.S.R. This anonymously edited anthology, like two others, is an outgrowth of that group. It contains 2 articles and 13 stories by Baku writers. One of the articles is on the scientific "predictions" of H. G. Wells; the other discusses several aspects of science and SF in a manner that would not seem out of place in *Analog.* Two stories by E. Makhmudov have been translated into Russian from Azerbaijani. These are quite competent stylistically, although the plot devices are predictably naïve (SF, a minority taste to begin with, rarely thrives in small linguistic communities). The remaining

stories, written in Russian, span a considerable range. The two by Valentina Zhuravleva, the title story and one translated into English as "The Brat," are more autobiography and speculation than SF, but still interesting and effective, as is a historical story about the Soviet fantasy writer Aleksandr Grin. The two "hardest" stories in the collection are adventures set respectively in the satellite systems of Jupiter and Saturn. Most of the rest take place on near-future Earth, but one fantasy involves a threatened robot takeover of heaven. The volume's physical format seems to suffer from its provincial publication, but on the whole the contents are up to Moscow or Leningrad standards.

*6-219. Fantastika 19— (from 1962; from 1969, title includes only last two digits of year). Moscow: Molodaia gvardiia.
A more or less annual anthology, although in the heady days of the mid-1960s, *Fantastika* twice issued three numbers (*vypuski*) in one year, and more recently it has sometimes put out double-numbered volumes and volumes dated earlier than the actual year of publication. Most recent number seen is *Fantastika-85*. Fiction in this anthology series is mostly Soviet (plus an occasional prerevolutionary find), usually original but including reprints from periodicals. (It is not Soviet practice to indicate such reprints.) *Fantastika* itself has some magazinelike attributes: for one thing, it is in large measure a market for beginning and lesser known writers. (Given this fact, American university librarians cannot form even a skeleton Soviet SF collection simply by acquiring *Fantastika* volumes, despite what some of them seem to think.) The quality of the fiction, not too surprisingly, varies considerably. Many of the better works have subsequently been included in single author collections or "fix-up" novels, or in retrospective anthologies. Again, as with many magazines, one of *Fantastika*'s greatest strengths has been in its nonfiction features. Of special interest was a series of year-by-year bibliographies of Soviet SF (see Žantovská-Murray [6-231] and Suvin [6-230] for details), but the nonfiction material in one volume or another also includes many critical articles, a readership poll and discussion, interviews, color plates of SF-related artwork, and, in recent years, some speculative science articles.

*6-220. Guminskii, V., ed. **Vzgliad skvoz' stoletie. Russkaia fantastika XVIII i pervoi poloviny XIX veka.** Moscow: Molodaia gvardiia, 1977.
A collection of 11 stories and excerpts dating from the 1780s to the 1840s, representing Shcherbatov, Senkovskii, Odoevskii, the obligatory Radishchev, and others. In still another Russian usage, in this title the elusive *fantastika* would seem to mean neither the as yet uninvented science fiction (the contents of *View* almost entirely antedate those of even Franklin's *Future Perfect* [1-36]), nor yet anything so broad as "fantasy" (the collection excludes fables and fairy or folk tales), but rather "proto-science fiction": those works, chiefly satires, utopias, and extraordinary voyages that most directly gave rise to modern SF. Russia at this time was no richer in such material than was the United States before Poe, and the editor has had to show some ingenuity to collect enough material to fill a volume. For instance, he excerpts two "dream" chapters from essentially nonspeculative works. Still, at worst, this illustrates the relative comprehensiveness of the collection (like anything Soviet, it favors "progressive" writers), which also includes scholarly apparatus, a rather nationalistic foreword by Aleksandr Kazantsev, and an after-

word by the editor. This considerably facilitates access to seminal works of Russian proto-SF. A companion volume filling in the period up to the Revolution is *Vechnoe solntse: Russkaia sotsial'naia utopiia i nauchnaia fantastika* (*vtoraia polovina XIX veka—nachalo XX veka*) (*The Eternal Sun: The Russian Social Utopia and Science Fiction of the Second Half of the Nineteenth Century and Early Twentieth Century*) (198?; not seen). In English, Fetzer's anthology (see the section on Other Sources on Soviet SF) overlaps both of these Soviet anthologies.

*6-221.   NF. Al'manakh nauchnoi fantastiki, 1964–1971. **NF. Sbornik nauchnoi fantastiki,** 1972– .Moscow: Znanie.
An anthology series issued somewhat irregularly, but very roughly on an annual basis. Most recent number actually seen is 27 (1982), but reportedly newer volumes have appeared. Number (*vypusk*) 20, 1979, has an index by issue of contents through number 19, 1978. Contents through number 12, 1972, are also listed in Liapunov, *V mire fantastiki* [6-229]. Thanks to an inconsistency between the title page and the block of publication data for libraries, this work is sometimes cataloged by its current or old subtitle.
    NF is broadly similar to *Fantastika 19—* [6-219], though smaller and more cheaply produced. A higher proportion of its contributing authors are already established professionals. *NF* also runs a varying proportion of translations, largely but not exclusively from English, and has sometimes devoted entire numbers to translated works. About three-quarters of *NF* issues, including all numbers from 15 on, have included some sort of nonfictional material, usually "self-contained" SF criticism or material on the relation of SF to science or society.

6-222.   Sokolov, O., ed. Mir "Iskatelia." Moscow: Molodaia gvardiia, 1973.
The Soviet SF and adventure magazine *Iskatel'* (*Explorer*) seems to be a very scarce item in the West, even though abroad it is available by subscription (it is retail-only in the U.S.S.R.). Given that the magazine emphasizes shorter works, of which only about half are SF, and that about half of the SF is translated foreign work, this scarcity is less than a tragedy for the Western researcher of Soviet SF. Even so, this more readily obtainable "best of" anthology is valuable as a sampler of, and guide to, the magazine's contents. Besides 11 adventure stories, this collection contains 4 Western SF works and 6 Soviet science fiction stories. Also included is an author index for *Iskatel'* from 1961 to 1972, divided into adventure and SF sections, and a brief article on *Iskatel'* and the adventure and SF genres. (The science fiction contents of *Iskatel'* are also indexed issue by issue through 1973 in Liapunov's *V mire fantastiki* [6-229].)

Nonfiction

6-223.   Brandis, Evgenii Pavlovich, and Vladimir Ivanovich Dmitrevskii. Cherez gory vremeni. Moscow and Leningrad: Sovetskii pisatel, 1963.
In English, the first book-length study of a post-Wellsian SF author seems to have been Panshin's *Heinlein in Dimension* (1969) [10-73]. This biography and literary study of Ivan Efremov had appeared in the U.S.S.R. six years earlier, no doubt prompted by the remarkable success of Efremov's *Andromeda* [3-152]. The authors deal briefly with Efremov's adventurous life and, while focusing on *Andromeda*, they discuss his entire literary corpus to that date. In an effort to set

Efremov in perspective, they also discuss Soviet SF in general, with particular attention to works that, like *Andromeda,* depict future communist societies. In this connection they even go abroad to treat the Polish Stanislaw Lem and the Czech Jan Weiss. A bit too adulatory and somewhat outdated by the rapid progress of Soviet SF and SF criticism through the 1960s, but still a useful starting point. Unfortunately, although after a late start collections or monographs devoted to a single SF author proliferated in the United States, only a few more followed in the Soviet Union. One such is Boris Valerianovich Liapunov, *Aleksandr Beliaev* (Moscow: Sovetskii pisatel, 1967). A monograph on Efremov also exists in English: G. V. Grebens, *Ivan Efremov's Theory of Soviet Science Fiction* (New York: Vantage Press, 1978). In intent this is a more scholarly work than *Cherez gory;* it examines scientific, philosophical, and aesthetic aspects of Efremov's work. Unfortunately, the work is disappointingly shallow and poorly organized, and it overstates the extent to which Efremov's views on SF have been accepted by other Soviet authors and critics, while at the same time it underrates Efremov's subtle divergences from Marxism-Leninism. On the other hand, Grebens's monograph does contain one or two interesting insights, and its extended discussion of Efremov's untranslated *Hour of the Bull* (*Chas Byka* [6-203]) should be useful to the researcher who cannot read Russian.

*6-224. Britikov, Anatolii Fedorovich. **Russkii sovetskii nauchno-fantasticheskii roman.** Leningrad: Nauka, 1970.

A survey and critical discussion of Russian science fiction to 1968, scholarly but readable. Its coverage is somewhat wider than the title suggests, since Britikov also briefly discusses prerevolutionary SF, and touches on short fiction, SF by Russian émigrés, and even a few works of Western SF. Organization is basically chronological, with some thematic grouping of works. Britikov does consider general trends, but he also devotes much space to discussion of individual titles, including his evaluation of them. His criteria, of course, conform to the official Soviet critical line for SF; within that limitation, Britikov comes across as a mild traditionalist, favoring the post-*Andromeda* revolution but drawing the line at absurdist fantasy or at any Soviet New Wave. Such disapproval may not be entirely consistent; Britikov, like virtually all Soviet critics except Ivan Efremov, places much less emphasis on rationality than do traditionalist American critics such as, say, James Gunn, and instead stresses the "arbitrary nature" (*uslovnost'*) of science fiction situations. As for other defects, Britikov makes numerous minor errors of fact about story details and shows distressing tendencies toward Lysenkoism and vitalism in his evaluations. Even so, this book remains the most exhaustive study and one of the most scholarly studies of Soviet SF. The volume's usefulness is considerably enhanced by an appendix by Boris Liapunov. This consists of a bibliography of Soviet SF and SF criticism to 1967, with 564 numbered entries for fiction and 296 for criticism. Liapunov aims at complete coverage of Russian Soviet SF novels and *povesti* (a *povest'* is a somewhat loose Russian literary category that usually corresponds to works of novelette through short novel length) published in magazines or books from 1917 to 1967. The bibliography also includes, without a claim of attempted completeness, pre-1917 works, some straight fantasy, translations into Russian from other Soviet languages, speculative sketches, and collections of short stories. The coverage of criticism is more selective but still sizable; in addition to the separate criticism entries, treatments of individual works are indicated under the relevant fiction entry. The bibliography lists contents of anthologies and is thoroughly cross-indexed. Commentary is indirectly supplied by Britikov's text. This is the most extensive bibliography of Soviet SF published to date, by itself more than sufficient reason to acquire the book. Before writing his monograph, Britikov had already covered much the same ground in his sections (*passim*) on SF in a general work on the Soviet novel, *Istoriia russkogo sovetskogo romana,* edited by the Institut russkoi literatury AN SSSR (2 vols., Moscow: Nauka, 1965). This earlier title was published at a slightly more liberal time and differs enough in detail to be worth consulting alongside Britikov's later study. Britikov discusses the Soviet SF short story in another collective book with a similar format, *Russkii sovetskii rasskaz,* edited by the Institut russkoi literatury AN SSSR (Leningrad: Nauka, 1970).

6-225. Gakov, Vl. **Chetyre puteshestviia na mashine vremeni (Nauchnaia fantastika i ee predvideniia).** Moscow: Znanie, 1983.
A lengthy introductory section plus four essays on the interrelation of fact and SF covering space travel; ecology; robots, androids, and computers; and "the final war." The approach somewhat resembles that of *Chto takoe fantastika?* [6-228], though on a less academic level. Rather over half the discussion is devoted to Western (mostly Anglo-American) fiction and nonfiction, but Russian/Soviet and East European works are also covered. The sections on space travel and on robots, etc., are both the longest and the best. The chapters on ecology and on apocalyptic war, while not devoid of useful insights, are marred by polemic on the moral superiority of Soviet ecological policy and "peace-loving foreign policy," with accompanying distortions in the selection of supporting evidence. Despite these drawbacks, the book remains a useful overview for the general Russian-speaking public, displaying impressive familiarity with, and access to, Western primary and secondary sources. The inclusion, alongside more familiar Western examples, of illustrations drawn from Soviet and East European work lends interest to the book for Western SF scholars, though for them the absence of a scholarly apparatus, or even of story titles in the original language, is a marked disadvantage.

6-226. Gurevich, Georgii Iosifovich. **Karta Strani Fantazii.** Moscow: Iskusstvo, 1970.
This is the first book-length study of Soviet SF to be authored by an actual SF writer. *Karta* is a basic book, written in an entertaining style and assuming virtually no background knowledge on the part of the reader. One aim in writing it was to educate the Soviet motion picture community in an attempt (largely unsuccessful, at least in the short run) to get them to make more and better SF films. Accordingly, Gurevich devotes considerable space to Soviet and Western cinematic fantasy and science fiction. (A more recent study of Western films is by Iurii Mironovich Khaniutin, *Real'nost fantisticheskogo mira,* Moscow: Iskusstvo, 1977.) Beyond this, Gurevich gives a quick history of the development of Soviet SF, enriched with his own recollections. He makes a useful effort to periodize and characterize this history and argues that there exist many different kinds of SF, with different critical standards appropriate to each. This sounds unexcep-

tionable, but Gurevich uses the point to defend certain subtypes (for example, the marvelous invention story) now regarded in the West as hopelessly outmoded. Compare de Camp's *Science Fiction Handbook* [13-14], especially the first edition. Gurevich uses a similar approach, down to the map, in *Besedy o nauchnoi fantastike: Kniga dlia uchashchikhsia* (Moscow: Prosveshchenie, 1983). This later book, probably based on the author's lectures at schools, deals mostly with pre–World War II SF and proto-SF, back to More and Swift. There is some mention of modern Soviet SF, but almost no reference to post-Wellsian Western work. Published by the state educational materials publisher, and thus symptomatic of at least marginal acceptance of SF by the official educational system.

*6-227. Heller, Leonid. **Vselennaia za predelom dogmy: Razmyshleniia o sovetskoi fantastike.** London: Overseas Publications Interchange, 1985.
A revised Russian-language version of the author's *De la science-fiction soviétique* (1979), perhaps hence the facing English title page in the Russian edition that reads simply, *Soviet Science Fiction*. Heller is an émigré now teaching at the University of Lausanne in Switzerland. At perhaps 150,000 words, this is by far the most comprehensive treatment of Soviet SF to appear in the West, and it is rivaled in the Soviet Union itself only by A. F. Britikov's book [6-224]. Heller's volume begins with a fairly detailed historical survey, goes on to inspect various aspects of the genre per se (heroes, plots, stylistics, etc.), then studies in detail the works of the Strugatskii brothers, Vladimir Savchenko, and Ivan Efremov, and concludes with a summary chapter on the golden age of SF of the late 1950s through the early 1970s and an updating chapter on the situation since then (some recent material has also, however, been incorporated into earlier chapters). The introduction indicates that Heller has dropped much of the discussion of literary theory to be found in the French edition; instead, he briefly explains that his starting point is an approach whereby pure genre SF is to be regarded as insignificant paraliterature, but where "true" literature can, for higher purposes, adopt genre elements to one degree or another. This turns out to be not nearly so condescending in practice as it sounds in principle, since Heller regards all those works commonly held to be important Soviet SF as "true" literature. The idea may, however, help to explain why, despite holding a fairly strict definition of SF, Heller feels free to devote much of his attention to peripheral areas such as the Strugatskiis' absurdist fantasy. Although Heller tries not to assume prior familiarity on the reader's part, he is highly interpretive, making little effort to start out with an "objective" overview of a given work. This is less objectionable in the Russian edition, where it can be assumed that the reader can consult the work referred to, than it must have been in the French edition. Many a reader will be grateful to have any sort of plausible interpretation to guide him through the thickets of absurdist fantasy, but on the more familiar ground of SF, Heller's interpretations often can be seen to be debatable. Somewhat similarly, Heller's perceptions of English-language SF, which he sometimes alludes to for comparison, are the rather quirky ones of the Francophone world—for example, very high ranking of Farmer and van Vogt. On the more positive side, Heller provides a wealth of background material useful to the Western reader, such as extensive comparisons with Soviet mainstream literature, discussion of the varying political

climate, and explanations of esoterica such as dialectical materialism. The bibliography is fairly extensive and there is an index of surnames.

6-228. Kagarlitskii, Iulii Iosifovich. **Chto takoe fantastika?** Moscow: Khudozhestvennaia literatura, 1974.
A collection of essays first published separately. Save for some passing comments on Soviet SF, these deal with Western (mostly British and American) science fiction and proto-SF and its relation to society, viewing SF alternately as a generator and as a mirror of social and technological ideas. Kagarlitskii takes a long view, starting with Swift, but he shows himself to be fairly familiar with the contemporary field, and even with the existence of such institutions as fandom and the SF Writers of America. Despite this acquaintance, and in contrast to the work of Western scholars with genre ties such as James Gunn or Susan Wood, Kagarlitskii takes a resolutely academic approach to his subject matter, one that may somewhat limit his appeal.

*6-229. Liapunov, Boris Valerianovich. **V mire fantastiki.** Moscow: Kniga, 1975.
This revision of *V mire mechty* (1970) provides a descriptive survey of Soviet SF, written in the form of a continuous narrative briefly describing the contents of books, with references to the bibliography in the back (or to footnotes for works outside the bibliography's scope) for publication data. Organization is roughly chronological and, within a given historical period, thematic. A name index covers not only the narrative but the bibliography, which helps to make up for the fact that anthology contents are entered under the volume's title. The bibliography includes Soviet, and (in a separate list) translated foreign, fantasy and SF books published in Russian by Moscow, Leningrad, and Union Republic publishers from 1958 through 1973. Periodicals are excluded except for *Iskatel'*, but anthology series, such as *Na sushche i na more* and *Mir prikliuchenii*, which run a few SF stories per issue, do have their SF contents listed. There is also a list of book-length works about SF. Along with the volumes of Britikov [6-224] and Heller [6-227], this is one of the three most valuable references for the foreign student of Soviet SF.

*6-230. Suvin, Darko (Yugoslavia). **Russian Science Fiction 1956–1974: A Bibliography.** Elizabethtown, NY: Dragon Press, 1976.
This 73-page cloth edition supersedes his 1971 booklet, *Russian Science Fiction Literature and Criticism, 1956–1970: A Bibliography.* For book fiction, Suvin claims to be more inclusive than Liapunov's *V mire fantastiki* [6-229], besides covering a few more years, but this advantage is for most purposes more than counterbalanced by lack of descriptions or of a listing of the contents of anthologies. Suvin's use of Library of Congress transliteration may, however, make this listing useful for, say, editors or proofreaders who cannot read Cyrillic script. Suvin also includes a useful list of book-length translations into English and French, happily now somewhat outdated in view of a new surge of translations. The single most useful part of the bibliography is a section on selected Soviet SF criticism, mostly in Russian but including titles in English, French, and German. Unlike the other sections, the criticism listing is annotated and includes items of less than book length. Since the once-feverish publication rate for discussions of SF in the U.S.S.R. has

dropped off a bit in recent years, the listing is still useful despite its datedness. An appendix covers criticism of works of Russian SF published before 1956.

6-231. Žantovská-Murray, Irena, and Darko Suvin. **"A Bibliography of General Bibliographies of SF Literature,"** *Science-Fiction Studies* 3 (November 1978): 271–286.

Includes, *passim*, annotations of bibliographies of Soviet SF. The majority of these works are either outdated or highly specialized, but the listing does include descriptions of the various installments of the running bibliography of Soviet SF in *Fantastika*, information particularly useful to the researcher without ready access to a complete run of the anthology series who might, say, be contemplating use of interlibrary loan. Alternatively, see the source notes in Tables 1–3 in McGuire's *Red Stars* [9-58]. This useful feature unfortunately stopped with the annotations for 1976–1977 in *Fantastika-79*.

Japanese SF

David Lewis

Its writers regularly top the best-seller lists. Its books are made into movies and win literary awards. Its publishers put out hundreds of titles each year, and thousands of avid fans gather from around the country for regular national and regional conventions. By any standard, Japan's science fiction community must rank as one of the most active in the world. Yet the works it has produced remain all but unknown beyond the nation's borders.

The problem is not just linguistic, although certainly the notorious difficulties of written Japanese have not helped. It is also a question of content. Much of what is most easily translated is derivative and of little interest to Western editors; much of what is most original is highly culture-bound, and could leave audiences puzzling over why it was labeled science fiction in the first place.

Japanese SF—the Japanese also call it SF, blithely adding the English acronym to their melange of Chinese characters and homegrown syllabaries—is so diverse, and so frequently devoid of the standard roadmarks of science fiction in other countries, that foreign readers might justifiably wonder if it belongs in the genre at all. One Japanese SF critic has defined science fiction in his country as anything written by a science fiction author. Indeed, *SF Magazine*, the flagship of Japanese science fiction publishing, has even run an article on the proper care of stuffed animals, presumably on the grounds that the author was a popular SF writer.

But while the net may be cast wider than in the West, science fiction does exist as a genre in the minds of Japanese readers and publishers. SF claims its own corners in bookstores, its own clique of writers trained and groomed in specialized fanzines and magazines, and its own hard-core, fanatically devoted readership. Its roots go back almost as far as science fiction in the West—some might say farther—while in its postwar incarnation it has already raised a third generation of writers thoroughly versed in the conventions of their peculiar trade.

Ironically, the Western reader has more exposure to the earliest origins of Japanese science fiction than to its modern incarnations. When the critic Ishikawa Takashi[1] took a lighthearted stab at listing the books Japanese SF fans "would want to call SF if they re-read them," he began, not surprisingly, with *Kojiki* (*Record of Ancient Matters*, 712), the oldest book in Japan. No one would seriously label *Kojiki* science fiction. The compendium of creation myths and implausible events in the history of Japan's imperial line is, by its own admission, a chronicle, an attempt at history when history had no choice but to dip occasionally into fiction.

But Ishikawa's point is clear. From the earliest times, the Japanese have found the fantastic a source of inspiration. Although the geography of East Asia has pushed it closer to the supernatural and mystic sensibilities of China than the hard-nosed logic of Western science, Japanese literature nonetheless abounds from its beginnings with what Ishikawa elsewhere terms *sōzō no bungaku*, the literature of the imagination. *Kojiki* may not be science fiction (although Richard Lupoff gladly mined it for *Sword of the Demon* (1977), but it is a mark of how readily the Japanese embrace the phantasmagorical.

Ishikawa's list of proto-science fiction continues to "Taketori Monogatari" ("The Woodcutter's Tale," 800), whose preternatural heroine eventually flies to the Moon. He touches, in fact, on much of early Japanese fiction and on much of the writing of succeeding eras. The bulk of these works, even into the Edo period (1600–1867), are fantastic adventures on the Chinese model. This is not due to lack of interest in science and technology, but is rather a reflection of Japan's historically limited exposure to the rest of the world. It is hardly surprising that the literature of the fantastic has found a more comfortable place in the mainstream of Japanese letters than has science fiction.

The works of some of Japan's most respected modern writers fit easily into the fantasy category. Akutagawa Ryūnosuke's (1892–1927) "Kappa" ("Water Sprite," 1927) is often claimed by SF aficionados, even as it is championed by mainstream critics as one of the masterpieces of Japanese short fiction. Izumi Kyōka (1873–1939) wrote numerous short stories in the supernatural tradition, and even Nobel prize-winning novelist Kawabata Yasunari's *Nemureru Bijo* (*The House of Sleeping Beauties*, 1961) has a premise that strikes a sympathetic chord with SF readers.

Mishima Yukio (1925–1970), the best known of all Japanese writers in the West, made reincarnation central to his final tetralogy, *Hōjō no Umi* (*Sea of Fertility*, 1969–1971) and wrote the allegorical SF novel *Utsukushii Hoshi* [6-266]. A similar SF orientation can be found in much of the work of novelist and dramatist Abé Kōbō (1924–   ), whose *Dai yon kampyo-ki* (*Inter Ice Age 4* [3-1]) was for years the only Japanese SF novel available in English. The average Japanese, however, would be surprised to hear Abé labeled as a science fiction writer, which goes as well for such powerful new voices as novelists Ōe Kenzaburō and Murakami Ryū, or even playwrights Kara Jūro and Noda Hideki, who continue to mine the lode of the fantastic in Japanese literature.

Yet while these authors constitute a virtual who's who of modern Japanese literature, SF per se for years occupied a peculiar literary ghetto of its own, cut off from its distinguished fellows in the public eye, its writers dismissed as nobodies by the literary establishment. Not until the 1960s did anyone from inside the genre, as opposed to outsiders toying with its themes, begin to win recognition in Japan's world of letters.

The reason lies largely in historical accident, in two periods of intense Western influence that built an SF audience more receptive to works from other countries than to the books of Japanese writers. Especially in the years following World War II, SF in Japan has meant not so much writing incorporating an orientation toward the future as a body of work aimed at audiences that crystallized around translations of Western SF. Japanese SF writers first appeared in magazines created to print translations of Asimov, Bradbury, and the like. Their novels came out as supplements to the book lists of publishing houses specializing in classic American and British SF.

Even today, this strong external orientation can be seen in the prestigious position of translators in the Japanese SF community, compared with their virtual anonymity in the United States. Postwar SF in Japan does not trace its roots to the *Kojiki* so much as to *Amazing*, or at best to turn-of-the-century Japanese novels that were themselves inspired by the first great influx of Western science fiction in the late 1800s.

In 1853, Commodore Matthew Perry's black ships dropped anchor in Uraga Bay. The new challenge was too much for the fossilized Tokugawa Shogunate, and power passed into the hands of progressives in the ruling class who had long been chafing under the central government's fear of change.

Urged on by the spectacle of China dismembered by Western military might, the new leadership forced modernization on Japan in a matter of decades. It was a desperate search for options that was felt throughout the society, from government-subsidized steel plants to the new intelligentsia.

With so many people restructuring their own futures, it was perhaps inevitable that a literature of possible tomorrows should prove particularly attractive to Japanese readers. When the floodgates were finally opened to Western books and ideas, science fiction was on the crest of the ensuing wave of translations.

It is suggestive of the spirit with which Japan took up the Western challenge that H. G. Wells proved second in popularity only to Shakespeare in the early years of Japan's modernization. It is remarkable that many of the great classics of Western thought came second to novels of utopian society, and that the scientific adventures of Jules Verne were as readily accepted as were mainstream classics of "enduring" literary worth. The Japanese approached Western literature as they approached Western science and society. They had definite ideas of what they were looking for and what purposes they hoped it would serve.

After an initial phase dominated by translations, Japanese writers began to use the newly digested ideas on their own. Most of these efforts took their cue from the likes of Bellamy's *Looking Backward* [1-8], utopias long on ideology and short on interest. But they did pave the way for a distinctly Japanese subgenre that deserves, in its parochial way, the label of Japan's first science fiction.

In 1900, three Tokyo publishing houses simultaneously released a book by a new writer that quickly became a best-seller. It was *Kaitei Gunkan* (*The Undersea Warship* [6-274]) by Oshikawa Shunrō (1876–1914). The advertising promised "incredible mysteries" and an astounding warship "crossing a thousand leagues beneath the sea."[2] Japanese readers snapped it up, and Oshikawa's militaristic novels with their mechanical marvels so reminiscent of Verne came to shape Japan's SF for decades to come.

Oshikawa had been preceded by ten years by Yano Ryūkei and his *Ukishiro Monogatari* (*Tale of the Floating Fortress*, 1890), but it was the Kaitei Gunkan series that went down in history. The warship, and its stalwart crew of ruddy-cheeked naval ensigns, were eventually joined by flying machines and other extravagant devices. It also shifted its gunsights from nameless Caucasian pirates to British, French, and, as the Russo-Japanese War broke out, czarist fleets.

Oshikawa started *Bōken Sekai* (*Adventure World*) magazine in 1908 to continue the tradition he had established. Although he died when only 38, his particular brand of science-fired military adventure continued to appear sporadically in later years, as in 1930s author Unno Jūza's *Ukabu Hikōtō* (*The Floating Airfield*, 1938). Much of the vigor had gone out of the field, however, and it receded into the then backwaters of juvenile fiction.

Ironically, this was when such mainstream fantasy writers as Akutagawa and Izumi were producing some of their most famous work. Other authors, notably Inagaki Taruho with his *Issenichibyō Monogatari* [6-246], were beginning more directly to try out SF themes. In 1929, the poet and surrealist novelist Satō Haruo took time away from his usual endeavors to compose a short story almost unique in Japanese SF literature. "Nonsharan Kiroku" [6-276] was a dystopian vision in the tradition of Huxley's *Brave New World* [2-47], satirical and critical of conservative futures. Even today it has few counterparts. But while Satō was widely admired, his brief tale of a grim future metropolis was a critical failure. The burden of putting science into fiction fell back on the popular press.

By 1929, that press was showing signs of life, with the arrival of the Japanese pulps. The first of these had been around since 1920. It was *Shinseinen* (*New Youth*), a descendant of *Bōken Sekai*. Three years later came *Kagaku Gahō* (*Science Pictorial*). *Shinseinen* began with the same colonialist ideals of its predecessor, but as years passed turned increasingly to mysteries and suspense. *Kagaku Gahō* began with nonfiction and over the years added short adventure stories. It was in this fashion that science fiction began to sneak into their pages, under the belief that it constituted a variation on mystery writing.

The early stories do not do much to alter that perception. Long on gadgetry and short on story, they were not far removed from Hugo Gernsback's "scientifiction." SF historian Shimamoto Mitsuaki suggests that some of the first issues of Gernsback's *Amazing* may even have reached the hands of Kosakai Fugi, who has been credited with writing some of the first true Japanese SF about 1926.[3]

Kosakai, an instructor in medicine at Tohoku University, wrote such stories as "Jinzō Shinzō" ("The Artificial Heart") and left no enduring work; his best writing was in the mystery field. But in 1927, *Kagaku Gahō* initiated a contest that did uncover a major talent.

The new writer was Unno Jūza (1897–1949), who appeared in the magazine's first *kagaku shosetsu* "science novel" competition, not with a story, but with an honorable mention notice. Later, a sister publication of *Kagaku Gahō* did publish Unno's "Nazo no Tanpa Musenkyoku" ("The Mysterious Shortwave Radio Station," 1928), but by then *Shinseinen* had given Unno his first sale, "Denkifuro no Kaishi" ("The Electric Bath Murder Affair," 1928).

Unno's stories do not hold up well to the test of time. They creak. But he was the major force in Japan's prewar SF community and is virtually the only prewar SF writer to have had any influence on his postwar successors.

Unno dealt with mysteries, mad-scientist humor, alien invasions, and eventually nationalistic militarism. But in his most serious work, such as "Jūhachiji no Ongakuyoku" ("The Six O'Clock Music Bath," 1937), he came to grips with totalitarianism with a vigor all the more surprising for its coming on the verge of Japan's incursion into China.

As the war effort intensified, Unno was recruited into the government's propaganda apparatus. The moral dilemma this raised at war's end was as devastating for him as it was for countless other Japanese intellectuals, and his postwar output was negligible. New Japanese SF writers would rely not on their predecessors for inspiration, but on a second influx of science fiction from the West.

The noted SF collector and translator Noda Masahiro has described his first encounter with a table piled high with discarded American pulp SF magazines in a used-book store in postwar Tokyo.[4] For Noda, it was the cover art of these castoffs from the American occupation army that started his collecting career; for others, the stories themselves proved the catalyst for their own writing or translation. Just as Japan's SF was beginning to develop a tradition of its own, the war and the American occupation flung it back into imitation, a phase it took nearly a quarter of a century to overcome.

Edogawa Rampo, the giant of modern Japanese supernatural and mystery stories, wrote in 1953 of his encounter with a young Japanese SF fan named Yano Tetsu.[5] Yano was going to America at the invitation of one Forrest Ackerman, and he had come to Edogawa for information on Japanese SF. Edogawa could only tell him it was bad. A series of anthologies based on *Amazing* had appeared shortly after the war, only to fail in seven volumes. SF lines from Muromachi and Kōdansha publishing companies both collapsed after a handful of volumes; the Gengensha SF series reached 20 before going under. True, several writers were producing SF-oriented stories at the time. Kayama Shigeru's *Oran-penteku no Fukushū* [6-254] was well received in 1946; his *Gojira* (*Godzilla*) came to the silver screen the year after Yano's journey. But these writers were for the most part specialists in mysteries with only inconstant interest in SF; when *Seiun* (*Nebula*), the first Japanese science fiction magazine, appeared in 1954 with testimonials from Robert Heinlein and Judith Merril, it disappeared after a single issue.

Yet the litany did not discourage Yano, who later went on to head the Nihon SF Sakka Kurabu (Japan SF Writers Club). Even while Edogawa was speculating that science fiction was not suited to the Japanese temperament, the nucleus of Japan's SF renaissance was beginning to take shape in clubs and modest fanzines.

The first club was Omega, established by Kiodomari Allan in 1957, but the movement really crystallized several months later in the first edition of *Uchūjin* (*Cosmic Dust*). Long the most professional Japanese fanzine, *Uchūjin* benefited from the editorship of translator and Japanese fandom's founding father Shibano Takumi. Virtually all the first, and even second, generation postwar Japanese SF writers first appeared in the pages of *Uchūjin*.[6]

The decisive year for postwar Japanese SF was 1957. That was the year Hayakawa Shobō, now Japan's most important SF publisher, began its successful series of SF translations. Encouraged by the response, it added original novels by Japanese authors, paving the way for the 1960 first issue of *SF Magajin* (*SF Magazine*). Hayakawa Shobō has now issued more than 1,200 SF titles, and *SF Magajin* remains the dominant publication in the field.

Sōgensha followed in 1963 with its own series of translated SF, and other publishing houses, including mainstream giants like Kadokawa Shoten and Shinchōsha, have gradually added the best-known Japanese SF writers to their lines, as well as occasional translated theme anthologies and movie novelizations. Only a few other publishers have tried their hands at SF specialty lines, however, most notably Asahi Sonorama, which has claimed the SF juvenile market for its own, and the giant greeting card company Sanrio, which launched a line of SF in translation in 1978.

In the magazine field, Yamano Kōichi's limited circulation *Kikan NW-SF* (*New Wave Science Fiction Quarterly*) appeared in 1970 to give *SF Magajin* its first competition in bookstores, but by the mid-1980s had all but ceased publication. *Kisō Tengai* (*Fantastic*), a small but ambitious effort showcasing Japanese writers, came out in 1975. It expired after ten issues, but was revived in 1976 for another brief run. In 1979, *Hōseki* (*Jewel*), Japan's premier mystery magazine, published by Kōbunsha, started the lavishly produced *SF Hōseki* under a special arrangement with *Isaac Asimov's Science Fiction Magazine,* but ceased publication after only a few years. It was supplanted by *SF Adventure,* another thick digest, that, with the backing of publishing company Tokuma Shoten, has gone on to surpass *SF Magajin* in circulation, although its contents often verge closer to adventure and mystery fiction than SF. The 1980s brought the first semi-prozines since *NW-SF* with the appearance of *SFism* (now out of print) and *SF no Hon* (*The Book of SF*), both journals of SF criticism and news published by a new generation of committed SF enthusiasts. Several steps below these magazines, with their limited bookstore circulation, are Japan's many fanzines, estimated by Shibano to number more than 100, ranging from crude facsimile publications to glossily produced pamphlets.

Even as science fiction publishing came into its own in Japan, major mainstream houses and magazines began to show more interest in SF writers. In the afterword to *75 Nihon SF Besuto Shūsei* [6-297], editor Tsutsui Yasutaka observed that SF authors, far from being brushed away as in the past, by the mid-1970s were beginning to receive preferential treatment by the editors of mass market fiction magazines. He suggested that SF might even disappear as a distinct genre in Japan in the near future.[7]

Tsutsui himself has gone on to prove the point; his collected works have been published, he has organized his own theater troupe, and he has won an established place in Japanese literary circles. A small number of other successful writers, most notably Komatsu Sakyō of *Nippon Chimbotsu* (*Japan Sinks*) fame, have won similar recognition. Literary magazines have taken up the genre in occasional special issues, as have literary prize committees. In 1960, short-short-story master Hoshi Shinichi became the first SF writer to be nominated for the prestigious Naoki Prize for popular literature. Since 1969, SF writers have been nominated almost every year, and in 1974 Hanmura Ryō won the coveted prize for his mainstream *Ame Yadori* (*Shelter from the Rain*). The young novelist Kurimoto Kaoru has won the Edogawa Rampo and Yoshikawa Eiji awards for her non–science fiction work.

Science fiction itself made it into the awards in 1973, when Hanmura's *Musubiyama Hiroku* [6-236] received the first Izumi Kyōka Award for "the literature of the imagination" in 1973. In 1980, Mayumura Taku received the Izumi Kyōka Award for his *Shōmetsu no Kōrin* [6-265], while that same year Tanaka Kōji received the Kadokawa Prize for *Chi to Ōgon* (*Blood and Gold*), joining Yamada Masaki as an SF recipient of the award administered by Kadokawa Shoten.

The audience for SF in Japan has likewise grown explosively in recent years. Japanese fandom has been active since the 1950s, and in 1962 Shibano organized the first Japanese SF convention in Tokyo. Some 200 fans attended the first convention; 4,000 came to the 1986 All Japan SF Convention in Osaka. Conventions are now held the length of Japan, with many becoming annual events. In recent years, Japanese fans and professionals have been in regular attendance at worldwide conventions as well, and foreign fans and writers are an increasingly common sight at conventions in Japan.

It is hard to get an exact figure for the size of the Japanese SF audience, as circulation figures are traditionally shrouded in secrecy. *Uchūjin* reaches about 1,000 hard-core fans; most fanzines consider a few hundred to be outstanding circulation. The professional magazines have circulations in the 50,000 range, while the average SF paperback runs around 30,000 copies.

These figures, however, do not take into account readers who do not consider themselves SF fans but who read and enjoy science fiction when it is presented to them by mainstream magazines and publishing houses. Komatsu's *Nippon Chimbotsu* [6-259] sold four million copies, as did Mayumura's *Shōmetsu no Kōrin* [6-265]. Both Hanmura and Tsutsui are on the best-seller list as often as they are off, indicating the receptiveness of the average Japanese reader to SF. The best-selling book in Japan in 1985 was Komatsu's two-volume *Shuto Shōshitsu* (*The Capital Vanishes*), a tale about the destruction of Tokyo that also claimed the year's Japan SF Prize, an annual book award started in 1980 by the Japan SF Writers Club in cooperation with Tokuma Shoten.

Even translated science fiction can occasionally make the best-seller list, but there the tide has clearly turned. In the 1950s and early 1960s, translations, particularly of Arthur Clarke, Ray Bradbury, and Isaac Asimov, enjoyed overwhelming popularity. But a 1977 poll of the subscribers to *Uchūjin* found Bradbury in fourth place after Tsutsui, Komatsu, and Hanmura. Hoshi, Hirai Kazumasa, and Mitsuse Ryū followed, with Clarke coming in a poor eighth.[8] Among the most popular Japanese writers are some, such as Tsutsui and Hanmura, whose distinctly Japanese sensibilities on occasion seem to defy translation. Clearly Japan has assimilated science fiction as it has assimilated so many other Western artifacts and is well on the way to molding it into a distinctly Japanese configuration. The time is past when Mishima felt compelled to chide his nation's SF writers for writing like American hard-boiled detective novelists and giving all their characters English names.[9]

It is possible to find in Japanese science fiction virtually all the themes and subject matter of SF in the West. But it is also possible to find certain areas that come in for comparatively greater attention, and some that are virtually ignored. There is, for example, the paucity of hard SF; Japanese writers have come to toss off "hyperspace" and "black hole" with the casual ease of many Western writers, yet without having passed through a phase of laboriously spelling out the mechanics of each and every scientific innovation.

This lack of interest in the science of science fiction is not necessarily a bad thing; more regrettable is the relative lack of interest in the future. There are no real equivalents to books like Herbert's *Dune* [4-268] or Le Guin's *Left Hand of Darkness* [4-327], with their anthropological interest in building future societies. Mitsuse's Canal City series of short stories or Mayumura's "Shiseikan" ("Governors of the Worlds") cycle perhaps comes closest. But Mitsuse's Mars is closer to that of Bradbury's *Martian Chronicles* [3-64]; neither author is as comprehensive, or as interested, in his efforts to construct coherent alien worlds. Indeed, even aliens get short shrift in Japanese SF; when they do appear they tend to be anthropomorphic.

What Japanese SF writers have turned to is the individual character rather than his or her environment, and moral dilemmas confronting modern Japanese rather than their offspring. There is an abiding interest in time travel stories and parallel universes. Toyota's *Taimu Surippu Daisensō* [6-281], with the World War II positions of Japan and the United States reversed by a temporal dislocation, is typical of the ideas that tickle the Japanese SF imagination.

Sociologists have often remarked on the extreme fascination of the Japanese with the question of their own identity. Japan is a remarkably homogeneous country. Perhaps more than any other large nation, it has grown up free of invasion, of polyglot immigration, of outside cultural influence except on its own terms. This may account for some of the national pastime of introspection; certainly Japan's SF has inherited the trait, using its repertory of techniques to pose in ever more controlled settings the question "Who are we now?" rather than "Who will we become?"

Komatsu's *Nippon Chimbotsu* [6-259] uses the destruction of the Japanese homeland as a test tube for observing the Japanese people under stress. Hanmura's work reaches the extreme of SF as introspection, virtual parallel-world histories of Japan so close to the original that most of the surface detail goes unchanged. It is no coincidence that Hanmura, Hoshi, and Mitsuse also write historical novels. Japanese SF writers share the national preoccupation with the past; their work does not seek a path to the future so much as the hidden trail to today.

This has resulted in some exceptionally powerful work, often charged with vivid images of destruction springing from firsthand experience in Japan's devastated cities during the war. But it has also cost Japanese SF many things. Although there is a plentitude of carefully constructed near futures and a number of excursions to the ends of time and space, there are very few well-realized futures that betray any difference in mores, social structure, and values from the present day. Along the same vein, there have been few utopian visions, and even fewer dystopian, since the turn of the century. The few writers that have tried seriously to consider where society, rather than the events impacting on it, will find itself in the years ahead tend to be from outside the field. Ishikawa's *Saigo no Kyōwakoku* [6-249] is one rare example; *Sanjūnengo (Thirty Years After,* 1918) by Hoshi Ichi, grandfather of Hoshi Shinichi, is another. More recently, women mainstream novelists Kurihashi Yumeko and Natsuki Shizuko have attracted attention with novels about the aftermath of nuclear war, a theme taken up only sporadically by the science fiction community.

In short, Japanese science fiction is disappointing in the goals to which it aspires. Mishima once wrote a letter to *Uchūjin* calling SF the one genre that could mount an effective challenge to "modern humanism."[10] In another letter to *NW-SF,* he said of science fiction that "if Japanese literature is to record any intellectual accomplishments, this may be the only method."[11]

But Mishima has found few takers in Japan (the same can be said of the West). A handful of mainstream writers—most notably Abé in *Dai yon kampyo-ki* [3-1] and Numa Shōzō in his remarkable *Kachikujin Yapū* [6-272]—have used SF techniques for more rigorous intellectual exercises, but the majority of SF writers per se have steered in a different direction. "Sense of wonder" and "good entertainment" remain buzz words in SF book reviews. Japanese SF has generally not been willing to take on the intellectual challenges of which it is capable.

The Japanese SF community, while still small by U.S. standards, has grown rapidly in recent years. Some of the preeminent names include the following:

Hoshi Shinichi (1926–   ) is an astonishingly prolific writer who has turned out 1,000 short-short stories. He was the first Japanese SF writer to achieve recognition outside the genre and was also the first to appear in English. "Bokko-chan" was printed in *Fantasy and Science Fiction* in June 1963. "Oi, Dette Koi!" ("He-y, Come on Ou-t") appeared in *F&SF* in November 1978. A collection of short fiction serialized in the English-language *Japan Times* appeared in 1978 as *The Spiteful Planet* [6-245].

Abé Kōbō (1924–   ) was one of the first Japanese authors to give respectability to SF themes with *Dai yon kampyo-ki,* translated as *Inter Ice Age 4* [3-1]. Most of his novels, and several of his plays and short stories, are available in English translation.

Komatsu Sakyō (1931–   ) is as prolific in novel-length fiction as Hoshi is in short stories. His *Nippon Chimbotsu,* translated as *Japan Sinks* [6-259], led Japanese SF out of the ghetto. In recent years he has turned increasingly to essays on futurology. His short story "Donyoku na Kuchi" ("The Savage Mouth") appears in *Rooms of Paradise,* edited by Lee Harding (1979). Komatsu has been called the Heinlein of Japan, but in many respects he more closely resembles Asimov, both in the tone of his work and in his unique position in the Japanese science fiction community.

Tsutsui Yasutaka (1934–   ) has long been active in the SF community; he was the prime mover behind the early fanzine *NULL*. He has polished a particular brand of slapstick satire, seen in such collections as *Betonamu Kankō Kōsha* (Vietnam Tourist Co., 1976), but his most successful work reflects a darker strain. A translation of his story "Tatazumu Hito" ("Standing Woman") appeared in *Omni,*

January 1981. His mystery "Nyōbō Satsudan" ("Perfectly Lovely Ladies") appears in *Ellery Queen's Japanese Golden Dozen,* published by Tuttle in 1978.

Hanmura Ryō (1933–) was first seen in print with a flying saucer story in *SF Magajin,* 1962. He has called that work the last piece of science fiction he wrote, and it was in fact the last story of any kind he wrote for ten years. After his return to writing, his prodigious output—averaging about four books a year—made him one of the wealthiest and most critically acclaimed SF writers. His atypical short-short "Bōru Bako" ("Cardboard Box") appeared in *Pacific Quarterly/Moana,* 4 (1979).

Kanbayashi Chōhei (1953–) is one of the most powerful writers to emerge on the science fiction scene in many years. There are resonances in his unsentimental, hard-edged stories with the spirit if not the details of the cyberpunk movement. In recent years he has largely monopolized the Nebula Award, a Japanese fan award patterned on the American Hugo Award and presented at the annual Japan Science Fiction Convention.

Kurimoto Kaoru (1953–) was the first woman writer to have a major impact on the field. Tremendously prolific, her work ranges from murder mysteries to hard SF short stories to plays for the Kabuki stage. The 25 books of her Guin Saga series have made her the guiding light of Japanese sword and sorcery.

Mitsuse Ryū (1928–) is one of the masters of Japanese SF who has failed to find a following outside the genre. He brings a lyrical style to stories with the trappings of hard science that depict the future history of humans in space. "Sunset 2217" appared in Frederik Pohl's *Best Science Fiction for 1972.*

Mayumura Taku (1934–) writes solid nuts-and-bolts science fiction about bureaucrats and diplomats in space, a kind of Japanese Retief without the slapstick. He did not, however, win wide public recognition until the publication of *Shōmetsu no Kōrin* [6-265]. He remains untranslated.

Yano Tetsu (1923–) is the patriarch of Japanese SF and one of its most colorful personalities. He has written a number of strong, surprisingly romantic novels, of which *Origami Uchūsen no Densetsu* [6-292] is the best, and the classic ninja adventure novel, *Kamui no Ken* (*Sword of Kamui,* 1984).

Writers like Hanmura and Tsutsui have created unique SF visions and even Komatsu, Hoshi, and others have taken on Western SF in its own territory and created books and stories that suffer not at all in comparison. It is the Western reader's loss that there has been so little interest in making this remarkable SF literature available in translation.[12] Although the language difficulties are formidable, more formidable has been the attitude of editors and readers that all they can expect from Japanese SF is imitation. That may have been true many years ago; it is now time for such thinking to change.

Notes

1. Ishikawa Takashi, "Nihon SF-shi no Kokoromi," in *SF no Jidai: Nihon SF no Taidō to Tenbō,* ed. by Ishikawa Takashi (Tokyo: Kisō Tengaisha, 1977), pp. 120–137.

   All names are given in Japanese, with the surname first and the given name second. Romanization throughout follows that used in the fourth edition of *Kenkyusha's New Japanese-English Dictionary,* with the exception of several writers (Kiodomari Allan, for example) who frequently sign their names in English using romanization systems of their own. The Chinese characters used in Japanese personal names are open to a wide range of often idiosyncratic readings. Wherever possible, I have used the readings given in the six-volume *Nihon Kindai Bungaku Daijiten* (*Dictionary of Modern Japanese Literature*) (Tokyo: Kōdansha, 1978).

2. Yokota Junya, "Nihon SF Koten Koten," *SF Magajin* 15 (September 1974): 102–112.
3. Shimamoto Mitsuaki, "Zoku: Gaisetsu Nihon SF-shi," *Uchūjin* 1 (1973): 4–23.
4. Noda Masahiro, "Korekuta Muzan!" in *'73 Nihon SF Besuto Shūsei*, ed. by Tsutsui Yasutaka (Tokyo: Tokuma Shoten, 1975), pp. 321–334.
5. Edogawa Rampo, "Kagaku Shōsetsu no Oni," reprinted in the *Cosmicon '77* program, ed. by Itoh Norio and Kazami Jun.
6. Published in Japanese, with the table of contents and notes on Japanese fandom appended in English. *Uchūjin*'s editorial address is 700 Ninomiya, Ninomiya-machi, Naka-gun, Kanagawa-ken, 259-01, Japan.
7. Tsutsui Yasutake, " '75 Nendoban Kaisetsu," in *'75 Nihon SF Besuto Shusei*, ed. by Tsutsui Yasutaka (Tokyo: Tokuma Shoten, 1976), pp. 321–334.
8. "Zenin Anketo Kekka Hōkoku," *Uchūjin* 1 (1977): 18–25. The same survey found the average *Uchūjin* reader to be male, in college, middle class, atheistic, and apolitical. Compare the detailed analysis of Albert I. Berger, "SF Fans in Socio-Economic Perspective: Factors in the Social Consciousness of a Genre," *Science-Fiction Studies* 4 (November 1977): 232–246.
9. Mishima Yukio, "Hitori SF Fan no Wagamama na Kibō, *Uchūjin*, September 1963.
10. Ibid.
11. Mishima Yukio, letter to Yamano Kōichi, *Kikan NW-SF*, no. 3, 1971.
12. English-language references to Japanese SF are few and far between. One of the earliest is Takumi Shibano's "Report on Japanese Science Fiction," *If Science Fiction* 18, no. 10 (October 1968). Shibano's entry on Japan in *The Science Fiction Encyclopedia* [8-30] is an excellent concise guide to the topic; his "Current Science Fiction in Japan," published in the program of the second World Science Fiction Writers Conference in June 1978, briefly introduces the major Japanese writers. Occasional reports on Japanese SF appear in *Locus*. "Science Fiction in Japan," *Foundation* 19 (June 1980), contains many errors in the romanization of book titles and authors' names, but is still one of the most comprehensive articles in English.

Bibliography

Individual Authors

Abé, Kōbō. **Inter Ice Age 4 (Dai yon kampyo-ki)** [see **3-1**].

6-232. Aramaki, Yoshio. **Shirokabe no Moji wa Sekiyō ni Haeru.** Tokyo: Hayakawa Shobō, 1972.

Six novellas representing the early work of architect, painter, and patron of the arts Aramaki Yoshio. Among them is "Yawarakai Tokei" ("Soft Clock"), in which a professional marriage arranger must find a suitable husband for the daughter of the reigning head of the Dali estate. The estate is on Mars, which has become a haven for neurotics and artists' colonies. This story with its unusual subject matter and baroque styling encapsulates much of Aramaki's work, which features a brooding romanticism and interest in mythology and the occult found in few other Japanese SF writers. Compare with Ray Bradbury's *The October Country* (1955) and the short fiction of Tanith Lee.

6-233. Arai, Motoko. **Zekku.** . . . Tokyo: Hayakawa Shobō, 1983.
Perhaps not Arai's best book, but the one that best sums up the Arai Motoko phenomenon. Following her discovery by Hoshi Shinichi at the age of 17, Arai quickly became the darling of the science fiction community and the recipient of the Nebula Award for, among other works, her excellent novella "Neptune." Arai writes in a flip, conversational style that was unheard of in Japan when it first appeared, and has strongly influenced the work of younger writers far beyond the confines of SF. *Zekku* . . . is pure Arai: she appoints herself the novel's first-person heroine as she deals with a succession of bad and beautific aliens. Arai's *Green Requiem* and *A Ship to the Stars* have been published in simplified texts for Japanese students of English.

6-234. Fukushima, Masami. **Fundarika.** Tokyo: Hayakawa Shobō, 1969.
Four novellas written during 1968 and 1969 represent the later work of Fukushima Masami (1929–1976), the first editor of *SF Magajin*. A producer of "illusion tapes," used around the clock in every corner of society, suffers nightmares of the Buddhist hell of fire. He finds no satisfaction in his work as the tapes come under increasing fire for their negative effects on society. Following a particularly heated conference, he is attacked and immolated by a girl armed with a Molotov cocktail, seeing in his last moments a double image of his nightmare and his own death. Fukushima repeatedly returned to the theme of created illusion versus an unpalatable reality in his work. His traditionally written short stories received less attention than his efforts to improve the respectability of SF in Japan, for which he became known as "Mr. SF."

*6-235. Hanmura, Ryō. **Ishi no Ketsumyaku.** Tokyo: Hayakawa Shobō, 1971.
Hanmura postulates a secret organization shaping the events the rest of the world takes for granted. The milieu is big business, the secret shapers inheritors of the vampire and wolf-man traditions of Europe. Both conditions are seen as symptoms of a disease transmitted through intercourse and requiring blood to sustain the process, which sends carriers into a fossilized "chrysalis" state. When they emerge hundreds of years later, they become immortal. In a gothic web of intrigue charged with occasionally lurid eroticism, Hanmura scathingly assaults the business world as captains of industry seek to become infected and guarantee their safety while in the fossil state. More popularly written than *Musubiyama Hiroku,* but still technically impressive. Compare with Matheson's *I Am Legend* [3-274].

*6-236. Hanmura, Ryō. **Musubiyama Hiroku.** Tokyo: Hayakawa Shobō, 1973. The finest single book by one of the best SF writers in Japan. *Musubiyama Hiroku* reinterprets Japanese history, and later world history, from the perspective of an in-bred clan possessing limited extrasensory powers and dedicated to preserving peace and stability. Their powers are augmented by artifacts left thousands of years before by aliens, from which they may themselves be descended. The novel details the gradual decline and loss of purpose of the Hi clan, counterpointed by efforts around the world to discover its secrets. The tight plotting for the most part avoids melodrama and is reinforced by Hanmura's vivid reconstructions of different periods in Japanese history as he ingeniously weaves together historical events and personalities to show how the Hi have shifted the scales of history. The almost frighteningly convincing book was the first recipient of the Izumi Kyōka Award for the "literature of the imagination." Compare with Shea and Wilson's *Illuminatus!* [4-490].

6-237. Hanmura, Ryō. **Sengoku Jieitai.** Tokyo: Hayakawa Shobō, 1971. A unit of the Japanese Self Defense Force is on maneuvers near the historical location of the domain of warlord Oda Nobunaga, who began the unification of war-wracked Japan in the sixteenth century, when it encounters a "time slip" and is transported to that crucial period in Japanese history. But the soldiers find themselves in a parallel world, where Oda is a petty castle holder. They use their dwindling stock of modern weaponry to replicate Oda's deeds, even as they take on the ways and customs of the era in which they find themselves. A deft turn-about on Japanese history in the style at which Hanmura excels, and the basis of the 1980 Kadokawa movie *Time Slip.* Compare with Toyota's *Taimu Surippu Daisensō* [6-281].

*6-238. Hanmura, Ryō. **Yōseiden.** Tokyo: Kōdansha, 1973. This seven-volume epic takes to its furthest extreme Hanmura's technique of reconstructing history from the inside, while leaving the exterior intact. It is also the author's most ambitious attempt to come to terms with violence and war in human history, and the human place in the face of time. A handful of disembodied aliens pass from host to host in seventeenth-century Japan, inciting violence and destruction where they pass. Hanmura lived through the firebombing of Tokyo. Self-taught, he has worked at jobs ranging from manual laborer to cabaret manager. His experience has been dark and is reflected directly in his fiction in the sense of outrage with which he sometimes writes and the painfully short life of what happiness his characters may find. *Yōseiden,* since its beginning in 1973, has become the vehicle for tying together the many threads of Hanmura's own life and is considered to be his masterpiece. Compare with Heinlein's *The Puppet Masters* [3-205].

6-239. Hirai, Kazumasa. **Ōkami no Monshō.** Tokyo: Hayakawa Shobō, 1971. The first thing that strikes a teacher at a Tokyo junior high about her newest student is the ferocious energy lurking behind his outwardly placid features. The new student soon runs afoul of student delinquents led by the son of a Yakuza gangster. When the hoodlums try to rape the teacher, she is saved by an enormous wolf. Before the end of the book, her student "wolfman" gorily dispatches all the delinquents. No single work quite explains Hirai, whose fans verge on the fanatical and who claims himself to speak in tongues. The Wolf Guy series already has more than a dozen titles. His even more immense Genma Taisen (the Genma Wars) series has more than 30 titles in its various subseries, and is still growing. His books are passionate but simplistic tales of characters of almost saintlike goodness at war with an ultimate evil. *Ōkami no Monshō* is available in English as *Wolfcrest* (Tokyo: Kōdansha, 1985). Compare with Williamson's *Darker Than You Think* [3-401].

6-240. Hirose, Tadashi. **Erosu.** Tokyo: Hayakawa Shobō, 1971.
A young girl at the beginning of Japan's modern Shōwa period (1926 to present) changes world history as she works her will through the career of a young electrical engineer. Hirose Tadashi (1924–1972) was one of the most promising Japanese SF novelists until his fatal heart attack. Although he published only three novels before his death, all were nominated for the prestigious Naoki Prize for popular literature. All his books were marked by nostalgia for the recent past. *Erosu* lovingly re-creates prewar Tokyo. Compare with Cowper's *Breakthrough* [4-152] in the use of parallel worlds.

*6-241. Hirose, Tadashi. **Mainasu Zero.** Tokyo: Kawade Shobō Shinsha, 1970.
Hirose's first and most famous novel opens with firebombs raining down on Tokyo. A junior high school student is asked by a dying neighbor to return to his house in 18 years. When he does, he finds the neighbor's daughter emerging, unchanged from 18 years before, from a bunker behind the house. The bunker contains a time machine. The protagonist flies back in time to before the neighbor moved into the house, but misjudges and arrives two years early. He invents the yoyo to earn some money and enjoys the good old days. But he is exiled on suspicion of being a communist before the neighbor appears, and cannot return until 1947, when he marries an aging actress now living in the house. By the time the story and the flurry of time machine flights are over, the protagonist has married the daughter, who is her own mother, and has died while telling himself to return to the house 18 years later. Compare with Robert Heinlein's "All You Zombies" and Gerrold's *The Man Who Folded Himself* [4-229].

*6-242. Hoshi, Shinichi. **Jinzō Bijin.** Tokyo: Shinchōsha, 1961.
Hoshi Shinichi in 1986 achieved his life goal of writing 1,000 short-short stories. This book, one of the most famous in Japanese SF history, contains the first of them. Now out of print, it became the first Japanese SF book to receive wide recognition outside the field when it was nominated for the forty-fifth Naoki Prize for popular literature. The lead story, "Bokko-chan," was translated under the same title in *Fantasy and Science Fiction* in June 1963. All the stories are included in Shinchōsha's 18-volume *Hōshi Shinichi no Sakuhinshū* (*Complete Works of Hoshi Shinichi,* 1974–1975).

6-243. Hoshi, Shinichi. **Koe no Ami.** Tokyo: Kōdansha, 1970.
One of Hoshi's two SF novels, *Koe no Ami* betrays its short-short heritage in the episodic nature of its many brief chapters. In a utopian future society, a computer handles all human routine chores. However, unexpected events begin to happen as people all over the world receive mysterious phone calls accurately predicting break-ins, tattling on adulterous affairs, and revealing all manner of se-

crets. Finally, a famous psychiatrist receives a call for consultation, from the computer itself. Compare Jones's *Colossus* [4-289] and Gerrold's *When Harlie Was One* [4-230].

6-244. Hoshi, Shinichi. **Muma no Hyōteki.** Tokyo: Hayakawa Shobō, 1964.
Kuruko, the ventriloquist narrator's dummy, suddenly takes on a life of its own. The dummy has become the avenue into this world for invaders from another dimension. The narrator tries hysterically to convince people of the danger, in the process winning new admirers for his "madman act." Meanwhile, Kuruko sets about laying the groundwork for the coming of the new masters. A bizarre and often amusing invasion tale, in which Hoshi shows his abundant but little-used talents as an SF novelist. Compare with Clifford Simak's *They Walked Like Men* (1962).

6-245. Hoshi, Shinichi. **The Spiteful Planet and Other Stories.** Tr. by Tomoyoshi Genkawa and Bernard Susser. Tokyo: Japan Times, 1978.
Thirty short-short stories culled from Shinchōsha's collection of Hoshi's works, *Hōshi Shinichi no Sakuhinshū* (1974–1975). Unfortunately, many of the translations are awkward, betraying the translators' lack of familiarity with science fiction and failing as well to convey the polished style of the originals. The book remains the first English-language collection of short fiction by a Japanese SF writer. It serves by default as the most complete introduction to one of the leading figures in Japanese SF.

6-246. Inagaki, Taruho. **Issenichibyō Monogatari.** Tokyo: Kinseidō, 1923.
Inagaki Taruho, born in 1900 and best known for his essays and mainstream fiction, has held a lifelong interest in machines, aviation, and the future. He entered the second science fiction contest sponsored by *Kagaku Gahō* magazine in 1930, and prior to that published this strongly SF-oriented "novel." *Issenichibyō Monogatari,* made up of 200 brief chapters, is a gentle takeoff on *The Thousand and One Nights* using SF motifs. One of the earliest forays into science fiction by a Japanese mainstream writer. Compare with *The Arabian Nights.*

6-247. Ishihara, Fujio. **Haiuei Wakusei.** Tokyo: Hayakawa Shobō, 1967.
A set of stories by one of the few hard SF writers in Japan, whose main work is in electronics. In the title story, his best-known work, Hino and Shioda of Planetary Development Consultants land on a planet covered with a complex highway network built, and apparently abandoned on a whim, by a vanished interstellar civilization. Life on the planet has adapted to the grid of pavement and rolls rather than walks. Hino and Shioda are captured by the natives and escape after numerous adventures. It is science fiction in the 1950s mode, but harks back as well to such early Japanese humor as Jippensha Ikku's *Hizakurige* (*Shank's Mare,* 1809).

6-248. Ishikawa, Eiské. **SF Suikoden.** Tokyo: Kōdansha, 1977.
When a colony planet society begins to go to pieces, nine heroes out of the fourteenth-century Chinese classic *Shi-hu Chuan* (*Tale of the Marshes*) materialize to put things right. The heroes, it turns out, have been constructed through genetic engineering by the computer on board the colony ship itself, which is still in orbit around the planet. The novel elaborates on the *Shui-hu Chuan,* adding science fiction elements and plot devices of Ishikawa's own. This contrasts with his earlier

SF Seiyūki (*SF Journey to the West*), a nearly direct translation of the sixteenth-century *Hsi-yu Chi* (*Journey to the West,* better known in the West as *The Monkey*) into science fiction terminology. Compare with Simak's *The Goblin Reservation* (1968) and Zelazny's *Lord of Light* [4-631].

6-249. Ishikawa, Tatsuzō. **Saigo no Kyōwakoku.** Serialized in *Chūō Kōron,* 1952.
Saigo no Kyōwakoku is the only foray into the science fiction field by one of Japan's foremost modern novelists, and is also one of a mere handful of dystopias depicted in Japanese SF literature (interestingly, virtually all are by mainstream writers). Written as a collection of newspaper clippings, transcripts of newscasts, office memos, and snatches of diary entries, the book chronicles the decline of world government and its eventual replacement by a society run by the robots that handled the dirty work of the old republic. The book contains clever moments—the court litigation arising from the manufacture of white robots in Brazil, when international law stipulates that robots be of a "pleasant color inoffensive to all races" is one—but the disjointed style is hard to sustain. The main interest of the author is not the future, but the present. Compare with Orwell's *Nineteen Eighty-Four* [3-302] and Huxley's *Brave New World* [2-47].

6-250. Kajio, Shinji. **Chikyū wa Plain Yogurt.** Tokyo: Hayakawa Shobō, 1979.
A collection of short fiction by a younger writer who is an anomaly in the Japanese science fiction world—he makes no attempt to mass produce stories, a trap into which most new Japanese writers fall. Kajio shows a tender, often almost sentimental, sensibility in his fiction, which invites comparison with Bradbury's romantic moods. One of the most technically proficient new Japanese writers.

*6-251. Kanbayashi, Chōhei. **Sentō Yōsei: Yukikaze.** Tokyo: Hayakawa Shobō, 1984.
One of the books that made Kanbayashi's formidable reputation as the top SF writer of his generation, the third since World War II. Actually a collection of linked short stories, the novel describes a war with aliens who have opened a hyperspace "doorway" to the Earth at the North Pole. The aliens are intelligent machines that consider all life forms on Earth to be parasites—they are only concerned with the planet's obvious masters, its machines. The antihero of the book is the high performance fighter, Yukikaze, the name borrowed from the most famous destroyer of the old Imperial Japanese Navy, which gradually outgrows its devoted pilot as its own machine intelligence is enhanced through repeated refits. In the end, the pilot is ejected from the cockpit to die when he encumbers Yukikaze in combat. Kanbayashi's bitterly cool point of view and his cynical fascination with the machine are new to Japanese SF; *Sentō Yōsei* won the Japanese Nebula. Compare with Gibson's *Neuromancer* [4-233].

6-252. Kanbe, Musashi. **Kessen: Nihon Shirizu.** Tokyo: Hayakawa Shobō, 1976.
When Osaka's two professional baseball teams, owned respectively by the Hanshin and Hankyū private railway companies, reach the finals of the Japan series, the usual rivalries between fans of the two teams explode into a slapstick catastrophe. Kanbe Musashi, born in 1948, is one of the New Wave of young Japanese SF writers who have been exposed to science fiction by Japanese writers rather than by Western writers in translation. Kanbe shows the direct influence of Tsutsui

Yasutaka's slapstick satire. "Kessen: Nihon Shirizu" was his first published story. This collection of early works has been followed by more collections and several novels, one of which won the 1986 Japan SF Prize. Compare with Tsutsui's *Tōkaidō Sensō* [6-285].

6-253. Kawamata, Chiaki. **Genshi-gari.** Tokyo: Chūōkōron-sha, 1984.

Kawamata is an up-and-coming writer who has populated his numerous stories with gun-slinging motorcycle gangs and murderous game machines used as clandestine recruiting tests by a conniving army. His first-person characters frequently die. *Genshi-gari,* however, is far more ambitious. A government thought control enforcer with a license to kill finds himself thrown off balance and ultimately converted by an encounter with surrealistic literature. In a parallel plot that intersects with the main story, French poet André Burton is similarly disoriented by a young man with a mysterious power over words. Winner of the Japan SF Prize. Compare with Bradbury's *Fahrenheit 451* [3-61].

6-254. Kayama, Shigeru. **Oran-penteku no Fukushū.** Tokyo: Iwatani Shoten, 1946.

Scientists discover a small tribe with extrasensory powers on Sumatra, and the contact with civilization leads to the eventual destruction of the natives. Kayama Shigeru was only one of the SF writers active immediately after the war, yet his work—although not his name—is probably better known to people around the world than any other Japanese science fiction. Kayama (1909–1975) was a bureaucrat in the Japanese Ministry of Finance, making all the more remarkable his most famous creation, Godzilla, the ultimate expression of Japanese SF's war-scarred nihilism. He also created the giant insect invader Mothra, and can thus be credited with almost single-handedly spawning the flood of Japanese SF monster movies that did so much to condition the public's response to "sci-fi" in the 1950s, and even now brings an almost Pavlovian reaction to any mention of Japanese SF. *Oran-penteku no Fukushū* and its two sequels are Kayama's best works, a serious concern with civilization's effect on the noble savage tempering the rampant melodrama and wooden characters brought so faithfully to the silver screen by the Tōhō movie company. Compare with Hawkes's *Providence Island* [3-195] and Phelps's *The Winter People* (1964).

6-255. Kiodomari, Allan (pseud.). **Hikari no Tō.** Tokyo: Hayakawa Shobō, 1962.

Mysterious invaders launch a ferocious attack on Earth's major cities in 2011, then proceed to build gigantic Spires of Light in every corner of the globe. Scientists finally devise a way of penetrating the towers' defenses, only to find that the invaders are actually survivors of a horrendous nuclear war in Earth's future. They have returned to the past in a desperate effort to change the course of history and avert the future Armageddon. Born in 1921, Kiodomari founded Japan's first SF fan group, the Omega Club, in 1957, and has been instrumental in the rise of postwar Japanese SF. An accomplished linguist, he incorporated carefully thought-out future slang and linguistically justifiable transformations in grammar and pronunciation for his invaders from the future that make for an interesting comparison with Burgess's *Clockwork Orange* [3-82]; see also de Camp's *Lest Darkness Fall* [3-135].

6-256. Komatsu, Sakyō. **Chi ni wa Heiwa o.** Tokyo: Hayakawa Shobō, 1963.
The 11 stories contained here represent Komatsu's earliest work; the title story marked his SF debut when it received an honorable mention in the 1961 science fiction contest sponsored by *SF Magajin*. The story postulates that World War II did not end on August 15, 1945, but continued on through the invasion of Japan. A "mad" scientist rebels at the thought that such grim history must be fixed and immutable and travels back in time to try to create a more palatable future. The story compares and contrasts two alternative paths of human history, placing it both in the main current of Komatsu's concerns (as seen most dramatically in *Hateshinaki Nagare no Hate ni* [6-258]) and in one of the most distinctive traditions of Japanese SF. Compare with Hanmura's *Sengoku Jieitai* [6-237], Hirose's *Mainasu Zero* [6-241], Kiodomari's *Hikari no Tō* [6-255], and Toyota's *Mongoru no Zankō* [6-280]. For an interesting contrast from the side that history favored in World War II, see Cyril Kornbluth's 1958 tale "Two Dooms."

6-257. Komatsu, Sakyō. **Fukkatsu no Hi.** Tokyo: Hayakawa Shobō, 1964.
A virus developed at a British bacteriological warfare research laboratory is accidentally exposed to the air by a Soviet spy, and the disease soon sweeps the world. The virus is dormant at temperatures below $-10°C$, however, and a small band of survivors sets up home in the Antarctic. New disaster threatens when seismologists predict a giant earthquake in Alaska that will trigger a doomsday missile system. A desperate mission is sent on a nuclear submarine to Washington to disconnect the device. Komatsu's second novel quickly brought him to apocalyptic themes in a mix of motifs seen elsewhere in Stewart's *Earth Abides* [3-358], Shute's *On the Beach* [3-344], and George's *Dr. Strangelove* [3-172]. The basis of the 1980 Kadokawa movie *Virus*.

*6-258. Komatsu, Sakyō. **Hateshinaki Nagare no Hate ni.** Tokyo: Hayakawa Shobō, 1966.
A mysterious sand clock—the sand drains as it is supposed to, but the quantity on either side never changes—leads scientists to study the ancient Japanese tumulus where it was found. All the researchers either perish or disappear, and the data are lost. Similar research is disrupted over succeeding centuries, revealing only the shadowy outlines of two opposing forces in the universe, one uplifting and the other opposing the progress of evolution. When life on Earth is threatened by an unprecedented solar flare-up, alien spaceships intervene to carry the population to safety. Some of the survivors are chosen to advance to the next evolutionary stage, and one of the chosen is given the task of tracking down the antilife force through time and parallel worlds. He fuses with the last of those he pursues, his own son, and at the end of time witnesses the stirrings of a new metalife. Reduced to a memoryless shell, he is returned to Japan 50 years after the novel's beginning. The most sweeping work of Japan's premier SF writer, *Hateshinaki Nagare no Hate ni* contains all of Komatsu's major themes—humans ripped from the womb, rewriting history for a better future, human evolutionary potential— that reappear in other books and numerous essays. Compare Stapledon's *Last and First Men* [2-109] and George Zebrowski's *Macrolife* [4-625].

*6-259. Komatsu, Sakyō. **Nippon Chimbotsu.** Tokyo: Kōbunsha, 1973.
Maverick geologist Tadokoro discovers evidence of a tectonic upheaval that will

destroy the Japanese islands. He pushes his views in the face of official skepticism and succeeds in forcing the government to begin preparations for evacuating the country. In the second half of the two-volume novel, the predicted upheaval occurs and the Japanese people struggle to survive long enough to escape their sinking homeland. *Nippon Chimbotsu* sold over four million copies and was translated in severely abridged form by Michael Gallagher in 1976 as *Japan Sinks* [4-305] (later reissued in paperback as *Death of the Dragon*). Also the basis of the 1973 movie *Nippon Chimbotsu*, which was severely cut and released as *Tidal Wave* by Roger Corman's New World company. Although the translation slashes the original's still thin characterization and its meticulous scientific underpinnings, the central character of the novel is really Japanese culture and its values. Komatsu displays his journalistic eye for detail (he worked for trade journals and broadcast companies before turning to fiction), along with his sure grasp of pacing and vivid if "popular" prose. Compare with Abe's *Inter Ice Age 4* [3-1] and John Christopher's *A Wrinkle in the Skin* (1965).

6-260. Komatsu, Sakyō. **Sayonara Jupiter.** Tokyo: Sankei Shuppan, 1982.
Komatsu returns to his earlier roots in hard science fiction to describe a grandiose scheme to ignite Jupiter and make the rest of the solar system inhabitable. A best-selling book that won the Japanese Nebula Award and was made into a film with the inane title *Bye-bye, Jupiter,* the book actually predates Clarke's *2010* [4-141] by several years.

6-261. Komatsu, Sakyō. **Shuto Shōshitsu.** Tokyo: Tokuma Shoten, 1985.
Continuing his tradition of using imagined near-future disasters to point up what he considers the weaknesses of modern Japan, Komatsu uses a sprawling, two-volume work to look at the vulnerability of Japan to the collapse of modern telecommunications and computer systems. Stupendous storms and other abnormal natural phenomena combine to abruptly cut off Tokyo from the rest of the country; deprived of its nerve center, the nation's economy and society try to get by, with mixed success. The book, which won the 1985 Japan SF Prize, was the year's top seller and the basis of a movie.

6-262. Kono, Tensei. **Machi no Hakubutsushi.** Tokyo: Hayakawa Shobō, 1974.
Kono began his career as a writer of tough private eye stories, but in his "city naturalist" series he has produced a set of delicately evocative short stories that rank among the best of any Japanese SF writer. In "Torikeratopsu" ("Triceratops"), a father and his young son can see back in time to when a herd of dinosaurs lived on the site of their subdivision. In "Pasutoraru" ("Pastoral"), a father is suddenly visited by the distraught boyfriend of his daughter. The boy is trying to save the girl in the midst of a nuclear attack, but when the apparition occurs, the child is only two years old. The boy vanishes, leaving the father with the knowledge of his child's grim future. In this and other meticulously crafted stories, Kono explores the cracks in the veneer of everyday life with a skill matching the best of Bradbury.

6-263. Kurimoto, Kaori (pseud.). **Hyōto no Kamen.** Tokyo: Hayakawa Shobō, 1979.
Japanese science fiction has had nothing to match the world building of J. R. R. Tolkien and other Western fantasy writers. Kurimoto (a pen name) set out to rectify that and more when she began plotting the *Guin Saga,* a story of swords, sorcery, and very human lives in a mythical land. The central character is the leopard-headed warrior Guin, all but invincible in battle. But there is also a huge cast of supporting characters, who now are a frequent sight at Japanese SF convention costume balls. The *Guin Saga* is supposed to run for 100 volumes. *Hyōto no Kamen* was the first book; by 1986, Hayakawa Shobō had published 31, all of which had made the best-seller list. Kurimoto, one of Japan's handful of woman SF writers, has also published collections of straight SF stories, but *Guin Saga* overshadows her other work in the field. Compare with Tolkien's *Lord of the Rings.*

6-264. Mayumura, Taku. **Expo '87.** Tokyo: Hayakawa Shobō, 1968.
One of the early classics of postwar Japanese SF, helping to herald increasingly nonderivative works with a distinctively Japanese viewpoint. Completed two years before the 1970 World's Fair in Osaka, *Expo '87* is industrial science fiction that takes its cue from the years Mayumura spent in the business world. Multinational corporations are usurping control of Japan's economy, spurring the rise of rightist nationalism among Japanese industrial groups. The 1987 World's Fair becomes the symbolic focus of the battle for Japan, Inc., with both sides marshaling their forces in the economy and the mass media to dominate the proceedings. An interesting contrast with Pohl and Kornbluth's *The Space Merchants* [3-313].

*6-265. Mayumura, Taku. **Shōmetsu no Kōrin.** Tokyo: Hayakawa Shobō, 1979.
Mase PPKA4 Yukio is an elite civil servant in training. As one of his final exercises, he is entrusted with the evacuation of a heavily industrialized colony world threatened by a nova. As his work progresses, he encounters stiffening resistance from powerful special-interest groups and from the planet's original inhabitants. He is relieved of his command for incompetency, but while wandering among the natives makes a profound discovery about human nature and perceptions of reality. *Shōmetsu no Kōrin* was serialized in 33 installments in *SF Magajin* between 1976 and 1978, and received the Izumi Kyōka Award for "the literature of the imagination." The culmination of Mayumura's Governors of the Worlds series of long and short fiction, it is the best novel of one of Japanese SF's steadiest craftsmen. The Governors of the Worlds series bears comparison with Asimov's Foundation trilogy [3-19].

*6-266. Mishima, Yukio. **Utsukushii Hoshi.** Tokyo: Shinchōsha, 1962.
The most celebrated postwar Japanese novelist, Mishima Yukio (1925–1970) also possessed a deep interest in flying saucers, and through them, science fiction. *Utsukushii Hoshi* is his one SF novel, although science fiction elements can be found in his final tetralogy, *Hōjō no Umi (Sea of Fertility,* 1969–1971). A family of four north of Tokyo become convinced that they are aliens entrusted with preserving and protecting the "beautiful planet" Earth. They advertise for members to join the "Outer Space Friendship League," but in the process attract the attention of a college professor, a barber shop owner, and a student, who are equally

certain they are on mission from Signet 61 to destroy the planet. There are some strikingly beautiful evocations of nuclear holocaust in this lesser Mishima novel, which contrasts interestingly with his other novels treating with delusion and conviction, as in *Kinkakuji* (*The Golden Pavilion*, 1956).

*6-267. Mitsuse, Ryū. **Hyakuoku no Hiru, Senoku no Yoru.** Tokyo: Hayakawa Shobō, 1966.

Human history from the origins of life on Earth to the entropic end of the universe is handled in this most far-reaching of Mitsuse's novels. Plato finds the creators of Atlantis to be aliens intent on suppressing any potential competition in the galaxy. They destroy the continent in an internecine feud, but Buddha later encounters the aliens again, and a greater power, in India. Christ himself is saved from the cross to become a tool of the aliens. As the galaxy slides down the entropic scale, the search for the ultimate power controlling human destiny moves to Andromeda and a transcendence of physical reality. Mitsuse's concern with the end of human aspirations is couched in beautiful, often poetic, language, but inappropriate space opera clichés continue to appear in even his most serious work. Compare with Stapledon's *Last and First Men* [2-109].

*6-268. Mitsuse, Ryō. **Tasogare ni Kaeru.** Tokyo: Hayakawa Shobō, 1964.

Scientists working to explain the disappearance of ships traveling through the solar system uncover an alien vessel, 500 meters in diameter, buried on Pluto 12 million years ago. The ship proves to be a cyborg based on a giant alien life form; it tells the scientists of an ancient intergalactic war, and a mysterious third power that came from nowhere to exterminate the two combatants. A second ship is discovered on Earth itself, and the entire planet is destroyed as scientists seek to determine if the solar system is slated for annihilation. The survivors set up a giant deep-space antenna grid to try to find the answer, but it is blown apart by the powerful surge of energy from what they contact. Humans can only wait for their fate, naked in the face of the universe. Much of Mitsuse's work strives consciously to push a "sense of wonder" to its farthest possible extreme. *Tasogare ni Kaeru,* one of Japan's SF masterpieces, is the strongest statement of his recurring theme on humans' minor place in space and time. Compare with Clarke's *The City and the Stars* [3-98].

*6-269. Miyazawa, Kenji. **Ginga Tetsudō no Yoru** in **Miyazawa Kenji Zenshu** Tokyo: Jūjiya, 1948.

One of the best-loved works by Japanese poet and novelist Miyazawa Kenji (1896–1933), this is a fantasy written for children, reaching great depths of emotion and philosophy. It was written about 1925 following the death of Miyazawa's younger sister, but was not published until after his own death. The Milky Way is seen as the path to the afterworld; the dead ride a small train, stopping at various "stations" (stars) along the route. Lyrical and moving, it makes an intriguing contrast with the afterworld in C. S. Lewis's *The Last Battle* (1956).

6-270. Noa, Azusa. **Hana Kariudo.** Tokyo: Hayakawa Shobō, 1984.

The protagonist visits a planet in search of his missing brother and finds it a peculiar mix of the highly advanced and the archaic. As he explores the planet, which is populated in part by a race of intelligent, flowerlike creatures, he witnesses a mysterious figure on horseback cutting off the heads of flowers. His search for his brother leads him toward the heart of the mystery. Simply reciting plots does not do justice to Noa's work, which has earned him a reputation as one of the most stimulating young writers in Japan. He is also one of the most technically proficient at a time when editors are likely to say younger writers would be good if only they could learn to write literate Japanese.

6-271. Noda, Masahiro. **Ginga Kojiki Gundan.** Tokyo: Hayakawa Shobō, 1892– .
A continuing series begun in 1982 by the translator of the Star Wars novelizations, and the premier champion in Japan of good old-fashioned space opera. The Beggar's Brigade is a band of intergalactic ne'er-do-wells, who in fact are some of the only people around with hearts of gold. Through the half-dozen books in the series, they battle with the intergalactic army, the intergalactic police, and big business to help and protect the downtrodden and the little guy in the big universe. Noda is a devotee of *The Skylark of Space* [2-104], as befits the nation's most famous pulp SF collector; but he is also an earthy writer who has invested what could be standard space opera fare with a uniquely Japanese sense of the picaresque that comes straight from the back alleys of Tokyo.

6-272. Numa, Shōzō (pseud.). **Kachikujin Yapū.** Tokyo: Toshi Shuppansha, 1970.
One of the most remarkable books in modern Japanese literature, taking its place beside the works of the Marquis de Sade. A Japanese student in Germany is discussing plans for marriage and a trip to see Mount Fujiyama with his beautiful Aryan girlfriend, when a saucer-shaped vehicle piloted by a stunning white woman materializes before them. She is from a sensual Caucasian matriarchy of the future and has lost her time coordinates while being masturbated by her Kurininga, a surgically reconstructed slave designed for female oral sex. In her society, blacks are hunted as game and Orientals are altered into living furniture and "appliances." The boy and girl are transported into the future, where she quickly embraces the mores of her new world, and he is castrated and surgically rebuilt into her personal slave. He worships her as his shining goddess, joyfully accepting the extinction of his personality, and accompanies her and her lover on a trip to Fujiyama. Both a stunning display of paranoia toward the West manifested less blindingly in books such as Yano's *Chikyū Reinen* [6-291], and the most extreme example of the assaults of conventional humanism advocated by such writers and radical philosophers as Mishima Yukio and Shibusawa Tatsuhiko. Compare with Sade's *Juliette* and the castle of the giant Minsk.

6-273. Ōhara, Mariko. **Ningen no Yō ni Aruita Neko.** Tokyo: Hayakawa Shobō, 1982.
Ōhara is a young woman writer who seems to be following the career path of Arai Motoko [6-233], but whose fiction could not be more different. The cat of the title story is not a fluffy Persian, but a genetically engineered intelligent life form (there was a cat somewhere back there) in a far-future galaxy populated with crowds of generally disagreeable aliens—not monsters, but just mean-minded soldiers and bureaucrats going about their daily rounds with a minimum of charity. Ōhara's cats and angel cats (the product of symbiotic relationships

with a breed of manmade flying creatures, part animal, mostly machine) are generally losers, and rarely good sports about it. Her hedonistic and hermaphroditic humans play fast and loose with their sexuality. When the mix of decadent lassitude and tech so high that its origins have been forgotten clicks, it really clicks. When it doesn't, it merely seems turgid and precocious. Compare with Gibson's *Neuromancer* [4-233] and *Blade Runner*.

*6-274.　Oshikawa, Shunrō. **Kaitei Gunkan.** Tokyo: Hakubunkan, 1900.
The book that brought science fiction to Japan. It was preceded by ten years by Yano Ryūkei's *Ukishiro Monogatari* (*Tale of the Floating Fortress*), but outclassed it in scope and popularity. A Japanese naval officer, disenchanted with the Japanese government's ineffectiveness in the face of Western imperialism, retires to an isolated island to prepare for the inevitable war with the whites. The star of his futuristic armory is the submersible battle cruiser *Denkōtei*, which battles anonymous Caucasian pirates in the first volume and proceeds to smash the Russians, British, French, and others in succeeding adventures. The mix of technology, militarism, and racism was tremendously popular at the time, earning Oshikawa (1876–1914) the title of grandfather of Japanese SF. Compare with Verne's *Twenty Thousand Leagues under the Sea* [1-95].

*6-275.　Ōtomo, Katsuhiro. **Dōmu.** Tokyo: Futabasha, 1983.
When the Japan SF Writers Club sat down to choose the best SF novel of 1983, they didn't. They chose Ōtomo's *Dōmu* instead, perhaps the most perfect science fiction comic yet published in Japan. The story of a psychic struggle between a young girl and a senile old man with paranormal powers in a vast, inhuman housing development in modern-day Tokyo, *Dōmu* caused a revolution in Japanese cartooning; Ōtomo clones have been appearing ever since. *Dōmu* is a visual novel that could not have been duplicated in print; the same can be said, to a lesser degree, of his other science fiction works, including a wry story of Japanese mercenaries in a Sino-Soviet war and a massive series about young people with paranormal powers in a postholocaust Japan.

6-276.　Satō, Haruo. **"Nonsharan Kiroku."** *Kaizō,* January 1929.
One of the earliest dystopias in Japanese SF literature, written by the famous poet Satō Haruo (1892–1964). The protagonist lives among the lowest classes of a future society, 300 feet underground at the footings of a towering metropolis. Satō sympathetically explores their painful existence in this novella and finds in the planting of a rose far beneath the surface of the Earth a symbol for indomitable human spirit. Contemporary Japanese society comes in for bitter satire. Critics found the story stylistically difficult, but it was one of only a few of Satō's many short stories that the poet chose for a collection of his own best works. Compare with Huxley's *Brave New World* [2-47].

6-277.　Suzuki, Izumi. **Onna to Onna no Yo no Naka ni.** Tokyo: Hayakawa Shobō, 1978.
This set of stories by one of Japan's first woman science fiction writers stays close to present-day themes and concerns, with a thin veneer of science fiction motifs. In "Amai Ohanashi" ("Just a Little Spoiled"), the heroine falls for an intense young man who claims to be an alien. She is never sure whether to believe him,

and they part without making love. Later she finds that he has somehow gotten her pregnant. Suzuki, who died in 1986, was best known for her suspense fiction and her celebrity appearances on Japanese television.

6-278. Tanaka, Kōji. **Daimetsubō.** Tokyo: Shōdensha, 1975.
A global outbreak of the red tide pushes an overpopulated world over the brink of famine. A euthanasia cult gains popularity in Japan, but a television director, in the process of putting together a documentary supporting the movement, stumbles on evidence of an unprecedented plot. Tanaka's first novel reflects his experience as a television director and adds yet another scenario to the long list of Japanese apocalypses. Interestingly, it also adds another superconspiracy to a growing list of giant plots found in such books as Hanmura's *Ishi no Ketsumyaku* [6-235] and Yamada's *Kamigari* [6-288]. Younger Japanese writers seem particularly drawn to the theme, with the CIA or its equivalents making frequent appearances in both Tanaka's and Yamada's books and short stories. Compare with Harrison's *Make Room! Make Room!* [4-257] and Brunner's *Stand on Zanzibar* [4-92].

6-279. Tanaka, Kōji. **Isei no Hito.** Tokyo: Hayakawa Shobō, 1976.
A free-lance journalist joins an expedition in search of prehistoric animals on the upper reaches of the Amazon. He weathers the perilous journey with preternatural composure, only to disappear without a trace on a mission of his own. He is later encountered in the Himalayas, in communes, in the Mexican desert, always observing the people around him with a stoic, clinical eye. He is actually an android dispatched to prepare a report on humanity that will determine Earth's fate. These eight interconnected stories are the classic statement of Tanaka's virile but detached heroes, and also show to advantage his tightly plotted adventures and rapid style, which is sometimes accused of reading like a translation. Tanaka was born in Seoul in 1942; his father was a follower of the postwar mainstream novelist Dazai Osamu, but also wrote some primitive SF before committing suicide at Dazai's grave. Since his debut in *Uchūjin* in 1973, Tanaka has become one of the most prolific Japanese SF writers, ranging from heroic fantasy to ocean adventures. Compare with Doyle's *The Lost World* [1-31].

6-280. Toyota, Aritsune. **Mongoru no Zankō.** Tokyo: Kadokawa Shoten, 1967.
In a world controlled by the descendants of the Mongol Empire, Shigurt Lorenson commits a murder and, as a Caucasian, is forced to go underground. Linking up with a secret quasi-religious organization, he learns how the Mongols conquered the Western world in the thirteenth and fourteenth centuries and resolves to change the course of history. He steals a Mongol time machine and journeys back in time, where his presence by itself is enough to begin to disrupt history as he knows it; the arrival of a member of a mysterious "Time Patrol" further accelerates the collapse of the empire. But a trip ahead in time shows only the spectacle of war and slaughter perpetrated this time by Caucasians, leaving the heroes to wonder what has been the point of their efforts. The most complete of Toyota's many time-patrol stories, this novel also hints at the author's strong interest in ethnology and cross-cultural contact, which has manifested itself in a number of powerful essays and short stories. Compare with Williamson's *The Legion of Time* [2-135].

6-281. Toyota, Aritsune. **Taimu Surippu Daisensō.** Tokyo: Kadokawa Shoten, 1975.
Transmissions reaching Japan in the wake of a light earthquake revert to those received just before the attack on Pearl Harbor. The tremor was not an earthquake, but a "timequake" in which Japan alone has slid back in time. Japan immediately breaks its ties with the Axis, but a suspicious America launches a surprise attack on Tokyo Harbor. Japan wins the war by dropping an atomic bomb on Washington, but another timequake sends the country back to the arrival of Commodore Perry in 1853. More quakes follow, gradually skidding the islands toward destruction. One of the representative works of a member of the hard core of postwar Japanese SF authors. Compare with Hanmura's *Sengoku Jieitai* [6-237] and Dickson's *Time Storm* [4-183].

*6-282. Tsutsui, Yasutaka. **Dassō to Tsuiseki no Samba.** Tokyo: Hayakawa Shobō, 1972.
Considered by many to be the best work of one of Japan's foremost modern writers, this is a slapstick commentary on the author's battles with space, time, and the "informational society." Lacking a coherent plot, the novel begins with the author's being found suitable to become an SF writer by a job-suitability testing office. He proceeds through the kidnapping of his wife and ultimately programs himself into a world-controlling computer. Tsutsui has created a small mountain of works ranging from juvenile adventure to humor magazines. At his humorous best, he invites comparison with Vonnegut; in his darker moods, with Malzberg, whose *Herovit's World* [4-356] makes an interesting contrast.

6-283. Tsutsui, Yasutaka. **Kazoku Hakkei.** Tokyo: Shinchōsha, 1972.
Nanachan is an 18-year-old maid who is able to read other people's minds. Her progress through a series of households in this book and two sequels sets the stage for Tsutsui to puncture the pretensions of modern Japanese life and fill out his own depiction of women as the source of humanity's life force and "godliness," albeit a jealous godliness. Nanachan's experiences grow more extravagant as the series progresses, and she is joined by a boyfriend who also has extrasensory powers. One of the most popular and penetrating of the author's satires on the human condition, and a Naoki Award nominee in 1972. Compare with Silverberg's treatment of ESP in *Dying Inside* [4-502].

6-284. Tsutsui, Yasutaka. **Kyojin-tachi.** Tokyo: Chūō Kōron-sha, 1981.
Tsutsui carries his preoccupation with writing significant literature, and his fascination with the French New Wave avant-garde, to an extreme. When the protagonist loses consciousness, for example, Tsutsui simply leaves the next few pages blank. But Tsutsui is too accomplished a writer to take such techniques too seriously. *Kyojin-tachi* is good at what it sets out to do, though it is not particularly interested in being science fiction. It is an interesting example of what happens when an accomplished SF writer moves upmarket. Compare with Vonnegut.

*6-285. Tsutsui, Yasutaka. **Tōkaidō Sensō.** Tokyo: Hayakawa Shobō, 1964.
The Tōkaidō is the narrow strip of land along the coast between Tokyo and Osaka; the war breaks out for no clear reason between Japanese Self Defense Forces stationed in the two respective regions. Thirteen short stories written be-

tween 1961 and 1964 can in retrospect be seen as giving clear indication of all the various themes Tsutsui would continue to explore in future work. Included are Darwinism, Freudian psychology, and Marxism, all dealt with in a hand both lightly satirical and on occasion grimly pessimistic. The title story expands easily into *Yonjūhachioku Oku no Mōsō* [6-286]. The best collection of early Tsutsui. Compares at one extreme with Goulart and Lafferty, and at the other with such Silverberg short stories as "When We Went to See the End of the World."

6-286. Tsutsui, Yasutaka. **Yonjūhachioku Oku no Mōsō.** Tokyo: Hayakawa Shobō, 1965.
Tsutsui's first novel is a slapstick look at the mass media. In the uncomfortably near future, television has become the dominant force in society and is constantly on the lookout for spectacles to cover. When a minor dispute arises between Japanese and South Korean fishermen, media personalities leap aboard a seiner and manage to escalate the argument into a full-scale war. Compare with Spinrad's media treatment in *Bug Jack Barron* [4-525].

*6-287. Unno, Jūza. **Chikyū Tōnan.** Tokyo: Popurasha, 1936.
Vacationing physicist Ozumi searches for a missing child, only to find the boy enlarged to giant size and confined on the estate of an eccentric scientist. The scientist is in the employ of aliens, who are scheming to pull Earth closer to their planet. Alerted by Ozumi's announcement of the plot, humanity puts aside its differences to unite and defeat the aliens. Unno (1897–1949) was the best-known prewar Japanese SF writer and one of only a handful to have influenced the postwar SF community. His novels were amateurish by modern standards, but some of his short fiction showed greater promise. "Jūhachiji no Ongakuyoku" ("The Six O'Clock Music Bath") leveled a bitter blast against authoritarianism and thought control on the brink of Japan's invasion of China. Compare with Burroughs's *The Moon Maid* [2-11].

6-288. Yamada, Masaki. **Kamigari.** Tokyo: Hayakawa Shobō, 1975.
Archaeologists excavating a Japanese tumulus find a mysterious inscription in an unknown language. Using linguistic computers to decipher the script, they find it is a metalanguage used by the Gods themselves—not quite omnipotent beings who have worked since the dawn of history to keep humans suppressed. The researchers must battle the CIA for their data, while resisting the assaults, both physical and psychic, of the Gods. The struggle to end the hegemony of the Gods continues through several sequels. The most ambitious work by one of the best of a new generation of Japanese SF writers (Yamada was born in 1950). His early books are clogged with technological gimmickry; *Kamigari* has higher ambitions, although a somewhat simplistic approach. He has gone on to become one of Japanese SF's strongest idea men, and has won several SF awards, including the Japan SF Prize for his *Saigo no Teki* (*The Last Enemy*). Compare with del Rey's "For I Am a Jealous People" (1954).

*6-289. Yamano, Kōichi. **X Densha de Ikō.** Tokyo: Shinshokan, 1965.
Seven of the earliest stories by Yamano, gathered in his first collection. The title story is one of the best Japanese SF short stories, dealing with the growing alienation of the misfit hero as he pursues an invisible train—or is it a misfit alien?—

racing at ever greater speed over Japan's entire rail system. At first aiding the authorities in their efforts to catch the "X Train," the protagonist comes to identify with the quarry, only to be abandoned by it as well in the end. Yamano, long Japan's leading SF iconoclast, is mainly interested in human "inner space," rather than outer space. Heavily influenced by Ballard and by his own experiences in the Japanese radical student movement, he was the leading Japanese proponent in Japan of the New Wave movement. More recent stories and novels dwell heavily on individual isolation within society. Compare with Ballard's *Low Flying Aircraft* (1976).

6-290. Yamao, Yūko. **Yume no Sumu Machi.** Tokyo: Hayakawa Shobō, 1978. Born in 1956, Yamao made a promising debut as one of the best of Japan's women SF writers, but several years later all but dropped out of sight. Her themes and techniques come as much from the Japanese avant-garde as from the science fiction community, and her sometimes excessively intellectual prose, thick with symbols, also reflects this allegiance. This first collection of her work nonetheless contains several powerful stories that systematically assault conventional wisdom, using surrealistic techniques and occasionally grotesque characters. Compare with Ballard's "The Sound Sweep" and *Vermilion Sands* [4-38].

6-291. Yano, Tetsu. **Chikyū Reinen.** Tokyo: Hayakawa Shobō, 1969.
Nuclear war breaks out between the superpowers, and when the fallout settles, Japan is one of the few industrialized nations left with some semblance of government, albeit *sans* Tokyo. The remnants of the United Nations direct Japan to restore law and order to the west coast of the United States and it does, as naked children beg chewing gum from Japanese soldiers in jeeps, and American women offer their bodies in exchange for chocolate bars. Yano is the patriarch of Japanese science fiction, a longtime head of the Japan SF Writers Club and the first fan to visit the United States after the war. While not the best of several hundred works Yano has penned or translated, *Chikyū Reinen* is a fascinatingly unabashed recounting of a popular Japanese SF fantasy (see Toyota's *Taimu Surippu Daisensō* [6-281]. It also reflects the Japanese SF preoccupation with "what if?" as opposed to "what will?" that turns the genre more toward time travel and parallel worlds than world building on the order of Herbert's *Dune* [4-268].

*6-292. Yano, Tetsu. **Origami Uchūsen no Densetsu.** Tokyo: Hayakawa Shobō, 1978.
From the opening pages, with paper airplanes made by the madwoman Osen drifting through the mist around a secluded Japanese mountain village, this book sets itself apart as one of Yano's most evocative and carefully crafted works. Osen may be a survivor from an alien spaceship stranded centuries before. She and her son Eimon possess extrasensory powers; when he moves to the city he finds another group of similarly gifted people. An alien arrives in search of the survivors of the ancient crash, one of whom was a psychotic killer. Yano's imagery is at its best in this novel, and the mystery of the aliens and Eimon's own descent is cleverly handled with clues placed in old Japanese folk songs and place-names. Compare with Clement's *Needle* [3-110] and Bester's *The Demolished Man* [3-30].

6-293. Yumemakura, Baku. **Genken Shōnen Kimaira.** Tokyo: Asahi Sonorama, 1982.

Yumemakura struck a gold mine when he hit on the idea of using demons from Buddhism and other Japanese and Eastern mythology to populate his books. In other particulars, they remain violent occult horror fantasies packed with lurid sex. The Kimaira series, for juvenile publisher Asahi Sonorama, started him in the business, and is relatively restrained. It is his adult books, frequently serialized in popular weekly magazines, that are constantly on the best-seller list. When snowed under by deadlines, this mild and unassuming writer has been known to churn out 1,000 manuscript pages a month.

6-294. Yumeno, Kyūsaku. **Dogura Magura.** Tokyo: Gendai Kyōyō Bunko, 1935.

Yumeno Kyūsaku (1889–1936) spent ten years writing *Dogura Magura;* he called it the book he was born to write. The narrator awakes in a hospital room unable to remember even his name. He is told he was being used in an experiment by a psychiatrist who has since died. As doctors work to restore his memory, he finds that he may have been an insane murderer and that he may or may not have died. Then the psychiatrist reappears. He says he had been conducting research into the transmigration of the soul, but the ambiguous ending leaves the narrator unsure whether he is himself real or merely an illusion. In its concern with reincarnation and communication with the dead, *Dogura Magura* stands in the line of the fantastic and supernatural in Japanese literature reaching back to the *Genji Monogatari* (*Tale of Genji,* A.D. c.1100) of Murasaki Shikibu and the *Makura Sōshi* (*Pillow Book,* A.D. c.1000) of Sei Shōnagon, and forward to Mishima Yukio's tetralogy *Hōjō no Umi* (see *Utsukushii Hoshi* [6-266]). Yumeno, however, combines these themes with a powerful indictment of the immorality of modern science. Compare with Philip José Farmer's *Traitor to the Living* (1973).

Anthologies

*6-295. Fukushima, Masami, and Takashi Ishikawa, eds. **Nihon no SF.** Tokyo: Hayakawa Shobō, 1969.

A two-volume anthology, one of the first ever issued of Japanese science fiction. The first volume deals with early Japanese science fiction, the second with works from the 1960s. The modern volume in particular is a good introduction to the early works of most of the SF writers prominent in Japan today, as well as some that are less well known. Included are Tsutsui's "Betonamu Kankō Kōsha," Ishihara's "Haiuei Wakusei," and Hanmura's "Shūkaku," his first published work. Also included among the 35 stories is "Akichi," by the major mainstream novelist Kita Morio (1927–), translated as "The Empty Field" in the Roger Elwood anthology *Omega* (1973). The two books are the last in the 35-volume Hyakawa Shobō *Sekai SF Zenshū* (*Complete World SF*).

*6-296. Hayakawa, Shobō, ed. **SF Magajin Serekushon.** Tokyo: Hayakawa Shobō.

With the demise of Tsutsui's *Best Japanese SF* anthologies, this new set of anthologies is the best thing around for readers without the time to read through mountains of magazines. The editors have selected the "best" of the fiction published in *SF Magajin* each year, beginning in 1981. In practice, however, this means the best story by any single writer during the year; quality by author is sometimes extremely uneven. Although the selection reflects only one magazine's editorial policy, the anthologies offer the best available overview of current tastes in Japanese SF.

*6-297. Tsutsui, Yasutaka, ed. **Nihon SF Besuto Shūsei.** Tokyo: Tokuma Shoten, 1976–1978.
This series of annual anthologies is still one of the most accessible sources of Japanese SF short stories for the foreign reader. Published editions cover the years 1971 to 1975, with a single volume devoted to the best of the 1960s. A typical year's edition contains eight to ten short stories, a pair of SF comic strips, and an essay by Tsutsui reviewing the year's developments and providing biographical background on each author or artist represented. Tsutsui has been chided for being too idiosyncratic in his choices, and also for including minor works or essays simply to give recognition to prominent people in the SF writing community or fandom. However, the series is invaluable as a rapid introduction to the range of SF available in Japan.

*6-298. Yokota, Junya, ed. **Sengo Shoki Nihon SF Besuto Shūsei.** Tokyo: Tokuma Shoten, 1978.
A two-volume anthology that does for the period 1945 to 1960 what Tsutsui Yasutaka's *Nihon SF Besuto Shūsei* [6-297] does for 1960 and beyond. Yokota is Japan's premier SF archaeologist; here he provides a representative story from each of the writers, many of them obscure, active in the formative period of postwar Japanese SF. Included is the Kayama Shigeru (see *Oran-penteku no Fukushū* [6-254]) short story that gave rise to Mothra of Tōhō movie fame. The format follows closely that established in Tsutsui's annual anthologies.

Nonfiction

6-299. Fukushima, Masami. **SF no Sekai.** Tokyo: Sanseidō, 1977.
The revised and updated version of Fukushima's 1965 *SF Nyūmon (Introduction to SF)*. The book devotes separate chapters to major science fiction themes, discussing possible scientific evidence in support of some of them and giving brief descriptions of significant novels and short stories where they have been used. A list of the "Best 100" SF novels available in Japanese, including some by Japanese writers, is appended. A serious, although now dated, effort to widen SF readership in Japan.

*6-300. Ishihara, Fujio. **SF Tosho Kaisetsu Sōmokuroku.** Tokyo: Shambleau Press, 1969– .
A monumental listing of all the science fiction published in Japan since World War II, both in translation and by Japanese authors. Prepared as a labor of love and updated in a second volume by the author, who is also a publishing science fiction author (see Ishihara's *Haiuei Wakusei* [6-247]). Published in a very limited edition, this valuable reference work is now almost impossible to find.

6-301. Ishikawa, Takashi. **SF no Jidai: Nihon SF no Taidō to Tenbō.** Tokyo: Kisō Tengaisha, 1977.
Critical essays and reprints of columns about Japanese SF by the country's lead-

ing science fiction critic. Ishikawa taught the first science fiction course at prestigious Tokyo University and has published several collections of his own short fiction, most notably *Sekai kara Kotoba o Hikeba* (*If You Took the Words from the World*, 1974). There are essays on important Japanese writers, Japanese SF history, and world SF, as well as a long section of monthly news columns and yearly reports from *SF Magajin* and literary yearbooks. The latter provide a valuable overview of recent Japanese SF history and also mention in passing articles on SF in other publications. The bulk of the material first appeared in the 1960s, but the book remains an excellent resource work on Japanese SF.

*6-302. Ishikawa, Takashi, and Norio Itoh, eds. **Sekai no SF Bungaku Sōkai-setsu.** Tokyo: Jiyū Kokuminsha, 1978. Rev., expanded ed., 1986.
Not as comprehensive as the title suggests, this remains an excellent reference work providing synopses and author information (up to two full pages for major works) on hundreds of novels, short-story collections, and outstanding single stories from around the world. Particularly valuable to a Western reader are the nearly 100 entries on works by Japanese authors. Ishikawa is Japan's leading SF critic; Itoh is close behind and is also one of Japan's best translators.

6-303. Kasai, Kiyoshi. **Kikai-jikake no Yume.** Tokyo: Kōdansha, 1982.
A work by one of a new generation of science fiction critics and a landmark in Japanese science fiction criticism, as it goes beyond endless discussions of the books themselves to offer occasionally provocative views on the place of science fiction in Western philosophy and history. Not everyone agrees with Kasai's views, but a great many Japanese SF aficionados have read them. He deals mainly with Western authors, from Verne to Le Guin, in this collection of essays.

6-304. SF Yearbook of Japan Editorial Committee, eds. **Nihon SF Nenkan.** Tokyo: Shinjidai-sha.
An annual overview of the year in science fiction, including lists of all SF books, short stories, comics, and plays published in Japan, both original and in translation; capsule reviews of important works; and summaries of fan activities. The first yearbook, published in 1981 and covering the events of 1980, was issued at the 1981 Japan Science Fiction Convention. It has since become the responsibility of the publishers of the SF critical journal *SF no Hon* (*The Book of SF*).

6-305. Yokota, Junya. **Nihon SF Koten Koten.** Tokyo: Hayakawa Shobō, 1980.
What will be a three-volume collection of essays, likely to remain for years the definitive resource book on early Japanese science fiction. Yokota Junya has spent years researching the authors, both prominent and obscure, who wrote SF in Japan prior to the postwar resurgence. This book is a compilation of a column that runs regularly in *SF Magajin*. Yokota's style is flip, and there is considerable extraneous information, but the material on the authors and their work is solid, interesting, and seemingly endless.

Italian SF

Gianni Montanari

According to Homer, "even where sleep is concerned, too much is a bad thing." That could refer to Italian science fiction—"the sleeping muse." With the exception of the last 30 years, Italian SF is largely unknown and unexplored, even by Italians. Much science fiction in its modern meaning has been published in Italy since the 1950s, but Italian critics of SF have enjoyed a sort of enchanted sleep.

Italian proto-SF incorporates the expected utopias and fantastic voyages and includes such works as Dante's *Commedia* (1307–1321), Sannazaro's *Arcadia* (1501–1504), Ariosto's *Orlando Furioso* (1516–1532), Folengo's *Baldus* (1517), Fracastoro's *Syphilis* (1530), Doni's *I Mondi* (1552–1553), and Agostini's *I Dialoghi dell'Infinito* (1583–1590). With the exception of these works and a very few others in the early seventeenth century, the period between 1650 and the second half of the nineteenth century is largely unexplored in terms of early SF. And when you consider that the cited works are well-known "literary" writings, discussed in many histories of Italian literature, you find also that nobody had to *look* for them; very rarely have Italian critics been inclined to search for examples of early SF during that period. A few have been unearthed, but how many still lie unknown in libraries?

The years immediately after 1860 mark a sort of temporary break in the political storm of the Risorgimento, and the fulfilled hope of an Italy at last partially

Editor's Note: Piergiorgio Nicolazzini provided some assistance for this section and wrote notes 8 and 9 and annotations 6-308, 6-315, 6-320, 6-321, 6-333, 6-338, 6-339, and 6-342.

restored and united gave encouragement to writers and printers. Not yet "scientific fiction," but more prone to utopian views and "fantastic" contacts with imaginary lands are some interesting works: Folliero de Luna's *I Misteri Politici della Luna* (1860) and Tarchetti's *Racconti Fantastici* (1860), Ghislanzoni's *Abrakadabra* (1864–1884), Dossi's *La Colonia Felice* [6-307], Grifoni's *Dalla Terra alle Stelle* [6-309], Emilio Salgari's *Duemila Leghe sotto l'America* (1888), and in 1897 Paolo Mantegazza's *L'Anno 3000* [6-314]. In 1884, *Il Giornale Illustrato dei Viaggi e delle Avventure di Terra e di Mare* began weekly publication in Milan and, shortly after, *Il Giornale Illustrato dei Viaggi.* Many French authors like Verne, Boussenard, and Aimard appeared in their pages, and their example was slowly imitated by Italian writers. These adventure magazines continued into the new century, which saw the appearance of many indigenous writers, especially after the founding of a famous weekly, *La Domenica del Corriere*[1] on January 8, 1899. Other new periodicals also began, many for young readers, such as *Letture per la Gioventù, Il Novellino,* and *Il Corriere dei Piccoli,* and there was an increasing interest in anticipatory fiction.

Enrico Novelli, better known under his pseudonym, Yambo, wrote many serials, such as *Atlantide* (1901), *Gli Esploratori dell'Infinito* (1906), and *La Colonia Lunare* (1908) for his juvenile audience; while Emilio Salgari returned with his masterpiece, *Le Meraviglie del Duemila* [6-323], as well as two other novels dealing with formidable airships, *I Figli dell'Aria* (1904) and *Il Re dell'Aria* (1907). One of his former collaborators, Luigi Motta, began his own career with novels that showed a genuine interest in scientific speculation, such as *L'Onda Turbinosa* (1910), *Il Tunnel Sottomarino* [6-319], and *Il Vascello Aereo* (1914), later followed by other works of interest.[2]

During these early years comics began to appear in Italian periodicals, but without balloons and with the text in the form of captions. SF comics in Italy began in the 1930s with *Brick Bradford, Buck Rogers,* and *Flash Gordon,* all of which had a deep influence on the Italian comic field.[3]

Between the two world wars, there was in Italy a relative abundance of SF having very little in common with the American and British types then appearing in the pages of magazines totally unknown in Italy.[4] The works of Wells and especially Verne, were, of course, known, as well as those of other French authors, but until the 1950s the whole of American SF was to remain without readers or fans in Italy. American comics, which were very popular in the second half of the 1930s until the Fascist regime decided to censor them, soon influenced their Italian counterparts,[5] but had little influence on fiction. Since their modern beginning, Italian writers preferred to deal with anticipation and speculation from a "softer" point of view, leaving out most "harder" approaches.

In 1952, American SF came to Italy, along with the first Italian magazine, *Scienza Fantastica,* and the first Italian series, I Romanzi di Urania. Magazines then and now had relatively brief lives, but publishers' series—collections of novels similar to DAW or Ace paperbacks—soon proliferated. From 1952 to 1979, Italy gave birth to 71 different SF series and 20 SF magazines with a total of 2,256 books and 427 issues.[6] From the beginning, every publisher and editor tried to gain readers with heavy cuts and adaptations of the original works, oversimplifying themes, and deleting whole passages deemed "too difficult" for an Italian readership unaccustomed to such stories. The very popular and "secluded" vision of speculative fiction adopted then was generally successful, but neatly left out all those Italian writers whose SF had a more literary flavor. Publishers insisted that works be very similar to American ones after cutting and adaptation, including the use of pseudonyms suggesting American authorship. The Italian "age of the alias" began with a startling wave of pseudo-American writers whose names were featured by almost every magazine or publisher series: from 1954 to 1967 (the year of the first great crisis, by which time only two series survived), specialized publishers printed 114 Italian SF novels, but only 11 with the real names of their authors (and sometimes these were foreign-sounding names).

Prolific pseudonymous writers were Roberta Rambelli (14 novels, 1959–1962, five pseudonyms), Luigi Naviglio (10 novels, 1963–1967, two pseudonyms), Gianfranco Briatore (7 novels, 1959–1962, three pseudonyms), Luigi Rapuzzi (best known as L. R. Johannis, 6 novels, 1954–1958, two pseudonyms), and Ugo Malaguti (4 novels, 1961–1965, as Hugh Maylon), whose later works were much better. Most of these works appeared in the series I Romanzi del Cosmo, which included 202 books in nine years; 42 were Italian novels under pseudonyms. Very rarely were they, and others written for an equally undemanding market, of any critical or thematic interest. Only some works of Rapuzzi, who launched in Italy the vogue of "archaeological" SF (soon imitated by Hugh Maylon), show some originality and interest.

The vogue for pseudonyms disappeared about 1968, when the SF market was already badly weakened—only two series survived alone for some years, Urania and Galassia—and few publishers seemed inclined to venture into it. But in the following decade, the practice ceased: from 1968 to 1979, all 30 Italian novels were published under the real names of their authors. Among the few who preferred their names untouched are Sandro Sandrelli, primarily a short-story writer, who started the fine *Interplanet* anthologies (seven books, 1962–1965) devoted to Italian SF, and Lino Aldani (although some of his stories appeared with the anagrammatical signature N. L. Janda), author of the first clear Italian survey of SF, *La Fantascienza* [6-329], one of the first analyses recognizing other European contributions to the field. Aldani also founded *Futuro* (eight issues, 1963–1964), the first magazine for Italian authors. Other writers retaining their own names included Mauro Miglieruolo, Piero Prosperi, Gilda Musa, and Gustavo Gasparini, all primarily writers of short fiction. Sandrelli and Aldani are probably the most appealing and successful authors of the first modern wave of Italian science fiction. Sandrelli, alas, abandoned fiction at the end of the 1960s, leaving many stories and two collections, *I Ritorni di Cameron MacClure* (1962, a short novel and nine stories) and *Caino dello Spazio* [6-324]. Aldani also left fiction during the same period and after a remarkable collection of 12 stories, *Quarta Dimensione* (1964), but luckily returned in 1976 with a wonderful novel, *Quando le Radici* [6-306] and other stories.

Meanwhile, Italian mainstream authors wrote SF,[7] but always denied that their works had anything in common with *fantascienza*, a world of ill-repute, a disdain that caused their works to be largely ignored by Italian SF fans, events having close parallels in the United States. After the deep crisis in 1967–1968, the early 1970s saw a partial revival led by Vittorio Curtoni and Gianni Montanari, whose Galassia series included—among many foreign works—seven novels, three anthologies, and one collection by Italian writers in the years 1970–1973.

These books revealed that a distinctively Italian science fiction was still alive and well, and also very different in theme and approach from American or British SF. Technology and hard SF, the inheritance of the Campbellian era, together with "gadget" or "gimmick" stories, were ignored in favor of an emphasis on changes in the social order and in humans, including political and psychological values. In this resulting "literature of change," the visions of the future were often dark. Among those who made their debut or who reappeared were Piero Prosperi, Mauro Miglieruolo, Vittorio Catani, Vittorio Curtoni, and Gianni Montanari. The second half of the 1970s was also to bring back the names Gilda Musa, Anna Rinonapoli, Giuseppe Pederiali, and Ugo Malaguti, with the more recent names Livio Horrakh, Remo Guerrini, Luigi Menghini, and Daniela Piegai.[8]

Italian critics of SF prefer to emphasize the relatively wide audience for space operas and help to reinforce the impression that SF in Italy has regressed to the 1950s, thanks also to a large exploitation of Japanese cartoons by Italian television. The only exception among the critics is Sergio Solmi, who devoted to SF some interesting and perceptive essays, later collected in *Della Favola, del Viaggio e di Altre Cose* [6-340]. In recent times, the academic world has also shown some interest in SF: Carlo Pagetti at the University of Pescara, Valerio Fissore and Ruggero Bianchi at Turin, and Luigi Russo at Palermo. But even their published essays and articles or introductions to books deal primarily or only with Anglo-American science fiction. Nobody has so far paid sufficient attention to Italian SF. The critics remain somnolent, and vindicating Homer.[9]

Notes

1. *La Domenica del Corriere* published many serial novels that have not been adequately surveyed. Among these works in the vein of the mysterious and the extraordinary: Virginio Appiani's *Le Straordinarie Avventure del Capitano José Cabral* (1901) and *I Segreti della Morta* (1902), Carlo Dadone's *Il Barbiere dei Morti* (1901), Maurizio Basso's *L'Invasione di Tricupi* (1902), Giustino L. Ferri's *La Fine del Secolo XX* (1906), Comandante X's *La Guerra d'Europa: 1921– 23* (1912), and G. P. Cerretti's *L'Impero del Cielo* (1918). Sometimes these novels were reprinted in the series Il Romanzo Mensile, which was founded in 1903 to collect the serials *La Domenica del Corriere* and the *Corriere della Sera*, the parent newspaper, anticipating by some decades the cheap paperbacks of today.
2. Luigi Motta (1881–1955) was one of the true forefathers of Italian science fiction. Other works include *Il Raggio Naufragatore* (1926), *La Principessa delle Rose* (1930), *I Giganti dell'Infinito* (1930) and the sequel *La Battaglia dei Ciclopi* (1935), *L'Isola di Ferro* (1936), and *Quando Si Fermò la Terra* (1956).
3. Among the better specimens: Nino Salvaneschi's *La Rivolta del 2023* (1924), Cesare Sacchetti's *Gli Uomini dell'Ombra* (1926), Armando Silvestri's *La Meravigliosa Avventura* (1927) and *Il Signore della Folgore* (1931), G. Stocco's *Il Riformatore del Mondo* (1927), Vittorio Bravetta's *La Mummia in Fondo al Mare* (1928), Edgardo Baldi's *La Macchina dai Raggi Blu* (1929), Giorgio Cicogna's *I Cechi e le Stelle* (1931), Calogero Ciancimino and Luigi Motta's *Il Prosciugamento del Mediterraneo* (1932), Ugo Berni Scotti's *Il Mago dell'Energia*

(1933), Gastone Simoni's *L'Idolo d'Acciaio* (1934), Calogero Ciancimino's *Il Pirata dell'Aria* (1935) and *Le Bare di Granito* (1935), Giorgio Scerbanenco's *Il Paese Senza Cielo* (1938), Gustavo Reisolo's *La Disfatta dei Mostri* (1940), Mario Soldati's *La Verità sul Caso Motta* (1941), Giovanni Bottinelli's *Fantasie Cosmiche* (1941), and Guido Pusinich's *La Fabbrica degli Uomini Alati* (1945).

4. Armando Silvestri, in what is perhaps the only essay of some interest on Italian science fiction before the 1950s ("La Narrativa Fantasica in Italia fino al 1945," an appendix to the anthology published by Fanucci, *Porte sul Futuro*, Rome, 1978), maintains that in the 1930s it was possible to buy American magazines at the international newsstands of the larger Italian cities, but their number was too few to have much influence.

5. Among the best Italian comics of this period were "S.K.1" (1935) by Guido Moroni Celsi, "Saturno Contro la Terra" (1937) by Zavattini-Pedrocchi-Scolari, and "Virus" (1939) by Pedrocchi-Molino-Canale.

6. Series from 1952 to 1966 equal 23 (with 951 books) and only three surviving today, Urania (the former I Romanzi di Urania), Galassia, and the S.F.B.C.; from 1968 to 1979 equal 51 (with 1,305 books until the end of 1979) and only 20 surviving today. Magazines from 1952 to 1967 equal 14 (with 327 issues) and only one, *Nova SF,* begun as a book club, occasionally active; then ten years of inactivity. From 1976 to 1979, a new outburst of six other magazines, all dead today with the exception of the Italian edition of *Isaac Asimov's Science Fiction Magazine* [14-25]. We might also add three series of books devoted to history and criticism: Futuro Saggi (Fanucci, Rome, 1976) with eight books up to 1979; S. F. Saggi (Editrice Nord, Milan, 1977) with three books; and Stella—Enciclopedia del Cinema Fantastico (Nebula Film, Rome, 1979) with one book. [Figures are correct only through late 1979. —Ed.]

7. For example, Tommaso Landolfi's *Cancroregina* (1950), Ennio Flaiano's *Un Marziano a Roma* (1960, a play extracted from a 1954 story), Dino Buzzati's *Il Grande Ritratto* (1960; tr. as *Larger Than Life*, 1962), Italo Calvino's *Le Cosmicomiche* (1965; tr. as *Cosmicomics*, 1968) and *Ti con Zero* (1967; tr. as *T zero*, 1969; British title: *Time and the Hunter*), Carlo Della Corte's *Pulsatilla Sexuata* (1962), Primo Levi's *Storie Nalturali* (1966, as Damiano Malabaila), and Luigi Santucci's *Il Mandragolo* (1979).

8. On the recent developments of Italian SF, see also George L. Williams, "Italian Science Fiction for the 1980s," *Extrapolation* 22 (Summer 1981): 191–195; and Fabio Calabrese, "Italian Science Fiction: Trends and Authors," *Foundation* 34 (Autumn 1985): 49–56.

9. On SF criticism in Italy, see the review article by Carlo Pagetti, "Twenty-five Years of Science Fiction Criticism in Italy (1953–1978)," *Science-Fiction Studies* 6 (November 1979): 320–326. Significant nonfiction books by Italian authors not annotated in the following section include Carlo Pagetti and Riccardo Valla, eds., *Nuova Presenza*, no. 37/38 (1970), special issue on J. G. Ballard; Ruggero Bianchi, *Asimov* (Florence: La Nuova Italia, 1977); Luigi Russo, ed., *Vent'anni di Fantascienza in Italia* (n.p.: La Nuova Presenza, 1978); Alberto Abruzzese, *La Grande Scimmia: Mostri, Vampiri, Automi, Mutanti* (Rome: Napoleone, 1979); Collettivo "Un'ambigua utopia," *Nei Labirinti della Fantascienza: Guida Critica* (Milan: Feltrinelli, 1979); Vita Fortunati, *La Letteratura Utopica Inglese* (Ravenna: Longo, 1979); Alessandro Monti, *Invito*

Alla Lettura di H. G. Wells (Milan: Mursia, 1982); Stefano Manferlotti, *Antiutopia: Huxley, Orwell, Burgess* (Palermo: Sellerio, 1984); Antonio Caronia, *Il Cyborg: Saggio sull'Uomo Artificiale* (Rome, Naples: Edizioni Theoria, 1985); Carlo Pagetti, *I Marziani alla Corte della Regina Vittoria* (Pescara: Tracce, 1986).

Bibliography

Individual Authors

*6-306. Aldani, Lino. **Quando le Radici.** Piacenza: La Tribuna, 1977.
In 1998, Italy has a president who is nominally a communist, but nothing else has changed in the politics and economics of the country, whose life is now concentrated in a group of ten megalopoli. While utter alienation devours every social and human value, a clerk tries to recover his inner roots by abandoning Rome and going back to his small native village on the river Po. Among a dozen old and colorful fellows still clinging to old ways in a semighost town, he discovers love and freedom by joining a band of Gypsies. As hackneyed as its plot may seem, a powerful and very well-written novel whose realism stands out without any imitations.

Calvino, Italo. **Cosmicomics (Le Cosmicomiche)** [see **4-108**].

6-307. Dossi, Carlo. **La Colonia Felice.** Milan: Perelli, 1874.
A strong utopian novel published in four different editions in nine years and often quoted in parliamentary speeches against the death penalty and for a more humane treatment of prisoners. In a near future—as usual in most utopias—dissenters (and not only criminal ones) are taken to desert islands. A group of 40 exiled men and women try to build a new kind of society, but they fail because their former establishment corrupted them to such a point that any redemption is now impossible. The utopian start comes to a dystopian end.

6-308. Filastò, Nino. **La Proposta.** Milan: Editrice Nord, 1984.
Western Megalops, a gigantic and multileveled city, is the central and powerful image of this novel set in a bleak and dehumanized near future. The protagonist, Degrado, is a sleuth who sets out to rescue a woman and a girl who have mysteriously disappeared in the bizarre and ghastly underworld of the great city, populated by an array of strange creatures: vagrants, urban terrorists, religious fanatics. His amazing adventures are paralleled by the power dreams and the private obsessions of an enigmatic and mighty figure, the Master of Glass, who entertains a sinister project: a "proposal" aimed at transforming into an actual social practice the well-known "modest proposal" of Jonathan Swift, that of slaying children and selling them as food to solve problems of overpopulation, famine, and violence. Serious dystopian concerns and a rich satirical vein blend successfully in a colorful and wacky adventure, full of memorable characters and events.

*6-309. Grifoni, Ulisse. **Dalla Terra alle Stelle.** Florence: Niccolai, 1887.
Leaving his literary studies and turning to chemistry after an unfortunate love affair, Alberto C., a young Florentine, casually mixes up a paint that can nullify the effects of gravity. With the help of a college teacher, he builds a ship to take both of them into space, and after some flights over Africa, they head for Mars. But here the novel ends, and the announced sequel, *Nelle Stelle,* never appeared. Since the story is told by a friend of Alberto as a flashback after the Florentine came back to Earth with two Lilliputian Martians and the spaceship sank in the sea near the North Pole, we are given some information on Mars, but not enough. Compare the antigravitational paint to Wells's use of Cavorite 14 years later in his *The First Men in the Moon* [1–98].

6-310. Guerrini, Remo. **Pelle d'Ombra.** Piacenza: La Tribuna, 1979.
Run by a computer known as The Cathedral is a city in the depths inhabited by the survivors of a ghastly atomic war and by the Sharks, humanoids whose origin from the fish kingdom keeps them in a well-secluded ghetto. A man is murdered, and the investigation is conducted by Lorna the Shark. Very soon Lorna and the killer, Omar Khayam (a "maker of dreams" who killed out of passion), enter into troublesome relations with the master of the city. They both eventually go to the shores of the surface world, where another sort of society has survived and can witness their last confrontation. Literary roots with echoes of Melville's *Moby Dick* and Thomas Mann's decadence as in *Der Tod in Venedig.*

6-311. Horrakh, Livio. **Grattanuvole.** Piacenza: La Tribuna, 1977.
In 2099, after the atomic holocaust, there survive a few million people in the unbreakable Cloudscrapers, buildings with 30,000 flats and 3,000 floors, 15,000 meters high. Earth's population has been steadily declining and the birth rate is now almost zero. Karel flees from his Cloudscraper, and with the help of the mutated and telephatic dogs circling in the desert sets out for a mythical destination, the legendary Home of Man, which seems to be the only alternative to the fears of year 3000. He discovers at last that it is but another Cloudscraper whose fertile inhabitants are using all the facilities of the same building to construct a spaceship. He joins them, since escape from Earth is now the only hope. Compare Silverberg's *The World Inside* [4-513] and James Ballard's *High-Rise* (1975).

6-312. Malaguti, Ugo. **Il Palazzo nel Cielo.** Bologna: Libra, 1970.
In a distant future, Earth is almost a desert, and a man without memory looks for a mythical eternal city created by God to shelter the "memories of time." His quest takes him to Mars and Venus—where somebody thinks he is a new Messiah—and after a very long series of recognitions, he discovers that he is but an incarnation of a mighty computer, which lives in the palace in the sky and chooses to descend among people to share their sad loneliness. Some tiresome and repetitive passages, but also many interesting ideas.

*6-313. Malaguti, Ugo. **Satana dei Miracoli.** Piacenza: La Tribuna, 1966.
A distant planet shelters a self-exiled group of Earth people looking for religious freedom after Earth has become a queer technocratic society where robots are trying to put heretics and witches to the stake. On this planet, Satan is "good" and

seems inclined to give a sign of his existence by destroying the robots who pursue the exiles. Satan soon assumes his traditional character, and his followers start to behave exactly like their robot persecutors against the indigenous life of their adopted planet. An ambiguous allegory with attempts at lyricism.

6-314. Mantegazza, Paolo. **L'Anno 3000: Sogno.** Milan: Treves, 1897.
Paolo and Maria, a young couple who after five happy years of a so-called love marriage and are now entitled to a "fecund" marriage (that is, one that allows the bearing of children), leave the United States of Europe for a new and long honeymoon across the world of the year 3000, carrying with them a strange book, *The Year 3000,* written in the twenty-first century but describing life in the year 3000. Europe is now a strongly secular and technocratic federation after four experimental and ill-fated generations of socialism, and their travel provides an amusing comparison between the reality and the fantasies in the book. Some countries visited and discussed are Tyrannopolis (led by a czar), Turazia (where socialism is victorious), and Logopolis (very similar to ancient England). But at last the whole story in the year 3000 is revealed to be a dream.

6-315. Menghini, Luigi. **L'Assedio.** Milan: Editrice Nord, 1981.
Professor Hoodlige is working to develop a device that will cure patients affected by mental diseases: the Probe. While the project is on the point of being accomplished, Hoodlige undertakes a series of harmless experiments on a group of undergraduates. But as soon as the Probe is put in action, all of them simultaneously begin to provide a coherent and realistic account of an event set in the remote past: the Trojan War; and from then on past and present intertwine in a fast-paced and skillfully plotted adventure. An intriguing treatment of the theme of telepathic communication through distant ages.

6-316. Miglieruolo, Mauro Antonio. **Come Ladro di Notte.** Piacenza: La Tribuna, 1972.
In a far future, the overpowering forces of the Congregation intend to bring about in the whole known universe the Second Coming of Christ and the following destruction of life in every form, with the help of many billions of supporters and millions of huge starships. But political machinations in the heart of the same Congregation make this operation long and difficult. A bleak mixture of satire and the grotesque, the novel combines religious and political symbols into a sort of philosophical space opera without any precedents (or followers, up to now). More than an indirect attack on the traditional SF theme of colonial exploitation of other planets by terrestrials, it is an anarchistic and direct attack on *every* form of oppression.

*6-317. Montanari, Gianni. **Daimon.** Milan: Longanesi, 1978.
The last human survivor, now with godlike powers, uses clones for his experiments to re-create humans on a far-away planet. One of these experiments takes place in Labula, a town almost completely isolated and where Master Jockan and his feudal subjects live to worship certain races of fantastic animals created (or so they believe) before the human race. Master Jockan and his small world undergo two "substitutions" at the end of each experimental cycle and each time are re-

placed with younger clones who obviously remember nothing. But at last the third Master Jockan succeeds in facing his own Master in the heart of the planet and, defeated, is put to another experimental use.

6-318. Montanari, Gianni. **La Sepoltura.** Piacenza: La Tribuna, 1972.
In the near future, the early 1980s, the world is disrupted by the uprising of mutants possessing uncontrollable paranormal powers and by the efforts of every government to eliminate these capabilities with brain surgery in suitable concentration camps. The bleak picture of this future Italy, by now a police state, pivots around a young man who, after eight years of self-exile, returns to kill his father, who had been the cause of his mutant mother's death in a camp. But the utter hopelessness of the situation, notwithstanding a glimpse of a possible future society of self-controlled mutants, brings him to suicide. Compare—with every caution—van Vogt's *Slan* [3-383], although in the Italian novel the key symbol is "incommunicability" among people.

6-319. Motta, Luigi. **Il Tunnel Sottomarino.** Milan: Treves, 1912.
One of the first works envisaging the construction of a transatlantic tunnel linking Europe to the United States, this novel offers a wide-ranging and very complex plot stuffed with moustached villains, submarines, pirates, sabotage, the discovery of the ruins of Atlantis, and many other oddities. Great passions and a greater bourgeois heroic determination, with detailed information and figures from the engineering designs. Compare Bernhard Kellerman's *Der Tunnel* (1913).

6-320. Pestriniero, Renato. **Sette Accadimenti in Venezia.** Chieti: Marino Solfanelli Editore, 1985.
Seven loosely connected stories set in the common framework of the city of Venice, where the author lives. In "Nodi," the protagonist encounters a mysterious "custodian" and becomes aware of intersecting parallel timelines and of unknowable creatures manipulating human destiny; his discovery of these "knots" in time condemns him to further displacements in slightly altered worlds and he never regains his spatiotemporal identity. Another story, "Quelli dei quadri," is set in a submerged and crumbling Venice of the future, where the True Venice Sightseeing Co. produces for the tourists artificial "pictures" of the past splendors of the city employing a group of artists-actors. Philosophical speculation on the nature of time, strong characterization, and a magical and fascinating atmosphere all combine to create seven original portraits of a Venice transfigured through space and time.

6-321. Piegai, Daniela. **Ballata per Lima.** Milan: Editrice Nord, 1980.
The bloody Night of Fires marks the beginning of a new social order for mankind and the rise of a totalitarian state. Rebels and deviates are savagely hunted by robot-guards and sent before the Machine, a huge computer located in the depths of Rock Mountains, which picks their minds, absorbing memories and increasing its own knowledge. Some misfits try to escape from this bleak and nightmarish world, and their hope is embodied by the planet Lima, which eventually welcomes a mixed army of refugees determined a start a new life and to restore

true and "natural" human values. An outstanding novel that shows an unusual gift for intense characterization and effective storytelling.

6-322. Prosperi, Piero. **Autocrisi.** Piacenza: La Tribuna, 1971.
How could Dakopi, a small planet 300 light-years from Earth, guess what kind of gifts Earth people would bear? The Dakopians are the only intelligent race so far discovered in the galaxy, and their planet is rich in denilium, a precious transuranium element necessary for hyperdrive flights. Since Dakopians are humanoids and unfamiliar with road building and motoring, Earth people seduce them into a deep—and dangerous—love of motorcars to obtain denilium for stocks of General Motors and Chrysler-Ford products. A witty satire of American commercial colonialism from an author who is at his best with fast-paced and intriguing stories.

*6-323. Salgari, Emilio. **Le Meraviglie del Duemila.** Turin: Viglongo, 1907.
A wealthy young American finds in a discovery of a good friend a way to escape boredom: thanks to the powers of an ancient plant known as "the flower of resurrection," they both undergo a 100-year suspended animation and are awakened in 2003 by a descendant of the friend. The friend is their host as they view the wonders of the new century, which rely heavily on an exhaustive exploitation of electricity and include electric car-boats, anticipations of radar, a final world war, restricted islands for criminals, and freedom from discomfort and everyday duties thanks to machines. Humans have a larger skull for a larger brain and are happily in touch with Martians, creatures very like small seals, and both races are developing spaceflight. But in the end the electricity now permeating the whole Earth is fatal to the two travelers and drives them insane. Compare—at least partially—Wells's *When the Sleeper Wakes* [1-106], set in 1899, but without any forewarning of the possible dangers of technology.

*6-324. Sandrelli, Sandro. **Caino dello Spazio.** Piacenza: La Tribuna, 1964.
Twenty stories and the title short novel dealing with the tragic necessity for a man to behave as a traitor to and torturer of his own race during a space war in order to have some of his people finally saved. Many stories are full of keen satire and wit by a writer playing tongue in cheek with many well-known themes. Seven of the stories had been published in magazines and anthologies between 1957 and 1962.

6-325. Soldati, Mario. **Lo Smeraldo.** Milan: Mondadori, 1974. Tr. as *The Emerald* by William Weaver (Harcourt, 1977).
After a meeting with a sort of psychic sensitive in New York, a rather autobiographical character looks for an ancient emerald formerly owned by his family; so starts a long and vivid dream of life in Italy in a near future. This world has been divided into two great confederations by the deadly sinusoidal line traced by satellites from both the U.S.S.R. and the United States, neatly parting the northern industrialized countries from the southern developing ones. Our hero—now an old painter in this dream—makes a difficult trip to southern Italy, and from the cold and tyrannical matter-of-factness of the Russian-dominated side falls into the torpid and messy life of the side ruled by Arabs. Although over-

written and somewhat illogical, the novel shows many interesting points in the shaping of both societies.

Anthologies

*6-326. Cremaschi, Inisero, ed. **Universo e Dintorni.** Milan: Garzanti, 1978.
Twenty-nine previously unpublished Italian stories. This anthology ranks high with well-known authors such as Aldani, Musa, Prosperi, and Sandrelli, some younger names—Curtoni, Guerrini, and Montanari—and many others (some making their professional debuts). Despite a variable quality, the themes and approaches are very dissimilar and give a wide view of the recent Italian field with stories ranging from outer to inner space. The anthology includes a short essay by the editor, dealing mostly with Italian literary SF.

*6-327. Curtoni, Vittorio, Gianfranco De Turris, and Gianni Montanari, eds. **Fanta-Italia: Sedici Mappe del Nostro Futuro.** Piacenza: La Tribuna, 1972.
Sixteen stories with the coming future of Italy as a central theme. Several different political and social views are considered, but their common feature is a bleak vision of any possible reality. Beside stories portraying blitz from right or left parties—and even an American invasion of Italy—are others exploring Mediterranean pollution (Cesare Falessi's "I Gamberi"), the excessive power of bureaucracy (Mauro Miglieruolo's "Dittico Burocratico") and that of the Catholic religion (G. L. Staffilano's "Stato delle Chiavi"). The anthology offers some amazing perspectives when reread in the 1980s.

6-328. Malaguti, Ugo, ed. **Nova SF Speciale.** Bologna: Libra, 1976.
This special issue of the magazine *Nova SF* includes two short novels (Vittorio Catani's *Attentato all'Utopia* and Mauro Miglieruolo's *Oniricon*) and seven short stories, all by Italian writers. Catani's work is a strong attack on the reactionary roots of utopia, staged by the contraposition in a far future of a rigid technocratic establishment and another that is rather anarchical. Miglieruolo's, by contrast, is the sparkling adventure—almost Brownian for its witty humor and satire—of a little man swinging from dream to reality and at last waking up in another world. Among the stories, the nice fantasy "Dove Sono le Nevi" by Adalberto Cersosimo, an author at his best in this kind of fiction.

Nonfiction

*6-329. Aldani, Lino. **La Fantascienza: Che Cos'è, Come è Sorta, Dove Tende.** Piacenza: La Tribuna, 1962.
Just ten years after science fiction had appeared in Italy with the name *fantascienza,* this book provided a succinct critical survey with its 192 pages (50 devoted to the first lists of Italian and foreign works published in specialized media). Twelve short chapters provide a historical overview, including a brief discussion of the American golden age, Russian examples, comics, cinema, and the Italian scene. Although limited primarily to foreign works published in Italy, it is still one of the most intelligent and astute introductions to the field.

*6-330. Bertoni, Alfio, and Gianluigi Missiaja. **Catalogo Generale della Fanta-scienza.** Venice: Edizioni CCSF, 1968.

This catalog covers most foreign and Italian SF—novels and stories, including utopias and fantasy—published in Italy since the sixteenth century. Authors are listed alphabetically, their works following the chronology of every Italian edition; titles included range from More's *Utopia* to those published until June 30, 1968, covering both books and magazines. A complete list of Italian magazines and series is given, together with a list of fanzines. Pseudonyms, both foreign and Italian, are given too. The first catalog of its kind in Italy, it stands unexcelled for the richness of information on works that appeared before the birth in 1952 of specialized SF in Italy.

*6-331. Curtoni, Vittorio. **Le Frontiere dell'Ignoto: Vent'anni di Fantascienza Italiana.** Milan: Nord, 1977.

Originally a graduation thesis, this should have been the first history of modern Italian science fiction, but it covers just the 20 years following the first magazines published in 1952. From the viewpoint of both the historical and the critical, it is a rather idiosyncratic book with many gaps and very personal choices. But especially for the 1960s and the early 1970s, a very interesting work.

6-332. Ferrini, Franco. **Che Cosa E' la Fantascienza.** Rome: Ubaldini, 1970.

A curious book, full of interesting and sometimes obscure intuitions and written in a similar manner. Thirteen chapters discuss thematically topics such as false ancestors of SF, science and poetry, natural miracles, and so forth, and look at science fiction from a Marxist point of view. A wider reading of SF books would have improved this study.

6-333. Giovannoli, Renato. **La Scienza della Fantascienza.** Milan: Editori Europei Associati, 1982. Espresso Strumenti 14.

A lively and insightful study on the interaction between SF and its scientific content. Much more concerned with the exploration of the genre as a source of autonomous scientific theories than with the plausibility of science in SF, Giovannoli assumes that the internal logic of SF develops through scientific revolutions and conflicting theories as they emerge from the different views expressed by SF authors in their works. So far as SF is not a closed system but a literary genre that absorbs fragments of actual scientific debate, then hard and soft sciences are not immune to the influence of SF lore as well. Subjects such as aliens, robots, supermen, spaceflight, alternate worlds, time travel, psychohistory, and the theory of games are discussed with reference to a wide variety of sources, almost exclusively drawn from American SF.

6-334. Guardamagna, Daniela. **Analisi dell'Incubo: L'Utopia Negativa da Swift alla Fantascienza.** Rome: Bulzoni, 1980.

An ingratiating study of dystopian thought starting with Swift and largely concentrating on Zamiatin, Wells, Orwell, and Huxley, but also discussing other science fiction writers. Both an analysis of patterns and themes and an impassioned defense of these "modern mythographs" who put under accusation the present with their works in the future tense.

6-335. Mongini, Giovanni. **Storia del Cinema di Fantascienza.** 2 vols. Rome: Fanucci, 1976–1977.
Dealing mainly with modern cinema, primarily that available on Italian screens and without giving too much attention to the early period (the forefathers from 1898 to 1929 are dealt with in eight pages by quoting just Méliès and Lang), the two volumes include plot summaries, information on directors and players, excerpts from screenplays, and many black-and-white stills. Chronologically listed, these items are far from being exhaustive for either foreign or Italian movies. A partial filmography is given for the most important ones. Up to now it is the only Italian work that includes Italian movies.

6-336. Montanari, Gianni. **Ieri, il Futuro: Origini e Sviluppo della Fantascienza Inglese.** Milan: Nord 1977.
Originally a graduation thesis, this affectionate and critical investigation of 75 years of British science fiction goes from the already well-established Wells to the end of *New Worlds* and after, examining the magazines and authors of those times. History is limited to the first four chapters, with the remaining five devoted to analyses of the writings of E. F. Russell, J. Wyndham, A. C. Clarke, F. Hoyle, and J. G. Ballard. Included are a photographic section (authors, magazines and books, comics), a bibliography of criticism, and a complete Italian bibliography of the five writers analyzed.

*6-337. Pagetti, Carlo. **Il Senso del Futuro: La Fantascienza nella Letteratura Americana.** Rome: Edizioni di Storia e Letteratura, 1970. Biblioteca di Studi Americani, 20.
The 12 chapters of this interesting literary study deal with American SF from the nineteenth century to 1968. Acknowledging the importance of SF—with the models of utopia and satire—simultaneous with the origins of American literature, the first seven chapters examine both thematically and historically the works of Poe, Hawthorne, Brockden Brown, and other early writers. Modern SF is studied in its main themes, repetitive models, and outstanding authors. Chapters are devoted to Bradbury, Sheckley, Dick, and Vonnegut, and to the writers of the "space age," Delany, Zelazny, Le Guin, and Disch. Two chapters—those on Bradbury and on Vonnegut—had already appeared in an academic review, *Studi Americani*, nos. 11 and 12, in 1965 and 1966.

*6-338. Pilo, Gianni. **Catalogo Generale della Fantascienza in Italia, Vol. 1: 1930–1979; Vol. 2: 1979–1982.** Rome: Fanucci, 1979, 1982.
This catalog is strictly limited to SF and fantasy (utopias are excluded), of both foreign and Italian authors, published only in specialized series, magazines, and fanzines. Notwithstanding its title, it covers only works that appeared from 1952 through 1982, since specialized books and magazines started only in 1952. It includes an alphabetical list of authors (with their works also alphabetically listed) and another for the titles in Italian; a complete list of series, magazines, and fanzines; lists of pseudonyms and awards; and also information on Italian people working in SF. Critical pieces are partially listed.

*6-339. Russo, Luigi, ed. **La Fantascienza e la Critica.** Milan: Feltrinelli, 1980.
A collection of selected essays from the International Conference on SF and

Criticism held in Palermo (Italy) in 1978. Twenty-seven articles divided into two main sections dealing, respectively, with theoretical and interdisciplinary approaches and with history and criticism of the genre. Foreign contributors include distinguished SF scholars such as Marc Angenot, Charles Elkins, Peter Fitting, Fredric Jameson, Darko Suvin, and many others. About half of the essays are by Italian contributors, often leading authorities in a variety of fields other than SF, thus offering a fresh and stimulating overview on the relations between SF and other disciplines—sociology, anthropology, semiotics, ethology, philosophy of science, and so on. Even though some articles have been reprinted elsewhere and in languages other than Italian, this is probably the best collection of essays on SF originally published in Italy to date.

6-340. Solmi, Sergio. **Della Favola, del Viaggio e di Altre Cose: Saggi sul Fantastico.** Milan, Naples: Ricciardi, 1971. Reprinted as *Saggi sul Fantastico: Dall'Antichità alle Prospettive del Futuro,* Turin: Einaudi, 1978.
These 11 essays originally appeared between 1931 and 1966. Four of them—and particularly "Divagazioni sulla Science-Fiction, l'Utopia e il Tempo" and "Ancora della Fantascienza"—are among the most perceptive short criticism to appear in Italy, thanks to the very open-minded approach of one of our best literary critics. One essay is a shrewd analysis of the virtues and shortcomings of Bradbury's fiction.

6-341. Utopia e Fantascienza. Turin: Giappichelli, 1975.
These eight essays by faculty of Turin's university discuss relations between utopia and Anglo-American science fiction. Subjects discussed include time travel, the limits of dystopia, Wells, Golding, Godwin's *Man in the Moone* [1-39], and utopia and SF in Flann O'Brien (an Irish writer). This collection is also significant because it is one of the first—and one of very few—offered by the Italian academic sector.

Journal

6-342. La Città e le Stelle. First issue: Winter 1981/Spring 1982. Annual. Ed: Carlo Pagetti (Editrice Nord, via Rubens 25, I-20148 Milan, Italy).
Published by Editrice Nord in cooperation with the Department of English of the G. D'Annunzio University in Pescara, this academic journal represents the first ambitious effort to promote a serious critical study and debate on SF in Italy, following the path traced in the United States, Canada, and Britain by established journals as *Science-Fiction Studies, Extrapolation,* and *Foundation.* Contributors include prominent scholars from various Italian universities and institutions who have published extensively on SF subjects. Each of the four issues published to date has a thematic concern that emphasizes the historical development of the genre: no. 1 on twentieth-century British SF, no. 2 on American SF in the 1970s (Philip K. Dick and women writers), no. 4 on Victorian SF, and no. 3 on the image of Earth as alien landscape, with essays on Swift, Dickens, Delany, Dick, Ballard, and others.

Danish SF

Niels Dalgaard

To talk of a literary tradition implies that the writers working within it are conscious of their forebears and that they feel they are continuing and/or renewing something that is already in existence. In that sense, it is not possible to talk of a Danish SF tradition until some time in the twentieth century. SF works written before that time are few and far between, and the authors who wrote them seldom saw themselves as a part of a separate area of literature.

Research in this area is complicated by many early SF works being published only under obscure circumstances and by the bibliographical knowledge in the area being less than complete. Some works are known, though, and they provide a general picture of Danish SF—a picture that may turn out to be distorted if and when further bibliographical research is undertaken.

So far as we know, the first Danish SF work was Ludvig Holberg's *Niels Klims underjordiske Reise* [6-346, 1-50], published in 1741. This novel, written in Latin, became very popular throughout Europe. Holberg may have been inspired by Cyrano, and certainly by Swift, but he himself did not become the starting point of a Danish SF tradition. A few pamphlets from the 1770s were inspired by his work and used its locale, but they were mostly narrowly satirical and of little interest to the SF scholar. The one exception is an anonymously published, and unfortunately unfinished, serial in a magazine in the first decade of the nineteenth century, relating the adventures of Peter Klim—a relative to Niels—on a voyage to the Moon.[1]

What little SF-like literature we find about 1800 is mostly satirical in intent, such as Johan Herman Wessel's play *Anno 7603* (published in 1785), a classical role-reversal story about a future in which women rule. Wessel was a great humorist and satirist, but this play, written just before his death, is a distinctly minor effort.

SF as a genre presupposes a rationalistic outlook, and so it is no surprise that with the coming of the romantics, the publishing of SF almost stops. Because an age is called "romantic" does not mean that every author of that period certainly wallows in inward-looking metaphysics, as many certainly did. However, the Danish romantics did not use the future or space as a locale for their stories, nor did they—with very few exceptions—use science as an inspiration, as Mary Shelley did. Instead, they wrote stories taking place in the unspoiled nature, in the age of the Vikings, or in exotic, far-off lands.

The periodicals of the first half of the nineteenth century carried a number of serials about travels to the Moon, but they were invariably satires, written as weekly installments in order to satirize the most recent events. They rarely ended but simply petered out when the author(s) lost interest in them.[2]

One romantic who came close to writing SF is the well-known Hans Christian Andersen, who was very fascinated by the rapid technological development of his time. He was also taken in by the philosophy of his friend, the scientist Hans Christian Ørsted (the discoverer of electromagnetism). Several of Andersen's stories are heavily influenced by Ørsted, and in a few of them he even touches on SF. The best of those is the short piece "Om Årtusinder" (1853), telling of a far future where Americans toured Europe by balloons. Apart from a few cases, however, the underlying mysticism in Ørsted's deeply romantic worldview prevented Andersen from writing any real SF.

A new enlightenment, a new fascination with technology and a belief in science, a modern breakthrough in naturalistic literature, and a general turning away from religion and metaphysics came about around 1870. Oddly enough, though there is much literary evidence of the fascination with technology, little SF came of it. A notable story in the best of the Vernian style is Vilhelm Bergsøe's "En Reise med Flyvefisken 'Prometheus.' " Published in 1869 in the upper-class slick magazine *Illustreret Tidende*, it tells of a transatlantic trip with a new sort of vehicle. Its author was a scientist himself, and one can only be sad that he didn't write more such stories. The fact that it was published in an upper-class magazine showed, however, that science was gaining wider acceptance (it was also reprinted in several magazines aimed at a broader readership).

If Bergsøe provided us with an example of SF in the Vernean style, F. C Sibbern represented the utopian novel. His *Meddelelser af Indholdet af et Skrift fra Aaret 2135* (two volumes, 1858 and 1872) tells of a future Christian-communist ideal society.

Original Danish production of SF in the second half of the nineteenth century was not great, and this is somewhat strange, because at least from 1870 on, translations flourished—authors like Verne, Andre Laurie, George Griffith, as well as mystics like Camille Flammarion.

The breakdown of values resulting from World War I resulted in several pessimistic and/or idealistic novels. Among them are Sophus Michaëlis's *Himmelskibet*, which was published in 1921 but was made into a film in 1917. Up through the 1920s and 1930s we have a number of dystopias warning against totalitarianism, as well as a number of paranoid racist novels. Besides these books, some maga-zine-published SF exists, about which very little is known. There were no special-ized magazines publishing SF, and the nonspecialized fiction magazines of the time are not well known. We know that Wells's short stories were published in translation in the 1920s and that considerable juvenile SF was translated in the 1920s and 1930s, but that is all.[3]

The 1920s saw the first organized publishing of SF for the mass market, most issued by Martin's Forlag. It specialized in juvenile fiction for some time, and what wasn't translated from English or German was written by Niels Meyn, an ex-tremely prolific author, not all of whose works are definitely known. Meyn wrote in many genres and under many pseudonyms, but he is almost the only person representing the Danish SF of the 1920s and 1930s. What he wrote was inspired by the likes of Hans Dominik, and Meyn's SF is full of bug-eyed monsters and in-terplanetary imperialism. The paranoia and racism of his books are such that one is not surprised to learn that he later joined the Nazi party.

After the Second World War, Denmark was exposed to a massive American in-fluence, as was most of Western Europe. This also included a strong literary influ-ence and imported literature. Among the things imported was American SF, though it did not really come into its own until the 1950s. Most of the translated stories were published in magazines and Sunday newspapers and it was also here that the first new experiments were done by Danish authors working within the American magazine SF idiom.

What was written—and what was translated—were two different kinds of SF: the optimistic, Campbellian kind, working from a fascination with technical devel-opment, and the pessimistic, Bradbury kind, based on a view of technology as in-herently bad and a nostalgia for a simpler past. The Campbellian kind got off on a good footing when the first publishing boom in SF took place from 1957 to 1959. The boom included the first Danish SF magazine, *Planetmagasinet* (six is-sues, 1958–1959), which was a Danish edition of *Astounding*. But it was Brad-bury's kind of SF which was to have the major influence on the small production of Danish genre SF. The most important Danish SF author, Niels E. Nielsen, is very heavily influenced by Bradbury. Nielsen, whose SF debut was with the novel *Der meldes fra Sahara* (1953), is still writing and has published more than 25 books of SF. Almost all of his SF deals with the responsibility of the individual in the face of uncontrolled technology and military logic. His books often end with a small group of survivors starting over, basing their new society on the old lost val-ues of the small town.[4]

Outside of genre publishing, the 1950s continued the trend of occasional dystopias, a tendency clearly made stronger by the nuclear bombs of 1945, but also by the experience of totalitarianism. These books continue to be written, nor is it unreasonable to keep warning about trends and developments.

In the 1960s, a number of mainstream authors discovered SF. Different groups of authors saw different things in the genre, and they took what they found useful for their own purposes. Thus we get a number of modernist, ex-perimental authors—prominently among them Svend Åge Madsen[5]—who use the distancing devices of SF to express their own estrangement from the text and the world. A novel like *Liget og Lysten* (1968) is a rather schematic combination of

SF, crime fiction, and pornography, taking place in minimal surroundings under a double sun.

We also get a number of new authors associated with the hippie culture (a number of them writing for the underground magazine *Superlove,* which also published Ballard) taking ideas from SF. What they used is mostly the "far-out" inventory of space travel, distant planets, weird extraterrestrials, and the like. Probably the best example of this kind of SF is Knud Holten's *Suma-X* [6-347A].

A third group of mainstream authors attracted to aspects of SF were those working toward a "new realism" (that is, a new naturalism). Working in opposition to the dominant modernist literature of the early 1960s, they produced such works as Anders Bodelsen's *Frysepunktet* [4-67]. They saw extrapolative writing of the near future as a continuation of their "realism" by other means.[6]

In the late 1960s and the early 1970s SF boomed in Denmark. The general public was getting more interested—partly because of events like the Apollo missions and partly because it was slowly becoming acceptable to deal with popular culture—and several specialized paperback series were published. Even highbrow publishers like Rhodos and Gyldendal began publishing SF. Jannick Storm did a lot to introduce SF to the Danish public (and the Danish publishers). He was a strong supporter of the New Wave, and this of course influenced what SF the Danish authors were writing.[7]

The boom in genre publishing peaked in the first half of the 1970s, with several paperback series, one of which published two volumes monthly (a lot by Danish standards), and even the most thorough attempt at a Danish SF magazine, *Månedens Bedste Science Fiction* (16 issues, 1975–1977), published much translated SF and much original Danish material as well (some would say too much, or rather, too indiscriminately). Editor Frits Remar was too kind in some ways, and among brilliant stories by new authors was a lot of trash that should never have seen print. The low quality of the Danish material in the magazine contributed to its downfall—a sad thing, since at its best it sold more than 10,000 copies per month. An attempt at a successor, *Science-Fiction Magasinet,* was run by amateurs and looked it to such a degree that it is a wonder it lasted seven issues (1977–1978).

In the mid-1970s, Danish SF fandom organized, and the fan union, Science Fiction Cirklen, or its associated company, Tangentforlaget, was behind a number of publications. It was also the Science Fiction Cirklen that published the latest attempt at a Danish SF magazine, *Nye Verdener* (ten issues, 1981–1983). A number of authors found in these and similar publications an outlet for stories in the (American) genre idiom. Names like Steen Knudsen, Niels Søndergaard, and Bjarne Lund-Jensen (who later published a short-story collection, *Sagaen om Xroc* [Odense: Forlaget Utopia, 1980]) come to mind in this connection. Most of them are still writing, but lack an outlet, as most publishing companies prefer SF-like products by established names to genre SF by the not-very-known.

By 1978, there was almost no genre publishing of SF in Denmark, but several other things were happening. Some of the trends from the 1960s were continuing in the mainstream, such as the near-future extrapolation. Authors like Jørgen Lindgreen protested against nuclear power. In *Atomer på næsset* (1975), for instance, he writes about a near future where Denmark has implemented nuclear power, with disastrous results. What's more, in the late 1970s, academe discovered SF. To be more precise, it mostly discovered the feminist utopia. A number of Danish women authors began writing utopias, such as Vibeke Grønfeldt, whose *Det fantastiske barn* (1982) is about cloning, among other things. There were also a few dystopian visions, such as Dorrit Willumsen's *Programmeret til kærlighed* [6-358]. Some problems resulted because a large proportion of critics propagandizing for this literature didn't know the first thing about the history and nature of the literary utopia—let alone SF. The general impression was that no women had written SF or utopian fiction before the 1970s.[8]

As of late 1986, genre publishing seems to be coming back, though as trade rather than mass market paperback series. There are currently three such series, and they seem to be doing fairly well, though they are publishing mostly translations. Furthermore, the tendency to regard SF forms and ideas as legitimate ingredients in "fine" literature has continued and is steadily growing. More and more mainstream authors (especially of juvenile fiction, but also of fiction for adults) set their books in the future or in space. While few of the authors writing SF-related literature for the adult market so far display any genre consciousness, the general feeling is that with everything changing so quickly, and with the future—even the near future—guaranteed to be markedly different from today, SF and SF-like forms are adequate and relevant means of discussing the human condition.

Notes

1. Surely the best discussion of *Niels Klims underjordiske Reise* is the introduction by A. Kragelund in his edition of the work (Copenhagen: Gad, 1970). A discussion of the work specifically relating to SF is Niels Dalgaard, "En konvolut med blandet indhold: Om Holbergs Niels Klim," *Proxima*, no. 35 (1984). The first, and most thorough, discussion of Holberg's influences is Julius Paludan, *Om Holbergs Niels Klim* (Copenhagen, 1878).
2. Most of these are discussed in Niels Dalgaard, "Science fiction i Danmark: 1839–1868," *Pulsar*, no. 7/8 (1979).
3. A first survey of a number of penny magazines from the beginning of the century (not specifically concerned with SF) is Knud Nielsen, *De gamle kulørte hæfter* (Copenhagen: privately printed, 1983). A detailed description of the SF content in a 1930s boys' magazine is Niels Dalgaard, "Science fiction i Danmark: Drengebladet 1930–36," *Proxima*, no. 37/38 (1984).
4. The only major study of Nielsen's work so far is Per Mikkelsen, *Kathastrofe og Katharsis: En narratologisk og tematisk analyse af Niels E. Nielsen's science fiction romaner* (Frederikshavn: International Grafik, 1984).
5. About Madsen's works and their relation to SF and other genres, see Renny Edal and Ole Nielsen, *Identitet og virkelighed: En tematisk læsning i Svend Åge Madsens forfatterskab* (Odense: Odense University, 1980). A specialized reading of the novel *Tugt og utugt i mellemtiden* is Birgitte Grundtvig and Gitte Jørgensen, "Virkelighed eller fiktion," *SILAU*, no. 14/15 (1983).
6. On Anders Bodelsen and *Frysepunktet*, see Geert A. Nielsen, *Anders Bodelsens realisme* (Copenhagen: Vinten, 1978).

7. A collection of Storm's writing about the genre is *Vor tids eventyr: Katastrofeområdet* (Copenhagen: Swing, 1978).
8. *Kvindestudier 5: Utopi og subkultur* (Copenhagen: Delta, 1981) is a collection of essays by feminist critics. Unlike a number of others, they are aware that utopias are part of an old genre, but like others, they work with some strange theories indeed.

Bibliography

Individual Authors

Bodelsen, Anders. **Freezing Down (Frysepunktet)** [see **4-67**].

*6-343. Eriksen, Inge. **Rummet uden tid.** 3 vols. Copenhagen, 1983, 1985, 1986.
This series, the name of which means space without time, consists of three volumes so far, with at least a fourth announced. At the center of the books is the crew of the spaceship *Jezabel II*. In the first volume, *Luderen fra Gomorra* (Copenhagen: Rhodos, 1983), the year is 4693 and all resources are spent, so mankind must move to other places. Only a few people want no part of the streamlined future in space and instead elect to stay on the old and tired Earth. In *Nord for tiden* (Copenhagen: Gyldendal, 1985), *Jezabel II* is sabotaged and must land on an unknown planet for repairs. This is unsettling, as the crew is sure that no uncharted planet remained in known space. What is more shocking, however, is that the planet is discovered to be the demolished Earth, some centuries in the future. In *Dinosaurernes morgen* (Copenhagen: Gyldendal, 1986), the crew attempts to reestablish contact between the lost, low technology Earth and the rest of the high tech federation. The first three volumes, totaling more than 1,000 pages, deal with important questions of our time relating to technology, ways of government, and so on. It is without doubt the most ambitious SF project undertaken by a Danish SF writer for the past 30 years, though it cannot be said to be entirely successful. Compare—especially as regards the first volume—Doris Lessing's *Shikasta* [4-334]; also compare Le Guin's *The Dispossessed* [4-324] and, with caution, Russ's *And Chaos Died* [4-456].

6-344. Eskestad, Tage. **Flygtninge fra himlen.** Copenhagen: Stig Vendelkærs Forlag, 1973.
This is the first and probably the best of several works by Eskestad, in which he seeks to transplant ancient myths and religious tales into SF. In this case he uses the Book of Enoch, one of the noncanonical books of the Old Testament, which tells of 200 fallen angels coming to Earth, with disastrous results. In Eskestad's version, 200 political refugees flee from a gruesome matriarchy on Mars and its colony planet Semjus (this is the planet that exploded and become the asteroids). Escaping to Earth many thousand years ago, they are viewed as gods by the primi-

tive natives, with whom they interbreed, creating a race of giants. This is the first Danish example of this kind of mythography, and it has held up rather well.

6-345. Eskestad, Tage. **Matriarkatet.** Copenhagen: Irlov-Regulus, 1976.
The boy Jacob is growing up in a future postcatastrophe society, where all technology and most knowledge of the past have disappeared entirely. Marx and Mao are worshiped as gods by the ruling matriarchy, without anybody knowing what their names stand for (much like the names Marx and Ford are used in Huxley's *Brave New World*). The position of a young boy is not easy in a society where the women who rule do so ruthlessly and totally without feeling. Males function primarily as studs or as slave labor. But Jacob gets to know an underground movement, the "blackfriars," who attempt to resurrect the lost knowledge and create a new technology. This ends with a violent conflict and the promise of a renaissance. Unfortunately, the people are clichés and the portrayals of the evil women and the good men are even more so. In this it has much in common with most other antifeminist role-reversal stories.

*6-346. Holberg, Ludvig. **Niels Klims underjordiske Reise.** Leipzig: privately printed, 1741; Copenhagen: privately printed, 1742. Recommended edition edited by A. Kragelund (Copenhagen: Gad, 1970), which not only has an excellent preface and notes, but also gives the text in parallel Latin and Danish versions. Several English translations, one of which (from 1742) is reprinted in *Gulliveriana IV* (Delmar, NY: Scholars' Facsimiles & Reprints, 1973).
Niels Klim as a young man from Bergen, Norway, who returns to his native country after having completed studies at Copenhagen University. During an expedition he falls into a hollow Earth, which contains an entire universe, complete with stars and planets. With this novel, Holberg emerged as the first utopian-cum-satirical writer in Scandinavia. He was well versed in the international literary movements of his time, including Swift's *Gulliver's Travels* [1-89] and More's *Utopia* [1-68], and he wrote his book in Latin so that it could gain a wide audience, which it did. It was the first fantastic voyage to take place inside a hollow Earth. Contrary to popular belief, the book was never banned in Denmark, though the religious powers of the time frowned upon it. Also annotated as [1-50] and [6-390].

*6-347. Holm, Sven. **Termush, Atlanterhavskysten.** Copenhagen: Gyldendal, 1967. (*Termush.* London: Faber, 1969.)
This short novel is in the form of a diary, written by a nameless protagonist. He and others are installed at a luxury resort somewhere on the Atlantic coast. The specially built resort is created so that well-to-do people might survive a nuclear war in pleasant surroundings and comes complete with fallout shelters. The nuclear war as such is not the issue, however, but rather a psychological study of people isolated and under stress. On the symbolic level, it thus also becomes a statement about modern alienated man.

6-347A. Holten, Knud. **Suma-X.** Copenhagen: Gyldendal, 1969.
This is the story of Ketel, a young free-lance secret agent, and his adventures on the strange and wonderful planet of Suma-X. He is sent there by his employer,

the immortal superhero Champ-1, to save an Earth princess. His ordeal is made much more difficult because the enemy constantly manipulates his experience of reality. This distortion is mirrored in the narrative, which is floating, poetic, and associational. An example of what the psychedelic writers of the late 1960s did with the imagery of SF. Compare some of Ron Goulart's novels.

Jensen, Johannes V(ilhelm). **The Long Journey: Fire and Ice** and **The Cimbrians (Den lange rejse)** [see 2-50].

6-348. Lundberg, Knud. **Det olympiske håb.** Copenhagen: Branner og Korch, 1955.
A short novel in which the narrator, writing in 2004, looks back upon the 800-meter race of the 1996 Olympics. Throughout the book tension builds as we near the finish. Two Americans, two Russians, one German, and one Dane compete for the gold. When the German comes in second, he shoots himself in disgrace. The novel is prefaced by many apologies for its being so fantastic, but whereas it may well have seemed so to the reader of 1955, today all too much of the insanely competitive world of international sports that is depicted has become reality. Also annotated as [3-265].

6-349. Madsen, Svend Åge. **Se dagens lys.** Copenhagen: Gyldendal 1980.
A future Denmark is organized so that people experience one day at a time before being moved and drugged. The next day they wake up with a new job, family, etc. This relieves everybody of the feeling of responsibility, and if one is not happy with a job, family, or other things, tomorrow may be better or at least different. This naturally makes for an increasing alienation and a growing lack of personal identity. When the protagonist falls in love with a woman and wants to meet her again, the search for a more meaningful life begins. The technology of the society depicted is ludicrous—people are moved on gigantic conveyor belts in the streets at night—and Madsen has stated that this was on purpose. His idea was not to depict a workable or likely future, but to protest against the modern alienated society.

*6-350. Madsen, Svend Åge. **Tugt og utugt i mellemtiden.** Copenhagen: Gyldendal, 1976.
A huge and complex work, operating on several levels simultaneously. On one level, it is a piece of crime fiction about a man imprisoned for 12 years for a murder he didn't commit and who seeks revenge for his sufferings when released. On a second level, it is a story about the strange ways in which our modern society works. And on a third level, it is a discussion of the relationship between a narrator and his text—a concern Madsen has been dealing with ever since he started writing experimental fiction in the early 1960s. The narrative is presented as written by a certain Ato Vari some time in the future. He has decided to produce his historical study of our times as a piece of fiction, something that is not known in his time. The distance between the narrator and the events he depicts makes for a number of amusing misunderstandings. To complicate things further, Ato Vari's narrative is commented upon by a historical expert from his own time—

who, of course, also makes a number of mistakes. Too complicated to summarize adequately, the novel is one of the outstanding SF books of the 1970s.

6-351. Neutzsky-Wulff, Erwin. **Anno Domini.** Copenhagen: Vinten, 1975.
Peter Jessen lands on an unexplored planet. In his diary, he tells of his explorations, his meetings with various kinds of native intelligences, and in great detail of how he learned their languages. He is on a power trip and wallows in primitivism—sexual and otherwise—and it comes as no major surprise when he at last meets both God and Satan. This final sequence is intended to question Jessen's, and the reader's, belief in modern science. Certainly not a major work, this novel is representative of most of Neutzsky-Wulff's SF, which gained quite a following in Denmark in the 1970s. The basic philosophy is that modern scientific advances alienate us from our true natures.

6-352. Nielsen, Niels E. **Akerons porte.** Copenhagen: Vinten, 1976.
This novel begins like a heroic fantasy set in ice-cold surroundings inspired by Old Norse mythology. This would be very unlike Nielsen, however, and in fact he is dealing with two future societies, both refugees from a new ice age. They have settled in central Europe, the city of Vaalheim on land, and the city of Akeron under the sea. Akeron is a technologically well-equipped and artistically interesting society, but lacks sunshine and certain minerals, and so is slowly dying. Vaalheim is agrarian, but lacks sufficient technology to produce a sufficient amount of food. The two cities are at war with each other, but the solution to their problems lies in cooperation. A nice moral tale, combined with perceptive technological extrapolation.

*6-353. Nielsen, Niels E. **Herskerne.** Copenhagen: Hasselbalch, 1970.
Esau is a professor of poetry at the university of the free city of San Ysabel. We are in a relatively affluent future, and the people of San Ysabel are free to pursue their artistic and humanistic interests. On Cap Sheba off the shore, however, is a colony of grotesque people, the results of abandoned experiments in genetic engineering. Esau gets involved in an attempt to get human status for these underpeople. The novel is about the horrible consequences of man experimenting with powers that he cannot control, but it is also a strong antiracist statement. It is remarkable for dealing with genetic engineering as early as 1970. Compare Wells's *The Island of Dr. Moreau* [1-100], and some of Cordwainer Smith's stories about the underpeople [3-354].

6-354. Nielsen, Niels E. **Hinsides Bjergene.** Copenhagen: Irlov-Regulus, 1976.
Twelve short stories, most of them originally published in the 1950s in newspapers and magazines. They present various aspects of the colonization of Mars by people from Earth, including American and Soviet astronauts. Both parties, each in their way, do what they can to ruin the ancient and peaceloving—but perhaps too old and tired—Martian civilization. As in several other of Nielsen's early short stories, the American cultural imperialism of the postwar period is treated negatively, as is the Soviet totalitarianism. The point, however, in both cases is that the invaders unthinkingly destroy a very fine and sophisticated culture. Compare Bradbury's *Martian Chronicles* [3-64].

*6-355. Nielsen, Niels E. **Troldmandens Svaerd.** Copenhagen: Hasselbalch, 1967.
Long after an ecological breakdown that has made life on the surface impossible, the remaining humanity lives in a huge, mostly underground, city. Life there is monotonous, resources are scarce, and everything is tightly controlled under the benevolent dictatorship of the mythical figure Tante Kluk (Aunt Cluck). The only people not living gray, regimented lives are the so-called "lucky children," children born illegally and not entitled to food rations. They live lives that are in some ways freer, but they also starve, and when they are caught, are publicly executed. The novel deals with such a figure from the underground and his fight against authority. He meets a citizen-girl, and when he demonstrates to her that Tante Kluk is nothing but a computer, her world breaks down. Together they escape to the surface, discovering it has recovered. Typical of Nielsen's better work, this novel discusses good intentions gone sour and modern technology abused to uphold a bankrupt power structure. Compare Forster's "The Machine Stops" [1-35].

*6-356. Nielsen, Niels E. **Vagabondernes planet.** Copenhagen: Hasselbalch, 1970.
An impending general breakdown in the early twenty-first century has forced scientists and technicians to take power and set things straight for a population numbering 18 billion. This results in a situation where about half a million live secluded lives in a distant retreat, while the rest spend their lives on the world-encompassing net of 80-track superhighways. These eternal travelers suffer from boredom, with various alarming results, such as killer gangs. The leader of one of these gangs unprecedently gets to visit the elite's resort, falls in love with a young "data" there, and proceeds to return to the roads in order to bring about peace and unspoiled nature again. He reforms his old gang and, through a series of gang wars, becomes the leader of a regular army. The road system and the retreat are destroyed, and the few survivors are left to start over. The novel deals with a number of concerns of the 1960s such as overpopulation and youth crime. It is also a story about good intentions turning into dictatorship or chaos.

6-357. Toubro, Michael. **Topman.** Copenhagen: Tellerup, 1984.
Shortly after the turn of the century is a repressive Norwegian-Danish-Polish Union. This system, building on genetic engineering and widespread use of computer technology, is a society where the only freedom is the freedom to consume. Security is everywhere, partly in the form of robots. Life is generally unbearable, and an underground movement has formed. One of the underground heroes is Topman, and he shows the way to freedom. A blend of dystopia and satire, with some very witty portraits of Danish politicians. Despite the sometimes uneasy blend of genres and intentions, well worth reading.

*6-358. Willumsen, Dorrit. **Programmeret til Kærlighed.** Copenhagen: Vindrose, 1981.
In the near future the woman engineer Liv ("life") is commissioned to create a female android, an ideal woman to solve one of the most widespread problems of modern society: women tire of a relationship much faster than men, walk out,

and leave the men lonely and, what is worse, do not work optimally. The construction of Bianca the android is depicted, intertwined with descriptions of Liv's own alienated life. Bianca is successful, but only to a degree, for at the root of the problem is the very inhumanity of which the robot itself is an expression. This rather bleak novel offers little hope. The only glimpse of a perhaps workable solution is in a letter from one of the runaway wives. She writes from a communal settlement where people live clean, healthy lives and care for one other. Willumsen is one of the accomplished modernist writers of the 1960s and 1970s, and here she has written a book somewhere between a modernist parable of alienation and a feminist utopia.

Anthologies

6-359. Barfoed, Niels, et al., eds. **14 danske science fiction noveller.** Copenhagen: Thaning & Appel, 1970.
Fourteen stories selected from several hundred entered in a SF short-story contest run by the Danish daily *Politiken* in 1969. The contest is a reflection of the growing public awareness of SF in the late 1960s, and the general quality is rather good (certainly by Danish standards). Among the contributors were well-known crime fiction authors such as Frits Remar and Poul-Henrik Trampe, as well as Merete Kruuse, who later became well known for her SF. But the rest of the authors have not written much SF since, which is to be deplored.

6-360. Bolt, Nina, et al., eds. **Athena'er i byen og brugt.** Copenhagen: Hekla, 1984.
This book is an indirect result of the boom in academic and feminist interest in utopias and SF in the late 1970s and early 1980s. Five women authors, none of whom had written SF before, write about the future in order to "express their fears" about it and thereby come to grips with it. Reflecting the views of a majority of Danish feminist utopianists and SF writers, they do not discriminate between SF and occult fantasy. One story is markedly better than the rest: Anette Tamborg's "C II," telling of a future where the center of Copenhagen is reserved for the well to do, while the suburban slum houses the proles.

6-361. Swiatek, Erik H., ed. **Elverhøj retur.** Copenhagen: Science Fiction Cirklen, 1980.
The Scandinavian SF conventions in 1977 and 1980 sponsored SF short-story contests. This volume contains the ten best stories from the 1980 competition, judged by SF experts from Denmark, Norway, and Sweden. It is important in showing what the writers of genre fiction were capable of at the time, but most of the stories are not good. The exceptions are stories by Niels Søndergaard, Steen Knudsen, and Bjarne Lund-Jensen, all of whom show flair for working within a mostly 1950s American SF idiom.

Nonfiction

6-362. Dollerup, Cay, ed. **Vølve: Scandinavian Views on Science Fiction.** Copenhagen: University of Copenhagen, Department of English, 1978. Anglica et Americana 4.

This paperback collects revised transcripts of panels and selected papers from the Scandinavian SF convention in 1977. Besides five papers dealing specifically with Danish conditions, there are panel discussions on SF's relation to mainstream literature, to computers, and to politics. Among the participants were Philip José Farmer and Brian W. Aldiss.

*6-363. Guld, Jens. **Bibliografi over litteratur på dansk om science fiction til og med 1984.** Copenhagen: Science Fiction Cirklen, 1985.
This is an updated and expanded version of the author's work from 1977, covering books and articles about the genre. The coverage is good, as both specialized periodicals and newspapers are covered. Each entry is annotated, giving a short description of the contents, as well as the length in words. Book reviews are not covered, but most everything else seems to be. A very useful tool for the researcher.

*6-364. Holm, Palle Juul. **Syzygy og den sorte stjerne: Temaer og motiver i science fiction.** Copenhagen: Notabene, 1975.
These 64 pages constitute the first and so far only book-length study of SF published in Danish. Holm discusses the nature of the genre as distinguished from "realistic" or mimetic fiction, and proceeds to give an overview of different themes and motifs used by SF writers. In his theoretical discussions, Holm owes much to Darko Suvin. The discussion of different themes and motifs is comprehensive, if necessarily schematic. To a reader reading only Danish, its major fault is that most of its examples had not then been published in Danish translation.

*6-365. Schiøler, Carsten, and Erik H. Swiatek. **Dansk Science Fiction Indeks 1742–1976.** Copenhagen: Science Fiction Cirklen, 1977.
This is a pioneering effort, the first and so far only bibliography of SF published in Danish, including translations. Besides the bibliography proper, the volume contains an introduction to the history of the genre and an index of SF comics published in Danish. The bibliography covers most SF published in book form through 1976, but excludes for the most part material published in magazines and newspapers. In addition, the index of original titles covers only stories published in anthologies, not those published in single author collections. Despite these reservations, it is an indispensable tool for those interested in the history of SF in Denmark.

Magazine

*6-366. Proxima. ISSN: 0105-9017. 1974. 4/yr. Niels Dalgaard, ed. (Subscriptions: Poul Poulsen, Skolegade 26, DK-4800 Nykøbing F., Denmark.)
Proxima is published by the Danish SF fan organization, the Science Fiction Cirklen. It began life at the same time as the organization, and was then—under the editorship of Carsten Schiøler—a general SF review, each issue containing a short story (original or translated), a few reviews, and a number of short articles. Currently it is probably the most serious review of SF in Scandinavia, occasionally publishing short stories, but in general leaning toward criticism and often quite long reviews. It is the only periodical of its kind in Denmark, with a circulation of about 500.

Swedish SF

Sam J. Lundwall

Apart from a few isolated examples, mostly political allegories involving some space travel, hollow Earth tales, alien visitors, and so on, in the seventeenth and eighteenth centuries, indigenous Swedish science fiction did not appear until the late nineteenth century, when science fiction exploded everywhere in Europe and even started to appear in North America. Being a small and somewhat isolated country, Sweden did not have the literary and cultural traditions of the rest of Europe, and I personally regard the starting point for SF in Sweden as 1867, when the first book ever about science fiction, Camille Flammarion's *Les Mondes imaginaires et les mondes réels* (first published in France in 1864) was translated into Swedish. This classic work, which mainly deals with stories of space travel, appears to have made a great impact in Swedish literary circles; it went through at least three printings in 1867, and was reprinted several times the next decade. Flammarion was the foremost propagandizer of the "plurality of worlds" idea, including a sort of forerunner to the famous "panspermia"—space spores—theory proposed by the Swedish scientist Svante Arrhenius later that century.

The idea of other inhabited worlds had of course been around for some time, as had the idea of stories based on or explaining scientific facts and fantasies. In 1842, the Swedish author, archbishop, and member of the Royal Swedish Academy Esaias Tegnér wrote to the scientist Jöns Jacob Berzelius, known today as the discoverer of selenium and as the leading chemical authority in the world in his time:

Tell me, why could not the forces that really are present in Nature also be treated in didactic Poetry? What is Poetry, if not a way of poetizing, that is, symbolizing, Nature? Is this not the innermost nature of Poetry? Is not Nature itself just a vast unconscious Poem, written by God, and should not Poetry describe this, fantasize about it, create panoramas of Nature and science as it perhaps not is but might be, should not Poetry imagine things that not are but perhaps could be?

—Tord Hall, *Naturvetenskap och poesi.* Bonniers, 1981, p. 7

Nine years later, in 1851, the British essayist William Wilson took up the thread in his book, *A Little Earnest Book upon a Great Old Subject,* in which Wilson not only gave better form to Tegnér's and others' diffuse thoughts, but also gave this new scientific poetry a name—"science fiction." This newfangled name for the genre was naturally not used in Sweden, where the French name, *voyages extraordinaires,* had been translated as *Fantastiska resor* or *Naturvetenskapliga historier* ("fantastic journeys" or "scientific tales"). This latter name for the genre was used in the heading for the first Swedish SF magazine, an ill-fated attempt that lasted only four issues, from April 1886 through August 1888. It was called *Stella,* after a well-known science fiction novel by Flammarion, who was the big name in science fiction in Sweden at this time, much more popular than Jules Verne or André Laurie, and appeared as a supplement to a popular Swedish weekly, *Svenska Familj-Journalen Svea,* but was sold separately from it. It published most of the leading science fiction authors of the time, including Kurd Lasswitz, E. T. A. Hoffmann, Claës Lundin, Maurus Jokai, and Jules Verne. Evidently it never became very popular, though, and it remains a footnote in the history of science fiction magazines.

The next development was already waiting in the wings, however. The Swedish mining engineer Otto Witt (1875–1923) returned in 1912 to Sweden after having worked in Germany for a number of years. It is fascinating to note that he had studied at the Technikum in Bingen, Germany, at the same time as Karl Hans Strobl (1877–1946), who later launched the Austrian science fiction magazine *Der Orchideengarten,* and Hugo Gernsback (1884–1967), who much later launched *Amazing Stories,* studied there. I cannot help wonder if these three ever met and perhaps decided to change the world through science fiction magazines, talking young Hugo into the venture, probably over many steins of German beer.

In any event, Otto Witt started his magazine before the others. It was *Hugin,* a rather strange magazine that appeared with one trial issue in 1916, then went on with 85 regular issues until 1920. Witt became chiefly known for his many science fiction novels, but his real love seems to have been spent on *Hugin* of which he wrote every word, including the paid advertisements for various big companies like Munktell and Nobel that were in the form of didactic short science fiction stories. Witt called these stories *Naturvetenskapliga berättelser* ("scientific fiction"), a term already in use on the Continent at this time, and he used his scientific fiction as vehicles for every harebrained idea he could think of, from gold making to growing potatoes by "animal elektricity." He also wrote reviews of science fiction films and books (usually very negative); and he once made a curious reference to "an amateur publication devoted to inventions and travels in space," which I have been unable to trace.

As a science fiction writer, Witt was almost as bad as Gernsback, and as editor he had remarkably little influence. Although *Hugin* appears to have been popular, with a circulation (according to Witt) exceeding 15,000 copies, the literary world regarded him as little more than a boisterous madman, perhaps for good reasons. Swedish authors who wrote science fiction at the time, like Ossian Elgström and Henning Berger, obviously drew no inspiration from him.

Witt wrote what was, or was purported to be, "hard science fiction," based on scientific facts, in effect didactic tales designed to impress the wonders of science upon the readers. The main development of Swedish science fiction took another road, that of social satire, mostly radical in nature. The first modern example of this was a novel by Claës Lundin, journalist and mentor of August Strindberg, *Oxygen och Aromasia* (*Oxygen and Aromasia*) [6-369], published in 1878, a boisterous and very funny tale from the year 2378 incorporating all the themes and ideas that already were standard fare in European science fiction—space travel, television, moving sidewalks, terrible Martians chasing the heroine, time travel, even a little time travel paradox. Basically a political tale, aimed at the reactionary society at the time, it was also very witty and an amusing satire. The fact that most of the fantastic ideas and much of the plot were lifted from a novel by Kurd Lasswitz, *Bilder aus der Zukunft* [6-23], perhaps also tells us something about Swedish science fiction at this time.

After the turn of the century, the enormous science fiction boom on the Continent finally caught up with Sweden. In 1901, 27 Swedish original science fiction novels were published, and although this peak was not surpassed until 1954, when 34 novels saw publication, the output of Swedish science fiction remained good. Quality, however, was another matter—mostly adventure stories of the usual sort, with spaceships, strange inventions, heroes and villains, adventures in the hollow Earth—and it was heavily influenced by French and German writers, including the well-known German space opera series *Kapitän Mors,* a forerunner to *Perry Rhodan,* which was very popular in Germany in the years before World War I. The Norwegian-born Øvre Richter-Frich wrote a long series of novels about strange inventions, mad scientists, and spaceships, and quite a number of writers wrote what we might call pulp science fiction novels, thinly disguised as thrillers and crime novels. Occasional lights emerged, like Nobel Prize winner Pär Lagerkvist with his collection of short stories, *Onda sagor* (*Evil Fairy Tales,* 1924), which expressed a disillusioned attitude toward the evils of life.

These stories used science fiction and fantasy as tools in describing the horrors of the near future, but the first truly modern dystopian Swedish novel did not appear until 1940. The novel was *Kallocain* [6-367] by Karin Boye (1900–1941), a dystopian novel that outdid all other anti-utopian tales of this time, including Huxley's *Brave New World* [2-47], and rather more effective as a brutal reminder of the bestiality lurking in man than Orwell's much overrated *Nineteen Eighty-Four.* Both these celebrated novels deal with totalitarian states, but whereas *Nineteen Eighty-Four* describes the usual boots-and-whips state of Nazi Germany, set in a near future, and Huxley described Coca-Cola imperialism in absurdum, *Kallocain* uses the more subtle way of a truth serum in a totalitarian state much worse than the one portrayed in *Nineteen Eighty-Four. Kallocain* is pitch black in its view of the future and can be seen as a testament of Karin Boye and the hopelessness that compelled her to commit suicide in 1941.

The great forerunner to *Kallocain,* and indeed still the best dystopian novel, was Zamiatin's famous novel *We* [2-147]. It is possible that Boye had read *We;* but it is much more probable that she attacked the same thing that Zamiatin attacked in his novel: Alexey Gastev's infamous "machinism," a robotization of people, which for a while actually was put into practice in Moscow. Gastev was one of the more unusual futurists and one who got a chance to put his theories into practice. Zamiatin had personal reasons to dislike Gastev intensely, and attacked him violently in *We*—with the result that Gastev spent the rest of his life in a penal colony. Karin Boye knew about Gastev; she had visited Moscow and what remained of his Central Work Institute, and *Kallocain* is actually a rather good description of the first phase of machinism.

The most celebrated example of modern Swedish science fiction, however, is of course the Nobel Prize winner Harry Martinson's *Aniara* [6-370], the moving book-length poem about the spaceship *Aniara,* which, thrown off course when fleeing to Mars from a devastated Earth, falls forever through space. It is chiefly known for the opera version made by Karl-Birger Blomdahl, performed all over the world and acclaimed as one of the great modern operas. Using the standard fare of pulp science fiction of the 1940s (Martinson was an avid science fiction reader), Martinson managed to heighten this space drama into something universal, a story not merely about the spaceship but about man and his place in the universe.

In 1940, Sweden got its first pulp adventure science fiction magazine of the sort then popular in English-language countries. *Jules Verne-Magasinet,* launched on October 16, 1940, was the first weekly SF magazine in the world (as far as is known), soon selling more than 50,000 copies per issue, which was a lot for Sweden—the equivalent of something like 1,500,000 copies a week in the United States. The stories came almost exclusively from U.S. magazines, and most of them were space opera stories of negligible merit. It should be noted, however, that some of the better American authors, like Isaac Asimov and Ray Bradbury, were first published in Sweden in this magazine. An entire generation of Swedish science fiction fans was reared on this fare of intergalactic struggles, invincible heroes, monsters, and so on, and until it folded in 1947 after 332 issues it was a source of great happiness to many young readers. *Jules Verne-Magasinet* was revived in 1969 by the journalist Bertil Falk, who published it as a "little magazine" until 1972, when it was made into a professional magazine, presenting SF from all parts of the world. It is still being published, on a bimonthly basis [6-376].

Unfortunately, the rather primitive science fiction presented in *Jules Verne-Magasinet* during the 1940s created a science fiction ghetto in Sweden, as it had done in English-language countries, and this became apparent when the next magazine appeared. *Häpna* was launched on March 1, 1954, and folded December 4, 1969, after 141 issues. First using mainly U.S. material, it soon turned increasingly to British and Swedish stories, with the result that quite a number of Swedish writers made their debut there. Even more important, *Häpna* encouraged the forming of clubs, which in their turn grew into a science fiction fandom with conventions, fanzines, and so on. Fandom is today very strong in Sweden, with hundreds of fanzines and about a half-dozen conventions each year.

Two more SF magazines have appeared in Sweden: *Galaxy,* in the early 1960s, a Swedish edition of the U.S. magazine; and *Nova Science Fiction* [6-377], which appeared in the early 1980s but now seems to have folded, with no issues published for almost a year.

The present generation of Swedish science fiction writers has sprung from the magazines, starting with Sture Lönnerstrand, whose novel *Rymdhunden (The Space Dog)* appeared in 1955. Other noted authors in the field are Dénis Lindbohm, Börje Crona, Carl Johan Holzhausen, Bertil Mårtensson, and myself. These are authors that mainly or solely write science fiction. Apart from these are of course a number of authors who write science fiction occasionally, like the late Per Wahlöö and P. C. Jersild—not to mention Astrid Lindgren, of *Pippi Longstocking* fame, whose last few novels have been fantasy, selling several hundred thousand copies each in hardcover, not bad for a country of 8 million.

As for present trends in Swedish science fiction, it seems that the genre has finally gotten out of the ghetto: space adventures are confined to cheap paperbacks and serious novels of literary merit are published under prestigious imprints in hardcover. The enormous success in Sweden of surrealist and magic realism authors like Borges, Cortazar, and Fuentes has opened new ways out of the ghetto, and a number of interesting new works have appeared lately.

Ideology is important in Europe, as well as in all American countries except the United States, where all science fiction appears rather right wing to European eyes. This is very apparent in Sweden, where there are at present two main publishers specializing in the genre. One is Delta, liberal as Europe goes, which I suspect would be dangerously left wing in Anglo-American eyes, publishing hardcover novels, mostly translations from various European languages, but also from American countries like Argentina, Brazil, and the United States; and Laissez Faire, which is just what the name implies, a company on the far, far right, politically committed to Anglo-American libertarian values, publishing mass market paperback space adventures translated from English. Delta's big name is the Strugatskii brothers; Laissez Faire prefers Ayn Rand. Swedish fandom is divided along these lines as well—one liberal side, one on the far right. The two sides even hold separate conventions. The situation is rather like the one in West Germany and Poland.

Bibliography

Individual Authors

6-367. Boye, Karin. **Kallocain.**   Stockholm: Bonnier, 1940. Tr. as *Kallocain* (Univ. of Wisconsin Press, 1966).
Noted dystopian novel describing a totalitarian state in which a new truth serum is introduced, and discussions about whether any government has a right to im-

pose such tyranny on its subjects. Related to Zamiatin's celebrated novel *We* [2-147]. Also annotated as [3-58].

6-368. Jersild, P. C. **En levande själ.** Stockholm: Bonnier, 1980.
The story of a brain in a laboratory, the result of an experiment, who learns to swim around in his nutrient solution with the aid of what remains of his ear muscles, and thinks about the where and whence of man and mankind. A rather funny novel, reminiscent in setting of *Donovan's Brain* [3-351], but of course with a very different tone in all respects.

6-369. Lundin, Claës. **Oxygen och Aromasia.** Seeligman, 1878; Lindqvist, 1974.
Commonly considered the first modern Swedish science fiction novel, a strongly political, utopian farce mainly based on Kurd Lasswitz's *Bilder aus der Zukunft* [6-23].

6-370. Martinson, Harry. **Aniara.** Stockholm: Bonnier, 1956.
A cycle of poems describing the spaceship *Aniara,* which leaves a devastated Earth with colonists for Mars. En route the ship is hit by meteorites; the course is altered, and the ship falls out into eternity. The songs describe the life within the ship, including revolts and the emergence of a ruthless dictator, until a generation later when the last people aboard die and the ship falls on into space as a giant coffin. Martinson's last major work, also made into a noted opera by Karl-Birger Blomdahl. A somewhat less than satisfactory translation into English has been published [3-272], but is not recommended. A good German translation is available (Munich: Nymphenburger Verlagshandlung, 1961).

6-371. Parling, Nils. **Korset.** Stockholm: Tiden, 1957.
In a near future, after the nuclear war, a religious fanatic starts a major revival and marches through Europe with a few hundred followers who drag with them an enormous U.S. atomic cannon, found in what used to be West Germany. The cannon assumes the importance of a relic, the last weapon from the war, and thousands of people die dragging it through Europe. Finally, pressed to prove the cannon is really the Hand of God, the preacher fires it and destroys the last bastion of learning in the world.

Nonfiction

6-372. Holmberg, John-Henri. **Drömmar om evigheten.** Stockholm: Askild & Kärnekull, 1974.
The history of science fiction from an English-language perspective, but with one chapter on Swedish SF.

6-373. Lundwall, Sam J. **Bibliografi över science fiction & fantasy.** Stockholm: Lindqvist, 1974; Delta, 1984.
Bibliography of more than 3,000 science fiction and fantasy books, including utopias, published in the Swedish language (many of them translations), divided into two volumes covering the years 1741–1973 and 1974–1983, respectively. Entries are in a single alphabet, with complete information in the author entries and cross-references from the titles to the authors.

6-374. Lundwall, Sam J. **Science fiction.** Stockholm: Sveriges Radios, 1969.
A history of science fiction from an European point of view. Very much liked in Europe, but met with a hostile reaction in the United States. Also annotated as [9-55].

6-375. Qvarnström, Gunnar. **Dikten och den nya vetenskapen.** Vällingby: Gleerup, 1961.
Doctoral thesis on space travel in literature, from Lucian and on. Summary in English. Compare Nicolson [9-69].

Magazines

6-376. Jules Verne-Magasinet. 1940– . ISSN: 0345-5599. 6/yr. Sam J. Lundwall, ed. (Box 17030, S-161 17 Bromma, Sweden).

6-377. Nova Science Fiction. 1982–1986(?). ISSN: 0280-3232. 4/yr. John-Henri Holmberg, ed. (Laissez Faire Produktion AB, Råsundavägen 129, S-171 30 Solna, Sweden).

Norwegian SF

Jon Bing

One popular comic book is titled *The Mighty Thor*, the heroes of which are the gods of Asgard, borrowed from Norse mythology. The mythology and the sagas, which in terse language describe fantastic and dramatic events, are some of the background of modern Norwegian literature and, of course, science fiction. A similar background is found in the oral tradition that was recorded at the end of the last century, and where the archetypal fantasy figures of the troll, the hulder (the beautiful maiden with the tail of a cow), and the draug (an ogre rowing a half-boat) are some of the central characters.

This rich tradition has been important for modern science fiction and fantasy, but no really national fantastic literature was forged from the material. Looking for the origins of Norwegian fantastic literature, one finds actually a rather learned work originally published in Latin—*Nicolai Klimii Iter Subterraneum*, or *The Subterranean Voyage of Nils Klim to the Planet Nazar* [6-390]. This book was published in 1741 by Ludvig Holberg (1684–1754), a Norwegian with a central position in the national literature. He was originally from Bergen, but was drawn to studies and a career in the capital of what at that time was the twin kingdoms of Denmark and Norway. Today he is best remembered for his comedies—he made himself into some sort of Nordic Molière, and his comedies are still on the repertoire of the major stages.

Holberg made use of the visit to the many strange countries of the planet Nazar in a way well known from satirical and utopian literature, criticizing and ridiculing the politics and the Pietism that at that time was invading Norway.

The utopian story of Nils Klim's visit to Nazar is a major work in the history of Norwegian literature. The other early example is all but forgotten, though the author, Johan Hermann Wessel (1742–1785), is remembered with fondness. He was a satirical poet with a flair for an elegant punch line, some of which have eroded into proverbs. He also wrote a few comedies, and the last of these has the title *Anno 7603*, published in 1781 and never staged (and even excluded from the editions of his collected works). The play is somewhat lacking in quality, but it is a very early example of a standard science fiction gambit—time travel. The two central characters, Leander and Julia, are transported by a fairy to a future where the sex roles are reversed: men are vain and flirting, the women battle and drink.

These are two interesting early examples of fantastic literature in Norway, both by influential authors. It becomes, however, difficult to find some strain in the development of literature in Norway in which this utopian or fantastic initiative is conserved. It is true that Henrik Wergeland (1804–1845), who is seen as the national poet of Norway after its separation from Denmark in 1814, wrote a comedy under the rather improbable pseudonym Siful Sifadda titled *De sidste Kloge* (1835), taking place among the last wise persons of the planet Terra Nova. It is also true that the first author who really tried to make a living from his books in Norway, Christopher Maurits Hansen (1794–1842), wrote several romantic and fantastic stories, like the story of the magic egg, "Hovedvandsægget" (1820). And, more important, one of the major authors of the last century, Jonas Lie, collected in two volumes (*Trold* I and II, 1891–1892) short stories in which the living tradition of supernatural beings and forces was emphasized. These stories succeeded in bridging the gap between, on the one hand, fairy tales and superstition, and on the other hand, the life of the fisherman and farmer in the dramatic landscape of the north of Norway, achieving a symbolic quality of psychological reality. But these are, nevertheless, rather incidental examples, and do not come together to make any tradition. The opposite is rather true—Norwegian prose was characterized by realism and down-to-earth topics.

When the rotary press brought cheap books and magazines to Norway, at about the turn of the century, there emerged a few, interesting pulp writers. One of them was Johan Vibe (1840–1897), who published a collection of fantastic stories (*Fantastiske fortællinger* [6-394]), including the rather strange story of Professor Buntiger's journey to Mars. Another was Sven Elvestad (better known under his pseudonym Stein Riverton), who was an impressive and prolific writer of crime fiction, but who also wrote the fantastic tale of *Professor Umbrosus* (1922). The undisputed king of this area was, however, Øvre Richter Frich (1872–1945). He created superheroes in his pulp fiction, foremost Jonas Fjeld, a blond and blue-eyed doctor who roamed the world for fantastic adventure, like his encounter with the snake blossoms of Magdala. Another of his heroes, Adrian Rocca, belonged to a league of criminals who, among other things, used an airplane that folded into a suitcase. In both these series, new inventions and fantastic adventure are prominent. And in one of Frich's novels (*Det yderste hav,* 1921), the plot takes the pilot of a novel aircraft to an unknown planet that probably is Mars, though Frich is not generous in sharing astronomical details with his readers. The fiction of Frich has remained popular and in print; in spite of a doubtful ideological and political foundation, it still captures the imagination of readers.

Influential also was the novel by James K. Anthony (a pseudonym for Christian Haugen, 1894–?) called *Reisen til Ken* [6-378] (first published in Swedish in Stockholm 1925, in 1926 in the original Norwegian). This is a true space romance, which caught the public interest sufficiently for the novel to be turned into a comic strip (drawings by Arent Christensen for *Arbeider-magasinet*, 1933–1934), a strip that was given a continuation by the same team, *Den tause verden* (1935–1936). Another excellent science fiction comic strip was produced for several years as *Ingeniør Knut Berg på eventyr (The Adventures of Engineer Knut Berg*, 18 vol., 1943–1960; text by Vingleik Vikli, drawings by Ronald Stone, pseudonyms for Hallvard Sandnes and Jostein Øverlid), in which several, rather standard science fiction gimmicks were employed with new twists. Like Jonas Fjeld, the bold engineer Knut Berg still survives in popular imagination.

In the postwar period, several well-established authors made use of science fiction for fun or irony. One of them was Torolf Elster (1911–   ), a prominent figure in the Social-Democratic party and, later, director of the state broadcasting company of Norway. (As a director of the broadcasting company, Elster later invited Brian Aldiss to give a series of radio lectures on science fiction. These later became the core of his *Billion Year Spree* [9-4].) He wrote a couple of short-story collections (*Klovnen*, 1953, and *Sjørøvere* [6-385]) in which his fantastic satire is turned toward conventionality and conservatism. Niels Christian Brøgger (1914–1966) (using the pseudonym Harald Gammeng) wrote a pastiche (*Stoppested i evigheten* [6-387]) where, regrettably, several of the stories were directly based on Ray Bradbury's *Martian Chronicles* [3-64]. More important was Hans Christian Sandbeck's *Atomene spiller* [6-393], a utopian novel trying to discuss the recent lesson learned by Hiroshima.

These are examples of authors using science fiction as convenient vehicles for their plots and ideas. It would be possible to give further examples, but they really do not come together as anything like a trend. They are interesting, often amusing, but contributed little to creating a national science fiction literature. One of the major authors working at this time, Sigurd Evensmo (1912–1978), also used science fiction for some of his discussions on the professional responsibility of scientists (*Gåten fra år null*, 1957, and *Mirakelet på Blindern*, 1966). These were perhaps the more important books at the end of the period where a utopian novel represented some sort of turning point.

The novel was *Epp* [6-391] by the young author Axel Jensen (1932–   ). Jensen had made a name for himself by that time, but *Epp* was a departure from his earlier novels. It is a utopian novel, describing the isolation of an old man in a modern, near automatic society. The style is terse, giving the rather depressing description some sort of poetic or symbolic attribute. The novel was widely acclaimed, and it was given the international Woursell Prize in 1966. It was actually the first international Norwegian science fiction book since the journey of Holberg's Nils Klim.

Epp was a turning point, but Jensen did not pursue science fiction further for some time. In 1967, however, Jon Bing (1944–   ) and Tor Åge Bringsværd (1939–   ) made some impact on the Norwegian literary scene. Working together, they started to edit and publish a large number of science fiction anthologies and have major foreign authors translated. Working under their joint byline of Bing and Bringsværd, they brought modern science fiction into Norway. They edited for the largest publishing house, Gyldendal Norsk Forlag, the Lanterne science fiction series, which continued to publish titles until 1980. This series brought for the first time major British and U.S. authors in Norwegian translations—authors like Bradbury, Bester, Clarke, Le Guin, Leiber, and others—as well as original Norwegian books. Until this series, translations had been very few and shoddily produced (with a few honorable exceptions). The series contains altogether some 60 titles and represents the majority of translated science fiction. After the Norwegian paperback market folded for economic reasons in the beginning of the 1980s, very few books were translated, an exception being the juvenile softcover series of Gyldendal, Luna, which brings well-known juvenile authors like Le Guin, Lewis, and others who write science fiction or fantasy.

In 1967 Bing and Bringsværd also published their first collection of short stories (*Rundt solen i ring*), including stories by both of them. Their first stage play (*Å miste et romskip*, 1970) was a comedy with a thin plot concerning three astronauts losing a spaceship. Their joint career has lately centered on dramatic productions, the best known probably being *Blindpassasjer* (1979), a three-part television series centered on the mystery of identifying who of five astronauts aboard a spaceship has been replaced by a biomat, a synthetic person.

Separately, they have published a large number of novels and short-story collections. Bringsværd is one of the more acclaimed contemporary writers. Of his more recent novels, one should mention *Ker Shus* [6-384], a story from a far future outlining the fate of man in symbols borrowed from science fiction and mythology alike. It would be difficult to box Bringsværd into a narrow definition of science fiction—his use of mythological topics, his poetic and finely tuned language, and his outrageous humor make his books vary greatly. His latest novel, *Gobi* (1985), is the first in a series of historic and fantastic novels—this first book confronting the Children's Crusade of medieval Europe with the life and policies of Genghis Khan. Jon Bing has a smaller production, but which includes a quartet of juvenile novels (1975–1986) describing the voyages of the library starship *Alexandria*, cruising the heavens at sublight speed, stopping at planets and solving problems by using the traditional tools of librarians, knowledge. His latest book, *Hvadata?* (1986), is a collection of short stories on computer crime and data protection.

Based on the activities of Bing and Bringsværd, a somewhat increased interest in science fiction made itself felt in Norway, and several new authors were launched. These authors often had a background in fandom, exploiting traditional themes and finding themselves in a double opposition to the literary establishment. Bing and Bringsværd had identified science fiction with a broad understanding, including fantasy and surrealistic fiction, often attacking what they found to be "space opera," trivial science fiction. The new authors wanted to defend some of the more traditional Anglo-American science fiction, and therefore found themselves at odds both with the literary establishment and the views held by those subscribing to Bing and Bringsværd. Many of them felt that a sort of monopoly had been created of science fiction, which they opposed and set out to break.

The most important of these undoubtedly is Øyvind Myhre, a fast paced storyteller in the tradition of Heinlein, with controversial and right wing political views. He has become in some sense the counterpoint to Bing and Bringsværd, and making his views known in a number of novels as well as essays. Two others of some interest are Dag Ove Johansen (1950–   ) and Ingar Knutsen, Jr. Both have been published mainly by small houses or fanzine presses, but Knutsen has some accomplished juvenile novels (*Tyrannosaurus Rex,* 1978; *Tova,* 1979; *Reisen til Jorda,* 1981).

These authors also became central in a revival of fandom, which started with the publishing of a science fiction magazine in 1971, the only magazine that has had any real impact in Norway. In the beginning, the magazine was simply titled *Science fiction magasinet,* but was renamed *Nova* in 1973. The magazine was founded, and in the beginning edited, by Terje W Wanberg, but a large number of active fans took part in its publishing—Øyvind Myhre served as editor from 1975 to 1977. The magazine was discontinued in 1978, but Wanberg has continued regularly to publish Norwegian books with his imprint, Stowa.

In 1966 a science fiction club, Aniara, was founded at the University of Oslo. This was stimulated by *Nova,* and was revived in 1974. Since then, Aniara has organized conferences, published the fanzine *Algernon,* and generally has been a focus of fandom.

More traditional writers also made use of—and are increasingly making use of—science fiction frames of reference in their work. One of the most popular writers of Norway, Knut Faldbakken (1941–   ), wrote a utopian duo (*Uår* and *Uår: Sweetwater* [6-386]), where the decline of Western society is seen from the perspective of a few people living on a garbage dump in the outskirts of a dying city. Marta Schumann (1919–   ) wrote in 1983 a vivid utopian story of the terror balance (*Våge å tenkje*). And Eirik Austey (pseudonym for the Marxist-Leninist political ideologue Tron Øgrim) created something quite rare, a Marxist utopian novel using a detailed and fictitious community to create the conflicts and developments that illustrate his political ideas (*Tyskeren mot Stretermish* [6-379]).

Finally, two unique writers should be mentioned. Peter Haars is originally German, but has been living in Norway for a long time. He started by publishing serious, pop-art comic books, but graduated into well-plotted and surrealistic novels concerned with the mass media and the way images are used in modern society. Thore Hansen (1942–   ) is a jack-of-all-trades, famous for his work as an illustrator, but also for writing successful fantastic novels bordering on traditional fairy tales like his latest story of the alien longing for the stars (*Han som lengtet til stjernene* [6-389]).

In the mid-1980s, few Norwegian science fiction authors are active. Bing and Bringsværd are still writing, and so is Myhre. There is a tendency to include fantastic and science fiction elements in the postmodernist literature, but the works of such authors are not recognized as science fiction, and the authors do not identify themselves with this literature. The Latin American magical realism tradition has a much larger influence than the Anglo-American tradition of science fiction. Translations are very few, only three or four annually. The fandom-based publisher Stowa maintains its publishing base with a book club, averaging approximately four titles annually, and of varying quality. But they are important for young authors, and the plans for reviving their old magazine, *Nova,* in 1987 is a hopeful sign.

Bibliography

Individual Authors

6-378. Anthony, James K. (pseud. of Christian Haugen). **Reisen til Ken.** Tønsberg forlag, 1926.

A journey through space in the space cruiser, *Tagan,* to the planet Ken. A space opera similar to U.S. romances of that time. The book has interest only as a period piece.

6-379. Austey, Eirik (pseud. of Tron Øgrim). **Tyskeren mot Stretermish.** Oslo: Aschehoug, 1985.

A complex utopian tale from a middle European country, centered on the class struggle and myths of the local people confronting the mining engineers and the authorities. The political arguments do not dominate, the descriptions are vivid and original. Compare Le Guin's *Malafrena* (1979).

6-380. Bing, Jon. **Alene, og fremtiden.** Oslo: Gyldendal, 1977.

A selection of 39 short stories published from 1967 to 1975 ranging from space tales to fictitious documents on Charles Babbage and Johannes Kepler.

*6-381. Bing, Jon. **Dobbeltgjengere.** Oslo: Gyldendal, 1984.

A novel using the doppelgänger motif to discuss the nature and impact of new technology, especially artificial intelligence, and the operation of internal organizations within this field.

6-382. Brekke, Toril. **Sølvfalken.** Oktober, 1986.

A novel that, through a multifaceted view of the world, describes the invisible suppression of creative and political potential—a new type of political science fiction. The language and visions are poetic in a book of considerable strength and courage.

6-383. Bringsværd, Tor Åge. **Karavane.** 2nd ed. Oslo: Gyldendal, 1982.

A collection of 36 of the Bringsværd's short stories, published 1968 through 1982, from the outrageous exploits of the "Cream Cake Man" to the poetry in the tale of the man who collected September 1, 1972. Bringsværd's humorous style has been compared to Vonnegut's, but his later stories are closer to French surrealism than Anglo-American science fiction.

*6-384. Bringsværd, Tor Åge. **Ker Shus.** Oslo: Gyldendal, 1983.

A poetic and taut novel of an Earth in the far future, where the ideals and errors of humanity are reflected in the symbols and myths of robots, rats, and men. The story has a lot of excitement and mystery, but the strong and poetic images of the future world are its best features.

3-385. Elster, Torolf. **Sjørøvere.** Oslo: Tiden, 1959.

A collection of 11 humorous short stories on conservatism and social policy in the form of fables and fantasy. The stories are rather traditional in form and content, but written with wit and insight into the Norwegian postwar society.

6-386. Faldbakken, Knut. **Uår** and **Uår: Sweetwater.** Oslo: Gyldendal, 1974–1976.
A two-volume novel of the decline of Western civilization, seen from the perspective of the erotic love and struggle for survival of a few people trying to eke out a living on a garbage dump at the outskirts of a dying city, Sweetwater. It is a utopian novel written by a powerful author, but also an author with little knowledge of prior utopias on the same basic theme. To a science fiction reader, the lack of innovation in ideas or images to a certain extent reduces the quality of the book.

6-387. Gammeng, Harald (pseud. of Niels Christian Brøgger). **Stoppested i evigheten.** Oslo: Aschehoug, 1954.
Short stories, in the form of chapters of a novel, based on U.S. models, several openly exploiting the plots (though not the style) of Ray Bradbury. The book is interesting as a distinct science fiction short-story collection in a period where science fiction was practically not written.

6-388. Haars, Peter (Germany). **Reisen til Ai-Po-Tu.** Oslo: Gyldendal, 1978.
A very complex utopian novel based in a future world where the citizens live in subterranean tunnels, seduced by the dreaming mirrors. The illusions are literally shattered in the search of the protagonist for his lost wife and the distant planet Ai-Po-Tu. The novel is characterized by its vivid and pregnant images and its open references to fantasy literature (such as the *Necronomicon*, invented by H. P. Lovecraft).

6-389. Hansen, Thore. **Han som lengtet til stjernene.** Oslo: Gyldendal, 1985.
A poetic novel of an alien isolated on Earth and shaping human history by his longing for his lost home among the stars. The story has a lot in common with the theme of the film *E.T.*, but it is given a personal treatment by Hansen.

*6-390. Holberg, Ludvig. **Nicolai Klimii Iter Subterrancum.** Hafniae & Lipsae: Jacob Prevssi, 1741.
A utopian voyage to the planet Nazar in the center of the Earth, attacking the politics and Pietism of the Norwegian-Danish kingdom and presenting a wealth of strange aliens and eccentric customs highlighting Holberg's political and philosophical ideas. Though more than 200 years old, the book still reads well and is being republished in modern translations. It is considered one of the great, classic utopian novels. Also annotated as [1-50] and [6-346].

*6-391. Jensen, Axel. **Epp.** Oslo: Cappelens, 1965. English tr. Chatto & Windus, 1967.
A major utopian novel, centered on an old man trying to make sense of a confusing, modern world in which he is treated as an invalid and in which technology and news contribute to exclude him. The book has an effective style, and an ironic character, making it some sort of pre-pop art novel. Compare Zamiatin's *We* [2-147].

6-392. Myhre, Øyvind. **Snøen på Nix Olympia.** Oslo: Cappelens, 1975.
A collection of short stories from Mars, confronting settlers with the bureaucracy

and disclosing the strong belief of the author in the individual. The stories are in the vein of the early Heinlein, emphasizing the plot.

6-393. Sandbeck, Hans Christian. **Atomene spiller.** Oslo: Tiden, 1945.
A utopian moral tale from the year 2250, discussing the lesson of the Nazi occupation of Norway and the threat and promise of the new nuclear technology. The novel is an example of science fiction verging on philosophy, a pale reflection of Wells.

6-394. Vibe, Johan. **Fantastike fortællinger.** Oslo: Alb. Cammenmeyer, 1891.
A number of fantastic tales in the pulp tradition, including the story of Professor Buntiger's incredible journey to Mars. Though dated, the stories are still fun to read, but only if one has an appetite for pulp.

Anthologies

6-395. Bing, Jon, and Tor Åge Bringsværd, eds. **Dragsug.** Oslo: Gyldendal, 1977.
Norwegian science fiction anthology of 24 original stories, including a history of Norwegian fandom (1954–1977) by Roar Ringdahl [6-398].

*6-396. Bing, Jon, and Tor Åge Bringsværd, eds. **Stella Polaris.** Oslo: Den norske Bokklubben, 1982.
An annotated and illustrated anthology of 60 Norwegian, Danish, Finnish, and Swedish science fiction stories (including poems and comics), from Holberg and Wessel to modern authors.

6-397. Bing, Jon, Tor Åge Bringsværd, and Sigmun Hoftun, eds. **Malstrøm.** Oslo: Gyldendal, 1972.
Anthology of 21 original science fiction stories, including an index of Norwegian science fiction literature by Ola Strøm [6-399].

Nonfiction

6-398. Ringdahl, Roar. **"Norsk science fiction fandom,"** in Jon Bing and Tor Åge Bringsværd, eds. **Dragsug.** Oslo: Gyldendal, 1977, pp. 136–150.
An informal history of fandom in Norway by one of the founders, giving details of clubs and fanzines.

6-399. Strøm, Ola. **"Science fiction av norske forfattere,"** in Jon Bing, Tor Åge Bringsværd, and Sigmun Hoftun, eds. **Malstrøm.** Oslo: Gyldendal, 1972, pp. 123–139.
A bibliography covering science fiction by Norwegian authors, both novels and short stories, up to 1971.

Dutch SF

J. A. Dautzenberg

Dutch and Flemish SF took shape in the 1960s, when several publishers began a SF series, SF fandom was organized, and some Dutch and Flemish authors began to write SF novels.* Before the 1960s, there were only some individual works (original or translated) but no coherent or continuous tradition of science fiction. The SF boom did not last long, however; in the 1980s, the market declined to figures of the late 1960s. Between 1975 and 1979, for instance, the established SF publishers together published almost 100 books a year, mainly translations of British and American books. In 1985 and 1986, these figures declined to some 40 books. (At the same time, SF movies did remarkably well in Holland and Flanders, paradoxically.) Several publishers discontinued their SF lines, and in 1986 only three publishers were active in the SF market (Meulenhoff, Spectrum, and Bruna).

So the situation is now as it has always been: science fiction (and fantasy and horror) consists of isolated works scattered over the whole literary field. Even in those literary periods when the fantastic was flowering everywhere (as in the romantic era and the fin de siècle) the quantity of Dutch and Flemish science fiction was very small. In the nineteenth century several writers produced utopian descriptions of a future Holland, mostly in the form of an imaginary voyage, but

---

*This chapter deals with Dutch-language SF in the Netherlands and the Dutch-speaking part of Belgium known as Flanders. I have deliberately permitted some overlap between this section and that on Belgian SF to give a dual perspective.—Ed.

all of them are totally forgotten now; even the most comprehensive histories of Dutch literature do not mention them. There is only one proto-SF work that deserves some attention: the short novel *Kort verhaal van eene aanmerkelijke luchtreis en nieuwe planeetontdekking* (*Short Narrative of a Remarkable Air-Voyage and Discovery of a New Planet*, 1813) by the then very famous poet and scholar Willem Bilderdijk.

In the early twentieth century there were a few isolated SF novels, such as *Gevleugelde daden* (*Winged Deeds*, 1905) by the important playwright Herman Heijermans, and *Het verstoorde mierennest* (*The Disturbed Ant-Hill*, 1916) by the minor novelist Kees van Bruggen. The first is a humorous account of future aviation, the second an end-of-the-world novel. In the 1920s, two anti-utopias of some importance were published: *C.R. 133* (1926) by Maurits Dekker, a description from a leftist point of view of a future Fascist Europe, and *Het einde der wereld* (*The End of the World*, 1929) by the Fleming Jef Scheirs, an attack on communism from a very orthodox religious point of view. Two years later, in 1931, the most important anti-utopia of Dutch literature appeared: the short novel *Blokken* (*Blocks*) by Ferdinand Bordewijk [6-401].

In the 1940s and early 1950s, no SF novel is worth mentioning. In the late 1950s and especially in the 1960s, some authors came to the fore who could be considered real SF writers. The most remarkable is the physicist Dionijs Burger, the writer of *Bolland* [6-402]. The two most prolific writers of SF are Felix Thijssen and the Fleming Eddy Bertin. The first, originally a writer of adventure fiction for the juvenile market, started to write SF in 1971, when the first volume of the so-called Mark Stevens cycle appeared. This is a run-of-the-mill space opera series, the first volumes of which seemed to be aiming at young adults, but which gradually grew more mature. The series ended with a good eighth volume, *De poorten van het paradijs* (*The Gates of Paradise*) in 1974. Later, Thijssen wrote several much more serious novels, the best of which are *Emmarg* [6-410] and *Pion* [6-411]. Eddy Bertin is the only modern Belgian author who has some reputation in the English-speaking world, thanks to his own English translations of several of his stories. He is an active fan who edits his own fanzine, *SF Gids*, and is as well an ardent bibliographer. In addition to SF, he has written numerous horror stories, which are perhaps the better part of his opus. His most important SF are the so-called Membrane Universe stories [6-400].

Two other writers deserve mention. One is the Fleming Paul van Herck, who came on the scene in 1965 with a collection of short stories, *De cirkels* (*The Circles*). His first and most important novel was *Sam of de pluterdag*, which won the first Europa Award in 1972 [6-404]. A similar but nastier Dutch work is *Duvels en oranjemoeren* (*Demons and Orange Dams*, 1968) by Grovis, the pseudonym of R. Groot and E. Visser, two SF editors. It is an attack on hypocritical Calvinist prudishness; numerous inside jokes make it incomprehensible for non-Dutch readers.

The most remarkable SF debut was the novel *De eersten van Rissan* [6-403] by the poet and dramatist Wim Gijsen (1980); a sequel, *De koningen van weleer*, appeared in 1981. In 1982 Gijsen published his third SF novel, *Iskander de dromendief* (*Iskander, Thief of Dreams*). Advertised as adult SF, it turned out to be young adult fantasy and was a disappointment, not only in this respect but also in the heavy use of all the worn-out SF and fantasy clichés. Later works by Gijsen are all in the same vein.

Beside these real SF writers there are a few mainstream authors who sometimes write science fiction. The Fleming Ward Ruyslinck wrote in 1964 the bitter dystopian novel, *Het reservaat* [6-409]. Hugo Raes, also from Flanders, wrote two imaginary voyages with SF elements, *De lotgevallen* and *Reizigers in de Anti-tijd* [6-407], and a more traditional SF novel, *De verwoesting van Hyperion* [6-408]. In comparison with Flanders, Dutch mainstream SF is less interesting. A very strange book is *Het carnarium* [6-412] by Leo Vroman. *De toekomst van gisteren*, by Harry Mulisch, contains the synopsis of an unwritten alternate world novel, with a very long essay about his reasons for not writing it [6-406]. *De man achter het raam*, by Gerrit Krol, is a novel about a thinking computer with a human personality [6-405].

There is hardly any Dutch and Flemish SF criticism. Aside from a few general introductory booklets and articles in the 1950s and 1960s, the first important work was a dissertation by Riemer Reinsma of the history of Dutch and Flemish utopian literature in 1970 [6-415]. The second appeared in 1977: a collection of original scholarly articles edited by the Belgian university teacher Luk De Vos [6-413]. Two years later, the first serious bibliography appeared [6-416]. The most important secondary works are three connected books, edited by De Vos and published by the small Flemish firm Exa [6-414].

Besides these works there are some others, but they are all very short and sometimes not very reliable. Moreover, most of them are purely introductory texts that are rather superfluous, given the number of foreign introductions that have been translated now—for example, Aldiss's *Billion Year Spree* [9-4], Ash's *The Visual Encyclopedia of Science Fiction* [9-7], Lundwall's *Science Fiction: What It's All About* [9-55], Rottensteiner's *The Science Fiction Book* [9-86], and Nicholls's *The Science in Science Fiction* [9-68].

In the Dutch literary journals nearly nothing has been published about science fiction. In fact, my own "SF en literatuurwetenschap: Geschiedenis, problemen, bibliografie" ("SF and Literary Scholarship: History, Problems, Bibliography") in *Forum der Letteren* 21 (1980), was the first—and is still the only—article about SF in such a journal. In the essay I provided the Dutch scholar a survey of modern SF scholarship, centered on the problems of SF as a genre, the history of SF, and an evaluation of it. In the same journal (vol. 22, 1981) I wrote the essay "Vertelruimte en fysische tijd in de literatuur" ("Narrative Space and Physical time in Literature"), the second half of which is about fiction in which time doesn't take the normal course, but runs backward, or in circles, etc.

A little more is to be found in the Flemish journals, especially in *Restant*, of which Lok De Vos is editor in chief. This journal, however has a very small circulation. Sometimes the general cultural magazine *Ons Erfdeel* also publishes essays about SF and fantasy. The most important of recent years is "Maatschappij tussen hervorming en nachtmerrie in het Zuidnederlandse utopische denken" ("Society between Reform and Nightmare in South-Netherlandic Utopian Fiction") (vol. 24, 1981) by Luk De Vos and Ludo Stynen, who unearthed a lot of forgotten utopias.

On the other hand, two Dutch magazines published special issues on SF and fantasy. In 1980 the November–December issue of the review magazine *Literair Paspoort* (vol. 31, whole no. 287) was devoted to SF. Besides some stories and reviews it contained nine very short articles, some of them embarrassingly bad.

The well-known literary magazine *De Revisor* (vol. 8, no. 5) devoted the October 1981 issue to "The Fantastic." It contained seven articles, all written by academics, about Henry James, French fantasy, horror movies, fantastic architecture, and gothic fiction by women writers. I wrote a general introduction to fantasy.

In March 1982, the University of Groningen organized a series of lectures on SF, and in connection with that produced a mimeographed reader of articles, called *Science fiction*. As far as I know, this was the first (and is still the only) university publication on SF in Holland. In 1984, the college Haagse Leergangen at The Hague organized a series of lectures about "The Future" (in the light of Orwell's *Nineteen Eighty-Four*). The series was published by Coutinho as *Met het oog op de toekomst* (*With a View to the Future*).

Dutch fandom has always been a quiet, polite affair and the fanzine *Holland SF*, under the editorship of Annemarie van Ewijck (formerly Annemarie Kindt), is now in its twentieth year. The Netherlandic Contact Center for SF (NCSF), of which *Holland SF* is the official organ, held a very successful convention in Rotterdam in 1981. It was the first convention that received national publicity, because it was officially opened by the Dutch secretary of culture. For this occasion, the August issue of *Boekblad*, the journal of Dutch booksellers, was devoted to SF.

Flemish fandom is much more intricate: it has always been victim to violent feuds, which are far too complicated (and too childish) to explain here. However, some facts deserve to be mentioned. In 1980, the organization SFAN (the Flemish counterpart of the Dutch NCSF), publisher of the fanzine *Rigel,* merged with the smaller organization Progressef, publisher of a fanzine of that name. The new organization was called SFAN and its magazine *Progressef*. It survived only four issues and was then mothballed. In May 1982, it was revived as a part of Eddy Bertin's personal *SF Gids,* which has existed since 1973. Gradually, however, every trace of it disappeared from Bertin's magazine. It is unclear if SFAN still exists. Bertin's *SF Gids* is, at the moment, the most serious and the most regular fanzine in Holland and Flanders.

Bibliography

Individual Authors

6-400. Bertin, Eddy (Belgium). **Eenzame bloedvogel.** Utrecht: Bruna, 1976.
Collection of stories, interspersed with lyrics, fake documents, editorial comment, timetables, and so on, which take place in the so-called Membrane Universe, Bertin's future history from 1970 to 3666. Its two sequels are *De sluimerende stranden van de geest* (Bruna, 1981) and *Het blinde doofstomme beest op de kale berg* (Bruna, 1983). Bertin's best works. Also annotated as [6-427].

*6-401. Bordewijk, F. **Blokken.** Utrecht: De Gemeenschap, 1931.
Short novel about a near-future state, set in Russia but with at the same time communist and Fascist characteristics. In part a pure description of the state, in part

a story about an unsuccessful revolt. A group of dissidents, the "Group-A," revolts against the "Council," but is mercilessly slaughtered. At the end it is suggested that revolutionary upheavals will continue until the state is destroyed. Very serious literary novella that is generally considered the best anti-utopia of Dutch literature. A warning not so much against communism or fascism as against every totalitarian government. Perhaps influenced by Zamiatin's *We* [2-147].

*6-402. Burger, Dionijs. **Bolland.** The Hague: Blommendaal, 1957.
Continuation and expansion of Abbott's *Flatland* [1-1]. As Abbott tried to demonstrate four-dimensional geometry by means of a story about two-dimensional creatures, so Burger tries to explain for the lay reader Einstein's theories about curved space and the expanding universe. The story takes place two generations after the events described by Abbott; the narrator is the grandson of "A Square." Abbott is of higher literary quality but Burger is more inventive and sometimes more humorous. A new edition was published in 1983 with an afterword by J. A. Dautzenberg (Utrecht: Veen). American translation as *Sphereland* (New York: Crowell, 1965).

*6-403. Gijsen, Wim. **De eersten van Rissan.** Amsterdam: Meulenhoff, 1980.
Lost colony novel about the descendants of mankind on the planet Rissan. After many centuries a group of historians and sociologists from Earth secretly try to investigate the new culture that has risen on Rissan. Their inquiry disturbs the social order: some inhabitants develop new ideas about their way of living, but the powerful caste of priests tries to restore the old situation. In the sequel, *De koningen van weleer* (1981), the new order is established after long struggles, and it is discovered that the mysterious "First of Rissan" from the title of the first book are descendants from "the Kings of Old" of Atlantis, Well-written novels that hold their own with the better American novels of this type.

6-404. Herck, Paul van (Belgium). **Sam of de Pluterdag.** Amsterdam: Meulenhoff, 1968.
Sam falls in love with a girl of a higher social level who has access to an additional day of the week, the "Pluterday." After many years, his son finds another girl and a ninth day. Funny satire. American translation as *Where Were You Last Pluterday?* (New York: DAW, 1973). First Europa Award, 1972. Compare MacDonald's *The Girl, the Gold Watch, and Everything* [3-267]. Also annotated as [6-436].

6-405. Krol, Gerrit. **De man achter het raam.** Amsterdam: Querido, 1982.
Adam, a thinking computer with a personality, contemplates the problem of what a human being really is. Adam has no body or soul, but grows gradually more human as he gets at least the impression of having a body and soul when he is further programmed in that way. When he has developed into a full human being, he underlies the fate of all human beings and dies. Very serious and difficult novel by a prominent modern Dutch novelist, who is also a noted computer expert. Not so much SF as a novel of ideas or a fictional study about problems of

identity and consciousness in the vein of Hofstadter's and Dennett's *The Mind's I* (1981).

6-406. Mulisch, Harry. **De toekomst van gisteren.** Amsterdam: De Bezige Bij, 1972.

Not a novel but a long essay in which the author explains why the eponymous novel was not written. The novel would have presented an alternate world in which the Germans won the Second World War; within that novel the protagonist is writing a novel about a world, alternative to him, in which the Germans had lost the war. A long synopsis of Mulisch's novel is included in the essay. What interests Mulisch is the difference between the real world in which the Germans lost the war and the imaginary world in which the same thing happens. So the novel as a whole had to become at the same time an alternative world novel and what is called in German literary theory a *Doppelroman* ("double novel"). Mulisch demonstrates in his essay that this combination is theoretically impossible. His arguments have to do with rather difficult questions of narrative, but they are very convincing. And even if they were not, the book would still make obligatory reading for any writer of alternative world novels. Compare and contrast Dick's *The Man in the High Castle* [3-142].

*6-407. Raes, Hugo (Belgium). **De lotgevallen.** Amsterdam: De Bezige Bij, 1968.

Imaginary voyage in an unknown land and unknown time. Four people—father, mother, daughter, and son—who serve as symbols of mankind, go through all kinds of adventure, some of them very horrible. In the end they lose each other in utter darkness. Sometimes they are called "fugitives," but it is unclear what they are fleeing from. In the sequel, *Reizigers in de Anti-tijd,* they find each other and try to escape from "Peace City." At the end, the four travel faster than light and become time travelers who land at the beginning of the first book. Very symbolic novels whose theme seems to be that man's life is an endless voyage and that there is no such thing as man's destination; there is only a destiny that signifies nothing. The sequel is annotated as [6-432].

6-408. Raes, Hugo (Belgium). **De verwoesting van Hyperion.** Amsterdam: De Bezige Bij, 1978.

Postcatastrophe novel about the near immortal descendants of mankind in the doomed city Hyperion and their fight with evolved rats. Hyperion is destroyed by the intelligent rats, but a few survivors find a way to kill the rats and a new Hyperion is built.

*6-409. Ruyslinck, Ward (Belgium). **Het reservaat.** Antwerp: Manteau, 1964.

In a near-future Belgium, all dissidents are put away in "reservations" disguised as psychiatric clinics. The totalitarian Belgian government is presented as right wing and as corrupted by the political and cultural imperialism of the United States. However, the reservations remind one more of the repression in present-day Russia. Essentially it is an attack on any modern repressive society, whether right wing or left wing. English translation as *The Reservation* (London: Owen, 1978). Compare Huxley's *Brave New World* [2-47].

6-410. Thijssen, Felix. **Emmarg.** Baarn: Fontein, 1976.
A female alien is stranded on Earth and tries desperately to save the life of her yet unborn child. Emmarg develops a telepathic bond with a human woman, who is also pregnant. Hunted by men, the alien implants her embryo in the woman before she dies. Moving novel with considerable emotional impact on the reader. The ending is reminiscent of Levin's *Rosemary's Baby* (1967).

6-411. Thijssen, Felix. **Pion.** Baarn: Fontein, 1979.
Adventure SF about a robot, designed by the Venusians, who alters the Earth's atmosphere so that eventually the Venusians can live here. At the same time an exciting thriller and a well-researched end-of-the-world novel.

Van Herck, Paul. **Sam of de Pluterdag** [see **6-404**].

6-412. Vroman, Leo. **Het carnarium.** Amsterdam: Querido, 1973.
In the course of a successful attempt to create meat in a biological laboratory, the meat in three test tubes take shape and grow into three green babies who mature unbelievably quickly and start traveling all over the world (in fact the various countries the author has lived in). At first glance, a mad scientist novel, but in fact, a satirical, witty novel (and occasionally very experimental in language and composition) by a distinguished Dutch poet who has a deep knowledge of biology (he lives in New York City and works at the Veterans Administration Hospital in Brooklyn).

Nonfiction

6-413. De Vos, Luk (Belgium), ed. **Science Fiction: Status of Status Quo?** Antwerp and Ghent: Restant, 1977.
Collection of scholarly essays about—among other topics—Zamiatin, Asimov's Foundation trilogy [3-19], Dick, Bulwer-Lytton's *The Coming Race* [1-61], the Strugatskii brothers, and Romanian SF. Also some stories by Dutch and Flemish authors. Very extensive bibliography by the editor. Also annotated as [6-438].

*6-414. De Vos, Luk (Belgium), ed. **Waar helden sterven.** Antwerp: Restant-Exa, 1984. **Laatst nog.** Antwerp: Restant-Exa, 1984. **Just the Other Day.** Antwerp: Restant-Exa, 1985.
Three connected volumes. The first is a collection of 15 short stories by Dutch and Flemish authers, mainly fans. The second contains 14 articles, mainly by Flemish scholars, about science fiction and fantasy in Dutch and Flemish literature. The huge third volume (556 pages) bears an English title and the 40 articles are written in English, French, German, and Dutch. Subjects range from detailed studies on works by such writers as David Lindsay, Doris Lessing, Hermann Hesse, Stanislaw Lem, Joanna Russ, Philip K. Dick, Italo Calvino, and E. E. Smith to more general surveys of Renaissance space voyages, eighteenth-century SF, and Scandinavian SF. There are also interviews with Pohl, Knight and Wilhelm, Priest, and Vance. Among the contributors are Darko Suvin, Michael R. Collings, Lyman Tower Sargent, and Marleen Barr. The editor wrote a theoretical introduction about "the suture of the future" and an essay on "the last man topos."

6-415. Reinsma, Riemer. **Van hoop naar waarschuwing.** Amsterdam: Academic Servide, 1970.

Dissertation on images of the future in Dutch and Flemish literature from 1777 to 1968. Central theme is the development from utopias to dystopias. First Dutch study on this subject and seriously suffering from the absence of other studies. The author had to confine himself to some very basic remarks, which need to be broadened, deepened, and sometimes corrected.

6-416. Spaink, A.; G. Gorremans; and R. Gaasbeek. **Fantasfeer: Bibliografie van science fiction en fantasy in het Nederlands.** Amsterdam: Meulenhoff, 1979.

Listing of all original and translated SF and fantasy (not horror) that has been published through 1978. The book is hampered by the near-total absence of previous checklists and indexes that could have served as its foundation. Especially weak in publications before 1914. Nevertheless, an important work. A second, revised and updated edition has been completed, but the authors have had trouble finding a publisher, since Meulenhoff has lost interest in the project. See my review in *Science-Fiction Studies* 8 (March 1981): 110–112.

Belgian SF

Danny De Laet

Belgium's population of about 10 million is divided into two major groups, the Flemings, who live in northern Belgium (called Flanders), speak Dutch, and make up about 55 percent of the population; and the Walloons, who live in southern Belgium (Walloonia), speak French, and are about 30 percent of the population. The Belgian dialect of Dutch was long called Flemish, a practice I follow in this chapter, but it is now officially referred to as Dutch. Language differences have often been a source of bitter friction between these two major groups. For convenience, I discuss the two literatures separately.

French Authors

Wallonia is more oriented in its literature to folklore and fantasy than to SF. The first important SF story, "Le coeur de Tony Wandel," was written by Georges Bekhoud (1854–1927), published in 1884 and reprinted in the short-story collection *Kermesses*. This novelette describes a heart transplant at a time when this was still SF. In 1901, Eugène Demolder (1862–1919) published *L'Agonie d'Albion* [6-417], a satirical novel set in the future. François Léonard wrote two novels, *Le Triomphe de l'homme* [6-421] in 1911 and *La Conquète de Londres* in 1919. Polmoss, a Brussels publisher, issued in 1913 the first and only volume of what may have been the first (if short-lived) SF series, *Le Roman scientifique*. This novel was Alex Pasquier's *Le Secret de ne jamais mourir*, about a scientist who becomes a mechanical man as he replaces each of his organs by a mechanical device (compare the amusing description by Charles Finney of the lawyer in *The Circus of Doctor Lao* [1935]).

The most important SF writer in Belgium was Henri-Jacques Proumen (1879–1962), who wrote three rather interesting novels: *Sur le chemin des Dieux* (1928), *Le Sceptre volé aux hommes* [6-422], and *La brèche d'enfer* (1946). Proumen, a physician, also published prehistoric novels, short stories, and poetry in addition to his scientific books, and used such themes as mutants, the danger of nuclear war, and mad scientists. The prolific Georges Simenon, writing as Georges Sim, wrote several novels, including *Le Secret des Lamas* (1928) and *Le Roi des glaces* (1928). In 1928, Albert Bailly was awarded the Prix Jules Verne for his novel *L'Ether-Alpha,* a simple description of a trip to and subsequent adventures on the Moon. Marcel Thiry (1897–1977), a well-known poet, wrote a more sophisticated novel, *Echec au temps* [6-425], and a novelette, "Concerto pour Anne Queur," in 1949.

Other SF was written by authors who wrote only one SF novel. Not until the 1960s was SF considered a serious form of writing rather than simply a form of philosophical discussion or satire, as in such works as Roger Avermaete's *La Conjuration des Chats* (where cats take over and dominate the world), José Vial with *Le Dernier dictateur,* Stéphane Hauthem with *Le retour au silence* (a satire), and Pierre Nothomb with *La Rédemption de Mars.*[1]

Henri Vernes (pen name of Charles Dewisme) was one of Europe's most popular juvenile authors. His modern hero, Bob Morane, had all kinds of SF adventures involving time and space travel, lost races and aliens, and regularly fought the archvillain, Mister Ming, an updated version of Fu Manchu. Some of the more than 100 novels were translated and published in England and the United States.

The revival of fantasy in the early 1960s did not help SF in Belgium, which lacked publishers or editors specializing in SF, although more and more comic-strip artists, script writers, and film directors turned toward SF.[2] In the 1970s some young authors tried to rejuvenate the SF field: Vincent Goffart, Paul Hanost, Yves Varende, and Jean-Claude Smit le Bénédicte, but Antwerp-born Jacques Sternberg (1923–   ) prove most successful in France. When the popular paperback publisher Marabout collapsed, newcomers had very few opportunities.

Fandom started in the 1960s, when Michael Grayne (pseudonym of Michel Englebert) launched *Atlanta,* with the help of Michel Feron, who in turn was responsible for at least a dozen different fanzines. Feron published a small survey of SF in Belgium.[3] Claude Dumont celebrated in 1986 his twenty-fifth year of fan activities and still publishes *Octa-zine,* Belgium's oldest fanzine. Very active in late 1986 was Bernard Goorden, editor and publisher of the fanzine *Ides et . . . autres* (1974–   ). He also publishes an annual survey of SF and fantasy published in French[4] and runs the International Center for Documentation about Literature of the Strange in Brussels. With the exception of *Atlanta,* which turned professional but lasted only 12 more issues, there was only one other professional magazine published in French-speaking Belgium, *Anticipations,* which lasted 14 issues (1945–1946). It acquainted the French public, long before the better-known *Fiction* and *Galaxie,* with translations of U.S. authors such as Jack Williamson, D. H. Keller, Wallace West, and many others.[5]

Jacques Van Herp (1923–   ) is a well-known Belgian critic and editor. He wrote the impressive *Panorama de la science fiction*,[6] as well as many essays, studies, and books on other authors, such as Jean Ray,[7] Lovecraft, and the lesser known Gustave Le Rouge, José Moselli, and Jean de la Hire. His personal library of French SF is one of the most complete.

Flemish Authors

Neither Verne nor Wells nor Kurd Lasswitz had any notable influence on the Flemish literature of the nineteenth century, even if there was now and then a slight interest in socialism and utopia.[8] Flemish SF started very slowly and rather late in the twentieth century with two interesting works: *Het Einde der Wereld* [6-433] by Jef Scheirs and *De Vredemensch in 't jaar 3000* [6-430] by Theo Huet. Scheirs's novel[9] even started a series of end-of-the-world novels, continued by Anton Van de Velde with *God en de Wormen* (1947), Felix Dalle with *De Bom* (1961), and Jan Christiaens with *De lachende krokodil* (1963).

More political and utopian minded SF was written by Frans Buyens in *Na ons de Monsters* [6-428], Cor Ria Leeman with *God in de Strop* (1955), Andre Claeys with *Grote Mungu* (1970), and even by a politician and former prime minister, Mark Eyskens, with *Brief aan de Anbrunetiers* (1978), but Anglo-American influence was still minimal before 1950.[10] Action-adventure SF was found in juvenile novels, starting with Leopold Vermeiren and his Bob and Steele series, two young heroes using a subterranean machine to discover lost races. A. M. Lamend sent her heroes in space to encounter aliens on Mars and Jupiter. Piet Mortelmans (pseudonym of Julien Van Remoortere) wrote a series about space pilot Jan Monter.

In the 1960s, American influence was at last noticeable in *De Cirkels,* Paul Van Herck's first collection of short stories, which reflects a number of influences and styles, such as Brown, Kuttner, Bradbury, and Sheckley. Van Herck combined a rare sense of humor and mild satire with a dazzling imagination that explores many familiar SF subjects, talents most of his colleagues lack. His novel *Sam of de Pluterdag* [6-436] was translated into English, Spanish, French, and Swedish, but he published only two more novels, *Apollo XXIII,* a novelization of one of his many radio serials, and *Caroline oh! Caroline* (1976), published in French only.

Some authors started in fanzines, such as Eddy C. Bertin, Julien C. Raasveld, and Guido Eeekhaut, and turned professional. Others succeeded immediately in publishing SF, such as John Vermeulen, next to Van Herck our most representative Flemish SF author, Bob Van Laerhoven, and Gust Van Brussel. With the increasing success of SF in the 1960s and early 1970s, some opportunities were given to newcomers such as William Vananderoye, Mark Wynants, and R. E. C. Willemyns. Some of these authors were even translated into French (Bertin, Van Brussel, Van Herck, and Vermeulen) or English (Van Herck, Bertin), and most of them retained close contacts with fandom. Even some mainstream authors, such as Hugo Claus, Ward Ruyslinck, and Hugo Raes, were interested in the potential of expression given them by SF.

It was soon clear that very few Belgian publishers were able to absorb this increasing wave of more or less commercial authors. Only two of them, DAP-Reinaert (Zele) and Soethoudt (Antwerp), took the risk to encourage new talents. For a short time DAP-Reinaert even awarded money every two years to the best

SF novel. But neither the publishers nor the authors were able to force a major breakthrough. Flemish authors, be they SF or mainstream, rarely manage to become popular in Holland, where the publishing market is much larger, and Flemish publishers constantly struggle with the problem of how to survive in a small country of only 6 million readers. After DAP-Reinaert disappeared and Soethoudt was sold, very few possibilities were left for Belgian SF writers. With most of the translated SF (mostly Anglo-American) coming from Holland, only a very few Belgian publishers, and a very reduced market for short stories, the golden age for Flemish SF ended. Young and upcoming authors are turning toward more profitable genres such as detective stories and fantasy. But the main reason why Flemish SF failed to become popular is that few authors have the ability to create new ideas in an original style. Lack of imagination killed the first real wave of Flemish SF in the 1970s. We have returned to the situation before 1965—SF will be written and published only occasionally whenever an author finds the urge to do so.

The same decline is also noticeable in fandom. Flemish fandom started in the 1950s when Antwerp-born fan Jan Jansen started a club and fanzine named *Alpha*. In the 1960s a few fanzines were issued and edited by myself, the most important being the critically oriented *Kosmos* and *Toekomst 1,* dedicated to short stories only. In 1969, a club was founded under the name SFAN, when Julien C. Raasveld and I joined efforts that culminated in the organization of the first Belgian SF convention, Sfancon, in Antwerp in 1970. Other interesting fanzines were *Parallax, Rigel, SF-Gids,* and *Survival;* only the last two are still published.[11] Flemish fandom was important and more literature minded than Dutch fandom throughout the 1960s and the 1970s when fans were active and drew attention to some interesting new talents.[12] Fandom peaked with the organization of the Orwellcon in 1983, but this very serious professional organization already marked the gap between a serious critical approach by professionals and more fan-oriented activities.

Notes

1. Jacques Van Herp, "La Science-fiction en Belgigue," *Fiction* 42 (May 1957): 125–129.
2. Danny De Laet, *Science fiction et fantastique dans le cinema belge* (Brussels: The Skull, 1976).
3. Danny De Laet and Michel Feron, "A Short Handbook of SF and Fantasy in Belgium," *Early Bird* 5 (January 1968); reprinted as *Science Fiction and Fantasy in Belgium* (Brussels: The Skull, 1971), no. 11, special issue for Noreascon.
4. Bernard Goorden, *Annuaire bibliographique de la SF et du fantastique* (Brussels: Recto Verso, Vol. I, 1984; Vol. II, 1985).
5. Jacques Van Herp, "Het eerste belgische SF tijdschrift," in *De Wereld van de SF* (Antwerp: CIC, 1972), pp. 17–18.
6. Jacques Van Herp, *Panorama de la science fiction* [6-196].
7. François Truchaud and Jacques Van Herp, eds., *Jean Ray* (Paris: Cahiers de l'herne, 1980). The first of a series of major biobibliographic studies of Jean Ray, alias John Flanders, two pseudonyms of Raymond Jean Marie De Kremer (1887–1964), Belgium's most popular writer of fantasy and SF.

8. Luk De Vos and L. Stynen, "Maatschappij tussen hervorming en nacht-merrie in het Zuidnederlandse utopische schrijven," in *Ons Erfdeel* 5 (November–December 1981): 683–696.
9. Jacques Van Herp, "Jef Scheirs' 'Het Einde der Wereld,' " in *De Wereld van de SF* (Antwerp: CIC, 1972), pp. 14–15.
10. Serge Bertran, "Le roman de SF néerlandais," *Kosmos* 5–6 (December 1967): 11–20; Danny De Laet, "De Science Fiction in België," in *De Wereld van de SF* (Antwerp: CIC, 1972), pp. 8–12.
11. Jozef Peeters, *Fanzines in Vlaanderen en Nederland* (Kessel-Lo: Icon, 1975); Luc Roelen and Dirk Lauwens, *Essefenzoo* (Kessel-Lo: Icon, 1977).
12. Albert Van Hageland, "De hedendaagse toestand von SF en Fantastiek in België," *De Periscoop* (December 1978): 3–4.

Bibliography

French Authors

6-417. Demolder, Eugène. **L'Agonie d'Albion.** Paris: Mercure de France, 1901.
The Boers defeat the British army in Africa and start an invasion of England while the king of England travels on the Continent, trying to raise money for a new army. Written in a satirical mood. Compare Chesney's *The Battle of Dorking* [1-21].

6-418. Duesberg, Raymond. **Les Grenouilles.** Paris: Plon, 1962.
More than 500 pages of a terrifying view of the future, A.D. 2976, written in dialogues and a flamboyant style. Lemuria is the last city on Earth, the inhabitants under dictatorial leadership. While questioning themselves about the meaning of life and searching for a new philosophy and religion, the Lemurians die of an incurable disease, and frogs take over.

6-419. Hanost, Paul. **Le Livre des Etoiles.** Paris: Le Masque, 1977.
The first book of the Sherk d'Acamar series relates how this half-human half-feline creature, being a slave, escapes from the mines to join the city of Achernar. Here he tries to gain the favor of Lokri, who commands the Lionmen. After becoming a mercenary, Sherk will in turn be the hunter or the hunted of the Galactic Empire. Interesting for its combination of human and animal mutations and also for its style of heroic fantasy, close to Charles and Nathalie Henneberg, which isn't that common in Europe.

6-420. Landoy, J. A. C. **Du Fond des ages.** Liege: Pro Arte, 1948.
Young people from a savage tribe are captured and enslaved by the warriors of Atlantis. Among them are Rorik, the leader of a clan, and Aëlle, his fiancée from another tribe. Ryétor, the high priest, falls in love with the girl, who has to submit her body and mind in order to save Rorik. She in turn becomes high priestess but can't avoid the continuous wars lead by a declining civilization, tampered by natural cataclysms. Flamboyant, fast-paced, and epic, almost sword and sorcery-like

novel, about a well-known theme. Compare Georges Bordonove's *Les Atlantes* (1965).

6-421. Léonard, François. **Le Triomphe de l'homme.** Brussels: Lamberty, 1911.
This novel of the future starts with a mad scientist as the hero who succeeds in tearing Earth out of the solar system. From that moment on our planet is like a spaceship on the loose until its final destruction. As rational as any Jules Verne novel but simultaneously full of original Gernsbackian ideas. The second part, where Earth becomes the sole hero, is more like a cosmic poem. Compare and contrast Jules Verne's *Hector Servadac* (1877).

6-422. Proumen, Henri-Jacques. **Le Sceptre volé aux hommes.** Paris: Renaissance du Livre, 1930.
On an unknown island in the Pacific, a race of mutants, the Hyperanthropes, kidnap and enslave about 200,000 people. Among them is an engineer and his friend who, subjugated by the scientific knowledge of their masters, become their loyal servants. A girl succeeds in setting up a revolt among the captive women, which leads to the massacre of the mutants. By freeing the atomic energy, the island sinks to the bottom of the ocean so that the mutants will be destroyed forever. Contrast Weinbaum's *The New Adam* [2-126].

6-423. Ray, Jean (pseud. of Raymond Jean Marie De Kremer). **Le Carrousel des Maléfices.** Verviers: Marabout, 1964.
Eighteen short stories and a novelette, "Le Formidable secret du Pôle" ("The Great Polar Secret"), that was initially published as a two-part serial in 1936 under the pen name John Flanders. It is a lost civilization story of remarkable brevity and impact. After several cataclysms, the survivors of Atlantis retired in a huge submarine cavern where the race became extinct. Many centuries later, Saint Brandan, the Irish monk and explorer, discovered the ship in Thule, but kept it hidden because of the many abominations he discovered aboard. In the twentieth century an English explorer discovers the ship in Greenland and by accident awakens the robots and devices that protect the vessel. He is forced to destroy and sink the ship in order to save his life and those of his companions. The short stories are a fair sample of Ray's stunning talent as a master of fantasy and SF, one of the very few European authors to be published in *Weird Tales* and *Terror Tales* in the 1930s.

6-424. Sternberg, Jacques. **Future without Future.** Seabury, 1974. Tr. by Frank Zero of *Futurs sans avenir*, 1971.
Four short stories and a novella that give a good sample of Sternberg's satirical wit, sometimes as sharp as Jonathan Swift, other times as ironic as Vonnegut. In the novella, *Fin de siècle*, the narrator keeps a diary of the year 1999, as a close witness of mankind, just before Earth is sent to oblivion on the very first second of the twenty-first century. Sternberg's view of our nearby future is funny and claustrophobic at the same time. For Sternberg, SF is not the description of ideas but rather of human relationships. Compare *Fin de siècle* with Orwell's *Nineteen Eighty-Four* [3-302] and Zamiatin's *We* [2-147]. Not all stories in the original are included in the translation.

6-425. Thiry, Marcel. **Echec au temps.** Paris: Nouvelle France, 1945.
Apparently Waterloo was a victory for Napoleon, as the narrator and his friend witness on their television that captures images from the past. At that moment their intervention will be decisive and alter time so that the French tyrant will be defeated after all. Compare Moore's *Bring the Jubilee* [3-291].

6-426. Varende, Yves (pseud. of Thierry Martens). **Le Gadget de l'apocalypse.** Paris: Albin Michel, 1978.
In this near-future tale, a gadget has become the new rage, for it allows people to imagine whatever they want. But the gadgets drain energy from the body. A weakened and apathetic population can't resist the alien invasion. Fine satire of contemporary civilization.

Flemish Authors

6-427. Bertin, Eddy C. **Eenzame Bloedvogel.** Utrecht: Bruna, 1976.
Nine short stories and one novel. With the latter, *Eenzame Bloedvogel*, Bertin started his cycle of Membrane stories. The membrane is an organ in the brain that works like a passage to inner and even outer space. Thus three different minds (one alien) are confronted in an inner trip. Bertin combines a New Wave style and ideas in a classic pattern of travel through space and time. The nine short stories are not related to the Membrane cycle, but give a fair sample of Bertin's complicated but sometimes brilliant SF. Also annotated as [6-400].

6-428. Buyens, Frans. **Na ons de Monsters.** Antwerp: Satiricus, 1957.
After a nuclear holocaust, started by the United States, survivors have to live in underground cities. In the year 2025, however, a (frozen) survivor of 1956 is discovered on the surface of Earth. This man, who calls himself Hoera Boera, is horrified at discovering the very dictatorial future world and is thrown in jail. Underwater creatures, the octorapuss, became dominant and eliminate the remains of mankind. A very satirical dystopia.

6-428A. De Laet, Danny, ed. **De Dageraad des Duivels.** Antwerp: Soethoudt, 1974.
Thirty-one short stories and an essay about the history of SF and fantasy in Flanders during the nineteenth and twentieth centuries. This was the first of a series of anthologies edited by either Danny De Laet, Albert Van Hageland, or Son Tyberg where most of the Flemish SF authors such as Hugo Raes, Paul Van Herck, Eddy C. Bertin, J. C. Raasveld, Jean Ray, were published.

6-429. De Laet, Danny, ed. **Tussen Tijd en Schaduw.** Antwerp: Soethoudt, 1979.
Eleven short stories and an introductory essay on the situation of SF in Flanders. The selection includes some of the best classical authors (Vermeulen, Van Herck), some remarkable debuts (De Rybel, Noens), and some New Wave tales (Raasveld, Vananderoye, Eekhaut). The best story is by Frans Buyens, "De ontwenningskuur" ("The Cure"), an Orwellian story of a loner who revolts against society.

Herck, Paul Van. **Sam of de Pluterdag** [see **6-436**].

6-430. Huet, Theo. **De Vredemensch in 't jaar 3000.** Antwerp: Techniek, 1933.
The United States of Europe, television, taxi-planes, contact with extraterrestrials and death rays are among the themes in this early work. When first contact is made with the planet Spanier, the great scientist Walter Kroes develops a serum to pacify the whole Earth population and becomes the peacemaker of the year 3000. Compare Gernsback's *Ralph 124C41 +* [1-37].

6-431. Jacques, Maria. **Morgen is Blond.** Brussels: DAP-Reinaert, 1974.
While the population on Earth is decimated, some surviving Europeans mingle with the local population in Tibet. These people are the Eutibs, who reached a high peak of civilization in the twenty-fifth century. Young Tinia discovers she is a mutant, for she is blonde and has blue eyes. When she finds other mutants like her, they must flee after one Eutib is murdered. It appears that "frozen" Europeans are regularly revived to revitalize the dying race of the Eutibs. SF and a love story combined with a detective novel. Compare and contrast van Vogt's *Slan* [3-383].

6-432. Raes, Hugo. **Reizigers in de Anti-tijd.** Amsterdam: Bezige Bij, 1971.
The narrator, his wife, and their two children are on a journey to the anti-time. On their way they meet friends and foes, must fight weird creatures, and encounter all kind of dangers. We don't know their goal nor why they flee, but almost every possible reason is mentioned without a word of explanation. A hallucination written soberly and precisely but almost without emotion. This is the best of the author's SF-oriented novels. The novel to which this is a sequel is annotated as [6-407].

6-433. Scheirs, Jef. **Het Einde der Wereld.** Dendermonde: Van Lantschoot-Moens, 1929.
This near-future, end-of-the-world novel tells how occult sciences overwhelm the population all over the world. Religion and mysticism seem to await the coming of a new Messiah, and reporter, Jean Malfaict, follows the events that finally lead the world to apocalypse. An astonishing novel that has even greater depth, mainly because of its anticlerical opinion, than Benson's similar novel, *Lord of the World* [1-9].

6-434. Van Baelen, Kamiel. **De Oude Symphonie van ons Hart.** Brugge: Kinkhoren, 1943.
Lou Anders (whose name means "otherwise") is on the verge of committing suicide when a famous surgeon proposes that Anders submit his body and mind to some fantastic experiments. The scientist will replace his heart and maybe he will have a different view about life. Anders agrees and submits his body five times, subsequently behaving as a financer, a tramp, a philosopher, and a madman. When at last he is given a steel mechanical heart, he doesn't survive the operation. In spite of its grotesque situation, this novel is rather optimistic in the protagonist's quest for happiness and also remarkable for its structure and style.

6-435. Van Brussel, Gust. **De Ring.** Leuven: Clauwaert, 1969.
The Moon has disintegrated and its remains circle Earth as a constant menace. Mankind hopes that the superintelligent elite of the colony on Venus will bring salvation, but meanwhile the danger of war on Earth is even greater than that of the lunar ring. Because of the overpopulation, Earth is divided into a dominant surface class and a lower class underground. The subsequent war between continents destroys all life on Earth more surely that could the lunar debris. Narrated in a sober, emotionless style, it is like a chronicle of a faraway future. Never again could this author recapture the overwhelming power of this narration that received the SFAN Award at the first Belgian SF convention in 1970.

6-436. Van Herck, Paul. **Sam of de Pluterdag.** Amsterdam: Meulenhoff, 1968. Tr. by Danny De Laet and Willy Magiels as *Where Were You Last Pluterday?* (DAW, 1973).
Sam, a rejected SF writer, falls in love with a girl of higher social level. He discovers that she has access to an additional day of the week. Once he penetrates this secret, he wins the girl and the use of the eighth day. Later, his son follows suit and finds another girl and a ninth day. Good satire. First Europa Award, 1972. Also annotated as [6-404].

6-437. Vermeulen, John. **De Binaire Joker.** Zele: DAP-Reinaert, 1979.
The starship *Squash* lands on a small, unknown planet where the crew is soon opposed in a fierce battle with an invisible alien that will ultimately be defeated by "Nestor," the ship's computer. A slick example of a perfect space opera that is enhanced by the wit and humor of the author. Compare and contrast Lem's *The Invincible* [3-260]. This novel was translated into French as *Le Bouffon binaire* (1983).

Nonfiction

6-438. De Vos, Luk, ed. **Science Fiction: Status of Status Quo?** Antwerp and Ghent: Restant, 1977.
Collection of 11 academic essays in Dutch about such various authors as Zamiatin, Dick, and the Strugatskii brothers; six short stories; and a selective bibliography on SF. Compare Clareson's *SF: The Other Side of Realism* [9-23]. Also annotated as [6-413].

6-439. Goorden, Bernard, and San Tewen (pseud. of Anne Wets). **SF, fantastique et ateliers créatifs.** Brussels: Cahiers Jeb, 1978.
The editors' intention was to provide a general survey of the study of SF, fantasy, and detective literature in South America and Europe. For this reason they founded the fanzine *Ides et . . . autres.* Chapter 5 provides an excellent, although incomplete, comparative bibliography of studies, essays, and fiction in these countries.

Romanian SF

Ion Hobana

SF in Romania dates from the nineteenth century, which is true for most countries. Among the earliest are Ion Heliade Rădulescu's poem "Santa Cetate" ("The Sacred Citadel," 1856) and the narratives of G. Meledon, "Un vis curioz" ("A Strange Dream," 1857); Enrich Winterhalder, "Trecutul, prezentul şi viitorul" ("The Past, the Present and the Future," 1858); Demetriu G. Ionnescu, "Spiritele anului 3000" ("The Spirits of the Year 3000," 1875); and Ion Ghica, "Insula Prosta" ("Prosta Island," 1885). All those anticipatory visions evidenced steady concern with the shape of future cities and societies.

The emergence and evolution of Romanian SF were stimulated by the atmosphere of ardent intellectual curiosity due to major personalities, especially the poet Alexandru Macedonski. In his prose piece "Palatul fermecat" ("The Enchanted Palace," 1881), he envisioned a cinema projection. The title character in "Nicu Dereanu" (1886) wanted to apply perpetual motion to railway engines. The main character of "Intre coteţe" ("Between Chicken Coops," 1888) experimented steadily in cross-breeding fowls with a view to resurrecting species long extinct. Macedonski's most elaborated SF text was "Oceania-Pacific-Dreadnought" (1913).[1]

Late nineteenth-century Romanian popular science magazines, like their counterparts elsewhere, also explored the borderline between science and fantasy, carrying articles on artificial man, Atlantis, perpetual motion, extraterrestrials, and the like. Astronomical theories inspired such novels as Henric Stahl's *Un român în lună* (*A Romanian in the Moon*) [6-457] and Victor Anestin's *O tragedie cerească* (*Tragedy in the Sky*) [6-441].

Popular magazines stimulated native SF by publishing translations of Verne, Wells, Louis Boussenard, Arthur Conan Doyle, J. H. Rosny aîné, Garrett P. Serviss, David H. Keller, and others. A few magazine covers illustrated such themes as "A Farm in 1950," "The Earth on Fire," "The Railways of the Future," and "The Inhabitants of Mars Studying the Earth and Communicating with the Earth." These provided models for writers and acquainted the public with some of the ideas, modalities, and media of early SF.

Many authors produced only one SF work: B. Brănişteanu, "Cîrma balonului" ("The Rudder of the Balloon," 1902); Amargo, "Un reporter în noua planetă Aurora" ("A Reporter on the New Planet Aurora," 1907); Alexandru Speranţă, "O călătorie în lună" ("A Trip to the Moon," 1907); and an important novel of this early period, *Un român în lună* [6-457] by Henric Stahl. There was, however, an exception: Victor Anestin, a self-taught astronomer and a polyglot, the founder of the first Romanian astronomical review, *Orion*. He wrote three SF novels: *În anul 4000 sau O călătorie la Venus* (*In the Year 4000 or A Trip to Venus*, 1899), *O tragedie cerească*, and *Puterea ştiinţei sau Cum a fost "omorît" Răsboiul European* (*The Power of Science or How the European War Was "Killed,"* 1916). World War I stimulated other works, for example, the story "Un asasinat patriotic" ("A Patriotic Murder," 1917), by the poet and dramatist Victor Eftimiu.[2] Mainstream authors contributed a handful of works, as Cezar Petrescu with his novel *Baletul mecanic* (*The Mechanical Ballet*), Felix Aderca with *Oraşele înecate*[3] (*Drowned Cities* [6-440]), and Victor Papilian with *Manechinul lui Igor* (*Igor's Dummy*).[4] But these works, it should be realized, were isolated examples and did not represent any sustained tradition of a distinct genre.

After World War II, SF did not have a very definite stature, being currently mistaken for romances, stories of adventure, or vulgarized science. The first national competition for SF writings was launched in 1955 by the magazine *Ştiinţă şi technică* (*Science and Technology*). Many of the entries for the competition were not exactly literature, yet their existence and variety offered an opportunity for setting up a literary supplement of that magazine, entitled *Povestiri ştiinţifico-fantastice* (*Science Fiction Tales*).[5] Its editor, Adrian Rogoz, the author of the novel *Omul şi năluca* (*The Man and the Phantasm*, 1965) and of short stories like "Preţul secant al genunii" ("The Secant Price of the Abyss" [6-456]), attracted well-known writers while lauching many talented beginners.

By the mid-1950s, the genre was undermined by the repetition of themes, rather linear plots, black-and-white characters, minute technicalities, and so on. On the other hand, it was the period when books were written by genuine men of letters such as Victor Kernbach, *Luntrea sublimă* (*The Sublime Rowing-Boat* [6-452]; Mihu Dragomir, *Povestiri deocamdată fantastice* (*Stories Fantastic for the Time Being* [6-446]); and Vladimir Colin, *A zecea lume* (*The Tenth World*, 1964). They were soon joined by young writers who have since achieved greater prominence—Horia Aramă, Voicu Bugariu, Constantin Cubleşan, Ion Hobana, Eduard Jurist, Mihnea Moisescu, Mircea Opriţă—or by authors who had made their mark in other domains—professor and critic O. S. Crohmălniceanu, dramatist Dorel Dorian, and fiction writers Mircea Şerbănescu and Radu Teodoru.

They all explored the SF universe of ideas, focusing their attention not on the miracles of technical-scientific progress, but on the latter's impact on the characters' conscience. The boldest hypotheses, on the border between the possible and the impossible, were used to widen and stimulate readers' awareness, to try to envision the evolution of the individual and of the community and their new relations with nature and society. Some authors used nonconventional narrative techniques, just as their Anglo-American New Wave counterparts did.

The integration of SF within the area of belles lettres also entailed a gradual change in the attitude toward such fiction. Critics have taken more interest in the new books and in the theoretical problems of the genre. Prestigious publications devote special issues, groups of stories, or permanent columns to SF. Well-deserved popularity is enjoyed by specialized broadcasts. SF novels, stories, and works of literary history and theory have been awarded prizes by the Union of Writers, by the Writers' Associations in the main Romanian cities, as well as by some newspapers, reviews, and magazines.

About 50 SF fan clubs are currently active; they issue fanzines, organize public debates, literary competitions, performances, and exhibitions of fine arts, and gather at national conventions, the sixteenth of which was held in 1986. Professional writers permanently assist young hopefuls, a few of whom have made their debut in book form in the Fantastic Club collection issued by the Albatros Publishing House (specializing in juveniles): Rodica Bretin, Mihail Grămescu, Lucian Ionică, Leonard Oprea, Sorin Ştefănescu, Alexandru Ungureanu.

These and other gifted authors who have come to the fore in recent years to a great extent embody not only the future but also the present of Romanian SF. Thoroughly conversant with foreign literatures, they breezily operate with the stock-in-trade themes and ideas specific to the genre, while remaining distinct artistic individuals. As for the representatives of the first wave (1955 to 1965), they have contributed less often to the genre, or, like me, have devoted their energies to books on the history and theory of Romanian and world SF.

Notes

1. The first version we know was published in the Paris review *L'Industrie vélocipédique et automobile* (November 4, 1911), under the title "Oceania-Pacific-Dreadnought-Cité."
2. He also wrote the sketch "Pămîntul a vorbit!" ("The Earth Has Spoken," 1909) and the comedy *Sfîrşitul pămîntului* (*The End of the Earth*, 1915).
3. The first version, serialized by the magazine *Realitatea ilustrată* (September 29–December 15, 1932) under the title *X-0, Romanul viitorului* (*X-0, The Novel of the Future*), was signed with the pseudonym Leone Palmantini. It was substantially revised on its publication as a book. The author changed its title to *Oraşele scufundate* (*Sunken Cities*) in a 1966 reprint.
4. We can add Ion Minulescu, "De vorbă cu necuratul" ("Talking with the Evil One," 1930); Gib Mihăescu, the novel *Braţul Andromedei* (*Andromeda's Arm*, 1930); Tudor Arghezi, "În preistorie" ("In Prehistory," 1933); Ion Biberi, "Sfîrşit" ("The End," 1937); and Mircea Eliade, "Secretul doctorului Honigberger" ("Doctor Honigberger's Secret") and "Nopţi la Serampore" ("Nights at Serampore," 1940).

5. The collection was published from October 1, 1955 to April 15, 1974 (466 issues with a circulation of about 35,000 copies each).

Bibliography

Individual Authors

6-440. Aderca, Felix. **Oraşele înecate.** Bucharest: Editura Vremea, 1937.
In the remote future, mankind has withdrawn to the oceans, trying to replace the heat of the dying Sun by that of the Earth. As conventional energy sources are exhausted, the latent conflict between the inhabitants of the various submarine cities will inevitably lead to revolt and destruction. An engineer discovers the final secret of nuclear power. With Olivia, he leaves the condemned planet on an aircraft propelled by "an atomic lamp," heading for another celestial body. Advanced technology serves as a background for new social and psychological realities. The novel compares well with the best foreign SF of the 1930s through the rigorous development of the initial hypothesis and the apt transposition of visual images. Similarities with *Brave New World* [2-47] are fortuitous, as the early version appeared in the *Realitatea Ilustrată* magazine the very same year as Huxley's novel.

6-441. Anestin, Victor. **O tragedie cerească.** Bucharest: Editura Tipografiei ziarului "Universul," 1914.
In the year 3000 a Venusian astronomer discovers a dark celestial body approaching the solar system. Mars is driven out of the solar system, and the Earth is subject to gigantic tides, wrested from its orbit, and catapulted beyond Saturn. Before they succumb, the Earth's inhabitants use the wireless telegraph to inform the Venusians about their scientific gains, foremost of which the discovery of "intra-atomic power." Despite its ingenuity, an undistinguished novel. Anestin seems to have have drawn upon Camille Flammarion's novel *La Fin du monde* (1893) and on Wells's story, "The Star" (1897).

6-442. Bugariu, Voicu. **Vocile Vikingilor.** Bucharest: Editura Albatros, 1970.
Thirteen stories and an afterword, in which this literary critic demonstrates the consonance of SF with the theory of open structures, of unsolved conflicts. The story "Discutînd despre mesaj" attempts to illustrate this theory, as does the author's novel *Sfera* (1973).

6-443. Colin, Vladimir. **Babel.** Bucharest: Editura Albatros, 1978.
The characters of the novel are an earthly poet distraught at his wife's death, a killer from Mars, and a woman from Venus. The devilish scientist Scat Mor tortures them psychically, forcing them to live in imagination alone—as doubles of their real beings—on the fictional planet Babel. Revolting at this kind of manipulation, they recover their original identities. The book is influenced by Lem's *Solaris* [3-261], but Colin treats his subject in an original manner, infusing it with authentic lyricism.

6-444. Crohmălniceanu, Ovid S. **Istorii insolite.** Bucharest: Editura Cartea Românească, 1980.
Twelve stories by a literary critic and historian. A voracious reader of SF, Crohmălniceanu lends peculiar colors to the motifs belonging to the common stock of the genre. Martin Neuhof, in "Tratatul de la Neuhof," is invaded by enigmatic microscopic entities that change his body into their own universe and impose upon mankind the conclusion of the treaty in the title, under the menace of unleashing a viral war. Other "histories" dwell on unwonted aspects of the process of artistic creation.

6-445. Dorian, Dorel. **Ficţiuni pentru revolver şi orchestră.** Bucharest: Editura Albatros, 1970.
The nine stories are inquests conducted by the cybernetic detective Teo Celan and the investigator super-robot S.H.12. For instance, in "Improbabilul Quasifer" they want to ascertain the possibility of the existence of a criminal universe (Quasifer), proceeding from the messages conveyed by pilot Luan Wo, who is detained in a prison where he is subjected to neuropsychiatric cross-examinations. The models for these detectives are found in Asimov's *The Caves of Steel* [3-16] and *The Naked Sun* (1957). Typical of the volume as a whole is the logically faultless, compelling demonstration as well as the inspired use of the paradoxes of cybernetics.

6-446. Dragomir, Mihu. **Povestiri deocamdată fantastice.** Bucharest: Editura Tineretului, 1962.
Six stories characterized by discreet lyricism, insight into complex frames of mind, and fertile bookish inspiration. The author's fascination with the enigmas of ancient civilizations and the hypothesis of the Earth's having been visited by beings from outer space produces the best story, "Legenda îngerilor."

6-447. Grămescu, Mihail. **Aporisticon.** Bucharest: Editura Albatros, 1981.
Forty-two very short narratives in the debut volume of a highly gifted member of an SF club. The great variety of themes and subjects has its counterpart in the wide range of artistic modalities. An interesting blend of metaphors, symbols, and paradoxes. Echoes from Jorge Luis Borges combine with original insights.

6-448. Hobana, Ion. **Oameni şi stele.** Bucharest: Editura Tineretului, 1963.
Nine stories divided into three cycles: the fascination of the aquatic universe, the psychosocial implications of space flight, and the exploration of time. The author's imagination moves within a coherent anticipatory framework, in connection with the data and hypotheses of science. "Cea mai bună dintre lumi," a story translated into several foreign languages, describes the drama of a galactic pilot crippled by loss of memory who rediscovers his home, the Earth. Critics have pointed out the author's care for the truthfulness of portrayal as well as the poignancy of his style.

6-449. Ionică, Lucian. **Ziua confuză.** Bucharest: Editura Albatros, 1983.
Eight tales collected in a promising debut volume. The characters are ordinary people confronted with exceptional situations. In "La marginea oraşului," a spaceship lands at the outskirts of a city, but is described with a certain amount of detachment, the author not being involved in the futile attempts at establishing

contact. Gradually, people lose interest in the ship, which disappears one night as mysteriously as it appeared.

6-450. Ionnescu, Demetriu G. **Spiritele anului 3000.** Bucharest: Revista Junimei, 1875, nos. 7–8.
Falling asleep, the author wakes up in the Bucharest of the year 3000. He learns that there are no more monarchies, religions, or wars. The "Confederation of the Human Race" is administered by a "General Congress elected by the various Republics." Dirigibles have become the common means of public transport. Climate has been improved by means of many canals and plantations. Deserts have been changed into seas. And everything is but a dream. Ionnescu was acquainted with Poe, and shared themes with Mercier's utopia *L'An deux mille quatre cent quarante* [1-63]. Noteworthy is the radical fervor of the 17-year-old author, who, as chance had it, was to become the leader of the Conservative party.

6-451. Jurist, Eduard. **Oul lui Columb.** Bucharest: Editura Tineretului, 1963.
In his first SF book, the author narrates the adventures of his favorite hero, Mike Smith, using humor, satire, and puns, while warning against the dangers of making cybernetics a fetish of modern civilization.

6-452. Kernbach, Victor. **Luntrea sublimă.** Bucharest: Editura Tineretului, 1961.
A spaceship from Mars, sent to investigate living conditions on Terra, lands on Atlantis. Urged by its crew, slaves rebel against the ruling caste. Subsequent events include the sinking of Atlantis as well as the destruction of Sodom and Gomorrah by the Martians, who build the terrace at Baalbek, a launching ramp to return home. Compare with *Aelita* [2-119] by Aleksei Tolstoi and *Poslednii chelovek iz Atlantidi* (1926) by A. Beliaev. The author's merit is to have managed to turn a myth into a convincing picture of the confrontation of two civilizations on different levels of development.

6-453. Macedonski, Alexandru. **Oceania-Pacific-Dreadnought,** in the magazine *Flacăra* (December 7, 1913).
In 1952, a Franco-Anglo-American corporation launches a gigantic ship, the *Oceania-Pacific-Dreadnought,* as vast as Paris. The huge ship links Europe to the United States, carrying one million passengers on each crossing of the ocean. Among the wonders on board are world television, "travelator avenues," and "season conditioning." But the profits generated by this extraordinary means of transportation make everybody rich, so nobody wants to work any more. To avoid consequent economic-social catastrophe, the vessel is blown up by the very bankers who had financed its construction. There are similarities with Verne's *L'Ile à hélice* (1895), but the story descends rather from Villiers de l'Isle-Adam's *Contes cruels,* as it is aimed not so much at praising technical-scientific progress, as at revealing the latter's nefarious consequences, in the absence of commensurate moral progress.

6-454. Opriţă, Mircea. **Figurine de ceară.** Cluj-Napoca: Editura Dacia, 1978.
Thirteen stories selected by the author from his previous books. They are characterized by realism in background, characters, and details, which enhances the intrusion of the fantastic into everyday life. Exemplary is "O falie în timp." Two

future men, father and son, on a pleasure flight over the Carpathians, are accidentally and temporarily flashed back to the year 1944, when they are captured by a German column retreating from Romania. The transition from the joy of the flight to the nightmare of the confrontation with the subhumans in gray uniforms is achieved quite credibly and smoothly.

6-455. Păun, Gheorghe. **Sfera paralelă.** Bucharest: Editura Albatros, 1984.
Twenty tales tackling widely different themes: robotics, parallel universes, contact between the Earth and other worlds, and time travel. "Protezozaurii" unfolds in a technocratic mercantile society. Under the law, if citizens transplant more than 25 kilograms of artificial organs, they lose their suffrage, and for more than 40 kilograms they are delivered to hospitals as depositories of organs. Those approaching such limits, like the manufacturers of organs, want to raise the quotas. A dystopia that warns against changing science into a source of illicit enrichment and against violence.

6-456. Rogoz, Adrian. **Prețul secant al genunii.** Bucharest: Editura Albatros, 1974.
Six narratives of unequal lengths, with the title story ranking among Romania's best. After long quests, superchampion Dav Bogar reaches the planet Techom, programmed by Kim Kerim to play chess. Its opponents are killed if they lose 20 matches but released if they manage to draw one. Dav is released several times but, haunted by the wish to win, returns to the chessboard again and again. When he eventually outplays the planet, he is at the very end of his life, during which he has sacrificed his love of Umna on the altar of a tyrannical obsession. The author is at his best in analyzing the hero's psychological processes and in building an eerie atmosphere.

6-457. Stahl, Henric. **Un român în lună.** Bucharest: self-published, 1914.
A bizarre flying machine falls to Earth. It contains the logbook of the Romanian who had reached the Moon, recording the unfolding of his space flight and his exploration of the Earth's satellite. The climax of the story is the encounter with a Martian, whose spherical spaceship was damaged while landing on the Moon. Because his own machine cannot carry both of them, the Romanian sends the Martian to Earth, while he remains on the Moon, together with his solar brother, to search the sphere and to attempt its repair, in order to save both. The author acknowledges Verne's *De la terre à la lune* [1-93] and Wells's *The First Men in the Moon* [1-98] as partial sources of inspiration. The naïveté of the novel is to a great extent redeemed through the fluency of the epic discourse and through the romantic pathos in the description of "the first contact."

Anthologies

6-458. Hobana, Ion, ed. **O falie în timp.** Bucharest: Editura Eminescu, 1976.
A collection of 20 narratives, an attempt at demonstrating the continuing preoccupation with a genre that has attracted foremost Romanian men of letters—Macedonski, Arghezi, Eftimiu, and others. From the modern period, the editor has selected texts by authors who have written both short fiction and book-length works: Aramă, Colin, Opriţă, Rogoz, and others.

6-459. Hobana, Ion, ed. **Vîrsta de aur a anticipaţiei româneşti.** Bucharest: Editura Tineretului, 1969.
The only historical anthology of pre–World War II Romanian SF—16 tales and excerpts from novels, each author and each text being accompanied by an introduction and notes. A starting point for a history of Romanian SF.

Nonfiction

6-460. Aramă, Horia. **Colecţionarul de insule.** Bucharest: Editura Cartea Românească, 1981.
A book about utopias, with many references to SF texts by Verne, Wells, Zamiatin, Čapek, Huxley, F. Aderca, I. Efremov, Bradbury, and so on, showing the links between SF and utopian ideas.

6-461. Hobana, Ion. **Imaginile posibilului.** Bucharest: Editura Meridiane, 1968.
A thematic history of SF films, including the following chapters: "The Age of Fairy-Tales," "Superman & Co.," "The Crazy Scientist," "Artificial Man," "The Robot," "The Lost World," "The Way to the Stars," "The War of the Worlds," "The End of the World," "Of Things to Come," "Implications in Thrillers and Romances," "Implications in Horror Films," "Perspectives." With a selective filmography, a bibliography, and 36 black-and-white illustrations.

6-462. Hobana, Ion. **Science fiction: Autori, cărti, idei.** Bucharest: Editura Eminescu, vol. 1, 1983; vol. 2, 1986.
The two volumes include studies of SF aspects in the works of writers like Poe, Villiers de l'Isle-Adam, Arthur Conan Doyle, Alexandru Macedonski, and Victor Anestin; analyses of landmarks of the genre (*Robur le Conquérant, Le Voyage à travers l'impossible,* and *Maître du Monde* by Verne, *The Time Machine* [1-103] by Wells); and essays on the emergence and evolution of certain themes and ideas, including the relation between reality and fantasy, the morphology of extraterrestrials, the myth of the invisible being, utopia and the shapes of future cities in nineteenth-century Romanian utopias, the man of the future, and the two faces of nuclear power.

6-463. Hobana, Ion. **Viitorul a început ieri.** Bucharest: Editura Tineretului, 1966.
A panorama of French SF, from the forerunners (Cyrano de Bergerac, Louis Sébastien Mercier, Restif de la Bretonne) down to specialized contemporary authors (Jacques Sternberg, Gérard Klein, Michel Demuth). History alternates with representative texts to show the evolution of the genre.

6-464. Manolescu, Florin. **Literatura SF.** Bucharest: Editura Univers, 1980.
An excellent introduction to SF. The author discusses the name, history, and definition of the genre, its relations with science, the fantastic and the fairy tale, and then surveys SF species (the space narrative, the anti-utopia, heroic fantasy), SF themes (space flight, the war of the worlds, the parallel universe), and specific personages (the scientist, the androids, the mutants). A substantial chapter is devoted to Romanian SF.

6-465. Opriţă, Mircea. **H. G. Wells. Utopia modernă.** Bucharest: Editura Albatros, 1983.

The first Romanian study of Wells. Proceeding from the observation that Wells's "early productions set the highest standard, while subsequent ones are irremediably on the downgrade, in literary terms," Opriţă replaces the "usual chronological approach" by "a somewhat uncommon insight into the oeuvre, from late writings to his youthful ones." The validity of the observation and of the method is questionable. But the book is remarkable in its capacity for analysis and graphic style.

Yugoslav SF

Alexander B. Nedelkovich

Yugoslavia is a federation of several republics that are ethnically different and in which different languages are spoken. This reflects directly on Yugoslav SF. No one can claim to have read everything science fictional ever published in all the republics, in all the languages. According to the figures from the latest population census (1981), there are nearly 22 million people in Yugoslavia—more than 8 million Serbs, more than 4.5 million Croats, less than 2 million of those who declare themselves of Islamic (Muslim) nationality, less than 2 million Slovenians, about 1.2 million Macedonians, half a million Montenegrins, half a million Hungarians, about 1.5 million Albanians, a quarter million who declare themselves of Yugoslav nationality, and dozens of other ethnic groupings. There is no official Yugoslav language. Serbs, Croats, Montenegrins, and many Muslims speak a single language (but in several variants, differing more than London cockney from a Texas drawl) and that language should officially be described as "Serbo-Croat or Croato-Serbian"—all five words are necessary to show the unity, to stress the components, and to hurt nobody's ethnic feelings. I personally estimate that at least 15 million Yugoslavs can use this language easily, close to three-quarters of the total population.

I believe that the Yugloslav languages in which most SF has appeared are Slovenian, Serbo-Croat or Croato-Serbian, Hungarian, and Macedonian. Of these, I speak only Serbo-Croat or Croato-Serbian, which is my native tongue, but I have reliable sources (and many translations) that allow me to comment with some confidence about all Yugoslav SF, past and present. I have written and published the only two books known to have been published in Yugoslavia about the subject—*Our 110 SF Years* and *The History of the Serbian Science Fiction Literature* [6-475].

From the Beginning to 1945

In the nineteenth century several proto-SF books and fragments of the literatures of nationalities and territories later included in Yugoslavia were published. It now seems that most of these were published in Slovenia, the westernmost republic. Perhaps the first effort was the novella "Micromega," by Simon Jenko in 1851, subtitled "Travel of Sirians to Saturn and to Earth" and published in a handwritten school newspaper called *Slavia*. The first known printed Slovenian book with a strong SF element seems to be *Dijak v Luni* by Andrej Volkar, signed, however, only by the letters "H. G." In that book, two young scientists travel by balloon to the Moon, where they find a utopia. Also utopian but with some SF elements is *Deveta dežela* by Josip Stritar in 1878. Then come parodies, *Indija komandija* by Anton Mahnič in 1884 and *4000* by Ivan Tavčar in 1891. There were perhaps five other Slovenian books with SF elements in the nineteenth century. In the twentieth century, up to World War II (which hit Yugoslavia in 1941, after which everything was suspended for four years), at least 12 more Slovenian books with strong SF elements were published.

The first known Serbian SF work is a drama by Dragutin J. Ilić, titled *Posle milion godina* (*A Million Years After*), published in the magazine *Kolo* in 1899 and never performed on stage; its premiere was in 1985, with a delay of "only" 96 years on the radio. I discovered this in an archive where it lay buried, and gave a photocopy to some radio broadcasters in Belgrade, who rather freely transformed it into a radio play. The next known Serbian SF work is the novel *Jedna ugašena zvezda* (*One Extinguished Star*) by Lazar Komarčić, printed in 1902, and somewhat similar to *Star Maker* [2-112]. And then, astonishingly, there came six decades of silence—60 years without known Serbian SF.

The first known Croatian books with SF elements are *Začarano ogledalo* (*Magical Mirror*) (1913) by Fran Galović and *Gospodin čovjek* (*A Gentleman*) (1932) by Mato Hanžeković, with no more Croatian SF published until the 1950s. No Hungarian, Macedonian, or any other Yugoslav SF is known from this period.

From 1945 to 1986

For the Yugoslavs, the war years meant an incredible, undreamt-of nightmare. It was an occupation by foreign powers big and small, east, west, north, and south; it was an ethnic war and a religious war—crusades crashing into jihads amid unimaginable whirlpools of blood; it was a political war; there was genocidal slaughter of entire provinces. There was a churchman who slit more than 1,000 throats a day, and another who blessed big baskets full of freshly plucked-out eyes of children. There were armed men publicly roasting and eating human flesh; they drank blood and ate brain-on-bread. Tito and the Communist party ended that with their total victory in 1945, and since that time, Yugoslavia has been a socialist country. When you think and talk of anything Yugoslav—SF included—beware of any simplifications; this is not eastern SF, nor western SF; this is not the same society as 41 years ago. Yugoslavia is a land of reforms and great complexities, always shifting and changing.

In Slovenia, there have been, since 1945, at least 20 SF books, most of them clearly and recognizably belonging to this genre. Several of them were written by Vid Pečjak and several by Miha Remec. In 1983, Bojan Meserko published his collection, *Igra in agonija* (*Game and Agony*).

In Serbia, between 1960 and 1986, about a dozen SF novels appeared, including two by the much-respected mainstream author (who lives in London) Borislav Pekić. In Croatia, since 1955, about 20 SF novels were published, including several by Zvonimir Furtinger and several by Predrag Raos.

In Macedonia, the first known book with SF elements was published in 1959— *Golemata avantura* (*Great Adventure*) by Lazo Naumoski, a juvenile. Since then, five more Macedonian SF books have appeared, including three by Stojmir Stojče Simjanoski: *Acela* (a female name), published in 1977; *Poslednata Eva* (*The Last Eve*), in 1980, and *Ќerkata na zvezdite* (*The Daughter of Stars*), in 1981. In 1986, a SF drama, *Kerubin 2096* (*Cherub 2096*), was performed in an open-air theater and also shown on TV. This drama shows men from the future who come to judge us harshly; they have automatic rifles in their hands, and they land on the stage in a *real* helicopter—with all the roar and dust thrown on the audience.

A number of Hungarian SF stories, translated into Serbo-Croat or Croato-Serbian, have been published, including those by Geza Czath, Atila Gere, and Robert Hasz—all since 1970. An occasional Yugoslav story is translated into English, such as the tales by Krsto Mažuranić and Goran Hudec, which were included in the 1986 international anthology edited by Sam Lundwall and published by Penguin.

Science Fiction Translations in Yugoslavia

The first foreign SF book to be translated and published in Yugoslavia was probably Verne's *From the Earth to the Moon* [1-93] (in Belgrade, in Serbo-Croat, 1873). Verne has since been strongly represented, more than all other French authors combined. Since 1900, one or two American and one or two Russian SF books were translated every decade; in the first ten postwar years, 18 Russian SF books were published, and only one American (this had something to do with politics). Then Americans caught up and went to 30 or 40 titles per decade, while Russians fell to about ten titles per decade. As for the British, it is mostly H. G. Wells and A. C. Clarke. Wells was first published in 1914, stayed in print with two to five titles every decade, increased to eight titles in the 1951–1960 decade, then fell to one or two. Clarke peaked in the decade 1971–1980 with 12 titles, then fell sharply.

If we include all domestic (Yugoslav) SF books, then we see that, of all the SF books printed in Yugoslavia since 1900, 22 percent were translations of American authors, 23 percent French, 17 percent Soviet (largely Beliaev), 14 percent British, 14 percent all other foreign, and about 9 percent domestic.

Yugoslav Science Fiction

Before 1945, there were perhaps less than a dozen SF or semi-SF stories published in Yugoslavia, but after 1955, probably more than 1,000. They appeared in several languages, in all sorts of magazines and newspapers, big and small, adult or juvenile, and often not announced as SF. I have compiled a bibliography with several hundred of them, but to identify them all would be the work of Hercules or of a twenty-second-century supercomputer. Some hundreds of Yugoslav SF stories have been published under English-sounding pseudonyms—still a widespread practice, and not only in SF. Publishers know that the public buys such works more readily. I doubt that we shall ever know who is hiding behind every "G. Blackman" and "F. Stanson" and a legion of other maybe-pseudonyms scattered throughout the years and hidden between millions of non-SF pages. Some hundreds of Yugoslav stories are for children. Some others are simply bad; I know a hack who has produced and published about a hundred short stories, almost all awful, and who is still at it.

Very little Yugoslav SF is set in Yugoslavia. Most writers apparently feel that SF should take place elsewhere: distance lends enchantment. Perhaps these authors haven't been impressed by Yugoslav scientific achievements, and if they want to write about scientific innovations, they typically locate the story in Louisiana rather than Belgrade. But because many Yugoslav authors know America only secondhand, through films and books, characters are often wooden, plots strained and unconvincing.

Another defect of too much Yugoslav SF is derived from a half-understood ideological exaggeration: capitalists with recognizably English-sounding names wreck the environment, start nuclear wars because they're madly militaristic, attack people on Earth or in space, and so on. Everyone else is angelic, and the reader is expected to cheer for The People against Those Americans. The trash produced by such misguided writers somewhat resembles two less successful novels of Le Guin, *The Eye of the Heron* [4-325] and *The Word for World Is Forest* [4-329].

Finally, because few writers have made any attempt to explore a specifically Yugoslav future, too many novels have a stagy, artificial quality. Not willing or unable to locate the dramatic action in any carefully realized society or country or smaller social milieu, the author opts for an abstract scientific institute or center, where a professor acts out of pure scientific curiosity, surrounded by dutiful, unquestioning assistants. What emerges are characters who are wooden, unconvincing, motiveless, absurd, sometimes even nameless, clumsily moving across an obviously artificial stage. In sharp contrast are the novels by Benford, *Timescape* [4-54], and Fred Hoyle's *Comet Halley* (1985). Their authors' knowledge and literary skills helped them create believable worlds with a complexity that permits social criticism and the exploration of economic, religious, ethnic, sexual, and other concerns.

Because of the lack of any significant tradition of specifically Yugoslav SF, little interest in the genre is taken by Yugoslav academics, who are more oriented to structuralist and semiotic studies of literature. Some authors of "literary" fantasy, such as Borges, are respected, but no writer of Yugoslav SF has approached the stature of, say, Le Guin. One well-known and respected mainstream writer, Borislav Pekić, tried his hand at SF in *1999* (1985), but the novel was not well received.

Aside from an occasional earlier work of distinction, the best Yugoslav SF has been published in a monthly magazine begun in 1976, *Sirius*. Edited by Borivoj

Jurković and published in Zagreb, *Sirius* is Yugoslavia's first and only SF magazine. Each 120- to 150-page monthly issue features mostly short fiction translations from the United States, England, and the U.S.S.R., with a few tales from Germany and France. The work of Yugoslav writers appears regularly, and a special issue was devoted solely to Yugoslav authors. Nearly 500 original Yugoslav stories have been published in its pages during its first decade. It was judged the best European magazine at the 1980 and 1984 Eurocons. Its approximate circulation of 30,000 is proportionately much larger than its American magazine counterparts. Its best stories could compete with the better American or British stories, and I have summarized a selection in the bibliography.

Sirius is a major outlet for Yugoslav writers, some of whom were and are SF fans. There have been several fan clubs during the past decade, and fan activities include the publication of fanzines, since self-publishing is legal here.

Bibliography

Individual Authors

6-466. Alargić, Danilo. **Antares.** Belgrade: Author, 1969.
Benevolent extraterrestrials, headquartered in South America, are examining the mind of a Yugoslav engineer who was seriously wounded in a car crash. The ETs attempt to save him.

6-467. Belča, Dušan. **Prijatelj sa daleke zvezde.** Novi Sad: Ćirpanov/Dnevnik, 1982.
In this novella, benevolent extraterrestrials capture a boy and his grandparents and dog and examine them telepathically. They conclude that the boy is good, and a friendship develops; but then bad ETs attack the Earth.

6-468. Ćurčić, Slobodan. **"Kiše, šume, grad i zvezde."** *Sirius* 89 (November 1983).
In a postholocaust world, decadent, rich dwellers in antiradiation domes are surrounded by poor, often malformed, dwellers of radioactive forests. A boy avoids robot guards to enter the dome-city.

6-469. Filipović, Dragan R. **"Trominutni preskoci."** *Sirius* 77 (November 1982).
A student in a large city discovers that time slips away from him when he blinks. The effect increases, and he travels in time to see the beginnings of life on Earth and the distant future.

6-470. Lavrek, Andrija. **"Nemačka 1942."** *Sirius* 91 (January 1984).
In this alternate history, Hitler was assassinated in 1938 and Nazi rule overthrown.

6-471. Marković, Milanče. **"Sejač."** *Sirius* 62 (August 1981).
Following a nuclear holocaust, the few fertile Serbian men become "sowers," paid to inseminate the many fertile young women.

6-472. Pihač, Branko. **"Problem."** *Sirius* 66 (December 1981).
A female politician complains of the misuse of android doubles, but secretly uses one herself. When the human dies, the double is routinely destroyed. When the politician's double is killed in an accident, she must accept death to avoid revealing her duplicity.

6-473. Rus, Zofija. **"Dobri stari svijet."** *Sirius* 75 (September 1982).
This tale, by a woman, is set in the far future in which Victorian prudery rules and erotic pictures from our age are burned or sold at high prices on the black market.

6-474. Tezeus, Konstantin. **"Mudraci Saurije."** *Sirius* 115 (January 1986).
Two sentient species live in the ancient world. The reptiles favor culture, education, art, and wisdom, leaving the material gains and crass, worldly matters to the human "monkey." Over the ages the reptiles amass countless books, while laying fewer and fewer eggs.

Nonfiction

6-475. Nedelkovich, Alexander B. **Istorija srpske naučno-fantastične književnosti.** Belgrade: Author, 1985.
A 46-page booklet based on primary research, covering the 1889–1985 period and listing the works of a dramatist, a poet, 11 novelists, and 23 short fiction writers.

6-476. Živković, Zoran. **Savremenici buducnosti.** Belgrade: Narodna knjiga, 1983.
An anthology containing a theoretical introduction and stories by ten authors (Simak, Sturgeon, Asimov, Blish, Pohl, Bradbury, Clarke, Lem, the Strugatskiis, and Le Guin), each accompanied by a biobibliographical article. Derived from the author's doctoral thesis, this study argues that SF grew from kitsch to respectability.

Hebrew SF

Nachman Ben-Yehuda

Different answers to the question of what SF in Israel *is* will result in somewhat different interpretative "histories." I considered those literary creations that were written in Hebrew as SF and recognized as such by the authors, critics, or SF fans. Choosing this narrow approach means that one has to cope with at least two problems.

The first problem has to do with the complex relations between Jewish writings in general (in Yiddish, other languages, or even Hebrew) and the extensive Jewish literary creations on mysticism and fantasy particularly and SF in Israel. Of special interest here are legends and stories about Jewish magic, occult, witchcraft, and the like (for example, the golem legends). For example, in 1982, Shalom Babayof published a book called *Kadur Ha'esh* (the title was translated into English by the author as *Fireball from Space*, Jerusalem: Iris), about an expert in the Kabbalah who marries his adopted daughter to an extraterrestrial.

The second problem has to do with Israel's geopolitical situation. The inception of the modern state of Israel, founded in 1948, had its beginnings in the Zionist movement in pre–World War I Europe. Papers and books were written then on the future Jewish state, among them portraits of a future Jewish utopia. B. Z. Herzl's book *Altneuland* (written between 1899 and 1902) and many of his other fictional writings (from the 1890s) are considered to have served as the "blueprint" for Israel. After Israel was established, there appeared many stories and books dealing with how Israel ought to be, criticizing many aspects of Israeli society and politics, frequently using themes of utopias and dystopias. The last book in this long line is Amos Keinan's *The Road to Ein Harod* (Tel Aviv: Am Oved, 1983), which uses techniques of speculative fiction to describe a future Israeli dictatorship. It is Keinan's second book on the same subject. In 1973 he published *Shoah 2 (Holocaust 2)*, in which he envisioned the destruction of the state of Israel following an endless future-history of continuous wars. While these two books have clear elements of SF, they were *not* recognized by Israeli SF fans, literary critics, booksellers, and indeed, not even by the publishers as SF. In repeated interviews Keinan deliberately avoided using the term SF to describe his work. In an interview that was given to the local SF magazine (*Fantasia 2000* 43 [June 1984]: 22–24), Keinan significantly avoids any identification of his books as SF proper.

Thus, the amount of literature dealing with (or using) Jewish mysticism, the occult (not to mention the Kabbalah), and Jewish utopias and dystopias is huge. Indeed, one may speculate that these types of literature may provide a fertile seedbed for the development of various fantasy and SF stories. The obvious conclusion is that for the sake of simplicity and clarity, one should adhere to a simple, perhaps somewhat crude, definition of SF—as was suggested earlier. The next section, however, will provide a deeper reason for this approach.

Attitudes Toward Science Fiction in Israel

The relation between modern Israeli general literature and SF is one that may range from majestic and deliberate ignorance and disregard through misunderstandings, and much more often to scorn and ridicule of the former toward the latter, not unlike the attitude toward SF in other countries.

The most obvious reason for this is that the Israeli literary establishment (authors, critics, poets, publishers) views SF scornfully and suspiciously. I suspect that there is another reason. In many people's minds in Israel, especially in the late 1970s and early 1980s, SF and fantasy have become associated with the imaginary and the unreal. The genre has become, to a large extent, identified with that which is "out there" and not with the "here and now," even in an indirect way. Even the modern translation of the words science fiction into Hebrew suggests that. Until 1978, the words "science fiction" were translated as *Mada Dimioni*, literally meaning "science fiction" (or "imaginary science"). From 1978 (and especially due to the efforts by *Fantasia 2000*), the words SF were translated as *Mada Bidioni. Mada* stands for "science," but *Bidioni* stands for "falsehood," "fabrication," "legend." The older term, *Dimioni*, carries a much more positive tone—it means "fiction." We can safely assume that for people who want to criticize Israel socially or politically by using the SF genre, it would be better *not* to identify their work with SF, lest they will not be taken too seriously. Strangely, utopian writings apparently enjoy a much higher degree of legitimacy. However, authors in this specific genre are extremely reluctant to be identified, even remotely, with SF. Thus, Keinan's book (as well as other similar books) were classified with many other fictional papers and books—using different techniques—that provide literary, social, political, and other criticism of Israel.

Science Fiction in the Late 1950s and Early 1960s

During this period, many science fiction movies (such as *Destination Moon, When Worlds Collide, The Day the Earth Stood Still, Forbidden Planet, War of the Worlds, The Angry Red Planet*) were brought to Israel. A new publisher, Mazpen (Compass), began and specialized in translating science fiction books, among them Heinlein's *The Puppet Masters*, Brown's *What Mad Universe*, Frank M. Robinson's *The Power*, and others. A few other publishers translated one or two books, but these were isolated cases and did not indicate a major commitment to translate and/or publish SF. As far as we know, no local, original science fiction was then written. Mazpen lost much money very quickly and went bankrupt. Other publishers did not continue translating SF. Strange as it may sound, an Israeli SF author, Mordechai Roshwald, published in this period two SF books in English, both by Heinemann (London). One was *Level 7* [3-319] and detailed the final radioactive destruction of Earth. The other was *A Small Armageddon* (1962). Neither was ever translated into Hebrew, suggesting they were never meant for the Israeli, Hebrew-reading audience. However, the author got contemporary positive exposure in the Israeli media. Thus, the only SF Israeli author at the time directed his writing to audiences outside the country.

This period gave rise to three different, low-quality magazines: *Cosmos: Science Fiction Stories, Flash Gordon,* and *Mada Dimioni*—all with anonymous editors. *Mada Dimioni* began in 1958 in Hebrew. The editor and publisher(s) of the 13 issues are unknown. *Mada Dimioni* was, apparently, a cheap publishing enterprise of SF stories, strongly emphasizing short action stories. Careful reading would enable the reader to identify some of the original authors, although no names of authors were given. Despite the lack of identification of authors and its cheap looks, the translation was of good quality. *Cosmos: Science Fiction Stories* began in 1958 in Hebrew, in Tel Aviv, and lasted four issues. It was entirely devoted to translations of mostly American SF, but translators were not indicated. *Flash Gordon* began in 1963 in Tel Aviv and lasted seven issues. *Flash Gordon* was a magazine thriller devoted to its eponymous hero, Flash Gordon. Written by H. L. Halder (pen name?), it could be described as an Israeli form of a space-western.

This early period is best characterized as a "lead" age. No SF magazines or books appeared in Israel until the late 1970s. Although there were some new translations of a few science fiction books through this period (such as Asimov's *I, Robot* [3-20] and *Nine Tomorrows* [1972]), especially following SF movies (Clarke's *2001: A Space Odyssey, The Adromeda Strain,* and so on), no magazines appeared and hardly any activity in science fiction existed. Organized fan activities were completely nonexistent.

Science Fiction in the Late 1970s and Early 1980s

The golden age of SF in Israel began in the late 1970s, when there was a tremendous increase in science fiction activity, both in publishing and in fan activity. From 1978 through 1982 more than 190 books were translated, including many of the so-called "classics." Such major book publishers in Israel as Am Oved, Masada, Ma'ariv, and Zmora-Bitan-Modan began regular SF lines. Other publishers such as Ledori, Or Am, Ramdor, Schocken, and Rav Mecher also started to translate SF. During these years no less than ten Israeli publishers were involved in translating and publishing SF. Most appeared in paperback, a few in hardcover. Most of the translations were of good quality, some even demonstrating outstanding quality (especially Am Oved's superb SF line), but some were very poor.

During this time four new science fiction magazines appeared: *Olam Hamachar, Cosmos, Mada Bidioni,* and *Fantasia 2000.* A single issue of *Olam Hamachar* (*The World of Tomorrow*) appeared in 1979, in Hebrew, edited by Amir Gavrieli and Jacob Or and published by Khotam (Tel Aviv). The translated stories indicated neither original authors nor translators. This issue included information and articles about the U.S. space shuttle, UFOs, robots, and cartoons.

Cosmos began in 1979 in Hebrew. The six issues were edited by D. Kol and published by Atid (Ramat Hasharon). *Cosmos* was the Hebrew translation of the *Isaac Asimov's Science Fiction Stories,* both stories and departments. The letters department was locally produced, and some issues of the magazine included original Israeli SF stories. Poor publicity, few subscriptions, and lack of advertising killed it. *Mada Bidioni*'s single issue appeared in 1982 in Hebrew, edited by Avi Katzman and published by Dvir-Katzman (Tel Aviv).

Fantasia 2000 began in December 1978, in Hebrew, lasting 44 issues through 1984. The editors were Eli Tene, Zippi and Aharon Hauptman, and Dov Lerer (issues 1–16), Aharon and Zippi Hauptman (17–31), and Gabi Peleg (32–44). E. Tene (Tel Aviv) published issues 1–15 (June 1980), the remaining issues by Hyperion (Tel Aviv). *Fantasia 2000* was by far the most important and professional science fiction magazine published in Israel. The magazine maintained a very high quality, both in technical terms (paper, graphics, colors, and the like) and in literary quality. It was the second most expensive magazine in Israel, and at its peak had a monthly circulation of about 6,000 copies. (Although I have no hard data, I suspect this figure may refer to copies printed, not copies sold.) The departments included letters, SF news in Israel and elsewhere, articles about futurism, profiles of major science fiction writers, a regular science column, and various articles about either SF or speculative science. The translated stories credited their authors and translators, and were supplemented by a few original Israeli stories. *Fantasia 2000* had a formal agreement with *The Magazine of Fantasy and Science Fiction,* which permitted it to translate stories. *Fantasia 2000* gave the Israeli reader, for the first time, a taste of good-quality science fiction.

Fantasia 2000 and the active role one of its founders and editor, Aharon Hauptman, assumed gave local writers a golden opportunity to start producing original Israeli SF, some of it excellent. Only a few stories had any Jewish or specific Israeli themes; most resembled their Anglo-American counterparts.

A few local authors wrote SF, but most only one or two stories. A few published three or four stories, and even SF poetry, of whom the best known were Shira Tamir, Shimon Rosenberg, Yavsam Azgad, Shmuel Vaakneen, and Shlomo Shuval (who developed a special style for SF poetry). None produced a full-length book. One noteworthy figure is Orzion Bartana, a lecturer in Ben Gurion University's literature department, one of those rare literary critics who likes SF and wrote a few stories himself.

While *Fantasia 2000* was the obvious outlet for SF writers, it could not afford to pay its authors. Some authors had short SF stories published in the regular daily newspapers, especially in the special supplements of the weekend editions. Israeli writers also wrote full-length SF. Some of these six to ten books were self-published, usually on low-grade paper with very poor technical quality, and usually no more than 200 to 300 copies. The literary quality was very low, with bad Hebrew, inconsistent plots, terrible style—almost unreadable.

Aside from the above-mentioned books, about six good-quality original Israeli books appeared during 1980–1984, all published by Israeli publishers:

Melamud, David. *Tzavua in Corundy (Hyena in Corundy)*. Tel Aviv: Tamuz, 1980. Seven unrelated short stories, reprinted from *Fantasia 2000* and newspapers. The stories are of very good quality.

Damron, Hillel. *Milchemet Haminim (The War of the Sexes)*. Jerusalem: Domino Press, 1982. In a female-dominated future, the males rebel and social catastrophe follows. Parts of the book were published in *Fantasia 2000*.

Blumert, Ruth. *Hatzariach (The Turret* or *The Tower)*. Jerusalem: Keter, 1983. This paperback was illustrated by a very famous Israeli artist, Yigal Tumarkin. The book's androgynous hero tries to construct an elevator from the turret's basement to its top. The turret is populated by devils and monsters. The book may be thought of as an allegory, a story of a fantastic self versus other forces. A strange fantasy, very close in atmosphere to Kafka's *The Trial*.

Moav, Ram. *Zirmat Hachamin (Genes for Geniuses, Inc.)*. Tel Aviv: Bitan, 1982. *Luna-Gan Eden Genety (Luna—The Genetic Paradise)*. Tel Aviv: Bitan, 1985. Written by Ram Moav (1930–1984), a geneticist who was terminally ill and wrote the two books during the last few years of his life. Both give clear expression to some speculative ideas about possible genetic improvements of humans and the possible social consequences of such genetic manipulation or of avoiding the use of such manipulations.

Boussidan, I. *Sod Harishonim* (title translated by the author as *They Came from Beyond,* but literally *The Secret of the Firsts)*. Haifa: Tamar, 1984. A complicated story about humans aiding (or aided by) alien(s) (not clear from the book) invading Earth.

Other Developments

The years 1979–1982 witnessed the first time in the history of SF in Israel that fans started to communicate with one another and to organize clubs. Fan clubs sprang up in Holon, Ashkelon, Eilat, Haifa, Tel Aviv, and Jerusalem. The one in Jerusalem was the most active. It organized the first SF con (called Jerusalem Mini con) in Israel on March 22, 1981. The meeting attracted between 750 and 900 fans from all over Israel. An international SF con, Jerucon 81, had to be cancelled due to low registration and the inefficiency of the organizer.

The Holon SF club produced the only genuine Israeli fanzine, *Olamot (Worlds)*, edited by Eli Hershtein. The two issues had ten mimeographed pages each, which included information about the Holon SF club, short original SF stories, book reviews, SF in the world, and UFOs.

Two Israeli SF movies were produced. The first was produced by Riki Shelach in 1978–1979. This 25-minute film, *Ishur Nehita* (*Permission to Land*), was shown on Israeli TV in February 1979. The movie describes a UFO attempting to land in Israel. The second movie was released in 1981. Based on a poem by David Avidan (Tel Aviv), he later expanded it into a screenplay for an 87-minute color motion picture called *Sheder Min Ha'atid* (*Message from the Future*). The movie has an English-language soundtrack and was apparently not meant for a Hebrew-speaking audience. It was produced by Jacob Katcky for 30th Century Productions in Israel. The movie details how a Japanese industrial giant in the year 1985 attempts to market telepathic amplifiers and invents an elaborate advertising campaign. In the campaign humans from the year 3005 come to visit 1985 Earth and bestow on its people some of their futuristic marvelous gadgets.

SF activities in Israel sharply declined in 1982. The last active fan club, Holon, had its last meeting on October 20, 1982 at which *Fantasia 2000* gave the first awards to be given in Israel for the best four SF stories published there. The first prize was won by Yigal Zemach for "An Elephant Is about to Run" (issue 3); second to Hillel Damron for "The Monster" (15); and third to Shmuel Vaakneen for "Perfect Timing" (29). Monica Cohen won the fourth prize for "The Riddle" (30).

After a long and bitter feud with the publisher of *Fantasia 2000*, Aharon Hauptman, who probably did more than anybody else in Israel to advance SF, quit his position as editor of the magazine in the summer of 1982. While *Fantasia 2000* continued its highly irregular appearance under a new editor, it simply ceased to exist in 1984.

Following the sharp drop in fan activity and the demise of *Fantasia 2000*, there was a sharp drop in translations of SF books in late 1982 and throughout 1983–1986. Only three publishers continued their SF lines in 1982, and only about six to nine translated books appeared during 1982–1983—most of these the result of earlier contracts. In 1986 this trend continued. No fan activity existed and only a few translated books came out, all of them by the three publishers which continued their involvement in, and commitment to, translate SF on a restricted level (Am Oved, Bitan, and Keter).

I have elsewhere ("Sociological Reflections on the History of Science Fiction in Israel," *Science-Fiction Studies* 13 [March 1986]: 64–78) developed a full sociological explanation for the fortunes of SF in Israel. In brief, though, one can claim that Israel simply does not provide the kind of psychological-sociological climate that is hospitable to the widespread popularity of subcultures, including that of SF. Without such a supporting subculture, there will be no popular acceptance or legitimation of the genre, both of which are requisite for getting SF, including mature and innovative works, into print. SF in Israel depends on the influx of individuals from the centerless outside world who have been seeking to recenter themselves through SF and have for the most part been attracted to Israel by the self same search for an elective identity. That is also why levels of SF activity in the country have dropped so dramatically immediately after these outsiders exit in significant numbers (disappointed, for various reasons, in their Israeli quest). As one American SF fan put it to me before she left the country: "Israel is not crazy enough" for SF to prosper there—that is, it does not have an indigenous population of "decentralized personalities" large enough to sustain an SF subculture.

Research Aids

7

Science Fiction Publishing and Libraries

Neil Barron

Although the annual number of original works of SF has remained relatively constant since the second edition of *Anatomy of Wonder* in 1981 (see Table 7-1), the secondary literature has grown explosively, requiring considerable enlargement and rearrangement of these chapters. The chapters devoted to fiction are very selective, but the secondary literature is treated much more comprehensively, even though several dozen works annotated in the second edition have been dropped. The many books now available required grouping those with similar contents to permit easy comparison and evaluation in longer annotations.

SF Publishing

Locus [14-37] has for some years provided the most complete news coverage of English-language (mostly American) SF and has more recently broadened its scope to include SF published in Europe, the U.S.S.R., Japan, and other countries. Table 7-1 shows books published or distributed in the United States, with some British books not distributed in the United States included since about 1984. Science fiction, fantasy, some horror fiction, and most secondary literature was counted, from trade, mass market, and specialty publishers.

The growth in SF book publishing in recent years reflects its far wider popularity, stimulated by films and television, which are now the principal entry

Table 7-1   Growth of U.S. Science Fiction and Fantasy Publishing

Category	1975	1979	1981	1982	1984	1985	1986
Hardcover							
Original	160	320	247	246	270	305	338
Reprint	149	132	77	70	92	84	100
Paperback							
Original	251	365	332	326	343	410	508
Reprint	330	471	397	405	471	533	556
All books							
Original	411	685	579	572	613	715	846
Reprint	479	603	474	475	563	617	656

Source: *Locus,* February 1987.

Table 7-2   Principal U.S. Publishers of Science Fiction and Fantasy

Mass Market Paperbacks	Trade Paperbacks	Trade Hardcover	Secondary Literature
Berkley*	Harcourt*	Arbor House	Greenwood Press
Ace*	Bluejay (defunct)*	Doubleday	Borgo Press
Baen*	Donning/Starblaze*	Tor	Starmont House
Ballantine/Del Rey*	Ballantine/Del Rey*	Atheneum	Southern Illinois
Signet/NAL*	Viking/Penguin*	Morrow	Univ. Pr.
Bantam/Spectra*	Tor*	Harper & Row	UMI Research
DAW*	Ace*	SF Book Club	Bowling Green
Warner/Popular	Berkley*	Bluejay (defunct)	Popular Pr.
Library/Questar*		Dutton	Scribner
Pocket Books*		Houghton Mifflin	G. K. Hall
Avon*		Ballantine/Del Rey	Harcourt
Zebra*		Putnam	Indiana Univ. Pr.
		Macmillan	Salem Press
			Scarecrow Press
			Ungar/Continuum
			McFarland

*Publishes reprints and reissues as well as original paperbacks.

points for many readers, who not too many years ago would have discovered SF on the newsstand or in the library. Science fiction novels routinely appear on best-seller lists, although critical acceptance, especially in the academy, is still very qualified.

Locus analyzed the 1986 original books by type with these results:

294 SF novels (including 35 young adult [YA], 8 "literary books with SF more as metaphor than setting," 18 "survivalist," 27 first novels, 7 translations)

263 fantasy novels (including 41 YA, 20 first novels, 61 horror/fantasy, 8 literary/magic realism, 4 translations)

69 reference, a mixture of criticism, bibliography, biography, film studies, and miscellaneous works

72 anthologies, 26 mostly original, 46 mostly reprint

67 single author collections

22 film novelizations

22 omnibus

30 art (including "graphic novels," cartoon books and pop-up books)

 8 miscellaneous

Locus noted that the percentage of SF novels has remained relatively constant from 1981 through 1986 at about one-third. If about half the anthologies, collections, and novelizations are added to the novels figure, the percentage of original SF books of all types is about 45 percent. Thus, dividing the figures in Table 7-1 by two will give an approximate figure for SF books, using an elastic definition.

Although many publishers issue SF, even if not so labeled, most of the original titles and reprints are published by a relatively few companies. Table 7-2 shows in approximate 1986 rank order by category the principal publishers of SF and fantasy fiction, based on tabulations in the February 1987 issue of *Locus*. The list of publishers issuing secondary works is not limited to 1986 books but reflects a particular strength or emphasis. See also the introduction to Chapter 10 for additional details on author series issued by selected publishers. Libraries collecting SF in any depth should pay particular attention to the books of these publishers.

Not listed in Table 7-2 are most of the specialty publishers whose output is small and that usually stress well-printed books on quality paper. Two editions are often issued, a limited, signed, numbered, often slip-cased edition for collectors, and an unnumbered trade edition. The principal specialty publishers active in late 1986 are as follows:

Advent Publishers, Box A3228, Chicago, IL 60690. History and criticism; fan-oriented.

Arkham House, Box 546, Sauk City, WI 53583. Mostly supernatural fiction, especially H. P. Lovecraft; some SF recently.

Borgo Press, Box 2845, San Bernardino, CA 92406. Criticism in the short monographs, Milford Series: Popular Writers of Today.

Cheap Street, Rte. 2, Box 293, New Castle, VA 24127. Original fiction hand set in very fine quality editions; special collections departments should investigate.

Corroboree Press, 2729 Bloomington Ave. S., Minneapolis, MN 55407. Fiction.

Dark Harvest, Box 48134, Niles, IL 60648. Fiction.

Donning Co/Publishers, 5659 Virginia Beach Blvd., Norfolk, VA 23502. Starblaze trade paperback fiction; some Donning nonfiction.

Chris Drumm, Box 445, Polk City, IA 50226. Pamphlet-size author bibliographies, good and inexpensive, plus some original pamphlet short stories (see Chapter 10).

Evening Star Press, 5078 S. 108, Suite 159, Omaha, NE 68137. Fiction.

Ferret Fantasy, 27 Beechcroft Rd., Upper Tooting, London SW17 7BX, England. Bibliographies by George Locke.

Galactic Central Publications, George Benson, Jr., Box 40494, Albuquerque, NM 87196. Pamphlet-length author bibliographies (see Chapter 10).

W. Paul Ganley, Box 149, Buffalo, NY 14226. Fiction, mainly horror and fantasy; publishes *Weirdbook Magazine*.

Donald M. Grant, West Kingston, RI 02892. Fiction, especially from the pulps; occasional nonfiction.

Land of Enchantment, Box 5360, Plymouth, MI 48170. Fiction.

Maclay & Associates, Box 16253, Baltimore, MD 21210. Fiction.

Necronomicon Press, 101 Lockwood St., West Warwick, RI 02893. Material by and about H. P. Lovecraft.

NESFA Press, Box G, MIT Branch PO, Cambridge, MA 02139. Indexes, convention books.

Nemo Press, 1205 Harney St., Omaha, NE 68102. Ellison-related materials.

Norstrilia Press, Box 91, Carlton, Victoria, Australia 3053. Australian fiction and nonfiction.

Owlswick Press, Box 8243, Philadelphia, PA 19101. Mostly nonfiction.

Phantasia Press, 5536 Crispin Way, West Bloomfield, MI 48033. Fiction.

Scream/Press, Box 481146, Los Angeles, CA 90048. Fiction, mostly horror fiction.

Serconia Press, Box 1786, Seattle, WA 98111. Essay collections, initially by Aldiss.

Space & Time Press, 138 W. 76 St., #4B, New York, NY 10023. Fiction.

Starmont House, Box 851, Mercer Island, WA 98040. Starmont Guides (short author monographs) and other nonfiction.

The Strange Co., Box 864, Madison, WI 53701. Fiction, nonfiction, supernatural emphasis.

Tiger Eyes Press, Box 172, Lemoyne, PA 17043. Fiction.

Oswald Train, Box 1891, Philadelphia, PA 19105. Nonfiction, occasional fiction.

Underwood-Miller, 651 Chestnut St., Columbia, PA 17512. Fiction and some nonfiction, emphasizing work of Jack Vance.

Whispers Press, 70 Highland Ave., Binghamton, NY 13905. Fiction, especially in his irregular serial *Whispers*.

Mark V. Ziesing, Box 806, Willimantic, CT 06226. Fiction.

Reviewing and Selection

The reviewing of SF books, especially when so labeled by publishers, is still very erratic. Of the more than 30,000 original books published or distributed annually in the United States in recent years, no magazine reviews more than a small fraction. *Choice*, published 11 times yearly by the Association of College and Research Libraries, succinctly reviews about 600 books per issue, an enormous number but still only about 22 percent of all original books. (The effective percentage is of course far higher, since the focus is on those books judged best for college, university, and larger public libraries.) Original fiction alone accounts for at least 4,000 titles each year, but few journals or newspapers review more than several dozen works of fiction each year.

General reviewing sources tend to regard SF as simply another form of category fiction, much like mystery/detective fiction, and sometimes provide omnibus reviews of a recent sampling, or run the reviews in an occasional or regular department, both practices a form of ghettoization and an implicit statement that SF is not regarded as "serious" fiction. This is why writers like Vonnegut insist that their books be published simply as fiction. What Vonnegut said in 1965 rings true today:

> I have been a sore-headed occupant of a file drawer labeled "science fiction" ever since [1952], and I would like out, particularly since so many serious critics regularly mistake the drawer for a tall white fixture in a comfort station [from Vonnegut's "Science Fiction," *New York Times Book Review*, September 5, 1965, p. 2].

Norman Spinrad, one of the SF field's better writers, pointedly noted:

> Science fiction writers have complained that serious literary critics automatically ignore their work, no matter what its merits, and sometimes have spun elaborate theories about the snobbishness of the "literary establishment." But after all, how *can* a serious, conscientious literary critic sort through the year's mountain-high pile of tacky-looking science fiction paperbacks to find a few real jewels buried in this heap of literary mediocrity? He knows what a potentially important book looks like as an artifact, as a physical package, because publishers have consistently packaged most of these books in an identifiable style. He may even realize that one soap box out of twenty contains breakfast cereal, but is he going to chomp through nineteen boxes of soap to find it? Certainly not. He's going to open a box labeled breakfast cereal [from *Modern Science Fiction*, Doubleday, 1974, p. 3].

The sheer number of books published each year means that no magazine or newspaper can review more than a small selection, and certainly not necessarily the most enduring. This fact alone, quite apart from the tackiness Spinrad notes, means that little SF will be reviewed in general review media. Library and book trade journals review more, and a few specialty magazines more still, as Table 7-3 shows, based on information compiled by H. W. Hall, who indexes these book reviews (see [8-18]).

The library and book trade journals usually provide pre- or on-publication reviews. Of the specialty magazines, only *Locus* [14-37] does this with any consistency. This is important because much of SF has been and is published as mass market original paperbacks, which rarely remain on the newsstands for more than a few weeks, although jobbers can usually supply them for at least several

Table 7-3   Science Fiction and Fantasy Book Reviewing

Magazine	Frequency	Est. No. of SF/Fantasy Books Reviewed Annually
General		
NY Times Book Review	Weekly	25
Booklist	Biweekly	150
Choice	Monthly	50
Kirkus	Semimonthly	200
Kliatt Young Adult Paperback Book Guide	8 issues/year	200
Library Journal	Biweekly	150
Publishers Weekly	Weekly	225
Voice of Youth Advocates (VOYA)	Quarterly	150
Specialty		
Analog	Monthly	200
Extrapolation	Quarterly	50
Fantasy Review	10 issues/year	600
Foundation	3 issues/year	100
Isaac Asimov's SF Magazine	13 issues/year	150–200
Locus	Monthly	175
Science Fiction Chronicle	Monthly	250
Science-Fiction Studies	3 issues/year	50
Vector (BSFA)	Bimonthly	80

months after publication. Specialty dealers can usually supply them for a much longer period and of course have a much larger depth in their stock.

In addition to making use of reviews, libraries with more than casual interest in developing an SF collection should subscribe to *Locus,* which lists in each issue all books received, originals as well as reprints/reissues, providing a continuing bibliography of American and some British SF. This monthly listing can be used for retrospective selection.

I attempted to provide relatively comprehensive coverage of original SF and fantasy fiction and the secondary literature in *Science Fiction & Fantasy Book Review* (Borgo Press, 13 issues, 1979–1980). This was revived under the auspices of the Science Fiction Research Association in 1982, which published 20 issues through December 1983. In January 1984, this review became the book review section of *Fantasy Review* [14-35], which now provides the most comprehensive reviewing of any single journal. Constraints of time and money normally preclude prepublication reviews, but what it lacks in currency it makes up with its relatively comprehensive scope.

Once selection decisions have been made, books must be ordered. If a library buys heavily—arbitrarily defined as three titles weekly, roughly 40 percent of the original English-language SF published each year (see Table 7-1)—a specialty dealer may be preferable to a regular library jobber, especially for mass market paperbacks. There are two major mail order dealers in the United States that I can recommend.

1. Robert & Phyllis Weinberg Books (15145 Oxford Dr., Oak Forest, IL 60452) publishes a very useful monthly catalog of new and forthcoming books and fanzines: SF, fantasy and horror, domestic and some imported, plus some detective/mystery fiction. Pulp magazines are a sideline (Robert Weinberg has written a history of *Weird Tales*).

2. L. W. Currey (Elizabethtown, NY 12933) is generally regarded as the foremost antiquarian dealer specializing in fantastic literature. He carries new original hardcover and paperback fiction and most nonfiction as well, including many of the short-discount titles often purchased by libraries. He also carries a large selection of out-of-print material, galleys, proof copies, and many rarities, all meticulously described in his frequent catalogs, which reflect his wide knowledge not only of fantastic literature but of scholarly bibliography (see [8-3A] for his standard author bibliography). All serious collectors know of him, and a large portion of his inventory is sold by quotes, never reaching his catalogs.

There are in addition many other mail order specialty dealers and a number of specialty retail bookstores in larger metropolitan areas. Some are strong in particular types of material, such as pulps, comics, artwork, or specific authors.

Anatomy of Wonder has always been a critical guide to the best or better works. Scarcity, rarity, or collectibility were and are not among the selection criteria. Although SF has always been collected, in recent years it has become big business, like SF generally. It is not surprising that various price guides have been issued, such as Jeff Rovin's *The Science Fiction Collector's Catalog* (A. S. Barnes, 1982). As any knowledgeable collector knows, such guides are misleading at best and would never be written by a professional book dealer, who recognizes their inherently suspect nature, particularly in as rapidly changing a field as SF. Most guides omit the points necessary to identify the collectible editions (Currey's bibliography [8-3A] is the standard in this area) and fail to note the crucial effect condition has on price. Rovin, for example, cited a first edition of *Dune* as having a market value of $20. A dealer I know said at that time a fine copy in a fine jacket would bring $600 and up. The most reliable guides are the current catalogs of respected and established dealers, such as Currey. All serious collectors, dealers, and most order librarians know *AB Bookman's Weekly*, long the bible of the American used/antiquarian book trade. From 1983 through 1986 *AB* published a special SF and fantasy issue each October, when the World Fantasy Convention is held. These issues contain a number of articles of interest to collectors and librarians.

Cataloging

Hardcovers are almost always cataloged, but paperbacks, even originals, often end up in a library limbo, frequently placed on shelves or spinner racks but all

too often uncataloged. Since a user has no way of determining the library's holdings of such uncataloged works, simple chance is likely to determine their being
found and used. With today's computer-assisted cataloging, there is rarely any excuse for not cataloging paperback originals or, at the least, organizing a paperback collection for more effective access. One recent guide to classifying SF and
fantasy [8-38] would be of value to catalogers who deal with any significant
amount of fantastic literature.

8

General Reference Works

Neil Barron

The reference works published in recent years have proved extremely helpful to the serious reader of SF as well as to libraries. Most of the works discussed in this chapter are those that would commonly be shelved in a reference rather than a circulating collection. Specialized reference works, such as an author bibliography or a film encyclopedia, are discussed in their appropriate chapters.

Bibliographies and Indexes

*8-1. Reginald, R. **Science Fiction and Fantasy Literature: A Checklist, 1700– 1974, with Contemporary Science Fiction Authors II.** 2 vols. Gale Research, 1979.

This major reference tool lists the first editions of 15,884 books published in English from 1700 through 1974, and includes a biographical directory of 1,443 modern SF and fantasy writers, including editors and critics, replacing his *Stella Nova* (1970), reprinted as *Contemporary Science Fiction Authors* (1974). This is likely to be the definitive bibliography for many years. The books listed were examined and, if necessary, read to determine if they fell within the bibliography's broad scope. More than 4,000 titles were rejected as unsuitable. The biographical directory was compiled from questionnaires completed by the authors or their estates, and includes most writers active after World War II, except a few who failed to complete a questionnaire (like Lem) or who have achieved more recent prominence. Some death dates as recent as 1979 are included. The traditional information—family, education, career, memberships—is often useful, supplemented by personal comments, often lengthy. Cross-references in the bibliography are made to the biographies. Reginald effectively supersedes Bleiler [8-2], Bradford M. Day's *The Checklist of Fantastic Literature in Paperbound Books* (1965) and *The Supplemental Checklist of Fantastic Literature* (1963), and Marshall B. Tymn's *American Fantasy and Science Fiction: Towards a Bibliography of Works Published in the United States, 1948–1973* (FAX, 1979). The awards listing is more comprehensive than that in Franson and DeVore [8-36] but is not as current. Compare Currey [8-3A] and Tuck [8-7]. *Science Fiction and Fantasy Literature: A Supplement, 1975–1986, with Contemporary Science Fiction and Fantasy Authors III* is in preparation for publication by Gale Research. This supplement will list approximately 10,000 titles, including secondary literature, an enormous number for only a decade. Corrections and additions to the earlier period will be included. All earlier biographies will be updated and several hundred added.

8-2. Bleiler, Everett F. **The Checklist of Science-Fiction and Supernatural Fiction.** Fireball Books, 1978.
Bleiler's 1948 work, *The Checklist of Fantastic Literature,* was for many years the standard bibliography of fantastic fiction. This revised edition deletes 600 presumably marginal or improper titles and adds 1,150. The coverage extends through 1948 and includes almost 5,600 titles by author with a title index, in most cases the first edition. New are subject codes to indicate dominant themes. Bleiler, Reginald [8-1], and Currey [8-3A], do not always agree on first editions (prefer Currey). Bleiler says approximately a thousand titles in his checklist are improperly omitted from Reginald. John Eggeling's valuable review of Bleiler, Clarke [8-14], and Sargent [8-54] in *Foundation* 17 (September 1979) illuminates the problems involved in the compilation of such bibliographies and is well worth the attention of scholars and librarians.

8-3. Dictionary Catalog of the J. Lloyd Eaton Collection of Science Fiction and Fantasy Literature. 3 vols. G. K. Hall, 1982.
The 35,700 cards representing the cataloged holdings of the Eaton collection were microfilmed in September 1981 and represent the original 7,500 volumes, 7,500 subsequently acquired books, and 4,500 magazine issues. Access is by author and title, with many cross-references, and subject headings where appropriate. (SF novels and collections are usually cataloged only by author and title.) The Eaton collection [15-9] has grown enormously, as has the uncataloged backlog. A $135,000 grant from the U.S. Office of Education in late 1986 was to be used to catalog an additional 10,000 titles. Almost all cataloging records have been or will be entered into the On-line Catalog Library Center (OCLC) online cataloging database, greatly enhancing bibliographic accessibility to this largest of public collections.

*8-3A. Currey, L. W., comp. **Science Fiction and Fantasy Authors: A Bibliography of First Printings of Their Fiction and Selected Nonfiction.** G. K. Hall, 1979 (now available only from L. W. Currey, see Chapter 7).
A comprehensive listing of more than 6,200 printings and editions through June 1977 of works by 215 authors, from Wells to contemporary writers, over 98 percent personally checked by the compiler, a well-known specialist dealer. Non-SF

books are listed, such as the traditional fiction of Wells. Significant reference material published throughout June 1979 is listed, a very valuable feature, since this includes many fugitive fan press items rarely recorded elsewhere. The detailed points indicating first printings or significant editions are shown. Slightly more current than Reginald [8-1] and sometimes differs as to first editions. Used as the primary authority for *Anatomy of Wonder*. Especially valuable for collectors who have heretofore often had to rely on inaccurate compilations by amateurs not familiar with scholarly bibliography. A revised and greatly enlarged edition, covering the work of approximately 423 authors, is in preparation. Compare Locke [8-4].

8-4. Locke, George (U.K.). **A Spectrum of Fantasy: The Bibliography and Biography of a Collection of Fantastic Literature.** Ferret Fantasy, 1980.
Locke is a collector, dealer, and bibliographer, and this work is a detailed bibliography of his personal collection of more than 3,100 books. Beyond the publication data, physical description (including the points important to the collector), and an annotation, often detailed, discussing the work's significance, there is a description of Locke's own copy, with fascinating notes. The emphasis is on relatively scarce works published in the nineteenth and early twentieth centuries. A useful supplement to Currey [8-3A] and still in print in late 1986 for $95.00 from the compiler. An addendum volume is in preparation.

8-5. Locke, George (U.K.). **Science Fiction First Editions: A Select Bibliography with Notes for the Collector.** Ferret Fantasy, 1978.
Locke's descriptive bibliography of about 200 books annotated in the 1976 edition of *Anatomy of Wonder* is a fascinating work for any bibliophile, providing abundant detail about the points that identify first editions and the varied and often esoteric practices of publishers. Although Currey [8-3A] lists most of these works, Locke provides far more detail, and collectors should own both.

8-6. Locke, George (U.K.). **Voyages in Space: A Bibliography of Interplanetary Fiction, 1801–1914.** Ferret Fantasy, 1975.
A descriptively annotated bibliography of 263 books and magazine stories, with a sampling of 13 titles prior to 1800. Each entry includes bibliographic information, with notes on various editions, and a brief summary indicating distinctive thematic elements. Provides more detail than Reginald [8-1]. Author index. Issued as *Ferret Fantasy's Christmas Annual for 1974*. Most of the titles listed here and others of a similar nature are in the author's much more comprehensive *A Spectrum of Fantasy* [8-4].

*8-7. Tuck, Donald H(enry) (Australia). **The Encyclopedia of Science Fiction and Fantasy through 1968.** Advent, Vol. 1, 1974; Vol. 2, 1978; Vol. 3, 1983.
The first two volumes include a who's who and works, with a 52-page book title index. Volume 3 provides magazine checklists, extensive paperback information, pseudonyms, series, sequels, and other information. Brief biographical information—some more recent than the 1968 cutoff—appears for almost all authors, some of them only tangentially connected with SF (such as cartoonist Charles Addams). Contents of anthologies and collections are shown, as are series and original magazine sources for many works. Descriptive and evaluative comments are

intermixed. Though becoming dated, this is still a major reference work, and the author is working on supplements. Compare Nicholls [8-30] and Reginald [8-1]. HW, 1984 (officially for Volume 3, but in fact for the set).

*8-8. Brown, Charles N., and William G. Contento, comps. **Science Fiction in Print—1985: A Comprehensive Bibliography of Books and Short Fiction Published in the English Language.** Locus Press (Box 13305, Oakland, CA 94661), 1986.

The first of a planned annual publication. Offset from neat computer printout, this clothbound, 8½-by-11 inch volume assembles and revises material that appeared mostly in the 1985 issues of *Locus* [14-37]. Editor Brown surveys the year. The author list includes complete contents of collections, anthologies, and magazine issues, with pagination shown, and with original sources of publication if reprinted. New books are identified; reprints and reissues are also listed. The title index is limited to books. Original 1985 publications are listed separately by author. A subject list of original publications is divided into SF novels, fantasy novels, novelizations, collections, anthologies, omnibus volumes, magazines, reference (i.e., nonfiction), art, associational, and miscellaneous. A separate author and title list includes short pieces (mostly fiction). Appendixes reprint the book, cinema, and magazine summaries from the February 1986 issue, along with recommended reading lists. A list of publisher addresses concludes the 228-page volume. Abbreviations occupy the endpapers and several sheets at the beginning and end of the volume. This annual begins with 1985 books, temporarily leaving a one-year gap between it and Contento's latest short story index [8-10]. This first annual, in a 500-copy edition, appeared in December, probably reflecting teething problems. It is hoped that future volumes will appear by the spring and ideally should include much more thorough listing of British and Australian books (as befits the title) as well as foreign-language SF.

*8-9. Contento, William G. **Index to Science Fiction Anthologies and Collections.** G. K. Hall, 1978.

*8-10. Contento, William G. **Index to Science Fiction Anthologies and Collections 1977–1983.** G. K. Hall, 1984.

8-11. Fletcher, Marilyn P. **Science Fiction Story Index 1950–1979.** American Library Association, 1981.

8-12. Tymn, Marshall B., et al. **Index to Stories in Thematic Anthologies of Science Fiction.** G. K. Hall, 1978.

Approximately 12,000 English-language stories by 2,500 authors in more than 1,900 anthologies and single-author collections published through June 1977 are indexed by author, editor, and story and book title [8-9]. Original source (magazine or original anthology) is also shown, relying on the magazine indexes annotated in Chapter 14. (Supersedes Walter Cole's *A Checklist of Science-Fiction Anthologies* [1964], Fred Siemon's *Science Fiction Story Index* [1971], and the incredibly shoddy work of Fletcher [8-11], which disgraces its publisher.) Especially valuable for locating a source for an elusive story. The supplement [8-10] indexes about 8,550 works of short fiction, as well as 348 general introductions, 506 poems, and 22 plays, by about 2,600 authors. Some pre-1978 books and some weird, horror, and suspense books are indexed. Continued in Brown and Contento [8-8]. The

181 thematic anthologies, mostly out of print today, are indexed under 50 subject headings, such as anthropology, history, superior powers, overpopulation [8-12]. Author/editor and anthology/story title indexes. Contento indexes 167 of these but does not provide thematic access. Useful for an instructor desiring short fiction to illustrate a subject.

8-12A. Clareson, Thomas D. **Science Fiction in America, 1870s–1930s: An Annotated Bibliography of Primary Sources.** Greenwood, 1984.
Annotates 838 books, heavily by American writers, although British and some European writers are represented (e.g., Haggard, Wells, Verne). Annotations average about 100 words, are primarily descriptive, rarely evaluative except to note the historical importance of the work. The annotations in Chapter 1 of this guide could be considered a condensed version of this bibliography. Intended as a companion to Clareson's narrative history, *Some Kind of Paradise* [9-24]. Compare Suvin [9-98] and Stableford [9-93], who discuss British writers.

8-13. Colombo, John Robert, et al., comps. **CDN SF & F: A Bibliography of Canadian Science Fiction and Fantasy.** Toronto: Hounslow Press, 1979.
This 85-page paperback descriptively annotates approximately 600 books published or set in Canada or by Canadians (including transplanted authors such as van Vogt). The listings are grouped in sections: SF, national disaster scenarios, polar worlds, fantasy and weird tales, French-language works, children's books, and some nonfiction. Many items are decidedly associational, and the book unforgivably lacks an author or title index. For the specialist.

8-14. Clarke, I(gnatius) F(rederick) (U.K.), comp. **Tale of the Future from the Beginning to the Present Day: An Annotated Bibliography.** 3rd ed. London: Library Association, 1978.
A chronological and briefly annotated listing by year from 1644 to 1976 of about 3,900 utopian, political, and scientific romance tales of the future published in Britain, excluding juveniles and serial publications. Clarke's definition excludes alternate histories or parallel-world tales unless set in the future. In spite of its omissions, the best such bibliography of its type. His narrative survey of the subject, *The Pattern of Expectation: 1644–2001* [9-26], usefully complements this bibliography. Author (including pseudonym) and title indexes and brief bibliography.

8-15. Newman, John, and Michael Unsworth. **Future War Novels: An Annotated Bibliography of Works in English Published since 1946.** Oryx Press, 1985.
Approximately 191 novels published between 1946 and 1983 are chronologically listed and annotated, with author and title indexes. The selection criteria restricted the choices to relatively plausible wars among existing nations, thus excluding wars in space, in alternate histories, in the future, etc. Derived from the Imaginary Wars Collection at the Colorado State University Library [15-11]. Clarke [9-27] is much preferable.

*8-16. Clareson, Thomas D. **Science Fiction Criticism: An Annotated Checklist.** Kent State, 1972.
A pioneer listing of more than 800 items from both popular and academic sources,

excluding fanzines and most European sources. The entries are grouped in nine chapters, such as General Studies, Literary Studies, Visual Arts, Classroom, and Library. The book reviews are from general magazines not indexed by Hall [8-18]. The annotations are primarily descriptive but sometimes evaluative. Continued by Tymn and Schlobin [8-17].

*8-17.   Tymn, Marshall B., and Roger C. Schlobin. **The Year's Scholarship in Science Fiction and Fantasy: 1972–1975.** Kent State, 1979.
A supplement to Clareson [8-16], this is a cumulation of listings that appeared in the spring issues of *Extrapolation* [14-33], beginning with those in the December 1975 issue. The descriptive annotations are grouped into four sections. Coverage is limited to American and British journals and selected fanzines as well as books and doctoral and selected master's theses. Supplements cover 1976 to 1979 (1983), 1980, 1981, 1982 (1983–1985), in which citations are grouped in ten, then seven, sections. All volumes have author and title indexes. Publishing economics forced the return to *Extrapolation* with the 1983 installment (in the summer 1985 issue), followed by the 1984 and 1985 installments. Annotations have been largely omitted with the return of journal publication. Compare Hall [8-20].

*8-18.   Hall, H. W., ed. **Science Fiction Book Review Index, 1923–1973.** Gale Research, 1975.
*8-19.   Hall, H. W., ed. **Science Fiction Book Review Index, 1974–1979.** Gale Research, 1981.
*8-20.   Hall, H. W., ed. **Science Fiction and Fantasy Book Review Index, 1980–1984.** Gale Research, 1985.
An exceptionally helpful reference aid providing access to almost 14,000 book reviews of about 6,900 books, with full bibliographic citations. The reviews appeared in SF magazines since 1923 and in general reviewing media, such as *Library Journal* and *Publishers Weekly*, since 1970. The editor has issued these indexes since 1970, and the first four annuals are included in this 50-year index. A valuable two-part index records full details for almost all English-language SF magazines, 1923–1973, with a title checklist of all magazines covered by the index. The 1974–1979 cumulation indexes 15,600 reviews of 6,220 books, more reviews than in the first volume. The 1980–1984 cumulation indexes 13,800 reviews from more than 70 journals in the first 345 pages. The *Science Fiction and Fantasy Research Index* began as an annual in 1980, and the first five years are cumulated in the second part of the 1980–1984 cumulation, providing 16,000 author and subject citations to more than 4,700 books and articles. This second part will be part of *Science Fiction and Fantasy Reference Index, 1878–1985* (Gale Research, 1987), which indexes 19,000 books, articles, interviews, and so on by author (16,000 citations) and subject (27,000 citations). This is the largest bibliography by far of secondary literature. Hall's research index heavily duplicates the contents of Tymn and Schlobin [8-17], although there are many unique entries in each. Large libraries should consider both. In the *Science Fiction Master Index of Names* (McFarland, 1986), Keith L. Justice has indexed, page by page, 132 nonfiction books and volumes 1–10 (1959–1969) of *Extrapolation* [14-33] to generate a list of more than 20,000 personal names, as subject or author. Coverage ranges from Bailey's *Pilgrims* [9-8] to a few 1982 books. Only 18

of the listed books lack indexes (or are self-indexed), and many of these are the brief Borgo Press author studies, for which Justice is no help (access by title of book/story discussed is needed). There is no way of telling a useful reference, such as to an essay, from a simple bibliographic listing or passing mention. Far more books are not indexed than are. The Tymn and Schlobin [8-17] and Hall [8-20] indexes provide adequate coverage of English-language secondary literature. Justice has devoted immense effort to provide inadequate answers to questions very few people will ever ask.

8-21. Tymn, Marshall B.; Roger C. Schlobin; and L. W. Currey. **A Research Guide to Science Fiction Studies: An Annotated Checklist of Primary and Secondary Sources for Fantasy and Science Fiction.** Garland, 1977.
Descriptive and some evaluative annotations for almost 400 works from the very general to the very specialized, published through 1976 in the United States and England. Subject bibliographies, anthology and magazine indexes, histories, and critical studies are among the types of works annotated. More than 400 doctoral dissertations are listed but not annotated, most of them very marginal to the study of SF. Lacks a subject index and badly dated.

8-22. Cottrill, Tim; Martin H. Greenberg; and Charles G. Waugh, comps. **Science Fiction and Fantasy Series and Sequels: A Bibliography. Volume 1: Books.** Garland, 1986.
Series and sequels are very common in category fiction. This compilation builds on the work of Reginald [8-1], Tuck [8-7], and others cited in the bibliography, and lists roughly 1,160 series and more than 6,600 books, many paperback originals, mostly published in the twentieth century. Author, title, year, publisher, and sequence in series are shown through 1985 works. Series and book title indexes enhance the book's usefulness. Because most libraries view popular fiction series with caution verging on suspicion, they will not own—or catalog—most of these books. But because readers often want more of the same, a moderately useful book for medium-size or large reference collections, and very useful for specialty booksellers.

8-23. Garber, Eric, and Lyn Paleo. **Uranian Worlds: A Reader's Guide to Alternative Sexuality in Science Fiction and Fantasy.** G. K. Hall, 1983.
In spite of the occasionally titillating pulp covers showing lightly clad maidens threatened with unimaginable miscegenation by bug-eyed monsters, sexuality was taboo in the pages of most SF pulps. Garber and Paleo annotate 568 novels and shorter stories published through 1979 containing "images of and attitudes toward homosexuality" in SF and fantasy. Arranged by author with title and chronological indexes, the annotations are both descriptive and evaluative, not only of the fiction but of the authors, and the compilers' own biases are all too evident. A unique work, even if flawed, and very specialized in its appeal. A chapter in Lundwall [9-55] provides a European perspective on the role of sex and women in SF.

8-24. King, Betty. **Women of the Future: The Female Main Character in Science Fiction.** Scarecrow, 1984.
A mechanical compilation, nominally for teachers and general readers. Arrange-

ment is chronological (1818–1929, thereafter by decades). Each annotation notes main character, physical and mental/emotional characteristics, and "story particulars." Each chapter includes 15 to 30 annotated titles with others simply listed as "additional readings." The basis for selecting annotated titles is not given. Appendixes list collections and anthologies, women in erotic SF, and amazon women. Minor bibliography of secondary literature. Indexes by author and title for all titles as well as to physical and mental characteristics and plot elements for approximately 100 annotated titles. Compare Schlobin [8-25].

8-25. Schlobin, Roger C. **Urania's Daughters: A Checklist of Women Science-Fiction Writers, 1692–1982.** Starmont, 1983.
An expansion and revision of a similar checklist in *Extrapolation* 23 (Spring 1982): 91–107. Schlobin claims 375 authors and 830 novels, collections, and anthologies are listed. Basic bibliographic information is shown but nothing else. Some careless errors (Voltaire is listed) and omissions make this a marginal item, especially for libraries having the *Extrapolation* issue. Compare King [8-24].

Biocritical Works

8-26. Ash, Brian (U.K.). **Who's Who in Science Fiction.** Elm Tree Press and Taplinger, 1976.
A biobibliogrphic directory of roughly 400 primarily SF writers from the earliest years, although some entries are decidedly odd. Essentially superseded by the far superior Nicholls encyclopedia [8-30] and the biographical section of Reginald [8-1]. Mike Ashley's *Who's Who in Horror and Fantasy Fiction* [8-45] is a companion volume, with some authors listed in both.

*8-27. Bleiler, Everett F., ed. **Science Fiction Writers: Critical Studies of the Major Authors from the Early Nineteenth Century to the Present Day.** Scribner, 1982.
Each of these 76 well-written and carefully edited essays provides biographical information, a critical analysis of the fiction and the author's historical importance in the development of SF, and a basic primary and secondary bibliography. The approaches of the 26 contributors vary, as they should. Both SF writers and writers of occasional SF (Huxley, C. S. Lewis, Orwell) are discussed. Only three of the writers are not Anglo-American: Verne, Čapek, and Lem. Detailed index. More critically acute and better edited than the similar work by Cowart and Wymer [8-28]. Compare the much shorter entries in Smith [8-32].

8-28. Cowart, David, and Thomas L. Wymer, eds. **Twentieth-Century American Science-Fiction Writers.** 2 vols. Gale Research, 1981. *Dictionary of Literary Biography*, Vol. 8.
Here are 90 alphabetically arranged biocritical essays about authors, 11 of them women, who began writing after 1900 and before 1970. Varying in length from 2 to 3 pages to 16 pages for prolific or more important authors, each essay includes biographical information, critical evaluation of major works, and a bibliography of books and other writings, including a brief secondary bibliography. Photos of the authors and pages of manuscript are reproduced. Some choices are odd, such as William Burroughs and George R. Stewart (solely for *Earth Abides* [3-

358]). Four writers—Effinger, Haldeman, Sargent, and Zebrowski—fall after the 1970 cutoff. Appendixes discuss the New Wave, the fusion of SF and fantasy into science fantasy, SF illustration, paperback SF, SF films, fandom, fanzines, the Science Fiction Writers of America, Hugo and Nebula winners through 1979/1980, a chronology of SF books 1818–1979, details on American and British SF magazines, and a five-page secondary bibliography. Large libraries will probably want both this and Bleiler [8-27], which is less than half the cost of this expensive set and is preferred for medium-size or small libraries.

*8-29. Magill, Frank N., ed. **Survey of Science Fiction Literature.** 5 vols. Salem Press, 1979.
A major reference and critical source, containing 513 essays averaging 2,000 words each. Novels and short fiction by 280 authors, a fourth of them foreign, are critically analyzed by about 130 contributors, their work coordinated by the actual editor, Keith Neilson. Each essay is preceded by basic information: year of first book publication, type of work (novel, etc.), time, locale, one-line summary, and principal characters. Essays are arranged by title with an author index. The references following the essays are mostly to reviews, an oversight corrected with a bibliographical supplement compiled by Marshall B. Tymn (1982) and now included with the set. A one-volume paperback, *Science Fiction: Alien Encounter* (1981), reprinted the essays dealing with its subject for classroom use. A companion set devoted to fantasy [8-48] slightly overlaps this set. An essential tool, although its price will limit it to larger libraries.

*8-30. Nicholls, Peter (U.K.), general ed. **The Science Fiction Encyclopedia.** Doubleday, 1979. British title: *The Encyclopedia of Science Fiction*, Granada, 1979.
Assisted by other editors and about 30 contributors, Nicholls has produced the first true English-language encyclopedia and one of the most useful reference works for SF ever published. Based on original research and primary sources are 1,817 entries for authors, editors, and critics, ancient to modern, with judicious evaluation mixed with succinct description. Citations to books and articles about the subject are provided. The 175 theme entries occupy roughly one-third of the 672 pages, range from 200 to 2,500 words, and in scope from the predictable to the surprising. This feature should prove especially valuable for the instructor wishing to trace a theme through time. Films get 286 entries (mostly written by Brosnan of *Future Tense* fame [11-13]), magazines 167 entries, TV 56 entries, and so on. No summary can suggest the readability and richness of this work, which has remarkably few errors considering its immense scope. An essential item for any library, regrettably out of print. HW, L, 1980.

8-31. Searles, Baird, et al. **A Reader's Guide to Science Fiction.** Avon, 1979.
Short sketches (one-fourth page to three pages in length) of 204 SF and fantasy authors and their best-known works, most currently active but including earlier figures such as England, Burroughs, and Taine. Cross-references link authors whose works are similar. Lengthy series listings. Informal and necessarily superficial, it lacks a title index or any listings of suitable nonfiction for the serious reader. Of possible use for selecting paperbacks for a popular fiction collection.

*8-32. Smith, Curtis C., ed. **Twentieth-Century Science-Fiction Writers.** 2nd ed. St. James Press, 1986.

Uniform with other volumes in the publisher's Twentieth-Century Writers series, this second edition adds 94 entries to and drops 51 from the 1981 first edition, leaving 614, of which 571 are English-language writers, 38 foreign-language, with the same five "major fantasy writers" (Dunsany, Eddison, Morris, Peake, and Tolkien). New to this edition is a 51-page title index to all novels and collections and named series designated SF in the author entries. Smith was assisted by 21 advisers and 163 contributors. Most living authors checked their entries and often added a short comment. This work has too many typos and retains some of the bibliographic inadequacies of the first edition, which were mercilessly examined by John Clute in *Foundation* 25 (June 1982). In the five-page unselective reading list following the preface are several phantom books, announced but never published. The lists of uncollected short stories are limited to those uncollected since the author's latest collection, an eccentric and misleading policy. Many of the authors are minor or known only for a single work, such as Stewart for *Earth Abides* [3-358], for whom all books unrelated to SF are listed. Coverage of authors specializing in young adult books is weak. (The October 1986 *Fantasy Review* [14-35] has a review by Brian Stableford summarizing additional defects.) Even with its shortcomings, a very helpful and current biocritical guide, whose bibliographies should be used with great care. *Contemporary Authors* (Gale Research) usefully supplements this volume.

8-33. Tymn, Marshall B., ed. **The Science Fiction Reference Book: A Comprehensive Handbook and Guide to the History, Literature, Scholarship, and Related Activities of the Science Fiction and Fantasy Fields.** Starmont, 1981.

Historical and critical chapters provide overviews of SF, history, children's fantasy and SF, SF illustration, film, nonfiction works, fandom, awards, periodicals, recommended reading lists, library collections, doctoral dissertations (1970–1979), SF organizations and societies, a directory of SF specialty publishers, and definitions of SF and fantasy by 59 authors. The contents partly duplicate earlier works but the volume usefully assembles a large amount of information. Fairly well indexed. Current through early 1980. A revised edition, *A Science Fiction Handbook for Teachers,* has been announced. Compare Wingrove [8-34].

8-34. Wingrove, David (U.K.), ed. **The Science Fiction Source Book.** Longman, 1984.

Most closely resembling Tymn [8-33], this work assembles a short history, an essay on SF themes, working habits of authors, magazines, the economics of SF book publishing, the secondary literature, and the core (58 percent) of the book, a consumer's guide to the principal works of 880 authors of SF (and some fantasy) whose works have been available in English since about 1960. These entries by 12 British contributors are unsigned and range from 50 to 500 words. Some works are briefly mentioned and/or evaluated in an introductory paragraph, and others are shown on a grid assessing by zero to five stars readability, characterization, idea content, and literary merit. About one-sixth of the authors aren't in Nicholls [8-30], mostly those who have achieved greater prominence since 1979, although often on the basis of a few minor books. The entries for important authors are far too brief to give much sense of the complexity and variety of their fictions. Nicholls is much preferable to this, and Smith [8-32] is more current. A novice in SF seeking basic guidance should consider the inexpensive guide by Searles [8-31].

*8-35. Wolfe, Gary K. **Critical Terms for Science Fiction and Fantasy: A Glossary and Guide to Scholarship.** Greenwood, 1986.

Academics from various disciplines began moving into SF criticism in the late 1950s, bringing their special vocabularies and backgrounds. Wolfe is the first to map this Tower of Babel (or flea market, as he calls it). A valuable introduction traces the historical development of fantasy and SF critical discourse. Approximately three-fourths of this book is composed of a glossary of almost 500 terms and concepts, ranging from brief definitions to short essays, keyed to a secondary bibliography and to authors of cited fiction. Clear and concise and a most welcome and long-overdue work that all libraries should consider.

Miscellaneous Reference Works

8-36. Franson, Donald, and Howard DeVore. **A History of the Hugo, Nebula, and International Fantasy Awards.** Misfit Press, 1987.

8-37. Reginald, R. **Science Fiction & Fantasy Awards.** Borgo, 1981.

The Franson/DeVore booklet is usually revised every two years, includes both winners and nominees, and shows the original sources for short fiction. Reginald excludes nominations and original sources but includes many additional awards, some foreign, as well as a checklist of world SF conventions, including guests of honor, and statistical tables. A revised edition is in preparation for 1987 publication. Franson and DeVore provide more detailed background on the awards in Tymn's reference guide [8-33]. The Nicholls encyclopedia [8-30] lists awards, and any annotated title in this guide shows awards and nominations through 1986. If a separate listing is desired, Franson and DeVore is the best choice.

8-38. Burgess, Michael. **A Guide to Science Fiction & Fantasy in the Library of Congress Classification Scheme.** Borgo, 1984.

Burgess is a cataloger and, under his alter ego (R. Reginald) a bibliographer [8-1]. Following AACR2, he provides subject headings used by the Library of Congress (LC), from Androids to World War III. Author main entries and their class numbers, when assigned (LC does not usually catalog mass market paperbacks), compose 54 of the guide's 86 pages. A final section shows LC classification schedules, primarily in the literature classes but including some peripheral areas, such as art, with an index to the schedules concluding this tool. A specialized work, mostly for librarians, but of value to the scholar using a large collection of LC-classed fantastic literature. A revised edition is scheduled for 1987. Fred Lerner, also a librarian, wrote "The Cataloging and Classification of Science Fiction Collections" in Hall [8-39].

8-39. Hall, H. W., ed. **Science/Fiction Collections: Fantasy, Supernatural and Weird Tales.** Haworth Press, 1983.

This is Volume 2, numbers 1/2 of *Special Collections*, guest edited by Hall. Detailed information is provided by specialists about the library collections of SF and fantasy at the Library of Congress, the Eaton collection [15-9], Texas A&M University [15-45], Eastern New Mexico University [15-30], Syracuse University [15-34], Toronto's Spaced Out Library [15-57], and MIT Science Fiction Society Library [15-26], plus the huge collections of Ackerman [15-64] and Moskowitz [15-77]. Bob Weinberg provides a brief history of SF specialty publishers, Marshall B. Tymn surveys attempts at bibliographic control of fantastic literature through 1981, Fred Lerner discusses cataloging and classification and provides his own Fantasy Collection Classification Scheme, and Hall lists names and addresses of 54 library SF research collections, based on the 1981 edition of *Anatomy of Wonder*. There are cross-references in Chapter 15 to these detailed descriptions. Larger libraries would probably have received this overpriced volume on subscription.

8-40. Aldiss, Brian W(ilson) (U.K.). **Science Fiction Quiz.** Weidenfeld & Nicholson, 1983.

8-41. Ashley, Mike (U.K.). **The Illustrated Book of Science Fiction Lists.** Virgin Books, 1982; Cornerstone/Simon & Schuster, 1983.

8-42. Jakubowski, Maxim, and Malcolm Edwards (U.K.). **The SF Book of Lists.** Berkley and Granada, 1983.

8-43. Gaiman, Neil, and Kim Newman (U.K.). **Ghastly beyond Belief.** Arrow Books, 1985.

These are reference books of a sort, although more likely to be part of a circulating collection. The 30 quizzes devised by Aldiss increase in difficulty and are intended to amuse; "the questions and quotes are chosen because they seem in themselves worth reading, even to readers who are not devotées of science fiction." His wit and wide reading are evident throughout the book, which will challenge veteran readers of SF. Ashley, a British fan/bibliographer, has assembled an interesting, sometimes amusing group of lists, many of the general format, "the (N best) award-winning/most popular novels/stories about . . . ," derived from assorted polls, judgments of SF writers and critics, and other sources. Many illustrations break up the text. The table of contents lists the complete contents of the three sections, but there is no index. Jakubowski and Edwards lacks both a table of contents and an index, and the lists seem more trivial than those in Ashley, even when laced with humor. Gaiman and Newman have mined books, magazines, and films to write "something like the Oxford Book of Serious Literary Quotations, only snappier." There is considerable hilarity here, most of it unintended, and even nonfans would enjoy this original paperback compilation of nutty quotations, grouped in various categories. No index, of course.

8-44. Inge, M. Thomas, ed. **Handbook of American Popular Culture.** 3 vols. Greenwood, 1979–1981.

This will provide an invaluable starting point for scholars of popular culture. The 15 chapters in Volume 1, each by an expert, give synoptic overviews of their subjects, which include the automobile, children's literature, comic art, popular music, radio, TV, sports, and so on. Marshall B. Tymn wrote the chapter on SF. Each chapter provides a historical outline and bibliographic essay discussing reference works, research collections and histories, criticism, and journals, concluding with a bibliography of books and journals. Cumulative name and subject index. Although a reference work, it is very readable, with a remarkable amount of fascinating lore. *Concise Histories of American Popular Culture* is a 1982 trade paperback edition designed for classroom use. Most of the 50 chapters were revised, although the bibliographies are more selective. An original essay discusses approaches to the study of popular culture.

Fantasy and Horror Fiction

Some critics have suggested that SF is a particular type of fantasy, although that view is not dominant. What is indisputable is that the readership for fantasy, including horror, and SF overlaps heavily, and many authors write in both fields. Science fantasy incorporates elements from both genres. Annotated below are a few key works dealing with fantasy that are likely to be of interest to this guide's readers. Since these books fall outside SF as such, they have not been included here as core collection selections, although all medium-size and larger libraries should consider their acquisition. See also Chapter 14 for annotations of indexes to fantasy and horror magazines.

8-45. Ashley, Mike. **Who's Who in Horror and Fantasy Fiction.** Elm Tree Press, 1977; Taplinger, 1978.
Approximately 400 writers, mostly Anglo-American, from the eighteenth century to the present are briefly profiled, with biographical and critical information intermixed. A chronology from *Gilgamesh* to 1977 books precedes the profiles. Appendixes index key stories and books, summarize highlights from weird-fiction anthologies, and list the principal horror fiction magazines and the Derleth and World Fantasy award winners. A useful ready reference.

8-46. Bleiler, Everett F., ed. **The Guide to Supernatural Fiction.** Kent State, 1983.
A major reference work based on extensive reading, which critically surveys more than 7,000 stories and novels from gothics to about 1960, including translations. There are 1,775 books, about 250 of them anthologies, covered, with each entry providing a plot synopsis and biocritical information. Indexed by author and title, with a motif index with more than 40,000 entries.

8-47. Bleiler, Everett F., ed. **Supernatural Fiction Writers: Fantasy and Horror.** 2 vols. Scribner, 1985.
The first major survey of its subject. More than 145 writers, from Apuleius to contemporary writers, are treated, many for the first time in such detail. American, British, French, and German writers are included. The carefully edited essays incorporate a variety of approaches, each including biography, description and evaluation of major works, and an assessment of the author's historical position. A selected bibliography of primary and secondary works concludes each essay. Thoroughly indexed. Bleiler's supernatural fiction guide [8-46] treats most of these writers and many others, some of whom wrote only a few, usually shorter, pieces of supernatural fiction.

8-48. Magill, Frank N., ed. **Survey of Modern Fantasy Literature.** 5 vols. Salem Press. 1983.
A companion to Magill's SF set [8-29], this contains about 500 essays devoted to

341 authors of fantasy and horror literature. Lesser titles receive about 1,000 words, most titles about 2,000, with series, trilogies, and major works receiving 3,000 to 10,000 words. Volume 5 contains 19 topical essays (European theories of fantasy, fantasy versus horror, fantasy genre poetry, etc.), a chronology from *The Castle of Otranto* (1764) through 1981, an annotated bibliography of secondary literature, a list of major anthologies, and a detailed index.

8-49. Schlobin, Roger C. **The Literature of Fantasy: A Comprehensive Annotated Bibliography of Modern Fantasy Fiction.** Garland, 1979.
"Over 800 authors, 100 editors, 721 novels, 244 collections, 100 anthologies, 3,610 short stories, and 165 author bibliographies are cited and indexed here" — figures that appear to be accurate. The arrangement is by author of novels or collections, then by anthology editor. Complete contents are shown, providing a supplement to Contento [8-9] for fantasy and more recent than Tuck [8-7]. The emphasis is on nominally adult fantasy, excluding supernatural/horror fiction. Most entries are concisely annotated, often evaluatively, with series usually discussed as a group. Many original paperbacks are annotated. Some books discussed fall into the fuzzy area of science fantasy.

8-50. Sullivan, Jack, ed. **The Penguin Encyclopedia of Horror and the Supernatural.** Viking, 1986.
Approximately 600 entries in these categories: persons (authors, artists, directors, actors, composers, and so on); individual film analyses (about 150); and essays (54) on topics such as B movies, ghosts, graveyard poetry, opera, sex, urban and pastoral horror, writers of today, and zombies. Approximately 300 monochrome illustrations accompany the text. Hundreds of cross-references enhance reference use. The author entries lack the depth and thoroughness of those in Bleiler [8-47], but the scope is much broader. The writing is lively and clear, and the book encourages browsing.

8-51. Tymn, Marshall B.; Kenneth J. Zahorski; and Robert H. Boyer. **Fantasy Literature: A Core Collection and Reference Guide.** Bowker, 1979.
Boyer and Zahorski wrote the full—sometimes overly long—annotations for 240 core titles of fantasy, either for adults or with adult appeal, written in prose English between 1858 and 1978. The emphasis is on "high" fantasy, and the annotations generally praise all listed works, many of them original paperbacks of the preceding decade. A long introductory chapter defines the subgenres of fantasy. Tymn provides an excellent, briefly annotated bibliography of books and articles about fantasy and lists of fantasy periodicals and societies, awards, library collections, and U.S. and British publishers. More narrowly focused than Waggoner [8-53] but somewhat more reliable bibliographically.

8-52. Tymn, Marshall B., ed. **Horror Literature: A Core Collection and Reference Guide.** Bowker, 1981.
Five chronological checklists contain about 1,100 annotated entries, from gothics to authors prominent by 1980. The horror pulps from 1933 to 1940 and supernatural verse in English receive chapters. Mike Ashley covers reference tools, periodicals, societies, awards, and library collections. Core collection checklist of approximately 300 titles, not sufficiently selective. A useful guide, al-

though idiosyncratic in its coverage of modern authors. Bleiler's guide [8-46] and two-volume survey [8-47] are more rigorously critical.

8-53. Waggoner, Diana. **The Hills of Faraway: A Guide to Fantasy.** Atheneum, 1978.
Although the discussion of SF is necessarily limited, this is a very helpful companion for readers of fantasy. The core of the book is the annotated bibliography of 996 entries, listing novels, collections, some short stories, and articles. Many works are nominally juveniles, although many have great adult appeal. Some reviewers justly criticized the bibliographic inaccuracies and idiosyncratic judgments, but Waggoner writes with clarity and vigor. Two chapters are devoted to theory and trends in fantasy fiction. Many of the works listed in the science fantasy section of an appendix are annotated in this guide.

Utopian Studies

The earliest work annotated in this guide is More's *Utopia* [1-68], which gave its name to a large literature, many examples of which are drawn from modern science fiction. The books below provide some guidance.

8-54. Sargent, Lyman Tower. **British and American Utopian Literature 1516– 1975: An Annotated Bibliography.** G. K. Hall, 1979.
Following a very useful and extensively documented introduction is an invaluable descriptively annotated bibliography of utopian literature from More's *Utopia* in 1516 to recent works. Representative short fiction, mostly SF, is included among the approximately 1,600 entries. Equally valuable are the unannotated entries for about 600 books and dissertations and 1,600 articles in various languages that deal with utopian literature. Studies of utopias and utopian thought are numerous. Among the better ones are Frank E. Manuel and Fritzie P. Manuel's *Utopian Thought in the Western World* (Harvard, 1979), perhaps the most comprehensive survey in English (almost 900 pages). Narrower in focus but insightful and well written is Kenneth M. Roemer's *The Obsolete Necessity: America in Utopian Writings, 1888–1900* (Kent State, 1976), whose annotated bibliography is excellent. More analytical and especially cogent is George Kateb's *Utopia and Its Enemies* (Free Press, 1963; rev. ed., Schocken, 1972).

8-55. Ruppert, Peter. **Reader in a Strange Land: The Activity of Reading Literary Utopias.** Univ. of Georgia Press, 1986.
"My purpose . . . is not to determine what utopias mean, but to examine how they can mean different things to different readers." Chapter 1 describes the contradictions inherent in utopian literature that result in different readings. Chapter 2 surveys how readers read utopias; Chapter 3 proposes a way of reading based on utopias' dialectical structures, with Chapter 4 examining a detailed reading of More's *Utopia*. Chapter 5 discusses the anti-utopia, including *We* [2-147]

and *Brave New World* [2-47], while Chapter 6 discusses the open-ended ambiguous utopias that engage the reader to consider alternatives, such as *A Modern Utopia* [1-101], *Walden Two* [3-352], Callenbach's *Ecotopia* [4-107], Piercy's *Woman on the Edge of Time* [4-411], and Le Guin's *The Dispossessed* [4-324]. The final chapter summarizes the ways utopias are read and suggests "the most productive way of deriving their significance." Like Kateb's *Utopia and Its Enemies* (1963), Ruppert's work rejects the disdain often surrounding utopian literature, based on a one-sided reading of the texts, and stresses the crucial role played by readers in determining their meaning and value. Persuasive and clearly written, this study should enrich any reader's understanding of utopian literature and, to a lesser degree, of science fiction.

9

History and Criticism

Neil Barron

Criticism of SF as a distinct type of writing could be said to have begun in the letters and review columns of the early pulps in the 1920s. The letters, in particular, plus the fanzines, show the passionate devotion and contentiousness of fans, some of whom later became professional SF writers. A few of them combined their fictional and analytical skills to become the first house critics, providing a running commentary on the field in their magazine columns and fanzines. Some of these pieces have been collected in the works of Blish, Knight, and Budrys, and by fan-scholars like Moskowitz.

When fans-turned-academics began to take an active interest in the field in the late 1950s, it was logical that they would found magazines and hold conventions to share their insights, as well as advance themselves professionally. The movement of academics into the field was frequently regarded with suspicion bordering on hostility by many fans and some writers, attitudes that linger today.

Many senior English faculty also viewed with alarm or disdain the concern for a popular literature they thought lacked any depth or "seriousness," even though this feeling was often based on ignorance. George Slusser, curator of the Eaton collection [15-9], who has a Harvard doctorate in comparative literature, was given the Pilgrim award in June 1986 for his contributions to the study and understanding of science fiction. His acceptance speech in the July/August 1986 issue of the Science Fiction Research Association (SFRA) *Newsletter* [14-40] clearly indicates that this suspicion by "mainstream" critics and by English faculty is widespread today, to the detriment of both sides.

609

The increasing although still qualified acceptance of SF by the American academy (although rarely abroad) as a suitable subject for scholarly study has resulted in a very large increase in the secondary literature, including many of the reference works discussed in Chapter 8 as well as the works discussed in this and the next chapter. University press imprints jostle with those of fan-oriented publishers (see Chapter 7 for lists of the major publishers). Academics, many of them former fans, till the soil, often to exhaustion. Editors of the scholarly journals such as *Extrapolation* [14-33] justly complain that too many papers focus on a limited number of writers, such as Le Guin or Dick, neglecting many who are equally interesting if perhaps not as distinguished. The indexes to the secondary literature abundantly document this, but they also demonstrate the wide variety of material now appearing in books and magazines. The material itself reflects the varied approaches used by critics from different disciplines or critical persuasions—Marxist, structuralist, historical, linguistic, feminist, and so on. Wolfe [8-35] provides a thorough discussion of the evolution of SF criticism.

This chapter surveys most of the book-length works of history and criticism, including the increasing number of conference proceedings. When *Anatomy of Wonder* first appeared in 1976, the secondary literature was thin, and some marginal titles were annotated. I have been forced to be more selective in this and related chapters, even though all the major and many less important English-language works published by late 1986 are annotated here. Arrangement is largely alphabetical by author, but similar books are annotated as a group, with conference proceedings grouped at the end.

9-1. Aldiss, Brian W. (U.K.). **This World and Nearer Ones: Essays Exploring the Familiar.** Weidenfeld & Nicolson, 1979.
All 30 pieces collected here have been revised from earlier appearances except for minor revision of the six book reviews. It is easy to see why Aldiss was awarded the James Blish Award for Excellence in SF Criticism in 1977 and the Pilgrim award in 1978 for his contributions to the field. Few writers, in SF or otherwise, have the catholicity of interests and expository skills of Aldiss. Among the SF people and topics discussed with wit and insight are Blish, Dick, Sheckley, Nesvadba, Verne, Vonnegut, SF in Britain, SF art, and the film *Solaris;* other essays deal with travel, literature, and other topics.

9-2. Aldiss, Brian W. (U.K.). **The Pale Shadow of Science.** Serconia, 1985.
9-3. Aldiss, Brian W. (U.K.). **. . . And the Lurid Glare of the Comet.** Serconia, 1986.
Pale Shadow (HN, 1986) collects 13 pieces from sources not readily accessible to an American audience. Three pieces are autobiographical and give insight to knowledgeable readers of Aldiss's fiction. Six briefer essays treat Shelley, Stapleton, *1984,* and other topics. The title piece was delivered to the British Association for the Advancement of Science and exhibits Aldiss's usual acuteness. An original essay discusses his recent Helliconia series [4-6]. *Comet* again demonstrates his wide interests, whether treating *In the Days of the Comet* (1906), his own *Barefoot in the Head* [4-3], or a tribute to Theodore Sturgeon. Especially interest-

ing is the long autobiographical essay "The Glass Forest," an expansion and revision of his account in *Hell's Cartographers* [10-188].

*9-4. Aldiss, Brian W., and David Wingrove (U.K.). **Trillion Year Spree: The History of Science Fiction.** Atheneum and Gollancz, 1986.

Billion Year Spree: The True History of Science Fiction (1973) was the first critical history of the field, written by a distinguished writer and critic of both SF and traditional fiction. *Trillion Year Spree* is a worthy successor and is informed by the same wide knowledge and wit that distinguished its predecessor. Attentive readers will note extensive revision throughout and substantial enlargement. A note of modesty is evident in the new subtitle. Where the earlier history treated the 1950s and 1960s rather sketchily, the coverage here is admirably current, even including many 1986 books. Aldiss notes that SF "is now an industry, not a genre," and he has enlisted the talents of Wingrove to serve as an industrial manager. "I felt I could not bring the same fresh eye to the books, films, and events of the startling last fifteen years as I did to previous ones." The collaboration has greatly strengthened the book. My only disappointment is that there is little mention of his own work, since he is the best British writer of SF since Wells. There is, however, ample discussion of Aldiss in other works (see Chapter 10). Also slighted is any significant discussion of foreign-language SF other than some paragraphs devoted to Verne, Lem, Nesvadba, and the Strugatskiis. Valuable and enjoyable for the general reader and the fan, it will also serve admirably as a classroom text, provided the instructor realizes that the book represents an informed but very personal view of SF, unlike the sober consensus account in Gunn's *Alternate Worlds* [9-41]. The Gollancz trade paperback is less costly than the Atheneum hardcover. Sixteen black-and-white photos, detailed notes, bibliography, and index. "It provides, as no other volume does, a synoptic grasp of the whole field, with as much neutrality and freedom from favouritism or prejudice as its authors can contrive between them." Indeed it does, and it's an essential purchase for all libraries.

*9-5. Amis, Kingsley (U.K.). **New Maps of Hell: A Survey of Science Fiction.** Harcourt, 1960.

Instrumental in gaining SF a wider and more thoughtful critical acceptance, this is one of the best of the earlier critical studies. Amis sees social criticism and satire as SF's major virtues, adventure and action as artifacts from the pulp era. The easy conversational tone and wit make it an especially worthwhile work. Index of names and titles. Amis has since written fantasy and SF novels, such as *The Alteration* [4-10], and edited an anthology, *The Golden Age of Science Fiction* (1981).

9-6. Armytage, W(alter) H(arry) G(reen) (U.K.). **Yesterday's Tomorrows: A Historical Survey of Future Societies.** Univ. of Toronto Press, 1968.

This wide-ranging survey "tries to show how, out of the long process of preparatory day-dreams, imagined encounters, wish-fulfillment and compensatory projections, a constructive debate about tomorrow is emerging, providing us with operational models of what tomorrow could, or should, be" (p. x). The analysis is roughly chronological and discusses with perception many of the books annotated in this guide, although Armytage is sometimes careless in his facts. He has read widely, as the 44 pages of notes indicate, and this book is very useful background study for futurologists and SF readers. Compare Clarke's *The Pattern of Expectation* [9-26], and the visions documented in Corn and Horrigan [9-28]. Not seen is Frederik L. Polak's *The Image of the Future* (1961).

9-7. Ash, Brian (U.K.), ed. **The Visual Encyclopedia of Science Fiction.** Pan Books and Harmony, 1977.
A moderately detailed chronology from 1805 to 1976 lists in tabular format key books, stories, films, television series, and fan events. Nineteen chapters, extensively illustrated, by well-known writers show how various themes have been used in fiction. Fandom and media are discussed in the final part. A moderately useful but somewhat dated survey. The theme essays in Nicholls [8-30] are far more comprehensive and analytical. A more detailed index would have improved this book's reference value. Compare Holdstock [9-45].

*9-8. Bailey, J(ames) O(sler). **Pilgrims through Space and Time: Trends and Patterns in Scientific and Utopian Fiction.** Argus, 1947.
Based on the author's dissertation, "Scientific Fiction in English, 1817–1914" (1934), which in turn developed from a master's thesis on Wells, this is the first scholarly and comprehensive study of what were then called scientific romances. Although the focus is on pre–World War I works, enough attention is paid to subsequent works to show the continuities in themes and methods. The Science Fiction Research Association's Pilgrim award, given to the individual who has advanced the scholarly endeavor, is named for this pioneering study. Bailey was the first recipient. The origin and development of this book are explored in Sam Moskowitz's essay in *Science Fiction Dialogues* [9-107].

9-9. Bainbridge, William S. **Dimensions of Science Fiction.** Harvard, 1986.
Bainbridge is a Harvard sociologist who previously examined the SF subculture in a chapter of his *The Spaceflight Revolution* (1976). Here he extends his analysis, using replies from almost 600 registrants at the 1978 world SF convention in Phoenix and from briefer surveys later. The questionnaires asked for demographic information, evaluation of 140 SF and fantasy authors, and preferences as to 40 "types" of literature. All data are shown in the appendix. He isolates three dimensions of SF—hard science, New Wave, and fantasy—competing ideological factions with differing agendas for the future. Other chapters explore the effects of SF, women in SF, and the extent to which SF expands consciousness. How much of this will be new to veteran SF readers is hard to say, but it is clearly written, with many interesting sidelights, and is one of the few thorough statistical analyses of the genre by someone obviously familiar with it. Medium-size and larger libraries should consider.

9-10. Barr, Marleen S., ed. **Future Females: A Critical Anthology.** Bowling Green, 1981.
Collects 15 essays, 13 of which are original, about women writers of, or characters in, SF. Various approaches are used by the essayists, who include Robert Scholes, Eric Rabkin, and Joanna Russ. Schlobin's bibliography was expanded as *Urania's Daughters* [8-25]. Compare Weedman [9-119].

9-11. Ben-Yehuda, Nachman (Israel). **Deviance and Moral Boundaries: Witchcraft, the Occult, Science Fiction, Deviant Sciences and Scientists.** Univ. of Chicago Press, 1985.

An Israeli sociologist explores heterodox (deviant) beliefs in societies subject to rapid social change, especially modern Western societies. Topics discussed include witchcraft and contemporary occult beliefs in astrology, parapsychology, reincarnation, and various unorthodox quasi-religious beliefs. SF and fantasy fiction often incorporate ideas not validated by orthodox science (time travel, telepathy, matter transmission, etc.), and these deviant beliefs sometimes lead to quasi-religions, e.g., Scientology. Ben-Yehuda does not distinguish between the pseudoscience in SF, where the author sincerely believes in demonstrably false (or highly unlikely) notions, and imaginary science, which authors use to advance their plots or to suggest that what now appears impossible may some day be realized, e.g., manned interstellar travel; see entries in Nicholls [8-30] under Imaginary Science and Pseudo-Science for amplification. Fans share widely diverse beliefs and most have no difficulty recognizing this distinction. See also Brunner's lecture in *Science Fiction at Large* [9-67], and *The Science in Science Fiction* [9-68].

9-12. Berger, Harold L. **Science Fiction and the New Dark Age.** Bowling Green, 1976.

Walsh's *From Utopia to Nightmare* [9-102] more effectively traced the shift from utopian to dystopian literature. Berger's more recent survey groups roughly 300 works in 12 thematic groups to show the variety of treatments. No work is treated in any detail, and the historical perspective is cursory, but the coverage is more inclusive than that of any other single study. Notes and index.

9-13. Blish, James (as William Atheling). **The Issue at Hand: Studies in Contemporary Magazine Science Fiction.** Advent, 1964.

Most of these essays appeared in long-defunct fanzines from 1952 to 1963 and are spirited reviews of stories appearing in the SF magazines of the time, many since reprinted. Many of the pieces are dated, but their concern with quality is not, and they often repay reading, although mainly by the specialist. Blish's criticism is informed and blunt, refreshingly different from the puffery and cronyism that often substitutes for criticism. Detailed index.

9-14. Blish, James (as William Atheling). **More Issues at Hand: Critical Studies in Contemporary Science Fiction.** Advent, 1970.

The emphasis here is on reviews of books rather than of short magazine fiction. His subjects include the early SF critical literature, Heinlein, Sturgeon, Algis Budrys, A. Merritt, and some New Wave writings of the late 1960s. Compare Budrys's *Benchmarks* [9-17].

9-15. Bretnor, Reginald, ed. **Modern Science Fiction: Its Meaning and Future.** 2nd ed. Advent, 1979.

One of the first comprehensive discussions of modern SF by editors (such as Campbell and Boucher), critics (Boucher, Bretnor, Fabun), and writers (Pratt, de Camp, Asimov, Clarke, Philip Wylie). The original edition dates from 1953, and most pieces are now badly dated and betray SF's defensive stance of the time. The second edition adds notes, corrections, and an index, but the appeal will be mainly to the historian.

9-16. Bretnor, Reginald, ed. **Science Fiction, Today and Tomorrow.** Harper, 1974.
Fifteen essays by well-known SF writers, editors, and critics provide a thorough survey of the field in the early 1970s, 21 years after the editor's earlier survey. The coverage is wide, occasionally uneven, but still interesting, although more today for the historian. Biographical sketches and bibliographies for each author, plus an annotated critical bibliography and index, enhance the work. Compare Nicholls's *Science Fiction at Large* [9-67].

9-17. Budrys, Algis. **Benchmarks: Galaxy Bookshelf.** Southern Illinois, 1985.
From February 1965 through the November–December 1971 issue of *Galaxy*, Budrys acted as an investment counselor, as he termed himself, advising readers on the merits of 161 books, many of them major works of that period. Budrys sometimes adds a note to the pieces, which are chronological, with a title list of books reviewed and a thorough index. Budrys, like James Blish and Damon Knight, is a skilled writer of fiction, and carries on their critical tradition with care and insight. Catherine McClenahan appraises Budrys as critic, and Frederik Pohl, Budrys's editor for several years, contributes a shrewd perspective. Budrys continued to review for *The Magazine of Fantasy and Science Fiction* and for newspapers and is one of the field's most perceptive critics. L, HN, 1986.

9-18. Budrys, Algis. **Nonliterary Influences on Science Fiction.** Drumm, 1983.
This essay originally appeared in severely abridged and edited form in *Science Fiction Dialogues* [9-107] as "Fiction in the Chain Mode: Nonliterary Influences on Science Fiction." This is ironic, for the subject is the editing and publishing practices of the SF pulp magazine chains, which often changed many details of stories for literally mechanical reasons. The Drumm pamphlet is about 12,000 words (versus 5,000 words). The full text restores some important details, but it is much more prolix and less clear. The essay in either form highlights an important topic little known by most scholars and urges caution in drawing confident conclusions from texts that were corrupted for nonliterary reasons.

*9-19. Carter, Paul A. **The Creation of Tomorrow: Fifty Years of Magazine Science Fiction.** Columbia, 1977.
A professor of history at the University of Arizona and an occasional SF writer tempers his obvious enthusiasm with unobtrusive scholarship in a very readable account, which relates the thematic concerns of SF magazine fiction to the wider world, unlike most fan histories. Each of the ten chapters centers on a specific theme. See also the histories and studies of magazines in Chapter 14 and Cioffi's *Formula Fiction?* [9-21].

9-20. Cawelti, John G. **Adventure, Mystery, and Romance: Formula Stories as Art and Popular Culture.** Univ. of Chicago Press, 1976.
Although contemporary SF may be somewhat less formulaic than in earlier years, it still shares many features of mysteries, western, and melodramatic fiction, the subject of Cawelti's astute and readable study, whose insights could be

profitably studied in a course devoted to popular literature in general or SF in particular. Gary K. Wolfe, a student of Cawelti, analyzed SF's images in his important study *The Known and the Unknown* [9-106].

9-21. Cioffi, Frank. **Formula Fiction? An Anatomy of American Science Fiction, 1930–1940.** Greenwood, 1982.
Derived in large part from Cawelti, this analysis is based on the first decade of *Astounding*, when formula reigned supreme until late in the decade, at which time Campbell moved the magazine in more creative directions. A number of theoretical formulations are proposed, illustrated by the usually undistinguished stories typical of the period. I did not find that Cioffi's rather abstract schema aided my understanding of either early pulp SF or formula fiction in general. Compare the far more lively study by Carter [9-19].

9-22. Clareson, Thomas D., ed. **Many Futures, Many Worlds: Theme and Form in Science Fiction.** Kent State, 1977.
These 14 essays, primarily by academics, are original or revised from earlier appearances. Among the topics discussed are science in SF, myth, computers and machines, lost-race fiction, women in SF, theology, and recurrent SF imagery. A varied sampling of modern criticism.

9-23. Clareson, Thomas D., ed. **SF: The Other Side of Realism—Essays on Modern Fantasy and Science Fiction.** Bowling Green, 1972.
Twenty-six essays, mostly from the 1960s, from academic, popular, and specialist sources. They discuss individual works and authors or provide critical discussions of the meaning and significance of SF in both books and mass media. A balanced collection of earlier criticism, still worth the attention of today's reader. Compare Knight's more uneven *Turning Points* [9-48].

*9-24. Clareson, Thomas D. **Some Kind of Paradise: The Emergence of American Science Fiction.** Greenwood, 1985.
The most comprehensive study of its subject, begun originally in his 1956 dissertation, this is a historical and analytical work that explores a field first treated more sketchily by Bailey [9-8]. Many of the works described in Clareson's *Science Fiction in America* [8-12A] are examined in the seven chapters. The first two trace the incorporation of the idea of technological change in fiction and the rationalization of gothic and supernatural ideas in SF. Other chapters treat the mad scientist/scientist as hero, utopias and dystopias, world catastrophes, future roles of women, imaginary voyages, lost-race tales, and travel to the Moon and planets. Less rigorously analytical than Suvin [9-98], it is usefully read in conjunction with such historical anthologies as Franklin [1-36], Hartwell [1-49], and Menville and Reginald [1-62].

9-25. Clareson, Thomas D., ed. **Voices for the Future: Essays on Major Science Fiction Writers.** Bowling Green, Vol. 1, 1976; Vol. 2, 1979; Vol. 3, 1983 (co-edited by Thomas L. Wymer, with subtitle *Essays on Major Science Fiction and Fantasy Writers*).
The essays in Volume 1 discuss major SF writers whose careers began in the 1930s and 1940s, such as Williamson, Stapledon, Kuttner, Simak, Asimov, Heinlein, Sturgeon, Bradbury, Clarke, and Vonnegut. Eight authors whose ca-

reers began in the 1950s and early 1960s are the subjects in Volume 2, and include Mack Reynolds, Farmer, Ballard, Silverberg, Walter Miller, Le Guin, Brunner, and Zelazny. SF writers treated in Volume 3 include Delany, Disch, Wolfe, Damon Knight, Cordwainer Smith, and Pohl, with additional essays on C. S. Lewis as mythmaker and the complex fantasies of Mervyn Peake. This series of original essays maintains a relatively high standard. No future volumes are planned.

*9-26. Clarke, I(gnatius) F(rederick) (U.K.). **The Pattern of Expectation: 1644– 2001.** Basic Books, 1979.
A detailed, wide-ranging, and fascinating history of fictional speculation about the future from eighteenth-century tales and nineteenth-century utopias to recent SF and futurology. The earlier belief in infinite progress through science and technology has eroded in this century, and visions have turned dark, but Clarke argues that technology is two-edged and still offers a sense of possibility and hope. The 57 plates genuinely illustrate the text. Notes and index. Clarke's *Tale of the Future* [8-14] serves as the bibliography for this. Compare Armytage [9-6].

9-27. Clarke, I(gnatius) F(rederick) (U.K.). **Voices Prophesying War: 1763– 1984.** Oxford, 1966.
A useful background study of fictional works predicting future wars, from the anonymous *The Reign of George VI, 1900–1925* [1-2] to contemporary works. The account is chronological, with an entire chapter devoted to Chesney's *Battle of Dorking* [1-21]. Chapter 5 briefly mentions a few SF works, and others are listed in the longest part of the three-part chronological bibliography. Illustrated. For a more recent study of this topic, see Newman and Unsworth [8-15].

9-28. Corn, Joseph J., and Brian Horrigan. **Yesterday's Tomorrows: Past Visions of the American Future.** Katherine Chambers, ed. Summit, 1984.
A companion to a traveling Smithsonian Institution exhibit, 1984–1986, divided into five chapters: general visions, communities, housing, transportation, and weapons. The many illustrations and accompanying text could be used in a history course. The curators note that the vision is one of American corporate control, with many illustrations drawn from the 1939 World's Fair. Here the future is celebrated, as it often was in the American SF pulps of the same period, but there is little mention of the darkening of visions in later years. Armytage [9-6] provides some useful comparisons.

9-29. del Rey, Lester. **The World of Science Fiction, 1926–1976: The History of a Subculture.** Ballantine and Garland, 1979.
Drawing on his 50-year involvement with SF as reader, writer, and editor, del Rey discusses the evolution of the genre primarily in the United States, a narrowness he regrets but that weakens his account. The history is divided into 12-year periods (1926–1937, for example) and largely ignores historical events outside the pulps. There is too much plot summary, too little critical analysis, and the entire account has an insider quality not helped by slack writing. Compare the autobiographical commentary in *Early del Rey* (1975). An appendix annotates 14 nonfiction works and lists recommended works by period, including the long out of

print Garland Library of Science Fiction, of which this history is the first, although it appeared four years later. Aldiss [9-4] and Gunn [9-41] are much preferable as histories, and Carter's account [9-19] is far more perceptive regarding the same period. A detailed and somewhat polemical analysis of this book and the views it embodies is presented by Christopher Priest in *Foundation* 21 (February 1981): 53–63.

9-30. Delany, Samuel R. **The American Shore: Meditations on a Tale of Science Fiction by Thomas M. Disch—Angouleme.** Dragon Press, 1978.
An extremely specialized linguistic study of a section of Disch's novel *334* [4-188], in which the text is divided into 287 units and subjected to very detailed analysis and commentary. Delany's audience is likely to be limited to structuralist critics and linguists.

9-31. Delany, Samuel R. **The Jewel-Hinged Jaw: Notes on the Language of Science Fiction.** Dragon Press, 1977.
A collection of 14 pieces written between 1966 and 1976 and revised here. The essay on *The Dispossessed* [4-324] is original. Other essays deal with critical methods, the writing of SF, Russ's Alyx series [4-455], Disch's *Camp Concentration* [4-184] and other stories, and some of Zelazny's fiction. The pieces are of varying difficulty and will be of greater value to an experienced SF reader.

9-32. Delany, Samuel R. **Starboard Wine: More Notes on the Language of Science Fiction.** Dragon Press, 1984.
Collects speeches, essays, introductions to Gregg Press reprints of others' novels. Delany is widely read in literary theory, especially evident in "Dichtung and Science Fiction," which states part of his critical credo. Like that of Darko Suvin, Delany's prose is complex, sometimes opaque, although academic critics agree that his analyses are usually worth the sustained attention they demand. Delany received the Pilgrim award in 1985 for his contributions to the study of SF.

9-33. Dunn, Thomas P., and Richard D. Erlich, eds. **The Mechanical God: Machines in Science Fiction.** Greenwood, 1982.
9-33A. Erlich, Richard D., and Thomas P. Dunn, eds. **Clockwork Worlds: Mechanized Environments in Science Fiction.** Greenwood, 1983.
The Mechanical God was the first volume in Greenwood's series Contributions to the Study of Science Fiction and Fantasy, and is a companion to *Clockwork Worlds*. Although nominally dealing with distinct if related subjects, there is considerable overlap, as is evident in the two bibliographies. The many essays are very uneven, and libraries would have been better served by a single volume containing the best essays.

9-34. Eshbach, Lloyd Arthur. **Over My Shoulder: Reflections on a Science Fiction Era.** Oswald Train, 1983.
Eshbach (1910–) began reading SF in 1919 and founded Fantasy Press, one of the more important postwar specialty presses, in 1947, the same year he edited the first book on writing SF, *Of Worlds Beyond* (1947). Here he recounts the history of the SF book publishing field from the 1930s to the 1950s, when fan presses dominated the then-small field. A chapter provides a bibliography of the books issued by most of these specialty presses. While useful for the historian of

the field, the account is rather rambling and anecdotal, and only larger libraries need consider.

9-35. Fischer, William B. **The Empire Strikes Out: Kurd Lasswitz, Hans Dominik and the Development of German Science Fiction.** Bowling Green Univ. Popular Press, 1984.
This revised doctoral thesis is devoted to two writers important in German SF, whose works are discussed more fully in Chapter 6. Lasswitz's major novel, *Two Planets* [6-22], was published in 1897 but not until 1971 in English. Dominik's works appeared between the wars and are more technically oriented, lacking the human quality of Lasswitz. Fischer judges Dominik a mediocre writer, even though he is still popular in Germany. Neither writer had any notable influence on post–World War II German SF, unlike writers such as Wells or Stapledon. Also annotated as [6-40].

9-36. Fredericks, Casey. **The Future of Eternity: Mythologies of Science Fiction and Fantasy.** Indiana Univ. Press, 1982.
A classics scholar, whose bibliography and notes show wide familiarity with SF and fantasy, aims this book at the general reader with no special knowledge of either mythology or SF. After showing the use of various myths in works from *Frankenstein* [1-84] to stories of the 1960s, he discusses the use of "estrangement" in myth and SF. Four chapters analyze SF's use of mythic ideas regarding creation, Norse heroes, supermen, and the appeal of the primitive. The analysis concludes by examining three types of confrontation, man/superman, man/machine, and human/alien, and their varied uses in SF. Fredericks's background in the classics provides an unusual perspective and a fruitful means of better understanding the links between science's analytical/critical mode of thinking and myth's mystical/visionary mode.

9-37. Glad, John. **Extrapolations from Dystopia: A Critical Study of Soviet Science Fiction.** Kingston Press, 1982.
A slightly altered 1970 New York University dissertation whose origin is not indicated. Patrick McGuire, who wrote the chapter on Russian SF for this guide, judges the audience of this now dated and out-of-print work to be those with a prior knowledge of Russian literature and history, of literary theory and the Russian language. Prefer McGuire's own *Red Stars* [9-58].

9-38. Goswami, Amit, and Maggie Goswami. **The Cosmic Dancers: Exploring the Physics of Science Fiction.** Harper, 1983.
An informal guide for the SF reader to some of the key topics of modern physics, such as gravity, cosmology, causality, quantum mechanics, and the physics of epistemology. Diagrams clarify the text, as do many quotes from SF works, listed in a five-page bibliography. The authors minimize the choices writers often have to make between scientific accuracy and fictional imperatives, although they cite some examples. A somewhat specialized account likely to be less useful than the much broader survey, *The Science in Science Fiction* [9-68].

9-39. Greenland, Colin (U.K.). **The Entropy Exhibition: Michael Moorcock and the British "New Wave" in Science Fiction.** Routledge, 1983.

Derived from a doctoral thesis but thankfully better written, this specialized account explores the development of a diffuse "movement" centered in the pages of *New Worlds* when Michael Moorcock assumed the editorship in 1964. Greenland devotes considerable space to three key figures, Moorcock, Aldiss, and Ballard. Other chapters discuss sex in SF, psychology, and "inner space," all within the context of the experiments with form and content urged by Moorcock. The book would be more understandable to an American audience if some space had been given to American spokespersons for these manifestos, such as Disch, Ellison, and Malzberg. Historians of SF will find this a useful account, but most readers should find sufficient the New Wave entry in the Nicholls encyclopedia [8-30] or the discussion in *Trillion Year Spree* [9-4].

9-40. Griffiths, John (U.K.). **Three Tomorrows: American, British and Soviet Science Fiction.** Barnes & Noble and Macmillan, 1980.

Griffiths composed the original version of this book in 1970, but it was never published. He then read intensively works from the 1970s, hoping that the changes in the decade would stand out more vividly. They don't seem to, although his final chapter unsuccessfully attempts to synthesize dominant patterns. The book's structure is conventional. Its limited value is its comparison of Anglo-American SF to Soviet SF (Griffiths reads Russian), but his comments are not especially insightful, and readers will learn far more from the current survey in this guide. Many minor errors mar the account.

*9-41. Gunn, James E. **Alternate Worlds: The Illustrated History of Science Fiction.** Prentice-Hall, 1975.

From the earliest precursors of SF to the early 1970s, this provides a readable and thorough historical analysis of the scientific, social, and philosophical influences that created and shaped SF. Hundreds of illustrations, many in color, including several hundred photographs of SF and fantasy authors. An appendix includes the Nebula and Hugo awards, a partial thematic index with examples, and a tabular history of science, technology, and SF from the earliest times. Detailed index, but no bibliography. The author's academic background in literature and his reputation as a well-regarded SF writer make this a key work, much more satisfactory than Rottensteiner's pictorial history [9-86], although lacking the latter's more detailed European and Soviet coverage. More of a consensus history than a critical study like Aldiss's *Trillion Year Spree* [9-4], but equally valuable, especially when supplemented by his four-volume text/anthology, *The Road to Science Fiction* [13-25]. Compare the much shorter, unillustrated account by Scholes and Rabkin [9-90].

9-42. Hartwell, David. **Age of Wonders: Exploring the World of Science Fiction.** Walker, 1984.

Although Hartwell, a long-time fan and influential SF editor, claims that his audience is the casually curious and neophyte reader, this is probably too detailed for such readers, although it will certainly appeal to the fan or would-be fan. Chatty, anecdotal, and self-congratulatory; Hartwell's range is broad but not deep: how fans develop, common ideas and themes, the impact of the New Wave in the 1960s, the consequences of the much greater popularity of SF, the role of academic criticism, and other topics. References to selected secondary literature are in the text, but there is no reading list. Index. Compare the quite different analysis by Bainbridge [9-9].

9-43. Hassler, Donald M. **Comic Tones in Science Fiction: The Art of Compromise with Nature.** Greenwood, 1982.
If you think this book deals in any way with humor in SF, forget it. For that, see the Humour entry in the Nicholls encyclopedia [8-30]. I confess to having had great trouble seeing through the murky prose. Much of the account deals only peripherally with SF, and comparisons between SF writers and writers of traditional fiction (Le Guin and Austen, for example) do not advance what there is of a coherent argument.

*9-44. Hillegas, Mark R(obert). **The Future as Nightmare: H. G. Wells and the Anti-Utopians.** Oxford, 1967.
A well-written, absorbing, and perceptive study of Wells and his influence on writers such as Foster, Čapek, Zamiatin, Huxley, Orwell, and Lewis. The anti-utopian tradition is also traced in the works of the better SF writers such as Bradbury, Clarke, Pohl and Kornbluth, and Vonnegut. Compare Walsh [9-102].

9-45. Holdstock, Robert (U.K.), ed. **Encyclopedia of Science Fiction.** Octopus Books, 1978.
Misleadingly titled, this is a series of colorfully illustrated essays by 11 British contributors that deal with major themes, films, machines, magazines, art, prophecy, SF in non–English speaking countries, the New Wave, and more. Over half the 223 oversize pages are illustrations, either original work by British illustrators or reproductions of book and magazine covers; they tend to overwhelm the text, which is competent and reasonably accurate. Only the text is indexed. Gunn's illustrated history [9-41] is much preferable to this book, which is similar to Kyle's coffee table books [9-49, 9-50].

9-46. Ketterer, David (Canada). **New Worlds for Old: The Apocalyptic Imagination, Science Fiction, and American Literature.** Anchor Press and Indiana Univ. Press, 1974.
Both a study of American literature and an analysis of SF, the book insists on the centrality of the apocalyptic vision in both American literature in general and SF in particular. Le Guin, Lem, Vonnegut, Poe, Twain, Melville, London, and Bellamy are among the authors whose works are examined in this scholarly study, parts of which were published earlier. Ketterer is best when his analysis is linked to specific texts.

9-47. Knight, Damon F(rancis). **In Search of Wonder: Essays on Modern Science Fiction.** 2nd ed., rev. and enl. Advent, 1967.
With James Blish [9-13, 9-14], Knight was the best of the early critics of SF, later achieving distinction as an editor and author. These book reviews from the 1952–1960 period, slightly amended from their original appearances in fanzines and *The Magazine of Fantasy and Science Fiction,* provide clear evidence of his stiletto wit and impatience with shoddy SF. Somewhat dated but still of interest.

Thorough bibliography and index. See *Benchmarks* [9-17] for the work of a successor working in the same tradition.

9-48. Knight, Damon F(rancis), ed. **Turning Points: Essays on the Art of Science Fiction.** Harper, 1977.
A veteran editor, critic, and author has assembled 23 essays written over a 30-year period. The authors include genre authors, academics, and writers better known for their non-SF writings, such as Kingsley Amis. Very uneven, often dated, but still a useful selection. Clareson's *SF: The Other Side of Realism* [9-23] is a more solid selection, and the lectures edited by Nicholls [9-67] provide a more current perspective.

9-49. Kyle, David A. **A Pictorial History of Science Fiction.** Hamlyn, 1976.
9-50. Kyle, David A. **The Illustrated Book of Science Fiction Ideas and Dreams.** Hamlyn, 1977.
These oversize, heavily illustrated books are by the founder of Gnome Press, who is knowledgeable, if often very careless about basic facts, and includes considerable text amid the illustrations, most of it rather superficial and fan-oriented. Similar to Holdstock [9-45]; compare Gunn's much better balanced history [9-41].

*9-51. Le Guin, Ursula K(roeber). **The Language of the Night: Essays on Fantasy and Science Fiction.** Putnam, 1979.
One of the most distinguished writers in SF and fantasy has collected 16 essays and several introductions. Susan Wood's headnotes and a checklist of Le Guin's writings are additional benefits. Le Guin's fictional gifts of subtlety, perception, and clarity are equally evident in these pieces. A superior collection. HN, 1980.

*9-52. Lem, Stanislaw (Poland). **Microworlds: Writings on Science Fiction and Fantasy.** Franz Rottensteiner, ed. Harcourt, 1985.
Ten reprinted essays by one of the most gifted European authors of cerebral SF. Lem's agent, Rotteinsteiner (who wrote the chapter on German SF in this guide), puts the essays and Lem's ideas in perspective. An autobiographical chapter is followed by carefully argued essays, sometimes polemical, dealing with the inadequacies of SF, Dick, time travel tales, Todorov's theory of the fantastic, Borges, and *Roadside Picnic* [4-542]. An important collection of viewpoints not often seen in North America.

9-53. Lerner, Frederick A. **Modern Science Fiction and the Literary Community.** Scarecrow, 1985.
About half this study's 325 pages are devoted to documentation—chapter notes, sources consulted, book reviews, articles, etc.—betraying its origin as a library science doctoral thesis. The coverage is from 1926 through 1976 and is limited to fiction originating in the American pulps. On the basis of magazine fiction, 102 authors were selected as representative of the period. Arthur Clarke is for some reason identified as American. Following four chronological chapters tracing the changing critical reception of SF, Lerner discusses SF in the classroom, in the library, and in relation to future studies. A plodding documentation of the trivial or the obvious, which would have been better as an article.

9-54. Lovisi, Gary. **Science Fiction Detective Tales: A Brief Overview of Futuristic Detective Fiction in Paperback.** Gryphon Books (Box 209, Brooklyn, NY 11228), 1986.
A self-published survey of about 100 books that explores the links between detective fiction and SF, illustrated with reproductions of many covers. Many of these works were previously serialized and/or published in hardcover, but Lovisi is rather casual about recording such information. Many typos and the lack of an index make this a choice only for the largest library or a fan of this hybrid fiction. Compare Pierce's *A Literary Symbiosis* [9-76].

9-55. Lundwall, Sam J. (Sweden). **Science Fiction: An Illustrated History.** Grosset, 1978.
Lundwall is as comfortable in the European literary tradition as in the American pulps, and this informal account benefits from his multilingual perspective. His understandable unhappiness with the traditional view of SF as a predominantly American phenomenon gives his history a sometimes strident tone. The chapter on the development of magazine SF was reprinted in *Foundation* 34 (Autumn 1985), and strongly and effectively rebutted by Sam Moskowitz in *Foundation* 36 (Summer 1986). A useful companion to the much more comprehensive illustrated survey by Gunn [9-41]. Brief multilingual bibliography; index. Lundwall had earlier written *Science Fiction: What It's All About* (1971), an informal survey for the neophyte, now badly dated.

*9-56. Malzberg, Barry. **The Engines of the Night: Science Fiction in the Eighties.** Doubleday, 1982.
Malzberg has written a number of interesting SF stories, although many of his subjects are decidedly unheroic and the tone downbeat, the humor black. In these 36 short essays, many revised from earlier appearances in genre sources, the same sensibility is evident. His major concern is with the SF writer as victim, especially of market pressures, which impose crushing constraints. In spite of the subtitle, which Malzberg explicitly repudiates in one essay, his pieces discuss SF of the 1940s through the 1970s from his highly personal perspective. Written for fellow writers and fans, and likely to annoy many of them with his Cassandra utterances. An important collection by a much underrated writer. HN, L, 1983.

*9-57. Manlove, C(olin) N(icholas) (U.K.). **Science Fiction: Ten Explorations.** Kent State and Macmillan, 1986.
Manlove challenges the notion that SF's value is as "a metaphor, myth or projection of our world . . . is only really worth considering when it tells us something about ourselves." While conceding some merit to this view, he focuses his essays on the fictional element in and creative impulse behind SF "and the strangeness of the worlds it puts before us." One book from each of ten authors—Asimov, Pohl, Aldiss, Herbert, Silverberg, Farmer, Clarke, Simak, Wolfe, and A. A. Attanasio—is analyzed, linked to the author's other works and sometimes to works of other authors. Manlove, of Edinburgh University's English department, has read widely, writes with grace and insight, and has written one of the best recent works of criticism. Notes, bibliography, index.

9-58. McGuire, Patrick. **Red Stars: Political Aspects of Soviet Science Fiction.** UMI Research Press, 1985.
The emphasis of this slightly revised 1977 dissertation is on the political context in which Soviet SF evolved from 1923 to 1976, much less on the literary aspects of the fiction. Useful tables show fluctuations in the number of original Soviet SF works published in the U.S.S.R. between 1923 and 1976. See the section on Russian SF in this guide for an updated summary of this important early study, which is more current and better written than the Glad thesis [9-37].

*9-59. Meyers, Walter E. **Aliens and Linguists: Language Study and Science Fiction.** Univ. of Georgia Press, 1980.
Meyers is a skilled linguist and an extremely knowledgeable and witty writer. He is understandably unhappy that linguistics is largely neglected in the sciences supposedly undergirding SF and genially records hundreds of imbecilic ideas in SF, such as automatic translators used in communicating with aliens. He draws mostly from Anglo-American SF since 1950 and shows the crucial role of communication in so much SF, whether the theme be time travel, alien contact, or psychic communication. The linguistic principles are clearly explained.

9-60. Mogen, David. **Wilderness Visions: Science Fiction Westerns, Vol. 1.** Borgo, 1982.
Based on a 1977 dissertation, "Frontier Themes in Science Fiction," this short account examines the tradition of the frontier in SF, mostly American SF, including the work of Heinlein, Asimov, and Le Guin. European SF is said to have little of the frontier metaphor, although Soviet SF, which he does not discuss, has a recurrent concern with frontiers. A specialized but interesting study.

9-61. Moskowitz, Sam. **The Immortal Storm: A History of Science Fiction Fandom.** Atlanta Science Fiction Organization Press, 1954; Hyperion, 1974.
Although there had been SF readers before Hugo Gernsback began *Amazing Stories* in 1926, fandom—an organized body of readers who share their interests through magazines (fanzines), letters, and meetings—did not exist. Gernsback largely created it as means of boosting circulation. Moskowitz, one of the older fans, wrote this account for a long-defunct fanzine, a very personal and specialized chronicle of the many feuds and other activities of fandom in the 1930s. Detailed index. Compare Knight's *The Futurians* [10-190] and Warner's later histories (see below).

9-62. Warner, Harry, Jr. **All Our Yesterdays: An Informal History of Science Fiction in the Forties.** Advent, 1969.
9-63. Warner, Harry, Jr. **A Wealth of Fable: The History of Science Fiction Fandom in the 1950s.** Fanhistorica Press, 1976–1977.
Few save older fans will benefit from these casual histories of fan activities, but the scholar may find them useful as supplementary reading. A glossary of neologisms common to the field in the 1940s volume clarifies matters for the uninitiated. *Wealth* was issued as three stapled mimeographed volumes totaling 233 pages, continuously paged. It is crippled by the lack of an index, and the paper is poor. The publisher of *Wealth*, Joe Siclari, wrote "Science Fiction Fandom, A His-

tory of an Unusual Hobby," for Tymn's *Science Fiction Reference Book* [8-33]. A shorter account by James Scott Hicks, "Science-Fiction Fandom and Conventions," is part of Appendix 3 of Cowart and Wymer [8-28].

9-64. Moskowitz, Sam. **Science Fiction in Old San Francisco: Vol. 1, History of the Movement from 1854 to 1890.** Donald Grant, 1980.
Another of Moskowitz's pioneering studies, this one of selected American writers from the second half of the nineteenth century—Robert Duncan Milne, William Henry Rhodes, W. C. Morrow, Emma Frances Dawson—and their association with figures better known, such as Bierce and R. L. Stevenson. Moskowitz unearthed considerable detail about these writers and their many tales. Volume 2 collects some of Milne's stories [1-64]. Volumes 3 and 4, in preparation, will explore the later years of this movement.

9-65. Moskowitz, Sam. **Strange Horizons: The Spectrum of Science Fiction.** Scribner, 1976.
Ten of the 11 chapters were revised from their earlier appearance in the pulps. Although socially conscious SF is often considered to have become prominent since 1950, Moskowitz's original research into nineteenth- and early twentieth-century stories suggests there is little new under even alien suns. Topics treated included civil rights, anti-Semitism, religion, matriarchies, birth control, psychiatry, crime, juvenile SF, war, Charles Fort and his followers, and a biographical sketch of Virgil Finlay, the illustrator. Among the lesser-known authors who are rarely treated elsewhere are George Griffith, S. Fowler Wright, David H. Keller, and M. P. Shiel. A useful if rather specialized account, well indexed. Compare Carter's analysis [9-19] of how related themes were treated in later years.

9-66. Myers, Robert E., ed. **The Intersection of Science Fiction and Philosophy: Critical Studies.** Greenwood, 1983.
The 17 essays grouped in eight thematic sections are written by professors of philosophy and instructors in other fields (thus, intersections). Most essays raise a philosophic issue and then show how it is treated in several stories. Attempting to avoid jargon, this is more likely to interest readers of SF than teachers of philosophy, although both can learn from it. Compare the text/anthologies in Chapter 13 [13-32], which have a similar goal.

*9-67. Nicholls, Peter (U.K.), ed. **Science Fiction at Large.** Harper, 1977. British reprint, 1978, as *Explorations of the Marvellous.*
A superior collection of 11 pieces for the neophyte, most of them speeches delivered in London in 1975 to a nonspecialist audience. Seven of the 10 speakers are SF writers, including Le Guin, Brunner, Harrison, Disch, Sheckley, and Dick. Le Guin's and the editor's essays are particularly good. Compare Bretnor's *Science Fiction, Today and Tomorrow* [9-16], which is aimed more at the regular SF reader.

*9-68. Nicholls, Peter; David Langford; and Brian Stableford (U.K.). **The Science in Science Fiction.** Knopf, 1983.
Libraries classify this as a popular science book, which it is, rather than in the literature classes. Most of the hard, and some of the rubbery, sciences used in SF over the years are discussed—space travel, energy, aliens, antimatter, time travel, parallel and alternate universes, assorted catastrophes, artificial intelligence, ge-

netic engineering, social conditioning, powers of the mind, invisibility, and other topics. Stories illustrating these sciences and concepts are discussed and usefully listed in chapter bibliographies, along with collateral nonfiction. Index. Clearly written, effectively illustrated, this is a useful and fascinating companion for the SF reader, particularly the more credulous reader who is unaware of the extent to which fictional imperatives ignore science. Compare the essays in Ash's *Visual Encyclopedia of Science Fiction* [9-7], the Goswamis' *The Cosmic Dancers* [9-38], and Bretnor's *Science Fiction, Today and Tomorrow* [9-16].

9-69. Nicolson, Marjorie Hope. **Voyages to the Moon.** Macmillan, 1948.
A useful background study for the historian of early SF but much narrower than the popular account by Roger Lancelyn Green, *Into Other Worlds: Space Flight in Fiction, from Lucian to Lewis* (1958). An epilogue briefly traces the historical debts of Poe, Verne, Wells, and C. S. Lewis. Bibliography of primary and secondary materials; plates. Far more specialized is Philip Babcock Gove's *The Imaginary Voyage in Prose Fiction: A History of Its Criticism and a Guide for Its Study, with an Annotated Check List of 215 Imaginary Voyages from 1700 to 1800* (1941), a few of whose works are annotated in Chapter 1 of this guide.

9-70. Palumbo, Donald, ed. **Eros in the Mind's Eye: Sexuality and the Fantastic in Art and Film.** Greenwood, 1986.
These 18 original essays investigate not literature but pictorial art and film. The essays are supplemented with 47 reproductions, most of them by nongenre artists (Fuseli, Magritte, Picasso, etc.). Part of the multipart bibliography is keyed to the papers. Index. The essays are generally more readable than those in most such collections. A companion to Palumbo's *Erotic Universe* [9-116].

9-71. Panshin, Alexei, and Cory Panshin. **SF in Dimension: A Book of Explorations.** Advent, 1976; rev. and enl. ed., 1980.
Twenty-two essays from the 1969–1980 period, grouped in five semithematic parts. Many are omnibus book reviews, often dated. Two treat Heinlein in detail. Often repetitious, and the underlying critical theory seems weak and unconvincing, but readers may find some pieces of continuing value. Many of the ideas in these essays have been reworked into Panshin's *The World Beyond the Hill,* a historical analysis of SF announced as a late 1987 book from J. P. Tarcher.

9-72. Parker, Helen N. **Biological Themes in Modern Science Fiction.** UMI Research Press, 1984.
This overpriced revision of a 1977 doctoral thesis provides plot summaries under four headings—evolutionary SF, genetic SF, manipulative biology in SF, and the biological parable. Parker shows little knowledge of either SF or biology, and her study is not helped by murky prose.

9-73. Parrinder, Patrick (U.K.), ed. **Science Fiction: A Critical Guide.** Longman, 1979.
The 12 original essays here are primarily by academics and emphasize British and European rather than American SF. Each includes notes and annotated bibliography. The literary background of SF, Verne, and Wells are the subject of three essays. Raymond Williams discusses utopia and SF, the editor, SF and the scientific worldview. The cold war in SF, SF and religion, two approaches to characteriza-

tion in SF, American SF since 1960, and British and European SF are the subjects of the other essays. The general level is high, and all scholars and larger libraries should consider. Compare the Clareson collections [9-22, 9-23, 9-24, 9-25].

9-74. Parrinder, Patrick (U.K.). **Science Fiction: Its Criticism and Teaching.** Methuen, 1980.
Following the introductory chapter discussing various definitions of SF are chapters on its sociology (as product, as social document, and as a message to its audience), and SF viewed as romance, as fable, and as epic. Chapter 6 analyzes the use of language in SF to generate verisimilitude and novelty and shows through many examples how linguistic devices are used. *Solaris* [3-261] is analyzed as romance, fable, epic, and parody. The concluding chapter is a perceptive study of the teaching of SF, emphasizing its philosophical dimension rather than mechanical aspects. Notes, excellent annotated bibliography, index. A clearly written, well-argued critical analysis, it should be especially valuable to an academic readership or the more serious reader. Also annotated as [13-6].

9-75. Philmus, Robert. **Into the Unknown: The Evolution of Science Fiction from Francis Godwin to H. G. Wells.** Univ. of California Press, 1970.
A scholarly survey of English SF in the eighteenth and nineteenth centuries. The author defines SF as a rhetorical technique using (then) plausible scientific explanation to persuade the reader to suspend disbelief in otherwise fantastic situations. He relates SF to utopian satire and an archetypal mythical view of literature, discussing such works as *Gulliver's Travels* [1-89], Voltaire's *Micromégas* (1753), and *Frankenstein* [1-84]. A valuable early study of SF's origins for the more devoted reader, who should have good knowledge of the period for full comprehension. A 1983 reprint added an introduction that notes the inadequacies of the original study, written when there were few prior published accounts exploring the early years of the field. Compare the much more accessible account in *Trillion Year Spree* [9-4] and the important study by Suvin [9-98].

9-76. Pierce, Hazel Beasley. **A Literary Symbiosis: Science Fiction/Fantasy Mystery.** Greenwood, 1983.
Apparently written for an SF reader with little knowledge of detective/mystery fiction, yet with many detailed plot summaries of SF tales. The survey of detective fiction is limited and neglects much of the contemporary work and the scholarship dealing with it. A somewhat incoherent account of very limited appeal. Compare Lovisi [9-54].

9-77. Porush, David. **The Soft Machine: Cybernetic Fiction.** Methuen, 1985.
William Burroughs, Vonnegut, and Pynchon are the principal authors used to illustrate the evolution of what Porush calls cybernetic fiction; distinguished by a conscious use of modern information theory as metaphor, it often requires readers to decode the texts. A densely written study for the specialist.

*9-78. Pringle, David. **Science Fiction: The 100 Best Novels—An English-Language Selection, 1949–1984.** Xanadu, 1985.
The editor of *Interzone* [14-24] and until recently of *Foundation* [14-36] provides two-page critical appraisals of 100 superior novels, almost all annotated in this guide. Pringle is well read and both his choices and analyses are intelligent. He

recognizes that short fiction is slighted, although he mentions author collections in many appraisals. Some major authors, such as Tiptree and Vance, are omitted entirely, partly because of taste, partly for reasons of space. Libraries could do far worse than to begin with this judicious guide, whose reference value is enhanced by an author/title index. Compare Anthony Burgess's similar work, *99 Novels: The Best in English since 1939* (1984), which includes a few of Pringle's choices.

9-79. Rabkin, Eric S.; Martin H. Greenberg; and Joseph D. Olander, eds. **The End of the World.** Southern Illinois, 1983.
Six essays, including longer versions of two chapters from Wagar's *Terminal Visions* [9-101], more valuable for being more detailed. Brian Stableford's "Man-Made Catastrophes" provides many examples and shrewd analyses. Gary Wolfe's essay offers a useful structural analysis of postholocaust stories, using many examples to show variations on the formula, with a detailed discussion of *Earth Abides* [3-358]. The essays are often jargon-ridden but repay careful attention. A much broader and far better written study is *Terminal Visions* [9-101].

9-80. Rabkin, Eric S.; Martin H. Greenberg; and Joseph D. Olander, eds. **No Place Else: Explorations in Utopian and Dystopian Fiction.** Southern Illinois, 1983.
Fourteen original essays of very uneven quality. Subjects include Wells's *The Shape of Things to Come* [2-130], *Last and First Men* [2-109], *We* [2-147], *Fahrenheit 451* [3-61], Golding's *Lord of the Flies* (1953), *The Dispossessed* [4-324], *Erewhon* [1-19], *The Coming Race* [1-61], *Brave New World* [2-47], *Nineteen Eighty-Four* [3-302], *Player Piano* [3-392], and Silverberg's *The World Inside* [4-513]. Only print works are considered, no films. The contributors, oddly, are not identified in any way.

9-81. Reilly, Robert, ed. **The Transcendent Adventure: Studies of Religion in Science Fiction/Fantasy.** Greenwood, 1984.
"The vast majority of SF writers do seem either opposed to or oblivious to most religious concerns," says a contributor of one of these 15 pieces. Among the topics discussed are the later religious novels of Dick; the work of Farmer, Herbert, and Doris Lessing; Tevis's *Mockingbird* [4-551]; Tolkien, C. S. Lewis, Walter Miller, and James Blish. Checklist of works containing religious themes or motifs and secondary bibliography. Some very weak pieces, a few good ones, in an overpriced book. The article on religion in the Nicholls encyclopedia [8-30] might be a better starting point.

9-82. Riley, Dick, ed. **Critical Encounters: Writers and Themes in Science Fiction.** Ungar, 1978.
This volume inaugurated Ungar's Recognitions series and contains nine original essays by academics and free-lance writers. Topics include Asimov's robots, Bradbury's invasion stories, Herbert's *Dune* [4-268], *Childhood's End* [3-97], *Einstein Intersection* [4-167], *Stranger in a Strange Land* [3-207], Le Guin's *Left Hand of Darkness* [4-327], SF by women, and Sturgeon's stories. Similar to Clareson's *Voices for the Future* [9-25] but written more for the layperson.

*9-83. Rose, Mark. **Alien Encounters: Anatomy of Science Fiction.** Harvard, 1981.
A relatively short, lucid analysis that focuses on some of the basic ideas that make SF distinctive in contrast to a specifically literary analysis. Rose argues that SF is "a form of the fantastic that denies it is fantastic," similar to Clareson's view of SF as another kind of realism. Rose begins with two chapters, "Genre" and "Paradigm," which explore his ideas of human versus nonhuman and science versus nature. The final four chapters discuss categories in which these ideas take literary shape. Literary examples are used throughout, but no text is discussed in any detail. Rose's categories and discussion are suggestive rather than dogmatic and provoke the reader to respond. Rose will be most helpful to readers with some knowledge of SF, who will be able to flesh out a somewhat general, abstract narrative.

9-84. Rose, Mark, ed. **Science Fiction: A Collection of Critical Essays.** Prentice-Hall, 1976.
Eleven reprinted essays cover backgrounds, theory, and approaches. Written originally from 1960 to 1975, they are well chosen and are not heavily duplicated in similar collections. Included are Suvin's oft-cited "On the Poetics of the Science Fiction Genre," Robert Conquest's "Science Fiction and Literature," C. S. Lewis's "On Science Fiction," and Sontag's "The Imagination of Disaster."

9-85. Rosinski, Natalie M. **Feminist Futures: Contemporary Women's Speculative Fiction.** UMI Research Press, 1984.
The first in the publisher's Studies in Speculative Fiction, this 1982 thesis uses feminist deconstructionist critical ideas to examine selected SF novels by women writing in the 1960s and 1970s, such as Le Guin, Russ, and Marge Piercy. Her critical stance and rather dense prose is likely to limit her audience to academic critics, especially those who share many of her views. Compare the essays in Weedman [9-119].

9-86. Rottensteiner, Franz (Austria). **The Science Fiction Book: An Illustrated History.** Seabury, 1975.
The multilingual editor of *Quarber Merkur* [14-39] provides a brief history whose illustrations, often from unfamiliar sources, somewhat overwhelm the rather choppy text and are not well integrated with it. The survey's main value is its international approach, although Rottensteiner has more recently assessed SF in Parrinder's collection [9-73]. Chronology from Lucian to Le Guin, a multilingual descriptive bibliography, and a list of Nebula and Hugo awards conclude the work, which lacks an index. Gunn's survey [9-41] is preferable. Compare the very similar and slightly better survey by Lundwall [9-55].

9-87. Sadler, Frank. **The Unified Ring: Narrative Art and the Science-Fiction Novel.** UMI Research Press, 1984.
Derived from a 1974 doctoral thesis and predictably ponderous. *The Einstein Intersection* [4-167], *Report on Probability A* [4-9], and *Slaughterhouse-Five* [4-578] are claimed to embody the outlook of today's mathematical physicists. Heavy with quotes and documentation and somewhat dated; only the largest libraries need consider.

9-88. Samuelson, David. **Visions of Tomorrow: Six Journeys from Outer to Inner Space.** Arno, 1974.
A 1969 University of Southern California doctoral thesis that provides a historical and theoretical overview of the field and intensively studies six modern works: *Childhood's End* [3-97], *The Caves of Steel* [3-16], *More Than Human* [3-362], *A Canticle for Leibowitz* [3-287], *Rogue Moon* [3-77], and *The Crystal World* [4-35]. A good example of earlier scholarship still of value, with an excellent bibliography.

*9-89. Scholes, Robert. **Structural Fabulation: An Essay on Fiction of the Future.** Univ. of Notre Dame Press, 1975. Ward-Phillips Lectures in English Language and Literature, 7.
Revised from four 1974 lectures, this work argues that traditional forms of fiction are moribund and "that the most appropriate kind of fiction that can be written in the present and the immediate future is fiction that takes place in the future." Following the first half's relatively theoretical but clear discussion, Scholes discusses selected works such as *Flowers for Algernon* [3-228] and *Star Maker* [2-112]. An entire lecture is devoted to Le Guin. Short bibliography. Comparable to Amis's *New Maps of Hell* [9-5] in gaining SF greater academic respectability. His later study, *Fabulation and Metafiction* (1979), is only peripherally concerned with SF.

*9-90. Scholes, Robert, and Eric S. Rabkin. **Science Fiction: History-Science-Vision.** Oxford, 1977.
An excellent introduction to the field for the layperson and a good choice for an introductory text. The succinct history occupies about half the volume. The sciences of SF are intelligently explained using stories as examples. Vision deals with forms and themes and includes four- to six-page analyses of ten representative novels. Very useful annotated bibliographies and well indexed. Also annotated as [13-9].

9-91. The Science Fiction Novel: Imagination and Social Criticism. Advent, 1959.
Following Basil Davenport's introduction are lectures delivered in 1957 by Heinlein, Kornbluth, Bester, and Robert Bloch. Their tone is critical, stressing the lack of social criticism in most SF of that earlier period and the preoccupation with gadgets and technology in a social vacuum. A dated work of interest mainly to the historian.

9-92. Stableford, Brian M. (U.K.). **Masters of Science Fiction: Essays on Six Science Fiction Authors.** Borgo, 1981.
Stableford has a catholicity of interest uncommon for a critic and does not confine his attention to canonized authors. His subjects here are Edmond Hamilton, Leigh Brackett, Mack Reynolds, Vonnegut, Silverberg, and Malzberg. An astringent style makes these essays pleasurable as well as enlightening.

*9-93. Stableford, Brian M. (U.K.). **Scientific Romance in Britain 1890–1950.** Fourth Estate, 1985.
Stableford uses the phrase "scientific romance" to refer to the distinctively British tradition of speculative fiction, which developed largely separate from Ameri-

can SF, which derived far more from popular magazines of the early twentieth century. He traces the use of the term by Charles Hinton and the massive influence of Wells on other British writers of speculative fiction. Stableford analyzes the many varieties of scientific romance, "from the heavily didactic and passionately earnest . . . to the deliberately frivolous and farcical," but always blending playful with more serious elements. The literary ancestors are discussed (utopian and evolutionary fantasies, imaginary wars, and so on), and the major writers in this tradition before and after World War I are examined, along with patterns and trends in these periods. Although the traditions of scientific romance and SF blended in the U.K. in the 1950s, British SF retains a distinctive flavor. A major historical and literary analysis based on considerable original research, written with clarity and vigor, and an essential purchase for anyone or any library with a serious interest in SF. Compare Suvin's *Victorian Science Fiction in the UK* [9-98]; contrast Clareson's *Some Kind of Paradise* [9-24].

9-94. Staicar, Tom, ed. **Critical Encounters II: Writers and Themes in Science Fiction.** Ungar, 1982.
This continues Riley [9-82] and focuses on the work of Clement, Zelazny, Silverberg, Ian Watson, Doris Piserchia, Vonda McIntyre, Richard Matheson, and the Strugatskiis (the last essay by this guide's Patrick McGuire). Eric Rabkin's "The Rhetoric of Science in Science Fiction" has applicability in and outside SF. Although academics contributed most of these original essays, they are writing for a more general audience. Not quite the equal of the similar *Voices for the Future* volumes [9-25].

9-95. Staicar, Tom, ed. **The Feminine Eye: Science Fiction and the Women Who Write It.** Ungar, 1982.
Nine essays by men and women explore the work of Cherryh, Charnas, Elgin, Brackett, Norton, Bradley, Vinge, Tiptree, and C. L. Moore. The essays are very uneven but none, even by female essayists, is notably feminist in its emphasis, unlike Rosinski's study [9-85]. Compare the Weedman volume [9-119].

9-96. Sussman, Herbert L. **Victorians and the Machine: The Literary Response to Technology.** Harvard, 1968.
Seven representative writers are studied: Carlyle, Dickens, Ruskin, William Morris, Samuel Butler, Kipling, and Wells. Examines the complex ways these and other writers tried to adjust to the emerging industrial age and how the machine came to hold an important symbolic place in Victorian literature. A very useful background study for understanding the early years of SF. Compare Philmus's *Into the Unknown* [9-75].

*9-97. Suvin, Darko (Yugoslavia). **Metamorphoses of Science Fiction: On the Poetics and History of a Literary Genre.** Yale, 1979.
Revised and expanded from an earlier French version, *Pour une poétique de la science-fiction* (Montreal, 1977), this is a heavy but important study written in Suvin's typically dense style, whose abstractness is too often compounded by not being tied to specific texts. The first part is heavily theoretical, amplifying and revising some of his journal articles. The second part is more readable and includes discussions of Čapek, Russian SF, *News from Nowhere* [1-69], and *The Time Machine*

[1-103]. The scholar knowledgeable in the field will find this useful and provocative even when disagreeing with the author. Multilingual bibliography.

*9-98. Suvin, Darko (Yugoslavia). **Victorian Science Fiction in the UK: The Discourses of Knowledge and of Power.** G. K. Hall, 1983.
In this major study, building on his earlier work, Suvin begins by providing an annotated bibliography of 360 books (excluding short fiction) published in the U.K., 1848–1900, which are properly SF, as well as some he thinks are improperly included by others (including a few annotated in Chapter 1). Then the social context of the books is discussed in detail, with a chapter by John Sutherland on publishing and bookselling during this period. Suvin then presents biographical information about 270 of the writers, stressing how their social class backgrounds shaped their outlooks and fictions, which are analyzed in detail. Critics may argue that Suvin's Marxist persuasion distorts his analyses and conclusions, but few will dispute the magnitude of his achievement. An essential study in understanding the origins and nature of SF, and valuable for Victorian literature specialists as well. Compare Stableford's study of the 1890–1950 period [9-93].

9-99. Tolley, Michael J., and Kirpal Singh, eds. **The Stellar Gauge: Essays on Science Fiction Authors.** Norstrilia Press, 1980.
Collects 12 essays by Australian, British, and American writers with an introduction and index. Subjects include *Twenty Thousand Leagues under the Sea* [1-95], Orwell's *Nineteen Eighty-Four* [3-302], Bester, Clarke, Pohl, Aldiss, Blish, Ballard, Dick, Silverberg, and Disch. Varied, usually clearly written, often insightful. Compare *Voices for the Future* [9-25].

9-100. Turner, George (Australia). **In the Heart or the Head: An Essay in Time Travel.** Norstrilia Press, 1984.
An Australian writer recounts his life and involvement in SF. It is a life with considerable adversity overcome by determination. The sections on SF provide background on Australian SF, a topic relatively unknown to American readers, as well as Turner's critical judgments about SF generally. An interesting account of rather specialized appeal. HN, 1985.

*9-101. Wagar, W. Warren. **Terminal Visions: The Literature of Last Things.** Indiana Univ. Press, 1982.
An intellectual historian provides a wide-ranging analysis of nineteenth- and twentieth-century eschatological fiction, citing about 300 works, from Grainville's *Le Dernier homme* (1805) to Hoban's *Riddley Walker* [4-272]. The detailed scenarios of those books have more immediacy than the predictable warnings of evangelists or most social scientists. He notes that prior to World War I, natural disasters outnumbered human-caused ones two to one; after 1914 the ratio is reversed, and since 1965 ecological catastrophes have become prominent. Because so many books are discussed, extended literary analysis isn't practical. Wagar is knowledgeable with broad interests, writes well, and has contributed a major study of a theme having wide appeal in an age of anxiety. For all libraries.

9-102. Walsh, Chad. **From Utopia to Nightmare.** Harper, 1962.
An excellent short survey from an unobtrusive Christian perspective of nineteenth- and twentieth-century utopian and dystopian thought, discussing or al-

luding to not only standard utopias but many falling within the SF mainstream. Especially good in analyzing the shift from utopian to dystopian literature, where sociology, psychology, political science, theology, and philosophy meet. Compare the less analytical but broader and more current survey by Berger [9-12].

9-103. Warrick, Patricia S. **The Cybernetic Imagination in Science Fiction.** MIT Press, 1980.
This account of artificial intelligence in the form of robots and especially computers is based on a reading of 225 short stories and novels published between 1930 and 1977, all briefly listed in the bibliography (author, title, and year, but no magazine or publisher cited). Warrick contrasts the "closed-system" model found in the vast majority of all stories, in which robots and computers are regarded as dehumanizing and destructive, with the brighter vision of human-machine symbiosis of writers adopting the "open-system" mode. She concludes that most SF "written since World War II is reactionary in its attitude toward computers and artificial intelligence. It is often ill informed about information theory and computer technology and lags behind present developments instead of anticipating the future" (p. xvii). Her claim that this is the first such study is only partly true. Abbe Mowshowitz's excellent text/anthology *Inside Information* (1977) explores how fiction has treated the serious social concerns arising from computers and is both technically and humanistically better informed; his annotated bibliography is also more useful than hers. The aesthetic theory she proposes shapes but distorts her evaluations. Compare the study by Porush [9-77] and some of the papers in Dunn and Erlich [9-33].

9-104. Weber, Ronald. **Seeing Earth: Literary Responses to Space Exploration.** Ohio Univ. Press, 1985.
Weber examines the years from Sputnik to today in the writings of poets, journalists, astronauts, novelists, and scholars, but excluding SF writers. He found a renewed appreciation and rediscovery of the starting place, Earth. Weber also gives space to spokespersons boosting space exploration, such as Carl Sagan, and those who regard it as technological hubris. The views Weber analyzes are not those commonly found in SF (Malzberg's works are an exception), and it would be instructive to see a comparison of the differing views in and out of SF.

9-105. Wendland, Albert. **Science, Myth and the Fictional Creation of Alien Worlds.** UMI Research Press, 1984.
A slightly revised 1980 thesis distinguishes between SF in the "conventional" and "experimental" modes, with the latter claimed to involve the reader more fully and seriously. This distinction is explored in the writings of Anderson, Lem, Clarke, Niven, Aldiss, Wolfe, and others. Heavy going and expensive.

*9-106. Wolfe, Gary K. **The Known and the Unknown: The Iconography of Science Fiction.** Kent State, 1979.
In this fascinating and exceptionally perceptive study, Wolfe explores the recurrent iconic images that SF writers have used with varying degrees of subtlety, complexity, and power. He suggests that the "sense of wonder" so often talked of is generated by the juxtaposition of the known and the unknown separated by a barrier. Among the iconic images explored in a wide-ranging selection of Ameri-

can and British stories are those of the spaceship, the city, the wasteland, the robot, and the monster. Wolfe transcends a purely formulaic analysis of SF to show how many works blend traditional images and sophisticated development that engage the reader on many levels. The novice will not have sufficient knowledge of SF to appreciate the breadth and subtlety of Wolfe's analyses, but fans and scholars cannot fail to have their insights enriched. A major study worthy of the widest readership.

9-107. Wolfe, Gary K., ed. **Science Fiction Dialogues.** Academy Chicago, 1982.
This is the second volume to collect papers presented at the annual Science Fiction Research Association (SFRA) conferences or written by members. Aldiss's original essay on *Frankenstein* [1-84], later collected in his *The Pale Shadow of Science* [9-2], is followed by letters between Stapledon and Wells, the edited version of Budrys's valuable essay [9-18], and pieces on *Galaxy*'s first editor, H. L. Gold, Hal Clement, Niven's *Ringworld* [4-392], Piercy's *Woman on the Edge of Time* [4-411], Gardner's *Grendel*, and feminist SF. Sam Moskowitz's 1981 Pilgrim acceptance speech on the development of Bailey's *Pilgrims through Space and Time* [9-8] is followed by several bibliographic pieces.

9-108. Wollheim, Donald A. **The Universe Makers: Science Fiction Today.** Harper, 1971.
An anecdotal, personal, and dated brief survey by a veteran editor and author who heads DAW Books. Compare the similar account by Lundwall [9-55]. Wollheim's sympathies lie with SF of a rather traditional sort, reflected in his successful publishing program.

9-109. Yoke, Carl B., and Donald M. Hassler, eds. **Death and the Serpent: Immortality in Science Fiction and Fantasy.** Greenwood, 1985.
The nominal subject of this collection of 19 essays is itself rather diffuse, as the bibliography of more than 300 items suggests. Essays often skirt the topic and deal with such disparate topics as vampires, Merlin, and elves. A rather uneven gathering.

Conference Proceedings

There are four major conferences at which papers are regularly presented, with many of them later collected as part of the conference proceedings, published in journals, or both. The Eaton conference is held in April at the University of California, Riverside, and is devoted to a single topic, with papers refereed before acceptance and the best papers edited for publication by Southern Illinois University Press. The International Association for the Fantastic in the Arts (IAFA) holds its conference each spring. It is easily the largest such conference, typically attracting more than 200 registrants, and all aspects of the fantastic are treated. Greenwood Press has published selected papers. The Science Fiction Research Association (SFRA) attracts 75–125 persons to its annual summer conference, the location changing each year. Some papers later appear in journals. The world SF convention, held over Labor Day in various metropolitan areas, has in recent years had an academic track as part of the programming, at which papers are presented and panel discussions held. The Popular Culture Association con-

ventions usually have a section devoted to SF and fantasy. The collections of essays annotated below and earlier in this chapter are indexed by Tymn and
Schlobin [8-17] and Hall [8-20].

9-110. Blackford, Jenny, et al. **Contrary Modes: Proceedings of the World Sci-
ence Fiction Conference, Melbourne, Australia, 1985.** Ebony Books, 1985.
Ten papers, hurriedly prepared for Aussiecon, treat Australian utopian fiction,
Gene Wolfe (the guest of honor), *Stranger in a Strange Land* [3-207], the two Mad
Max films, and women in SF. Valuable for the Australian perspective.

9-111. Collings, Michael R., ed. **Reflections on the Fantastic: Selected Essays
from the Fourth International Conference on the Fantastic in the Arts.** Greenwood, 1986.
A dozen papers from the 1983 conference, two on theoretical approaches (would
you believe "Swiss Animal Satire as Psychological Safety Valve"?), the remainder
discussing works of fantasy and SF by authors such as Peter Beagle, Alain Robbe-
Grillet, Felix Labisse, Amado Nervo, Aldiss, and Pohl.

9-112. Collins, Robert A., and Howard D. Pearce, eds. **The Scope of the Fantastic: Vol. 1: Theory, Technique, Major Authors; Vol. 2: Culture, Biography,
Themes, Children's Literature.** Greenwood, 1985.
The first International Conference on the Fantastic in the Arts was held in Florida in 1980, and these two volumes select several dozen of the more than 200 papers presented, with emphases suggested by the subtitles, weighted more toward
fantasy than SF. For large collections.

9-113. Coyle, William, ed. **Aspects of Fantasy: Selected Essays from the Second
International Conference on the Fantastic.** Greenwood, 1986.
The 25 essays here, about a tenth of those presented at the conference, cover a
broad range of fantastic literature, from less commonly studied authors to classical epics, the pastoral, the Tarot in Calvino's work, and Twain's deficiencies as a
fantasist.

9-114. Hassler, Donald, ed. **Patterns of the Fantastic: Academic Programming
at Chicon IV.** Starmont, 1983.
9-114A. Hassler, Donald, ed. **Patterns of the Fantastic II: Academic Proceedings at Constellation.** Starmont, 1984.
The 12 papers presented in 1982 at the world SF convention in Chicago are by
academics from various disciplines. *Dahlgren* [4-165], *2001*, female SF writers, SF
conventions and fandom, Stephen King, and Robin Cook are among the subjects. The second volume collects 10 essays, 4 exploring the nature of SF, including its relation to so-called mainstream literature, 2 essays on computers in SF,
and other pieces. Fairly typical academic fare, mostly by SFRA members.

9-115. Hokenson, Jan, and Howard Pearce, eds. **Forms of the Fantastic: Selected Essays from the Third International Conference on the Fantastic in Literature and Film.** Greenwood, 1986.
Still another multidisciplinary collection with insights drawn from linguistics, philosophy, comparative literature, film, and other fields. The essays are arranged
thematically, and major themes and key works are indexed; short bibliography.

9-116. Palumbo, Donald, ed. **Erotic Universe: Sexuality and Fantastic Literature.** Greenwood, 1986.
Most of these 15 essays were presented at conventions, unlike the original essays in *Eros in the Mind's Eye* [9-70]. Four essays stress theoretical issues, five focus on themes (sex and death, sexual comedy, sex with aliens, homosexuality in SF and fantasy), another five present feminist views, with one on "Star Trek" fanzines. The annotated bibliography of fiction, film, and TV is keyed to the papers and provides unannotated citations. Both volumes explore areas relatively little investigated.

9-117. Slusser, George E.; George R. Guffey; and Mark Rose, eds. **Bridges to Science Fiction.** Southern Illinois, 1980.
Harry Levin's keynote paper portrays the varying literary responses to science. Among the better pieces are Stephen Potts's examination of the limits of human reason in SF, notably Lem's works; Gregory Benford's related discussion of how most aliens are heavily anthropocentric in conception, although *Solaris* [3-261] suggests the essential unknowability of a true alien; Robert Hunt's comparison of the use of visionary states in the works of Ian Watson, Dick, and Silverberg; Eric Rabkin's suggestion of parallels between fairy tales and SF; and Thomas Keeling's rejection of surface similarities that erroneously link SF to gothic fiction. Notes, index. These ten essays were originally presented at the first Eaton conference, 1979, and are better read than heard.

9-118. Slusser, George E., and Eric S. Rabkin, eds. **Hard Science Fiction.** Southern Illinois, 1986.
English, history, and science are the specialties of the participants at the 1983 Eaton conference. The 16 essays explore many facets of this frequently discussed topic with insight and concern. Several of the papers are by some of the field's more gifted hard SF writers—Brin, Benford, and Forward—who enliven the discussion. One of the best of the Eaton collections. Notes and index. Compare some of the essays in Bretnor's *The Craft of Science Fiction* [13-13].

9-119. Weedman, Jane B., ed. **Women Worldwalkers: New Dimensions of Science Fiction and Fantasy.** Texas Tech Press, 1985.
Sixteen papers, revised from their original delivery at a comparative literature symposium at Texas Tech in 1983. Delany and Bradley were invited speakers, whose papers are included. The emphasis is on women in/and SF, feminist concerns, and writers such as Wilhelm, Russ (Delany's subject), Herbert, Dick, Shelley, Lessing, Elgin, and Bradley. One paper, "The Brass Brassiere" (the reference is to the sort of illustration popularized by Earle Bergey's pulp covers in the 1940s), showed imagination by using slides of covers and interior illustrations, not reproduced here. Abstracts but no index (which it should have had). Compare the collections of essays edited by Palumbo [9-70, 9-116] and Rosinski's *Feminist Futures* [9-85].

10
Author Studies

Neil Barron

This chapter surveys books devoted to individual authors, collective biographies, and collections of interviews. The biocritical reference works annotated in Chapter 8 should also be consulted, for they discuss hundreds of authors who have not been (and will not be) the subject of treatments longer than essays. Many of the works of history and criticism discussed in Chapter 9 provide valuable insights into specific authors or their works. See also the author/subject index.

Coverage is limited to SF writers and some other writers who wrote at least one work important in the history of SF, such as Orwell or C. S. Lewis. In the latter case, only books dealing with the author's nominally science fiction writings are annotated (a book discussing Lewis's specifically religious beliefs, for example, would be excluded).

Writers whose works are recognized as suitable for study in university curricula, such as Wells, have been the subject of book-length studies and are regularly written about in magazines of general literary criticism. Until recently, relatively few authors known primarily or only for their SF have been the subjects of articles or books outside the fanzines or books issued by fan publishers such as Advent. But as SF has gained greater acceptance, the better-known or better writers and their works have become the subjects of articles and books from both inside and outside the field.

Several publishers have specialized series devoted to authors. The summaries below, arranged alphabetically by publisher, should be read in conjunction with the annotations, which do not repeat the information given here.

Borgo Press's The Milford Series: Popular Writers of Today, initially focused on SF and fantasy writers, beginning with Slusser's Heinlein volumes [10-74, 10-75] in 1977. A few other titles in the series are collections of interviews. These studies are typically 64 pages, comprising a 25,000–30,000 word critical essay and a chronological primary bibliography of books only, but no index. The structure of each essay varies according to author. They tend more to the analytical than do the more conventional Starmont guides. Borgo's more recent series, Bibliographies of Modern Authors, has included several authors of fantastic fiction.

Gordon Benson, Jr., who uses the name Galactic Central Publications for his booklets, will have about 25 author bibliographies in print by mid-1987. These are available as 5½-by-8½-inch saddle-stapled pamphlets or in 8½-by-11-inch format in paper covers or with plastic pressure strips. Most have been updated at least once (only the latest revision is mentioned in the annotations). As Benson would admit, they aren't very thorough and are properly designated first draft or working bibliographies. For authors not included in other bibliographies, they can be a useful starting point, since their cost is very modest ($1.00–$2.50 for most). They are usually arranged with short fiction in one alphabet, followed by books, both alphabetically.

Chris Drumm's publications include mini-booklet bibliographies arranged chronologically, usually with a title index. Material by and about the authors is intermixed. They have roughly the same virtues, including modest cost, and limitations as Benson's pamphlets.

The most ambitious continuing series by far is Greenwood Press's Contributions to the Study of Science Fiction and Fantasy, which began in 1982 and included 24 volumes by the end of 1986. Most are criticism, often collections of essays, but several have been devoted to individual writers, such as H. P. Lovecraft and Robert E. Howard. Greenwood has also published several microform series (see Chapter 14).

G. K. Hall's Masters of Science Fiction and Fantasy include 14 volumes, 1979–1984, all with the generic title, [name]: A Primary and Secondary Bibliography. Each volume is offset from typescript. Following an introduction, sometimes lengthy, is the primary bibliography, divided into categories such as fiction, poetry, nonfiction, and miscellaneous media, and a secondary bibliography. Both bibliographies are arranged chronologically and are selectively annotated. The two indexes permit alphabetical access by author and title. Appendixes often include nominations, awards, manuscripts, and papers. Coverage is usually limited to English-language materials. No future volumes are planned. G. K. Hall has also published other valuable reference books, such as the Contento indexes [8-9, 8-10].

The prestigious imprint of Oxford University Press appeared on four volumes in the short-lived Science-Fiction Writers series, edited by Robert Scholes of Brown University. Subjects were selected because their works have "proved substantial, durable and influential" (Asimov, Heinlein, Stapledon, and Wells), and each volume provides a general overview of the writer's life and works and critical interpretations of the major works. A few earlier Oxford University Press volumes, such as Franklin [1-36], have been devoted to SF.

The Alternatives series from Southern Illinois University Press has since 1980 included collections of fiction (often of marginal value), selected papers from the annual Eaton conferences dealing with topics in both SF and fantasy, and one collection of autobiographical essays [10-189].

Starmont House had published about 30 numbered Starmont Reader Guides by the end of 1986, with another four dozen contracted for. The format is largely standardized: chronology of life and works, a biographical chapter, a discussion of the principal works, a summary chapter, annotated primary and secondary bibliographies, and an index. The 5½-by-8½-inch paperbacks range in length from roughly 60 pages to about twice that, the length apparently unrelated to the writer's importance or volume of work (Wells is 79 pages, Bradley 138). Most studies appear to have been completed several years before they were published.

Taplinger's collections of critical essays were published in the now discontinued Writers of the 21st Century series. Bradbury, Dick, Heinlein, Le Guin, and Vance are the subjects. Taplinger has also published a few other titles of interest outside the series.

Twayne's long-running monographic series, Twayne's English Author Series (TEAS) and U.S. Authors Series (TUSAS), have included several studies of authors of fantastic fiction, such as Stapledon, Wells, Le Guin, E. R. Burroughs, and John Collier. These are often excellent starting points.

Underwood-Miller has specialized in quality editions of Jack Vance but has also published several attractive and useful author bibliographies devoted to de Camp, Dick, Vance, and Zelazny, plus essay collections devoted to Stephen King.

Frederick Ungar's Recognitions series included seven SF author monographs by the end of 1986 along with three essay collections. These are apparently designed for the general, relatively undemanding reader and tend more toward appreciation than careful critical evaluation.

Finally, University Microfilms International's UMI Research Press has published a severely overpriced series, Studies in Speculative Fiction, revisions of doctoral theses selected by Robert Scholes, 14 of which had been issued by the end of 1986.

Most of these studies or bibliographies of individual authors share a potential weakness: they have been published while their subjects are still active, sometimes relatively early in their careers, and will therefore date fairly rapidly. On the other hand, living authors have sometimes assisted their critics/bibliographers, giving the studies greater immediacy. That should be understood as an implicit comment in most of the evaluations that follow.

Individual Authors

Brian W. Aldiss

10-1. Collings, Michael R. **Brian W. Aldiss.** Starmont, 1986.
10-2. Griffin, Brian, and David Wingrove. **Apertures: A Study of the Writings of Brian W. Aldiss.** Greenwood, 1984.
10-3. Mathews, Richard. **Aldiss Unbound: The Science Fiction of Brian W. Aldiss.** Borgo, 1977.
Collings provides a relatively comprehensive overview in 115 pages. He discerns a unity in Aldiss through his use of map-making imagery, how characters ex-

plore their environment, discovering it and themselves. The guideposts are usually symbolic; the reader must interpret and understand them. The novels are discussed chronologically through the Helliconia series, showing their interconnections and the way they relate to other works. Short fiction and criticism are then assessed, followed by a selectively annotated primary and critical bibliography and an awkwardly designed index. Collings does not explore to any extent the links to literature generally, unlike *Apertures*, or Aldiss's place in SF, but this is the best short account of its subject currently available. *Apertures* is the most detailed study, from Aldiss's earliest work through *Life in the West* (1980), with brief mention of the Helliconia series, then being written. Nonfiction and traditional fiction are also discussed. Particularly valuable in showing the complex linkages among Aldiss's widely varied writings and the many writers (and painters) whose works influenced him as his mastery grew. Some of these linkages are rather tenuous and suggest not necessarily influence but simply shared ideas. Further, although Aldiss has written SF for more than 30 years, there is little effort to compare his works with those of fellow SF writers, as distinct from mainstream writers. The study also slights the wit and humor so evident in even his most serious works. Chapter notes, bibliography, index. Mathews provided the first extended study (64 pages) of Aldiss, which shows his growing richness and complexity and briefly explores influences on his writings, many of which are succinctly analyzed. Mathews is still well worth reading.

Poul Anderson

10-4. Benson, Gordon, Jr. **Poul Anderson: Myth-Master and Wonder-Weaver; An Interim Bibliography (1947–1986).** 4th rev. ed. Author, 1986.
10-5. Miesel, Sandra. **Against Time's Arrow: The High Crusade of Poul Anderson.** Borgo, 1978.
Miesel explores the concept of entropy in a selection of Anderson's voluminous writings, including both SF and fantasy, short fiction, and novels. Whether the leitmotiv of entropy adequately explains or links Anderson's large and varied output is questionable, and Miesel is too admiring of her subject and his philosophy. Benson provides a relatively thorough listing in his pamphlet, not only of fiction but of awards, honors, series, and chronologies of the Technic civilization and the Psychotechnic series.

Piers Anthony

10-6. Collings, Michael R. **Piers Anthony.** Starmont, 1983.
The first book-length study of this prolific author discusses some of Anthony's more important earlier fictions, suggests ways of reading Anthony generally, and shows how his life is loosely linked to his work. Chronology, annotated bibliographies, index. Helpful as a starting point but destined to be rapidly dated.

Isaac Asimov

10-7. Asimov, Isaac. **In Memory Yet Green: The Autobiography of Isaac Asimov, 1920–1954.** Doubleday, 1979.

10-8. Asimov, Isaac. **In Joy Still Felt: The Autobiography of Isaac Asimov, 1954–1978.** Doubleday, 1980.

10-9. Fiedler, Jean, and Jim Mele. **Isaac Asimov.** Ungar, 1982.

10-10. Gunn, James. **Isaac Asimov: The Foundations of Science Fiction.** Oxford, 1982.

10-11. Olander, Joseph D., and Martin H. Greenberg, eds. **Isaac Asimov.** Taplinger, 1977.

10-12. Patrouch, Joseph F., Jr. **The Science Fiction of Isaac Asimov.** Doubleday, 1974.

Asimov is one of the most prolific of contemporary writers, with almost 350 books published by the end of 1986. Only about 10 percent are SF, from juveniles by "Paul French" to his continuing Foundation series. His autobiography recounts his life in more than 1,500 pages, providing valuable information for the SF historian and determined reader. Indexes add to their reference value. HN for each volume. Fiedler and Mele provide a short overview of Asimov's SF for the neophyte, heavy on plot summary but with little sense of how Asimov has developed as a writer. Much less satisfactory than the Gunn study. Gunn, as befits an SF writer whose work was published about the same time as Asimov's, stresses Asimov's relationship with editors and markets. Individual chapters treat the Foundation series, the robot novels, short fiction, and the other novels. There is a great deal of plot summary, which Gunn defends, along with biographical material. Although a friend of his subject, Gunn offers a fair assessment, given his methodology and shared values. Checklist of SF, brief annotated secondary bibliography, index. The best single study of Asimov (HW, 1983). Nine original essays by academics compose the Olander and Greenberg collection and discuss Asimov's major works, characterization, his SF mysteries, and his use of technical metaphors. Bibliography through 1976. Patrouch's study covers most of Asimov's fiction, tracing patterns of development, contrasting stories with one another. The analysis and evaluation emphasize the craft—the mechanics of the stories and how they work or don't—and is clearly understandable by anyone who knows Asimov's fiction.

J. G. Ballard

*10-13. Brigg, Peter (Canada). **J. G. Ballard.** Starmont, 1985.

10-14. Goddard, James, and David Pringle (U.K.). **J. G. Ballard: The First Twenty Years.** Bran's Head Books, 1976.

10-15. Pringle, David (U.K.). **Earth Is the Alien Planet: J. G. Ballard's Four-Dimensional Nightmare.** Borgo, 1979.

10-16. Pringle, David (U.K.). **J. G. Ballard: A Primary and Secondary Bibliography.** G. K. Hall, 1984.

10-17. Vale, Vane, and Andrea Juno. **Re/Search No. 8/9: J. G. Ballard.** Re/Search Publications (20 Romolo St., Suite B, San Francisco, CA 94133), 1984.

Brigg's study is the most thorough and current appraisal. Ballard's early (1956–1969) short fiction is first discussed, then the global disaster quartet, *The Atrocity Exhibition* [4-33], the urban disaster trilogy, his more recent short fiction and novels, and his autobiographical *Empire of the Sun* (1984). Chronological, selectively annotated bibliographies of fiction, interviews, essays, letters, reviews, and the secondary literature. Although Brigg recognizes Ballard's failings—repetition, obsessive concerns, thin characterization—he clearly shows the sources of Ballard's strengths and powers as "one of the vital mythmakers of modern science fiction." The Goddard and Pringle collaboration includes a long 1975 interview, seven critical pieces, and a detailed bibliography, later replaced by the comprehensive 1984 bibliography. *Earth Is the Alien Planet* provides a sensible and perceptive appraisal, unavoidably limited by the constraints of the Milford series (63 pages). The sources of Ballard's recurrent images of decay, death, and despair are examined in his novels and short fiction, which is more appreciated in France than in the U.K. or the United States. The 1984 bibliography contains an essay on Ballard and a weak 1979 interview. The Vale and Juno volume is an odd collection of fiction, criticism, interviews, quotes, autobiographical fragments, and many photographs. Far different from the typical collection of essays, this is more for the Ballard enthusiast and scholar.

Alfred Bester

10-18. Wendell, Carolyn. **Alfred Bester.** Starmont, 1980.
Bester has always been harshly critical of SF, with good reason, and his own SF writings have been relatively few, perhaps because of this. The biographical section of this study draws on his account in *Hell's Cartographers* [10-188]. The other chapters discuss *The Demolished Man* [3-30], *The Stars My Destination* [3-32], *The Computer Connection* (1975), and his short fiction. Mostly summary; little critical analysis; moderately useful.

James Blish

10-19. Stableford, Brian M. (U.K.). **A Clash of Symbols: The Triumph of James Blish.** Borgo, 1979.
Blish continually exhorted his fellow SF writers to achieve greater things and was equally demanding of himself (see his own criticism [9-13, 9-14]). Stableford provides an acute and excellent appraisal of Blish's most significant works, analyzing his use of religion and historical philosophy in his fiction and how this differs from that in works by Asimov and Heinlein. A superior introduction. David Ketterer's *Imprisoned in a Tessaract: The Life and Work of James Blish* was announced as a spring 1987 title by Kent State.

Leigh Brackett

10-20. Benson, Gordon, Jr. **Leigh Douglass Brackett & Edmond Hamilton: A Working Bibliography.** Author, 1986.
10-21. Carr, John L. **Leigh Brackett: American Writer.** Drumm, 1986.
10-22. Arbur, Rosemarie. **Leigh Brackett, Marion Zimmer Bradley, Anne McCaffrey: A Primary and Secondary Bibliography.** G. K. Hall, 1982.
Brackett and her husband, Edmond Hamilton, died in 1977 and 1978, respectively. She wrote not only popular SF in the late 1940s and early 1950s but screenplays and other novels. Hamilton, a veteran pulpster and creator of Captain Future, is best known for his space operas. Benson's pamphlet cannot compete with the comprehensive Arbur bibliography. Carr's booklet is presumably part of a dissertation due summer 1986 at Ohio State, the first chapter of a book-length

study of Brackett and Hamilton. A very well-written account, which shows how her temperament, her life, and her writings were linked. Brackett wrote many filmscripts, the last for George Lucas for *The Empire Strikes Back,* which she did not live to see.

Marion Zimmer Bradley

10-23. Arbur, Rosemarie. **Marion Zimmer Bradley.** Starmont, 1985.
Bradley is best known among SF readers for her Darkover series [4-77]. Arbur is a fan of Bradley and it shows, although she sometimes distances herself by her critical judgments. The survey is heavy with plot summaries of the Darkover series, her other SF, and her fantasies, including the best-seller *The Mists of Avalon.* Annotated primary and secondary bibliographies, which omit some of her pseudonymously authored paperbacks. A more thorough bibliography is in [10-22].

Ray Bradbury

10-24. Greenberg, Martin H., and Joseph D. Olander, eds. **Ray Bradbury.** Taplinger, 1980.
10-25. Johnson, Wayne L. **Ray Bradbury.** Ungar, 1980.
10-26. Nolan, William F. **The Ray Bradbury Companion: A Life and Career History, Photolog, and Comprehensive Checklist of Writers, with Facsimiles from Ray Bradbury's Unpublished and Uncollected Work in All Media.** Gale Research, 1975.
10-27. Slusser, George Edgar. **The Bradbury Chronicles.** Borgo, 1977.
10-28. Touponce, William F. **Ray Bradbury and the Poetics of Reverie: Fantasy, Science Fiction and the Reader.** UMI Research Press, 1984.
The Taplinger collection includes eight original and two reprinted essays that focus on the frontier myth and religion in Bradbury's works, *The Martian Chronicles* [3-64], his attitudes toward children, his imagery, and *Fahrenheit 451* [3-61]. Bibliography, index. Although Johnson admires Bradbury, his judgment is somewhat harsh: "Generally speaking, Bradbury's handling of a given theme in an early story as compared to a later story is essentially the same. That is, his themes do not display a growth in emotional depth or logical complexity as time goes on" (p. x). Seven of the ten chapters treat the themes of the many stories, but there are so many that the account has a fragmented quality and thus lacks any coherent view of Bradbury's achievement, unlike Slusser's more focused study. Notes, bibliography, index. Nolan's subtitle provides a good summary of his book. Although not a complete or formal bibliography, it provides a kaleidoscopic view of a talented and widely praised writer, whose published work far transcends the limits of SF. The coverage is from 1936 through 1973. Slusser stresses Bradbury's sources and place in the American literary tradition and explores his dark visions and later affirmation. The stories are first examined as they evolve and then as they are combined into more complex works. A persuasive and valuable short study. The Touponce work is heavily theoretical for most of its length, as befits a doctoral thesis, and uses something called reader response critical methods to examine a few short fictions and *Fahrenheit 451* [3-61]. Very specialized and overpriced.

John Brunner

10-29. De Bolt, Joe, ed. **The Happening Worlds of John Brunner: Critical Explorations in Science Fiction.** Kennikat, 1975.

10-30. Benson, Gordon, Jr. **John Killian Houston Brunner.** Rev. ed. Author, 1985.

Eight original essays on Brunner's works, including a lengthy career biography by the editor. The approach is interdisciplinary. Includes a preface by James Blish and a final chapter in which Brunner responds. Bibliography of his professional works and name and title index. A valuable overview of an important contemporary SF writer. The Benson booklet updates the De Bolt bibliography.

Algis Budrys

10-31. Drumm, Chris. **An Algis Budrys Checklist.** Drumm, 1983.

A booklet chronologically listing works from 1952 through 1982, with a title index. Citations to essays and interviews and reviews of his books are included, but not his many book reviews. A jumbled compilation.

Edgar Rice Burroughs

10-32. Holtsmark, Erling B. **Edgar Rice Burroughs.** Twayne, 1986. TUSAS 499.

10-33. Lupoff, Richard A. **Barsoom: Edgar Rice Burroughs and the Martian Vision.** Mirage Press, 1976.

10-34. Lupoff, Richard A. **Edgar Rice Burroughs: Master of Adventure.** 2nd rev. ed. Ace, 1975.

*10-35. Porges, Irwin. **Edgar Rice Burroughs: The Man Who Created Tarzan.** Brigham Young, 1975.

Holtsmark provides a useful current survey of one of the most popular of all twentieth-century writers. He includes a short biography and a discussion of the Mars, Tarzan, Pellucidar, and Venus series; discusses literary background and themes; and offers a final assessment. Notes, bibliography, index. Holtsmark admits to being a "devoted fan," but he is also fair in his assessments. His earlier specialized study draws on his academic specialty to argue that the Tarzan books gained part of their popularity from their use of classical elements (*Tarzan and Tradition: Classical Myth in Popular Literature*, 1981). Lupoff's 1975 book treats the entire range of Burroughs's writings, from Tarzan in 1914 to posthumous works issued in the 1960s. Chapter 19, "A Basic Burroughs Library," will be helpful to libraries, which usually reject the works of this author. A balanced study that lacks an index. *Barsoom* analyzes and evaluates the Martian books "on a number of levels and in a number of contexts, other than the obvious one, i.e., that of a series of romantic adventure tales set in exotic surroundings." Published on the one hundredth anniversary of Burroughs's birth, Porges is the authorized and definitive biography, over 800 pages, including more than 250 photos and illustrations. The sources of Burroughs's popularity and the entire scope of his works and life are discussed in detail by Porges, who has relied on many primary sources not previously available. Holtsmark is the most readily available study.

Italo Calvino

10-36. Carter, Albert Howard, III. **Italo Calvino: Metamorphoses of Fantasy.** UMI Research Press, 1986.

Calvino (1923–1985) was one of the most respected writers in Italian literature. Through William Weaver's distinguished translations he has become known to English-language readers. His *t zero* and *Cosmicomics* [4-108] blend fantasy with elements of SF. This revision of a 1971 doctoral thesis is a thorough survey of Calvino's varied writings, probably too detailed for most readers. The bibliography provides ample supplemental sources.

John W. Campbell, Jr.

10-37. Campbell, John W., Jr. **The John W. Campbell Letters.** Vol. 1. AC Projects (Box 137, Franklin, TN 37064), 1985.

Campbell (1910–1971) was unquestionably the most influential magazine editor SF has known. His major influence extended from 1938, when he assumed the editorship of *Astounding* (now *Analog*), to the early 1950s, when *Astounding*'s dominance was challenged by other magazines and Campbell rode his pseudoscientific hobbyhorses into a bog. Unfortunately, only five letters date from the pre-1950 period, sometimes called the golden age. Further, the nominal editors provide no editorial apparatus whatever—who the correspondents are, what they said in letters to which Campbell is replying, etc. Thus, only someone knowledgeable about Campbell will be able to make much sense of the correspondence. Weak sales make future volumes unlikely. A careful study of Campbell would be a major contribution to the history of SF (Berger's profile of *Astounding/Analog* in Tymn and Ashley [14-18] is a start). HN, 1986.

A. Bertram Chandler

10-38. Benson, Gordon, Jr. **Arthur Bertram Chandler.** Rev. ed. Author, 1985. A 14-page pamphlet listing the many books and stories of this Australian merchant mariner, who drew on his seafaring experience for many of his fast-moving stories.

Arthur C. Clarke

10-39. Hollow, John. **Against the Night, the Stars: The Science Fiction of Arthur C. Clarke.** Harcourt, 1983.
10-40. Olander, Joseph D., and Martin H. Greenberg, eds. **Arthur C. Clarke.** Taplinger, 1977.
10-41. Rabkin, Eric S. **Arthur C. Clarke.** 2nd ed., rev. Starmont, 1980.
10-42. Samuelson, David N. **Arthur C. Clarke: A Primary and Secondary Bibliography.** G. K. Hall, 1984.
10-43. Slusser, George Edgar. **The Space Odysseys of Arthur C. Clarke.** Borgo, 1978.

Writing for a general audience, Hollow sees Clarke working in the tradition of Wells but retaining a degree of hope for humankind. Most of Clarke's novels and short fiction are discussed, but only *Childhood's End* [3-97] and *2001* [4-140] in any detail. Clarke is linked to Stapledon and Wells, but there is little mention of

Clarke's contemporaries in SF, as if he worked in a literary vacuum. Hollow's account is sober and cautious, well suited to the neophyte, but adds relatively little to earlier studies. Partial bibliography of Clarke's fiction, secondary bibliography, but no index. The 1968 film *2001* greatly enhanced Clarke's popularity, and he has been the subject of extensive critical scrutiny. The nine essays in the Taplinger collection explore various facets of Clarke's achievements as a hard SF writer who infuses many of his works with a mysticism most prominent in *Childhood's End* [3-97], the subject of several essays; primary and secondary bibliography. Slusser's short monograph rejects the fragmentary approach and attempts to show that all Clarke's stories exhibit an archetypal "Odyssey pattern." Rabkin devotes chapters to the major novels and short fiction. Samuelson's bibliography is current through 1980; omits foreign-language editions and citations to most book reviews. Clarke's *The View from Serendip* (1977) is autobiographical.

Hal Clement

10-44. Benson, Gordon, Jr. **Hal Clement (Harry Clement Stubbs).** Rev. ed. Author, 1985.

10-45. Drumm, Chris. **A Hal Clement Checklist: Notes toward a Bibliography.** Drumm, 1980.

10-46. Hassler, Donald M. **Hal Clement.** Starmont, 1982.

Clement is the quintessential "hard" SF enthusiast, and Hassler competently surveys his work from his first story in 1942 through *The Nitrogen Fix* in 1980. Clement's fiction is relatively straightforward and neither lends itself to nor requires "deep" analysis. Hassler's 64-page study is quite sufficient. Primary and secondary bibliography. Drumm's pamphlet adds little to Hassler; Benson's pamphlet is a bit more current.

L. Sprague de Camp

10-47. Laughlin, Charlotte, and Daniel J. H. Levack, comps. **De Camp: An L. Sprague de Camp Bibliography.** Underwood-Miller, 1983.

The 822 entries, many annotated, for books, articles, and other items, supplemented by reproductions of many magazine and book covers, show the variety and extent of de Camp's writings, from a book on inventions in 1937 to his many Conan books, based on fragments by Robert E. Howard. De Camp is the subject of a forthcoming Starmont guide.

Samuel R. Delany

10-48. Barbour, Douglas. **Worlds Out of Words: The SF Novels of Samuel R. Delaney.** Bran's Head Books, 1979.

10-49. McEvoy, Seth. **Samuel R. Delany.** Ungar, 1983.

10-50. Peplow, Michael W., and Robert S. Bravard. **Samuel R. Delany: A Primary and Secondary Bibliography, 1962–1979.** G. K. Hall, 1980.

10-51. Slusser, George Edgar. **The Delany Intersection: Samuel R. Delany Considered as a Writer of Semi-Precious Words.** Borgo, 1977.

10-52. Weedman, Jane Branhan. **Samuel R. Delany.** Starmont, 1982.

Delany is one of the most studied SF writers and is himself one of the more significant critics in the field (he received the Pilgrim award in 1985). Barbour's careful and detailed study is derived from his 1976 doctoral thesis, parts of which appeared earlier in specialty magazines. Barbour uses four general approaches in examining the novels (short fiction is only lightly touched upon). The quest pattern is central and usually explicit in most of the novels, and one chapter discusses this. Others discuss Delany's frequent use of literary, cultural, and mythological allusions, his creation of complex and believable other cultures, and the style and structure of his works. *Dhalgren* [4-165] and *Triton* [4-170] each receive a chapter. Informative notes and a dated bibliography conclude this atrociously proofread study from a long-defunct publisher. Slusser's structuralist analysis, drawing on Scholes [9-89], considers both fiction and criticism. The latter is often complex and intimidating, and Slusser's explication is often as jargon-filled as that of his subject, but his approach differs from that of Barbour. McEvoy adds little to the understanding of the general reader, the apparent audience for his book; the analysis is simplistic and repetitious and betrays little knowledge of previous scholarship. Weedman does what she can in 79 pages, discussing Delany's critical concepts and focusing on three major thematic areas: science (especially cultural anthropology), race (Delany is one of the very few black SF writers), and sex (Delany is gay, and sexual identity is a recurrent theme in his work). Peplow and Bravard supply a valuable 61-page introduction, based on extensive correspondence, followed by an annotated bibliography of fiction; a secondary bibliography; appendixes listing juvenilia, unpublished speeches, and nonfiction; and descriptions of two manuscript collections. The indexes are to works by and about Delany.

Philip K. Dick

10-53. Benson, Gordon, Jr. **Philip Kindred Dick: A Preliminary Working Bibliography.** Author, 1986.

10-54. Gillespie, Bruce (Australia), ed. **Philip K. Dick: Electric Shepherd.** Norstrilia Press, 1975.

*10-55. Greenberg, Martin H., and Joseph D. Olander, eds. **Philip K. Dick.** Taplinger, 1983.

10-56. Pierce, Hazel. **Philip K. Dick.** Starmont, 1982.

10-57. Rickman, Gregg. **Philip K. Dick: In His Own Words.** Fragments West, 1984. Rickman, Gregg. **Philip K. Dick: The Last Testament.** Fragments West, 1985.

10-58. Robinson, Kim Stanley. **The Novels of Philip K. Dick.** UMI Research Press, 1984.

10-59. Williams, Paul. **Only Apparently Real: The World of Philip K. Dick.** Arbor House, 1986.

10-60. Levack, Daniel J. H., comp. **PKD: A Philip K. Dick Bibliography.** Underwood-Miller, 1981. With annotations by Steven Owen Godersky.

Dick was one of the most idiosyncratic and complex writers in SF, and he and his works have been the subject of many essays, including almost all of the March 1975 issue of *Science-Fiction Studies*. The pieces in Gillespie's 106-page paperback appeared originally in his defunct fanzine. Gillespie wrote three essays, Dick contributed two letters and his 1972 speech, "The Android and the Human," and Lem praised Dick in "Science Fiction: A Hopeless Case—with Exceptions." A useful brief survey. The Taplinger volume collects ten essays, three original, in a volume assembled not long after Dick's death in 1982. Following Malzberg's introduction and Dick's introduction to his 1980 collection, *The Golden Man*, are essays treating *Solar Lottery* [3-144], *Martian Time-Slip* [3-143], *Ubik* [4-178], and *The Man in the High Castle* [3-142], plus essays covering other aspects of Dick's work. Pierce provides a chronology, overview, and chapters on four major novels, short fiction, criticism, and two of the 1980s novels, all in 64 pages, much too short to do more than suggest Dick's complexity. Rickman knew Dick for about a year (beginning in 1981) and recorded five conversations totaling about 16 hours, which, along with other materials, is the basis for these two books. Topics include Dick's life, his writing habits, and his response to critics, and comments on each of his published novels. Rickman's interviews lack much bite because of his liking for Dick, and they tend to ramble. A third volume, *Philip K. Dick: A Life*, has been announced for late 1987. Poorly proofread; of value to the serious Dick student. Robinson is much better known for his fiction, and rightly so. His literary skills are evident in this clearly written revision of his 1982 doctoral thesis. In 150 pages Robinson cannot possibly do justice to 42 novels, since part of the text discusses other matters. But there are many useful insights into Dick's writings, and large libraries should consider this overpriced book. The bibliography and appendix on Dick scholarship are notably deficient. Williams's short paperback is an expansion of a 1975 *Rolling Stone* interview by the executor of Dick's estate, largely concerned with a break-in at Dick's northern California home in 1971. The disturbed and paranoic nature of many of his fictional creations is mirrored in Dick's own obsessional outpourings in this transcription of the interview, supplemented with additional material. An appendix listing Dick's 50 published novels in approximate order of creation should be of considerable value to critics of this often studied author. Levack provides a comprehensive bibliography through mid-1981, extensively illustrated. The two largest sections list books and stories alphabetically, with other sections devoted to unpublished manuscripts, connected stories, an index to nonfiction, a chronological list, and a 5-page secondary bibliography. Godersky's annotations—mostly plot summaries—are helpful. Benson's pamphlet is more current, but he admits not having seen the Levack work.

Gordon R. Dickson

10-61. Thompson, Raymond H. **Gordon R. Dickson: A Primary and Secondary Bibliography.** G. K. Hall, 1982.

10-62. Benson, George, Jr. **Gordon Rupert Dickson: First Dorsai.** Rev. ed. Author, 1986.

Dickson is a prolific author but has rarely been the subject of extended critical scrutiny, which Thompson provides in his introduction. His coverage is through early 1981. Benson's 20-page pamphlet has a slight edge in currency but doesn't acknowledge Thompson. A forthcoming Starmont guide is devoted to Dickson.

Thomas R. Disch

10-63. Drumm, Chris. **A Tom Disch Checklist: Notes toward a Bibliography.** Drumm, 1983.

Disch's work is not limited to SF, and this booklet lists several of his poetry collections as well. A December 1982 letter from Disch is reproduced, listing more items, published or forthcoming. Addendum lists additional items. Title index.

Harlan Ellison

10-64. Slusser, George Edgar. **Harlan Ellison: Unrepentant Harlequin.** Borgo, 1977.

In spite of his many awards, some from outside the SF field, Ellison has been surprisingly neglected as a subject of criticism, perhaps because his sometimes prickly personality has intimidated would-be critics. Slusser analyzes Ellison's journalism, fantasy, and myth to show how his anger and fury led to a mood of reconciliation in his later works and a maturing of his artistry. A good although dated introduction to the work of an important modern writer who deserves more critical attention. Ellison's essays tend too often to the polemical, and his shrillness and contempt for his subjects are not likely to persuade the reader. Some of these essays are collected in *Sleepless Nights in the Procrustean Bed,* edited by Marty Clark (Borgo, 1984), and *An Edge in My Voice* (Donning, 1985), 61 pieces from the *L.A. Weekly* and other sources.

Philip José Farmer

10-65. Brizzi, Mary T. **Philip José Farmer.** Starmont, 1980.
10-66. Chapman, Edgar L. **The Magic Labyrinth of Philip José Farmer.** Borgo, 1985.

Following a chronology of Farmer's life and works, Brizzi provides a 6-page biography (through mid-1978). Most of the 61 pages of the rest of the book explore his technique and imagery, and concepts in his key works, notably *The Lovers* [3-159], *Night of Light* [3-160], and others. Alphabetical bibliography, 2-page secondary bibliography, and index. Chapman is more detailed and current than Brizzi, who is one of a number of omissions from the bibliography. Chapman explores many facets of Farmer's works—sexuality, religion, mythology, popular culture, and his use of parody and satire.

James Gunn

10-67. Drumm, Chris. **A James Gunn Checklist.** Drumm, 1984.
Following a four-page introduction by colleague Stephen Goldman is a chronological listing from 1949 through early 1984, with a title index. A May 1984 letter from Gunn cites forthcoming work.

H. Rider Haggard

10-68. Etherington, D. S. **Rider Haggard.** Twayne, 1984. TEAS 383.
Although earlier studies of Haggard had discussed his fiction, including Morton
Cohen's *Rider Haggard: His Life and Works* (1960) and D. S. Higgins's *Rider Haggard: A Biography* (1983), this is the first book-length study to focus on his fiction,
although his life is not ignored. Etherington is an Australian historian who has
written widely on Africa and British colonialism, and he brings a valuable perspective on Haggard's many novels, including those discussed in Chapter 1.

Joe Haldeman

10-69. Gordon, Joan. **Joe Haldeman.** Starmont, 1980.
Haldeman (1943–   ) seems a bit young and his writings too few to appear in this
series. Gordon, who is not identified, bases much of her survey on conversation
and correspondence with Haldeman, for whom his year in Vietnam has provided the basis for his writings: *War Year* (1972), a semiautobiographical war
novel; *The Forever War* [4-247]; *Mindbridge* (1976); *All My Sins Remembered* (1977);
and *Infinite Dreams* (1978). Since little save reviews has discussed Haldeman's
works, this largely descriptive survey should be moderately useful.

Harry Harrison

10-70. Benson, Gordon, Jr. **Harry Harrison.** Rev. ed. Author, 1985.
The prolific Harrison helped Benson to complete this 16-page pamphlet.

Robert A. Heinlein

*10-71. Franklin, H(oward) Bruce. **Robert A. Heinlein: America as Science Fiction.** Oxford, 1980.
10-72. Olander, Joseph D., and Martin H. Greenberg, eds. **Robert A. Heinlein.**
Taplinger, 1978.
10-73. Panshin, Alexei. **Heinlein in Dimension.** Advent, 1968.
10-74. Slusser, George Edgar. **The Classic Years of Robert A. Heinlein.** Borgo,
1977.
10-75. Slusser, George Edgar. **Robert A. Heinlein: Stranger in His Own Land.**
2nd ed. Borgo, 1977.
Franklin's perspective is that of a Marxist, for whom history is destiny. He divides Heinlein's stories into five periods (1939–1946, 1947–1959, 1961–1968,
1970–1973, and 1980), relating the stories to contemporary American history.
He is effective—if a trifle dogmatic—in showing how the contradictions in
American society and monopoly capitalism are reflected and refracted in
Heinlein's tales. The familiar Heinlein dualisms of authoritarianism/anarchism,
futuristic realism/nostalgia, and hardheaded rationalism/mysticism are carefully
explored in Heinlein's entire output, through *The Number of the Beast* (1980).
But the focus is too narrow and almost wholly neglects the larger field in which
most of his work appeared (SF) and the wider field of popular fiction generally.
Nevertheless, an important study of a seminal writer in SF. Notes, chronology,
excellent bibliography, index. The nine original essays in the Taplinger collection treat Heinlein's juveniles, his future history series, *Stranger in a Strange*

Land [3-207], and *Time Enough for Love* [4-264]. Other essays discuss his preoccupation with techniques for human survival, human sexuality, and social Darwinism in his fiction. Primary and secondary bibliography; index. A useful synoptic survey and starting point. Panshin's study was the first detailed critical work, revised from its original appearance in *Riverside Quarterly*. Balanced and detailed, although dated, the study assesses Heinlein's subjects, plots, literary qualities, militaristic heroes, and influence. Alexei and Cory Panshin devote additional space to Heinlein in their *SF in Dimension* [9-71]. Slusser examines Heinlein's works of the 1940s and 1950s in his first study, with the second, extensively revised from the 1976 edition, focusing on his later work. Both studies attempt to explore the central dynamics underlying the surface themes, conventions, and doctrines and how they generate the formal structures of the stories. They are especially valuable for their close readings, which challenge many of the conventional critical notions about Heinlein. Both have brief bibliographies of Heinlein's books.

Frank Herbert

10-76. McNelly, Willis E., comp. **The Dune Encyclopedia.** Berkley, 1984.
10-77. Miller, David M. **Frank Herbert.** Starmont, 1980.
10-78. O'Reilly, Timothy. **Frank Herbert.** Ungar, 1981.
After a slow start, the Dune series is now one of the most popular of all SF series [4-268]. McNelly and his 43 contributors have not merely provided a companion to *Dune* and some of its successors but, with Herbert's "delighted approval," have composed many fictional entries, embroidering an already complex novel. Probably essential for Dune series fans but for few others (HN, 1985). Miller departs from Starmont's general pattern. The biographical details are sparse. The analyses of stories are genuinely critical, often harshly so, and are unified by Miller's concept of dynamic homeostasis, which he argues is central to an understanding of Herbert's works, each of which receive 2 to 4 pages. Miller's 70-page study cannot begin to approach the thoroughness of O'Reilly's, which is three times as long. Later books in the Dune series undercut some of the statements in both studies. O'Reilly explores the philosophical ideas underlying and linking Herbert's fiction, not only the Dune series. Herbert was a journalist before he became a novelist, and his varied interests are reflected in his idea-laden novels.

Aldous Huxley

10-79. Firchow, Peter Edgerly. **The End of Utopia: A Study of Aldous Huxley's Brave New World.** Bucknell Univ. Press, 1984.
Huxley's novel and *Nineteen Eighty-Four* are the archetypal nightmares of the twentieth century. Firchow's detailed study assembles three rewritten essays and two new chapters to "elucidate *Brave New World* literarily, historically, socially, politically, scientifically." A valuable study of one of the most important dystopias, whose relevance to our own era steadily increases.

Stephen King

10-80. Collings, Michael R. **The Films of Stephen King.** Starmont, 1986.

10-81. Collings, Michael R. **Stephen King as Richard Bachman.** Starmont, 1985.

10-82. Collings, Michael R. **The Many Facets of Stephen King.** Starmont, 1986.

10-83. Collings, Michael R. **The Annotated Guide to Stephen King: A Primary and Secondary Bibliography of the Works of America's Premier Horror Writer.** Starmont, 1986.

10-84. Collings, Michael R., and David Engebretson. **The Shorter Works of Stephen King.** Starmont, 1985.

10-85. Schweitzer, Darrell, ed. **Discovering Stephen King.** Starmont, 1985.

10-86. Underwood, Tim, and Chuck Miller, eds. **Fear Itself: The Horror Fiction of Stephen King.** Underwood-Miller, 1982.

10-87. Underwood, Tim, and Chuck Miller, eds. **Kingdom of Fear: The World of Stephen King.** Underwood-Miller, 1986.

10-88. Winter, Douglas E. **Stephen King: The Art of Darkness.** NAL, 1984; rev. and enl. ed., Plume/NAL, 1986.

Like Tolkien in the 1960s, King in the 1980s has become a cottage industry—a brand name, as King himself has remarked. Although he uses SF devices such as psychokinesis and precognition, horror and terror are at the dark heart of most of his fiction. A lawyer/critic and good friend, Winter wrote the first book-length study, *Stephen King* (Starmont, 1982), revised and greatly expanded for the NAL hardcover and revised still further for the 1986 Plume trade paperback. Multiple perspectives on King are provided in the two Underwood and Miller and the Schweitzer volumes. Starmont, whose Winter study is out of print, is heavily courting King fans with its series of studies by Collings, which naturally overlap one another to varying degrees and provide exhaustive detail on their topics, far more than all save King fanatics will want. Starmont plans still more books—a concordance by Engebretson, Collings's *The Stephen King Phenomenon*, and casebooks devoted to each of King's novels. Libraries should begin with the latest Winter volume, perhaps supplemented by either or both of the Underwood and Miller volumes.

R. A. Lafferty

10-89. Drumm, Chris. **An R. A. Lafferty Checklist: A Bibliographical Chronology with Notes and Index.** Drumm, 1983.

Drumm has published several booklets of fiction by Lafferty, a quirky, underappreciated writer who profiles himself in *Fantastic Lives* [10-189]. This checklist covers 1959–1980 publications, mostly by, occasionally about, Lafferty.

Ursula K. Le Guin

10-90. Bloom, Harold, ed. **Ursula K. Le Guin.** Chelsea House, 1986.

10-91. Bucknall, Barbara J. **Ursula K. Le Guin.** Ungar, 1981.

10-92. Cogell, Elizabeth C. **Ursula K. Le Guin: A Primary and Secondary Bibliography.** G. K. Hall, 1983.

*10-93. De Bolt, Joe, ed. **Ursula K. Le Guin: Voyager to Inner Lands and to Outer Space.** Kennikat, 1979.

10-94. Olander, Joseph D., and Martin H. Greenberg, eds. **Ursula K. Le Guin.** Taplinger, 1979.

10-95. Slusser, George Edgar. **The Farthest Shores of Ursula K. Le Guin.** Borgo, 1976.

*10-96. Spivack, Charlotte. **Ursula K. Le Guin.** Twayne, 1984. TUSAS 453.

Few other writers of SF have inspired as much admiration and analysis as Le Guin, the subject of a very large and growing body of exegesis, such as the November 1975 issue of *Science-Fiction Studies* and the fall 1980 issue of *Extrapolation*. De Bolt's collection provides a valuable overview of her achievements, and his biographical account is very useful, relating her life to her works. James Bittner's helpful survey of Le Guin criticism notes that its growth has been explosive since the first serious piece in 1969. The remaining seven essays discuss both specific works and the subtle and complex elements that enrich her varied work. The nine original essays by academics in the Taplinger book do not equal those in De Bolt's, although they are of value to the specialist. Slusser's long essay blends intelligent praise with careful analysis of her major works, arguing for a constancy of philosophy throughout her works, which have become increasingly complex in content and style. Le Guin herself articulately expresses her own judgments in *The Language of the Night* [9-51]. The Bloom work is part of the publisher's Modern Critical Views series and the only volume devoted to an SF author; it collects 16 previously published essays and one original piece, but omits all the essays' notes, seriously weakening the book. The bibliography is incomplete, the chronology stops at 1981, and some of Le Guin's more important books are not discussed. Bucknall explores the fiction in chronological order, with notes, selective primary and secondary bibliography, and index. Her audience is the general reader, and the text is heavy with plot summaries and routine analysis, not helped by Bucknall's excessive admiration for her subject. Spivack provides a sound, balanced survey. Chronology, life and intellectual background, influences, and a moderately detailed discussion of all Le Guin's key works, fiction, essays, and poetry, through about 1981. The critical analyses are clear and are not limited to plot summaries. Bibliography, index. The best starting point. Cogell provides the most complete listing of works by and about Le Guin through about 1980, plus indexes and a useful introductory essay.

Fritz Leiber

10-97. Frane, Jeff. **Fritz Leiber.** Starmont, 1980.

10-98. Staicar, Tom. **Fritz Leiber.** Ungar, 1983.

Leiber has won awards for both his SF and his fantasy, but, although the general level of his work is relatively high, he is not known for one or several really outstanding pieces. Frane's short study provides a useful overview of his life and works, with chapters devoted to his major novels, the Fafhrd and Gray Mouser series, and other short fiction. The annotated bibliographies are current through mid-1980. Frane's attempt to cover most of Leiber's fiction in a short space precludes detailed critical analysis. Staicar's study, although twice the length of Frane's, is more elementary. A biographical chapter gives the father's birthdate (a publisher's error), with successive chapters devoted to various groups of fiction, and a brief concluding chapter summarizing Leiber's basic themes. Heavy on plot summaries, weak on critical analysis, with little sense of Leiber's development.

Stanislaw Lem

10-99. Ziegfeld, Richard E. **Stanislaw Lem.** Ungar, 1985.
The first English-language book-length study of an important Polish writer read worldwide but respected rather than popular, and more in Europe than in the United States. A short biography is followed by analyses of Lem's major works of fiction in 12 chapters. A final chapter assesses Lem's achievement. A primary and secondary bibliography through 1982 and an index conclude this introductory survey, whose publication was delayed by several years. Ziegfeld praises but does not discuss Lem's major works of nonfiction, nor does he give any examples of his "frequent veiled criticism of Socialist practices," which has not prevented Lem from receiving several Polish literary prizes. Usefully read with Lem's own essays in *Microworlds* [9-52]. Lem is the subject of an interesting article by John Tierney, "A Mundane Master of Cosmic Vision," *Discover* 7 (December 1986): 56–66. *Science-Fiction Studies* 13 (November 1986) is largely devoted to Lem and his many works and includes a long review of Ziegfeld's study, calling it "a vapid and confused book, combining pedestrian analysis with tone-deaf prose." There is also a review of a 1986 German study of Lem, which the reviewer says is only one of six cited books on Lem published in West Germany.

C. S. Lewis

10-100. Murphy, Brian C. **C. S. Lewis.** Starmont, 1983.
Lewis was one of Christianity's most gifted defenders, and his religious beliefs are strongly evident in his writings, fiction and otherwise. Within SF, he is best known for his "space trilogy" [3-263], which is the focus of Murphy's 95-page study. He surveys Lewis's life and thought, the trilogy, and his last works, and includes a primary and annotated secondary bibliography. The last will guide the reader to some of the many other studies of Lewis, about whom a great deal has been written.

David Lindsay

10-101. Sellin, Bernard. **The Life and Works of David Lindsay.** Tr. by Kenneth Gunnell. Cambridge, 1981.
10-102. Wilson, Colin. **The Haunted Man: The Strange Genius of David Lindsay.** Borgo, 1979.
Lindsay is best known for one book, *A Voyage to Arcturus* [2-63], a complex, demanding novel that in recent years has gained greater recognition. Sellin's revision of his dissertation is not likely to attract more Lindsay enthusiasts, although it does provide new information and detailed interpretation. Wilson's short study (65 pages) is clear and readable, a personal account of how he discovered and responded to Lindsay's works.

Jack London

10-103. Beauchamp, Gorman. **Jack London.** Starmont, 1986.
London was a prolific author, but only three novels, a novella, and some short fiction are SF or fantasy, and it is these Beauchamp examines. He provides synopses for the reader unfamiliar with London's SF and shows his familiarity with London's other, more important (or popular) work. A useful if necessarily partial view of a writer more fully discussed in many other studies, such as Earle Labor's *Jack London* (1974) in the Twayne U.S. Authors Series.

H. P. Lovecraft

10-104. Burleson, Donald R. **H. P. Lovecraft: A Critical Study.** Greenwood, 1983.
10-105. Joshi, S. T. **H. P. Lovecraft.** Starmont, 1982.
10-106. Joshi, S. T. **H. P. Lovecraft: Four Decades of Criticism.** Ohio Univ. Press, 1980.
10-107. Joshi, S. T. **H. P. Lovecraft and Lovecraft Criticism.** Kent State, 1981.
10-108. Joshi, S. T., and L. D. Blackmore. **H. P. Lovecraft and Lovecraft Criticism: An Annotated Bibliography, Supplement 1980–1984.** Necronomicon Press, 1984.
Lovecraft (1890–1937) is usually considered a writer of horror fiction. Although some of his fiction uses many of the narrative conventions and plot elements of SF, the dominant mood is one of menace or horror. Burleson provides the most detailed critical analysis, using a variety of approaches (formal, Jungian, structural, etc.) to elucidate the peculiar and continuing appeal of this Rhode Island recluse. He provides adequate plot summaries for readers not familiar with Lovecraft's many stories and defends them against the many criticisms (purple prose, formulaic writing, racism), even when recognizing faults. Thorough, balanced, and recommended to anyone wanting more detail than Joshi can provide in his 80-page Starmont study. He is the foremost Lovecraft advocate and scholar, having edited the four volumes of the revised and corrected editions of Lovecraft issued by Arkham House. He groups Lovecraft's fiction into three categories, which is not a very satisfactory approach for the beginning reader, for whom the Starmont guides are prepared and who may be somewhat confused by the many plot summaries and the discussion. The concluding chapter provides a useful analysis of the major themes and narrative devices used by Lovecraft. The essay collections [10-106, 10-107] provide an overview of Lovecraft and his contribution to American literature. Most pieces are laudatory, but Joshi is fair-minded enough to include a piece by Edmund Wilson, who remarked, "The only real horror of these fictions is the horror of bad taste and bad art." The standard biography is by L. Sprague de Camp, *Lovecraft* (1975). The two volumes of bibliography are essentially exhaustive and will remain the standard for many years.

Julian May

10-109. Dikty, T. E., and R. Reginald. **The Work of Julian May: An Annotated Bibliography and Guide.** Borgo, 1985.
May is the wife of Dikty, owner of Starmont House, and best known for her tetral-

ogy, "Saga of the Pliocene Exile" [4-366]. After the publication of "Dune Roller" in 1951, May left SF to write encyclopedia articles and more than 250 books for younger readers, all listed in this semi-vanity bibliography.

Anne McCaffrey

10-110. Benson, Gordon, Jr. **Anne Inez McCaffrey: Dragonlady and More; A Working Bibliography.** Rev. ed. Author, 1986.
10-111. Fonstad, Karen Wynn. **The Atlas of Pern.** Ballantine, 1984.
McCaffrey's Pern is a fairly complex world, for which Fonstad serves as a cartographer and guide. An appendix provides a glossary of geographical locations, with page references to the Ballantine editions of McCaffrey's books. Benson's nine-page pamphlet is slightly more current than the far more complete bibliography in [10-22].

A. Merritt

10-112. Merritt, Abraham. **Reflections in the Moon Pool.** Sam Moskowitz, ed. Oswald Train, 1985.
Merritt was the author of many romantic fantasies (see Chapter 2), some with SF elements. Moskowitz assembles fiction, poetry, essays, fragments, and letters of Merritt, along with photographs. A 50,000-word biography, based on interviews, should be useful to anyone seeking to link Merritt's life with his works, which have often been reprinted. Moskowitz is obviously fond of his subject, but his praise is too undiscriminating, his style somewhat rambling, and his account likely to appeal mainly to Merritt fans.

Larry Niven

10-113. Drumm, Chris. **A Larry Niven Checklist.** Drumm, 1983.
A 24-page chronological bibliography through late 1983 with a title index. Drumm relied on Niven's own bibliography. Numbered items are designated by type of writing (article, novel, etc.) and whether part of one of Niven's many series.

Andre Norton

10-114. Schlobin, Roger C. **Andre Norton: A Primary and Secondary Bibliography.** G. K. Hall, 1980.
A retired children's librarian, Norton is a popular and prolific author of both SF and fantasy, books usually marketed for young adults but read by all ages. In addition to the usual primary and secondary bibliographies, there is a series listing and an indication of whether the work is SF or fantasy.

George Orwell

10-115. Crick, Bernard, ed. **George Orwell: Nineteen Eighty-Four.** Clarendon Press, 1984.
10-116. Howe, Irving, ed. **Orwell's Nineteen Eighty-Four: Text, Sources, Criticism.** Harcourt, 1963; 2nd ed. Harcourt, 1982.
10-117. Stansky, Peter, ed. **Nineteen Eighty-Four.** W. H. Freeman, 1984.
The Crick volume reprints the novel, based on Peter Davison's edition (Harcourt, 1984), but the accompanying background material is the reason to consider—a 136-page introduction, eight appendixes, and indexes. Crick is one of Orwell's major biographers, and his knowledge is well displayed here. Howe's Harbrace Sourcebook is one of the more useful classroom/library resources, providing not only the complete unannotated novel, but sources (essays by Orwell, Huxley, Zamiatin) and critical essays. The second edition adds essays, including an original and perceptive piece by Michael Harrington. Stansky coauthored an Orwell biography and here assembles 22 essays by Stanford University faculty, organized into four parts, which use many approaches to illuminate Orwell's novel. Howe is a better choice for classroom or library.

Edgar Pangborn

10-118. Benson, Gordon, Jr. **Edgar Pangborn: A Bibliography.** Rev. ed. Author, 1985.
A dozen books (one never published) and 33 stories by Pangborn (1909–1976) are listed in this brief pamphlet.

H. Beam Piper

10-119. Benson, Gordon, Jr. **Henry Beam Piper.** Rev. ed. Author, 1985.
Five-page pamphlet listing books and stories by Piper, several books by others based on Piper's stories, and three articles about Piper.

Frederik Pohl

10-120. Pohl, Frederik. **The Way the Future Was: A Memoir.** Ballantine, 1978.
Pohl has been one of the most influential editors, writers, and agents in SF. Not much of a stylist either here or in his fiction, as a raconteur his prose is clear and sensible, reflecting his own temperament. The non-SF reader may find this account interesting, for Pohl doesn't limit his memoir to SF activities, but its primary appeal will be to fans and historians. An index would have helped. Compare Knight's *The Futurians* [10-190] for a different viewpoint.

Mack Reynolds

10-121. Drumm, Chris, and George Flynn. **A Mack Reynolds Checklist: Notes toward a Bibliography.** Drumm, 1983.
Compiled just before Reynolds's death in January 1983, this chronological bibliography has 242 numbered entries, 1950–1983, with an addendum sheet and title index. Reynolds was a militant socialist for many years, and a number of his stories have sociopolitical ideas at their centers, although they are not polemical or didactic. He is one of the few SF writers with such a background.

Eric Frank Russell

10-122. Stephensen-Payne, Phil, and Gordon Benson, Jr. **Eric Frank Russell: A Working Bibliography.** Benson, 1986.
Russell (1905–1978) is a British writer relatively little read today. In addition to the books and short fiction, articles, and nonfiction by him, articles about Russell and reviews are also listed in this 19-page pamphlet.

Margaret St. Clair

10-123. Benson, Gordon, Jr. **Margaret St. Clair.** Rev. ed. Author, 1986.
Eleven books and 114 stories by a woman who also wrote as Idris Seabright. She wrote one of the essays in *Fantastic Lives* [10-189].

Bob Shaw

10-124. Nelson, Chris, and Gordon Benson, Jr. **Bob Shaw: A Bibliography.** Rev. ed. Benson, 1986.
An eight-page pamphlet listing works by this British author.

Mary Shelley

10-125. Florescu, Radu. **In Search of Frankenstein.** New York Graphic Society, 1975.
10-126. Glut, Donald F. **The Frankenstein Legend: A Tribute to Mary Shelley and Boris Karloff.** Scarecrow, 1973.
*****10-127.** Levine, George, and V. C. Knoepflmacher, eds. **The Endurance of Frankenstein: Essays on Mary Shelley's Novel.** Univ. of California Pres, 1979.
10-128. Small, Christopher (U.K.). **Mary Shelley's "Frankenstein": Tracing the Myth.** Univ. of Pittsburgh Press, 1973. British title: *Ariel Like a Harpy: Shelley, Mary and Frankenstein,* Gollancz, 1972.
*****10-129.** Tropp, Martin. **Mary Shelley's Monster: The Story of Frankenstein.** Houghton Mifflin, 1976.
10-130. Veeder, William. **Mary Shelley & Frankenstein: The Fate of Androgyny.** Univ. of Chicago Press, 1986.
Aldiss calls Shelley's *Frankenstein* [1-84] "the first great myth of the industrial age" in his history of SF, *Billion Year Spree* [9-4]. Few novels have had such wide influence, and the literature about the novel and its many descendants is voluminous, as one can learn by reading the useful survey "Recent Works on Mary Shelley and *Frankenstein*" by Aija Ozolins, *Science-Fiction Studies* 3 (July 1976): 187–202. Annotated here are a few of the best studies, several of which have detailed bibliographies. General studies or bibliographies of Mary Shelley are omitted. Small traces the "myth" of Frankenstein from its origin in Shelley's imagination to its current forms in film and SF and literature generally. He focuses on the genesis of the novel, especially as influenced by her poet-husband and his works. Chapter 13, "Robots and Resurrection," explores the use of robots in fiction, from Čapek's coinage of the word in *R.U.R.* [2-15] to Asimov. Glut's more popular account provides a thorough coverage of the modern—and usually debased—versions of the myth in film, TV, and recent literature from comics to pornography. A more recent study of Shelley's sources, based

on firsthand investigation, is presented by Florescu, whose conclusions are often based on unproven assumptions. His audience is popular rather than scholarly. Written by and presumably for fellow academics are the 12 essays grouped in five parts in the Levine book, which deal with sources, the relations between Shelley's life and the novel, the social and literary contexts in which she wrote, the language of the novel, and dramatic and film spin-offs. Annotated bibliography of works by Shelley and about *Frankenstein*. Tropp's intent "is to understand how the dream of a 19-year-old woman could become the myth of technology." He traces the genesis of the novel through Shelley's life and provides a perceptive chronicle of the many influences of this seminal novel, especially in film. A particularly well-written study appealing to both the lay reader and the specialist. Twenty-four pages of plates, useful notes, chronology with cast credits of Frankenstein films 1911–1974, a valuable guide to further reading, and index. Veeder "examines Mary and her fiction in light of the psychological model she and Percy looked upon as the ideal, the androgyne." His closely reasoned and thoroughly documented study combines biography and close analysis. "Dissenting from the critical consensus that Mary's female characters are simple stereotypes, I present her women and herself in light of the ideal of androgyny and the threat of bifurcation" (pp. 16, 17). A variant reading likely to appeal to the Shelley specialist.

M. P. Shiel

10-131. Morse, A. Reynolds, ed. **Shiel in Diverse Hands: A Collection of Essays.** A. Reynolds Morse Foundation, Cleveland, 1983. Dist. by J. D. S. Books (Box 67 MCS, Dayton, OH 45402).
Shiel (1865–1947) was a prolific writer best known for his *The Purple Cloud* (1901). This is the last of four volumes by and about Shiel and collects more than 30 pieces treating his short fiction, his novels, and many of his sometimes eccentric ideas. Specialists may find this of interest, but most libraries should find sufficient the section in Stableford [9-92] and the chapter in Bleiler [8-27].

Robert Silverberg

10-132. Clareson, Thomas D. **Robert Silverberg.** Starmont, 1983.
10-133. Clareson, Thomas D. **Robert Silverberg: A Primary and Secondary Bibliography.** G. K. Hall, 1983.
Clareson has written on Silverberg in several essays, reworked for the short Starmont study. The approach is mostly chronological, from his fiction factory years in the 1950s and 1960s to his more "serious" work in the 1970s and later, with 11 novels discussed (about three pages each). The shorter fiction (1969–1974) and the Majipoor series in the 1980s are also discussed. Annotated bibliography and index. Clareson provides a balanced assessment of one of the field's major figures, who continues to produce distinguished work. Clareson lists and often annotates Silverberg's extensive writings, many for young readers in past years, as well as providing a secondary bibliography. An expensive, specialized bibliography.

Clifford D. Simak

10-134. Becker, Muriel R. **Clifford Simak: A Primary and Secondary Bibliography.** G. K. Hall, 1980.
An introduction, brief interview, and thorough primary bibliography are followed by a 193-item secondary bibliography, only three items of which are actual essays, according to David Pringle's review. A forthcoming Starmont guide will be devoted to Simak.

Cordwainer Smith

10-135. Lewis, Anthony R. **Concordance to Cordwainer Smith.** NESFA Press, 1984.
Paul Linebarger (1913–1966), who wrote as Cordwainer Smith, created relatively complex worlds in his fictions. Lewis indexes this private universe, suggesting the derivation of the many names and places.

E. E. Smith

10-136. Ellik, Ron, and Bill Evans. **The Universes of E. E. Smith.** Advent, 1966.
10-137. Sanders, Joe. **E. E. "Doc" Smith.** Starmont, 1986.
Smith (1890–1965) acquired a doctorate in chemistry, giving him his nickname. The initial book-length study of his work is a concordance to his popular Lensman and Skylark series of space operas, with a bit of critical comment and a bibliography. Sanders's guide, the first critical study, "is intended to explain Smith's popularity while countering some of the unthinking aversion Smith's work has received." Sanders quotes Stableford's assessment of Smith's writings as "aesthetically and intellectually vacuous," but also cites Heinlein, Pohl, and Williamson in Smith's support. A useful defense, even if I remain among the plaintiffs.

Olaf Stapledon

10-138. Fiedler, Leslie A. **Olaf Stapledon: A Man Divided.** Oxford, 1983.
10-139. Kinnaird, John. **Olaf Stapledon.** Starmont, 1986.
*10-140. McCarthy, Patrick A. **Olaf Stapledon.** Twayne, 1982. TEAS 340.
10-141. Satty, Harvey, and Curtis C. Smith. **Olaf Stapledon: A Bibliography.** Greenwood, 1984.
10-142. Stapledon, Olaf. **Far Future Calling: Uncollected Science Fiction and Fantasies.** Sam Moskowitz, ed. Oswald Train, 1980.
Fiedler has long had an interest in SF and edited a 1975 historical/critical anthology, *In Dreams Awake.* He is as interested in Stapledon the man as in his works, unlike McCarthy, for whom the texts are more important. Fiedler is often careless of his facts but his interpretations, which have a Freudian flavor, are fascinating, even when idiosyncratic, as they often are. Kinnaird suggests in his first chapter that Stapledon's works can best be understood as products of four periods of his life, which are examined in moderate detail. Later chapters survey five major novels and the later fiction. Annotated primary and secondary bibliographies, index. Not as balanced or as detailed as McCarthy, who wrote the first published book-length study. Balanced, fair, and clearly written; all the major and most of the minor works are discussed, showing many of the influences on Stapledon's

thought, although neglecting his influence on the American pulp SF tradition. Selective primary and secondary bibliography, chronology, and index; the best single study. Stapledon was not a prolific author, with fewer than 20 books, plus essays, pamphlets, etc. Satty and Smith's exhaustive, descriptively annotated bibliography would be needed only by Stapledon specialists. Moskowitz's edited volume collects five short fictions, the eponymous unproduced radio play, an address to the British Interplanetary Society in 1948, and a 55-page biographical study of Stapledon, based on original research, the first detailed (if limited) study of the man H. Bruce Franklin suggested is the Milton of SF.

Theodore Sturgeon

10-143. Diskin, Lahna. **Theodore Sturgeon.** Starmont, 1981.
10-144. Diskin, Lahna. **Theodore Sturgeon: A Primary and Secondary Bibliography.** G. K. Hall, 1980.
10-145. Menger, Lucy. **Theodore Sturgeon.** Ungar, 1981.
Diskin's bibliography is actually more current than her 72-page 1981 study because of Starmont's delay in publishing. It has a feature the other Hall bibliographies should emulate: all criticism about a given work is indexed as a group. Her brief study of Sturgeon is moderately useful, though she overpraises her subject, a failing Menger shares. Menger begins with a short biography, then examines Sturgeon's fiction chronologically, although very selectively (the rationale for inclusion isn't explained), emphasizing four novels and about 25 shorter tales. Sturgeon was an important if erratic SF author, and he and his works deserve a better book-length assessment than either of these studies provides.

William Tenn

10-146. Benson, Gordon, Jr. **William Tenn (Philip Klass).** Rev. ed. Author, 1985.
A seven-page pamphlet listing the books and stories by Tenn, who became an English instructor after writing most of his SF, the last more than a decade ago.

James Tiptree, Jr.

10-147. Siegel, Mark. **James Tiptree, Jr.** Starmont, 1986.
Alice Sheldon came late to SF, her first SF story having been published at age 54 under her now well-known pseudonym. A frequent award winner and nominee. Her work has attracted considerable praise and scrutiny, although this is the first book-length study (89 pages), but one hopes not the last. Now in her seventies, she continues to write her perceptive stories about the difficulties of human understanding.

Bob Tucker

10-148. Benson, Gordon, Jr. **Arthur Wilson "Bob" Tucker.** Author, 1985.
Tucker's 15 SF books, 11 mysteries, short fiction, and a handful of pieces about Tucker comprise this five-page bibliography.

Jack Vance

10-149. Levack, Daniel J. H., and Tim Underwood, comps. **Fantasms: A Bibliography of the Literature of Jack Vance.** Underwood-Miller, 1978.
Underwood-Miller originally specialized in issuing Vance's work, and *Fantasms* was their first author bibliography. Coverage includes all known English-language writings through early 1978, both book-length and shorter fiction, including the pseudonymous works and the mysteries written under his real name, John Holbrook Vance. Cover reproductions of all first editions are included. Series and connected stories, chronological listing, and a list of his "Captain Video" scripts. The eight essays, several reprinted, treat various facets of Vance's SF and fantasy. Marshall B. Tymn's bibliography lists secondary literature as well as a slightly more current primary bibliography. A useful survey of Vance's varied fictions. Announced for 1987 was the study by Jack Rawlins, *Demon Prince: The Dissonant Worlds of Jack Vance* (Borgo).

Jules Verne

10-150. Allot, Kenneth (U.K.). **Jules Verne.** Cresset Press, 1940.
10-151. Chesneaux, Jean (France). **The Political and Social Ideas of Jules Verne.** Thames & Hudson, 1972. Tr. by Thomas Wikeley of *Une Lecture politique de Jules Verne*, 1971.
10-152. Costello, Peter (Ireland). **Jules Verne: Inventor of Science Fiction.** Scribner, 1978.
10-153. Jules-Verne, Jean (France). **Jules Verne: A Biography.** Taplinger, 1976. Tr. and adapted by Roger Greaves of *Jules Verne*, 1973.
10-154. Gallagher, Edward J.; Judith A. Misticelli; and John A. Van Eerde. **Jules Verne: A Primary and Secondary Bibliography.** G. K. Hall, 1980.
The literature on Verne is very large and growing. English-language scholarship has been far more limited than French, perhaps because the English translations of Verne have been generally wretched, erroneously labeling him a boy's adventure writer. Walter James Miller's annotated editions published by Crowell may rectify this, but the French editions should be read for accurate texts, especially the now out-of-print Rencontre editions published in Switzerland. The general SF histories annotated in Chapter 9 will usually provide an adequate account of his role in the development of SF. Annotated below are a sampling of the better English-language works for the more ambitious reader. French literary criticism of Verne is usefully surveyed by Marc Angenot in "Jules Verne and French Literary Criticism," *Science-Fiction Studies* 1 (Spring 1973): 333–337. Allot was for many years the standard English-language biography, leaning heavily on the discreet biography by Verne's niece, Marguerite Allotte de la Füye's *Jules Verne—sa vie, son oeuvre* (1928). Verne destroyed most of his personal papers before his death, and the Verne family's archives are relatively inaccessible to outsiders. Allot's chronological biography is competent but now largely superseded by two more recent biographies. Chesneaux's examination of Verne's many *voyages extraordinaires* as elements in his political view of the world argues that Verne's view is far wider and more unorthodox than Verne's bourgeois upbringing would suggest. Forty-one engravings from original editions of the novels enliven the text. Costello presents "Verne in relation to the science, technology, and geographical discoveries of his

time," tracing his sources and how he used them. His main theme, Verne's gradual loss of faith and growing disillusionment, makes Verne a modern figure of great interest, "far removed from the shallow-minded romancer of popular fame." Costello's account draws on the earlier scholarship, cited in his multilingual bibliography, and is the most balanced biography available. Eight pages of plates, chronological list of the *voyages extraordinaires,* index. Verne's grandson drew on material in the family archives to provide a detailed picture of this major figure in the evolution of SF. He elucidates Verne's experiences and reveals in Verne's own words how many of his stories actually evolved. Like Chesneaux, he places Verne's works and ideas in the larger context of his times. Twenty-four pages of plates, good bibliography, index. Although Jules-Verne's biography is the first in many years by a family member with access to private family records, Costello's biography is preferable, although both are valuable. Costello says the Greaves translation of the 1973 French original is abridged and much less satisfactory than the original (not seen). Gallagher's work, the longest by far of the Hall bibliographies (408 pages), includes a preface, an introduction, and a five-part bibliography, each chronological. Verne's 106 pieces of fiction from 1858 to 1970 are listed in Part A, French originals and English translations only. Part B lists the librettos and songs Verne wrote while studying law in Paris. Part C lists nonfiction works (a few book-length) and a few letters. Part D annotates critical studies in English (100 pages), Part E critical studies in French (190 pages). An index to Verne's works and to author or title and subjects of all secondary literature completes the volume. The secondary bibliographies are comprehensive through 1978, selective through 1979. The secondary literature is limited to English and French. Scholars needing access to this literature and that in other languages should consult Jean-Michael Margot's *Bibliographie documentaire sur Jules Verne* (Author, 1978), which cites—but doesn't annotate—about 1,300 critical studies in many languages.

Kurt Vonnegut

10-155. Giannone, Richard. **Vonnegut: A Preface to His Novels.** Kennikat, 1977.

10-156. Klinkowitz, Jerome, and Donald L. Lawler, eds. **Vonnegut in America: An Introduction to the Life and Work of Kurt Vonnegut.** Delacorte, 1977.

10-157. Klinkowitz, Jerome, and John Somer, eds. **The Vonnegut Statement.** Delacorte, 1972.

10-158. Lundquist, James. **Kurt Vonnegut.** Ungar, 1977.

10-159. Mayo, Clark. **Kurt Vonnegut: The Gospel from Outer Space (Or, Yes, We Have No Nirvanas).** Borgo, 1977.

10-160. Pieratt, Asa B.; Julie Huffman-Klinkowitz; and Jerome Klinkowitz, eds. **Kurt Vonnegut: A Comprehensive Bibliography.** Shoestring, 1987.

10-161. Schatt, Stanley. **Kurt Vonnegut, Jr.** Twayne, 1976. TUSAS 276.

Vonnegut's reluctance to be considered an SF writer (see Chapter 7) and his obvious literary gifts have made him a popular subject of articles, and the scholarly mills are grinding him fine indeed (the 1977 Klinkowitz collection cites 16 doctoral dissertations; so it goes). Here are several of the best full-length studies. Giannone discusses "thematic affinities among the novels before taking up the texts singly to show how Vonnegut's recurring subjects are realized in particular fictions." A sensible, clear introduction. The 1972 Klinkowitz book has 13 pieces, some revised from earlier publication, mostly by academics. They focus on Vonnegut's popular and academic acceptance, his literary experience and development, and the theses and techniques in his novels and many shorts. One essay argues that Vonnegut is not an SF writer in the traditional (pulp) sense, but is "a writer who uses the techniques of that form to delineate human experience—a human experience of necessity broadened to include within its scope the technology which forms a goodly part of that experience." The nine original essays in the 1977 Klinkowitz book "show how Vonnegut's posture as a writer seems to grow out of his realization of the possibilities of our common American culture with its disparate energies and its eclectic forms." The pieces study various facets of Vonnegut's fiction. McNelly's "Kurt Vonnegut as a Science-Fiction Writer" argues that, contrary to what Vonnegut may insist, he *does* write science fiction. Twelve pages of photos, 39-page primary and secondary bibliography (updating that in the earlier collection), index. Lundquist's short monograph provides a discursive, informal introduction to Vonnegut's "cosmic irony" and how this is embodied in his stories. Mayo's long essay emphasizes the novels, examining them in sequence, but not in any great detail. Schatt's monograph is the most satisfactory of the four. He tries "to trace the development of (Vonnegut's style and philosophy) simultaneously since Vonnegut's medium is often closely related to its message." The treatment is roughly chronological, from *Player Piano* [3-392] to *Slapstick*, with separate chapters on the short stories, the plays, and the "public man." Announced for early 1987 is a revision of the Pieratt-Klinkowitz bibliography issued by Shoestring in 1974.

Manly Wade Wellman

10-162. Benson, Gordon, Jr. **Manly Wade Wellman: Gentleman from Chapel Hill; A Memorial Working Bibliography.** Author, 1986.
Prepared shortly after Wellman's death in April 1986. Wellman's SF is generally poor, but his fantasy writings proved very popular, incorporating his southern regionalism into his best work. This 17-page booklet is one of Benson's longer efforts.

H. G. Wells

10-163. Batchelor, John (U.K.). **H. G. Wells.** Cambridge, 1985.
*10-164. Bergonzi, Bernard (U.K.). **The Early H. G. Wells: A Study of the Scientific Romances.** Manchester Univ. Press, 1961.
10-165. Bergonzi, Bernard (U.K.). **H. G. Wells: A Collection of Critical Essays.** Prentice-Hall, 1976.
10-166. Borrello, Alfred. **H. G. Wells: Author in Agony.** Southern Illinois, 1972.
10-167. Costa, Richard Hauer. **H. G. Wells.** Rev. ed. Twayne, 1985. TEAS 43.
10-168. Crossley, Robert. **H. G. Wells.** Starmont, 1986.
10-169. Haynes, Roslynn D. **H. G. Wells: Discoverer of the Future: The Influence of Science on His Thought.** New York Univ. Press, 1980.
10-170. Huntington, John. **The Logic of Fantasy: H. G. Wells and Science Fiction.** Columbia, 1982.

*10-171. MacKenzie, Norman Ian, and Jean MacKenzie (U.K.). **H. G. Wells: A Biography.** Simon & Schuster, 1973. British title: *The Time Traveller.*
10-172. McConnell, Frank. **The Science Fiction of H. G. Wells.** Oxford, 1981.
10-173. Parrinder, Patrick (U.K.). **H. G. Wells.** Oliver & Boyd, 1970.
*10-174. Parrinder, Patrick, ed. (U.K.). **H. G. Wells: The Critical Heritage.** Routledge, 1972.
*10-175. Suvin, Darko (Yugoslavia), and Robert M. Philmus, eds. **H. G. Wells and Modern Science Fiction.** Bucknell Univ. Press, 1977.
10-176. Wagar, W. Warren. **H. G. Wells and the World State.** Yale, 1961.
10-177. Wells, H. G. (U.K.). **H. G. Wells: Early Writings in Science and Science Fiction.** Robert M. Philmus and David Y. Hughes, eds. Univ. of California, 1975.
10-178. Williamson, Jack. **H. G. Wells: Critic of Progress.** Mirage, 1973.

In his 1941 essay "Wells, Hitler and the World State," Orwell remarks: "I doubt whether anyone who was writing books between 1900 and 1920, at any rate in the English language, influenced the young so much. The minds of all of us, and therefore the physical world, would be perceptibly different if Wells had never existed . . . here was this wonderful man who . . . *knew* that the future was not going to be what respectable people imagined." Aldiss [9-4] called him the Shakespeare of science fiction with good reason, and few writers, then or now, are his equal in imaginative scope and power. The literature about Wells is very large. The annotated bibliography by David Y. Hughes, "Bergonzi and After in the Criticism of Wells' SF," *Science-Fiction Studies* 3 (July 1976): 165–174, provides a useful overview of recent significant criticism. Many bibliographies of Wells's works exist. J. R. Hammond's *Herbert George Wells: An Annotated Bibliography of His Works* (Garland, 1977) is usually considered the most definitive to date. For most purposes, the annotated bibliographies of his science journalism, 1887–1901, by David Y. Hughes and Robert Philmus, and his books and pamphlets, by R. D. Mullen, both in the Suvin and Philmus compilation, should meet the needs of almost anyone primarily concerned with Wells's SF and his thought generally. Annotated below are the better book-length studies that examine Wells's influential scientific romances. The works in Chapter 9 often treat Wells, some of them in detail, notably that of Hillegas [9-44]. Bergonzi provides the most detailed and one of the most important studies of the works SF readers usually cite. The Victorian world shaped by tradition and the uncertain new world dominated by science and technology are bridged by Wells. Bergonzi relates Wells's early works to the nineteenth-century *fin de siècle* attitudes common at that time. Hillegas [9-44] relates these romances to similar works by later writers. The Bergonzi collection assembles ten essays published since Wells's death in 1946, most since 1960, but emphasizing the 1895–1910 period "when he published most of the fiction that has endured." The earliest piece is by V. S. Pritchett on the scientific romances. The editor's essay on *The Time Machine* [1-103] is taken from his longer 1961 study, above. Two essays discuss *Tono-Bungay* (1909). Not as comprehensive as the Parrinder collection [10-174] but usefully complements it with more recent criticism. Borrello provides a capable survey of recent criticism of Wells rather than an original analysis. The recurrent themes of qualified optimism and unrelieved despair are traced through all his works. Wells's early life as a shopkeeper's son is described, then his education, and his career in and out of literature, in the MacKenzies' balanced and detailed study, which relies on primary sources and is the best biography yet written of this influential figure. Parrinder's admirably judicious short study (102 pages for the text proper in the British edition) [10-173] emphasizes the intellectual and imaginative qualities of Wells's work and relies on recent criticism listed in the excellent 11-page primary and secondary bibliography, updated for the 1977 Putnam edition. Human failure to understand and control the environment is a theme developed throughout Wells's works. Although a chapter is devoted to the scientific romances, the most detailed analyses are of his best social novels, *Tono-Bungay* (1909) and *The History of Mr Polly* (1910). An excellent overview. The Parrinder compilation reprints reviews of selected books by Wells originally published 1895–1946 by such writers as Conrad, Forster, Henry James, Virginia Woolf, Leavis, Eliot, and others, including Zamiatin's entire short book on Wells (1922). Among the books reviewed are *The Time Machine* [1-103], *The Island of Dr. Moreau* [1-100], *The Plattner Story and Others* (1897), *The Invisible Man* (1897), *The War of the Worlds* [1-105], *The Food of the Gods* [1-99], *A Modern Utopia* [1-101], and *In the Days of the Comet* (1906). Parrinder's introduction and notes are excellent. A bibliography lists selected criticism, including the most detailed study of the critical reception of Wells's works, *H. G. Wells and His Critics* (1962) by Ingvald Raknem. A most useful collection. Suvin and Philmus assemble 11 essays, some revised from earlier publications or presented as papers at a 1971 Montreal symposium. The pieces range from detailed analyses of individual works to more general essays, such as Parrinder's comparison of Wells and Zamiatin or Komatsu's study of Wells's influence on Japanese SF. The two bibliographic essays mentioned above are especially valuable. A major compilation for Wells specialists. The Wagar study was rewritten from a doctoral dissertation and argues that Wells conditioned his readers to think in terms of the entire world, tried to expand the parochial late-nineteenth-century worldview to a view Wells felt was essential for understanding the future. He shows (as Williamson did later) that Wells was not a believer in inevitable progress and that he understood the mixed blessings of science and technology. Williamson's study is "devoted to the premise that Wells' early science fiction presents searching and significant criticism of the idea of progress," which the author claims contradicts the stereotype of Wells as "the deluded prophet of a crassly materialistic progress." This revision of a doctoral dissertation by the well-known SF writer was partially anticipated by several of the other works cited above. Philmus and Hughes collected 28 previously unreprinted writings of the 1880s and 1890s dealing with science and the sciences. They show how Wells retained both the cosmic and the human perspective in his writings, although he progressively shifted from the former to the latter. Excellent introduction and notes that link the pieces to one another and to his other writings, notably his scientific romances. A valuable selective bibliography of 95 pieces of his science journalism, 1887–1901, with abstracts, concludes the volume. Title and name indexes. A most useful compilation that collects fugitive pieces providing insights into Wells's attitudes toward human status and destiny. Batchelor's introductory survey provides a balanced consensus survey of Wells's life and work. Only two chapters discuss the scientific romances in any detail. Costa's revision of his earlier study reflects the critical reassessment to which Wells has been subjected since the 1960s. The revised edition has a chapter devoted to the SF (almost ignored in the original edition). A useful synthesis and starting point. In spite of Wells's importance in SF, Crossley's 79-page introduction is much shorter than Starmont guides to the work of far lesser writers. Perhaps he recognized that there was little he could do to add to the many longer studies listed in his annotated secondary bibliography. In McConnell, two chapters provide the biographical and historical setting, followed by detailed discussions of seven of the major works of SF, with a final chapter devoted to the later Wells. Chronology, chronological checklist of works, selected annotated secondary bibliography, index. McConnell is perceptive in his discussion of both the literary and the political ideas of Wells, and his survey is one of the better recent studies of this seminal writer. Haynes characterizes herself as "a scientist who defected to the literary camp." Her scientific training proves very helpful in her detailed analysis of how crucial Wells's science training was in shaping his works, not only his SF but his themes, methods of characterization, even his style. Wells was experienced enough to distinguish between science (a method of inquiry) and technology, his fictions reflecting their shifting relationship. A useful study of aspects of Wells slighted by critics whose analyses focus largely on literary concerns. Huntington provides a rigorously argued, complex analysis of the formal intellectual structures and rhetorical devices in the scientific romances, broadening his coverage beyond the works investigated in Bergonzi's pioneering study, which Huntington enriches.

James White

10-179. Benson, Gordon, Jr. **James White: Doctor to Aliens, A Working Bibliography.** Rev. ed. Author, 1986.
The nine pages list 66 stories, 20 books, and 16 articles, interviews, etc., by this Belfast-born writer.

Jack Williamson

10-180. Benson, Gordon, Jr. **Jack (John Stewart) Williamson: Child and Father of Wonder.** Rev. ed. Author, 1985.
10-181. Myers, Robert E. **Jack Williamson: A Primary and Secondary Bibliography.** G. K. Hall, 1980.
10-182. Williamson, Jack. **Wonder's Child: My Life in Science Fiction.** Bluejay, 1984.
Aptly titled, Williamson's very personal autobiography reveals a life begun in poverty in the Southwest and leading to his election as a Grand Master by fellow writers. Williamson triumphed over poverty, inadequate education, and emotional problems and continues to publish almost 80 years after his birth. Compare the less narrowly focused *The Way the Future Was* by Pohl [10-120] and Asimov's massive autobiography [10-7, 10-8]. HW, 1985. The Myers bibliography benefited from the compiler's access to Williamson's library and is therefore more complete than other Hall bibliographies. Benson acknowledges Myers and includes Williamson's nonfiction in his 14-page pamphlet.

John Wyndham

10-183. Stephensen-Payne, Phil, and Gordon Benson, Jr. **John Wyndham Parkes Lucas Benyon Harris.** Benson, 1985.
The 19 pages of the bibliography proper are supplemented by 14 pages of photo-copies of American and British paperback covers.

Roger Zelazny

10-184. Krulik, Theodore. **Roger Zelazny.** Ungar, 1986.
10-185. Levack, Daniel J. H. **Amber Dreams: A Roger Zelazny Bibliography.** Underwood-Miller, 1983.
10-186. Sanders, Joseph L. **Roger Zelazny: A Primary and Secondary Bibliography.** G. K. Hall, 1980.
10-187. Yoke, Carl B. **Roger Zelazny.** Starmont, 1979.
Krulik surveys the work of a popular writer, using his letters at Syracuse University as well as a 1982 interview. He is best when linking biography to fiction, but the book is heavy with plot summaries, often ineptly written (or edited), and stops with 1983. Notes, primary and secondary bibliography, index. Yoke, a longtime friend, surveys Zelazny's work through 1977 writings, with selectively annotated primary and secondary bibliographies. The major novels and important shorter fiction are discussed with greater insight than Krulik's work. Following a useful introduction surveying Zelazny's life and career, Sanders provides a bibliography of fiction, poetry, and nonfiction, with a long section devoted to secondary literature, much of it appearing in relatively obscure fanzines, with the latter annotated. Appendixes list nominations, awards, honors, foreign-language editions, and detailed descriptions of the Zelazny papers and manuscripts at Syracuse and the University of Maryland. Indexes to primary and secondary literature. More recent than Sanders, Levack extends coverage through 1982. The audience for this is the collector, although the scholar will also find it useful. Fiction entries are annotated; secondary literature is not. Includes a list of works in series or with common characters. Many reproductions of covers.

Collective Biography

As modern science fiction "ages," some of its veteran practitioners have been prompted to compose autobiographical essays. These rarely reach the elephantine bulk of Asimov's two-volume work [10-7, 10-8]. *Foundation* [14-36] has published a useful series called "The Profession of SF," with almost three dozen pieces having appeared by the end of 1986. The collections here are placed in this section as a matter of convenience, although they might be equally at home in Chapter 9.

10-188. Aldiss, Brian W. (U.K.), and Harry Harrison, eds. **Hell's Cartographers: Some Personal Histories of Science Fiction Writers.** Harper, 1976.
Autobiographical essays by Robert Silverberg, Alfred Bester, Damon Knight, Frederik Pohl, and the editors. Bester (1913–) is the oldest writer, Silverberg (1935–) the youngest, and as the annotations of their books indicate, they are all veteran and distinguished writers. A supplement includes brief accounts of their working habits and selected bibliographies. Aldiss wrote a quasi-diary for a

month in 1969, published it as *The Shape of Further Things* (1970), and has an auto-biographical essay in his . . . *And the Lurid Glare of the Comet* [9-3]. Pohl later wrote a full-length autobiography [10-120], and Knight's account is amplified in *The Futurians* [10-190]. The pieces range from the uncomfortably personal (Knight) to the thoughtful and moving (Silverberg and Aldiss) and will be of primary inter-est to readers familiar with their works.

10-189. Greenberg, Martin H., ed. **Fantastic Lives: Autobiographical Essays by Notable Science Fiction Writers.** Southern Illinois, 1981.
Inspired by *Hell's Cartographers,* Greenberg chose nine contributors "who have made major contributions to the field of science fiction," which is certainly not true for some. Ellison discusses the genesis and reception of his famous tale "I Have No Mouth, and I Must Scream." Farmer describes his life until 1952. The quirky R. A. Lafferty includes autobiographical fragments amid his outspoken comments on the generally confused state of SF. The little-known Katherine Mac-Lean, one of the earlier female SF writers, talks of the influence of SF (especially of Wells) on her childhood. Malzberg reprints the introduction from his *Down Here in the Dream Quarter* (1976), a review of a 1974 book, and adds a postscript, all of a piece with his later essays collected in *The Engines of the Night* [9-56]. Mack Reynolds accurately titles his piece "Science Fiction and Socioeconomics," and ex-plains why much of his SF has explored the political economies of future soci-eties. Margaret St. Clair muses on her SF, little known today, and Spinrad re-counts his experiences in Hollywood as a scriptwriter and some of his skirmishes in publishing. Anyone interested in the odd mechanics of his stories should read van Vogt's final piece. Not nearly the equal of *Hell's Cartographers* but of some value.

10-190. Knight, Damon F(rancis). **The Futurians: The Story of the Science Fic-tion "Family" of the 30's That Produced Today's Top SF Writers and Editors.** John Day, 1977.
The Futurian Society was founded in 1938 and never numbered more than 20 members. Among those better known today are Knight, Asimov, Blish, Korn-bluth, Judith Merril, Pohl, and Wollheim. Most of those Knight writes of were liv-ing in 1977, and he includes material about their personal lives that I judge quite unwarranted. This account should interest the historian of SF but few others.

10-191. Moskowitz, Sam. **Explorers of the Infinite: Shapers of Science Fiction.** World, 1963.
Revised from earlier magazine publication, this is a largely uncritical history of writers from the seventeenth century through the 1930s. Chapters are arranged chronologically and are devoted to Cyrano de Bergerac, Mary Shelley's proto-SF, Poe, Fitz-James O'Brien, Verne, Edward Everett Hale, Lu Senarens and his Franke Reade series, Wells, M. P. Shiel, A. C. Doyle, Burroughs, Merritt, Čapek, Gernsback, Lovecraft, Stapledon, Philip Wylie, and Weinbaum. The develop-ment of the term *science fiction* is discussed in another chapter, and a superficial and dated survey of developments since the 1930s concludes the book. Name in-dex. Although little attempt is made to relate the works of these authors to wider literary traditions or social history, some of the essays are the first extended dis-

cussion of their subjects in book form, and the specialist may therefore find this account of some value.

10-192. Moskowitz, Sam. **Seekers of Tomorrow: Masters of Modern Science Fiction.** World, 1966.
This account covers the post-1940 period to 1965. Twenty-one mostly genre writers are profiled, with a chapter devoted to Superman and his creators and one briefly treating a number of writers Moskowitz judges of lesser importance (such as Vonnegut). The same inbred quality vitiates both his works, and his critical estimates should be judged accordingly. In spite of these serious weaknesses, he deserves credit for providing a reasonably accurate biographical survey of early and modern SF writers.

Interviews

Letters in the early American SF pulps led to correspondence among fans and the development of fandom, a fascinating, often inbred subculture with its own language and codes. Conventions increasingly brought fans and writers together (the first "world" SF convention was held in 1939), a tradition that continues today on a major scale. Interviews have been conducted at such meetings or by mail, and it is not surprising that many have been published, usually initially in fanzines, some of them later collected as books. A generic limitation of most such interviews is the relatively uncritical stance taken by the fan-interviewer, which can result in superficiality or lack of focus. More probing might avoid the blandness so common in published interviews, in which there are often two intersecting monologues but little real dialogue. These interviews are a form of oral history and can sometimes provide genuine insight into an author's works, although they lack the depth of something like the *Paris Review* interviews. Annotated below are the principal collections of interviews published to date.

10-193. Elliot, Jeffrey M. **Science Fiction Voices #2: Interviews with Science Fiction Writers.** Borgo, 1979.
10-194. Elliot, Jeffrey M. **Science Fiction Voices #4: Interviews with Modern Science Fiction Writers.** Borgo, 1982.
10-195. Elliot, Jeffrey M. **Pulp Voices, or Science Fiction Voices #6: Interviews with Pulp Magazine Writers and Editors.** Borgo, 1983.
Elliot, a professor of political science, is thoroughly prepared for his interviews, which are sometimes lengthier than the usual. His first collection is amusingly introduced by Richard Lupoff, who suggests the rationale for and value of well-conducted interviews. The subjects in number 2 are Niven, Bradbury, van Vogt, Anderson, and Silverberg. Number 4 profiles Charles D. Hornig, editor of *Wonder Stories* in the 1930s, Bob Shaw, Frank Kelly Freas (the illustrator), and Brian Stableford. Number 6 includes interviews of Jack Williamson, H. L. Gold of *Galaxy*, Stanton A. Coblentz, C. L. Moore, and Raymond Z. Gallun.

10-196. Schweitzer, Darrell. **Science Fiction Voices #1: Interviews with Science Fiction Writers.** Borgo, 1979.
Reprinted from fanzines, 1975–1979, are interviews with Sturgeon (the best

piece), Bester, Pohl, Gunn, Leiber, Clement, and de Camp, apparently at conventions, the interviews ranging from 5 to 14 pages. Schweitzer's control is sometimes unsure (he ran out of questions for Bester), and the pieces have a fragmentary quality.

10-197. Schweitzer, Darrell. **Science Fiction Voices #5: Interviews with American Science Fiction Writers of the Golden Age.** Borgo, 1981.
Published originally from 1976 through 1979 are interviews with Asimov, Lin Carter, del Rey, Hamilton/Brackett, Frank Belknap Long, Simak, Wilson Tucker, and Jack Williamson.

10-198. Walker, Paul. **Speaking of Science Fiction: The Paul Walker Interviews.** Luna Press (655 Orchard St., Oradell, NJ 07649), 1978.
Walker conducted interviews by mail with 31 contemporary SF and fantasy authors, from the well to the lesser known. They were originally published from 1971 to 1979 in the defunct *LUNA Monthly*. In spite of the limitations imposed by mail and the consequent lack of spontaneity, many interviews remain interesting and often give some insight into the works of the writers.

10-199. Lane, Daryl; William Vernon; and David G. Carson. **The Sound of Wonder: Interviews from "The Science Fiction Radio Show."** 2 vols. Oryx Press, 1985.
This program was nationally syndicated from 1980 to 1983. The interviewers assume more knowledge of the authors' works than most listeners probably had, but their questions are intelligent. The interviews average 20 pages and are apparently unedited and therefore repetitious. The emphasis is on each writer's subjects, writing habits, and specific books. Volume 1 includes interviews with Stephen Donaldson, Cherryh, Clement, Harness, Sturgeon, Howard Waldrop, Williamson, Rudy Rucker, and illustrator Michael Whelan. Volume 2 includes interviews with Anthony, Edward Bryant, Farmer, Wollheim, James Hogan, Bradley, Roger Ebert (the film critic), Wolfe, Dickson, and George R. R. Martin. The interviewers elicit more facts than does Platt [10-200, 10-201], who is more concerned with the authors' philosophy and personal characteristics. Overpriced trade paperbacks.

*10-200. Platt, Charles (U.K.). **Dream Makers.** Berkley, 1980. British title: *Who Writes Science Fiction?* Savoy, 1980. Reprinted as *Dream Makers* (Xanadu, 1986).
*10-201. Platt, Charles (U.K.). **Dream Makers II.** Berkley, 1983.
Platt is a novelist and short fiction writer usually identified with the New Wave movement of the late 1960s. He is also a skilled interviewer, as these volumes prove (both were Hugo nominees, 1981 and 1984, and the second volume won the *Locus* award poll). The 1980 collection has 28 interviews plus a self-profile. (The British edition adds an interview with Ben Bova.) The 1983 volume collects another 28, plus an interview with Platt by Douglas Winter. Most subjects are SF writers, but Platt includes interviews with Vonnegut, Wiliam Burroughs, D. M. Thomas, Alvin Toffler, and Stephen King. Platt thankfully does not follow the formula question-and-answer format used by the other interviewers. As a consequence his subjects are far more human, with the warts and rough edges showing. As he puts it: "I have tried to be . . . balanced. Neither obsequious nor snide;

not too inquisitive; but not too discreet. I never demanded information that an author was reluctant to give, and I only dwelled on topics that were relevant to an author's published work." He is notably successful, even if judged as occasionally poorly prepared (his admission before the Herbert interview that he was repeatedly unsuccessful in reading *Dune* is honest and hilarious). Useful bibliographical notes. A selection from both volumes was published in 1987 as *Dream Makers: Science Fiction and Fantasy Writers at Work* (Ungar). Platt's iconoclastic temperament surfaced in his *The Patchin Review* (seven issues, 1981–1985), which was succeeded by a personal seminewsletter called *REM*. A sample copy can be had by sending $1.00 to the author (594 Broadway, Suite 1208, New York, NY 10012).

11
Science Fiction on Film and Television

Neil Barron

When the first edition of *Anatomy of Wonder* was published in 1976, there was no separate chapter devoted to SF in nonprint media. Only five annotated books were devoted to SF cinema, one of them emphasizing horror films. The second edition devoted a separate chapter to the topic, annotating or mentioning about a dozen studies. This expanded chapter acknowledges the remarkable popularity of SF in today's cinema. Peter Nicholls explains why:

> In 1971, fantastic cinema accounted for only 5 per cent of American box-office takings, if we can accept *Variety*'s findings. By 1982 this figure had risen close to an amazing 50 per cent. There is, therefore, a vast amount of money at stake in making fantastic movies, especially since their very nature often means that they are extremely expensive to produce.[1]

The listing in the January 14, 1987, issue of *Variety* indicates that of the top 20 all-time theatrical rental films in the United States and Canada, SF films occupied places 1, 2, 3, 4, 10, 15, and 16. (See Table 11-2 for additional rankings.)

SF in film or on TV is for many people their initial introduction to the field, a major change from earlier years. James Gunn, a professor of English at the University of Kansas and SF writer, including the TV series "The Immortals," made this remark.

When it comes to the student of science fiction, there are virtually no good films that are good science fiction. The problem with the science-fiction film is that it adds nothing to science fiction except concreteness of image—and this may be more of a drawback than an asset.[2]

Whatever one's opinion, SF films are increasingly common and occasionally distinguished, much like printed SF.

Science fiction has been part of cinema from the earliest years, beginning with the lengthy 21-minute film (when most films were 1 to 3 minutes) by Georges Méliès, *Le Voyage dans la lune* (1902). Similarly, SF on TV dates from the earliest years when TV became more than a laboratory curiosity. Older readers may recall the "electronic wizard, master of time and space and guardian of the safety of the world," Captain Video, whose 1949 series began an unending sequence of scientific superheroes and equally supervillains, sometimes extraterrestrial in origin.

Science fiction and horror cinema, which often share common elements (*Alien* is a good example), are standard film genres in film texts such as Stuart M. Kaminsky's *American Film Genres* (2nd ed., 1985). Science fiction films range from the atrocious (*Plan Nine from Outer Space*, a deserved Golden Turkey award) to the sentimental (*E.T.*) to the cautionary (*Dr. Strangelove, A Clockwork Orange*). Of the approximately 1,200 SF films described in Hardy [11-1] and released through 1983, only two have won Academy Awards for acting: Cliff Robertson in *Charly*, based on *Flowers for Algernon* [3-228], and Frederic March in the 1932 version of *Dr. Jekyll and Mr. Hyde* [1-86].

Because of the development of videocassette recorders, owned by more than 40 percent of all American households by fall 1986, a very large number of films of all types can be viewed, either taped off the air or cable or rented. While videotapes are not entirely adequate substitutes for 35mm motion pictures in a theater, their widespread availability, convenience, and low rental cost have contributed to their great popularity. Videotape rentals in 1986 totaled $3.4 billion; movie ticket sales about $4 billion. *Video Marketing Newsletter* reported 1.04 billion videotapes rented in 1986 vs. 1.02 billion film tickets sold. Libraries routinely acquire videotapes of theatrical films. To assist them in selection, Tables 11-1A and 11-1B present a list of SF films judged best or most significant by various sources. Table 11-1A lists the SF films alphabetically by title and Table 11-1B lists these same films by number of votes (and then alphabetically by title).

Variety publishes an annual list of all-time theatrical rental champs, which records distributors' receipts, not ticket sales, in the United States and Canada only, and notes that rentals outside North America "sometimes equal or slightly surpass American and Canadian rentals." The listing from the January 14, 1987, issue (see Table 11-2) shows these as the top 50 SF films.

Not all films in Tables 11-1A, 11-1B, and 11-2 are universally judged SF, e.g., *King Kong, The China Syndrome, Blue Thunder*. Three titles in the top-ten rental list, between *The Empire Strikes Back* and *Back to the Future*, might be included: *Ghostbusters* (1984), *Raiders of the Lost Ark* (1981), and *Indiana Jones and the Temple of Doom* (1984). The purpose of the lists is to provide guidance in selecting SF films for libraries, relying on a rough critical consensus as well as box office popularity.

The range in quality for books about SF film parallels that for the fiction itself, from atrocious to superb. Because of the popularity—and profitability—of

Table 11-1A   SF Films Judged Best or Most Significant*

Votes	Title, Year	Votes	Title, Year
6	Alien, 1979	4	King Kong, 1933
3	Alphaville, 1965	4	Mad Max 2 [Road Warrior], 1981
1	Android, 1982	1	The Man in the White Suit, 1951
1	The Andromeda Strain, 1971	6	The Man Who Fell to Earth, 1976
1	Back to the Future, 1985	6	Metropolis, 1926
1	Barbarella, 1967	1	Night of the Living Dead, 1968
2	The Birds, 1963	1	Nineteen Eighty-Four, 1956
4	Blade Runner, 1982	2	Not of This Earth, 1957
3	Bride of Frankenstein, 1935	3	On the Beach, 1959
1	The Brood, 1979	3	The Parasite Murders, 1974
1	Capricorn One, 1977	2	Planet of the Apes, 1968
2	Charly, 1968	1	Quatermass and the Pit, 1967
4	A Clockwork Orange, 1971	2	Quatermass 2, 1957
6	Close Encounters of the Third Kind, 1977	1	The Quatermass Xperiment, 1955
4	Dark Star, 1974	1	Quest for Fire, 1981
1	The Day the Earth Caught Fire, 1960	2	Quintet, 1979
		1	Repo Man, 1985
1	Death Race 2000, 1975	1	Robinson Crusoe on Mars, 1964
1	Dr. Cyclops, 1940	1	Scanners, 1981
3	Dr. Strangelove, 1964	1	Seconds, 1966
1	Duel, 1971	1	Silent Running
2	The Empire Strikes Back, 1980	2	Sleeper, 1971
3	E.T., 1982	2	Solaris, 1971
1	The Fabulous World of Jules Verne, 1958	1	Star Trek—The Motion Picture, 1979
3	Fahrenheit 451, 1966	6	Star Wars, 1977
1	Fail Safe, 1964	1	Strange Invaders, 1983
1	Fantastic Planet [Planète Sauvage], 1973	2	Superman—The Movie, 1978
		1	The Terminator, 1985
1	Fantastic Voyage, 1966	3	Them!, 1954
2	Flash Gordon, 1936	6	The Thing, 1951
4	Forbidden Planet, 1956	2	The Thing, 1982
2	Frankenstein, 1931	6	Things to Come, 1936
1	Gladiatorerna, 1969	2	The Island Earth, 1955
1	God Told Me To!, 1976	1	THX-1138, 1970
1	Der Grosse Verhau, 1970	1	The Time Machine, 1960
1	The Illustrated Man, 1968	1	20,000 Leagues under the Sea, 1954
7	The Incredible Shrinking Man, 1957		
1	Invaders from Mars, 1953	8	2001, 1968
8	Invasion of the Body Snatchers, 1956	1	Videodrome, 1982
1	Invasion of the Body Snatchers, 1978	1	Village of the Damned, 1960
1	The Invisible Man, 1933	3	War of the Worlds, 1953
1	It Came from Outer Space, 1953	4	Westworld, 1973
1	It's Alive!, 1973	1	Who?, 1974
2	Je T'Aime, Je T'Aime, 1967	1	Zardoz, 1973
1	La Jetée, 1963		

*Sources for Tables 11-1A and 11-1B: Hardy [11-1], nine critics' lists, pp. 388–391; Baird Searles, in Ashley [8-41], p. 86; David Pringle, *Vector* 114 (June 1983) and personal letter; David Pringle, Brian Aldiss, Michael Klossner, outside readers.

674

Table 11-1B   SF Films Judged Best or Most Significant by Vote

Votes	Title	Votes	Title
8	Invasion of the Body Snatchers (1956)	1	Barbarella
		1	The Brood
8	2001	1	Capricorn One
7	The Incredible Shrinking Man	1	The Day the Earth Caught Fire
6	Alien	1	Death Race 2000
6	Close Encounters of the Third Kind	1	Dr. Cyclops
6	The Man Who Fell to Earth	1	Duel
6	Metropolis	1	The Fabulous World of Jules Verne
6	Star Wars		
6	The Thing (1951)	1	Fail Safe
6	Things to Come	1	Fantastic Planet [Planète Sauvage]
5	[None]	1	Fantastic Voyage
4	Blade Runner	1	Gladiatorerna
4	A Clockwork Orange	1	God Told Me To!
4	Dark Star	1	Der Grosse Verhau
4	Forbidden Planet	1	The Illustrated Man
4	King Kong	1	Invaders from Mars
4	Mad Max 2 [Road Warrior]	1	Invasion of the Body Snatchers (1978)
4	Westworld		
3	Alphaville	1	The Invisible Man
3	Bride of Frankenstein	1	It Came from Outer Space
3	Dr. Strangelove	1	It's Alive
3	E.T.	1	La Jetée
3	Fahrenheit 451	1	The Man in the White Suit
3	On the Beach	1	Night of the Living Dead
3	The Parasite Murders	1	Nineteen Eighty-Four
3	Them!	1	Quatermass and the Pit
3	War of the Worlds	1	The Quatermass Xperiment
2	The Birds	1	Quest for Fire
2	Charly	1	Repo Man
2	The Empire Strikes Back	1	Robinson Crusoe on Mars
2	Flash Gordon	1	Scanners
2	Frankenstein	1	Seconds
2	Je T'aime, Je T'aime	1	Silent Running
2	Not of This Earth	1	Sleeper
2	Planet of the Apes	1	Star Trek—The Motion Picture
2	Quatermass 2	1	Strange Invaders
2	Quintet	1	The Terminator
2	Solaris	1	THX-1138
2	Superman—The Movie	1	The Time Machine
2	The Thing (1982)	1	20,000 Leagues under the Sea
2	This Island Earth	1	Videodrome
1	Android	1	Village of the Damned
1	The Andromeda Strain	1	Who?
1	Back to the Future	1	Zardoz

Table 11-2 Top 50 Rental Films

Rank	Title, Year	$ (Thousands)
1	E.T., 1982	228,379
2	Star Wars, 1977	193,500
3	Return of the Jedi, 1983	168,002
4	The Empire Strikes Back, 1980	141,600
5	Back to the Future, 1985	101,956
6	Superman, 1978	82,800
7	Close Encounters of the Third Kind, 1977/1980	82,750
8	Superman II, 1980	65,100
9	Star Trek—The Motion Picture, 1979	56,000
10	Star Trek IV—The Voyage Home, 1986	45,000
11	Aliens, 1986	42,500
12	Alien, 1979	40,300
13	Star Trek II: The Wrath of Khan, 1982	40,000
14	Cocoon, 1985	40,000
15	Star Trek III: The Search for Spock, 1984	39,000
16	Young Frankenstein, 1974	38,823
17	War Games, 1983	37,938
18	Superman III, 1983	37,200
19	Octopussy, 1983	34,024
20	Moonraker, 1979	33,917
21	Never Say Never Again, 1983	28,000
22	Thunderball, 1965	26,912
23	For Your Eyes Only, 1981	26,536
24	The Black Hole, 1979	25,437
25	The China Syndrome, 1979	25,342
26	A View to a Kill, 1985	25,236
27	Firefox, 1982	25,000
28	The Spy Who Loved Me, 1977	24,350
29	2001—A Space Odyssey, 1968	24,100
30	The Love Bug, 1969	23,150
31	Goldfinger, 1964	22,981
32	Blue Thunder, 1983	21,953
33	2010, 1984	20,115
34	Diamonds Are Forever, 1971	19,717
35	Time Bandits, 1981	19,488
36	You Only Live Twice, 1967	19,388
37	Mad Max Beyond Thunderdome, 1985	17,900
38	Red Dawn, 1984	17,832
39	The Fly, 1986	17,500
40	A Clockwork Orange, 1971	17,000
41	Herbie Rides Again, 1974	17,000
42	The Terminator, 1984	16,956
43	Tron, 1982	16,704
44	Dune, 1984	16,080
45	Live and Let Die, 1973	15,919
46	Flash Gordon, 1980	15,404
47	Planet of the Apes, 1968	15,000
48	Modern Problems, 1981	14,800
49	Blade Runner, 1982	14,800
50	Coma, 1978	14,500

Source: Variety, January 14, 1987.

many SF films, there has been a relatively large increase in the number of books devoted to them. I have restricted coverage to books whose principal subject was science fiction in film or on TV, thus excluding those that focus more on horror or fantasy films, also popular categories that are often treated with SF cinema. Film novelizations are little more than mementos of the film and rarely have any literary merit. Neither I nor the contributors to Chapters 3 and 4 judged novelizations worth annotating. The principal English-language journal devoted to fantastic cinema is *Cinefantastique* [14-30]. The indexes to the secondary literature by Hall [8-20] and Tymn and Schlobin [8-17] list many of the growing number of articles and books devoted to SF on film and TV. The Nicholls encyclopedia [8-30] provides succinct evaluations of 286 films.

Notes

1. Nicholls [11-16], p. 6.
2. From his valuable chapter, "The Tinsel Screen: Science Fiction and the Movies," in Williamson's *Teaching Science Fiction* [13-11], pp. 205–206.

Bibliography

Reference Works

*11-1. Hardy, Phil, ed. **Science Fiction [Film Encyclopedia].** Morrow, 1984. British title: *Aurum Film Encyclopedia,* Vol. 2. Aurum Press, 1984.
This second volume of a multivolume film encyclopedia describes and evaluates about 1,200 films from 1897 through 1983 from 25 countries. Annotations range from 100 to 1,000 words, depending on the film's interest or historical importance. Arrangement is chronological, with each decade introduced by a short overview. Each entry provides variant titles, studio, year of release, running time, color or black-and-white, and selected credits, including at least six leading players, plot synopsis, and critical evaluation. Silent and animated films are included. Excluded are made-for-TV films and films of the lost-world subgenre, such as *King Kong.* Six appendixes provide useful statistical information, critics' lists, lists of awards, and a bibliography. About 450 well-chosen black-and-white stills and 16 pages of color stills supplement the text. The title index, in rather small type, includes cross-references from variant titles. The annotations by Hardy and his contributors are succinct and intelligent. The most useful reference work devoted to the SF film and essential for most larger libraries. Volume 3, devoted to horror films, includes discussion of many films closely related to SF films, and a number of the same films are discussed in both volumes.

11-2. Lee, Walt. **Reference Guide to Fantastic Films: Science Fiction, Fantasy, and Horror.** 3 vols. Chelsea-Lee Books, 1972–1974.
Three sturdy 8½-by-11-inch paperbacks list over 20,000 films from more than 50 countries released since about 1900. The information is presented in title sequence, four columns per page, with cross-references from variant titles. Date of release, country of production, length, cast, credits, brief content note, source of film story, and references to reviews are among the elements shown for most ti-

tles. Almost 150 stills complement the text, as does a list of exclusions (films apparently but not actually within the scope of the book), one of "problems," and an extensive bibliography. Easily the most complete such filmography for its period.

11-3. Warren, Bill, and Bill Thomas. **Keep Watching the Skies! American Science Fiction Movies of the Fifties.** Vol. 1, 1950–1957; Vol. 2, 1958–1962. McFarland, 1982, 1986.

Warren says he's "just a movie fan," not a film scholar, which is very unfair, for his analytical skills are well developed. He was growing up when the 133 films in Volume 1 were released, and his detailed discussions go well beyond the nostalgic. Even when recognizing that most of these films were schlock, Warren is astute enough to see merit in many, and he makes a genuine contribution to film and cultural history. The 151 films in Volume 2 include some British and Japanese imports, and he notes a decline in quality in this period. The 1,300 pages in these volumes provide as definitive analyses as we're likely to get (or need) of this period. The 4-page selected bibliography stars especially recommended titles. Science fiction film fans and libraries with large film collections should consider. Compare the heavily analytical account of roughly the same period by Sobchack [11-36].

11-4. Willis, Donald. **Horror and Science Fiction Films.** Scarecrow, Vol. I, 1972; Vol. II, 1982; Vol. III, 1984.

Volume I provides an alphabetical listing by title of approximately 4,400 films, 1913–1971, giving reasonably complete production information: alternate titles, producing company, country of origin, year, length, director, story source, and so on, with a brief plot synopsis and comment. Volume II lists about 2,350 films from 16 countries, of which about half are from the 1972–1981 period, 300 are missed titles from the earlier period, 350 are revised from the first volume, and a final 500, a mixture of short, usually animated films and made-for-TV films; 750 films are designated peripheral (some fantastic elements) or problem (too little information available). A few theme entries (Bermuda Triangle, Dracula, Mummies, and so on) are in the title listing. Volume III has 760 entries from late 1981 to late 1983, titles missed, and additions to entries in earlier volumes. Critical commentary in one volume is thus sometimes separated from film credits in another. As the number of films discussed in each successive volume has decreased, the length of the annotations has greatly increased. Willis tends toward fannish criticism, not necessarily uninformed but rather parochial. Most entries include citations to film reviews, a valuable feature. Few save film buffs and very large cinema collections need consider. Hardy [11-1], while more selective, is a far better reference guide.

11-5. Willis, Donald, ed. **Variety's Complete Science Fiction Reviews.** Garland, 1986.

Reviews of approximately 1,000 films, 1907–1984, are reprinted from the pages of a standard trade journal. The sequence is by date of publication, followed by a title index. The reviewers often saw the films at foreign film festivals or studio screenings and are knowledgeable, often witty, and emphasize the films' box office potential. If the reviews lack historical perspective, their immediacy offsets this. Useful for reference and for casual browsing.

11-6. Lentz, Harris M., III, comp. **Science Fiction, Horror & Fantasy Film & Television Credits.** 2 vols. McFarland, 1983.
The compiler claims there are more than 10,000 actors, actresses, directors, producers, and makeup, special effects, costume, and other people in Volume 1, whose entries show films, year of birth and death, and name of character. Volume 2 has two alphabets, one for theatrical films, the other for made-for-TV films/series. Each entry lists title, alternate title, year of release or date of broadcast, director, and principal cast and their characters' names. A remarkably thorough compilation, especially for TV, whose specialized appeal is further limited by relatively high cost. For large reference collections.

11-7. Strickland, A. W., and Forrest J. Ackerman. **A Reference Guide to American Science Fiction Films.** Vol. 1, 1897–1929. TIS Publications, 1981.
Approximately 220 films, including serials, released from 1897 through 1929, almost all silent, are described. Year of release, producing company, silent or sound, length (in feet, usually), category (SF, SF-comedy, etc.), references (keyed to a six-page bibliography of books, magazines, and newspapers), and cast precede the largely descriptive summaries, which are sometimes accompanied by quotes from contemporary reviews. Brief overviews precede the decades, which are followed by listings by category and releasing company, with cumulative indexes and a master filmography. Approximately 25 percent of the 400 pages are full-page stills. Of some historical interest, but the 61 pages in Hardy [11-1] devoted to the same period provide international coverage (including *Metropolis*, 1926) and better critical assessments. TIS says contractual problems preclude any additional volumes.

11-8. Weldon, Michael. **The Psychotronic Encyclopedia of Film.** Ballantine, 1983.
More than 3,000 films "often treated with indifference or contempt by other guides" (and with good reason), from the 1930s to the 1980s but emphasizing the 1950s and 1960s. The uncounted hours of late-night TV viewing, which obviously constituted much of the research for this book, has not (yet) turned Weldon's brains to mush. He writes with wit and humor and an unabashed devotion to schlock, only some of which are fantastic films. Similar works include Danny Peary's *Cult Movies* (1981) and *Cult Movies 2* (1983), which together analyze 150 films, about a fourth of them fantastic. For popular collections as demand dictates.

11-9. Wingrove, David, ed. **The Science Fiction Film Source Book.** Longman, 1985.
The core of this 312-page book is the listing of approximately 1,350 films in 251 pages, each briefly described and evaluated, mostly by the editor. As with his *Science Fiction Source Book* [8-34], four elements are used for evaluation, in this case using zero to four stars for plot, technical merit, enjoyment, and artistic merit. Wingrove provides a 10-page history; a list of SF serials; about 300 brief profiles of actors, special effects specialists, cinematographers, and directors; a 6-page list

of books used for films; a short account by John Brosnan on special effects; and a bibliography. Wingrove sees more merit in many of these films than I do, overrating plodding obscurities like *Stalker*. Less expensive than but far inferior to Hardy [11-1], and not recommended.

11-10. Wright, Gene. **The Science Fiction Image: The Illustrated Encyclopedia of Science Fiction in Film, Television, Radio and the Theater.** Facts on File, 1983.
Wright claims more than 1,000 entries, with films the largest category, followed by entries for actors, actresses, directors, special effects technicians, awards, and assorted oddities like an entry for kryptonite. There are many important omissions (no mention whatever of theater, for example), blind cross-references, all suggesting extreme haste or carelessness. The black-and-white and color stills add little. Heavy on trivia and strictly for the remainder tables.

General Surveys

11-11. Baxter, John (U.K.). **Science Fiction in the Cinema.** A. S. Barnes, 1970.
An early British survey of the field, emphasizing the aesthetics of the SF film, with some attention to its social significance. The account is roughly chronological, but combines shrewd thematic analysis and a thorough knowledge of filmmaking. Baxter's scope is international and includes a now dated chapter on SF on TV. As in Brosnan [11-13], the illustrations genuinely complement the text. Notes and bibliography. The filmography of 161 titles gives principal credits and page references to the discussion in the main text. The best survey then available and still worth reading.

11-12. Benson, Michael. **Vintage Science Fiction Films, 1896–1949.** McFarland, 1985.
A choppy, anecdotal account of silents, sound films, and serials. The 53-page filmography is arranged by title, showing year, producing company, color or black-and-white, running time (or length in feet), and production and acting credits for about 400 films. Detailed name and title index. The bibliography is weak and fails to list the Strickland-Ackerman survey [11-7]. A minor work.

*****11-13.** Brosnan, John (U.K.). **Future Tense: The Cinema of Science Fiction.** Macdonald, 1978.
Brosnan is a very knowledgeable British critic who has written excellent studies of special effects in the cinema [11-26] and of the horror film industry, as well as most film entries in the Nicholls encyclopedia [8-30]. This chronological account of approximately 400 films is easily the best critical history of SF films, blending technical knowledge, lively history, personal anecdotes, and considerable wit. The illustrations, all black-and-white and usually small, genuinely illustrate. Brosnan retains a critical perspective that nicely balances intelligent appreciation and enthusiasm. Chronological summary of the principal U.S. and British television films and series, much more fully treated by Gerani and Schulman [11-27]. Name and film title index, list of references, but no bibliography.

11-14. Menville, Douglas, and R. Reginald. **Things to Come: An Illustrated History of the Science Fiction Film.** Times Books, 1977.
11-15. Menville, Douglas, and R. Reginald. **Futurevision: The New Golden Age of the Science Fiction Film.** Newcastle, 1985.
Two chronological histories, heavily illustrated with black-and-white stills. The text consists of hundreds of plot summaries with short critical comments. The 1985 book includes some made-for-TV and cable films. Both books include selected bibliographies and indexes. There is little sustained critical analysis to provide historical perspective. Brosnan [11-13], although not as current, is much preferable to these thin accounts. Strick [11-22] remains the best pictorial history.

*11-16. Nicholls, Peter. **The World of Fantastic Films: An Illustrated Survey.** Dodd Mead, 1984. British title: *Fantastic Cinema,* Ebury, 1984.
Nicholls emphasizes the post-*2001* (1968) period, although 86 of the 700 films discussed are from the 1897–1967 period. Thirteen key directors are profiled, and three chapters analyze SF, horror, and fantasy films since 1968. A 42-page filmography provides details on 700 films, some discussed only briefly in the filmography, the others more fully in the text. One to five stars denote quality, one to three skulls the squeamish factor, i.e., the amount and explicitness of violent and/or disgusting imagery. Exceptionally well organized, unusually broad coverage, and shrewd and fair analyses, sometimes dissenting from the prevailing consensus, make this the best current critical survey available.

11-17. Rovin, Jeff. **A Pictorial History of Science Fiction Films.** Citadel, 1975.
11-18. Meyers, Richard. **S-F 2: A Pictorial History of Science Fiction Films from "Rollerball" to "Return of the Jedi."** Citadel, 1984.
Rovin's first book "is an entertainment, rather than a lofty critical document. It is informal, hardly pedantic, and created solely for the enjoyment of the lay reader and interested fan," says its author. About 450 black-and-white stills overwhelm the simple-minded text. Meyers's sequel covers many U.S. and a few foreign films from the 1975–1983 period. Many plot synopses, production details, and illustrations, but little sustained analysis; no index. Not even for coffee tables.

11-19. Parish, James Robert, and Michael R. Pitts. **The Great Science Fiction Pictures.** Scarecrow, 1977.
Provides plot summaries, credits, and excerpts from reviews for about 350 "great" SF/fantasy/monster films. Irrelevant bibliography. Hardy [11-1] provides all the needed factual data and succinct appraisals, and Brosnan [11-13] provides the historical and critical context.

11-20. Pohl, Frederik, and Frederik Pohl IV. **Science Fiction Studies in Film.** Ace, 1981.
An informal account arranged chronologically from Méliès to 1979 films, with the text interspersed with quotes from many people interviewed by the authors or from printed sources, both acknowledged in chapter notes. Film credits appear in blocs adjacent to the commentary. Many black-and-white stills of little value. An appendix is devoted to the development of increasingly sophisticated special effects, which have not been paralleled by sophistication or subtlety in plot

or acting. Pohl and son are both knowledgeable and distinguish between commit-tee-designed junk "sci-fi" and more thoughtful "sf" films. Inexcusably lacking an index, which reduces its value greatly. Prefer Brosnan [11-13].

11-21. Shipman, David (U.K.). **A Pictorial History of Science Fiction Films.** Hamlyn, 1985.
A popular coffee table history, heavily illustrated, by a critic with some odd pref-erences. Coverage ranges from silents to today's films and includes some out-right fantasy. Better than several of the similar pictorial works evaluated here but much inferior to Nicholls [11-16].

11-22. Strick, Philip (U.K.). **Science Fiction Movies.** Octopus Books, 1976.
The best pictorial history by a critic very knowledgeable in both film and SF films. The oversize book's 160 pages do not permit detailed analyses of any of the more than 500 films listed in the index (few warrant such analysis), but this the-matic survey provides a useful contrast to the chronological approach taken by Brosnan [11-13]. The many stills, some in color, are well chosen and intelligently complement the text. More current coverage is provided by Nicholls [11-16].

Other Studies

11-23. Adler, Alan, ed. **Science Fiction and Horror Movie Posters in Full Color.** Dover, 1977.
This is the only book reproducing film posters reasonably close to their original size. Here are 44 from the 1950s to 1973, each with a brief, intelligent annota-tion. Deliberately garish and eye-catching, they are sometimes better than the films they promote.

11-24. Agel, Jerome, ed. **The Making of Kubrick's 2001.** Signet, 1970.
A thick paperback containing Arthur C. Clarke's original source story, "The Sen-tinel," articles about and reviews of the film, interviews with Kubrick and others, production details, and a 96-page photo insert. A multifaceted look at what may be the most ambitious SF film ever attempted, and one of the best. Clarke's screenplay was published as *2001: A Space Odyssey* [4-140], and his later account of the film appeared as *The Lost Worlds of "2001"* (Signet, 1972). Carolyn Geduld's *Filmguide to "2001: A Space Odyssey"* (Indiana Univ. Press, 1973) is an 87-page guide designed for classroom use, placing Kubrick's films in perspective and providing a reading list for further examination of this major film.

11-25. Anderson, Craig W. **Science Fiction Films of the Seventies.** McFarland, 1985.
Derived from fanzines, this long-winded, ineptly written account discusses 50 films, all save one (*Solaris*) British or American. Heavy on plot synopses, thin on analysis or insight. The preface refers to a nonexistent bibliography. A very weak title from a publisher whose books on film are usually praiseworthy.

11-26. Finch, Christopher. **Special Effects: Creating Movie Magic.** Abbeville Press, 1984.
Tracing the history of cinematic special effects from the 1890s, Finch devotes chapters to *King Kong, Star Wars, 2001,* and other SF films, a chapter to TV com-

mercials, with briefer mention of special effects in nonfantastic cinema. Half the book explains the complex techniques now used in special effects, with three chapters devoted to computer graphics. Many color and some black-and-white stills. The entire oversize book is printed on expensive coated stock, making it somewhat pricey for libraries. Much more reasonably priced is John Brosnan's *Movie Magic* (1974). *Cinefex* [14-31] is devoted exclusively to special effects. Many additional books, from popular to technical, treat special effects, whose use is most prominent in fantastic cinema.

11-27. Gerani, Gary, and Paul H. Schulman. **Fantastic Television.** Harmony, 1977.
A useful survey of all types of "fantastic" programs on American TV, although British TV programs are briefly discussed. The coverage ranges from 1949 to 1976 programs and is knowledgeable and balanced. Each of 13 major series receives a chapter (introduction plus a summary of each episode, including credits), followed by briefer discussion of 65 American and 14 British lesser series, children's shows, and made-for-TV films. Lentz [11-6] provides more current and more complete information.

11-28. Harryhausen, Ray. **Film Fantasy Scrapbook.** 3rd ed., rev. & enl. A. S. Barnes, 1981.
A minor revision of the 1972 and 1974 editions, adding a 16-page color insert devoted to *Clash of the Titans*, a 1981 film, suggesting a book/film tie-in. The aptly named scrapbook contains preproduction drawings, enlarged frames, publicity stills, and film posters from Harryhausen's puppet shorts from the 1940s to 1981. The black-and-white photos are poorly reproduced, and Harryhausen's commentary is surprisingly uninformative and rather dull. He was a pioneer in stop-motion animation, but special effects have become immensely more sophisticated in recent years, making this fragmented account of historical interest only.

11-29. Hickman, Gail Morgan. **The Films of George Pal.** A. S. Barnes, 1977.
A fan's uncritical account of Pal's career, beginning with his Puppetoons in the 1940s. A chapter is devoted to each of 14 feature SF and fantasy films, from *The Great Rupert* (1949) through *Doc Savage* (1975), the last released five years before Pal's death. Pal is better known for his special effects than for the quality of acting or scripts of his films and was one of the best-known directors specializing in fantastic cinema.

11-30. Johnson, William, ed. **Focus on the Science Fiction Film.** Prentice-Hall, 1972.
Essays by and interviews of American, British, and European critics about the origin and development of the SF film, its relation to other kinds of film and to SF writing, and its aesthetic value. A number of individual films are also discussed. The essays, in four chronological periods, span the years 1895 to 1970 and include pieces by Wells, Clarke, and Heinlein, but the most valuable essays are by European critics. Chronology showing scientific developments in SF writing and films, filmography, briefly annotated bibliography, index. Especially valuable for its breadth of coverage and one of the best collections of SF film criticism. Compare Peary [11-33].

11-31. Larson, Randall D. **Musique Fantastique: A Survey of Film Music in the Fantastic Cinema.** Scarecrow, 1985.
A massive study by the editor of *CinemaScore* covering about 55 years of film music. Individual chapters discuss John Williams, Bernard Herrmann, Miklos Rozsa, and Jerry Goldsmith. Others provide chronological or thematic surveys. Considerable material was derived from interviews. The filmography is arranged by composer (more than 1,300 of them), the discography by film title. The index includes only composers and musical titles in the narrative chapters. No musical examples are given; Larson attempts by text alone to characterize the music, a difficult task. A valuable study of a meagerly treated topic, although mainly for the specialist and large film collection. There are some entries devoted to music in Sullivan's encyclopedia [8-50].

11-32. Lofficier, Jean-Marc. **The Doctor Who Programme Guide.** 2 vols. W. H. Allen, 1981.
Compiled with the assistance of the BBC's "Doctor Who" production office and a fan club, this provides details on all the stories from November 1963, when the series began, through March 1981, covering adventures of the first four doctors. Volume 1 contains plot synopses and cast/technical credits; Volume 2 lists characters, species, and places, referenced to specific shows, and other information. A useful compilation for fans of a TV series that rivals "Star Trek" in popularity and to which many books have been devoted.

11-33. Peary, Danny, ed. **Omni's Screen Flights/Screen Fantasies: The Future according to Science Fiction Cinema.** Doubleday, 1984.
The original essays are in three parts. The first features more general pieces. The second deals with individual films such as *Metropolis, Things to Come, THX 1138,* and *Soylent Green,* the pieces by both SF writers and film critics. Part three provides mostly interviews, some by Peary, of figures like George Miller (*Road Warrior*) and Kubrick. A checklist includes about a thousand films. The editor should have caught some careless errors in this sampling, which is much better than uncritical fan works and more accessible than the heavier academic studies. Compare the collections by Johnson [11-30] and Slusser and Rabkin [11-35].

11-34. Schow, David J., and Jeffrey Frentzen. **The Outer Limits: The Official Companion.** Ace, 1986.
One of the more popular TV shows among SF fans was "The Outer Limits," whose 49 episodes, originally broadcast 1963–1965, are still in syndication. Many skilled actors, directors, and writers contributed their talents. The authors are enthusiastic but genuinely critical and provide ample detail about each episode, with extensive quotes from the show's participants. The many illustrations are small and poorly reproduced. *Fantastic Television* [11-27] devotes four pages, photos plus episode summaries and credits, to this series, which is oriented far more toward SF than is *The Twilight Zone.* (Annotation based on review by Michael Klossner.)

11-35. Slusser, George Edgar, and Eric S. Rabkin, eds. **Shadows of the Magic Lamp: Fantasy and Science Fiction in Film.** Southern Illinois, 1985.
Each Eaton conference is devoted to a single topic, and the 14 papers here are

from the fourth (1982) conference. They include those dealing with genre questions, distinctions between SF and horror films, special effects (a particularly good piece), bleak visions of the future, political ideology and sexual politics in SF cinema, and other topics. In spite of an occasional overdose of jargon, the general level is high, and libraries with larger cinema collections should consider carefully.

11-36. Sobchack, Vivian. **Screening Space: The American Science Fiction Film.** Ungar, 1986.

Originally published as *The Limits of Infinity: The American Science Fiction Film 1950–75* (A. S. Barnes, 1980), this retitled edition adds a new preface, an 83-page fourth chapter, and an updated, selective bibliography. The initial chapter attempts to define the essential elements of SF films, showing how the creature in SF films is distinct from the monster in horror films—"Ultimately the horror film evokes fear, the SF film interest." The long second chapter analyzes how the content and presentation of specifically visual images make the SF film uniquely itself. Familiar icons such as the alien are examined, as is the "visual subversion of the familiar" (as in films like *Invasion of the Body Snatchers*). The third chapter treats uses of dialogue in SF films, music, and sound effects. This original material repays the close attention required for full comprehension and provides analytic insights into SF cinema. The new chapter borrows heavily from a left-wing essay by Fredric Jameson and is crippled by a jargon that overwhelms the reader and will limit the audience to academic film genre critics. The enlarged edition is little improvement.

11-37. Titelman, Carol, ed. **The Art of Star Wars.** Ballantine, 1979.

Of the uncounted spin-offs from *Star Wars,* this is more substantial and valuable than most. The complete shooting script is illustrated by hundreds of sketches, storyboards, production and matte paintings, and photographs, all of which illustrate the film's enormous technical complexity. The poster art used for publicity is reproduced, as are cartoons and children's drawings based on the film. Subsequent similar volumes include *The Art of the Empire Strikes Back,* text by Vic Bulluck and Valerie Hoffman, edited by Deborah Call (Ballantine, 1980), and *The Art of Return of the Jedi* (Ballantine, 1983), which includes the complete filmscript. Expensive mementos for fans, but of possible value to libraries collecting intensively in modern cinema.

11-38. Trimble, Bjo. **On the Good Ship Enterprise: My Fifteen Years with Star Trek.** Donning, 1983.

11-39. Gerrold, David. **The World of Star Trek.** Rev. ed. Bluejay, 1984.

Trimble provides an autobiographical reminiscence of her relationship with the cast, the TV shows, the films, and the fans. Heavily anecdotal, but useful to the historian of one of the most popular TV series. Trimble also wrote *The Star Trek Concordance* (Ballantine, 1976), which provided plot summaries of all episodes, a dictionary of characters, locations, special terms, etc. Gerrold revised his 1973 edition using footnotes, new text, and many new photos. The original ideas, the people involved, the development of the fan cult, and the theatrical films are all discussed. He wrote "Star Trek" episodes and other TV fare, and this account is mostly for fans.

11-40. Von Gunden, Kenneth, and Stuart H. Stock. **Twenty All-Time Great Science Fiction Films.** Arlington House, 1982.

An unpromising title for a book that transcends the coffee table category. All films are American or British and, except for *Things to Come* (1936), were released between 1950 and 1971 (why they stopped in 1971 is not explained). The detailed plot synopses are supplemented by production details, information about the filmmakers and cast, discussion of SF themes, and of course many black-and-white illustrations, including design sketches. The commentary is sensible if not especially penetrating, and the selections predictable. Compare the more exhaustive analyses by Warren and Thomas [11-3].

11-41. Zicree, Marc Scott. **The Twilight Zone Companion.** Bantam, 1982.

From 1959 through 1964, 151 episodes of "The Twilight Zone" were telecast and are still seen in syndication. Many of them qualify rather loosely as SF. Profiles of anecdotes about Rod Serling (1924–1975) and other writers and producers, detailed episode summaries, more than 200 photos, with an index to episodes and key writers and producers. Zicree honestly states the deficiencies as well as the achievements of the series, which was followed by "Night Gallery." Most libraries would find the summary chapter in Gerani and Schulman [11-27] adequate. Lentz [11-6] lists casts only.

12
Science Fiction Illustration

Neil Barron

Illustration is an integral and significant part of the field of science fiction. Just as the writer must use words to suggest and accustom us to worlds or beings outside ordinary human experience, so the illustrator provides a pictorial frame of reference, often intensifying strangeness to provoke wonder or awe.

The familiar icons of SF, such as spaceships, tentacled aliens, and futuristic hardware, have adorned SF magazines and books for decades. The content is shaped more by the need for newsstand and bookstore sales and fictional conventions than by the traditions of fine art, although European illustration is markedly different from its Anglo-American counterpart. Because of this, the term *illustration* rather than *art* is used, since the usual intent is to suggest a scene or the general nature of a story. Some SF writers have written stories based on the cover illustration, reversing the usual sequence. Although today's SF illustration is perhaps more technically proficient than that on the covers of pulps from the 1930s, its basic purpose remains unchanged.

Until recent years the illustrators sold all rights to their work and rarely even had their originals returned, so many of the early originals were lost, often discarded by publishers. Although these illustrations are popular with private collectors and often sold at conventions, established museums have usually ignored such work, perhaps judging it commercial hack work of no "serious" artistic merit (but see Chapter 15 for holdings by libraries and private collectors).

Recognition has come mostly from within the field, most commonly in the form of the Hugo to the best professional artist awarded each year at the "world"

Table 12-1 Hugo Professional Artist Winners
and Nominees, 1955–1986

Illustrator	Winners × 2 +	Nominations	= Rank
Frank Kelly Freas, 1922–	10	11	31
Michael Whelan, 1950–	7	2	16
Jack Gaughan, 1930–1985	2	8	12
John Schoenherr, 1935–	1	10	12
Vincent Di Fate, 1945–	1	10	12
Ed Emshwiller (Emsh), 1925–	3	5	11
Virgil Finlay, 1914–1971	1	6	8
Stephen E. Fabian, 1930–	0	7	7
Rick Sternbach, 1951–	2	3	7
Frank Frazetta, 1928–	1	4	6
Don Maitz, 1953–	0	5	5
Rowena Morrill, 1944–	0	5	5
Leo and Diane Dillon, both 1933–	1	2	4
Barclay Shaw, 1949–	0	4	4
Mel Hunter, 1929–	0	3	3
Roy Krenkel, 1918–	1	1	3
Gray Morrow, 1934–	0	3	3
Jeff Jones, 1944	0	3	3
Boris Vallejo (Boris), 1941–	0	3	3
Wally Wood, 1927–1981	0	2	2
Hannes Bok, 1914–1964	1	0	2
Vaughn Bode	0	2	2
Eddie Jones, 1935–	0	2	2
George Barr, 1937–	0	2	2
Paul Lehr, 1930–	0	2	2
Val Lakey Lindahn	0	2	2
H. R. Van Dongen	0	2	2
Alex Schomburg, 1905–	0	1	1
Chesley Bonestell, 1888–1986	0	1	1
Mike Hinge	0	1	1
Tim Kirk, 1947–	0	1	1
David Hardy, 1936–	0	1	1
Alicia Austin, 1942–	0	1	1
Carl Lundgren, 1947–	0	1	1
Darrell Sweet	0	1	1
Tom Kidd, 1955–	0	1	1

SF convention. Work by many of the illustrators listed in Table 12-1 is found in the annotated books, although few illustrators have had books devoted solely to their work. Because the fans who vote the award often do not see British or European illustration, the individuals listed are mostly American. (My thanks to Bob Weinberg for providing birth and death dates for some of the illustrators [some dates were unavailable], approximately 375 of whom will be profiled in his *Biographical Dictionary of Science Fiction and Fantasy Artists,* forthcoming from Greenwood Press.)

The books annotated here suggest the range of Anglo-American SF and fantasy illustration. The distinctions between SF and fantasy are even more blurred in illustration than in fiction, and many illustrators, like many writers, work in both fields. The work of foreign illustrators is largely absent in these books. See the foreign-language chapters, especially Wilfert's *Tor zu den Sternen* [6-49], and the surveys by Rottensteiner [9-86] and Lundwall [9-55]. Many other books are extensively illustrated, such as Gunn [9-41], Holdstock [9-45], and Kyle [9-49, 9-50]. A useful, brief illustrated survey is provided by Vincent Di Fate in his chapter "Science Fiction Art: Some Contemporary Illustrators" in Tymn's *Science Fiction Reference Book* [8-33]. Gary K. Wolfe perceptively discusses "The Iconography of Science-Fiction Art" in Volume 2 of Cowart and Wymer [8-28]. He is especially valuable in tracing the changes in SF illustration resulting from changes in the market, and his selection of illustrations makes his points well.

Excluded from this chapter are books devoted to comic art, a world all its own, and traditional artists of the fantastic, such as Bosch or Rackham. Unlike traditional "fine" art books, few of the annotated titles below include size of original, medium, or present location.

Bibliography

*12-1. Aldiss, Brian W. (U.K.). **Science Fiction Art.** Crown, 1975.
An oversized (10½ by 14¾ inches) 128-page paperback, which presents the work of 30 American and British SF magazine illustrators from the 1920s to the 1970s, showing, describing, and contrasting their individual techniques and strengths. Their work is seen further in short chapters dealing with common themes—catastrophes, machines, robots, spaceships, and so on. A magazine gallery of 79 titles with covers in color and black-and-white provides a useful sampling. Index of artists and magazines. Garish and repetitive though they are, the illustrations, Aldiss argues, stimulated youthful readers as much as did the text. An excellent survey, but possibly awkward for libraries because of its size. Compare Frewin [12-18], whose historical scope is broader, and the more anecdotal work of Sadoul [12-30]. See also Adler's collection of film posters [11-23].

*12-2. Barlowe, Wayne Douglas, and Ian Summers. **Barlowe's Guide to Extraterrestrials.** Workman, 1979.
Barlowe is the Audubon for aliens. These color drawings are meticulous and lovingly rendered, and are carefully derived from a wide variety of stories, such as the Puppeteers from Niven's *Ringworld* [4-392] or the likable Mesklinites from Clement's *Mission of Gravity* [3-109]. The text describes the physical characteristics, habitat, culture, and reproductive systems of 50 aliens. Compare Holdstock and Edwards [12-23] for a similar account of fictional worlds. HN, L, 1980.

12-3. Barr, George. **Upon the Winds of Yesterday and Other Explorations.** Donald Grant, 1976.
Barr began as a commercial illustrator in Utah, had work published in fanzines,

and won the 1968 Hugo for best fan artist. His professional SF work was first published in the early 1960s, and he has had much work published since. More than 50 pieces are reproduced on glossy stock, a number of them first published here. Most are ballpoint pen and watercolor, a technique explained by Stuart Schiff in his introduction. Barr's illustrations favor fantasy more than SF and tend toward whimsy.

12-4. Bova, Ben. **Vision of the Future: The Art of Robert McCall.** Abrams, 1982.
McCall (1919–   ) has had his work published in popular magazines for many years, with aviation and aerospace almost his sole subjects. His work is in the Johnson Space Center and the National Air and Space Museum. Included here are sketches, rough drafts, watercolors, oils, and acrylics. Bova is a long-time space booster and contributes a laudatory text. Resolutely high tech, his work lacks any sense of the mystery found in the work collected in *Space Art* [12-26].

12-5. Burns, Jim (U.K.). **Lightship.** Text by Chris Evans. Paper Tiger, 1986.
Welsh-born Burns (1948–   ) uses an airbrush with great flair. This book collects 125 color and nine black-and-white illustrations, many used as covers for British and American books. His subjects are varied and include people, androids, and machines, all lovingly rendered in vivid color and careful detail. He extensively illustrated the odd novel by Harry Harrison, *Planet Story* (Pierrot, 1979).

12-6. Cartier, Edd. **Edd Cartier: The Known and the Unknown.** Gerry de la Ree, 1977.
One of the most popular illustrators for *Unknown* and *Astounding* in the 1940s and early 1950s was Cartier, whose work with brush and lithographic pencil is immediately recognizable. Much of his work has a whimsical quality, and he was especially skilled at depicting gnomes and aliens. This is one of de la Ree's out-of-print series of limited editions devoted mostly to fantasy artists such as Finlay and Fabian.

12-7. Dean, Martyn, ed. (U.K.). **The Guide to Fantasy Art Techniques.** Paper Tiger, 1984.
Not a how-to book, as the title suggests, but interviews with eight American and British fantasy illustrators, including Boris Vallejo, Syd Mead, Jim Burns, Chris Foss, and Patrick Woodroffe. Their lives, ideas, and attitudes are clearly brought out by Dean's interviews, effectively rewritten by Chris Evans. More than 100 color and 23 black-and-white illustrations.

12-8. Dean, Roger (U.K.). **Views.** Dragon's Dream, 1975.
12-9. Dean, Roger, and Martyn Dean (U.K.). **Magnetic Storm.** Paper Tiger, 1984.
Dean's work in a variety of media is showcased here. *Views* shows his varied interests and methods, and the reproductions range from preliminary sketches to finished work. Book and record jackets, architectural and stage designs, are among the types of work shown, with the emphasis more on fantasy than SF. The text is by Dominy Hamilton and Carl Capalbo. *Magnetic Storm* shows the work of the brothers during the past decade in architecture, film, TV, album covers, posters, and even video games. The interesting text is by Colin Greenland.

12-10. Di Fate, Vincent, and Ian Summers. **Di Fate's Catalog of Science Fiction Hardware.** Workman, 1980.
Di Fate works in the tradition of Frank R. Paul (1884–1963), whose work was featured in the pulps from the 1920s on and who was the guest of honor at the first world SF convention in 1939. Human figures are depicted infrequently and usually as accessories to the dominant machine. Approximately 50 works from the 1974–1980 period are reproduced here, along with engineering drawings, grouped by subject (transportation, environments, weapons, etc.). Compare the similar work by Robert McCall [12-4]; contrast the colorful airbrushed work of British illustrators like Chris Foss [12-14]. HW, 1981.

12-11. Dixon, Dougal (U.K.). **After Man: A Zoology of the Future.** St. Martin's, 1981.
A paleogeologist specializing in evolution plausibly speculates on probable fauna 50 million years hence, when plate tectonic movement has fused Eurasia, Australia, and North America and turned South America into an island. The text is careful, the speculation linked to known and probable principles of animal evolution. The author's sketches have been turned into beautiful color renderings by six British illustrators, each animal species given its Latin name. An imaginative tour de force of value to any library's biology collection. Compare Barlowe's creatures [12-2].

*12-12. Durant, Frederick, III, and Ron Miller. **Worlds Beyond: The Art of Chesley Bonestell.** Donning, 1983.
Bonestell (1888–1986) was the dean of astronomical artists, his paintings having a remarkable photographic realism. His first book, *The Conquest of Space* (1949), collected 48 paintings. Some are repeated here, along with landscapes, seascapes, and many other quasi-photographic paintings that originally appeared in *Life* and other magazines. He has painted murals for the Boston Museum of Science and the Flandrau planetarium of the University of Arizona. He has received various awards but none from traditional fine art museums. Selections from his work and from many others working in astronomical art are collected in *Space Art* [12-26].

12-13. Elson, Peter, and Chris Moore (U.K.). **Parallel Lines: The Science Fiction Illustrations of Peter Elson & Chris Moore.** Dragon's Dream, 1981.
Two British illustrators working in the tradition of Chris Foss [12-14], largely limited to space hardware. Pat Vincent's introduction suggests Elson is the more romantic of the two, but I found their work almost indistinguishable. Many similar books emphasizing space hardware have been published in the past few years, almost all designed as instant remainders and largely interchangeable.

*12-14. Foss, Chris (U.K.). **21st Century Foss.** Dragon's Dream, 1978.
12-15. Foss, Chris (U.K.). **Science Fiction Art.** Text by Brian Aldiss. Hart-Davis, 1976.
21st Century Foss provides an extensive selection of work by one of the most popular British artists, who has done production sketches for films, such as *Dune, Superman,* and *Alien.* His colorful space vehicles and other machines—humans rarely appear—have influenced the work of many contemporary British illustrators. Most work reproduced here appeared on the covers of British books, which

are identified. The 1976 collection has ten 11-by-18-inch plates. Both celebrate a hurtling high tech world.

12-16. Frazetta, Frank. **The Fantastic Art of Frank Frazetta.** 1975. **Frank Frazetta, Books 2–5.** Peacock Press, 1977, 1978, 1980, 1985.

These books collect Frazetta's work over many years, from his 20 years illustrating comic books and comic strips beginning in the 1940s, to Tarzan books in the 1960s. He is perhaps best known for his paperback covers for Robert E. Howard's Conan novels. Many illustrations, from doodlings to finished work, reflect all these periods. His muscular heroes and top-heavy, wide-hipped, often subjugated women are unabashedly melodramatic. His paintings lack the lushness and gloss of Vallejo's but are more vigorous and varied.

*12-17. Freas, Frank Kelly. **The Art of Science Fiction.** Donning, 1977.
12-17A. Freas, Frank Kelly. **A Separate Star.** Greenswamp, 1984.

Probably the best known of all SF illustrators is Freas, winner of ten Hugos. His initial work appeared in the early 1950s in the magazines—notably *Analog*—and has been featured extensively since in magazines and paperbacks. People are the center of his art, in contrast to the hardware emphasis of other illustrators. His anecdotal text clearly explains the development of each illustration. The self-published *Separate Star* collects more recent work, from preliminary sketches to finished work. His commentary might be useful to aspiring illustrators.

12-18. Frewin, Anthony (U.K.). **One Hundred Years of SF Illustration, 1840–1940.** Pyramid, 1975.

Because the early pulps are seldom seen today, this work provides a useful survey of SF illustration. The fascinating work of Grandville and Robida, two prolific nineteenth-century French artists, begins the book, followed by selected illustrations from editions of Verne and Wells. The emphasis is on illustrations in the SF pulps from the 1920s and 1930s—Frank R. Paul, Eliot Dold, and others known only to aficionados. Over 40 covers are reproduced in color, some full size, some reduced. All illustrations have captions, and the remaining text, while succinct, is intelligent and helpful, putting SF illustration in a wider historical context. A very good introduction to the early years of SF illustration. Not quite the equal of the Aldiss survey [12-1], but preferable to Sadoul [12-30].

12-19. Giger, H. R. **H. R. Giger's Necronomicon.** Big O, 1978.
12-20. Giger, H. R. **H. R. Giger's Necronomicon 2.** Editions C, 1985.

Giger (1940–   ) is a Swiss artist and illustrator who achieved prominence with his set designs for the 1979 film *Alien,* for which he and others won an Oscar for visual effects. The autobiographical account in the 1978 volume reveals a preoccupation with death, the fantastic, and the morbid, evident in all his work. He strikingly juxtaposes or blends the human figure with mechanical structures to create biomechanoid images of great power, in which a decadent eroticism is prevalent. The 1985 collection is more of the same, unsettling and visceral in its impact. Giger is one of the more important artists working in nongenre fantastic art, and libraries with large art collections should consider one of his oversized collections.

12-21. Gustafson, Jon. **Chroma: The Art of Alex Schomburg.** Father Tree Press (5 Reno Rd., Poughkeepsie, NY 12603), 1986.
Schomberg (1905–) is one of the oldest illustrators still active in SF and worked for, corresponded with, and dealt with Hugo Gernsback for almost 40 years, from the 1920s to the 1950s. His airbrushed work appeared on the covers of many pulps in the 1950s and 1960s as well as in comics, notably the Marvel line. Appreciations by Harlan Ellison, Stan Lee, Vincent Di Fate, Brian Aldiss, George Barr, and Frank Kelly Freas. Schomburg has received various awards but not a Hugo, for which he was nominated in 1962.

12-22. Hildebrandt, Greg, and Tim Hildebrandt. **The Art of the Brothers Hildebrandt.** Text by Ian Summers. Ballantine, 1978.
Best known for their Tolkien calendars, many images from which are reproduced here, and a *Star Wars* poster. They have also illustrated many fantasy and some SF works, including their own illustrated novel, *Ushurak* (Bantam, 1979). Some of their most interesting work in this collection is unpublished. Greg Hildebrandt's *From Tolkien to Oz* (Unicorn, 1985) is almost entirely fantasy.

12-23. Holdstock, Robert, and Malcolm Edwards (U.K.). **Alien Landscapes.** Mayflower, 1979.
A variety of British artists have illustrated ten fictional worlds, from Clarke's Rama to Herbert's Arrakis to McCaffrey's Pern. A pseudoencyclopedic text accompanies the pictures, which are large and colorful but far less credible than the detailed exactness of Barlowe's work [12-2]. Wingrove [12-38] is a companion.

12-24. Lehmkuhl, Donald (U.K.). **The Flights of Icarus.** Martyn Dean and Roger Dean, eds. Dragon's World, 1977.
This oversize compilation features the work of 32 illustrators, mostly young Britons, much of which appeared on book covers and record jackets. The text is minimal and banal. The Holdstock and Edwards survey [12-23] includes a wider range of illustrators and emphasizes SF rather than fantasy, and has useful essays as well. Similar to but not nearly as good as the Summers compilation [12-32].

12-25. Mathews, Rodney (U.K.). **In Search of Forever.** Paper Tiger, 1985.
Born in 1945, Mathews early developed an interest in nature and still prefers drawing animals—often very fantastic animals—to people. Some of his work has a playful quality. It has been featured in several calendars and on many posters, and has illustrated many works of Michael Moorcock. He uses various media— ink, ink and gouache, and watercolor—for his books, LP jackets and posters, logos and alphabets. The text by Mathews and Nigel Suckling provides interesting details about Mathew's work, which heavily favors the fantastic, with typical SF icons uncommon.

12-26. Miller, Ron, comp. **Space Art.** Starlog Magazine, 1978.
The former art director of the Smithsonian's National Air and Space Museum provides a comprehensive collection of astronomical art from the nineteenth century to the present, featuring the work of about 60 artists. The work is semiphotographic in most cases, but the best pieces share the same central concern as traditional religious art—mystery. As landscape and religious paintings are recog-

nized genres, so space art in a secular age may take its place. See also the collection of Bonestell's work [12-12].

12-27. Morrill, Rowena. **The Fantastic Art of Rowena.** Pocket Books, 1983.
Morrill's vivid oil paintings have appeared on many books, mostly mass market fantasy paperback covers, and 26 are reproduced here in color without overprinting, with brief text on the facing page. She describes her meticulous techniques, and the evolution of one painting from same-size drawing to finished work is shown. Her work resembles that of Vallejo, who contributed an introduction, but is more varied if not as popular. HN, 1984.

12-28. Perret, Patti. **The Faces of Science Fiction.** Bluejay, 1984.
Because of the close relationship between fans and SF writers, a work like this was probably inevitable. Eighty-five writers, well and lesser known, are the subjects, with usually banal comments on the facing page. The wittiest photo is of Tom Disch, but most photos are undistinguished and rarely reveal character. Gunn's *Alternate Worlds* [9-41] has several hundred postage-stamp-size photos. HN, 1985.

12-29. Powers, Richard. **Spacetimewarp.** Nelson Doubleday, 1983.
This portfolio of 16 loose plates, 13 of them book covers, was a premium of the SF Book Club. Powers has illustrated hundreds of books in many fields but, perhaps because of the variety of his work, has never received great acclaim for his paintings in the SF/fantasy fields. These plates, about 11 by 14 inches, showcase his talents well. His images tend toward the abstract/surrealistic, unlike the hard-edge photographic realism favored by many SF illustrators.

12-30. Sadoul, Jacques (France). **2000 A.D.: Illustration from the Golden Age of Science Fiction Pulps.** Regnery, 1975. Tr. of *Hier, l'an 2000,* 1973.
This affectionate study clearly reproduces several hundred black-and-white interior illustrations as well as many covers in full color, all with artist and issue indicated, from the 1926–1953 pulps. All the names familiar to fans and collectors are here. The illustrations are grouped in eight theme chapters, each introduced by a brief commentary. Frewin [12-18], although his coverage stops at 1940, has better-quality illustrations, more in color, and a livelier text. Much less satisfactory is Lester del Rey's *Fantastic Science-Fiction Art, 1926–1954* (Ballantine, 1975), which reproduces 40 pulp covers in color, 18 by Frank Paul, an imbalance not helped by a routine eight-page introduction.

12-31. [Sherwin, Mary; Ellen Asher, and Joe Miller, eds.] **The New Visions: A Collection of Modern Science Fiction Art.** Doubleday, 1982.
Reproduces jacket paintings commissioned for SF Book Club editions: 46 images without the overprinted text, by 23 contemporary illustrators, who provide brief biographical notes often linked to the specific painting reproduced, which is always identified by the author and title of the book.

*12-32. Summers, Ian, ed. **Tomorrow and Beyond: Masterpieces of Science Fiction Art.** Workman, 1978.
The former art director of Ballantine has assembled over 300 color reproductions from 67 primarily American illustrators. Much of the work depicted ap-

peared on mass market paperback covers of the 1970s, as well as on LP jackets, in articles, and the like. No biographical information on the illustrators, nor are media and size of original shown. Yet the survey is a broad one and valuable for larger collections devoted to contemporary book illustration.

12-33. Thole, Karel. **Visionen des Unwirklichen: Die phantastischen Bilder des Karel Thole.** Munich: Wilhelm Heyne Verlag, 1982.
Published under license from Mondadari, the Italian publisher, this large paperback collects 77 color covers from the last 20 years of C.A.M. ("Karel") Thole (1914–), born in the Netherlands and a resident of Italy since 1958. Trained in poster and book jacket illustration, he came to SF illustration by chance. His paintings are usually symbolic rather than literal and display an excellent sense of design. Rejecting the acrylics and airbrushes of many illustrators, he works with an opaque, casein-based tempera, giving a subdued but precise look to his pictures, which are rarely seen outside Europe. (Annotation based on review by Helmut Pesch in *Science Fiction & Fantasy Book Review* 12 [March 1983].)

12-34. Vallejo, Boris. **The Fantastic Art of Boris Vallejo.** Ballantine, 1978.
12-35. Vallejo, Boris. **Mirage.** Ballantine, 1982.
12-36. Vallejo, Boris. **Fantasy Art Techniques.** Dragon's Dream, 1985.
Peruvian-born Boris, as he signs his paintings, is one of the more popular illustrators (a three time nominee), especially in the field of heroic fantasy/sword and sorcery. His first collection includes 40 color plates, along with early paintings, pen-and-ink drawings, and cartoons. *Mirage* assembles 11 black-and-white drawings with commentary by Boris, and 29 color plates with bad poetry by his wife, Doris, on the facing page. The techniques volume, while nominally aimed at would-be art students, collects many examples of Vallejo's work, preliminary sketches, Polaroid photos of models, and finished paintings. His figures are carefully posed and relatively static (compare the vigor of Frazetta), the men are almost impossibly muscled, the women almost caricatures, heavy breasted, slim waisted, and clones of one another.

*12-37. Whelan, Michael. **Wonderworks: Science Fiction and Fantasy Art.** Polly Freas and Kelly Freas, eds. Donning, 1979.
Whelan (1950–) is one of the best of today's illustrators, and this retrospective compilation reproduces both working sketches and the finished art, usually much larger than the American paperback covers it adorned. Comments by six writers whose work he illustrated praise his skill in capturing key aspects of their works. HN, 1980.

12-38. Wingrove, David (U.K.). **The Immortals of Science Fiction.** Pierrot, 1980.
Wingrove's mock-encyclopedic text discusses the central characters from the works of ten authors, such as Susan Calvin in Asimov's robot tales [3-20], Slippery Jim Digriz in Harrison's Stainless Steel Rat series [3-193], and others. The British illustrators are identified only as Young Artists. Colorful, little more. Intended as a companion to *Alien Landscapes* [12-23].

12-39. Woodroffe, Patrick (U.K.). **Mythopoeikon: Fantasies, Monsters, Daydreams.** Dragon's World, 1976.

Born in Yorkshire in 1940, Woodroffe has developed a variety of techniques to explore his extremely imaginative and varied worlds. He is skilled in the use of pen and ink, oils, acrylic gouache, and crayon, and many published and unpublished examples of his work are included, from book covers to record jackets. *A Closer Look* (Dragon's Dream, 1986) is an extensively illustrated book that explores his many techniques.

13
Teaching Materials

Muriel Rogow Becker

In 1970, the Science Fiction Research Association (SFRA) was organized "to improve classroom teaching; to encourage and assist scholarship; and to evaluate and publicize new books, teaching methods and materials." In that spirit, this chapter has been designed. Retained from the eight "better or typical" teaching aids in the 1976 edition of *Anatomy of Wonder* are two teacher's guides, a writing guide, and a film series. Continued from the 1981 edition are an additional three teacher's guides, six text-anthologies, four writing guides, and eight classroom aids. The original plan was to annotate only material currently for sale or rent since the general rule with texts and audiovisual (AV) materials is that once the item is out of print, it is rarely reprinted. My work for this chapter, however, revealed that AV materials and writing guides have had longer lives than text-anthologies or teaching guides. Thus, while all items in the classroom aids section are available, a few primary out-of-print distinctive entries are annotated and included in the core collection: three instructional guides [13-2, 13-2A, and 13-10], three writing guides [13-13, 13-16, and 13-20], and three classroom texts [13-22, 13-37, and 13-38]. If necessary, it is worth the effort to obtain these through interlibrary loan systems. Accessibility of teaching materials has been a constant problem for instructors organizing courses in modern science fiction because faculty frequently assign supplemental readings from paperback novels, many of which are not kept in stock in bookstores. Chapter 7 provides the names and addresses of specialty SF booksellers from whom class sets may be purchased when normal ordering patterns fail.

Exclusive of the myriad sound recordings, the 53 entries in this chapter refer to over 100 book and nonbook educational items, keyed to the applicable grade level: E, elementary; M, middle school; J, junior high; S, high school; C, college; and A, adult reader.

The first section, Instructional Guides, annotates works addressed primarily to elementary, secondary, and college teachers organizing units and courses in SF. Although there is no specific methodology text, both beginning and experienced teachers should find material suitable for application to classroom practice. For all educational levels, there are works that suggest general approaches to SF, promote specific themes, provide analyses of well-known novels, offer suggestions for primary and supplementary reading, detail activities and units, address pedagogical problems, explain the science undergirding SF, and report a variety of experience in teaching. Other chapters, although not designed with the teacher in mind, suggest titles for creating a basic desk collection. In addition to this volume, an instructor could shelve for ready reference Peter Nicholls's *The Science Fiction Encyclopedia* [8-30], Gene Wright's *The Science Fiction Image* [11-10], Brian Aldiss's *Trillion Year Spree* [9-4], James Gunn's *Alternate Worlds* [9-41], Jacques Sadoul's *2000 A.D.* [12-30] and any one of several fine SF filmographies. A subscription to *Locus: The Newspaper of the Science Fiction Field* [14-37] would bring current news of fandom, publishing, and the marketplace. The quarterly *Extrapolation* [14-33], available by subscription or by membership in SFRA, contains many articles applicable to teaching and annually publishes "The Year's Scholarship in Science Fiction and Fantasy," an annotated bibliography that includes Teaching Resources as a subject heading. Just for fun in the classroom, one could add a work like Maxim Jakubowski and Malcolm Edwards's *The SF Book of Lists* [8-42]. Alternatively, for intellectual pleasure there is Walter E. Meyers's *Aliens and Linguists* [9-59]. This work can sensitize teachers to the many options for integrating the study of language into the SF course.

A different way to increase expertise is by attending SF academic sessions at conferences and/or teaching workshops. The subject of SF appears not only on programs of SFRA and on the academic track at world conventions but also on those of the Popular Culture Association, the National Council of Teachers of English (NCTE), and the Modern Language Association. Specific teaching workshops also exist. One is held annually in conjunction with the early spring conference of the International Association for the Fantastic in the Arts (IAFA) (contact Marshall Tymn, IAFA President, 721 Cornell, Ypsilanti, MI 48197). Another, a three-week credit-bearing summer session course on the teaching of SF offered by the University of Kansas Center for the Study of Science Fiction, is in temporary suspension (contact James Gunn, English Department, The University of Kansas, Lawrence, KS 66045).

Writing courses and writing development are the concerns of the second section. From the earliest years, successful SF writers have always been willing to help aspiring writers. Indeed, some feel only they can. Therefore, they often are the instructors at general and teaching conferences throughout the United States—conferences sponsored by colleges, bookstores, SF writers' associations, and fan groups. Also, for six weeks each summer, the Clarion Writers' Workshop, taught by acknowledged writers, accepts selected students, many of whom go on to become well known themselves—eventually returning as instructors.

There are other honors as well. Publishers sometimes announce monetary or publication awards for first novels. Each year at the Center for the Study of Science Fiction at the University of Kansas, the John W. Campbell Award publicizes the work of the best new writers who have had a first professional SF publication within the last two calendar years. The latest evidence of the desire in the SF community to support writing talent appears in the L. Ron Hubbard contest. Seventeen thousand words or less of speculative fiction may bring a novice writer a quarterly prize of $500, $750, or $1,000; an annual prize of $4,000; and top rates for limited publication rights in a Writers of the Future anthology [4-639] (contact Writers of the Future Contest, 2210 Wilshire Blvd., Suite 343, Santa Monica, CA 90403). Indeed, markets for SF do exist. These are described in such annual guides as *Writer's Market* or *Literary Market Place* and in such SF monthlies as *Locus* [14-37] and *Science Fiction Chronicle* [14-38].

For those individuals unable to take advantage of workshops, the nine entries below, annotating ten books on writing, offer advice and practice. Again there is no specific methodological work; however, various individuals of distinction discuss their methods and philosophy in Bretnor [13-13], Jarvis [13-15], and the Science Fiction Writers of America (SFWA) [13-17]. De Camp and de Camp [13-14] and Longyear [13-16] work well as classroom texts. Bova [13-12], Scithers, Schweitzer, and Ford [13-18], and Wilson [13-20] include full-length stories as models for analyzing the craft. Several chapters in some of the preceding and in Spinrad and Curtis [both 13-19] expose many of the problems of the marketplace. Also of value to the prospective writer who is following self-study programs are the presentations of manuscript formats in Bova, de Camp, Scithers, and especially Longyear.

For the purposes of the third section, a classroom text is defined as any book used as the basis or partial basis of study that gives instruction in the principles of SF. This excludes novels and those anthologies without ancillary materials, although an exception has been made for the frequently adopted *Science Fiction Hall of Fame* [13-36]. All but three of the textbooks annotated here are text-anthologies, containing supplementary apparatus: teacher's guides, introductions, headnotes, commentary, biographies, bibliographies, questions, suggested reading lists, writing topics for discussion and research, and prereading and/or postreading activities. Sixteen use SF to teach subjects in the sciences, the social sciences, and general humanities. A half dozen function to improve reading ability and/or reduce frustration of some adult nonreaders. Two emphasize values clarification. Nine use the historical approach, either beginning with Gilgamesh, Cyrano de Bergerac, or Shelley or surveying the nineteenth or twentieth century. Several employ the formalist, sociological, thematic, or generic approaches. The remainder contain short stories and excerpts the individual editors judged quality SF.

Despite this variety, many instructors do not use text-anthologies. Classroom texts have as poor a record for remaining in print as do teaching guides. Also, many teachers disdain teaching paraphernalia. They would argue that exemplary and prototypical SF (short stories, novelettes, novellas, and serialized novels) should be studied in their originally published form—an impossible goal. As a compromise, instructors who select the texts for their courses often choose the aforementioned *Hall of Fame* volumes, a work like *Dangerous Visions* [4-650], or one or more of the annual collections of prizewinning or best SF. There is no one best curriculum, no one best method for presenting material, and, definitely, no one best textbook. Those annotated here offer choices to instructors.

Scholes [13-9] begins his chapter "Science Fiction in Other Media" by claiming that "science fiction has appeared in every medium of artistic creation, from the popular song 'The One-Eyed, One-Horned, Flying Purple People Eater' to Frankenstein's Monster Halloween masks." He goes on to discuss the dialectic that ensues as one medium creates interest in another, which, in turn, places demands on still other media. Assuredly, the popularity of SF best-sellers and films has increased the interest in SF, resulting in students eager to study its content in the classroom. They expect an impact similar to that experienced when viewing spectacular films or exciting television programs. Some students, too, are totally dedicated to one specific program, to a particular comic, or even to old-time radio. Few educational productions can compete with commercial ones. There is little place in this electronic world for story boards, posters, silent filmstrips, records, teleplays, 16mm films, or filmstrip/cassette programs, the traditional classroom aids. Long-playing (LP) records are now offered as cassettes and 16mm films may be rented as videos. Yet only one of the entries following, *Return to Reading Software* [13-49], utilizes a new technology, and only one, *Science Fiction: Jules Verne to Ray Bradbury* [13-51], has changed its form from slide/tape to videocassette. Most of the others are filmstrip/cassette programs produced in the 1970s. These are identified as fs/cs. Addresses of the relevant producers and/or distributors and the 1986 prices are noted. Shipping and handling charges are common.

The use of media as teaching aids cannot succeed if limited to audiovisual materials or treated as a gimmick. On the other hand, classroom aids, properly utilized, increase visual literacy, motivate reluctant students, quickly survey the history of SF, enrich the study of well-known novels and authors, and generally deepen understanding of SF forms and themes. The bimonthly *Media & Methods* regularly reviews instructional products, SF among them. Media can supply ideas and reinforce concepts. The technology should become so familiar to students that they themselves will respond by analyzing, discussing, writing, filming, recording, programming—by themselves creating.

This chapter is concerned primarily with the teacher, the writer, and the classroom, although other persons, particularly those who remain students throughout their lives, will find certain entries of interest: Williamson [13-11] on teaching; Bretnor [13-13] on writing; Asimov [13-22] for reading scientifically based stories; Gunn [13-25] for stories chronologically arranged; and the Hall of Fame series [13-36] for retrospective Nebulas. There is also the nostalgic *Radio's Golden Age of Science Fiction* [13-48], recommended selected short films [13-52], and sound recordings and reference sources [13-53]. Elementary, middle, and junior high school teachers will find teaching ideas in the instructional guides [13-3, 13-4, and 13-11], classroom texts [13-27, 13-29, 13-31, 13-34, and 13-36]; filmstrip/cassette programs [13-40, 13-41, 13-44, 13-45, and 13-47]; computer diskettes [13-49]; and suggestions for the use of short films and sound recordings [13-52 and 13-53]. Instructors of advanced high school SF classes and introductory college SF courses can select from a variety of instructional guides [13-2, 13-2A, 13-3, 13-5, 13-7, and 13-11]; use writing guides

[13-12 and 13-16]; and/or choose a classroom text [13-22, 13-23, 13-26, 13-28, 13-30, or 13-36]. College instructors in the sciences can examine Scholes and Rabkin [13-9]; Asimov [13-22] and Nicholls, Langford, and Stableford [9-68]; and Rabkin [13-35]. Social science instructors could look at classroom texts [13-21, 13-23, 13-28, and 13-33] and pay special attention to several aids [13-42 and 13-50]. Teachers of philosophy are directed to one entry [13-32]. Teachers of literature will find innumerable ideas and illustrative matter in all the entries: those teaching upper-level college or graduate courses in either a historical or a formalist manner should evaluate Riley [13-8], Wilson [13-20], Franklin [13-24], Gunn [13-25], and Wymer [13-39].

Since Sam Moskowitz offered the first course in SF at the City College of New York in fall 1953, where he featured guest lectures by well-known writers and editors, the use of SF for educational purposes has varied as much as schools and teachers themselves. For the last 30 years, educational journals (*Education Digest, Elementary English, English Journal, Scholastic Teacher, Science Education, Science Teacher,* and *Social Studies*) have had articles suggesting ways to use SF in the public schools to achieve other purposes. In the middle of the 1980s, one finds courses in colleges and universities originating from departments in the humanities, the sciences, and the social sciences. For enrichment, supplementary reading, and reading improvement and/or writing development in the high schools, SF appears in single lessons, in units of varying lengths, and in elective courses in a number of disciplines.

While it is unlikely that SFRA or any individual will receive funds to survey public schools, colleges, and universities to determine the number of SF courses being taught, in my college town in New Jersey in late 1986, SF teaching is omnipresent. In the elementary schools, some fourth-graders are researching UFOs while a fifth-grade class reads *A Wrinkle in Time* [5-96]. In the middle and junior high schools, one social studies/language arts class investigates ecology through SF while an English class reports on weird animals in novels and films. In the high school, one class discusses individual SF short stories included in its literature text, another reads SF novels to supplement in-class thematic study, while a third responds in writing to *Anthem* [3-315]. At the college, students in an introductory course in political science are completing assignments in three SF texts in the library reserve room. In a flyer, the physics department is enticing nonscientists to The Science in Science Fiction course described as "an exploration of some of the scientific and mathematical principles which underlie the speculative fiction of this century, including astronomy, causality, chemistry, cosmology, computers, entropy, genetics, relativity and modern mathematics." The English department, in addition to its yearly SF course, has scheduled a literature and women's studies seminar. Their advertisement indicates that Speculative Fiction by Women "will focus on SF and utopian fiction written by women in the last fifteen years, will discuss five novels and selected short stories which suggest the new direction taken by the female imagination in contemporary literature." At the same time, in multiple sections of the required introductory literature courses, students are reading SF by well-known writers in a variety of recently published anthologies.

The battle for acceptance in academe in the 1960s and the 1970s has been won. Scholarly journals publish special SF issues; university presses print SF scholarship; prestigious academic organizations regularly include SF on their programs; and college literature texts include modern SF. Those who fought so hard for acceptance in the 1960s would not have speculated that the current cry might be that those early academic detractors and their successors are today co-opting SF. Perhaps the issue for the 1990s will be the one raised by a panelist at the teaching session of the 1986 SFRA annual convention at San Diego State University. Should SF be taught in regular literature courses with no distinction made between it and the mainstream? The issue is unimportant. It will have no effect, for wherever SF is taught, from the earliest grades to graduate school, no other literature is so informative, so exciting, or so demanding.

Instructional Guides

13-1. Acquino, John. **Science Fiction as Literature.** National Education Association, 1976. J/S.
This 64-page pamphlet briefly defines SF and provides a rationale for its teaching. "Zero Hour" by Bradbury, "The Star" by Wells, *Childhood's End* [3-97] by Clarke, and "Queen of Air and Darkness" by Poul Anderson are the examples used to detail each of four possible approaches to SF. The practical suggestions, the recommended classroom materials, the list of noteworthy antecedents of SF, and the annotations of a few well-known film adaptations and TV programs may ease entry for those new to teaching SF. Tymn, in Jarvis [13-15], specifically addressing the new teacher, takes a similar approach to teaching SF; however, for the experienced or long-term SF teacher/reader, neither generates new ideas. In contrast, Everest in Spann and Culp [13-10] and the many contributors to Williamson [13-11] describe innumerable creative activities and offer a wide range of approaches.

*13-2. Allen, L. David. **Science Fiction: An Introduction.** Cliffs Notes, 1973. S/C.
*13-2A. Allen, L. David. **Science Fiction Reader's Guide.** Centennial Press, 1974. S/C.
Allen categorizes SF as hard SF, soft SF, science fantasy, and fantasy. The works he analyzes include two scientific romances (Wells and Verne); ten well-known novels of the 1950s and 1960s; and Niven's *Ringworld* [4-392], 1970 Nebula and Hugo winner. The 1974 version added *The Foundation Trilogy* [3-19] and *Stranger in a Strange Land* [3-207]. Allen defines SF and, in swift order, uses *Dune* [4-268] to address the problems in reading SF, provides 15 guidelines for reading SF, briefly discusses verisimilitude in SF, lists novel and short fiction award winners, recommends supplementary reading, annotates works about SF, and includes an index. Five of the same novels are analyzed by Scholes and Rabkin [13-9] from a literary/scientific stance, again not a substitute for the works themselves. These are handy, inexpensive means of providing students with prereading and postreading activities. Barron's, Cliffs, and Monarch have guides for the works of such well-established writers as Shelley, Robert Louis Stevenson, Orwell, Huxley, and Vonnegut. Only Cliffs has had guides to the works of Asimov, Heinlein, Herbert, and Tolkien. To popularize its own young adult literature, Ballantine offers teaching guides for several novels by Lester del Rey, Heinlein, and Norton.

13-3. Antczak, Janice. **Science Fiction: The Mythos of a New Romance.** Neal-Schuman, 1985. E/M/J/S/C.

Archetypal criticism undergirds this analysis of SF literature for the 8- to 14-year-old. Fourteen self-explanatory figures illustrate such concerns as how the comic and tragic visions reveal the human/machine relationship or to which category alien animals belong. A selective bibliography highlights the authority from which the myth criticism, SF substance, and children's literature derive. The treatment of symbols, of the hero and minor characters, and of the presentation of SF as "A New Romance" supports Antczak's view that through SF young people will face the future with excitement and understanding. Discussions of young adult works by Christopher, Heinlein, McCaffrey, Norton, and many others appear to limit the audience to elementary or middle-school teachers. Yet all interested in what children read will find value here. Its premises transfer easily to archetypally oriented college SF. This book is also discussed in the introduction to Chapter 5.

*13-4. Donelson, Kenneth, ed. **Science Fiction in the English Class.** NCTE, 1972. M/J/S.

Middle-school and junior and senior high school teachers will find a rich variety of materials, approaches, plans, and objectives in this 120-page reprint from the *Arizona English Bulletin*. Among the 19 articles, several deal with the nature of SF and the rationale for teaching it; one with utopias and dystopias; six with creative techniques for teaching SF; and others with films, magazines, authors, themes, or uses of old radio programs. The references, bibliographies, and filmographies are now dated. In conjunction with the many ideas that can be derived from Williamson [13-11], the use of this work will ensure a creative sequence from grade 6 through college.

13-5. Magill, Frank N., ed. **Science Fiction Alien Encounter.** Salem Press, 1981. S/C.

Excerpted from *Survey of Science Fiction Literature* [8-29] are 75 essays, arranged alphabetically by title from *Andromeda Strain* [4-156] to *The Word for World Is Forest* [4-329]. The introduction validates the use of the alien for a thematic treatment in the classroom. The essays can initiate well-planned units on aliens, suggest supplementary readings, and offer students many research ideas.

13-6. Parrinder, Patrick (U.K.). **Science Fiction: Its Criticism and Teaching.** Methuen, 1980. C.

Although the title indicates equality between criticism and teaching, only the final chapter, "The SF Course," addresses classroom concerns specifically. Such inclusions as the list of the books Hillegas used at Colgate in 1962 or of the dozen most popular texts found in the Williamson survey of 1974 trivialize the "generic identity" of SF established in the earlier six chapters. Nonetheless, Parrinder's open-mindedness has pedagogical merit. In well-reasoned arguments, he implores teachers to set aside the two-cultures debate and the American-versus-European discord and, instead, "clearly set out [one's] own assumptions and, where possible, initiate full discussion of the issues involved." The annotated bibliography and the index increase the value of this clearly written analysis and survey. Both the academic readership and the more serious SF reader will find

Parrinder's elucidation of narrative technique worth studying and/or incorporating into SF courses. Also annotated as [9-74].

13-7. Pringle, David (U.K.). **Science Fiction: The 100 Best Novels—An English-Language Selection, 1949–1984.** Xanadu, 1985. S/C.
In fewer than 1,000 words for each, Pringle selects the best post–World War II SF novels—a third of which he believes may meet the test of time. Many persons, including Michael Moorcock, who introduces the work, would not agree. Yet a number of the works listed do appear on syllabi of courses taught in high schools and colleges. The last 25 entries, from the 1974–1984 period, can encourage instructors to include recent novels in the classroom. The brief biobibliographic information and thematic identifications enhance the plot descriptions. A quick and useful source for novel selection. Also annotated as [9-78].

*13-8. Riley, Dick, ed. **Critical Encounters: Writers and Themes in Science Fiction.** Ungar, 1978. C.
These unpretentious critical essays, addressed to serious readers and fans, are particularly valuable for teaching. The novels cited, generally standard works that remain in print, are frequently taught. Even the progression of the chapters is suggestive of an undergraduate syllabus, with much material adaptable to high school units or courses. For example, in "Sisters, Daughters and Aliens" by Catherine Podojil, traditional sex roles, questioned in the 1950s, are contrasted with more recent treatments. Its impact is increased by appearing directly after "Androgynes in Outer Space," in which Le Guin's *Left Hand of Darkness* [4-327] is discussed. Other chapters give clear treatments of the mythic *Childhood's End* [3-97], the allegorical *Einstein Intersection* [4-167], and the messianic *Stranger in a Strange Land* [3-207]. Compare Williamson [13-11]. Also annotated as [9-82].

13-9. Scholes, Robert, and Eric S. Rabkin. **Science Fiction: History-Science-Vision.** Oxford, 1977. C.
This critical survey that approaches SF as an aspect of the history of fiction in general, annotated elsewhere [9-90], can function as a supplementary text in the classroom but would best be evaluated as an instructional guide. The first part highlights the interdisciplinary nature of SF; the second offers scientific concepts necessary for understanding much SF; the third is a succinct, intelligent description of forms and themes in SF with analyses of ten representative SF novels by European, British, and American writers. Although five of the novels in this final section were treated by Allen [13-2, 13-2A], the remainder—*Frankenstein* [1-84], *We* [2-147], *The Shockwave Rider* [4-91], and particularly *A Voyage to Arcturus* [2-63] and *Star Maker* [2-112]—are nowhere else so clearly set forth. Compare the text-anthology edited by Rabkin [13-35].

*13-10. Spann, Sylvia, and Mary Beth Culp, eds. **Thematic Units in Teaching English and the Humanities.** NCTE, 1975, 1977, 1980. S.
It is worth the effort to borrow these out-of-print books. Among the units in the first compilation (1975) is possibly the most detailed and balanced approach to organizing a 22-day unit ever published: "The Future Arrives before the Present Has Left" by Jane Everest. In the attachments, for example, Everest considers techniques for drawing inferences in SF, provides provocative questions for the

seven major stories studied, and attaches a list of imaginative student projects. Everest also provides a 15-day unit for an eleventh-grade class: "Is Anyone Out There?" It maintains the general format of introductory comments, overview, general objectives, evaluation, materials, daily plans and activities, bibliography, and attachments. The projects and the imaginative assignments ensure a clear visualization. The second supplement (1977) offers "Futurism: Framework and Composition" by Leah A. Marquis and Elizabeth Carros Keroach, 25 lessons supported by essays, magazines, short stories, the novels *Brave New World* [2-47] and *Nineteen Eighty-Four* [3-302], and *You and Science Fiction* [13-28].

*13-11. Williamson, Jack, ed. **Teaching Science Fiction: Education for Tomorrow.** Owlswick Press, 1980. E/M/J/S/C.
Every SF teacher, no matter how experienced, should read this definitive guidebook. It is packed with informed, useful commentary from well-known scientists, writers, editors, teachers, and researchers, plus an artist and a publisher. Williamson, himself a teacher as well as an SF writer, recipient of both the Grand Master award of the Science Fiction Writers of America and the Pilgrim award of the Science Fiction Research Association, is an ideal editor. Carl Sagan introduces the varied essays. Seven address the topic of SF: its origins, evolution, influences, and teaching values—the last by Le Guin. Another four deal with the tools for teaching: the use of SF films, fandom, twentieth-century fiction, and reference sources. In the major section of the guide, which comprises half the volume, are 14 multilevel, interdisciplinary reports of experiences ranging from the primary grades to graduate schools, from science classes to language arts classes, and a Clarion Writers' Workshop. This is an essential work for any SF scholar/teacher.

Writing Guides

13-12. Bova, Ben. **Notes to a Science Fiction Writer.** Rev. ed. Houghton Mifflin, 1981. J/S/C/A.
The former editor of *Analog*, and current editor of *Omni*, suggests that the dearth of publishable SF short stories results from potential writers never having been taught to construct a story or to submit it in any publishable form. Bova discusses four essentials of short story writing: character development, background, conflict, and plot. After a theoretical explanation, he presents one of his own stories, and examines that story as it relates to the four aspects. The colloquial tone is pleasing, but Bova's analyses of his own stories are simplistic; in no way do they approach the depth and objectivity of some self-critiques in Bretnor [13-13] and most in Wilson [13-20].

*13-13. Bretnor, Reginald, ed. **The Craft of Science Fiction.** Harper, 1976. C/A.
In "Yes, Well But . . . ," a review in *This World and Nearer Ones* [9-1], Brian Aldiss takes Bretnor to task for implying in the introduction that a reader could find therein solutions to writing problems. Aldiss argues that this can happen only from within, never from reading what others have found, and offers detailed explanations for his judgments. Interestingly, he points out that of the 15 writers in

this book only Poul Anderson and Jack Williamson talk acceptably about their own writing. For gaining knowledge of the subjects themselves, he recommends Ellison on writing for television, Brunner on basic plots, Clement on the hard sciences and technology, Anderson on epics and sagas, and, as particularly good, Pournelle on constructing believable societies. This is a work that should be read in a leisurely manner. Potential subjects for research are myriad. Of greater import are insights into the methods and philosophies of such writers as Sturgeon or Katherine MacLean. It should be on the supplementary reading list of any course in SF writing and on the want lists of serious SF readers. Compare the volume sponsored by the Science Fiction Writers of America (SFWA) [13-17].

13-14. de Camp, L. Sprague, and Catherine Crook de Camp. **Science Fiction Handbook, Revised.** McGraw-Hill, 1977. C/A.
Rewritten from the admirable 1953 handbook for the writing of imaginative fiction, this handbook, subtitled *How to Write and Sell Imaginative Stories,* continues to offer aspiring SF writers practical information about both the creative and the business aspects of writing SF. Two chapters describe the history of SF; two more survey the readers, writers, editors, and publishers. Because of its "nuts-and-bolts" approach, it could be a primary text in an SF writing course or a supplementary text in any writing course. The bibliographies of fiction, criticism, and reference in SF/fantasy and those in science history and technology, in myth and legend, and in basic references broaden its use. It is less idiosyncratic than Bova [13-12] or Scithers, Schweitzer, and Ford [13-18].

13-15. Jarvis, Sharon, ed. **Inside Outer Space: Science Fiction Professionals Look at Their Craft.** Ungar, 1985. C/A.
Ten essays treat subjects as diverse as George Alec Effinger's "Writing through Adversity" and Lloyd Biggle, Jr.'s "Taxicab Tour of SF History" and as related as Marion Zimmer Bradley's approval of fandom and Carter Scholz's description of the SF ghetto. Each contributor offers a personal view of the world of SF. Although this guide is not written with the same objectives as the more text-oriented de Camp and de Camp [13-14] or Scithers, Schweitzer, and Ford [13-18], most of the essayists do address the contemporary problems of SF writers, editors, and publishers.

*****13-16.** Longyear, Barry B. **Science Fiction Writer's Workshop I: An Introduction to Fiction Mechanics.** Owlswick Press, 1980. S/C/A.
The suggested exercises and the practical assignments in this text designed for workshop sessions, the classroom, or self-instruction on constructing a short story are the best available. What Longyear terms "the direct, illustrated approach" is readily adaptable to any level. The essential references, the practical glossary, the varied organizational plans for possible workshops, and the graphic illustrations are bonus items in this introduction to the craft of writing. No other writer's guide compares. The others talk about writing; this provides hands-on experience.

13-17. Science Fiction Writers of America. **Writing and Selling Science Fiction.** Writer's Digest, 1976. C/A.

C. L. Grant introduces the light, whimsical rules and regulations for SF writers by SF writers Poul Anderson, Gardner Dozois, James Gunn, George R. R. Martin, Thomas F. Monteleone, Andrew J. Offutt, Jerry Pournelle, Tom Purdom, Gene Snyder, and Kate Wilhelm. Underlying the light tone of "You Are What You Eat" or of "Recipes for Believable Aliens" is the strong demand that the prospective SF writer, whether creating an alien, visualizing a future society, or enhancing the language, should discipline the mind, the emotions, and especially the typing fingers. Compare Jarvis [13-15].

13-18. Scithers, George H.; Darrell Schweitzer; and John M. Ford. **On Writing Science Fiction: The Editors Strike Back.** Owlswick Press, 1981. C/A.
Former editors of *Isaac Asimov's Science Fiction Magazine* present their views of idea, conflict, character, plot, background, science, tragedy and futility, and humor—each as specifically necessary in SF. Among the appendixes are "The Rules" and "Manuscript Format." Not only is there an annotated bibliography and an index but there is also the "Special Index to the Rules in the Text." There is humor in "Laws Not Wisely Broken," and the use of models—illustrations from one or two first-sale stories—for each of the aspects of writing adds relevance for the would-be writer in a course or in a home-study program.

13-19. Spinrad, Norman. **Staying Alive: A Writer's Guide.** Donning, 1983. C/A.
These slightly revised columns from *Locus* [14-37], published between 1979 and 1981, and a final original section derive from Spinrad's experiences as a writer (mostly of SF), a negotiator, and a past president of SFWA. The SFWA model paperback contract is reproduced and explained, and suggestions for maximizing income have impact. This work's anecdotal nature, its lack of an index, and the rapid changes in American publishing diminish its value. Both Bova [13-12] and de Camp and de Camp [13-14] write about the marketplace. For a hard-nosed, systematic guide to publishing as a business, the best source, also from the pages of *Locus,* is the poorly titled *How to Be Your Own Literary Agent* (Houghton Mifflin, 1983) by Richard Curtis. Without Spinrad's personalized voice, Curtis, himself a literary agent, explains the unavoidably adversarial relations between writers and publishers.

*13-20. Wilson, Robin Scott, ed. **Those Who Can: A Science Fiction Reader.** Mentor, 1973. C.
For each of the following story elements—plot, character, setting, theme, point of view, and style—two authors provide a story and a critical analysis. The contrasts are often interesting, and the dozen essays are analytic enough for a writer's guide and for upper-level or graduate SF classes. All the contributors and the editor are themselves well-known writers who have functioned as teachers at the various Clarion Writers' Workshops. They include Delany, Ellison, Gunn, Daniel Keyes, Damon Knight, Le Guin, Pohl, Russ, Silverberg, Kate Wilhelm, Williamson, and Wilson. Not only do these sophisticated analyses serve literary purposes; their sources of imagination and their attention to craft become an inspiration.

Classroom Texts

*13-21. Allen, Dick, ed. **Science Fiction: The Future.** 2nd ed. Harcourt, 1983. C.

Poetry, stories, and critical essays cluster in a classroom text designed to provide source material for college SF courses, futurology studies, and freshman English. Opening with James Dickey's "Apollo," the first part introduces SF and writers who react in their works both optimistically and pessimistically to our current life. Part 2 offers four stories reflecting estrangement. Part 3 collects 13 stories, all set in the future, that speculate on the effects on society of technological change, including two not generally anthologized: John Varley's "Air Raid" and William Harrison's "Roller Ball Murder." In this edition, but not in the original 1971 text, are familiar favorites: Godwin's "Cold Equations," Ellison's "Jefty Is Five," and Silverberg's "A Happy Day in 2381." Questions follow each of the 23 selections and the 6 critical essays in the fourth (final) part. The work concludes with over 100 topics for discussion and/or research and a four-part SF bibliography. This one-volume classroom text-anthology has more extensive teaching apparatus than Volumes 3 or 4 of Gunn's series [13-25].

*13-22. Asimov, Isaac, ed. **Where Do We Go from Here?** Fawcett, 1972. S/C.

Both high school teachers who emphasize the sciences in SF and college instructors of introductory science taught through SF must have mourned the passing from print status of this incomparable text. Among the 17 fine stories are "Night" by Campbell, Heinlein's "—And He Built a Crooked House—," Asimov's "Pate de Foie Gras," and, in their short story forms, Blish's "Surface Tension" [3-41], Clarke's "The Deep Range" (1954), and Niven's "Neutron Star" [4-390]. Each, followed by commentary and by questions and suggestions for discussion and writing, illustrates a science such as meteorology, geometry, topology, biology, or physics. The bibliography of collateral reading in nonfiction could be easily updated. No substitute exists. Consider for class use the recent *Science in Science Fiction* [9-68], in which advanced high school students, college students, and the sophisticated adult reader can enjoy 12 chapters of clearly written and well-depicted scientific information.

13-23. Clem, Ralph S.; Martin H. Greenberg; and Joseph D. Olander, eds. **No Room for Man: Population and the Future through Science Fiction.** Roman & Littlefield, 1979. S/C.

Useful as a supplementary text in a social science class or as a resource for senior high or college research. The succinct introductions and suggested readings provide a sound basis for further exploration of our ability to find living space as the population explosion continues. "The Social Consequences of Overpopulation," "World Food Problems," "Impact on the Environment and Resources," and "Solutions" provide a focus for the 11 excellent short stories. Included is the original story from which the movie *Soylent Green* was derived and stories by Aldiss, Ballard, Silverberg, and others. An afterword relieves the overwhelmingly pessimistic speculations with two delightful, optimistic short shorts. The suggested readings are primarily from the 1960s and 1970s, but include Malthus's "Essay on the Principle of Population." By the same editors, *The City 2000 A.D.* (1976), an anthology with no teaching matter other than an introduction, narrows the focus to the future nightmares of many real and imagined cities—New York, Chicago, Urbmon. *Sociology through Science Fiction,* edited by Milstead and others (cited in [13-33]) investigates population as only one concern of sociology.

13-24. Franklin, H. Bruce, ed. **Future Perfect: American Science Fiction of the Nineteenth Century.** Rev. ed. Oxford, 1978. C.
Succinct introductions to each topic provide a focus for college instruction. The samples of works of Irving, Poe, Hawthorne, Melville, Twain, Bierce, Bellamy, and London prove that every major nineteenth-century American writer wrote SF or utopian romance. More important, through the use of nineteenth-century SF in the classroom, one can address the movements of social history as the source matter for our own age. While both Gunn [13-25] and Rabkin [13-35] include nineteenth-century works in their texts, Franklin's focus is narrower but has greater depth. Also annotated as [1-36].

*13-25. Gunn, James, ed. **The Road to Science Fiction.** 4 vols. Mentor, 1977, 1979, 1982. C/A.
The four volumes in this series form the finest SF text-anthology yet produced. The editor is well known as a scholar, SF author and editor, and professor of English. The first three volumes are arranged chronologically. Lengthy introductions, read in conjunction with the detailed story headnotes, develop a coherent historical perspective of SF and its precursors. Commentary accentuates the cultural and scientific topicality of SF. Volume 1, *From Gilgamesh to Wells,* identifies the dreams and fears that inform SF from "Gilgamesh" to Wells's imaginative reaction to invention and discovery in "The Star." Volume 2, *From Wells to Heinlein,* appends a chronology of key SF works. Volume 3, *From Heinlein to Here* contains an author-title-subject index to the first three volumes. A teacher's guide for all three by Gunn and Stephen H. Goldman provides substantiation for the selections, questions that could apply to any story, and suggestions for using the texts in other than chronological order. Volume 4, *From Here to Forever,* retains the introductions and headnotes but departs from the chronological arrangement. Science fiction pieces drawn from 1951 to 1981 "emphasize the quality of the writing rather than the quality of the visions." With more than 100 stories or selections in over 2,100 pages, combined with informed, lucid commentary, these four volumes are an essential acquisition for the general reader, the library, and the classroom. As of late 1986, not all volumes were in print.

13-26. Heintz, Bonnie L., et al., eds. **Tomorrow, and Tomorrow, and Tomorrow. . . .** Holt, 1974. S/C.
The editors state they chose the short stories and novellas from those that many high school and college teachers and students declared "interesting, important, exciting, and challenging." A sampling of one story in each of the nine categories could provide the following list: Wells's "Star," Clarke's "Rescue Party," Bradbury's "Veldt," Brown's "Arena," Ellison's "'Repent, Harlequin!' Said the Ticktockman," Sheckley's "Perfect Woman," Simak's "Desertion," Silverberg's "Sundance," and Asimov's "Singing Bell." The topical approach used here compares to the subdivision of the genre categories in Lawler [13-30].

13-27. Hipple, Theodore W., and Robert G. Wright, eds. **The Worlds of Science Fiction.** Allyn & Bacon, 1979. M/J/S.
Interesting full-page black-and-white illustrations; wide margins. Both recall and conceptual questions and writing topics follow each well-written, highly motivational story in this fine text for grades 6–12. Edgar Allan Poe's "Cask of Amontillado" is paired with Ray Bradbury's "Usher II." Asimov, Clarke, Vonnegut, and others treat subjects that are suitable for bright preteen students and for reluctant high school readers. In the accompanying teacher's guide, the editors explain their rationale for selecting stories to fit six broad categories: social issues, the future, time travel, space travel, aliens, and computers. They discuss the methodology for teaching any short story and for planning related activities. These are then applied to SF. There are teaching suggestions for the specific stories, both prereading and postreading discussion or activities, and recommendations of related stories. Middle-school and high school teachers planning SF units and mini- or semester-length courses with a more advanced reading level than that in Potter [13-34] or a more traditional approach than in Hollister [13-28] will find an abundance of material.

*13-28. Hollister Bernard. **You and Science Fiction.** National Textbook, 1976. S.
Reissued in 1985. The new cover blazons the names of Asimov, Ballard, Bradbury, Dickson, Henderson, Pohl, Silverberg, and Simak. As it was in Hollister's earlier texts for SF and futurology in the high school, *Grokking the Future: Science Fiction in the Classroom* (1973) and *Another Tomorrow: Science Fiction Anthology* (1974), the humanistic approach is at the core. Strong motivational devices urge students to respond creatively to change, possibly achieving personal growth. Four sections, each with its own introduction, each subdivided into such topics as occupations, leisure, sexual roles, family, friends, generations, justice, bio-ethics, and so on, ask the overwhelming questions: Who am I? How do I relate to others? What kind of society do I want? What kind of world do I seek? Interesting illustrated "projections" precede each story and "probes" follow. A 20-page teacher's guide suggests alternative activities. This is the most thought-provoking student-oriented high school text currently in print, unique in its use of SF for values clarification.

13-29. Kelley, Leo P. **Space Adventure Series.** Fearon Education and David S. Lake Publishers, 1979. E/M/J/S.
Fearon Education publishes primarily ESL, literacy, special education, and high-interest/easy-reading materials. In the latter category, SF is used. Six titles each in the Space Police and Galaxy 5 series, each 5 by 7 inches and about 60 pages, provide an interest level of 6–12/ABE and a reading level of 1.8–3.0. For each title, there are teaching notes and skill-builders for the students. Three drama cassettes are available to accompany the Galaxy series. Although the stories are of the cops-and-robbers or hero-and-villain variety, they are action-packed and do serve the needs and interests of a special population in the schools. Recently added to their SF listings are ten fastbacks. These are 27-page, 4 1/4-by-5 1/2-inch books with a reading level of 4.5–5.0 and an interest level of 7–12/ABE. At a second-grade reading level with an interest level of 5–12/ABE are pacemaker

classics, abridgments of such SF works as *Frankenstein* [1-84], *The Time Machine* [1-103], and *Twenty Thousand Leagues under the Sea* [1-95]. Fearon's illustrated pocket classics series offers regular adult-size paperbacks, abridged with comic-style printing for ease in reading. These can be used in the classroom by individuals or groups. Compare to Potter [13-34], who abridges, adapts, and selects.

13-30. Lawler, Donald L., ed. **Approaches to Science Fiction.** Houghton Mifflin, 1978. S/C.
A thoughtful introduction, accompanied by a 10-page "time capsule" listing events from the printing press of 1450 to the use of commercial laser in 1976, provides a historical perspective for this 560-page text, designed for college or advanced high school classes. Each of the 26 excellent selections, 5 from the nineteenth century and the remainder mostly post–World War II, is preceded by a succinct biographical sketch of the writer and a historical commentary. An interesting discussion of themes and subgenres appears in the instructor's manual. The text organization, however, is atypical and may create a problem; nonetheless, the excellent questions following each piece can ease the burden of teachers new to teaching SF. The second and third volumes of Gunn [13-25] provide similar scope.

13-31. Liebman, Arthur, ed. **The Worlds of Science Fiction Series.** Rosen, 1979, 1980, 1981. J/S.
Each of the three volumes in this series briefly annotates significant fiction, Hugo award winners to 1976, magazines, scholarly works, films, and film criticism. Lists of books for thematic reading and addresses of film distributors are also included. One-page biographical/literary comments precede each short story. Each also introduces the period surveyed. For example, *Science Fiction: Creators and Pioneers* surveys the history of SF from the myth of Icarus to Voltaire's "Micromégas." Nine stories, including Mary Shelley's "Mortal Immortal" and Jack London's "Shadow and the Flash," appear. *Science Fiction: The Best of Yesterday* introduces the pulp explosion and offers works by Edgar Rice Burroughs, E. E. Smith, Jack Williamson, and others primarily from the 1930s. *Science Fiction: Masters of Today* considers the influence of the editors in the 1940s and 1950s, the New Wave of the 1960s, and the public acceptance of the 1970s. The selections are from the best-known writers of these decades. The series would be a fine addition for a secondary classroom or school library. For college-track students, a one-volume alternative—from Shelley through Wilhelm—is Lawler [13-30].

13-32. Miller, Fred D., Jr., and Nicholas D. Smith, eds. **Thought Probes: Philosophy through Science Fiction.** Prentice-Hall, 1981. C.
Suitable for introductory philosophy courses, with the possibility of interdisciplinary course work in philosophy and literature. Basic issues related to philosophical concepts are considered, conceptualized (by means of SF), analyzed, and discussed in each of the eight chapters. Suggestions for further reading in SF, in philosophy, and in related nonfiction end each chapter. Several of the selections have rarely been anthologized. The familiar ones clearly relate to the philosophical questions addressed: Godwin's "Cold Equations" to exemplify whether one can know what is right or wrong; Heinlein's "All You Zombies" to question the feasibility of time travel; Zelazny's "For a Breath I Tarry" to exam-

ine differences between men and machines. If the relationships are not as clear in others, the programmed questions termed "probes" do challenge students' intellectual capabilities.

A more recent text-anthology, *Philosophy and Science Fiction*, edited by Michael Philips (Prometheus, 1984), relies more heavily on the instructor's presentation and explanation. It uses two or three somewhat antiquated, illustrative stories for each of five philosophical issues and has very brief introductions.

A third possibility for course organization is to use a critical work either alone or as supplementary to either of the texts discussed above. *Philosophers Look at Science Fiction*, edited by Nicholas D. Smith (Nelson-Hall, 1982), contains 12 essays and, to illustrate the possibility of time travel, a short story by a philosopher. Fine SF exemplifies the issues: *Stranger in a Strange Land* [3-207] conceptualizes the issue of ethics while Le Guin's "Nine Lives" and Stapledon's *Last and First Men* [2-109] support the possibility of a group mind. The essayists on linguistic philosophy support their arguments with *Solaris* [3-261], Piper's "Omnilingual" (1957), and *Babel-17* [4-164]. An index to both the fiction and the nonfiction is badly needed.

13-33. Olander, Joseph D.; Martin H. Greenberg; and Patricia Warrick, eds. **School and Society through Science Fiction.** Univ. Press of America, 1982. C. The purposes of education, teaching and learning in society, school and society, technology and education, and critical issues in contemporary education are chapter subjects. Each has its own introduction; 3–5 carefully chosen SF stories, preceded by a headnote and 4–6 questions; and a selected bibliography. Stories like Henry Slesar's "Examination Day," Howard Fast's "First Men," and Zenna Henderson's "Pottage" contain enough substance to confront the human issues and to speculate on possible solutions. Instructors will find it easy to motivate students, to rearrange the subjects to fit their own course formats, or to use the stories as models to criticize complex situations in modern schools. The bibliography of this reprint of the 1974 Rand-McNally edition was not updated.

Theoretically, many general education requirements could be met through SF. Currently available are Miller and Smith [13-32] for introduction to philosophy, Clem, Greenberg, and Olander [13-23] for urban sociology, and this text. Placed on reserve, the following out-of-print texts, all coedited by Martin H. Greenberg, could support other courses: Greenberg and Joseph D. Olander, *International Relations through Science Fiction* (New Viewpoints, 1978); *Criminal Justice through Science Fiction* (New Viewpoints, 1977); and *Run to Starlight: Sports through Science Fiction* (Delacorte, 1975); by Greenberg and Patricia Warrick, *Political Science Fiction* (Prentice-Hall, 1974); by Harvey A. Katz, Warrick, and Greenberg, *Introductory Psychology through Science Fiction* (Rand-McNally, 1974); by Carol Mason, Greenberg, and Warrick, *Anthropology through Science Fiction* (St. Martin's, 1974); by John W. Milstead, Greenberg, Olander, and Warrick, *Sociology through Science Fiction* (St. Martin's, 1974); and *Science Fiction: Contemporary Mythology* (Harper, 1978) by Warrick, Greenberg, and Olander.

13-34. Potter, Robert R., ed. **Beyond Time and Space.** Globe, 1978. M/J/S. High interest/easy reading for middle, junior, and senior high school students can be attained either by careful selection of stories with low-level vocabulary and straightforward syntax or by adapting difficult material. Both systems were used to create this excellent developmental reading text. Each story is preceded by "Word Warm-Up" and followed by questions that check understanding, the making of inferences, and the building of vocabulary. A final set of questions allows students to consider matters beyond the story itself. Hipple and Wright [13-27], also for grades 6–12, has a higher reading level.

*13-35. Rabkin, Eric S., ed. **Science Fiction: A Historical Anthology.** Oxford, 1983. C.
Representative excerpts and short stories from Cyrano de Bergerac's "Other Worlds" (1657) to Le Guin's "Vaster Than Empires and More Slow" (1971) provide a well-balanced historical approach to SF for the interested adult and the serious college student. A general introduction, essays for each of the five chronological divisions, and headnotes for each story provide an abundance of intelligent commentary. This is the best text surveying a period of more than 300 years for which class sets can be obtained. The comparable volumes in Gunn [13-25] are not currently available.

*13-36. Science Fiction Hall of Fame. Editors vary. Vol. 1, Doubleday, 1971; Vols. 2A and 2B, Doubleday, 1974. J/S/C/A.
Fully annotated elsewhere [3-455]. No examination of classroom text-anthologies would be complete without the inclusion of the short stories in Volume 1 of this series, edited by Robert Silverberg, or of the novelettes and novellas in the two volumes edited by Ben Bova. While later volumes contain ongoing Nebula-winning selections, the first three represent the choices of the then more than 400 professionals of SFWA for retrospective pre-1966 awards. Published for the general SF reader, not the student, so there is no teaching apparatus; yet Jack Williamson's survey [13-11] reports Volume 1 the only anthology among the dozen most popular titles used in the classroom—and, as a scanning of modern anthologies annotated in Chapters 3 and 4 reveals, there were many to choose from. A later survey, a report given at a SFRA conference held at Midland, Michigan, in 1983, revealed that SFRA members choose one or more volumes of Gunn [13-25] as their first choice but close seconds continue to be *Hall of Fame* 1 and/or 2A.

*13-37. Silverberg, Robert ed. **The Mirror of Infinity: A Critics' Anthology of Science Fiction.** Harper, 1970. C.
Successfully combining the fiction with criticism by leading SF critics is a unique feat; this work, although now out of print, should not be weeded from any library collection. Each "unit" has sketches of the author and the critic, most of whom are themselves SF writers. Criticism and then the story itself follow. All but two—Wells's "Star" and Borges's "Library of Babel"—appeared in American or British SF magazines. In effect, the development of the whole modern period up to the late 1960s is summarized here, including the increasing efforts at SF criticism and the rise of academic interest in the genre.

*13-38. Spinrad, Norman, ed. **Modern Science Fiction.** Anchor, 1974. C.
The second edition of *Anatomy of Wonder* identified this out-of-print book as "one of the best of the anthologies published in the 1970s." One need not treasure it

for the included stories, for most appear in *Hall of Fame* [13-36] and/or Gunn [13-25]. It is appreciated for the general introduction to the work in its entirety, for the essays that introduce the periods into which Spinrad has divided modern SF, and for the value of studying the viewpoints of this well-known short story writer, novelist, and critic. See also his writer's guide [13-19].

*13-39. Wymer, Thomas L., et al. **Intersections: The Elements of Fiction in Science Fiction.** Bowling Green, 1978. C.

In Appendix A is "A Bibliography of Short Fiction and Poetry Cited with Location Notes," the items keyed to 34 anthologies and collections, among which are the non-SF Norton anthology and the *Science Fiction Hall of Fame* volumes [13-36]. Thus, there is a good possibility of obtaining class sets of primary material for which *Intersections* becomes the explanatory text. This offers an ideal arrangement for an introduction to literature courses using SF to present fundamental literary elements of plot, character, setting, point of view, language, tone, theme and value, and symbol and myth. Referred to are *Caves of Steel* [3-16], *Demolished Man* [3-30], *Martian Chronicles* [3-64], and *Starship Troopers* [3-206]. Like Scholes and Rabkin [13-9], the works addressed need not be the primary material selected, and like Wilson [13-20], there is possible application to SF writing courses. Wymer differs in presuming no special literary knowledge.

Classroom Aids

13-40. Best of Bradbury Sound Filmstrips. 1976–1980. 4 fs/4 cs, study guide. Boxed. Listening Library. $115.00. **The Future Worlds of Ray Bradbury.** 1976–1980. 3 fs/3 cs, study guide. Boxed. Listening Library. $109.00. Dist. by A. W. Peller (Box 106, Hawthorne, NJ 07507) or Perfection Form (1000 N. 2nd Ave., Logan, IA 51546). E/M/J/S/C.

Much ancillary material exists for individual titles and in varying packaging combinations for the works of Ray Bradbury. *Future Worlds* contains *Fahrenheit 451* [3-61] (2 fs/2 cs, $55.00), narrated by Bradbury, and (1 fs/1 cs, $32.00) "Frost and Fire" and "There Will Come Soft Rains." The *Best of Bradbury* includes "The Fog Horn," "The Illustrated Man," "A Sound of Thunder," and "The Veldt." For each, and for "The Dwarf" and "Usher II," the teacher's guide provides critical commentary and ten provocative questions. The vibrant drawings, dramatic presentation, and careful abridgments will appeal to upper-elementary as well as college students. In addition, from Perfection Form, one can obtain a suitable elementary school edition of "The Veldt," with related reading and writing developmental questions and activities. For "The Illustrated Man" there are tests for students and notes for teachers. *The Martian Chronicles* [3-64] (3 fs/3 cs/book, $116.50), from the actual motion picture and soundtrack, is an option for those without stop-frame projectors or pause capability. Other references to Bradbury appear throughout this section.

13-41. Broadcast Theater. 1 cs/1 or more scripts per title. The Silver Sounds of Radio and Nostalgia Broadcasting. $9.95 ea./$.99 ea. Dist. by Perfection Form (1000 N. 2nd Ave., Logan, IA 51546). J/S/C.

A Connecticut Yankee by Mark Twain [1-25], *Lost Horizon* by James Hilton [2-43], and *Nineteen Eighty-Four* by George Orwell [3-302], the last starring David Niven and providing an intermission remark from James Hilton, are among the memorable hour-long radio programs of the past, complete with good music and realistic sound effects. People in literature and writing classes, in acting courses, in radio and TV work, at fan conferences, and elsewhere will enjoy the more active involvement made possible by the accompanying "Readeo." Other dramatizations without accompanying read-along scripts are readily available from various producers/distributors. Cassette Productions (2561 S. 1560 West, Suite B, Woods Cross, UT 84087) lists six tapes of 13 dramatizations based on stories written by Ray Bradbury, each $6.95. For younger readers, Cassette Book Co. (Box 7111, Pasadena, CA 91109) offers *Dr. Jekyll and Mr. Hyde* [1-86]. Mind's Eye (Box 6727, San Francisco, CA 94101) has dramatizations of two of H. G. Wells's novels. Appreciative listening and oral interpretation are but two objectives for using such material. Examine also the entry for recordings [13-53].

13-42. Classics of Science Fiction. 1975. 4 fs/4 cs, teacher's guide. Boxed. $154.00. **Future Imperfect: The Utopian Novel.** 1974. 2 fs/2 cs, teacher's guide. Boxed. $77.00. **Tales of Time and Space.** 1978. 4 fs/4 cs, library kit, discussion guide. $154.00. Educational Dimensions Group (Box 126, Stamford, CT 06904). S/C.
Each cassette/filmstrip in the three programs depicts a theme that affects the human condition. In the first program, although the visuals vary from static to exciting, the narrative voice and script for *Childhood's End* [3-97], *Fahrenheit 451* [3-61], *R.U.R.* [2-15], and *The Time Machine* [1-103] clearly exemplify the epic vision and offer warnings about the future. The program is discounted when purchased with *Future Imperfect: The Utopian Novel*, where well-chosen background music reinforces the loss of humanity from differing kinds of conditioning portrayed in *Nineteen Eighty-Four* [3-302] and *Brave New World* [2-47]. Each teacher's guide includes an introduction, the transcript of the narration, relevant bibliographies, an explanation of the theme, suggested assignments with opportunities to develop comparison/contrast techniques, and—for each novel—4–10 topics suitable for discussion or for individual research. *Tales of Time and Space* is less satisfying than the other two, but is the only currently available program that focuses on SF short stories. The abstracts and line drawings please, but the teacher's guide is little more than a transcript; however the admirable short stories ("Vintage Season" by Kuttner and Moore, Niven's "Neutron Star," and Asimov's "Nightfall") do reveal how SF writers "can make a profound, human statement utilizing fictional and scientific principles." Any one of these can be used by the college student for individual instruction or review and by the high school student for either remediation or enrichment.

13-43. Favorite Book Filmstrips. 1978. 1 fs/l cs, 1 cover craft book, 1 discussion guide per title. Boxed. Center for Literary Review and Current Affairs Multimedia (Box 426, Ridgefield, CT 06877). $34.95. S.
Brave New World [2-47], *Flowers for Algernon* [3-228], and *Nineteen Eighty-Four* [3-302] are the three SF novels chosen to motivate high school students to read. Each discussion guide is thorough, providing biographical information, study questions with possible answers, a list of related activities, a selected bibliography, and the choice of two full-period tests. Each spoken analysis is sound and does

stimulate thinking; the background music is appropriate, but the quality of the visuals is substandard. Although some photographs and works of art related to utopia and/or the modern world appear intermittently in *Nineteen Eighty-Four,* in *Brave New World* only the beginning frames depicting utopias of the past are interesting; the static nature of the remainder only emphasizes the amateurish acting. For more advanced students, a better choice for a study of dystopian novels is *Future Imperfect* [13-42]. To stimulate leisure reading activity by reluctant high school students, a program collateral to *Getting Hooked on Science Fiction* [13-44] exists: *Suspense Classics* (#04006-690: sound slides, $209.00/sound fs, $189.00; teacher's guide, library kit, four student activity books, and four comic-style paperbacks of nineteenth-century SF classics).

*13-44. Getting Hooked on Science Fiction. 1976. 1 fs/1 LP or cs, teacher's guide, catalog cards. Boxed. Guidance Associates (Communications Park, Box 3000, Mount Kisco, NY 10549). $47.00. M/J.
The quality of the books chosen should motivate upper-elementary and middle-school children to explore some if not all of the ten titles. The 12-page teacher's guide includes a filmscript, a discussion of objectives, a brief summary of each plot and theme, a selected bibliography of related professional reading, and, of particular value, a section entitled "Student Guide." Here are thoughtful, imaginative questions and activities for discussion, writing, drawing, dramatizing, constructing, taping, and so forth. The novels are Verne's *Twenty Thousand Leagues under the Sea* [1-95], Clarke's *Dolphin Island* (1963), Cameron's *Wonderful Flight to the Mushroom Planet* [5-23], del Rey's *Runaway Robot* [5-49], Nourse's *Star Surgeon* [5-125], Norton's *Moon of Three Rings* (1966), L'Engle's *Wrinkle in Time* [5-96], Christopher's *White Mountains* [5-32], Engdahl's *Enchantress from the Stars* [5-47], and O'Brien's *Mrs. Frisby and the Rats of NIMH* [5-126]. Excellence is evident in every aspect of this 17-minute program from The Reading for the Fun of It series, the finest for grades 5–9. Consider as well the use of the software program [13-49] with junior high students.

13-45. Literature of Science Fiction: An Overview. 1974. 2 fs/2 cs, discussion guide. $77.00. S/C. Educational Dimensions Group (Box 126, Stamford, CT 06904). **What Is Science Fiction?** 1975. 2 fs/2 cs or LPs, teacher's guide. Guidance Associates (Communications Park, Box 3000, Mount Kisco, NY 10549). $97.00. J/S.
Two programs try to deepen the understanding of SF and its value for study. For junior high and high school students, SF is defined, with examples from Wells and Clarke, as that literature which "wonders on the basis of scientific law or fact." Works of Bradbury, Herbert, Le Guin, and others exemplify character, plot, and setting. *A Canticle for Leibowitz* [3-287] and *Earthman, Come Home* [3-43] underscore the concern for humanity's place in the universe. The teacher's guide includes a transcript of the text, good vocabulary lists, and activities for before and after viewing. The more advanced *Literature of SF* first traces SF from its beginnings in Greek literature to the middle of the twentieth century and the golden age of SF. The second part, using selected works of Asimov, Bradbury, Clarke, Wyndham, Nevil Shute, Silverberg, and Vonnegut, emphasizes the problems of our time, reflects on biological catastrophes or nuclear warfare, and re-

veals the absurdity of man. The bibliography is the same as that in *Classics of Science Fiction* [13-42]; the projects are different. Not as comprehensive or visually effective as *Science Fiction and Fantasy* [13-50] or *Science Fiction: Jules Verne to Ray Bradbury* [13-51], but stresses current concerns.

13-46. Literature of Science Fiction: A Filmed Lecture Series. 1970–1975. 1½" VHS or ¾" U-matic videocassettes. Univ. of Kansas AV Center (746 Massachusetts Ave., Lawrence, KS 66044). Sale $250.00–$275.00/rental $20.00–$27.00. C.
Hosted by writer/educator James Gunn. Eleven filmed talks and discussions with outstanding writers/editors, critics, and a historian were pioneer attempts to provide enrichment for introductory college courses in SF. Two, "The Early History of SF" and "The History of SF from 1938 to the Present," can be recommended. Certainly Isaac Asimov, James Gunn, and Damon Knight are qualified to discuss SF history. Thus, while the series suffers from its low budget and unsophisticated recording techniques, nowhere else will a serious SF student find John W. Campbell building a story with Gordon Dickson and Harry Harrison, Harlan Ellison interacting with James Gunn and other seminar participants, or Forrest Ackerman discoursing on SF films in his own museum/home so full of SF film paraphernalia. Other guests are Poul Anderson, John Brunner, Frederik Pohl, and Clifford D. Simak. Opportunities for original research lie hidden here. The collections of interviews in Chapter 10, short film entries [13-52], and sound recordings [13-53] can provide further source material for study of modern SF authors.

13-47. Meet the Authors. 1985. 1 fs/cs each, teacher's guide. Boxed. January Productions. $24.00 each title. Dist. by A. W. Peller (Box 106, Hawthorne, NJ 07507). M/J/S.
More than 50 frames introduce either Jules Verne or H. G. Wells. The script appears in each teacher's guide, where there are also suggested projects and activities and comprehension questions. Whether these, or indeed any filmstrip in this age of sophisticated TV interviews, will inspire students "to read classic world literature" is arguable: in this program it is not helped by the patronizing voice of the narrator nor by the resemblance to a poorly illustrated children's text of the stills in the Wells program. Nonetheless, the two programs function to place Verne and Wells in their historical period, a necessity when teaching younger students. It is much easier to introduce still-living writers. For example, Ray Bradbury himself narrates a 15-minute fs/cs program, *Ray Bradbury: The Man in the Wonderful Ice Cream Suit* (dist. by Perfection Form, 1000 N. 2nd Ave., Logan, IA 51546; $29.95). Among the 145 frames are some of his personal pictures, a fine device for "meeting" an author.

*13-48. Radio's Golden Age of Science Fiction. 1978. 4 cs/8-track/reel-to-reel. Library boxed. Satellite Broadcasting (Box 5364, Rockville, MD 20851). $9.95 ($11.95 for the 8-track). E/M/J/S/C/A.
A comprehensive program of excerpts from over 100 SF radio shows from the late 1940s provides four full hours of high-quality, carefully edited portions from such radio classics as *X Minus One, Superman, Buck Rogers, Dimension X, Captain Jupiter, Exploring Tomorrow, Host Planet Earth* (BBC), *Tarzan, 2000 Plus, The Hermit's Cave,* and *CBS Science Fiction.* Background music from the shows them-

selves and knowledgeable comments by the narrator spark the imagination. As motivation for reading science fiction, as a primary resource for the study of SF radio, or as pure delight, this is a "best buy" for the classroom or for an individual. The catalog lists hundreds of incomparable full-length SF programs.

*13-49. Return to Reading Software. 1983–1984. 2 diskettes per novel. Apple II or II Plus. Teacher's guide, activity sheets. Media Basics Courseware (Larchmont Plaza, Larchmont, NY 10533). $70.00. J/S.

Computer programs and accompanying study guides are available for seven novels: *Brave New World* [2-47], *Dracula* (1897), *Fahrenheit 451* [3-61], *Flowers for Algernon* [3-228], *The Martian Chronicles* [3-64], *Mrs. Frisby and the Rats of NIMH* [5-126], and *A Wrinkle in Time* [5-96]. Designed for students in grades 7–12, the menu permits a student to choose whether to respond personally to the novel with no grades recorded, to prove an understanding of the total work, to become involved in stimulating related activities, and/or to explore related readings. Bonus questions, commendations for correct answers, and feedback responses (second chances to produce a correct answer) reflect the best ideas in learning theory. The reproducible activity sheets, a response journal, and a sentence-combining worksheet reinforce the courseware objectives in reading, writing, language, research, and, of greatest importance, thinking. The teacher password accesses up to 20 scores (40 if the backup diskette is also used). While the activity sheets are definitely secondary level, the program itself could serve as a college review for *Brave New World* or *Fahrenheit 451*. The only limitation to the courseware is its being limited to the Apples.

13-50. Science Fiction and Fantasy. 1976. 2 fs/2 cs or LPs, teacher's notes. Educational Audio Visual (17 Marble Ave., Pleasantville, NY 10570). $92.00. S/C.

Within the context of the history of the science and accompanied by appropriate illustrations or documentary visuals, the commentary, prepared by Ben Bova, first considers the evolution of SF from Cyrano de Bergerac to World War II. The second part emphasizes social, political, and ethical issues in films and in the writings of the golden age and New Wave writers. The teacher's notes include the credits, the complete transcript, study aids with 13 clearly stated objectives, and a sound reading list organized by topic. Notwithstanding that some of the expressed views are now dated, the 40-minute filmstrip could be used as an overview of future coursework or as a review for a final exam either in high school or college. The use of original illustrations from early SF publications and the expressed concerns reinforce the role of SF as a reflection of society. To trace the history of SF back to the Greeks, this thorough program could be supplemented by the *Literature of Science Fiction* [13-45].

*13-51. Science Fiction: Jules Verne to Ray Bradbury. 1974. 240 slides in 3 carousels/3 cs or LPs or slides on video, library kit, teacher's guide. Center for Humanities (Communications Park, Box 1000, Mount Kisco, NY 10549). $209.00. S/C.

Surveying major writers from Lucian to Wells, Part 1 concludes with the influence of Wells on Orwell. In Part 2, contemporary themes in the pulps and in the media, the development of robotics, and the rise of dystopian writing are explored. Part 3 continues the consideration of dystopias; it treats, as well, religion and the environment. The narration and musical background are exceptionally well done. Dick Allen, who edited the fine text-anthology [13-21], prepared the teacher's guide. It includes not just the text of the narration but notations of the accompanying visuals and the sources of the musical background. Further, any one of the parts may be used alone, and all references are to standard SF fiction. The appeal is such that any interested adult would enjoy the excursion to the past and the future. Now offered as a video, the program remains the most comprehensive introduction to SF and the most satisfying audio-visual aid for supplementing introductory SF courses in either high school or college.

13-52. Short Films. E/M/J/S/C/A.
The feature-length films that are the subject of the books annotated in Chapter 11 may be too lengthy or expensive for routine classroom use. Instructors should investigate the short film. They will find interviews and biographies or talks, most more expensively produced than *Literature of Science Fiction: A Filmed Lecture Series* [13-46]. There are also many filmed short stories, a most useful aid in the classroom. What may be as exciting as was Méliès's film in 1902 are the several short SF art films created in the last few decades—films still available through purchase, rent, or interlibrary/media loan. A few recommendations in each category follow.

For an effective, straightforward film interview, try *Arthur C. Clarke: Starglider* (Films for the Humanities, sale/rental). Clarke talks about his life, works, ideas, and plans for 53 minutes. For an autobibliograpy/critical analysis/60-minute talk, try *Kurt Vonnegut, Jr.: "Deadeye Dick"* (Arts International, dist. by Wombat, 16mm, 3/4″ video, 1/2″). For story into film, there is the 26-minute award-winning *Ugly Little Boy* (Learning Corp., sale/rental), based on a story of the same name by Isaac Asimov. Also from Learning Corp. of America (sale/rental) are two from Ray Bradbury; the first, 28 minutes, is based on "All Summer in a Day," and the second, retitled *The Electric Grandmother* (32 minutes), derives from "I Sing the Body Electric." Each is excellent. Equally suitable for the classroom, or elsewhere, are the short films with original stories: the 15-minute version of *THX* for which George Lucas won the 1967 grand prize at the National Student Film Festival or the film *00173* (Poland, 1969, 9 min./color, dist. by Contemporary) with its depiction of the total dehumanization of man in a machine-worshiping dystopia. Most haunting of them all, and one with myriad SF themes, is *La Jetée* (France, 1963, 29 min./b&w, dist. by Pyramid, English narration). No single class period is long enough to moderate the many student responses generated by any of the preceding.

13-53. Sound Recordings. E/M/J/S/C/A.
There are now several hundred spoken word recordings of SF. This fairly recent development can give delight to fans, provide greater variety of experiences for the blind than that discussed in Chapter 15, and enhance the teaching of SF at every level of education.

A handful of recordings discussing SF exist. Chapter 10 details collections of interviews. A fair number of recordings are dramatizations like those of the old radio series and shows noted earlier [13-41 and 13-48]. For unabridged recordings of novels or story collections, typically on multiple cassettes, producers use professional readers or actors who vitalize the fiction with appropriate accents and inflections. Leonard Nimoy (Mr. Spock) reading Bradbury and Heinlein packaged with William Shatner (Captain Kirk) reading Kuttner and Asimov bring out high motivational factors for teaching. Most commonly found is fiction read by the authors themselves. Caedmon currently catalogs 38 recordings in its SF/fantasy section, 26 performed by the author on single cassettes. The short stories are complete; the novels are abridged or excerpted. Caedmon retains its reputation as the oldest ongoing producer of SF recordings; yet others are creating interesting material. Readers, instructors, and/or librarians should consult the following sources to determine what is available.

On Cassette: A Comprehensive Bibliography of Spoken Word Audio Cassettes. Bowker, 1985; 2nd ed., 1986. The most comprehensive listing, with the second edition listing almost twice as many entries as the first. See under Literature and Fiction—Fantasy and Science Fiction/Mystery and Suspense/Short Stories and Essays, for most recordings. The author index should be checked for recordings not typically identified as by SF authors, such as Kingsley Amis or Anthony Burgess. Approximately 22,000 entries from about 250 American cassette producers and distributors are indexed, with cross-references to specific and main titles. Six indexes permit multiple access.

Words on Tape: An International Guide to Recorded Books. Meckler Publishing, 1986. First published in 1984, now an annual. The 1986 edition lists nearly 10,000 titles from more than 300 publishers. Collections are individually indexed, and there are author and subject indexes to the main (title) listings. Also available through BRS as an online database, updated quarterly.

Schwann Record & Tape Guide. ABC Schwann Publications, Boston. A monthly since 1949 and a standard tool in retail stores and libraries. The Spoken & Miscellaneous section appears in the four complete quarterly issues. Most SF recordings are listed under Poetry, Prose, Speech in this section and are largely limited to recordings likely to be found in or available through larger record dealers such as the Caedmon or Spoken Arts labels.

14

Science Fiction Magazines

H. W. Hall

Science fiction, even when not so identified, has been published in magazines and newspapers since the early nineteenth century, becoming more common as steam-driven presses and cheap printing made available popular magazines around the time of the American Civil War. Many of the stories probably remain undiscovered in the yellowing pages of American and British (and probably European) magazines and newspapers. Science fiction stories were common in magazines like *Argosy* and *All-Story* early in the twentieth century, less common in their European counterparts. By general consensus, the first magazine to publish SF exclusively was *Amazing Stories* [14-22], still published 60 years later. The development of the American SF pulps provided an outlet for many writers but simultaneously resulted in a ghettoization of American SF. As Chapter 2 indicates, this did not happen in England or on the Continent, and the quality of SF published outside the United States between the two world wars was generally better as well as more serious in its concerns.

The early history of English-language SF magazines is chronicled in a variety of books. Sam Moskowitz's historical anthologies *Science Fiction by Gaslight* [1-70] and *Under the Moons of Mars* [1-71] explore the 1891–1920 period. Carter's *The Creation of Tomorrow* [9-19] critically surveys the first five decades of SF magazine history. A number of histories of popular magazines have briefly discussed the SF pulps. *The Fiction Factory* (1955) by Quentin Reynolds devotes a chapter to *Astounding*. Harold Hersey, who edited Street and Smith's *Thrill Book* (1919) and assisted in the founding of *Astounding*, wrote *Pulpwood Editor* (1937). Tony Goodstone's *The Pulps: 50 Years of American Pop Culture* (1970) contains over 50 complete stories, poems, features, articles, and advertisements, and many covers in color, with one chapter devoted to the SF pulps. Ron Goulart's *Cheap Thrills: An Informal History of the Pulp Magazines* (1972) provides some coverage of SF pulps. R. K. Jones's *The Shudder Pulps* (1975) touches on the SF and fantasy magazines. Robert Sampson's *Yesterday's Faces: Vol. 1, Glory Figures* and *Vol. 2, Strange Days* [14-17] provide an interesting look at the content of the pulps.

The early history of the pulps and their writers is often revealed in interviews. J. M. Elliot's *Pulp Voices: Interviews with Pulp Magazine Writers and Editors* [10-195] is a compact source of several interviews. Bill Blackbeard's chapter on the pulps in Volume 1 of Inge's *Handbook of American Popular Culture* [8-44] provides a good introduction to the study of this literature. The more general histories annotated in Chapter 9 discuss the important role of the magazines. *The Science Fiction Encyclopedia* [8-30] has succinct entries for 207 fiction magazines as well as entries for many of the editors. Pierre Versins's *Encyclopédie de l'utopie, des voyages extraordinaires et de la science-fiction* [6-197] profiles the French magazines and selected other titles.

By far the most important work on the SF magazines is Tymn and Ashley's *Science Fiction, Fantasy, and Weird Fiction Magazines* [14-18]. It is the first point of reference for any study of the magazines.

SF and fantasy magazines have been well indexed since 1952, when Donald B. Day's pioneering work [14-4] appeared. The indexes and studies annotated in this chapter provide a basis for access and study of the SF magazines. With the increasing but still limited availability of the SF magazines in microform, and the efficiency of interlibrary loan, these indexes have increasing value for all libraries with clientele requiring access to primary source materials. Other indexes to the magazine exist, sometimes duplicating the coverage of the works annotated, but most are out of print or relatively rare. William Contento's essential indexes [8-9, 8-10] provide access to several thousand reprints of the stories from the magazines.

Today, relatively few of the more than 175 science fiction magazines published during the past 50 years survive, and in the early 1970s an important change occurred: the paperback and hardcover book became the most important source of original science fiction. In the past five years, several attempts have been made to start new SF magazines, or to revive old titles. Of these, the majority were announced but never published. The best source of information on new magazines, and of an annual survey of the current magazine scene, is *Locus* [14-37]. *Locus* lists all new magazine issues received, with considerable detail on volume numbers, dates, addresses, and descriptive notes, and covers American and some foreign magazines. The annual survey evaluates the major American magazines, and provides factual information, including circulation figures.

The preservation of the SF magazines (and of paperbound books) is a matter of serious concern to scholars and libraries. Some of the problems of preservation are described by George Tuttle in *Problems in the Pulps: A Study of Special Collections in Pulp Magazines* (ERIC ED 249 989). The most reliable method of preservation today is microfilming. Greenwood Press has two series of SF magazines in 35mm microfilm, and Micro Information Concepts started an extensive filming project in 1984. The Greenwood project was filmed with issues missing. The Micro Information Concepts effort is a model project, providing the issues in microfiche, with a separate set of the magazines' covers only in color microfiche. Some libraries are involved in internal preservation microfilming. One such effort is described in "Science Fiction Microfilming Project at the New York Public Library" by Alice Dowd (*Microfilm Review* 14 [Winter 1985]: 15–20). Texas A&M University sity filmed the longer runs of several fanzines held in its collections. The concluding section of this chapter provides information on SF magazines available in microform. University Microfilms (UMI) owns the microfilming rights to a number of magazines that have never been filmed. Listed in the UMI catalogs, these titles carry a notation that filming has not been done. When and if sufficient firm orders have been received, UMI will film the titles.

Indexes and Checklists

14-1. Ashley, Mike. **Complete Index to Astounding/Analog.** Weinberg, 1981. This volume is the definitive index to *Astounding/Analog* for 1930–1979. An issue-by-issue listing of the contents of the magazine is followed by indexes by author, title, artist, and writer of letters published in the letter column. A basic reference tool because of the importance of this magazine in the history of SF.

14-2. Boyajian, Jerry, and Kenneth R. Johnson. **Index to the Science Fiction Magazines.** Twaci Press, 1981–1986. These indexes provide access by author and title to SF magazines. Citation is to month only. A valuable feature is the appendix "SF in Miscellaneous Magazines." Volumes available: 1977, 1978, 1979, 1980, 1981, 1982, 1983, 1984. Indexing of magazines was continued in Brown and Contento [8-8].

14-3. Boyajian, Jerry, and Kenneth R. Johnson. **Index to the Semi-Professional Fantasy Magazines.** Twaci Press, 1983–1986. The only available indexing for some of the magazines covered. Volumes available: 1982, 1983. These volumes follow the same format as *Index to the Science Fiction Magazines* (above). No longer being published, they are available from the compilers (Box 87, MIT Branch Sta., Cambridge, MA 02139).

*14-4. Day, Donald B. **Index to the Science Fiction Magazines, 1926–1950.** Rev. ed. G. K. Hall, 1982. The pioneering SF magazine index, this remains the only comprehensive index for English-language magazines for the period covered. Day provides access by author and title of stories, and includes a checklist of magazines indexed. The 1982 revised edition corrects and updates the original 1952 volume. A basic reference tool.

14-5. Hall, H. W. **The Science Fiction Magazines: A Bibliographical Checklist of Titles and Issues through 1982.** Borgo Press, 1984. This is the most comprehensive checklist of SF magazines available, showing titles, title variations, publishers, publisher variations, volume and issue data, exact point of title changes, numbering errors, and other data of interest to the scholar and the collector.

14-6. Jaffery, Sheldon, and Fred Cook. **Collector's Index to Weird Tales.** Bowling Green Univ. Popular Press, 1985.
Jaffery and Cook have compiled a variety of indexes in this volume, including an issue-by-issue checklist, an index by author, an author index to poetry, an index to cover artists, and several appendixes, most dealing with *Oriental Stories/Magic Carpet.* The indexes have the common failing of not providing inclusive pagination, a feature valuable to the scholar seeking particular items, and as an indicator of the length of the contribution. *Monthly Terrors* [14-8] provides a checklist showing all issues, with an author index.

14-7. Metcalf, Norman. **Index of Science Fiction Magazines, 1951–1965.** J. Ben Stark, 1968.
Indexes the English-language magazines by author and title. Artists and editors are also indexed, and a checklist of magazines indexed is provided. Although Metcalf covers some items not included in Strauss [14-9], the latter is preferred for its ease of use and format compatible with the New England Science Fiction Association (NESFA) indexes [14-10, 14-11].

14-8. Parnell, Frank H., and Mike Ashley, comps. **Monthly Terrors: An Index to the Weird Fantasy Magazines Published in the United States and Great Britain.** Greenwood, 1985.
Parnell and Ashley extensively, but not comprehensively, index 1,733 issues of 168 "weird fantasy" magazines published from 1919 to 1983 that included more than 50 percent weird fantasy in the magazine run. Magazines devoted to science fiction, such as *The Magazine of Fantasy and Science Fiction,* are excluded, as are horror magazines and sado-sexual magazines. An issue-by-issue checklist for each title covered is followed by an author index, an artist index (both cover and interior art), an editor index, and appendixes: index to series and connected stories; honorable mentions (magazines that almost qualified for inclusion); chronological listing of magazines; geographical listing of magazines. A valuable tool, providing indexing to many titles not otherwise indexed. Librarians may regret the compiler's failure to include inclusive pagination of stories.

*14-9. Strauss, Irwin S., comp. **The MIT Science Fiction Society's Index to the SF Magazines, 1951–1965.** MIT Science Fiction Society, 1966.
One of the earliest computer-generated indexes to science fiction; access is by author and title for stories. A useful feature is an issue-by-issue checklist of each magazine. Continues the coverage provided by Donald B. Day's index [14-4], and is continued by the NESFA indexes [14-10, 14-11]. A basic reference tool.

*14-10. New England Science Fiction Association. **Index to the Science Fiction Magazines 1966–1970.** NESFA, 1971.
*14-11. New England Science Fiction Association. **The NESFA Index: Science Fiction Magazines and Original Anthologies.** NESFA, 1973–   . Volumes available: 1971–1972, 1973, 1974, 1975, 1976, 1977, 1978, 1979–1980, 1981, 1982, 1983.
The NESFA indexes continue the format and arrangement of Strauss's 1951–1965 index almost exactly, providing author and title access to stories, and an issue-by-issue checklist of the magazines. With the 1971–1972 index, coverage

was expanded to include original anthologies. A basic reference tool, but one that could be improved by being more current and cumulated for the 1966–1985 period.

Studies

14-12. Ashley, Mike. **The History of the Science Fiction Magazines.** New English Library, 1974–1978. Part 1, 1926–1934; Part 2, 1936–1945; Part 3, 1946–1955; Part 4, 1956–1965.
This set features the most complete history of the SF magazines worldwide yet undertaken. Part 1 covers in detail those magazines featuring SF prior to 1926, then surveys the beginnings of the specialty SF magazines. Each succeeding volume includes the magazines published in the decade covered. A checklist of the titles included in each volume gives title, a chart of publication history, and total issues published during that period. A valuable glossary of magazine editors is included. Each volume also includes a representative sampling of ten stories drawn from the period, usually one from each year. Partially superseded by Tymn and Ashley's *Science Fiction, Fantasy, and Weird Fiction Magazines* [14-18], this set remains useful for its integrated look at the world magazine scene.

14-13. Gallagher, Edward J. **Annotated Guide to Fantastic Adventures.** Starmont, 1985.
14-14. Gammell, Leon L. **The Annotated Guide to Startling Stories.** Starmont, 1986.
Following a 17-page survey of the publication period of *Fantastic Adventures*, Gallagher presents a comprehensive annotated story guide, featuring a 70- to 100-word annotation for each story. Appendixes include a list of issues, lists of departments, biographies, illustrators, editorial personnel, authors, and titles. Annotations are descriptive, not critical. Gammell annotates novels that appeared in *Startling Stories* with 70- to 250-word annotations. Shorter fiction is also covered, but the annotations are too brief to be useful. No indexes are provided; in short, it is essentially valueless for any serious user. Both the magazines covered were of generally poor quality, and only pulp enthusiasts will find these guides useful.

14-15. Rogers, Alva. **Requiem for Astounding.** Advent, 1964.
This book is the only full-length treatment of *Astounding* from 1930 to February 1960. It is not a critical study, but is valuable for the detail included and for the anecdotes, which provide some insight into the editors and writers. Supplemented by Ashley's *Complete Index to Astounding/Analog* [14-1], with its issue-by-issue contents listings, and a variety of statistics, and Carter's *The Creation of Tomorrow* [9-19]. Because of the magazine's historical importance, scholars should find this book of value. Most libraries will find the careful analytical history by Albert Berger in Tymn and Ashley [14-18] more than adequate.

14-16. Rosheim, David L. **Galaxy Magazine: The Dark and the Light Years.** Advent, 1986.
Unlike *Astounding/Analog*, *Galaxy* stressed the social impact of technology, with less emphasis on the hardware. After H. L. Gold's ill health forced his retire-

ment, Frederik Pohl capably edited the magazine until 1970. This account is a tedious recital of stories, plot summaries, and comments on illustrations, mixed with cover reproductions and bits of commentary, all slackly written. A bibliography and index are included. Libraries should find the 20-page account by Donald Lawler in Tymn and Ashley [14-18] quite sufficient. (Annotation by editor.)

14-17. Sampson, Robert. **Yesterday's Faces: A Study of Series Characters in the Early Pulp Magazines, Vol. 1, Glory Figures; Vol. 2, Strange Days.** Bowling Green Univ. Popular Press, 1983–1984.
The first two of four projected volumes, exploring the origins of the pulp heroes of the 1930s and 1940s in the popular fiction of the preceding 40 years, which is analyzed in detail. Volume 2 discusses several "scientific detectives," Tarzan and John Carter, and Smith's Skylark series [2-104].

*14-18. Tymn, Marshall B., and Mike Ashley. **Science Fiction, Fantasy, and Weird Fiction Magazines.** Greenwood, 1985.
The definitive treatment of the English-language magazines of the world. Coverage ranges from less than a page to over 40 pages for a title like *Astounding/Analog*. The essays are comprehensive and informative. Each includes a bibliography, sources where indexed, reprints, selective locations, and details on publication. Separate chapters cover critical magazines, serial English-language anthologies, major fanzines, foreign-language magazines, an index to major cover artists, a chronology (1882–1983), and a valuable bibliography. For a unified perspective on the worldwide magazine scene, see Ashley's *History of the Science Fiction Magazines* [14-12].

14-19. Weinberg, Robert. **The Weird Tales Story.** Fax, 1977.
Weird Tales is important as a science fiction source because it carried some SF, but more because many SF writers also appeared there. This volume is the only history of *Weird Tales,* written by a long-time fan and collector. It is valuable for its historical coverage, and for the personal reflections by various authors featured. Hundreds of covers and interior illustrations are reproduced in black-and-white. A color microfiche set of covers from *Weird Tales* has been produced by Micro Information Concepts. Jaffery and Cook [14-6] and Parnell and Ashley [14-8] indexed *Weird Tales.*

14-20. Wertham, Fredric. **The World of Fanzines: A Special Form of Communication.** Southern Illinois, 1973.
Wertham presents the only extended study of fanzines to date, based on a random sample of donated fanzines. He identifies characteristics and contents of the fanzines, concluding that fanzine publishing is a healthy, creative form of communication. A useful book, but limited in both its sample and its treatment. An expansion of the whole fan topic is found in Beverly Friend's dissertation, "The Science Fiction Fan Cult" (Northwestern Univ., 1975), and a good bit of commentary is provided in Sam Moskowitz's *The Immortal Storm* [9-61] and in Harry Warner, Jr.'s, *All Our Yesterdays* [9-62] and *A Wealth of Fable* [9-63]. A chapter in Tymn and Ashley [14-18] provides abundant detail on many fanzines.

Magazines

Annotated below are currently published magazines featuring science fiction in English and a selection of the better magazines about SF likely to have research value. Subscription prices are omitted because of frequent changes. Factual information is current as of fall 1986. Magazines featuring fiction are annotated first, followed by those about SF.

Magazines Featuring Fiction

14-21. Aboriginal SF. ISSN: 0888-3475. 1986. Bimonthly. Charles C. Ryan, ed. (Box 2449, Woburn, MA 01801.)
This new entry into the SF magazine field is edited by Charles C. Ryan, formerly associated with *Galileo* magazine. The initial issue, a tabloid format (11 by 17 inches), features five stories, a book review column, a movie column, and an article by Hal Clement. Sold by subscription only. Obtain a sample issue and evaluate quality at the time of selection.

14-22. Amazing Science Fiction Stories. ISSN: 0279-1706. 1926. Bimonthly. Patrick L. Price, ed. (Box 110, Lake Geneva, WI 53147.) Circ.: 13,183.
Amazing survives changes in editors and publishers, and circulation decreases. A recent change in editors and a March 1986 report in *Locus* indicate that the publisher, TSR, Inc., plans a revamping of the magazine and a major subscription push. The quality of fiction has been generally good, but more variable than that in other magazines. A second choice for libraries.

*14-23. Analog Science Fiction/Science Fact. ISSN: 0161-2328. 1930. 13 issues per year. Stanley Schmidt, ed. (Davis Publications, 380 Lexington Ave., New York, NY 10017.) Circ.: 98,123.
For most of the time from 1930 to 1971, *Astounding/Analog* ranked as the best and most influential magazine in the field, a reflection of the tremendous influence of its editor, John W. Campbell, Jr. Each issue features 6–9 stories, often including a serialized novel, one or two articles, a book review column, a games column, an editorial, and letters. Heavily mined for anthologies from the mid-1940s, its pages have featured the work of many of the best-known SF writers. The historical run of the journal is an essential purchase for any SF research collection. Since Campbell's death in 1971, editorial direction has varied somewhat. One of the best SF magazines, and a core title for any library with an active SF reader group.

14-24. Interzone. ISSN: 0264-3596. 1982. Quarterly. Simon Ounsley; Judith Hanna; and David Pringle, eds. (124 Osborne Rd., Brighton BN1 6LU, England.) Circ.: 4,000.
Interzone is the only British SF magazine, and features 5–7 stories from 2,000 to 8,000 words, one or two articles, a film column, and book reviews. The quality of the fiction is good, including a 1984 World Fantasy Award novella. *Interzone*'s tone is quite unlike that of American magazines, having echoes of the Moorcock-edited *New Worlds* in its emphasis on nontraditional SF and fantasy. *Interzone: The First Anthology* [4-643] reprints 13 tales from the first few years.

*14-25. Isaac Asimov's Science Fiction Magazine. ISSN: 0162-2188. 1976. 13 issues per year. Gardner Dozois, ed. (Davis Publications, 380 Lexington Ave., New York, NY 10017.) Circ.: 79,389.

Asimov's continues to be one of the most popular of the SF magazines. It is well edited, featuring good short stories and novelettes, thoughtful articles, and interesting columns. Each digest-size 190-page issue features 5–9 stories, an Asimov editorial, a book review column covering 6–10 books, an article, and assorted shorter material. A core title for research collections and for libraries with a strong SF clientele.

*14-26. The Magazine of Fantasy and Science Fiction. ISSN: 0024-984X. 1949. Monthly. Edward L. Ferman, ed. (Mercury Press, Box 56, Cornwall, CT 06753.) Circ.: 56,470.

One of the best SF magazines, as its many Hugo awards indicate. Each digest-size 160-page issue features 6–10 stories, a perceptive book review column by Algis Budrys (one of the field's leading critics), an interesting film/media column by Harlan Ellison, and a long-running science column by Isaac Asimov. The fiction is consistently among the best in the field, and frequently features well-known writers. A core journal.

14-27. Omni. ISSN: 0149-8711. 1978. Monthly. Ellen Datlow, fiction ed. (1965 Broadway, New York, NY 10023.) Circ.: 903,014.

Omni is a popular science magazine that regularly features science fiction. Issues typically carry one or two pieces of fiction, frequently by big-name authors, and usually of high quality. Several articles typically focus on science or space technology, and one or two futuristic pictorial features. Regular departments include "Earth" (environmental notes), "Life" (anthropological notes), "Body" (biomedical notes), "Stars" (astronomy), "Continuum" (a science news column of 8–10 pages), "Games" (challenging science-oriented games), and a section on the arts: books, films, or music. Aimed at the reader interested in the future and the effects of scientific progress, *Omni* should appeal to many SF readers, although probably not to readers with a more serious interest in science. A good choice for general patron appeal, but a second choice for pure science fiction.

14-28. SF International. 1986. William H. Wheeler, ed. (99 Teardrop Court, Newbury Park, CA 91320.)

The first issue is not adequate for evaluation and annotation; obtain a sample and evaluate for purchase.

14-29. Worlds of IF. 1986. Clifford R. Hong, ed. (Box 93, Hicksville, NY 11802.)

Worlds of IF is a reincarnation of the original magazine of that title, and picks up the volume numbering with Vol. 23, No. 1. The magazine is digest size, and repeats the format of the original magazine. The one issue published to date does not allow adequate evaluation; obtain a sample and evaluate for purchase.

Magazines about Science Fiction

*14-30. Cinefantastique. ISSN: 0145-6032. 1970. Quarterly. Frederick S. Clarke, ed. (Box 270, Oak Park, IL 60303.) Circ.: 21,000.

14-31. Cinefex. ISSN: 0198-1056. Quarterly. Don Shay, ed. (Box 20027, Riverside, CA 92516.) Circ.: 15,000.

14-32. Starlog. ISSN: 0191-4626. 1976. Monthly. David McDonnel, ed. (475 Park Ave. S., New York, NY 10016.) Circ.: 350,000.

Cinefantastique is the premier magazine on the fantastic cinema. Issues range in length from 60–90 pages and feature color photographs. Each 8 1/2-by-11-inch issue includes 3–5 features ranging from in-depth treatments of motion pictures and television shows to interviews with personalities. A "Reviews" section features 6–8 long reviews of current releases, and a "Short Notices" section covering 6–8 additional titles. "Coming" provides notes on forthcoming releases. *Cinefantastique*'s frank treatment has more than once antagonized the studios. *Cinefex* is the technical journal of special effects, and features long articles with complete descriptions, illustrated with full-color photographs of scenes and details. Issues are 70–80 pages in length, and feature from 1–4 articles per issue. An excellent journal for the specialist. *Starlog* covers the same general material as *Cinefantastique,* but is aimed at the less-discriminating film fan. It features more coverage of the cast of movies than does *Cinefantastique,* and features valuable episode guides to television series. Additional features in each issue cover individual movies and special effects.

*14-33. Extrapolation. ISSN: 0014-5483. 1959. Quarterly. Thomas D. Clareson, ed. (Kent State Univ. Press, Kent, OH 44242.) Circ.: 1,500.

The oldest critical journal in the field, *Extrapolation* offers critical articles, bibliographies, and occasional articles on teaching. An annual bibliography, the "Year's Scholarship in Science Fiction, Fantasy, and Horror," has returned to *Extrapolation* after three years as a monographic publication, but lacking the annotations that had been cited as its primary value. Articles are refereed. A Science Fiction Research Association (SFRA) membership benefit.

14-34. Fantasy Commentator. 1943. Annual. A. Langley Searles, ed. (48 Highland Circle, Bronxville, NY 10708.)

Fantasy Commentator is an important historical and critical magazine, begun in 1943. The editor published 28 quarterly issues before the magazine was suspended. In 1978, publication was resumed on an annual basis. The magazine features lengthy historical and critical articles by well-known names in the study of science fiction and fantasy, including Sam Moskowitz, John J. Pierce, and the editor. The major strength of the journal is the historical material, and criticism of older SF and fantasy works, but recent material is covered also, especially in the book reviews. A core journal for research collections.

14-35. Fantasy Review. 1978. 10 issues per year. Robert A. Collins, ed. (Meckler Publishing, 11 Ferry Lane, Westport, CT 06880.) Circ.: 3,000.

Fantasy Review began as *Fantasy Newsletter* and was originally what that name suggests. The current title dates from January 1984, but the contents had been more varied for several years previously. Issues typically feature 4–6 articles on science fiction and fantasy, a number of short pieces, and news notes. A major feature is the extensive book review section covering 50–60 books per issue, which continues the tradition of *Science Fiction and Fantasy Book Review*, originally published by Borgo Press, then by SFRA, and absorbed by *Fantasy Review*. A long-running feature is Jack Chalker's series on specialty presses. Sections covering new books and magazines round out each issue. Feature articles cover a variety of topics, including authors, interviews, and historical items.

*14-36. Foundation. ISSN: 0306-4964. 1972. 3 issues per year. Edward James, ed. (Science Fiction Foundation, North East London Polytechnic, Longbridge Rd., Dagenham RM8 2AS, England.) Circ.: 1,200.
Foundation is the primary source of non-American SF and fantasy criticism, and often offers a valuable perspective on SF quite different from that found in American criticism. Each 100- to 120-page issue features critical articles on SF, interviews, commentary by SF writers (including a valuable autobiographical series, "The Profession of Science Fiction"), and a lengthy book review section. Articles are generally more readable than those found in *Extrapolation* or *Science-Fiction Studies*.

*14-37. Locus: The Newspaper of the Science Fiction Field. ISSN: 0047-4959. 1968. Monthly. Charles N. Brown, ed. (Locus Publications, Box 13305, Oakland, CA 94661.) Circ.: 8,000.
14-38. Science Fiction Chronicle: The Monthly SF and Fantasy Newsmagazine. ISSN: 0195-5365. 1979. Monthly. Andrew I. Porter, ed. (Algol Press, Box 4175, New York, NY 10163.) Circ.: 5,000.
Locus is the oldest and the best of the existing news magazines of the SF field and provides broad, up-to-date coverage of the field. Each 50- to 70-page issue contains well-written, illustrated coverage of the field, including increasingly good international coverage. Other features include publishing notes, obituaries, book reviews (8–15 per issue), letters, a briefly annotated listing of new books received (comprehensive for U.S., selective for British), best-seller lists, convention reports, columns, and convention listings. Reporting is accurate, complete, and primarily factual. The quality of *Locus* is indicated by its many Hugo awards and nominations, and by the high percentage of paid advertising. *Science Fiction Chronicle* is similar to *Locus* in size, format, and coverage, but carries more extensive news of fans and fan topics. Other features include obituaries, reviews, columns, letters, and special features. Book reviews in *Science Fiction Chronicle* are greater in number but shorter and less analytical than those in *Locus,* and are all written by Don D'Ammassa. Ed Naha's Hollywood column, the "London Report," and "Releases," which lists forthcoming books, are regular features. A market report is featured several times each year.

Locus offers stronger and broader news coverage, more extensive international coverage, and an important bibliographic record of book publishing. Book reviews in both are indexed in *Science Fiction and Fantasy Book Review Index, 1980–1984* [8-20]. News items and articles are indexed in *Science Fiction and Fantasy Book Review Index, 1980–1984* [8-20] and selectively in *The Year's Scholarship in Science Fiction and Fantasy* [8-17]. The historical file of both titles is indexed in *Science Fiction and Fantasy Reference Index* [8-20], forthcoming from Gale Research in

1987. Research collections should have both titles; *Locus* is preferred where only one title is needed.

14-39. Quarber Merkur. 1963. Semiannual. Franz Rottensteiner, ed. (Subscriptions: Hans Joachim Alpers, D-285 Bremerhaven, Weissenburger Str. 6, BDR.) *Quarber Merkur* is an important critical journal in SF and fantasy. Rottensteiner is a perceptive editor, who attracts serious and significant articles from a wide range of authors, with a surprising geographic and topical breadth of coverage. The review column features informed critical reviews of books published in German, French, English, Spanish, Polish, Russian, and Hungarian. At its best, *Quarber Merkur* rivals *Foundation* [14-36] and *Extrapolation* [14-33] in quality of content. By far the most international critical magazine available, this is a core title for research collections. An anthology of 15 articles selected from *Quarber Merkur* has been published, edited by Franz Rottensteiner and titled *Quarber Merkur* (Frankfurt: Suhrkamp, 1979). Also annotated as [6-50].

14-40. Science Fiction Research Association Newsletter. ISSN: 0048-9646. 1971. 10 issues per year. Richard W. Miller, ed. (Membership inquiries: Charlotte P. Donsky, Treas., 1265 S. Clay, Denver, CO 80219.) Circ.: 400.
The official news organ for SFRA, the *Newsletter* is highly variable in content, including news notes on forthcoming books, research in progress, association business reports, and Pilgrim award speeches. Currently of marginal value, the *Newsletter* comes as a benefit of SFRA membership, along with *Extrapolation* [14-33], *Fantasy Review* [14-35], and a membership directory.

*14-41. Science-Fiction Studies. ISSN: 0091-7729. 1973. 3 issues per year. Robert M. Philmus and Charles Elkins, eds. (McGill Univ. Arts Bldg., 853 Sherbrooke St. W., Montreal, Quebec H3A 2T6, Canada.) Circ.: 1,200.
This is the most "academic" of the SF critical magazines. The prose too often reads like a typical dissertation. A distinct leftist/Marxist flavor has been discerned by some critics. Eight to ten articles, each with abstracts in English and French, are featured in each 110- to 120-page issue. Issues frequently focus on a single author or topic, for example, Le Guin, Lem, or nuclear war. Of particular value is the international scope of articles and reviews. *Science-Fiction Studies* is the best source of information on non–English-language criticism and bibliography, along with *Quarber Merkur*. The "Notes" section frequently features material not available from other sources. An essential critical journal, included in SFRA membership. Two volumes of selected articles were reprinted by Gregg Press as *Science Fiction Studies: First Series 1973–1975* (1976) and *Second Series 1976–1977* (1978).

14-42. SFWA Bulletin. ISSN: 0036-1364. 1965. Bimonthly. George Zebrowski and Pamela Sargent, eds. (Box 486, Johnson City, NY 13790.) Circ.: 900.
The *Bulletin* of the Science Fiction Writers of America (SFWA) is the trade publication of the genre. Each digest-size 60- to 80-page issue contains articles of interest to SF writers, reports on grievances (such as problems with publishers), market reports, model contracts, news reports, and book reviews. An invaluable source for news of the SF writers' world, and a valuable title for any fledgling writer. Much of the pragmatic content on contracts, writing tips, and such from

past issues has been condensed in the *SFWA Handbook,* available from the same address for $5.00. A basic title for research collections. The *Bulletin* is a benefit of membership in SFWA and is also available by subscription.

14-43. Thrust. ISSN: 0198-0686. Semiannual. Douglas Fratz, ed. (8217 Langport Terrace, Gaithersburg, MD 20877.) Circ.: 1,800.

Thrust is an excellent example of the best of the fanzine field, featuring articles and interviews that are well written and knowledgeable, plus columns and book reviews. The feature articles make the magazine valuable for the scholar, and the columns and letters give a good view of the fan phenomenon. A good choice where SF readership is large and active.

14-44. Vector. ISSN: 0505-0448. 1958. Bimonthly. David V. Barrett, ed. (23 Oakfield Rd., Croydon, Surrey CRO 2UD, England.) Circ.: 900.

Vector is the official journal of the British Science Fiction Association (BSFA) and provides a literate and perceptive view of SF and fantasy. Typical issues feature an editorial, two or three articles or interviews on the field, and a book review column covering 10–15 books. At their best, the articles and interviews equal those found in *Foundation.* The book reviews are well written and informed, offering good coverage of British imprints. A valuable supplement to *Foundation* and a required title for research collections. Membership in BSFA also brings other benefits, including *Paperback Inferno,* a bimonthly paperback book review magazine; *Focus,* a semiannual magazine for writers; *Matrix,* a newsletter; and *SF Published in Great Britain,* an irregular checklist.

Science Fiction Magazines in Microform

Greenwood Press. 88 Post Road W., Westport, CT 06881. 35mm.

Amazing Stories. Vols. 1–19, 1926–1945, $1,235.00; vols. 20–49, 1946–1975, $1,895.00.

Amazing Stories. 1927. $25.00.

Amazing Stories Quarterly. Vols. 1–7, 1928–1934, $150.00.

Astonishing Stories. Vols. 1–4, 1940–1943, $70.00.

Comet. Vol. 1, 1940–1941, $30.00.

Cosmic Stories. Vol. 1, 1941, $25.00.

Dynamic Science Stories. Vol. 1, 1939, $25.00.

Extrapolation. Vols. 1–15, 1958–1974, $75.00; vols. 16–19, 1974–1978, $30.00.

Fantastic Adventures. Vols. 1–7, 1939–1945, $395.00.

Fantastic Stories. Series I, vols. 8–15, 1946–1953, and Series II, vol. 2, nos. 3–24, 1953–1975, $1,795.00.

Miracle Stories. Vol. 1, 1931, $30.00.

Planet Stories. Vols. 1–2, 1939–1945, $135.00.

Science Fiction. Vols. 1–3, 1939–1943, $65.00.

Science Fiction Quarterly. Nos. 1–10, 1940–1943, $60.00.

Science Wonder Stories/Wonder Stories/Thrilling Wonder Stories. Vols. 1–7, 1929–1936, $445.00; vols. 8–44, 1936–1955, $545.00.

Science Wonder Quarterly/Wonder Stories Quarterly. Vols. 1–4, 1929–1933, $85.00.

Startling Stories. Vols. 1–33, 1939–1955, $545.00.

Stirring Science Stories. Vol. 1, 1941–1942, $35.00.

Micro Information Concepts. Box 2163, Dallas, TX 75221. Micro Information Concepts has some material in print. Inquire for current stocks and prices.

Oxford Microform Publications. c/o Microforms International Marketing Corp., Maxwell House, Fairview Park, Elmsford, NY 10523. Microfiche.
Impulse. Nos. 1–12, 1966–1967, $70.00.
New Worlds. Nos. 138(?)–200, 1964–1971, $180.00.
Speculation. Nos. 1–33, 1963–1973, $80.00.
Vector (BSFA). Nos. 1–74, 1958–197?, $150.00.

University Microfilms. 300 N. Zeeb Rd., Ann Arbor, MI 48106. Primarily 35mm; some titles are available in 16mm or on microfiche. Prices are as of fall 1986.
Algol. Vols. 20–23, 1973–1974, $11.80/year; vols. 30– , 1978– , $11.80/year. Continued by *Starship.*
Alien Critic. Vols. 2–3, 1973–1974, $26.80. See also *Science Fiction Review.*
Analog. Vols. 64–88, Feb. 1960–Feb. 1972, $411.00; vols. 89–104, Mar. 1972–Dec. 1984, $39.70/year; vol. 105, 1985, $29.80; vols. 106– , 1986– , $30/year. British edition, vols. 17–18, 1971–1972, $29.00.
Astounding. Vols. 1–65, 1930–1960, $1,089.00.
Extrapolation. Vols. 20–25, 1979–1984, $26.80/year; vol. 26, 1985, $20.40; vols. 27– , 1986– , $21.50/year.
Isaac Asimov's Science Fiction Magazine. Vols. 1–2, 1977–1978, $16.60/year; vols. 3–8, 1979–1984, $37.50/year; vols. 9– , 1985– , $28.70/year.
Locus. Nos. 131–182, 1973–1975, $26.80/year; vols. 9–17, 1976–1984, $26.80/year; vol. 18, 1985, $24.40; vols. 19– , 1986– , $21.50/year.
Magazine of Fantasy and Science Fiction. Vols. 1–39, 1949–1970, $468.20 (16mm); vols. 40–67, 1971–1984, $20.00/year; vols. 68–69, 1985, $20.40/year; vols. 70– , 1986– , $24.50/year.
Omni. Vols. 1–2, 1978–1980, $61.60/year; vols. 3–7, 1980–1985, $30.80/year; vol. 8, 1985/1986, $23.60; vols. 9– , 1986– , $24.80/year.
Riverside Quarterly. Vols. 1–4, 1964–1971, $47.40; vols. 5–6, 1971–1977, $26.80/year; vols. 7– , 1980–1983, $26.80/year.
SFWA Bulletin. 1974–1984, $26.80/year; 1985, $20.40; 1986– , $21.50/year.
Science Fiction Chronicle. Vols. 1–6, 1979–1985, $11.80/year; vol. 7, 1985, $9.40; vols. 8– , 1986– , $9.90/year.
Science Fiction Review. Vols. 4–13, 1975–1984, $26.80/year; vol. 14, 1985, $20.40; vol. 15, 1986, $21.50.
Starship. Vols. 16–20, 1979–1984, $11.80/year.

15
Library and Private Collections of Science Fiction and Fantasy

H. W. Hall

The serious collecting of science fiction and fantasy by libraries is a relatively recent phenomenon, even though many libraries have purchased SF and fantasy for their reading collections for decades. Only since 1970 has there been widespread, intensive development of large research collections. Efforts such as those listed here are to be applauded, but there is clearly a need for several libraries to emphasize the development of comprehensive SF and fantasy research collections to support the growing interest in this genre. Evidence suggests that the existing collections, with a few exceptions, are not maintaining their collection building even to the level of acquiring most of the current output of science fiction and fantasy, nor are serious efforts to acquire historical and associational material apparent.

Certain general statements may be made about the collections identified here. Collections are primarily found in university libraries and are intended for research rather than for recreational reading. University library collections are frequently in closed stacks in special collections or in rare-book rooms. Few of those listed here exhibit strength in all the major categories: magazines, books, and amateur magazines (fanzines). In particular, significant, accessible fanzine collections are rare. SF magazines are generally retained unbound; complete collections of American and British magazines are few. Active collection of foreign-language magazines and books is rare. Few libraries support their magazine collections with the available microform editions. Cataloging of SF collections has improved since the second edition of *Anatomy of Wonder,* but many still have large blocks of uncataloged material. Published catalogs or descriptions of the collections are infrequent; internal catalogs or finding aids are frequently available in the library.

Interlibrary loans and photocopies are the exception. Institutions offering these services are indicated by the notations "Photocopies" and "ILL." Even when available, interlibrary loan is frequently limited to monographs. Photocopy service always implies "if condition of the material allows."

Many libraries buy reading collections of SF. This listing focuses on those libraries that go further, either in building major research collections or in building extensive circulating collections. In general, collections of under 1,000 items are excluded. Researchers should note that almost all large metropolitan public libraries have significant SF holdings; the Dallas Public Library listing [15-43] is typical of that type library both in size and in the problems noted. Other collections, such as those devoted to C. S. Lewis and J. R. R. Tolkien at Wheaton College, are not listed because of their specialized nature or because the library requested exclusion from this listing.

Collections for the blind and physically handicapped are generally limited to regional centers devoted to that special service. Holdings of SF in these collections vary from a few items to large collections. Access is generally limited to the blind and physically handicapped, and frequently limited to residents of individual states. The Iowa Commission for the Blind Library, Des Moines, previously listed in *Anatomy of Wonder,* is an example of the best of such regional collections, but the scope and direction have changed to deemphasize "recreational reading" and the science fiction and fantasy collection is decreasing in size as the materials wear out. This library requested omission from the current edition. Contact state or local groups for access to the regional center in a given geographic area.

Services to the blind and visually impaired have been available for many years, and materials offered include considerable science fiction. Two major organizations offer these services.

1. The National Library Service (NLS) for the Blind and Physically Handicapped (1291 Taylor St. N.W., Washington, DC 20542) is the primary service. Call 1-800-424-9100 toll free and give them your name, address, and telephone number, and you will be referred to the nearest of the 160 regional and subregional libraries. NLS publishes *Talking Book Topics* and *Braille Book Review* (both bimonthly) and the catalogs *Talking Books, Press Braille,* and *Cassette Books* (all biennially). *Analog* is available each month on disc, and *Isaac Asimov's Science Fiction Magazine* in braille. The booklet *Science Fiction: A Selected List of Books That Have Appeared in Talking Book Topics and Braille Book Review* was issued in 1979 and is still available through NLS or its regional libraries. This is a descriptive listing of 135 disc recordings, 59 cassettes, and 92 braille editions of novels, anthologies, and young adult stories, arranged by author with title indexes. The booklet is itself available

in large print, disc, and braille formats. NLS furnishes regional libraries with a master index on microfiche each quarter, listing not only NLS recordings but the recordings done by the regional libraries as well. The number of SF works available through the system may be about 2,000, with NLS and the regional libraries contributing roughly 100 each year. Readers can request SF mini-bibliographies through the regional libraries.

2. Recording for the Blind (RFB) (20 Roszel Rd., Princeton, NJ 98540; 1-800-221-4793 toll free) is a national nonprofit service providing recorded educational books to anyone who cannot read standard print materials. Approximately 60,000 titles are in the master tape library, with 3,500 added each year through the efforts of about 500 volunteers in 28 studios nationwide. RFB books are recorded on the standard 15/16 ips, 4 track cassettes (one-half the speed of commercial cassettes), each containing four hours of text, and requiring special players. Only entire books are recorded; no partial recordings, chapters, articles, magazines, etc., are included. All subjects are covered, from highly specialized to popular fiction, although the emphasis is on books useful to students from elementary grades through college. Approximately 1,600 pages of the 2,200-page catalog, *Learning through Listening,* are devoted to the main entries, listed in Dewey class number order. Author, title, added entry, and series indexes permit ready access. Several dozen books of criticism are available, from Aldiss's *Billion Year Spree* [9-4] to Franson and DeVore's awards listings [8-36]. The two-volume 1984/1985 catalog lists between 1,000 and 2,000 SF novels, collections, and anthologies.

In addition to these two major organizations, SF fans have themselves been active. Ed Meskys (RFD No. 1, Box 63, Center Harbor, NH 03226) operates Science Fiction and Fantasy for the Blind, an informal service that distributes recordings of fiction and nonfiction requested by fans and recorded by volunteers. Selections from fanzines comprise the recorded *Fanzine,* and short fiction is recorded for *Anthology.* Meskys says he is a one-man operation and sometimes slow to reply.

Mary Lou Lacefield (413 Atwood, Louisville, KY 40217) produces a talking fanzine, *Si Fi Cee,* consisting of author interviews at conventions, plus authors reading from their fiction.

Volunteers of Vacaville (Box 670, Vacaville, CA 95696) has about 200 recorded SF titles in its library and adds about two titles monthly. One of its four book clubs is devoted to SF, with titles suggested by the members, who supply a reading copy for recording.

An increasing selection of recorded SF is available from a variety of publishers. See Chapter 13 for details about commercially available spoken word recordings.

The most significant development in making all types of material available to the visually impaired is the Kurzweil Reading Machine (KRM), a sophisticated computer scanner and speech generation system that works directly from the printed book, and requires no assistance to the user beyond the mandatory training period. KRM scans the text, analyzes the letters, and synthesizes speech. The speech sounds, to quote a KRM representative, "like an East European who learned English in his native country." The machine is available in many larger public libraries and college and university libraries. Although it requires the user to come to it, with its use there are virtually no limitations on the material available to the blind and visually impaired. KRM is not perfect, but it does offer a tremendous improvement over previous service to this special audience.

Special note should be made of the addition of significant major collections from outside the United States. These collections highlight the point that interest in SF is international and that major resources are becoming available worldwide to support research. Of particular note are the University of Sydney collection [15-54], the Science Fiction Foundation collection (London) [15-61], the Spaced Out Library (Toronto) [15-57], and the Maison d'Ailleurs (Switzerland) [15-63]. The scope and influence of French SF may be best studied through the resources of the Maison d'Ailleurs.

The Science Fiction Writers of America (SFWA) has fostered interest in collecting SF through its regional depository system, in which SFWA donates books to designated depositories. As of December 1986, the SFWA depository libraries are: American Philosophical Society Library (Philadelphia); Brigham Young University Library; California State University Library, Fullerton; Eastern New Mexico University; MIT Science Fiction Society Library; Michigan State University Library; North East London Polytechnic; Northern Illinois University Library; State University College (Fredonia, N.Y.); Texas A&M University Library; University of Dayton (Ohio); University of Kansas Library; University of New Brunswick Library (Canada); University of Sydney (Australia); and Uniao Cultural Brasil-Estados Unidos (São Paulo, Brazil).

Two other depository arrangements should be noted. SFWA has established an oral history project to record and preserve interviews, speeches, and panels involving SF personalities. The project, begun in 1977, now has some 350 tapes. This archive is housed at the Vincent Voice Library, Michigan State University. The Science Fiction Research Association (SFRA) has established its archives at the University of Kansas. This archive should become a significant resource for the study of science fiction.

Additions or corrections to this listing should be sent to the editor, whose address is shown in the list of contributors.

Arrangement here is by state, then by country, followed by privately owned collections arranged in the same manner. The information about private collections was compiled and written by Neil Barron. (Some libraries did not provide updated information since the 1981 edition of *Anatomy of Wonder*.)

Library Collections

Arizona

15-1. University of Arizona Library. Science Fiction Collection, Special Collections, Tucson, AZ 85721. 602-621-6423.

Holdings: Fiction, 18,000 volumes; reference/critical, 200 volumes. Magazines: English language, 140+ titles; foreign language, 15 titles; critical, 10 titles; fanzines, 1,300+ titles.

Based on the individual collections of Margaret Brown, Archibald Hanna, and Anthony Boucher; complete runs of most American SF magazines, including strong holdings of the early SF pulps (1923–1943); current acquisitions restricted to SF; actively collect all major authors.

Status: Active, adding 200 titles annually. *Access:* 95 percent cataloged, with special author catalog. Photocopies.

California

15-2. California State University Library, Fullerton. Archives and Special Collections, Science Fiction Collection, Box 4150, Fullerton, CA 92634. 714-773-3444.

Holdings: Fiction, 6,650 volumes; reference/critical, 150 volumes. Magazines: English language, 156 titles; fanzines, 70 titles. Audiovisuals: audio recordings, 30. Manuscripts: Avram Davidson, Philip K. Dick, Harry Harrison, Zenna Henderson, Frank Herbert, Ray Bradbury, Robert Moore Williams; 25 others.

The SF collection consists of materials housed throughout the library. The Special Collections section houses manuscripts and papers of more than 30 SF writers, 3,900 periodical issues, audiovisual material, and an SFWA Depository Collection. The circulating collection contains more than 1,500 hardcover books, and 5,100 paperbacks are in the Reserve Book Room. The Philip Dick holdings are described in "Philip K. Dick Manuscripts and Books: The Manuscripts and Papers at Fullerton," *Science-Fiction Studies* 2, no. 1 (March 1975): 4–5.

Status: Inactive, gifts accepted. *Access:* 5 percent cataloged; inventory or holdings lists. Photocopies.

15-3. Huntington Library. 1151 Oxford Rd., San Marino, CA 91108. 818-405-2100.

The Huntington Library has a small collection of SF, supplemented by the following collections of correspondence: Brian Aldiss, 107 letters to his publishers, 1965–1973; Poul Anderson, 79 letters to his publishers, 1960–1977; Philip K. Dick, 61 pieces, including letters, outlines, and photographs; Frederik Pohl, 91 letters, 1959–1975; Robert Silverberg, 1,144 pieces, 1953–1982, including notes, drafts of short stories, and letters; Clifford D. Simak, 20 letters, 1961–1974. This information was accurate as of 1979.

15-4. Los Angeles Science Fantasy Society Library. 11513 Burbank Blvd., North Hollywood, CA 91601. 818-760-9234.

Holdings: Fiction, 7,000+ volumes; reference/critical, 200 volumes. Magazines: English language, 120+ titles; fanzines, 2,000+ titles; microform, 3 titles.

A SF club collection primarily for club members' use. The prospective user should call first to make arrangements to use the collection. Major strengths lie in the fairly large book collection (mostly paperbacks), the American pulp magazines, and the large fanzine collection.

Status: Active, adding 500 items annually. *Access:* 60 percent cataloged; computer listing of fiction and reference available for cost of printing and postage. Cataloging of magazines in progress.

15-5. San Diego State University Library. Special Collections, San Diego, CA 92182. 619-265-6791.

Holdings: Fiction, 4,000 volumes; reference/critical, 20 volumes. Magazines: English language, 34 titles; critical, 2 titles; fanzines, 2 titles. Audiovisuals:

audiotapes, 25; phonodiscs, 10; films, 1; graphics (posters, etc.), 50. Manuscripts (linear feet): Joan Vinge (8), Suzette Haden Elgin (2), Elizabeth Chater (2), and Jeff Sutton (9).

Chater donated her 2,500-item collection in 1977. Other gifts and purchases, including many autographed editions, have strengthened the collection.

Status: Active, adding 100+ books annually. *Access:* Fully cataloged; printed index to short stories in anthologies.

15-6. San Francisco Academy of Comic Art Library. 2850 Ulloa St., San Francisco, CA 94116. 415-681-1737.

Holdings: Fiction: 10,000 volumes. Magazines: extensive collection; statistics not available.

This specialty collection includes extensive holdings of SF comic strips, and both American and foreign comic books. Associated collections include extensive SF holdings. Special strengths in the SF collection include dime novels and their precursors, including many items in the Frank Reade and Tom Wright series. A large collection of pulps includes such special features as the only known complete run of *Thrill Book* in a public collection, *Argosy*, and *Weird Tales*. Over 12 file cabinets of SF fanzines dating back to the 1930s is an additional strength. About 100 videotapes of little-known SF movies.

Status: Active. *Access:* Alphabetic. Use of the collection is by appointment only. Photocopies, ILL.

15-7. San Francisco Public Library. McComas Collection of Fantasy and Science Fiction, Civic Center, San Francisco, CA 94102. 415-558-3511.

Holdings: Fiction: 2,800 volumes. Magazines: 92 titles.

Started with a small gift by anthologist and author J. Francis McComas, the collection now has over 2,800 volumes and complete runs of 92 U.S. science fiction magazines, and is a reference/research collection for scholarly study.

Status: Active, adding 60 books annually. *Access:* Fully cataloged.

15-8. University of California at Los Angeles. Special Collections, A1713 University Research Library, University of California, Los Angeles, CA 90024. 213-825-4988.

Holdings: Fiction, 10,500 volumes; reference/critical, 50 volumes. Magazines: English language, 140+ titles (about 5,000 issues). Manuscripts: Ray Bradbury (1.5 linear feet); Jean Aroeste (one box Star Trek scripts); one manuscript each of Henry Kuttner, Ward Moore, Margaret St. Clair, Fritz Leiber, and G. C. Edmondson.

The Nitka Collection of Fantastic Fiction comprises extensive holdings of English-language magazines and a strong book collection, including 3,000 paperbacks. The book collection is strongest in the 1950–1975 period, and includes over 400 early editions of the works of H. Rider Haggard. Oral histories of Ray Bradbury and A. E. van Vogt are included.

Status: Active. *Access:* Fully cataloged.

15-9. University of California, Riverside Library. Eaton Collection, Box 5900, Riverside, CA 92507. 714-787-3233.

Holdings: Fiction, 40,000 volumes; reference/critical, 3,000–4,000 volumes.

Magazines: English language, 175 titles; foreign language, 100 titles (including bandes déssinées); critical, 100 titles; fanzines, 100 titles; microform, 50 titles. Audiovisuals: audio recordings, 200; films, 25; videotapes, 450–500. Manuscripts: Gregory Benford (35 boxes); Colin Wilson (25 boxes); Robert Forward (50 boxes).

Presently 40,000 volumes and growing at a rate of 3,000–4,000 volumes annually with standing orders for all new/reprinted American SF/fantasy/horror in hardcover and paperback; all British imprints; all original German-language SF (including East German). Recent acquisitions include utopian and imaginary voyage fiction, seventeenth–nineteenth century, in English, French, German, Spanish, and Dutch; SF/fantasy film shooting scripts (200); French bandes déssinées, 1,000 titles; French SF from Verne to 1945, 100 titles; and a massive collection of critical material in all languages. An associated collection of Anglo-American boys' books contains many "proto-SF" materials. The university was awarded a Title II-C grant in 1986 to catalog the SF collection, which is described in more detail in Hall [8-39]. A printed card catalog of the collection, *Dictionary Catalog of the J. Lloyd Eaton Collection of Science Fiction and Fantasy Literature* [8-3], reflects holdings when the collection was far smaller. The library has issued two publications, *Introduction to the J. Lloyd Eaton Collection of Science Fiction and Fantasy*, by Clifford Wurfel (1979), and *Space Voyages, 1591–1920*, by L. S. Smith (1979).

Status: Active, adding 3,000–4,000 items annually. *Access:* 60 percent cataloged. Photocopies.

15-10. University of California, Santa Cruz. Library, Special Collections, Santa Cruz, CA 95064. 408-429-2547.

Holdings: Manuscripts: Robert A. Heinlein (44 boxes); Eric Temple Bell (7 boxes).

The Robert A. Heinlein Archive is primarily a manuscript collection, but does contain printed versions of Heinlein's work. Heinlein periodically adds to the collection. Some correspondence is sealed and unavailable for research.

Status: Active. *Access:* Uncataloged; a brief listing of collection contents is available. Information current as of 1980.

Colorado

15-11. Colorado State University Library. Imaginary Wars Collection, Fort Collins, CO 80523. 303-491-1844.

Holdings: Fiction, 1,000 volumes; reference/critical, 30.

The Imaginary Wars Collection includes novels, short stories, and other fictional treatments of future wars, hypothetical wars, and people and societies who survive such wars. Descriptions and bibliographies appear in *Extrapolation* (Dec. 1974 and May 1975), *Alternative Futures* (Fall 1978), and *Bulletin of Bibliography* (Oct./Dec. 1978). *Future War Novels* [8-15] was based on this collection.

Status: Active. *Access:* 95 percent cataloged; book catalogs, Photocopies, ILL.

15-12. University of Colorado Library. Reference Division, Boulder, CO 80302.

Holdings: Fiction, 1,200 volumes; reference/critical, 30–50 volumes. Magazines: English language, 8–9 titles; fanzines, 6 titles.

A collection of representative titles is being developed in the general collection. *Status:* Active, adding 50–100 items annually. *Access:* 80–90 percent cataloged. Photocopies.

Florida

15-13. Florida International University Library. Tamiami Trail, Miami, FL 33199. 305-552-2461.

Holdings: Fiction, 1,500 volumes; reference/critical, 40 volumes. Magazines: English language, 15 titles in microform.

Not a separate research collection. All materials are in the circulating collections. Includes the reprint collections from Gregg Press and Arno Press, plus modern SF books.

Status: Active. *Access:* Fully cataloged. ILL.

Georgia

15-14. University of Georgia Libraries. Reference Division, Athens, GA 30602. 404-542-7463.

Holdings: Fiction, 5,350 volumes; reference, 100. Magazines: English language, 140 titles; foreign language, 1 title. Audiovisuals: videotapes, 23. Manuscripts: Michael Bishop (9 boxes), Brad Strickland (2 boxes), Sharon Webb (21 boxes).

Major strength is an extensive collection of pulps from 1926 to 1950. Holdings include 87 percent of the core collection listed in the 1976 edition of *Anatomy of Wonder*. Books are part of the circulating collection. The collection is described in "New Worlds at the Library," *Southeastern Librarian* 31, no. 2 (Summer 1981): 65–67.

Status: Active, adding 150 items annually. *Access:* Cataloged; titles acquired after 1980 appear in the University of Georgia Libraries online catalog. Photocopies.

Illinois

15-15. Northern Illinois University Library. Special Collections, DeKalb, IL 60115. 815-753-0255.

Holdings: Fiction, 71 volumes; reference/critical, 5 volumes. Magazines: English language, 105. Manuscripts: H. P. Lovecraft (a few letters).

Complete runs of many major American magazine titles. Some H. P. Lovecraft material and a dime novel collection complement the SF magazine collection.

Status: Active, adding 20 items annually. *Access:* 99 percent cataloged; list of magazine titles. Photocopies.

15-16. University of Illinois Library at Urbana-Champaign. Rare Book Room, H. G. Wells Collection/Jaffe Collection, Urbana, IL 61801. 217-333-0790.

Holdings: H. G. Wells Collection: 1,000+ volumes including Wells's SF with an almost complete file of English editions, inscribed and corrected by Wells; correspondence to and from Wells; 145 manuscript boxes, 24 boxes of SF-related material. Jaffe Collection: 200+ modern-period titles.

SF is distributed in various departmental library locations, including the general stacks and the undergraduate library. No figures exist on total collection size.

Status: Active, adding 25 items annually. *Access:* Fully cataloged; Wells items described in *The Rare Book Room Catalog of the University of Illinois,* vol. 11 (G. K. Hall, 1972). Photocopies.

Indiana

15-17. Indiana University. Lilly Library, Bloomington, IN 47405. 812-337-2452.

The Lilly Library has no separate SF/fantasy collections, but has extensive holdings in these areas. Authors' papers in the library include those of Anthony Boucher, Fritz Leiber, August Derleth, and Robert Bloch. Correspondence from many SF/fantasy writers is scattered throughout the collections, especially in publishers' files such as those of Bobbs-Merrill and Capra Press. First edition collections of many authors are held, including Wells, Verne, Haggard, Chesterton, Derleth, and Lovecraft. A separate catalog of the collection is available. An exhibition catalog highlights some of the SF/fantasy holdings (*Science Fiction and Fantasy,* David R. Randell, S. C. Fredericks, and Tim Mitchell, comps. Lilly Library, 1975).

Status: Active. *Access:* Fully cataloged.

Iowa

15-18. Waterloo Public Library. 415 Commercial St., Waterloo, IA 50501. 319-291-4482.

Holdings: Fiction, 1,253 volumes. Magazines: 59 titles (1,327 issues).

This collection is strongest for the period from 1941 to 1986, particularly in the paperback books and the magazines, which are in excellent condition. The collection was donated by Elmer Moeller in 1985, and is housed as a separate research collection.

Status: Active, by gift. *Access:* Computer printout by author and title.

Kansas

15-19. University of Kansas Kenneth Spencer Research Library. Dept. of Special Collections, Lawrence, KS 66045. 913-864-4334.

Holdings: Fiction, 6,000+ volumes; reference/critical, 80 volumes. Magazines: English language, 110 titles; foreign language, 5 titles; critical, 2 titles; fanzines, large uncataloged collection. Audiovisuals: audio recordings, 280; miscellaneous convention literature, buttons, posters, prospectuses, etc. Manuscripts (linear feet, most uncataloged): James E. Gunn (20), Lloyd Biggle (16), Cordwainer Smith (10.5), J. Hunter Holly (4), Algis Budrys (.25), T. L. Sherred (3), P. Schuyler Miller (2.5), A. E. van Vogt (.5).

Begun in 1969, the collection has been built primarily through gifts. The Biggle and Gunn materials are deposits only. The collection is the official repository for the archives of the Science Fiction Research Association (2.5 linear feet) and the Science Fiction Oral History Association. The Gunn material contains some SFWA official papers, from the term of his presidency. The collection is the North American Repository for World SF, which deposits non–English-language books, and is the depository for the papers of SFRA. The collection is described in "Library of the Future: Science Fiction and the Department of Special Collections," *Books and Libraries at the University of Kansas* (Spring 1976): 1–5.

Status: Active, by gift, adding 400 items annually. *Access:* 30 percent cataloged; donor lists, shelf arrangement. Photocopies.

Kentucky

15-20. University of Kentucky Library. Special Collections, Lexington, KY 40506. 606-257-8611.

Holdings: Fiction, 1,485 volumes. Magazines: English language, 54 titles; foreign language, 1 title; fanzines, 4 titles.

The core of this minor collection was donated to the library and consists mostly of paperbacks, with a few hardcover books.

Status: Active, growth by donation only, adding 10 items annually. *Access:* Minimum-level cataloging; approximately 10 percent in OCLC. Photocopies.

15-21. University of Louisville Library. Patterson Room, Louisville, KY 40208. 502-588-6762.

Holdings: 20,000 items by and related to Edgar Rice Burroughs. Magazines: 10,000 pulp magazines, mostly SF and fantasy; foreign language, 13 titles; critical magazines, 35 titles; fanzines, 35 titles, plus scattered items with Burroughs material. Audiovisuals: films, 20; videotapes, 12.

The basic collection is a 20,000-item Edgar Rice Burroughs collection, cited as the largest of its kind in any institutional library. The collection includes English-language and foreign-language first editions, most in dust wrappers; personal memorabilia; scrapbooks, Burroughs's school textbooks, comics, posters, photos, manuscripts, fanzines, toys, movies, and related material about Burroughs. A recent acquisition is a complete file of all syndicated Sunday and daily comic strips of Tarzan, 1928 to the present, and all but two or three of the Tarzan motion pictures, some with scripts. With the movies are several home movies of Burroughs and his family. Manuscripts, papers, and letters are included (25 boxes). The collection is described by George McWhorter, "Edgar Rice Burroughs: King of Dreams," *Library Review* (Univ. of Louisville), no. 30 (May 1980): 3–25.

Status: Active, adding 600 items annually. *Access:* Local card catalog, including a subject index to the collection (four catalog drawers).

Louisiana

15-22. Louisiana State University. Middleton Library, The Clarence J. Laughlin Library of the Arts, Baton Rouge, LA 70803. 504-388-6572.

Holdings: Fiction, 11,000 volumes; reference/critical, 500 volumes. Magazines: 200 titles; fanzines, 50.

The Clarence J. Laughlin Library of the Arts is an extensive collection of the literary output of major American and British trade publishers from the late nineteenth century to the mid-twentieth century. From that point, the focus narrowed to science fiction, fantasy, and mystery fiction. The collection is based heavily on Bleiler's *The Checklist of Fantastic Literature* [8-2]. The large fiction holdings, the runs of many pulps, and the output of specialty presses such as Gnome Press and Arkham House make this a major resource collection.

Status: Inactive. *Access:* In process; much of the collection is still boxed.

15-23. Tulane University Library. Special Collections, New Orleans, LA 70118. 504-865-6695.

Holdings: Fiction, 850 volumes; reference/critical, 8 volumes. Magazines: English language, 38 titles.

The Brown collection consists of 847 books and 924 issues of 38 periodical titles. The Heinlein collection consists of 31 first editions, many signed, and a copy of the typescript *I Will Fear No Evil* (1970). Information current as of 1980.

Maryland

15-24. University of Maryland, Baltimore County. Albin O. Kuhn Library and Gallery, Arzriel Rosenfeld Science Fiction Research Collection, 5401 Wilkens Ave., Catonsville, MD 21228. 301-455-2353.

Holdings: Fiction, 7,400 volumes; reference/critical, 600 volumes. Magazines: English language, 102 titles; critical, 15 titles; fanzines, 11,100 issues. Audiovisuals: audio recordings, 42; films, 10; videotapes, 7 (TV show episodes); art, 50 items. Manuscripts: Roger Zelazny (5 books), Charles L. Harness (3 books), Brian M. Stableford (4 books), E. C. Tubb (2 books), single items from 18 other authors.

The major strength of this impressive collection consists of the large Walter Coslet fanzine collection, mostly pre-1960, including many from the 1930–1950 period, and the large pulp collection. A catalog of the fanzine collection is available in the library.

Status: Active, adding 300 items annually. *Access:* 99 percent of hardcover books in OCLC; paperbacks, separate card catalog; fanzines, pulps, artwork—lists. Photocopies.

Massachusetts

15-25. Boston University. Mugar Memorial Library, Twentieth Century Archives, Dept. of Special Collections, 771 Commonwealth Ave., Boston, MA 02215. 617-353-3696.

Holdings: Fiction, 1,286 volumes; reference/critical, few. Magazines: English language, 1 title. Manuscripts (linear feet): Isaac Asimov (190), Marion Zimmer Bradley (36), Arthur C. Clarke (2), L. Sprague de Camp (45), Samuel R. Delany (36), Alan Nourse (40), Edgar Pangborn (18), Curt Siodmak (10), Jack Vance (John Holbrook Vance) (10). (*Note:* Total size of manuscript holdings, not size of SF portion.)

Status: Active, adding 100 items annually. *Access:* Manuscripts, 60–75 percent cataloged; control file by author for books; accession cards with volume, brief description of manuscripts. Photocopies.

15-26. MIT Science Fiction Society Library. MIT Student Center, Rm. 420-421, Cambridge, MA 02139. 617-253-1000, ext. 5-9144.

Holdings: Fiction, 17,500 volumes; reference/critical, 300 volumes. Magazines:

English language, 138 titles; foreign language, 65 titles; fanzines, 1,000 issues; microforms, 68.

Primarily a circulating collection for recreational reading of the members. The 32,000-item collection has an almost complete file of American and British SF magazines. A particular strength is the extensive collection of foreign-language magazines, especially German and Italian. A large group of foreign translations is held. The collection is available to scholars; inquire first as to restrictions and hours. A copy of the catalog is available at the requester's cost. Not an official part of the Massachusetts Institute of Technology. The collection is described in Hall [8-39].

Status: Active, adding 2,000 items per year. *Access:* Fully cataloged (listed) for access; computerized bibliography available. Information current as of 1980.

Michigan

15-27. Michigan State University Library. Special Collections, East Lansing, MI 48824. 517-355-3770.

Holdings: Fiction, 8,600 volumes. Magazines: English language, 71 titles; fanzines, 2,500 issues. Audiovisuals: audio recordings, 350. Manuscripts: 1,500+.

The science fiction section is part of the Russell B. Nye Popular Culture Collections in the Special Collections Department. A major strength lies in the magazines since 1940, and in the fanzines, supplemented by the fiction collection. The manuscripts from the Clarion Workshop from 1973 to the present are held, including the original story, critiques by participants, and revisions. The fanzine collection is accessible by editor or title. The Vincent Voice Library is the repository for the SFWA Oral History Project, which now numbers over 350 tapes.

Status: Active, SFWA depository and donations primarily; some large collections purchased as available. *Access:* 90 percent cataloged; listing of fanzines; computerized holdings list by author. Photocopies.

15-28. University of Michigan. Harlan Hatcher Graduate Library, Dept. of Rare Books and Special Collections, Hubbard Collection of Imaginary Voyages, Ann Arbor, MI 48109. 313-764-9377.

Holdings: Fiction, 2,898 volumes; reference/critical, 129 volumes.

The collection consists of over 3,000 volumes, largely various editions, translations, adaptations, abridgments, and imitations of *Robinson Crusoe* and *Gulliver's Travels*. A few books by such authors as Verne, Bellamy, and Cyrano de Bergerac are included. Almost entirely limited to imaginary voyages on Earth, with few interplanetary trips.

Status: Active, adding 1–2 items annually. *Access:* Fully cataloged. Photocopies.

Minnesota

15-29. University of Minnesota Libraries. Manuscripts Division, Star Trek Collection, 826 Berry St., St. Paul, MN 55714. 612-376-7271.

Holdings: Fiction, 50 volumes; reference/critical, 95 volumes; unpublished scripts, 11 volumes; research material, 11 volumes of other unpublished story treatments, etc. Audiovisuals: discs, 9. Manuscripts (8 linear feet total): Gordon

R. Dickson (60 boxes), Clifford D. Simak (17 boxes), Thomas Disch (18 boxes), Carl Jacobi (5 boxes), E. Hoffman Price (1 box), H. P. Lovecraft (17 items).

The focus of the collection is authors having Minnesota connections, either by birth or residence (exceptions are Price and Lovecraft). An attempt is also being made to collect materials from the old pulp writers, such as Price and Jacobi. Collections contain notes, correspondence, manuscript drafts, and some galley proofs. The Hess Collection in the Special Collections Department includes over 40,000 dime novels, selected pulp magazines, and related material, some of which is SF. The Kerlan Collection emphasizes twentieth-century children's literature and includes many of the juvenile titles annotated in this guide. A "Star Trek" collection is included.

Status: Active, by gift only. *Access:* Fully cataloged. Photocopies.

New Mexico

15-30. Eastern New Mexico University. Golden Library, Special Collections, Williamson Library, Portales, NM 88130. 505-562-2636.

Holdings: Fiction, 8,072 volumes; reference/critical, 638 volumes. Magazines: English language, 181 titles; foreign language, 24 titles; critical, 36 titles; fanzines, 469 titles; microform, 1 title; 9,934 total magazine issues. Audiovisuals: audio recordings, 319; films, 3; videotapes, 1; photographs/personal papers (1 linear foot); artists illustrations (.5 linear foot); various plaques/trophies (visual, 1 linear foot). Manuscripts (linear feet): Jack Williamson, includes some SFWA files during his term as president (47), Leigh Brackett (8), Edmond Hamilton (4), Forrest J. Ackerman (13.5), Piers Anthony (1), *Analog* files, 1954–1975 (21), James Blish, SFWA Presidential (1), Marcia Howl (1), Woody Wolfe (1).

The collection originated with gifts from Jack Williamson and now consists of more than 18,000 items. Strengths include the pulp magazine collection, old editions of "classics," and the manuscript holdings. The *Analog* files, 1954–1975, include copy-edited manuscripts from many authors. The collection is an SFWA and Science Fiction Oral History Association depository. It is listed in the *National Catalog of Manuscript Collections.* Articles on the collection include "Eastern Dedicates Williamson Library," *New Mexico Library Association Newsletter* 10 (June 1982): 5; "Fantastic Tale: Science Fiction at Eastern New Mexico University," *Extrapolation* 14 (May 1973): 126–128; and "Out of the Closet: Science Fiction at Eastern New Mexico," in Hall [8-39].

Status: Active, mainly gifts from Williamson and SFWA deposits; adding 200 items annually. *Access:* Books, fully cataloged; personal papers, 60 percent cataloged; catalog cards for oral histories and photos; registers and indexes for personal papers. Photocopies.

15-31. University of New Mexico Library. Zimmerman Library, Albuquerque, NM 87131. 505-277-4241.

Holdings: Magazines: English language, 61 titles.

The Donald Day SF Collection consists of a virtually complete collection of 52 American and 3 British SF magazines published between 1926 and 1950. The magazines are those indexed in Donald B. Day's *Index to the Science Fiction Magazines, 1926–1950* [14-4]. The collection includes Day's original card index.

Status: Inactive. Information current as of 1980.

New York

15-32. New York Public Library. General Research Division, 42 St. & Fifth Ave., New York, NY 10018. 212-930-0671.

Holdings: Fiction, 6,500 volumes; reference/critical, 46 volumes on open shelf, 348 volumes on closed shelf. Magazines: English language, 146 titles; foreign language, 9 titles; critical, 12 titles; fanzines, representative selection on film; microform, 79 titles.

There is no separate SF collection. Holdings are strong, however, particularly in pre-1960 material.

Status: Active, adding 500 items annually. *Access:* fully cataloged. Photocopies.

15-33. State University of New York, Albany. University Library, Special Collections, 1400 Washington Ave., Albany, NY 12222. 518-442-3543.

Holdings: Fiction, 2,800 volumes; reference/critical, 100 volumes. Magazines: English language, 23 titles; critical, 2 titles. Audiovisuals: audio recordings, 2.

This monographic collection is strongest for the 1951–1975 period.

Status: Active, adding 150 items annually. *Access:* Title entry in main catalog; author entry in Special Collection Catalog. Photocopies.

15-34. Syracuse University. George Arents Research Library, Manuscript Division, Syracuse, NY 13244. 315-423-2585.

Holdings: Fiction, 3,100 volumes; reference/critical, 150 volumes. Magazines: English language, 5,800 issues; fanzines, 50 titles. Manuscripts (linear feet): Forrest J. Ackerman (79), Piers Anthony (4.7), Hal Clement (Harry C. Stubbs) (2.5), Galaxy Publishing Corporation (31.8), Hugo Gernsback (33), Gnome Press (.5), William F. Jenkins (35), David Keller (5), Damon Knight (10), David A. Kyle (.5), Keith Laumer (8.5), Anne McCaffrey (1.8), Mercury Press (20), Andre Norton (16.25), Frederik Pohl (6.5), Robert Silverberg (2.5), Universal Publishing Corporation (.8), Kate Wilhelm (6), Richard Wilson (17.25), Donald A. Wollheim (.25), Roger Zelazny (3.5).

This major collection is split between the Manuscript Division and the Rare Book Room. It is particularly strong in the area of manuscripts and correspondence. Of particular note are the files of Galaxy Publishing Corporation, Mercury Press, and Gnome Press. The supporting collections of more than 8,900 book and magazine items add strength to the collection. A pamphlet, *Science Fiction Collections in the George Arents Research Library at Syracuse University,* compiled by Philip F. Mooney (Syracuse, undated, ca. 1968), offers some access to the collection. A further description of the collection, "Syracuse University," by Fred Lerner, appears in Hall [8-39]. Researchers should contact the library in advance for an appointment and information on restrictions.

Status: Active, primarily through gifts. *Access:* Uncataloged; processed manuscript collections have inventories available in the library.

North Carolina

15-35. Duke University Library. Dept. of Rare Books, Durham, NC 27706. 919-684-4134.

Holdings: Fiction, 1,600 volumes.

The basic description of the Negley collection is found in Glen Negley's *Uto-*

pian Literature: A Bibliography, with a Supplementary Listing of Works Influential in Utopian Thought (1978). (*Note:* The frequently cited Folcroft edition is reprinted from a partial checklist and should be avoided, according to the Library.) One of the major utopian collections.

Status: Active, adding 15–20 items annually. *Access:* Fully cataloged; separate catalog available.

Ohio

15-36. Bowling Green State University. Popular Culture Library, Bowling Green, OH 43403. 419-372-2450.

Holdings: Fiction, 5,000 volumes; reference/critical, 150 volumes. Magazines: English language, 500 titles; fanzines, 1,000 issues; pulps, 1,700 issues. Manuscripts (linear feet): Daniel Cohen (18), Alexei Panshin (19.5), Joanna Russ (7.5). The separate Bradbury collection includes many Bradbury manuscripts.

The special strength of the collection is American magazines, 1926–1960; pulp magazines and fanzines. Especially notable are the Michael L. Cook Collection of fanzines (including rare issues of *Flying Saucers, Twilight Zone,* and *Spacecraft Digest*) and the H. James Horvitz SF Collection of pulp magazines (including runs of *Amazing Stories, Tales of Magic and Mystery,* and *Weird Tales,* among others). The Ray Bradbury collection consists of over 700 books and 15 linear feet of nonbook materials. There are a number of rare Bradbury pamphlets, comic book adaptations, original art by Bradbury, tapes, phonodiscs, cassettes, maps, broadsides, photographs, galley proofs, scripts, programs, screenplays, diary notes, posters, promotional material, interviews, speeches, and over 400 periodicals. The centerpiece of the manuscript collection is the heavily revised 221-page typed draft of *Fahrenheit 451*. Also included are 120 manuscripts in 160 drafts of Bradbury short stories and verse. An unusual item is a 135,000-word manuscript transcribed from tapes forming a complete Bradbury autobiography.

Status: Active, adding 200–1,000 items annually. *Access:* 75 percent cataloged. Some indexed by item, some by collection; some await processing. Photocopies.

15-37. Kent State University Libraries. Kent, OH 44242. 216-672-2270.

Holdings: Fiction, 800 volumes. Manuscripts: Stephen R. Donaldson (11 boxes).

The strength of the collection is the Donaldson books and manuscripts; the fiction is mostly paperback, 1950–1980.

Status: Active, gifts only. *Access:* Uncataloged; separate checklist in the library.

15-38. Ohio State University Libraries. Special Collections, 1858 Neil Avenue, Columbus, OH 43210. 614-422-5938.

Holdings: Magazines: English language, 105 titles; fanzines, "11 cubic feet" of sample titles from the 1950s and the 1970s.

The collection consists of an extensive file of American and British SF magazines from 1926 to the present, including a nearly complete set of *Weird Tales.* Supplementing the magazine collection is a sample collection of fanzines, a collection of 4,000 paperback books, an extensive collection of Arkham House imprints, and a representative collection of fiction in the regular collections of the library.

Status: Active. *Access:* Cataloged. Photocopies.

Oregon

15-39. Multinomah County Library. 801 S.W. Tenth St., Portland, OR 97205. 503-223-7201.

Holdings: Fiction, 1,600 volumes. Audiovisuals: films, 16; videotapes, 10.

A representative collection, strongest from 1951 to 1980, integrated into the circulating collection.

Status: Active, adding 100 items annually. *Access:* Fully cataloged except paperbacks.

Pennsylvania

15-40. Pennsylvania State University. Pattee Library, Special Collections, Science Fiction Collection, University Park, PA 16802. 814-865-1793.

Holdings: Fiction, 3,000 volumes; reference/critical, 150 volumes. Magazines: English language, 145; critical, 10 titles.

The strength of the collection is in the 3,000-issue magazine collection, which includes complete runs of many titles. The monograph collection includes a near-complete file of Arkham House books, and a utopian collection of 1,700 items.

Status: Active, adding 10 items annually. *Access:* Bibliography available for $10 (Utopian Collection); 35 percent cataloged; author/title access through computer system. Photocopies, ILL.

15-41. Temple University Libraries. Special Collections, Philadelphia, PA 19122. 215-787-8230.

Holdings: Fiction, 7,543 volumes; reference/critical, 494 volumes. Magazines: English language, 125 titles; foreign language, 3 titles; critical, 21 titles; fanzines, 1,000+ issues. Audiovisuals: audio recordings, 12. Manuscripts: (linear feet): Ben Bova (32), Gardner Dozois (7), Lloyd A. Eshbach/Fantasy Press (5.8), Jack Dann (12), Tom Purdom (4), Pamela Sargent (13), George Zebrowski (14), Michael Bishop (15), Felix Gotschalk (1), John Varley (2), Oswald Train/Prime Press (2), Miriam DeFord (.5), Richard Peck (.5), assorted authors (6).

The David C. Paskow Collection was established in 1972 as a research collection, and is strongest for the 1951–1980 period. Current publications are received through standing orders. Manuscript collections are a particular strength, especially the archives of Fantasy Press and Prime Press.

Status: Active, adding 500 items per year. *Access:* 90 percent cataloged; temporary cards and computer files for uncataloged books; inventories for manuscripts.

Rhode Island

15-42. Brown University. John Hay Library, Providence, RI 02912. 401-863-2146.

Holdings: Fiction, 550 volumes; reference/critical, 50 volumes. Magazines: English language, 10 titles; foreign, 2 titles; fanzines, 24 titles. Audiovisuals: audiotapes, 1; phonodiscs, 4. Manuscripts: H. P. Lovecraft; Clark Ashton Smith.

The Lovecraft collection contains more than 700 printed items by and about Lovecraft, supplementing more than 5,000 manuscripts/typescripts, including essays, letters, poems, and stories by Lovecraft, and more than 3,000 essays, letters, and the like by 200 of his correspondents, including August Derleth, Frank Belknap Long, C. L. Moore, E. Hoffman Price, and Clark Ashton Smith. The Smith collection contains more than 5,000 manuscripts/typescripts (1893–1972) of essays, fiction, poetry, and miscellaneous material by Smith and more than 5,000 letters to Smith, many from well-known writers and publishers.

Status: Active, adding 25 items annually. *Access:* Uncataloged. Information current as of 1980.

Texas

15-43. Dallas Public Library. Science Fiction and Fantasy Collection, 1954 Commerce St., Dallas, TX 75201. 214-749-4261.

Holdings: Fiction, 13,000+ volumes; reference/critical: 400+ volumes. Magazines: English language, 50 titles; foreign language: 1 title; critical, 8 titles; fanzines, 12 titles; microform, 25 titles. Audiovisuals: audio recordings, 225; films, 3. Manuscripts: In addition to above, the Brian Aldiss Collection consists of 2,350 volumes of fantasy and SF, 187 fantasy and SF periodical titles, personal correspondence, photographs, speeches, illustrations, introductions, posters and cover art, book and film reviews, radio plays, and notes and typescripts for short stories, novels, and poetry.

Since 1974, the Dallas Public Library has been committed to developing a research collection of science fiction. Multiple copies of primary and secondary source material are routinely added to the collection, and attempts are made to fill gaps from previous years. The personal library and archives of Brian Aldiss were purchased and are now open to researchers.

Status: Active. *Access:* 90–95 percent cataloged; uncataloged materials are inventoried. Photocopies. ILL.

15-44. Sam Houston State University. Thomason Room (Special Collection), Huntsville, TX 77341. 409-294-1619.

A collection of all H. G. Wells first editions, including books and pamphlets. Also collects Texas science fiction.

Status: Active. *Access:* 95 percent cataloged. Photocopies.

15-45. Texas A&M University Library. Science Fiction Research Collection, College Station, TX 77843. 409-845-1951.

Holdings: Fiction, 20,000+ volumes; reference/critical, 500+ volumes. Magazines: English language, 200+ titles; foreign language, 20 titles; critical, 19 titles; fanzines, 6,000 issues; microforms, 20 titles. Audiovisuals: audiotapes, 20; phonodiscs, 4; videocassettes, 1. Manuscripts (16 linear feet): Moorcock, Sladek, Silverberg, Davidson, Burgess.

Begun in 1970, the collection now exceeds 25,000 items. The core of the collection is the pulp magazine collection, which contains 95 percent of the American and British SF magazines from 1923 to the present, plus a growing sample of foreign-language titles, including near complete runs of *Fiction* (France), *Galactika* (Hungary), and *Robot* (Italy). The monograph collection is strongest from 1950 to the present, but includes much pre-1950 material. A special effort is made to collect all historical, critical, and reference materials in all languages, including master's theses and doctoral dissertations. A particularly valuable segment of the collection is the "Science Fiction: Collected Papers" file, consisting of more than 10,000 pages of articles about SF collected by a local professor in his research. A representative collection of more than 6,000 fanzine issues is maintained, providing a sampling of this important but little-used segment of the literature of SF. The collection is described in Hall [8-39] and in "Announcing the Future: Science Fiction at Texas A&M University," *Texas Library Journal* 50 (December 1974): 221–223, 257. The library issued a pamphlet, *Announcing the Future,* in 1974.

Status: Active, adding 800–1,200 items annually. *Access:* 50 percent cataloged; card files by author for books and anthologized stories. Photocopies.

15-46. The University of Texas, Austin. Harry Ransom Humanities Research Center, The L. W. Currey Science Fiction and Fantasy Collection, Box 7219, Austin, TX 78713. 512-471-9119.

Holdings: Fiction, 6,300 volumes; reference/critical, 108 volumes. Magazines: English language, 111 titles; critical, 3 titles; fanzines, 400 + titles.

The core of the collection is the L. W. Currey collection of first editions, which was the basis for his book on SF first editions [8-3A]. Supplementing the Currey collection is the Selznik Archive, which includes extensive material on *King Kong* and other fantastic films, and a large collection of motion picture promotional material and lobby cards. The Harry Ransom Humanities Research Center has hundreds of letters to or from SF writers scattered throughout its collections, by Ambrose Bierce, Stapledon, Čapek, Lewis, Orwell, and many others. Manuscript collections include Arthur Conan Doyle (23 boxes), Lord Dunsany (6 boxes), Arthur Machen (23 boxes), Ernest Bramah Smith (25 boxes), and T. H. White (36 boxes).

Status: Active, adding 500 items annually. *Access:* 50 percent cataloged; short title catalog of Currey collection. Photocopies.

Utah

15-47. Brigham Young University. Lee Library, Science Fiction/Fantasy Collection, Provo, UT 84602. 801-378-6735.

Holdings: Fiction, 6,409 volumes; reference/critical, 459 volumes. Magazines: English language, 43 titles; critical, 11 titles; fanzines, 7 titles; microform, 2 titles.

The SF collection originated in 1964 with the purchase of a large collection, and is used in support of university SF classes. Special interests include Arkham House publications, Edgar Rice Burroughs first editions, and SF Book Club editions. The collection is an SFWA depository.

Status: Active, adding 300 items annually. *Access:* Fully cataloged; separate catalog also available in the library. Photocopies, ILL.

Virginia

15-48.   University of Virginia Library. James Branch Cabell Collection, Manuscripts Dept., Charlottesville, VA 22903. 804-924-3025.

The James Branch Cabell Collection covers the years 1886–1958, and is especially rich in the period 1920–1940. The collections include the manuscripts of 23 books and a number of articles and stories. Original correspondence numbers about 1,500 items; photocopies or microfilm of an additional 800 items are held.

Status: Active. Manuscripts are described in Matthew J. Bruccoli, *Notes on the Cabell Collections at the University of Virginia* (Charlottesville: Univ. of Virginia Press, 1957).

Washington

15-48A.   Washington State University. Holland Library, Pullman, WA 99164. 509-335-5517.

The Nuclear War Fiction Collection consists of approximately 750 titles, hardcover and paperback, including novels, short fiction, and plays, and is growing steadily. In addition to war fiction as such, including fiction based on the bombing of Hiroshima and Nagasaki, postnuclear war fiction is also included. Coverage is limited to works in English, including translations. Although there is no separate catalog for the collection, it is based on an annotated bibliography by a member of the Washington State University English faculty, *Nuclear Holocausts: Atomic War in Fiction 1895–1984* (Kent State, 1987), compiled by Paul Brians. The works are shelved with the regular fiction collection, and all save a few works circulate. Photocopies, ILL.

Wisconsin

15-49.   State Historical Society. August Derleth Papers, 816 State St., Madison, WI 53706. 608-463-6594.

The August Derleth pulp collection is composed of fantasy and SF pulp magazines, together with many detective and genre pulps to which Derleth contributed. Roughly two-thirds of the pulp collection is SF and fantasy. The collection also includes most Arkham House books and the bulk of Derleth's manuscripts and personal papers, but not the papers of Arkham House. The collection can be examined in the Archives Reading Room. No appointment is necessary, but it is recommended that researchers call ahead or write.

15-50.   University of Wisconsin, La Crosse. Murphy Library, La Crosse, WI 54601. 608-785-8511.

Holdings: Fiction, 1,100 volumes.

The Paul W. Skeeters Collection of fantasy, SF, and horror literature contains more than 1,000 items ranging from 1764 to the mid-1960s. Primarily first editions. Authors include Aiken, Wharton, Burroughs, Rohmer, and Thayer. Greatest strength is in the 1900–1926 period, and in Arkham House books, about 100 titles.

Status: Active, adding 5 items annually. *Access:* Fully cataloged. Photocopies.

15-51. University of Wisconsin, Milwaukee. Golda Meir Library, Special Collections, Box 604, Milwaukee, WI 53201. 414-963-6119.

Holdings: Magazines: English language, 57 titles.

The collection consists of 1,500 magazine issues, 1926–1953, received by gift.

Status: Inactive. *Access:* Fully cataloged. Photocopies.

Wyoming

15-52. University of Wyoming Library. American Heritage Center, Laramie, WY 82071. 307-766-4114.

Holdings: Fiction, 6,000 volumes; reference/critical, 500 volumes. Magazines: English language, 12 titles; foreign language, 4 titles; critical, 2 titles; fanzines, 1 title; microform, 5 titles. Audiovisuals: audio recordings, 200; videotapes, 50. Manuscripts (boxes): Robert Bloch (234+), Sam Peeples (222), Forrest J. Ackerman (140+), Martin Caidin (54+), Fritz Lang (30), H. L. Prosser (19), Donald A. Wollheim (14), Michael Kurland (8), Hugo Gernsback (6), Philip J. Farmer (6), A. E. van Vogt (3), Stanley B. Hough (2); 1 box each of Joseph Payne Brennan, William Brittain, James Byrne, George Pal, William G. Wilson, Jr.; plus Michael Avallone (1 item), Michael Porjes (1 item), Edmund Cooper (1 item), James McQuade (1 book).

The collections contain books, correspondence, magazines, and fan material collected by Wollheim, Bloch, Shea, and Ackerman. Of particular note in the Wollheim material are much data on early fan movements in the United States and voluminous correspondence relating to Wollheim's editorial experience, extremely valuable in the study of the development of the anthology. The correspondence also reflects important aspects of the market conditions for SF over a long period. Much correspondence with well-known SF writers is included. Some material is restricted.

Status: Active, adding 500 items annually. *Access:* 60 percent cataloged; finding aids for remainder. Photocopies, ILL.

Australia

15-53. Murdoch University Library. Box 14, Willetton, Western Australia 6155.

Holdings: Fiction, 2,500 volumes; reference/critical, 150 volumes. Magazines: English language, 40 titles; critical, 10 titles; fanzines, 300 titles (primarily Australian); microforms, 7 titles. Audiotapes, 2.

Murdoch's collections arose from a need for resources in course work and to support a Ph.D. candidate. Most of the collection has come by donation; fanzines are acquired by active fanzine participation by a staff member. Emphasis is from 1965 to 1975. A major strength is in Australian fanzines, 1940– , with over 300 titles represented, and in associated international fanzines.

Status: Adding 450 items annually. *Access:* Cataloging in process. Photocopies, ILL. Information current as of 1980.

15-54. University of Sydney Library. Rare Books and Special Collections, Science Fiction and Fantasy Collection, Sydney, N.S.W. 2006, Australia. (02)692-4162.

Holdings: Fiction, 42,000 volumes; reference/critical, 650 volumes. Magazines: English language, 150–200 titles; foreign language, 40+ titles; critical, 14+ titles; fanzines, 2,000 titles; comics, 1,257 titles. Audiovisuals: audio recordings, 25; films, 11; videotapes, 2. Manuscripts (10 boxes): Aldiss, Brunner, Chandler, Cowper, Ellison, Lovecraft, Priest, Tubb, Wilhelm, Wollheim.

The collection was established in 1974 as a research collection for scholars. In 1979, holdings were greatly increased with the donation of the Ron Graham SF Collection, one of the largest private collections in the world. Holdings for most major SF magazines are complete; a representative collection of English-language fanzines is also held. Primary strength in the monograph collection lies after 1945, but the earlier period is well covered. The collection includes a comprehensive comic collection, specializing in titles related to the weird or fantastic.

Status: Active, adding 70–100 items annually. *Access:* 10 percent cataloged; items accessible by author and/or title. The Graham collection has a card catalog devised by Graham. Photocopies.

Canada

15-55. McGill University. McLennan Library, 3459 McTavish St., Montreal, Quebec H3A 1Y1.

Holdings: Fiction, 600 volumes; reference/critical, 850 volumes. Magazines: English language, 9 titles; critical, 16 titles; microform, 19 titles.

The SF materials are in the general humanities collection. Strength of the holdings is in the period 1950–1975; heavy collecting was started in 1975, focusing on 25 representative authors, who are collected in depth. All available critical material is collected. Authors collected are Asimov, Ballard, Bradbury, Čapek, Clarke, Clement, Compton, Dick, Disch, Heinlein, Knight, Kornbluth, Kuttner, Le Guin, Miller, Pohl, Sheckley, Simak, Smith, Stapledon, Sturgeon, van Vogt, Verne, Vonnegut, Wyndham, and Zamiatin. McGill continues to collect science fiction, but now emphasizes other collecting interests. The McGill collection is typical of those of many large university libraries in its size and activity.

Status: Active, adding 100 items annually. *Access:* Fully cataloged. Photocopies, ILL.

15-56. Queen's University. Douglas Library, Special Collections, Kingston, Ontario K7L 5C4.

Holdings: Fiction, 1,600 volumes. Magazines: English language, 2,500 issues. Manuscripts: H. P. Lovecraft (.5 linear feet).

The Gothic-Fantasy Collection of more than 4,000 items is most heavily concentrated in the SF end of the gothic-fantasy spectrum, and is strongest in American SF magazines. The Lovecraft collection contains some manuscripts and letters, as well as books and bibliographic and biographical material.

Status: Inactive. *Access:* Fully cataloged; checklist for serials. Information current as of 1980.

15-57. Spaced Out Library. Toronto Public Library, 40 St. George St., Toronto, Ontario M5S 2E4. 416-593-5351.

Holdings: Fiction, 16,000 volumes; reference/critical, 1,058 volumes. Magazines: English language, 56 titles; foreign language, 13 titles; critical, 8 titles; fanzines, 1,000+ titles. Audiovisuals: audio recordings, 314; stamp collection made up of stamps with space themes; original art by Emshwiller, Ellis, and Freas. Manuscripts: Andre Norton MS title, *Quest for Kolder,* published as *Web of the Witch World;* Eric Frank Russell original and British title, *With a Strange Device,* published as *The Mindwarpers;* Donald H. Tuck, carbon copy of typescript of Volume 2 of his encyclopedia [8-7]; Poul Anderson, MS of *Earthman Go Home!*

Established in 1970 with the donation of Judith Merril's 5,000-item collection, the holdings now number more than 20,000 items, including novels, plays, poetry, criticism, tapes, art, and periodicals. In addition to the strong book and periodical holdings, a Verne collection is maintained. The fanzine collection includes issues of more than 1,000 titles, many in complete runs, and is indexed by author and subject. It is without doubt the most accessible fanzine collection extant. The collection is described in Hall [8-39], and in "Toronto's Spaced Out Library: A Science Fiction Collection," *Ontario Library Review* 57 (September 1973): 167–170.

Status: Active, adding 1,000 books and 1,200 periodical items annually. *Access:* Monographs and short story collections, fully cataloged; periodicals, subject index; fanzines, alphabetical listing, some by subject. Photocopies.

15-58. University of New Brunswick. Ward Chipman Library, Box 5050, St. John, New Brunswick E2L 4L5. 506-648-5703.

Holdings: Fiction, 13,862 volumes; reference/critical, 1,266 + 75 on microfilm. Magazines: English language, 312 titles; foreign language, 10 titles; critical, 65 titles; fanzines, 221 titles; microform, 10 titles. Audiovisuals: audio recordings, 89; 56 art books, 11 volumes poetry, 20 calendars, small slide collection. Manuscripts: John Wyndham, 3 short stories; Alexei Panshin, *Rite of Passage.*

The SF collection began in 1966 and now consists of more than 15,000 books and more than 6,700 magazine issues, including 96 percent of all indexed SF material. The collection is an SFWA depository.

Status: Active, adding 500 items annually. *Access:* Books, fully cataloged; serials, 95 percent cataloged; vertical file index. Photocopies.

15-59. University of Winnipeg Library. 515 Portage Ave., Winnipeg, Manitoba R3B 2E9.

Holdings: Fiction, 1,840 volumes; reference/critical, 90 volumes. Magazines: English language, 8 titles; microform, 3 titles.

The collection consists of more than 1,900 items, primarily SF, and microfilmed SF magazines. The complete works of many major SF writers are included.

Status: Active, adding 60 items annually. *Access:* Fully cataloged. Photocopies, ILL.

England

15-60. Bodleian Library. Oxford University, Oxford, England.

Holdings: Papers of James Blish, Michael Moorcock, and Brian Aldiss, plus a large general collection of SF received through copyright deposit.

15-61. Science Fiction Foundation Research Library. North East London Polytechnic, Longbridge Rd., Dagenham, Essex RM8 2AS, England.

Holdings: Fiction, 12,000 volumes; reference/critical, 1,100 volumes. Magazines: English language, 85 titles; foreign, 10 titles; critical, 25 titles; fanzines, "many"; microforms, 11 titles. Audiovisuals: audiotapes, 50+. Manuscripts (15 boxes total): John Wyndham, Ian Watson, Bob Shaw, Christopher Priest, Brian Stableford, Arthur Sellings, Barrington J. Bayley.

The major collection in England, and important worldwide. Of special note are the strong book and magazine collections and the manuscripts. Greatest strength is from 1951 to present.

Status: Active. *Access:* Internal catalog. Photocopies.

15-62. University of Liverpool. Special Collections, Sydney Jones Library, Liverpool L69 3DA, England.

The Olaf Stapledon collection includes first editions of Stapledon's works, presentation copies from other authors, books from Stapledon's personal library, manuscripts, typescripts, scrapbooks, letters, and miscellaneous other primary material. A 73-page catalog of the collection is available in the library. Additional details are in the *SFRA Newsletter* no. 117 (December 1983): 8–10.

Switzerland

15-63. Maison d'Ailleurs. Musée de l'Utopie, des Voyages Extraordinaires et de la Science Fiction, Rue du Four 5, 1400 Yverdon-les-Bains, Switzerland.

Holdings: Fiction, 20,000–25,000 volumes (34 original language, translations from 16 others); reference/critical, 1,000+ volumes. Magazines: English language, 150+ titles; other languages, 50+ titles; critical, 40–50 titles; fanzines, 300+ titles. Audiovisuals: audio recordings, 350+; films, 2; videotapes, 220+; some 1,000 slides; animation cels, 14. Manuscripts: "Nearly every French author is represented (at least some pages) and some English," according to Pascal Ducommun, the part-time curator.

More properly a museum than a library, the Maison D'Ailleurs contains more than 50,000 items, about one-third of them printed material. The remainder includes posters, paintings, music, postage stamps, toys, games, comics, art, autographs, calendars, photographs, and much more, all relating to science fiction. The collection was amassed by Pierre Versins and Martine Thome, and is the essential collection for the study of French or European SF. Inquire regarding hours and appointments. The collection is also discussed in "La Maison d'Ailleurs Opens," *Science Fiction Review* 19 (June 1982): 18–19.

Status: Active. *Access:* Partially cataloged.

Private Collections

Many of the largest collections of SF and fantasy materials are still in the hands of private collectors, some of whom are dealers as well. The collections described below are listed with the explicit permission of their owners, primarily for the use of libraries and serious scholars only. Although no collectors listed in the 1981 edition reported any problems, several did not respond to requests for updated information, and these collectors have been dropped. Several other collections have been sold.

Certain stringent rules apply in all cases: (1) answers to *brief* inquiries may be attempted, but only if a self-addressed stamped envelope is provided; (2) no lending of materials will normally be permitted, nor will personal visits be allowed without prior approval of the collector. These collections are listed primarily to provide libraries and their scholarly clientele with possible help in locating bibliographic or other information on rare materials not found elsewhere. They may prove helpful to larger libraries seeking to acquire a large collection intact, thus providing collectors who may wish to sell or donate their collections the names of possible buyers or recipients. Where no address is shown, to protect the privacy of the collector, queries will be forwarded by the editor who compiled this information, whose address is shown in the list of contributors. Arrangement is by state, then by country.

California

15-64. Forrest J. Ackerman. 2495 Glendower Ave., Los Angeles, CA 90027.

Probably the largest private collection (ca. 300,000 items), acquired during more than 50 years by a long-time fan, editor, and agent. Comprehensive holdings of hardcover and paperback books, complete runs of all SF and fantasy magazines and many other pulps, such as the Munsey titles. Most fanzines, 1930–date. Much original/fantasy illustration. Extensive correspondence and clipping files from 1930. Many original MSS. Exceptionally strong holdings of film memorabilia (ca. 125,000 stills, 18,000 lobby cards, film posters, props, and more). Ackerman's generosity in assisting researchers and fans is well known, and he and his collection have been profiled often in both fan and general publications. A number of the higher priced collectible books have been sold, leaving an estimated 36,000 books. Ackerman was seeking a buyer in early 1987. Described in detail in Hall [8-39].

15-65. Roy Lavender. 2507 E. 17 St., Long Beach, CA 90804.

About 1,500 hardcovers, 2,000 original paperbacks, 2,000 reprints; strong in books by Eric Frank Russell (including correspondence); most of book collection in storage. Original illustrations by Hannes Bok and George Barr. Several thousand slides from conventions, especially costume shows. Complete file of *Doubt* (Fortean Society magazine).

15-66. Samuel A. Peeples. Southern California.

Essentially complete holdings of the SF pulps and the popular magazines of the 1900–1925 period. Approximately 8,000 volumes of hardcover books, 1,500 original paperbacks. Very strong Burroughs collection with many rarities.

Strong collection of western and detective fiction. Has donated many materials to the University of Wyoming [15-52].

15-67. Stuart A. Teitler. 625 Cornell Ave., Albany, CA 94706.

Approximately 2,500 hardcover books, many rare, plus 400 books, pamphlets, and ephemera, mostly from the nineteenth century. Specializes in lost-race works from seventeenth century to date and has an encyclopedic knowledge of this field, evident in his well-annotated catalogs.

15-68. Dan Temianka. 1032 Via Nogales, Palos Verdes Estates, CA 90274.

All materials related to Jack Vance: about 170 original and reprint hardcover volumes, 150 paperbacks, both including some foreign editions; about 100 magazine issues with first appearances of stories; some manuscripts, letters, proofs, audiotapes of radio shows and interviews; other material. Indexed on Macintosh computer.

Florida

15-69. Joseph K. Wilcoxen. Largo, FL.

About 15,000 SF paperbacks. Very strong Vance collection, strong Burroughs collection.

Illinois

15-69A. Chicago Area.

Complete SF magazines, including *Weird Tales;* incomplete British magazines. Very strong Munsey and Popular Publications magazine collections. Many other associational pulps. Total magazine collection exceeds 15,000 issues. About 3,000 volumes original hardcovers, including all specialty press books from 1930. About 12,000 paperbacks, especially 1939–1965, not all SF. Selected fanzine runs. More than 200 pieces SF art by Finlay, Bok, Freas, Paul, Cartier (last especially strong). Strong in ephemera.

Indiana

15-70. Ray Beam. 2209 S. Webster St., Kokomo, IN 46902.

About 75 SF/fantasy magazine runs, 1926–date, 1,000 volumes original hardcovers (especially specialty presses), 700 volumes original paperbacks. Strong in fanzines, 1946–1959. Manuscripts by Bloch (*Psycho*), E. F. Russell, E. E. Smith; art by Binkley, Cartier, Dollens, Finlay, others.

Kansas

15-71. Robert R. Barrett. 2040 Salina, Wichita, KS 67203.

Primarily holdings of Burroughs and Farmer (first editions and reprints, including all magazine appearances, plus fanzines about these writers), plus books by Merritt, Howard, and Hodgson, and illustrations by Frank Frazetta (mostly of Burroughs stories), J. Allen St. John, and Michael Whelan. Strong holdings in illustrations of Burroughs stories, plus original illustrations by all Hugo winners except Leo and Diane Dillon.

Maryland

15-72. Robert A. Madle. 4406 Bestor Dr., Rockville, MD 20853.

All SF and fantasy pulps and many related magazines. Several thousand fanzines, particularly complete in the 1930–1940 period. Roughly 1,500 volumes of original hardcovers, including almost all works from the specialty publishers, many signed. Much memorabilia dating from his initial fan activities in 1933. Active dealer; catalogs on request.

15-73. Lester Mayer. Silver Spring, MD.

Almost complete collection of American SF/fantasy magazines plus thousands of additional pulps, such as the Munsey line and British titles, many dating from the nineteenth century. About 3,000 hardcover books, 5,000 paperbacks.

Michigan

15-74. Howard DeVore. 4705 Weddel St., Dearborn Heights, MI 48125.

Comprehensive magazine holdings, including some British and European titles. Many fanzines, 1933–date, plus representative book collection, including most books from specialty publishers. Active fan and dealer.

New Jersey

15-75. Gerry de la Ree. 7 Cedarwood La., Saddle River, NJ 07458.

About 10,000 issues of all SF and fantasy magazines. Comprehensive book collection (9,000 hardcover, 5,000 paperback, plus about 1,000 reprints), heavy in Burroughs, Poe, Haggard, Lovecraft, Clark Ashton Smith, Dunsany, Wells, Coppard, Griffith, Stoker, Machen, and other early twentieth-century fantasy authors, plus early (late nineteenth-century) interplanetary voyage books. More than 600 original SF fantasy pieces of artwork by Finlay, Bok, Fabian, Cartier, and others, used for his hardcover fantasy art books published since 1972. Active also as a dealer. His home was designed partly to display his large collection, which is indexed by author.

15-76. Stephen T. Miller. One Heatherwood Ct., Medford, NJ 08035.

Complete runs of all SF/fantasy magazines, plus nearly complete runs of earlier popular magazines (*Argosy, All-Story,* and others), and the hero and adventure pulps. British and Australian magazines. Modest hardcover collection but strong in paperbacks, 1920s to date, including sets of the specialty publishers. Strong Lovecraft collection.

15-77. Sam Moskowitz. 361 Roseville Ave., Newark, NJ 07107.

An enormous collection comparable to Ackerman's (see under California). Massive magazine holdings, not only all SF/fantasy magazines, including foreign-language titles, but dozens of other pulps (adventure, detective, British and American popular magazines, many from the nineteenth century). Exhaustive fanzine collection, 1930–1950, selective thereafter, with all associated indexes. About 1,000 dime novels, 1878–1923, containing SF/fantasy, including associated reference aids. About 6,000 hardcover books, including comprehensive holdings of all major and many minor authors, both SF and fantasy/supernatural. Comprehensive original paperback collection. Comprehensive reference collection, including all standard and many fugitive works, plus personally compiled indexes to his collection. Very large clipping file, extensive correspondence (notably Gernsback, D. H. Keller, W. H. Hodgson, Eando Binder), dealer catalogs since 1950, originals of many SF magazine covers (especially those by Frank R. Paul), more than 1,000 photographs of people associated with SF/fantasy. Many MSS, especially by Gernsback, Hodgson, Keller, Binder, plus extensive other files, all well organized for effective access and added to constantly. Moskowitz has drawn on his collection for his many books. Hourly fee charged; inquire. Collection described in more detail in Hall [8-39].

New York

15-78. New York City Region.
About 6,000 hardcover books (nearly half signed, 1926–date), 1,500 original paperbacks, plus 1,000 reprints, emphasizing post-1926 works, but solid collection of earlier works of SF/fantasy, some supernatural. Modest magazine holdings, some MSS, plus a good reference collection.

15-79. Southeastern Area. New York.
Select collection including *Astounding/Analog, Magazine of Fantasy and Science Fiction,* and *Unknown,* all complete, plus complete runs of major fanzines, pre-1950. Book collection emphasizes pre-1960 imprints, especially weird/supernatural. Extensive correspondence with August Derleth, Matthew Onderdonk, Thyril Ladd. Photographs of Lovecraft family.

15-80. Stuart David Schiff. Whispers Press, 70 Highland Ave., Binghamton, NY 13905.
Specializes in fantasy and supernatural/horror materials. About 2,500 issues of magazines, 4,000 books (some SF, especially from the specialty publishers), comprehensive holdings of material dealing with Lovecraft. Publishes *Whispers,* a professional magazine reflecting his collecting interests.

15-81. Donald A. Wollheim. 66-17 Clyde St., Rego Park, NY 11374.
Approximately 15,000 hardcover and 6,000 original paperback books, plus a good selection of foreign-language SF, notably French and Russian. Magazines and fanzines sold to Ronald Graham, now in University of Sydney Library [15-54].

15-82. Claude Held. Box 515, Buffalo, NY 14225.
Complete runs of 15 major pulps, about 1,000 original hardcovers, including Haggard, Mundy, Merritt, and Dennis Wheatley. Dealer; has sold many of his books and magazines.

North Carolina

15-83. Terry A. Murray. 2540 Chapel Hill Rd., Durham, NC 27707.
Complete runs of all nonreprint American SF magazines, 1926–date; *Weird Tales,* 1934–1954. Strong collection of pre-1967 British SF/fantasy magazines. About 7,000 paperbacks, mostly first paperback editions.

Ohio

15-84. James "Rusty" Hevelin. Box 112, Dayton, OH 45401.

All American and some British magazines, plus other associational pulps. About 3,000 volumes original hardcovers, 4,000 original paperbacks, plus reprints. Fanzines, 1938–1948, 1968–1986. Query by telephone: 513-236-0728.

15-85. Sheldon Jaffery. 1525 Leader Bldg., Cleveland, OH 44114.

Unknown, complete; about 1,000 assorted issues of other pulps. About 2,500 volumes of original hardcovers, many rare, 500 original paperbacks, heavy in the specialty presses, notably Arkham House. Major emphasis on weird/supernatural and horror pulps. Author of *Horrors and Unpleasantries: A Bibliographical History & Collector's Guide to Arkham House* (1982) and coauthor of *Collector's Index to Weird Tales* [14-6].

15-86. Lynn A. Hickman. 413 Ottokee St., Wauseon, OH 43567.

Uncataloged collection estimated to total about 20,000 books and magazine issues. Strong magazine holdings, including many issues of non-SF magazines containing SF/fantasy stories. Some original illustrations from the 1925–1970 period.

Pennsylvania

15-87. Clarence B. Hyde. Pennsylvania.

Major collection of E. R. Burroughs—magazines, fanzines, books (many foreign editions), original art, comic strips and books, film memorabilia.

15-88. Oswald Train. 1129 W. Wingohocking St., Philadelphia, PA 19140.

Strong magazine collection, including some British and Australian titles. Approximately 5,500 hardcovers, 4,000–5,000 paperbacks. Old photographs, slides, selected artwork. Perhaps finest collection of Haggard in the United States, including about 40 letters, photographs, and signed and inscribed first editions. Strong collections of Dunsany, Burroughs, Doyle, Cummings, Stapledon, Rohmer, and others.

Tennessee

15-89. Darrell C. Richardson. 899 Stonewall, Memphis, TN 38107.

Very comprehensive magazine collection, including all SF/fantasy and early pulps. Books total about 29,000 volumes, of which 11,000 are hardcover, 6,000 original paperbacks, 2,000 reprints, not only in SF and fantasy, but adventure, lost-race, ancient civilizations, and Western Americana. Strong on first editions and fine copies, with more than 100 authors covered completely, including many foreign editions. Heavy British coverage. One of the largest Burroughs collections, plus heavy in western fiction. Very strong collection of early fanzines, roughly 7,500 issues, 1930–1950. More than 300 original illustrations from books and magazines, many letters. Approximately 7,000 comics, mostly Tarzan, Flash Gordon, Buck Rogers. Card indexes to books and magazines.

15-90. Larry D. Woods. 121 17th Ave. S., Nashville, TN 37203.

Complete runs of *Magazine of Fantasy and Science Fiction, Galaxy, If,* plus *Astound-*

ing/Analog, 1943–date. Complete collection of hardcover, magazine, and fanzine first editions by Zelazny, and similar holdings for Le Guin, Clarke, Farmer, Herbert, King, Haldeman, Niven, Varley, McIntyre, Delany, and Heinlein. Most first editions by many other writers, including those of every Hugo, Nebula, International Fantasy, *Locus,* Campbell, and Jupiter award winners.

15-91. Dalvan M. Coger. 1433 W. Crestwood Dr., Memphis, TN 38119.

About 40 SF magazine titles, mostly complete runs. About 3,000 original hardcovers, 2,500 original paperbacks, 1,000 reprints. Photos of Michigan Fandom Group, notably E. E. Smith.

Texas

15-92. John N. Marx. 4412 18th, Lubbock, TX 79416.

Near complete runs of almost all U.S. and British SF/fantasy magazines. About 600 original hardcovers, 12,000 original paperbacks, 6,000 reprints.

Canada

15-93. Chester D. Cuthbert. 1104 Mulvey Ave., Winnipeg, Manitoba R3M 1J5, Canada.

About 60 complete magazine runs, 1926–1965, scattered holdings thereafter. Roughly 2,000 hardcover, 1,000 paperback books, 4,000 reprints. Fantasy books by Canadian authors a specialty, plus works by Merritt, Blackwood, and Lovecraft.

England

15-94. George Locke. Ferret Fantasy Ltd., 27 Beechcroft Rd., Upper Tooting, London SW17 7BX, England.

The approximately 4,100 nineteenth- and twentieth-century books collected for more than 30 years are described in detail in the author's *A Spectrum of Fantasy* [8-4]. Locke's interests center on interplanetary voyages to 1914 [8-6], future wars to 1945, lost-race, pre-1914 books (although roughly 20 percent of the collection is post–World War II). His dealership specializes in early works, but has recently added proof copies of SF and fantasy and manuscripts.

France

15-95. Jacques Sadoul. Editions J'ai Lu, 27 rue Cassette, Paris 75006, France.

The 2,500 issues are pre–World War II American and British magazines and all French SF magazines since the war. The uncounted book collection is mostly in French, including first editions of Verne. Many photographs taken at European conventions, correspondence from contemporary SF authors, and original illustrations by European artists. The collector is also a prominent editor of French SF and author of a French history of SF [6-194].

16
Core Collection Checklist

Neil Barron

This best-books listing is derived from three sources.

1. First-purchase recommendations by this guide's contributors, which are identified by an asterisk preceding the author's name, both here and in the numbered annotations.

2. Books that were nominated for or won one of the four principal awards shown below. The abbreviations follow the title and are also included in the annotations. These awards apply only to books in Chapters 3 and 4 and a few books in Chapters 8, 9, and 10.

 HW—Hugo award winner
 HN—Hugo nominee
 JWC—John W. Campbell Memorial Award winner
 L—*Locus* award winner
 NN—Nebula award nominee
 NW—Nebula award winner

The Science Fiction Achievement Awards, informally called Hugos, have been given each year at the "world" SF conventions since 1953. Although awards are given in many categories, only novels and a few nonfiction books are included here. Hugos measure popularity as much as literary merit. About 1,200 mail ballots were counted for the 1986 novel awards. Nebulas are voted by roughly half of the 500 members of the SF Writers of America. The first awards were given in

1966. A small group of writers and academics select the Campbell award winner, given since 1973. The annual *Locus* awards currently reflect the judgments of approximately 1,000 active readers.

3. Books selected by these knowledgeable outside readers, whose initials follow the book titles:

EB—Everett F. Bleiler, editor of *Science Fiction Writers* [8-27] and other major reference works

JC—John Clute, critic, associate editor of *The Science Fiction Encyclopedia* [8-30]

SM—Sam Moskowitz, author of many studies, Pilgrim award winner

PN—Peter Nicholls, editor of *The Science Fiction Encyclopedia* [8-30]

FP—Frederik Pohl, author, editor, critic

GW—Gary K. Wolfe, author of *The Known and the Unknown* [9-106]

In a few instances these readers selected books not annotated in this guide, although some of them are mentioned in the introductory essays. These are identified by a year of publication following the title. Outside readers evaluated English-language books only; and some categories were not evaluated by all readers (notably children's SF and teaching materials). Core collection listings were not received for Swedish, Belgian, and Romanian science fiction. The Yugoslav section is not included in this core collection and Hebrew SF does not have an annotated bibliography and, therefore, no core collection listings.

The entries listed here are in chapter and entry sequence.

The Emergence of Science Fiction

Abbott, Edwin A. *Flatland* (EB)
Allen, Grant. *The British Barbarians* (1895) (EB)
Bellamy, Edward. *The Blindman's World and Other Stories* (EB)
*———. *Looking Backward* (EB, JC, SM, PN, FP, GW)
*Beresford, John Davys. *The Hampdenshire Wonder* (EB, JC, SM, PN, GW)
Bergerac, Cyrano Savinien de. *The Comical History of the States* . . . (PN)
Besant, Walter. *The Inner House* (1888) (EB)
Briusov, Valerii. *The Republic of the Southern Cross* (1918) (EB)
*Burroughs, Edgar Rice. *At the Earth's Core* (JC, PN, GW)
*———. *A Princess of Mars* (EB, JC, SM, PN, FP, GW)
———. *Tarzan of the Apes* (PN)
*Butler, Samuel. *Erewhon* (EB, JC, SM, PN, FP, GW)
———. *Erewhon Revisited* (JC)
*Chesney, Sir George. *The Battle of Dorking* (EB, JC, SM, GW)
*Childers, Erskine. *The Riddle of the Sands* (EB, JC, GW)
*Clemens, Samuel Langhorne. *A Connecticut Yankee in King Arthur's Court* (EB, JC, FP, GW)
———. *Mark Twain's Which Was the Dream? and Other Symbolic Writings of the Later Years* (1966) (EB)
Cook, William Wallace. *A Round Trip to the Year 2000* (1925) (EB)
*De Mille, James. *A Strange Manuscript Found in a Copper Cylinder* (JC, SM, PN)
*Donnelly, Ignatius. *Caesar's Column* (EB, JC, SM, PN, GW)

Doyle, Arthur Conan. *The Doings of Raffles Haw* (1892) (EB)
*————. *The Lost World* (EB, JC, SM, PN, FP, GW)
*————. *The Poison Belt* (EB, JC, SM, PN, FP, GW)
Dudbroke (pseud.). *The Prots* (1903) (EB)
Flammarion, Camille. *Omega* (1894) (EB)
Flecker, James Elroy. *The Last Generation* (1908) (EB)
*Forster, E. M. "The Machine Stops" (EB, JC, SM, PN, GW)
*Franklin, H. Bruce. *Future Perfect* (JC, SM, PN, GW)
*Gilman, Charlotte Perkins. *Herland* (EB, JC, SM, PN, GW)
*Greg, Percy. *Across the Zodiac* (EB, JC, SM, PN, GW)
Griffith, George. *Olga Romanoff* (PN)
Griffith, Mary. "Three Hundred Years Hence" (EB)
Haggard, H. Rider. *Allan Quatermain* (EB)
*————. *She* (EB, JC, SM, PN, GW)
Hodson, William Hope. *The House on the Borderland and Other Novels* (1908, 1946)
    (EB)
*Holberg, Ludwig. *A Journey to the World Under-Ground* (JC, SM, PN, GW)
Hudson, W. H. *A Crystal Age* (EB)
Jefferies, Richard. *After London* (EB, PN)
*Kepler, Johannes. *Somnium* (EB, JC, SM, PN, GW)
Le Queux, William. *The Invasion of 1910* (EB)
Locke, Richard Adams. *The Moon Hoax* (1859) (EB)
*London, Jack. *Before Adam* (JC, PN, GW)
————. *The Iron Heel* (EB)
*————. *The Science Fiction of Jack London* (EB, JC, SM, PN, GW)
*Lytton, Edward Bulwer. *The Coming Race* (EB, JC, SM, PN, GW)
Mackaye, Harold S. *The Panchronicon* (1904) (EB)
Milne, Robert D. *Into the Sun & Other Stories* (EB)
Mitchell, Edward Page. *The Crystal Man* (EB)
*More, Thomas. *Utopia* (EB, JC, SM, PN, FP, GW)
Morris, William. *News from Nowhere* (EB, PN)
Moskowitz, Sam. *Science Fiction by Gaslight* (EB)
*O'Brien, Fitz-James. *The Fantastic Tales of Fitz-James O'Brien* (EB, JC, SM, PN)
*Poe, Edgar Allan. *The Narrative of Arthur Gordon Pym of Nantucket* (EB, JC, PN,
    GW)
*————. *The Science Fiction of Edgar Allan Poe* (EB, JC, SM, PN, FP, GW)
Pope, Gustavus W. *Journey to Mars* (SM, GW)
*Rhodes, W. H. *Caxton's Book* (SM, GW)
Rosny aîné, J. H. *The Xipéhuz* (PN)
Rousseau, Victor. *The Messiah of the Cylinder* (1917) (EB)
*Seaborn, Adam. *Symzonia* (EB, JC, SM, PN, GW)
Senarans, Luis. *The Frank Reade Library* (1876–1913) (EB)
*Serviss, Garrett P. *Edison's Conquest of Mars* (PN, GW)
*————. *The Second Deluge* (EB, SM, GW)
*Shelley, Mary Wollstonecraft. *Frankenstein* (EB, JC, SM, PN, FP, GW)
Shiel, M. P. *The Purple Cloud* (1901) (PN)
*Stevenson, Robert Louis. *The Strange Case of Dr. Jekyll and Mr. Hyde* (EB, JC, SM,
    PN, GW)

Stockton, Frank. *The Great Stone of Sardis* (EB)
———. *The Great War Syndicate* (EB)
*Swift, Jonathan. *Gulliver's Travels* (EB, JC, SM, PN, FP, GW)
Train, Arthur Cheyney, and Robin William Wood. *The Man Who Rocked the Earth*
  (EB)
Verne, Jules. *Castle of the Carpathians* (1893) (EB)
———. *The Clipper of the Clouds* (1895) (JC)
———. *From the Earth to the Moon* (EB, PN)
*———. *A Journey to the Center of the Earth* (EB, JC, SM, PN, FP, GW)
———. *Master of the World* (1904) (JC)
*———. *Twenty Thousand Leagues under the Sea* (EB, JC, SM, PN, FP, GW)
———. *Yesterday and Tomorrow* (1910) (EB)
Villiers de l'Isle Adam, Jean. *Tomorrow's Eve* (1885) (EB)
Voltaire, François-Marie Arouet. *Micromégas* (1753) (EB)
Wells, H. G. *The First Men in the Moon* (JC, PN)
———. *The Food of the Gods* (PN)
———. *In the Days of the Comet* (1906) (FP)
———. *The Invisible Man* (1897) (EB)
———. *The Island of Doctor Moreau* (FP, PN)
*———. *A Modern Utopia* (JC, PN, FP)
*———. *The Short Stories of H. G. Wells* (EB, JC, SM, PN, FP, GW)
*———. *The Time Machine* (EB, JC, SM, PN, FP, GW)
———. *The War in the Air* (PN)
*———. *The War of the Worlds* (EB, JC, SM, PN, FP, GW)
———. *When the Sleeper Wakes* (EB)
*White, Stewart Edward, and Samuel Hopkins Adams. *The Mystery*
*White, Stewart Edward. *The Sign at Six* (EB)

Science Fiction between the Wars: 1918–1938

*Asimov, Isaac. *Before the Golden Age* (JC, SM, PN, GW)
*Bell, Neil (as "Miles"). *The Seventh Bowl* (EB)
*Burroughs, Edgar Rice. *The Land That Time Forgot* (EB, JC, SM, PN, GW)
———. *The Moon Maid* (EB)
*Čapek, Karel. *The Absolute at Large* (EB, JC, PN, FP, GW)
*———. *Krakatit* (EB, JC, PN)
*———. *R.U.R.* (EB, JC, SM, PN, FP, GW)
*———. *War with the Newts* (EB, JC, SM, PN, FP, GW)
Collier, John. *Tom's a-Cold* (1933) (EB, JC)
Connington, J. J. *Nordenholt's Million* (EB)
Cox, Erle. *Out of the Silence* (1925) (EB)
*Cummings, Ray. *The Girl in the Golden Atom* (EB, JC, SM, PN, GW)
*Dent, Guy. *Emperor of the If* (EB, JC, GW)
Doyle, Arthur Conan. *The Maracot Deep and Other Stories* (PN)
*Farrère, Claude. *Useless Hands* (EB)
Flint, Homer Eon. *The Devolutionist* and *The Emancipatrix* (EB)
Gail, Otto Willi. *By Rocket to the Moon* (1930) (EB)
*Gloag, John. *To-Morrow's Yesterday* (EB, JC, SM, PN, GW)

*————. *Winter's Youth* (PN)

Gregory, Owen. *Meccania* (EB)

Hamilton, Edmond. *Crashing Suns* (EB)

*Huxley, Aldous. *Brave New World* (EB, JC, SM, PN, FP, GW)

*Karinthy, Frigyes. *Voyage to Faremido and Capillaria*

Knox, Ronald. *Other Eyes Than Ours* (1926) (EB)

*Large, E. C. *Sugar in the Air* (SM, PN, FP)

*Lindsay, David. *A Voyage to Arcturus* (EB, JC, SM, PN, GW)

Llewellan, Alun. *The Strange Invaders* (JC)

Lovecraft, H. P. *At the Mountains of Madness and Other Novels*

*Maurois, André. *The Weigher of Souls* (EB, PN, GW)

Merritt, A. *Dwellers in the Mirage* (1932) (EB)

————. *The Metal Monster* (PN)

————. *The Moon Pool* (EB)

Moore, C. L. *Northwest of Earth* (EB)

————. *Shambleau* (JC)

Mundy, Talbot. *Jimgrim* (1931) (EB)

*Odle E. V. *The Clockwork Man* (EB, JC, PN, GW)

O'Neill, Joseph. *Land under England* (EB, PN)

Read, Herbert. *The Green Child* (EB)

Shanks, Edward. *The People of the Ruins* (EB)

*Shaw, George Bernard. *Back to Methuselah* (EB, JC, PN, FP, GW)

*Shiel, M. P. *The Young Men Are Coming!* (JC)

*Smith, E. E., and Lee Hawkins Garby. *The Skylark of Space* (EB, JC, SM, FP, GW)

*Stapledon, Olaf. *Last and First Men* (EB, JC, SM, PN, FP, GW)

*————. *Odd John* (EB, JC, SM, PN, FP, GW)

*————. *Sirius* (EB, JC, SM, PN, FP, GW)

*————. *Star Maker* (EB, JC, SM, PN, FP, GW)

Taine, John. *The Crystal Horde* (PN)

————. *The Purple Sapphire* (1924) (EB)

*————. *The Time Stream* (EB, SM, PN, FP, GW)

*Weinbaum, Stanley G. *A Martian Odyssey and Other Science Fiction Tales* (EB, JC, SM, PN, FP, GW)

*————. *The New Adam*

Wells, H. G. *Men like Gods* (EB, FP)

————. *Mr. Blettsworthy on Rampole Island* (1928) (EB)

*————. *The Shape of Things to Come* (JC, PN, FP, GW)

Williamson, Jack. *The Legion of Space* (PN)

*————. *The Legion of Time* (JC, PN, FP, GW)

*Wright, S. Fowler. *Deluge* (EB, PN, FP, GW)

*————. *The New Gods Lead* (EB, PN)

*————. *The World Below* (EB, JC, SM, PN, FP, GW)

*Wylie, Philip. *Gladiator* (EB, JC, SM, PN, GW)

————, and Edwin Balmer. *When Worlds Collide* (EB, PN)

*Zamiatin, Evgenii. *We* (EB, JC, SM, PN, FP, GW)

The Early Modern Period: 1938–1963

*Aldiss, Brian W. *Best Science Fiction Stories of Brian W. Aldiss* (EB, JC, SM, PN, FP)
*———. *The Long Afternoon of Earth* (HW) (EB, JC, PN, FP, GW)
———. *Non-Stop* (1958) (JC, PN)
*Anderson, Poul. *Brain Wave* (EB, JC, PN, FP, GW)
*———. *The Enemy Stars* (HN) (FP, PN, GW)
*———. *The High Crusade* (HN) (EB, JC, SM, PN)
*Asimov, Isaac. *The Caves of Steel* (EB, JC, SM, PN, FP, GW)
———. *The End of Eternity* (JC, PN)
*———. *The Foundation Trilogy* (special H) (EB, JC, SM, PN, FP, GW)
*———. *I, Robot* (EB, JC, SM, PN, FP, GW)
*———. *Nightfall and Other Stories*
*Bester, Alfred. *The Demolished Man* (HW) (EB, JC, SM, PN, FP, GW)
*———. *Starlight* (EB, JC, PN, GW)
*———. *The Stars My Destination* (EB, JC, SM, PN, FP, GW)
Blish, James. *The Best of James Blish* (PN)
*———. *A Case of Conscience* (HW) (JC, PN, FP, GW)
*———. *Cities in Flight* (EB, FP, PN, GW)
*———. *The Seedling Stars* (JC, PN, FP, GW)
*Boulle, Pierre. *Planet of the Apes* (SM, PN, FP, GW)
*Brackett, Leigh. *The Long Tomorrow* (JC, PN, FP, GW)
*Bradbury, Ray. *Fahrenheit 451* (EB, JC, SM, PN, FP, GW)
*———. *The Illustrated Man* (EB, JC, SM, PN, GW)
*———. *The Martian Chronicles* (EB, JC, SM, PN, FP, GW)
*Brown, Fredric. *Honeymoon in Hell* (SM, FP, GW)
*———. *The Lights in the Sky Are Stars* (EB, JC, PN, FP)
———. *What Mad Universe* (EB, PN)
*Brunner, John. *Out of My Mind*
———. *The Squares of the City* (HN) (EB, PN, FP, GW)
*———. *The Whole Man* (HN) (PN, GW)
*Budrys, Algis. *Rogue Moon* (HN) (EB, JC, PN, FP, GW)
*———. *The Unexpected Dimension* (JC, PN, GW)
———. *Who?* (HN) (PN, FP, GW)
*Burgess, Anthony. *A Clockwork Orange* (EB, JC, SM, PN, FP, GW)
*Campbell, John W. *Who Goes There?* (EB, JC, SM, PN, FP, GW)
*Christopher, John. *The Death of Grass* (EB, JC, SM, PN, FP, GW)
———. *The Long Winter* (PN)
*Clarke, Arthur C. *Childhood's End* (EB, JC, SM, PN, FP, GW)
*———. *The City and the Stars* (EB, JC, SM, PN, FP, GW)
———. *Expedition to Earth* (EB)
———. *A Fall of Moondust* (HN)
*———. *The Other Side of the Sky* (JC, GW)
*———. *Prelude to Space* (GW)
*Clement, Hal. *Mission of Gravity* (JC, SM, PN, FP, GW)
*———. *Needle* (EB, SM, GW)
———. *Starlight* (HN)
*Clifton, Mark, and Frank Riley. *They'd Rather Be Right* (HW) (JC, PN, GW)

Cogswell, Theodore R. *The Wall around the World* (PN)
*Condon, Richard. *The Manchurian Candidate* (JC, PN, FP)
*Daniel, Yuli. *This Is Moscow Speaking, and Other Stories* (GW)
*Davidson, Avram. *Or All the Seas with Oysters* (EB, JC, PN, GW)
*de Camp, L. Sprague. *The Best of L. Sprague de Camp* (EB, JC, SM, PN, GW)
*————, and Fletcher Pratt. *The Incomplete Enchanter* (JC, SM, PN, GW)
*de Camp, L. Sprague. *Lest Darkness Fall* (JC, SM, PN, FP, GW)
*del Rey, Lester. *And Some Were Human* (JC, SM, PN, FP, GW)
*————. *Nerves* (JC, SM, PN, FP, GW)
Dick, Philip K. *Eye in the Sky* (PN)
*————. *The Man in the High Castle* (HW) (EB, JC, SM, PN, FP, GW)
————. *Time Out of Joint* (1959) (JC)
*Dickson, Gordon R. *Dorsai!* (EB, SM, PN, FP, GW)
————. *The Genetic General* (HN) (JC, PN)
*Drury, Allen. *Advise and Consent* (series) (FP)
Duncan, David. *Occam's Razor* (PN)
*Farmer, Philip José. *The Lovers* (EB, JC, SM, PN, FP, GW)
————. *Night of Light* (NN)
*————. *Strange Relations* (JC, SM, PN, FP, GW)
*Finney, Jack. *The Body Snatchers* (SM, PN, FP, GW)
*Frank, Pat. *Alas, Babylon* (JC, PN, FP, GW)
*Galouye, Daniel F. *Dark Universe* (HN) (JC, PN, GW)
Gordon, Rex. *No Man Friday* (PN)
*Graves, Robert. *Seven Days in New Crete* (EB, JC, FP, GW)
Harness, Charles L. *Flight into Yesterday* (JC, PN)
————. *The Rose* (PN)
*Harrison, Harry. *Deathworld* (HN) (PN, FP, GW)
————. *Planet of the Damned* (HN) (GW)
Heard, H. F. *Doppelgangers* (EB)
Heinlein, Robert A. *The Door into Summer* (PN)
*————. *Double Star* (HW) (EB, JC, PN, FP, GW)
————. *Glory Road* (HN)
————. *Have Space Suit—Will Travel* (HN) (JC)
————. *Orphans of the Sky* (PN)
*————. *The Past through Tomorrow* (JC, PN, GW)
————. *The Puppet Masters* (PN)
*————. *Starship Troopers* (HW) (JC, SM, PN, FP, GW)
*————. *Stranger in a Strange Land* (HW) (EB, SM, PN, FP, GW)
*Henderson, Zenna. *Pilgrimage* (SM, GW)
Herbert, Frank. *The Dragon in the Sea* (PN)
*Hersey, John. *The Child Buyer* (FP, GW)
*Hesse, Hermann. *The Glass Bead Game* (EB, GW)
*Hoyle, Fred. *The Black Cloud* (EB, JC, PN, FP, GW)
————. *Ossian's Ride* (PN)
*Hubbard, L. Ron. *Final Blackout* (JC, SM, PN, FP, GW)
*Huxley, Aldous. *After Many a Summer Dies the Swan* (PN, FP, GW)
————. *Ape and Essence* (JC)
————. *Island* (GW)

Jones, Raymond F. *This Island Earth* (PN)
*Karp, David. *One* (PN, FP, GW)
*Kelley, William Melvin. *A Different Drummer* (GW)
*Keyes, Daniel. *Flowers for Algernon* (HN, NW) (JC, SM, PN, FP, GW)
Kneale, Nigel. *Quatermass and the Pit* (PN)
*Knight, Damon F. *Far Out* (EB, JC, PN, GW)
*————. *In Deep* (JC, PN, GW)
*Kornbluth, C. M. *The Best of C. M. Kornbluth* (EB, JC, SM, PN, FP, GW)
*————. *Not This August* (JC, PN, FP, GW)
*Kuttner, Henry. *The Best of Henry Kuttner* (EB, JC, SM, PN, FP, GW)
*————, and C. L. Moore. *Mutant* (JC, PN, FP, GW)
Kuttner, Henry. *Robots Have No Tails* (EB)
*Leiber, Fritz. *The Big Time* (HW) (EB, JC, PN, FP, GW)
*————. *Gather, Darkness!* (JC, SM, PN, GW)
*————. *The Wanderer* (HW) (EB, SM, PN, FP)
*Leinster, Murray. *The Best of Murray Leinster* (EB, JC, SM, FP, GW)
*————. *Colonial Survey* (SM, GW)
————. *The Pirates of Zan* (HN)
————. *Sidewise in Time* (1950) (JC)
*Lem, Stanislaw. *Solaris* (EB, JC, SM, PN, FP, GW)
*Lewis, C. S. "Space Trilogy" (series) (EB, JC, PN, GW)
Matheson, Richard. *Born of Man and Woman* (EB)
*————. *I Am Legend* (EB, JC, SM, PN, FP, GW)
————. *The Shrinking Man* (GW)
*McIntosh, J. T. *One in Three Hundred* (JC, SM, PN, GW)
*McKenna, Richard M. *Casey Agonistes and Other Science Fiction and Fantasy Stories*
   (EB, JC, PN, GW)
*Merril, Judith. *Shadow on the Hearth* (EB, FP, GW)
Miller, Walter M., Jr. *The Best of Walter M. Miller, Jr.* (PN)
*————. *A Canticle for Leibowitz* (EB, JC, SM, PN, FP, GW)
Mitchison, Naomi. *Memoirs of a Spacewoman* (PN, GW)
*Moore, C. L. *The Best of C. L. Moore* (EB, JC, SM, PN, FP, GW)
Moore, Ward. *Bring the Jubilee* (PN, GW)
Norton, Andre. *Witch World* (1963) (HN)
Oliver, Chad. *Another Kind* (EB)
————. *Shadows in the Sun* (GW)
*Orwell, George. *Nineteen Eighty-Four* (EB, JC, SM, PN, FP, GW)
Pangborn, Edgar. *Davy* (HN) (SM)
*————. *A Mirror for Observers* (JC, SM, PN, GW)
Phillips, Mark. *Brain Twister* (HN)
Piper, H. Beam. *Little Fuzzy* (HN)
*Pohl, Frederik. *The Best of Frederik Pohl* (EB, JC, SM, PN, FP, GW)
————, and C. M. Kornbluth. *Gladiator-at-Law* (PN)
*————. *The Space Merchants* (EB, JC, SM, PN, FP, GW)
————. *Wolfbane* (PN)
*Rand, Ayn. *Anthem* (SM, GW)
*Russell, Eric Frank. *The Great Explosion* (PN, GW)
————. *Wasp* (PN)

St. Clair, Margaret. *Change the Sky and Other Stories* (EB)
————. *Sign of the Labrys* (PN)
*Sarban. *The Sound of His Horn* (EB, JC, PN, FP, GW)
Schmitz, James H. *The Witches of Karres* (HN) (JC, SM, PN, FP, GW)
Sheckley, Robert. *Immortality, Inc.* (HN) (JC, PN, FP, GW)
*————. *Pilgrimage to Earth* (JC, SM, PN, GW)
*————. *Untouched by Human Hands* (EB, JC, PN, GW)
Shiras, Wilmar H. *Children of the Atom* (PN)
*Shute, Nevil. *On the Beach* (JC, SM, PN, FP, GW)
*Simak, Clifford D. *City* (EB, JC, SM, PN, FP, GW)
————. *Time Is the Simplest Thing* (HN) (SM, PN, GW)
*————. *Way Station* (JC, SM, PN, FP, GW)
————. *The Worlds of Clifford Simak* (PN)
Smith, Cordwainer. *The Best of Cordwainer Smith* (1975) (GW)
————. *Norstrilia* (EB, JC, SM, PN, FP, GW)
————. *The Planet Buyer* (HN)
*————. *You Will Never Be the Same* (JC, PN)
*Smith, E. E. *The Lensman Series* (EB, JC, SM, PN, FP, GW)
*Stewart, George R. *Earth Abides* (JC, SM, PN, GW)
*Sturgeon, Theodore. *E Pluribus Unicorn* (JC, SM, PN, GW)
*————. *More Than Human* (EB, JC, SM, PN, FP, GW)
————. *A Touch of Strange* (EB)
————. *Venus Plus X* (HN) (PN, FP, GW)
*————. *Without Sorcery* (JC, SM, PN, GW)
*Tenn, William. *Of All Possible Worlds* (EB, JC, SM, PN, FP, GW)
*Tevis, Walter S. *The Man Who Fell to Earth* (JC, PN, GW)
*Tucker, Wilson. *The Long Loud Silence* (SM, PN, GW)
Vance, Jack. *Big Planet* (1957) (PN)
————. *The Blue World* (NN) (PN, GW)
*————. *The Dragon Masters*
————. *The Dying Earth* (JC, PN)
————. *The Eyes of the Overworld* (NN) (PN, GW)
*————. *The Languages of Pao* (EB, JC, SM, PN, FP)
van Vogt, A. E. *Away and Beyond* (EB)
————. *Destination Universe* (1952) (EB)
————. *The Players of Null-A* (JC)
*————. *Slan* (EB, JC, SM, PN, FP, GW)
————. *The Voyage of the Space Beagle* (PN)
————. *The Weapon Makers* (JC)
————. *The Weapon Shops of Isher* (JC, PN)
*————. *The World of Null-A* (EB, JC, SM, PN, FP, GW)
Vercors. *Sylva* (NN)
Vonnegut, Kurt, Jr. *Cat's Cradle* (EB, PN)
*————. *Player Piano* (EB, JC, PN, FP, GW)
————. *The Sirens of Titan* (HN) (EB, JC, SM, PN, FP, GW)
White, James. *The Escape Orbit* (NN)
————. *Hospital Station* (NN) (JC, SM, PN, GW)
————. *Second Ending* (NN) (PN, GW)

*Williamson, Jack. *Darker Than You Think* (EB, JC, SM, PN, GW)
*———. *The Humanoids* (EB, JC, SM, PN, FP, GW)
Wolfe, Bernard. *Limbo* (JC, PN, GW)
Wright, Austin Tappan. *Islandia* (PN)
*Wylie, Philip. *The Disappearance* (EB, SM, PN, FP, GW)
*Wyndham, John. *The Day of the Triffids* (EB, JC, SM, PN, FP, GW)
*———. *The Midwich Cuckoos* (EB, JC, SM, PN, FP, GW)
———. *Re-Birth* (PN)

Anthologies
Amis, Kingsley, and Robert Conquest. *Spectrum* (PN)
*Asimov, Isaac, and Martin H. Greenberg. *Isaac Asimov Presents the Great Science Fiction Stories* (JC, FP, GW)
*Bleiler, Everett, and T. E. Dikty. *The Best Science-Fiction Stories* (EB, JC, SM, PN, FP, GW)
*Boucher, Anthony, and J. Francis McComas. *The Best from Fantasy and Science Fiction* (EB, JC, PN, FP, GW)
*Boucher, Anthony. *A Treasury of Great Science Fiction* (EB, JC, PN, GW)
*Campbell, John W., Jr. *The Astounding Science Fiction Anthology* (EB, JC, SM, PN, FP, GW)
*Conklin, Groff. *The Best of Science Fiction* (EB, JC, SM, PN, GW)
———. *The Big Book of Science Fiction* (EB)
———. *The Omnibus of Science Fiction* (EB)
Derleth, August. *Beyond Time and Space* (1950) (EB)
*Gold, H. L. *Galaxy Reader of Science Fiction* (EB, JC, SM, PN, FP, GW)
*Healy, Raymond J., and J. Francis McComas. *Adventures in Time and Space* (EB, JC, SM, PN, GW)
*Knight, Damon F. *A Century of Science Fiction* (EB, JC, SM, PN, GW)
*Merril, Judith. *SF: The Year's Greatest Science-Fiction and Fantasy* (EB, JC, PN, FP, GW)
*Pohl, Frederik. *Star Science Fiction Stories* (EB, JC, PN, FP, GW)
Science Fiction Hall of Fame (JC, SM, PN, FP, GW)

The Modern Period: 1964–1986

*Aldiss, Brian W. *Barefoot in the Head* (EB, JC, GW)
———. *Frankenstein Unbound* (JC)
*———. *Greybeard* (EB, JC, GW)
———. *Helliconia Spring* (NN, JWC) (JC, SM, PN, FP, GW)
———. *Helliconia Summer* (JC, GW)
———. *Helliconia Winter* (NN) (JC, SM, PN, GW)
*———. *Hothouse* (HW) (EB, JC, SM, PN, FP, GW)
Amis, Kingsley. *The Alteration* (JWC) (EB)
*Anderson, Poul. *The Avatar* (JC, GW)
———. *The Byworlder* (NN)
———. *Fire Time* (HN) (EB, JC, GW)
———. *Midsummer Tempest* (1974) (NN)
———. *People of the Wind* (HN, NN)

————. *The Star Fox* (1965) (NN) (JC, GW)

*————. *Tau Zero* (HN) (EB, JC, PN, FP, GW)

————. *There Will Be Time* (HN)

*Anthony, Piers. *Chthon* (HN, NN) (JC, SM, PN, GW)

————. *Macroscope* (HN) (JC, GW)

————. *Orn* (EB)

Asimov, Isaac. *Fantastic Voyage* (1966) (NN) (SM)

————. *Foundation's Edge* (HW, NN) (EB, SM, GW)

*————. *The Gods Themselves* (HW, NW, L) (JC, GW)

————. *The Robots of Dawn* (HN) (SM, GW)

Attanasio, A. A. *Radix* (NN) (SC, GW)

*Ballard, J. G. *Chronopolis and Other Stories* (EB, JC, PN, GW)

————. *Crash* (1973) (JC)

*————. *The Crystal World* (NN) (JC, SM, PN, GW)

————. *Day of Forever* (1967) (EB)

*————. *The Drought* (JC)

*————. *The Drowned World* (JC, PN, FP)

————. *Low-Flying Aircraft and Other Stories* (1976) (GW)

————. *The Unlimited Dream Company* (1979) (GW)

————. *Vermilion Sands* (PN)

Barth, John. *Giles Goat-Boy* (EB)

Bass, T. J. *The Godwhale* (NN) (PN)

————. *Half Past Human* (NN) (JC, GW)

Batchelor, John Calvin. *The Birth of the People's Republic of Antarctica* (JC)

*Bayley, Barrington J. *The Knights of the Limits* (JC)

*Bear, Greg. *Blood Music* (HN, NN) (JC, SM, PN, GW)

————. *Eon* (EB, JC, PN)

Benford, Greg. *Against Infinity* (NN) (PN, GW)

————. *In the Ocean of Night* (NN) (PN, GW)

*————. *Timescape* (NW, JWC) (JC, SM, PN, FP, GW)

Bester, Alfred. *The Computer Connection* (1975) (HN, NN) (EB)

Biggle, Lloyd, Jr. *Watchers of the Dark* (1966) (NN)

Bishop, Michael. *Blooded on Arachne* (PN)

*————. *Catacomb Years* (JC)

————. *A Funeral for the Eyes of Fire* (1975) (NN) (PN, GW)

*————. *No Enemy but Time* (JC, SM, PN, GW)

————. *Transfigurations* (JC)

Blish, James. *Black Easter* (NN) (JC, PN)

Bradley, Marion Zimmer. *The Forbidden Tower* (HN) (SM)

————. *The Heritage of Hastur* (NN) (PN, GW)

————. *The Sword of Aldones* (HN)

Brin, David. *The Postman* (HN, JWC) (FP, GW)

*————. *Startide Rising* (HW, NW) (JC, SM, PN, GW)

Brunner, John. *The Jagged Orbit* (NN) (JC, GW)

————. *The Productions of Time* (1967) (NN)

*————. *The Sheep Look Up* (NN) (EB, JC, PN, FP, GW)

*————. *Stand on Zanzibar* (HW, NN) (EB, JC, SM, PN, FP, GW)

Budrys, Algis. *Michaelmas* (EB, PN)

*Bunch, David R. *Moderan* (EB, JC, GW)
Burroughs, William S. *Nova Express* (NN) (JC, SM, PN, GW)
Calvino, Italo. *Invisible Cities* (1974) (NN) (JC, SM, PN, GW)
Card, Orson Scott. *Ender's Game* (HW, NW) (JC, SM, GW)
———. *Songmaster* (EB)
———. *Speaker for the Dead* (EB)
*Carr, Jayge. *Leviathan's Deep* (GW)
Carr, Terry. *Cirque* (NN)
———. *The Light at the End of the Universe* (1976) (PN)
*Carter, Angela. *The Infernal Desire Machines of Doctor Hoffman* (JC, PN, GW)
Cherryh, C. J. *Cuckoo's Egg* (HN)
*———. *Downbelow Station* (HW) (JC, SM, GW)
———. *The Faded Sun: Kesrith* (HN, NN) (PN, GW)
*Clarke, Arthur C. *The Fountains of Paradise* (NW, HW) (SM, GW)
*———. *Rendezvous with Rama* (HW, NW, JWC, L) (EB, JC, SM, PN, FP, GW)
*Compton, D. G. *The Continuous Katherine Mortenhoe* (PN)
———. *The Electric Crocodile* (NN) (SM, PN, GW)
Coney, Michael G. *The Celestial Steam Locomotive* (PN)
Cover, Arthur Bryon. *Autumn Angels* (NN)
*Cowper, Richard. *The Road to Corlay* (NN) (JC, PN, GW)
———. *The Twilight of Briareus* (1974) (PN)
*Crowley, John. *Engine Summer* (JC, SM, PN, GW)
———. *Little, Big* (1981) (JC, PN)
Dann, Jack. *The Man Who Melted* (NN) (JC)
Davidson, Avram. *Rogue Dragon* (1965) (NN) (JC)
*Delany, Samuel R. *Babel-17* (HN, NW) (EB, JC, PN, FP)
*———. *Dhalgren* (NN) (EB, SM, PN, FP, GW)
*———. *The Einstein Intersection* (HN, NW) (EB, JC, PN, FP, GW)
*———. *Nova* (HN) (JC, PN, FP, GW)
———. *Triton* (NN) (SM, PN, FP, GW)
Dick, Philip K. *The Divine Invasion* (EB)
*———. *Do Androids Dream of Electric Sheep?* (NN) (EB, JC, SM, PN, FP, GW)
———. *Dr. Bloodmoney* (NN) (JC, PN)
———. *Flow My Tears, the Policeman Said* (HN, NN, JWC) (EB, JC, SM, PN, GW)
———. *A Maze of Death* (JC)
———. *The Three Stigmata of Palmer Eldritch* (NN) (EB, JC, PN, GW)
*———. *Ubik* (EB, JC, PN, GW)
Dickson, Gordon R. *Time Storm* (HN) (PN, FP, GW)
*Disch, Thomas M. *Camp Concentration* (EB, JC, SM, PN, FP, GW)
———. *Fundamental Disch* (EB)
———. *The Genocides* (NN) (PN, GW)
*———. *On Wings of Song* (HN, NN, JWC) (EB, JC, GW)
*———. *334* (NN) (EB, JC, PN, GW)
Doctorow, E. L. *Ragtime* (1975) (NN)
Dozois, Gardner. *Strangers* (NN) (JC, PN)
Durrell, Lawrence. *Nunquam* and *Tunc* (EB)
Edmondson, G. C. *The Ship That Sailed the Time Stream* (NN) (GW)
Effinger, George Alec. *What Entropy Means to Me* (NN) (JC, PN, GW)

*Ellison, Harlan. *Alone against Tomorrow* (JC, PN, GW)
*———. *Deathbird Stories* (EB, JC, SM, PN, FP, GW)
———. *Stalking the Nightmare* (1982) (EB)
———. *Strange Wine* (1978) (EB)
Farmer, Philip José. *The Fabulous Riverboat* (EB)
*———. *To Your Scattered Bodies Go* (HW) (EB, JC, SM, PN, FP, GW)
*———. *The Unreasoning Mask* (GW)
Finney, Jack. *Time and Again* (PN)
Garrett, Randall. *Too Many Magicians* (1967) (HN)
Gerrold, David. *The Man Who Folded Himself* (HN, NN) (GW)
———. *Moonstar Odyssey* (1977) (NN)
———. *When Harlie Was One* (HN, NN)
Gibson, William. *Burning Chrome* (1986) (EB)
*———. *Neuromancer* (HW, NW, JWC) (EB, JC, PN, GW)
Gray, Alaisdair. *Lanark* (1981) (JC, PN)
*Gunn, James E. *The Listeners* (EB, JC, PN, FP, GW)
*Haldeman, Joe. *The Forever War* (HW, NW, L) (EB, JC, SM, PN, FP, GW)
———. *Mindbridge* (1976) (HN) (FP, GW)
*Harrison, Harry. *Make Room! Make Room!* (NN) (JC, SM, PN, FP, GW)
———. *Winter in Eden* (1986) (EB)
Heinlein, Robert A. *Friday* (HN, NN) (EB, GW)
*———. *The Moon Is a Harsh Mistress* (HN, HW, NN) (EB, JC, SM, FP, GW)
———. *Time Enough for Love* (HN, NN) (EB, GW)
Helprin, Mark. *Winter's Tale* (JC)
Herbert, Frank. *Children of Dune* (HN) (EB, JC, PN, GW)
*———. *Dune* (HW, NW) (EB, JC, SM, PN, GW)
———. *Dune World* (HN) (magazine title of *Dune*)
———. *The Eyes of Heisenberg* (1966) (NN) (PN, GW)
Hoban, Russell. *Riddley Walker* (NN, JWC) (JC, SM, PN, GW)
Holdstock, Robert. *Mythago Wood* (1984) (PN)
Holland, Cecilia. *Floating Worlds* (1976) (JC)
Howard, Hayden. *The Eskimo Invasion* (1967) (NN) (SM)
*Kavan, Anna. *Ice* (GW)
*Kingsbury, Donald. *Courtship Rite* (HN) (JC)
Lafferty, R. A. *The Devil Is Dead* (1971) (NN) (SM)
*———. *Fourth Mansions* (NN) (PN, GW)
*———. *Nine Hundred Grandmothers* (PN, FP, GW)
———. *Past Master* (HN, NN) (EB, JC, GW)
———. *Strange Doings* (EB)
Laumer, Keith. *Earthblood* (1966) (NN) (GW)
———. *A Plague of Demons* (1965) (NN) (JC, SM, PN)
Lee, Tanith. *The Birthgrave* (1975) (NN) (JC, PN, GW)
*Le Guin, Ursula K. *Always Coming Home* (GW)
*———. *The Dispossessed* (HW, NW, L) (EB, JC, SM, PN, FP, GW)
———. *The Lathe of Heaven* (HN, NN, L)
*———. *The Left Hand of Darkness* (HW, NW) (EB, JC, SM, PN, FP, GW)
*———. *The Wind's Twelve Quarters* (JC, PN, GW)
———. *The Word for World Is Forest* (HW, NN) (PN, GW)

Lem, Stanislaw. *Memoirs Found in a Bathtub* (1971) (EB)
Lupoff, Richard A. *Sword of the Demon* (1977) (NN)
MacLean, Katherine. *The Missing Man* (NN) (GW)
Malzberg, Barry N. *Beyond Apollo* (JWC) (EB, JC, GW)
*———. *Cross of Fire*
*———. *Galaxies* (PN)
———. *Guernica Night* (1975) (NN) (PN, GW)
———. *Herovit's World* (EB)
———. *The Remaking of Sigmund Freud* (NN) (JC, GW)
Martin, George R. R. *Dying of the Light* (HN) (JC, SM, GW)
Masson, David I. *The Caltraps of Time* (PN)
May, Julian. *The Many-Colored Land* (HN, NN) (SM, GW)
McCaffrey, Anne. *Dragonquest* (HN) (SM, PN, GW)
———. *Moreta, Dragonlady of Pern* (HN) (GW)
———. *The White Dragon* (HN)
McIntyre, Vonda N. *Dreamsnake* (HW, NW, L) (SM, PN, GW)
———. *The Exile Waiting* (1975) (NN) (GW)
McKillip, Patricia. *Harpist in the Wind* (1979) (HN) (PN, GW)
*Merle, Robert. *Malevil* (JWC) (GW)
*Moorcock, Michael. *Behold the Man* (JC, SM, GW)
———. *The Cornelius Chronicles* (JC, PN)
———. *Gloriana* (1978) (JWC) (JC, PN, GW)
Niven, Larry. *Inferno* (1975) (HN, NN)
———. *The Integral Trees* (HN, NN) (SM, FP, GW)
*———. *The Long ARM of Gil Hamilton* (PN)
———. *Neutron Star* (PN)
———. *Protector* (HN)
*———. *Ringworld* (HW, NW, L) (EB, JC, JM, PN, FP, GW)
———. *World of Ptavvs* (1966) (NN) (JC, PN, FP)
———, and Jerry Pournelle. *Footfall* (HN) (EB)
———. *Lucifer's Hammer* (HN)
———. *The Mote in God's Eye* (HN, NN)
Palmer, David R. *Emergence* (HN) (GW)
*Panshin, Alexei. *Rite of Passage* (HN, NW) (JC, SM, PN, GW)
*Piercy, Marge. *Woman on the Edge of Time*
Pohl, Frederik. *The Age of the Pussyfoot* (1969) (NN) (FP)
———. *Beyond the Blue Event Horizon* (HN, NN) (PN, FP, GW)
*———. *Gateway* (HW, NW, JWC, L) (EB, JC, SM, PN, FP, GW)
———. *JEM* (HN, NN) (EB, JC, FP, GW)
*———. *Man Plus* (HN, NW) (JC, SM, PN, FP, GW)
———. *The Years of the City* (JWC) (JC, FP)
*Powers, Tim. *The Anubis Gates* (PN, GW)
———. *Dinner at Deviant's Palace* (NN)
Priest, Christopher. *Inverted World* (HN) (JC, SM, PN, GW)
Pynchon, Thomas. *Gravity's Rainbow* (NN) (JC, SM, GW)
Randall, Marta. *Islands* (NN) (GW)
Reamy, Tom. *Blind Voices* (HN, NN) (PN, GW)
Rice, Anne. *Interview with a Vampire* (1976) (JC)

*Roberts, Keith. *Pavane* (JC, PN, GW)
*Robinson, Kim Stanley. *The Memory of Whiteness* (GW)
———. *The Wild Shore* (NN) (JC, GW)
*Rucker, Rudy. *Software* (PN, GW)
Russ, Joanna. *Alyx* (EB, JC, PN, GW)
———. *And Chaos Died* (NN) (PN)
*———. *The Female Man* (NN) (JC, FP, GW)
———. *Picnic on Paradise* (NN)
———. *The Zanzibar Gate* (1986) (EB)
Ryman, Geoff, *The Unconquered Country* (1986) (JC, PN)
Sargent, Pamela. *Venus of Dreams* (EB)
Schenck, Hilbert. *At the Eye of the Ocean* (PN)
*———. *A Rose for Armageddon* (JC, PN)
Shaw, Bob. *Orbitsville* (JC, PN, GW)
*———. *Other Days, Other Eyes* (JC, PN, GW)
Shea, Michael. *Nifft the Lean* (1982) (PN)
Shepherd, Lucius. *Green Eyes* (JC)
Silverberg, Robert. *The Book of Skulls* (1971) (HN, NN) (JC)
*———. *Downward to the Earth* (JC, GW)
*———. *Dying Inside* (HN, NN) (EB, JC, PN, GW)
———. *The Masks of Time* (NN) (JC, PN)
———. *Shadrach in the Furnace* (1976) (HN, NN) (JC, PN, FP, GW)
———. *Stochastic Man* (1975) (HN, NN) (JC, GW)
———. *Thorns* (HN, NN) (JC, SM)
———. *A Time of Changes* (HN, NW) (JC, PN)
———. *Tom o'Bedlam* (JC)
———. *Tower of Glass* (1970) (HN, NN) (EB)
———. *Up the Line* (HN, NN) (PN)
*———. *The World Inside* (HN [withdrawn]) (JC, GW)
Simak, Clifford D. *All Flesh Is Grass* (1975) (NN) (JC, GW)
*———. *A Choice of Gods* (GW)
———. *Goblin Reservation* (1968) (HN)
*Sladek, John T. *Roderick* and *Roderick at Random* (JC, PN, GW)
Smith, E. E. *Skylark DuQuesne* (1966) (HN) (FP)
Spinrad, Norman. *Bug Jack Barron* (HN, NN) (EB, JC, SM, PN, FP, GW)
*———. *Child of Fortune* (GW)
*———. *The Iron Dream* (NN) (JC, FP, GW)
*———. *The Void Captain's Tale* (GW)
*Sterling, Bruce. *Schismatrix* (JC, PN, GW)
*Strugatskiis. *Roadside Picnic & The Tale of the Troika* (JC, SM, PN, FP, GW)
Swann, Thomas Burnett. *Day of the Minotaur* (1966) (HN) (SM, PN)
Thomas, Theodore L. *The Clone* (1965) (NN) (PN)
Tiptree, James, Jr. *Ten Thousand Light Years from Home* (PN)
———. *Up the Walls of the World* (HN [withdrawn]) (EB, JC, SM, GW)
———. *Warm Worlds and Otherwise* (JC, PN)
*Tucker, Wilson. *The Year of the Quiet Sun* (HN, NN, JWC [retrospective]) (PN)
Van Scyoc, Sydney. *Cloudcry* (1977) (EB)
*Varley, John. *Millennium* (EB, JC, GW)

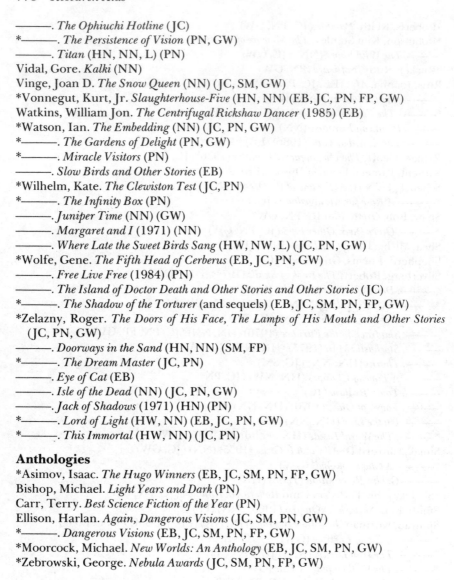

————. *The Ophiuchi Hotline* (JC)
*————. *The Persistence of Vision* (PN, GW)
————. *Titan* (HN, NN, L) (PN)
Vidal, Gore. *Kalki* (NN)
Vinge, Joan D. *The Snow Queen* (NN) (JC, SM, GW)
*Vonnegut, Kurt, Jr. *Slaughterhouse-Five* (HN, NN) (EB, JC, PN, FP, GW)
Watkins, William Jon. *The Centrifugal Rickshaw Dancer* (1985) (EB)
*Watson, Ian. *The Embedding* (NN) (JC, PN, GW)
*————. *The Gardens of Delight* (PN, GW)
*————. *Miracle Visitors* (PN)
————. *Slow Birds and Other Stories* (EB)
*Wilhelm, Kate. *The Clewiston Test* (JC, PN)
*————. *The Infinity Box* (PN)
————. *Juniper Time* (NN) (GW)
————. *Margaret and I* (1971) (NN)
————. *Where Late the Sweet Birds Sang* (HW, NW, L) (JC, PN, GW)
*Wolfe, Gene. *The Fifth Head of Cerberus* (EB, JC, PN, GW)
————. *Free Live Free* (1984) (PN)
————. *The Island of Doctor Death and Other Stories and Other Stories* (JC)
*————. *The Shadow of the Torturer* (and sequels) (EB, JC, SM, PN, FP, GW)
*Zelazny, Roger. *The Doors of His Face, The Lamps of His Mouth and Other Stories*
    (JC, PN, GW)
————. *Doorways in the Sand* (HN, NN) (SM, FP)
*————. *The Dream Master* (JC, PN)
————. *Eye of Cat* (EB)
————. *Isle of the Dead* (NN) (JC, PN, GW)
————. *Jack of Shadows* (1971) (HN) (PN)
*————. *Lord of Light* (HW, NN) (EB, JC, PN, GW)
*————. *This Immortal* (HW, NN) (JC, PN)

Anthologies

*Asimov, Isaac. *The Hugo Winners* (EB, JC, SM, PN, FP, GW)
Bishop, Michael. *Light Years and Dark* (PN)
Carr, Terry. *Best Science Fiction of the Year* (PN)
Ellison, Harlan. *Again, Dangerous Visions* (JC, SM, PN, GW)
*————. *Dangerous Visions* (EB, JC, SM, PN, FP, GW)
*Moorcock, Michael. *New Worlds: An Anthology* (EB, JC, SM, PN, GW)
*Zebrowski, George. *Nebula Awards* (JC, SM, PN, FP, GW)

Children's and Young Adult Science Fiction

*Anthony, Piers. *Race against Time* (SM, GW)
*Benford, Greg. *Jupiter Project* (SM, GW)
*Bethancourt, T. Ernesto. *The Mortal Instruments* (and sequel)
*Bond, Nancy. *The Voyage Begun*
*Bova, Ben. *Exiled from Earth* (SM, GW)
*Christopher, John. *The Guardians* (SM, PN, GW)
*————. *The White Mountains* (and sequels) (JC, SM, PN, GW)

Claudy, Carl H. *Adventures in the Unknown* (1933–1934) (FP)
*Corlett, William. *Return to the Gate* (GW)
*Cross, John Keir. *The Angry Planet* (JC, SM, GW)
Dickinson, Peter. *Heartsease* (JC)
*———. *The Weathermonger* (JC, PN, GW)
*du Bois, William Pene. *The Twenty-One Balloons* (JC, GW)
*Engdahl, Sylvia Louise. *Enchantress from the Stars* (GW)
*Fisk, Nicholas. *Trillions* (JC, PN, GW)
Garner, Alan. *Elidor* (1965) (PN)
———. *Red Shift* (1973) (PN)
*Hamilton, Virginia. *Justice and Her Brothers*
*Harding, Lee. *Misplaced Persons*
Heinlein, Robert A. *Citizen of the Galaxy* (JC, PN)
———. *Farmer in the Sky* (PN)
*———. *Rocket Ship Galileo* (JC, FP, GW)
———. *The Rolling Stones* (PN)
*———. *Starman Jones* (JC, SM, PN, FP, GW)
*———. *Tunnel in the Sky* (JC, SM, PN, FP, GW)
*Hoover, H. M. *Another Heaven, Another Earth* (GW)
*———. *The Rains of Eridan* (GW)
*Huddy, Delia. *Time Piper* (PN, GW)
Jones, Diana Wynne. *The Homeward Bounders* (1981) (PN)
*Karl, Jean E. *The Turning Place* (GW)
*L'Engle, Madeleine. *A Wrinkle in Time* (and sequels) (SM, FP, GW)
*Mayne, William. *Earthfasts* (PN, GW)
*McCaffrey, Anne. *Dragonsong* (and sequels) (SM, GW)
*McKillip, Patricia. *Moon-Flash* (SM, GW)
*North, Eric. *The Ant Men* (SM, GW)
Norton, Andre. *Catseye* (PN)
*———. *Operation Time Search* (SM, PN, GW)
*———. *Star Man's Son: 2250 A.D.* (SM, PN, GW)
*Nourse, Alan E. *Star Surgeon* (SM, PN, GW)
*O'Brien, Robert C. *Mrs. Frisby and the Rats of NIMH* (JC, PN, GW)
*———. *Z for Zachariah* (PN)
*Pesek, Ludek. *Trap for Perseus* (GW)
*Randall, Florence Engel. *A Watcher in the Woods* (PN)
*Sargent, Pamela. *Earthseed* (GW)
*Schlee, Ann. *The Vandal*
Silverberg, Robert. *Lost Race of Mars* (1960) (FP)
*Sleator, William. *House of Stairs*
*Snyder, Zilpha Keatley. *Below the Root* (and sequels)
*Stone, Josephine Rector. *The Mudhead*
*Stoutenberg, Adrien. *Out There* (GW)
*Suddaby, Donald. *Village Fanfare*
*Swindells, Robert. *Brother in the Land*
*Vinge, Joan D. *Psion* (GW)
*Westall, Robert. *Futuretrack 5*
White, T. H. *The Master* (PN)

Wilder, Cherry. *The Luck of Brin's Five* (PN)
*Yep, Laurence. *Sweetwater* (JC, PN, GW)
*Zebrowski, George. *Sunspacer* (SM, GW)

Foreign-Language Science Fiction

German

*Braun, Joanna, and Günter Braun. *Der Fehlfaktor*
*———. *Der Irrtum des Grossen Zauberers*
*Döblin, Alfred. *Berge, Meere und Giganten*
*Franke, Herbert W. *Der Elfenbeinturm*
*———. *Ypsilon minus*
*Fühmann, Franz. *Saiäns Fiktschen*
*Gurk, Paul. *Tuzub 37*
*Lasswitz, Kurd. *Bilder aus der Zukunft*
*Schattschneider, Peter. *Singularitäten*
*Scheerbart, Paul. *Die grosse Revolution*
*Steinmüller, Angela, and Karlheinz Steinmüller. *Der Traum vom Grossen Roten Fleck*

German: Nonfiction

*Bloch, Robert N. *Bibliographie der utopischen und phantastischen Literatur 1750– 1950*
*Heidtmann, Horst. *Utopisch-phantastische Literatur in der DDR*
*Körber, Joachim. *Bibliographisches Lexikon der utopisch-phantastischen Literatur*
*Krysmanski, Hans-Jürgen. *Die utopische Methode*
*Lem, Stanislaw. *Phantastik und Futurologie, I and II*
*Nagl, Manfred. *Science Fiction in Deutschland*

French

*Andrevon, Jean-Pierre. *Le Désert du monde*
*Barjavel, René. *Ashes, Ashes*
*Curval, Philippe. *Cette chère humanité*
*Drode, Daniel. *Surface de la planète*
*Henneberg, Nathalie C., and Charles Henneberg. *La Rosée du soleil*
*Jeury, Michel. *Le Temps incertain*
*———. *Les Yeux géants*
*Ray, Jean. *Malpertuis*
*Renard, Maurice. *Le Péril bleu*
*Rosny aîné, J. H. *La Force mystérieuse*
*Ruellan, André. *Tunnel*
*Sternberg, Jacques. *La Sortie est au fond de l'espace*
*Vian, Boris. *L'Automne à Pékin*

French: Anthologies

*Jeury, Michel. *Utopies 75*
*Klein, Gérard. *Anthologie de la science-fiction Française*

French: Nonfiction

Eizykman, Boris. *Science fiction et capitalisme*

*Goimard, Jacques. *L'Année de la science fiction et du fantastique*
*Méheust, Bertrand. *Science-fiction et soucoupes volantes*
*Versins, Pierre. *Encyclopédie de l'utopie, des voyages extraordinaires et de la science-fiction*

Russian
*Bogdanov, Aleksandr Aleksandrovich. *Krasnaia zvezda*
*Bulychev, Kir. *Posledniaia voina*
*Efremov, Ivan Antonovich. *Chas Byka*
*Larionovna, Ol'ga Nikolaevna. *Ostrov muzhestva*
*Martynov, Georgii Sergeevich. *Gost' iz bezdny*
*Mikhailov, Vladimir Dmitrievich. *Togda pridite, i rassudim*
*Snegov, Sergei. *Liudi kak bogi*

Russian: Anthologies
*Brandis, Evgenii Pavlovich, and Vladimir Ivanovich Dmitrevskii. *Kol'tso obratnogo vremeni*
Fantastika 19—
*Guminskii, V. *Vzgliad skvoz' stoletie*
NF

Russian: Nonfiction
*Britikov, Anatolii Fedorovich. *Russkii sovetskii nauchno-fantasticheskii roman*
*Heller, Leonid. *Vselennaia za predelom dogmy*
*Liapunov, Boris Valer'ianovich. *V mire fantastiki*
*Suvin, Darko. *Russian Science Fiction 1956–1974*

Japanese
*Hanmura, Ryó. *Ishi no Ketsumyaku*
*———. *Musubiyama Hiroku*
*———. *Yōseiden*
*Hirose, Tadashi. *Mainasu Zero*
*Hoshi, Shinichi. *Jinzō Bijin*
*Kanbayashi, Chōhei. *Sentō Yōsei*
*Komatsu, Sakyō. *Hateshinaki Nagare no Hate ni*
*———. *Nippon Chimbotsu*
*Mayumura, Taku. *Shōmetsu no Kōrin*
*Mishima, Yukio. *Utsukushii Hoshi*
*Mitsuse, Ryū. *Hyakuoku no Hiru, Senoku no Yoru*
*———. *Tasogare ni Kaeru*
*Miyazawa, Kenji. *Ginga Tetsudō no Yoru*
*Oshikawa, Shunrō. *Kaitei Gunkan*
*Ōtomo, Katsuhiro. *Dōmu*
*Tsutsui, Yasutaka. *Dassō to Tsuiseki no Samba*
*———. *Tōkaidō Sensō*
*Unno, Jūza. *Chikyū Tōnan*
*Yamano, Kōichi. *X Densha de Ikō*
*Yano, Tetsu. *Origami Uchūsen no Densetsu*

Japanese: Anthologies
*Fukushima, Masimi, and Takashi Ishikawa. *Nihon no SF*
*Hayakawa, Shobō. *SF Magajin Serekushon*
*Tsutsui, Yasutaka. *Nihon SF Besuto Shūsei*
*Yokota, Junya. *Sengo Shoki Nihon SF Besuto Shūsei*

Japanese: Nonfiction
*Ishihara, Fujio. *SF Tosho Kaisetsu Sōmokuroku*
*Ishikawa, Takashi, and Norio Itoh. *Sekai no SF Bungaku Sōkaisetsu*

Italian
*Aldani, Lino. *Quando le Radici*
*Grifoni, Ulisse. *Dalla Terra alle Stelle*
*Malaguti, Ugo. *Satana dei Miracoli*
*Montanari, Gianni. *Daimon*
*Salgari, Emilio. *Le Meraviglie del Duemila*
*Sandrelli, Sandro. *Caino dello Spazio*

Italian: Anthologies
*Cremaschi, Inisero. *Universo e Dintorni*
*Curtoni, Vittorio, Gianfranco De Turris, and Gianni Montanari. *Fanta-Italia*

Italian: Nonfiction
*Aldani, Lino. *La Fantascienza*
*Bertoni, Alfio, and Gianlvigi Missiaja. *Catalogo Generale della Fantascienza*
*Curtoni, Vittorio. *Le Frontiere dell'Ignoto*
*Pagetti, Carlo. *Il Senso del Futuro*
*Pilo, Gianni. *Catalogo Generale della Fantascienza in Italia*
*Russo, Luigi. *La Fantascienza e la Critica*

Danish: Fiction
*Eriksen, Inge. *Rummet uden tid*
*Holberg, Ludvig. *Niels Klims underjordiske Reise*
*Holm, Sven. *Termush*
*Madsen, Svend Åge. *Tugt og utugt i mellemtiden*
*Nielsen, Niels E. *Herskerne*
*———. *Troldmandens sværd*
*———. *Vagabondernes planet*
*Willumsen, Dorrit. *Programmeret til kærlighed*

Danish: Nonfiction
*Guld, Jens. *Bibliografi over litteratur på dansk om science fiction til og med 1984*
*Holm, Palle Juul. *Syzygy og den sorte stjerne*
*Schiøler, Carsten, and Erik H. Swiatek. *Dansk Science Fiction Indeks 1742–1976*
Proxima

Norwegian: Fiction
*Bing, Jon. *Dobbeltgjengere*
*Bringsværd, Tor Åge. *Ker Shus*
*Holberg, Ludvig. *Nicolai Klimii Iter Subterraneum*
*Jensen, Axel. *Epp*

Norwegian: Anthology
*Bing, Jon, and Tor Åge Bringsværd. *Stella Polaris*

Dutch: Fiction
*Bordewijk, F. *Blokken*
*Gijsen, Wim. *De eersten van Rissan*
*Burger, Dionijs. *Bolland*
*Raes, Hugo. *De lotgevallen*
*Ruyslinck, Ward. *Het reservaat*

Dutch: Nonfiction
*De Vos, Luk. *Waar helden sterven*

General Reference Works

Bibliographies and Indexes
*Reginald, R. *Science Fiction and Fantasy Literature* (EB, JC, SM, PN, GW)
Bleiler, Everett F. *The Checklist of Science-Fiction and Supernatural Fiction* (EB)
*Currey, L. W. *Science Fiction and Fantasy Authors* (EB, JC, SM, PN, GW)
*Tuck, Donald H. *The Encyclopedia of Science Fiction and Fantasy through 1968* (EB, JC, SM, PN, GW)
*Brown, Charles N., and William G. Contento. *Science Fiction in Print* (EB, JC, SM, PN, GW)
*Contento, William G. *Index to Science Fiction Anthologies and Collections* (EB, JC, SM, PN, GW)
Clareson, Thomas D. *Science Fiction in America, 1870s–1930s* (GW)
*———. *Science Fiction Criticism* (EB, JC, PN, GW)
*Tymn, Marshall B., and Roger C. Schlobin. *The Year's Scholarship in Science Fiction and Fantasy* (EB, JC, PN, GW)
*Hall, H. W. *Science Fiction and Fantasy Book Review Index* (EB, JC, SM, PN, GW)

Biocritical Works
*Bleiler, Everett F. *Science Fiction Writers* (EB, JC, SM, PN, GW)
*Magill, Frank N. *Survey of Science Fiction Literature* (EB, JC, SM, PN, GW)
*Nicholls, Peter. *The Science Fiction Encyclopedia* (EB, JC, SM, PN, FP, GW)
*Smith, Curtis C. *Twentieth-Century Science-Fiction Writers* (EB, JC, SM, PN, GW)
*Wolfe, Gary K. *Critical Terms for Science Fiction and Fantasy* (EB, PN, GW)

History and Criticism

*Aldiss, Brian W., and David Wingrove. *Trillion Year Spree* (EB, JC, SM, PN, FP, GW)
*Amis, Kingsley. *New Maps of Hell* (EB, JC, PN, FP, GW)
*Bailey, J. O. *Pilgrims through Space and Time* (EB, SM, GW)
*Carter, Paul A. *The Creation of Tomorrow* (SM, GW)
*Clareson, Thomas D. *Some Kind of Paradise* (EB, SM, PN, FP, GW)
*Clarke, I. F. *The Pattern of Expectation* (JC, GW)
Delany, Samuel R. *The Jewel-Hinged Jaw* (GW)
Fredericks, Casey. *The Future of Eternity* (GW)
*Gunn, James E. *Alternate Worlds* (EB, JC, SM, PN, FP, GW)

*Hillegas, Mark R. *The Future as Nightmare* (JC, GW)
King, Stephen. *Danse Macabre* (1981) (HW, L) (JC)
Knight, Damon F. *Turning Points* (GW)
*Le Guin, Ursula K. *The Language of the Night* (NN) (JC, GW)
*Lem, Stanislaw. *Microworlds* (GW)
*Malzberg, Barry. *The Engines of the Night* (JC, PN, GW)
*Manlove, C. N. *Science Fiction: Ten Explorations* (EB, JC, FP, GW)
*Meyers, Walter E. *Aliens and Linguists* (GW)
*Nicholls, Peter. *Science Fiction at Large* (EB, JC, PN, GW)
*———, David Langford, and Brian Stableford. *The Science in Science Fiction* (EB, PN)
*Pringle, David. *Science Fiction: The 100 Best Novels* (JC, GW)
*Rose, Mark. *Alien Encounters* (JC, PN, GW)
*Scholes, Robert. *Structural Fabulation* (EB, JC, PN, GW)
*———, and Eric S. Rabkin. *Science Fiction: History-Science-Vision* (JC, PN, GW)
*Stableford, Brian M. *Scientific Romance in Britain 1890–1950* (EB, JC, SM, PN, GW)
*Suvin, Darko. *Metamorphoses of Science Fiction* (EB, JC, PN, GW)
*———. *Victorian Science Fiction in the UK* (JC, SM, PN, GW)
*Wagar, W. Warren. *Terminal Visions* (JC, GW)
*Wolfe, Gary K. *The Known and the Unknown* (EB, JC, PN, GW)

Author Studies

Griffin, Brian, and David Wingrove. *Apertures* (GW)
Asimov, Isaac. *In Memory Yet Green* (HN) (EB, SM)
———. *In Joy Still Felt* (HN, L) (EB, SM)
Gunn, James. *Isaac Asimov* (HW) (EB, SM, GW)
*Brigg, Peter. *J. G. Ballard* (JC, SM, GW)
Lupoff, Richard A. *Edgar Rice Burroughs* (JC, PN)
*Porges, Irwin. *Edgar Rice Burroughs* (EB, SM, GW)
Campbell, John W., Jr. *The John W. Campbell Letters* (GW)
Barbour, Douglas. *Worlds Out of Words* (GW)
*Greenberg, Martin H., and Joseph D. Olander. *Philip K. Dick* (JC, GW)
*Franklin, H. Bruce. *Robert A. Heinlein* (JC, SM, PN, GW)
McNelly, Willis E. *The Dune Encyclopedia* (EB)
*De Bolt, Joe. *Ursula K. Le Guin* (SM, GW)
Slusser, George Edgar. *The Farthest Shores of Ursula K. Le Guin* (EB)
*Spivack, Charlotte. *Ursula K. Le Guin* (GW)
de Camp, L. Sprague. *Lovecraft* (EB)
Pohl, Frederik. *The Way the Future Was* (FP)
*Levine, George, and V. C. Knoepflmacher. *The Endurance of Frankenstein* (SM, PN, GW)
*Tropp, Martin. *Mary Shelley's Monster* (GW)
Fiedler, Leslie A. *Olaf Stapledon* (GW)
*McCarthy, Patrick A. *Olaf Stapledon* (SM, GW)
Jules-Verne, Jean. *Jules Verne* (EB)
*Bergonzi, Bernard. *The Early H. G. Wells* (EB, JC, SM, GW)

*MacKenzie, Norman Ian, and Jean MacKenzie. *H. G. Wells: A Biography* (JC, SM, PN, GW)
*Parrinder, Patrick. *H. G. Wells: The Critical Heritage* (JC, PN, GW)
*Suvin, Darko, and Robert M. Philmus. *H. G. Wells and Modern Science Fiction*

Collective Biography
Aldiss, Brian W., and Harry Harrison. *Hell's Cartographers* (EB)

Interviews
*Platt, Charles. *Dream Makers* (HN) (JC, SM, PN, GW)
*———. *Dream Makers II* (HN, L) (JC, SM, PN, GW)

Science Fiction on Film and Television

Reference Works
*Hardy, Phil. *Science Fiction [Film Encyclopedia]* (JC, SM, PN, GW)
Warren, Bill, and Bill Thomas. *Keep Watching the Skies!* (PN, GW)

General Survey
*Brosnan, John. *Future Tense* (JC, SM, PN, GW)
*Nicholls, Peter. *The World of Fantastic Films* (JC, PN, GW)
Strick, Philip. *Science Fiction Movies* (PN)

Other Studies
Sobchack, Vivian. *Screening Space* (GW)

Science Fiction Illustration

*Aldiss, Brian W. *Science Fiction Art* (PN, GW)
*Barlowe, Wayne Douglas, and Ian Summers. *Barlowe's Guide to Extraterrestrials* (HN, L)
Di Fate, Vincent, and Ian Summers. *Di Fate's Catalog of Science Fiction Hardware* (HW)
The Art of Leo & Diane Dillon (1981) (HN) (GW)
*Durant, Frederick, III, and Ron Miller. *Worlds Beyond*
*Foss, Chris. *21st Century Foss* (PN, GW)
*Freas, Frank Kelly. *The Art of Science Fiction* (PN, GW)
Morrill, Rowena. *The Fantastic Art of Rowena* (HN)
Perret, Patti. *The Faces of Science Fiction* (HN) (SM, GW)
*Summers, Ian. *Tomorrow and Beyond* (PN, GW)
*Whelan, Michael. *Wonderworks* (HN) (PN, GW)

Teaching Materials

Instructional Guides
*Allen, L. David. *Science Fiction: An Introduction*
*———. *Science Fiction Reader's Guide.*
*Donelson, Kenneth. *Science Fiction in the English Class*
*Riley, Dick. *Critical Encounters* (SM)
*Spann, Sylvia, and Mary Beth Culp. *Thematic Units in Teaching English and the Humanities*
*Williamson, Jack. *Teaching Science Fiction* (SM, GW)

Writing Guides
*Bretnor, Reginald. *The Craft of Science Fiction* (PN, GW)
*Longyear, Barry B. *Science Fiction Writer's Workshop I* (GW)
*Wilson, Robin Scott. *Those Who Can* (GW)

Classroom Texts
*Allen, Dick. *Science Fiction: The Future* (SM, GW)
*Asimov, Isaac. *Where Do We Go from Here?* (GW)
*Gunn, James. *The Road to Science Fiction* (EB, SM, PN, GW)
*Hollister, Bernard. *You and Science Fiction*
*Rabkin, Eric S. *Science Fiction: A Historical Anthology* (SM, PN)
**Science Fiction Hall of Fame* (SM, PN, GW)
*Silverberg, Robert. *The Mirror of Infinity* (PN, GW)
*Spinrad, Norman. *Modern Science Fiction* (PN, GW)
*Wymer, Thomas L. *Intersections* (GW)

Classroom Aids
**Getting Hooked on Science Fiction*
**Radio's Golden Age of Science Fiction*
**Return to Reading Software*
**Science Fiction: Jules Verne to Ray Bradbury* (GW)

Science Fiction Magazines

Indexes and Checklists
*Day, Donald B. *Index to the Science Fiction Magazines, 1926–1950* (EB, SM, PN, GW)
*Strauss, Irwin S. *The MIT Science Fiction Society's Index to the SF Magazines, 1951–1965* (EB, SM, PN, GW)
*New England Science Fiction Association. *Index to the Science Fiction Magazines 1966–1970* (EB, SM, PN, GW)
*————. *The NESFA Index: Science Fiction Magazines and Original Anthologies*

Studies
*Tymn, Marshall B., and Mike Ashley. *Science Fiction, Fantasy, and Weird Fiction Magazines* (SM)

Magazines
**Analog Science Fiction/Science Fact* (EB, SM, PN, GW)
**Isaac Asimov's Science Fiction Magazine* (EB, SM, PN, GW)
**The Magazine of Fantasy and Science Fiction* (EB, SM, GW)
**Cinefantastique* (EB, SM, PN, GW)
**Extrapolation* (EB, SM, PN, GW)
**Foundation* (EB, SM, PN, GW)
**Locus* (EB, SM, PN, GW)
**Science-Fiction Studies* (EB, SM, PN, GW)

Author/Subject Index

This index includes all entries from the title index, except for those works lacking named authors (such as audiovisual materials in Chapter 13), thereby permitting rapid scanning of all books and some short fiction by an author, or materials about an author. Annotations are cited by entry numbers, easily identified by the hyphen, such as 3-231 (meaning entry 231 in Chapter 3). All other references, such as to introductory essays, are cited by "no-hyphen" page numbers, such as 475. Annotated books are listed under the author's most common name even if it is a pseudonym. A few name cross-references are included where there might be some question; for example, for compound last names, or where two names might be equally known, e.g., Henry Kuttner and Lewis Padgett. In order to make this index as useful as possible, and keep it to a reasonable length, only substantive references (defined as having at least minimal descriptive or critical comment) to authors or to titles are included. References to authors as subjects follow the author's name; author collections mentioned in Chapter 15, "Library and Private Collections of Science Fiction and Fantasy," are indexed. Coauthors and coeditors are indexed and can be identified by the principal author's or editor's name in parentheses following the title.

Subject indexing includes some general categories, for example, fantasy fiction, recordings, and utopian literature, and such headings are typeset in caps and small caps.

Certain types of material were not indexed: (1) references to authors or titles with no substantive content, e.g., mentions of stories in a collection or anthology (Contento in his *Index to Science Fiction Anthologies and Collections* [8-9 and 8-10] thoroughly indexes these); (2) mentions of authors and titles in the compare and contrast statements; (3) passing references to authors as subjects, such as in essay collections (such secondary literature is indexed by Tymn and Schlobin [8-17] and Hall [8-18, 8-19, and 8-20]); (4) magazine editors in Chapter 14; (5) translators; (6) foreign-language titles of translated books; (7) film titles.

Abbott, Edwin A.
  Flatland, 1-1
Abé, Kobo, 475, 482
  Inter Ice Age 4, 3-1
Abrashkin, Raymond
  Danny Dunn and the Homework Machine (Williams), 5-171

Ackerman, Forrest J., 15-30, 15-34, 15-52
  A Reference Guide to American Science Fiction Films (Strickland), 11-7
Acquino, John
  Science Fiction as Literature, 13-1
Adams, Douglas
  The Hitch-Hiker's Guide to the Galaxy, 4-1

Life, the Universe and Everything, 4-1
The Restaurant at the End of the Universe, 4-1
So Long, and Thanks for All the Fish, 4-1
Adams, Samuel Hopkins
The Mystery (White), 1-107
Aderca, Felix
Oraşele înecate, 6-440
Adler, Alan
Science Fiction and Horror Posters in Full Color, 11-23
"A.E." *See* Russell, George William
Agel, Jerome
The Making of Kubrick's 2001, 11-24
Aiken, Conrad, 15-50
Alargić, Danilo
Antares, 6-466
Aldani, Lino
La Fantascienza, 6-329
Quando le Radici, 6-306
Aldiss, Brian W., 10-1, 10-2, 10-3, 15-3, 15-43, 15-54, 15-60
An Age, 4-2
. . . And the Lurid Glare of the Comet, 9-3
The Astounding-Analog Reader (Harrison), 3-426, 3-437
Barefoot in the Head, 4-3
Best Science Fiction of Brian W. Aldiss, 3-2
Billion Year Spree, 9-4
Cryptozoic!, 4-2
Decade: The 1940s, 3-418
Decade: The 1950s, 3-418
Decade: The 1960s, 3-418
Evil Earths, 3-419
Frankenstein Unbound, 4-4
Galactic Empires, 3-419
Galaxies Like Grains of Sand, 3-3
Greybeard, 4-5
Helliconia Spring, 4-6
Helliconia Summer, 4-6
Helliconia Winter, 4-6
Hell's Cartographers, 10-188
Hothouse, 3-4, 4-7
An Island Called Moreau, 4-4
Last Orders and Other Stories, 4-8
Life in the West, 4-6
The Long Afternoon of Earth, 3-4, 4-7
The Moment of Eclipse, 4-8
Moreau's Other Island, 4-4
Non-stop, 3-6
The Pale Shadow of Science, 9-2
The Penguin World Omnibus of Science Fiction, 4-633
Perilous Planets, 3-419
Report on Probability A, 4-9

The Saliva Tree and Other Strange Growths, 3-5
Science Fiction Art, 12-1
Science Fiction Quiz, 8-40
Seasons in Flight, 4-8
Space Odysseys, 3-419
Space Opera, 3-419
Starship, 3-6
This World and Nearer Ones, 9-1
Trillion Year Spree, 9-4
Who Can Replace a Man?, 3-2
Aldrich, Thomas Bailey
"The Queen of Sheba," 11
Allard, Yvon
Paralittératures, 6-177
Allen, Dick
Science Fiction: The Future, 13-21
Allen, L. David
Science Fiction: An Introduction, 13-2
Science Fiction Reader's Guide, 13-2A
Allighan, Garry
Verwoerd—The End, 3-7
Allot, Kenneth
Jules Verne, 10-150
Allum, Tom
Boy beyond the Moon, 5-1
Emperor of Space, 501
Alpers, Hans Joachim
Lexikon der Science Fiction Literatur, 6-36
Reclams Science-Fiction-Führer, 6-37
Science Fiction aus Deutschland, 6-34
Amery, Carl
Der Untergang der Stadt Passau, 6-1
Ames, Mildred
Anna to the Infinite Power, 5-2
Is There Life on a Plastic Planet?, 5-3
Amis, Kingsley
The Alteration, 4-10
New Maps of Hell, 9-5
Russian Hide and Seek, 4-11
Spectrum, 3-420
Anderson, Chester
The Butterfly Kid, 4-12
Anderson, Craig W.
Science Fiction Films of the Seventies, 11-25
Anderson, Poul, 10-4, 10-5, 15-3, 15-57
The Avatar, 4-13
Brain Wave, 3-8
The Byworlder, 4-14
Earthman's Burden, 3-9
The Enemy Stars, 3-10
Fire Time, 4-15
The High Crusade, 3-11
Hoka!, 3-9
Maurai and Kith, 4-16
Orion Shall Rise, 4-16

People of the Wind, 4-17
The Star Fox, 3-12
Star Prince Charlie, 3-9
Tau Zero, 4-18
There Will Be Time, 4-19
Time and Stars, 3-13
Trader to the Stars, 3-14
Vault of the Ages, 5-4
Anderson, Susan Janice
Aurora (McIntyre), 4-653
Andrae, Johann V.
Christianopolis, 5
Andrevon, Jean-Pierre, 412
Avenirs à la dérive, 6-169
Compagnons en terre étrangère, 6-168
Le Désert du monde, 6-53
Le Livre d'or de Jean-Pierre Andrevon, 6-55
Retour à la terre, 6-169
Le Travail du Furet à l'intérieur du Poulailler, 6-56
Anestin, Victor
O tragedie cerească, 6-441
Anet, Claude
The End of a World, 56
Anonymous
The Reign of George VI, 1900–1925, 8, 1-2
Antczak, Janice
Science Fiction: The Mythos of a New Romance, 13-3
Anthony, James K.
Reisen til Ken, 539, 6-378
Anthony, Piers, 15-30, 15-34
Battle Circle, 4-20
Bearing an Hourglass, 4-23
Chaining the Lady, 4-22
Chthon, 4-21
Cluster, 4-22
Faith of Tarot, 4-23
God of Tarot, 4-23
Kirlian Quest, 4-22
Macroscope, 4-23
Neq the Sword, 4-20
Omnivore, 4-24
On a Pale Horse, 4-23
Orn, 4-24
Ox, 4-24
Phthor, 4-21
Race against Time, 5-5
Sos the Rope, 4-20
Thousandstar, 4-22
Var the Stick, 4-20
Vicinity Cluster, 4-22
Viscous Circle, 4-22
Vision of Tarot, 4-23
With a Tangled Skein, 4-23
Appleton, Victor

Tom Swift and His Electric Rifle, 5-6
Arai, Motoko
Zekku . . . , 6-233
Aramă, Horia
Colecţionarul de insule, 6-460
Aramaki, Yoshio
Shirokabe no Moji wa Sekiyo ni Haeru, 6-232
Arbur, Rosemarie
Leigh Brackett, Marion Zimmer Bradley, Anne McCaffrey, 10-22
Marion Zimmer Bradley, 10-23
Arlen, Michael
Man's Mortality, 2-1
Armytage, W. H. G.
Yesterday's Tomorrows, 9-6
Arnaud, G. J.
La Compagnie des glaces, 6-57
Arnold, Edwin L.
Lieut. Gullivar Jones, 18
Aroeste, Jean, 15-8
Ash, Brian
The Visual Encyclopedia of Science Fiction, 9-7
Who's Who in Science Fiction, 8-26
Asher, Ellen
The New Visions (Sherwin), 12-31
Ashley, Mike
Complete Index to Astounding/Analog, 14-1
The History of the Science Fiction Magazines, 14-12
The Illustrated Book of Science Fiction Lists, 8-41
Monthly Terrors (Parnell), 14-8
Science Fiction, Fantasy, and Weird Fiction Magazines (Tymn), 14-18
Who's Who in Horror and Fantasy Fiction, 8-45
Ashton, Francis Leslie
Alas, That Great City, 3-15
Asimov, Isaac, 10-7, 10-8, 10-9, 10-10, 10-11, 10-12, 15-25, 15-55
Amazing Stories, 3-425
Before the Golden Age, 2-2
The Bicentennial Man and Other Stories, 4-25
The Caves of Steel, 3-16
David Starr: Space Ranger, 5-7
The Early Asimov, 3-17
The End of Eternity, 3-18
Foundation, 3-19
Foundation and Earth, 4-26
Foundation and Empire, 3-19
The Foundation Trilogy, 3-19
Foundation's Edge, 4-26
The Gods Themselves, 4-27
The Hugo Winners, 4-634

I, Robot, 3-20
In Joy Still Felt, 10-8
In Memory Yet Green, 10-7
Isaac Asimov Presents the Great Science
    Fiction Stories, 3-421
Machines That Think, 4-635
The Man Who Upset the Universe, 3-19
The Martian Way and Other Stories, 3-
    21
Nightfall and Other Stories, 3-21
The 1000 Year Plan, 3-19
Pebble in the Sky, 3-22
The Rest of the Robots, 3-20
Robots and Empire, 4-28
The Robots of Dawn, 4-28
Second Foundation, 3-19
The 13 Crimes of Science Fiction, 3-460
Where Do We Go from Here?, 13-22
The Winds of Change and Other Sto-
    ries, 4-25
Asprin, Robert
    The Cold Cash War, 4-29
Astor, John Jacob
    A Journey in Other Worlds, 1-3
Atherton, Gertrude
    Black Oxen, 2-3
Atkins, John
    Tomorrow Revealed, 3-23
Attanasio, A. A.
    Radix, 4-30
Atterley, Joseph
    A Voyage to the Moon, 6, 1-4
Atwood, Margaret
    The Handmaid's Tale, 4-31
Aubrey, Frank
    The Devil Tree of El Dorado, 1-5
    A Queen of Atlantis, 1-5
AUDIOVISUAL MATERIALS, 714-719
Auel, Jean M.
    The Clan of the Cave Bear, 4-32
    The Mammoth Hunters, 4-32
    The Valley of Horses, 4-32
Austey, Eirik
    Tyskeren mot Stretermish, 6-379
Austin, F. Britten
    Tomorrow, 62
Avallone, Michael, 15-52
Aziza, Claude
    Encyclopédie de poche de la science-
        fiction, 6-178

Bacon, Francis
    The New Atlantis, 5
Baen, James
    The Best from Galaxy, 3-436
    The Best from If, 3-436
    Far Frontiers (Pournelle), 4-662

Galaxy: The Best of My Years, 3-436
Bahnson, Agnew H., Jr.
    The Stars Are Too High, 3-24
Bailey, Charles W., II
    Seven Days in May (Knebel), 3-232
Bailey, J. O.
    Pilgrims through Space and Time, 9-8
Bainbridge, William S.
    Dimensions of Science Fiction, 9-9
Ballard, J. G., 10-13, 10-14, 10-15, 10-16,
    10-17, 15-55
    The Atrocity Exhibition, 4-33, 412
    The Best Short Stories of J. G. Ballard,
        4-34
    The Burning World, 4-36
    Chronopolis and Other Stories, 4-34
    The Crystal World, 4-35
    The Drought, 4-36
    The Drowned World, 4-37
    Love and Napalm: Export U.S.A., 4-33
    Vermilion Sands, 4-38
Ballou, Arthur W.
    Bound for Mars, 5-8
Balmer, Edwin
    After Worlds Collide (Wylie), 2-146
    When Worlds Collide (Wylie), 2-146
Barbour, Douglas
    Worlds Out of Words, 10-48
Barbusse, Henri
    Chains, 56, 60
Barets, Stan
    Catalogue des âmes et cycles de la sci-
        ence fiction, 6-179
Barfoed, Niels
    14 danske science fiction noveller, 6-359
Barjavel, René, 409
    Ashes, Ashes, 3-25, 6-58
    Le Díable l'emporte, 6-59
    Future Times Three, 6-60
Barlowe, Wayne Douglas
    Barlowe's Guide to Extraterrestrials, 12-2
Barnes, Arthur K.
    Interplanetary Hunter, 3-26
Barnes, Steven
    The Descent of Anansi (Niven), 4-394
    Dream Park (Niven), 4-395
    Streetlethal, 4-38A
Barney, J. Stewart
    L.P.M.: The End of the Great War, 14,
        1-6
Barnouw, Dagmar
    Die versuchte Realität oder von der
        Möglichkeit, glücklichere Welten zu
        denken, 6-38
Barr, George, 15-65
    Upon the Winds of Yesterday and Other
        Explorations, 12-3
Barr, Marleen S.

Future Females, 9-10
Barrett, Neal, Jr.
 Aldair in Albion, 4-39
 Stress Pattern, 4-39
Barth, John
 Giles Goat-Boy, 4-40
Bass, T. J.
 The Godwhale, 4-41
 Half Past Human, 4-41
Batchelor, John
 H. G. Wells, 10-163
Batchelor, John Calvin
 The Birth of the People's Republic of
  Antarctica, 4-42
 The Further Adventures of Halley's
  Comet, 4-43
Battestine, Monique
 Les Lolos de Venus, 6-170
Baum, L. Frank
 The Master Key, 5-9
Baxter, John
 Science Fiction in the Cinema, 11-11
Bayley, Barrington J., 15-61
 The Fall of Chronopolis, 4-44
 The Knights of the Limits, 4-45
 The Rod of Light, 4-46
 The Seed of Evil, 4-45
 Soul of the Robot, 4-46
 Star Winds, 4-47
 The Zen Gun, 4-48
Bear, Greg
 Beyond Heaven's River, 4-49
 Blood Music, 4-50
 Eon, 4-51
 Eternity, 4-51
Beatty, Jerome, Jr.
 Matthew Looney's Voyage to the Earth,
  5-10
Beauchamp, Gorman
 Jack London, 10-103
Becker, Muriel R.
 Clifford Simak, 10-134
Begouen, Max
 Bison of Clay, 56
Belča, Dušan
 Prijatelj sa daleke zvezde, 6-467
Beliaev, Aleksandr, 444, 446
 The Amphibian, 2-4, 444
 The Struggle in Space, 2-4, 444
Bell, Clare
 Ratha's Creature, 5-11
Bell, Neil
 The Lord of Life, 2-5
 Precious Porcelain, 2-6
 The Seventh Bowl, 2-7
Bell, William Dixon
 The Moon Colony, 5-12
Bellamy, Edward

Equality, 1-7
 Looking Backward, 1-8
 "To Whom This May Come," 1-7
Benford, Gregory, 15-9
 Across the Sea of Suns, 4-53
 Against Infinity, 4-52
 The Heart of the Comet, 4-55
 Hitler Victorious, 4-636
 If the Stars Are Gods, 4-56
 In the Ocean of Night, 4-53
 Jupiter Project, 5-13
 Timescape, 4-54
Bennett, Margot
 The Long Way Back, 3-21
Benoit, Pierre
 L'Atlantide, 23
Bensen, Donald R.
 And Having Writ . . . , 4-57
Benson, Gordon, Jr.
 Anne Inez McCaffrey, 10-110
 Arthur Bertram Chandler, 10-38
 Arthur Wilson "Bob" Tucker, 10-148
 Bob Shaw (Nelson), 10-124
 Edgar Pangborn, 10-118
 Eric Frank Russell (Stephensen-Payne),
  10-122
 Gordon Rupert Dickson, 10-62
 Hal Clement (Harry Clement Stubbs),
  10-44
 Harry Harrison, 10-70
 Henry Beam Piper, 10-119
 Jack (John Stewart) Williamson, 10-180
 James White, 10-179
 John Killian Houston Brunner, 10-30
 John Wyndham Parkes Lucas Benyon
  Harris (Stephensen-Payne), 10-183
 Leigh Douglass Brackett & Edmond
  Hamilton, 10-20
 Manly Wade Wellman, 10-162
 Margaret St. Clair, 10-123
 Philip Kindred Dick, 10-51
 Poul Anderson, 10-4
 William Tenn (Philip Klass), 10-146
Benson, Michael
 Vintage Science Fiction Films, 1896–
  1949, 11-12
Benson, Robert Hugh
 The Dawn of All, 1-9
 Lord of the World, 1-9
Ben-Yehuda, Nachman
 Deviance and Moral Boundaries, 9-11
Beresford, John Davys
 Goslings, 1-10
 The Hampdenshire Wonder, 11, 1-11
 The Riddle of the Tower, 3-28
 What Dreams May Come . . . , 52
 The Wonder, 1-11
 A World of Women, 1-10

Berger, Harold L.
  Science Fiction and the New Dark Age,
    9-12
Bergerac, Cyrano Savinien de, 406
  Histoire comique des États et Empires
    de la lune, 5, 1-12
Bergonzi, Bernard
  The Early H. G. Wells, 10-164
  H. G. Wells, 10-165
Bernal, J. D.
  "The World, the Flesh and the Devil,"
    55
Berry, James R.
  Dar Tellum, 5-14
Bersianik, Louky
  The Euguélionne, 6-66
Berthelot, Francis
  La Line noire d'orion, 6-62
Bertin, Eddy, 546
  Eenzame bloedvogel, 6-400, 6-427
Bertoni, Alfio
  Catalogo Generale della Fantascienza, 6-
    330
Best, Herbert
  The Twenty-fifth Hour, 3-29
Bester, Alfred, 10-18
  The Demolished Man, 3-30
  Starlight, 3-31
  The Stars My Destination, 3-32
  Tiger! Tiger!, 3-32
Bethancourt, T. Ernesto
  Instruments of Darkness, 5-15
  The Mortal Instruments, 5-15
Bialkowski, Stanislaw
  Krieg im All, 6-2
Biemiller, Carl L.
  Escape from the Crater, 5-16
  Follow the Whales, 5-16
  The Hydronauts, 5-16
Bierce, Ambrose, 15-46
  "The Damned Thing," 1-13
  "Moxon's Master," 1-13
Biggle, Lloyd, Jr., 15-19
  The Metallic Muse, 3-33
  Monument, 3-34
  The Still Small Voice of Trumpets, 4-58
  The World Menders, 4-58
Bilenkin, Dmitrii Aleksandrovich
  Antologiia sovetskoi fantastiki, 6-215
  Marsianskii priboi, 6-199
  Noch'kontrabandoi, 6-199
  Proverka na razumnost', 6-199
Billon, Pierre
  L'enfant du cinquième nord, 6-63
Binder, Eando, 15-77
  Adam Link: Robot, 3-35
  Puzzle of the Space Pyramids, 3-36
Binder, Earl Andrew. See Binder, Eando

Binder, Otto Oscar. See Binder, Eando
Bing, Jon, 539–540
  Alene, og fremtiden, 6-380
  Dobbeltgjengere, 6-381
  Dragsug, 6-395
  Malstrøm, 6-397, 6-399
  Stella Polaris, 6-396
Bingenheimer, Heinz
  Katalog der deutschsprachigen
    utopischphantistichen Literatur aus
    fünf Jahrhunderten 1460–1960, 379,
    6-36, 6-39
Bioy Casares, Adolfo
  The Invention of Morel and Other Sto-
    ries, 3-37
Birkenhead, Earl of
  The World in 2030 A.D., 54
Bischoff, David
  Mandala, 4-59
Bishop, Michael, 15-14, 15-41
  Ancient of Days, 4-60
  Blooded on Arachne, 4-61
  Catacomb Years, 4-62
  Close Encounters with the Deity, 4-61
  Light Years and Dark, 4-637
  A Little Knowledge, 4-62
  No Enemy but Time, 4-63
  One Winter in Eden, 4-61
  Transfigurations, 4-64
  Under Heaven's Bridge (Watson), 4-592
Bixby, Jerome
  Space by the Tale, 3-38
Blackburn, John F.
  A Scent of New-Mown Hay, 3-39
Blackford, Jenny
  Contrary Modes, 9-110
Blackwood, Algernon, 15-93
Blaine, John
  The Rocket's Shadow, 5-17
Blake, Stacey
  Beyond the Blue, 53
Blanc, Bernard
  Pourquois J'ai tué Jules Verne, 6-180
Blaylock, James P.
  The Digging Leviathan, 4-65
  Homunculus, 4-66
Bleiler, Everett
  The Best Science-Fiction Stories, 3-422
  The Checklist of Fantastic Literature, 8-2
  The Checklist of Science-Fiction and Su-
    pernatural Fiction, 8-2
  The Guide to Supernatural Fiction, 8-46
  Science Fiction Omnibus, 3-422
  Science Fiction Writers, 8-27
  Supernatural Fiction Writers, 8-47
  The Year's Best Science Fiction Novels,
    3-422
BLIND, SCIENCE FICTION FOR, 735–737

Blish, James, 10-19, 15-30, 15-60
Anywhen, 3-40
The Best of James Blish, 3-41
Black Easter, 3-42
A Case of Conscience, 3-42
Cities in Flight, 3-43
A Clash of Cymbals, 3-43
The Day after Judgment, 3-42
Doctor Mirabilis, 3-42
The Duplicated Man, 3-44
Earthman, Come Home, 3-43
ESP-er, 3-46
Galactic Cluster, 3-45
The Issue at Hand, 9-13
Jack of Eagles, 3-46
A Life for the Stars, 3-43
Mission to the Heart Stars, 5-18
More Issues at Hand, 9-14
The Seedling Stars, 3-47
They Shall Have Stars, 3-43
A Torrent of Faces, 3-48
The Triumph of Time, 3-43
Year 2018!, 3-43
Bloch, Robert, 15-17, 15-52, 15-70
Fear Today, Gone Tomorrow, 3-49
Bloch, Robert N.
Bibliographie der utopischen und
phantastichen Literatur 1750–1950, 6-
39
Bloom, Harold
Ursula K. Le Guin, 10-90
Bodelsen, Anders
Freezing Down, 4-67
Freezing Point, 4-67
Bogdanoff, Grichka
Clefs pour la science-fiction, 6-181
Bogdanoff, Igor
Clefs pour la science-fiction, 6-181
Bogdanov, Aleksandr Aleksandrovich
Engineer Menni, 6-200
Inzhener Menni, 442, 6-200
Krasnaia zvezda, 442, 6-200
Red Star, 6-200
Boireau, Jacques
Les Années de sable, 6-64
Bok, Hannes, 15-65, 15-69A, 15-75
The Blue Flamingo, 2-43
Bolt, Nina
Athena'er i byen og brugt, 6-360
Bolton, Charles E.
The Harris-Ingram Experiment, 21
Bond, Nancy
The Voyage Begun, 5-19
Bond, Nelson S.
Exiles of Time, 3-50
Lancelot Biggs: Spaceman, 3-51
Bonestell, Chesley
Worlds Beyond (Durant), 12-12

Bonham, Frank
The Forever Formula, 5-20
BOOK REVIEWING, 588–590
BOOK SELECTION, 588–590
Bordewijk, F.
Blokken, 6-401
Borges, Jorge Luis
El Aleph, 3-52
Ficciones, 3-52
Labyrinths, 3-52
Borrello, Alfred
H. G. Wells, 10-166
Boucher, Anthony, 15-17
The Best from Fantasy and Science Fic-
tion, 3-423
Far and Away, 3-53
A Treasury of Great Science Fiction, 3-
424
Boulle, Pierre
Garden on the Moon, 3-54
Planet of the Apes, 3-55
Time Out of Mind, 3-56
Bova, Ben, 15-41
Analog 9, 3-426
The Analog Science Fact Reader, 3-426
The Best of Analog, 3-426
Colony, 4-68
End of Exile, 5-21
Exiled from Earth, 5-21
Flight of Exiles, 5-21
Kinsman, 4-68
Millennium, 4-68
Notes to a Science Fiction Writer, 13-12
Privateers, 4-69
Science Fiction Hall of Fame (Silver-
berg), 3-455
Test of Fire, 4-78
Vision of the Future, 12-4
Voyagers, 4-71
The Winds of Altair, 5-22
Bowen, John
After the Rain, 3-57
Boyajian, Jerry
Index to the Science Fiction Magazines,
14-2
Index to the Semi-Professional Fantasy
Magazines, 14-3
Boyce, Chris
Catchworld, 4-72
Boyd, John
The Last Starship from Earth, 4-73
The Pollinators of Eden, 4-74
Sex and the High Command, 4-75
Boye, Karin
Kallocain, 3-58, 532, 6-367
Boyer, Robert H.
Fantasy Literature (Tymn), 8-51
Boyett, Stephen R.

The Architect of Sleep, 4-76
Brackett, Leigh, 10-20, 10-21, 10-22, 15-30
    The Best of Leigh Brackett, 3-59
    The Best of Planet Stories #1, 3-425
    The Long Tomorrow, 3-60
Bradbury, Ray, 10-24, 10-25, 10-26, 10-27,
        10-28, 15-2, 15-8, 15-36, 15-55
    Fahrenheit 451, 3-61
    The Golden Apples of the Sun, 3-62
    The Illustrated Man, 3-63
    The Martian Chronicles, 3-64
    The Silver Locusts, 3-64
    The Stories of Ray Bradbury, 3-62
Bradley, Marion Zimmer, 10-23, 15-25
    City of Sorcery, 4-77
    Darkover series, 4-77
    Free Amazons of Darkover, 4-77
    The Heritage of Hastur, 4-77
    Sharra's Exile, 4-77
    The Sword of Aldones, 4-77
Bradshaw, William Richard
    The Goddess of Atvatabar, 1-14
Brandis, Evgenii Pavlovich
    Cherez gory vremeni, 6-223
    Ellinskii sekret, 6-216
    Kol'tso obratnogo vremeni, 6-217
Braun, Günter, 387
    Der Fehlfaktur, 6-3
    Der Irrtum des Grossen Zauberers, 6-4
Braun, Johanna, 387
    Der Fehlfaktor, 6-3
    Der Irrtum des Grossen Zauberers, 6-4
Brautigan, Richard
    The Hawkline Monster, 4-78
Bravard, Robert S.
    Samuel R. Delany (Peplow), 10-50
Brekke, Toril
    Sølvfalken, 6-382
Brennan, Joseph Payne, 15-52
Bretnor, Reginald
    The Craft of Science Fiction, 13-13
    The Future at War, 4-663
    Modern Science Fiction, 9-15
    The Schimmelhorn File, 4-79
    Schimmelhorn's Gold, 4-79
    Science Fiction, Today and Tomorrow,
        9-16
    See also Briarton, Grendel
Breuer, Miles J.
    Paradise and Iron, 2-8
Briarton, Grendel
    The Complete Feghoot, 3-65
    Through Time and Space with Ferdi-
        nand Feghoot, 3-65
Bridenne, Jean-Jacques
    La Littérature Française d'imagination
        scientifique, 6-182
Brigg, Peter

J. G. Ballard, 10-13
Brin, David
    The Heart of the Comet (Benford), 4-55
    The Postman, 4-80
    The Practice Effect, 4-81
    Startide Rising, 4-82
    Sundiver, 4-83
    The Uplift War, 4-82
Bringsværd, Tor Åge, 539–540
    Dragsug (Bing), 6-395
    Karavane, 6-383
    Ker Shus, 6-384
    Malstrøm (Bing), 6-397
    Stella Polaris (Bing), 6-396
Britikov, Anatolii Fedorovich
    Russkii sovetskii nauchno-
        fantasticheskiis roman, 6-224
Brittain, William, 15-52
Briusov, Valerii
    Respublik Iuzhnogo Kresta, 442
Brizzi, Mary T.
    Philip José Farmer, 10-65
Broderick, Damien
    The Dreaming Dragons, 4-84
    The Judas Mandala, 4-85
    Strange Attractors, 4-638
Brooke-Rose, Christine
    Xorandor, 4-86
Brosnan, John
    Future Tense, 11-13
Brown, Charles N.
    Science Fiction in Print—1985, 8-8
Brown, Fredric
    Angels and Spaceships, 3-66
    Honeymoon in Hell, 3-67
    The Lights in the Sky Are Stars, 3-68
    Project Jupiter, 3-68
    Space on My Hands, 3-69
    What Mad Universe, 3-70
Brunner, John, 10-29, 10-30, 15-54
    The Crucible of Time, 4-87
    The Jagged Orbit, 4-88
    No Future in It, 3-71
    Out of My Mind, 3-72
    Quicksand, 4-89
    The Sheep Look Up, 4-90
    The Shockwave Rider, 4-91
    The Squares of the City, 3-73
    Stand on Zanzibar, 4-92
    Telepathist, 4-94
    Total Eclipse, 4-93
    The Whole Man, 3-74, 4-94
Brunt, Samuel
    A Voyage to Cacklogallinia, 6
Bruss, B. R.
    Apparition des surhommes, 6-65
    Les Espaces enchevêtrés, 6-66
    Et la planète sauta, 6-67

Brussolo, Serge, 412
  Portrait du diable en chapeau melon, 6-68
  Vue en coupe d'une ville malade, 6-69
Bryant, Edward
  Cinnabar, 4-95
Bryne, James, 15-52
Bucknall, Barbara J.
  Ursula K. Le Guin, 10-91
Budrys, Algis, 10-31, 15-19
  Benchmarks, 9-17
  Blood and Burning, 3-75
  Budrys' Inferno, 3-76
  The Furious Future, 3-76
  L. Ron Hubbard Presents: Writers of the Future, 4-639
  Michaelmas, 4-96
  Nonliterary Influences on Science Fiction, 9-18
  Rogue Moon, 3-77
Bugariu, Voicu
  Vocile Vikingilor, 6-442
Bulgakov, Mikhail
  "The Fatal Eggs," 57, 2-9
  Heart of a Dog, 2-9
Bulmer, Kenneth
  New Writings in SF, 4-640
  Stained-Glass World, 4-97
  The Ulcer Culture, 4-97
Bulychev, Kir
  Letnee utro, 6-201
  Posledniaia voina, 453, 6-202
Bunch, David R.
  Moderan, 4-98
Burdick, Eugene L.
  Fail-Safe, 3-81
Burger, Dionijs
  Bolland, 6-402
  Sphereland, 6-402
Burgess, Anthony, 15-45
  A Clockwork Orange, 3-82
  1985, 3-302
  The Wanting Seed, 3-83
Burgess, Michael
  A Guide to Science Fiction & Fantasy in the Library of Congress Classification Scheme, 8-38
Burgoyne, A. H.
  The Great Naval War of 1887 (Clowes), 12
  Trafalgar Refought (Clowes), 12
Burleson, Donald R.
  H. P. Lovecraft, 10-104
Burns, Jim
  Lightship, 12-5
Burroughs, Edgar Rice, 10-32, 10-33, 10-34, 10-35, 15-21, 15-47, 15-50, 15-66, 15-69, 15-71, 15-75, 15-87, 15-88, 15-89

At the Earth's Core, 19, 1-15
The Gods of Mars, 1-17
The Land That Time Forgot, 2-10
The Monster Men, 19
The Moon Maid, 2-11
Pirates of Venus, 1-16
A Princess of Mars, 18, 1-17
Tarzan of the Apes, 1-18
Under the Moons of Mars, 1-17
The Warlord of Mars, 1-17
Burroughs, William S.
  Cities of the Red Night, 4-99
  Nova Express, 4-100
Busby, F. M.
  Star Rebel, 4-101
Butler, Octavia
  Clay's Ark, 4-102
  Kindred, 4-104
  Mind of My Mind, 4-103
  Patternmaster, 4-103
  Wild Seed, 4-104
Butler, Samuel
  Erewhon, 1-19
  Erewhon Revisited Twenty Years Later, 1-19
Buyens, Frans
  Na ons de Monsters, 6-428
Bywater, Hector C.
  The Great Pacific War, 14

Cabell, James Branch, 15-48
Caidin, Martin, 15-52
  Cyborg, 4-105
Caldwell, Taylor
  The Devil's Advocate, 3-84
Calisher, Hortense
  Journal from Ellipsia, 4-106
Callenbach, Ernest
  Ecotopia, 4-107
  Ecotopia Emerging, 4-107
Calvino, Italo, 10-36
  Cosmicomics, 4-108
  t zero, 4-108
Cameron, Eleanor
  Mr. Bass's Planetoid, 5-23
  A Mystery for Mr. Bass, 5-23
  Stowaway to the Mushroom Planet, 5-23
  Time and Mr. Bass, 5-23
  The Wonderful Flight to the Mushroom Planet, 5-23
Campanella, Tommaso
  The City of the Sun, 5
  Civitas Solis, 1-20
Campbell, John W., Jr., 54, 10-37
  Analog 1–8, 3-426

The Astounding Science Fiction Anthology, 3-426
The Best of John W. Campbell, 3-85
The Black Star Passes, 2-12
Collected Editorials from Analog, 3-426
Invaders from the Infinite, 2-12
Islands of Space, 2-12
The John W. Campbell Letters, 10-37
Prologue to Analog, 3-426
Who Goes There?, 3-86
Canal, Richard
La Malédiction de l'ephemère, 6-70
Čapek, Karel, 57–58, 15-46, 15-55
The Absolute at Large, 2-13
Krakatit, 2-14
R.U.R., 2-15
War with the Newts, 2-16
Capon, Paul
Flight of Time, 5-24
Lost: A Moon, 5-25
The Other Side of the Sun, 3-87
Phobos, the Robot Planet, 5-25
Card, Orson Scott
Ender's Game, 4-109
A Planet Called Treason, 4-110
Songmaster, 4-111
Speaker for the Dead, 4-109
Carlson, Dale
The Shining Pool, 5-26
Carmer, Carl
The Year after Tomorrow (del Rey), 5-42
Carnell, E. J.
The Best from New Worlds Science Fiction, 3-427
Lambda 1 and Other Stories, 3-427
Carr, Jayge
Leviathan's Deep, 4-112
Navigator's Syndrome, 4-113
The Treasure in the Heart of the Maze, 4-113
Carr, John Dickson
Fire, Burn!, 3-88
Carr, John F.
The Endless Frontier (Pournelle), 4-662
There Will Be War (Pournelle), 4-663
Carr, John L.
Leigh Brackett, 10-21
Carr, Robert Spencer
Beyond Infinity, 3-89
Carr, Terry
Best Science Fiction Novellas of the Year, 4-641
Best Science Fiction of the Year, 4-641
Cirque, 4-114
Classic Science Fiction, 3-452
An Exaltation of Stars, 4-665
Universe, 4-642
Carsac, Francis

Ce monde est nôtre, 6-71
Ceux de nulle part, 6-72
Pour patrie l'espace, 6-73
Terre en fuite, 6-74
Carson, David G.
The Sound of Wonder (Lane), 10-199
Carter, Albert Howard, III
Italo Calvino, 10-36
Carter, Angela
Heroes and Villains, 4-115
The Infernal Desire Machines of Doctor Hoffman, 4-116
The Passion of New Eve, 4-117
The War of Dreams, 4-116
Carter, Lin
Time War, 4-118
The Valley Where Time Stood Still, 4-118
Carter, Paul A.
The Creation of Tomorrow, 9-19
Cartier, Edd, 15-69A, 15-70, 15-75
Edd Cartier, 12-6
Carver, Jeffrey A.
The Infinity Link, 4-119
Case, Tom
Cook, 4-120
CATALOGING, 591–592, 8-38
Cawelti, John G.
Adventure, Mystery, and Romance, 9-20
Cerf, Christopher
The Vintage Anthology of Science Fantasy, 3-428
Chalker, Jack L.
Dancers in the Afterglow, 4-121
Downtiming the Night Side, 4-122
Exiles at the Well of Souls, 4-123
Midnight at the Well of Souls, 4-123
Quest for the Well of Souls, 4-123
The Return of Nathan Brazil, 4-123
Twilight at the Well of Souls, 4-123
Chambers, Robert W.
The Green Mouse, 11
Some Ladies in Haste, 11
Chandler, A. Bertram, 10-38, 15-54
The Rim of Space, 3-90
The "Rim World" series, 3-90
Road to the Rim, 3-90
The Ship from Outside, 3-90
The Wild Ones, 4-124
Chapman, Edgar L.
The Magic Labyrinth of Philip José Farmer, 10-66
Charbonneau, Louis
The Sentinel Stars, 3-91
Charnas, Suzy McKee
Motherlines, 4-125
Walk to the End of the World, 4-125
Chater, Elizabeth, 15-5

Chayevsky, Paddy
  Altered States, 4-126
Chernyshevsky, N., 57
Cherryh, C. J.
  Cuckoo's Egg, 4-127
  Downbelow Station, 4-128
  The Faded Sun: Kesrith, 4-129
  The Faded Sun: Kutath, 4-129
  The Faded Sun: Shon'Jir, 4-129
  Merchanter's Luck, 4-129A
  Port Eternity, 4-130
  The Pride of Chanur, 4-131
  Serpent's Reach, 4-132
  Visible Light, 4-133
  Voyager in Night, 4-134
Chesneaux, Jean
  The Political and Social Ideas of Jules
    Verne, 10-151
Chesney, George Tomkyns
  "The Battle of Dorking," 11, 1-21
Chester, George Randolph
  The Jingo, 1-22
Chesterton, G. K., 15-17
  The Napoleon of Notting Hill, 1-23
Childer, Erskine
  The Riddle of the Sands, 12, 1-24
Chilton, Charles
  Journey into Space, 5-27
Christin, Pierre
  Les Prédateurs enjolivés, 6-75
Christopher, John
  Beyond the Burning Lands, 5-31
  The City of Gold and Lead, 5-32
  The Death of Grass, 3-92
  Dragon Dance, 5-29
  Empty World, 5-28
  Fireball, 5-29
  The Guardians, 5-30
  The Long Winter, 3-93
  New Found Land, 5-29
  No Blade of Grass, 3-92
  The Pool of Fire, 5-32
  The Possessors, 3-94
  The Prince in Waiting, 5-31
  The Ragged Edge, 3-95
  The Sword of the Spirits, 5-31
  The White Mountains, 5-32
  The World in Winter, 3-93
  Wrinkle in the Skin, 3-95
Churchill, R. C.
  A Short History of the Future,
    3-96
Cioffi, Frank
  Formula Fiction?, 9-21
Clareson, Thomas D.
  Many Futures, Many Worlds, 9-22
  Robert Silverberg, 10-132, 10-133
  Science Fiction Criticism, 8-16

Science Fiction in America, 1870s–
    1930s, 8-12A
  SF: The Other Side of Realism, 9-23
  Some Kind of Paradise, 9-24
  Voices for the Future, 9-25
Clark, Ronald
  Queen Victoria's Bomb, 4-135
Clarke, Arthur C., 10-39, 10-40, 10-41, 10-
    42, 10-43, 15-25, 15-55, 15-90
  Against the Fall of Night, 3-98
  Childhood's End, 3-97
  The City and the Stars, 3-98
  The Deep Range, 3-99
  Dolphin Island, 5-33
  Expedition to Earth, 3-100, 3-102
  A Fall of Moondust, 3-101
  The Fountains of Paradise, 4-136
  From the Ocean, from the Stars, 3-98
  Imperial Earth, 4-137
  Islands in the Sky, 5-34
  The Other Side of the Sky, 3-102
  Prelude to Space, 3-103
  Reach for Tomorrow, 3-102, 3-104
  Rendezvous with Rama, 4-138
  The Songs of Distant Earth, 4-139
  Tales from the White Hart, 3-102, 3-105
  2001: A Space Odyssey, 4-140
  2010: Odyssey Two, 4-141
  The Wind from the Sun, 3-106
Clarke, I. F.
  The Pattern of Expectation, 9-26
  Tale of the Future from the Beginning
    to the Present Day, 8-14
  Voices Prophesying War: 1763-1984, 9-
    27
Clarke, Joan B.
  The Happy Planet, 5-35
CLASSIFICATION, 592, 8-38
Claudy, Carl H.
  Adventures in the Unknown, 5-36
Clem, Ralph S.
  No Room for Man, 13-23
Clemens, Samuel Langhorne
  A Connecticut Yankee in King Arthur's
    Court, 1-25
  "The Curious Republic of Gondour," 1-
    25
  "From the 'London Times' of 1904," 1-
    25
  "The Great Dark," 10, 1-25
  The Science Fiction of Mark Twain, 1-
    25
Clement, Hal, 10-44, 10-45, 10-46, 15-34,
    15-55
  The Best of Hal Clement, 3-107
  Close to Critical, 3-109
  Cycle of Fire, 3-108
  From Outer Space, 3-110

Mission of Gravity, 3-109
Needle, 3-110
Starlight, 3-109
Through the Eye of a Needle, 3-110
Clifton, Mark
Eight Keys to Eden, 3-111
The Forever Machine, 3-113
The Science Fiction of Mark Clifton, 3-112
They'd Rather Be Right, 3-113
Clingerman, Mildred
A Cupful of Space, 3-114
Clouston, J. Storer
Button Brains, 2-17
The Man in Steel, 2-17
Clowes, William Laird
The Great Naval War of 1887, 12
Trafalgar Refought, 12
Clute, John
Interzone: The First Anthology, 4-643
Coates, Robert M.
The Eater of Darkness, 2-18
Coblentz, Stanton A.
After 12,000 Years, 2-19
Hidden World, 2-19
In Caverns Below, 2-19
The Sunken World, 2-19
Cogell, Elizabeth C.
Ursula K. Le Guin, 10-92
Cogswell, Theodore R.
The Wall around the World, 3-115
Cohen, Daniel, 15-36
Cole, Everett B.
The Philosophical Corps, 3-116
Colerus, Egmont
Wielder wandert Bebemoth, 6-5
Colin, Vladimir
Babel, 6-443
Collings, Michael R.
The Annotated Guide to Stephen King, 10-83
Brian W. Aldiss, 10-1
The Films of Stephen King, 10-80
The Many Facets of Stephen King, 10-82
Piers Anthony, 10-6
Reflections on the Fantastic, 9-111
The Shorter Works of Stephen King, 10-84
Stephen King as Richard Bachman, 10-81
Collins, Hunt
Tomorrow and Tomorrow, 3-117
Tomorrow's World, 3-117
Collins, Paul
Distant Worlds, 4-644
Envisaged Worlds, 4-644
Frontier Worlds, 4-644

Collins, Robert A.
The Scope of the Fantastic, 9-112
Colomb, Philip Howard
The Great War of 189-, 1-26
Colombo, John Robert
CDN SF & F, 8-13
Compton, D. G., 15-55
Ascendancies, 4-142
The Continuous Katherine Mortenhoe, 4-143
Death Watch, 4-143
The Electric Crocodile, 4-144
The Steel Crocodile, 4-144
Synthajoy, 4-145
The Unsleeping Eye, 4-143
Windows, 4-143
Comte, Jean-François
Sylvie et les vivisecteurs, 6-76
Condon, Richard
The Manchurian Candidate, 3-118
Coney, Michael G.
Cat Karina, 4-146
The Celestial Steam Locomotive, 4-146
Gods of the Greataway, 4-146
Hello Summer, Goodbye, 4-147
Conklin, Groff
The Best of Science Fiction, 3-429
The Big Book of Science Fiction, 3-431
Great Science Fiction by Scientists, 3-451
Invaders of Earth, 3-430
The Omnibus of Science Fiction, 3-431
A Treasury of Science Fiction, 3-431
Connington, J. J.
Nordenholt's Million, 2-20
Connolly, Ray
Invasion from the Air (McIlraith), 2-75
Conquest, Robert
Spectrum (Amis), 3-420
A World of Difference, 3-119
Conrad, Michael George
In purpurner Finsternis, 382
Constantine, Murray
Swastika Night, 2-21
Contento, William G.
Index to Science Fiction Anthologies and Collections, 8-9
Index to Science Fiction Anthologies and Collections 1977–1983, 8-10
Science Fiction in Print—1985 (Brown), 8-8
Cook, Fred
Collector's Index to Weird Tales (Jaffery), 14-6
Cooper, Edmund, 15-52
Deadly Image, 3-120
A Far Sunset, 4-148
Seed of Light, 3-121
The Uncertain Midnight, 3-120

Coppard, A. E., 15-75
Coppel, Alfred
  Dark December, 3-122
Cordesse, Gerard
  La Nouvelle science-fiction Américaine,
   6-183
Corlett, William
  The Gate of Eden, 5-37
  The Land Beyond, 5-37
  Return to the Gate, 5-37
Corn, Joseph J.
  Yesterday's Tomorrows, 9-28
Correy, Lee
  Manna, 4-149
Costa, Richard Hauer
  H. G. Wells, 10-167
Costello, Peter
  Jules Verne, 10-152
Cottrill, Tim
  Science Fiction and Fantasy Series and
   Sequels, 8-22
Coulson, Juanita
  Tomorrow's Heritage, 4-150
Cover, Arthur Byron
  Autumn Angels, 4-151
  An East Wind Coming, 4-151
  The Platypus of Doom and Other Nihil-
   ists, 4-151
Cowan, Frank
  Revi-Lona, 1-27
Cowart, David
  Twentieth-Century American Science-
   Fiction Writers, 8-28
Cowper, Richard, 15-54
  Breakthrough, 4-152
  Clone, 4-153
  The Custodians and Other Stories, 4-
   154
  A Dream of Kinship, 4-155
  Out There Where the Big Ships Go, 4-
   154
  Profundis, 4-153
  The Road to Corlay, 4-155
  A Tapestry of Time, 4-155
  The Tithonian Factor and Other Stories,
   4-154
  The Web of the Magi and Other Stories,
   4-154
Coyle, William
  Aspects of Fantasy, 9-113
Craigie, David
  The Voyage of the Luna 1, 5-38
Crane, Robert
  Hero's Walk, 3-123
Cremaschi, Inisero
  Universo e Dintorni, 6-326
Crichton, Michael
  The Andromeda Strain, 4-156

The Terminal Man, 4-156
Crick, Bernard
  George Orwell: Nineteen Eighty-Four,
   10-115
Crispin, Edmund
  Best SF, 3-432
Crohmălniceanu, Ovid S.
  Istorii insolite, 6-444
Cromie, Robert
  For England's Sake, 12
  The Next Crusade, 12
Cross, John Keir
  The Angry Planet, 5-39
Crossley, Robert
  H. G. Wells, 10-168
Crowley, John
  Beasts, 4-157
  Engine Summer, 4-158
Culp, Beth
  Thematic Units in Teaching English and
   the Humanities (Spann), 13-10
Cummings, Ray, 15-88
  The Girl in the Golden Atom, 10, 2-22
  Into the Fourth Dimension, 2-22
  The Man Who Mastered Time, 2-24
  The Princess of the Atom, 2-23
  The Shadow Girl, 2-24
Cunis, Reinmar
  Livesendung, 6-35
Ćurčić, Slobodan
  "Kiše, šume, grad i zvezde," 6-468
Currey, L. W.
  The Battle of the Monsters and Other
   Stories (Hartwell), 1-49
  A Research Guide to Science Fiction
   Studies (Tymn), 8-21
  Science Fiction and Fantasy Authors, 8-
   3A
Curtis, Jean-Louis
  The Neon Halo, 3-124
Curtis, Richard
  How to Be Your Own Literary Agent,
   13-19
Curtoni, Vittorio
  Fanta-Italia, 6-327
  Le Frontiere dell'Ignoto, 6-331
Curval, Philippe, 411
  Brave Old World, 4-159, 6-77
  Cette chère humanité, 4-159, 6-77
  Le Dormeur s'éveillera-t-il?, 6-78
  En Souvenir du futur, 6-79
  La Face cachée du désir, 6-80
  Futurs au présent, 6-176
  L'Homme à rebours, 6-81
  Le Livre d'or de Philippe Curval,
   6-82
  Les Sables de Falun, 6-83
  Y a quelqu'un?, 6-84

Dake, Charles Romyn
  A Strange Discovery, 9
Dalos, Gyorgy
  1985, 4-160
Daniel, Yuri
  This Is Moscow Speaking, and Other Sto-
    ries, 3-125
Dann, Jack, 15-41
  The Man Who Melted, 4-161
  More Wandering Stars, 4-645
  Wandering Stars, 4-645
Datlow, Ellen
  The Third Omni Book of Science Fic-
    tion, 4-646
Daumann, Rudolf Heinrich
  Abenteuer mit der Venus, 6-6
Davenport, Benjamin Rush
  Anglo-Saxons Onward, 14
Davidson, Avram, 15-2, 15-45
  The Best from Fantasy and Science Fic-
    tion (Boucher), 3-423
  The Best of Avram Davidson, 3-126
  Clash of Star-Kings, 3-127
  Joyleg, 3-128
  Or All the Seas with Oysters, 3-129
  Strange Seas and Shores, 3-130
Davis, Gerry
  Brainrack (Pedler), 4-407
  The Dynostar Menace (Pedler), 4-407
  Mutant 59 (Pedler), 4-407
Day, Donald B.
  Index to the Science Fiction Magazines,
    1926–1950, 14-4
Dean, Martyn
  The Guide to Fantasy Art Techniques,
    12-7
  Magnetic Storm, 12-9
Dean, Roger
  Magnetic Storm, 12-9
  Views, 12-8
De Bolt, Joe
  The Happening Worlds of John
    Brunner, 10-29
  Ursula K. Le Guin, 10-93
de Camp, Catherine Crook
  Science Fiction Handbook, Revised, 13-
    14
de Camp, L. Sprague, 10-47, 15-25
  The Best of L. Sprague de Camp,
    3-131
  The Castle of Iron, 3-134
  The Compleat Enchanter, 3-134
  Divide and Rule, 3-132
  Genus Homo, 3-133
  The Incomplete Enchanter, 3-134
  Lest Darkness Fall, 3-135
  Lovecraft, 10-104
  Rogue Queen, 3-136

  Science Fiction Handbook, Revised, 13-
    14
  Wall of Serpents, 3-134
De Carnin, Camilla
  Worlds Apart, 4-649
Defoe, Daniel
  The Consolidator, 6
Defontenay, Charles
  Star ou psi de Cassiopée, 406
DeFord, Miriam Allen, 15-41
  Space, Time and Crime, 3-460
  Xenogenesis, 3-137
Deighton, Len
  SS-GB, 4-162
Dekker, Maurits
  C.R., 546
De Laet, Danny
  De Dageraad des Duivels, 6-428A
  Tussen Tijd en Schaduw, 6-429
Delaney, Joseph H.
  Valentina, 4-163
del'Antonio, Eberhard
  Heimkehr der Vorfahren, 6-7
  Titanus, 6-7
Delany, Samuel R., 10-48, 10-49, 10-50,
    10-51, 10-52, 15-25, 15-90
  The American Shore, 9-30
  Babel-17, 4-164
  Dhalgren, 4-165
  Distant Stars, 4-166
  Driftglass, 4-166
  The Einstein Intersection, 4-167
  Empire Star, 4-166
  The Jewel-Hinged Jaw, 9-31
  Nova, 4-168
  Starboard Wine, 9-32
  Stars in My Pocket like Grains of Sand,
    4-169
  Triton, 4-170
Delmas, Henri
  Le Rayon SF, 6-184
del Rey, Lester
  And Some Were Human, 3-138
  The Eleventh Commandment, 3-139
  Fantastic Science-Fiction Art, 12-30
  The Infinite Worlds of Maybe, 5-40
  Nerves, 3-140
  Preferred Risk (McCann), 3-275A
  Step to the Stars, 5-41
  The World of Science Fiction, 9-29
  The Year after Tomorrow, 5-42
De Mille, James
  A Strange Manuscript Found in a Cop-
    per Cylinder, 16, 1-28
Demolder, Eugène
  L'Agonie d'Albion, 6-417
Demuth, Michel
  Les Galaxiales, 6-85

Dent, Guy
  Emperor of the If, 2-25
Derleth, August William, 15-17, 15-42, 15-49, 15-79
  The Other Side of the Moon, 3-433
  Strange Ports of Call, 3-434
Desmond, Shaw
  Black Dawn, 2-26
  Chaos, 2-26
  Ragnarok, 2-26
De Turris, Gianfranco
  Fanta-Italia, 6-327
DeVore, Howard
  A History of the Hugo, Nebula, and International Fantasy Awards (Franson), 8-36
De Vos, Luk
  Just the Other Day, 6-414
  Laatst nog, 6-414
  Science Fiction: Status of Status Quo?, 6-413
  Waar helden sterven, 6-414
Dewdney, A. K.
  The Planiverse, 4-171
Dick, Philip K., 10-51, 10-52, 10-53, 10-54, 10-55, 10-56, 10-57, 10-58, 10-59, 10-60, 15-3, 15-55
  The Divine Invasion, 4-172
  Do Androids Dream of Electric Sheep?, 4-173
  Dr. Bloodmoney, 4-174
  Eye in the Sky, 3-141
  Flow My Tears, the Policeman Said, 4-175
  Galactic Pot-Healer, 4-176
  The Man in the High Castle, 3-142
  Martian Time-Slip, 3-143
  A Maze of Death, 4-176
  Now Wait for Last Year, 4-175
  Our Friends from Frolix-8, 4-176
  A Scanner Darkly, 4-177
  Solar Lottery, 3-144
  The Three Stigmata of Palmer Eldritch, 4-175
  The Transmigration of Timothy Archer, 4-172
  Ubik, 4-178
  VALIS, 4-179
  We Can Build You, 4-173
  World of Chance, 3-144
Dickinson, Peter
  The Devil's Children, 5-43
  Heartsease, 5-43
  The Weathermonger, 5-43
Dicks, Terrance
  Doctor Who and the Day of the Daleks, 5-44
Dickson, Gordon R., 10-61, 10-62, 15-29

The Alien Way, 3-145
Dorsai!, 3-146
The Dorsai Companion, 3-146
Earthman's Burden (Anderson), 3-9
The Final Encyclopedia, 4-181
The Forever Man, 4-182
The Genetic General, 3-146
Gordon R. Dickson's SF Best, 3-147
Lost Dorsai, 3-146
Necromancer, 3-146
No Room for Man, 3-146
Soldier, Ask Not, 3-148
Space Winners, 5-45
The Spirit of Dorsai, 3-146
Tactics of Mistake, 3-146
Time Storm, 4-183
Di Fate, Vincent
  Di Fate's Catalog of Science Fiction Hardware, 12-10
Dikty, T. E.
  The Best Science-Fiction Stories, 3-422
  Science Fiction Omnibus (Bleiler), 3-422
  The Work of Julian May, 10-109
  The Year's Best Science Fiction Novels (Bleiler), 3-422
Disch, Thomas M., 10-63, 15-29, 15-55
  Bad Moon Rising, 4-647
  Camp Concentration, 4-184
  Fun with Your New Head, 4-186
  Fundamental Disch, 4-186
  The Genocides, 4-185
  Getting Into Death, 4-186
  The Man Who Had No Idea, 4-186
  New Constellations, 4-647
  The New Improved Sun, 4-647
  On Wings of Song, 4-187
  One Hundred and Two H Bombs, 4-186
  The Ruins of Earth, 4-647
  Strangeness, 4-647
  334, 4-188
  Under Compulsion, 4-186
  White Fang Goes Dingo and Other Funny SF Stories, 4-186
Diskin, Lahna
  Theodore Sturgeon, 10-143, 10-144
Dixon, Dougal
  After Man, 12-11
Dmitrevskii, Vladimir Ivanovich
  Cherez gory vremeni (Brandis), 6-223
  Ellinskii sekret (Brandis), 6-216
  Kol'tso obratnogo vremeni (Brandis), 6-217
Dneprov, Anatolii, 449
Döblin, Alfred
  Berge, Meere und Giganten, 382, 6-8
Dobzynski, Charles
  Taromancie, 6-86
Dollens, Morris Scott, 15-70

Dollerup, Cay
    Vølve, 6-362
Dominik, Hans, 57, 383
    Atomgewicht 500, 6-9
    Der Brand der Cheopspyramide, 6-10
Donaldson, Stephen R., 15-37
Donelson, Kenneth
    Science Fiction in the English Class, 13-4
Donnelly, Ignatius
    Atlantis, 19
    Caesar's Column, 1-28
Dooner, Pierpont W.
    The Last Days of the Republic, 14, 1-29
Dorémieux, Alain
    Le Livre d'or d'Alain Dorémieux, 6-87
Dorian, Dorel
    Ficţiuni pentru revolver şi orchestră, 6-445
Dossi, Carlo
    La Colonia Felice, 6-307
Douay, Dominique
    Cinq Solutions pour en finir, 6-88
    L'Impasse-temps, 6-89
    Strates, 6-90
    La Vie comme une course de chars à voile, 6-96
Douglas, Carole Nelson
    Probe, 4-189
Doyle, Arthur Conan, 15-46, 15-88
    The Best Science Fiction of Arthur Conan Doyle, 1-31
    The Land of Mist, 52, 2-27
    The Lost World, 20, 21, 1-31
    The Maracot Deep, 2-25
    The Poison Belt, 21, 1-32
    "When the World Screamed," 2-28
Dozois, Gardner, 15-41
    Strangers, 4-190
    The Year's Best Science Fiction, 4-648
Dragomir, Mihu
    Povestiri deocamdată fantastice, 6-446
Drake, David
    Birds of Prey, 4-192
    Bridgehead, 4-191
    Cross the Stars, 4-192
    Forlorn Hope, 4-192
    Hammer's Slammers, 4-192
    Ranks of Bronze, 4-192
Drayton, Henry
    In Oudemon, 17
Driant, E. A.
    La Guerre en ballon, 13
    La Guerre en forteresse, 13
    La Guerre en rase campagne, 13
Drode, Daniel
    Surface de la planète, 6-92
Drumm, Chris
    An Algis Budrys Checklist, 10-31

A Hal Clement Checklist, 10-45
A James Gunn Checklist, 10-67
A Larry Niven Checklist, 10-113
A Mack Reynolds Checklist, 10-121
An R. A. Lafferty Checklist, 10-89
A Tom Disch Checklist, 10-63
Drury, Allen
    Advise and Consent, 3-149
    Capable of Honor, 3-149
    Come Nineveh, Come Tyre, 3-149
    Preserve and Protect, 3-149
    The Promise of Joy, 3-149
    A Shade of Difference, 3-149
du Bois, William Pene
    The Twenty-One Balloons, 5-46
Dudintsev, Vladimir
    A New Year's Tale, 3-150
Duesberg, Raymond
    Les Grenouilles, 6-418
Duffy, Maureen
    Gor Saga, 4-193
Duits, Charles
    Ptah Hotep, 6-93
Duncan, David
    Occam's Razor, 3-151
Dunn, Thomas P.
    Clockwork Worlds (Erlich), 9-33A
    The Mechanical God, 9-33
Dunsany, Lord, 15-46, 15-75, 15-88
Durant, Frederick, III
    Worlds Beyond, 12-12
Durrell, Lawrence
    Nunquam, 4-194
    The Revolt of Aphrodite, 4-194
    Tunc, 4-194
Duvic, Patrice
    Naissez, nous ferons le reste!, 6-94
    Poisson-pilote, 6-95
Dvorkin, David
    Time for Sherlock Holmes, 4-195

Earnshaw, Brian
    Planet in the Eye of Time, 4-196
Edmondson, G. C., 15-8
    The Man Who Corrupted Earth, 4-197
    The Ship That Sailed the Time Stream, 4-198
    To Sail the Century Sea, 4-198
Edwards, Gawain
    The Earth Tube, 14
Edwards, Malcolm
    Alien Landscapes (Holdstock), 12-23
    The SF Book of Lists (Jakubowski), 8-42
Effinger, George Alec
    Relatives, 4-199
    What Entropy Means to Me, 4-199
    The Wolves of Memory, 4-199

Efremov, Ivan Antonovich, 447–448
  Andromeda, 3-152
  Chas Byka, 6-203
Ehrlich, Max
  The Big Eye, 3-153
Eisenstein, Phyllis
  Shadow of Earth, 4-200
Eizykman, Boris
  Inconscience fiction, 6-185
Eklund, Gordon
  All Times Possible, 4-201
  If the Stars Are Gods (Benford), 4-56
Eldridge, Paul
  My First Two Thousand Years
    (Viereck), 62
Elgin, Suzette Haden, 15-5
  At the Seventh Level, 4-202
  Communipath Worlds, 4-202
  The Communipaths, 4-202
  Furthest, 4-202
  Star Anchored, Star Angered, 4-202
  Yonder Comes the Other End of Time,
    4-202
Ellik, Ron
  The Universe of E. E. Smith, 10-136
Elliot, Jeffrey M.
  Kindred Spirits, 4-649
  Pulp Voices, 10-195
  Science Fiction Voices #2, 10-193
  Science Fiction Voices #4, 10-194
Elliot, John
  A for Andromeda (Hoyle), 3-215
Elliott, Sumner Locke
  Going, 4-203
Ellison, Harlan, 10-64, 15-54
  Again, Dangerous Visions, 4-650
  Alone Against Tomorrow, 4-204
  Dangerous Visions, 4-650
  Deathbird Stories, 4-205
  An Edge in My Voice, 10-64
  Medea, 4-651
  Shatterday, 4-206
  Sleepless Nights in the Procrustean Bed,
    10-64
Elson, Peter
  Parallel Lines, 12-13
Elster, Torolf, 539
  Sjørøvere, 6-385
Elvestad, Sven, 538
Elwood, Roger
  Future City, 3-443
Emelina, Jean
  Actes du premier colloque international
    de science-fiction de Nice (1983), 6-
    187
  Actes du deuxième colloque interna-
    tional de science-fiction de Nice
    (1985), 6-188

Emtsev, Mikhail
  World Soul, 3-154
Engdahl, Sylvia Louise
  Enchantress from the Stars, 5-47
  The Far Side of Evil, 5-48
Engebretson, David
  The Shorter Works of Stephen King
    (Collings), 10-84
Engel, Leonard
  The World Aflame, 3-155
England, George Allan
  Darkness and Dawn, 1-33
Eriksen, Inge
  Dinosaurernes morgen, 6-343
  Luderen fra Gomorra, 6-343
  Nord for tiden, 6-343
  Rummet uden tid, 6-343
Erlich, Richard D.
  Clockwork Worlds, 9-33A
  The Mechanical God (Dunn), 9-33
Eshbach, Lloyd Arthur, 15-41
  Over My Shoulder, 9-34
Eskestad, Tage
  Flygtninge fra himlen, 6-344
  Matriarkatet, 6-345
Etherington, D. S.
  Rider Haggard, 10-68
Evans, Bill
  The Universes of E. E. Smith (Ellik), 10-
    136
Evans, Christopher
  The Insider, 4-207
Evensmo, Sigurd, 539

Fabian, Stephen, 15-75
Fairman, Paul W.
  The Runaway Robot, 5-49
Faldbakken, Knut
  Uår, 541, 6-386
FANTASY FICTION, 605–607
Farjeon, J. Jefferson
  Death of a World, 3-156
Farley, Ralph Milne
  The Omnibus of Time, 2-29
  The Radio Man, 52, 2-29
Farmer, Philip José, 10-65, 10-66, 15-52,
    15-71, 15-90
  The Alley God, 3-157
  The Dark Design, 4-210
  Dayworld, 4-208
  Doc Savage, 4-209
  The Fabulous Riverboat, 4-210
  Father to the Stars, 3-160
  Gods of Riverworld, 4-210
  The Green Odyssey, 3-158
  Jesus on Mars, 4-209
  The Lovers, 3-159

The Magic Labyrinth, 4-210
Night of Light, 3-160
River of Eternity, 4-210
Riverworld and Other Stories, 4-210
Strange Relations, 3-161
Tarzan Alive, 4-209
To Your Scattered Bodies Go, 4-210
The Unreasoning Mask, 4-211
Farrère, Claude
  Useless Hands, 2-30
Fast, Howard
  The Edge of Tomorrow, 3-162
Fawcett, Edgar
  Solarion, 11, 1-34
Felice, Cynthia
  Godsfire, 4-212
  Water Witch, 4-213
FEMINIST SF, 219, 9-10, 9-85, 9-95, 9-119
Ferman, Edward
  Arena: Sports SF, 3-435
  The Best from Fantasy and Science Fic-
    tion, 3-423, 4-652
  The Magazine of Fantasy and Science
    Fiction, 3-423
Ferrini, Franco
  Che Cosa E'la Fantascienza, 6-332
Feyerabend, Paul
  Against Method, 220
Fiedler, Jean
  Isaac Asimov, 10-9
Fiedler, Leslie A.
  Olaf Stapledon, 10-138
Filastò, Nino
  La Proposta, 6-308
Filipović, Dragan R.
  "Tominutni presckoci", 6-469
FILMS, SF, 672–686, 13-52
Finch, Christopher
  Special Effects, 11-26
Finlay, Virgil, 15-69A, 15-70, 15-75
Finney, Jack
  The Body Snatchers, 3-163
  The Clock of Time, 3-164
  Invasion of the Body Snatchers, 3-163
  The Third Level, 3-164
  Time and Again, 4-214
Firchow, Peter Edgerly
  The End of Utopia, 10-79
Fischer, William B.
  The Empire Strikes Out, 6-40, 9-35
Fisk, Nicholas
  A Rag, A Bone and a Hank of Hair, 5-
    50
  Space Hostages, 5-51
  Time Trap, 5-52
  Trillions, 5-53
Fitz Gibbon, Constantine
  When the Kissing Had to Stop, 3-165

Flammarion, Camille
  Les Mondes imaginaires et les mondes
    réels, 530
Fletcher, Marilyn P.
  Science Fiction Story Index 1950–1979,
    8-11
Flint, Homer Eon, 52
  The Blind Spot, 2-31
  The Devolutionist, 2-31
  The Emancipatrix, 2-31
Florescu, Radu
  In Search of Frankenstein, 10-125
Flynn, George
  A Mack Reynolds Checklist (Drumm),
    10-121
Foeldeak, Hans
  Neuere Tendenzen der sowjetischen Sci-
    ence Fiction, 6-47
Fonstad, Karen Wynn
  The Atlas of Pern, 10-111
Forbes, Caroline
  The Needle on Full, 4-215
Ford, John M.
  On Writing Science Fiction (Scithers),
    13-18
  Web of Angels, 4-216
Forester, C. S.
  The Peacemaker, 2-32
Forman, James D.
  Call Back Yesterday, 5-54
Forster, E. M.
  "The Machine Stops," 1-35
Forward, Robert L., 15-9
  Dragon's Egg, 4-217
  The Flight of the Dragonfly, 4-218
  Starquake!, 4-217
Foss, Chris
  Science Fiction Art, 12-15
  21st Century Foss, 12-14
Foster, Alan Dean
  Bloodhype, 4-220
  The End of the Matter, 4-220
  For Love of Mother-Not, 4-220
  Icerigger, 4-219
  Mission to Moulokin, 4-219
  Nor Crystal Tears, 4-220
  Orphan Star, 4-220
  The Tar-Aiym Krang, 4-220
Foster, M. A.
  The Morphodite, 4-221
  Preserver, 4-221
  Transformer, 4-221
  Waves, 4-222
Frane, Jeff
  Fritz Leiber, 10-97
Frank, Pat
  Alas, Babylon, 3-166
  Mr. Adam, 3-167

Franke, Herbert W., 385
  Der Elfenbeinturm, 6-11
  The Orchid Cage, 3-168
  Ypsilon minus, 6-12
Franklin, H. Bruce
  Countdown to Midnight, 4-660
  Future Perfect, 1-36, 13-24
  Robert A. Heinlein, 10-71
Franson, Donald
  A History of the Hugo, Nebula, and International Fantasy Awards, 8-36
Franson, Robert W.
  The Shadow of the Ship, 4-223
Frayn, Michael
  A Very Private Life, 4-224
Frazetta, Frank, 15-71
  The Fantastic Art of Frank Frazetta, 12-16
Freas, Frank Kelly, 15-69A
  The Art of Science Fiction, 12-17
  A Separate Star, 12-17A
Fredericks, Casey
  The Future of Eternity, 9-36
Freeman, Gaail
  Alien Thunder, 5-55
Freksa, Friedrich
  Druso, 383
Frentzen, Jeffrey
  The Outer Limits (Schow), 11-34
Frewin, Anthony
  One Hundred Years of SF Illustration, 12-18
Frich, Øvre Richter, 538
Friend, Oscar J.
  From Off This World (Margulies), 2-69
  My Best Science Fiction Story (Margulies), 3-448
Fuchs, Werner
  Reclams Science-Fiction-Führer (Alpers), 6-37
Fühmann, Franz
  Saiäns Fiktschen, 6-13
Fukushima, Masami
  Fundarika, 6-234
  Nihon no SF, 6-295
  SF no Sekai, 6-299

Gaasbeck, R.
  Fantasfeer (Spaink), 6-416
Gail, Otto Willi, 383
  Der Schuss ins All, 57, 2-33
  The Shot Into Infinity, 57, 2-33
Gaiman, Neil
  Ghastly beyond Belief, 8-43
Gakov, Vladimir
  Chetyre puteshestviia na mashine vremeni, 6-225

World Spring, 3-447
GALAXY PUBLISHING CORP., 15-34
Galileo
  Sidereus Nuncius, 5
Gallagher, Edward J.
  Annotated Guide to Fantastic Adventures, 14-13
  Jules Verne, 10-154
Gallun, Raymond Z.
  The Best of Raymond Z. Gallun, 3-169
  The Eden Cycle, 4-225
Galouye, Daniel F.
  Dark Universe, 3-170
Gammell, Leon L.
  The Annotated Guide to Startling Stories, 14-14
Gammeng, Harald
  Stoppested i evigheten, 6-387
Garber, Eric
  Uranian Worlds, 8-23
  Worlds Apart (De Carnin), 4-649
Garby, Lee Hawkins
  The Skylark of Space (Smith), 2-104
Garnett, David S.
  Mirror in the Sky, 4-226
Garrett, Randall
  Brain Twister (Phillips), 3-306
  Takeoff!, 3-171
Gary, Romain
  The Gasp, 4-227
Gaskell, Jane
  A Sweet, Sweet Summer, 4-228
Gegouen, Max
  Les Bisons d'argile, 56
George, Peter
  Dr. Strangelove, 3-172
  Red Alert, 3-172
Gerani, Gary
  Fantastic Television, 11-27
Gernsback, Hugo, 53, 15-34, 15-52, 15-77
  Ralph 124C41+, 21, 1-37
Gerrold, David
  The Man Who Folded Himself, 4-229
  When Harlie Was One, 4-230
  The World of Star Trek, 11-39
Geston, Mark S.
  Lords of the Starship, 4-231
  Out of the Mouth of the Dragon, 4-231
Giannone, Richard
  Vonnegut, 10-155
Gibbons, Floyd
  The Red Napoleon, 2-34
Gibson, William
  Burning Chrome, 4-232
  Count Zero, 4-232
  Neuromancer, 4-233
Giesy, J. U.
  All for His Country, 14

"Palos" trilogy, 52
Giger, H. R.
    H. R. Giger's Necronomicon, 12-19
    H. R. Giger's Necronomicon 2, 12-20
Gijsen, Wim, 546
    De eersten van Rissan, 6-403
    De koningen van weleer, 6-403
Gillespie, Bruce
    Philip K. Dick, 10-54
Gilman, Charlotte Perkins
    Herland, 1-38
Ginsburg, Mirra
    The Ultimate Threshold, 3-447, 4-670
Giuliani, Pierre
    Les Frontières d'Oulan-Bator, 6-96
Glad, John
    Extrapolations from Dystopia, 455, 9-37
Gladilin, Anatolii Tikhonovich
    FSSR, 6-204
Glaskin, G. M.
    A Change of Mind, 3-173
Gloag, John
    The New Pleasure, 2-35
    99%, 2-36
    To-Morrow's Yesterday, 2-37
    Winter's Youth, 2-38
Glut, Donald F.
    The Frankenstein Legend, 10-126
GNOME PRESS, 15-34
Goddard, James
    J. G. Ballard, 10-14
Godfrey, Hollis
    The Man Who Ended War, 14
Godwin, Francis
    The Man in the Moone, 5, 1-39
Godwin, Tom
    The Survivors, 3-174
Goimard, Jacques
    L'Année de la science fiction et du
        fantastique, 6-189
    Encyclopédie de poche de la science-
        fiction (Aziza), 6-178
Gold, H. L.
    Bodyguard and Four Other Short Nov-
        els, 3-436
    Galaxy Reader of Science Fiction, 3-436
    Mind Partner and Eight Other Novelets
        from Galaxy, 3-436
    The Old Die Rich and Other Science Fic-
        tion Stories, 3-175
    What Will They Think of Last?, 3-436
    The World That Couldn't Be and Eight
        Other Novelets from Galaxy, 3-436
Goldin, Stephen
    The Eternity Brigade, 4-234
Golding, William
    The Brass Butterfly, 3-176
    The Inheritors, 20, 2-79

Goldstein, Lisa
    The Dream Years, 4-235
Goodstone, Tony
    The Pulps, 722
Goorden, Bernard
    SF, fantastique et ateliers créatifs,
        6-439
Gordon, Joan
    Joe Haldeman, 10-69
Gordon, Rex
    First on Mars, 3-177
    No Man Friday, 3-177
Gordon, Stuart
    Smile on the Void, 4-236
Gorremans, G.
    Fantasfeer (Spaink), 6-416
Goswami, Amit
    The Cosmic Dancers, 9-38
Goswami, Maggie
    The Cosmic Dancers, 9-38
Gotschalk, Felix, 15-41
Gottlieb, Hinko
    The Key to the Great Gate, 3-178
Goulart, Ron
    After Things Fell Apart, 4-237
    Cheap Thrills, 722
Gove, Philip Babcock
    The Imaginary Voyage in Prose Fiction,
        9-69
Goy, Philip
    Le Livre machine, 6-97
Graham, P. A.
    The Collapse of Homo Sapiens, 51
Grainville, Jean-Baptiste Cousin de
    Le Dernier Homme, 9, 406
Grămescu, Mihael
    Aporisticon, 6-447
Grant, Charles L.
    Ascension, 4-238
    Legion, 4-238
    The Shadow of Alpha, 4-238
Gratacap, Louis P.
    The Certainty of a Future Life on Mars,
        18
Graves, Robert
    Seven Days in New Crete, 3-179
    Watch the Northwind Rise, 3-179
Gray, Curme
    Murder in Millennium VI, 3-180
Green, Jan
    Despatches from the Frontiers of the Fe-
        male Mind, 4-653
Green, Roger Lancelyn
    Into Other Worlds, 9-69
Green, Roland
    Clan and Crown (Pournelle), 4-421
Greenberg, Martin H.
    Amazing Stories (Asimov), 3-425

The Arbor House Treasury of Great Science Fiction Short Novels, 3-457
The Arbor House Treasury of Modern Science Fiction (Silverberg), 3-457
The Arbor House Treasury of Science Fiction Masterpieces (Silverberg), 3-457
The End of the World (Rabkin), 9-79
Fantastic Lives, 10-189
Hitler Victorious (Benford), 4-636
Isaac Asimov (Olander), 10-11
Isaac Asimov Presents the Great Science Fiction Stories (Asimov), 3-421
Machines That Think (Asimov), 4-635
Mysterious Visions (Waugh), 3-460
No Place Else (Rabkin), 9-80
No Room for Man (Clem), 13-23
Philip K. Dick, 10-55
Ray Bradbury, 10-24
Robert A. Heinlein (Olander), 10-72
School and Society through Science Fiction (Olander), 13-33
Science Fiction and Fantasy Series and Sequels (Cottrill), 8-22
Science Fiction of the Fifties, 3-452
Science Fiction of the Forties (Pohl), 3-452
The 13 Crimes of Science Fiction (Asimov), 3-460
Ursula K. Le Guin (Olander), 10-94
Greenland, Colin
   The Entropy Exhibition, 9-39
   Interzone: The First Anthology (Clute), 4-643
Greg, Percy
   Across the Zodiac, 1-40
Gregory, Owen
   Meccania, 2-39
Griffin, Brian
   Apertures, 10-2
Griffin, Russell M.
   The Blind Men and the Elephant, 4-239
   Century's End, 4-240
Griffith, George, 15-75
   The Angel of the Revolution, 1-41
   Olga Romanoff, 1-42
Griffith, Mary
   "Three Hundred Years Hence," 8, 1-43
Griffiths, John
   Three Tomorrows, 9-40
Grifoni, Ulisse
   Dalla Terra alle Stelle, 6-309
Groc, Léon
   L'Univers vagabond, 6-98
Grunert, Carl
   Der Marsspion und andere Novellen, 6-14
Guardamagna, Daniela

Analisi dell'Incubo, 6-334
Guerard, Albert Joseph
   Night Journey, 3-181
Guerrini, Remo
   Pelle d'Ombra, 6-310
Guffey, George R.
   Bridges to Science Fiction (Slusser), 9-117
Guin, Wyman
   Beyond Bedlam, 3-182
   Living Way Out, 3-182
   The Standing Joy, 4-241
Guld, Jens
   Bibliografi over litteratur på dansk om science fiction til og med 1984, 6-363
Guminskii, V.
   Vzgliad skvoz' stoletie, 6-220
Gunn, James E., 10-67, 15-19
   Alternate Worlds, 9-41
   Crisis!, 4-242
   The Dreamers, 4-243
   Future Imperfect, 3-184
   The Immortal, 3-183
   The Immortals, 3-183
   Isaac Asimov, 10-10
   The Joy Makers, 3-185
   The Listeners, 4-244
   The Road to Science Fiction, 13-25
   Some Dreams Are Nightmares, 3-185
Gurevich, Georgii Iosifovich
   Karta Strani Fantazii, 6-226
Gurk, Paul
   Tuzub 37, 6-15
Gustafson, Jon
   Chroma, 12-21
Gutteridge, Lindsay
   Cold War in a Country Garden, 2-60

Haars, Peter
   Reisen til Ai-Po-Tu, 541, 6-388
Hackett, John
   The Third World War: August 1985, 4-245
   The Third World War: The Untold Story, 4-245
Hadley, Arthur T.
   The Joy Wagon, 3-186
Haggard, H. Rider, 17, 10-68, 15-8, 15-17, 15-75, 15-82, 15-88
   Allan Quatermain, 1-44
   King Solomon's Mines, 1-45
   She, 1-46
   When the World Shook, 1-47
Hahn, Ronald M.
   Reclams Science-Fiction-Führer (Alpers), 6-37

Science Fiction aus Deutschland
  (Alpers), 6-34
Haiblum, Isidore
  Nightmare Express, 4-246
Halacy, D. S.
  Return from Luna, 5-56
Haldane, Charlotte
  Man's World, 59
Haldane, J. B. S.
  Daedalus, 54
  "The Last Judgment," 55
  Possible Worlds, 55
Haldeman, Joe, 10-69, 15-90
  The Forever War, 4-247
  Worlds, 4-248
  Worlds Apart, 4-248
Hale, Edward Everett
  "The Brick Moon," 1-48
Hall, Austin
  The Blind Spot (Flint), 2-31
  People of the Comet, 2-31
  The Spot of Life, 2-31
Hall, H. W.
  Science Fiction and Fantasy Book Re-
    view Index, 1980–1984, 8-20
  Science Fiction and Fantasy Reference
    Index, 1978–1985, 8-20
  Science Fiction Book Review Index,
    1923–1973, 8-18
  Science Fiction Book Review Index,
    1974–1979, 8-19
  Science/Fiction Collections, 8-39
  The Science Fiction Magazines, 14-5
Hamilton, Cicely
  Lest Ye Die, 2-40
  Theodore Savage, 2-40
Hamilton, Edmond, 10-20, 15-30
  The Best of Edmond Hamilton, 3-187
  The Horror on the Asteroid, 2-41
  Outside the Universe, 2-41
  The Star of Life, 3-188
Hamilton, Virginia
  Dustland, 5-57
  The Gathering, 5-57
  Justice and Her Brothers, 5-57
Hammond, J. R.
  Herbert George Wells, 10-163
Hancock, Harrie Irving
  The Invasion of the United States, 5-58
Handley, Max
  Meanwhile, 4-249
Hanmura, Ryō, 483
  Ishi no Ketsumyaku, 6-235
  Musubiyama Hiroku, 6-236
  Sengoku Jieitai, 6-237
  Yōseiden, 6-238
Hanost, Paul
  Le Livre des Etoiles, 6-419

Hansen, Thore, 541
  Han som lengtet til stjernene, 6-389
Hanstein, Otfrid von. See von Hanstein,
  Otfrid
Harbou, Thea von. See von Harbou, Thea
Harcourt, Glen A.
  Palimpsests, 4-479
Harding, Lee
  Displaced Person, 5-59
  Misplaced Persons, 5-59
Hardy, Phil
  Aurum Film Encyclopedia, 11-1
  Science Fiction [Film Encyclopedia],
    11-1
Hargrave, John
  Harbottle, 2-42
  The Imitation Man, 2-42
Harness, Charles L., 15-24
  The Catalyst, 4-250
  Firebird, 4-252
  Flight Into Yesterday, 3-189
  The Paradox Men, 3-189
  Redworld, 4-251
  The Ring of Ritornel, 4-252
  The Rose, 3-190
Harper, Vincent
  The Mortgage on the Brain, 11
Harrington, Alan
  Paradise I, 4-254
Harrison, Harry, 10-70, 15-2
  Apeman, Spaceman (Stover), 3-459
  The Astounding-Analog Reader, 3-426,
    3-437
  Bill, the Galactic Hero, 4-255
  The California Iceberg, 5-60
  The Daleth Effect, 4-256
  Deathworld, 3-191
  Deathworld 2, 3-191
  Deathworld 3, 3-191
  Decade: The 1940s (Aldiss), 3-418
  Decade: The 1950s (Aldiss), 3-418
  Decade: The 1960s (Aldiss), 3-418
  The Ethical Engineer, 3-191
  Hell's Cartographers (Aldiss), 10-188
  In Our Hands, the Stars, 4-256
  The Light Fantastic, 3-438
  Make Room! Make Room!, 4-257
  Planet of No Return, 3-192
  Planet of the Damned, 3-192
  SF: Authors' Choice, 3-448
  Sense of Obligation, 3-192
  The Stainless Steel Rat, 3-193
  West of Eden, 4-258
  Winter in Eden, 4-258
Harrison, M. John
  The Centauri Device, 4-259
  The Floating Gods, 4-260
  In Viriconium, 4-260

The Pastel City, 4-260
A Storm of Wings, 4-260
Viriconium Nights, 4-260
Harryhausen, Ray
Film Fantasy Scrapbook, 11-28
Hartley, L. P.
Facial Justice, 3-194
Hartwell, David
Age of Wonders, 9-42
The Battle of the Monsters and Other
Stories, 1-49
Hassler, Donald M.
Comic Tones in Science Fiction, 9-43
Death and the Serpent (Yoke), 9-109
Hal Clement, 10-46
Patterns of the Fantastic, 9-114
Patterns of the Fantastic II, 9-114A
Hawel, Rudolf
Im Reiche der Homunkuliden, 6-16
Hawkes, Jacquetta
Providence Island, 3-195
Hayakawa Shōbō
SF Magajin Serekushon, 6-296
Haynes, Roslynn D.
H. G. Wells, 10-169
Healy, Raymond J.
Adventures in Time and Space, 3-439
Famous Science Fiction Stories, 3-439
New Tales of Space and Time, 3-440
Heard, H. F.
Doppelgangers, 3-196
Heidtmann, Horst
Utopisch-phantastiche Literatur in der
DDR, 6-41
Heijermans, Herman
Gevleugelde daden, 546
Heinlein, Robert A., 10-71, 10-72, 10-73,
10-74, 10-75, 15-10, 15-23, 15-55, 15-
90
Beyond This Horizon, 3-197
The Cat Who Walks Through Walls, 4-
261
Citizen of the Galaxy, 5-61
The Door Into Summer, 3-198
Double Star, 3-199
Farmer in the Sky, 5-62
Friday, 4-262
Glory Road, 3-200
The Green Hills of Earth, 3-204
Have Space Suit—Will Travel, 3-201
The Man Who Sold the Moon, 3-204
The Menace from Earth, 3-202
Methuselah's Children, 3-204
The Moon Is a Harsh Mistress, 4-263
The Past Through Tomorrow, 3-204
The Puppet Masters, 3-205
Revolt in 2100, 3-204
Rocket Ship Galileo, 5-63

The Rolling Stones, 5-64
Starman Jones, 5-65
Starship Troopers, 3-206
Stranger in a Strange Land, 3-207
Time Enough for Love, 4-264
Tunnel in the Sky, 5-66
Heintz, Bonnie L.
Tomorrow, and Tomorrow, and Tomor-
row, 13-26
Held, S. S.
The Death of Iron, 56
Heller, Leonid
Vselennaia za predelom dogmy, 6-227
Helprin, Mark
Winter's Tale, 4-265
Henderson, Zenna, 15-2
The People: No Different Flesh, 3-208
Pilgrimage, 3-208
Henneberg, Charles, 411
Le Chant des Astronautes, 6-99
La Naissance des dieux, 6-100
La Plaie, 6-101
La Rosée du soleil, 6-102
Henneberg, Nathalie C., 411
Le Dieu foudroyé, 6-101
The Green Gods, 3-209
La Plaie, 6-101
La Rosée du soleil, 6-102
Herbert, Brian
Man of Two Worlds, 4-271
Sudanna, Sudanna, 4-266
Herbert, Frank, 10-76, 10-77, 10-78, 15-2,
15-90
Chapter House: Dune, 4-268
Children of Dune, 4-268
Destination: Void, 4-267
The Dragon in the Sea, 3-210
Dune, 4-268
Dune Messiah, 4-268
God-Emperor of Dune, 4-268
Hellstrom's Hive, 4-269
Heretics of Dune, 4-268
The Jesus Incident, 4-267
The Lazarus Effect, 4-267
Man of Two Worlds, 4-271
21st Century Sub, 3-210
Under Pressure, 3-210
The White Plague, 4-270
Herck, Paul van, 546
Sam of de Pluterdag, 6-404, 6-436
Hersey, Harold
Pulpwood Editor, 721
Hersey, John
The Child Buyer, 3-211
Hesse, Hermann
The Glass Bead Game, 3-212, 382
Hext, Harrington. See Phillpotts, Eden
Hey, Richard

Im Jahr 95 nach Hiroshima, 6-17
Hickman, Gail Morgan
  The Films of George Pal, 11-29
Hicks, Granville
  The First to Awaken, 3-213
Higon, Albert
  Aux étoiles de destin, 6-103
Hildebrandt, Greg
  The Art of the Brothers Hildebrandt,
    12-22
  From Tolkien to Oz, 12-22
Hildebrandt, Tim
  The Art of the Brothers Hildebrandt,
    12-22
Hill, Douglas
  Alien Citadel, 5-68
  Day of the Starwind, 5-67
  Galactic Warlord, 5-67
  The Huntsman, 5-68
  Planet of the Warlord, 5-67
  Warriors of the Wasteland, 5-68
Hillegas, Mark Robert
  The Future as Nightmare, 9-44
Hilton, James
  Lost Horizon, 2-43
Hingley, Ronald
  Up Jenkins!, 3-214
Hipple, Theodore W.
  The Worlds of Science Fiction, 13-27
Hirai, Kazumasa
  Okami no Monshō, 6-239
  Wolfcrest, 6-239
Hirose, Tadashi
  Erosu, 6-240
  Mainasu Zero, 6-241
Hoban, Russell
  Riddley Walker, 4-272
Hobana, Ion
  Imaginile posibilului, 6-461
  O falie în timp, 6-458
  Oameni şi stele, 6-448
  Science fiction: Autori, cărti, idei, 6-462
  Viitorul a inceput ieri, 6-463
  Virsta de aur a anticipaţiei româneşti, 6-
    459
Hobson, Pearson
  "If War Should Come," 14
Hodder-Williams, Christopher
  The Chromosome Game, 4-273
Hodgson, William Hope, 15-71, 15-77
Hoftun, Sigmun
  Malstrøm (Bing), 6-397, 6-399
Hogan, James P.
  Code of the Lifemaker, 4-274
  The Genesis Machine, 4-275
  The Gentle Giants of Ganymede, 4-276
  Giants' Star, 4-276
  Inherit the Stars, 4-276

  The Minervan Experiment, 4-276
  Voyage from Yesteryear, 4-277
Hokenson, Jan
  Forms of the Fantastic, 9-115
Holberg, Ludvig
  Nicolai Klimii Iter Subterraneum, 7, 1-
    50, 6-346, 537, 6-390
  Niels Klims underjordiske Reise, 518, 6-
    346
  A Journey to the World Under-Ground,
    7, 1-50, 6-346, 537, 6-390
Holdstock, Robert
  Alien Landscapes, 12-23
  Encyclopedia of Science Fiction, 9-45
  When Time Winds Blow, 4-278
Hollister, Bernard
  You and Science Fiction, 13-28
Hollow, John
  Against the Night, the Stars, 10-39
Holly, J. Hunter, 15-19
Holm, Palle Juul
  Syzygy og den sorte stjerne, 6-364
Holm, Sven
  Termush, 6-347
Holmberg, John-Henri
  Drömmar om evigheten, 6-372
Holmes, Bruce T.
  Anvil of the Heart, 4-279
Holmes, Oliver Wendell
  Elsie Venner, 11
Holten, Knud
  Suma-X, 6-347A
Holtsmark, Erling B.
  Edgar Rice Burroughs, 10-32
  Tarzan and Tradition, 10-32
Hoover, H. M.
  Another Heaven, Another Earth, 5-69
  Children of Morrow, 5-70
  The Lost Star, 5-71
  The Rains of Eridan, 5-72
  Return to Earth, 5-73
  The Shepherd Moon, 5-74
  Treasures of Morrow, 5-70
Horrakh, Kivio
  Grattanuvole, 6-311
Horrigan, Brian
  Yesterday's Tomorrows (Corn), 9-28
HORROR FICTION, 605–607
Hoshi, Shinichi, 480, 482
  Jinzō Bijin, 6-242
  Koe no Ami, 6-243
  Muma no Hyōteki, 6-244
  The Spiteful Planet and Other Stories,
    6-245
Hoskins, Robert
  The Liberated Future, 3-441
Hough, Stanley B., 15-52
Houghton, Claude

This Was Ivor Trent, 2-44
Hougron, Jean
La Naguen, 6-104
La Signe du chien, 6-105
Houssin, Joël
Les Vautours, 6-106
Howard, Robert E., 20, 15-71
Howe, Irving
Orwell's Nineteen Eighty-Four, 10-116
Hoyle, Fred
A for Andromeda, 3-215
The Black Cloud, 3-216
Ossian's Ride, 3-217
Hoyne, Thomas Temple
Intrigue on the Upper Level, 2-45
Hubbard, L. Ron
Battlefield Earth, 4-280
Black Genesis, 4-280
The Enemy Within, 4-280
Final Blackout, 3-218
Mission Earth: The Invaders Plan, 4-280
Hubert, Jean-Pierre
Le Champ du rêveur, 6-107
Les Faiseurs d'orage, 6-108
Mort a l'étouffée, 6-109
Scènes de guerre civile, 6-110
Huddy, Delia
The Humboldt Effect, 5-75
Time Piper, 5-76
Hudson, W. H.
A Crystal Age, 1-51
Huet, Theo
De Vredemensch in 't jaar 3000, 6-430
Huffman-Klinkowitz, Julie
Kurt Vonnegut (Pieratt), 10-160
Hughes, Monica
The Guardian of Isis, 5-77
The Isis Pedlar, 5-77
The Keeper of the Isis Light, 5-77
The Tomorrow City, 5-78
Hunter, Evan
Find the Feathered Serpent, 5-79
Hunter, Norman
The Incredible Adventures of Professor Branestawn, 5-80
Hunting, Gardner
The Vicarion, 2-46
Huntington, John
The Logic of Fantasy, 10-170
Huxley, Aldous
After Many a Summer, 3-219
After Many a Summer Dies the Swan, 3-219
Ape and Essence, 3-220
Brave New World, 2-47, 10-79
Brave New World Revisited, 2-47
Island, 3-221
Hyams, Edward

Morrow's Ants, 4-281
Hyne, Cutliffe
The Lost Continent, 1-52

Ikin, Van
Australian Science Fiction, 4-638
Illing, Werner
Utopolis, 6-18
Inagaki, Taruho
Issenichibyō Monogatari, 6-246
Ing, Dean
Soft Targets, 4-282
Systemic Shock, 4-283
Inge, M. Thomas
Concise Histories of American Popular Culture, 8-44
Handbook of American Popular Culture, 8-44
Ionică, Lucian
Ziua confuză, 6-449
Ionnescu, Demetriu G.
Spiritele anului 3000, 6-450
Ishihara, Fujio
Haiuei Wakusei, 6-247
SF Tosho Kaisetsu Sōmokuroku, 6-300
Ishikawa, Eiské
SF Seiyūki, 6-248
SF Suikoden, 6-248
Ishikawa, Takashi
Nihon no SF (Fukushima), 6-295
SF no Jidai, 6-301
Sekai no SF Bungaku Sōkaisetsu, 6-302
Ishikawa, Tatsuzō
Saigo no Kyōwakoku, 6-249

Jackson, Jacqueline
The Endless Pavement, 5-81
Jacobi, Carl, 15-29
Jacques, Maria
Morgen is Blond, 6-431
Jaeger, Muriel
The Man with Six Senses, 2-48
Jaffery, Sheldon
Collector's Index to Weird Tales, 14-6
Jakes, John
On Wheels, 4-284
Jakobsson, Ejler
The Best from Galaxy, 3-436
Jakubowski, Maxim
The SF Book of Lists, 8-42
Travelling towards Epsilon, 4-654
James, Dakota
Milwaukee the Beautiful, 4-285
James, Henry
"Maud Evelyn," 10
"The Turn of the Screw," 10

Jane, Frederick T.
  Blake of the 'Rattlesnake,' 12
Janifer, Laurence M.
  Brain Twister (Phillips), 3-306
Jarvis, Sharon
  Inside Outer Space, 13-15
Jean, Albert
  Blind Circle (Renard), 2-92
Jeffries, Richard
  After London, 1-53
Jenkins, William Fitzgerald. *See* Leinster,
  Murray
Jensen, Axel
  Epp, 539, 6-391
Jensen, Johannes V.
  The Long Journey, 2-50
Jersild, P. C.
  En levande själ, 6-368
Jeschke, Wolfgang
  Das Auge des Phoenix, 6-35
  The Last Day of Creation, 4-286, 6-19
  Der letzte Tag der Schöpfung, 4-286, 6-
  19
  Der Zeiter, 6-20
Jeter, K. W.
  Dr. Adder, 4-287
Jeury, Michel, 411
  Aux étoiles de destin (Higon), 6-103
  Chronolysis, 4-288, 6-114
  Le Livre d'or de Michel Jeury, 6-111
  L'orbe et la roue, 6-112
  Planète socialiste, 6-172
  Poney-Dragon, 6-113
  Les Singes du temps, 6-113
  Soleil chaud poisson des profondeurs, 6-
  113
  Le Temps incertain, 4-288, 6-114
  Le Territoire humain, 6-115
  Utopies 75, 6-173
  Les Yeux géants, 6-116
Johnson, Annabel
  Prisoner of PSI, 5-82
Johnson, Edgar
  Prisoner of PSI, 5-82
Johnson, George Clayton
  Logan's Run (Nolan), 4-400
Johnson, Kenneth R.
  Index to the Science Fiction Magazines
  (Boyajian), 14-2
  Index to the Semi-Professional Fantasy
  Magazines (Boyajian), 14-3
Johnson, Owen
  The Coming of the Amazons, 2-51
Johnson, Wayne L.
  Ray Bradbury, 10-25
Johnson, William
  Focus on the Science Fiction Film, 11-30
Jones, D. F.

Colossus, 4-289
Colossus and the Crab, 4-289
The Fall of Colossus, 4-289
Jones, Langdon
  The Eye of the Lens, 4-290
  The Nature of the Catastrophe
  (Moorcock), 4-382
Jones, McClure
  Cast Down the Stars, 5-83
Jones, Neil R.
  Planet of the Double Sun, 2-52
Jones, R. K.
  The Shudder Pulps, 722
Jones, Raymond F.
  This Island Earth, 3-222
  The Toymaker, 3-223
  The Year When Stardust Fell, 5-84
Joseph, M. K.
  The Hole in the Zero, 4-291
Joshi, S. T.
  H. P. Lovecraft, 10-105
  H. P. Lovecraft and Lovecraft Criticism,
  10-107, 10-108
  H. P. Lovecraft: Four Decades of Criti-
  cism, 10-106
Jouanne, Emmanuel
  Damiers imaginaires, 6-117
  Nuage, 6-118
Jules-Verne, Jean
  Jules Verne, 10-153
Julian, Alain
  Le Rayon SF (Delmas), 6-184
Jünger, Ernst
  Gläserne Bienen
  Heliopolis, 382
Juno, Andrea
  Re/Search No. 8/9: J. G. Ballard (Vale),
  10-17
Jurist, Eduard
  Oul lui Columb, 6-451
Justice, Keith L.
  Science Fiction Master Index of Names,
  8-20

Kagarlitskii, Iulii Iosifovich
  Chto takoe fantastika?, 6-228
Kahn, James
  Time's Dark Laughter, 4-292
  World Enough and Time, 4-292
Kajio, Shinji
  Chikyu wa Plain Yogurt, 6-250
Kanbayashi, Chōhei, 483
  Sentō Yōssei: Yikikaze, 6-251
Kanbe, Mushashi
  Kessen: Nihon Shirizu, 6-252
Kantor, MacKinlay

If the South Had Won the Civil War, 3-224

Karinthy, Frigyes
Voyage to Faremido and Capillaria, 2-53

Karl, Jean E.
But We Are Not of Earth, 5-85
The Turning Place, 5-86

Karp, David
Escape to Nowhere, 3-225
One, 3-225

Kasai, Kiyoshi
Kikai-jikake no Yume, 6-303

Kateb, George
Utopia and Its Enemies, 8-54

Kaul, Fedor
Contagion to This World, 2-54
Die Welt ohne Gedächtnis, 2-54

Kavan, Anna
Ice, 4-293

Kawamata, Chiaki
Genshi-gari, 6-253

Kayama, Shigeru
Oran-penteku no Fukushū, 6-254

Keller, David H., 54, 15-34, 15-77
Life Everlasting . . . , 2-55
The Metal Doom, 2-106
Tales from Underwood, 2-55

Kellermann, Bernhard
Der Tunnel, 382

Kelley, Leo P.
Space Adventure Series, 13-29

Kelley, William Melvin
A Different Drummer, 3-226

Kelly, Frank K.
Starship Invincible, 2-56

Kendall, John
Unborn Tomorrow, 59

Kepler, Johann
Somnium, 5, 1-54

Keppel-Jones, Arthur
When Smuts Goes, 3-227

Kernbach, Victor
Luntrea sublimă, 6-452

Kerr, Stephen
A Bibliographical Guide to Soviet Fantasy and Science Fiction, 1957–1968, 455

Kestaven, G. R.
The Pale Invaders, 5-87

Ketterer, David
Imprisoned in a Tessaract, 10-19
New Worlds for Old, 9-46
The Science Fiction of Mark Twain (Clemens), 1-25

Key, Alexander
Escape to Witch Mountain, 5-88
The Forgotten Door, 5-89
Return from Witch Mountain, 5-88

Keyes, Daniel
Flowers for Algernon, 3-228

Kilian, Crawford
Eyas, 4-294

Killough, Lee
Aventine, 4-295

Kilworth, Garry
The Night of Kadar, 4-296
The Songbirds of Pain, 4-297
A Theatre of Timesmiths, 4-298

King, Betty
Women of the Future, 8-24

King, Stephen, 10-80, 10-81, 10-82, 10-83, 10-84, 10-85, 10-86, 10-87, 10-88, 15-90
Carrie, 4-299
The Dead Zone, 4-300

Kingsbury, Donald
Courtship Rite, 4-301
Geta, 4-301

Kingsmill, Hugh
The Return of William Shakespeare, 2-57

Kinnaird, John
Olaf Stapledon, 10-139

Kiodomari, Allan
Hikari no Tō, 6-255

Kipling, Rudyard
"As Easy as A.B.C.," 1-55
"With the Night Mail," 1-55

Kippax, John
The Neutral Stars (Morgan), 4-384
Seed of Stars (Morgan), 4-384
A Thunder of Stars (Morgan), 4-384
Where No Stars Guide, 4-384

Kirst, Hans Hellmut
No One Will Escape, 3-229
The Seventh Day, 3-229

Klein, Gérard, 411
Anthologie de la science-fiction Française, 6-174
The Day before Tomorrow, 4-302
Histoires comme si, 6-119
Le Livre d'or de Gérard Klein, 6-120
Malaise dans la science-fiction, 6-190
Starmaster's Gambit, 3-230
Temps n'a pas odeur, 4-302

Kline, Otis Adelbert
Venus series, 52

Klinkowitz, Jerome
Kurt Vonnegut (Pieratt), 10-160
Vonnegut in America, 10-156
The Vonnegut Statement, 10-157

Kneale, Nigel
Quatermass and the Pit, 3-231
The Quatermass Experiment, 3-231
Quatermass II, 3-231

Knebel, Fletcher

Night of Camp David, 3-232
Seven Days in May, 3-232
Knight, Damon F., 15-34, 15-55
Analogue Men, 3-234
A Century of Great Short Science Fiction Novels, 3-442
A Century of Science Fiction, 3-442
Cities of Wonder, 3-443
CV, 4-303
Far Out, 3-233
The Futurians, 10-190
Hell's Pavement, 3-234
In Deep, 3-235
In Search of Wonder, 9-47
The Man in the Tree, 4-304
One Hundred Years of Science Fiction, 3-442
Orbit, 4-655
A Science Fiction Argosy, 3-444
Science Fiction of the Thirties, 2-58
Thirteen French Science-Fiction Stories, 3-445
Turning On, 3-236
Turning Points, 9-48
Knight, Norman L.
A Torrent of Faces (Blish), 3-48
Knoepflmacher, V. C.
The Endurance of Frankenstein (Levine), 10-127
Knott, William C.
Journey across the Third Planet, 5-90
Koestler, Arthur
The Age of Longing, 3-237
Twilight Bar, 3-237
Komatsu, Sakyō, 479, 482
Chi ni wa Heiwa o, 6-256
Fukkatsu no Hi, 6-257
Hateshinaki Nagare no Hate ni, 6-258
Japan Sinks, 4-305
Nippon Chimbotsu, 481, 6-259
Sayonara Jupiter, 6-260
Shuto Shōshitsu, 6-261
Kono, Tensei
Machi no Hakubutsushi, 6-262
Koontz, Dean R.
Beastchild, 4-306
Körber, Joachim
Bibliographisches Lexikon der utopisch-phantastichen Literatur, 6-42
Kornbluth, C. M., 15-55
The Best of C. M. Kornbluth, 3-238
Christmas Eve, 3-239
Gladiator-at-Law (Pohl), 3-311
Not This August, 3-239
The Space Merchants (Pohl), 3-313
The Syndic, 3-240
Takeoff, 3-241
Wolfbane (Pohl), 3-314

Kossak-Raytenau, Karl L.
Die Welt am laufenden Band, 6-21
Kraft, Robert, 380
Krasnov, P. N.
Za chertopolokhom, 445
Kremnov, Iv
Puteshestvie moego brata Alekseiia v stranu krestianskoi utopii, 445, 6-205
Krol, Gerrit
De man achter het raam, 6-405
Krulik, Theodore
Roger Zelazny, 10-184
Krysmanski, Hans-Jürgen
Die utopische Methode, 6-43
Kube-McDowell, Michael P.
Emprise, 4-307
Enigma, 4-307
Kuhn, Thomas
The Structure of Scientific Revolutions, 220
Kurimoto, Kaori, 483
Hyōto no Kamen, 6-263
Kurland, Michael, 15-52
The Princes of Earth, 5-91
The Unicorn Girl, 4-12
Kuttner, Henry, 15-8, 15-55
The Best of Henry Kuttner, 3-242
Chessboard Planet, 3-246
Destination Infinity, 3-243
The Far Reality, 3-246
Fury, 3-243
Mutant, 3-244
Robots Have No Tales, 3-245
Tomorrow and Tomorrow and The Fairy Chessman, 3-246
Kyle, David A., 15-34
The Illustrated Book of Science Fiction Ideas and Dreams, 9-50
A Pictorial History of Science Fiction, 9-49

Ladd, Thyril, 15-79
Lafferty, R. A., 10-89
Annals of Klepsis, 4-308
Apocalypses, 4-309
Does Anyone Else Have Something Further to Add?, 4-311
Fourth Mansions, 4-310
Nine Hundred Grandmothers, 4-311
Past Master, 4-312
Ringing Changes, 4-311
Space Chantey, 4-313
Strange Doings, 4-311
The Three Armageddons of Enniscorthy Sweeny, 4-309
Where Have You Been, Sandaliotis?, 4-309

Lahana, Jacqueline
 Les Mondes parallèles de la science fiction sovietique, 6-191
Laidlaw, Marc
 Dad's Nuke, 4-314
Lake, David J.
 The Man Who Loved Morlocks, 4-315
 The Right Hand of Dextra, 4-316
Landoy, J. A. C.
 Du Fond des ages, 6-420
Lane, Daryl
 The Sound of Wonder, 10-199
Lane, Mary E. Bradley
 Mizora, 1-56
Lang, Fritz, 15-52
Langford, David
 The Science in Science Fiction (Nicholls), 9-68
 The Space Eater, 4-317
 The Third Millennium (Stableford), 4-534
Lanier, Sterling E.
 Hiero's Journey, 4-318
 The Unforsaken Hiero, 4-318
Large, E. C.
 Asleep in the Afternoon, 2-59
 Sugar in the Air, 2-59
Larionova, Ol'ga Nikolaevna
 Leopard s vershiny Kilimandzharo, 449, 6-206
 Ostrov muzhestva, 6-206
Larson, Randall D.
 Musique Fantastique, 11-31
Lasswitz, Kurd
 Auf zwei Planeten, 383, 6-22
 Bilder aus der Zukunft, 383, 6-23
Latham, Philip
 Missing Men of Saturn, 5-92
Laughlin, Charlotte
 De Camp, 10-47
Laumer, Keith, 15-34
 Assignment in Nowhere, 3-248
 Beyond the Imperium, 3-248
 Envoy to New Worlds, 3-247
 The Infinite Cage, 4-319
 The Other Side of Time, 3-248
 Star Colony, 4-320
 Worlds of the Imperium, 3-248
Laurance, Alice
 Cassandra Rising, 4-653
Lavrek, Andrija
 "Nemačka 1942," 6-470
Lawler, Donald L.
 Approaches to Science Fiction, 13-30
 Vonnegut in America (Klinkowitz), 10-156
Lawrence, Louise
 Children of the Dust, 5-93

The Power of Stars, 5-94
Lebar, John
 The Devil's Highway (Wright), 2-137
Lee, Tanith
 Sabella, 4-321
 The Silver Metal Lover, 4-322
Lee, Walt
 Reference Guide to Fantastic Films, 11-2
Leek, Sybil
 The Tree That Conquered the World, 5-96
Lefanu, Sarah
 Despatches from the Frontiers of the Female Mind (Green), 4-653
Le Guin, Ursula K., 10-90, 10-91, 10-92, 10-93, 10-94, 10-95, 10-96, 15-55, 15-90
 Always Coming Home, 4-323
 The Dispossessed, 4-324
 The Eye of the Heron, 4-325
 The Language of the Night, 9-51
 The Lathe of Heaven, 4-326
 The Left Hand of Darkness, 4-327
 The Wind's Twelve Quarters, 4-328
 The Word for World Is Forest, 4-329
Lehmkuhl, Donald
 The Flights of Icarus, 12-24
Leiber, Fritz, 10-97, 10-98, 15-8, 15-17
 The Big Time, 3-249
 The Change War, 3-249
 Gather, Darkness!, 3-250
 The Green Millennium, 3-251
 The Mind Spider, 3-249
 The Silver Eggheads, 3-252
 The Wanderer, 3-253
Leinster, Murray, 15-34
 The Best of Murray Leinster, 3-254
 Colonial Survey, 3-255
 The Forgotten Planet, 2-60, 3-256
 The Murder of the U.S.A., 3-257
 The Mutant Weapon, 3-258
 The Pirates of Zan, 3-258
 The Planet Explorer, 3-255
Lem, Stanislaw, 10-99
 The Cyberiad, 4-330
 The Futurological Congress, 4-331
 His Master's Voice, 4-332
 The Investigation, 3-259
 The Invincible, 3-260
 Memoirs of a Space Traveller, 4-331
 Microworlds, 9-52
 Phantastik und Futurologie, 6-44
 Solaris, 3-261
 The Star Diaries, 4-331
L'Engle, Madeleine
 A Swiftly Tilting Planet, 5-96
 A Wind in the Door, 5-96
 A Wrinkle in Time, 5-96

Lentz, Harris M., III
 Science Fiction, Horror & Fantasy Films
  & Television Credits, 11-6
Léonard, François
 Le Triomphe de l'homme, 6-421
Le Queux, William
 The Great War in England in 1897, 13,
  1-57
 The Invasion of 1910, 13
 The Terror of the Air, 52
Lerner, Frederick A.
 Modern Science Fiction and the Literary
  Community, 9-53
Le Rouge, Gustave, 408
 La Conspiration des milliardaires, 6-121
 La Guerre des vampires, 6-123
 Le Mystérieux Docteur Cornélius, 6-122
 Le Prisonnier de la planète Mars, 6-123
Leroux, Gaston
 The Machine to Kill, 2-61
Lessing, Doris
 The Making of the Representative for
  Planet 8, 4-334
 The Memoirs of a Survivor, 4-333
 The Marriages between Zones Three,
  Four and Five, 4-334
 The Sentimental Agents in the Volyen
  Empire, 4-334
 Shikasta, 4-334
 The Sirian Experiments, 4-334
Levack, Daniel J. H.
 Amber Dreams, 10-185
 De Camp (Laughlin), 10-47
 Fantasms, 10-149
 PKD, 10-60
Leven, Jeremy
 Satan, 4-336
Levin, Ira
 The Boys from Brazil, 4-337
 This Perfect Day, 4-338
Levine, George
 The Endurance of Frankenstein, 10-127
Lewis, Anthony R.
 Concordance to Cordwainer Smith, 10-
  135
Lewis, C. S., 10-100, 15-46
 The Dark Tower and Other Stories, 3-
  262
 Out of the Silent Planet, 3-263
 Perelandra, 3-263
 That Hideous Strength, 3-263
 The Tortured Planet, 3-263
 Voyage to Venus, 3-263
Lewis, Sinclair
 It Can't Happen Here, 2-62
Lewis, Tony
 The Best of Astounding, 3-426
Liapunov, Boris Valer'ianovich

 V mire fantastiki, 6-229
Lichtenberg, Jacqueline
 Dushau, 4-339
 Farfetch, 4-339
 Outreach, 4-339
Liebman, Arthur
 The Worlds of Science Fiction Series,
  13-31
Lightner, A. M.
 The Day of the Drones, 5-97
 Doctor to the Galaxy, 5-98
 The Space Ark, 5-99
 The Space Plague, 5-99
Ligny, Jean-Marc
 Temps blancs, 6-124
Lindsay, David, 60, 10-101, 10-102
 Devil's Tor, 2-63
 The Violet Apple, 2-63
 A Voyage to Arcturus, 2-63
Llewellyn, Alun
 The Strange Invaders, 2-64
Llewellyn, Edward
 Salvage and Destroy, 4-340
Locke, George
 Science Fiction First Editions, 8-5
 A Spectrum of Fantasy, 8-4
 Voyages in Space, 8-6
Locke, Richard Adams
 "The Moon Hoax," 6
Lofficier, Jean-Marc
 The Doctor Who Programme Guide, 11-
  32
Logsdon, Syd
 A Fond Farewell to Dying, 4-341
London, Jack, 10-103
 Before Adam, 20, 1-58
 "The Red One," 1-60
 "A Relic of the Pliocene," 1-60
 The Scarlet Plague, 1-60
 The Science Fiction of Jack London, 1-
  60
 The Star Rover, 11
 "The Unparalleled Invasion," 1-60
Long, Frank Belknap, 15-42
 The Early Long, 3-264
Longyear, Barry B.
 Manifest Destiny, 4-342
 Science Fiction Writer's Workshop I, 13-
  16
 The Tomorrow Testament, 4-342
Lord, Beman
 The Day the Spaceship Landed, 5-101
 The Day the Spaceship Returns, 5-101
Lovecraft, H. P., 10-104, 10-105, 10-106,
  10-107, 10-108, 15-15, 15-17, 15-42,
  15-54, 15-55, 15-75, 15-79, 15-80, 15-
  93
 At the Mountains of Madness . . . , 2-65

The Dunwich Horror and Others, 2-65
Lovisi, Gary
  Science Fiction Detective Tales, 9-54
Low, A. M.
  Our Wonderful World, 54
Lowndes, Robert
  The Duplicated Man (Blish), 3-44
Lucian
  True History, 5
Lukod'ianov, Isai Borisovich
  Plesk zvezdnykh morei (Voiskunskii),
    452, 6-213
Lundberg, Knud
  The Olympic Hope, 3-265, 6-348
  Det olympiske håb, 3-265, 6-348
Lundin, Claës
  Oxygen och Aromasia, 532, 6-369
Lundwall, Sam J.
  Bibliografi över science fiction & fan-
    tasy, 6-373
  The Penguin World Omnibus of Science
    Fiction (Aldiss), 4-633
  Science Fiction: An Illustrated History,
    9-55
  Science Fiction: What It's All About, 6-
    374, 9-55
  2018 A.D., 4-343
Lupoff, Richard A.
  Barsoom, 10-33
  Circumpolar!, 4-344
  Countersolar!, 4-344
  Edgar Rice Burroughs, 10-34
  Space War Blues, 4-345
  Sun's End, 4-346
  What If?, 3-446
Lynn, Elizabeth A.
  A Different Light, 4-347
  The Sardonyx Net, 4-348
Lytton, Edward Bulwer
  The Coming Race, 1-61

MacArthur, David
  The Thunderbolt Men, 5-102
Macaulay, Rose
  What Not, 2-66
McCaffrey, Anne, 10-110, 15-34
  The Crystal Singer, 4-367
  Dragondrums, 5-110
  Dragonflight, 4-368
  Dragonquest, 4-368
  The Dragonriders of Pern, 4-368
  Dragonsinger, 5-110
  Dragonsong, 5-110
  Moreta, Dragonlady of Pern, 4-368
  Nerilka's Story, 4-368
  The Ship Who Sang, 4-369
  The White Dragon, 4-368

McCall, Robert
  Vision of the Future (Bova), 12-4
McCann, Edison
  Preferred Risk, 3-275A
McCarthy, Patrick A.
  Olaf Stapledon, 10-140
McClary, Thomas Calvert
  Rebirth, 2-74
McComas, J. Francis
  Adventures in Time and Space, 3-439
  The Best from Fantasy and Science Fic-
    tion (Boucher), 3-423
  Famous Science Fiction Stories, 3-439
McConnell, Frank
  The Science Fiction of H. G. Wells, 10-
    172
MacDonald, John D.
  Ballroom of the Skies, 3-266
  The Girl, the Gold Watch, and Every-
    thing, 3-267
  Planet of the Dreamers, 3-268
  Wine of the Dreamers, 3-268
Mace, Elizabeth
  Out There, 5-103
Macedonski, Alexandru
  Oceania-Pacific-Dreadnought, 6-453
McEvoy, Seth
  Samuel R. Delany, 10-49
MacGregor, Ellen
  Miss Pickerell Goes to Mars, 5-104
McGuire, Patrick L.
  Red Stars, 455, 9-58
Machen, Arthur, 15-46, 15-75
McHugh, Vincent
  I Am Thinking of My Darling, 3-276
McIlraith, Frank
  Invasion from the Air, 2-75
McIntosh, J. T.
  One in Three Hundred, 3-278
McIntyre, Vonda N., 15-90
  Aurora, 4-653
  Dreamsnake, 4-370
  Superluminal, 4-371
MacIsaac, Fred
  The Hothouse World, 2-67
McKenna, Richard M.
  Casey Agonistes and Other Science Fic-
    tion and Fantasy Stories, 3-279
MacKenzie, Jean
  H. G. Wells, 10-171
  The Time Traveller, 10-171
MacKenzie, Norman Ian
  H. G. Wells, 10-171
  The Time Traveller, 10-171
McKillip, Patricia
  The Moon and the Face, 5-111
  Moon-Flash, 5-111
MacLean, Katherine

The Missing Man, 4-349
MacLeod, Sheila
　Xanthe and the Robots, 4-350
McLuhan, Marshall
　Understanding Media, 210
McNelly, Willis F.
　The Dune Encyclopedia, 10-76
McQuade, James, 15-52
McQuay, Mike
　Lifekeeper, 4-372
MacVicar, Angus
　The Lost Planet, 5-105
Madden, Samuel
　Memoirs of the Twentieth Century, 8
Madlee, Dorothy
　Star Ka'at (Norton), 5-119
　Star Ka'at World (Norton), 5-119
　Star Ka'ats and the Winged Warriors
　　(Norton), 5-119
Madsen, Svend Åge
　Se dagens lys, 6-349
　Tugt og utugt i mellemtiden, 6-350
Magidoff, Robert
　Russian Science Fiction, 3-447
Magill, Frank N.
　Science Fiction Alien Encounter, 13-5
　Survey of Modern Fantasy Literature, 8-
　　48
　Survey of Science Fiction Literature, 8-
　　29
Maine, Charles Eric
　Count-Down, 3-264
　Fire Past the Future, 3-264
Malaguti, Ugo
　Nova SF Speciale, 6-328
　Il Palazzo nel Cielo, 6-312
　Satana dei Miracoli, 6-313
Malamud, Bernard
　God's Grace, 4-351
Malzberg, Barry N.
　Arena: Sports SF (Ferman), 3-435
　Beyond Apollo, 4-352
　Bug-Eyed Monsters (Pronzini), 3-454
　Chorale, 4-353
　Cross of Fire, 4-354
　Dark Sins, Dark Dreams, 3-460
　Down Here in the Dream Quarter, 4-
　　357
　Dwellers of the Deep, 4-356
　The End of Summer, 3-452
　The Engines of the Night, 9-56
　Galaxies, 4-355
　Gather in the Hall of the Planets, 4-356
　Herovit's World, 4-356
　The Man Who Loved the Midnight
　　Lady, 4-357
　The Remaking of Sigmund Freud, 4-
　　358

Manlove, C. N.
　Science Fiction: Ten Explorations, 9-57
Mann, Philip
　The Eye of the Queen, 4-359
Manning, Laurence
　The Man Who Awoke, 2-68
Manolescu, Florin
　Literatura SF, 6-464
Mantegazza, Paolo
　L'Anno 3000: Sogno, 6-314
Manuel, Frank E.
　Utopian Thought in the Western World,
　　8-54
Manuel, Fritzie P.
　Utopian Thought in the Western World,
　　8-54
Manvell, Roger
　The Dreamers, 3-270
March, William
　The Bad Seed, 3-271
Margot, Jean-Michael
　Bibliographie documentaire sur Jules
　　Verne, 10-150
Margulies, Leo
　From Off This World, 2-69
　My Best Science Fiction Story, 3-448
Mark, Jan
　The Ennead, 5-106
Marković, Milanče
　"Sejač," 6-471
Marsten, Richard
　Rocket to Luna, 5-107
Martel, Suzanne
　The City under Ground, 5-108
Martin, George R. R.
　Dying of the Light, 4-360
　The John W. Campbell Awards, 4-656
　New Voices, 4-656
　Nightflyers, 4-361
　Sandkings, 4-361
　A Song for Lya and Other Stories, 4-361
　Wild Cards, 4-657
　Windhaven, 4-362
Martinson, Harry
　Aniara, 3-272, 533, 6-370
Martynov, Georgii Sergeevich
　Gianeia, 450, 6-207
　Gost' iz bezdny, 449, 6-208
　Kallisto, 449
Marvell, Andrew
　Minimum Man, 2-70
　Three Men Make a World, 2-70
Masson, David I.
　The Caltraps of Time, 4-363
Matheson, Richard
　Bid Time Return, 4-364
　Born of Man and Woman, 3-273
　I Am Legend, 3-274

The Shrinking Man, 3-275
Third from the Sun, 3-273
The Twilight Zone (Greenberg),
3-4
Mathews, Richard
Aldiss Unbound, 10-3
Mathews, Rodney
In Search of Forever, 12-25
Matschatt, Cecile
The Year after Tomorrow (del Rey), 5-42
Matson, Norman
Doctor Fogg, 2-71
Maupassant, Guy de
"Le Horla," 10
Maurois, André, 56
The Thought-Reading Machine, 2-72
The Weigher of Souls, 2-73
Maxwell, Ann
Timeshadow Rider, 4-365
May, Julian, 10-109
The Adversary, 4-366
The Golden Torc, 4-366
The Many-Colored Land, 4-366
The Nonborn King, 4-366
The Pliocene Companion, 4-366
Mayhar, Ardath
Golden Dream, 3-308
Mayne, William
Earthfasts, 5-109
Mayo, Clark
Kurt Vonnegut, 10-159
Mayumura, Taku, 483
Expo '87, 6-264
Shōmetsu no Kōrin, 6-265
Mead, Harold
The Bright Phoenix, 3-280
Mead, Shepherd
The Big Ball of Wax, 3-281
Meek, S. P., 53
Méheust, Bertrand
Science-fiction et soucoups volantes, 6-192
Mele, Jim
Isaac Asimov (Fiedler), 10-9
Mendelson, Drew
Pilgrimage, 4-373
Menger, Lucy
Theodore Sturgeon, 10-145
Menghini, Luigi
L'Assedio, 6-315
Menville, Douglas
Ancestral Voices, 1-62
Futurevision, 11-15
Things to Come, 11-14
Mercier, Louis Sebastian
L'An deux mille quatre cent quarante, 1-63, 406

Memoirs of the Year Two Thousand
Five Hundred, 8, 1-63
Meredith, Richard C.
Run, Come See Jerusalem, 4-374
We All Died at Breakaway Station, 4-375
Merle, Robert
Malevil, 4-376
Merril, Judith
The Best of Judith Merril, 3-282
Daughters of Earth, 3-283
Path Into the Unknown, 3-447
SF: The Year's Greatest Science-Fiction
and Fantasy, 3-449
Shadow on the Hearth, 3-284
Tesseracts, 4-658
Merritt, Abraham, 53, 10-112, 15-71, 15-82, 15-93
Dwellers in the Mirage, 2-43
The Metal Monster, 2-76
The Moon Pool, 2-77
Reflections in the Moon Pool, 10-112
Messac, Régis, 409
La Cité des asphyxiés, 6-125
Quinzinzinsili, 6-126
Metcalf, Norman
Index of Science Fiction Magazines,
1951–1965, 14-7
Meyers, Richard
S-F 2, 11-18
Meyers, Walter E.
Aliens and Linguists, 9-59
Mielke, Thomas R. P.
Grand Orientale 3301, 6-35
Miglieruolo, Mauro Antonio
Come Ladro di Notte, 6-316
Mikhailov, Vladimir Dmitrievich
Togda pridite, i rassudim, 453, 6-209
Miklowitz, Gloria
After the Bomb, 5-112
"Miles." *See* Bell, Neil
Milesi, Raymond
Mouvance, 6-175
Miller, Chuck
Fear Itself (Underwood), 10-86
Kingdom of Fear (Underwood), 10-87
Miller, David M.
Frank Herbert, 10-77
Miller, Fred D., Jr.
Thought Probes, 13-32
Miller, Joe
The New Visions (Sherwin), 12-31
Miller, P. Schuyler, 15-19
Genus Homo (de Camp), 3-133
The Titan, 3-285
Miller, Ron
Space Art, 12-26
Worlds Beyond (Durant), 12-12
Miller, Walter M., Jr., 15-55

The Best of Walter M. Miller, Jr., 3-286
A Canticle for Leibowitz, 3-287
Conditionally Human, 3-286
The Science Fiction Stories of Walter M.
    Miller, Jr., 3-286
View from the Stars, 3-286
Mills, Robert
    The Best from Fantasy and Science Fic-
        tion (Boucher), 3-423
    A Decade of Fantasy and Science Fic-
        tion, 3-423
Milne, Robert Duncan
    Into the Sun & Other Stories, 1-64
Mishima, Yukio
    Utsukushii Hoshi, 6-266
Missiaja, Gianluigi
    Catalogo Generale della Fantascienza
        (Bertoni), 6-330
Misticelli, Judith A.
    Jules Verne (Gallagher), 10-154
Mitchell, Adrian
    The Bodyguard, 4-377
Mitchell, Edward Page
    The Crystal Man, 1-65
Mitchell, J. A.
    The Last American, 1-66
Mitchell, J. Leslie
    Gay Hunter, 2-78
    Three Go Back, 60, 2-79
Mitchison, Naomi
    Memoirs of a Spacewoman, 3-258
    Not by Bread Alone, 4-378
Mitsuse, Ryū, 481, 483
    Hyakuoku no Hiru, Senoku no Yoru, 6-
        267
    Tasogare ni Kaeru, 6-268
Miyazawa, Kenji
    Ginga Tetsudō no Yoru, 6-269
Moffett, Cleveland
    The Conquest of America, 13, 1-67
Mogen, David
    Wilderness Visions, 9-60
Mohs, Mayo
    Other Worlds, Other Gods, 4-665
Mongini, Giovanni
    Storia del Cinema di Fantascienza,
        6-335
Montanari, Gianni
    Daimon, 6-317
    Fanta-Italia, 6-327
    Ieri, il Futuro, 6-336
    La Sepoltura, 6-318
Monteleone, Thomas F.
    The Time-Swept City, 4-379
Montgomery, Richard B.
    A Sheet of Blotting Paper, 20
Moorcock, Michael, 15-45, 15-60
    The Adventures of Una Persson and

Catherine Cornelius in the Twentieth
    Century, 4-382
An Alien Heat, 4-383
Behold the Man, 4-380
The Best of New Worlds, 3-427
Best SF Stories from New Worlds, 3-
    427, 4-659
The Black Corridor, 4-381
The Condition of Muzak, 4-382
The Cornelius Chronicles, 4-382
A Cure for Cancer, 4-382
The Dancers at the End of Time, 4-383
Elric at the End of Time, 4-383
The End of All Songs, 4-383
The English Assassin, 4-382
The Entropy Tango, 4-382
The Final Programme, 4-382
The Hollow Lands, 4-383
Legends from the End of Time, 4-383
The Lives and Times of Jerry Cornelius,
    4-382
Messiah at the End of Time, 4-383
The Nature of the Catastrophe, 4-382
New Worlds, 4-659
The Opium General and Other Stories,
    4-382
The Transformation of Miss Mavis
    Ming, 4-383
Moore, C. L., 15-42
    The Best of C. L. Moore, 3-289
    Destination Infinity (Kuttner), 3-243
    The Far Reality (Kuttner), 3-246
    Fury (Kuttner), 3-243
    Judgment Night, 3-290
    Mutant (Kuttner), 3-244
    Scarlet Dream, 2-80
    Tomorrow and Tomorrow and The
        Fairy Chessman (Kuttner), 3-246
Moore, Chris
    Parallel Lines (Elson), 12-13
Moore, Ward, 15-8
    Bring the Jubilee, 3-291
    Greener Than You Think, 3-292
    Joyleg (Davidson), 3-128
More, Thomas
    Utopia, 1-68
Morgan, Dan
    The Neutral Stars, 4-384
    Seed of Stars, 4-384
    A Thunder of Stars, 4-384
Morressy, John
    The Drought on Ziax II, 5-113
    The Humans of Ziax II, 5-113
    The Windows of Forever, 5-114
Morrill, Rowena
    The Fantastic Art of Rowena, 12-27
Morris, Janet
    Afterwar, 4-660

Morris, William
A Dream of John Ball, 1-69
News from Nowhere, 1-69
Morrow, James
The Continent of Lies, 4-385
This Is the Way the World Ends, 4-386
Morse, A. Reynolds
Shiel in Diverse Hands, 10-131
Moselli, Jose
La Fin d'illa, 6-127
Moskowitz, Sam
Explorers of the Infinite, 10-191
Far Future Calling (Stapledon), 10-142
The Immortal Storm, 9-61
Modern Masterpieces of Science Fiction, 3-450
Reflections in the Moon Pool (Merritt), 10-112
Science Fiction by Gaslight, 1-70
Science Fiction in Old San Francisco, 9-64
Seekers of Tomorrow, 10-192
Strange Horizons, 9-65
Under the Moons of Mars, 1-71
Moszkowski, Alexandr
The Isles of Wisdom, 2-81
Motta, Luigi
Il Tunnel Sottomarino, 6-319
MOVIES, 672–686, 13-52
Mowshowitz, Abbe
Inside Information, 9-103
Moxley, F. Wright
Red Snow, 2-82
Mrozek, Slawomir
The Ugupu Bird, 3-293
Mulisch, Harry
De toekomst van gisteren, 6-406
Mundy, Talbot, 15-82
Murphy, Brian C.
C. S. Lewis, 10-100
Myers, Alan
Bibliography of Russian Science Fantasy 1917–1966, 455
Myers, Robert E.
The Intersection of Science Fiction and Philosophy, 9-66
Jack Williamson, 10-181
Myhre, Øyvind, 539-540
Snøen på Nix Olympia, 6-392
Myrus, Don
The Best of Omni Science Fiction, 4-646

Nagl, Manfred
Science Fiction in Deutschland, 379, 6-45
Nathan, Robert
Portrait of Jennie, 3-294

Naylor, Charles
New Constellations (Disch), 4-647
Strangeness (Disch), 4-647
Nearing, Homer, Jr.
The Sinister Researches of C. P. Ransom, 3-295
Nedelkovich, Alexander B.
Istorija srpske naučno-fantastične književnosti, 6-475
Neilson, Keith
Survey of Science Fiction Literature (Magill), 8-29
Nelson, Chris
Bob Shaw, 10-124
Nelson, Ray Faraday
Blake's Progress, 4-387
The Prometheus Man, 4-387
Then Beggars Could Ride, 4-387
Timequest, 4-387
Nesvadba, Josef
In the Footsteps of the Abominable Snowman, 3-296
The Lost Face, 3-296
Neutzsky-Wulff, Erwin
Anno Domini, 6-351
Neville, Kris
Bettyann, 3-297
New England Science Fiction Association
Index to the Science Fiction Magazines 1966–1970, 14-10
The NESFA Index, 14-11
NEW WAVE SF, 211
Newcomb, Simon
His Wisdom: The Defender, 14
Newman, John
Future War Novels, 8-15
Newman, Kim
Ghastly beyond Belief (Newman), 8-43
Nicholls, Peter
The Encyclopedia of Science Fiction, 8-30
Explorations of the Marvellous, 9-67
Fantastic Cinema, 11-16
Science Fiction at Large, 9-67
The Science Fiction Encyclopedia, 8-30
The Science in Science Fiction, 9-68
The World of Fantastic Films, 11-16
Nicolson, Marjorie Hope
Voyages to the Moon, 9-69
Nielsen, Niels E., 520
Akerons porte, 6-352
Herskerne, 6-353
Hinsides Bjergene, 6-354
Troldmandens Svaerd, 6-355
Vagabondernes planet, 6-356
Niemann, August
The Coming Conquest of England, 13
Nikol'skii, V.

Cherez tysiachu let, 445
Niven, Larry, 10-113, 15-90
  All the Myriad Ways, 4-390
  The Descent of Anansi, 4-394
  Dream Park, 4-395
  Footfall, 4-396
  A Gift from Earth, 4-389
  A Hole in Space, 4-390
  Inconstant Moon, 4-390
  The Integral Trees, 4-388
  Limits, 4-390
  The Long ARM of Gil Hamilton, 4-389
  Lucifer's Hammer, 4-397
  The Mote in God's Eye, 4-398
  Neutron Star, 4-390
  Oath of Fealty, 4-399
  The Patchwork Girl, 4-389
  Protector, 4-391
  Ringworld, 4-392
  Ringworld Engineers, 4-392
  The Shape of Space, 4-390
  The Smoke Ring, 4-388
  Tales of Known Space, 4-390
  A World out of Time, 4-393
Noa, Azusa
  Hana Karido, 6-270
Noda, Masahiro
  Ginga Kojiki Gundan, 6-271
Nolan, William F.
  Logan's Run, 4-400
  Logan's Search, 4-400
  Logan's World, 4-400
  The Ray Bradbury Companion, 10-26
Nolane, Richard D.
  Terra SF, 4-661
Norman, John
  Tarnsman of Gor, 4-401
North, Eric
  The Ant Men, 5-115
Norton, Andre, 10-114, 15-34, 15-57
  Catseye, 5-116
  Crosstime Agent, 5-118
  Daybreak 2250 A.D., 5-120
  Operation Time Search, 5-117
  Ordeal in Otherwhere, 5-122
  Quest Crosstime, 5-118
  Space Police, 3-460
  Star Born, 5-121
  Star Ka'at, 5-119
  Star Ka'at World, 5-119
  Star Ka'ats and the Planet People, 5-119
  Star Ka'ats and the Winged Warriors, 5-119
  Star Man's Son, 5-120
  The Stars Are Ours, 5-121
  Storm over Warlock, 5-122
Norton, Roy
  The Vanishing Fleets, 14

Nourse, Alan E., 15-25
  Beyond Infinity, 3-298
  The Bladerunner, 5-123
  The Mercy Men, 5-124
  Star Surgeon, 5-125
  Tiger by the Tail and Other Science Fiction Stories, 3-298
Nowlan, Philip Francis
  Armageddon 2419 A.D., 2-83
Numa, Shōzō
  Kachikujin Yapū, 6-272

O'Brien, Fitz-James
  "The Diamond Lens," 10, 1-72
  "What Was It?," 1-72
O'Brien, Robert C.
  Mrs. Frisby and the Rats of NIMH, 5-126
  Z for Zachariah, 5-127
Obruchev, Vladimir
  Plutoniia, 442
Odle, E. V.
  The Clockwork Man, 2-84
O'Duffy, Eimar
  The Spacious Adventures of the Man in the Street, 2-85
O'Donnell, K. M. See Malzberg, Barry N.
O'Donnell, Kevin, Jr.
  Mayflies, 4-402
  ORA:CLE, 4-403
O'Donnell, Lawrence. See Kuttner, Henry; Moore, C. L.
Offutt, Andrew J.
  The Galactic Rejects, 5-128
Ōhara, Mariko
  Ningen no Yō ni Aruita Neko, 6-273
Okunev, Iakov
  Griaduschii mir, 445
Olander, Joseph D.
  Arthur C. Clarke, 10-40
  The End of the World (Rabkin), 9-79
  Isaac Asimov, 10-11
  Mysterious Visions (Waugh), 3-460
  No Place Else (Rabkin), 9-80
  No Room for Man (Clem), 13-23
  Philip K. Dick (Greenberg), 10-55
  Ray Bradbury (Greenberg), 10-24
  Robert A. Heinlein, 10-72
  School and Society through Science Fiction, 13-33
  Science Fiction of the Fifties (Greenberg), 3-452
  Science Fiction of the Forties (Pohl), 3-452
  Ursula K. Le Guin, 10-94
Oliver, Chad
  Another Kind, 3-299

The Edge of Forever, 3-300
Mists of Dawn, 5-129
Shadows in the Sun, 3-301
Ollier, Claude
La Vie sur Epsilon, 6-128
Onderdonk, Matthew, 15-79
O'Neill, Joseph
Day of Wrath, 2-86
Land Under England, 2-86
Onions, Oliver
The New Moon, 2-87
Opriţă, Mircea
Figurine de ceară, 6-454
H. G. Wells. Utopia modernă, 6-465
O'Reilly, Timothy
Frank Herbert, 10-78
Orwell, George, 10-115, 10-116, 10-117,
15-46
Nineteen Eighty-Four, 3-302
Oshikawa, Shunrō, 477
Kaitei Gunkan, 6-274
Ōtomo, Katsuhiro
Dōmu, 6-275

Pachter, Josh
Top Science Fiction, 3-448
Padgett, Lewis. *See* Kuttner, Henry
Pagetti, Carlo
Il Senso del Futuro, 6-337
Paine, Albert Bigelow
The Great White Way, 17
The Mystery of Evelin Delorme, 11
Pal, George, 11-29, 15-52
Paleo, Lyn
Uranian Worlds (Garber), 8-23
Worlds Apart (De Carnin), 4-649
Pallander, Edwin
Adventures of a Micro-Man, 2-60
Pallen, Condé B.
Crucible Island, 59
Palmer, David R.
Emergence, 4-404
Palmer, Jane
The Watcher, 4-405
Palmer, John
The Hesperides, 2-88
Paltock, Robert
The Life and Adventures of Peter Wilkins, 7, 1-73
Palumbo, Donald
Eros in the Mind's Eye, 9-70
Erotic Universe, 9-116
Pangborn, Edgar, 10-118, 15-25
The Company of Glory, 3-303
Davy, 3-303
A Mirror for Observers, 3-304
Still I Persist in Wondering, 3-303

West of the Sun, 3-305
Panshin, Alexei, 15-36
Heinlein in Dimension, 10-73
Rite of Passage, 4-406, 15-58
SF in Dimension, 9-71
The World Beyond the Hill, 9-71
Panshin, Cory
SF in Dimension, 9-71
Pantell, Dora
Miss Pickerell on the Moon, 5-104
Parish, James Robert
The Great Science Fiction Pictures, 11-19
Parker, Helen N.
Biological Themes in Modern Science Fiction, 9-72
Parker, Richard
The Hendon Fungus, 5-130
Parkinson, H. F.
They Shall Not Die, 2-89
Parling, Nils
Korset, 6-371
Parnell, Frank H.
Monthly Terrors, 14-8
Parnov, Eremei
World Soul (Emtsev), 3-154
Parrinder, Patrick
H. G. Wells, 10-173, 10-174
Science Fiction: A Critical Guide, 9-73
Science Fiction: Its Criticism and Teaching, 9-74, 13-6
Patchett, Mary E.
Adam Troy: Astroman, 5-131
Patrouch, Joseph F., Jr.
The Science Fiction of Isaac Asimov, 10-12
Paul, Frank R., 15-69A
Păun, Gheorghe
Sfera paralelă, 6-453
Pearce, Howard
Forms of the Fantastic (Hokenson), 9-115
The Scope of the Fantastic (Collins), 9-112
Peary, Danny
Cult Movies, 11-8
Omni's Screen Flights/Screen Fantasies, 11-33
Peck, Richard, 15-41
Pedler, Kit
Brainrack, 4-407
The Dynostar Menace, 4-407
Mutant 59, 4-407
Peeples, Sam, 15-52
Pelot, Pierre
Delirium circus, 6-129
Foetus-party, 6-130
Les Iles de Vacarme, 6-131

Transit, 6-132
Peplow, Michael W.
    Samuel R. Delany, 10-50
Percy, Walker
    Love in the Ruins, 4-408
Perlmutter, William
    The Endless Pavement (Jackson), 5-81
Perret, Patti
    The Faces of Science Fiction, 12-28
Pesek, Ludek
    The Earth Is Near, 4-409, 5-132
    Trap for Perseus, 4-410, 5-133
Pestriniero, Renato
    Sette Accadimenti in Venezia, 6-320
Pettigrew, Jean
    L'Année de la science-fiction et du
        fantastique Québécois, 6-193
Philips, Michael
    Philosophy and Science Fiction, 13-32
Phillips, Mark
    Brain Twister, 3-306
    The Impossibles, 3-306
    Supermind, 3-306
Phillpotts, Eden
    Address Unknown, 2-90
    Number 87, 2-90
    Saurus, 2-90
Philmus, Robert M.
    H. G. Wells and Modern Science Fiction
        (Suvin), 10-175
    Into the Unknown, 9-75
Piegai, Daniela
    Ballata per Lima, 6-321
Pieratt, Asa B.
    Kurt Vonnegut, 10-160
Pierce, Hazel Beasley
    A Literary Symbiosis, 9-76
    Philip K. Dick, 10-56
Piercy, Marge
    Woman on the Edge of Time, 4-411
Pihač, Branko
    "Problem," 6-472
Piller, Emanuel S.
    The World Aflame (Engel), 3-155
Pilo, Gianni
    Catalogo Generale della Fantascienza in
        Italia, 6-338
Piper, H. Beam, 10-119
    Federation, 3-307
    Fuzzies and Other People, 3-308
    Fuzzy Sapiens, 3-308
    Little Fuzzy, 3-308
    The Other Human Race, 3-308
Piserchia, Doris
    Earthchild, 4-412
    Mister Justice, 4-413
    Star Rider, 4-412
Pitts, Michael R.

The Great Science Fiction Pictures, 11-
    19
Platt, Charles
    Dream Makers, 10-200
    Dream Makers II, 10-201
    Who Writes Science Fiction?, 10-200
Poe, Edgar Allan, 15-75
    "The Balloon Hoax," 1-75
    "The Black Cat," 10
    "The Conversation of Eiros and
        Charmion," 1-75
    "The Facts in the Case of M.
        Waldemar," 1-75
    "Mellonta Tauta," 1-75
    "MS Found in a Bottle," 1-75
    The Narrative of Arthur Gordon Pym
        of Nantucket, 9, 1-74
    "The Tell-Tale Heart," 10
    "The Unparalleled Adventures of One
        Hans Pfaall," 6, 1-75
    "William Wilson," 1-75
Pohl, Frederik, 10-120, 15-3, 15-34, 15-55
    The Annals of the Heechee, 4-415
    The Best of Frederik Pohl, 3-309
    Beyond the Blue Event Horizon, 4-415
    The Coming of the Quantum Cats, 4-
        414
    Drunkard's Walk, 3-310
    The Expert Dreamers, 3-451
    Galaxy Magazine, 3-436
    Gateway, 4-415
    Gladiator-at-Law, 3-311
    Heechee Rendezvous, 4-415
    JEM, 4-416
    Man Plus, 4-417
    The Merchant's War, 3-313
    Midas World, 4-418
    Not This August (Kornbluth), 3-239
    Preferred Risk (McCann), 3-275A
    Science Fiction of the Forties, 3-452
    Science Fiction Studies in Film, 11-20
    Slave Ship, 3-312
    The Space Merchants, 3-313
    Star Science Fiction Stories, 3-453
    Starburst, 4-419
    Time Waits for Winthrop and Four
        Other Short Novels from Galaxy, 3-
        436
    The Way the Future Was, 10-120
    Wolfbane, 3-314
    The Years of the City, 4-420
Pohl, Frederik IV
    Science Fiction Studies in Film, 11-20
Polak, Frederick
    The Image of the Future, 58
Pope, Gustavus W.
    Journey to Mars, 1-76
    Wonderful Adventures on Venus, 18

Porges, Irwin
  Edgar Rice Burroughs, 10-35
Porjes, Michael, 15-52
Porush, David
  The Soft Machine, 9-77
Potter, Robert R.
  Beyond Time and Space, 13-34
Pournelle, Jerry
  Clan and Crown, 4-421
  The Endless Frontier, 4-662
  Far Frontiers, 4-662
  Footfall (Niven), 4-396
  Janissaries, 4-421
  Lucifer's Hammer (Niven), 4-397
  The Mercenary, 4-421
  The Mote in God's Eye (Niven), 4-398
  Oath of Fealty (Niven), 4-399
  There Will Be War, 4-663
  West of Honor, 4-421
Powers, Richard
  Spacetimewarp, 12-29
Powers, Tim
  The Anubis Gates, 4-422
  Dinner at Deviant's Palace, 4-423
Pragnell, Festus
  The Green Man of Graypec, 53
  The Green Man of Kilsona, 53
Pratchett, Terry
  Strata, 4-424
Pratt, Fletcher
  The Castle of Iron (de Camp), 3-134
  The Compleat Enchanter (de Camp), 3-134
  The Incomplete Enchanter (de Camp), 3-134
  Wall of Serpents (de Camp), 3-134
Preuss, Paul
  Broken Symmetries, 4-425
  Human Error, 4-426
Price, E. Hoffman, 15-29, 15-42
Priest, Christopher, 15-54, 15-61
  The Affirmation, 4-427
  Darkening Island, 4-428
  Fugue for a Darkening Island, 4-428
  The Glamour, 4-429
  An Infinite Summer, 4-430
  Inverted World, 4-431
Pringle, David
  Earth Is the Alien Planet, 10-15
  Interzone: The First Anthology, 4-643
  J. G. Ballard, 10-16
  J. G. Ballard (Goddard), 10-14
  Science Fiction: The 100 Best Novels, 9-78, 13-7
Prokop, Gert
  Wer stiehlt schon Unterschenkel?, 6-24
Pronzini, Bill
  Bug-Eyed Monsters, 3-454

Dark Sins, Dark Dreams (Malzberg), 3-460
The End of Summer (Malzberg), 3-452
Prosperi, Piero
  Autocrisi, 6-322
Prosser, H. L., 15-52
Proumen, Henri-Jacques
  Le Sceptre volé aux hommes, 6-422
PUBLISHING OF SF, 585–588, 9-34
Purdom, Tom, 15-41
Pynchon, Thomas
  Gravity's Rainbow, 4-432

Qvarnström, Gunnar
  Dikten och den nya vetenskapen, 6-375

Rabkin, Eric S.
  Arthur C. Clarke, 10-41
  The End of the World, 9-79
  Hard Science Fiction (Slusser), 9-118
  No Place Else, 9-80
  Science Fiction: A Historical Anthology, 13-35
  Science Fiction: History-Science-Vision (Scholes), 9-90, 13-9
  Shadows of the Magic Lamp (Slusser), 11-35
Raes, Hugo
  De lotgevallen, 6-407
  Reizigers in de anti-tijd, 6-407, 6-432
  De verwoesting van Hyperion, 6-408
Raknem, Ingvald
  H. G. Wells and His Critics, 10-163
Rand, Ayn
  Anthem, 3-315
  Atlas Shrugged, 3-316
Randall, Florence Engel
  A Watcher in the Woods, 5-134
Randall, Marta
  Islands, 4-433
  Journey, 4-434
  New Dimensions, 4-664
Rank, Heiner
  Die Ohnmacht der Allmächtigen, 6-25
Ransom, Bill
  The Jesus Incident (Herbert), 4-267
  The Lazarus Effect (Herbert), 4-267
Ray, Jean
  Le Carrousel des Maléfices, 6-423
  Malpertuis, 6-133
Read, Herbert
  The Green Child, 2-91
  Reason and Romanticism, 2-91
Reamy, Tom
  Blind Voices, 4-435
RECORDINGS, 719–720

Reed, Kit
Armed Camps, 4-436
The Killer Mice, 4-436
Other Stories, and the Attack of the Giant Baby, 4-436
The Revenge of the Senior Citizens ∗∗ Plus, 4-436
Reeve, Arthur B., 21
The Silent Bullet, 1-77
Reginald, R.
Ancestral Voices (Menville), 1-62
Futurevision (Menville), 11-15
Science Fiction and Fantasy Literature, . 8-1
Science Fiction and Fantasy Literature: A Supplement, 1975–1986, 8-1
Things to Come (Menville), 11-14
The Work of Julian May (Dikty), 10-109
Rehn, Jens
Die Kinder des Saturn, 6-26
Reilly, Robert
The Transcendent Adventure, 9-81
Reinsma, Riemer
Van hoop naar waarschuwing, 6-415
Rémy, Ada
La Maison du cygne, 6-134
Rémy, Yves
La Maison du cygne, 6-134
Renard, Christine
Le Temps des cerises, 6-135
Renard, Maurice, 409
Blind Circle, 2-92
Le Péril bleu, 6-136
Resnick, Mike
Santiago, 4-437
Restif de la Bretonne
La Découverte australe, 406
Les Posthumes, 406
REVIEWING, BOOK, 588–590
Reynolds, Alfred
Kiteman of Karanga, 5-135
Reynolds, Mack, 10-121
After Utopia, 4-439
The Best of Mack Reynolds, 3-317
Chaos in Lagrangia, 4-438
Commune 2000, 4-439
Equality in the Year 2000, 4-439
Lagrange Five, 4-438
The Lagrangists, 4-438
Looking Backward from the Year 2000, 4-439
Perchance to Dream, 4-439
Rolltown, 4-439
The Towers of Utopia, 4-439
Trojan Orbit, 4-438
Reynolds, Quentin
The Fiction Factóry, 721
Rhodes, William H.

Caxton's Book, 15, 1-78
Rickman, Gregg
Philip K. Dick: In His Own Words, 10-57
Philip K. Dick: The Last Testament, 10-57
Riley, Dick
Critical Encounters, 9-82, 13-8
Riley, Frank
The Forever Machine (Clifton), 3-113
They'd Rather Be Right (Clifton), 3-113
Ringdahl, Roar
"Norsk science fiction fandom," 6-398
Ritter, Claus
Anno Utopia oder So var die Zukunft, 6-46
Kampf um Utopolis, 6-46
Start nach Utopolis, 6-46
Roberts, Keith
The Chalk Giants, 4-440
The Grain Kings, 4-442
Kiteworld, 4-441
Ladies from Hell, 4-442
The Lordly Ones, 4-442
Machines and Men, 4-442
Molly Zero, 4-443
Pavane, 4-444
Robertson, E. Arnot
Three Came Unarmed, 2-93
Robida, Albert
Le Vingitième siècle, 6-137
Robinson, Frank M.
The Power, 3-318
Robinson, Jeanne
Stardance, 4-449
Robinson, Kim Stanley
Icehenge, 4-445
The Memory of Whiteness, 4-446
The Novels of Philip K. Dick, 10-58
The Wild Shore, 4-447
Robinson, Spider
Callahan's Crosstime Saloon, 4-448
Callahan's Secret, 4-448
Stardance, 4-449
Time Travelers Strictly Cash, 4-448
Rockwood, Roy
Through the Air to the North Pole, 5-136
Roemer, Kenneth M.
The Obsolete Necessity, 8-54
Roger, Noëlle
The New Adam, 2-94
Rogers, Alva
Requiem for Astounding, 14-15
Rogoz, Adrian
Pretul secant al genunii, 6-456
Rohan, Mike Scott
Run to the Stars, 4-450

Rohmer, Sax, 15-50, 15-88
Rose, Mark
  Alien Encounters, 9-83
  Bridges to Science Fiction (Slusser), 9-117
  Science Fiction: A Collection of Critical Essays, 9-84
Rosheim, David L.
  Galaxy Magazine, 14-16
Roshwald, Mordecai
  Level 7, 3-319
Rosinski, Natalie M.
  Feminist Futures, 9-85
Rosny aîné, J. H., 56, 408
  The Death of the Earth, 1-79
  L'Etonnant voyage de Hareton Ironcastle, 2-95
  La Force mystérieuse, 6-138
  The Giant Cat, 2-95
  Ironcastle, 2-95
  Les Navigateurs de l'infini, 6-139
  Quest for Fire, 1-79, 2-95
  Quest of the Dawn Man, 2-95
  Récits de science fiction, 6-140
  The Xiphéhuz, 1-79
Rotsler, William
  Patron of the Arts, 4-451
Rottensteiner, Franz
  The Science Fiction Book, 9-86
  View from Another Shore, 4-661
Rovin, Jeff
  A Pictorial History of Science Fiction Films, 11-17
Rucker, Rudy
  The 57th Franz Kafka, 4-452
  The Secret of Life, 4-454
  The Sex Sphere, 4-454
  Software, 4-453
  White Light, 4-454
Ruellan, André
  Aux armes d'Ortog (Steiner), 6-148
  Brebis galeuses (Steiner), 6-147
  Les Chiens, 6-141
  Ortog et les ténèbres (Steiner), 6-148
  Un Passe-temps (Steiner), 6-149
  Le 32 Juillet (Steiner), 6-150
  Tunnel, 6-142
Rullkoetter, Bernd
  Die Wissenschaftliche Phantastik der Sowjetunion, 6-47
Ruppert, Peter
  Reader in a Strange Land, 8-55
Rus, Zofija
  "Dobri stari svijet," 6-473
Russ, Joanna, 15-36
  The Adventures of Alyx, 4-455
  Alyx, 4-455
  And Chaos Died, 4-456

Extra(ordinary) People, 4-457
  The Female Man, 4-458
  Picnic on Paradise, 4-455
  The Two of Them, 4-455
Russell, Alan K.
  Science Fiction by the Rivals of H. G. Wells, 1-80
Russell, Bertrand
  Icarus, 54
  Nightmares of Eminent Persons and Other Stories, 3-320
Russell, Eric Frank, 10-122, 15-57, 15-65, 15-70
  The Great Explosion, 3-321
  Men, Martians, and Machines, 3-322
  Sinister Barrier, 3-323
  Wasp, 3-324
Russell, George William
  The Avatars, 60
Russen, David
  Iter Lunare, 6
Russo, Luigi
  La Fantascienza e la Critica, 6-339
Ruyslinck, Ward
  The Reservation, 6-409
Ryan, Alan
  Perpetual Light, 4-665
Ryan, Thomas J.
  The Adolescence of P-1, 4-459

Saberhagen, Fred
  Berserker, 4-460
  Berserker Base, 4-460
  Berserker: Blue Death, 4-460
  Berserker Man, 4-460
  The Berserker Throne, 4-460
  The Berserker Wars, 4-460
  Berserker's Planet, 4-460
  Brother Assassin, 4-460
  Brother Berserker, 4-460
  A Century of Progress, 4-461
  Earth Descended, 4-460
  Octagon, 4-462
  The Ultimate Enemy, 4-460
Sadler, Frank
  The Unified Ring, 9-87
Sadoul, Jacques
  Histoire de la science-fiction moderne, 6-194
  2000 A.D., 12-30
Sagan, Carl
  Contact, 4-463
Saha, Arthur W.
  The 1986 Annual World's Best SF (Wollheim), 4-672
St. Clair, Margaret, 10-123, 15-8

Change the Sky and Other Stories, 3-325
Sign of the Labrys, 3-326
St. John, J. Allen, 15-71
Salgari, Emilio
  Le Meraviglie del Duemila, 6-323
Sallis, James
  A Few Last Words, 4-464
Sampson, Robert
  Yesterday's Faces, 14-17
Samuelson, David
  Arthur C. Clarke, 10-42
  Visions of Tomorrow, 9-88
Sanborn, Robin
  The Book of Stier, 4-465
Sanders, Joseph L.
  E. E. "Doc" Smith, 10-137
  Roger Zelazny, 10-186
Sanders, Lawrence
  The Tomorrow File, 4-466
Sanders, Scott Russell
  Terrarium, 4-467
Sandrelli, Sandro
  Caino dello Spazio, 6-324
Sandt, Emil
  Cavete!, 6-27
Santesson, Hans Stefan
  Crime Prevention in the 30th Century, 3-460
Sapir, Richard Ben
  The Far Arena, 4-468
Sarban
  The Sound of His Horn, 3-327
Sargent, Lyman Tower
  British and American Utopian Literature 1516-1975, 8-54
Sargent, Pamela, 15-41
  Afterlives, 4-666
  The Alien Upstairs, 4-469
  Cloned Lives, 4-470
  Earthseed, 5-137
  The Golden Space, 4-471
  Venus of Dreams, 4-472
  Women of Wonder, 4-653
Satō, Haruo
  "Nonsharan Kiroku," 477, 6-276
Satty, Harvey
  Olaf Stapledon, 10-141
Saxton, Josephine
  The Power of Time, 4-473
  The Travails of Jane Saint and Other Stories, 4-475
Schatt, Stanley
  Kurt Vonnegut, Jr., 10-161
Schattschneider, Peter
  Singularitäten, 6-28
Scheerbart, Paul
  Die grosse Revolution, 6-29

Lesabèndio, 382
Scheirs, Jef
  Het Einde der Wereld, 546, 6-433
Schenck, Hilbert
  At the Eye of the Ocean, 4-476
  A Rose for Armageddon, 4-477
Schiøler, Carsten
  Dansk Science Fiction Indeks 1742–1976, 6-365
Schlee, Ann
  The Vandal, 5-138
Schlobin, Roger C.
  Andre Norton, 10-114
  The Literature of Fantasy, 8-49
  A Research Guide to Science Fiction Studies (Tymn), 8-21
  Urania's Daughters, 8-25
Schmidt, Arno
  The Egghead Republic, 383
  Kaff, auch Mare Crisium, 383
Schmidt, Stanley
  Lifeboat Earth, 4-478
  The Sins of the Fathers, 4-478
Schmitz, James H.
  The Lion Game, 3-328
  The Telzey Toy, 3-328
  The Universe against Her, 3-328
  The Witches of Karres, 3-329
Schochet, Victoria
  The Berkley Showcase, 4-667
Scholes, Robert
  Science Fiction: History-Science-Vision, 9-90
  Structural Fabulation, 9-89
Scholz, Carter
  Palimpsests, 4-479
Schomburg, Alex
  Chroma (Gustafson), 12-21
Schow, David J.
  The Outer Limits, 11-34
Schulman, Paul H.
  Fantastic Television (Gerani), 11-27
Schumann, Marta
  Våge å tenkje, 541
Schweitzer, Darrell
  Discovering Stephen King, 10-85
  On Writing Science Fiction (Scithers), 13-18
  Science Fiction Voices #1, 10-196
  Science Fiction Voices #5, 10-197
Schwonke, Martin
  Vom Staatsroman zur Science Fiction, 6-48
Science Fiction Writers of America
  Writing and Selling Science Fiction, 13-17
SF Yearbook of Japan Editorial Committee
  Nihon SF Nenkan, 6-304

Scithers, George H.
  On Writing Science Fiction, 13-18
Scott, Jody
  I, Vampire, 4-480
  Passing for Human, 4-480
Scrymsour, Ella
  The Perfect World, 2-96
Seaborn, Adam
  Symzonia, 7, 1-81
Searles, Baird
  A Reader's Guide to Science Fiction, 8-31
Sellin, Bernard
  The Life and Works of David Lindsay, 10-101
Sellings, Arthur, 15-61
  Junk Day, 4-481
  The Long Eureka, 3-330
  The Silent Speakers, 3-331
  Telepath, 3-331
  The Uncensored Man, 3-332
Sériel, Jérome
  Le Sub-espace, 6-143
Serling, Rod
  More Stories from the Twilight Zone, 3-333
  New Stories from the Twilight Zone, 3-333
  Stories from the Twilight Zone, 3-333
Serviss, Garrett P.
  The Second Deluge, 1-83
Severn, David
  The Future Took Us, 5-139
Shanks, Edward
  The People of the Ruins, 2-97
Shaw, Bob, 15-61
  Ground Zero Man, 4-485
  Orbitsville, 4-482
  Orbitsville Departure, 4-482
  Other Days, Other Eyes, 4-483
  The Palace of Eternity, 4-484
  The Peace Machine, 4-485
  The Ragged Astronauts, 4-486
  The Two-Timers, 4-487
  Vertigo, 4-488
  Who Goes Here?, 4-489
Shaw, George Bernard
  Back to Methuselah, 60, 2-98
Shcherbatov, Mikhail
  Puteshestvie v zemliu Ofirskuiu, 441
Shea, Michael
  A Quest for Simbilis, 3-380
Shea, Robert
  Illuminatus!, 4-490
Sheckley, Robert, 15-55
  After the Fall, 4-668
  Can You Feel Anything When I Do This?, 4-492

Citizen in Space, 3-334
Dimension of Miracles, 4-491
Dramocles, 4-491
Immortality Delivered, 3-335
Immortality, Inc., 3-335
Is That What People Do?, 4-492
Journey beyond Tomorrow, 3-336
Notions: Unlimited, 3-337
Options, 4-491
The People Trap, 4-492
Pilgrimage to Earth, 3-338
The Robot Who Looked Like Me, 4-492
The Same to You Doubled, 4-492
Untouched by Human Hands, 3-339
The Wonderful World of Robert Scheckley, 4-492
Sheffield, Charles
  Between the Strokes of Night, 4-493
  Hidden Variables, 4-494
  The McAndrew Chronicles, 4-494
  Sight of Proteus, 4-495
  The Web between the Worlds, 4-496
Shelley, Mary, 10-125, 10-126, 10-127, 10-128, 10-129, 10-130
  Frankenstein, 9, 1-84
  The Last Man, 9, 1-85
Shepard, Lucius
  Green Eyes, 4-497
Sherred, T. L., 15-19
  First Person, Peculiar, 3-340
Sherriff, R. C.
  The Cataclysm, 3-341
  The Hopkins Manuscript, 3-341
Sherwin, Mary
  The New Visions, 12-31
Shiel, M. P., 10-131
  The Young Men Are Coming!, 52, 2-99
Shipman, David
  A Pictorial History of Science Fiction Films, 11-21
Shiras, Wilmar H.
  Children of the Atom, 3-342
Shirley, John
  Eclipse, 4-498
  Three-Ring Psychus, 4-499
Shute, Nevil
  In the Wet, 3-343
  On the Beach, 3-344
Siegel, Mark
  James Tiptree, Jr., 10-147
Silverberg, Robert, 10-132, 10-133, 15-3, 15-34, 15-45
  Across a Billion Years, 5-140
  The Arbor House Treasury of Great Science Fiction Short Novels, 3-457
  The Arbor House Treasury of Modern Science Fiction, 3-457

The Arbor House Treasury of Science
 Fiction Masterpieces, 3-457
Beyond the Safe Zone, 4-500
Born with the Dead, 4-500
The Conglomeroid Cocktail Party, 4-500
Downward to the Earth, 4-501
Dying Inside, 4-502
The Feast of St. Dionysus, 4-500
The Gate of Worlds, 5-141
Hawksbill Station, 4-503
The Masks of Time, 4-504
The Mirror of Infinity, 13-37
Moonferns and Starsongs, 4-500
New Dimensions (Randall), 4-664
Nightwings, 4-505
The Reality Trip and Other
 Implausibilities, 4-500
Science Fiction Hall of Fame, 3-455
The Second Trip, 4-506
Son of Man, 4-507
Star of Gypsies, 4-508
The Stochastic Man, 4-502
Thorns, 4-509
A Time of Changes, 4-510
Time of the Great Freeze, 5-142
Tom o'Bedlam, 4-511
Tower of Glass, 4-504
Up the Line, 4-512
Vornan-19, 4-504
The World Inside, 4-513
Simak, Clifford D., 10-134, 15-3, 15-29,
 15-55
All Flesh Is Grass, 3-350
A Choice of Gods, 4-514
City, 3-345
First He Died, 3-347
The Marathon Photograph and Other
 Stories, 4-515
Project Pope, 4-516
Ring around the Sun, 3-346
Time and Again, 3-347
Time Is the Simplest Thing, 3-348
The Visitors, 4-517
Way Station, 3-349
The World of Clifford Simak, 3-350
Sinclair, Upton
The Millennium, 2-100
Singer, Melissa
The Berkley Showcase (Schochet), 4-667
Singh, Kirpal
The Stellar Gauge (Tolley), 9-99
Siodmak, Curt, 57, 15-25
Donovan's Brain, 3-351
F.P.1. Does Not Reply, 2-101
Hauser's Memory, 3-351
Skal, David J.
When We Were Good, 4-518
Skinner, B. F.

Walden Two, 3-352
Sladek, John T., 15-45
Alien Accounts, 4-519
Keep the Giraffe Burning, 4-519
The Lunatics of Terra, 4-519
Mechasm, 4-521
The Müller-Fokker Effect, 4-520
The Reproductive System, 4-521
Roderick, 4-522
Roderick at Random, 4-522
The Steam-Driven Boy and Other
 Strangers, 4-519
Tik-Tok, 4-523
Sleator, William
House of Stairs, 5-143
Singularity, 5-144
Sloane, William
The Edge of Running Water, 2-102
To Walk the Night, 2-102
Slobodkin, Louis
Round Trip Space Ship, 5-145
The Space Ship in the Park, 5-145
The Space Ship Returns to the Apple
 Tree, 5-145
The Space Ship under the Apple Tree,
 5-145
The Three-Seated Space Ship, 5-145
Slusser, George Edgar
The Bradbury Chronicles, 10-27
Bridges to Science Fiction, 9-117
The Classic Years of Robert A. Heinlein,
 10-74
The Delany Intersection, 10-51
The Farthest Shores of Ursula K. Le
 Guin, 10-95
Hard Science Fiction, 9-118
Harlan Ellison, 10-64
Robert A. Heinlein (Slusser), 10-75
Shadows of the Magic Lamp, 11-35
The Space Odysseys of Arthur C.
 Clarke, 10-43
Small, Christopher
Ariel Like a Harpy, 10-128
Mary Shelley's "Frankenstein," 10-128
Smith, Clark Ashton, 15-42, 15-75
"The Eternal World," 62
Zothique, 2-103
Smith, Cordwainer, 10-135
The Best of Cordwainer Smith, 3-354
Norstrilia, 3-353
The Planet Buyer, 3-353
Space Lords, 3-354
The Underpeople, 3-353
You Will Never Be the Same, 3-354
Smith, Curtis C.
Olaf Stapledon (Satty), 10-141
Twentieth-Century Science-Fiction Writ-
 ers, 8-32

Smith, E. E., 10-136, 10-137, 15-55, 15-70, 15-91
 Children of the Lens, 3-355
 First Lensman, 3-355
 Gray Lensman, 3-355
 The Lensmen Series, 3-355
 Second Stage Lensman, 3-355
 The Skylark of Space, 2-104
 Triplanetary, 3-355
 The Vortex Blaster, 3-355
Smith, Ernest Bramah, 15-46
Smith, Garret
 Between Worlds, 2-105
Smith, George O.
 The Brain Machine, 3-356
 The Complete Venus Equilateral, 3-357
 The Fourth "R," 3-356
 Venus Equilateral, 3-357
Smith, Martin Cruz
 The Indians Won, 4-524
Smith, Nicholas D.
 Philosophers Look at Science Fiction, 13-32
 Thought Probes (Miller), 13-32
Smith, Wayland
 The Machine Stops, 2-106
Snegov, Sergei
 Liudi kak bogi, 449, 6-210
Snell, Edmund
 Kontrol, 2-107
Snyder, Zilpha Keatley
 And All Between, 5-146
 Below the Root, 5-146
 Until the Celebration, 5-146
Sobchack, Vivian
 The Limits of Infinity, 11-36
 Screening Space, 11-36
Sokolov, O.
 Mir "Iskatelia," 6-222
Soldati, Mario
 Lo Smeraldo, 6-325
Solmi, Sergio
 Della Favola, del Viaggio e di Altre Cose, 6-340
 Saggi sul Fantastico, 6-340
Solzhenitsyn, Aleksandr
 Candle in the Wind, 3-357A
 Sveča na vetru, 3-357A
Somer, John
 The Vonnegut Statement (Klinkowitz), 10-157
Spaink, A.
 Fantasfeer, 6-416
Spann, Sylvia
 Thematic Units in Teaching English and the Humanities, 13-10
Spinrad, Norman
 Bug Jack Barron, 4-525

Child of Fortune, 4-526
The Iron Dream, 4-527
The Last Hurrah of the Golden Horde, 4-528
Modern Science Fiction, 13-38
No Direction Home, 4-528
Songs from the Stars, 4-529
The Star-Spangled Future, 4-528
Staying Alive, 13-19
The Void Captain's Tale, 4-530
A World Between, 4-531
Spitz, Jacques, 409
 La Guerre des mouches, 6-144
 L'Homme élastique, 6-145
 L'Oeil du purgatoire, 6-146
Spivack, Charlotte
 Ursula K. Le Guin, 10-96
Squire, J. C.
 If, 2-108
Stableford, Brian M., 15-24, 15-61
 A Clash of Symbols, 10-19
 Man in a Cage, 4-532
 Masters of Science Fiction, 9-92
 The Science in Science Fiction (Nicholls), 9-68
 Scientific Romance in Britain 1890–1950, 9-93
 The Third Millennium, 4-534
 The Walking Shadow, 4-533
Stahl, Henric
 Un român în lună, 6-457
Staicar, Tom
 Critical Encounters II, 9-94
 The Feminine Eye, 9-95
 Fritz Leiber, 10-98
Stansky, Peter
 Nineteen Eighty-Four, 10-117
Stapledon, Olaf, 61, 10-138, 10-139, 10-140, 10-141, 10-142, 15-46, 15-55, 15-62, 15-88
 Far Future Calling, 10-142
 Last and First Men, 2-109
 Nebula Maker, 2-112
 Odd John, 2-110
 Sirius, 2-111
 Star Maker, 2-112
"STAR TREK," 213, 15-29
Steele, Linda
 Ibis, 4-535
Steiner, Kurt
 Aux armes d'Ortog, 6-148
 Brebis galeuses, 6-147
 Ortog, 6-148
 Ortog et les ténèbres, 6-148
 Un Passe-temps, 6-149
 Le 32 Juillet, 6-150
Steinmüller, Angela

Der Traum vom Grossen Roten Fleck, 6-30

Steinmüller, Karlheinz
Der Traum vom Grossen Roten Fleck, 6-30

Stephan, Bernard
Mouvance (Milesi), 6-175

Stephensen-Payne, Phil
Eric Frank Russell, 10-122
John Wyndham Parkes Lucas Benyon Harris, 10-183

Stephenson, Andrew M.
The Wall of Years, 4-536

Sterling, Bruce
The Artificial Kid, 4-537
Mirrorshades, 4-669
Schismatrix, 4-538

Sternberg, Jacques, 411
Future without Future, 6-424
La Sortie est au fond de l'espace, 6-151

Stevens, Francis
The Heads of Cerberus, 2-113

Stevenson, Robert Louis
The Strange Case of Dr. Jekyll and Mr. Hyde, 1-86

Stewart, George R.
Earth Abides, 3-358

Stiegler, Marc
Valentina, 4-163

Stine, Hank
Season of the Witch, 4-539

Stock, Stuart H.
Twenty All-Time Great Science Fiction Films (Von Gunden), 11-40

Stockton, Frank
The Great Stone of Sardis, 1-87
The Great War Syndicate, 14, 1-88

Stoker, Bram, 15-75

Stolze, Pierre
Marilyn Monroe et les samouraïs du Père Noël, 6-152

Stone, Josephine Rector
The Mudhead, 5-147
Praise All the Moons of Morning, 5-148

Stong, Phil
The Other Worlds, 3-458

Stoutenburg, Adrien
Out There, 5-149

Stover, Leon E.
Apeman, Spaceman, 3-459

Strauss, Irwin S.
The MIT Science Fiction Society's Index to the SF Magazines, 1951–1965, 14-9

Strete, Craig
The Bleeding Man and Other Science Fiction Stories, 5-150

Strick, Philip
Science Fiction Movies, 11-22

Strickland, A. W.
A Reference Guide to American Science Fiction Films, 11-7

Strickland, Brad, 15-14

Strobl, Hans
Der Orchideengarten, 531

Strøm, Ola
"Science fiction av norske forfattere," 6-399

Strugatskii, Arkadii and Boris, 449–452
Beetle in the Anthill, 4-540
Definitely Maybe, 4-541
Noon: 22nd Century, 4-670
Roadside Picnic & The Tale of the Troika, 4-542
The Snail on the Slope, 4-543
Strana bagrovykh tuch, 6-211
The Time Wanderers, 6-212
The Ugly Swans, 4-544
Volny gasiat veter, 6-212

Stuart, Don A. *See* Campbell, John W., Jr.

Sturgeon, Theodore, 10-143, 10-144, 10-145, 15-55
Aliens 4, 3-359
The Dreaming Jewels, 3-360
E Pluribus Unicorn, 3-361
Godbody, 4-545
More Than Human, 3-362
New Soviet Science Fiction, 4-670
Not Without Sorcery, 3-366
The Synthetic Man, 3-360
Thunder and Roses, 3-365
A Touch of Strange, 3-363
Venus Plus X, 3-364
A Way Home, 3-365
Without Sorcery, 3-366

Sucharitkul, Somtow
The Aquiliad, 4-546
The Darkling Wind, 4-547
Light on the Sound, 4-547
Mallworld, 4-548
Starship and Haiku, 4-549
The Throne of Madness, 4-547
Utopia Hunters, 4-547

Suddaby, Donald
Village Fanfare, 5-151

Sullivan, Jack
The Penguin Encyclopedia of Horror and the Supernatural, 8-50

Summers, Ian
Barlowe's Guide to Extraterrestrials (Barlowe), 12-2
Di Fate's Catalog of Science Fiction Hardware (Di Fate), 12-10
Tomorrow and Beyond, 12-32

SUPERNATURAL FICTION, 605–607

Sussman, Herbert L.
Victorians and the Machine, 9-96

Sutton, Jean
The Programmed Man, 5-153
Sutton, Jeff, 15-5
Beyond Apollo, 5-152
The Programmed Man, 5-153
Suvin, Darko
"A Bibliography of General Bibliographies of SF Literature," (Žantovská-Murray), 6-231
H. G. Wells and Modern Science Fiction, 10-175
Metamorphoses of Science Fiction, 9-97
Other Worlds, Other Seas, 4-670
Russian Science Fiction 1956–1974, 6-230
Victorian Science Fiction in the UK, 9-98
Suzuki, Izumi
Onna to Onna no Yo no Naka ni, 6-277
Swanwick, Michael
In the Drift, 4-550
Swayne, Martin
The Blue Germ, 2-114
Swiatek, Erik H.
Dansk Science Fiction Indeks 1742–1976 (Schiøler), 6-365
Elverhøj retur, 6-361
Swift, Jonathan
Gulliver's Travels, 1-89, 15-28
Swindells, Robert
Brother in the Land, 5-154
Symmes, John Cleves, 7

Taine, John, 54
Before the Dawn, 2-115
The Crystal Horde, 2-116
The Iron Star, 2-117
Seeds of Life, 2-117
The Time Stream, 2-118
White Lily, 2-116
Tanaka, Kōji
Daemetsubō, 6-278
Isei no Hito, 6-279
Tarde, Gabriel de
Underground Man, 1-90
Taylor, Robert Lewis
Adrift in a Boneyard, 3-367
Temple, William F.
The Four-sided Triangle, 3-368
Tenn, William, 10-146
The Human Angle, 3-369
Of All Possible Worlds, 3-370
Of Men and Monsters, 3-371
The Wooden Star, 3-372
Terrel, Denise
Actes du premier colloque international

de science-fiction de Nice (1983) (Emelina), 6-187
Actes du deuxième colloque international de science-fiction de Nice (1985) (Emelina), 6-188
Tevis, Walter S.
The Man Who Fell to Earth, 3-373
Mockingbird, 4-551
Steps of the Sun, 4-551
Tewen, San
SF, fantastique et ateliers créatifs (Goorden), 6-439
Tezeus, Konstantin
"Mudraci Saurije," 6-474
Thayer, Tiffany, 15-50
Thijssen, Felix, 546
Emmarg, 6-410
Pion, 6-411
Thiry, Marcel
Echec au temps, 6-425
Thole, Karel
Visionen des Unwirklichen, 12-33
Thomas, Bill
Keep Watching the Skies! (Warren), 11-3
Thomas, Louis-Vincent
Civilisations et divagations, 6-195
Thomas, Theodore L.
The Clone, 3-374
Thompson, Raymond H.
Gordon R. Dickson, 10-61
Thurston, Robert
Q Colony, 4-552
Tinker, Chauncey
The Crystal Button, 20
Tiptree, James, Jr., 10-147
Brightness Falls from the Air, 4-553
Out of the Everywhere and Other Extraordinary Visions, 4-554
Star Songs of an Old Primate, 4-554
The Starry Rift, 4-553
Ten Thousand Light Years from Home, 4-554
Up the Walls of the World, 4-555
Warm Worlds and Otherwise, 4-554
Titelman, Carol
The Art of Star Wars, 11-37
Tolkien, J. R. R.
Lord of the Rings, 212
Tolley, Michael J.
The Stellar Gauge, 9-99
Tolstoi, Aleksei
Aelita, 2-119, 444
The Death Box, 2-119, 444
The Garin Death Ray, 2-119, 444
Torgeson, Roy
Chrysalis, 4-671
Toubro, Michael

Topman, 6-357
Touponce, William F.
  Ray Bradbury and the Poetics of Reverie, 10-28
Townsend, John Rowe
  The Creatures, 5-155
  Noah's Castle, 5-156
  The Visitors, 5-157
Toyota, Aritsune
  Mongoru no Zankō, 6-280
  Taimu Surippu Daisensō, 481, 6-281
Train, Arthur Cheyney
  The Man Who Rocked the Earth, 14, 1-91
  The Moon Maker, 1-91
Train, Oswald, 15-41
Trimble, Bjo
  On the Good Ship Enterprise, 11-38
Tropp, Martin
  Mary Shelley's Monster, 10-129
Tsiolkovsky, Konstantin, 57, 442
  Beyond the Planet Earth, 2-120
  The Call of the Cosmos, 2-120
Tsutsui, Yasutaka, 479, 482
  Dassō to Tsuiseki no Samba, 6-282
  Kazoku Hakkei, 6-283
  Kyojin-tachi, 6-284
  Nihon SF Besutu Shūsei, 6-297
  Tōkaidō Sensō, 6-285
  Yonjūnhachioku Oku no Mōsō, 6-286
Tubb, E. C., 15-24, 15-54
  Gath, 4-556
  The Winds of Gath, 4-556
Tuck, Donald H., 15-57
  The Encyclopedia of Science Fiction and Fantasy through 1968, 8-7
Tucker, Wilson, 10-148
  The Long Loud Silence, 3-375
  Man from Tomorrow, 3-376
  Wild Talent, 3-376
  The Year of the Quiet Sun, 4-557
Tung, Lee
  The Wind Obeys Lama Toru, 4-558
Tuning, William
  Fuzzy Bones, 3-308
Turner, George
  Beloved Son, 4-559
  In the Heart or the Head, 9-100
  Vaneglory, 4-559
  Yesterday's Men, 4-559
Tuttle, Lisa
  Windhaven (Martin), 4-362
Twain, Mark. *See* Clemens, Samuel Langhorne
Tymn, Marshall B.
  Fantasy Literature, 8-51
  Horror Literature, 8-52
  Index to Stories in Thematic Anthologies of Science Fiction, 8-12
  A Research Guide to Science Fiction Studies, 8-21
  Science Fiction, Fantasy, and Weird Fiction Magazines, 14-18
  The Science Fiction Reference Book, 8-33
  The Year's Scholarship in Science Fiction and Fantasy, 8-17

Ulbrich, Bernd
  Der unsichtbare Kreis, 6-31
Underwood, Tim
  Fantasms (Levack), 10-149
  Fear Itself, 10-86
  Kingdom of Fear, 10-87
Unno, Jūza, 478
  Chikyū Tōnan, 6-287
Unsworth, Michael
  Future War Novels (Newman), 8-15
UTOPIAN LITERATURE, 607–608

Vale, Vane
  Re/Search No. 8/9: J. G. Ballard, 10-17
Vallejo, Boris
  The Fantastic Art of Boris Vallejo, 12-34
  Fantasy Art Techniques, 12-36
  Mirage, 12-35
Van Baelen, Kamiel
  De Oude Symphonie van ons Hart, 6-434
van Bruggen, Kees
  Het verstoode mierennest, 546
Van Brussel, Gust
  De Ring, 6-435
Vance, Jack, 10-149, 15-68, 15-69
  The Best of Jack Vance, 3-377
  The Blue World, 3-378
  Cugel's Saga, 3-380
  The Dragon Masters, 3-379
  The Dying Earth, 3-380
  Emphyrio, 4-560
  The Languages of Pao, 3-381
  The Last Castle, 4-561
  Rhialto the Marvelous, 3-380
  Vandals of the Void, 5-158
Van Eerde, John A.
  Jules Verne (Gallagher), 10-154
Van Greenaway, Peter
  graffiti, 4-562
Van Herp, Jacques
  Panorama de la science fiction, 6-196
Van Lhin, Eric
  Battle on Mercury, 5-159
Van Scyoc, Sydney J.

Bluesong, 4-564
Darkchild, 4-564
Daughters of the Sunstone, 4-564
Starsilk, 4-564
van Vogt, A. E., 15-8, 15-19, 15-52, 15-55
    The Anarchistic Colossus, 4-565
    Away and Beyond, 3-382
    The Battle of Forever, 4-566
    Cosmic Encounter, 4-567
    Mission: Interplanetary, 3-384
    Null-A Three, 3-386
    One Against Eternity, 3-385
    The Pawns of Null-A, 3-386
    Slan, 3-383
    The Voyage of the Space Beagle, 3-384
    The Weapon Makers, 3-385
    The Weapon Shops of Isher, 3-385
    The World of Null-A, 3-386
Varende, Yves
    Le Gadget de l'apocalypse, 6-426
Varley, John, 15-41, 15-90
    The Barbie Murders and Other Stories,
        4-570
    Demon, 4-571
    In the Hall of the Martian Kings, 4-570
    Millennium, 4-568
    The Ophiuchi Hotline, 4-569
    The Persistence of Vision, 4-570
    Titan, 4-571
    Wizard, 4-571
Veeder, William
    Mary Shelley & Frankenstein, 10-130
Veillot, Claude
    La Machine de Balmer, 6-153
Veinburg, B. P.
    "K dvukhdesiatitysiacheletiu nachala
        rabot po osushcheniiu okeanov," 445
Vercors
    Borderline, 3-388
    The Murder of the Missing Link, 3-388
    Sylva, 3-387
    You Shall Know Them, 3-388
Vermeulen, John
    De Binaire Joker, 6-437
Verne, Jules, 15, 406–408, 10-150, 10-151,
        10-152, 10-153, 10-154, 15-17, 15-55,
        15-95
    Adventures of Captain Hatteras, 1-92
    An Antarctic Mystery, 9
    Five Weeks in a Balloon, 15
    From the Earth to the Moon, 15, 16, 1-
        93
    A Journey to the Center of the Earth, 1-
        94
    Round the Moon, 16, 1-93
    Twenty Thousand Leagues under the
        Sea, 16, 1-95
Vernon, William

The Sound of Wonder (Lane), 10-199
Verrill, A. Hyatt, 53
Versins, Pierre
    Encyclopédie de l'utopie, des voyages
        extraordinaires et de la science-fiction,
        6-197
    Les Transhumains, 6-154
Vian, Boris, 409
    L'Automne à Pékin, 6-155
    L'Herbe rouge, 6-156
Vibe, Johan
    Fantastike fortællinger, 6-394
Vidal, Gore
    Kalki, 4-572
    Messiah, 3-389
    Visit to a Small Planet, 3-390
Viereck, George
    My First Two Thousand Years, 62
Villemur, Alain
    63 Auteurs, 6-198
Vinge, Joan D., 15-5
    Eyes of Amber and Other Stories, 4-573
    Fireship, 4-572
    Phoenix in the Ashes, 4-573
    Psion, 5-160
    The Snow Queen, 4-574
    World's End, 4-574
Vinge, Vernor
    Marooned in Real Time, 4-575
    The Peace War, 4-575
    True Names, 4-576
Vivian, E. Charles
    Star Dust, 2-121
Voiskunskii, Evgenii L'vovich
    Plesk zvezdnykh morei, 452, 6-213
Vol'f, Sergei Evgen'evich
    Zavtra utrom, za chaem, 452, 6-214
Volkoff, Vladimir
    Metro pour l'enfer, 6-157
Volodine, Antoine
    Biographie comparée de Jorian
        Murgrave, 6-158
    Le navire de nulle part, 6-158
Von Gunden, Kenneth
    Twenty All-Time Great Science Fiction
        Films, 11-40
von Hanstein, Otfrid, 57
    Electropolis, 2-122
von Harbou, Thea
    Metropolis, 2-133
    The Rocket to the Moon, 2-133
Vonnegut, Kurt, Jr., 10-155, 10-156, 10-
        157, 10-158, 10-159, 10-160, 10-161,
        15-55
    Canary in a Cat House, 3-394
    Cat's Cradle, 3-391
    Galapagos, 4-577
    Player Piano, 3-392

The Sirens of Titan, 3-393
Slaughterhouse-Five, 4-578
Utopia 14, 3-392
Welcome to the Monkey House, 3-394
Vroman, Leo
    Het carnarium, 6-412

Wagar, W. Warren
    H. G. Wells and the World State, 10-176
    Terminal Visions, 9-101
Waggoner, Diana
    The Hills of Faraway, 8-53
Wait, Froma Eunice
    Yermah the Dorado, 20
Waldrop, Howard
    Howard Who?, 4-579
    Them Bones, 4-579
Walker, Paul
    Speaking of Science Fiction, 10-198
Wallace, Ian
    Croyd, 4-580
    Deathstar Voyage, 4-581
    Dr. Orpheus, 4-580
    Heller's Leap, 4-581
    The Lucifer Comet, 4-582
    The Purloined Prince, 4-581
    The Sign of the Mute Medusa, 4-581
Walsh, Chad
    From Utopia to Nightmare, 9-102
Walsh, Jill Paton
    The Green Book, 5-161
Walters, Hugh
    Destination Mars, 5-162
    The Mohole Mystery, 5-163
Walther, Daniel, 412
    L'Epouvanté, 6-159
    Requiem pour demain, 6-160
    Les Soleils noirs d'Arcadie, 6-176
Walton, Bryce
    Sons of the Ocean Deeps, 5-164
Wandrei, Donald
    "Colossus," 62
Warner, Harry, Jr.
    All Our Yesterdays, 9-62
    A Wealth of Fable, 9-63
Warner, Rex
    The Wild Goose Chase, 59
Warren, Bill
    Keep Watching the Skies!, 11-3
Warrick, Patricia
    The Cybernetic Imagination in Science
        Fiction, 9-103
    Machines That Think (Asimov), 4-635
    School and Society through Science Fic-
        tion (Olander), 13-33
Waterloo, Stanley
    Armageddon, 14

A Son of the Ages, 20, 1-96
The Story of Ab, 20, 1-97
Waters, T. A.
    The Probability Pad, 4-12
Watkins, William Jon
    What Rough Beast, 4-583
Watson, Ian, 15-61
    Afterlives (Sargent), 4-666
    Alien Embassy, 4-589
    The Book of Being, 4-584
    The Book of the River, 4-584
    The Book of the Stars, 4-584
    Chekhov's Journey, 4-585
    Deathhunger, 4-590
    The Embedding, 4-586
    The Gardens of Delight, 4-587
    The Jonah Kit, 4-588
    The Martian Inca, 4-589
    Miracle Visitors, 4-589
    Queenmagic, Kingmagic, 4-590
    Slow Birds and Other Stories, 4-591
    Sunstroke and Other Stories, 4-591
    Under Heaven's Bridge, 4-592
    The Very Slow Time Machine, 4-591
Watson, Simon
    No Man's Land, 5-165
Waugh, Charles G.
    Mysterious Visions, 3-460
    Science Fiction and Fantasy Series and
        Sequels (Cottrill), 8-22
    The 13 Crimes of Science Fiction (Asi-
        mov), 3-460
Waugh, Evelyn
    Love Among the Ruins, 3-395
Webb, Sharon, 15-14
    Earth Song, 5-166
    Earthchild, 5-166
    Ram Song, 5-166
Weber, Ronald
    Seeing Earth, 9-104
Weedman, Jane Branhan
    Samuel R. Delany, 10-52
    Women Worldwalkers, 9-119
Weinbaum, Stanley G., 54
    The Black Flame, 2-124
    A Martian Odyssey . . . , 2-125
    The New Adam, 2-126
    The Red Peri, 2-125
Weinberg, Robert
    The Weird Tales Story, 14-19
Weisser, Michael
    Syn-Code-7, 6-32
Weldon, Michael
    The Psychotronic Encyclopedia of Film,
        11-8
Wellman, Manly Wade, 10-162
Wells, H. G., 21–22, 10-163, 10-164, 10-
        165, 10-166, 10-167, 10-168, 10-169,

10-170, 10-171, 10-172, 10-173, 10-174, 10-175, 10-176, 10-177, 10-178, 15-16, 15-17, 15-44, 15-75
The Autocracy of Mr. Parham, 51
"The Country of the Blind," 1-102
The Croquet Player, 2-127
"The Empire of the Ants," 1-102
The First Men in the Moon, 1-98
"The Flowering of a Strange Orchid," 1-102
The Food of the Gods, 11, 1-99
H. G. Wells: Early Writings in Science and Science Fiction, 10-177
The Holy Terror, 2-128
"In the Avu Observatory," 1-102
The Island of Dr. Moreau, 22, 1-100
Men like Gods, 51, 2-129
Mr. Blettsworthy on Rampole Island, 51
"The Sea Raiders," 21, 1-102
The Shape of Things to Come, 51, 2-130
The Short Stories of H. G. Wells, 1-102
"The Star," 21, 1-102
Star-Begotten, 51, 2-131
"A Story of Days to Come," 1-102
"A Story of the Stone Age," 1-102
The Time Machine, 21–22, 1-103
The Undying Fire, 51
The War in the Air, 13, 1-104
The War of the Worlds, 22, 1-105
When the Sleeper Wakes, 1-106
The World Set Free, 13
Wendell, Carolyn
Alfred Bester, 10-18
Wendland, Albert
Science, Myth and the Fictional Creation of Alien Worlds, 9-105
Werfel, Franz, 382
Star of the Unborn, 3-396
Wertham, Fredric
The World of Fanzines, 14-20
Wessel, Johan Hermann
Anno 7603, 538
Westall, Robert
Futuretrack 5, 5-167
Wharton, Edith, 15-50
Wheatley, Dennis, 15-82
Wheeler, Harvey
Fail-Safe (Burdick), 3-81
Whelan, Michael, 15-71
Wonderworks, 12-37
White, James, 10-179
The Aliens Among Us, 3-398
All Judgment Fled, 4-594
Ambulance Ship, 3-398, 4-594
The Dream Millennium, 4-593
The Escape Orbit, 3-397
Futures Past, 3-398

Hospital Station, 3-398
Major Operation, 3-398
Second Ending, 3-399
Sector General, 3-398
Star Healer, 3-398, 4-594
Star Surgeon, 3-398
The Watch Below, 4-594
White, Stewart Edward
The Mystery, 1-107
The Sign at Six, 1-108
White, T. H., 15-46
The Master, 5-168
White, Ted
By Furies Possessed, 4-595
The Jewels of Elsewhen, 4-596
Wibberly, Leonard
Encounter near Venus, 5-169
Wicks, Mark
To Mars Via the Moon, 18
Wilder, Cherry
The Luck of Brin's Five, 5-170
The Nearest Five, 5-170
Second Nature, 4-597
Wilfert, Peter
Tor zu den Sternen, 6-49
Wilhelm, Kate, 15-34, 15-54
Abyss, 4-600
The Clewiston Test, 4-598
The Clone (Thomas), 3-374
The Downstairs Room, 4-600
Huysman's Pets, 4-599
The Infinity Box, 4-600
Juniper Time, 4-601
Listen, Listen, 4-600
Somerset Dreams and Other Fictions, 4-600
Welcome, Chaos, 4-602
Where Late the Sweet Birds Sang, 4-603
Wilkins, John
A Discourse Concerning a New World and Another Planet, 5
Williams, Charles, 60
Many Dimensions, 2-132
Williams, Jay
Danny Dunn and the Homework Machine, 5-171
The People of the Ax, 5-172
The Time of the Kraken, 5-173
Williams, Paul
Only Apparently Real, 10-59
Williams, Paul O.
An Ambush of Shadows, 4-604
The Breaking of Northwall, 4-604
The Dome in the Forest, 4-604
The Ends of the Circle, 4-604
The Fall of the Shell, 4-604
The Song of the Axe, 4-604
Williams, Robert Moore, 15-2

The Day They H-Bombed Los Angeles,
3-400
Doomsday Eve, 3-400
Williams, Walter Jon
Knight Moves, 4-606
Williamson, Jack, 10-180, 10-181, 10-182,
15-30
The Cometeers, 2-134
Darker Than You Think, 3-401
Firechild, 4-607
The Green Girl, 2-133
H. G. Wells, 10-178
The Humanoid Touch, 3-402
The Humanoids, 3-402
The Legion of Space, 2-134
The Legion of Time, 2-135
Lifeburst, 4-608
Manseed, 4-609
The Queen of the Legion, 2-134
Seetee Ship, 3-403
Seetee Shock, 3-403
Teaching Science Fiction, 13-11
Trapped in Space, 5-174
Wonder's Child, 10-182
Willis, Connie
Fire Watch, 4-610
Water Witch (Felice), 4-213
Willis, Donald
Horror and Science Fiction Films, 11-4
Variety's Complete Science Fiction Re-
views, 11-5
Willumsen, Dorrit
Programmeret til Kærlighed, 6-358
Wilson, Colin, 15-9
The Haunted Man, 10-102
The Mind Parasites, 4-611
The Philosopher's Stone, 4-611
The Space Vampires, 4-611
Wilson, Richard, 15-34
Wilson, Robert Anton
Illuminatus! (Shea), 4-490
Schrödinger's Cat, 4-612
Wilson, Robin Scott
Those Who Can, 13-20
Wilson, Snoo
Inside Babel, 4-613
Spaceache, 4-613
Wilson, William G., Jr., 15-52
Wingrove, David
Apertures (Griffin), 10-2
The Immortals of Science Fiction, 12-38
The Science Fiction Film Source Book,
11-9
The Science Fiction Source Book, 8-34
Trillion Year Spree (Aldiss), 9-4
Winsor, G. MacLeod
Station X, 2-136
Winter, Douglas E.

Stephen King, 10-88
Winterfeld, Henry
Star Girl, 5-175
Wintrebert, Joëlle
Chromoville, 6-161
Les Maîtres-feu, 6-162
Les Olympiades truquées, 6-163
Witt, Otto
Hugin, 531
Wolfe, Bernard
Limbo, 3-404
Limbo 90, 3-404
Wolfe, Gary K.
Critical Terms for Science Fiction and
Fantasy, 8-35
The Known and the Unknown, 9-106
Science Fiction Dialogues, 9-107
Wolfe, Gene
The Citadel of the Autarch, 4-616
The Claw of the Conciliator, 4-616
The Fifth Head of Cerberus, 4-614
Gene Wolfe's Book of Days, 4-615
The Island of Doctor Death and Other
Stories and Other Stories, 4-615
The Shadow of the Torturer, 4-616
The Sword of the Lictor, 4-616
Wollheim, Donald A., 15-34, 15-52, 15-54
The Best from the Rest of the World, 4-
661
The 1986 Annual World's Best SF, 4-
672
The Pocket Book of Science Fiction, 3-
461
The Secret of Saturn's Rings, 5-176
The Secret of the Martian Moons, 5-177
The Universe Makers, 9-108
Wood, Robert William
The Man Who Rocked the Earth (Train)
14, 1-91
The Moon Maker (Train), 1-91
Woodroffe, Patrick
A Closer Look, 12-39
Mythopoeikon, 12-39
Wouk, Herman
The "Lomokome" Papers, 3-405
Wright, Austin Tappan
Islandia, 3-406
Wright, Gene
The Science Fiction Image, 11-10
Wright, Harold Bell
The Devil's Highway, 2-137
Wright, Robert G.
The Worlds of Science Fiction (Hipple),
13-27
Wright, S. Fowler
The Adventures of Wyndham Smith, 2-
138
The Amphibians, 2-144

Deluge, 2-139
Dream, 2-140
The Dwellers, 2-144
Four Days War, 2-143
The Island of Captain Sparrow, 2-141
Megiddo's Ridge, 2-143
The New Gods Lead, 2-142
Prelude in Prague, 2-143
Spider's War, 2-140
The Throne of Saturn, 2-142
Vengeance of Gwa, 2-140
The World Below, 2-144
Wrightson, Patricia
Down to Earth, 5-178
Wul, Stefan
Niourk, 6-164
Noö, 6-165
Oms en série, 6-166
Temple of the Past, 3-407
Terminus 1, 6-167
Wylie, Philip
After Worlds Collide, 2-146
The Disappearance, 3-408
The End of the Dream, 4-617
Gladiator, 2-145
Tomorrow!, 3-409
Triumph, 3-409
When Worlds Collide, 2-146
Wymer, Thomas L.
Intersections, 13-39
Twentieth-Century American Science-
Fiction Writers (Cowart), 8-28
Voices for the Future (Clareson), 9-25
Wyndham, John, 10-183, 15-55, 15-58, 15-
61
Chocky, 3-410
The Chrysalids, 3-414
The Day of the Triffids, 3-411
The Kraken Wakes, 3-412
Midwich Cuckoos, 3-413
Out of the Deeps, 3-412
Re-Birth, 3-414
Revolt of the Triffids, 3-411
Tales of Gooseflesh and Laughter, 3-415
Trouble with Lichen, 3-416
Village of the Damned, 3-413
Wynne-Tyson, Esme
The Riddle of the Tower (Beresford), 3-
21

Yamada, Masaki
Kamigari, 6-288
Yamano, Kōichi
X Densha de Ikō, 6-289
Yamao, Yūko
Yume no Sumu Machi, 6-290
Yano, Tetsu, 483

Chikyū Reinen, 6-291
Origami Uchūsen no Densetsu, 6-292
Yarbro, Chelsea Quinn
False Dawn, 4-618
Hyacinths, 4-619
Yefremov, Ivan Antonovich. *See* Efremov,
Ivan Antonovich
Yep, Laurence
Sweetwater, 5-179
Yermakov, Nicholas
Epiphany, 4-620
Jehad, 4-620
Last Communion, 4-620
Yershov, Peter
Science Fiction and Utopian Fantasy in
Soviet Literature, 455
Yoke, Carl B.
Death and the Serpent, 9-109
Roger Zelazny, 10-187
Yokota, Junya
Nihon SF Koten Koten, 6-305
Sengo Shoki Nihon SF Besuto Shūsei, 6-
298
Young, Robert F.
The Last Yggdrasil, 4-621
Starfinder, 4-622
The Worlds of Robert F. Young, 3-417
Yulsman, Jerry
Elleander Morning, 4-623
Yumemakura, Baku
Genken Shōnen Kimaira, 6-293
Yumeno, Kyūsaku
Dogura Magura, 6-294

Zahn, Timothy
A Coming of Age, 4-624
Zahorski, Kenneth J.
Fantasy Literature (Tymn), 8-51
Zamiatin, Evgenii, 57, 445, 15–55
Herbert Wells, 22
My, 2-147
We, 2-147
Žantovská-Murray, Irena
"A Bibliography of General Bibliogra-
phies of SF Literature," 6-231
Zauner, Georg
Die Enkel der Raketenbauer, 6-35
Zebrowski, George, 15-41
Macrolife, 4-625
Nebula Awards, 4-673
Sunspacer, 5-180
Zelazny, Roger, 10-184, 10-185, 10-186,
10-187, 15-24, 15-34, 15-90
Creatures of Light and Darkness, 4-631
The Doors of His Face, The Lamps of
His Mouth and Other Stories, 4-626
Doorways in the Sand, 4-627

The Dream Master, 4-628
Eye of Cat, 4-629
Four for Tomorrow, 4-626
Isle of the Dead, 4-630
The Last Defender of Camelot, 4-626
Lord of Light, 4-631
My Name Is Legion, 4-626
This Immortal, 4-632
Zicree, Marc Scott
The Twilight Zone Companion, 11-41
Ziegfeld, Richard E.
Stanislaw Lem, 10-99
Ziegler, Thomas
Die Stimmen der Nacht, 6-33
Živković, Zoran
Savremenici buducnosti, 6-476
Zorn, Jacqueline
L'Univers vagabond (Groc), 6-98

Title Index

This index was prepared to allow direct access to a title when the user does not know or is unsure of the author's name. The Author/Subject Index includes most of the information in this Title Index and should be consulted when the author's name is known. Short fiction is not normally indexed for reasons explained in the introductory note to the Author/Subject Index (see page 787). Indexed short fiction and essay titles are shown in quotation marks. Variant titles, sequels, and books in series are indexed for the sake of completeness. Works not translated into English are indexed only by their foreign titles, since readers of foreign languages would normally search under such titles. Translated books are indexed only by their translated title. Subtitles are included when it is necessary to distinguish works having the same title. SF is alphabetized as if spelled Science Fiction; alphabetization is word-by-word.

A for Andromeda, 3-215
Abenteuer mit der Venus, 6-6
Aboriginal SF, 14-21
The Absolute at Large, 2-13
Abyss, 4-600
Across a Billion Years, 5-140
Across the Sea of Suns, 4-53
Across the Zodiac, 1-40
Actes du [premier] deuxième colloque international de science-fiction de Nice (1983–1985), 6-187, 6-188
Adam Link: Robot, 3-35
Adam Troy: Astroman, 5-131
Address Unknown, 2-90
The Adolescence of P-1, 4-459
Adrift in a Boneyard, 3-367
Adventure, Mystery, and Romance, 9-20
Adventures in the Unknown, 5-36
Adventures in Time and Space, 3-439
Adventures of a Micro-Man, 2-60
The Adventures of Alyx, 4-455

Adventures of Captain Hatteras, 1-92
The Adventures of Una Persson and Catherine Cornelius in the Twentieth Century, 4-382
The Adventures of Wyndham Smith, 2-138
The Adversary, 4-366
Advise and Consent, 3-149
Aelita, 2-119, 444
The Affirmation, 4-427
After London, 1-53
After Man, 12-11
After Many a Summer, 3-219
After Many a Summer Dies the Swan, 3-219
After the Bomb, 5-112
After the Fall, 4-668
After the Rain, 3-57
After Things Fell Apart, 4-237
After 12,000 Years, 2-19
After Utopia, 4-439

After Worlds Collide, 2-146
Afterlives, 4-666
Afterwar, 4-660
Again, Dangerous Visions, 4-650
Against Infinity, 4-52
Against Method, 220
Against the Fall of Night, 3-98
Against the Night, the Stars, 10-39
An Age, 4-2
The Age of Longing, 3-237
Age of Wonders, 9-42
L'Agonie d'Albion, 6-417
Akerons porte, 6-352
Alas, Babylon, 3-166
Alas, That Great City, 3-15
Aldair in Albion, 4-39
Aldiss Unbound, 10-3
Alene, og fremtiden, 6-380
El Aleph, 3-52
Alfred Bester, 10-18
An Algis Budrys Checklist, 10-31
Alien Accounts, 4-519
Alien Citadel, 5-68
Alien Embassy, 4-589
Alien Encounters, 9-83
An Alien Heat, 4-383
Alien Landscapes, 12-23
Alien Thunder, 5-55
The Alien Upstairs, 4-469
The Alien Way, 3-145
The Aliens Among Us, 3-398
Aliens and Linguists, 9-59
Aliens 4, 3-359
All Flesh Is Grass, 3-350
All for His Country, 14
All Judgment Fled, 4-594
All Our Yesterdays, 9-62
All the Myriad Ways, 4-390
All Times Possible, 4-201
Allan Quatermain, 1-44
The Alley God, 3-157
Alone Against Tomorrow, 4-204
The Alteration, 4-10
Altered States, 4-126
Alternate Worlds, 9-41
Always Coming Home, 4-323
Alyx, 4-455
Amazing Science Fiction Stories, 14-22
Amazing Stories, 3-425
Amber Dreams, 10-185
Ambulance Ship, 3-398, 4-594
An Ambush of Shadows, 4-604
The American Shore, 9-30
The Amphibian, 2-4, 444
L'An deux mille quatre cent quarante, 1-63, 406
Analisi dell'Incubo, 6-334
Analog, 3-426

The Analog Science Fact Reader, 3-426
Analog Science Fiction/Science Fact, 14-23
Analogue Men, 3-234
The Anarchistic Colossus, 4-565
Ancestral Voices, 1-62
Ancient of Days, 4-60
And All Between, 5-146
And Chaos Died, 4-456
And Having Writ . . . , 4-57
And Some Were Human, 3-138
. . . And the Lurid Glare of the Comet, 9-3
Andre Norton, 10-114
Andromeda, 3-152
The Andromeda Strain, 4-156
The Angel of the Revolution, 1-41
Angels and Spaceships, 3-66
Anglo-Saxons Onward, 14
The Angry Planet, 5-39
Aniara, 3-272, 533, 6-370
Anna to the Infinite Power, 5-2
Annals of Klepsis, 4-308
The Annals of the Heechee, 4-415
Anne Inez McCaffrey, 10-110
L'Année de la science fiction et du fantastique, 6-189
L'Année de la science-fiction et du fantastique Québécois, 6-193
Les Années de sable, 6-64
Anno Domini, 6-351
Anno 7603, 538
L'Anno 3000: Sogno, 6-314
Anno Utopia oder So var die Zukunft, 6-46
Annotated Guide to Fantastic Adventures, 14-13
The Annotated Guide to Startling Stories, 14-14
The Annotated Guide to Stephen King, 10-83
Another Heaven, Another Earth, 5-69
Another Kind, 3-299
The Ant Men, 5-115
An Antarctic Mystery, 9
Antares, 6-466
Anthem, 3-315
Anthologie de la science-fiction Française, 6-174
Antologiia sovetskoi fantastiki, 6-215
The Anubis Gates, 4-422
Anvil of the Heart, 4-279
Anywhen, 3-40
Ape and Essence, 3-220
Apeman, Spaceman, 3-459
Apertures, 10-2
Apocalypses, 4-309
Aporisticon, 6-447
Apparition des surhommes, 6-65
Approaches to Science Fiction, 13-30

The Aquiliad, 4-546
The Arbor House Treasury of Great Science Fiction Short Novels, 3-457
The Arbor House Treasury of Modern Science Fiction, 3-457
The Arbor House Treasury of Science Fiction Masterpieces, 3-457
The Architect of Sleep, 4-76
Arena: Sports SF, 3-435
Ariel Like a Harpy, 10-128
Armageddon, 14
Armageddon 2419 A.D., 2-83
Armed Camps, 4-436
The Art of Science Fiction, 12-17
The Art of Star Wars, 11-37
The Art of the Brothers Hildebrandt, 12-22
Arthur Bertram Chandler, 10-38
Arthur C. Clarke, 10-40, 10-41, 10-42
Arthur Wilson "Bob" Tucker, 10-148
The Artificial Kid, 4-537
"As Easy as A.B.C.," 1-55
Ascendancies, 4-142
Ascension, 4-238
Ashes, Ashes, 3-25, 6-58
Asleep in the Afternoon, 2-59
Aspects of Fantasy, 9-113
L'Assedio, 6-315
Assignment in Nowhere, 3-248
The Astounding Science Fiction Anthology, 3-426
The Astounding-Analog Reader, 3-426, 3-437
At the Earth's Core, 19, 1-15
At the Eye of the Occan, 4-476
At the Mountains of Madness . . . , 2-65
At the Seventh Level, 4-202
Athena'er i byen og brugt, 6-360
L'Atlantide, 23
Atlantis, 19
The Atlas of Pern, 10-111
Atlas Shrugged, 3-316
Atomgewicht 500, 6-9
The Atrocity Exhibition, 4-33, 412
Auf zwei Planeten, 383, 6-22
Das Auge des Phoenix, 6-35
Aurora, 4-653
Aurum Film Encyclopedia, 11-1
Australian Science Fiction, 4-638
The Autocracy of Mr. Parham, 51
Autocrisi, 6-322
L'Automne à Pékin, 6-155
Autumn Angels, 4-151
Aux armes d'Ortog, 6-148
Aux étoiles de destin, 6-103
The Avatar, 4-13
The Avatars, 60
Avenirs à la dérive, 6-169

Aventine, 4-295
Away and Beyond, 3-382

Babel, 6-443
Babel-17, 4-164
Back to Methuselah, 60, 2-98
Bad Moon Rising, 4-647
The Bad Seed, 3-271
Ballata per Lima, 6-321
"The Balloon Hoax," 1-75
Ballroom of the Skies, 3-266
The Barbie Murders and Other Stories, 4-570
Barefoot in the Head, 4-3
Barlowe's Guide to Extraterrestrials, 12-2
Barsoom, 10-33
Battle Circle, 4-20
"The Battle of Dorking," 11, 1-21
The Battle of Forever, 4-566
The Battle of the Monsters and Other Stories, 1-49
Battle on Mercury, 5-159
Battlefield Earth, 4-280
Bearing an Hourglass, 4-23
Beastchild, 4-306
Beasts, 4-157
Beetle in the Anthill, 4-540
Before Adam, 20, 1-58
Before the Dawn, 2-115
Before the Golden Age, 2-2
Behold the Man, 4-380
Beloved Son, 4-559
Below the Root, 5-146
Benchmarks, 9-17
Berge, Meere und Giganten, 382, 6-8
The Berkley Showcase, 4-667
Berserker, 4-460
Berserker Base, 4-460
Berserker: Blue Death, 4-460
Berserker Man, 4-460
The Berserker Throne, 4-460
The Berserker Wars, 4-460
Berserker's Planet, 4-460
The Best from Fantasy and Science Fiction, 3-423, 4-652
The Best from Galaxy, 3-436
The Best from If, 3-436
The Best from New Worlds Science Fiction, 3-427
The Best from the Rest of the World, 4-661
The Best of Analog, 3-426
The Best of Astounding, 3-426
The Best of Avram Davidson, 3-126
Best of Bradbury Sound Filmstrips, 13-40
The Best of C. L. Moore, 3-289
The Best of C. M. Kornbluth, 3-238

The Best of Cordwainer Smith, 3-354
The Best of Edmond Hamilton, 3-187
The Best of Frederik Pohl, 3-309
The Best of Hal Clement, 3-107
The Best of Henry Kuttner, 3-242
The Best of Jack Vance, 3-377
The Best of James Blish, 3-41
The Best of John W. Campbell, 3-85
The Best of Judith Merril, 3-282
The Best of L. Sprague de Camp
The Best of Leigh Brackett, 3-59
The Best of Mack Reynolds, 3-317
The Best of Murray Leinster, 3-254
The Best of New Worlds, 3-427
The Best of Omni Science Fiction, 4-646
The Best of Planet Stories #1, 3-425
The Best of Raymond Z. Gallun, 3-169
The Best of Science Fiction, 3-429
The Best of Walter M. Miller, Jr., 3-286
Best SF, 3-432
Best Science Fiction Novellas of the Year,
    4-641
The Best Science Fiction of Arthur Conan
    Doyle, 1-31
Best Science Fiction of Brian W. Aldiss,
    3-2
Best Science Fiction of the Year, 4-641
The Best Science-Fiction Stories, 3-422
Best SF Stories from New Worlds, 3-427,
    4-659
The Best Short Stories of J. G. Ballard, 4-
    34
Bettyann, 3-297
Between the Strokes of Night, 4-493
Between Worlds, 2-105
Beyond Apollo, 4-352, 5-152
Beyond Bedlam, 3-182
Beyond Heaven's River, 4-49
Beyond Infinity, 3-89, 3-298
Beyond the Blue, 53
Beyond the Blue Event Horizon, 4-415
Beyond the Burning Lands, 5-31
Beyond the Imperium, 3-248
Beyond the Planet Earth, 2-120
Beyond the Safe Zone, 4-500
Beyond This Horizon, 3-197
Beyond Time and Space, 13-34
Bibliografi over litteratur på dansk om sci-
    ence fiction til og med 1984, 6-363
Bibliografi över science fiction & fantasy,
    6-373
A Bibliographical Guide to Soviet Fantasy
    and Science Fiction, 1957–1968, 455
Bibliographie der utopischen und
    phantastichen Literatur 1750–1950, 6-
    39
Bibliographie documentaire sur Jules
    Verne, 10-150

Bibliographisches Lexikon der utopisch-
    phantastichen Literatur, 6-42
"A Bibliography of General Bibliographies
    of SF Literature," 6-231
Bibliography of Russian Science Fantasy
    1917–1966, 455
The Bicentennial Man and Other Stories,
    4-25
Bid Time Return, 4-364
The Big Ball of Wax, 3-281
The Big Book of Science Fiction, 3-431
The Big Eye, 3-153
The Big Time, 3-249
Bilder aus der Zukunft, 383, 6-23
Bill, the Galactic Hero, 4-255
Billion Year Spree, 9-4
De Binaire Joker, 6-437
Biographie comparée de Jorian Murgrave,
    6-158
Biological Themes in Modern Science Fic-
    tion, 9-72
Birds of Prey, 4-192
The Birth of the People's Republic of Ant-
    arctica, 4-42
Bison of Clay, 56
Les Bisons d'argile, 56
"The Black Cat," 10
The Black Cloud, 3-216
The Black Corridor, 4-381
Black Dawn, 2-26
Black Easter, 3-42
The Black Flame, 2-124
Black Genesis, 4-280
Black Oxen, 2-3
The Black Star Passes, 2-12
The Bladerunner, 5-123
Blake of the 'Rattlesnake,' 12
Blake's Progress, 4-387
The Bleeding Man and Other Science Fic-
    tion Stories, 5-150
Blind Circle, 2-92
The Blind Men and the Elephant, 4-239
The Blind Spot, 2-31
Blind Voices, 4-435
Blokken, 6-401
Blood and Burning, 3-75
Blood Music, 4-50
Blooded on Arachne, 4-61
Bloodhype, 4-220
The Blue Flamingo, 2-43
The Blue Germ, 2-114
The Blue World, 3-378
Bluesong, 4-564
Bob Shaw, 10-124
The Body Snatchers, 3-163
The Bodyguard, 4-377
Bodyguard and Four Other Short Novels,
    3-436

Bolland, 6-402
The Book of Being, 4-584
The Book of Stier, 4-465
The Book of the River, 4-584
The Book of the Stars, 4-584
Borderline, 3-388
Born of Man and Woman, 3-273
Born with the Dead, 4-500
Bound for Mars, 5-8
Boy beyond the Moon, 5-1
The Boys from Brazil, 4-337
The Bradbury Chronicles, 10-27
The Brain Machine, 3-356
Brain Twister, 3-306
Brain Wave, 3-8
Brainrack, 4-407
Der Brand der Cheopspyramide, 6-10
The Brass Butterfly, 3-176
Brave New World, 2-47, 10-79
Brave New World Revisited, 2-47
Brave Old World, 4-159, 6-77
The Breaking of Northwall, 4-604
Breakthrough, 4-152
Brebis galeuses, 6-147
Brian W. Aldiss, 10-1
"The Brick Moon," 1-48
Bridgehead, 4-191
Bridges to Science Fiction, 9-117
The Bright Phoenix, 3-280
Brightness Falls from the Air, 4-553
Bring the Jubilee, 3-291
British and American Utopian Literature 1516-1975, 8-54
Broadcast Theater, 13-41
Broken Symmetries, 4-425
Brother Assassin, 4-460
Brother Berserker, 4-460
Brother in the Land, 5-154
Budrys' Inferno, 3-76
Bug-Eyed Monsters, 3-454
Bug Jack Barron, 4-525
Burning Chrome, 4-232
The Burning World, 4-36
But We Are Not of Earth, 5-85
The Butterfly Kid, 4-12
Button Brains, 2-17
By Furies Possessed, 4-595
The Byworlder, 4-14

C. S. Lewis, 10-100
Caesar's Column, 1-28
Caino dello Spazio, 6-324
The California Iceberg, 5-60
Call Back Yesterday, 5-54
The Call of the Cosmos, 2-120
Callahan's Crosstime Saloon, 4-448
Callahan's Secret, 4-448

The Caltraps of Time, 4-363
Camp Concentration, 4-184
Can You Feel Anything When I Do This?, 4-492
Canary in a Cat House, 3-394
Candle in the Wind, 3-357A
A Canticle for Leibowitz, 3-287
Capable of Honor, 3-149
Carrie, 4-299
Le Carrousel des Maléfices, 6-423
A Case of Conscience, 3-42
Casey Agonistes and Other Science Fiction and Fantasy Stories, 3-279
Cassandra Rising, 4-653
Cast Down the Stars, 5-83
The Castle of Iron, 3-134
Cat Karina, 4-146
The Cat Who Walks Through Walls, 4-261
The Cataclysm, 3-341
Catacomb Years, 4-62
Catalogo Generale della Fantascienza, 6-330
Catalogo Generale della Fantascienza in Italia, 6-338
Catalogue des âmes et cycles de la science fiction, 6-179
The Catalyst, 4-250
Catchworld, 4-72
Cat's Cradle, 3-391
Catseye, 5-116
The Caves of Steel, 3-16
Cavete!, 6-27
Caxton's Book, 15, 1-78
CDN SF & F, 8-13
Ce monde est nôtre, 6-71
The Celestial Steam Locomotive, 4-146
The Centauri Device, 4-259
A Century of Great Short Science Fiction Novels, 3-442
A Century of Progress, 4-461
A Century of Science Fiction, 3-442
Century's End, 4-240
The Certainty of a Future Life on Mars, 18
Cette chère humanité, 4-159, 6-77
Ceux de nulle part, 6-72
Chaining the Lady, 4-22
Chains, 56, 60
The Chalk Giants, 4-440
Le Champ du rêveur, 6-107
A Change of Mind, 3-173
Change the Sky and Other Stories, 3-325
The Change War, 3-249
Le Chant des Astronautes, 6-99
Chaos, 2-26
Chaos in Lagrangia, 4-438
Chapter House: Dune, 4-268
Chas Byka, 6-203
Che Cosa E' la Fantascienza, 6-332

Cheap Thrills, 722
The Checklist of Fantastic Literature, 8-2
The Checklist of Science-Fiction and Super-
    natural Fiction, 8-2
Chekhov's Journey, 4-585
Cherez gory vremeni, 6-223
Cherez tysiachu let, 445
Chessboard Planet, 3-246
Chetyre puteshestviia na mashine vremeni,
    6-225
Chi ni wa Heiwa o, 6-256
Les Chiens, 6-141
Chikyū Reinen, 6-291
Chikyū Tōnan, 6-287
Chikyu wa Plain Yogurt, 6-250
The Child Buyer, 3-211
Child of Fortune, 4-526
Childhood's End, 3-97
Children of Dune, 4-268
Children of Morrow, 5-70
Children of the Atom, 3-342
Children of the Dust, 5-93
Children of the Lens, 3-355
Chocky, 3-410
A Choice of Gods, 4-514
Chorale, 4-353
Christianopolis, 5
Christmas Eve, 3-239
Chroma, 12-21
The Chromosome Game, 4-273
Chromoville, 6-161
Chronolysis, 4-288, 6-114
Chronopolis and Other Stories, 4-34
The Chrysalids, 3-414
Chrysalis, 4-671
Chthon, 4-21
Chto takoe fantastika?, 6-228
Cinefantastique, 14-30
Cinefex, 14-31
Cinnabar, 4-95
Cinq Solutions pour en finir, 6-88
Circumpolar!, 4-344
Cirque, 4-114
The Citadel of the Autarch, 4-616
La Cité des asphyxiés, 6-125
Cities in Flight, 3-43
Cities of the Red Night, 4-99
Cities of Wonder, 3-443
Citizen in Space, 3-334
Citizen of the Galaxy, 5-61
La Città e le Stelle, 6-342
City, 3-345
The City and the Stars, 3-98
The City of Gold and Lead, 5-32
City of Sorcery, 4-77
The City of the Sun, 5
The City under Ground, 5-108
Civilisations et divagations, 6-195

Civitas Solis, 1-20
Clan and Crown, 4-421
The Clan of the Cave Bear, 4-32
A Clash of Cymbals, 3-43
Clash of Star-Kings, 3-127
A Clash of Symbols, 10-19
Classic Science Fiction, 3-452
The Classic Years of Robert A. Heinlein,
    10-74
Classics of Science Fiction, 13-42
The Claw of the Conciliator, 4-616
Clay's Ark, 4-102
Clefs pour la science-fiction, 6-181
The Clewiston Test, 4-598
Clifford Simak, 10-134
The Clock of Time, 3-164
The Clockwork Man, 2-84
A Clockwork Orange, 3-82
Clockwork Worlds, 9-33A
Clone, 4-153
The Clone, 3-374
Cloned Lives, 4-470
Close Encounters with the Deity, 4-61
Close to Critical, 3-109
A Closer Look, 12-39
Cluster, 4-22
Code of the Lifemaker, 4-274
The Cold Cash War, 4-29
Cold War in a Country Garden, 2-60
Colecționarul de insule, 6-460
The Collapse of Homo Sapiens, 51
Collected Editorials from Analog, 3-426
Collector's Index to Weird Tales, 14-6
La Colonia Felice, 6-307
Colonial Survey, 3-255
Colony, 4-68
Colossus, 4-289
"Colossus," 62
Colossus and the Crab, 4-289
Come Ladro di Notte, 6-316
Come Nineveh, Come Tyre, 3-149
The Cometeers, 2-134
Comic Tones in Science Fiction, 9-43
The Coming Conquest of England, 13
A Coming of Age, 4-624
The Coming of the Amazons, 2-51
The Coming of the Quantum Cats, 4-414
The Coming Race, 1-61
Commune 2000, 4-439
Communipath Worlds, 4-202
The Communipaths, 4-202
La Compagnie des glaces, 6-57
Compagnons en terre étrangère, 6-168
The Company of Glory, 3-303
The Compleat Enchanter, 3-134
The Complete Feghoot, 3-65
Complete Index to Astounding/Analog,
    14-1

The Complete Venus Equilateral, 3-357
Concise Histories of American Popular Culture, 8-44
Concordance to Cordwainer Smith, 10-135
The Condition of Muzak, 4-382
Conditionally Human, 3-286
The Conglomeroid Cocktail Party, 4-500
A Connecticut Yankee in King Arthur's Court, 1-25
The Conquest of America, 13, 1-67
The Consolidator, 6
La Conspiration des milliardaires, 6-121
Contact, 4-463
Contagion to This World, 2-54
The Continent of Lies, 4-385
The Continuous Katherine Mortenhoe, 4-143
Contrary Modes, 9-110
"The Conversation of Eiros and Charmion," 1-75
Cook, 4-120
The Cornelius Chronicles, 4-382
The Cosmic Dancers, 9-38
Cosmic Encounter, 4-567
Cosmicomics, 4-108
Count-Down, 3-264
Count Zero, 4-232
Countdown to Midnight, 4-660
Countersolar!, 4-344
"The Country of the Blind," 1-102
Courtship Rite, 4-301
C.R., 546
The Craft of Science Fiction, 13-13
The Creation of Tomorrow, 9-19
The Creatures, 5-155
Creatures of Light and Darkness, 4-631
Crime Prevention in the 30th Century, 3-460
Crisis!, 4-242
Critical Encounters, 9-82, 13-8
Critical Encounters II, 9-94
Critical Terms for Science Fiction and Fantasy, 8-35
The Croquet Player, 2-127
Cross of Fire, 4-354
Cross the Stars, 4-192
Crosstime Agent, 5-118
Croyd, 4-580
Crucible Island, 59
The Crucible of Time, 4-87
Cryptozoic!, 4-2
A Crystal Age, 1-51
The Crystal Button, 20
The Crystal Horde, 2-116
The Crystal Man, 1-65
The Crystal Singer, 4-367
The Crystal World, 4-35
Cuckoo's Egg, 4-127

Cugel's Saga, 3-380
Cult Movies, 11-8
A Cupful of Space, 3-114
A Cure for Cancer, 4-382
"The Curious Republic of Gondour," 1-25
The Custodians and Other Stories, 4-154
CV, 4-303
The Cyberiad, 4-330
The Cybernetic Imagination in Science Fiction, 9-103
Cyborg, 4-105
Cycle of Fire, 3-108

Dad's Nuke, 4-314
Daedalus, 54
Daemetsubō, 6-278
De Dageraad des Duivels, 6-428A
Daimon, 6-317
The Daleth Effect, 4-256
Dalla Terra alle Stelle, 6-309
Damiers imaginaires, 6-117
"The Damned Thing," 1-13
The Dancers at the End of Time, 4-383
Dancers in the Afterglow, 4-121
Dangerous Visions, 4-650
Danny Dunn and the Homework Machine, 5-171
Dansk Science Fiction Indeks 1742–1976, 6-365
Dar Tellum, 5-14
Dark December, 3-122
The Dark Design, 4-210
Dark Sins, Dark Dreams, 3-460
The Dark Tower and Other Stories, 3-262
Dark Universe, 3-170
Darkchild, 4-564
Darkening Island, 4-428
Darker Than You Think, 3-401
The Darkling Wind, 4-547
Darkness and Dawn, 1-33
Darkover series, 4-77
Dassō to Tsuiseki no Samba, 6-282
Daughters of Earth, 3-283
Daughters of the Sunstone, 4-564
David Starr: Space Ranger, 5-7
Davy, 3-303
The Dawn of All, 1-9
The Day after Judgment, 3-42
The Day before Tomorrow, 4-302
The Day of the Drones, 5-97
Day of the Starwind, 5-67
The Day of the Triffids, 3-411
Day of Wrath, 2-86
The Day the Spaceship Landed, 5-101
The Day the Spaceship Returns, 5-101
The Day They H-Bombed Los Angeles, 3-400

Daybreak 2250 A.D., 5-120
Dayworld, 4-208
De Camp, 10-47
The Dead Zone, 4-300
Deadly Image, 3-120
Death and the Serpent, 9-109
The Death Box, 2-119, 444
Death of a World, 3-156
The Death of Grass, 3-92
The Death of Iron, 56
The Death of the Earth, 1-79
Death Watch, 4-143
Deathbird Stories, 4-205
Deathhunger, 4-590
Deathstar Voyage, 4-581
Deathworld, 3-191
Deathworld 2, 3-191
Deathworld 3, 3-191
A Decade of Fantasy and Science Fiction,
    3-423
Decade: The 1940s, 3-418
Decade: The 1950s, 3-418
Decade: The 1960s, 3-418
La Découverte australe, 406
The Deep Range, 3-99
Definitely Maybe, 4-541
The Delany Intersection, 10-51
Delirium circus, 6-129
Della Favola, del Viaggio e di Altre Cose,
    6-340
Deluge, 2-139
The Demolished Man, 3-30
Demon, 4-571
Le Dernier Homme, 9, 406
The Descent of Anansi, 4-394
Le Désert du monde, 6-53
Despatches from the Frontiers of the Fe-
    male Mind, 4-653
Destination Infinity, 3-243
Destination Mars, 5-162
Destination: Void, 4-267
Deviance and Moral Boundaries, 9-11
The Devil Tree of El Dorado, 1-5
The Devil's Advocate, 3-84
The Devil's Children, 5-43
The Devil's Highway, 2-137
Devil's Tor, 2-63
The Devolutionist, 2-31
Dōmu, 6-275
Dhalgren, 4-165
Di Fate's Catalog of Science Fiction Hard-
    ware, 12-10
Le Diable l'emporte, 6-59
"The Diamond Lens," 10, 1-72
Dictionary Catalog of the J. Lloyd Eaton
    Collection of Science Fiction and Fantasy
    Literature, 8-3
Le Dieu foudroyé, 6-101

A Different Drummer, 3-226
A Different Light, 4-347
The Digging Leviathan, 4-65
Dikten och den nya vetenskapen, 6-375
Dimension of Miracles, 4-491
Dimensions of Science Fiction, 9-9
Dinner at Deviant's Palace, 4-423
Dinosaurernes morgen, 6-343
The Disappearance, 3-408
A Discourse Concerning a New World and
    Another Planet, 5
Discovering Stephen King, 10-85
Displaced Person, 5-59
The Dispossessed, 4-324
Distant Stars, 4-166
Distant Worlds, 4-644
Divide and Rule, 3-132
The Divine Invasion, 4-172
Do Androids Dream of Electric Sheep?, 4-
    173
Dobbeltgjengere, 6-381
"Dobri stari svijet," 6-473
Doc Savage, 4-209
Dr. Adder, 4-287
Dr. Bloodmoney, 4-174
Doctor Fogg, 2-71
Doctor Mirabilis, 3-42
Dr. Orpheus, 4-580
Dr. Strangelove, 3-172
Doctor to the Galaxy, 5-98
Doctor Who and the Day of the Daleks, 5-
    44
The Doctor Who Programme Guide, 11-32
Does Anyone Else Have Something Fur-
    ther to Add?, 4-311
Dogura Magura, 6-294
Dolphin Island, 5-33
The Dome in the Forest, 4-604
Donovan's Brain, 3-351
Doomsday Eve, 3-400
The Door Into Summer, 3-198
The Doors of His Face, The Lamps of His
    Mouth and Other Stories, 4-626
Doorways in the Sand, 4-627
Doppelgangers, 3-196
Le Dormeur s'éveillera-t-il?, 6-78
Dorsai!, 3-146
The Dorsai Companion, 3-146
Double Star, 3-199
Down Here in the Dream Quarter, 4-357
Down to Earth, 5-178
Downbelow Station, 4-128
The Downstairs Room, 4-600
Downtiming the Night Side, 4-122
Downward to the Earth, 4-501
Dragon Dance, 5-29
The Dragon in the Sea, 3-210
The Dragon Masters, 3-379

Dragondrums, 5-110
Dragonflight, 4-368
Dragonquest, 4-368
The Dragonriders of Pern, 4-368
Dragon's Egg, 4-217
Dragonsinger, 5-110
Dragonsong, 5-110
Dragsug, 6-395
Dramocles, 4-491
Dream, 2-140
Dream Makers, 10-200
Dream Makers II, 10-201
The Dream Master, 4-628
The Dream Millennium, 4-593
A Dream of John Ball, 1-69
A Dream of Kinship, 4-155
Dream Park, 4-395
The Dream Years, 4-235
The Dreamers, 3-270, 4-243
The Dreaming Dragons, 4-84
The Dreaming Jewels, 3-360
Dreamsnake, 4-370
Driftglass, 4-166
Drömmar om evigheten, 6-372
The Drought, 4-36
The Drought on Ziax II, 5-113
The Drowned World, 4-37
Drunkard's Walk, 3-310
Druso, 383
Du Fond des ages, 6-420
Dune, 4-268
The Dune Encyclopedia, 10-76
Dune Messiah, 4-268
The Dunwich Horror and Others, 2-65
The Duplicated Man, 3-44
Dushau, 4-339
Dustland, 5-57
The Dwellers, 2-144
Dwellers in the Mirage, 2-43
Dwellers of the Deep, 4-356
The Dying Earth, 3-380
Dying Inside, 4-502
Dying of the Light, 4-360
The Dynostar Menace, 4-407

E. E. "Doc" Smith, 10-137
E Pluribus Unicorn, 3-361
The Early Asimov, 3-17
The Early H. G. Wells, 10-164
The Early Long, 3-264
Earth Abides, 3-358
Earth Descended, 4-460
The Earth Is Near, 4-409, 5-132
Earth Is the Alien Planet, 10-15
Earth Song, 5-166
The Earth Tube, 14
Earthchild, 4-412, 5-166

Earthfasts, 5-109
Earthman, Come Home, 3-43
Earthman's Burden, 3-9
Earthseed, 5-137
An East Wind Coming, 4-151
The Eater of Darkness, 2-18
Echec au temps, 6-425
Eclipse, 4-498
Ecotopia, 4-107
Ecotopia Emerging, 4-107
Edd Cartier, 12-6
The Eden Cycle, 4-225
Edgar Pangborn, 10-118
Edgar Rice Burroughs, 10-32, 10-34, 10-35
An Edge in My Voice, 10-64
The Edge of Forever, 3-300
The Edge of Running Water, 2-102
The Edge of Tomorrow, 3-162
Eenzame bloedvogel, 6-400, 6-427
De eersten van Rissan, 6-403
The Egghead Republic, 383
Eight Keys to Eden, 3-111
The Einstein Intersection, 4-167
The Electric Crocodile, 4-144
Electropolis, 2-122
The Eleventh Commandment, 3-139
Der Elfenbeinturm, 6-11
Elleander Morning, 4-623
Ellinskii sekret, 6-216
Elric at the End of Time, 4-383
Elsie Venner, 11
Elverhøj retur, 6-361
The Emancipatrix, 2-31
The Embedding, 4-586
Emergence, 4-404
Emmarg, 6-410
Emperor of Space, 501
Emperor of the If, 2-25
Emphyrio, 4-560
"The Empire of the Ants," 1-102
Empire Star, 4-166
The Empire Strikes Out, 6-40, 9-35
Emprise, 4-307
Empty World, 5-28
En levande själ, 6-368
En Souvenir du futur, 6-79
Enchantress from the Stars, 5-47
Encounter near Venus, 5-169
Encyclopedia of Science Fiction, 9-45
The Encyclopedia of Science Fiction, 8-30
The Encyclopedia of Science Fiction and
    Fantasy through 1968, 8-7
Encyclopédie de l'utopie, des voyages
    extraordinaires et de la science-fiction,
    6-197
Encyclopédie de poche de la science-
    fiction, 6-178
The End of a World, 56

The End of All Songs, 4-383
The End of Eternity, 3-18
End of Exile, 5-21
The End of Summer, 3-452
The End of the Dream, 4-617
The End of the Matter, 4-220
The End of the World, 9-79
The End of Utopia, 10-79
Ender's Game, 4-109
The Endless Frontier, 4-662
The Endless Pavement, 5-81
The Ends of the Circle, 4-604
The Endurance of Frankenstein, 10-127
The Enemy Stars, 3-10
The Enemy Within, 4-280
L'enfant du cinquième nord, 6-63
Engine Summer, 4-158
Engineer Menni, 6-200
The Engines of the Night, 9-56
The English Assassin, 4-382
Enigma, 4-307
Die Enkel der Raketenbauer, 6-35
The Ennead, 5-106
The Entropy Exhibition, 9-39
The Entropy Tango, 4-382
Envisaged Worlds, 4-644
Envoy to New Worlds, 3-247
Eon, 4-51
Epiphany, 4-620
L'Epouvanté, 6-159
Epp, 539, 6-391
Equality, 1-7
Equality in the Year 2000, 4-439
Erewhon, 1-19
Erewhon Revisited Twenty Years Later, 1-19
Eric Frank Russell, 10-122
Eros in the Mind's Eye, 9-70
Erosu, 6-240
Erotic Universe, 9-116
Escape from the Crater, 5-16
The Escape Orbit, 3-397
Escape to Nowhere, 3-225
Escape to Witch Mountain, 5-88
Les Espaces enchevêtrés, 6-66
ESP-er, 3-46
Et la planète sauta, 6-67
"The Eternal World," 62
Eternity, 4-51
The Eternity Brigade, 4-234
The Ethical Engineer, 3-191
Eti udivitel'nye zvezdy, 6-218
L'Etonnant voyage de Hareton Ironcastle, 2-95
The Euguélionne, 6-66
Evil Earths, 3-419
An Exaltation of Stars, 4-665
Exiled from Earth, 5-21

Exiles at the Well of Souls, 4-123
Exiles of Time, 3-50
Expedition to Earth, 3-100, 3-102
The Expert Dreamers, 3-451
Explorations of the Marvellous, 9-67
Explorers of the Infinite, 10-191
Expo '87, 6-264
Extra(ordinary) People, 4-457
Extrapolation, 14-33
Extrapolations from Dystopia, 455, 9-37
Eyas, 4-294
Eye in the Sky, 3-141
Eye of Cat, 4-629
The Eye of the Heron, 4-325
The Eye of the Lens, 4-290
The Eye of the Queen, 4-359
Eyes of Amber and Other Stories, 4-573

The Fabulous Riverboat, 4-210
La Face cachée du désir, 6-80
The Faces of Science Fiction, 12-28
Facial Justice, 3-194
"The Facts in the Case of M. Waldemar," 1-75
The Faded Sun, 4-129
Fahrenheit 451, 3-61
Fail-Safe, 3-81
Les Faiseurs d'orage, 6-108
Faith of Tarot, 4-23
The Fall of Chronopolis, 4-44
The Fall of Colossus, 4-289
A Fall of Moondust, 3-101
The Fall of the Shell, 4-604
False Dawn, 4-618
Famous Science Fiction Stories, 3-439
Fanta-Italia, 6-327
La Fantascienza, 6-329
La Fantascienza e la Critica, 6-339
Fantasfeer, 6-416
Fantasms, 10-149
The Fantastic Art of Boris Vallejo, 12-34
The Fantastic Art of Frank Frazetta, 12-16
The Fantastic Art of Rowena, 12-27
Fantastic Cinema, 11-16
Fantastic Lives, 10-189
Fantastic Science-Fiction Art, 12-30
Fantastic Television, 11-27
Fantastika 19–, 6-219
Fantastike fortællinger, 6-394
Fantasy Art Techniques, 12-36
Fantasy Commentator, 14-34
Fantasy Literature, 8-51
Fantasy Review, 14-35
Far and Away, 3-53
The Far Arena, 4-468
Far Frontiers, 4-662
Far Future Calling, 10-142

Far Out, 3-233
The Far Reality, 3-246
The Far Side of Evil, 5-48
A Far Sunset, 4-148
Farfetch, 4-339
Farmer in the Sky, 5-62
The Farthest Shores of Ursula K. Le Guin, 10-95
"The Fatal Eggs," 57, 2-9
Father to the Stars, 3-160
Favorite Book Filmstrips, 13-43
Fear Itself, 10-86
Fear Today, Gone Tomorrow, 3-49
The Feast of St. Dionysus, 4-500
Federation, 3-307
Der Fehlfaktor, 6-3
The Female Man, 4-458
The Feminine Eye, 9-95
Feminist Futures, 9-85
A Few Last Words, 4-464
Ficciones, 3-52
Fiction 411, 15-45
The Fiction Factory, 721
Ficţiuni pentru revolver şi orchestră, 6-445
The Fifth Head of Cerberus, 4-614
The 57th Franz Kafka, 4-452
Figurine de ceară, 6-454
Film Fantasy Scrapbook, 11-28
The Films of George Pal, 11-29
The Films of Stephen King, 10-80
La Fin d'illa, 6-127
Final Blackout, 3-218
The Final Encyclopedia, 4-181
The Final Programme, 4-382
Find the Feathered Serpent, 5-79
Fire, Burn!, 3-88
Fire Past the Future, 3-264
Fire Time, 4-15
Fire Watch, 4-610
Fireball, 5-29
Firebird, 4-252
Firechild, 4-607
Fireship, 4-572
First He Died, 3-347
First Lensman, 3-355
The First Men in the Moon, 1-98
First on Mars, 3-177
First Person, Peculiar, 3-340
The First to Awaken, 3-213
Five Weeks in a Balloon, 15
Flatland, 1-1
Flight Into Yesterday, 3-189
Flight of Exiles, 5-21
The Flight of the Dragonfly, 4-218
Flight of Time, 5-24
The Flights of Icarus, 12-24
The Floating Gods, 4-260

Flow My Tears, the Policeman Said, 4-175
"The Flowering of a Strange Orchid," 1-102
Flowers for Algernon, 3-228
Flygtninge fra himlen, 6-344
Focus, 14-44
Focus on the Science Fiction Film, 11-30
Foetus-party, 6-130
Follow the Whales, 5-16
A Fond Farewell to Dying, 4-341
The Food of the Gods, 11, 1-99
Footfall, 4-396
For England's Sake, 12
For Love of Mother-Not, 4-220
La Force mystérieuse, 6-138
The Forever Formula, 5-20
The Forever Machine, 3-113
The Forever Man, 4-182
The Forever War, 4-247
The Forgotten Door, 5-89
The Forgotten Planet, 2-60, 3-256
Forlorn Hope, 4-192
Forms of the Fantastic, 9-115
Formula Fiction?, 9-21
Foundation, 3-19, 14-36
Foundation and Earth, 4-26
Foundation and Empire, 3-19
The Foundation Trilogy, 3-19
Foundation's Edge, 4-26
The Fountains of Paradise, 4-136
Four Days War, 2-143
Four for Tomorrow, 4-626
The Four-sided Triangle, 3-368
14 danske science fiction noveller, 6-359
Fourth Mansions, 4-310
The Fourth "R," 3-356
F.P.1. Does Not Reply, 2-101
Frank Herbert, 10-77, 10-78
Frankenstein, 9, 1-84
The Frankenstein Legend, 10-126
Frankenstein Unbound, 4-4
Free Amazons of Darkover, 4-77
Freezing Down, 4-67
Freezing Point, 4-67
Friday, 4-262
Fritz Leiber, 10-97, 10-98
From Off This World, 2-69
From Outer Space, 3-110
From the Earth to the Moon, 15, 16, 1-93
"From the 'London Times' of 1904," 1-25
From the Ocean, from the Stars, 3-98
From Tolkien to Oz, 12-22
From Utopia to Nightmare, 9-102
Frontier Worlds, 4-644
Le Frontiere dell'Ignoto, 6-331
Les Frontières d'Oulan-Bator, 6-96
FSSR, 6-204
Fugue for a Darkening Island, 4-428

Fukkatsu no Hi, 6-257
Fun with Your New Head, 4-186
Fundamental Disch, 4-186
Fundarika, 6-234
The Furious Future, 3-76
The Further Adventures of Halley's
    Comet, 4-43
Furthest, 4-202
Fury, 3-243
The Future as Nightmare, 9-44
The Future at War, 4-663
Future City, 3-443
Future Females, 9-10
Future Imperfect, 3-184
Future Imperfect: The Utopian Novel, 13-
    42
The Future of Eternity, 9-36
Future Perfect, 1-36, 13-24
Future Tense, 11-13
Future Times Three, 6-60
The Future Took Us, 5-139
Future War Novels, 8-15
Future without Future, 6-424
Futures Past, 3-398
Futuretrack 5, 5-167
Futurevision, 11-15
The Futurians, 10-190
The Futurological Congress, 4-331
Futurs au présent, 6-176
Fuzzies and Other People, 3-308
Fuzzy Bones, 3-308
Fuzzy Sapiens, 3-308

Le Gadget de l'apocalypse, 6-426
Galactic Cluster, 3-45
Galactic Empires, 3-419
Galactic Pot-Healer, 4-176
The Galactic Rejects, 5-128
Galactic Warlord, 5-67
Galapagos, 4-577
Les Galaxiales, 6-85
Galaxies, 4-355
Galaxies Like Grains of Sand, 3-3
Galaxy Magazine, 3-436, 14-16
Galaxy Reader of Science Fiction, 3-436
Galaxy: The Best of My Years, 3-436
Garden on the Moon, 3-54
The Gardens of Delight, 4-587
The Garin Death Ray, 2-119, 444
The Gasp, 4-227
The Gate of Eden, 5-37
The Gate of Worlds, 5-141
Gateway, 4-415
Gath, 4-556
Gather, Darkness!, 3-250
Gather in the Hall of the Planets, 4-356
The Gathering, 5-57

Gay Hunter, 2-78
Gene Wolfe's Book of Days, 4-615
The Genesis Machine, 4-275
The Genetic General, 3-146
Genken Shōnen Kimaira, 6-293
The Genocides, 4-185
Genshi-gari, 6-253
The Gentle Giants of Ganymede, 4-276
Genus Homo, 3-133
George Orwell: Nineteen Eighty-Four, 10-
    115
Geta, 4-301
Getting Hooked on Science Fiction, 13-44
Getting Into Death, 4-186
Gevleugelde daden, 546
Ghastly beyond Belief, 8-43
Gianeia, 450, 6-207
The Giant Cat, 2-95
Giants' Star, 4-276
A Gift from Earth, 4-389
Giles Goat-Boy, 4-40
Ginga Kojiki Gundan, 6-271
Ginga Tetsudō no Yoru, 6-269
The Girl in the Golden Atom, 10, 2-22
The Girl, the Gold Watch, and Everything,
    3-267
Gladiator, 2-145
Gladiator-at-Law, 3-311
The Glamour, 4-429
The Glass Bead Game, 3-212, 382
Glory Road, 3-200
God-Emperor of Dune, 4-268
God of Tarot, 4-23
Godbody, 4-545
The Goddess of Atvatabar, 1-14
God's Grace, 4-351
The Gods of Mars, 1-17
Gods of Riverworld, 4-210
Gods of the Greataway, 4-146
The Gods Themselves, 4-27
Godsfire, 4-212
The Godwhale, 4-41
Going, 4-203
The Golden Apples of the Sun, 3-62
Golden Dream, 3-308
The Golden Space, 4-471
The Golden Torc, 4-366
Gor Saga, 4-193
Gordon R. Dickson, 10-61
Gordon R. Dickson's SF Best, 3-147
Gordon Rupert Dickson, 10-62
Goslings, 1-10
Gost' iz bezdny, 449, 6-208
graffiti, 4-562
The Grain Kings, 4-442
Grand Orientale 3301, 6-35
Grattanuvole, 6-311
Gravity's Rainbow, 4-432

Gray Lensman, 3-355
"The Great Dark," 10, 1-25
The Great Explosion, 3-321
The Great Naval War of 1887, 12
The Great Pacific War, 14
Great Science Fiction by Scientists, 3-451
The Great Science Fiction Pictures, 11-19
The Great Stone of Sardis, 1-87
The Great War in England in 1897, 13, 1-57
The Great War of 189-, 1-26
The Great War Syndicate, 14, 1-88
The Great White Way, 17
The Green Book, 5-161
The Green Child, 2-91
Green Eyes, 4-497
The Green Girl, 2-133
The Green Gods, 3-209
The Green Hills of Earth, 3-204
The Green Man of Graypec, 53
The Green Man of Kilsona, 53
The Green Millennium, 3-251
The Green Mouse, 11
The Green Odyssey, 3-158
Greener Than You Think, 3-292
Les Grenouilles, 6-418
Greybeard, 4-5
Griaduschii mir, 445
Die grosse Revolution, 6-29
Ground Zero Man, 4-485
The Guardian of Isis, 5-77
The Guardians, 5-30
La Guerre des mouches, 6-144
La Guerre des vampires, 6-123
La Guerre en ballon, 13
La Guerre en forteresse, 13
La Guerre en rase campagne, 13
The Guide to Fantasy Art Techniques, 12-7
A Guide to Science Fiction & Fantasy in the Library of Congress Classification Scheme, 8-38
The Guide to Supernatural Fiction, 8-46
Gulliver's Travels, 1-89, 15-28

H. G. Wells, 10-163, 10-165, 10-166, 10-167, 10-168, 10-169, 10-171, 10-173, 10-174, 10-178
H. G. Wells and His Critics, 10-163
H. G. Wells and Modern Science Fiction, 10-175
H. G. Wells and the World State, 10-176
H. G. Wells: Early Writings in Science and Science Fiction, 10-177
H. G. Wells. Utopia modernă, 6-465
H. P. Lovecraft, 10-104, 10-105

H. P. Lovecraft and Lovecraft Criticism, 10-107, 10-108
H. P. Lovecraft: Four Decades of Criticism, 10-106
H. R. Giger's Necronomicon, 12-19
H. R. Giger's Necronomicon 2, 12-20
Haiuei Wakusei, 6-247
Hal Clement, 10-46
A Hal Clement Checklist, 10-45
Hal Clement (Harry Clement Stubbs), 10-44
Half Past Human, 4-41
Hammer's Slammers, 4-192
The Hampdenshire Wonder, 11, 1-11
Han som lengtet til stjernene, 6-389
Hana Karido, 6-270
Handbook of American Popular Culture, 8-44
The Handmaid's Tale, 4-31
Häpna, 533
The Happening Worlds of John Brunner, 10-29
The Happy Planet, 5-35
Harbottle, 2-42
Hard Science Fiction, 9-118
Harlan Ellison, 10-64
The Harris-Ingram Experiment, 21
Harry Harrison, 10-70
Hateshinaki Nagare no Hate ni, 6-258
The Haunted Man, 10-102
Hauser's Memory, 3-351
Have Space Suit—Will Travel, 3-201
The Hawkline Monster, 4-78
Hawksbill Station, 4-503
The Heads of Cerberus, 2-113
Heart of a Dog, 2-9
The Heart of the Comet, 4-55
Heartsease, 5-43
Heechee Rendezvous, 4-415
Heimkehr der Vorfahren, 6-7
Heinlein in Dimension, 10-73
Heliopolis, 382
Heller's Leap, 4-581
Helliconia Spring, 4-6
Helliconia Summer, 4-6
Helliconia Winter, 4-6
Hello Summer, Goodbye, 4-147
Hell's Cartographers, 10-188
Hell's Pavement, 3-234
Hellstrom's Hive, 4-269
The Hendon Fungus, 5-130
Henry Beam Piper, 10-119
L'Herbe rouge, 6-156
Herbert George Wells, 10-163
Herbert Wells, 22
Heretics of Dune, 4-268
The Heritage of Hastur, 4-77
Herland, 1-38

Heroes and Villains, 4-115
Hero's Walk, 3-123
Herovit's World, 4-356
Herskerne, 6-353
The Hesperides, 2-88
Het carnarium, 6-412
Het Einde der Wereld, 546, 6-433
Het verstoode mierennest, 546
Hidden Variables, 4-494
Hidden World, 2-19
Hiero's Journey, 4-318
The High Crusade, 3-11
Hikari no Tō, 6-255
The Hills of Faraway, 8-53
Hinsides Bjergene, 6-354
His Master's Voice, 4-332
His Wisdom: The Defender, 14
Histoire comique des États et Empires de
   la lune, 5, 1-12
Histoire de la science-fiction moderne, 6-
   194
Histoires comme si, 6-119
A History of the Hugo, Nebula, and Inter-
   national Fantasy Awards, 8-36
The History of the Science Fiction Maga-
   zines, 14-12
The Hitch-Hiker's Guide to the Galaxy, 4-
   1
Hitler Victorious, 4-636
Hoka!, 3-9
A Hole in Space, 4-390
The Hole in the Zero, 4-291
The Hollow Lands, 4-383
The Holy Terror, 2-128
L'Homme à rebours, 6-81
L'Homme élastique, 6-145
Homunculus, 4-66
Honeymoon in Hell, 3-67
The Hopkins Manuscript, 3-341
"Le Horla," 10
Horror and Science Fiction Films, 11-4
Horror Literature, 8-52
The Horror on the Asteroid, 2-41
Hospital Station, 3-398
Hothouse, 3-4, 4-7
The Hothouse World, 2-67
House of Stairs, 5-143
How to Be Your Own Literary Agent, 13-
   19
Howard Who?, 4-579
Hugin, 531
The Hugo Winners, 4-634
The Human Angle, 3-369
Human Error, 4-426
The Humanoid Touch, 3-402
The Humanoids, 3-402
The Humans of Ziax II, 5-113
The Humboldt Effect, 5-75

The Huntsman, 5-68
Huysman's Pets, 4-599
Hyacinths, 4-619
Hyakuoku no Hiru, Senoku no Yoru, 6-
   267
The Hydronauts, 5-16
Hyōto no Kamen, 6-263

I Am Legend, 3-274
I Am Thinking of My Darling, 3-276
I, Robot, 3-20
I, Vampire, 4-480
Ibis, 4-535
Icarus, 54
Ice, 4-293
Icehenge, 4-445
Icerigger, 4-219
Ieri, il Futuro, 6-336
If, 2-108
If the South Had Won the Civil War, 3-
   224
If the Stars Are Gods, 4-56
"If War Should Come," 14
Les Iles de Vacarme, 6-131
Illuminatus!, 4-490
The Illustrated Book of Science Fiction
   Ideas and Dreams, 9-50
The Illustrated Book of Science Fiction
   Lists, 8-41
The Illustrated Man, 3-63
Im Jahr 95 nach Hiroshima, 6-17
Im Reiche der Homunkuliden, 6-16
The Image of the Future, 58
The Imaginary Voyage in Prose Fiction, 9-
   69
Imaginile posibilului, 6-461
The Imitation Man, 2-42
The Immortal, 3-183
The Immortal Storm, 9-61
Immortality Delivered, 3-335
Immortality, Inc., 3-335
The Immortals, 3-183
The Immortals of Science Fiction, 12-38
Imperial Earth, 4-137
The Impossibles, 3-306
Imprisoned in a Tessaract, 10-19
In Caverns Below, 2-19
In Deep, 3-235
In Joy Still Felt, 10-8
In Memory Yet Green, 10-7
In Oudemon, 17
In Our Hands, the Stars, 4-256
In purpurner Finsternis, 382
In Search of Forever, 12-25
In Search of Frankenstein, 10-125
In Search of Wonder, 9-47
"In the Avu Observatory," 1-102

In the Drift, 4-550
In the Footsteps of the Abominable Snowman, 3-296
In the Hall of the Martian Kings, 4-570
In the Heart or the Head, 9-100
In the Ocean of Night, 4-53
In the Wet, 3-343
In Viriconium, 4-260
The Incomplete Enchanter, 3-134
Inconscience fiction, 6-185
Inconstant Moon, 4-390
The Incredible Adventures of Professor Branestawn, 5-80
Index of Science Fiction Magazines, 1951–1965, 14-7
Index to Science Fiction Anthologies and Collections, 8-9
Index to Science Fiction Anthologies and Collections 1977–1983, 8-10
Index to Stories in Thematic Anthologies of Science Fiction, 8-12
Index to the Science Fiction Magazines, 14-2
Index to the Science Fiction Magazines 1926–1950, 14-4
Index to the Science Fiction Magazines 1966–1970, 14-10
Index to the Semi-Professional Fantasy Magazines, 14-3
The Indians Won, 4-524
The Infernal Desire Machines of Doctor Hoffman, 4-116
The Infinite Cage, 4-319
An Infinite Summer, 4-430
The Infinite Worlds of Maybe, 5-40
The Infinity Box, 4-600
The Infinity Link, 4-119
Inherit the Stars, 4-276
The Inheritors, 20, 2-79
Inside Babel, 4-613
Inside Information, 9-103
Inside Outer Space, 13-15
The Insider, 4-207
Instruments of Darkness, 5-15
The Integral Trees, 4-388
Inter Ice Age 4, 3-1
Interplanetary Hunter, 3-26
The Intersection of Science Fiction and Philosophy, 9-66
Intersections, 13-39
Interzone, 14-24
Interzone: The First Anthology, 4-643
Into Other Worlds, 9-69
Into the Fourth Dimension, 2-22
Into the Sun & Other Stories, 1-64
Into the Unknown, 9-75
Intrigue on the Upper Level, 2-45
Invaders from the Infinite, 2-12

Invaders of Earth, 3-430
Invasion from the Air, 2-75
The Invasion of 1910, 13
Invasion of the Body Snatchers, 3-163
The Invasion of the United States, 5-58
The Invention of Morel and Other Stories, 3-37
Inverted World, 4-431
The Investigation, 3-259
The Invincible, 3-260
Inzhener Menni, 442, 6-200
The Iron Dream, 4-527
The Iron Star, 2-117
Ironcastle, 2-95
Der Irrtum des Grossen Zauberers, 6-4
Is That What People Do?, 4-492
Is There Life on a Plastic Planet?, 5-3
Isaac Asimov, 10-9, 10-10, 10-11
Isaac Asimov Presents the Great Science Fiction Stories, 3-421
Isaac Asimov's Science Fiction Magazine, 14-25
Isei no Hito, 6-279
Ishi no Ketsumyaku, 6-235
The Isis Pedlar, 5-77
Island, 3-221
An Island Called Moreau, 4-4
The Island of Captain Sparrow, 2-141
The Island of Doctor Death and Other Stories and Other Stories, 4-615
The Island of Dr. Moreau, 22, 1-100
Islandia, 3-406
Islands, 4-433
Islands in the Sky, 5-34
Islands of Space, 2-12
Isle of the Dead, 4-630
The Isles of Wisdom, 2-81
Issenichibyō Monogatari, 6-246
The Issue at Hand, 9-13
Istorii insolite, 6-444
Istorija srpske naučno-fantastične književnosti, 6-475
It Can't Happen Here, 2-62
Italo Calvino, 10-36
Iter Lunare, 6

J. G. Ballard, 10-13, 10-14, 10-16
Jack (John Stewart) Williamson, 10-180
Jack London, 10-103
Jack of Eagles, 3-46
Jack Williamson, 10-181
The Jagged Orbit, 4-88
A James Gunn Checklist, 10-67
James Tiptree, Jr., 10-147
James White, 10-179
Janissaries, 4-421
Japan Sinks, 4-305

Jehad, 4-620
JEM, 4-416
The Jesus Incident, 4-267
Jesus on Mars, 4-209
The Jewel-Hinged Jaw, 9-31
The Jewels of Elsewhen, 4-596
The Jingo, 1-22
Jinzō Bijin, 6-242
Joe Haldeman, 10-69
John Killian Houston Brunner, 10-30
The John W. Campbell Awards, 4-656
The John W. Campbell Letters, 10-37
John Wyndham Parkes Lucas Benyon Harris, 10-183
The Jonah Kit, 4-588
Journal from Ellipsia, 4-106
Journey, 4-434
Journey across the Third Planet, 5-90
Journey beyond Tomorrow, 3-336
A Journey in Other Worlds, 1-3
Journey into Space, 5-27
Journey to Mars, 1-76
A Journey to the Center of the Earth, 1-94
A Journey to the World Under-Ground, 7, 1-50, 6-346, 537, 6-390
The Joy Makers, 3-185
The Joy Wagon, 3-186
Joyleg, 3-128
The Judas Mandala, 4-85
Judgment Night, 3-290
Jules Verne, 10-150, 10-152, 10-153, 10-154
Jules Verne-Magasinet, 533, 6-376
Juniper Time, 4-601
Junk Day, 4-481
Jupiter Project, 5-13
Just the Other Day, 6-414
Justice and Her Brothers, 5-57

"K dvukhdesiatitysiacheletiu nachala rabot po osushcheniiu okeanov," 445
Kachikujin Yapū, 6-272
Kaff, auch Mare Crisium, 383
Kaitei Gunkan, 6-274
Kalki, 4-572
Kallisto, 449
Kallocain, 3-58, 532, 6-367
Kamigari, 6-288
Kampf um Utopolis, 6-46
Kapitän Mors, 380
Karavane, 6-383
Karta Strani Fantazii, 6-226
Katalog der deutschsprachigen utopischphantistichen Literatur aus fünf Jahrhunderten 1460–1960, 379, 6-36, 6-39

Kazoku Hakkei, 6-283
Keep the Giraffe Burning, 4-519
Keep Watching the Skies!, 11-3
The Keeper of the Isis Light, 5-77
Ker Shus, 6-384
Kessen: Nihon Shirizu, 6-252
The Key to the Great Gate, 3-178
Kikai-jikake no Yume, 6-303
The Killer Mice, 4-436
Die Kinder des Saturn, 6-26
Kindred, 4-104
Kindred Spirits, 4-649
King Solomon's Mines, 1-45
Kingdom of Fear, 10-87
Kinsman, 4-68
Kirlian Quest, 4-22
"Kiše, šume, grad i zvezde," 6-468
Kiteman of Karanga, 5-135
Kiteworld, 4-441
Knight Moves, 4-606
The Knights of the Limits, 4-45
The Known and the Unknown, 9-106
Koe no Ami, 6-243
Kol'tso obratnogo vremeni, 6-217
De koningen van weleer, 6-403
Kontrol, 2-107
Korset, 6-371
Krakatit, 2-14
The Kraken Wakes, 3-412
Krasnaia zvezda, 442, 6-200
Krieg im All, 6-2
Kurt Vonnegut, 10-159, 10-160, 10-161
Kyojin-tachi, 6-284

L. Ron Hubbard Presents: Writers of the Future, 4-639
Laatst nog, 6-414
Labyrinths, 3-52
Ladies from Hell, 4-442
Lagrange Five, 4-438
The Lagrangists, 4-438
Lambda 1 and Other Stories, 3-427
Lancelot Biggs: Spaceman, 3-51
The Land Beyond, 5-37
The Land of Mist, 52, 2-27
The Land That Time Forgot, 2-10
Land Under England, 2-86
The Language of the Night, 9-51
The Languages of Pao, 3-381
A Larry Niven Checklist, 10-113
The Last American, 1-66
Last and First Men, 2-109
The Last Castle, 4-561
Last Communion, 4-620
The Last Day of Creation, 4-286, 6-19
The Last Days of the Republic, 14, 1-29

The Last Defender of Camelot, 4-626
The Last Hurrah of the Golden Horde, 4-528
"The Last Judgment," 55
The Last Man, 9, 1-85
Last Orders and Other Stories, 4-8
The Last Starship from Earth, 4-73
The Last Yggdrasil, 4-621
The Lathe of Heaven, 4-326
The Lazarus Effect, 4-267
The Left Hand of Darkness, 4-327
Legends from the End of Time, 4-383
Legion, 4-238
The Legion of Space, 2-134
The Legion of Time, 2-135
Leigh Brackett, 10-21
Leigh Brackett, Marion Zimmer Bradley, Anne McCaffrey, 10-22
Leigh Douglass Brackett & Edmond Hamilton, 10-20
The Lensmen Series, 3-355
Leopard s vershiny Kilimandzharo, 449, 6-206
Lesabèndio, 382
Lest Darkness Fall, 3-135
Lest Ye Die, 2-40
Letnee utro, 6-201
Der letzte Tag der Schöpfung, 4-286, 6-19
Level 7, 3-319
Leviathan's Deep, 4-112
Lexikon der Science Fiction Literatur, 6-36
The Liberated Future, 3-441
Lieut. Gullivar Jones, 18
The Life and Adventures of Peter Wilkins, 7, 1-73
The Life and Works of David Lindsay, 10-101
Life Everlasting . . . , 2-55
A Life for the Stars, 3-43
Life in the West, 4-6
Life, the Universe and Everything, 4-1
Lifeboat Earth, 4-478
Lifeburst, 4-608
Lifekeeper, 4-372
The Light Fantastic, 3-438
Light on the Sound, 4-547
Light Years and Dark, 4-637
The Lights in the Sky Are Stars, 3-68
Lightship, 12-5
Limbo, 3-404
Limbo 90, 3-404
Limits, 4-390
The Limits of Infinity, 11-36
La Line noire d'orion, 6-62
The Lion Game, 3-328
Listen, Listen, 4-600
The Listeners, 4-244
A Literary Symbiosis, 9-76

Literatura SF, 6-464
The Literature of Fantasy, 8-49
Literature of Science Fiction, 13-46
La Littérature Française d'imagination scientifique, 6-182
Little Fuzzy, 3-308
A Little Knowledge, 4-62
Liudi kak bogi, 449, 6-210
The Lives and Times of Jerry Cornelius, 4-382
Livesendung, 6-35
Living Way Out, 3-182
Le Livre des Etoiles, 6-419
Le Livre d'or d'Alain Dorémieux, 6-87
Le Livre d'or de Gérard Klein, 6-120
Le Livre d'or de Jean-Pierre Andrevon, 6-55
Le Livre d'or de Michel Jeury, 6-111
Le Livre d'or de Philippe Curval, 6-82
Le Livre machine, 6-97
Lo Smeraldo, 6-325
Locus, 14-37
Logan's Run, 4-400
Logan's Search, 4-400
Logan's World, 4-400
The Logic of Fantasy, 10-170
Les Lolos de Venus, 6-170
The "Lomokome" Papers, 3-405
The Long Afternoon of Earth, 3-4, 4-7
The Long ARM of Gil Hamilton, 4-389
The Long Eureka, 3-330
The Long Journey, 2-50
The Long Loud Silence, 3-375
The Long Tomorrow, 3-60
The Long Way Back, 3-21
The Long Winter, 3-93
Looking Backward, 1-8
Looking Backward from the Year 2000, 4-439
The Lord of Life, 2-5
Lord of Light, 4-631
Lord of the Rings, 212
Lord of the World, 1-9
The Lordly Ones, 4-442
Lords of the Starship, 4-231
Lost: A Moon, 5-25
The Lost Continent, 1-52
Lost Dorsai, 3-146
The Lost Face, 3-296
Lost Horizon, 2-43
The Lost Planet, 5-105
The Lost Star, 5-71
The Lost World, 20, 21, 1-31
De lotgevallen, 6-407
Love Among the Ruins, 3-395
Love and Napalm: Export U.S.A., 4-33
Love in the Ruins, 4-408
Lovecraft, 10-104

The Lovers, 3-159
L.P.M.: The End of the Great War, 14, 1-6
The Lucifer Comet, 4-582
Lucifer's Hammer, 4-397
The Luck of Brin's Five, 5-170
Luderen fra Gomorra, 6-343
The Lunatics of Terra, 4-519
L'Univers vagabond, 66, 6-98
Luntrea sublimă, 6-452

Machi no Hakubutsushi, 6-262
La Machine de Balmer, 6-153
The Machine Stops, 2-106
"The Machine Stops," 1-35
The Machine to Kill, 2-61
Machines and Men, 4-442
Machines That Think, 4-635
A Mack Reynolds Checklist, 10-121
Macrolife, 4-625
Macroscope, 4-23
The Magazine of Fantasy and Science Fiction, 3-423, 14-26
The Magic Labyrinth, 4-210
The Magic Labyrinth of Philip José Farmer, 10-66
Magnetic Storm, 12-9
Mainasu Zero, 6-241
La Maison du cygne, 6-134
Les Maîtres-feu, 6-162
Major Operation, 3-398
Make Room! Make Room!, 4-257
The Making of Kubrick's 2001, 11-24
The Making of the Representative for Planet 8, 4-334
Malaise dans la science-fiction, 6-190
La Malédiction de l'ephemère, 6-70
Malevil, 4-376
Mallworld, 4-548
Malpertuis, 6-133
Malstrøm, 6-397, 6-399
The Mammoth Hunters, 4-32
De man achter het raam, 6-405
Man from Tomorrow, 3-376
Man in a Cage, 4-532
The Man in Steel, 2-17
The Man in the High Castle, 3-142
The Man in the Moone, 5, 1-39
The Man in the Tree, 4-304
Man of Two Worlds, 4-271
Man Plus, 4-417
The Man Who Awoke, 2-68
The Man Who Corrupted Earth, 4-197
The Man Who Ended War, 14
The Man Who Fell to Earth, 3-373
The Man Who Folded Himself, 4-229
The Man Who Had No Idea, 4-186
The Man Who Loved Morlocks, 4-315

The Man Who Loved the Midnight Lady, 4-357
The Man Who Mastered Time, 2-24
The Man Who Melted, 4-161
The Man Who Rocked the Earth, 14, 1-91
The Man Who Sold the Moon, 3-204
The Man Who Upset the Universe, 3-19
The Man with Six Senses, 2-48
The Manchurian Candidate, 3-118
Mandala, 4-59
Manifest Destiny, 4-342
Manly Wade Wellman, 10-162
Manna, 4-149
Man's Mortality, 2-1
Man's World, 59
Manseed, 4-609
Many Dimensions, 2-132
The Many Facets of Stephen King, 10-82
Many Futures, Many Worlds, 9-22
The Many-Colored Land, 4-366
The Maracot Deep, 2-25
The Marathon Photograph and Other Stories, 4-515
Margaret St. Clair, 10-123
Marilyn Monroe et les samouraïs du Père Noël, 6-152
Marion Zimmer Bradley, 10-23
Marooned in Real Time, 4-575
The Marriages between Zones Three, Four and Five, 4-334
Marsianskii priboi, 6-199
Der Marsspion und andere Novellen, 6-14
The Martian Chronicles, 3-64
The Martian Inca, 4-589
A Martian Odyssey . . . , 2-125
Martian Time-Slip, 3-143
The Martian Way and Other Stories, 3-21
Mary Shelley & Frankenstein, 10-130
Mary Shelley's "Frankenstein," 10-128
Mary Shelley's Monster, 10-129
The Masks of Time, 4-504
The Master, 5-168
The Master Key, 5-9
Masters of Science Fiction, 9-92
Matriarkatet, 6-345
Matrix, 14-44
Matthew Looney's Voyage to the Earth, 5-10
"Maud Evelyn," 10
Maurai and Kith, 4-16
Mayflies, 4-402
A Maze of Death, 4-176
The McAndrew Chronicles, 4-494
Meanwhile, 4-249
Meccania, 2-39
The Mechanical God, 9-33
Mechasm, 4-521
Medea, 4-651

Meet the Authors, 13-47
Megiddo's Ridge, 2-143
"Mellonta Tauta," 1-75
Memoirs of a Space Traveller, 4-331
Memoirs of a Spacewoman, 3-258
The Memoirs of a Survivor, 4-333
Memoirs of the Twentieth Century, 8
Memoirs of the Year Two Thousand Five
   Hundred, 8, 1-63
The Memory of Whiteness, 4-446
Men like Gods, 51, 2-129
Men, Martians, and Machines, 3-322
The Menace from Earth, 3-202
Le Meraviglie del Duemila, 6-323
The Mercenary, 4-421
Merchanter's Luck, 4-129A
The Merchant's War, 3-313
The Mercy Men, 5-124
Messiah, 3-389
Messiah at the End of Time, 4-383
The Metal Doom, 2-106
The Metal Monster, 2-76
The Metallic Muse, 3-33
Metamorphoses of Science Fiction, 9-97
Methuselah's Children, 3-204
Metro pour l'enfer, 6-157
Metropolis, 2-133
Michaelmas, 4-96
Microworlds, 9-52
Midas World, 4-418
Midnight at the Well of Souls, 4-123
Midwich Cuckoos, 3-413
Millennium, 2-100, 4-68, 4-568
Milwaukee the Beautiful, 4-285
Mind of My Mind, 4-103
The Mind Parasites, 4-611
Mind Partner and Eight Other Novelets
   from Galaxy, 3-436
The Mind Spider, 3-249
The Minervan Experiment, 4-276
Minimum Man, 2-70
Mir "Iskatelia," 6-222
Miracle Visitors, 4-589
Mirage, 12-35
A Mirror for Observers, 3-304
Mirror in the Sky, 4-226
The Mirror of Infinity, 13-37
Mirrorshades, 4-669
Misplaced Persons, 5-59
Miss Pickerell Goes to Mars, 5-104
Miss Pickerell on the Moon, 5-104
The Missing Man, 4-349
Missing Men of Saturn, 5-92
Mission Earth: The Invaders Plan, 4-280
Mission: Interplanetary, 3-384
Mission of Gravity, 3-109
Mission to Moulokin, 4-219
Mission to the Heart Stars, 5-18

Mr. Adam, 3-167
Mr. Bass's Planetoid, 5-23
Mr. Blettsworthy on Rampole Island, 51
Mister Justice, 4-413
Mrs. Frisby and the Rats of NIMH, 5-126
Mists of Dawn, 5-129
The MIT Science Fiction Society's Index to
   the SF Magazines, 1951–1965, 14-9
Mizora, 1-56
Mockingbird, 4-551
Moderan, 4-98
Modern Masterpieces of Science Fiction, 3-
   450
Modern Science Fiction, 9-15, 13-38
Modern Science Fiction and the Literary
   Community, 9-53
The Mohole Mystery, 5-163
Molly Zero, 4-443
The Moment of Eclipse, 4-8
Les Mondes imaginaires et les mondes
   réels, 530
Les Mondes parallèles de la science fiction
   sovietique, 6-191
Mongoru no Zankō, 6-280
The Monster Men, 19
Monthly Terrors, 14-8
Monument, 3-34
The Moon and the Face, 5-111
The Moon Colony, 5-12
"The Moon Hoax," 6
The Moon Is a Harsh Mistress, 4-263
The Moon Maid, 2-11
The Moon Maker, 1-91
The Moon Pool, 2-77
Moonferns and Starsongs, 4-500
Moon-Flash, 5-111
More Issues at Hand, 9-14
More Soviet Science Fiction, 3-447
More Stories from the Twilight Zone, 3-
   333
More Than Human, 3-362
More Wandering Stars, 4-645
Moreau's Other Island, 4-4
Moreta, Dragonlady of Pern, 4-368
Morgen is Blond, 6-431
The Morphodite, 4-221
Morrow's Ants, 4-281
Mort a l'étouffée, 6-109
The Mortal Instruments, 5-15
The Mortgage on the Brain, 11
The Mote in God's Eye, 4-398
Motherlines, 4-125
Mouvance, 6-175
"Moxon's Master," 1-13
"MS Found in a Bottle," 1-75
The Mudhead, 5-147
"Mudraci Saurije," 6-474
The Müller-Fokker Effect, 4-520

Muma no Hyōteki, 6-244
Murder in Millennium VI, 3-180
The Murder of the Missing Link, 3-388
The Murder of the U.S.A., 3-257
Musique Fantastique, 11-31
Musubiyama Hiroku, 6-236
Mutant, 3-244
Mutant 59, 4-407
The Mutant Weapon, 3-258
My Best Science Fiction Story, 3-448
My First Two Thousand Years, 62
My Name Is Legion, 4-626
Le Mystérieux Docteur Cornélius, 6-122
Mysterious Visions, 3-460
The Mystery, 1-107
A Mystery for Mr. Bass, 5-23
The Mystery of Evelin Delorme, 11
Mythopoeikon, 12-39

Na ons de Monsters, 6-428
La Naguen, 6-104
La Naissance des dieux, 6-100
Naissez, nous ferons le reste!, 6-94
The Napoleon of Notting Hill, 1-23
The Narrative of Arthur Gordon Pym of
    Nantucket, 9, 1-74
The Nature of the Catastrophe, 4-382
Les Navigateurs de l'infini, 6-139
Navigator's Syndrome, 4-113
Le navire de nulle part, 6-158
The Nearest Five, 5-170
Nebula Awards, 4-673
Nebula Maker, 2-112
Necromancer, 3-146
Needle, 3-110
The Needle on Full, 4-215
"Nemačka 1942," 6-470
The Neon Halo, 3-124
Neq the Sword, 4-20
Nerilka's Story, 4-368
Nerves, 3-140
The NESFA Index, 14-11
Neuere Tendenzen der sowjetischen Sci-
    ence Fiction, 6-47
Neuromancer, 4-233
The Neutral Stars, 4-384
Neutron Star, 4-390
The New Adam, 2-94, 2-126
The New Atlantis, 5
New Constellations, 4-647
New Dimensions, 4-664
New Found Land, 5-29
The New Gods Lead, 2-142
The New Improved Sun, 4-647
New Maps of Hell, 9-5
The New Moon, 2-87
The New Pleasure, 2-35

New Soviet Science Fiction, 4-670
New Stories from the Twilight Zone, 3-333
New Tales of Space and Time, 3-440
The New Visions, 12-31
New Voices, 4-656
New Worlds, 4-659
New Worlds for Old, 9-46
New Writings in SF, 4-640
A New Year's Tale, 3-150
News from Nowhere, 1-69
The Next Crusade, 12
NF, 6-221
Nicolai Klimii Iter Subterraneum, 7, 1-50,
    6-346, 537, 6-390
Niels Klims underjordiske Reise, 518, 6-
    346
Night Journey, 3-181
Night of Camp David, 3-232
The Night of Kadar, 4-296
Night of Light, 3-160
Nightfall and Other Stories, 3-21
Nightflyers, 4-361
Nightmare Express, 4-246
Nightmares of Eminent Persons and Other
    Stories, 3-320
Nightwings, 4-505
Nihon no SF, 6-295
Nihon SF Besutu Shūsei, 6-297
Nihon SF Koten Koten, 6-305
Nihon SF Nenkan, 6-304
Nine Hundred Grandmothers, 4-311
1985, 3-302, 4-160
Nineteen Eighty-Four, 3-302, 10-117
The 1986 Annual World's Best SF, 4-672
99%, 2-36
Ningen no Yō ni Aruita Neko, 6-273
Niourk, 6-164
Nippon Chimbotsu, 481, 6-259
No Blade of Grass, 3-92
No Direction Home, 4-528
No Enemy but Time, 4-63
No Future in It, 3-71
No Man Friday, 3-177
No Man's Land, 5-165
No One Will Escape, 3-229
No Place Else, 9-80
No Room for Man, 3-146, 13-23
Noah's Castle, 5-156
Noch'kontrabandoi, 6-199
The Nonborn King, 4-366
Nonliterary Influences on Science Fiction,
    9-18
"Nonsharan Kiroku," 477, 6-276
Non-stop, 3-6
Noö, 6-165
Noon: 22nd Century, 4-670
Nor Crystal Tears, 4-220
Nord for tiden, 6-343

Nordenholt's Million, 2-20
"Norsk science fiction fandom," 6-398
Norstrilia, 3-353
Not by Bread Alone, 4-378
Not This August, 3-239
Not Without Sorcery, 3-366
Notes to a Science Fiction Writer, 13-12
Notions: Unlimited, 3-337
La Nouvelle science-fiction Américaine, 6-183
Nova, 4-168
Nova Express, 4-100
Nova Science Fiction, 6-377
Nova SF Speciale, 6-328
The Novels of Philip K. Dick, 10-58
Now Wait for Last Year, 4-175
Nuage, 6-118
Null-A Three, 3-386
Number 87, 2-90
Nunquam, 4-194

O falie în timp, 6-458
O tragedie cerească, 6-441
Oameni şi stele, 6-448
Oath of Fealty, 4-399
The Obsolete Necessity, 8-54
Occam's Razor, 3-151
Oceania-Pacific-Dreadnought, 6-453
Octagon, 4-462
Odd John, 2-110
L'Oeil du purgatoire, 6-146
Of All Possible Worlds, 3-370
Of Men and Monsters, 3-371
Die Ohnmacht der Allmächtigen, 6-25
Okami no Monshō, 6-239
Olaf Stapledon, 10-138, 10-139, 10-140, 10-141
The Old Die Rich and Other Science Fiction Stories, 3-175
Olga Romanoff, 1-42
Les Olympiades truquées, 6-163
The Olympic Hope, 3-265, 6-348
Det olympiske håb, 3-265, 6-348
Omni, 14-27
The Omnibus of Science Fiction, 3-431
The Omnibus of Time, 2-29
Omni's Screen Flights/Screen Fantasies, 11-33
Omnivore, 4-24
Oms en série, 6-166
On a Pale Horse, 4-23
On the Beach, 3-344
On the Good Ship Enterprise, 11-38
On Wheels, 4-284
On Wings of Song, 4-187
On Writing Science Fiction, 13-18
One, 3-225

One Against Eternity, 3-385
One Hundred and Two H Bombs, 4-186
One Hundred Years of Science Fiction, 3-442
One Hundred Years of SF Illustration, 12-18
One in Three Hundred, 3-278
The 1000 Year Plan, 3-19
One Winter in Eden, 4-61
Only Apparently Real, 10-59
Onna to Onna no Yo no Naka ni, 6-277
Operation Time Search, 5-117
The Ophiuchi Hotline, 4-569
The Opium General and Other Stories, 4-382
Options, 4-491
Or All the Seas with Oysters, 3-129
ORA:CLE, 4-403
Oran-penteku no Fukushū, 6-254
Oraşele înecate, 6-440
L'orbe et la roue, 6-112
Orbit, 4-655
Orbitsville, 4-482
Orbitsville Departure, 4-482
The Orchid Cage, 3-168
Der Orchideengarten, 531
Ordeal in Otherwhere, 5-122
Origami Uchūsen no Densetsu, 6-292
Orion Shall Rise, 4-16
Orn, 4-24
Orphan Star, 4-220
Ortog, 6-148
Ortog et les ténèbres, 6-148
Orwell's Nineteen Eighty-Four, 10-116
Ossian's Ride, 3-217
Ostrov muzhestva, 6-206
Other Days, Other Eyes, 4-483
The Other Human Race, 3-308
The Other Side of the Moon, 3-433
The Other Side of the Sky, 3-102
The Other Side of the Sun, 3-87
The Other Side of Time, 3-248
Other Stories, and the Attack of the Giant Baby, 4-436
The Other Worlds, 3-458
Other Worlds, Other Gods, 4-665
Other Worlds, Other Seas, 4-670
Oul lui Columb, 6-451
De Oude Symphonie van ons Hart, 6-434
Our Friends from Frolix-8, 4-176
Our Wonderful World, 54
Out of My Mind, 3-72
Out of the Deeps, 3-412
Out of the Everywhere and Other Extraordinary Visions, 4-554
Out of the Mouth of the Dragon, 4-231
Out of the Silent Planet, 3-263
Out There, 5-103, 5-149

Out There Where the Big Ships Go, 4-154
The Outer Limits, 11-34
Outreach, 4-339
Outside the Universe, 2-41
Over My Shoulder, 9-34
Ox, 4-24
Oxygen och Aromasia, 532, 6-369

The Palace of Eternity, 4-484
Il Palazzo nel Cielo, 6-312
The Pale Invaders, 5-87
The Pale Shadow of Science, 9-2
Palimpsests, 4-479
"Palos" trilogy, 52
Panorama de la science fiction, 6-196
Paperback Inferno, 14-44
Paradise and Iron, 2-8
Paradise I, 4-254
The Paradox Men, 3-189
Paralittératures, 6-177
Parallel Lines, 12-13
Un Passe-temps, 6-149
Passing for Human, 4-480
The Passion of New Eve, 4-117
Past Master, 4-312
The Past Through Tomorrow, 3-204
The Pastel City, 4-260
The Patchwork Girl, 4-389
Path Into the Unknown, 3-447
Patron of the Arts, 4-451
The Pattern of Expectation, 9-26
Patternmaster, 4-103
Patterns of the Fantastic, 9-114
Patterns of the Fantastic II, 9-114A
Pavane, 4-444
The Pawns of Null-A, 3-386
The Peace Machine, 4-485
The Peace War, 4-575
The Peacemaker, 2-32
Pebble in the Sky, 3-22
Pelle d'Ombra, 6-310
The Penguin Encyclopedia of Horror and
    the Supernatural, 8-50
The Penguin World Omnibus of Science
    Fiction, 4-633
The People: No Different Flesh, 3-208
The People of the Ax, 5-172
People of the Comet, 2-31
The People of the Ruins, 2-97
People of the Wind, 4-17
The People Trap, 4-492
Perchance to Dream, 4-439
Perelandra, 3-263
The Perfect World, 2-96
Le Péril bleu, 6-136
Perilous Planets, 3-419
Perpetual Light, 4-665

Perry Rhodan, 381
The Persistence of Vision, 4-570
Phantastik und Futurologie, 6-44
Philip José Farmer, 10-65
Philip K. Dick, 10-54, 10-55, 10-56
Philip Kindred Dick, 10-51
Philosophers Look at Science Fiction, 13-
    32
The Philosopher's Stone, 4-611
The Philosophical Corps, 3-116
Philosophy and Science Fiction, 13-32
Phobos, the Robot Planet, 5-25
Phoenix in the Ashes, 4-573
Phthor, 4-21
Picnic on Paradise, 4-455
A Pictorial History of Science Fiction, 9-49
A Pictorial History of Science Fiction
    Films, 11-17, 11-21
Piers Anthony, 10-6
Pilgrimage, 3-208, 4-373
Pilgrimage to Earth, 3-338
Pilgrims through Space and Time, 9-8
Pion, 6-411
Pirates of Venus, 1-16
The Pirates of Zan, 3-258
PKD, 10-60
La Plaie, 6-101
The Planet Buyer, 3-353
A Planet Called Treason, 4-110
The Planet Explorer, 3-255
Planet in the Eye of Time, 4-196
Planet of No Return, 3-192
Planet of the Apes, 3-55
Planet of the Damned, 3-192
Planet of the Double Sun, 2-52
Planet of the Dreamers, 3-268
Planet of the Warlord, 5-67
Planète socialiste, 6-172
The Planiverse, 4-171
The Platypus of Doom and Other Nihilists,
    4-151
Player Piano, 3-392
Plesk zvezdnykh morei, 452, 6-213
The Pliocene Companion, 4-366
Plutoniia, 442
The Pocket Book of Science Fiction, 3-461
The Poison Belt, 21, 1-32
Poisson-pilote, 6-95
The Political and Social Ideas of Jules
    Verne, 10-151
The Pollinators of Eden, 4-74
Poney-Dragon, 6-113
The Pool of Fire, 5-32
Port Eternity, 4-130
Portrait du diable en chapeau melon, 6-68
Portrait of Jennie, 3-294
Posledniaia voina, 453, 6-202
The Possessors, 3-94

Possible Worlds, 55
Les Posthumes, 406
The Postman, 4-80
Poul Anderson, 10-4
Pour patrie l'espace, 6-73
Pourquois J'ai tué Jules Verne, 6-180
Povestiri deocamdată fantastice, 6-446
The Power, 3-318
The Power of Stars, 5-94
The Power of Time, 4-473
The Practice Effect, 4-81
Praise All the Moons of Morning, 5-148
Precious Porcelain, 2-6
Les Prédateurs enjolivés, 6-75
Preferred Risk, 3-275A
Prelude in Prague, 2-143
Prelude to Space, 3-103
Preserve and Protect, 3-149
Preserver, 4-221
Prețul secant al genunii, 6-456
The Pride of Chanur, 4-131
Prijatelj sa daleke zvezde, 6-467
The Prince in Waiting, 5-31
The Princes of Earth, 5-91
A Princess of Mars, 18, 1-17
The Princess of the Atom, 2-23
Prisoner of PSI, 5-82
Le Prisonnier de la planète Mars, 6-123
Privateers, 4-69
The Probability Pad, 4-12
Probe, 4-189
"Problem," 6-472
Profundis, 4-153
The Programmed Man, 5-153
Programmeret til Kærlighed, 6-358
Project Jupiter, 3-68
Project Pope, 4-516
Prologue to Analog, 3-426
The Prometheus Man, 4-387
The Promise of Joy, 3-149
La Proposta, 6-308
Protector, 4-391
Proverka na razumnost', 6-199
Providence Island, 3-195
Proxima, 6-366
Psion, 5-160
The Psychotronic Encyclopedia of Film,
    11-8
Ptah Hotep, 6-93
Pulp Voices, 10-195
The Pulps, 722
Pulpwood Editor, 721
The Puppet Masters, 3-205
The Purloined Prince, 4-581
Puteshestvie moego brata Alekseiia v
    stranu krestianskoi utopii, 445, 6-205
Puteshestvie v zemliu Ofirskuiu, 441
Puzzle of the Space Pyramids, 3-36

Q Colony, 4-552
Quando le Radici, 6-306
Quarber Merkur, 6-50, 14-39
Quatermass and the Pit, 3-231
The Quatermass Experiment, 3-231
Quatermass II, 3-231
A Queen of Atlantis, 1-5
"The Queen of Sheba," 11
The Queen of the Legion, 2-134
Queen Victoria's Bomb, 4-135
Queenmagic, Kingmagic, 4-590
Quest Crosstime, 5-118
Quest for Fire, 1-79, 2-95
A Quest for Simbilis, 3-380
Quest for the Well of Souls, 4-123
Quest of the Dawn Man, 2-95
Quicksand, 4-89
Quinzinzinsili, 6-126

An R. A. Lafferty Checklist, 10-89
Race against Time, 5-5
The Radio Man, 52, 2-29
Radio's Golden Age of Science Fiction, 13-
    48
Radix, 4-30
A Rag, a Bone and a Hank of Hair, 5-50
The Ragged Astronauts, 4-486
The Ragged Edge, 3-95
Ragnarok, 2-26
The Rains of Eridan, 5-72
Ralph 124C41+, 21, 1-37
Ram Song, 5-166
Ranks of Bronze, 4-192
Ratha's Creature, 5-11
Ray Bradbury, 10-24, 10-25
Ray Bradbury and the Poetics of Reverie,
    10-28
The Ray Bradbury Companion, 10-26
Le Rayon SF, 6-184
Reach for Tomorrow, 3-102, 3-104
Reader in a Strange Land, 8-55
A Reader's Guide to Science Fiction, 8-31
The Reality Trip and Other
    Implausibilities, 4-500
Reason and Romanticism, 2-91
Rebirth, 2-74
Re-Birth, 3-414
Récits de science fiction, 6-140
Reclams Science-Fiction-Führer, 6-37
Red Alert, 3-172
The Red Napoleon, 2-34
"The Red One," 1-60
The Red Peri, 2-125
Red Snow, 2-82
Red Star, 6-200
Red Stars, 455, 9-58
Redworld, 4-251

A Reference Guide to American Science Fiction Films, 11-7
Reference Guide to Fantastic Films, 11-2
Reflections in the Moon Pool, 10-112
Reflections on the Fantastic, 9-111
The Reign of George VI, 1900–1925, 8, 1-2
Reisen til Ai-Po-Tu, 541, 6-388
Reisen til Ken, 539, 6-378
Reizigers in de anti-tijd, 6-407, 6-432
Relatives, 4-199
"A Relic of the Pliocene," 1-60
The Remaking of Sigmund Freud, 4-358
Rendezvous with Rama, 4-138
Report on Probability A, 4-9
The Reproductive System, 4-521
Requiem for Astounding, 14-15
Requiem pour demain, 6-160
A Research Guide to Science Fiction Studies, 8-21
Re/Search No. 8/9: J. G. Ballard, 10-17
The Reservation, 6-409
Respublik Iuzhnogo Kresta, 442
The Rest of the Robots, 3-20
The Restaurant at the End of the Universe, 4-1
Retour à la terre, 6-169
Return from Luna, 5-56
Return from Witch Mountain, 5-88
The Return of Nathan Brazil, 4-123
The Return of William Shakespeare, 2-57
Return to Earth, 5-73
Return to Reading Software, 13-49
Return to the Gate, 5-37
Revi-Lona, 1-27
Revolt in 2100, 3-204
The Revolt of Aphrodite, 4-194
Revolt of the Triffids, 3-411
Rhialto the Marvelous, 3-380
The Riddle of the Sands, 12, 1-24
The Riddle of the Tower, 3-21, 3-28
Riddley Walker, 4-272
Rider Haggard, 10-68
The Right Hand of Dextra, 4-316
The Rim of Space, 3-90
The "Rim World" series, 3-90
De Ring, 6-435
Ring around the Sun, 3-346
The Ring of Ritornel, 4-252
Ringing Changes, 4-311
Ringworld, 4-392
Ringworld Engineers, 4-392
Rite of Passage, 4-406, 15-58
River of Eternity, 4-210
Riverworld and Other Stories, 4-210
The Road to Corlay, 4-155
The Road to Science Fiction, 13-25
Road to the Rim, 3-90

Roadside Picnic & The Tale of the Troika, 4-542
Robert A. Heinlein, 10-71, 10-72, 10-75
Robert Silverberg, 10-132, 10-133
The Robot Who Looked Like Me, 4-492
Robots and Empire, 4-28
Robots Have No Tales, 3-245
The Robots of Dawn, 4-28
Rocket Ship Galileo, 5-63
Rocket to Luna, 5-107
The Rocket to the Moon, 2-133
The Rocket's Shadow, 5-17
The Rod of Light, 4-46
Roderick, 4-522
Roderick at Random, 4-522
Roger Zelazny, 10-184, 10-186, 10-187
Rogue Moon, 3-77
Rogue Queen, 3-136
The Rolling Stones, 5-64
Rolltown, 4-439
Un român în lună, 6-457
The Rose, 3-190
A Rose for Armageddon, 4-477
La Rosée du soleil, 6-102
Round the Moon, 16, 1-93
Round Trip Space Ship, 5-145
The Ruins of Earth, 4-647
Rummet uden tid, 6-343
Run, Come See Jerusalem, 4-374
Run to the Stars, 4-450
The Runaway Robot, 5-49
R.U.R., 2-15
Russian Hide and Seek, 4-11
Russian Science Fiction, 3-447
Russian Science Fiction 1956–1974, 6-230
Russkii sovetskii nauchno-fantasticheskiis roman, 6-224

Sabella, 4-321
Les Sables de Falun, 6-83
Saggi sul Fantastico, 6-340
Saiäns Fiktschen, 6-13
Saigo no Kyōwakoku, 6-249
The Saliva Tree and Other Strange Growths, 3-5
Salvage and Destroy, 4-340
Sam of de Pluterdag, 6-404, 6-436
The Same to You Doubled, 4-492
Samuel R. Delany, 10-49, 10-50, 10-52
Sandkings, 4-361
Santiago, 4-437
The Sardonyx Net, 4-348
Satan, 4-336
Satana dei Miracoli, 6-313
Saurus, 2-90
Savremenici buducnosti, 6-476
Sayonara Jupiter, 6-260

A Scanner Darkly, 4-177
Scarlet Dream, 2-80
The Scarlet Plague, 1-60
Scènes de guerre civile, 6-110
A Scent of New-Mown Hay, 3-39
Le Sceptre volé aux hommes, 6-422
The Schimmelhorn File, 4-79
Schimmelhorn's Gold, 4-79
Schismatrix, 4-538
School and Society through Science Fiction, 13-33
Schrödinger's Cat, 4-612
Der Schuss ins All, 57, 2-33
Science Fiction: A Collection of Critical Essays, 9-84
Science Fiction: A Critical Guide, 9-73
Science Fiction: A Historical Anthology, 13-35
Science Fiction Alien Encounter, 13-5
Science Fiction: An Illustrated History, 9-55
Science Fiction: An Introduction, 13-2
Science Fiction and Fantasy, 13-50
Science Fiction and Fantasy Authors, 8-3A
Science Fiction and Fantasy Book Review Index, 1980–1984, 8-20
Science Fiction and Fantasy Literature, 8-1
Science Fiction and Fantasy Reference Index, 1978–1985, 8-20
Science Fiction and Fantasy Series and Sequels, 8-22
Science Fiction and Horror Posters in Full Color, 11-23
Science Fiction and the New Dark Age, 9-12
Science Fiction and Utopian Fantasy in Soviet Literature, 455
A Science Fiction Argosy, 3-444
Science Fiction Art, 12-1, 12-15
Science Fiction as Literature, 13-1
Science Fiction at Large, 9-67
Science Fiction aus Deutschland, 6-34
SF: Authors' Choice, 3-448
Science fiction: Autori, cărti, idei, 6-462
"Science fiction av norske forfattere," 6-399
The Science Fiction Book, 9-86
The SF Book of Lists, 8-42
Science Fiction Book Review Index, 1923–1973, 8-18
Science Fiction Book Review Index, 1974–1979, 8-19
Science Fiction by Gaslight, 1-70
Science Fiction by the Rivals of H. G. Wells, 1-80
Science Fiction Chronicle, 14-38
Science/Fiction Collections, 8-39
Science Fiction Criticism, 8-16

Science Fiction Detective Tales, 9-54
Science Fiction Dialogues, 9-107
The Science Fiction Encyclopedia, 8-30
Science-fiction et soucoups volantes, 6-192
SF, fantastique et ateliers créatifs, 6-439
Science Fiction, Fantasy, and Weird Fiction Magazines, 14-18
Science Fiction [Film Encyclopedia], 11-1
The Science Fiction Film Source Book, 11-9
Science Fiction Films of the Seventies, 11-25
Science Fiction First Editions, 8-5
Science Fiction Hall of Fame, 3-455, 13-36
Science Fiction Handbook, Revised, 13-14
Science Fiction: History-Science-Vision, 9-90, 13-9
Science Fiction, Horror & Fantasy Films & Television Credits, 11-6
The Science Fiction Image, 11-10
Science Fiction in America, 1870s–1930s, 8-12A
Science Fiction in Deutschland, 379, 6-45
SF in Dimension, 9-71
Science Fiction in Old San Francisco, 9-64
Science Fiction in Print–1985, 8-8
Science Fiction in the Cinema, 11-11
Science Fiction in the English Class, 13-4
SF International, 14-28
Science Fiction: Its Criticism and Teaching, 9-74, 13-6
Science Fiction: Jules Verne to Ray Bradbury, 13-51
SF Magajin Serekushon, 6-296
The Science Fiction Magazines, 14-5
Science Fiction Master Index of Names, 8-20
Science Fiction Movies, 11-22
SF no Jidai, 6-301
SF no Sekai, 6-299
The Science Fiction Novel, 9-91
The Science Fiction of H. G. Wells, 10-172
The Science Fiction of Isaac Asimov, 10-12
The Science Fiction of Jack London, 1-60
The Science Fiction of Mark Clifton, 3-112
The Science Fiction of Mark Twain, 1-25
Science Fiction of the Fifties, 3-452
Science Fiction of the Forties, 3-452
Science Fiction of the Thirties, 2-58
Science Fiction Omnibus, 3-422
SF Published in Great Britain, 14-44
Science Fiction Quiz, 8-40
Science Fiction Reader's Guide, 13-2A
The Science Fiction Reference Book, 8-33
Science Fiction Research Association Newsletter, 14-40
SF Seiyūki, 6-248
The Science Fiction Source Book, 8-34

Science Fiction: Status of Status Quo?, 6-413
The Science Fiction Stories of Walter M. Miller, Jr., 3-286
Science Fiction Story Index 1950–1979, 8-11
Science-Fiction Studies, 14-41
Science Fiction Studies in Film, 11-20
SF Suikoden, 6-248
Science Fiction: Ten Explorations, 9-57
Science Fiction: The Future, 13-21
Science Fiction: The Mythos of a New Romance, 13-3
Science Fiction: The 100 Best Novels, 9-78, 13-7
SF: The Other Side of Realism, 9-23
SF: The Year's Greatest Science-Fiction and Fantasy, 3-449
Science Fiction Times, 6-51
Science Fiction, Today and Tomorrow, 9-16
SF Tosho Kaisetsu Sōmokuroku, 6-300
Science Fiction Voices #1, 10-196
Science Fiction Voices #5, 10-197
Science Fiction: What It's All About, 6-374, 9-55
Science Fiction Writers, 8-27
Science Fiction Writer's Workshop I, 13-16
The Science in Science Fiction, 9-68
Science, Myth and the Fictional Creation of Alien Worlds, 9-105
Scientific Romance in Britain 1890–1950, 9-93
The Scope of the Fantastic, 9-112
Screening Space, 11-36
Se dagens lys, 6-349
"The Sea Raiders," 21, 1-102
Season of the Witch, 4-539
Seasons in Flight, 4-8
The Second Deluge, 1-83
Second Ending, 3-399
Second Foundation, 3-19
Second Nature, 4-597
Second Stage Lensman, 3-355
The Second Trip, 4-506
The Secret of Life, 4-454
The Secret of Saturn's Rings, 5-176
The Secret of the Martian Moons, 5-177
Sector General, 3-398
The Seed of Evil, 4-45
Seed of Light, 3-121
Seed of Stars, 4-384
The Seedling Stars, 3-47
Seeds of Life, 2-117
Seeing Earth, 9-104
Seekers of Tomorrow, 10-192
Seetee Ship, 3-403
Seetee Shock, 3-403

"Sejač," 6-471
Sekai no SF Bungaku Sōkaisetsu, 6-302
Sengo Shoki Nihon SF Besuto Shūsei, 6-298
Sengoku Jieitai, 6-237
Sense of Obligation, 3-192
Il Senso del Futuro, 6-337
Sentō Yōssei: Yikikaze, 6-251
The Sentimental Agents in the Volyen Empire, 4-334
The Sentinel Stars, 3-91
A Separate Star, 12-17A
La Sepoltura, 6-318
Serpent's Reach, 4-132
Sette Accadimenti in Venezia, 6-320
Seven Days in May, 3-232
Seven Days in New Crete, 3-179
The Seventh Bowl, 2-7
The Seventh Day, 3-229
Sex and the High Command, 4-75
The Sex Sphere, 4-454
S-F 2, 11-18
Sfera paralelă, 6-453
SFWA Bulletin, 14-42
A Shade of Difference, 3-149
The Shadow Girl, 2-24
The Shadow of Alpha, 4-238
Shadow of Earth, 4-200
The Shadow of the Ship, 4-223
The Shadow of the Torturer, 4-616
Shadow on the Hearth, 3-284
Shadows in the Sun, 3-301
Shadows of the Magic Lamp, 11-35
The Shape of Space, 4-390
The Shape of Things to Come, 51, 2-130
Sharra's Exile, 4-77
Shatterday, 4-206
She, 1-46
The Sheep Look Up, 4-90
A Sheet of Blotting Paper, 20
The Shepherd Moon, 5-74
Shiel in Diverse Hands, 10-131
Shikasta, 4-334
The Shining Pool, 5-26
The Ship from Outside, 3-90
The Ship That Sailed the Time Stream, 4-198
The Ship Who Sang, 4-369
Shirokabe no Moji wa Sekiyō ni Haeru, 6-232
The Shockwave Rider, 4-91
Shōmetsu no Kōrin, 6-265
A Short History of the Future, 3-96
The Short Stories of H. G. Wells, 1-102
The Shorter Works of Stephen King, 10-84
The Shot Into Infinity, 57, 2-33
The Shrinking Man, 3-275

The Shudder Pulps, 722
Shuto Shōshitsu, 6-261
Sidereus Nuncius, 5
Sight of Proteus, 4-495
The Sign at Six, 1-108
Sign of the Labrys, 3-326
The Sign of the Mute Medusa, 4-581
La Signe du chien, 6-105
The Silent Bullet, 1-77
The Silent Speakers, 3-331
The Silver Eggheads, 3-252
The Silver Locusts, 3-64
The Silver Metal Lover, 4-322
Les Singes du temps, 6-113
Singularitäten, 6-28
Singularity, 5-144
Sinister Barrier, 3-323
The Sinister Researches of C. P. Ransom,
   3-295
The Sins of the Fathers, 4-478
The Sirens of Titan, 3-393
The Sirian Experiments, 4-334
Sirius, 2-111
63 Auteurs, 6-198
Sjørøvcre, 6-385
The Skylark of Space, 2-104
Slan, 3-383
Slaughterhouse-Five, 4-578
Slave Ship, 3-312
Sleepless Nights in the Procrustean Bed,
   10-64
Slow Birds and Other Stories, 4-591
Smile on the Void, 4-236
The Smoke Ring, 4-388
The Snail on the Slope, 4-543
Snøen på Nix Olympia, 6-392
The Snow Queen, 4-574
So Long, and Thanks for All the Fish, 4-1
The Soft Machine, 9-77
Soft Targets, 4-282
Software, 4-453
Solar Lottery, 3-144
Solarion, 11, 1-34
Solaris, 3-261
Solaris-Almanach, 6-52
Soldier, Ask Not, 3-148
Soleil chaud poisson des profondeurs, 6-
   113
Les Soleils noirs d'Arcadie, 6-176
Some Dreams Are Nightmares, 3-185
Some Kind of Paradise, 9-24
Some Ladies in Haste, 11
Somerset Dreams and Other Fictions, 4-
   600
Somnium, 5, 1-54
Son of Man, 4-507
A Son of the Ages, 20, 1-96
A Song for Lya and Other Stories, 4- 361

The Song of the Axe, 4-604
The Songbirds of Pain, 4-297
Songmaster, 4-111
Songs from the Stars, 4-529
The Songs of Distant Earth, 4-139
Sons of the Ocean Deeps, 5-164
La Sortie est au fond de l'espace, 6-151
Sos the Rope, 4-20
Soul of the Robot, 4-46
The Sound of His Horn, 3-327
The Sound of Wonder, 10-199
Soviet Science Fiction, 3-447
Space Adventure Series, 13-29
The Space Ark, 5-99
Space Art, 12-26
Space by the Tale, 3-38
Space Chantey, 4-313
The Space Eater, 4-317
Space Hostages, 5-51
Space Lords, 3-354
The Space Merchants, 3-313
Space Odysseys, 3-419
The Space Odysseys of Arthur C. Clarke,
   10-43
Space on My Hands, 3-69
Space Opera, 3-419
The Space Plague, 5-99
Space Police, 3-460
The Space Ship in the Park, 5-145
The Space Ship Returns to the Apple
   Tree, 5-145
The Space Ship under the Apple Tree, 5-
   145
Space, Time and Crime, 3-460
The Space Vampires, 4-611
Space War Blues, 4-345
Space Winners, 5-45
Spaccache, 4-613
Spacetimewarp, 12-29
The Spacious Adventures of the Man in
   the Street, 2-85
Speaker for the Dead, 4-109
Speaking of Science Fiction, 10-198
Special Effects, 11-26
Spectrum, 3-420
A Spectrum of Fantasy, 8-4
Sphereland, 6-402
Spider's War, 2-140
The Spirit of Dorsai, 3-146
Spiritele anului 3000, 6-450
The Spiteful Planet and Other Stories, 6-
   245
The Spot of Life, 2-31
The Squares of the City, 3-73
SS-GB, 4-162
Stained-Glass World, 4-97
The Stainless Steel Rat, 3-193
Stand on Zanzibar, 4-92

The Standing Joy, 4-241
Stanislaw Lem, 10-99
"The Star," 21, 1-102
Star Anchored, Star Angered, 4-202
Star Born, 5-121
Star Colony, 4-320
The Star Diaries, 4-331
Star Dust, 2-121
The Star Fox, 3-12
Star Girl, 5-175
Star Healer, 3-398, 4-594
Star Ka'at, 5-119
Star Ka'at World, 5-119
Star Ka'ats and the Planet People, 5-119
Star Ka'ats and the Winged Warriors, 5-119
Star Maker, 2-112
Star Man's Son, 5-120
Star of Gypsies, 4-508
The Star of Life, 3-188
Star of the Unborn, 3-396
Star ou psi de Cassiopée, 406
Star Prince Charlie, 3-9
Star Rebel, 4-101
Star Rider, 4-412
The Star Rover, 11
Star Science Fiction Stories, 3-453
Star Songs of an Old Primate, 4-554
The Star-Spangled Future, 4-528
Star Surgeon, 3-398, 5-125
Star Winds, 4-47
Star-Begotten, 51, 2-131
Starboard Wine, 9-32
Starburst, 4-419
Stardance, 4-449
Starfinder, 4-622
Starlight, 3-31, 3-109
Starlog, 14-32
Starman Jones, 5-65
Starmaster's Gambit, 3-230
Starquake!, 4-217
The Starry Rift, 4-553
The Stars Are Ours, 5-121
The Stars Are Too High, 3-24
Stars in My Pocket like Grains of Sand, 4-169
The Stars My Destination, 3-32
Starship, 3-6
Starship and Haiku, 4-549
Starship Invincible, 2-56
Starship Troopers, 3-206
Starsilk, 4-564
Start nach Utopolis, 6-46
Startide Rising, 4-82
Station X, 2-136
Staying Alive, 13-19
The Steam-Driven Boy and Other Strangers, 4-519

The Steel Crocodile, 4-144
Stella Polaris, 6-396
The Stellar Gauge, 9-99
Step to the Stars, 5-41
Stephen King, 10-88
Stephen King as Richard Bachman, 10-81
Steps of the Sun, 4-551
Still I Persist in Wondering, 3-303
The Still Small Voice of Trumpets, 4-58
Die Stimmen der Nacht, 6-33
Sølvfalken, 6-382
The Stochastic Man, 4-502
Stoppested i evigheten, 6-387
Storia del Cinema di Fantascienza, 6-335
Stories from the Twilight Zone, 3-333
The Stories of Ray Bradbury, 3-62
A Storm of Wings, 4-260
Storm over Warlock, 5-122
The Story of Ab, 20, 1-97
"A Story of Days to Come," 1-102
"A Story of the Stone Age," 1-102
Stowaway to the Mushroom Planet, 5-23
Strana bagrovykh tuch, 6-211
Strange Attractors, 4-638
The Strange Case of Dr. Jekyll and Mr. Hyde, 1-86
A Strange Discovery, 9
Strange Doings, 4-311
Strange Horizons, 9-65
The Strange Invaders, 2-64
A Strange Manuscript Found in a Copper Cylinder, 16, 1-28
Strange Ports of Call, 3-434
Strange Relations, 3-161
Strange Seas and Shores, 3-130
Strangeness, 4-647
Stranger in a Strange Land, 3-207
Strangers, 4-190
Strata, 4-424
Strates, 6-90
Streetlethal, 4-38A
Stress Pattern, 4-39
Structural Fabulation, 9-89
The Structure of Scientific Revolutions, 220
The Struggle in Space, 2-4, 444
Le Sub-espace, 6-143
Sudanna, Sudanna, 4-266
Sugar in the Air, 2-59
Suma-X, 6-347A
Sundiver, 4-83
The Sunken World, 2-19
Sun's End, 4-346
Sunspacer, 5-180
Sunstroke and Other Stories, 4-591
Superluminal, 4-371
Supermind, 3-306
Supernatural Fiction Writers, 8-47

Surface de la planète, 6-92
Survey of Modern Fantasy Literature, 8-48
Survey of Science Fiction Literature, 8-29
The Survivors, 3-174
Sveča na vetru, 3-357A
Swastika Night, 2-21
A Sweet, Sweet Summer, 4-228
Sweetwater, 5-179
A Swiftly Tilting Planet, 5-96
The Sword of Aldones, 4-77
The Sword of the Lictor, 4-616
The Sword of the Spirits, 5-31
Sylva, 3-387
Sylvie et les vivisecteurs, 6-76
Symzonia, 7, 1-81
Syn-Code-7, 6-32
The Syndic, 3-240
Synthajoy, 4-145
The Synthetic Man, 3-360
Systemic Shock, 4-283
Syzygy og den sorte stjerne, 6-364

t zero, 4-108
Tactics of Mistake, 3-146
Taimu Surippu Daisensō, 481, 6-281
Takeoff, 3-171, 3-241
Tale of the Future from the Beginning to
    the Present Day, 8-14
The Tale of the Troika, 4-542
Tales from the White Hart, 3-102, 3-105
Tales from Underwood, 2-55
Tales of Gooseflesh and Laughter, 3-415
Tales of Known Space, 4-390
Tales of Time and Space, 13-42
A Tapestry of Time, 4-155
The Tar-Aiym Krang, 4-220
Tarnsman of Gor, 4-401
Taromancie, 6-86
Tarzan Alive, 4-209
Tarzan and Tradition, 10-32
Tarzan of the Apes, 1-18
Tasogare ni Kaeru, 6-268
Tau Zero, 4-18
Teaching Science Fiction, 13-11
Telepath, 3-331
Telepathist, 4-94
"The Tell-Tale Heart," 10
The Telzey Toy, 3-328
Temple of the Past, 3-407
Temps blancs, 6-124
Le Temps des cerises, 6-135
Le Temps incertain, 4-288, 6-114
Temps n'a pas odeur, 4-302
Ten Thousand Light Years from Home, 4-554
The Terminal Man, 4-156
Terminal Visions, 9-101

Terminus 1, 6-167
Termush, 6-347
Terra SF, 4-661
Terrarium, 4-467
Terre en fuite, 6-74
Le Territoire humain, 6-115
The Terror of the Air, 52
Tesseracts, 4-658
Test of Fire, 4-78
Tōkaidō Sensō, 6-285
That Hideous Strength, 3-263
A Theatre of Timesmiths, 4-298
Them Bones, 4-579
Thematic Units in Teaching English and
    the Humanities, 13-10
Then Beggars Could Ride, 4-387
Theodore Savage, 2-40
Theodore Sturgeon, 10-143, 10-144, 10-145
There Will Be Time, 4-19
There Will Be War, 4-663
They Shall Have Stars, 3-43
They Shall Not Die, 2-89
They'd Rather Be Right, 3-113
Things to Come, 11-14
Third from the Sun, 3-273
The Third Level, 3-164
The Third Millennium, 4-534
The Third Omni Book of Science Fiction, 4-646
The Third World War: August 1985, 4-245
The Third World War: The Untold Story, 4-245
The 13 Crimes of Science Fiction, 3-460
Thirteen French Science-Fiction Stories, 3-445
This Immortal, 4-632
This Is Moscow Speaking, and Other Stories, 3-125
This Is the Way the World Ends, 4-386
This Island Earth, 3-222
This Perfect Day, 4-338
This Was Ivor Trent, 2-44
This World and Nearer Ones, 9-1
Thorns, 4-509
Those Who Can, 13-20
Thought Probes, 13-32
The Thought-Reading Machine, 2-72
Thousandstar, 4-22
The Three Armageddons of Enniscorthy
    Sweeny, 4-309
Three Came Unarmed, 2-93
Three Go Back, 60, 2-79
334, 4-188
"Three Hundred Years Hence," 8, 1-43
Three Men Make a World, 2-70

The Three Stigmata of Palmer Eldritch, 4-175
Three Tomorrows, 9-40
Three-Ring Psychus, 4-499
The Three-Seated Space Ship, 5-145
The Throne of Madness, 4-547
The Throne of Saturn, 2-142
Through the Air to the North Pole, 5-136
Through the Eye of a Needle, 3-110
Through Time and Space with Ferdinand Feghoot, 3-65
Thrust, 14-43
Thunder and Roses, 3-365
A Thunder of Stars, 4-384
The Thunderbolt Men, 5-102
Tiger by the Tail and Other Science Fiction Stories, 3-298
Tiger! Tiger!, 3-32
Tik-Tok, 4-523
Time and Again, 3-347, 4-214
Time and Mr. Bass, 5-23
Time and Stars, 3-13
Time Enough for Love, 4-264
Time for Sherlock Holmes, 4-195
Time Is the Simplest Thing, 3-348
The Time Machine, 21–22, 1-103
A Time of Changes, 4-510
Time of the Great Freeze, 5-142
The Time of the Kraken, 5-173
Time Out of Mind, 3-56
Time Piper, 5-76
Time Storm, 4-183
The Time Stream, 2-118
The Time-Swept City, 4-379
Time Trap, 5-52
Time Travelers Strictly Cash, 4-448
The Time Traveller, 10-171
Time Waits for Winthrop and Four Other Short Novels from Galaxy, 3-436
The Time Wanderers, 6-212
Time War, 4-118
Timequest, 4-387
Time's Dark Laughter, 4-292
Timescape, 4-54
Timeshadow Rider, 4-365
The Titan, 3-285
Titan, 4-571
Titanus, 6-7
The Tithonian Factor and Other Stories, 4-154
To Mars Via the Moon, 18
To Sail the Century Sea, 4-198
To Walk the Night, 2-102
"To Whom This May Come," 1-7
To Your Scattered Bodies Go, 4-210
De toekomst van gisteren, 6-406
Togda pridite, i rassudim, 453, 6-209
A Tom Disch Checklist, 10-63

Tom o'Bedlam, 4-511
Tom Swift and His Electric Rifle, 5-6
"Tominutni presckoci", 6-469
Tomorrow, 62, 3-409
Tomorrow and Beyond, 12-32
Tomorrow and Tomorrow, 3-117
Tomorrow and Tomorrow and The Fairy Chessman, 3-246
Tomorrow, and Tomorrow, and Tomorrow, 13-26
The Tomorrow City, 5-78
The Tomorrow File, 4-466
Tomorrow Revealed, 3-23
The Tomorrow Testament, 4-342
Tomorrow's Heritage, 4-150
Tomorrow's World, 3-117
To-Morrow's Yesterday, 2-37
Top Science Fiction, 3-448
Topman, 6-357
Tor zu den Sternen, 6-49
A Torrent of Faces, 3-48
The Tortured Planet, 3-263
Total Eclipse, 4-93
A Touch of Strange, 3-363
Tower of Glass, 4-504
The Towers of Utopia, 4-439
The Toymaker, 3-223
Trader to the Stars, 3-14
Trafalgar Refought, 12
The Transcendent Adventure, 9-81
Transfigurations, 4-64
The Transformation of Miss Mavis Ming, 4-383
Transformer, 4-221
Les Transhumains, 6-154
Transit, 6-132
The Transmigration of Timothy Archer, 4-172
Trap for Perseus, 4-410, 5-133
Trapped in Space, 5-174
Der Traum vom Grossen Roten Fleck, 6-30
Le Travail du Furet à l'intérieur du Poulailler, 6-56
The Travails of Jane Saint and Other Stories, 4-475
Travelling towards Epsilon, 4-654
The Treasure in the Heart of the Maze, 4-113
Treasures of Morrow, 5-70
A Treasury of Great Science Fiction, 3-424
A Treasury of Science Fiction, 3-431
The Tree That Conquered the World, 5-96
Le 32 Juillet, 6-150
Trillion Year Spree, 9-4
Trillions, 5-53
Le Triomphe de l'homme, 6-421

Triplanetary, 3-355
Triton, 4-170
Triumph, 3-409
The Triumph of Time, 3-43
Trojan Orbit, 4-438
Troldmandens Svaerd, 6-355
Trouble with Lichen, 3-416
True History, 5
True Names, 4-576
Tugt og utugt i mellemtiden, 6-350
Tunc, 4-194
Der Tunnel, 382
Tunnel, 6-142
Tunnel in the Sky, 5-66
Il Tunnel Sottomarino, 6-319
"The Turn of the Screw," 10
Turning On, 3-236
The Turning Place, 5-86
Turning Points, 9-48
Tussen Tijd en Schaduw, 6-429
Tuzub 37, 6-15
Twentieth-Century American Science-
    Fiction Writers, 8-28
Twentieth-Century Science-Fiction Writ-
    ers, 8-32
Twenty All-Time Great Science Fiction
    Films, 11-40
21st Century Foss, 12-14
21st Century Sub, 3-210
Twenty Thousand Leagues under the Sea,
    16, 1-95
The Twenty-fifth Hour, 3-29
The Twenty-One Balloons, 5-46
Twilight at the Well of Souls, 4-123
Twilight Bar, 3-237
The Twilight Zone Companion, 11-41
The Two of Them, 4-455
2000 A.D., 12-30
2001: A Space Odyssey, 4-140
2010: Odyssey Two, 4-141
2018 A.D., 4-343
The Two-Timers, 4-487
Tyskeren mot Stretermish, 6-379

Uår, 541, 6-386
Ubik, 4-178
The Ugly Swans, 4-544
The Ugupu Bird, 3-293
The Ulcer Culture, 4-97
The Ultimate Enemy, 4-460
The Ultimate Threshold, 3-447, 4-670
Unborn Tomorrow, 59
The Uncensored Man, 3-332
The Uncertain Midnight, 3-120
Under Compulsion, 4-186
Under Heaven's Bridge, 4-592
Under Pressure, 3-210

Under the Moons of Mars, 1-17
Underground Man, 1-90
The Underpeople, 3-353
Understanding Media, 210
The Undying Fire, 51
The Unforsaken Hiero, 4-318
The Unicorn Girl, 4-12
The Unified Ring, 9-87
Universe, 4-642
The Universe against Her, 3-328
The Universe Makers, 9-108
The Universe of E. E. Smith, 10-136
Universo e Dintorni, 6-326
"The Unparalleled Adventures of One
    Hans Pfaall," 6, 1-75
"The Unparalleled Invasion," 1-60
The Unreasoning Mask, 4-211
Der unsichtbare Kreis, 6-31
The Unsleeping Eye, 4-143
Der Untergang der Stadt Passau, 6-1
Until the Celebration, 5-146
Untouched by Human Hands, 3-339
Up Jenkins!, 3-214
Up the Line, 4-512
Up the Walls of the World, 4-555
The Uplift War, 4-82
Upon the Winds of Yesterday and Other
    Explorations, 12-3
Uranian Worlds, 8-23
Urania's Daughters, 8-25
Ursula K. Le Guin, 10-90, 10-91, 10-92,
    10-93, 10-94, 10-96
Useless Hands, 2-30
Utopia, 1-68
Utopia and Its Enemies, 8-54
Utopia e Fantascienza, 6-341
Utopia 14, 3-392
Utopia Hunters, 4-547
Utopian Thought in the Western World,
    8-54
Utopies 75, 6-173
Utopisch-phantastiche Literatur in der
    DDR, 6-41
Die utopische Methode, 6-43
Utopolis, 6-18
Utsukushii Hoshi, 6-266

V mire fantastiki, 6-229
Vagabondernes planet, 6-356
Valentina, 4-163
VALIS, 4-179
The Valley of Horses, 4-32
The Valley Where Time Stood Still, 4- 118
Van hoop naar waarschuwing, 6-415
The Vandal, 5-138
Vandals of the Void, 5-158
Vaneglory, 4-559

The Vanishing Fleets, 14
Var the Stick, 4-20
Variety's Complete Science Fiction Reviews, 11-5
Vault of the Ages, 5-4
Les Vautours, 6-106
Vector, 14-44
Våge å tenkje, 541
Vengeance of Gwa, 2-140
Venus Equilateral, 3-357
Venus of Dreams, 4-472
Venus Plus X, 3-364
Venus series, 52
Vermilion Sands, 4-38
Die versuchte Realität oder von der Möglichkeit, glücklichere Welten zu denken, 6-38
Vertigo, 4-488
Verwoerd—The End, 3-7
De verwoesting van Hyperion, 6-408
A Very Private Life, 4-224
The Very Slow Time Machine, 4-591
The Vicarion, 2-46
Vicinity Cluster, 4-22
Victorian Science Fiction in the UK, 9-98
Victorians and the Machine, 9-96
La Vie comme une course de chars à voile, 6-96
La Vie sur Epsilon, 6-128
View from Another Shore, 4-661
View from the Stars, 3-286
Views, 12-8
Viitorul a inceput ieri, 6-463
Village Fanfare, 5-151
Village of the Damned, 3-413
Le Vingitième siècle, 6-137
The Vintage Anthology of Science Fantasy, 3-428
Vintage Science Fiction Films, 1896–1949, 11-12
The Violet Apple, 2-63
Viriconium Nights, 4-260
Virsta de aur a anticipației românești, 6-459
Viscous Circle, 4-22
Visible Light, 4-133
Vision of Tarot, 4-23
Vision of the Future, 12-4
Visionen des Unwirklichen, 12-33
Visions of Tomorrow, 9-88
Visit to a Small Planet, 3-390
The Visitors, 4-517, 5-157
The Visual Encyclopedia of Science Fiction, 9-7
Vocile Vikingilor, 6-442
Voices for the Future, 9-25
Voices Prophesying War: 1763-1984, 9-27
The Void Captain's Tale, 4-530

Volny gasiat veter, 6-212
Vølve, 6-362
Vom Staatsroman zur Science Fiction, 6-48
Vonnegut, 10-155
Vonnegut in America, 10-156
The Vonnegut Statement, 10-157
Vornan-19, 4-504
The Vortex Blaster, 3-355
The Voyage Begun, 5-19
Voyage from Yesteryear, 4-277
The Voyage of the Luna 1, 5-38
The Voyage of the Space Beagle, 3-384
A Voyage to Arcturus, 2-63
A Voyage to Cacklogallinia, 6
Voyage to Faremido and Capillaria, 2-53
A Voyage to the Moon, 6, 1-4
Voyage to Venus, 3-263
Voyager in Night, 4-134
Voyagers, 4-71
Voyages in Space, 8-6
Voyages to the Moon, 9-69
De Vredemensch in 't jaar 3000, 6-430
Vselennaia za predelom dogmy, 6-227
Vue en coupe d'une ville malade, 6-69
Vzgliad skvoz' stoletie, 6-220

Waar helden sterven, 6-414
Walden Two, 3-352
Walk to the End of the World, 4-125
The Walking Shadow, 4-533
The Wall around the World, 3-115
Wall of Serpents, 3-134
The Wall of Years, 4-536
The Wanderer, 3-253
Wandering Stars, 4-645
The Wanting Seed, 3-83
The War in the Air, 13, 1-104
The War of Dreams, 4-116
The War of the Worlds, 22, 1-105
War with the Newts, 2-16
The Warlord of Mars, 1-17
Warm Worlds and Otherwise, 4-554
Warriors of the Wasteland, 5-68
Wasp, 3-324
The Watch Below, 4-594
Watch the Northwind Rise, 3-179
The Watcher, 4-405
A Watcher in the Woods, 5-134
Water Witch, 4-213
Waves, 4-222
A Way Home, 3-365
Way Station, 3-349
The Way the Future Was, 10-120
We, 2-147
We All Died at Breakaway Station, 4-375
We Can Build You, 4-173

A Wealth of Fable, 9-63
The Weapon Makers, 3-385
The Weapon Shops of Isher, 3-385
The Weathermonger, 5-43
The Web between the Worlds, 4-496
Web of Angels, 4-216
The Web of the Magi and Other Stories, 4-154
The Weigher of Souls, 2-73
The Weird Tales Story, 14-19
Welcome, Chaos, 4-602
Welcome to the Monkey House, 3-394
Die Welt am laufenden Band, 6-21
Die Welt ohne Gedächtnis, 2-54
Wer stiehlt schon Unterschenkel?, 6-24
West of Eden, 4-258
West of Honor, 4-421
West of the Sun, 3-305
What Dreams May Come . . . , 52
What Entropy Means to Me, 4-199
What If?, 3-446
What Mad Universe, 3-70
What Not, 2-66
What Rough Beast, 4-583
"What Was It?," 1-72
What Will They Think of Last?, 3-436
When Harlie Was One, 4-230
When Smuts Goes, 3-227
When the Kissing Had to Stop, 3-165
When the Sleeper Wakes, 1-106
"When the World Screamed," 2-28
When the World Shook, 1-47
When Time Winds Blow, 4-278
When We Were Good, 4-518
When Worlds Collide, 2-146
Where Do We Go from Here?, 13-22
Where Have You Been, Sandaliotis?, 4-309
Where Late the Sweet Birds Sang, 4-603
Where No Stars Guide, 4-384
The White Dragon, 4-368
White Fang Goes Dingo and Other Funny SF Stories, 4-186
White Light, 4-454
White Lily, 2-116
The White Mountains, 5-32
The White Plague, 4-270
Who Can Replace a Man?, 3-2
Who Goes Here?, 4-489
Who Goes There?, 3-86
Who Writes Science Fiction?, 10-200
The Whole Man, 3-74, 4-94
Who's Who in Horror and Fantasy Fiction, 8-45
Who's Who in Science Fiction, 8-26
Wielder wandert Bebemoth, 6-5
Wild Cards, 4-657
The Wild Goose Chase, 59
The Wild Ones, 4-124

Wild Seed, 4-104
The Wild Shore, 4-447
Wild Talent, 3-376
Wilderness Visions, 9-60
William Tenn, 10-146
"William Wilson," 1-75
The Wind from the Sun, 3-106
A Wind in the Door, 5-96
The Wind Obeys Lama Toru, 4-558
Windhaven, 4-362
Windows, 4-143
The Windows of Forever, 5-114
The Winds of Altair, 5-22
The Winds of Change and Other Stories, 4-25
The Winds of Gath, 4-556
The Wind's Twelve Quarters, 4-328
Wine of the Dreamers, 3-268
Winter in Eden, 4-258
Winter's Tale, 4-265
Winter's Youth, 2-38
Die Wissenschaftliche Phantastik der Sowjetunion, 6-47
The Witches of Karres, 3-329
With a Tangled Skein, 4-23
"With the Night Mail," 1-55
Without Sorcery, 3-366
Wizard, 4-571
Wolfbane, 3-314
Wolfcrest, 6-239
The Wolves of Memory, 4-199
Woman on the Edge of Time, 4-411
Women of the Future, 8-24
Women of Wonder, 4-653
Women Worldwalkers, 9-119
The Wonder, 1-11
Wonderful Adventures on Venus, 18
The Wonderful Flight to the Mushroom Planet, 5-23
The Wonderful World of Robert Sheckley, 4-492
Wonder's Child, 10-182
Wonderworks, 12-37
The Wooden Star, 3-372
The Word for World Is Forest, 4-329
The Work of Julian May, 10-109
The World Aflame, 3-155
The World Below, 2-144
A World Between, 4-531
The World Beyond the Hill, 9-71
World Enough and Time, 4-292
The World in 2030 A.D., 54
The World in Winter, 3-93
The World Inside, 4-513
The World Menders, 4-58
World of Chance, 3-144
The World of Clifford Simak, 3-350
A World of Difference, 3-119

The World of Fantastic Films, 11-16
The World of Fanzines, 14-20
The World of Null-A, 3-386
The World of Science Fiction, 9-29
The World of Star Trek, 11-39
A World of Women, 1-10
A World out of Time, 4-393
The World Set Free, 13
World Soul, 3-154
World Spring, 3-447
The World That Couldn't Be and Eight
   Other Novelets from Galaxy, 3-436
"The World, the Flesh and the Devil,"
   55
Worlds, 4-248
Worlds Apart, 4-248, 4-649
Worlds Beyond, 12-12
World's End, 4-574
Worlds of IF, 14-29
The Worlds of Robert F. Young, 3-417
The Worlds of Science Fiction, 13-27
The Worlds of Science Fiction Series, 13-
   31
Worlds of the Imperium, 3-248
Worlds Out of Words, 10-48
Wrinkle in the Skin, 3-95
A Wrinkle in Time, 5-96
Writing and Selling Science Fiction, 13-
   17

X Densha de Ikō, 6-289
Xanthe and the Robots, 4-350
Xenogenesis, 3-137
The Xiphéhuz, 1-79
Xorandor, 4-86

Y a quelqu'un?, 6-84
Year 2018!, 3-43
The Year after Tomorrow, 5-42
The Year of the Quiet Sun, 4-557
The Year When Stardust Fell, 5-84
The Year's Best Science Fiction, 4-648
The Year's Best Science Fiction Novels, 3-
   422
The Years of the City, 4-420
The Year's Scholarship in Science Fiction
   and Fantasy, 8-17
Yermah the Dorado, 20
Yesterday's Faces, 14-17
Yesterday's Men, 4-559
Yesterday's Tomorrows, 9-6, 9-28
Les Yeux géants, 6-116
Yōseiden, 6-238
Yonder Comes the Other End of Time, 4-
   202
Yonjūnhachioku Oku no Mōsō, 6-286
You and Science Fiction, 13-28
You Shall Know Them, 3-388
You Will Never Be the Same, 3-354
The Young Men Are Coming!, 52, 2-99
Ypsilon minus, 6-12
Yume no Sumu Machi, 6-290

Z for Zachariah, 5-127
Za chertopolokhom, 445
Zavtra utrom, za chaem, 452, 6-214
Der Zeiter, 6-20
Zekku . . . , 6-233
The Zen Gun, 4-48
Ziua confuză, 6-449
Zothique, 2-103